WILKINSON'S

ROAD TRAFFIC OFFENCES

WILKINSON'S
ROAD TRAFFIC OFFENCES

Fourteenth Edition

VOLUME 2

Prepared by PAUL H NIEKIRK, MA
of Gray's Inn, Barrister

Consultant Editor
HIS HONOUR JUDGE HALNAN

General Editor
PETER WALLIS
Solicitor, Clerk to the Ashford and Tenterden and Dover and East Kent Justices

ISBN 2 Vols: 0 85121 519 X
Vol 1: 0 85121 597 1
Vol 2: 0 85121 599 8

First published 1953
Fourteenth edition 1989

Published by
Longman Group UK Ltd
21–27 Lamb's Conduit Street
London WC1N 3NJ
ENGLAND

Associated offices:
Australia, Hong Kong, Malaysia, Singapore, USA.

A CIP catalogue record for this book is available from
the British Libary.

Computerset by Promenade Graphics Ltd, Cheltenham
Printed and bound in Great Britain by
The Bath Press, Bath

Contents

Table of Statutes

Table of Statutory Instruments

Table of European Provisions

EEC Regulations

ECE Regulations

EEC Treaty

International Agreements

Table of Destinations

Note. In the following table the references to the provisions repealed or revoked by the Road Traffic (Consequential Provisions) Act 1988 are to substantive provisions as amended. In consequence, references to provisions which are purely amending provisions have been omitted from the table, except for certain amendments which have not yet been brought into force. Provisions applicable only in Scotland have been included in outline.

Provision	*Road Traffic Act 1988*	*Road Traffic Offenders Act 1988*	*Road Traffic (Consequential Provisions) Act 1988*
Road Traffic Act 1972			
s 1	s 1		
s 2	s 2		
s 3	s 3		
s 4	*		
s 5(1), (2)	s 4(1), (2)		
s 5(3)	s 4(3), (4)		
s 5(4)–(7)	s 4(4)–(8)		
s 6(1)	s 5(1)		
s 6(2)	s 5(2), (3)		
s 7(1)–(8)	s 6(1)–(8)		
s 8(1)–(5)	s 7(1)–(5)		
s 8(6)	s 8(1), (2)		
s 8(7), (8)	s 7(6), (7)		
s 8(9)	s 8(3)		
s 9(1), (2)	s 9(1), (2)		
s 10(1)		s 15(1)	
s 10(2)		s 15(2), (3)	
s 10(3)		s 16(1)	
s 10(4)		ss 15(4), 16(2)	
s 10(5)		s 16(3), (4)	
s 10(6)		s 15(5)	
s 10(7)–(9)		s 16(5)–(7)	
s 11	s 10(1)–(3)		
s 12(1)–(4)	s 11(1)–(4)		
s 13		s 5	
s 14	s 12(1), (2)		
s 15(1)–(3)	s 13(1)–(4)		
s 16	s 23(1)–(3)		

* Denotes a provision which was repealed by an earlier enactment.

Provision	*Road Traffic Act 1988*	*Road Traffic Offenders Act 1988*	*Road Traffic (Consequential Provisions) Act 1988*
Road Traffic Act 1972 *ctd*			
s 17	s 28		
s 18	s 29		
s 19(1)	s 30(1)		
s 19(2)		s 5	
s 19(3)	*		
s 19(4)	s 30(1)		
s 19(5)	s 30(3)		
s 20(1)–(3)	s 31(1)–(3)		
s 20(4)	s 31(4), (5)		
s 20(5)	s 31(6)		
s 21	s 24(1)–(3)		
s 22(1)	ss 35(1), 36(1)		
s 22(2), (3)	s 36(2), (3)		
s 22(4)		s 21(1), (3)	
s 22A(1), (2)	ss 35(2), 36(4)		
s 22A(3)	s 35(2)		
s 22A(4)	s 35(3)		
s 23	s 37		
s 24	s 22		
s 25(1)	s 170(1), (2)		
s 25(2)	s 170(3), (6)†		
s 25(3)	s 170(8)		
s 25(4)	s 170(4)		
s 26(1)	s 181(1)		
s 26(2)	s 181(2), (3)		
s 26(3), (4)	s 181(4), (5)		
s 27(1), (2)	s 182(1), (2)		
s 28	*		
s 29	s 25		
s 30(1), (2)	s 26(1), (2)		
s 31(1)	s 27(1)		
s 31(2)	s 27(2), (3)		
s 31(3)–(5)	s 27(4)–(6)		
s 31(6)		s 4(2)	
s 31(7)	s 27(7)		
s 31(8)	s 27(8)		
s 32(1)	s 16(1)		
s 32(2)	s 16(3)		
s 32(2A)	s 16(2)		
s 32(3)	s 16(4)		
s 33(1)–(3)	s 17(1)–(3)		Sched 2 para 31
s 33(4)		s 4(1)	

Provision	*Road Traffic Act 1988*	*Road Traffic Offenders Act 1988*	*Road Traffic (Consequential Provisions) Act 1988*
Road Traffic Act 1972 *ctd*			
s 33(5), (6)	s 17(4), (5)		
s 33AA(1), (2)	s 18(1), (2)		
s 33AA(3)–(5)	s 18(3)–(5)		
s 33AA(6)		s 4(1)	
s 33AA(7)	s 18(6), Sched 1		
s 33AA(8)	s 18(8)		
s 33A(1)–(3)	s 14(1)–(3)		
s 33A(4)	s 14(4), (5)		
s 33A(5)	s 14(6)		
s 33B(1), (2)	s 15(1), (2)		Sched 5
s 33B(3)	s 15(5)		para 1
s 33B(4)	s 15(9)		
s 33C(1), (2)	s 15(3), (4)		para 1
s 33C(3), (4)	s 15(5), (6)		para 1
s 33C(5)	s 15(7), (8)		para 1
s 33C(6)	s 15(9)		
s 34‡	†		
s 35(1)–(5)	s 33(1)–(5)		
s 36(1)–(4)	s 34(1)–(4)		
s 36A(1)–(3)	s 19(1)–(3)		
s 36A(3A), (3B)			Sched 2 para 21
s 36A(4)	s 19(4)		
s 36A(5)–(11)	s 20(1)–(7)		
s 36B			para 22(1)
s 37(1)–(9)	s 38(1)–(9)		
s 38(1)–(2A)	s 39(1)–(3)		
s 38(3), (4)	*		
s 38(5)	s 39(4)		
s 38(6)‡			
s 39	s 40		
s 40(1)	s 41(1), (2)		
s 40(2), (2A)	s 41(3), (4)		
s 40(3), (4)	s 41(5), (6)		
s 40(5), (6)	s 42(1), (2)		
s 40(7)	s 41(7)		
s 41(1)–(4)	s 43(1)–(4)		
s 42(1), (2)	s 44(1), (2)		

* Denotes a provision which was repealed by an earlier enactment.
† Denotes a provision in which a Law Commission recommendation is implemented.
‡ Not re-enacted.

Provision	*Road Traffic Act 1988*	*Road Traffic Offenders Act 1988*	*Road Traffic (Consequential Provisions) Act 1988*
Road Traffic Act 1972 *ctd*			
s 42(3), (4)	s 44(3)		
s 43(1)–(3)	s 45(1)–(3)		
s 43(4)	s 45(4), (5)		
s 43(5)	s 45(6)		
s 43(6)	ss 45(7), 46		Sched 2 *ctd* para 32
s 43(7)	s 45(8)		
s 44(1)	s 47(1)		
s 44(2)	s 47(2)		
s 44(3)	s 47(4)		para 23
s 44(4)	s 47(5)		
s 44(5)	s 47(9)		
s 44(6), (7)	s 47(6), (7)		
s 44(8)–(10)	s 48(1)–(3)		
s 44(10A)	s 48(4)–(6)		
s 44(11)	s 47(8)		
s 44(12)‡			
s 44(13)	s 47(1)		
s 45(1)	s 49(1)–(3)		
s 45(2)	s 49(4)		
s 45(3)	s 50(1), (2)		
s 45(4)	s 50(3), (4)		
s 45(5)	s 50(5)		
s 45(6), (7)	s 51(1), (2)		
s 45(8), (9)	s 52(1), (2)		
s 45(9A)	s 49(3)		
s 45(10)	ss 51(3), 68(2)		
s 46(1)–(5)	s 53(1)–(5)		
s 47(1)–(3)	s 54(1)–(3), (6)		
s 47(4)	s 55(1)–(3)		
s 47(5)–(7)	s 57(1)–(3)		
s 47(8)	s 58(1), (2)		
s 47(9)	ss 55(4), (5), 57(4), 58(3)		
s 47(10)	s 55(6)		
s 47(11)	s 58(4), (5)		
s 47(12)	s 58(6)		
s 47(13)	ss 55(8), 58(7)		
s 48(1)	s 56(1)		
s 48(2)–(5)	s 59(1)–(4)		
s 48(6), (7)	s 56(2), (3)		
s 49(1), (2)	s 60(1)		
s 49(3)	s 60(1), (2)		

Provision	*Road Traffic Act 1988*	*Road Traffic Offenders Act 1988*	*Road Traffic (Consequential Provisions) Act 1988*
Road Traffic Act 1972 *ctd*			
s 49(4)	s 60(2)		
s 49A(1)	s 54(4)		
s 49A(2)	ss 54(4), (5), 55(7), 57(5), 59(4)		
s 50(1)	s 61(1), (2)		
s 50(2)	s 61(3)		
s 50(3), (4)	s 62(1), (2)		
s 50(5)	s 61(4)		
s 50(6)	ss 61, 62(3)†, 68		
s 51(1)–(5)	s 63(1)–(5)		
s 51A	s 63A		
s 52(1)	s 66(1), (2)		
s 52(2)	s 66(3)–(6)		
s 52(3)–(5)	s 66(7)–(9)		
s 53(1)	s 67(1)–(3)		
s 53(2)	s 67(4), (5)		Sched 2 *ctd* para 24
s 54			para 25
s 55			para 25
s 56(1)	s 68(1), (2)		
s 56(2)–(5)	s 68(3)–(6)		
s 57(1)–(4A)	s 69(1)–(5)		
s 57(5), (6)	s 69(6), (7)		
s 57(7)	s 70(1)–(3)		
s 57(7A), (7B)	s 70(4), (5)		
s 57(8)	s 73(1), (4)		
s 57(9), (10)	s 71(1), (2)		
s 57(11), (12)	s 73(2), (3)		
s 58(1)	s 72(1)		
s 58(2)	s 72(2), (3)		
s 58(2A)	s 72(4)		
s 58(3)	s 72(5), (6)		
s 58(4)	s 72(7)		
s 58(5)	s 72(8)		
s 58(5A)	s 72(9)		
s 58(6), (7)	s 72(10), (11)		
s 59(1)–(4)	s 74(1)–(4)		
s 59(5)		s 14	
s 60(1)	s 75(1)–(3)		

† Denotes a provision in which a Law Commission recommendation is implemented.
‡ Not re-enacted.

Provision	*Road Traffic Act 1988*	*Road Traffic Offenders Act 1988*	*Road Traffic (Consequential Provisions) Act 1988*
Road Traffic Act 1972 *ctd*			
s 60(2)–(6)	s 75(4)–(8)		
s 60A(1), (2)	s 76(1), (2)		
s 60A(3)	s 76(3), (4)		
s 60A(4)	s 76(5)		
s 60A(5)	s 76(5), (6)		
s 60A(6)–(8)	s 76(7)–(10)		
s 61(1)	s 77(1), (2), (4)		
s 61(1A)	s 77(2)–(4)		
s 61(2)	s 77(5)		
s 61(3)	s 77(6)		
s 62(1)	s 65(1), (2)		
s 62(2), (3)	s 65(3), (4)		
s 63(1)–(4)	s 80(1)–(4)		
s 64(1)–(4)		s 17(1)–(4)	
s 65	*		
s 66(1)	s 81(1), (2)		
s 66(2)–(5)	s 81(3)–(6)		
s 67(1)–(4)	s 82(1)–(4)		
ss 68–80	*		
s 81(1)	*		
s 81(2)	s 83		
s 82(1)	ss 85, 86		
s 82(2)			Sched 2 *ctd* para 17
s 83(1)‡			
s 83(2)–(5)	s 84(1)–(4)		
s 84(1), (2)	s 87(1), (2)		
s 84(3)	s 88(7)		
s 84(4)	s 88(1), (2)		
s 84(4A)	s 88(3), (4)		
s 84(5)	s 88(5), (6)		
s 85(1)	s 89(1), (2)		
s 85(2)	s 89(3), (4)		
s 85(3)	s 90(1), (2)		
s 85(4)	s 89(6), (7)		
s 85(5)	s 89(7)		
s 85(6), (7)	s 89(8), (9)		
s 86	s 91		
s 87(1)	s 92(1), (2)		
s 87(2), (3)	s 92(3), (4)		
s 87(4)	s 92(5)–(7)		
s 87(5)	s 93(1), (3)		

Provision	*Road Traffic Act 1988*	*Road Traffic Offenders Act 1988*	*Road Traffic (Consequential Provisions) Act 1988*
Road Traffic Act 1972 *ctd*			
s 87(5A)	s 93(2), (3)		
s 87(6)	s 92(2), (8)		Sched 4 para 7(1)
s 87(7)	s 92(9)		
s 87A(1)	s 94(1), (2)		
s 87A(2)	s 94(4), (5)		
s 87A(3)–(6)	s 94(6)–(9)		
s 87A(7)	s 92(2)		
s 88(1)	s 97(1), (3), (4)		
s 88(2)	s 97(2), (3)		
s 88(2A), (2B)	s 97(5), (6)		
s 88(3)	s 98(1)		
s 88(4)	s 98(2), (3)		
s 88(4A)	s 98(4)		
s 88(5)	s 98(2)		
s 88(6)	ss 97(7), 98(5)		
s 89(1), (1A)	s 99(1), (2)		
s 89(2)	s 99(3)		
s 89(3)	s 99(4), (5)		
s 89(4)	s 99(7), (8)		
s 90(1)	s 100(1), (2)		
s 90(2)	s 100(3)		
s 91(1)	s 96(1)		
s 91(2)	s 96(2), (3)		
s 92(1)		s 22(1), (2)	
s 92(2)	s 95(1)		
s 92(3)‡			
s 93(1)		ss 34(1), 97(1)	
s 93(2)		ss 34(2), 97(2)	
s 93(3)		*	
s 93(3A)		s 34(4)	
s 93(4)		s 34(3)	
s 93(5)		*	
s 93(6)		s 34(5)	
s 93(7)		s 36(1)–(3)	
s 93(8)		s 46(3)†	
s 94(1)		s 38(1)	
s 94(2)		s 39(1)	
s 94(3)		ss 38(2), 39(2)	

* Denotes a provision which was repealed by an earlier enactment.
† Denotes a provision in which a Law Commission recommendation is implemented.
‡ Not re-enacted.

Provision	*Road Traffic Act 1988*	*Road Traffic Offenders Act 1988*	*Road Traffic (Consequential Provisions) Act 1988*
Road Traffic Act 1972 *ctd*			
s 94(3A)		s 39(3), (4)	
s 94(4)		s 43	
s 94A(1)–(6)		s 40(1)–(6)	
s 94A(7)		s 40(7), (8)	
s 94B		s 41	
s 95(1)		s 42(1), (2)	
s 95(2)–(4)		s 42(3)–(5)	
s 95(5)		s 42(6)	Sched 4 *ctd* para 7(5)
s 96(1)–(5)	s 101(1)–(5)		
s 97	s 102		
s 98(1)		s 37(1), (2)	
s 98(2)	s 103(2)		
s 98(3)		s 37(3)	para 7(5)
s 99	s 103(1)		
s 100	s 103(3)		
s 101(1)		ss 31(4), 44(1), 96(1)	
s 101(2)		s 44(2)	
s 101(3)		s 45(1)	
s 101(4)		ss 7, 27(1), (3)	
s 101(4A)		s 31(1)	
s 101(5)–(7)		s 45(2)–(4)	
s 101(7A)		s 45(5)–(7)	
s 101(8)–(8B)		ss 31, 32	
s 101(9)		s 46(3)†	
s 102		s 46(1), (2)	
s 103(1)		s 26(1)	
s 103(2)		s 26(2), (3)	
s 103(3)		s 26(5)	
s 103(4)		s 27(2)	
s 103(5), (6)		s 26(6), (7)	
s 103(7)‡			
s 104(1)		s 25(1)	
s 104(2)		ss 8, 25(2)	
s 104(3)		s 25(4)	
s 104(4)		s 25(3)	
s 104(5)		s 25(5), (6)	
s 104(6)		s 8	
s 105(1)–(3)		s 47(1)–(3)	
s 105(4)		s 36(4)	Sched 4 *ctd* para 7(5)
s 105(5)		s 47(4)	

Provision	*Road Traffic Act 1988*	*Road Traffic Offenders Act 1988*	*Road Traffic (Consequential Provisions) Act 1988*
Road Traffic Act 1972 *ctd*			
s 106(1), (2)	s 104(1), (2)		
s 107(1)	s 105(1), (2), (5)		
s 107(2), (3)	s 105(3), (4)		
s 108(1), (2)	s 106(1), (2)		
s 109	s 107	s 25(7)	
s 110(1)	s 108(1)	s 98(1)	
s 110(2), (3)	s 108(2), (3)		
s 111(1)	s 109(1), (2)		
s 111(2)	s 109(3), (4)		
s 111(3)	s 109(5)		
s 112(1)–(4)	s 110(1)–(4)		
s 113(1), (2)	s 111(1), (2)		
s 114(1)	s 112(1)		
s 114(1A)–(1C)	s 112(2)–(4)		
s 114(2)–(4)	s 112(5)–(7)		
s 115(1)	s 113(1), (2)		
s 115(1A)	s 113(3)		
s 115(2), (3)	s 113(4), (5)		
s 115(4)	s 113(6)		
s 116(1)	s 114(1)		
s 116(1A)	s 114(2)		
s 116(2)	s 114(3), (6)		
s 116(3)	s 114(4)		
s 116(4)	s 114(5), (6)		
s 117	s 115(1), (2)		
s 118(1)	s 116(1)		
s 118(2)	s 116(2), (3)		
s 118(3), (4)	s 116(4), (5)		
s 119(1)	s 117(1), (2)		
s 119(2), (3)	s 117(4), (5)		
s 120(1)–(3)	s 118(1)–(3)		
s 120(4)‡			
s 121	s 119		
s 122	*		
s 123		s 3(1)	
s 124	ss 112(8), 117(3), 120		
s 125(1)–(4)	s 121(1)–(4)		
s 125(5)‡			
s 126(1), (1A)	s 123(1), (2)		

* Denotes a provision which was repealed by an earlier enactment.
† Denotes a provision in which a Law Commission recommendation is implemented.
‡ Not re-enacted.

Provision	*Road Traffic Act 1988*	*Road Traffic Offenders Act 1988*	*Road Traffic (Consequential Provisions) Act 1988*
Road Traffic Act 1972 *ctd*			
s 126(2)–(4A)	s 123(3)–(6)		
s 126(5)	s 123(7)		
s 127(1)–(3)	s 124(1)–(3)†		Sched 4 *ctd* para 7(2)
s 128(1)	s 125(1)–(3)		
s 128(1A)	s 125(4)		
s 128(2)–(5)	s 125(5)–(8)		
s 128(6), (7)	s 126(1)–(3)		
s 129(1)	s 127(1)–(3)		para 7(2)
s 129(2)	s 127(4)		
s 129(3)	s 127(5), (6)		
s 129(4)	ss 127(7), (8), 128(7), 130(6)		
s 129(5)	s 126(1)		
s 130(1)	s 128(1)–(3)		para 7(2)
s 130(2)	s 128(4), (5)		
s 130(3)	s 128(6), (7)		
s 131(1)	s 129(1), (2)		
s 131(2)–(5)	s 129(3)–(6)		
s 131(6)	s 129(7), (8)		
s 131(7)	s 130(1)–(4)		para 7(2)
s 131(8)	s 130(5), (6)		
s 132(1)	s 131(1), (2)		
s 132(2)	s 131(3), (4)		
s 132(3)	s 131(5)		
s 133(1)	s 132(1), (2)		
s 133(2)	s 133(1), (2)		
s 133(3)	s 133(3)		
s 134	s 134		
s 135(1)	s 135(1)		
s 135(2)	s 135(2), (3)		
s 136	s 136		
s 137(1)–(4)	s 137(1)–(4)		
s 138(1), (2)		s 18(1), (2)	
s 139	s 138		
s 140(1), (2)	s 139(1), (2)		
s 141(1)‡			
s 141(2)	s 140		
s 142	s 141		
s 143(1)	s 143(1), (2)		
s 143(2), (3)	s 143(3), (4)		
s 144(1), (2)	s 144(1), (2)†		

Provision	*Road Traffic Act 1988*	*Road Traffic Offenders Act 1988*	*Road Traffic (Consequential Provisions) Act 1988*
Road Traffic Act 1972 *ctd*			
s 145(1)	s 145(1)		
s 145(2)	ss 95(2), 145(2), (5)		
s 145(3), (4)	s 145(3), (4)		
s 146(1), (2)	s 146(1), (2)		
s 146(3)	s 146(3), (4)		
s 147(1)–(3)	s 147(1)–(3)		
s 147(4)	s 147(4), (5)		
s 148(1)	s 148(1)–(4)		
s 148(2)	s 148(5), (6)		
s 148(3)	s 149(1)–(4)		
s 148(4)	s 148(7)		
s 148(5), (6)	s 150(1), (2)		
s 148(7)	s 150(3), (4)		
s 149(1)–(1E)	s 151(1)–(6)		
s 149(2)	s 152(1)		
s 149(3)	s 152(2)–(4)		
s 149(4), (4A)	s 151(7)		
s 149(4B)	s 151(8)		
s 149(5)	s 151(9)		
s 149(6)	ss 151(10), 152(3)		
s 150(1)	s 153(1)–(3)		
s 150(2)	s 153(2)		
s 151(1), (2)	s 154(1), (2)		
s 152(1)	s 155(1)		
s 152(2)	s 155(2), (3)		
s 153	s 156		
s 154(1)	s 157(1), (2)		
s 154(2)	s 157(3)		
s 155(1)	s 158(1), (2)		
s 155(2), (3)	s 158(3), (4)		
s 156(1)	s 159(1)		
s 156(2)	s 159(2), (3)		
s 156(3)‡			
s 156(4), (5)	s 159(4), (5)		
s 157	s 160(1), (2)		
s 158(1)	ss 160(1), 161(1)		
s 158(2), (3)	s 161(2), (3)		
s 159	s 163(1)–(3)		

† Denotes a provision in which a Law Commission recommendation is implemented.
‡ Not re-enacted.

Provision	*Road Traffic Act 1988*	*Road Traffic Offenders Act 1988*	*Road Traffic (Consequential Provisions) Act 1988*
Road Traffic Act 1972 *ctd*			
s 160(1)	s 78(1), (3), (4), (8)		
s 160(1A)	s 78(5)		
s 160(1B)	s 78(2), (3)		
s 160(2)	s 78(6)		
s 160(2A)	s 78(7)		
s 160(3)	s 79(1)		
s 160(4)	s 79(2), (3)		
s 160(5), (6)	s 79(4), (5)		
s 160(7)	s 78(8)		
s 161(1)	s 164(1), (2), (11)		
s 161(2)–(3A)	s 164(3)–(5)		
s 161(4), (4A)	s 164(6), (8)		
s 161(5), (6)	s 164(9), (10)		
s 162(1)	s 165(1)–(3)		
s 162(2)	s 165(4)		
s 162(3)	s 165(5), (6)		
s 162(4)	s 165(7)		
s 163	s 166		
s 164(1)	s 168		
s 164(2)	*		
s 165	s 169		
s 166(1)	s 170(1), (5), (6)†		
s 166(2)	s 170(7)		
s 167(1)	s 171(1), (2)		
s 167(2)	s 171(3)		
s 168(1), (2)	s 172(1), (2)		Sched 2 paras 22(2), 26
s 168(3)	s 172(3), (4)		
s 169(1)–(3)	s 173(1)–(3)		para 12
s 170(1)–(3)	s 174(1)–(3)		
s 170(4)			para 27
s 170(5)	s 174(4)		
s 170(5A)	s 94(3)	s 3(2)	
s 170(6)	s 174(5)		
s 170(7)		s 17(2)	
s 171	s 175		
s 172	s 64(1), (2)		
s 173(1)	s 176(1)–(3)		
s 173(2)	s 176(4)–(7)		
s 173(3)	s 176(5)		
s 174	s 177		
s 175	s 178		

Provision	*Road Traffic Act 1988*	*Road Traffic Offenders Act 1988*	*Road Traffic (Consequential Provisions) Act 1988*
Road Traffic Act 1972 *ctd*			
s 176‡			
s 177(1)		ss 9, 33, 96, 97	
s 177(2)		ss 9, 33, 96, 97	
s 177(3)		ss 96, 97	
s 177(4)–(6)‡			
s 178		s 91	Sched 2 *ctd* para 28
s 179(1)		s 1(4)	
s 179(2)		s 1(1)	
s 179(3)		s 1(3)	
s 179(3A)		s 2(1)	
s 179(4)		s 2(3)	
s 180		s 6(1)–(4), (6)	
s 181(1)		s 11(1), (5)	
s 181(2)–(4)		s 11(2)–(4)	
s 182(1)		s 13(1), (2)	para 20
s 182(2), (2A)		s 13(3), (4)	
s 182(3)		s 13(5)	
s 183		s 12(1), (2)	
s 184‡			
s 185(1)		*	
s 185(2)		s 95	para 29
s 186	s 179		
s 187(1)	s 180(1), (2)		
s 187(2)	s 180(3)		
s 188(1)	s 183(1)	s 92	
s 188(2)	s 183(7), (8)		
s 188(3)	s 183(5)		
s 188(4)	s 183(2), (3)		
s 188(5)	*		
s 188(6), (7)	s 183(4), (6)		
s 188(8)		s 94(1), (2)	
s 188(9)		s 94(3)	
s 189(1)	s 184(1)	s 93(1)	
s 189(2), (3)	s 184(2), (3)		
s 190(1)–(8)	ss 185(1), (2), 186(1)	s 98(2)	
s 190(9), (10)	s 186(2), (3)	s 98(2)	
s 190(11)	s 186(4)–(6)		

* Denotes a provision which was repealed by an earlier enactment.
† Denotes a provision in which a Law Commission recommendation is implemented.
‡ Not re-enacted.

Provision	*Road Traffic Act 1988*	*Road Traffic Offenders Act 1988*	*Road Traffic (Consequential Provisions) Act 1988*
Road Traffic Act 1972 *ctd*			
s 191(1)–(4)	s 187(1)–(4)		
s 192(1), (2)	s 188(1), (2)		
s 192(3)			Sched 4 para 8
s 193(1), (2)	s 189(1), (2)		
s 194	s 190(1), (2)		
s 195	s 191		
s 196(1)	s 192(1)	s 98(1)	Sched 2 para 19
s 196(2)	s 192(3)		
s 196(3)‡			
s 197	*		
s 198(1)	Sched 4, paras 1, 2		
s 198(2), (3)	Sched 4, paras 3, 4		
s 198(4)	Sched 4, paras 5, 6		
s 198(5)	Sched 4, para 7		
s 198(6)	Sched 4, paras 8, 9		
s 198(7), (8)	Sched 4, paras 10, 11		
s 199(1), (2)	s 195(1), (2)		
s 199(2A)‡			
s 199(3)	s 195(3)	s 13(6)	Sched 5 para 1
s 199(4)	s 195(4)		para 1
s 195(5)	s 195(5)		
s 200(1)	s 196(1)		
s 200(2)	s 196(2), (3)		
s 200(3)	s 196(4)		
s 201			Sched 3 para 1
s 202	s 122		
s 203(1)‡			
s 203(2)	*		
ss 204–206‡			
s 207			s 7
s 208‡			
s 209‡			
s 209(2)	s 197(3)	s 99(7)	
Sched 1	Sched 1		
para 1(1)	para 1(1), (2)		
para 1(2)	para 1(3)		
para 1(3)	para 2(1), (2)		

Provision	*Road Traffic Act 1988*	*Road Traffic Offenders Act 1988*	*Road Traffic (Consequential Provisions) Act 1988*
Road Traffic Act 1972 *ctd*			
Sched 1 *ctd*			
para 2(1)–(4)	para 3(1)–(4)		
para 3(1), (2)	para 4(1), (2)		
para 4(1)–(4)	para 5(1)–(4)		
para 5(1)–(3)	para 6(1)–(3)		
Sched 2	*		
Sched 3	Sched 2		
para 1	para 1 †		
paras 2–4	paras 2–4		
para 5	para 5(1), (2)		
Sched 4			Sched 2
Part I		Sched 1 †, Sched 2, Part I	para 22(3)
			paras 22(4), 30
Part II		Sched 2, Part II	
Part III			
paras 1–3		Sched 2, Part II	
paras 4–8		*	
Part IV			
para 1		s 23 †	
para 2		s 23 †	
para 3		*	
para 3A (1), (2)		s 24(1), (2)	
para 4		s 24(3), (4)	
paras 5–7		s 2(4)–(6)	
para 8		s 23 †	
Part V‡			
Sched 5	*		
Sched 6	Sched 3		
para 1	para 1		
para 2(1)	para 2(1)–(3)		
para 2(2)–(4)	para 2(4)–(6)		
para 3	para 3(1), (2)		
para 4	para 4(1), (2)		
para 5	para 5		
Sched 7‡			
Sched 8			Sched 2
para 1			para 23

* Denotes a provision which was repealed by an earlier enactment.
† Denotes a provision in which a Law Commission recommendation is implemented.
‡ Not re-enacted.

Provision	*Road Traffic Act 1988*	*Road Traffic Offenders Act 1988*	*Road Traffic (Consequential Provisions) Act 1988*
Road Traffic Act 1972 *ctd*			
Sched 8 *ctd*			Sched 2 *ctd*
para 2			para 25
paras 3–5‡			
Road Traffic Act 1974			
s 9(4)(*a*)‡			
s 9(4)(*b*)			Sched 4 para 3(1)
s 9(5)			para 3(2)
s 9(6)			para 3(3)
s 20(3)	s 145(6)		
Criminal Procedure (Scotland) Act 1975			
s 289F		s 91†	
s 289G		s 91†	
Road Traffic (Drivers' Ages and Hours of Work) Act 1976			
Sched 2			Sched 4
para 1‡			
para 2			para 4
paras 3, 4‡			
Criminal Justice (Scotland) Act 1980			
s 7(2)		s 10	
s 26(8)		s 19	

Provision	*Road Traffic Act 1988*	*Road Traffic Offenders Act 1988*	*Road Traffic (Consequential Provisions) Act 1988*
Transport Act 1981			
s 19(1)		ss 28(1), (2), 44(1)	
s 19(2)		s 35(1)	
s 19(3)		s 29(1), (2)	
s 19(4)–(6)		s 35(2)–(4)	
s 19(7)			Sched 4 para 7(3)
s 19(8)		s 28(3)	
s 19(9)		s 35(5)	
s 20			para 7(6)
s 21		s 49	
s 23(6)	ss 89(5), 90(3)		
s 24(2)	s 32(1), (2)		
s 24(3)		Sched 2	
s 25(4)		Sched 2	
Sched 7		Sched 2	
Transport Act 1982			
s 27(1)		s 54(1), (2)	
s 27(2)		s 62(1)	
s 27(3)		s 54(3)	
s 27(4)		s 62(1)	
s 27(5), (6)		s 51(1), (2)	
s 27(7)‡			
s 27(8)		s 52(1)	
s 27(9)		s 96	
s 28(1)–(4)		s 54(4)–(7)	
s 29(1)		ss 52(3), 78(1)	
s 29(2)		s 51(3)	
s 29(3)–(5)		s 53(1)–(3)	
s 29(6)		s 52(2)–(4)	
s 29(7)		s 62(2), Sched 2	
s 30(1)–(3)		s 55(1)–(3)	
s 31(1)–(4)		s 63(1)–(4)	
s 31(5)		s 64(4)	
s 31(6)		s 64(1)	
s 31(7)		s 64(5)	
s 31(8)		s 64(6)	

† Denotes a provision in which a Law Commission recommendation is implemented.
‡ Not re-enacted.

Provision	*Road Traffic Act 1988*	*Road Traffic Offenders Act 1988*	*Road Traffic (Consequential Provisions) Act 1988*
Transport Act 1982 *ctd*			
s 31(9)		s 63(5)	
s 32(1)		s 65(2)	
s 32(2)		s 64(2)	
s 32(3)		s 63(6)	
s 32(4)		s 65(1)	
s 32(5)		s 63(7)	
s 32(6)		s 65(4)	
s 33(1)		ss 69(1), 82(1)	
s 33(2)		s 69(4)	
s 33(3)		s 69(2), (3)	
s 33(4)		s 80	
s 33(5)		s 78(2)	
s 33(6)		s 65(3)	
s 33(7), (8)		s 82(2), (3)	
s 34(1), (2)		s 57(1), (2)	
s 34(3)		s 54(7)	
s 34(4)–(6)		s 57(3)–(5)	
s 34(7), (8)		s 58(1), (2)	
s 34(9)		s 83(1), (2)	
s 34(10)		s 57(6)	
s 35(1)–(3)		s 56(1)–(3)	
s 35(4)		s 27(4)†	
s 35(5)		s 26(4)	
s 35(6)	s 164(7)		
s 35(7)	ss 93(4), 99(6)		
s 36(1), (2)		s 70(1), (2)	
s 36(3)		ss 70(3), 71(3)	
s 36(4), (5)		s 70(4), (5)	
s 36(6)		s 71(1), (2)	
s 36(7)		s 71(4), (5)	
s 36(8)		s 71(6)	
s 36(9)		s 71(9)	
s 36(10), (11)		s 71(7), (8)	
s 37(1)		ss 72(1), 73(1)	
s 37(2)		s 72(2)	
s 37(3)		s 73(2)	
s 37(4)–(6)		s 72(3)–(5)	
s 37(7)–(10)		s 73(3)–(6)	
s 38(1)		s 72(6)	
s 38(2)		s 73(7)	
s 38(3)		s 74(1)	
s 38(4)		s 74(4)	

Provision	*Road Traffic Act 1988*	*Road Traffic Offenders Act 1988*	*Road Traffic (Consequential Provisions) Act 1988*
Transport Act 1982 *ctd*			
s 38(5)		s 74(2), (3)	
s 38(6)		ss 72(7), 73(8)	
s 38(7)		s 74(5), (6)	
s 38(8)		s 74(7)	
s 39(1)–(6)		s 59(1)–(6)	
s 40(1)		s 60(1), (2)	
s 40(2)–(5)		s 60(3)–(6)	
s 41(1)–(3)		s 61(1)–(3)	
s 41(4)		s 61(4), (5)	
s 42		ss 75†, 76†	
s 43		ss 77†, 83(1)	
s 44(1)–(4)		s 30(1)–(3)	
s 45(1)–(8)		s 66(1)–(8)	
s 46(1)		s 67, Sched 2	
s 46(2), (3)		s 6(1), (2), Sched 1, para 2†	
s 46(4)		s 6(5)†	
s 46(5)		s 6(3), (4)	
s 47(1)–(4)		s 79(1)–(4)	
s 47(5)		s 79(5), (6)	
s 47(6), (7)		s 81(1), (2)	
s 47(8)		s 79(7)	
s 48		ss 10, 35(6)†, 44(3)†, 50	
s 49(1)		s 84	
s 49(2), (3)		s 68(1), (2)	
s 49(4)–(7)		s 85(1)–(4)	
s 49(8)		ss 85(5), 89(2)	
s 49(9), (10)		s 68(3), (4)	
s 49(11)		s 86(1)	
s 49(12)		s 2(2)	
s 49(13)		s 64(7)	
s 50(1), (2)		s 89(1), (2)	
s 50(3)		s 86(2)	
s 50(4)		s 89(1)	
s 50(5)		s 98(4)	
s 50(6)		s 90	
s 51		s 87	

† Denotes a provision in which a Law Commission recommendation is implemented.

Provision	*Road Traffic Act 1988*	*Road Traffic Offenders Act 1988*	*Road Traffic (Consequential Provisions) Act 1988*
Transport Act 1982 *ctd*			
s 73(3)		s 88(2)	
Sched 1		Sched 3	Sched 2 para 22(5)
Sched 2		Sched 5	
Sched 3		Sched 4	
Sched 5			
para 10(*a*)			para 15(*a*)
para 11			para 17
para 12			para 16
para 13(1)‡			
para 13(2)–(4)			Sched 4 para 7(4)
			Sched 2
para 14			para 20
para 15			para 18
para 16			para 19
para 26‡			
Cycle Tracks Act 1984			
s 2(1)	s 21(1)	Sched 2	
s 2(2), (3)	s 21(2), (3)		
Road Traffic Regulation Act 1984			
s 35(8)		s 4(3)	
s 47(7)		s 4(4)	
s 53(7)		s 4(5)	
s 78‡			
s 90		s 20	
s 98(1), (2)		ss 9, 33(1), 34(1), 44	
s 98(3)‡			
s 98(4)		s 33(2)	
s 113(1)		s 11(1), Sched 1, para 3	
s 113(2)–(4)		s 11(2)–(4)	
s 114		s 12(3)	

Provision	*Road Traffic Act 1988*	*Road Traffic Offenders Act 1988*	*Road Traffic (Consequential Provisions) Act 1988*
Road Traffic Regulation Act 1984 *ctd*			
s 118		s 91†	
s 120(1), (2)		s 21(1), (2)	
s 121		s 95	
s 130(4)		s 94(1), (2)	
s 130(5)		s 94(3)	
Sched 7		Sched 2	
Sched 10 para 12‡			
Motor Vehicles (Wearing of Rear Seat Belts by Children) Act 1988			
s 3(2)			Sched 5 para 1
Motor Vehicles (Tests) (Extension) Order 1982 (SI 1982 No 1550)	s 47(2), (3)		
Road Vehicles (Construction and Use) Regulations 1986 (SI 1986 No 1078)			
reg 91†‡			

† Denotes a provision in which a Law Commission recommendation is implemented.
‡ Not re-enacted.

Provision	*Road Traffic Act 1988*	*Road Traffic Offenders Act 1988*	*Road Traffic (Consequential Provisions) Act 1988*
Road Traffic Accidents (Payments for Treatment) Order 1987 (SI 1987 No 353)			
art 4			Sched 4 para 6

Levels of Fines on the Standard Scale

The standard scale of fines is set out in the Criminal Justice Act 1982, s 37, as amended. The levels on the standard scale were increased in respect of offences committed after 30 April 1984 by the Criminal Penalties etc (Increase) Order 1984 (SI 1984 No 447). For convenience, the current levels are set out below:

Level on the standard scale	*Amounts*
1	£50
2	£100
3	£400
4	£1000
5	£2000

SI 1984 No 447 increased the amount of the prescribed sum (see the Magistrates' Courts Act 1980, s 32(9)) payable on conviction of any offence triable either way to £2000.

The scale of fines applicable before 1 May 1984 and the prescribed sum applicable before that date are referred to in the notes to the Criminal Justice Act 1982, s 37, and the Magistrates' Courts Act 1980, s 32(*qv*), respectively.

General Note

Volume 2 of this book contains only a selection of statutory provisions and the omission of any provision does not necessarily imply that it is not operative.

Reference to page numbers in the tables and in contents lists in this volume are references to Volume 2.

Section A

Statutes

The Agriculture Act 1947

(10 & 11 Geo 6 c 48)

An Act to make further provision for agriculture.

[6th August 1947]

* * *

109. Interpretation

(1), (2) *[Omitted.]*

(3) In this Act the following expressions have the meanings hereby respectively assigned to them, that is to say:—

'agriculture' includes horticulture, fruit growing, seed growing, dairy farming and livestock breeding and keeping, the use of land as grazing land, meadow land, osier land, market gardens and nursery grounds, and the use of land for woodlands where that use is ancillary to the farming of land for other agricultural purposes, and 'agricultural' shall be construed accordingly;

. . . .

(4)–(6) *[Omitted.]*

[The definition of agriculture in s 109(3) is incorporated by reference into the Transport Act 1968, s 103 (qv).]

* * *

The Airports Act 1986

(1986 c 31)

An Act to . . . provide for the regulation of the use of airports . . . and for connected purposes.

[8th July 1986]

* * *

63. Airport byelaws

(1) Where an airport is either—

(*a*) designated for the purposes of this section by an order made by the Secretary of State, or

(*b*) managed by the Secretary of State,

the airport operator (whether the Secretary of State or some other person) may make byelaws for regulating the use and operation of the airport and the conduct of all persons while within the airport.

(2) Any such byelaws may, in particular, include byelaws—

(*a*)–(*c*) *[Omitted.]*

(*d*) for regulating vehicular traffic anywhere within the airport, except on roads within the airport to which the road traffic enactments apply, and in particular (with that exception) for imposing speed limits on vehicles within the airport and for restricting or regulating the parking of vehicles or their use for any purpose or in any manner specified in the byelaws;

(*e*) for prohibiting waiting by hackney carriages except at standings appointed by such person as may be specified in the byelaws;

(*f*) –(*k*) *[Omitted.]*

(3) In paragraph (*d*) of subsection (2) 'the road traffic enactments' means the enactments (whether passed before or after this Act) relating to road traffic, including the lighting and parking of vehicles, and any order or other instrument having effect by virtue of any such enactment.

(4)–(8) *[Omitted.]*

* * *

65. Control of road traffic at designated airports

(1) Subject to the provisions of this section, the road traffic enactments shall apply in relation to roads which are within a designated airport but to which the public does not have access as they apply in relation to roads to which the public has access.

(2) The Secretary of State may by order direct that in their application to roads within such an airport the road traffic enactments shall have effect subject to such modifications as appear to him necessary or expedient for the purpose of, or in consequence of, conferring—

(*a*) on the airport operator functions exercisable under those enactments by a highway authority or local authority; or

(*b*) on the chief officer of any airport constabulary functions so exercisable by a chief officer of police.

(3) An order under subsection (2) may exempt from the application of the road traffic enactments particular roads or lengths of road to which the public does not have access and may require the airport operator to indicate the roads or lengths of roads so exempted in such manner as may be specified in the order.

(4) Before making an order under this section in relation to any airport (other than one managed by the Secretary of State) the Secretary of State shall consult the airport operator.

(5) Any road or place within an airport in the metropolitan police district shall be deemed to be a street or place within the meaning of section 35 of the London Hackney Carriage Act 1831.

(6) In this section—

'airport constabulary' means, in relation to an airport owned or managed by the Secretary of State, the special constables appointed under section 57 of the 1982 Act and, in relation to any airport owned or managed by a local authority, any body of constables which the authority have power to maintain at that airport;

'designated airport' means an airport which is designated for the purposes of this section by an order made by the Secretary of State; and

'the road traffic enactments' has the meaning given by section 63(3).

(7) *[Applies to Scotland.]*

[The reference to the '1982 Act' is a reference to the Civil Aviation Act 1982; Airports Act 1986, s 82(1).]

* * *

The Banking and Financial Dealings Act 1971

(1971 c 80)

An Act to make new provision in place of the Bank Holidays Act 1871 . . . and for purposes connected therewith

[16th December 1971]

* * *

SCHEDULE 1

Bank Holidays

1. The following are to be bank holidays in England and Wales:—
Easter Monday.
The last Monday in May.
The last Monday in August.
26th December, if it be not a Sunday.
27th December in a year in which 25th or 26th December is a Sunday.

2. *[Applies to Scotland.]*

3. *[Applies to Northern Ireland.]*

[Days may be substituted for or added to the above list by royal proclamation. In recent years 1 (or 2) January and the first Monday in May have been so added.

The above definition of 'bank holiday' has been incorporated by reference into the Motor Vehicles (Authorisation of Special Types) (General) Order 1979 (SI 1979 No 1198), art 3(1), the Public Service Vehicles (Operators' Licences) Regulations 1986 (SI 1986 No 1668), reg 22, and the Road Vehicles (Construction and Use) Regulations 1986 (SI 1986 No 1078), Sched 12, para 1 (qv).]

* * *

The Car Tax Act 1983

(1983 c 53)

An Act to consolidate the enactments relating to car tax.

[26th July 1983]

* * *

7. Remission of tax on certain vehicles

(1) Where the Commissioners are satisfied that a vehicle—

(*a*) has been exported; or

(*b*) is to be exported under arrangements approved by them,

they shall remit the tax on the vehicle or, if the tax has been paid, repay it (subject in the case of a vehicle registered before exportation, to such conditions as they think fit); but where such a vehicle is imported after having been exported the provisions of this Act shall apply in relation to it as they apply in relation to a vehicle made outside the United Kingdom and not previously imported.

(2) Where it is shown to the satisfaction of the Commissioners that a person who acquires a chargeable vehicle is only temporarily in the United Kingdom or is about to become resident outside the United Kingdom the Commissioners may, subject to such conditions as they think necessary for the protection of the revenue, remit the tax on the vehicle or, if the tax has been paid and the vehicle is unused, repay the tax.

(3) If—

(*a*) tax has been remitted or repaid on a vehicle under subsection (2) above, and

(*b*) the vehicle is found in the United Kingdom after the date by which the Commissioners directed, as a condition of the remission or repayment, that it should be exported, or any other condition imposed by the Commissioners under that subsection is not complied with, and

(*c*) the presence of the vehicle in the United Kingdom after that date or the non-observance of that condition has not been authorised for the purposes of this subsection by the Commissioners,

then the tax which would have been payable but for the remission or, as the case may be, an amount of tax equal to that repaid shall become payable forthwith by the person by whom the vehicle was acquired or by any other person in whose possession the vehicle is found in the United Kingdom, and shall be recoverable as a debt due to the Crown, unless, or except to the extent that, the Commissioners see fit to waive payment of the whole or part of it.

(4)–(7) *[Omitted.]*

[Vehicles which satisfy the requirements of subss (1)–(3) of s 7 may be exempt from the requirements of the Motor Vehicles (Type Approval for Goods Vehicles) (Great Britain) Regulations 1982 (SI 1982 No 1271) (see reg 3(2)(b)) and the Motor Vehicles (Type Approval) (Great Britain) Regulations 1984 (SI 1984 No 981) (see reg 3(2)(f)), below.]

* * *

The Chronically Sick and Disabled Persons Act 1970

(1970 c 44)

An Act to make further provision with respect to the welfare of chronically sick and disabled persons; and for connected purposes.

[29th May 1970]

* * *

20. Use of invalid carriages on highways

(1) In the case of a vehicle which is an invalid carriage complying with the prescribed requirements and which is being used in accordance with the prescribed conditions—

(*a*) no statutory provision prohibiting or restricting the use of footways shall prohibit or restrict the use of that vehicle on a footway;

(*b*) if the vehicle is mechanically propelled, it shall be treated for the purposes of the [Road Traffic Regulation Act [1984] and [the Road Traffic Act 1988 and the Road Traffic Offenders Act 1988]] as not being a motor vehicle; and

(*c*) whether or not the vehicle is mechanically propelled, it shall be exempted from the requirements of [section 83 of the said Act of 1988].

(2) In this section—

'footway' means a way which is a footway, footpath or bridleway within the meaning of [the Highways Act 1980];

'invalid carriage' means a vehicle, whether mechanically propelled or not, constructed or adapted for use for the carriage of one person, being a person suffering from some physical defect or disability;

'prescribed' means prescribed by regulations made by the [Secretary of State for Transport];

'statutory provision' means a provision contained in, or having effect under, any enactment.

(3) *[Omitted.]*

[Section 20 is printed as amended by the Secretary of State for the Environment Order 1970 (SI 1970 No 1681); the Road Traffic Act 1972, s 203(1) and Sched 7; the Secretary of State for Transport Order 1976 (SI 1976 No 1775); the Minister of Transport Order 1979 (SI 1979 No 571); the Highways Act 1980, s 343(2) and Sched 24, para 19; the Transfer of Functions (Transport) Order 1981 (SI 1981 No 238); the Road Traffic Regulation Act 1984, s 146(a) and Sched 13, para 10; the Road Traffic (Consequential Provisions) Act 1988, s 4 and Sched 3, para 7.

Words relating expressly and exclusively to Scotland have been omitted from the definition of 'footway'.

The Use of Invalid Carriages on Highways Regulations 1988 (SI 1988 No 2268) (qv) have been made under this section.]

21. Badges for display on motor vehicles used by disabled persons

(1)–(7E) *[Omitted.]*

(8) The local authorities for the purposes of this section shall be the common council of the City of London, the council of a county . . . [or metropolitan district] in England or Wales or of a London borough; and in this section 'motor vehicle' has the same meaning as in the Road Traffic Regulation Act [1984].

(9) *[Omitted.]*

[The definition of 'local authority' is by implication incorporated into the Disabled Persons (Badges for Motor Vehicles) Regulations 1982 (SI 1982 No 1740), reg 3(1), qv.

Subsection (8) is printed as amended by the Local Government Act 1972, s 272(1) and Sched 30; the Road Traffic Regulation Act 1984, s 146(a) and Sched 13, para 11; the Local Government Act 1985, s 8 and Sched 5, Part I, para 1.

Words relating expressly and exclusively to Scotland have been omitted from subs (8) above.]

* * *

The Civil Aviation Act 1982

(1982 c 16)

An Act to consolidate certain enactments relating to civil aviation.

[27th May 1982]

*   *   *

105. General interpretation

(1) In this Act, except where the context otherwise requires—

. . .

'aerodrome' means any area of land or water designated, equipped, set apart or commonly used for affording facilities for the landing and departure of aircraft and includes any area or space, whether on the ground, on the roof of a building or elsewhere, which is designed, equipped, or set apart for affording facilities for the landing and departure of aircraft capable of descending or climbing vertically;

. . .

(2)–(7) *[Omitted.]*

(8) *[Repealed.]*

[The definition of 'aerodrome' is incorporated by reference into the Community Drivers' Hours and Recording Equipment (Exemptions and Supplementary Provisions) Regulations 1986 (SI 1986 No 1456), Schedule (qv) and the Goods Vehicles (Plating and Testing) Regulations 1988 (SI 1988 No 1478), Sched 2 (qv).]

*   *   *

The Civil Defence Act 1948

(12, 13 & 14 Geo 6 c 5)

An Act to make further provision for civil defence.

[16th December 1948]

*　*　*

9. Interpretation, etc

(1) In this Act, except where the context otherwise requires—

'civil defence' does not include the provision or maintenance of a shelter which is used or intended to be used wholly or mainly by naval, military or air forces but, save as aforesaid, includes any measures not amounting to actual combat for affording defence against any form of hostile attack by a foreign power or for depriving any form of hostile attack by a foreign power of the whole or part of its effect, whether the measures are taken before, at or after the time of the attack;

. . .

(2), (3) *[Omitted.]*

[The definition of 'civil defence' is incorporated by reference into the Vehicles (Excise) Act 1971, s 7 (qv).]

*　*　*

The Civil Evidence Act 1968

(1968 c 64)

An Act to amend the law of evidence in relation to civil proceedings . . . .
[25th October 1968]

* * *

10. Interpretation of Part I, and application to arbitrations, etc

(1) In this Part of this Act—

. . .

'document' includes, in addition to a document in writing—

(*a*) any map, plan, graph or drawing;

(*b*) any photograph;

(*c*) any disc, tape, sound track or other device in which sounds or other data (not being visual images) are embodied so as to be capable (with or without the aid of some other equipment) of being reproduced therefrom; and

(*d*) any film, negative, tape or other device in which one or more visual images are embodied so as to be capable (as aforesaid) of being reproduced therefrom;

. . .

'statement' includes any representation of fact, whether made in words or otherwise.

(2) In this Part of this Act any reference to a copy of a document includes—

(*a*) in the case of a document falling within paragraph (*c*) but not (*d*) of the definition of 'document' in the foregoing subsection, a transcript of the sounds or other data embodied therein;

(*b*) in the case of a document falling within paragraph (*d*) but not (*c*) of that definition, a reproduction or still reproduction of the image or images embodied therein, whether enlarged or not;

(*c*) in the case of a document falling within both those paragraphs, such a transcript together with such a still reproduction; and

(*d*) in the case of a document not falling within the said paragraph (*d*) of which a visual image is embodied in a document falling within that paragraph, a reproduction of that image, whether enlarged or not,

and any reference to a copy of the material part of a document shall be construed accordingly.

(3), (4) *[Omitted.]*

[The above provisions are incorporated by reference into the Road Traffic Offenders Act 1988, s 13, and the Vehicles (Excise) Act 1971, s 31 (qv).]

The Companies Act 1985

(1985 c 6)

An Act to consolidate the greater part of the Companies Acts.

[11th March 1985]

* * *

735. 'Company' etc

(1) In this Act—

(*a*) 'company' means a company formed and registered under this Act, or an existing company;

(*b*) 'existing company' means a company formed and registered under the former Companies Acts, but does not include a company registered under the Joint Stock Companies Acts, the Companies Act 1862 or the Companies (Consolidation) Act 1908 in what was then Ireland;

(*c*) 'the former Companies Acts' means the Joint Stock Companies Acts, the Companies Act 1862, the Companies (Consolidation) Act 1908, the Companies Act 1929 and the Companies Acts 1948 to 1983.

(2) 'Public company' and 'private company' have the meanings given by section 1(3).

(3) 'The Joint Stock Companies Acts' means the Joint Stock Companies Act 1856, the Joint Stock Companies Acts 1856, 1857, the Joint Stock Banking Companies Act 1857 and the Act to enable Joint Stock Banking Companies to be formed on the principle of limited liability, or any one or more of those Acts (as the case may require), but does not include the Joint Stock Companies Act 1844.

(4) The definitions in this section apply unless the contrary intention appears.

[See the note to s 736, below.]

736. 'Holding company' 'subsidiary' and 'wholly-owned subsidiary'

(1) For the purposes of this Act, a company is deemed to be a subsidiary of another if (but only if)—

(*a*) that other either—

(i) is a member of it and controls the composition of its board of directors, or

(ii) holds more than half in nominal value of its equity share capital, or

(*b*) the first-mentioned company is a subsidiary of any company which is that other's subsidiary.

The above is subject to subsection (4) below in this section.

(2) For purposes of subsection (1), the composition of a company's board of directors is deemed to be controlled by another company if (but only if) that other company by the exercise of some power exercisable by it without the consent or

concurrence of any other person can appoint or remove the holders of all or a majority of the directorships.

(3) For purposes of this last provision, the other company is deemed to have power to appoint to a directorship with respect to which any of the following conditions is satisfied—

(*a*) that a person cannot be appointed to it without the exercise in his favour by the other company of such a power as is mentioned above, or

(*b*) that a person's appointment to the directorship follows necessarily from his appointment as director of the other company, or

(*c*) that the directorship is held by the other company itself or by a subsidiary of it.

(4) In determining whether one company is a subsidiary of another—

(*a*) any shares held or power exercisable by the other in a fiduciary capacity are to be treated as not held or exercisable by it,

(*b*) subject to the two following paragraphs, any shares held or power exercisable—

(i) by any person as nominee for the other (except where the other is concerned only in a fiduciary capacity), or

(ii) by, or by a nominee for, a subsidiary of the other (not being a subsidiary which is concerned only in a fiduciary capacity),

are to be treated as held or exercisable by the other,

(*c*) any shares held or power exercisable by any person by virtue of the provisions of any debentures of the first-mentioned company or of a trust deed for securing any issue of such debentures are to be disregarded,

(*d*) any shares held or power exercisable by, or by a nominee for, the other or its subsidiary (not being held or exercisable as mentioned in paragraph (*c*)) are to be treated as not held or exercisable by the other if the ordinary business of the other or its subsidiary (as the case may be) includes the lending of money and the shares are held or the power is exercisable as above mentioned by way of security only for the purposes of a transaction entered into in the ordinary course of that business.

(5) For purposes of this Act—

(*a*) a company is deemed to be another's holding company if (but only if) the other is its subsidiary, and

(*b*) a body corporate is deemed the wholly-owned subsidiary of another if it has no members except that other and that other's wholly-owned subsidiaries and its or their nominees.

(6) In this section 'company' includes any body corporate.

[Sections 735 and 736 of this Act are incorporated by reference into the Transport Act 1968, s 99 (qv), and the Goods Vehicles (Operators' Licences, Qualifications and Fees) Regulations 1984 (SI 1984 No 176), reg 3(1) (qv).]

The Consumer Credit Act 1974

(1974 c 39)

An Act to establish for the protection of consumers a new system . . . of licensing and other control of traders concerned with the provision of credit, or the supply of goods on hire or hire-purchase, and their transactions . . . .

[31st July 1974]

* * *

189. Definitions

(1) In this Act, unless the context otherwise requires—

. . .

'conditional sale agreement' means an agreement for the sale of goods or land under which the purchase price or part of it is payable by instalments, and the property in the goods or land is to remain in the seller (notwithstanding that the buyer is to be in possession to the goods or land) until such conditions as to the payment of instalments or otherwise as may be specified in the agreement are fulfilled;

. . .

'hire purchase agreement' means an agreement, other than a conditional sale agreement, under which—

(*a*) goods are bailed or (in Scotland) hired in return for periodical payments by the person to whom they are bailed or hired, and

(*b*) the property in the goods will pass to that person if the terms of the agreement are complied with and one or more of the following occurs—

(i) the exercise of an option to purchase by that person,

(ii) the doing of any other specified act by any party to the agreement,

(iii) the happening of any other specified event;

. . .

(2)–(7) *[Omitted.]*

[The above definition of 'hire-purchase agreement' (itself dependent in part on the definition of 'conditional sale agreement') is incorporated by reference into the Road Traffic Regulation Act 1984, s 109, and the Transport Act 1982, s 45 (qv).]

The Criminal Attempts Act 1981

(1981 c 47)

An Act to amend the law of England and Wales . . . and . . . to repeal the provisions of section 4 of the Vagrancy Act 1824 which apply to suspected persons and reputed thieves; to make provision against unauthorised interference with vehicles . . .

[27th July 1981]

*   *   *

PART II

SUSPECTED PERSONS ETC

8. Abolition of offence of loitering etc with intent

The provisions of section 4 of the Vagrancy Act 1824 which apply to suspected persons and reputed thieves frequenting or loitering about the places described in that section with the intent there specified shall cease to have effect.

[In the Vagrancy Act 1824, s 4, the words from 'every suspected person' to 'arrestable offence' were formally repealed by s 10 of and Part II of the Schedule to this Act.]

9. Interference with vehicles

(1) A person is guilty of the offence of vehicle interference if he interferes with a motor vehicle or trailer or with anything carried in or on a motor vehicle or trailer with the intention that an offence specified in subsection (2) below shall be committed by himself or some other person.

(2) The offences mentioned in subsection (1) above are—

(*a*) theft of the motor vehicle or trailer or part of it;

(*b*) theft of anything carried in or on the motor vehicle or trailer; and

(*c*) an offence under section 12(1) of the Theft Act 1968 (taking and driving away without consent);

and, if it is shown that a person accused of an offence under this section intended that one of those offences should be committed, it is immaterial that it cannot be shown which it was.

(3) A person guilty of an offence under this section shall be liable on summary conviction to imprisonment for a term not exceeding three months or to a fine not exceeding [level 4 on the standard scale] or to both.

(4) . . .

(5) In this section 'motor vehicle' and 'trailer' have the meanings assigned to them by [section 185(1) of the Road Traffic Act 1988 [*qv*]].

[Section 9 is printed as amended by the Criminal Justice Act 1982, s 46(1); the Police and Criminal Evidence Act 1984, s 119(2) and Sched 7, Part I; the Road Traffic (Consequential Provisions) Act 1988, s 4 and Sched 3, para 23.]

* * *

The Criminal Justice Act 1982

(1982 c 48)

An Act to make further provision as to the sentencing and treatment of offenders (including provision as to . . . the standardisation of fines and of certain other sums specified in enactments relating to the powers of criminal courts) . . .

[28th October 1982]

* * *

Introduction of standard scale of fines

37. The standard scale of fines for summary offences

(1) There shall be a standard scale of fines for summary offences, which shall be known as 'the standard scale'.

(2) The scale *at the commencement of this section* is shown below.

Level on the scale	*Amount of fine*
1	[£50]
2	[£100]
3	[£400]
4	[£1000]
5	[£2000]

(3) Where any enactment (whether contained in an Act passed before or after this Act) provides—

(*a*) that a person convicted of a summary offence shall be liable on conviction to a fine or a maximum fine by reference to a specified level on the standard scale; or

(*b*) confers power by subordinate instrument to make a person liable on conviction of a summary offence (whether or not created by the instrument) to a fine or maximum fine by reference to a specified level on the standard scale,

it is to be construed as referring to the standard scale for which this section provides as that standard scale has effect from time to time by virtue either of this section or of an order under section 143 of the Magistrates' Courts Act 1980.

[Section 37 is printed as amended by the Criminal Penalties etc (Increase) Order 1984 (SI 1984 No 447) so far as it relates to offences committed after 30 April 1984. On the substitution of the new rates the words in italics have in effect lapsed.

Article 1(2) of SI 1984 No 447 reads:

'This Order shall not affect the amount of any fine imposed, nor the amount of any compensation order made, in respect of any offence committed before 1st May 1984 nor the amount of any fine imposed in respect of any act or omission taking place before that date.'

Before 1 May 1984 the levels of fines were as follows:

level 1	*£25*
level 2	*£50*
level 3	*£200*
level 4	*£500*
level 5	*£1000.*]

* * *

The Criminal Justice Act 1988

(1988 c 33)

An Act . . . to amend the law with regard to the jurisdiction and powers of criminal courts . . . and for connected purposes.

[29th July 1988]

* * *

PART V

JURISDICTION, IMPRISONMENT, FINES, ETC

Jurisdiction

* * *

40. Power to join in indictment count for common assault etc

(1) A count charging a person with a summary offence to which this section applies may be included in an indictment if the charge—

(*a*) is founded on the same facts or evidence as a count charging an indictable offence; or

(*b*) is part of a series of offences of the same or similar character as an indictable offence which is also charged,

but only if (in either case) the facts or evidence relating to the offence were disclosed in an examination or deposition taken before a justice in the presence of the person charged.

(2) Where a count charging an offence to which this section applies is included in an indictment, the offence shall be tried in the same manner as if it were an indictable offence; but the Crown Court may only deal with the offender in respect of it in a manner in which a magistrates' court could have dealt with him.

(3) The offences to which this section applies are—

(*a*) common assault;

(*b*) an offence under section 12(1) of the Theft Act 1968 [*qv*] (taking motor vehicle or other conveyance without authority etc);

(*c*) an offence under [section 103(1)(*b*) of the Road Traffic Act 1988] [*qv*] (driving a motor vehicle while disqualified);

(*d*) an offence mentioned in the first column of Schedule 2 to the Magistrates' Courts Act 1980 (criminal damage etc.) which would otherwise be triable only summarily by virtue of section 22(2) of that Act; and

(*e*) any summary offence specified under subsection (4) below.

(4) The Secretary of State may by order made by statutory instrument specify for the purposes of this section any summary offence which is punishable with imprisonment or involves obligatory or discretionary disqualification from driving.

(5) *[Statutory instruments subject to negative resolution procedure.]*

[Section 40 came into operation on 12 October 1988; see the Criminal Justice Act 1988 (Commencement No 2) Order 1988 (SI 1988 No 1676).

Section 40 is printed as amended by the Road Traffic (Consequential Provisions) Act 1988, s 4 and Sched 3, para 39.]

41. Power of Crown Court to deal with summary offence where person committed for either way offence

(1) Where a magistrates' court commits a person to the Crown Court for trial on indictment for an offence triable either way or a number of such offences, it may also commit him for trial for any summary offence with which he is charged and which—

(*a*) is punishable with imprisonment or involves obligatory or discretionary disqualification from driving; and

(*b*) arises out of circumstances which appear to the court to be the same as or connected with those giving rise to the offence, or one of the offences, triable either way,

whether or not evidence relating to that summary offence appears on the depositions or written statements in the case; and the trial of the information charging the summary offence shall then be treated as if the magistrates' court had adjourned it under section 10 of the Magistrates' Courts Act 1980 and had not fixed the time and place for its resumption.

(2) Where a magistrates' court commits a person to the Crown Court for trial on indictment for a number of offences triable either way and exercises the power conferred by subsection (1) above in respect of a summary offence, the magistrates' court shall give the Crown Court and the person who is committed for trial a notice stating which of the offences triable either way appears to the court to arise out of circumstances which are the same as or connected with those giving rise to the summary offence.

(3) A magistrates' court's decision to exercise the power conferred by subsection (1) above shall not be subject to appeal or liable to be questioned in any court.

(4) The committal of a person under this section in respect of an offence to which section 40 above applies shall not preclude the exercise in relation to the offence of the power conferred by that section; but where he is tried on indictment for such an offence, the functions of the Crown Court under this section in relation to the offence shall cease.

(5) If he is convicted on the indictment, the Crown Court shall consider whether the conditions specified in subsection (1) above were satisfied.

(6) If it considers that they were satisfied, it shall state to him the substance of the summary offence and ask him whether he pleads guilty or not guilty.

(7) If he pleads guilty, the Crown Court shall convict him, but may deal with him in respect of that offence only in a manner in which a magistrates' court could have dealt with him.

(8) If he does not plead guilty, the powers of the Crown Court shall cease in respect of the offence except as provided by subsection (9) below.

(9) If the prosecution inform the Court that they would not desire to submit evidence on the charge relating to the summary offence, the Court shall dismiss it.

(10) The Crown Court shall inform the clerk of the magistrates' court of the outcome of any proceedings under this section.

(11) Where the Court of Appeal allows an appeal against conviction of an offence triable either way which arose out of circumstances which were the same as or connected with those giving rise to a summary offence of which the appellant was convicted under this section—

(*a*) it shall set aside his conviction of the summary offence and give the clerk of the magistrates' court notice that it has done so; and

(*b*) it may direct that no further proceedings in relation to the offence are to be undertaken;

and the proceedings before the Crown Court in relation to the offence shall thereafter be disregarded for all purposes.

(12) A notice under subsection (11) above shall include particulars of any direction given under paragraph (*b*) of that subsection in relation to the offence.

(13) The references to the clerk of the magistrates' court in this section are to be construed in accordance with section 141 of the Magistrates' Courts Act 1980 [*qv*].

[Section 41 came into operation on 12 October 1988; see the Criminal Justice Act 1988 (Commencement No 2) Order 1988 (SI 1988 No 1676).]

* * *

The Customs and Excise Management Act 1979

(1979 c 2)

An Act to consolidate the enactments relating to the collection and management of the revenues of customs and excise and in some cases to other matters in relation to which the Commissioners of Customs and Excise for the time being perform functions, with amendments to give effect to recommendations of the Law Commission and the Scottish Law Commission.

[22nd February 1979]

* * *

102. Payment for excise licences by cheque

(1) Any government department or local authority having power to grant an excise licence may, if they think fit, grant the licence upon receipt of a cheque for the amount of the duty payable thereon.

(2) Where a licence is granted to any person on receipt of a cheque and the cheque is subsequently dishonoured, the licence shall be void as from the time when it was granted, and the department or authority who granted it shall send to that person, by letter sent by registered post or the recorded delivery service and addressed to him at the address given by him when applying for the licence, a notice requiring him to deliver up the licence within the period of 7 days from the date when the notice was posted.

(3) If a person who has been required under subsection (2) above to deliver up a licence fails to comply with the requirement within the period mentioned in that subsection he shall be liable on summary conviction to a penalty of the following amount, that is to say—

(*a*) *[Refers to gaming/gaming machine licences.]*

[(*aa*) where the licence is a licence under the Vehicles (Excise) Act 1971, a penalty of whichever is the greater of—

(i) level 3 on the standard scale, or

(ii) an amount equal to five times the annual rate of duty that was payable on the grant of the licence or would have been so payable if it had been taken out for a period of twelve months.]

(*b*) *[Refers to any other case.]*

[Section 102 is printed as amended by the Finance Act 1987, s 2(6) and (8)(c) and Sched 1, Part III, para 20.]

* * *

The Fatal Accidents Act 1976

(1976 c 30)

An Act to consolidate the Fatal Accidents Acts.

[22nd July 1976]

* * *

[1A. Bereavement

(1) An action under this Act may consist of or include a claim for damages for bereavement.

(2) A claim for damages for bereavement shall only be for the benefit—

(*a*) of the wife or husband of the deceased; and

(*b*) where the deceased was a minor who was never married—

(i) of his parents, if he was legitimate; and

(ii) of his mother, if he was illegitimate.

(3) Subject to subsection (5) below, the sum to be awarded as damages under this section shall be £3,500.

(4) Where there is a claim for damages under this section for the benefit of both the parents of the deceased, the sum awarded shall be divided equally between them (subject to any deduction falling to be made in respect of costs not recovered from the defendant).

(5) *[Power to alter sum specified in s 1A(3) by order.]*]

[Section 1A was inserted by the Administration of Justice Act 1982, s 3(1).
This section is incorporated by reference into the Powers of Criminal Courts Act 1973, s 35 (qv).]

* * *

The Finance Act 1971

(1971 c 68)

An Act to grant certain duties, to alter other duties . . . and to make further provision in connection with finance.

[5th August 1971]

*   *   *

7. Disabled passengers—vehicles excise duty

A mechanically propelled vehicle . . . [suitable] for use by persons having a particular disability that so incapacitates them in the use of their limbs that they have to be driven and cared for by a full-time constant attendant and registered in the name of such a disabled person under the Vehicles (Excise) Act 1971 shall not be chargeable with any duty under that Act by reason of its use by or for the purposes of that disabled person or by reason of its being kept for such use where— . . .

(*c*) . . . the disabled person is sufficiently disabled to be eligible under the [National Health Service Act 1977] for an invalid tricycle but too disabled to drive it; [and

(*d*) no vehicle exempted from duty under section 7(2) of the Vehicles (Excise) Act 1971 is (or by virtue of that provision is deemed to be) registered in his name under that Act;]

and where regulations under section 23 of the Vehicles (Excise) Act 1971 require a person to furnish particulars as to a vehicle exempted from duty by this section, they may require him to furnish in addition such evidence of the facts giving rise to the exemption as is prescribed by the regulations.

[Section 7 is printed as amended by the Finance Act 1972, ss 128(2), 134(7) and Sched 28, Part XII; the Finance Act 1974, s 50; the National Health Service Act 1977, s 129 and Sched 15; the Finance Act 1978, s 8(3).]

*   *   *

The Harbours Act 1964

(1964 c 40)

An Act to . . . make . . . provision respecting the construction, improvement, maintenance and management of harbours . . . .

[10th June 1964]

* * *

57. Interpretation

(1) In this Act, unless the context otherwise requires, the following expressions have the meanings hereby assigned to them respectively, that is to say:–

. . .

'harbour', except where used with reference to a local lighthouse authority, means any harbour whether natural or artificial, and any port, haven, estuary, tidal or other river or inland waterway navigated by sea-going ships, and includes a dock, a wharf and where used with reference to such an authority has the meaning assigned to it by section 742 of the Merchant Shipping Act 1894 [ie 'Harbour' includes harbours properly so called, whether natural or artificial, estuaries, navigable rivers, piers, jetties, and other works in or at which ships can obtain shelter, or ship and unship goods or passengers];

'harbour authority' means any person in whom are vested under this Act, by another Act or by an order or other instrument (except a provisional order) made under another Act or by a provisional order powers or duties of improving, maintaining or managing a harbour;

. . .

'harbour operations' means,—

(*a*) the making or lighting of a harbour or any part thereof;

(*b*) the berthing or dry docking of a ship;

(*c*) the warehousing, sorting, weighing or handling of goods on harbour land or at a wharf;

(*d*) the movement of goods or passengers within the limits within which the person engaged in improving, maintaining or managing a harbour has jurisdiction or on harbour land;

(*e*) in relation to a harbour (which expression for the purposes of this paragraph does not include a wharf)—

(i) the towing, or moving of a ship which is in or is about to enter or has recently left the harbour;

(ii) the loading or unloading of goods, or embarking or disembarking of passengers, in or from a ship which is in the harbour or the approaches thereto;

(iii) the lighterage or handling of goods in the harbour; and

(*f*) in relation to a wharf,—

(i) the towing or moving of a ship to or from the wharf;

(ii) the loading or unloading of goods, or the embarking or disembarking of passengers, at the wharf in or from a ship;

. . .

(2)–(5) *[Omitted.]*

[The definitions of 'harbour' and 'harbour authority' are incorporated by reference into the Community Drivers' Hours and Recording Equipment (Exemptions and Supplementary Provisions) Regulations 1986 (SI 1986, No 1456), Schedule (qv). The definitions of 'harbour' and 'harbour operations' have been incorporated by reference into the Road Traffic Act 1988, s 78(8) (qv).

Words applicable expressly and exclusively to Scotland have been omitted from the definition of 'harbour' above.]

* * *

The Highways Act 1980

(1980 c 66)

An Act to consolidate the Highways Act 1959 to 1971 and related enactments, with amendments to give effect to recommendations of the Law Commission.

[13th November 1980]

* * *

137. Penalty for wilful obstruction

(1) If a person, without lawful authority or excuse, in any way wilfully obstructs the free passage along a highway he is guilty of an offence and liable to a fine not exceeding [level 3 on the standard scale].

(2) *[Repealed.]*

[Section 137 is printed as amended by the Criminal Justice Act 1982, ss 38, 46(1); the Police and Criminal Evidence Act 1984, s 119(2) and Sched 7, Part I.

As to the application of the fixed penalty procedure to offences under s 137, see the Road Traffic Offenders Act 1988, Sched 3, below.]

* * *

329. Further provision as to interpretation

(1) In this Act, except where the context otherwise requires—

. . .

'bridge' does not include a culvert, but, save as aforesaid, means a bridge or viaduct which is part of a highway, and includes the abutments and any other part of a bridge but not the highway carried thereby;

'bridleway' means a highway over which the public have the following, but no other, rights of way, that is to say, a right of way on foot and a right of way on horseback or leading a horse, with or without a right to drive animals of any description along the highway;

. . .

'carriageway' means a way constituting or comprised in a highway, being a way (other than a cycle track) over which the public have a right of way for the passage of vehicles;

. . .

'cycle track' means a way constituting or comprised in a highway, being a way over which the public have the following, but not other, rights of way, that is to say, a right of way on pedal cycles [(other than pedal cycles which are motor vehicles within the meaning of [the Road Traffic Act 1988])] with or without a right of way on foot;

. . .

'footpath' means a highway over which the public have a right of way on foot only, not being a footway;

'footway' means a way comprised in a highway which also comprises a carriageway, being a way over which the public have a right of way on foot only;

. . .

'the Minister', subject to subsection (5) below, means as respects England, the Minister of Transport and as respects Wales, the Secretary of State; and in section 258 of, and paragraphs 7, 8(1) and (3), 14, 15(1) and (3), 18(2), 19 and 21 of Schedule 1 to, this Act, references to the Minister and the Secretary of State acting jointly are to be construed, as respects Wales, as references to the Secretary of State acting alone;

. . .

'proposed highway' means land on which, in accordance with plans made by a highway authority, that authority are for the time being constructing or intending to construct a highway shown in the plans;

. . .

'sewerage authority' means a water authority in their capacity as an authority exercising functions under or by virtue of section 14 of the Water Act 1973;

. . .

'special road' means a highway, or a proposed highway, which is a special road in accordance with section 16 above;

. . .

'statutory undertakers' means persons authorised by any enactment to carry on any of the following undertakings:—

(*a*) a railway, tramway, road transport, water transport, canal, inland navigation, dock, harbour, pier or lighthouse undertaking, or

(*b*) an undertaking for the supply of electricity, . . . water or hydraulic power,

and 'statutory undertaking' is to be construed accordingly;

'street' includes any highway and any road, lane, footpath, square, court, alley or passage, whether a thoroughfare or not, and includes any part of a street;

. . .

'trunk road' means a highway, or a proposed highway, which is a trunk road by virtue of section 10(1) or section 19 above or by virtue of an order or direction under section 10 above or under any other enactment;

. . .

(2)–(5) *[Omitted.]*

[Only selected definitions from s 329(1) are set out above.

The definition of 'cycle track' is printed as amended by the Cycle Tracks Act 1984, s 1(1) and the Road Traffic (Consequential Provisions) Act 1988, s 4 and Sched 3, para 21(2).

The definition of 'statutory undertakers' is printed as amended by the Gas Act 1986, s 67(4) and Sched 9, Part I. By ibid, s 67(1) and Sched 7, para 2(1)(xl), a public gas supplier is deemed to be a statutory undertaker for the purpose of the Highways Act 1980.

The Water Act 1973, s 14 (to which reference is made in the definition of 'sewerage authority' in s 329(1)), requires water authorities to provide public sewers as necessary and to make provision for effectually dealing with the contents of their sewers.

Section 10 of this Act (to which reference is made in the definition of 'trunk road' in s 329(1)) provides that all highways which were trunk roads under the earlier legislation should continue to be trunk roads and s 19 provides that a special road to be provided under a scheme will (unless otherwise provided in the scheme) become a trunk road.

Subsection (5) of s 329 relates to functions in relation to part of a particular road (as to which, see further the Transfer of Functions (Transport) Order 1981 (SI 1981 No 238), art 3(1)).

The functions of the Minister of Transport were transferred to the Secretary of State for Transport by the Transfer of Functions (Transport) Order 1981 (including the functions exercisable jointly with the Secretary of State under the provisions listed in the definition of 'the Minister' above); ibid, art 2 and Schedule.]

* * *

SCHEDULE 4

Classes of Traffic for Purposes of Special Roads

Class I:

Heavy and light locomotives, motor tractors, heavy motor cars, motor cars and motor cycles whereof the cylinder capacity of the engine is not less than 50 cubic centimetres, and trailers drawn thereby, which comply with general regulations as to construction and use made, or having effect as if made, under [section 41 of the Road Traffic Act 1988] and in the case of which the following conditions are satisfied:—

(i) that the whole weight of the vehicle is transmitted to the road surface by means of wheels;

(ii) that all wheels of the vehicle are equipped with pneumatic tyres;

(iii) that the vehicle is not controlled by a pedestrian;

(iv) that the vehicle is not a vehicle chargeable with duty under paragraph 2 of Part I of Schedule 3 to the Vehicles (Excise) Act 1971; and

(v) in the case of a motor vehicle, that it is so constructed as to be capable of attaining a speed of 25 miles per hour on the level under its own power, when unladen and not drawing a trailer.

Class II:

Motor vehicles and trailers the use of which for or in connection with the conveyance of abnormal indivisible loads is authorised by order made, or having effect as if made, by the Minister under [section 44(1) of the Road Traffic Act 1988].

Motor vehicles and trailers constructed for naval, military, air force or other defence purposes, the use of which is authorised by order made, or having effect as if made, by the Minister under [section 44(1) of the Road Traffic Act 1988].

Motor vehicles and trailers, to which any of the following Articles of the Motor Vehicles (Authorisation of Special Types) General Order 1973, namely Article 16 (which relates to vehicles for moving excavated material), Article 17 (which relates inter alia to vehicles constructed for use outside the United Kingdom) and Article 21 (which relates to engineering plant) relate and which are authorised to be used by any of those Articles of the said order or by any other [order made, or having effect as if made, under section 44(1) of the Road Traffic Act 1988], the said motor vehicles being vehicles in respect of which the following condition is satisfied, that is to say, that the vehicle is so constructed as to be capable of attaining a speed of 25 miles per hour on the level under its own power, when unladen and not drawing a trailer.

Class III:

Motor vehicles controlled by pedestrians.

Class IV:

All motor vehicles (other than invalid carriages and motor cycles whereof the cylinder capacity of the engine is less than 50 cubic centimetres) not comprised in Class I, Class II or Class III.

Class V:
Vehicles drawn by animals.

Class VI:
Vehicles (other than pedal cycles, perambulators, push-chairs and other forms of baby carriages) drawn or propelled by pedestrians.

Class VII:
Pedal cycles.

Class VIII:
Animals ridden, led or driven.

Class IX:
Pedestrians, perambulators, push-chairs and other forms of baby carriages and dogs held on a lead.

Class X:
Motor cycles whereof the cylinder capacity of the engine is less than 50 cubic centimetres.

Class XI:
Invalid carriages.

In this Schedule any expression defined for the purposes of [the Road Traffic Act 1988] has the same meaning as in that Act and the expression 'abnormal indivisible load' has the same meaning as in the Motor Vehicles (Authorisation of Special Types) General Order 1973.

[Schedule 4 is printed as amended by the Road Traffic (Consequential Provisions) Act 1988, s 4 and Sched 3, para 21(3).

Schedule 4 refers to the Motor Vehicles (Authorisation of Special Types) General Order 1973 (SI 1973 No 1101). This order was, however, revoked and replaced on 1 November 1979 by the Motor Vehicles (Authorisation of Special Types) General Order 1979 (SI 1979 No 1198). The provisions in the 1979 Order which relate to vehicles for moving excavated material, vehicles constructed for use outside the United Kingdom, and engineering plant, are arts 15, 16 and 19 respectively; see below.

For the Vehicles (Excise) Act 1971, Sched 3, Part I, and the Road Traffic Act 1988, s 44(1), see below.]

The Insurance Companies Act 1982

(1982 c 50)

An Act to consolidate the Insurance Companies Acts 1974 and 1981.
[28th October 1982]

* * *

SCHEDULE 2

General Business

PART I

Classes

Number	Description	Nature of Business
1	Accident	Effecting and carrying out contracts of insurance providing fixed pecuniary benefits or benefits in the nature of indemnity (or a combination of both) against risks of the person insured or, in the case of a contract made by virtue of section 140, 140A or 140B of the Local Government Act 1972, a person for whose benefit the contract is made— (*a*) sustaining injury as the result of an accident or of an accident of a specified class, or (*b*) dying as the result of an accident or of an accident of a specified class, or (*c*) becoming incapacitated in consequence of disease or of disease of a specified class, inclusive of contracts relating to industrial injury and occupational disease but exclusive of contracts falling within class 2 below or within class IV in Schedule I to this Act (permanent health).
*	* * *	* * *
3	Land vehicles	Effecting and carrying out contracts of insurance against loss or damage to vehicles used on land, including motor vehicles but excluding railway rolling stock.
*	* * *	* * *

Number	Description	Nature of Business
7	Goods in transit	Effecting and carrying out contracts of insurance against loss of or damage to merchandise, baggage and all other goods in transit, irrespective of the form of transport
*	* * *	* * *
10	Motor vehicle liability	Effecting and carrying out contracts of insurance against damage arising out of or in connection with the use of motor vehicles on land, including third-party risks and carrier's liability.
*	* * *	* * *

PART II

GROUPS OF CLASSES

Number	Description	Composition
*	* * *	* * *
2	Motor	Class 1 (to the extent that the relevant risks are risks of the person insured sustaining injury, or dying, as the result of travelling as a passenger) and classes 3, 7 and 10.
*	* * *	* * *

[Schedule 2 (reproduced in part only) is incorporated by reference into the Road Traffic Act 1988, ss 95(2) and 145(5), below.

The Local Government Act 1972, ss 140, 140A and 140B (referred to in class 1 in the table in Part I) deal with the following subject-matter: s 140 (as amended), contracts of insurance within class 1 entered into by a local authority in respect of members of the authority while engaged on business of the authority; s 140A (together with s 140B, added by the Local Government (Miscellaneous Provisions) Act 1982), contracts of insurance entered into by a local authority in respect of (inter alia) personal accidents suffered by voluntary assistants of the authority while engaged as such; and s 140B, contracts of insurance entered into by county councils in respect of (inter alia) personal accidents suffered by voluntary assistants of relevant probation committees while engaged as such.

Class 2 of Part I of Sched 2 (also referred to in class 1 in the table in Part I), is sickness insurance (ie loss attributable to sickness or infirmity).]

* * *

The International Road Haulage Permits Act 1975

(1975 c 46)

An Act to make further provision with respect to the forgery, carriage and production of licences, permits, authorisations and other documents relating to the international carriage of goods by road; and for purposes connected therewith.

[1st August 1975]

1. Carriage on United Kingdom vehicles, and production, of international road haulage permits

(1) The Secretary of State may by regulations made by statutory instrument provide that—

(*a*) a goods vehicle registered in the United Kingdom, or

(*b*) a trailer drawn by a vehicle registered in the United Kingdom, or

(*c*) an unattached trailer which is for the time being in the United Kingdom,

may not be used on a journey to which the regulations apply, being a journey—

(i) for or in connection with the carriage or haulage of goods either for hire or reward or for or in connection with any trade or business carried on by the user of the vehicle, and

(ii) either between a place in the United Kingdom and a place outside the United Kingdom or, if the journey passes through any part of the United Kingdom, between places both of which are outside the United Kingdom,

unless a document of a description specified in the regulations is carried on the vehicle or, in the case of a trailer, is carried either on the vehicle drawing it or by a person in charge of it.

(2) If it appears to an examiner that a goods vehicle registered in the United Kingdom or a trailer is being used in such circumstances that, by virtue of regulations under subsection (1) above, a document of a description specified in the regulations is required to be carried as mentioned in that subsection he may, on production if so required of his authority,—

(*a*) require the driver of the goods vehicle concerned or, in the case of a trailer, the driver of the vehicle drawing it or the person in charge of it to produce a document of the description in question and to permit the examiner to inspect and copy it,

(*b*) detain the goods vehicle or trailer concerned for such time as is requisite for the purpose of inspecting and copying the document,

(*c*) at any time which is reasonable having regard to the circumstances of the case enter any premises on which he has reason to believe that there is kept a vehicle (whether a goods vehicle or a trailer) which is being used on a journey to which regulations under subsection (1) above apply, and

(*d*) at any time which is reasonable having regard to the circumstances of the case enter any premises in which he has reason to believe that any document of a description specified in regulations under subsection (1) above is to be found and inspect and copy any such document which he finds there.

(3) If, without reasonable excuse, any person uses a goods vehicle or trailer in contravention of regulations under subsection (1) above he shall be liable on summary conviction to a fine not exceeding [level 4 on the standard scale].

(4) If the driver of a goods vehicle which is being used in such circumstances as are specified in subsection (2) above or the person in charge of, or the driver of a vehicle drawing, a trailer which is being so used—

(*a*) without reasonable excuse refuses or fails to comply with a requirement under subsection (2) above, or

(*b*) wilfully obstructs an examiner in the exercise of his powers under that subsection,

he shall be liable on summary conviction to a fine not exceeding [level 3 on the standard scale].

(5) If any person (other than a person specified in subsection (4) above) wilfully obstructs an examiner in the exercise of his powers under paragraph (*d*) of subsection (2) above, he shall be liable on summary conviction to a fine not exceeding [level 3 on the standard scale].

(6) For the purposes of this section a motor vehicle which for the time being has exhibited on it a licence or trade plates issued—

(*a*) under the Vehicles (Excise) Act 1971 or under an enactment repealed by that Act, or

(*b*) under the Vehicles (Excise) Act (Northern Ireland) 1972 or under any enactment of the Parliament of Northern Ireland repealed by the Act,

shall be presumed, unless the contrary is proved, to be registered in the United Kingdom.

(7) *[Omitted.]*

(8) Any reference in this section to a person using a vehicle (whether a goods vehicle or a trailer) shall be construed as if this section were included in Part V of the Transport Act 1968.

(9) In this section—

'examiner' means an examiner appointed under section 56(1) of the Road Traffic Act 1972 [or section 68(1) of the Road Traffic Act 1988];

'goods vehicle' means a motor vehicle constructed or adapted for use for the carriage of goods or burden or any description;

'trailer' means a trailer so constructed or adapted;

and for the purposes of this subsection 'motor vehicle' and 'trailer' have the same meaning as [in the Road Traffic Act 1988].

[Section 1 is printed as amended by the Criminal Justice Act 1982, ss 37, 38 and 46; the Road Traffic (Consequential Provisions) Act 1988, s 4 and Sched 3, para 13. References to Northern Ireland legislation have been omitted from the text of s 1(8) and (9).

The Goods Vehicles (International Road Haulage) Regulations 1975 (SI 1975 No 2234) have been made under this section.]

2. Power to prohibit vehicle or trailer being taken out of the United Kingdom

(1) If it appears to an examiner:—

(*a*) that a goods vehicle or a trailer is being used in such circumstances as are specified in subsection (2) of section 1 above, and

(*b*) that, without reasonable excuse, the driver of the goods vehicle or, as the case may require, the person in charge of, or the driver of a vehicle drawing, the trailer has refused or failed to comply with a requirement under that subsection,

the examiner may prohibit the removal of the goods vehicle or trailer out of the United Kingdom, either absolutely or for a specified purpose, and either for a specified period or without limitation of time.

(2) Where an examiner prohibits the removal of a goods vehicle or trailer out of the United Kingdom under subsection (1) above, he shall forthwith give notice in writing of the prohibition to the driver of the goods vehicle or, as the case may require, to the person in charge of, or the driver of the vehicle drawing, the trailer, specifying—

(*a*) the circumstances in consequence of which the prohibition is imposed,

(*b*) whether the prohibition applies absolutely or for a specified purpose, and

(*c*) whether the prohibition is for a specified period or without limit of time,

and the prohibition under subsection (1) above shall come into force as soon as notice thereof is given under this subsection.

(3) Where an examiner is satisfied, with respect to a goods vehicle or trailer to which a prohibition under subsection (1) above relates,—

(*a*) that the goods vehicle or trailer is being used on a journey to which regulations under section 1(1) above do not apply, or

(*b*) that there is carried on the goods vehicle or, in the case of a trailer, on the vehicle drawing it or by a person in charge of it a document of a description specified in those regulations,

he may remove the prohibition and, where he does so, shall forthwith give notice in writing of the removal of the prohibition to the driver of the goods vehicle or, as the case may require, to the person in charge of, or the driver of the vehicle drawing, the trailer and the prohibition shall cease to have effect on the giving of that notice.

(4) Unless the person to whom a notice is given under subsection (2) or subsection (3) above is the person using the vehicle concerned, as soon as practicable after such a notice has been given, the examiner who gave it shall take steps to bring the contents of the notice to the attention of the person using the vehicle.

(5) In the exercise of his functions under this section, an examiner shall act in accordance with any general directions given by the Secretary of State.

(6) Any person who, without reasonable excuse,—

(*a*) removes a goods vehicle or trailer out of the United Kingdom in contravention of a prohibition under subsection (1) above, or

(*b*) causes or permits a goods vehicle or trailer to be removed out of the United Kingdom in contravention of such a prohibition,

shall be guilty of an offence and liable on summary conviction to a fine not exceeding [level 4 on the standard scale].

(7) Subsections (8) and (9) of section 1 above shall apply in relation to this section as they apply in relation to that.

[Section 2 is printed as amended by the Criminal Justice Act 1982, ss 37, 38 and 46.]

3–5. *[Omitted.]*

The Interpretation Act 1978

(1978 c 30)

An Act to consolidate the Interpretation Act 1889 and certain other enactments relating to the construction and operation of Acts of Parliament and other instruments, with amendments to give effect to recommendations of the Law Commission and the Scottish Law Commission.

[20th July 1978]

* * *

5. Definitions

In any Act, unless the contrary intention appears, words and expressions listed in Schedule 1 to this Act are to be construed according to that Schedule.

* * *

7. References to service by post

Where an Act authorises or requires any document to be served by post (whether the expression 'serve' or the expression 'give' or 'send' or any other expression is used) then, unless the contrary intention appears, the service is deemed to be effected by properly addressing, pre-paying and posting a letter containing the document and, unless the contrary is proved, to have been effected at the time at which the letter would be delivered in the ordinary course of post.

* * *

SCHEDULE 1

WORDS AND EXPRESSIONS DEFINED

* * *

['The standard scale', with reference to a fine or penalty for an offence triable only summarily,—

(*a*) in relation to England and Wales, has the meaning given by section 37 of the Criminal Justice Act 1982 [*qv*];

(*b*) *[Applies to Scotland]*

(*c*) *[Applies to Northern Ireland]*]

* * *

['Statutory maximum', with reference to a fine or penalty on summary conviction for an offence,—

(*a*) in relation to England and Wales, means the prescribed sum within the meaning of section 32 of the Magistrates' Courts Act 1980 [*qv*];

(*b*) *[Applies to Scotland]*

(*c*) *[Applies to Northern Ireland]*]

* * *

[The definitions of 'the standard scale' and 'statutory maximum' were added to Sched 1 by the Criminal Justice Act 1988, s 170(1) and Sched 15, para 58.]

* * *

The Justices of the Peace Act 1979

(1979 c 55)

An Act to consolidate certain enactments relating to justices of the peace (including stipendiary magistrates) . . .

[6th December 1979]

* * *

4. Petty sessions areas

(1) The following areas outside Greater London are petty sessions areas, that is to say—

(*a*) every non-metropolitan county which is not divided into petty sessional divisions;

(*b*) every petty sessional division of a non-metropolitan county;

(*c*) every metropolitan district which is not divided into petty sessional divisions; and

(*d*) every petty sessional division of a metropolitan district.

(2) In the following provisions of this Act 'petty sessions area' means any of the following, that is to say—

(*a*) any of the areas outside Greater London specified in subsection above;

[(*b*) the inner London area if it is not divided into petty sessional divisions;]

[(*c*) any petty sessional division of the inner London area;]

[(*d*) any outer London borough which is not divided into petty sessional divisions;]

[(*e*) any petty sessional division of an outer London borough; and]

[(*f*) the City of London.]

[Section 4 is incorporated by reference into the Magistrates' Courts Act 1980, s 150(1) (qv), and thereby into the Road Traffic Act 1988, s 192, and the Road Traffic Offenders Act 1988, s 89, below. It is printed as amended by the Local Government Act 1985, s 12(2).]

* * *

The Local Government Act 1972

(1972 c 70)

An Act to make provision with respect to local government and the functions of local authorities in England and Wales . . . .

[26th October 1972]

* * *

262. Local Acts and instruments

(1)–(12) *[Omitted.]*

(13) In subsection (12) above 'local authority' means—

(*a*) the council of an administrative county, urban district or rural district;

(*b*) the municipal corporation of a borough acting by the council of that borough;

(*c*) any commissioners, trustees or other persons invested by any local Act with powers of town government or rating;

(*d*) any local board constituted in pursuance of the Public Health Act 1848, the Local Government Act 1858, the Local Government (1858) Amendment Act 1861 or the Local Government Amendment Act 1863; or

(*e*) without prejudice to the foregoing any body of persons constituted or designated as an urban or rural sanitary authority under the Public Health Act 1875;

and 'statutory undertaking' means any railway, light railway, tramway, road transport, water transport, canal, inland navigation, ferry, dock, harbour, pier or lighthouse undertaking, any telephone undertaking, any market undertaking or any undertaking for the supply of electricity, gas, hydraulic power, . . . or district heating.

[The definition of 'statutory undertaking' is incorporated by reference into the Road Vehicles (Construction and Use) Regulations 1986 (SI 1986 No 1078), reg 3(2) (qv). Subsection (13) of s 262 is printed as amended by the Water Act 1973, s 40(3) and Sched 9.]

* * *

270. General provisions as to interpretation

(1) In this Act, except where the context otherwise requires, the following expressions have the following meanings respectively, that is to say—

. . .

'local authority' means a county council . . . a district council, a London borough council or a parish or community council;

. . .

(2)–(5) *[Omitted.]*

[The above definition is applied by the Public Passenger Vehicles Act 1982, s 82 (qv). The definition is printed as amended by the Local Government Act 1985, s 102(2) and Sched 17.]

The Local Government (Miscellaneous Provisions) Act 1976

(1976 c 57)

An Act to make amendments for England and Wales of provisions of the law which relates to local authorities or highways and is commonly amended by local Acts . . .

[15th November 1976]

ARRANGEMENT OF SECTIONS

PART I

General

Supplemental

44. Interpretation etc of Part I

(1), (2) *[Omitted.]*

(3) When an offence under this Part of this Act (including an offence under byelaws made by virtue of section 12 of this Act) which has been committed by a body corporate is proved to have been committed with the consent or connivance of, or to be attributable to any neglect on the part of, any director, manager, secretary or other similar officer of the body corporate or any person who was purporting to act in any such capacity, he as well as the body corporate shall be guilty of that offence and be liable to be proceeded against and punished accordingly.

Where the affairs of a body corporate are managed by its members the preceding provisions of this subsection shall apply in relation to the acts and defaults of a member in connection with his functions of management as if he were a director of the body corporate.

(4)–(6) *[Omitted.]*

[Section 44(3) is expressly applied to offences under Part II of this Act by s 72(2).]

PART II

Hackney Carriages and Private Hire Vehicles

45. Application of Part II

(1) The provisions of this Part of this Act, except this section, shall come into force in accordance with the following provisions of this section.

(2) If the Act of 1847 is in force in the area of a district council, the council may resolve that the provisions of this Part of this Act, other than this section, are to apply to the relevant area; and if the council do so resolve those provisions shall come into force in the relevant area on the day specified in that behalf in the resolution (which must not be before the expiration of the period of one month beginning with the day on which the resolution is passed).

In this subsection 'the relevant area', in relation to a council, means—

(*a*) if the Act of 1847 is in force throughout the area of the council, that area; and

(*b*) if the Act of 1847 is in force for part only of the area of the council, that part of that area.

(3) A council shall not pass a resolution in pursuance of the foregoing subsection unless they have—

(*a*) published in two consecutive weeks, in a local newspaper circulating in their area, notice of their intention to pass the resolution; and

(*b*) served a copy of the notice, not later than the date on which it is first published in pursuance of the foregoing paragraph, on the council of each parish or community which would be affected by the resolution or, in the case of such a parish which has no parish council, on the chairman of the parish meeting.

(4) If after a council has passed a resolution in pursuance of subsection (2) of this section the Act of 1847 comes into force for any part of the area of the council for which it was not in force when the council passed the resolution, the council may pass a resolution in accordance with the foregoing provisions of this section in respect of that part as if that part were included in the relevant area for the purposes of subsection (2) of this section.

46. Vehicle drivers' and operators' licences

(1) Except as authorised by this Part of this Act—

(*a*) no person being the proprietor of any vehicle, not being a hackney carriage [or London cab] in respect of which a vehicle licence is in force, shall use or permit the same to be used in a controlled district as a private hire vehicle without having for such a vehicle a current licence under section 48 of this Act;

(*b*) no person shall in a controlled district act as driver of any private hire vehicle without having a current licence under section 51 of this Act;

(*c*) no person being the proprietor of a private hire vehicle licensed under this Part of this Act shall employ as the driver thereof for the purpose of any hiring any person who does not have a current licence under the said section 51;

(*d*) no person shall in a controlled district operate any vehicle as a private hire vehicle without having a current licence under section 55 of this Act;

(*e*) no person licensed under the said section 55 shall in a controlled district operate any vehicle as a private hire vehicle—

(i) if for the vehicle a current licence under the said section 48 is not in force, or

(ii) if the driver does not have a current licence under the said section 51.

(2) If any person knowingly contravenes the provisions of this section he shall be guilty of an offence.

[Section 46 is printed as amended by the Transport Act 1985, s 139(2) and Sched 7, para 17(1).]

47. Licensing of hackney carriages *[Omitted.]*

48. Licensing of private hire vehicles

(1)–(4) *[Omitted.]*

(5) Where a district council grant under this section a vehicle licence in respect of a private hire vehicle they shall issue a plate or disc identifying that vehicle as a private hire vehicle in respect of which a vehicle licence has been granted.

(6) (*a*) Subject to the provisions of this Part of this Act, no person shall use or permit to be used in a controlled district as a private hire vehicle a vehicle in respect of which a licence has been granted under this section unless the plate or disc issued in

accordance with subsection (5) of this section is exhibited on the vehicle in such manner as the district council shall prescribe by condition attached to the grant of the licence.

(*b*) If any person without reasonable excuse contravenes the provisions of this subsection he shall be guilty of an offence.

(7) *[Omitted.]*

49. Transfer of hackney carriages and private hire vehicles

(1) If the proprietor of a hackney carriage or of a private hire vehicle in respect of which a vehicle licence has been granted by a district council transfers his interest in the hackney carriage or private hire vehicle to a person other than the proprietor whose name is specified in the licence, he shall within fourteen days after such transfer give notice in writing thereof to the district council specifying the name and address of the person to whom the hackney carriage or private hire vehicle has been transferred.

(2) If a proprietor without reasonable excuse fails to give notice to a district council as provided by subsection (1) of this section he shall be guilty of an offence.

50. Provisions as to proprietors

(1) Without prejudice to the provisions of section 68 of this Act, the proprietor of any hackney carriage or of any private hire vehicle licensed by a district council shall present such hackney carriage or private hire vehicle for inspection and testing by or on behalf of the council within such period and at such place within the area of the council as they may by notice reasonably require:

Provided that a district council shall not under the provisions of this subsection require a proprietor to present the same hackney carriage or private hire vehicle for inspection and testing on more than three separate occasions during any one period of twelve months.

(2) The proprietor of any hackney carriage or private hire vehicle—

(*a*) licensed by a district council under the Act of 1847 or under this Part of this Act; or

(*b*) in respect of which an application for a licence has been made to a district council under the Act of 1847 or under this Part of this Act;

shall, within such period as the district council may by notice reasonably require, state in writing the address of every place where such hackney carriage or private hire vehicle is kept when not in use, and shall if the district council so require afford to them such facilities as may be reasonably necessary to enable them to cause such hackney carriage or private hire vehicle to be inspected and tested there.

(3) Without prejudice to the provisions of [section 170 of the Act of 1988], the proprietor of a hackney carriage or of a private hire vehicle licensed by a district council shall report to them as soon as reasonably practicable, and in any case within seventy-two hours of the occurrence thereof, any accident to such hackney carriage or private hire vehicle causing damage materially affecting the safety, performance or appearance of the hackney carriage or private hire vehicle or the comfort or convenience of persons carried therein.

(4) The proprietor of any hackney carriage or of any private hire vehicle licensed by a district council shall at the request of any authorised officer of the council produce for inspection the vehicle licence for such hackney carriage or private hire vehicle

and the certificate of the policy of insurance or security required by [Part VI of the Act of 1988] in respect of such hackney carriage or private hire vehicle.

(5) If any person without reasonable excuse contravenes the provisions of this section, he shall be guilty of an offence.

[Section 50 is printed as amended by the Road Traffic (Consequential Provisions) Act 1988, s 4 and Sched 3, para 16(2).]

51. Licensing of drivers of private hire vehicles *[Omitted.]*

52. Appeals in respect of drivers' licences *[Omitted.]*

53. Drivers' licences for hackney carriages and private hire vehicles

(1) (*a*) Every licence granted by a district council under the provisions of this Part of this Act to any person to drive a private hire vehicle shall remain in force for three years from the date of such licence or for such lesser period as the district council may specify in such licence.

(*b*) Notwithstanding the provisions of the Public Health Act 1875 and the Town Police Clauses Act 1889, every licence granted by a district council under the provisions of the Act of 1847 to any person to drive a hackney carriage shall remain in force for three years from the date of such licence or for such lesser period as they may specify in such licence.

(2) Notwithstanding the provisions of the Act of 1847, a district council may demand and recover for the grant to any person of a licence to drive a hackney carriage, or a private hire vehicle, as the case may be, such a fee as they consider reasonable with a view to recovering the costs of issue and administration and may remit the whole or part of the fee in respect of a private hire vehicle in any case in which they think it appropriate to do so.

(3) The driver of any hackney carriage or of any private hire vehicle licensed by a district council shall at the request of any authorised officer of the council or of any constable produce for inspection his driver's licence either forthwith or—

(*a*) in the case of a request by an authorised officer, at the principal offices of the council before the expiration of the period of five days beginning with the day following that on which the request is made;

(*b*) in the case of a request by a constable, before the expiration of the period aforesaid at any police station which is within the area of the council and is nominated by the driver when the request is made.

(4) If any person without reasonable excuse contravenes the provisions of this section, he shall be guilty of an offence.

54. Issue of drivers' badges

(1) When granting a driver's licence under section 51 of this Act a district council shall issue a driver's badge in such a form as may from time to time be prescribed by them.

(2) (*a*) A driver shall at all times when acting in accordance with the driver's licence granted to him wear such badge in such position and manner as to be plainly and distinctly visible.

(*b*) If any person without reasonable excuse contravenes the provisions of this subsection, he shall be guilty of an offence.

55. Licensing of operators of private hire vehicles *[Omitted.]*

56. Operators of private hire vehicles

(1) For the purposes of this Part of this Act every contract for the hire of a private hire vehicle licensed under this Part of this Act shall be deemed to be made with the operator who accepted the booking for that vehicle whether or not he himself provided the vehicle.

(2) Every person to whom a licence in force under section 55 of this Act has been granted by a district council shall keep a record in such form as the council may, by condition attached to the grant of the licence, prescribe and shall enter therein, before the commencement of each journey, such particulars of every booking of a private hire vehicle invited or accepted by him, whether by accepting the same from the hirer or by undertaking it at the request of another operator, as the district council may by condition prescribe and shall produce such record on request to any authorised officer of the council or to any constable for inspection.

(3) Every person to whom a licence in force under section 55 of this Act has been granted by a district council shall keep such records as the council may, by condition attached to the grant of the licence, prescribe of the particulars of any private hire vehicle operated by him and shall produce the same on request to any authorised officer of the council or to any constable for inspection.

(4) A person to whom a licence in force under section 55 of this Act has been granted by a district council shall produce the licence on request to any authorised officer of the council or any constable for inspection.

(5) If any person without reasonable excuse contravenes the provisions of this section, he shall be guilty of an offence.

57. Power to require applicants to submit information

(1) A district council may require any applicant for a licence under the Act of 1847 or under this Part of this Act to submit to them such information as they may reasonably consider necessary to enable them to determine whether the licence should be granted and whether conditions should be attached to any such licence.

(2) Without prejudice to the generality of the foregoing subsection—

(*a*) a district council may require an applicant for a driver's licence in respect of a hackney carriage or a private hire vehicle—

(i) to produce a certificate signed by a registered medical practitioner to the effect that he is physically fit to be the driver of a hackney carriage or a private hire vehicle; and

(ii) whether or not such a certificate has been produced, to submit to examination by a registered medical practitioner selected by the district council as to his physical fitness to be the driver of a hackney carriage or a private hire vehicle;

(*b*) a district council may require an applicant for an operator's licence to submit to them such information as to—

(i) the name and address of the applicant;

(ii) the address or addresses whether within the area of the council or not from which he intends to carry on business in connection with private hire vehicles licensed under this Part of this Act;

(iii) any trade or business activities he has carried on before making the application;

(iv) any previous application he has made for an operator's licence;
(v) the revocation or suspension of any operator's licence previously held by him;
(vi) any convictions recorded against the applicant;

as they may reasonably consider necessary to enable them to determine whether to grant such licence;

(*c*) in addition to the information specified in paragraph (*b*) of this subsection, a district council may require an applicant for an operator's licence to submit to them—

(i) if the applicant is or has been a director or secretary of a company, information as to any convictions recorded against that company at any relevant time; any trade or business activities carried on by that company; any previous application made by that company for an operator's licence; and any revocation or suspension of an operator's licence previously held by that company;
(ii) if the applicant is a company, information as to any convictions recorded against a director or secretary of that company; any trade or business activities carried on by any such director or secretary; any previous application made by any such director or secretary for an operator's licence; and any revocation or suspension of an operator's licence previously held by such director or secretary;
(iii) if the applicant proposes to operate the vehicle in partnership with any other person, information as to any convictions recorded against that person; any trade or business activities carried on by that person; any previous application made by that person for an operator's licence; and any revocation or suspension of an operator's licence previously held by him.

(3) If any person knowingly or recklessly makes a false statement or omits any material particular in giving information under this section, he shall be guilty of an offence.

58. Return of identification plate or disc on revocation or expiry of licence etc

(1) On—

(*a*) the revocation or expiry of a vehicle licence in relation to a hackney carriage or private hire vehicle; or

(*b*) the suspension of a licence under section 68 of this Act;

a district council may by notice require the proprietor of that hackney carriage or private hire vehicle licensed by them to return to them within seven days after the service on him of that notice the plate or disc which—

(*a*) in the case of a hackney carriage, is required to be affixed to the carriage as mentioned in section 38 of the Act of 1847; and

(*b*) in the case of a private hire vehicle, was issued for the vehicle under section 48(5) of this Act.

(2) If any proprietor fails without reasonable excuse to comply with the terms of a notice under subsection (1) of this section—

(*a*) he shall be guilty of an offence and liable on summary conviction to a fine not exceeding [level 3 on the standard scale] and to a daily fine not exceeding [level 1 on the standard scale]; and (*b*) any authorised officer of the council or constable shall be entitled to remove and retain the said plate or disc from the said hackney carriage or private hire vehicle.

[Section 58 is printed as amended by the Criminal Justice Act 1982, ss 38 and 46.]

59. Qualifications for drivers of hackney carriages *[Omitted.]*

60. Suspension and revocation of vehicle licences *[Omitted.]*

61. Suspension and revocation of drivers' licences

(1) *[Omitted.]*

(2) (*a*) Where a district council suspend, revoke or refuse to renew any licence under this section they shall give to the driver notice of the grounds on which the licence has been suspended or revoked or on which they have refused to renew such licence within fourteen days of such suspension, revocation or refusal and the driver shall on demand return to the district council the driver's badge issued to him in accordance with section 54 of this Act.

(*b*) If any person without reasonable excuse contravenes the provisions of this section he shall be guilty of an offence and liable on summary conviction to a fine not exceeding [level 1 on the standard scale].

(3) *[Omitted.]*

[Section 61 is printed as amended by the Criminal Justice Act 1982, ss 38 and 46.]

62. Suspension and revocation of operators' licences *[Omitted.]*

63. Stands for hackney carriages *[Omitted.]*

64. Prohibition of other vehicles on hackney carriage stands

(1) No person shall cause or permit any vehicle other than a hackney carriage to wait on any stand for hackney carriages during any period for which that stand has been appointed, or is deemed to have been appointed, by a district council under the provisions of section 63 of this Act.

(2) Notice of the prohibition in this section shall be indicated by such traffic signs as may be prescribed or authorised for the purpose by the Secretary of State in pursuance of his powers under [section 64 of the Road Traffic Regulation Act 1984].

(3) If any person without reasonable excuse contravenes the provisions of this section, he shall be guilty of an offence.

(4) In any proceedings under this section against the driver of a public service vehicle it shall be a defence to show that, by reason of obstruction to traffic or for other compelling reason, he caused his vehicle to wait on a stand or part thereof and that he caused or permitted his vehicle so to wait only for so long as was reasonably necessary for the taking up or setting down of passengers.

[Section 64 is printed as amended by the Road Traffic Regulation Act 1984, s 146(a) and Sched 13, para 36.]

65. Fixing of fares for hackney carriages *[Omitted.]*

66. Fares for long journeys *[Omitted.]*

67. Hackney carriages used for private hire *[Omitted.]*

68. Fitness of hackney carriages and private hire vehicles

Any authorised officer of the council in question or any constable shall have power at all reasonable times to inspect and test, for the purpose of ascertaining its fitness any hackney carriage or private hire vehicle licensed by a district council, or any taximeter affixed to such a vehicle, and if he is not satisfied as to the fitness of the hackney carriage or private hire vehicle or as to the accuracy of its taximeter he may by notice in writing require the proprietor of the hackney carriage or private hire vehicle to make it or its taximeter available for further inspection and testing at such reasonable time and place as may be specified in the notice and suspend the vehicle licence until such time as such authorised officer or constable is so satisfied:

Provided that, if the authorised officer or constable is not so satisfied before the expiration of a period of two months, the said licence shall, by virtue of this section, be deemed to have been revoked and subsections (2) and (3) of section 60 of this Act shall apply with any necessary modifications.

69. Prolongation of journeys *[Omitted.]*

70. Fees for vehicle and operators' licences *[Omitted.]*

71. Taximeters *[Omitted.]*

72. Offences due to fault of other person

(1) Where an offence by any person under this Part of this Act is due to the act or default of another person, then, whether proceedings are taken against the first-mentioned person or not, that other person may be charged with and convicted of that offence, and shall be liable on conviction to the same punishment as might have been imposed on the first-mentioned person if he had been convicted of the offence.

(2) Section 44(3) of this Act shall apply to an offence under this Part of this Act as it applies to an offence under Part I of this Act.

73. Obstruction of authorised officers

(1) Any person who—

(*a*) wilfully obstructs an authorised officer or constable acting in pursuance of this Part of this Act or the Act of 1847; or

(*b*) without reasonable excuse fails to comply with any requirement properly made to him by such officer or constable under this Part of this Act; or

(*c*) without reasonable cause fails to give such an officer or constable so acting any other assistance or information which he may reasonably require of such person for the purpose of the performance of his functions under this Part of this Act or the Act of 1847;

shall be guilty of an offence.

(2) If any person, in giving any such information as is mentioned in the preceding subsection, makes any statement which he knows to be false, he shall be guilty of an offence.

74. Saving for certain businesses

Where any provision of this Part of this Act coming into operation on a day fixed by resolution under section 45 of this Act requires the licensing of a person carrying on any business, or of any vehicle used by a person in connection with any business, it shall be lawful for any person who—

(*a*) immediately before that day was carrying on that business; and

(*b*) had before that day duly applied for the licence required by that provision:

to continue to carry on that business until he is informed of the decision with regard to his application and, if the decision is adverse, during such further time as is provided under section 77 of this Act.

75. Saving for certain vehicles etc

(1) Nothing in this Part of this Act shall—

(*a*) apply to a vehicle used for bringing passengers or goods within a controlled district in pursuance of a contract for the hire of the vehicle made outside the district if the vehicle is not made available for hire within the district;

(*b*) apply to a vehicle used only for carrying passengers for hire or reward under a contract for the hire of the vehicle for a period of not less than seven days;

(*c*) apply to a vehicle while it is being used in connection with a funeral or a vehicle used wholly or mainly, by a person carrying on the business of a funeral director, for the purpose of funerals;

[(*cc*) apply to a vehicle while it is being used in connection with a wedding;]

(*d*) require the display of any plate, disc or notice in or on any private hire vehicle licensed by a council under this Part of this Act during such period that such vehicle is used for carrying passengers for hire or reward—

. . .

(ii) under a contract for the hire of the vehicle for a period of not less than 24 hours.

(2) Paragraphs (*a*), (*b*) and (*c*) of section 46(1) of this Act shall not apply to the use or driving of a vehicle or to the employment of a driver of a vehicle while the vehicle is used as a private hire vehicle in a controlled district if a licence issued under section 48 of this Act by the council whose area consists of or includes another controlled district is then in force for the vehicle and a driver's licence issued by such a council is then in force for the driver of the vehicle.

(3) Where a licence under section 48 of this Act is in force for a vehicle, the council which issued the licence may, by a notice in writing given to the proprietor of the vehicle, provide that paragraph (*a*) of subsection (6) of that section shall not apply to the vehicle on any occasion specified in the notice or shall not so apply while the notice is carried in the vehicle; and on any occasion on which by virtue of this subsection that paragraph does not apply to a vehicle section 54(2)(*a*) of this Act shall not apply to the driver of the vehicle.

[Section 75 is printed as amended by the Transport Act 1985, s 139(2) and Sched 7, para 17(2). (A further amendment, which applies only in Scotland, has not been incorporated.)]

76. Penalties

Any person who commits an offence against any of the provisions of this Part of this Act in respect of which no penalty is expressly provided shall be liable on summary conviction to a fine not exceeding [level 3 on the standard scale].

[Section 76 is printed as amended by the Criminal Justice Act 1982, ss 38 and 46.]

77. Appeals (against decisions of district councils) *[Omitted.]*

78. Application of provisions of Act of 1936 *[Omitted.]*

79. Authentication of licences *[Omitted.]*

80. Interpretation of Part II

(1) In this Part of this Act, unless the subject or context otherwise requires—

'the Act of 1847' means the provisions of the Town Police Clauses Act 1847 with respect to hackney carriages;

'the Act of 1936' means the Public Health Act 1936;

. . .

'authorised officer' means any officer of a district council authorised in writing by the council for the purposes of this Part of this Act;

'contravene' includes fail to comply;

'controlled district' means any area for which this Part of this Act is in force by virtue of a resolution passed by a district council under section 45 of this Act;

'daily fine' means a fine for each day during which an offence continues after conviction thereof;

'the district', in relation to a district council in whose area the provisions of this Part of this Act are in force, means—

(*a*) if those provisions are in force throughout the area of the council, that area; and

(*b*) if those provisions are in force for part only of the area of the council, that part of that area;

'driver's badge' means, in relation to the driver of a hackney carriage, any badge issued by a district council under byelaws made under section 68 of the Act of 1847 and, in relation to the driver of a private hire vehicle, any badge issued by a district council under section 54 of this Act;

'driver's licence' means, in relation to the driver of a hackney carriage, a licence under section 46 of the Act of 1847 and, in relation to the driver of a private hire vehicle, a licence under section 51 of this Act;

'hackney carriage' has the same meaning as in the Act of 1847 [*qv*];

'hackney carriage byelaws' means the byelaws for the time being in force in the controlled district in question relating to hackney carriages;

['London cab' means a vehicle which is a hackney carriage within the meaning of the Metropolitan Public Carriage Act 1869 [*qv*];]

'operate' means in the course of business to make provision for the invitation or acceptance of bookings for a private hire vehicle;

'operator's licence' means a licence under section 55 of this Act;

'private hire vehicle' means a motor vehicle constructed or adapted to seat [fewer than nine passengers], other than a hackney carriage or public service vehicle [or a London cab], which is provided for hire with the services of a driver for the purpose of carrying passengers;

'proprietor' includes a part-proprietor and, in relation to a vehicle which is the subject of a hiring agreement or hire-purchase agreement, means the person in possession of the vehicle under that agreement;

'public service vehicle' has the same meaning as in [the Public Passenger Vehicles Act 1981];

'taximeter' means any device for calculating the fare to be charged in respect of any journey in a hackney carriage or private hire vehicle by reference to the distance travelled or time elapsed since the start of the journey, or a combination of both; and

'vehicle licence' means in relation to a hackney carriage a licence under sections 37 to 45 of the Act of 1847 [in relation to a London cab a licence under section 6 of the Metropolitan Public Carriage Act 1869] and in relation to a private hire vehicle means a licence under section 48 of this Act.

(2) In this Part of this Act references to a licence, in connection with a controlled district, are references to a licence issued by the council whose area consists of or includes that district, and 'licensed' shall be construed accordingly.

(3) Except where the context otherwise requires, any reference in this Part of this Act to any enactment shall be construed as a reference to that enactment as applied, extended, amended or varied by, or by virtue of, any subsequent enactment including this Act.

[Section 80 is printed as amended by the Transport Act 1980, s 43(1) and Sched 5, Part II; the Public Passenger Vehicles Act 1981, s 88(2) and Sched 7, para 20; the Transport Act 1985, s 139(2) and Sched 7, para 17(3); the Road Traffic (Consequential Provisions) Act 1988, s 3(1) and Sched 1, Part I.]

* * *

The London Regional Transport Act 1984

(1984 c 32)

An Act to make provision with respect to transport in and around greater London and for connected purposes.

[26th June 1984]

*   *   *

68. Interpretation

In this Act—

. . .

'subsidiary' (subject to section 62 of this Act) means, in relation to any body corporate, a body corporate which is a subsidiary of the first-mentioned body corporate as defined by [section 736 of the Companies Act 1985 [*qv*]] (taking references in that section to a company as being references to a body corporate);

. . .

'wholly owned subsidiary' means a subsidiary all the securities of which are owned by a body of which it is a subsidiary, or by one or more other wholly owned subsidiaries of that body, or partly by that body and partly by any wholly owned subsidiary of that body.

[The definition of 'wholly owned subsidiary' is incorporated by reference into the Community Drivers' Hours and Recording Equipment (Exemptions and Supplementary Provisions) Regulations 1986 (SI 1986 No 1456), Schedule, Part I (qv).

The text above is printed as amended by the Companies Consolidation (Consequential Provisions) Act 1985, s 31(6).

Section 62 of the London Regional Transport Act 1984 (to which reference is made in the definition of 'subsidiary' above) relates to joint subsidiaries of London Regional Transport and the Railways Board.]

*   *   *

The Magistrates' Courts Act 1980

(1980 c 43)

An Act to consolidate certain enactments relating to the jurisdiction of, and the practice and procedure before, magistrates' courts . . . .

[1st August 1980]

* * *

32. Penalties on summary conviction for offences triable either way

(1) *[Omitted.]*

(2) For any offence triable either way which is not listed in Schedule 1 to this Act, being an offence under a relevant enactment, the maximum fine which may be imposed on summary conviction shall by virtue of this subsection be the prescribed sum unless the offence is one for which by virtue of an enactment other than this subsection a larger fine may be imposed on summary conviction.

(3)–(8) *[Omitted.]*

(9) In this section—

'fine' includes a pecuniary penalty but does not include a pecuniary forfeiture or pecuniary compensation;

'the prescribed sum' means [£2,000] or such sum as is for the time being substituted in this definition by an order in force under section 143(1) below;

'relevant enactment' means an enactment contained in the Criminal Law Act 1977 or in any Act passed before, or in the same Session as, that Act.

[Section 32 is printed as amended by the Criminal Penalties etc (Increase) Order 1984 (SI 1984 No 447).

The definition of the 'prescribed sum' in this section has been incorporated by reference into the Interpretation Act 1978, Sched 1 (qv).

None of the offences listed in Sched 1 to this Act (to which s 32(2) refers) is a road traffic offence.

Article 1(2) of SI 1984 No 447 reads:

'This Order shall not affect the amount of any fine imposed, nor the amount of any compensation order made, in respect of any offence committed before 1st May 1984 nor the amount of any fine imposed in respect of any act or omission taking place before that date.'

Before 1 May 1984 the amount of the prescribed sum was £1,000.]

40. Restriction on amount payable under compensation order of magistrates' court

(1) The compensation to be paid under a compensation order made by a magistrates' court in respect of any offence of which the court has convicted the offender shall not exceed [£2,000]; and the compensation or total compensation to be paid under a compensation order or compensation orders made by a magistrates' court in respect of any offence or offences taken into consideration in determining sentence

shall not exceed the difference (if any) between the amount or total amount which under the preceding provisions of this subsection is the maximum for the offence or offences of which the offender has been convicted and the amount or total amounts (if any) which are in fact ordered to be paid in respect of that offence or those offences.

(2) In subsection (1) above 'compensation order' has the meaning assigned to it by section 35(1) of the Powers of Criminal Courts Act 1973 [*qv*].

[Section 40 is printed as amended by the Criminal Penalties etc (Increase) Order 1984 (SI 1984 No 447).]

* * *

141. Clerks to justices

(1) Any reference in this Act to a clerk of any magistrates' court shall be construed as a reference to the clerk to the justices for the petty sessions area for which the court is acting, or was acting at the relevant time.

(2) Where there is more than one clerk to the justices for any petty sessions area, anything that this Act requires or authorises to be done by or to the clerk to the justices shall or may be done by or to any of the clerks or by or to such of the clerks as the magistrates' courts committee having power over the appointment of clerks to justices for that area generally or in any particular case or cases may direct.

(3) Subsections (1) and (2) above shall apply to the justices' clerks for the inner London area as if the reference in subsection (2) to the magistrates' courts committee were a reference to the committee of magistrates.

[Section 141 is incorporated by reference into s 41(13) of the Criminal Justice Act 1988, qv.]

* * *

148. 'Magistrates' court'

(1) In this Act the expression 'magistrates' court' means any justice or justices of the peace acting under any enactment or by virtue of his or their commission or under the common law.

(2) *[Omitted.]*

[The definition in subs (1) is incorporated by reference into the Public Passenger Vehicles Act 1981, s 82, below.]

* * *

150. Interpretation of other terms

(1) In this Act, unless the context otherwise requires, the following expressions have the meanings hereby assigned to them, that is to say—

. . .

['petty sessions area' has the same meaning as in the Justices of the Peace Act 1979;]

. . .

(2)–(7) *[Omitted.]*

[The above definition is incorporated by reference into the Road Traffic Act 1988, s 192, and the Road Traffic Offenders Act 1988, s 89 (qv). It is printed as substituted by the Local Government Act 1985, s 12(11).]

* * *

The Metropolitan Public Carriage Act 1869

(32 & 33 Vict c 115)

An Act for amending the law relating to hackney and stage carriages within the Metropolitan Police District.

[11th August 1869]

*   *   *

2. Limits of Act

The limits of this Act shall be the metropolitan police district, and the city of London and the liberties thereof.

*   *   *

4. Interpretation

In this Act 'stage carriage' shall mean any carriage for the conveyance of passengers which plies for hire in any public street, road, or place within the limits of this Act, and in which the passengers or any of them are charged to pay separate and distinct or at the rate of separate and distinct fares for their respective places or seats therein.

'Hackney carriage' shall mean any carriage for the conveyance of passengers which plies for hire within the limits of this Act, and is not a stage carriage.

'Prescribed' shall mean prescribed by order of one of Her Majesty's Principal Secretaries of State.

[The definition of 'hackney carriage' in this Act is incorporated by reference into s 80 of the Local Government (Miscellaneous Provisions) Act 1976 (qv).]

The Police Act 1964

(1964 c 48)

An Act to re-enact with modifications certain enactments relating to police forces in England and Wales . . . .

[10th June 1964]

* * *

SCHEDULE 8

MEANING OF POLICE AREA, &C

Police area	Police authority	Chief Officer of Police
The City of London	The Common Council	The Commissioner of City of London Police
The metropolitan police district	The Secretary of State	The Commissioner of Police of the metropolis
[A non-metropolitan county	The police committee	The chief constable]
[A metropolitan county	The metropolitan county police authority	The chief constable]
[The Northumbria police area	The Northumbria police authority	The chief constable]
A combined area	The combined police authority	The chief constable
. . .	. . .	. . .

[The meanings of 'chief officer of police' and 'police area' are incorporated by reference into the Motor Vehicles (Authorisation of Special Types) General Order 1979 (SI 1979 No 1198), art 3, the Road Vehicles (Construction and Use) Regulations 1986 (SI 1986 No 1078), Sched 12, para 1, and the Road Vehicles Lighting Regulations 1984 (SI 1984 No 812), reg 3(2) (qv). The text of Sched 8 (restricted to those items) is printed as amended by the Statute Law (Repeals) Act 1971; the Local Government Act 1972, s 272 and Sched 30; the Local Government Act 1985, s 37 and Sched 11.]

* * *

The Police and Criminal Evidence Act 1984

(1984 c 60)

An Act to make further provision in relation to the powers and duties of the police . . .
[31st October 1984]

ARRANGEMENT OF PARTS

*   *   *

PART I

Powers to Stop and Search

1. Power of constable to stop and search persons, vehicles etc

(1) A constable may exercise any power conferred by this section—

(*a*) in any place to which at the time when he proposes to exercise the power the public or any section of the public has access, on payment or otherwise, as of right or by virtue of express or implied permission; or

(*b*) in any other place to which people have ready access at the time when he proposes to exercise the power but which is not a dwelling.

(2) Subject to subsections (3) to (5) below, a constable—

(*a*) may search—

(i) any person or vehicle;

(ii) anything which is in or on a vehicle,

for stolen or prohibited articles [or any article to which subsection (8A) below applies]; and

(*b*) may detain a person or vehicle for the purpose of such a search.

(3) This section does not give a constable power to search a person or vehicle or anything in or on a vehicle unless he has reasonable grounds for suspecting that he will find stolen or prohibited articles [or any article to which subsection (8A) below applies].

(4) *[Omitted.]*

(5) If a vehicle is in a garden or yard occupied with and used for the purposes of a dwelling or on other land so occupied and used, a constable may not search the vehicle or anything in or on it in the exercise of the power conferred by this section unless he has reasonable grounds for believing—

(*a*) that the person in charge of the vehicle does not reside in the dwelling; and

(*b*) that the vehicle is not in the place in question with the express or implied permission of a person who resides in the dwelling.

(6) If in the course of such a search a constable discovers an article which he has reasonable grounds for suspecting to be a stolen or prohibited article [or an article to which subsection (8A) below applies], he may seize it.

(7) An article is prohibited for the purposes of this Part of this Act if it is—

(*a*) an offensive weapon; or

(*b*) an article—

(i) made or adapted for use in the course of or in connection with an offence to which this sub-paragraph applies; or

(ii) intended by the person having it with him for such use by him or by some other person.

(8) The offences to which subsection (7)(*b*)(i) above applies are—

(*a*) burglary;

(*b*) theft;

(*c*) offences under section 12 of the Theft Act 1968 (taking motor vehicle or other conveyance without authority); and

(*d*) offences under section 15 of that Act (obtaining property by deception).

[(8A) *[Applies to offence of having article with blade or point in public place.]*]

(9) In this Part of this Act 'offensive weapon' means any article—

(*a*) made or adapted for use for causing injury to persons; or

(*b*) intended by the person having it with him for such use by him or by some other person.

[Section 1 is printed as amended by the Criminal Justice Act 1988, s 140(1), with effect from 29 September 1988 (see ibid, s 170(6)).

Guidance on what constitutes 'reasonable grounds for suspicion' that particular articles are being carried for the purpose of the exercise of a statutory power of stopping and searching (eg as in s 1(3)) is given in Annex B to the code of practice on the exercise by police officers of statutory powers of stop and search, issued by the Home Secretary under s 66 of this Act. Annex B reads as follows:

'1 Reasonable suspicion does not require *certainty* that an unlawful article is being carried; nor does the officer concerned have to be satisfied of this beyond reasonable doubt. Reasonable suspicion, in contrast to *mere* suspicion, must be founded on fact. There must be some concrete basis for the officer's suspicion, related to the individual person concerned, which can be considered and evaluated by an objective third person. Mere suspicion, in contrast, is a hunch or instinct which cannot be explained or justified to an objective observer. An officer who has such a hunch or instinct may well be justified in continuing to keep the person under observation or speak to him, but additional grounds which bring up mere suspicion to the level of reasonable suspicion are needed before he may exercise the powers dealt with in this code.

2 Reasonable suspicion may arise from the nature of the property observed or being carried or suspected of being carried coupled with other factors including the time, the place or the suspicious behaviour of the person concerned or those with him. The decision to search must be based on all the facts which, to a careful officer, bear on the likelihood that an article of a certain kind will be found, and not only on what can be seen at the time. So an officer with prior knowledge of the behaviour of someone he sees in a certain situation, or acting on information received (such as a description of a suspected offender) may have reasonable grounds for searching him although another officer would not.

3 Reasonable suspicion cannot be supported on the basis simply of a higher than average chance that the person has committed or is committing an offence, for example because he belongs to a group within which offenders of a certain kind are relatively common, or because of a combination of factors such as these. For example, a person's colour of itself can never be a reasonable ground for suspicion. The mere fact alone that a person is carrying a particular kind of property or is dressed in a certain way or has a certain hairstyle is likewise not of itself sufficient. Nor is the fact that a person is known to have a previous conviction for unlawful possession of an article.

4 The degree or level of suspicion required to establish the reasonable grounds justifying the exercise of powers of stop and search is no less than the degree or level of suspicion required to effect an arrest without warrant for any of the suspected offences to which these powers relate. The powers of stop and search provide an opportunity to establish the commission or otherwise of certain kinds of offences without arrest and may therefore render arrest unnecessary.

5 Paragraph 4 above is subject to the principle that where a police officer has reasonable grounds to suspect that a person is in *innocent* possession of a stolen or prohibited article, the power of stop and search exists notwithstanding that there would be no power of arrest. However every effort should be made to secure the voluntary production of the article before the power is resorted to.']

2. Provisions relating to search under section 1 and other powers

(1) A constable who detains a person or vehicle in the exercise—

(*a*) of the power conferred by section 1 above; or

(*b*) of any other power—

(i) to search a person without first arresting him; or

(ii) to search a vehicle without making an arrest,

need not conduct a search if it appears to him subsequently—

(i) that no search is required; or

(ii) that a search is impracticable.

(2) If a constable contemplates a search, other than a search of an unattended vehicle, in the exercise—

(*a*) of the power conferred by section 1 above; or

(*b*) of any other power, except the power conferred by section 6 below and the power conferred by section 27(2) of the Aviation Security Act 1982—

(i) to search a person without first arresting him; or

(ii) to search a vehicle without making an arrest,

it shall be his duty, subject to subsection (4) below, to take reasonable steps before he commences the search to bring to the attention of the appropriate person—

(i) if the constable is not in uniform, documentary evidence that he is a constable; and

(ii) whether he is in uniform or not, the matters specified in subsection (3) below;

and the constable shall not commence the search until he has performed that duty.

(3) The matters referred to in subsection (2)(ii) above are—

(*a*) the constable's name and the name of the police station to which he is attached;

(*b*) the object of the proposed search;

(*c*) the constable's grounds for proposing to make it; and

(*d*) the effect of section 3(7) or (8) below, as may be appropriate.

(4) A constable need not bring the effect of section 3(7) or (8) below to the attention of the appropriate person if it appears to the constable that it will not be practicable to make the record in section 3(1) below.

(5) In this section 'the appropriate person' means—

(*a*) if the constable proposes to search a person, that person; and

(*b*) if he proposes to search a vehicle, or anything in or on a vehicle, the person in charge of the vehicle.

(6) On completing a search of an unattended vehicle or anything in or on such a vehicle in the exercise of any such power as is mentioned in subsection (2) above a constable shall leave a notice—

(*a*) stating that he has searched it;

(*b*) giving the name of the police station to which he is attached;

(*c*) stating that an application for compensation for any damage caused by the search may be made to that police station; and

(*d*) stating the effect of section 3(8) below.

(7) The constable shall leave the notice inside the vehicle unless it is not reasonably practicable to do so without damaging the vehicle.

(8) The time for which a person or vehicle may be detained for the purposes of such a search is such time as is reasonably required to permit a search to be carried out either at the place where the person or vehicle was first detained or nearby.

(9) Neither the power conferred by section 1 above nor any other power to detain and search a person without first arresting him or to detain and search a vehicle without making an arrest is to be construed—

(*a*) as authorising a constable to require a person to remove any of his clothing in public other than an outer coat, jacket or gloves; or

(*b*) as authorising a constable not in uniform to stop a vehicle.

(10) This section and section 1 above apply to vessels, aircraft and hovercraft as they apply to vehicles.

3. Duty to make records concerning searches

(1) Where a constable has carried out a search in the exercise of any such power as is mentioned in section 2(1) above, other than a search—

(*a*) under section 6 below; or

(*b*) under section 27(2) of the Aviation Security Act 1982,

he shall make a record of it in writing unless it is not practicable to do so.

(2)–(6) *[Omitted.]*

(7) If a constable who conducted a search of a person made a record of it, the person who was searched shall be entitled to a copy of the record if he asks for one before the end of the period specified in subsection (9) below.

(8) If—

(*a*) the owner of a vehicle which has been searched or the person who was in charge of the vehicle at the time when it was searched asks for a copy of the record of the search before the end of the period specified in subsection (9) below; and

(*b*) the constable who conducted the search made a record of it,

the person who made the request shall be entitled to a copy.

(9) The period mentioned in subsections (7) and (8) above is the period of 12 months beginning with the date on which the search was made.

(10) The requirements imposed by this section with regard to records of searches of vehicles shall apply also to records of searches of vessels, aircraft and hovercraft.

4. Road checks

(1) This section shall have effect in relation to the conduct of road checks by police officers for the purpose of ascertaining whether a vehicle is carrying—

(*a*) a person who has committed an offence other than a road traffic offence or a vehicles excise offence;

(*b*) a person who is a witness to such an offence;

(*c*) a person intending to commit such an offence; or

(*d*) a person who is unlawfully at large.

(2) For the purposes of this section a road check consists of the exercise in a locality of the power conferred by [section 163 of the Road Traffic Act 1988] in such a way as to stop during the period for which its exercise in that way in that locality continues all vehicles or vehicles selected by any criterion.

(3) Subject to subsection (5) below, there may only be such a road check if a police officer of the rank of superintendent or above authorises it in writing.

(4) An officer may only authorise a road check under subsection (3) above—

(*a*) for the purpose specified in subsection (1)(*a*) above, if he has reasonable grounds—

(i) for believing that the offence is a serious arrestable offence; and

(ii) for suspecting that the person is, or is about to be, in the locality in which vehicles would be stopped if the road check were authorised;

(*b*) for the purpose specified in subsection (1)(*b*) above, if he has reasonable grounds for believing that the offence is a serious arrestable offence;

(*c*) for the purpose specified in subsection (1)(*c*) above, if he has reasonable grounds—

(i) for believing that the offence would be a serious arrestable offence; and

(ii) for suspecting that the person is, or is about to be, in the locality in which vehicles would be stopped if the road check were authorised;

(*d*) for the purpose specified in subsection (1)(*d*) above, if he has reasonable grounds for suspecting that the person is, or is about to be, in that locality.

(5) An officer below the rank of superintendent may authorise such a road check if it appears to him that it is required as a matter of urgency for one of the purposes specified in subsection (1) above.

(6) If an authorisation is given under subsection (5) above, it shall be the duty of the officer who gives it—

(*a*) to make a written record of the time at which he gives it; and

(*b*) to cause an officer of the rank of superintendent or above to be informed that it has been given.

(7) The duties imposed by subsection (6) above shall be performed as soon as it is practicable to do so.

(8) An officer to whom a report is made under subsection (6) above may, in writing, authorise the road check to continue.

(9) If such an officer considers that the road check should not continue, he shall record in writing—

(*a*) the fact that it took place; and

(*b*) the purpose for which it took place.

(10) An officer giving an authorisation under this section shall specify the locality in which vehicles are to be stopped.

(11) An officer giving an authorisation under this section, other than an authorisation under subsection (5) above—

(*a*) shall specify a period, not exceeding seven days, during which the road check may continue; and

(*b*) may direct that the road check—

(i) shall be continuous; or

(ii) shall be conducted at specified times,

during that period.

(12) If it appears to an officer of the rank of superintendent or above that a road check ought to continue beyond the period for which it has been authorised he may, from time to time, in writing specify a further period, not exceeding seven days, during which it may continue.

(13) Every written authorisation shall specify—

(*a*) the name of the officer giving it;

(*b*) the purpose of the road check; and

(*c*) the locality in which vehicles are to be stopped.

(14) The duties to specify the purposes of a road check imposed by subsections (9) and (13) above include duties to specify any relevant serious arrestable offence.

(15) Where a vehicle is stopped in a road check, the person in charge of the vehicle at the time when it is stopped shall be entitled to obtain a written statement of the purpose of the road check if he applies for such a statement not later than the end of the period of twelve months from the day on which the vehicle was stopped.

(16) Nothing in this section affects the exercise by police officers of any power to stop vehicles for purposes other than those specified in subsection (1) above.

[Section 4 is printed as amended by the Road Traffic (Consequential Provisions) Act 1988, s 4 and Sched 3, para 27(1).

'Serious arrestable offences' are described in s 116 of and Sched 5 to this Act (qv).]

* * *

6. Statutory undertakers etc

(1) A constable employed by statutory undertakers may stop, detain and search any vehicle before it leaves a goods area included in the premises of the statutory undertakers.

(2) In this section 'goods area' means any area used wholly or mainly for the storage or handling of goods.

(3), (4) *[Omitted.]*

[The application of the code of practice for the exercise by police officers of statutory powers of stop and search issued under s 66 of the Act to this section is expressly excluded; see para 1.4(ii) of the code.]

7. Part I—supplementary

(1), (2) *[Omitted.]*

(3) In this Part of this Act 'statutory undertakers' means persons authorised by any enactment to carry on any railway, light railway, road transport, water transport, canal, inland navigation, dock or harbour undertaking.

* * *

PART III

ARREST

24. Arrest without warrant for arrestable offences

(1) The powers of summary arrest conferred by the following subsections shall apply—

(*a*) to offences for which the sentence is fixed by law;

(*b*) to offences for which a person of 21 years of age or over (not previously convicted) may be sentenced to imprisonment for a term of five years (or might be so sentenced but for the restrictions imposed by section 33 of the Magistrates' Courts Act 1980); and

(*c*) to the offences to which subsection (2) below applies, and in this Act 'arrestable offence' means any such offence.

(2) The offences to which this subsection applies are—

(*a*) offences for which a person may be arrested under the Customs and Excise Acts, as defined in section 1(1) of the Customs and Excise Management Act 1979;

(*b*) offences under the Official Secrets Acts 1911 and 1920 that are not arrestable offences by virtue of the term of imprisonment for which a person may be sentenced in respect of them;

(*c*) offences under section 14 (indecent assault on a woman), 22 (causing prostitution of women) or 23 (procuration of girl under 21) of the Sexual Offences Act 1956;

(*d*) offences under section 12(1) (taking motor vehicle or other conveyance without authority etc) or 25(1) (going equipped for stealing, etc) of the Theft Act 1968; and

(*e*) *[Repealed.]*

(3) Without prejudice to section 2 of the Criminal Attempts Act 1981, the powers of summary arrest conferred by the following subsections shall also apply to the offences of—

(*a*) conspiring to commit any of the offences mentioned in subsection (2) above;

(*b*) attempting to commit any such offence [other than an offence under section 12(1) of the Theft Act 1968];

(*c*) inciting, aiding, abetting, counselling or procuring the commission of any such offence;

and such offences are also arrestable offences for the purposes of this Act.

(4) Any person may arrest without a warrant—

(*a*) anyone who is in the act of committing an arrestable offence;

(*b*) anyone whom he has reasonable grounds for suspecting to be committing such an offence.

(5) Where an arrestable offence has been committed, any person may arrest without a warrant—

(*a*) anyone who is guilty of the offence;

(*b*) anyone whom he has reasonable grounds for suspecting to be guilty of it.

(6) Where a constable has reasonable grounds for suspecting that an arrestable offence has been committed, he may arrest without a warrant anyone whom he has reasonable grounds for suspecting to be guilty of the offence.

(7) A constable may arrest without a warrant—

(*a*) anyone who is about to commit an arrestable offence;

(*b*) anyone whom he has reasonable grounds for suspecting to be about to commit an arrestable offence.

[Section 24 is printed as amended by the Criminal Justice Act 1988, s 170(1) and (2) and Sched 15, para 98, and Sched 16 (the amendment to s 24(3)(b) took effect on 29 July 1988 and the amendment to s 24(2)(e) took effect on 29 September 1988; see ibid, s 171(5) and (6)).

Section 33 of the Magistrates' Courts Act 1980 (to which s 24(1)(b) refers) restricts the sentence which a court may impose in relation to certain criminal damage offences.

For the Theft Act 1968, ss 12 and 25, see below.]

25. General arrest conditions

(1) Where a constable has reasonable grounds for suspecting that any offence which is not an arrestable offence has been committed or attempted, or is being committed or attempted, he may arrest the relevant person if it appears to him that service of a summons is impracticable or inappropriate because any of the general arrest conditions is satisfied.

(2) In this section 'the relevant person' means any person whom the constable has

reasonable grounds to suspect of having committed or having attempted to commit the offence or of being in the course of committing or attempting to commit it.

(3) The general arrest conditions are—

(*a*) that the name of the relevant person is unknown to, and cannot be readily ascertained by, the constable;

(*b*) that the constable has reasonable grounds for doubting whether a name furnished by the relevant person as his name is his real name;

(*c*) that—

(i) the relevant person has failed to furnish a satisfactory address for service; or

(ii) the constable has reasonable grounds for doubting whether an address furnished by the relevant person is a satisfactory address for service;

(*d*) that the constable has reasonable grounds for believing that arrest is necessary to prevent the relevant person—

(i) causing physical injury to himself or any other person;
(ii) suffering physical injury;
(iii) causing loss of or damage to property;
(iv) committing an offence against public decency; or
(v) causing an unlawful obstruction of the highway;

(*e*) that the constable has reasonable grounds for believing that arrest is necessary to protect a child or other vulnerable person from the relevant person.

(4) For the purposes of subsection (3) above an address is a satisfactory address for service if it appears to the constable—

(*a*) that the relevant person will be at it for a sufficiently long period for it to be possible to serve him with a summons; or

(*b*) that some other person specified by the relevant person will accept service of a summons for the relevant person at it.

(5) Nothing in subsection (3)(*d*) above authorises the arrest of a person under sub-paragraph (iv) of that paragraph except where members of the public going about their normal business cannot reasonably be expected to avoid the person to be arrested.

(6) This section shall not prejudice any power of arrest conferred apart from this section.

26. Repeal of statutory powers of arrest without warrant or order

(1) Subject to subsection (2) below, so much of any Act (including a local Act) passed before this Act as enables a constable—

(*a*) to arrest a person for an office without a warrant; or

(*b*) to arrest a person otherwise than for an offence without a warrant or an order of a court,

shall cease to have effect.

(2) Nothing in this subsection (1) above affects the enactments specified in Schedule 2 to this Act.

[The enactments originally listed in Sched 2 to this Act included ss 5(5), 7 and 10 of the Road

Traffic Act 1972; reference to these provisions in Sched 2 was repealed by the Road Traffic (Consequential Provisions) Act 1988, s 3(1) and Sched 1, Part I.]

* * *

31. Arrest for further offence

Where—

(*a*) a person—

(i) has been arrested for an offence; and

(ii) is at a police station in consequence of that arrest; and

(*b*) it appears to a constable that, if he were released from that arrest, he would be liable to arrest for some other offence,

he shall be arrested for that other offence.

* * *

PART IV

Detention

Detention—conditions and duration

34. Limitations on police detention

(1) A person arrested for an offence shall not be kept in police detention except in accordance with the provisions of this Part of this Act.

(2) Subject to subsection (3) below, if at any time a custody officer—

(*a*) becomes aware, in relation to any person in police detention, that the grounds for the detention of that person have ceased to apply; and

(*b*) is not aware of any other grounds on which the continued detention of that person could be justified under the provisions of this Part of this Act,

it shall be the duty of the custody officer, subject to subsection (4) below, to order his immediate release from custody.

(3) No person in police detention shall be released except on the authority of a custody officer at the police station where his detention was authorised or, if it was authorised at more than one station, a custody officer at the station where it was last authorised.

(4) A person who appears to the custody officer to have been unlawfully at large when he was arrested is not to be released under subsection (2) above.

(5) A person whose release is ordered under subsection (2) above shall be released without bail unless it appears to the custody officer—

(*a*) that there is need for further investigation of any matter in connection with which he was detained at any time during the period of his detention; or

(*b*) that proceedings may be taken against him in respect of any such matter,

and, if it so appears, he shall be released on bail.

(6) For the purposes of this Part of this Act a person arrested under [section 6(5) of the Road Traffic Act 1988] is arrested for an offence.

[Section 34 is printed as amended by the Road Traffic (Consequential Provisions) Act 1988, s 4 and Sched 3, para 27(2).]

35. Designated police stations

(1) The chief officer of police for each police area shall designate the police stations in his area which, subject to section 30(3) and (5) above, are to be the stations in that area to be used for the purpose of detaining arrested persons.

(2), (3) *[Omitted.]*

(4) In this Act 'designated police station' means a police station for the time being designated under this section.

36. Custody officers at police stations

(1) One or more custody officers shall be appointed for each designated police station.

(2) A custody officer for a designated police station shall be appointed—

(*a*) by the chief officer of police for the area in which the designated police station is situated; or

(*b*) by such other police officer as the chief officer of police for that area may direct.

(3) No officer may be appointed a custody officer unless he is of at least the rank of sergeant.

(4) An officer of any rank may perform the functions of a custody officer at a designated police station if a custody officer is not readily available to perform them.

(5) Subject to the following provisions of this section and to section 39(2) below, none of the functions of a custody officer in relation to a person shall be performed by an officer who at the time when the function falls to be performed is involved in the investigation of an offence for which that person is in police detention at that time.

(6) Nothing in subsection (5) above is to be taken to prevent a custody officer—

(*a*) performing any function assigned to custody officers—

(i) by this Act; or

(ii) by a code of practice issued under this Act;

(*b*) carrying out the duty imposed on custody officers by section 39 below;

(*c*) doing anything in connection with the identification of a suspect; or

(*d*) doing anything under [sections 7 and 8 of the Road Traffic Act 1988].

(7) Where an arrested person is taken to a police station which is not a designated police station, the functions in relation to him which at a designated police station would be the functions of a custody officer shall be performed—

(*a*) by an officer who is not involved in the investigation of an offence for which he is in police detention, if such an officer is readily available; and

(*b*) if no such officer is readily available, by the officer who took him to the station or any other officer.

(8) References to a custody officer in the following provisions of this Act include references to an officer other than a custody officer who is performing the functions of a custody officer by virtue of subsection (4) or (7) above.

(9) Where by virtue of subsection (7) above an officer of a force maintained by a

police authority who took an arrested person to a police station is to perform the functions of a custody officer in relation to him, the officer shall inform an officer who—

(*a*) is attached to a designated police station; and

(*b*) is of at least the rank of inspector,

that he is to do so.

(10) The duty imposed by subsection (9) above shall be performed as soon as it is practicable to perform it.

[Section 36 is printed as amended by the Road Traffic (Consequential Provisions) Act 1988, s 4 and Sched 3, para 27(3).]

37. Duties of custody officer before charge

(1) Where—

(*a*) a person is arrested for an offence—

(i) without a warrant; or

(ii) under a warrant not endorsed for bail, or

(*b*) a person returns to a police station to answer to bail,

the custody officer at each police station where he is detained after his arrest shall determine whether he has before him sufficient evidence to charge that person with the offence for which he was arrested and may detain him at the police station for such period as is necessary to enable him to do so.

(2) If the custody officer determines that he does not have such evidence before him, the person arrested shall be released either on bail or without bail, unless the custody officer has reasonable grounds for believing that his detention without being charged is necessary to secure or preserve evidence relating to an offence for which he is under arrest or to obtain evidence by questioning him.

(3) If the custody officer has reasonable grounds for so believing, he may authorise the person arrested to be kept in police detention.

(4)–(6) *[Written record of grounds for detention.]*

(7) Subject to section 41(7) below, if the custody officer determines that he has before him sufficient evidence to charge the person arrested with the offence for which he was arrested, the person arrested—

(*a*) shall be charged; or

(*b*) shall be released without charge, either on bail or without bail.

(8) Where—

(*a*) a person is released under subsection (7)(*b*) above; and

(*b*) at the time of his release a decision whether he should be prosecuted for the offence for which he was arrested has not been taken,

it shall be the duty of the custody officer so to inform him.

(9) If the person arrested is not in a fit state to be dealt with under subsection (7) above, he may be kept in police detention until he is.

(10) *[Duty under s 37(1) to be performed as soon as practicable.]*

(11)–(14) *[Arrested juveniles.]*

(15) *[Definitions.]*

[In s 37, subss (11) to (14) have not yet been brought into operation; Police and Criminal Evidence Act 1984 (Commencement No 3) Order 1985 (SI 1985 No 1934), art 2 and Schedule.]

38. Duties of custody officer after charge *[Omitted.]*

39. Responsibilities in relation to persons detained

(1) Subject to subsections (2) and (4) below, it shall be the duty of the custody officer at a police station to ensure—

(*a*) that all persons in police detention at that station are treated in accordance with this Act and any code of practice issued under it and relating to the treatment of persons in police detention; and

(*b*) that all matters relating to such persons which are required by this Act or by such codes of practice to be recorded are recorded in the custody records relating to such persons.

(2) If the custody officer, in accordance with any code of practice issued under this Act, transfers or permits the transfer of a person in police detention—

(*a*) to the custody of a police officer investigating an offence for which that person is in police detention; or

(*b*) to the custody of an officer who has charge of that person outside the police station,

the custody officer shall cease in relation to that person to be subject to the duty inposed on him by subsection (1)(*a*) above; and it shall be the duty of the officer to whom the transfer is made to ensure that he is treated in accordance with the provisions of this Act and of any such codes of practice as are mentioned in subsection (1) above.

(3) If the person detained is subsequently returned to the custody of the custody officer, it shall be the duty of the officer investigating the offence to report to the custody officer as to the manner in which this section and the codes of practice have been complied with while that person was in his custody.

(4) If an arrested juvenile is transferred to the care of a local authority in pursuance of arrangements made under section 38(6) above, the custody officer shall cease in relation to that person to be subject to the duty imposed on him by subsection (1) above.

(5) It shall be the duty of a local authority to make available to an arrested juvenile who is in the authority's care in pursuance of such arrangements such advice and assistance as may be appropriate in the circumstances.

(6) Where—

(*a*) an officer of higher rank than the custody officer gives directions relating to a person in police detention; and

(*b*) the directions are at variance—

(i) with any decision made or action taken by the custody officer in the performance of a duty imposed on him under this Part of this Act; or

(ii) with any decision or action which would but for the directions have been made or taken by him in the performance of such a duty,

the custody officer shall refer the matter at once to an officer of the rank of superintendent or above who is responsible for the police station for which the custody officer is acting as custody officer.

40. Review of police detention *[Omitted.]*

41. Limits on period of detention without charge

(1) Subject to the following provisions of this section and to sections 42 and 43 below, a person shall not be kept in police detention for more than 24 hours without being charged.

(2) The time from which the period of detention of a person is to be calculated (in this Act referred to as 'the relevant time')—

(*a*) in the case of a person to whom this paragraph applies, shall be—

(i) the time at which that person arrives at the relevant police station, or

(ii) the time 24 hours after the time of that person's arrest,

whichever is the earlier;

(*b*) in the case of a person arrested outside England and Wales, shall be—

(i) the time at which that person arrives at the first police station to which he is taken in the police area in England and Wales in which the offence for which he was arrested is being investigated; or

(ii) the time 24 hours after the time of that person's entry into England and Wales,

whichever is the earlier;

(*c*) in the case of a person who—

(i) attends voluntarily at a police station; or

(ii) accompanies a constable to a police station without having been arrested,

and is arrested at the police station, the time of his arrest;

(*d*) in any other case, except where subsection (5) below applies, shall be the time at which the person arrested arrives at the first police station to which he is taken after his arrest.

(3) Subsection (2)(*a*) above applies to a person if—

(*a*) his arrest is sought in one police area in England and Wales;

(*b*) he is arrested in another police area; and

(*c*) he is not questioned in the area in which he is arrested in order to obtain evidence in relation to an offence for which he is arrested;

and in sub-paragraph (i) of that paragraph 'the relevant police station' means the first police station to which he is taken in the police area in which his arrest was sought.

(4) Subsection (2) above shall have effect in relation to a person arrested under section 31 above as if every reference in it to his arrest or his being arrested were a reference to his arrest or his being arrested for the offence for which he was originally arrested.

(5) If—

(*a*) a person is in police detention in a police area in England and Wales ('the first area'); and

(*b*) his arrest for an offence is sought in some other police area in England and Wales ('the second area'); and

(*c*) he is taken to the second area for the purposes of investigating that offence, without being questioned in the first area in order to obtain evidence in relation to it, the relevant time shall be—

(i) the time 24 hours after he leaves the place where he is detained in the first area; or

(ii) the time at which he arrives at the first police station to which he is taken in the second area,

whichever is the earlier.

(6) When a person who is in police detention is removed to hospital because he is in need of medical treatment, any time during which he is being questioned in hospital or on the way there or back by a police officer for the purpose of obtaining evidence relating to an offence shall be included in any period which falls to be calculated for the purposes of this Part of this Act, but any other time while he is in hospital or on his way back shall not be so included.

(7) Subject to subsection (8) below, a person who at the expiry of 24 hours after the relevant time is in police detention and has not been charged shall be released at that time either on bail or without bail.

(8) Subsection (7) above does not apply to a person whose detention for more than 24 hours after the relevant time has been authorised or is otherwise permitted in accordance with section 42 or 43 below.

(9) A person released under subsection (7) above shall not be re-arrested without a warrant for the offence for which he was previously arrested unless new evidence justifying a further arrest has come to light since his release.

* * *

PART V

Questioning and Treatment of Persons by Police

* * *

56. Right to have someone informed when arrested

(1) Where a person has been arrested and is being held in custody in a police station or other premises, he shall be entitled, if he so requests, to have one friend or relative or other person who is known to him or who is likely to take an interest in his welfare told, as soon as is practicable except to the extent that delay is permitted by this section, that he has been arrested and is being detained there.

(2) Delay is only permitted—

(*a*) in the case of a person who is in police detention for a serious arrestable offence; and

(*b*) if an officer of at least the rank of superintendent authorises it.

(3) In any case the person in custody must be permitted to exercise the right conferred by subsection (1) above within 36 hours from the relevant time, as defined in section 41(2) above.

(4) An officer may give an authorisation under subsection (2) above orally or in writing but, if he gives it orally, he shall confirm it in writing as soon as is practicable.

(5) An officer may only authorise delay where he has reasonable grounds for believing that telling the named person of the arrest—

(*a*) will lead to interference with or harm to evidence connected with a serious arrestable offence or interference with or physical injury to other persons; or

(*b*) will lead to the alerting of other persons suspected of having committed such an offence but not yet arrested for it; or

(*c*) will hinder the recovery of any property obtained as a result of such an offence.

[(5A) *[Applies to drug trafficking offences.]*]

(6) If a delay is authorised—

(*a*) the detained person shall be told the reason for it; and

(*b*) the reason shall be noted on his custody record.

(7) The duties imposed by subsection (6) above shall be performed as soon as is practicable.

(8) The rights conferred by this section on a person detained at a police station or other premises are exercisable whenever he is transferred from one place to another; and this section applies to each subsequent occasion on which they are exercisable as it applies to the first such occasion.

(9) There may be no further delay in permitting the exercise of the right conferred by subsection (1) above once the reason for authorising delay ceases to subsist.

(10), (11) *[Apply to terrorism provisions.]*

57. Additional rights of children and young persons

[Amends the Children and Young Persons Act 1933, s 34.]

58. Access to legal advice

(1) A person arrested and held in custody in a police station or other premises shall be entitled, if he so requests, to consult a solicitor privately at any time.

(2) Subject to subsection (3) below, a request under subsection (1) above and the time at which it was made shall be recorded in the custody record.

(3) Such a request need not be recorded in the custody record of a person who makes it at a time while he is at a court after being charged with an offence.

(4) If a person makes such a request, he must be permitted to consult a solicitor as soon as is practicable except to the extent that delay is permitted by this section.

(5) In any case he must be permitted to consult a solicitor within 36 hours from the relevant time, as defined in section 41(2) above.

(6) Delay in compliance with a request is only permitted—

(*a*) in the case of a person who is in police detention for a serious arrestable offence; and

(*b*) if an officer of at least the rank of superintendent authorises it.

(7) An officer may give an authorisation under subsection (6) above orally or in writing, but, if he gives it orally, he shall confirm it in writing as soon as is practicable.

(8) An officer may only authorise delay where he has reasonable grounds for believing that the exercise of the right conferred by subsection (1) above at the time when the person detained desires to exercise it—

(*a*) will lead to interference with or harm to evidence connected with a serious arrestable offence or interference with or physical injury to other persons; or

(*b*) will lead to the alerting of other persons suspected of having committed such an offence but not yet arrested for it; or

(*c*) will hinder the recovery of any property obtained as a result of such an offence.

[(8A) *[Applies to drug trafficking offences.]*]

(9) If delay is authorised—

(*a*) the detained person shall be told the reason for it; and

(*b*) the reason shall be noted on his custody record.

(10) The duties imposed by subsection (9) above shall be performed as soon as is practicable.

(11) There may be no further delay in permitting the exercise of the right conferred by subsection (1) above once the reason for authorising delay ceases to subsist.

(12) The reference in subsection (1) above to a person arrested includes a reference to a person who has been detained under the terrorism provisions.

(13)–(18) *[Persons arrested or detained under terrorism provisions.]*

[The term 'serious arrestable offence' is defined in s 116, below.]

* * *

PART VIII

EVIDENCE IN CRIMINAL PROCEEDINGS—GENERAL

* * *

Miscellaneous

78. Exclusion of unfair evidence

(1) In any proceedings the court may refuse to allow evidence on which the prosecution proposes to rely to be given if it appears to the court that, having regard to all the circumstances, including the circumstances in which the evidence was obtained, the admission of the evidence would have such an adverse effect on the fairness of the proceedings that the court ought not to admit it.

(2) Nothing in this section shall prejudice any rule of law requiring a court to exclude evidence.

79. Time for taking accused's evidence

If at the trial of any person for an offence—

(*a*) the defence intends to call two or more witnesses to the facts of the case; and

(*b*) those witnesses include the accused,

the accused shall be called before the other witness or witnesses unless the court in its discretion otherwise directs.

* * *

PART VIII Supplementary

82. Part VIII—interpretation

(1) In this Part of this Act—

'confession', includes any statement wholly or partly adverse to the person who made it, whether made to a person in authority or not and whether made in words or otherwise;

'court-martial' means a court-martial constituted under the Army Act 1955, the Air Force Act 1955 or the Naval Discipline Act 1957 or a disciplinary court constituted under section 50 of the said Act of 1957;

'proceedings' means criminal proceedings, including—

(*a*) proceedings in the United Kingdom or elsewhere before a court-martial constituted under the Army Act 1955 or the Air Force Act 1955;

(*b*) proceedings in the United Kingdom or elsewhere before the Courts-Martial Appeal Court—

(i) on an appeal from a court-martial so constituted or from a court-martial constituted under the Naval Discipline Act 1957; or

(ii) on a reference under section 34 of the Courts-Martial (Appeals) Act 1968; and

(*b*) proceedings before a Standing Civilian Court; and

'Service court' means a court-martial or a Standing Civilian Court.

(2) In this Part of this Act references to conviction before a Service court are references—

(*a*) as regards a court-martial constituted under the Army Act 1955 or the Air Force Act 1955, to a finding of guilty which is, or falls to be treated as, a finding of the court duly confirmed;

(*b*) as regards—

(i) a court-martial; or

(ii) a disciplinary court,

constituted under the Naval Discipline Act 1957, to a finding of guilty which is, or falls to be treated as, the finding of the court;

and 'convicted' shall be construed accordingly.

(3) Nothing in this Part of this Act shall prejudice any power of a court to exclude evidence (whether by preventing questions from being put or otherwise) at its discretion.

PART XI

MISCELLANEOUS AND SUPPLEMENTARY

* * *

116. Meaning of 'serious arrestable offence'

(1) This section has effect for determining whether an offence is a serious arrestable offence for the purpose of this Act.

(2) The following arrestable offences are always serious—

(*a*) an offence (whether at common law or under any enactment) specified in Part I of Schedule 5 to this Act; and (*b*) an offence under an enactment specified in Part II of that Schedule.

(3) Subject to subsections (4) and (5) below, any other arrestable offence is serious only if its commission—

(*a*) has led to any of the consequences specified in subsection (6) below; or

(*b*) is intended or is likely to lead to any of those consequences.

(4) An arrestable offence which consists of making a threat is serious if carrying out the threat would be likely to lead to any of the consequences specified in subsection (6) below.

(5) An offence under section 1, 9 or 10 of the Prevention of Terrorism (Temporary Provisions) Act 1984 is always a serious arrestable offence for the purposes of section 56 or 58 above, and an attempt or conspiracy to commit any such offence is also always a serious arrestable offence for those purposes.

(6) The consequences mentioned in subsections (3) and (4) above are

(*a*) serious harm to the security of the State or to public order;

(*b*) serious interference with the administration of justice or with the investigation of offences or of a particular offence;

(*c*) the death of any person;

(*d*) serious injury to any person;

(*e*) substantial financial gain to any person; and

(*f*) serious financial loss to any person.

(7) Loss is serious for the purposes of this section if, having regard to all the circumstances, it is serious for the person who suffers it.

(8) In this section 'injury' includes any disease and any impairment of a person's physical or mental condition.

[The term 'arrestable offence' is defined in s 24(1) of this Act (qv).]

* * *

SCHEDULE 5

Serious Arrestable Offences

PART I

Offences Mentioned in Section 116(2)(*a*)

* * *

PART II

Offences Mentioned in Section 116(2)(*b*)

Explosive Substances Act 1883 (c 3)

1. Section 2 (causing explosion likely to endanger life or property).

Sexual Offences Act 1956 (c 69)

2. Section 5 (intercourse with a girl under the age of 13).

Firearms Act 1968 (c 27)

3. Section 16 (possession of firearms with intent to injure).
4. Section 17(1) (use of firearms and imitation firearms to resist arrest).
5. Section 18 (carrying firearms with criminal intent).

6. *[Repealed.]*

Taking of Hostages Act 1982 (c 28)

7. Section 1 (hostage-taking).

Aviation Security Act 1982 (c 36)

8. Section 1 (hi-jacking).

[Criminal Justice Act 1988 (c 33)

9. Section 134 (torture).]

[Road Traffic Act 1988 (c 52)

Section 1 (causing death by reckless driving).]

[Schedule 5 is printed as amended by the Criminal Justice Act 1988, s 170(1) and Sched 15, para 102, on 29 July 1988 (see ibid, s 171(5)); the Road Traffic (Consequential Provisions) Act 1988, ss 3(1) and 4, and Sched 1, Part I, and Sched 3, para 27(5).]

* * *

The Powers of Criminal Courts Act 1973

(1973 c 62)

An Act to consolidate certain enactments relating to the powers of courts to deal with offenders and defaulters, to the treatment of offenders and to arrangements for persons on bail.

[25th October 1973]

* * *

Compensation orders

35. Compensation orders against convicted persons

[(1) Subject to the provisions of this Part of this Act and to section 40 of the Magistrates' Courts Act 1980 (which imposes a monetary limit on the powers of a magistrates' court under this section), a court by or before which a person is convicted of an offence, instead of or in addition to dealing with him in any other way, may, on application or otherwise, make an order (in this Act referred to as 'a compensation order') requiring him to pay compensation for any personal injury, loss or damage resulting from that offence or any other offence which is taken into consideration by the court in determining sentence] [or to make payments for funeral expenses or bereavement in respect of a death resulting from any such offence, other than a death due to an accident arising out of the presence of a motor vehicle on a road; and a court shall give reasons, on passing sentence, if it does not make such an order in a case where this section empowers it to do so.]

[(1A) Compensation under subsection (1) above shall be of such amount as the court considers appropriate, having regard to any evidence and to any representations that are made by or on behalf of the accused or the prosecutor.]

(2) In the case of an offence under the Theft Act 1968, where the property in question is recovered, any damage to the property occurring while it was out of the owner's possession shall be treated for the purposes of subsection (1) above as having resulted from the offence, however and by whomsoever the damage was caused.

[(3) A compensation order may only be made in respect of injury, loss or damage (other than loss suffered by a person's dependants in consequence of his death) which was due to an accident arising out of the presence of a motor vehicle on a road, if—

(*a*) it is in respect of damage which is treated by subsection (2) above as resulting from an offence under the Theft Act 1968; or

(*b*) it is in respect of injury, loss or damage as respects which—

(i) the offender is uninsured in relation to the use of the vehicle; and

(ii) compensation is not payable under any arrangements to which the Secretary of State is a party;

and, where a compensation order is made in respect of injury, loss or damage due to such an accident, the amount to be paid may include an amount representing the whole or part of any loss of or reduction in preferential rates of insurance attributable to the accident.]

[(3A) A vehicle the use of which is exempted from insurance by [section 144 of the Road Traffic Act 1988] is not uninsured for the purposes of subsection (3) above.]

[(3B) A compensation order in respect of funeral expenses may be made for the benefit of anyone who incurred the expenses.]

[(3C) A compensation order in respect of bereavement may only be made for the benefit of a person for whose benefit a claim for damages for bereavement could be made under section 1A of the Fatal Accidents Act 1976 [*qv*].]

[(3D) The amount of compensation in respect of bereavement shall not exceed the amount for the time being specified in section 1A(3) of the Fatal Accidents Act 1976.]

(4) In determining whether to make a compensation order against any person, and in determining the amount to be paid by any person under such an order, the court shall have regard to his means so far as they appear or are known to the court.

[(4A) Where the court considers—

(*a*) that it would be appropriate both to impose a fine and to make a compensation order; but

(*b*) that the offender has insufficient means to pay both an appropriate fine and appropriate compensation,

the court shall give preference to compensation (though it may impose a fine as well).]

(5) *[Repealed.]*

[Section 35 is printed as amended by the Interpretation Act 1978, s 17(2)(a); the Magistrates' Courts Act 1980, s 154(3) and Sched 9; the Criminal Justice Act 1982, s 67; and (from 12 October 1988) by the Criminal Justice Act 1988, ss 104(1) and (2) (see the Criminal Justice Act 1988 (Commencement No 2) Order 1988 (SI 1988 No 1676)). With effect from a date to be announced, s 35 will be further amended by the Criminal Justice Act 1988, ss 170(1) and 171(1) and Sched 15, para 40; when these provisions are brought into force the following text will be substituted for s 35(4) above:

[(4) In determining whether to make a compensation order against any person, and in determining the amount to be paid by any person under such an order, it shall be the duty of the court—

(*a*) to have regard to his means so far as they appear or are known to the court; and

(*b*) in a case where it is proposed to make against him both a compensation order and a confiscation order under Part VI of the Criminal Justice Act 1988, also to have regard to its duty under section 72(7) of that Act (duty where the court considers that the offender's means are insufficient to satisfy both orders in full to order the payment out of sums recovered under the confiscation order of sums due under the compensation order).]*]*

[36. Enforcement and appeals

(1) A person in whose favour a compensation order is made shall not be entitled to receive the amount due to him until (disregarding any power of a court to grant leave to appeal out of time) there is no further possibility of an appeal on which the order could be varied or set aside.

(2) *[Rule-making power.]*

(3) *[Powers of Court of Appeal.]*

(4) *[Power of House of Lords.]*

(5) Where a compensation order has been made against any person in respect of an offence taken into consideration in determining his sentence—

(*a*) the order shall cease to have effect if he successfully appeals against his conviction of the offence or, if more than one, all the offences, of which he was convicted in the proceedings in which the order was made;

(*b*) he may appeal against the order as if it were part of the sentence imposed in respect of the offence or, if more than one, any of the offences, of which he was so convicted.]

[Section 36 is printed as substituted (with effect from 12 October 1988) by the Criminal Justice Act 1988, ss 105 and 171(1) (see the Criminal Justice Act 1988 (Commencement No 2) Order 1988 (SI 1988 No 1676)).]

[37. Review of compensation orders

At any time before the person against whom a compensation order has been made has paid into court the whole of the compensation which the order requires him to pay, but at a time when (disregarding any power of a court to grant leave to appeal out of time) there is no further possibility of an appeal on which the order could be varied or set aside, the magistrates' court for the time being having functions in relation to the enforcement of the order may, on the application of the person against whom it was made, discharge the order, or reduce the amount which remains to be paid, if it appears to the court—

(*a*) that the injury, loss or damage in respect of which the order was made has been held in civil proceedings to be less than it was taken to be for the purposes of the order; or

(*b*) in the case of an order in respect of the loss of any property, that the property has been recovered by the person in whose favour the order was made; or

(*c*) that the means of the person against whom the order was made are insufficient to satisfy in full both the order and a confiscation order under Part VI of the Criminal Justice Act 1988 made against him in the same proceedings; or

(*d*) that the person against whom the order was made has suffered a substantial reduction in his means which was unexpected at the time when the compensation order was made, and that his means seem unlikely to increase for a considerable period;

but where the order was made by the Crown Court, a magistrates' court shall not exercise any power conferred by this section in a case where it is satisfied as mentioned in paragraph (*c*) or (*d*) above unless it has first obtained the consent of the Crown Court.]

[Section 37 is printed as substituted (with effect from 12 October 1988) by the Criminal Justice Act 1988, ss 105 and 171(1) (see the Criminal Justice Act 1988 (Commencement No 2) Order 1988 (SI 1988 No 1676)).]

* * *

43. Power to deprive offender of property used, or intended for use, for purposes of crime

[(1) Subject to the following provisions of this section, where a person is convicted of an offence and—

(*a*) the court by or before which he is convicted is satisfied that any property which has been lawfully seized from him or which was in his possession or under his control at the time when he was apprehended for the offence or when a summons in respect of it was issued—

(i) has been used for the purpose of committing, or facilitating the commission of, any offence; or

(ii) was intended by him to be used for that purpose; or

(*b*) the offence, or an offence which the court has taken into consideration in determining his sentence, consists of unlawful possession of property which—

(i) has been lawfully seized from him; or

(ii) was in his possession or under his control at the time when he was apprehended for the offence of which he has been convicted or when a summons in respect of that offence was issued,

the court may make an order under this section in respect of that property, and may do so whether or not it also deals with the offender in respect of the offence in any other way and without regard to any restrictions on forfeiture in an enactment contained in an Act passed before the Criminal Justice Act 1988.]

[(1A) In considering whether to make such an order in respect of any property a court shall have regard—

(*a*) to the value of the property; and

(*b*) to the likely financial and other effects on the offender of the making of the order (taken together with any other order that the court contemplates making).]

(2) Facilitating the commissioning of an offence shall be taken for the purposes of this section and section 44 of this Act to include the taking of any steps after it has been committed for the purpose of disposing of any property to which it relates or of avoiding apprehension or detection, and references in this or that section to an offence punishable with imprisonment shall be construed without regard to any prohibition or restriction imposed by or under any enactment on the imprisonment of young offenders.

(3) An order under this section shall operate to deprive the offender of his rights, if any, in the property to which it relates, and the property shall (if not already in their possession) be taken into the possession of the police.

(4) The Police (Property) Act 1897 shall apply, with the following modifications, to property which is in the possession of the police by virtue of this section—

(*a*) no application shall be made under section 1(1) of that Act by any claimant of the property after the expiration of six months from the date on which the order in respect of the property was made under this section; and

(*b*) no such application shall succeed unless the claimant satisfies the court either that he had not consented to the offender having possession of the property [or, where an order is made under subsection (1)(*a*) above, that he did not know, and had no reason to suspect, that the property was likely to be used for the purpose mentioned in that paragraph].

(5) In relation to property which is in the possession of the police by virtue of this section, the power to make regulations under section 2(1) of the Police (Property) Act 1897 (disposal of property in cases where the owner of the property has not been ascertained and no order of a competent court has been made with respect thereto) shall include power to make regulations for disposal in cases where no application by

a claimant of the property has been made within the period specified in subsection (4)(*a*) above or no such application has succeeded.

[Section 43 is printed as amended by the Criminal Justice Act 1988, ss 69(1) and 170(1) and Sched 15, para 41.

The text of s 43(1) was substituted and that of s 43(1A) was inserted by the 1988 Act with effect from 29 September 1988; see ibid, s 171(6). The text of s 43(4)(b) was substituted with effect from 12 October 1988; see ibid, s 171(1) and the Criminal Justice Act 1988 (Commencement No 2) Order 1988 (SI 1988 No 1676).]

[43A. Application of proceeds of forfeited property

(1) Where a court makes an order under section 43 above in a case where—

(*a*) the offender has been convicted of an offence which has resulted in a person suffering personal injury, loss or damage; or

(*b*) any such offence is taken into consideration by the court in determining sentence,

the court may also make an order that any proceeds which arise from the disposal of the property and which do not exceed a sum specified by the court shall be paid to that person.

(2) The court may only make an order under this section if it is satisfied that but for the inadequacy of the means of the offender it would have made a compensation order under which the offender would have been required to pay compensation of an amount not less than the specified amount.

(3) An order under this section has no effect—

(*a*) before the end of the period specified in section 43(4)(*a*) above; or

(*b*) if a successful application under section 1(1) of the Police (Property) Act 1897 has been made.]

[Section 43A was inserted (with effect from 12 October 1988) by the Criminal Justice Act 1988, ss 107 and 171(1) (see the Criminal Justice Act 1988 (Commencement No 2) Order 1988 (SI 1988 No 1676)).

The Police (Property) Act 1897, s 1(1) (to which reference is made in s 43A above but which is not reproduced in this work), empowers a magistrates' court to make an order for the delivery of certain property in the hands of the police to the person appearing to the court to be the owner, or otherwise disposing of the property.]

44. Driving disqualification where vehicle used for purposes of crime

(1) This section applies where a person is convicted before the Crown Court of an offence punishable on indictment with imprisonment for a term of two years or more or, having been convicted by a magistrates' court of such an offence, is committed under [section 38 of the Magistrates' Courts Act 1980] to the Crown Court for sentence.

(2) If in a case to which this section applies the Crown Court is satisfied that a motor vehicle was used (by the person convicted or by anyone else) for the purpose of committing, or facilitating the commission of, the offence in question (within the meaning of section 43 of this Act), the court may order the person convicted to be disqualified, for such period as the court thinks fit, for holding or obtaining a licence to drive a motor vehicle granted under [Part III of the Road Traffic Act 1988].

(3) A court which makes an order under this section disqualifying a person for

holding or obtaining any such licence as is mentioned in subsection (2) above shall require him to produce any such licence held by him; and—

(*a*) if he does not produce the licence as required he shall be guilty of an offence under [section 27(3) of the Road Traffic Offenders Act 1988] (failure to produce licence for endorsement); and

(*b*) if he applies under [section 42] of that Act for the disqualification to be removed and the court so orders, [subsection (5)] of that section shall not have effect so as to require particulars of the order to be endorsed on the licence, but the court shall send notice of the order to the [Secretary of State for Transport] and [section 47(4) of that Act] (procedure for sending notice to [Secretary of State for Transport]) shall apply to the notice.

[Section 44 is printed as amended by the Minister of Transport Order 1979 (SI 1979 No 571); the Magistrates' Courts Act 1980, s 154(1) and Sched 7, para 122; the Transfer of Functions (Transport) Order 1981 (SI 1981 No 238); the Road Traffic (Consequential Provisions) Act 1988, s 4 and Sched 3, para 11.]

* * *

The Prosecution of Offences Act 1985

(1985 c 23)

An Act to provide for the establishment of a Crown Prosecution Service for England and Wales; to make provision as to costs in criminal cases . . . .

[23rd May 1985]

ARRANGEMENT OF SECTIONS

* * *

* * *

PART I

The Crown Prosecution Service

Constitution and functions of Service

* * *

3. Functions of the Director

(1), (2) *[Omitted.]*

(3) In this section—

. . .

'police force' means any police force maintained by a police authority under the Police Act 1964 and any other body of constables for the time being specified by order made by the Secretary of State for the purposes of this section;

. . .

[The definition of 'police force' in subs (3) is incorporated by reference into s 17 [qv].]

PART II

Costs in Criminal Cases

Award of costs out of central funds

16. Defence costs

(1) Where—

(*a*) an information laid before a justice of the peace for any area, charging any person with an offence, is not proceeded with;

(*b*) a magistrates' court inquiring into an indictable offence as examining justices determines not to commit the accused for trial;

(*c*) a magistrates' court dealing summarily with an offence dismisses the information;

that court or, in a case falling within paragraph (*a*) above, a magistrates' court for that area, may make an order in favour of the accused for a payment to be made out of central funds in respect of his costs (a 'defendant's costs order').

(2) Where—

(*a*) any person is not tried for an offence for which he has been indicted or committed for trial; or

[(*aa*) *[Relates to complex cases of serious fraud.]*]

(*b*) any person is tried on indictment and acquitted on any count in the indictment;

the Crown Court may make a defendant's costs order in favour of the accused.

(3) Where a person convicted of an offence by a magistrates' court appeals to the Crown Court under section 108 of the Magistrates' Courts Act 1980 (right of appeal against conviction of sentence), and, in consequence of the decision on appeal—

(*a*) his conviction is set aside; or

(*b*) a less severe punishment is awarded;

the Crown Court may make a defendant's costs order in favour of the accused.

(4) Where the Court of Appeal—

(*a*) allows an appeal under Part I of the Criminal Appeal Act 1968 against—

(i) conviction;

(ii) a verdict of not guilty by reason of insanity; or

(iii) a finding under section 4 of the Criminal Procedure (Insanity) Act 1964 that the appellant is under disability; or

[(*aa*) directs under section 8(1B) of the Criminal Appeal Act 1968 the entry of a judgment and verdict of acquittal;]

(*b*) on an appeal under that Part against conviction—

(i) substitutes a verdict of guilty of another offence;

(ii) in a case where a special verdict has been found, orders a different conclusion on the effect of that verdict to be recorded; or

(iii) is of the opinion that the case falls within paragraph (*a*) or (*b*) of section 6(1) of that Act (cases where the court substitutes a finding of insanity or unfitness to plead); or

(*c*) on an appeal under that Part against sentence, exercises its power under section 11(3) of that Act (powers where the court considers that the appellant should be sentenced differently for an offence for which he was dealt with by the court below);

the court may make a defendant's costs order in favour of the accused.

[(4A) *[Relates to complex cases of serious fraud.]*]

(5) Where—

(*a*) any proceedings in a criminal cause or matter are determined before a Divisional Court of the Queen's Bench Division;

(*b*) the House of Lords determines an appeal, or application for leave to appeal, from such a Divisional Court in a criminal cause or matter;

(*c*) the Court of Appeal determines an application for leave to appeal to the House of Lords under Part II of the Criminal Appeal Act 1968; or

(*d*) the House of Lords determines an appeal, or application for leave to appeal, under Part II of that Act;

the court may make a defendant's costs order in favour of the accused.

(6) A defendant's costs order shall, subject to the following provisions of this section, be for the payment out of central funds, to the person in whose favour the order is made, of such amount as the court considers reasonably sufficient to compensate him for any expenses properly incurred by him in the proceedings.

(7) Where a court makes a defendant's costs order but is of the opinion that there are circumstances which make it inappropriate that the person in whose favour the order is made should recover the full amount mentioned in subsection (6) above, the court shall—

(*a*) assess what amount would, in its opinion, be just and reasonable; and

(*b*) specify that amount in the order.

(8) *Where a defendant's costs order is made in favour of a legally assisted person, any expenses incurred on his behalf pursuant to the legal aid order in question shall be disregarded in determining (for the purposes of this section) the amount of the expenses incurred by him in the proceedings.*

(9) Subject to subsection (7) above, the amount to be paid out of central funds in pursuance of a defendant's costs order shall—

(*a*) be specified in the order, in any case where the court considers it appropriate for the amount to be so specified and the person in whose favour the order is made agrees the amount; and

(*b*) in any other case, be determined in accordance with regulations made by the Lord Chancellor for the purposes of this section.

(10) Subsection (6) above shall have effect, in relation to any case falling within subsection (1)(*a*) or (2)(*a*) above, as if for the words 'in the proceedings' there were substituted the words 'in or about the defence'.

(11) Where a person ordered to be retried is acquitted at his retrial, the costs which may be ordered to be paid out of central funds under this section shall include—

(*a*) any costs which, at the original trial, could have been ordered to be so paid under this section if he had been acquitted; and

(*b*) if no order was made under this section in respect of his expenses on appeal, any sums for the payment of which such an order could have been made.

[Section 16 is printed as amended by the Criminal Justice Act 1988, s 170(1) and Sched 15, para 103; the amendment took effect on 29 July 1988 (see ibid, s 171(5)). Section 16(8) has been prospectively repealed (from a date to be announced) by the Legal Aid Act 1988, s 45(2) and Sched 6.]

17. Prosecution costs

(1) Subject to subsection (2) below, the court may—

(*a*) in any proceedings in respect of an indictable office; and

(*b*) in any proceedings before a Divisional Court of the Queen's Bench Division or the House of Lords in respect of a summary offence;

order the payment out of central funds of such amount as the court considers reasonably sufficient to compensate the prosecutor for any expenses properly incurred by him in the proceedings.

(2) No order under this section may be made in favour of—

(*a*) a public authority; or

(*b*) a person acting—

(i) on behalf of a public authority; or

(ii) in his capacity as an official appointed by such an authority.

(3) Where a court makes an order under this section but is of the opinion that there are circumstances which make it inappropriate that the prosecution should recover the full amount mentioned in subsection (1) above, the court shall—

(*a*) assess what amount would, in its opinion, be just and reasonable; and

(*b*) specify that amount in the order.

(4) Subject to subsection (3) above, the amount to be paid out of central funds in pursuance of an order under this section shall—

(*a*) be specified in the order, in any case where the court considers it appropriate for the amount to be so specified and the prosecutor agrees the amount; and

(*b*) in any other case be determined in accordance with regulations made by the Lord Chancellor for the purposes of this section.

(5) Where the conduct of proceedings to which subsection (1) above applies is taken over by the Crown Prosecution Service, that subsection shall have effect as if it

referred to the prosecutor who had the conduct of the proceedings before the intervention of the Service and to expenses incurred by him up to the time of intervention.

(6) In this section 'public authority' means—

(*a*) a police force within the meaning of section 3 of this Act;

(*b*) the Crown Prosecution Service or any other government department;

(*c*) a local authority or other authority or body constituted for purposes of—

(i) the public service or of local government; or

(ii) carrying on under national ownership any industry or undertaking or part of an industry or undertaking; or

(*d*) any other authority or body whose members are appointed by Her Majesty or by any Minister of the Crown or government department or whose revenues consist wholly or mainly of money provided by Parliament.

Award of costs against accused

18. Award of costs against accused

(1) Where—

(*a*) any person is convicted of an offence before a magistrates' court;

(*b*) the Crown Court dismisses an appeal against such a conviction or against the sentence imposed on that conviction; or

(*c*) any person is convicted of an offence before the Crown Court;

the court may make such order as to the costs to be paid by the accused to the prosecutor as it considers just and reasonable.

(2) Where the Court of Appeal dismisses—

(*a*) an appeal or application for leave to appeal under Part I of the Criminal Appeal Act 1968; or

(*b*) an application by the accused for leave to appeal to the House of Lords under Part II of this Act;

[(*c*) *[Relates to complex cases of serious fraud.]*]

it may make such order as to the costs to be paid by the accused, to such person as may be named in the order, as it considers just and reasonable.

(3) The amount to be paid by the accused in pursuance of an order under this section shall be specified in the order.

(4) Where any person is convicted of an offence before a magistrates' court and—

(*a*) under the conviction the court orders payment of any sum as a fine, penalty, forfeiture or compensation; and

(*b*) the sum so ordered to be paid does not exceed £5;

the court shall not order the accused to pay any costs under this section unless in the particular circumstances of the case it considers it right to do so.

(5) Where any person under the age of seventeen is convicted of an offence before a magistrates' court, the amount of any costs ordered to be paid by the accused under this section shall not exceed the amount of any fine imposed on him.

(6) Costs ordered to be paid under subsection (2) above may include the reasonable costs of any transcript of a record of proceedings made in accordance with rules of court made for the purposes of section 32 of the Criminal Appeal Act 1968.

Other awards

19. Provisions for orders as to costs in other circumstances

(1)–(3A) *[Regulation-making powers.]*

(4) The Court of Appeal may order the payment out of central funds of such sums as appear to it to be reasonably sufficient to compensate an appellant who is not in custody and who appears before it on, or in connection with, his appeal under Part I of the Criminal Appeal Act 1968.

(5) *[Regulation-making powers.]*

Supplemental

20. Regulations *[Omitted.]*

21. Interpretation, etc

(1) In this Part—

'defendant's costs order' has the meaning given in section 16 of this Act;

'legal aid order' means an order under any provision of section 28 of the Legal Aid Act 1974 and includes, in relation to proceedings in a Divisional Court of the Queen's Bench Division, any certificate or other instrument under which legal aid is given;

'legally assisted person' means a person to whom aid is ordered to be given by a legal aid order;

'proceedings' includes—

(*a*) proceedings in any court below; and

(*b*) in relation to the determination of an appeal by any court, any application made to that court for leave to bring the appeal; and

'witness' means any person properly attending to give evidence, whether or not he gives evidence or is called at the instance of one of the parties or of the court, but does not include a person attending as a witness to character only unless the court has certified that the interests of justice required his attendance.

(2) Except as provided by or under this Part no costs shall be allowed on the hearing or determination of, or of any proceedings preliminary or incidental to, an appeal to the Court of Appeal under Part I of the Criminal Appeal Act 1968.

(3) Subject to rules of court made under section 53(1) of the Supreme Court Act 1981 (power by rules to distribute business of Court of Appeal between its civil and criminal divisions), the jurisdiction of the Court of Appeal under this Part, or under regulations made under this Part, shall be exercised by the criminal division of that Court; and references in this Part to the Court of Appeal shall be construed as references to that division.

(4) For the purposes of sections 16 and 17 of this Act, the costs of any party to proceedings shall be taken to include the expense of compensating any witness for the expense, trouble or loss of time, properly incurred in or incidental to his attendance.

[(4A) Where one party to any proceedings is a legally assisted person then—

(*a*) for the purposes of sections 16 and 17 of this Act, his costs shall be taken not to include either the expenses incurred on his behalf by the Legal Aid Board or the Lord Chancellor or, if he is liable to make a contribution under section 23 of the Legal Aid Act 1988, any sum paid or payable by way of contribution; and

(*b*) for the purposes of sections 18 and 19 of this Act, his costs shall be taken to include the expenses incurred on his behalf by the Legal Aid Board or the Lord Chancellor (without any deduction on account of any contribution paid or payable under section 23 of the Legal Aid Act 1988) but, if he is liable to make such a contribution, his costs shall be taken not to include any sum paid or payable by way of contribution.]

(5) Where, in any proceedings in a criminal cause or matter or in either of the cases mentioned in subsection (6) below, an interpreter is required because of the accused's lack of English, the expenses properly incurred on his employment shall not be treated as costs of any party to the proceedings.

(6) The cases are—

(*a*) where an information charging the accused with an offence is laid before a justice of the peace for any area but not proceeded with and the expenses are incurred on the employment of the interpreter for the proceedings on the information; and

(*b*) where the accused is committed for trial but not tried and the expenses are incurred on the employment of the interpreter for the proceedings in the Crown Court.

[Section 21 is printed as prospectively amended by the Legal Aid Act 1988; the definition of 'legal aid order' in s 21(1) has been prospectively repealed (as from a date to be announced) by the Legal Aid Act 1988, s 45(2) and Sched 6; also from a date to be announced, the definition of 'legally assisted person' in s 21(1) will be replaced (see ibid, s 45(4) and Sched 7, para 14) by the following:

['legally assisted person', in relation to any proceedings, means a person to whom representation under the Legal Aid Act 1988 has been granted for the purposes of the proceedings;]

Section 21(4A) (which was prospectively inserted by the Legal Aid Act 1988, s 45(4) and Sched 7, para 15) will take effect from a date to be announced.]

* * *

The Public Passenger Vehicles Act 1981

(1981 c 14)

An Act to consolidate certain enactments relating to public passenger vehicles.
[15th April 1981]

ARRANGEMENT OF SECTIONS

PART I

PRELIMINARY

Definition and classification of public service vehicles

PART II

GENERAL PROVISIONS RELATING TO PUBLIC SERVICE VEHICLES

Fitness of public service vehicles

Public service vehicle operators' licences

Drivers' licences

22. Drivers' licences

. . . .

Regulation of conduct etc of drivers, inspectors, conductors and passengers

24. Regulation of conduct of drivers, inspectors and conductors
25. Regulation of conduct of passengers
26. Control of number of passengers

Supplementary provisions

27. Returns to be provided by persons operating public service vehicles

. . . .

* * *

PART IV

Modification of Requirements of Part II in Relation to Certain Vehicles and Areas

Fare-paying passengers on school buses

46. Fare-paying passengers on school buses

* * *

PART V

Miscellaneous and Supplementary

* * *

60. General power to make regulations for purposes of Act

* * *

Provisions relating to offences and legal proceedings

65. Forgery and misuse of documents
66. False statements to obtain licence etc

. . . .

67. Penalty for breach of regulations
68. Defences available for persons charged with certain offences
69. Restriction on institution in England and Wales of proceedings under Part II
70. Duty to give information as to identity of driver in certain cases
71. Evidence by certificate
72. Proof in summary proceedings of identity of driver of vehicle
73. Time within which summary proceedings for certain offences may be commenced
74. Offences by companies

* * *

* * *

SCHEDULES

* * *

PART I

PRELIMINARY

Definition and classification of public service vehicles

1. Definition of 'public service vehicle'

(1) Subject to the provisions of this section, in this Act 'public service vehicle' means a motor vehicle (other than a tramcar) which—

(*a*) being a vehicle adapted to carry more than eight passengers, is used for carrying passengers for hire or reward; or

(*b*) being a vehicle not so adapted, is used for carrying passengers for hire or reward at separate fares in the course of a business of carrying passengers.

(2) For the purposes of subsection (1) above a vehicle 'is used' as mentioned in paragraph (*a*) or (*b*) of that subsection if it is being so used or if it has been used as mentioned in that paragraph and that use has not been permanently discontinued.

(3) A vehicle carrying passengers at separate fares in the course of a business of carrying passengers, but doing so in circumstances in which the conditions set out in Part I, . . . or III of Schedule 1 to this Act are fulfilled, shall be treated as not being a public service vehicle unless it is adapted to carry more than eight passengers.

(4) For the purposes of this section a journey made by a vehicle in the course of which one or more passengers are carried at separate fares shall not be treated as made in the course of a business of carrying passengers if—

(*a*) the fare or aggregate of the fares paid in respect of the journey does not exceed the amount of the running costs of the vehicle for the journey; and

(*b*) the arrangements for the payment of fares by the passenger or passengers so carried were made before the journey began;

and for the purposes of paragraph (*a*) above the running costs of a vehicle for a journey shall be taken to include an appropriate amount in respect of depreciation and general wear.

(5) For the purposes of this section, . . . and Schedule 1 to this Act—

(*a*) a vehicle is to be treated as carrying passengers for hire or reward if payment is made for, or for matters which include, the carrying of passengers, irrespective of the person to whom the payment is made and, in the case of a transaction effected by or on behalf of a member of any association of persons (whether incorporated or not) on the one hand and the association or another member thereof on the other hand, notwithstanding any rule of law as to such transactions;

(*b*) a payment made for the carrying of a passenger shall be treated as a fare notwithstanding that it is made in consideration of other matters in addition to the journey and irrespective of the person by or to whom it is made;

(*c*) a payment shall be treated as made for the carrying of a passenger if made in consideration of a person's being given a right to be carried, whether for one or more journeys and whether or not the right is exercised.

(6) Where a fare is paid for the carriage of a passenger on a journey by air, no part of that fare shall be treated for the purposes of subsection (5) above as paid in consideration of the carriage of the passenger by road by reason of the fact that, in case of mechanical failure, bad weather or other circumstances outside the operator's control, part of that journey may be made by road.

[Section 1 is printed as amended by the Transport Act 1985, s 139(3) and Sched 8.]

2. *[Repealed.]*

* * *

PART II

General Provisions Relating to Public Service Vehicles

Fitness of public service vehicles

6. Certificate of initial fitness (or equivalent) required for use as public service vehicles

(1) A public service vehicle adapted to carry more than eight passengers shall not be used on a road unless—

(*a*) a certifying officer [or an authorised inspector] has issued a certificate (in this Act referred to as a 'certificate of initial fitness') that the prescribed conditions as to fitness are fulfilled in respect of the vehicle; or

(*b*) a certificate under section 10 of this Act has been issued in respect of the vehicle; or

(*c*) there has been issued in respect of the vehicle a certificate under section 47 of the Road Traffic Act 1972 [or sections 55 to 58 of the Road Traffic Act 1988 [*qv*]] (type approval) of a kind which by virtue of regulations is to be treated as the equivalent of a certificate of initial fitness.

[(1A) *[Omitted.]*]

(2) Subject to section 68(3) of this Act, if a vehicle is used in contravention of subsection (1) above, the operator of the vehicle shall be liable on summary conviction to a fine not exceeding [level 4 on the standard scale].

[Section 6 is printed as amended by the Criminal Justice Act 1982, ss 37 and 46; the Road Traffic (Consequential Provisions) Act 1988, s 4 and Sched 3, para 22. The words in s 6(1)(a) printed inside square brackets were added by the Transport Act 1982, s 10(3), and will take effect from a date to be announced. Section 6(1A) was added by the Transport Act 1982, s 10(8), and will also take effect from a date to be announced.

The application of ss 6, 12, 18 and 22 of this Act to certain vehicles is excluded (and in some cases a modified version of s 12 is applied) by the Road Transport (International Passenger Services) Regulations 1984 No 748), regs 4 to 12 (inclusive) (qv).]

7. Certifying officers and public service vehicle examiners

(1) For the purpose of the provisions of this Act with respect to the certification of fitness of vehicles, the Secretary of State may with the approval of the Minister for the Civil Service appoint such officers (in this Act referred to as 'certifying officers') as he thinks fit, and those officers shall perform such duties in relation to the examination of vehicles, the issue of certificates of initial fitness and otherwise, as the Minister may require.

(2) The Secretary of State may, with the approval of the Minister for the Civil Service, appoint as public service vehicle examiners such persons as he considers necessary for the purpose of the inspection of public service vehicles within the several traffic areas and for the purpose of the discharge of such other duties as he considers can conveniently be discharged by persons acting as such examiners, and for that purpose may, with the concurrence of the Secretary of State concerned, make arrangements with any police authority for the appointment of members of their police force for this purpose.

(3) A certifying officer or public service vehicle examiner shall, in exercising any of the functions of such an officer or examiner, act under the general directions of the Secretary of State.

(4) There shall be paid to or in respect of certifying officers and public service vehicle examiners such remuneration and such salaries or allowances, if any, as the Secretary of State may, with the consent of the Minister for the Civil Service, determine.

8. Powers of, and facilities for, inspection of public service vehicles

(1) A certifying officer or public service vehicle examiner, on production if so required of his authority—

(*a*) may at any time inspect any public service vehicle, and for that purpose—

(i) may enter the vehicle; and

(ii) may detain the vehicle during such time as is required for the inspection;

(*b*) may at any time which is reasonable having regard to the circumstances of the case enter any premises on which he has reason to believe that there is a public service vehicle.

[(1A) For the purposes of subsection (1)(*b*) above, a vehicle which is used to carry passengers for hire or reward only under a permit granted under section 19 or 22 of the Transport Act 1985 (permits relating to the use of vehicles by educational and other bodies or in providing community bus services) shall be treated as not being a public service vehicle.]

(2) A person who intentionally obstructs a certifying officer or public service vehicle examiner acting in the exercise of his powers under subsection (1) above shall be liable on summary conviction to a fine not exceeding [level 3 on the standard scale].

(3) The Secretary of State may—

(*a*) provide and maintain stations where inspections of public service vehicles for the purposes of this Act may be carried out;

(*b*) designate premises as stations where such inspections may be carried out; and

(*c*) provide and maintain apparatus for the carrying out of such inspections;

and in this Act 'official PSV testing station' means a station provided, or any premises for the time being designated, under this subsection.

[Section 8 is printed as amended by the Criminal Justice Act 1982, ss 37 and 46; the Transport Act 1985, s 139(2) and Sched 7, para 21(2).]

9. Power to prohibit driving of unfit public service vehicles

(1) If on any inspection of a public service vehicle it appears to a certifying officer or public service vehicle examiner [or an authorised inspector] that owing to any defects therein the vehicle is, or is likely to become, unfit for service, he may prohibit the driving of the vehicle on a road either—

(*a*) absolutely; or

(*b*) for one or more specified purposes; or

(*c*) except for one or more specified purposes.

(2) A prohibition under subsection (1) above may be imposed with a direction making it irremovable unless and until the vehicle has been inspected at an official PSV testing station.

(3) Where a certifying officer or examiner [or authorised inspector] prohibits the driving of a vehicle under subsection (1) above, he shall forthwith give notice in writing of the prohibition to the person in charge of the vehicle at the time of the inspection—

(*a*) specifying the defects which occasioned the prohibition;

(*b*) stating whether the prohibition is on all driving of the vehicle or driving it for one or more specified purposes or driving it except for one or more specified purposes (and, where applicable, specifying the purpose or purposes in question); and

(*c*) stating whether the prohibition is to come into force immediately or at the end of a specified period.

(4) If the person to whom written notice of a prohibition is given under subsection (3) above as being the person in charge of the vehicle at the time of the inspection is not—

(*a*) the operator of the vehicle; or

(*b*) if there is no operator at that time, the owner of the vehicle,

the officer or examiner [or authorised inspector] shall as soon as practicable take steps to bring the contents of the notice to the attention of the said operator or owner.

(5) If, in the opinion of the certifying officer or examiner [or authorised inspector] concerned, the defects in the vehicle in question are such that driving it, or driving it for any purpose prohibited by the notice given to the person in charge of it, would involve danger to *the driver or to passengers or other members of the public*, the prohibition under subsection (1) above with respect to the vehicle shall come into force as soon as that notice has been given.

(6) In any other case a prohibition under subsection (1) above shall come into force at such time not later than ten days from the date of the inspection as seems appropriate to the certifying officer or examiner [or authorised inspector] having regard to all the circumstances.

(7) Where a notice has been given under subsection (3) above, any certifying officer or public service vehicle examiner [or an authorised inspector] may—

(*a*) grant an exemption in writing for the use of the vehicle in such manner, subject to such conditions and for such purpose or purposes as may be specified in the exemption;

(*b*) by endorsement on the notice vary its terms and, in particular—

(i) alter the time at which the prohibition is to come into force, or suspend it if it has come into force; or

(ii) cancel a direction under subsection (2) above with which the prohibition was imposed.

(8) *[Omitted.]*

(9) Except in such cases as may be prescribed, a person who—

(*a*) knowingly drives a vehicle in contravention of a prohibition under subsection (1) above; or

(*b*) subject to section 68(3) of this Act, causes or permits a vehicle to be driven in contravention of such a prohibition,

shall be liable on summary conviction to a fine not exceeding [level 5 on the standard scale].

[(10) Any removal of a prohibition under subsection (1) above shall be made by notice in writing.]

[Section 9 is printed as amended by the Criminal Justice Act 1982, ss 37 and 46. The references to 'authorised inspector' were added by the Transport Act 1982, s 10(3), and will take effect from a date to be announced. The words in italics will be replaced under the Transport Act 1982, s 74 and Sched 5, para 21, by the words 'any person' from a date to be announced. Section 9(10), which was added by the Transport Act 1982, s 74 and Sched 5, para 21, will take effect from a date to be announced.

For s 68(3) of this Act, see below.

The Public Passenger Vehicles (Exemptions, and Appeals against Refusals to Issue Certificates or Remove Prohibitions) Regulations 1987 (SI 1987 No 1150) (qv) were made in part under s 9(9) above.]

9A. Extensions of sections 8 and 9 to certain passenger vehicles other than public service vehicles

(1) Section 8 of this Act shall apply, with the omission of subsection (1)(*b*), to any motor vehicle (other than a tramcar) which is adapted to carry more than eight passengers but is not a public service vehicle as it applies to a public service vehicle.

(2) Section 9 of this Act shall apply to any such motor vehicle as it applies to a public service vehicle with the omission of subsection (4).]

[Section 9A was inserted by the Transport Act 1985, s 33.]

10. Approval of type vehicle and effect thereof *[Omitted.]*

11. Modification of section 6 in relation to experimental vehicles

(1) Where it appears to the Secretary of State expedient to do so for the purpose of the making of tests or trials of a vehicle or its equipment, he may by order made in respect of that vehicle for the purposes of section 6 of this Act dispense with such of

the prescribed conditions as to fitness referred to in subsection (1)(*a*) of that section as are specified in the order.

(2) While such an order is in force in respect of a vehicle, section 6 of this Act shall have effect in relation to the vehicle as if the prescribed conditions as to fitness referred to in subsection (1)(*a*) of that section did not include such of those conditions as are dispensed with by the order.

(3) An order under this section shall specify the period for which it is to continue in force, and may contain, or authorise the imposition of, requirements, restrictions or prohibitions relating to the construction, equipment or use of the vehicle to which the order relates.

(4) Where an order under this section in respect of a vehicle is revoked or otherwise ceases to have effect, any certificate of initial fitness issued under section 6 of this Act in respect of the vehicle while the order was in force shall, for the purposes of that section as regards any use of the vehicle after the order has ceased to have effect, be deemed never to have been issued.

Public service vehicle operators' licences

12. PSV operators' licences

[(1) A public vehicle shall not be used on a road for carrying passengers for hire or reward except under a PSV operator's licence granted in accordance with the following provision of this Part of this Act.]

(2)–(4) *[Omitted.]*

(5) Subject to section 68(3) of this Act, if a vehicle is used in contravention of subsection (1) above, the operator of the vehicle shall be liable on summary conviction to a fine not exceeding [level 4 on the standard scale].

[Section 12 is printed as amended by the Criminal Justice Act 1982, ss 37 and 46; the Transport Act 1985, s 1(3) and Sched 1, para 4.

For s 68(3) of this Act, see below.

The application of this section to certain vehicles is excluded (or a modified version of the section is applied); see further the notes to s 6 of this Act.]

* * *

16. Conditions attached to licences

(1) [Subject to subsection (1A) below and section 12(7) of the Transport Act 1985 a traffic commissioner] on granting a PSV operator's licence shall attach to it one or more conditions specifying the maximum number of vehicles (being vehicles having their operating centre in the area of [that commissioner]) which the holder of the licence may at any one time use under the licence.

[(1A) In the case of a restricted licence, the number specified as the maximum in any condition imposed under subsection (1) above shall not, except in any prescribed case or class of case, exceed two.]

(2) Conditions attached under subsection (1) above to a PSV operator's licence may specify different maximum numbers for different descriptions of vehicle.

(3) [A traffic commissioner] may (whether at the time when the licence is granted or at any time thereafter) attach to a PSV operator's licence granted by [him] such

conditions or additional conditions as [he thinks] fit for restricting or regulating the use of vehicles under the licence, being conditions of any prescribed description.

(4) Without prejudice to the generality of the power to prescribe descriptions of conditions for the purposes of subsection (3) above, the descriptions which may be so prescribed include conditions for regulating the places at which vehicles being used under a PSV operator's licence may stop to take up or set down passengers.

(5), (6) *[Omitted.]*

(7) Subject to section 68(3) of this Act, if a condition attached to a PSV operator's licence is contravened, the holder of the licence shall be liable on summary conviction to a fine not exceeding [level 3 on the standard scale].

(8) Compliance with any condition attached to a PSV operator's licence . . . [(other than a condition so attached under subsection (1A) above)] may be temporarily dispensed with by the traffic commissioner by whom the licence was granted if [he is] satisfied that compliance with the condition would be unduly onerous by reason of circumstances not foreseen when the condition was attached or, if the condition has been altered, when it was last altered.

(9) It is hereby declared that the conditions attached under subsection (1) [or (1A)] above to a PSV operator's licence granted by the traffic commissioner for any area do not affect the use by the holder of the licence of a vehicle—

(*a*) under a PSV operator's licence granted to him by the traffic commissioner for another area; or

(*b*) in circumstances such that another person falls to be treated as the operator of the vehicle (for example, by virtue of regulations under section 81(1)(*a*) of this Act).

[Section 16 is printed as amended by the Criminal Justice Act 1982, ss 37 and 47; the Transport Act 1985, ss 3(5), 24(1), 139(2) and (3), Sched 2, Part II, para 4(7), Sched 7, para 21(4), and Sched 8.

For ss 68(3) and 81(1)(a) of this Act, see below.

The Public Service Vehicles (Operators' Licences) Regulations 1986 (SI 1986 No 1668) below were in part made under this section.]

17. Revocation, suspension etc of licences *[Omitted.]*

18. Duty to exhibit operator's disc

(1) Where a vehicle is being used in circumstances such that a PSV operator's licence is required, there shall be fixed and exhibited on the vehicle in the prescribed manner an operator's disc issued under this section showing particulars of the operator of the vehicle and of the PSV operator's licence under which the vehicle is being used.

(2) [A traffic commissioner] on granting a PSV operator's licence shall supply the person to whom the licence is granted with a number of operators' discs equal to the maximum number of vehicles which he may use under the licence in accordance with the condition or conditions attached to the licence under section 16(1) [or (1A)] of this Act; and if [(in the case of any condition or conditions attached under section 16(1)] that maximum number is later increased on the variation of one or more of those conditions, the traffic [commissioner] on making the variation shall supply him with further operators' discs accordingly.

(3) Regulations may make provision—

(*a*) as to the form of operators' discs and the particulars to be shown on them;

(*b*) with respect to the custody and production of operators' discs;

(*c*) for the issue of new operators' discs in place of those lost, destroyed or defaced;

(*d*) for the return of operators' discs on the revocation or expiration of a PSV operators' licence or in the event of a variation of one or more conditions attached to a licence under section 16(1) of this Act having the effect of reducing the maximum number of vehicles which may be used under the licence.

(4) Subject to section 68(3) of this Act, if a vehicle is used in contravention of subsection (1) above, the operator of the vehicle shall be liable on summary conviction to a fine not exceeding [level 3 on the standard scale].

[Section 18 is printed as amended by the Criminal Justice Act 1982, ss 37 and 46; the Transport Act 1985, ss 3(5), 24(2), and Sched 2, Part II, para 4(9).

The Public Service Vehicles (Operators' Licences) Regulations 1986 (SI 1986 No 1668) below were in part made under this section.

For s 68(3) of this Act, see below.

The application of this section to certain vehicles is excluded; see further the notes to s 6 of this Act.]

19. Duty to inform traffic commissioners of relevant convictions etc

(1) A person who has applied for a PSV operator's licence shall forthwith notify the traffic [commissioner] to whom the application was made if, in the interval between the making of the application and the date on which it is disposed of, a relevant conviction occurs of the applicant, or any employee or agent of his, or of any person proposed to be engaged as transport manager whose repute and competence are relied on in connection with the application.

(2) It shall be the duty of the holder of a PSV operator's licence to give notice in writing to the traffic [commissioner] by whom the licence was granted of—

(*a*) any relevant conviction of the holder; and

(*b*) any relevant conviction of any officer, employee or agent of the holder for an offence committed in the course of the holder's road passenger transport business,

and to do so within 28 days of the conviction in the case of a conviction of the holder or his transport manager and within 28 days of the conviction coming to the holder's knowledge in any other case.

(3) It shall be the duty of the holder of a PSV operator's licence within 28 days of the occurrence of—

(*a*) the bankruptcy or liquidation of the holder, or the sequestration of his estate [or the making of an administration order under Part II of the Insolvency Act 1986 in relation to the holder] or the appointment of a receiver, manager or trustee of his road passenger transport business; or

(*b*) any change in the identity of the transport manager of the holder's road passenger transport business,

to give notice in writing of that event to the traffic [commissioner] by whom the licence was granted.

(4) [A traffic commissioner] on granting or varying a PSV operator's licence, or at any time thereafter, may require the holder of the licence to inform [him] forthwith or within a time specified by [him] of any material change specified by [him] in any of

[the holder's] circumstances which were relevant to the grant or variation of the licence.

(5) Subject to section 68(1) of this Act, a person who fails to comply with subsection (1), (2) or (3) above or with any requirement under subsection (4) above shall be liable on summary conviction to a fine not exceeding [level 3 on the standard scale].

[Section 19 is printed as amended by the Criminal Justice Act 1982, ss 37 and 46; the Insolvency Act 1985, s 235(1) and Sched 8, para 34; the Transport Act 1985, s 3(5) and Sched 2, Part II, para 4(10); the Insolvency Act 1986, s 439(2) and Sched 14.

For s 68(1) of this Act, see below.]

20. Duty to give traffic commissioners information about vehicles

(1) It shall be the duty of the holder of a PSV operator's licence, on the happening to any public service vehicle owned by him of any failure or damage of a nature calculated to affect the safety of occupants of the public service vehicle or of persons using the road, to report the matter as soon as is practicable to the [Secretary of State].

(2) It shall be the duty of the holder of a PSV operator's licence, on any alteration otherwise than by replacement of parts being made in the structure or fixed equipment of any public service vehicle owned by him, to give notice of the alteration as soon as is practicable to the [Secretary of State].

(3) The traffic [commissioner] by whom a PSV operator's licence was granted may—

(*a*) require the holder of the licence to supply [him] forthwith or within a specified time with such information as [he] may reasonably require about the public service vehicles owned by [the holder] and normally kept at an operating centre within the area of [that commissioner], and to keep up to date information supplied by [the holder] under this paragraph; or

(*b*) require the holder or former holder of the licence to supply [him] forthwith or within a specified time with such information as [he] may reasonably require about the public service vehicles owned by [the holder or former holder] at any material time specified by [him] which were at that time normally kept at an operating centre within the area of [that commissioner].

In this subsection 'material time' means a time when the PSV operator's licence in question was in force.

(4) Subject to section 68(1) of this Act, a person who fails to comply with the provisions of subsection (1) or (2) above or with any requirement under subsection (3) above shall be liable on summary conviction to a fine not exceeding [level 3 on the standard scale].

(5) A person who in purporting to comply with any requirement under subsection (3) above supplies any information which he knows to be false or does not believe to be true shall be liable on summary conviction to a fine not exceeding [level 4 on the standard scale].

(6) Where a certifying officer or public service vehicle examiner [or an authorised inspector] imposes or removes a prohibition on the driving of a public service vehicle, he shall forthwith give notice of that fact to the traffic [commissioner] who granted the PSV operator's licence under which the vehicle was last used before the prohibition was imposed.

[Section 20 is printed as amended by the Criminal Justice Act 1982, ss 37 and 46; the Transport Act 1982, s 10(3); the Transport Act 1985, ss 3(5) and 29, Sched 2, Part II, para 4(11).

The reference in s 20(6) to an authorised inspector (words printed inside square brackets) were inserted by the Transport Act 1982, s 10(3), and will take effect from a date to be announced. Section 10(9) of the 1982 Act inserted the following subsection prospectively into s 20 and also added a reference to the new subsection at the end of s 20(1) and (2) (but it seems that the new subsection may not be brought into operation):

[(2A) Regulations may make provision—

(*a*) for any report or notice required under subsection (1) or (2) above to be made or given to the Secretary of State or to the prescribed testing authority;

(*b*) for requiring a public service vehicle to be submitted for examination in the event of any such failure or damage as is mentioned in subsection (1) above or any such alteration as is mentioned in subsection (2) above; and

(*c*) for the examinations to be carried out under the regulations and, in particular, for authorising any such examination to be carried out by or under the direction of a public service vehicle examiner or an authorised inspector.]

For s 68(1) of this Act, see below.]

21. Certificates of qualification *[Omitted.]*

Drivers' licences

22. Drivers' licences

(1) A person—

(*a*) shall not drive a public service vehicle on a road unless he is licensed for the purpose under this section; and

(*b*) shall not employ a person who is not so licensed for the purpose to drive a public service vehicle on a road.

Notwithstanding section 1(1) of this Act, in this section and in sections 23 to 26 of this Act 'public service vehicle' shall be construed as meaning [a public service vehicle being used on a road for carrying passengers for hire or reward].

(2) The authority having power to grant under this section a licence to a person to drive a public service vehicle shall be [the traffic commissioner for the traffic area in which that person resides at the time when he applies for a licence].

(3) A person shall be disqualified for obtaining a licence to drive a public service vehicle unless he fulfils such conditions as may be prescribed.

(4) A licence to drive a public service vehicle may be limited to such type or types of vehicles as may be specified in the licence.

(5) A licence to drive a public service vehicle may at any time be suspended or revoked by the authority by whom it was granted upon the ground that, by reason of his conduct or physical disability, the holder is not a fit person to hold such a licence; and a licence suspended under this subsection shall during the time of suspension be of no effect.

(6) A licence to drive a public service vehicle shall, unless previously revoked, continue in force for five years from the date on which it is expressed to take effect.

(7) Without prejudice to section 23(3) of this Act if, on the date on which an application is made for a licence to drive a publice service vehicle, the applicant is the

holder of such a licence, the existing licence shall, notwithstanding anything in subsection (6) above, continue in force until the application is disposed of.

(8) A licence granted under this section to a person resident in any traffic area shall be valid in every other traffic area.

(9) Subject to section 68(1) and (3) of this Act, a person who contravenes subsection (1)(*a*) or (*b*) above shall be liable on summary conviction to a fine not exceeding [level 4 on the standard scale].

[Section 22 is printed as amended by the Criminal Justice Act 1982, ss 37 and 46; the Transport Act 1985, ss 1(3) and 139(2), Sched 1, para 5, and Sched 7, para 21(7).
The Public Service Vehicles (Drivers' Licences) Regulations 1985 (SI 1985 No 214) were made in part under this section.
For s 68(1) and (3) of this Act, see below.
The application of this section to certain vehicles is excluded; see further the notes to s 6 of this Act.]

23. Appeals to courts of summary jurisdiction in connection with drivers' licences *[Omitted.]*

Regulation of conduct etc of drivers, inspectors, conductors and passengers

24. Regulation of conduct of drivers, inspectors and conductors

(1) Regulations may make provision for regulating the conduct, when acting as such, of—

(*a*) persons licensed to act as drivers of public service vehicles, and

(*b*) inspectors and conductors of such vehicles.

(2) Subject to section 68(1) of this Act, if a person to whom regulations having effect by virtue of this section apply contravenes, or fails to comply with, any of the provisions of the regulations, he shall be liable on summary conviction to a fine not exceeding [level 2 on the standard scale] and, in the case of an offence by a person acting as driver, the court by which he is convicted may, if it thinks fit, cause particulars of the conviction to be endorsed upon the licence granted to that person under section 22 of this Act.

(3) The person who has the custody of the licence shall, if so required by the convicting court, produce the licence within a reasonable time for the purpose of endorsement, and, subject to section 68(1) of this Act, if he fails to do so, shall be liable on summary conviction to a fine not exceeding [level 3 on the standard scale].

(4) In this section and in section 25 of this Act 'inspector', in relation to a public service vehicle, means a person authorised to act as an inspector by the holder of the PSV operator's licence under which the vehicle is being used.

[Section 25 is printed as amended by the Criminal Justice Act 1982, ss 37 and 46.
For s 68(1) of this Act, see below.]

25. Regulation of conduct of passengers

(1) Regulations may make provision generally as to the conduct of passengers on public service vehicles and in particular (but without prejudice to the generality of the foregoing provision) for—

(*a*) authorising the removal from a public service vehicle of a person infringing the regulations by the driver, inspector or conductor of the vehicle or on the request of the driver, inspector or conductor by a police constable;

(*b*) requiring a passenger in a public service vehicle who is reasonably suspected by the driver, inspector or conductor thereof of contravening the regulations to give his name and address to the driver, inspector or conductor on demand;

(*c*) requiring a passenger to declare, if so requested by the driver, inspector or conductor, the journey he intends to take or has taken in the vehicle, and to pay the fare for the whole of that journey and to accept any ticket provided therefor;

(*d*) requiring, on demand being made for the purpose by the driver, inspector or conductor, production during the journey and surrender at the end of the journey by the holder thereof of any ticket issued to him;

(*e*) requiring a passenger, if so requested by the driver, inspector or conductor, to leave the vehicle on the completion of the journey the fare for which he has paid;

(*f*) requiring the surrender by the holder thereof on the expiry of the period for which it is issued of a ticket issued to him.

(2) . . .

(3) Subject to section 68(1) of this Act, if a person contravenes, or fails to comply with, a provision of regulations having effect by virtue of this section, he shall be liable on summary conviction to a fine not exceeding [level 3 on the standard scale].

(4) *[Applies to Scotland.]*

[Section 25 is printed as amended by the Criminal Justice Act 1982, ss 37 and 46; the Police and Criminal Evidence Act 1984, s 119(2) and Sched 7, Part I.

The Public Service Vehicles (Conduct of Drivers, Conductors and Passengers) Regulations 1936 (S R & O 1936 No 619) (qv) have effect in part as if made under this section.

For s 68(1) of this Act, see below.]

26. Control of number of passengers

(1) Regulations may make provision with respect to public service vehicles for—

(*a*) the determination by or under the regulations of the number of the seated passengers and standing passengers respectively for whom a vehicle is constructed or adapted and fit to carry;

(*b*) the determination by or under the regulations of the number of such passengers respectively who may be carried in a vehicle;

(*c*) the marks to be carried on a vehicle showing those numbers and the manner in which those marks are to be carried.

(2) Subject to section 68(1) and (3) of this Act, if a person contravenes, or fails to comply with, a provision of regulations having effect by virtue of this section, he shall be liable on summary conviction to a fine not exceeding [level 2 on the standard scale].

[Section 26 is printed as amended by the Criminal Justice Act 1982, ss 37, 39(1), 46, and Sched 2.

For s 68(1) and (3) of this Act, see below.

The Public Service Vehicles (Carrying Capacity) Regulations 1984 (SI 1984 No 1406) (qv) were made in part under this section.]

Supplementary provisions

27. Returns to be provided by persons operating public service vehicles

(1) It shall be the duty of a person carrying on the business of operating public service vehicles to keep such accounts and records in relation thereto and to make to the Secretary of State such financial and statistical returns, and in such manner and at such times, as the Secretary of State may from time to time require.

(2) Subject to section 68(3) of this Act, if a person fails to comply with the requirements of subsection (1) above, he shall be liable on summary conviction to a fine not exceeding [level 3 on the standard scale].

(3) This section shall not apply to the British Railways Board or [London Regional Transport or to any subsidiary of London Regional Transport (within the meaning of the London Regional Transport Act 1984)].

[Section 27 is printed as amended by the Criminal Justice Act 1982, ss 37 and 46; the London Regional Transport Act 1984, s 71(3) and Sched 6, para 22.
For s 68(3) of this Act, see below.]

* * *

PART IV

MODIFICATION OF REQUIREMENTS OF PART II IN RELATION TO CERTAIN VEHICLES AND AREAS

Fare-paying passengers on school buses

46. Fare-paying passengers on school buses

(1) Subject to subsection (2) below, a local education authority may—

(*a*) use a school bus, when it is being used to provide free school transport, to carry as fare-paying passengers persons other than those for whom the free school transport is provided;

(*b*) use a school bus belonging to the authority, when it is not being used to provide free school transport, to provide a local . . . service;

and sections 6, 8, 9, 12(1) and 22 of this Act shall not apply to a school bus belonging to a local education authority in the course of its use by the authority in accordance with this subsection.

(2) Subsection (1) above does not affect the duties of a local education authority in relation to the provision of free school transport or authorise a local education authority to make any charge for the carriage of a pupil on a journey which he is required to make in the course of his education at a school maintained by such an authority.

(3) In this section—

'free school transport' means transport provided by a local education authority in pursuance of arrangements under section 55(1) of the Education Act 1944 for the purpose of facilitating the attendance of pupils at a place of education;

. . .

'school bus', in relation to a local education authority, means a motor vehicle which is used by that authority to provide free school transport.

(4) *[Applies to Scotland.]*

[Section 46 is printed as amended by the Transport Act 1986, ss 1(3) and 139(3), Sched 1, para 6, and Sched 8.]

* * *

PART V

MISCELLANEOUS AND SUPPLEMENTARY

* * *

60. General power to make regulations for purposes of Act

(1) *[Omitted.]*

(2) In this Act 'prescribed' means prescribed by regulations and 'regulations' means regulations made under this section.

(3) *[Repealed.]*

* * *

Provisions relating to offences and legal proceedings

65. Forgery and misuse of documents

(1) This section applies to the following documents and other things, namely—

(*a*) a licence under Part II . . . of this Act;

(*b*) a certificate of initial fitness under section 6 of this Act;

[(*bb*) a notice removing a prohibition under section 9 of this Act;]

(*c*) a certificate under section 10 of this Act that a vehicle conforms to a type vehicle;

(*d*) an operator's disc under section 18 of this Act;

(*e*) a certificate under section 21 of this Act as to the repute, financial standing or professional competence of any person;

(*f*) a document evidencing the appointment of a person as a certifying officer or public service vehicle examiner.

(2) A person who, with intent to deceive—

(*a*) forges or alters, or uses or lends to, or allows to be used by, any other person, a document or other thing to which this section applies; or

(*b*) makes or has in his possession any document or other thing so closely resembling a document or other thing to which this section applies as to be calculated to deceive,

shall be liable—

(i) on conviction on indictment, to imprisonment for a term not exceeding two years;

(ii) on summary conviction, to a fine not exceeding the statutory maximum.

(3) In the application of this section to England and Wales—

['forges' means makes a false document or other thing in order that it may be used as genuine];

'statutory maximum' [in relation to a fine on summary conviction for an offence in England and Wales means the prescribed sum within the meaning of section 32 of the Magistrates' Courts Act 1980 [*qv*]].

(4) *[Applies to Scotland.]*

[Section 65 is printed as amended by the Forgery and Counterfeiting Act 1981, s 12; the Transport Act 1982, s 23(4) (which added s 65(1)(bb) from a day to be announced); and the Transport Act 1985, s 139(3) and Sched 8.

As to references in ss 65(1)(a) and 66(a) to a licence under any part of this Act, see the Road Transport (International Passenger Services) Regulations 1984 (SI 1984 No 748), reg 21, below.]

66. False statements to obtain licence etc

A person who knowingly makes a false statement for the purpose of—

(*a*) obtaining the grant of a licence under Part II . . . of this Act to himself or any other person, obtaining the variation of such licence, preventing the grant or variation of any such licence or procuring the imposition of a condition or limitation in relation to any such licence;

(*b*) obtaining the issue of a certificate of initial fitness under section 6 of this Act;

(*c*) obtaining the issue of a certificate under section 10 of this Act that a vehicle conforms to a type vehicle;

(*d*) obtaining the issue of an operator's disc under section 18 of this Act; or

(*e*) obtaining the issue of a certificate under section 21 of this Act as to the repute, financial standing or professional competence of any person;

shall be liable on summary conviction to a fine not exceeding [level 4 on the standard scale].

[Section 66 is printed as amended by the Criminal Justice Act 1982, ss 37 and 46; the Transport Act 1985, s 139(3) and Sched 8.

See further the note to s 65.]

[66A. Issue of false documents] *[Omitted.]*

67. Penalty for breach of regulations

Subject to section 68(1) of this Act, if a person acts in contravention of, or fails to comply with, any regulations made by the Secretary of State under this Act . . . and contravention thereof, or failure to comply therewith, is not made an offence under any other provision of this Act, he shall for each offence be liable on summary conviction to a fine not exceeding [level 2 on the standard scale].

[Section 67 is printed as amended by the Criminal Justice Act 1982, ss 37 and 46; the Transport Act 1985, s 139(3) and Sched 8.]

68. Defences available to persons charged with certain offences

(1) It shall be a defence for a person charged with an offence under any of the provisions of this Act mentioned in subsection (2) below to prove that there was a reasonable excuse for the act or omission in respect of which he is charged.

(2) The provisions referred to in subsection (1) above are—

(*a*) sections 19(5), 20(4), 24(2) and (3), 25(3), 26(2), . . . 67 and 70(3); and

(*b*) so much of section 22(9) as relates to contravention of section 22(1)(*a*).

(3) It shall be a defence for a person charged with an offence under any of the provisions of this Act mentioned in subsection (4) below to prove that he took all reasonable precautions and exercised all due diligence to avoid the commission of any offence under that provision.

(4) The provisions referred to in subsection (3) above are—

(*a*) sections 6(2), 9(9)(*b*), 12(5), 16(7), 18(4), 26(2), [and 27(2)]; and

(*b*) so much of section 22(9) as relates to contravention of section 22(1)(*b*).

[Section 68 is printed as amended by the Transport Act 1985, ss 1(3) and 139(3), Sched 1, para 11, and Sched 8.]

69. Restriction on institution in England and Wales of proceedings under Part II

(1) Subject to the provisions of this section proceedings for an offence under Part II . . . of this Act shall not, in England and Wales, be instituted except by or on behalf of the Director of Public Prosecutions or by a person authorised in that behalf by [a traffic commissioner], a chief officer of police, or the council of a county or district.

(2) Subsection (1) above shall not apply to proceedings for the breach of regulations having effect by virtue of section 25 or 26 of this Act.

(3) Subsection (1) above shall not prevent the institution by or on behalf of the Secretary of State of proceedings for an offence under section 27 of this Act.

[Section 69 is printed as amended by the Transport Act 1985, ss 3(5) and 139(3), Sched 2, Part II, para 4(19), and Sched 8.]

70. Duty to give information as to identity of driver in certain cases

(1) Where the driver of a vehicle is alleged to be guilty of an offence under Part II . . . of this Act—

(*a*) the person keeping the vehicle shall give such information as to the identity of the driver as he may be required to give by or on behalf of a chief officer of police, and

(*b*) any other person shall if required as aforesaid give any information which it is in his power to give and may lead to the identification of the driver.

(2) A person who fails to comply with the requirement of paragraph (*a*) of subsection (1) above shall, unless he shows to the satisfaction of the court that he did not know and could not with reasonable diligence ascertain who the driver of the vehicle was, be liable on summary conviction to a fine not exceeding [level 3 on the standard scale].

(3) Subject to section 68(1) of this Act, a person who fails to comply with the requirement of paragraph (*b*) of subsection (1) above shall be liable on summary conviction to a fine not exceeding [level 3 on the standard scale].

[Section 70 is printed as amended by the Criminal Justice Act 1982, s 38(1), (6) and (8) (it being assumed that the s 70 offence, being a re-enactment of an offence in the Road Traffic Act

1960, was a summary offence created not later than 29 July 1977 and hence within the scope of s 38(1) of the 1982 Act); the Transport Act 1985, s 139(3) and Sched 8.]

* * *

71. Evidence by certificate

(1) In any proceedings in England or Wales for an offence under Part II . . . of this Act a certificate in the prescribed form, purporting to be signed by a constable and certifying that the person specified in the certificate stated to the constable—

(*a*) that a particular motor vehicle was being driven or used by, or belonged to, that person on a particular occasion; or

(*b*) that a particular motor vehicle on a particular occasion was used by or belonged to a firm in which that person also stated that he was at the time of the statement a partner; or

(*c*) that a particular motor vehicle on a particular occasion was used by or belonged to a company of which that person also stated that he was at the time of the statement a director, officer or employee,

shall be admissible as evidence for the purpose of determining by whom the vehicle was being driven or used or to whom it belonged, as the case may be, on that occasion.

(2) Nothing in subsection (1) above shall be deemed to make a certificate admissible as evidence in proceedings for an offence except in a case where and to the like extent to which oral evidence to the like effect would have been admissible in those proceedings.

(3) Nothing in subsection (1) above shall be deemed to make a certificate admissible as evidence in proceedings for an offence—

(*a*) unless a copy thereof has, not less than seven days before the hearing or trial, been served in the prescribed manner on the person charged with the offence; or

(*b*) if that person, not later than three days before the hearing or trial or within such further time as the court may in special circumstances allow, serves a notice in the prescribed form and manner on the prosecutor requiring attendance at the trial of the person who signed the certificate.

(4) In this section 'prescribed' means prescribed by rules made by the Secretary of State by statutory instrument.

[Section 71 is printed as amended by the Transport Act 1985, s 139(3) and Sched 8.

No rules have been prescribed under s 71(3). This section re-enacts the Road Traffic Act 1960, s 242, without, however, repealing it. Hence the Evidence by Certificate Rules 1961 (SI 1961 No 248), as amended, rr 2, 3 and Schedule, made under the 1960 Act may not, strictly, be applicable under s 71; cf the Interpretation Act 1978, s 17(2)(b) (which applies where an Act 'repeals and re-enacts a previous enactment').]

72. Proof in summary proceedings of identity of driver of vehicle

Where on a summary trial in England or Wales of an information for an offence under Part II . . . of this Act—

(*a*) it is proved to the satisfaction of the court, on oath or in a manner prescribed by rules made under [section 144 of the Magistrates' Courts Act 1980], that a requirement under subsection (1) of section 70 of this Act to give information as to the identity of the driver of a particular vehicle on the particular occasion to which the information relates has been served on the accused by post; and

(*b*) a statement in writing is produced to the court purporting to be signed by the accused that the accused was the driver of that vehicle on that occasion,

the court may accept that statement as evidence that the accused was the driver of that vehicle on the occasion.

[Section 72 is printed as amended by the Magistrates' Courts Act 1980, s 154(2) and Sched 8, para 5 (which came into operation after this Act had received the royal assent but before this Act came into operation); the Transport Act 1985, s 139(3) and Sched 8.]

73. Time within which summary proceedings for certain offences may be commenced

Summary proceedings for an offence under section 65 or 66 of this Act may be brought within a period of six months from the date on which evidence sufficient in the opinion of the prosecutor to warrant the proceedings came to his knowledge; but no such proceedings shall be brought by virtue of this section more than three years after the commission of the offence.

For the purposes of this section a certificate by or on behalf of the prosecutor and stating the date on which such evidence as aforesaid came to his knowledge shall be conclusive evidence of that fact; and a certificate stating that matter and purporting to be so signed shall be deemed to be so signed unless the contrary is proved.

74. Offences by companies

(1) Where an offence under Part II . . . of this Act committed by a company is proved to have been committed with the consent or connivance of, or to be attributable to any neglect on the part of, any director, manager, secretary or other similar officer of the company, or any person who was purporting to act in any such capacity, he, as well as the company, shall be guilty of that offence and be liable to be proceeded against and punished accordingly.

(2) Where the affairs of a company are managed by its members, subsection (1) above shall apply in relation to the acts and defaults of a member in connection with his functions of management as if he were a director of the company.

[Section 74 is printed as amended by the Transport Act 1985, s 139(3) and Sched 8.]

* * *

81. Interpretation of references to the operator of a vehicle or service

(1) For the purposes of this Act—

(*a*) regulations may make provision as to the person who is to be regarded as the operator of a vehicle which is made available by one holder of a PSV operator's licence to another under a hiring arrangement; and

(*b*) where regulations under paragraph (*a*) above do not apply, the operator of a vehicle is—

(i) the driver, if he owns the vehicle; and

(ii) in any other case, the person for whom the driver works (whether under a contract of employment or any other description of contract personally to do work).

(2) *[Repealed.]*

[Section 81 is printed as amended by the Transport Act 1985, s 1(3) and Sched 1, para 12.]

82. General interpretation provisions

(1) In this Act, unless the context otherwise requires—

'certificate of initial fitness' has the meaning given by section 6;

'certifying officer' means an officer appointed under section 7(1);

. . .

'company' means a body corporate;

. . .

'contravention', in relation to any condition or provision, includes a failure to comply with the condition or provision, and 'contravene' shall be construed accordingly;

'director', in relation to a company, includes any person who occupies the position of a director, by whatever name called;

'driver', where a separate person acts as steersman of a motor vehicle, includes that person as well as any other person engaged in the driving of the vehicle, and 'drive' shall be construed accordingly;

. . .

'fares' include sums payable in respect of a contract ticket or a season ticket;

'international operation' means a passenger transport operation starting or terminating in the United Kingdom and involving an international journey by the vehicle concerned, whether or not any driver leaves or enters the United Kingdom with that vehicle;

'local authority' means—

(*a*) in relation to England and Wales, any local authority within the meaning of the Local Government Act 1972;

(*b*) *[Applies to Scotland.]*

['local service' has the same meaning as in the Transport Act 1985;]

'magistrates' court' and 'petty sessions area' have the same meanings as in the Magistrates' Courts Act 1980;

'modification' includes addition, omission and alteration, and related expressions shall be construed accordingly;

'motor vehicle' means a mechanically propelled vehicle intended or adapted for use on roads;

'national operation' means a passenger transport operation wholly within the United Kingdom;

'official PSV testing station' has the meaning given by section 8(3);

'operating centre', in relation to a vehicle, means the base or centre at which the vehicle is normally kept;

'operator' has the meaning given by section 81;

'owner', in relation to a vehicle which is the subject of an agreement for hire, hire-purchase, conditional sale or loan, means the person in possession of the vehicle under that agreement, and references to owning a vehicle shall be construed accordingly;

'prescribed' has the meaning given by section 60(2);

['prescribed testing authority' means such person authorised by the Secretary of

State under section 8 of the Transport Act 1982 to carry on a vehicle testing business within the meaning of Part II of that Act as may be prescribed;]

'PSV operator's licence' means a PSV operator's licence granted under the provisions of Part II of this Act;

'public service vehicle' has the meaning given by section 1;

'relevant conviction' means a conviction (other than a spent conviction) of any offence prescribed for the purposes of this Act, or an offence under the law of Northern Ireland, or of a country or territory outside the United Kingdom, corresponding to an offence so prescribed;

'restricted licence' means such a PSV operator's licence as is mentioned in section 13(3);

'road' means any highway and any other road to which the public has access, and includes bridges over which a road passes;

. . .

'standard licence' means a PSV operator's licence which is not a restricted licence;

'statutory provision' means a provision contained in an Act or in subordinate legislation within the meaning of the Interpretation Act 1978;

['traffic commissioner' means the person appointed to be the commissioner for a traffic area constituted for the purposes of this Act;]

'tramcar' includes any carriage used on any road by virtue of an order made under the Light Railways Act 1896;

'transport manager', in relation to a business, means an individual who, either alone or jointly with one or more other persons, has continuous and effective responsibility for the management of the road passenger transport operations of the business;

. . .

[(1A) References in any provision of this Act to an authorised inspector are references to an authorised inspector under section 8 of the Transport Act 1982 and, where the function to which that provision relates is one of those specified in section 9 of that Act (testing and surveillance functions), are limited to an authorised inspector authorised under section 8 to exercise that function.]

(2) Any reference in this Act to a Community instrument or to a particular provision of such an instrument—

(*a*) is a reference to that instrument or provision as amended from time to time, and

(*b*) if that instrument or provision is replaced, with or without modification, shall be construed as a reference to the instrument or provision replacing it.

[Section 82 is printed as amended by the Transport Act 1982, s 74(1) and Sched 5, para 23; the Transport Act 1985, ss 1(3), 3(5) and 139(3), Sched 1, para 13, Sched 2, Part II, para 4(2), and Sched 8.

The definition of 'prescribed testing authority' (in s 82(1) and s 82(1A)), which were inserted by the Transport Act 1982, s 74(1) and Sched 5, para 23, will take effect from a date to be announced.]

83. Construction of references in other Acts etc to public service vehicles, licensing authorities etc

(1) A provision of an Act other than this Act or of an instrument having effect under an enactment not repealed by this Act which (however expressed) defines 'public service vehicle' . . . by reference to the Road Traffic Act 1930 or the Road Traffic

Act 1960 shall have effect as if it provided that that expression should be construed in like manner as if it were contained in this Act.

(2) *[Repealed.]*

[Section 83 is printed as amended by the Transport Act 1983, ss 1(3) and 139(3), Sched 1, para 14, and Sched 8.]

*   *   *

SCHEDULE 1

Public Service Vehicles: Conditions Affecting Status for Classification

PART I

Sharing of Taxis and Hire-Cars

1. The making of the agreement for the payment of separate fares must not have been initiated by the driver or by the owner of the vehicle, by any person who has made the vehicle available under any arrangement, or by any person who receives any remuneration in respect of the arrangements for the journey.

2.—(1) The journey must be made without previous advertisement to the public of facilities for its being made by passengers to be carried at separate fares, except where the local authorities concerned have approved the arrangements under which the journey is made as designed to meet the social and welfare needs of one or more communities, and their approvals remain in force.

(2) In relation to a journey the local authorities concerned for the purposes of this paragraph are those in whose area any part of the journey is to be made; and in this sub-paragraph 'local authority' means—

(*a*) in relation to England and Wales, [the council of a county, metropolitan district or London borough and the Common Council of the City of London];

(*b*) *[Applies to Scotland.]*

3. *[Repealed.]*

PART II

Parties of Overseas Visitors

4. *[Repealed.]*

PART III

Alternative Conditions Affecting Status for Classification

5. Arrangements for the bringing together of all the passengers for the purpose of making the journey must have been made otherwise than by, or by a person acting on behalf of—

(*a*) the holder of the PSV operator's licence under which the vehicle is to be used, if such a licence is in force.

(*b*) the driver or the owner of the vehicle or any person who has made the vehicle available under any arrangement, if no such licence is in force,

and otherwise than by any person who receives any remuneration in respect of the arrangements.

6. The journey must be made without previous advertisement to the public of the arrangements therefor.

7. All passengers must, in the case of a journey to a particular destination, be carried to, or to the vicinity of, that destination, or, in the case of a tour, be carried for the greater part of the journey.

8. No differentiation of fares for the journey on the basis of distance or of time must be made.

PART IV

SUPPLEMENTARY

9. For the purposes of paragraphs 2 and 6 above no acount shall be taken of any such advertisement as follows, that is to say—

(*a*) a notice displayed or announcement made—

(i) at or in any place of worship for the information of persons attending that place of worship;

(ii) at or in any place of work for the information of persons who work there; or

(iii) by any club or other voluntary association at or in any premises occupied or used by the club or association;

(*b*) a notice contained in any periodical published for the information of, and circulating wholly or mainly among—

(i) persons who attend or might reasonably be expected to attend a particular place of worship or a place of worship in a particular place; or

(ii) persons who work at a particular place of work or at any of two or more particular places of work; or

(iii) the members of a club or other voluntary association.

[Schedule 1 is printed as amended by the Local Government Act 1985, s 8(1) and Sched 5, para 3(7); the Transport Act 1985, s 139(2) and (3), Sched 7, para 21(12), and Sched 8.]

* * *

The Refuse Disposal (Amenity) Act 1978

(1978 c 3)

An Act to consolidate certain enactments relating to abandoned vehicles and other refuse

[23rd March 1978]

* * *

3. Removal of abandoned vehicles

(1) Where it appears to a local authority that a motor vehicle in their area is abandoned without lawful authority on any land in the open air or on any other land forming part of a highway, it shall be the duty of the authority, subject to the following provisions of this section, to remove the vehicle.

(2) Where it appears to a local authority that the land on which a motor vehicle is abandoned as aforesaid is occupied by any person, the authority shall give him notice . . . that they propose to remove the vehicle in pursuance of subsection (1) above but shall not be entitled to remove it if he objects to the proposal . . . within the prescribed period.

(3) A local authority shall not be required by virtue of subsection (1) above to remove a vehicle situated otherwise than on a carriageway within the meaning of [the Highways Act 1980] if it appears to them that the cost of its removal to the nearest convenient carriageway within the meaning of that Act would be unreasonably high.

(4) *[Applies to Scotland.]*

(5) Where in pursuance of this section a local authority propose to remove a vehicle which in their opinion is in such a condition that it ought to be destroyed they shall, not less than the prescribed period before removing it, cause to be affixed to the vehicle a notice stating that the authority propose to remove it for destruction on the expiration of that period.

[(6) Any vehicle removed under this section by the council of a London borough whose area is included in the area of a London waste disposal authority, or by the council of a metropolitan district whose area is included in the area of the Greater Manchester Waste Disposal Authority or the Merseyside Waste Disposal Authority, shall be delivered by them to the authority in question in accordance with such arrangements (including arrangements as to the sharing of any expenses incurred or sums received by the council and the authority under this Act) as may be agreed between the council and the authority or, in default of agreement, as may be determined by arbitration.]

(7) Any vehicle removed by the council of [a non-metropolitan district in England] under this section shall be delivered by them to the county council in accordance with such arrangements (including arrangements as to the sharing of any expenses incurred or sums received by the district council and the county council under this Act) as may be agreed between the district council and the county council or, in default of agreement, as may be determined by arbitration.

(8) While a vehicle, other than a vehicle to which a notice was affixed in accordance with subsection (5) above, is in the custody of a local authority [, a London waste disposal authority, the Greater Manchester Waste Disposal Authority, the Merseyside Waste Disposal Authority] . . . or the council of a county in England in pursuance of this section, it shall be the duty of that body to take such steps as are reasonably necessary for the safe custody of the vehicle.

(9) Subsections (5) and (6) of section 1 above shall apply to the duties imposed by subsections (1) and (2) above as if—

(*a*) for any reference to the duty imposed by that section there were substituted a reference to the duties aforesaid; and

(*b*) for any reference to a local authority within the meaning of that section there were substituted a reference to a local authority within the meaning of this section.

[(10) In this section and section 5 the area of the Greater Manchester Waste Disposal Authority is the metropolitan county of Greater Manchester excluding the metropolitan district of Wigan.]

[Section 3 is printed as amended by the Local Government, Planning and Land Act 1980, s 194 and Sched 34, Part III; the Highways Act 1980, s 343(2) and Sched 24, para 30; the Local Government Act 1985, ss 9 and 102, and Sched 6, para 4(3), and Sched 17; the Waste Regulation and Disposal (Authorities) Order 1985 (SI 1985 No 1884).

Section 3 is expressly applied by the Road Traffic Regulation Act 1984, s 104 (qv), the Motor Vehicles (Tests) Regulations 1981 (SI 1981 No 1694), reg 6(2) (qv), and the Goods Vehicles (Plating and Testing) Regulations 1988 (SI 1988 No 1478), reg 44(1).]

* * *

11. Interpretation

(1) In this Act, unless the contrary intention appears, the following expressions have the following meanings, that is to say—

'the Common Council' means the Common Council of the City of London;

'licence' means, in relation to a vehicle, a licence issued for the vehicle under the Vehicles (Excise) Act 1971;

'local authority' means—

(*a*) in relation to England, a district council, London borough council or the Common Council;

(*b*) *[Applies to Scotland.]*; and

(*c*) in relation to Wales, a district council;

['London waste disposal authority' means an authority established by Part II, III IV or V of Schedule 1 to the Waste Regulation and Disposal (Authorities) Order 1985;]

'motor vehicle' means a mechanically propelled vehicle intended or adapted for use on roads, whether or not it is in a fit state for such use, and includes any trailer intended or adapted for use as an attachment to such a vehicle, any chassis or body, with or without wheels, appearing to have formed part of such a vehicle or trailer and anything attached to such a vehicle or trailer;

'owner', in relation to a motor vehicle which is the subject of a hiring agreement or hire-purchase agreement, includes the person entitled to possession of the vehicle under the agreement;

'prescribed' means prescribed by regulations made by the Secretary of State;

'the relevant date' has the meaning given to it by section 13(3) below.

(2) Any reference in this Act to an enactment is a reference to it as amended or applied by or under any other enactment, including this Act.

[Section 11 is printed as amended by the Waste Regulation and Disposal (Authorities) Order 1985 (SI 1985 No 1884).

A definition relating exclusively and expressly to Scotland has been omitted from s 11(1).]

The Road Traffic Act 1988

(1988 c 52)

An Act to consolidate certain enactments relating to road traffic with amendments to give effect to recommendations of the Law Commission and the Scottish Law Commission.

[15 November 1988]

ARRANGEMENT OF SECTIONS

PART I

PRINCIPAL ROAD SAFETY PROVISIONS

Driving offences

Tests of certain classes of goods vehicles

Approval of design, construction, equipment and marking of vehicles

Conditions for grant of excise licence

. . . .

Testing vehicles on roads

Maintenance and loading of goods vehicles

Miscellaneous provisions about vehicles and vehicle parts

PART IV

Licensing of Drivers of Heavy Goods Vehicles

Requirement for HGV licence

Grant, duration and revocation of licences

Appeals and review of tests

General and supplemental

PART V

Driving Instruction

Instructors to be registered or licensed

Registration

Licences

Appeals

Examinations and tests

General and supplemental

. . . .

135. Power to prescribe form of certificate of registration, etc.
136. Surrender of certificates and licences
137. Production of certificates and licences to constables and authorised persons
138. Offences by corporations

. . . .

142. Index to Part V

PART VI

Third-Party Liabilities

Compulsory insurance or security against third-party risks

143. Users of motor vehicles to be insured or secured against third-party risks
144. Exceptions from requirement of third-party insurance or security
145. Requirements in respect of policies of insurance

. . . .

147. Issue and surrender of certificates of insurance and of security
148. Avoidance of certain exceptions to policies or securities
149. Avoidance of certain agreements as to liability towards passengers
150. Insurance or security in respect of private use of vehicle to cover use under car-sharing arrangements

. . . .

154. Duty to give information as to insurance or security where claim made

. . . .

Payments for treatment of traffic casualties

157. Payment for hospital treatment of traffic casualties
158. Payment for emergency treatment of traffic casualties
159. Supplementary provisions as to payments for treatment

General

. . . .

161. Interpretation
162. Index to Part VI

PART VII

Miscellaneous and General

Powers of constables and other authorised persons

163. Power of police to stop vehicles
164. Power of constables to require production of driving licence and in certain cases statement of date of birth
165. Power of constables to obtain names and addresses of drivers and others, and to require production of evidence of insurance or security and test certificates
166. Powers of certifying officers and examiners as respects goods vehicles

. . . .

Duty to give name and address

Duties in case of accident

Other duties to give information or documents

Forgery, false statements, etc.

Offences in Scotland

. . . .

Inquiries

. . . .

Application to the Crown

Interpretation

Supplementary

. . . .

SCHEDULES

PART 1

Principal Road Safety Provisions

Driving offences

1. Causing death by reckless driving

A person who causes the death of another person by driving a motor vehicle on a road recklessly is guilty of an offence.

[The offence under s 1 is expressly excluded from the application of the Criminal Justice Act 1982, s 32 (early release of prisoners); see Part II of Sched 1 to that Act, as amended by the Road Traffic (Consequential Provisions) Act 1988, s 4 and Sched 3, para 24.

An offence under s 1 is designated as a 'serious arrestable offence' by the Police and Criminal Evidence Act 1984, s 116(2) and Sched 5, Part II, as amended by the Road Traffic (Consequential Provisions) Act 1988, s 4 and Sched 3, para 27(5).]

2. Reckless driving

A person who drives a motor vehicle on a road recklessly is guilty of an offence.

3. Careless, and inconsiderate, driving

If a person drives a motor vehicle on a road without due care and attention, or without reasonable consideration for other persons using the road, he is guilty of an offence.

Motor vehicles: drink and drugs

4. Driving, or being in charge, when under influence of drink or drugs

(1) A person who, when driving or attempting to drive a motor vehicle on a road or other public place, is unfit to drive through drink or drugs is guilty of an offence.

(2) Without prejudice to subsection (1) above, a person who, when in charge of a motor vehicle which is on a road or other public place, is unfit to drive through drink or drugs is guilty of an offence.

(3) For the purposes of subsection (2) above, a person shall be deemed not to have been in charge of a motor vehicle if he proves that at the material time the circumstances were such that there was no likelihood of his driving it so long as he remained unfit to drive through drink or drugs.

(4) The court may, in determining whether there was such a likelihood as is mentioned in subsection (3) above, disregard any injury to him and any damage to the vehicle.

(5) For the purposes of this section, a person shall be taken to be unfit to drive if his ability to drive properly is for the time being impaired.

(6) A constable may arrest a person without warrant if he has reasonable cause to suspect that that person is or has been committing an offence under this section.

(7) For the purpose of arresting a person under the power conferred by subsection (6) above, a constable may enter (if need be by force) any place where that person is or where the constable, with reasonable cause, suspects him to be.

(8) Subsection (7) above does not extend to Scotland, and nothing in that subsection affects any rule of law in Scotland concerning the right of a constable to enter any premises for any purpose.

[The code of practice for the identification of persons by police officers issued under s 66 of the Police and Criminal Evidence Act 1984 does not to affect any procedure under ss 4–11 of this Act; see para 1.13(i) of the code.]

5. Driving or being in charge of a motor vehicle with alcohol concentration above prescribed limit

(1) If a person—

(*a*) drives or attempts to drive a motor vehicle on a road or other public place, or

(*b*) is in charge of a motor vehicle on a road or other public place,

after consuming so much alcohol that the proportion of it in his breath, blood or urine exceeds the prescribed limit he is guilty of an offence.

(2) It is a defence for a person charged with an offence under subsection (1)(*b*) above to prove that at the time he is alleged to have committed the offence the circumstances were such that there was no likelihood of his driving the vehicle whilst the proportion of alcohol in his breath, blood or urine remained likely to exceed the prescribed limit.

(3) The court may, in determining whether there was such a likelihood as is mentioned in subsection (2) above, disregard any injury to him and any damage to the vehicle.

[See the note to s 4 above.]

6. Breath tests

(1) Where a constable in uniform has reasonable cause to suspect—

(*a*) that a person driving or attempting to drive or in charge of a motor vehicle on a road or other public place has alcohol in his body or has committed a traffic offence whilst the vehicle was in motion, or

(*b*) that a person has been driving or attempting to drive or been in charge of a motor vehicle on a road or other public place with alcohol in his body and that that person still has alcohol in his body, or

(*c*) that a person has been driving or attempting to drive or been in charge of a motor vehicle on a road or other public place and has committed a traffic offence whilst the vehicle was in motion,

he may, subject to section 9 of this Act, require him to provide a specimen of breath for a breath test.

(2) If an accident occurs owing to the presence of a motor vehicle on a road or other public place, a constable may, subject to section 9 of this Act, require any person who he has reasonable cause to believe was driving or attempting to drive or in charge of the vehicle at the time of the accident to provide a specimen of breath for a breath test.

(3) A person may be required under subsection (1) or subsection (2) above to provide a specimen either at or near the place where the requirement is made or, if the requirement is made under subsection (2) above and the constable making the requirement thinks fit, at a police station specified by the constable.

(4) A person who, without reasonable excuse, fails to provide a specimen of breath when required to do so in pursuance of this section is guilty of an offence.

(5) A constable may arrest a person without warrant if—

(*a*) as a result of a breath test he has reasonable cause to suspect that the proportion of alcohol in that person's breath or blood exceeds the prescribed limit, or

(*b*) that person has failed to provide a specimen of breath for a breath test when required to do so in pursuance of this section and the constable has reasonable cause to suspect that he has alcohol in his body,

but a person shall not be arrested by virtue of this subsection when he is at a hospital as a patient.

(6) A constable may, for the purpose of requiring a person to provide a specimen of breath under subsection (2) above in a case where he has reasonable cause to suspect that the accident involved injury to another person or of arresting him in such a case under subsection (5) above, enter (if need be by force) any place where that person is or where the constable, with reasonable cause, suspects him to be.

(7) Subsection (6) above does not extend to Scotland, and nothing in that subsection shall affect any rule of law in Scotland concerning the right of a constable to enter any premises for any purpose.

(8) In this section 'traffic offence' means an offence under—

(*a*) any provision of Part II of the Public Passenger Vehicles Act 1981 [*qv*],

(*b*) any provision of the Road Traffic Regulation Act 1984 [*qv*],

(*c*) any provision of the Road Traffic Offenders Act 1988 [*qv*] except Part III, or

(*d*) any provision of this Act except Part V.

[See the note to s 4 above.]

7. Provision of specimens for analysis

(1) In the course of an investigation into whether a person has committed an offence under section 4 or 5 of this Act a constable may, subject to the following provisions of this section and section 9 of this Act, require him—

(*a*) to provide two specimens of breath for analysis by means of a device of a type approved by the Secretary of State, or

(*b*) to provide a specimen of blood or urine for a laboratory test.

(2) A requirement under this section to provide specimens of breath can only be made at a police station.

(3) A requirement under this section to provide a specimen of blood or urine can only be made at a police station or at a hospital; and it cannot be made at a police station unless—

(*a*) the constable making the requirement has reasonable cause to believe that for medical reasons a specimen of breath cannot be provided or should not be required, or

(*b*) at the time the requirement is made a device or a reliable device of the type mentioned in subsection (1)(*a*) above is not available at the police station or it is then for any other reason not practicable to use such a device there, or

(*c*) the suspected offence is one under section 4 of this Act and the constable making the requirement has been advised by a medical practitioner that the condition of the person required to provide the specimen might be due to some drug;

but may then be made notwithstanding that the person required to provide the specimen has already provided or been required to provide two specimens of breath.

(4) If the provision of a specimen other than a specimen of breath may be required in pursuance of this section the question whether it is to be a specimen of blood or a specimen of urine shall be decided by the constable making the requirement, but if a medical practitioner is of the opinion that for medical reasons a specimen of blood cannot or should not be taken the specimen shall be a specimen of urine.

(5) A specimen of urine shall be provided within one hour of the requirement for its provision being made and after the provision of a previous specimen of urine.

(6) A person who, without reasonable excuse, fails to provide a specimen when required to do so in pursuance of this section is guilty of an offence.

(7) A constable must, on requiring any person to provide a specimen in pursuance of this section, warn him that a failure to provide it may render him liable to prosecution.

[In Note 6C of the notes for guidance in the code of practice for the detention, treatment and questioning of persons by police officers issued under s 66 of the Police and Criminal Evidence Act 1984, it is stated that procedures under s 7 of this Act do not constitute interviewing for the purposes of the code. Note 6C is appended to para 6.6 of the code which states that a solicitor may only be required to leave an interview if his conduct is such that the interviewing officer is unable properly to put questions to the suspect. Paragraph 6.6 appears in the section of the code dealing with the right of a suspect to legal advice. The notes for guidance are expressly stated not to be provisions of the code.

The code of practice for the identification of persons by police officers (also issued under s 66) is expressed not to affect any procedure under ss 4–11 of this Act; see para 1.13(i) of the code.]

8. Choice of specimens of breath

(1) Subject to subsection (2) below, of any two specimens of breath provided by any person in pursuance of section 7 of this Act that with the lower proportion of alcohol in the breath shall be used and the other shall be disregarded.

(2) If the specimen with the lower proportion of alcohol contains no more than 50 microgrammes of alcohol in 100 millilitres of breath, the person who provided it may claim that it should be replaced by such specimen as may be required under section 7(4) of this Act and, if he then provides such a specimen, neither specimen of breath shall be used.

(3) The Secretary of State may by regulations substitute another proportion of alcohol in the breath for that specified in subsection (2) above.

9. Protection for hospital patients

(1) While a person is at a hospital as a patient he shall not be required to provide a specimen of breath for a breath test or to provide a specimen for a laboratory test unless the medical practitioner in immediate charge of his case has been notified of the proposal to make the requirement; and—

(*a*) if the requirement is then made, it shall be for the provision of a specimen at the hospital, but

(*b*) if the medical practitioner objects on the ground specified in subsection (2) below, the requirement shall not be made.

(2) The ground on which the medical practitioner may object is that the requirement or the provision of a specimen or, in the case of a specimen of blood or urine, the warning required under section 7(7) of this Act, would be prejudicial to the proper care and treatment of the patient.

[See the note to s 4 above.]

10. Detention of persons affected by alcohol or a drug

(1) Subject to subsections (2) and (3) below, a person required to provide a specimen of breath, blood or urine may afterwards be detained at a police station until it appears to the constable that, were that person then driving or attempting to drive a motor vehicle on a road, he would not be committing an offence under section 4 or 5 of this Act.

(2) A person shall not be detained in pursuance of this section if it appears to a constable that there is no likelihood of his driving or attempting to drive a motor vehicle whilst his ability to drive properly is impaired or whilst the proportion of alcohol in his breath, blood or urine exceeds the prescribed limit.

(3) A constable must consult a medical practitioner on any question arising under this section whether a person's ability to drive properly is or might be impaired through drugs and must act on the medical practitioner's advice.

[See the note to s 4 above.]

11. Interpretation of sections 4 to 10

(1) The following provisions apply for the interpretation of sections 4 to 10 of this Act.

(2) In those sections—

'breath test' means a preliminary test for the purpose of obtaining, by means of a device of a type approved by the Secretary of State, an indication whether the proportion of alcohol in a person's breath or blood is likely to exceed the prescribed limit,

'drug' includes any intoxicant other than alcohol,

'fail' includes refuse,

'hospital' means an institution which provides medical or surgical treatment for in-patients or out-patients,

'the prescribed limit' means, as the case may require—

(*a*) 35 microgrammes of alcohol in 100 millilitres of breath,

(*b*) 80 milligrammes of alcohol in 100 millilitres of blood, or

(*c*) 107 milligrammes of alcohol in 100 millilitres of urine, or such other proportion as may be prescribed by regulations made by the Secretary of State.

(3) A person does not provide a specimen of breath for a breath test or for analysis unless the specimen—

(*a*) is sufficient to enable the test or the analysis to be carried out, and

(*b*) is provided in such a way as to enable the objective of the test or analysis to be satisfactorily achieved.

(4) A person provides a specimen of blood if and only if he consents to its being taken by a medical practitioner and it is so taken.

[The devices which have been approved for use in England and Wales under s 11(2) are the following:

Alcotest 80	(see the Breath Test Device (Approval) (No 1) Order 1968)
Alcotest 80A	(see the Breath Test Device (Approval) (No 1) Order 1975)
Alcolyser	(see the Breath Test Device (Approval) (No 1) Order 1979)
Alcolmeter	(see the Breath Test Device (Approval) (No 2) Order 1979)
Alert	(see the Breath Test Device (Approval) (No 1) Order 1980),
and	
Alcolmeter S-L2A	(see the Breath Test Device Approval 1987), dated 7 September 1987

See further the note to s 4 above.]

Motor racing and motoring events on public ways

12. Motor racing on public ways

(1) A person who promotes or takes part in a race or trial of speed between motor vehicles on a public way is guilty of an offence.

(2) In this section 'public way' means, in England and Wales, a public highway.

[Words relating exclusively and expressly to Scotland have been omitted from s 12(2).]

13. Regulation of motoring events on public ways

(1) A person who promotes or takes part in a competition or trial (other than a race or trial of speed) involving the use of motor vehicles on a public way is guilty of an offence unless the competition or trial—

(*a*) is authorised, and

(*b*) is conducted in accordance with any conditions imposed,

by or under regulations under this section.

(2) The Secretary of State may by regulations authorise, or provide for authorising, the holding of competitions or trials (other than races or trials of speed) involving the use of motor vehicles on public ways either—

(*a*) generally, or

(*b*) as regards any area, or as regards any class or description of competition or trial or any particular competition or trial,

subject to such conditions, including conditions requiring the payment of fees, as may be imposed by or under the regulations.

(3) Regulations under this section may—

(*a*) prescribe the procedure to be followed, and the particulars to be given, in connection with applications for authorisation under the regulations, and

(*b*) make different provision for different classes or descriptions of competition or trial.

(4) In this section 'public way' means, in England and Wales, a public highway.

[Words relating exclusively and expressly to Scotland have been omitted from s 13(4).]

Protective measures: seat belts, helmets, etc

14. Seat belts: adults

(1) The Secretary of State may make regulations requiring, subject to such exceptions as may be prescribed, persons who are driving or riding in motor vehicles on a road to wear seat belts of such description as may be prescribed.

(2) Regulations under this section—

(*a*) may make different provision in relation to different classes of vehicles, different descriptions of persons and different circumstances,

(*b*) shall include exceptions for—

(i) the users of vehicles constructed or adapted for the delivery of goods or mail to consumers or addresses, as the case may be, while engaged in making local rounds of deliveries,

(ii) the drivers of vehicles while performing a manoeuvre which includes reversing,

(iii) any person holding a valid certificate signed by a medical practitioner to the effect that it is inadvisable on medical grounds for him to wear a seat belt,

(*c*) may make any prescribed exceptions subject to such conditions as may be prescribed, and

(*d*) may prescribe cases in which a fee of a prescribed amount may be charged on an application for any certificate required as a condition of any prescribed exception.

(3) A person who drives or rides in a motor vehicle in contravention of regulations under this section is guilty of an offence; but, notwithstanding any enactment or rule of law, no person other than the person actually committing the contravention is guilty of an offence by reason of the contravention.

(4) If the holder of any such certificate as is referred to in subsection (2)(*b*) above is informed by a constable that he may be prosecuted for any offence under subsection (3) above, he is not in proceedings for that offence entitled to rely on the exception afforded to him by the certificate unless—

(*a*) it is produced to the constable at the time he is so informed, or

(*b*) it is produced—

(i) within seven days after the date on which he is so informed, or

(ii) as soon as is reasonably practicable,

at such police station as he may have specified to the constable, or

(*c*) where it is not produced at such police station, it is not reasonably practicable for it to be produced there before the day on which the proceedings are commenced.

(5) For the purposes of subsection (4) above, the laying of the information or, in Scotland, the service of the complaint on the accused shall be treated as the commencement of the proceedings.

(6) Regulations under this section requiring the wearing of seat belts by persons riding in motor vehicles shall not apply to children under the age of fourteen years.

[The fixed penalty procedure applies to offences under s 14; see the Road Traffic Offenders Act 1988, Sched 3.

The Motor Vehicles (Wearing of Seat Belts) Regulations 1982 (SI 1982 No 1203) (qv) have effect as if made under s 14.]

15. Restriction on carrying children not wearing seat belts in motor vehicles

(1) Except as provided by regulations, where a child under the age of fourteen years is in the front of a motor vehicle, a person must not without reasonable excuse drive the vehicle on a road unless the child is wearing a seat belt in conformity with regulations.

(2) It is an offence for a person to drive a motor vehicle in contravention of subsection (1) above.

(3) Except as provided by regulations, where a child under the age of fourteen years is in the rear of a motor vehicle and any seat belt is fitted in the rear of that vehicle, a person must not without reasonable excuse drive the vehicle on a road unless the child is wearing a seat belt in conformity with regulations.

(4) It is an offence for a person to drive a motor vehicle in contravention of subsection (3) above.

(5) Provision may be made by regulations—

(*a*) excepting from the prohibition in subsection (1) or (3) above children of any prescribed description, vehicles of a prescribed class or the driving of vehicles in such circumstances as may be prescribed,

(*b*) defining in relation to any class of vehicle what part of the vehicle is to be regarded as the front of the vehicle for the purposes of subsection (1) above or as the rear of the vehicle for the purposes of subsection (3) above,

(*c*) prescribing for the purposes of subsection (1) or (3) above the descriptions of seat belt to be worn by children of any prescribed description and the manner in which such seat belt is to be fixed and used.

(6) Regulations made for the purposes of subsection (3) above shall include an exemption for any child holding a valid certificate signed by a medical practitioner to the effect that it is inadvisable on medical grounds for him to wear a seat belt.

(7) If the driver of a motor vehicle is informed by a constable that he may be prosecuted for an offence under subsection (4) above, he is not in proceedings for that offence entitled to rely on an exception afforded to a child by a certificate referred to in subsection (6) above unless—

(*a*) it is produced to the constable at the time he is so informed, or

(*b*) it is produced—

(i) within seven days after the date on which he is so informed, or

(ii) as soon as is reasonably practicable,

at such police station as he may have specified to the constable, or

(*c*) where it is not produced at such police station, it is not reasonably practicable for it to be produced there before the day on which the proceedings are commenced.

(8) For the purposes of subsection (7) above, the laying of the information shall be treated as the commencement of the proceedings.

(9) In this section—

'regulations' means regulations made by the Secretary of State under this section, and

'seat belt' includes any description of restraining device for a child and any reference to wearing a seat belt is to be construed accordingly.

(10) This section is affected by Schedule 5 to the Road Traffic (Consequential Provisions) Act 1988 (transitory modifications).

[Words relating exclusively and expressly to Scotland have been omitted from s 5(8).
The fixed penalty procedure applies to offences under s 15(2); see the Road Traffice Offenders Act 1988, Sched 3.
The Motor Vehicles (Wearing of Seat Belts by Children) Regulations 1982 (SI 1982 No 1342) (qv) have effect as if made under s 15.
Until the day appointed by the Secretary of State, s 15 has effect as if subss (3), (4) and (6) to (8) were omitted; as if the words 'or (3)' were omitted from s 5(5)(a) and (c); and as if the words 'or as the rear of the vehicle for the purposes of subsection (3) above' were omitted from s 15(5)(b); see subs (10) above and the Road Traffic (Consequential Provisions) Act 1988, s 6 and Sched 5, para 1, below.]

16. Wearing of protective headgear

(1) The Secretary of State may make regulations requiring, subject to such exceptions as may be specified in the regulations, persons driving or riding (otherwise than in side-cars) on motor cycles of any class specified in the regulations to wear protective headgear of such description as may be so specified.

(2) A requirement imposed by regulations under this section shall not apply to any follower of the Sikh religion while he is wearing a turban.

(3) Regulations under this section may make different provision in relation to different circumstances.

(4) A person who drives or rides on a motor cycle in contravention of regulations under this section is guilty of an offence; but notwithstanding any enactment or rule of law no person other than the person actually committing the contravention is guilty of an offence by reason of the contravention unless the person actually committing the contravention is a child under the age of sixteen years.

[The fixed penalty procedure applies to offences under s 16; see the Road Traffic Offenders Act 1988, Sched 3.
The Motor Cycles (Protective Helmets) Regulations 1980 (SI 1980 No 1279) (qv) have effect as if made in part under s 16.]

17. Protective helmets for motor cyclists

(1) The Secretary of State may make regulations prescribing (by reference to shape, construction or any other quality) types of helmet recommended as affording protection to persons on or in motor cycles, or motor cycles of different classes, from injury in the event of accident.

(2) If a person sells, or offers for sale, a helmet as a helmet for affording such protection and the helmet is neither—

(*a*) of a type prescribed under this section, nor

(*b*) of a type authorised under regulations made under this section and sold or offered for sale subject to any conditions specified in the authorisation,

subject to subsection (3) below, he is guilty of an offence.

(3) A person shall not be convicted of an offence under this section in respect of the sale or offer for sale of a helmet if he proves that it was sold or, as the case may be, offered for sale for export from Great Britain.

(4) The provisions of Schedule 1 to this Act shall have effect in relation to contraventions of this section.

(5) In this section and that Schedule 'helmet' includes any head-dress, and references in this section to selling or offering for sale include respectively references to letting on hire and offering to let on hire.

[As to the institution of proceedings under s 17, see the Road Traffic Offenders Act 1988, s 4(1) below.

The Motor Cycles (Protective Helmets) Regulations 1980 (SI 1980 No 1279) (qv) have effect as if made in part under this section.

From a date to be announced, s 17(2) will be amended by the substitution for the words from 'neither' to 'authorisation' of the words 'not of a type prescribed under this section'; see the Road Traffic (Consequential Provisions) Act 1988, ss 4 and 8(3) and Sched 2, Part IV, para 31.]

18. Authorisation of head-worn appliances for use on motor cycles

(1) The Secretary of State may make regulations prescribing (by reference to shape, construction or any other quality) types of appliance of any description to which this section applies as authorised for use by persons driving or riding (otherwise than in side-cars) on motor cycles of any class specified in the regulations.

(2) Regulations under this section—

(*a*) may impose restrictions or requirements with respect to the circumstances in which appliances of any type prescribed by the regulations may be used, and

(*b*) may make different provision in relation to different circumstances.

(3) If a person driving or riding on a motor cycle on a road uses an appliance of any description for which a type is prescribed under this section and that appliance—

(*a*) is not of a type so prescribed, or

(*b*) is otherwise used in contravention of regulations under this section,

he is guilty of an offence.

(4) If a person sells, or offers for sale, an appliance of any such description as authorised for use by persons on or in motor cycles, or motor cycles of any class, and that appliance is not of a type prescribed under this section as authorised for such use, he is, subject to subsection (5) below, guilty of an offence.

(5) A person shall not be convicted of an offence under this section in respect of the sale or offer for sale of an appliance if he proves that it was sold or, as the case may be, offered for sale for export from Great Britain.

(6) The provisions of Schedule 1 to this Act shall have effect in relation to contraventions of subsection (4) above.

(7) This section applies to appliances of any description designed or adapted for use—

(*a*) with any headgear, or

(*b*) by being attached to or placed upon the head,

(as, for example, eye protectors or earphones).

(8) References in this section to selling or offering for sale include respectively references to letting on hire and offering to let on hire.

[As to the institution of proceedings under s 18, see the Road Traffic Offenders Act 1988, s 4(1) below.

The Motor Cycle (Eye Protectors) Regulations 1985 (SI 1985 No 1593) (qv) have effect as if made under s 18.]

Stopping on verges, etc, or in dangerous positions, etc

19. Prohibition of parking of HGVs on verges, central reservations and footways

(1) Subject to subsection (2) below, a person who parks a heavy commercial vehicle (as defined in section 20 of this Act) wholly or partly—

(*a*) on the verge of a road, or

(*b*) on any land situated between two carriageways and which is not a footway, or

(*c*) on a footway,

is guilty of an offence.

(2) A person shall not be convicted of an offence under this section in respect of a vehicle if he proves to the satisfaction of the court—

(*a*) that it was parked in accordance with permission given by a constable in uniform, or

(*b*) that it was parked in contravention of this section for the purpose of saving life or extinguishing fire or meeting any other like emergency, or

(*c*) that it was parked in contravention of this section but the conditions specified in subsection (3) below were satisfied.

(3) The conditions mentioned in subsection (2)(*c*) above are—

(*a*) that the vehicle was parked on the verge of a road or on a footway for the purpose of loading or unloading, and

(*b*) that the loading or unloading of the vehicle could not have been satisfactorily performed if it had not been parked on the footway or verge, and

(*c*) that the vehicle was not left unattended at any time while it was so parked.

[(3A) The Secretary of State may by regulations provide that, in relation to vehicles of such classes as may be specified in the regulations, subsection (1) above shall not apply or shall apply subject to such conditions as may be so specified.]

[(3B) In England and Wales, the council of a county, district or London borough or the Common Council of the City of London may institute proceedings for an offence under this section committed in relation to the verge of a road, land or a footway in their area.]

(4) In this section 'carriageway' and 'footway', in relation to England and Wales, have the same meanings as in the Highways Act 1980.

[Section 19 is printed as prospectively amended by the Road Traffic (Consequential Provisions) Act 1988, s 4 and Sched 2, Part II, para 21. Subsections (3A) and (3B) (which were added by those provisions) will be brought into force on a date to be announced; see ibid, s 8(3) below.

The fixed penalty procedure applies to offences under s 19; see the Road Traffic Offenders Act 1988, Sched 3 below.

The terms 'carriageway' and 'footway' are defined in s 329(1) of the Highways Act 1980 (qv).]

19A. Prohibition of parking of vehicles on verges, central reservations and footways

(1) Subject to the provisions of this section, a person who parks a vehicle, other than a heavy commercial vehicle (as defined in section 20 of this Act) wholly or partly—

(*a*) on the verge of an urban road, or

(*b*) on any land which is situated between two carriageways of an urban road and which is not a footway, or

(*c*) on a footway comprised in an urban road,

is guilty of an offence.

(2) A person shall not be convicted of an offence under this section with respect to a vehicle if he proves to the satisfaction of the court—

(*a*) that it was parked in accordance with permission given by a constable in uniform, or

(*b*) that it was parked in contravention of this section for the purpose of saving life or extinguishing fire or meeting any other like emergency, or

(*c*) that it was parked in contravention of this section but the conditions specified in subsection (3) below were satisfied.

(3) The conditions mentioned in subsection (2)(*c*) above are—

(*a*) that the vehicle was parked on a verge or footway for the purpose of loading or unloading, and

(*b*) that the loading or unloading of the vehicle could not have been satisfactorily performed if it had not been parked on the footway or verge, and

(*c*) that the vehicle was not left unattended at any time while it was so parked.

(4) The Secretary of State may by regulations provide that, in relation to vehicles of such classes as may be specified in the regulations, subsection (1) above shall not apply or shall apply subject to such conditions as may be so specified.

(5) The authority having power, otherwise than by virtue of Part I of Schedule 9 to the Road Traffic Regulation Act 1984 (reserve powers of Secretary of State), to make an order under section 1 or section 6 of that Act (orders for regulating traffic) in relation to a road may by order specifying that road provide that the provisions of subsection (1) above shall not apply in relation to it or to any part of it specified in the order, either at all times or during periods so specified.

(6) In England and Wales, the council of a county, district or London borough or the Common Council of the City of London may institute proceedings for an offence under this section committed in relation to the verge of a road, land or a footway in their area.

(7) Section 125 of the Road Traffic Regulation Act 1984 (boundary roads) applies for the purposes of subsection (5) above as it applies for the purposes of sections 1(1) and 6(1) of that Act; and Parts I (reserve powers of Secretary of State), III (procedure as to certain orders), IV (variation or revocation of certain orders) and VI (validity of certain orders) of Schedule 9 to that Act shall apply in relation to orders under subsection (5) above as they apply in relation to orders under any provision of section 1 or 6 of that Act.

(8) Section 122 of the Road Traffic Regulation Act 1984 (manner of exercise of functions by local authorities) applies to functions conferred by subsections (1) and (5) above as it applies to functions conferred by that Act.

(9) In this section—

'footway', in relation to England and Wales, has the same meaning as in the Highways Act 1980, and

'urban road' means a road which—

(i) is a restricted road for the purposes of section 81 of the Road Traffic Regulation Act 1984 (30 mph speed limit), or

(ii) is subject to an order under section 84 of that Act imposing a speed limit not exceeding 40 mph, or

(iii) is subject to a speed limit not exceeding 40 mph which is imposed by or under any local Act.]

[Section 19A(1)–(4) and (9) is prospectively inserted by the Road Traffic (Consequential Provisions) Act 1988, s 4 and Sched 2, Part II, para 22(1). Those provisions will be brought into force on a date to be announced; see ibid, s 8(3), below. (Section 19A(5)–(8) came into force on 15 May 1989; see ibid, s 8(2) and (3)(b), below.)

The fixed penalty procedure applies to offences under s 19A; see the Road Traffic Offenders Act 1988, Sched 3, below.

The term 'footway' is defined in s 329(1) of the Highways Act 1980 (qv).]

20. Definition of 'heavy commercial vehicle' for the purposes of section 19

(1) In section 19 of this Act, 'heavy commercial vehicle' means any goods vehicle which has an operating weight exceeding 7.5 tonnes.

(2) The operating weight of a goods vehicle for the purposes of this section is—

(*a*) in the case of a motor vehicle not drawing a trailer or in the case of a trailer, its maximum laden weight,

(*b*) in the case of an articulated vehicle, its maximum laden weight (if it has one) and otherwise the aggregate maximum laden weight of all the individual vehicles forming part of that articulated vehicle, and

(*c*) in the case of a motor vehicle (other than an articulated vehicle) drawing one or more trailers, the aggregate maximum laden weight of the motor vehicle and the trailer or trailers attached to it.

(3) In this section 'articulated vehicle' means a motor vehicle with a trailer so attached to it as to be partially superimposed upon it; and references to the maximum laden weight of a vehicle are references to the total laden weight which must not be exceeded in the case of that vehicle if it is to be used in Great Britain without contravening any regulations for the time being in force under section 41 of this Act.

(4) In this section, and in the definition of 'goods vehicle' in section 192 of this Act as it applies for the purposes of this section, 'trailer' means any vehicle other than a motor vehicle.

(5) The Secretary of State may by regulations amend subsections (1) and (2) above (whether as originally enacted or as previously amended under this subsection)—

(*a*) by substituting weights of a different description for any of the weights there mentioned, or

(*b*) in the case of subsection (1) above, by substituting a weight of a different description or amount, or a weight different both in description and amount, for the weight there mentioned.

(6) Different regulations may be made under subsection (5) above as respects different classes of vehicles or as respects the same class of vehicles in different circum-

stances and as respects different times of the day or night and as respects different localities.

(7) Regulations under subsection (5) above shall not so amend subsection (1) above that there is any case in which a goods vehicle whose operating weight (ascertained in accordance with subsection (2) above as originally enacted) does not exceed 7.5 tonnes is a heavy commercial vehicle for any of the purposes of section 19 of this Act.

21. Prohibition of driving or parking on cycle tracks

(1) Subject to the provisions of this section, any person who without lawful authority, drives or parks a motor vehicle wholly or partly on a cycle track is guilty of an offence.

(2) A person shall not be convicted of an offence under subsection (1) above with respect to a vehicle if he proves to the satisfaction of the court—

(*a*) that the vehicle was driven or (as the case may be) parked in contravention of that subsection for the purpose of saving life, or extinguishing fire or meeting any other like emergency, or

(*b*) that the vehicle was owned or operated by a highway authority or by a person discharging functions on behalf of a highway authority and was driven or (as the case may be) parked in contravention of that subsection in connection with the carrying out by or on behalf of that authority of any of the following, that is, the cleansing, maintenance or improvement of, or the maintenance or alteration of any structure or other work situated in, the cycle track or its verges, or

(*c*) that the vehicle was owned or operated by statutory undertakers and was driven or (as the case may be) parked in contravention of that subsection in connection with the carrying out by those undertakers of any works in relation to any apparatus belonging to or used by them for the purpose of their undertaking.

(3) In this section—

(*a*) 'cycle track' and other expressions used in this section and in the Highways Act 1980 have the same meaning as in that Act,

(*b*) in subsection (2)(*c*) above 'statutory undertakers' means any body who are statutory undertakers within the meaning of the Highways Act 1980, any sewerage authority within the meaning of that Act or the operator of a telecommunications code system (as defined by paragraph 1(1) of Schedule 4 to the Telecommunications Act 1984 [*qv*]), and in relation to any such sewerage authority 'apparatus' includes sewers or sewerage disposal works.

(4) This section does not extend to Scotland.

[The terms 'cycle track', 'statutory undertakers' and 'sewerage authority' are defined in s 329(1) of the Highways Act 1980 (qv).]

22. Leaving vehicles in dangerous positions

If a person in charge of a vehicle causes or permits the vehicle or a trailer drawn by it to remain at rest on a road in such a position or in such condition or in such circumstances as to be likely to cause danger to other persons using the road, he is guilty of an offence.

[The fixed penalty procedure applies to offences under s 22; see the Road Traffic Offenders Act 1988, Sched 3, below.]

Other restrictions in interests of safety

23. Restriction of carriage of persons on motor cycles

(1) Not more than one person in addition to the driver may be carried on a two-wheeled motor cycle.

(2) No person in addition to the driver may be carried on a two-wheeled motor cycle otherwise than sitting astride the motor cycle and on a proper seat securely fixed to the motor cycle behind the driver's seat.

(3) If a person is carried on a motor cycle in contravention of this section, the driver of the motor cycle is guilty of an offence.

[The fixed penalty procedure applies to offences under s 23; see the Road Traffic Offenders Act 1988, Sched 3, below.]

24. Restriction of carriage of persons on bicycles

(1) Not more than one person may be carried on a road on a bicycle not propelled by mechanical power unless it is constructed or adapted for the carriage of more than one person.

(2) In this section—

(*a*) references to a person carried on a bicycle include references to a person riding the bicycle, and

(*b*) 'road' includes bridleway.

(3) If a person is carried on a bicycle in contravention of subsection (1) above, each of the persons carried is guilty of an offence.

25. Tampering with motor vehicles

If, while a motor vehicle is on a road or on a parking place provided by a local authority, a person—

(*a*) gets on to the vehicle, or

(*b*) tampers with the brake or other part of its mechanism,

without lawful authority or reasonable cause he is guilty of an offence.

[Offences under s 25 and any other offences of which persons may have been convicted in the same proceedings may be recorded in national police records; see the National Police Records (Recordable Offences) Regulations 1985 (SI 1985 No 1941.]

26. Holding or getting on to vehicle in order to be towed or carried

(1) If, for the purpose of being carried, a person without lawful authority or reasonable cause takes or retains hold of, or gets on to, a motor vehicle or trailer while in motion on a road he is guilty of an offence.

(2) If, for the purpose of being drawn, a person takes or retains hold of a motor vehicle or trailer while in motion on a road he is guilty of an offence.

27. Control of dogs on roads

(1) A person who causes or permits a dog to be on a designated road without the dog being held on a lead is guilty of an offence.

(2) In this section 'designated road' means a length of road specified by an order in that behalf of the local authority in whose area the length of road is situated.

(3) The powers which under subsection (2) above are exercisable by a local auth-

ority in England and Wales are, in the case of a road part of the width of which is in the area of one local authority and part in the area of another, exercisable by either authority with the consent of the other.

(4) An order under this section may provide that subsection (1) above shall apply subject to such limitations or exceptions as may be specified in the order, and (without prejudice to the generality of this subsection) subsection (1) above does not apply to dogs proved—

(*a*) to be kept for driving or tending sheep or cattle in the course of a trade or business, or

(*b*) to have been at the material time in use under proper control for sporting purposes.

(5) An order under this section shall not be made except after consultation with the chief officer of police.

(6) The Secretary of State may make regulations—

(*a*) prescribing the procedure to be followed in connection with the making of orders under this section, and

(*b*) requiring the authority making such an order to publish in such manner as may be prescribed by the regulations notice of the making and effect of the order.

(7) In this section 'local authority' means—

(*a*) in relation to England and Wales, the council of a county, metropolitan district or London borough or the Common Council of the City of London, and

(*b*) *[Applies to Scotland.]*

(8) The power conferred by this section to make an order includes power, exercisable in like manner and subject to the like conditions, to vary or revoke it.

[As to the institution of proceedings under s 27, see the Road Traffic Offenders Act 1988, s 4(2), below.]

Cycling offences and cycle racing

28. Reckless cycling

A person who rides a cycle on a road recklessly is guilty of an offence.

In this section 'road' includes a bridleway.

29. Careless, and inconsiderate, cycling

If a person rides a cycle on a road without due care and attention, or without reasonable consideration for other persons using the road, he is guilty of an offence.

In this section 'road' includes a bridleway.

30. Cycling when under influence of drink or drugs

(1) A person who, when riding a cycle on a road or other public place, is unfit to ride through drink or drugs (that is to say, is under the influence of drink or a drug to such an extent as to be incapable of having proper control of the cycle) is guilty of an offence.

(2) *[Applies to Scotland.]*

(3) In this section 'road' includes a bridleway.

31. Regulation of cycle racing on public ways

(1) A person who promotes or takes part in a race or trial of speed on a public way between cycles is guilty of an offence, unless the race or trial—

(*a*) is authorised, and

(*b*) is conducted in accordance with any conditions imposed,

by or under regulations under this section.

(2) The Secretary of State may by regulations authorise, or provide for authorising, for the purposes of subsection (1) above, the holding on a public way other than a bridleway—

(*a*) of races or trials of speed of any class or description, or

(*b*) of a particular race or trial of speed,

in such cases as may be prescribed and subject to such conditions as may be imposed by or under the regulations.

(3) Regulations under this section may—

(*a*) prescribe the procedure to be followed, and the particulars to be given, in connection with applications for authorisation under the regulations, and

(*b*) make different provision for different classes or descriptions of race or trial.

(4) Without prejudice to any other powers exercisable in that behalf, the chief officer of police may give directions with respect to the movement of, or the route to be followed by, vehicular traffic during any period, being directions which it is necessary or expedient to give in relation to that period to prevent or mitigate—

(*a*) congestion or obstruction of traffic, or

(*b*) danger to or from traffic,

in consequence of the holding of a race or trial of speed authorised by or under regulations under this section.

(5) Directions under subsection (4) above may include a direction that any road or part of a road specified in the direction shall be closed during the period to vehicles or to vehicles of a class so specified.

(6) In this section 'public way' means, in England and Wales, a public highway and, in Scotland, a public road and includes a bridleway but not a footpath.

32. Electrically assisted pedal cycles

(1) An electrically assisted pedal cycle of a class specified in regulations made for the purposes of section 189 of this Act and section 140 of the Road Traffic Regulation Act 1984 shall not be driven on a road by a person under the age of fourteen.

(2) A person who—

(*a*) drives such a pedal cycle, or

(*b*) knowing or suspecting that another person is under the age of fourteen, causes or permits him to drive such a pedal cycle,

in contravention of subsection (1) above is guilty of an offence.

Use of motor vehicles away from roads

33. Control of use of footpaths and bridleways for motor vehicle trials

(1) A person must not promote or take part in a trial of any description between motor vehicles on a footpath or bridleway unless the holding of the trial has been authorised under this section by the local authority.

(2) A local authority shall not give an authorisation under this section unless satisfied that consent in writing to the use of any length of footpath or bridleway for the purposes of the trial has been given by the owner and by the occupier of the land over which that length of footpath or bridleway runs, and any such authorisation may be given subject to compliance with such conditions as the authority think fit.

(3) A person who—

(*a*) contravenes subsection (1) above, or

(*b*) fails to comply with any conditions subject to which an authorisation under this section has been granted,

is guilty of an offence.

(4) The holding of a trial authorised under this section is not affected by any statutory provision prohibiting or restricting the use of footpaths or bridleways or a specified footpath or bridleway; but this section does not prejudice any right or remedy of a person as having any interest in land.

(5) In this section 'local authority'—

(*a*) in relation to England and Wales, means the council of a county, metropolitan district or London borough, and

(*b*) *[Applies to Scotland.]*

34. Prohibition of driving motor vehicles elsewhere than on roads

(1) Subject to the provisions of this section, if without lawful authority a person drives a motor vehicle—

(*a*) on to or upon any common land, moorland or land of any other description, not being land forming part of a road, or

(*b*) on any road being a footpath or bridleway,

he is guilty of an offence.

(2) It is not an offence under this section to drive a motor vehicle on any land within fifteen yards of a road, being a road on which a motor vehicle may lawfully be driven, for the purpose only of parking the vehicle on that land.

(3) A person shall not be convicted of an offence under this section with respect to a vehicle if he proves to the satisfaction of the court that it was driven in contravention of this section for the purpose of saving life or extinguishing fire or meeting any other like emergency.

(4) *[Saving for s 193 of the Law of Property Act 1925 and byelaws and law of trespass.]*

[The fixed penalty procedure applies to offences under s 34; see the Road Traffic Offenders Act 1988, Sched 3, below.]

Directions to traffic and to pedestrians and traffic signs

35. Drivers to comply with traffic directions

(1) Where a constable is for the time being engaged in the regulation of traffic in a road, a person driving or propelling a vehicle who neglects or refuses—

(*a*) to stop the vehicle, or

(*b*) to make it proceed in, or kept to, a particular line of traffic,

when directed to do so by the constable in the execution of his duty is guilty of an offence.

(2) Where—

(*a*) a traffic survey of any description is being carried out on or in the vicinity of a road, and

(*b*) a constable gives to a person driving or propelling a vehicle a direction—

(i) to stop the vehicle,

(ii) to make it proceed in, or keep to, a particular line of traffic, or

(iii) to proceed to a particular point on or near the road on which the vehicle is being driven or propelled,

being a direction given for the purposes of the survey (but not a direction requiring any person to provide any information for the purposes of a traffic survey),

the person is guilty of an offence if he neglects or refuses to comply with the direction.

(3) The power to give such a direction as is referred to in subsection (2) above for the purposes of a traffic survey shall be so exercised as not to cause any unreasonable delay to a person who indicates that he is unwilling to provide any information for the purposes of the survey.

[The fixed penalty procedure applies to offences under s 35; see the Road Traffic Offenders Act 1988, Sched 3, below.]

36. Drivers to comply with traffic signs

(1) Where a traffic sign, being a sign—

(*a*) of the prescribed size, colour and type, or

(*b*) of another character authorised by the Secretary of State under the provisions in that behalf of the Road Traffic Regulation Act 1984,

has been lawfully placed on or near a road, a person driving or propelling a vehicle who fails to comply with the indication given by the sign is guilty of an offence.

(2) A traffic sign shall not be treated for the purposes of this section as having been lawfully placed unless either—

(*a*) the indication given by the sign is an indication of a statutory prohibition, restriction or requirement, or

(*b*) it is expressly provided by or under any provision of the Traffic Acts that this section shall apply to the sign or to signs of a type of which the sign is one;

and, where the indication mentioned in paragraph (*a*) of this subsection is of the general nature only of the prohibition, restriction or requirement to which the sign relate, a person shall not be convicted of failure to comply with the indication unless he has failed to comply with the prohibition, restriction or requirement to which the sign relates.

(3) For the purposes of this section a traffic sign placed on or near a road shall be deemed—

(*a*) to be of the prescribed size, colour and type, or of another character authorised by the Secretary of State under the provisions in that behalf of the Road Traffic Regulation Act 1984, and

(*b*) (subject to subsection (2) above) to have been lawfully so placed,

unless the contrary is proved.

(4) Where a traffic survey of any description is being carried out on or in the vicinity of a road, this section applies to a traffic sign by which a direction is given—

(*a*) to stop a vehicle,

(*b*) to make it proceed in, or keep to, a particular line of traffic, or

(*c*) to proceed to a particular point on or near the road on which the vehicle is being driven or propelled,

being a direction given for the purposes of the survey (but not a direction requiring any person to provide any information for the purposes of the survey).

(5) Regulations made by the Secretary of State for Transport, the Secretary of State for Wales and the Secretary of State for Scotland acting jointly may specify any traffic sign for the purposes of column 5 of the entry in Schedule 2 to the Road Traffic Offenders Act 1988 relating to offences under this section (offences committed by failing to comply with certain signs involve discretionary disqualification).

[The fixed penalty procedure applies to offences under s 36; see the Road Traffic Offenders Act 1988, Sched 3, below.]

37. Directions to pedestrians

Where a constable in uniform is for the time being engaged in the regulation of vehicular traffic in a road, a person on foot who proceeds across or along the carriageway in contravention of a direction to stop given by the constable in the execution of his duty, either to persons on foot or to persons on foot and other traffic, is guilty of an offence.

Promotion of road safety

38. The Highway Code

(1) The Highway Code shall continue to have effect, subject however to revision in accordance with the following provisions of this section.

(2)–(6) *[Revision and publication of the Highway Code.]*

(7) A failure on the part of a person to observe a provision of the Highway Code shall not of itself render that person liable to criminal proceedings of any kind but any such failure may in any proceedings (whether civil or criminal, and including proceedings for an offence under the Traffic Acts, the Public Passenger Vehicles Act 1981 [*qv*] or sections 18 to 23 of the Transport Act 1985 [*qv*]) be relied upon by any party to the proceedings as tending to establish or negative any liability which is in question in those proceedings.

(8) In this section 'the Highway Code' means the code comprising directions for the guidance of persons using roads issued under section 45 of the Road Traffic Act 1930, as from time to time revised under this section or under any previous enactment.

(9) *[Further provision as to the revision of the Highway Code.]*

39. Powers of Secretary of State and local authorities as to giving road safety information and training *[Omitted.]*

40. Powers of Secretary of State to subsidise bodies other than local authorities for giving road safety information and training *[Omitted.]*

PART II

CONSTRUCTION AND USE OF VEHICLES AND EQUIPMENT

General regulation of construction, use etc

41. Regulation of construction, weight, equipment and use of vehicles

(1) The Secretary of State may make regulations generally as to the use of motor vehicles and trailers on roads, their construction and equipment and the conditions under which they may be so used.

Subsections (2) to (4) below do not affect the generality of this subsection.

(2) *[Particular provisions which may be included in regulations.]*

(3) *[Provisions as to goods vehicles which may be included in regulations.]*

(4) *[Provisions as to lighting equipment and reflectors which may be included in regulations.]*

(5) *[Power to make different regulations for different classes of vehicles, etc.]*

(6) In framing regulations under this section prescribing a weight of any description which is not to be exceeded in the case of goods vehicles of a class for which a certificate of conformity or Minister's approval certificate may be issued under section 57 or 58 of this Act the Secretary of State must have regard to the design weight of the like description determined by virtue of section 54 of this Act for vehicles of that class and must secure that the first-mentioned weight does not exceed the design weight.

(7) In this Part of this Act—

'construction and use requirements' means requirements, whether applicable generally or at specified times or in specified circumstances, imposed under this section,

'plated particulars' means such particulars as are required to be marked on a goods vehicle in pursuance of regulations under this section by means of a plate,

'plated weights' means such weights as are required to be so marked.

[The regulations which have effect as if made under s 41 include the Minibus (Conditions of Fitness, Equipment and Use) Regulations 1977 (SI 1977 No 2103), the Community Bus Regulations 1978 (SI 1978 No 1313), the Public Service Vehicles (Conditions of Fitness, Equipment, Use and Certification) Regulations 1981 (SI 1981 No 257) qv, the Road Transport (International Road Services) Regulations 1984 (SI 1984 No 748) qv, the Road Vehicles Lighting Regulations 1984 (SI 1984 No 812) qv, and the Road Vehicles (Construction and Use) Regulations 1986 (SI 1986 No 1078) qv.]

42. Offence where regulations are contravened, etc

(1) Subject to subsection (2) below and sections 43 and 44 of this Act, a person who—

(*a*) contravenes or fails to comply with any regulations under section 41 of this Act, or

(*b*) uses on a road a motor vehicle or trailer which does not comply with any such regulations or causes or permits a vehicle to be so used,

is guilty of an offence.

(2) In any proceedings for an offence under subsection (1) above in which there is alleged a contravention of or failure to comply with a construction and use requirement relating to any description of weight applicable to a goods vehicle, it shall be a defence to prove either—

(*a*) that at the time when the vehicle was being used on the road—

(i) it was proceeding to a weighbridge which was the nearest available one to the place where the loading of the vehicle was completed for the purpose of being weighed, or

(ii) it was proceeding from a weighbridge after being weighed to the nearest point at which it was reasonably practicable to reduce the weight to the relevant limit, without causing an obstruction on any road, or

(*b*) in a case where the limit of that weight was not exceeded by more than 5 per cent.—
(i) that limit was not exceeded at the time when the loading of the vehicle was originally completed, and
(ii) that since that time no person has made any addition to the load.

[The fixed penalty procedure applies to offences under s 42; see the Road Traffic Offenders Act 1988, Sched 3, below.]

43. Temporary exemption (contained in regulations) from application of regulations under section 41 *[Omitted.]*

44. Authorisation of use on roads of special vehicles not complying with regulations under section 41

(1) The Secretary of State may be order authorise, subject to such restrictions and conditions as may be specified by or under the order, the use on roads—

(*a*) of special motor vehicles or trailers, or special types of motor vehicles or trailers, which are constructed either for special purposes or for tests or trials,

(*b*) of vehicles or trailers, or types of vehicles or trailers, constructed for use outside the United Kingdom,

(*c*) of new or improved types of motor vehicles or trailers, whether wheeled or wheelless, or of motor vehicles or trailers equipped with new or improved equipment or types of equipment, and

(*d*) of vehicles or trailers carrying loads of exceptional dimensions,

and nothing in sections 41 and 42 of this Act shall prevent the use of such vehicles, trailers, or types in accordance with the order.

(2) The Secretary of State may by order make provision for securing that, subject to such restrictions and conditions as may be specified by or under the order, regulations under section 41 of this Act shall have effect in their application to such vehicles, trailers and types of vehicles and trailers as are mentioned in subsection (1) above subject to such modifications or exceptions as may be specified in the order.

(3) The powers conferred by this section on the Secretary of State to make orders shall be exercisable by statutory instrument except in the case of orders applying only to specified vehicles or to vehicles of specified persons, but in that excepted case (as in others) the order may be varied or revoked by subsequent order of the Secretary of State.

[The orders made by statutory instrument which have effect as if made under s 44 include the Motor Vehicles (Authorisation of Special Types) General Order 1979 (SI 1979 No 1198) qv.]

Tests of vehicles other than goods vehicles to which section 49 applies

45. Tests of satisfactory condition of vehicles

(1) This section applies to motor vehicles other than goods vehicles which are required by regulations under section 49 of this Act to be submitted for a vehicle test under that section and has effect for the purpose of ascertaining whether the prescribed statutory requirements relating to the construction and condition of motor vehicles or their accessories or equipment are complied with.

(2) The Secretary of State may by regulations make provision—

(*a*) for the examination of vehicles submitted for examination under this section, and

(*b*) for the issue, where it is found on such an examination that the requirements mentioned in subsection (1) above are complied with, of a certificate (in this Act referred to as a 'test certificate') that at the date of the examination the requirements were complied with in relation to the vehicle.

(3) *[Examinations to be carried out by authorised examiners and others.]*

(4) *[Refusal of test certificate.]*

(5) *[Appeal against refusal of test certificate.]*

(6) *[Examination stations and equipment.]*

(7) *[Power to make regulations.]*

(8) In its application to vehicles in which recording equipment is required by Article 3 of the Community Recording Equipment Regulation to be installed and used, this section shall have effect as if any reference to prescribed statutory requirements relating to the construction and condition of motor vehicles or their accessories or equipment included a reference to the prescribed requirements of so much of that Regulation as relates to the installation of recording equipment and the seals to be fixed to such equipment.

[The Motor Vehicles (Tests) Regulations 1981 (SI 1981 No 1694) (qv) have effect as if made in part under s 45.]

46. Particular aspects of regulations under section 45 *[Omitted.]*

47. Obligatory test certificates

(1) A person who uses on a road at any time, or causes or permits to be so used, a motor vehicle to which this section applies, and as respects which no test certificate has been issued within the appropriate period before that time, is guilty of an offence.

In this section and section 48 of this Act, the 'appropriate period' means a period of twelve months or such shorter period as may be prescribed.

(2) Subject to subsections (3) and (5) below, the motor vehicles to which this section applies at any time are—

(*a*) those first registered under the Vehicles (Excise) Act 1971, the Vehicles (Excise) Act 1962, the Vehicles (Excise) Act 1949 or the Roads Act 1920, not less than three years before that time, and

(*b*) those which, having a date of manufacture not less than three years before that time, have been used on roads (whether in Great Britain or elsewhere) before being registered under the Vehicles (Excise) Act 1971 or the Vehicles (Excise) Act 1962,

being, in either case, motor vehicles other than goods vehicles which are required by regulations under section 49 of this Act to be submitted for a goods vehicle test.

(3) As respects a vehicle being—

(*a*) a motor vehicle used for the carriage of passengers and with more than eight seats, excluding the driver's seat, or

(*b*) a taxi (as defined in section 64(3) of the Transport Act 1980 [*qv*]), being a vehicle licensed to ply for hire, or

(*c*) an ambulance, that is to say, a motor vehicle which is constructed or adapted, and primarily used, for the carriage of persons to a place where they will receive, or from a place where they have received, medical or dental treatment, and which, by reason of design, marking or equipment is readily identifiable as a vehicle so constructed or adapted, subsection (2)(*a*) above shall have effect as if for the period there mentioned there were substituted a period of one year.

(4) For the purposes of subsection (2)(*b*) above, there shall be disregarded the use of a vehicle before it is sold or supplied by retail [or before it is registered by the Secretary of State under paragraph (*b*) of section 19(1) of the Vehicles (Excise) Act 1971 (registration when Secretary of State receives from a motor dealer particulars of a vehicle to which the dealer has assigned a mark under section 20 of that Act) and after a mark is assigned to it under section 20 of that Act.]

(5) This section does not apply to vehicles of such classes as may be prescribed.

(6) The Secretary of State may by regulations exempt from subsection (1) above the use of vehicles for such purposes as may be prescribed.

(7) The Secretary of State may by regulations exempt from subsection (1) above the use of vehicles in any such area as may be prescribed.

(8) For the purposes of this section the date of manufacture of a vehicle shall be taken to be the last day of the year during which its final assembly is completed, except where after that day modifications are made to the vehicle before it is sold or supplied by retail, and in that excepted case shall be taken to be the last day of the year during which the modifications are completed.

(9) The Secretary of State may by order made by statutory instrument direct that subsection (2) above shall have effect with the substitution, for three years (in both places), of such other period (not being more than ten years) as may be specified in the order.

An order under this subsection shall not have effect unless approved by resolution of each House of Parliament.

[Section 47 is printed as prospectively amended by the Road Traffic (Consequential Provisions) Act 1988, s 4 and Sched 2, Part III, para 23. The words printed inside square brackets in s 47(4) will be brought into force on a date to be announced; see ibid, s 8(3), below.

The Motor Vehicles (Tests) Regulations 1981 (SI 1981 No 1694) have effect as if made in part under s 47.]

48. Supplementary provisions about test certificates

(1) *[Regulations changing length of appropriate period and period under s 47(2).]*

(2) Where—

(*a*) within the appropriate period after a test certificate is issued or treated for the purposes of section 47 of this Act as issued, but

(*b*) not earlier than one month before the end of that period,

a further test certificate is issued as respects the same vehicle, the further certificate shall be treated for the purposes of that section as if issued at the end of the appropriate period.

(3) Where the particulars contained in a test certificate in accordance with regulations made under section 45 of this Act include a date of expiry falling later, but not more than one month later, than the end of the appropriate period after the date on which it is issued—

(*a*) the certificate shall be deemed to have been issued in respect of the same vehicle as an earlier test certificate, and

(*b*) the date on which it was issued shall be deemed to have been a date falling within the last month of the appropriate period after the date on which that earlier certificate was issued or treated for the purposes of section 47 of this Act as issued;

and any date of expiry contained in a test certificate shall be deemed to have been entered in accordance with regulations under section 45 of this Act unless the contrary is proved.

(4) The Secretary of State may by regulations make provision for the issue, in such circumstances as may be prescribed, of a certificate of temporary exemption in respect of a public service vehicle adapted to carry more than eight passengers, exempting that vehicle from the provisions of section 47(1) of this Act for such period as may be specified in the certificate.

(5) In relation to any public service vehicle so adapted—

(*a*) subsections (2) and (3) above shall have effect as if for 'one month' (in both places) there were substituted 'two months', and

(*b*) subsection (3) above shall have effect as if for 'last month' there were substituted 'last two months'.

(6) In subsections (4) and (5) above 'public service vehicle' has the same meaning as in the Public Passenger Vehicles Act 1981.

[The term 'public service vehicle' is defined in s 1 of the Public Passenger Vehicles Act 1981 (qv).]

Tests of certain classes of goods vehicles

49. Tests of satisfactory condition of goods vehicles and determination of plated weights, etc

(1) The Secretary of State may by regulations make provision for the examination of goods vehicles of any prescribed class—

(*a*) for the purpose of selecting or otherwise determining plated weights or other plated particulars for goods vehicles of that class, or

(*b*) for the purpose of ascertaining whether any prescribed construction and use requirements (whether relating to plated particulars or not) are complied with in the case of goods vehicles of that class,

or for both purposes.

(2) In particular the regulations may make provision—

(*a*) for the determination, according to criteria or by methods prescribed by or determined under the regulations, of the plated particulars for a goods vehicle (including its plated weights), on an examination of the vehicle for the purpose, and for the issue on such an examination, except as provided by regulations made by virtue of paragraph (*c*) of this subsection, of a certificate (in this Act referred to as a 'plating certificate') specifying those particulars,

(*b*) for the issue, for a goods vehicle which has been found on examination for the purpose to comply with the prescribed construction and use requirements, of a certificate (in this Act referred to as a 'goods vehicle test certificate') stating that the vehicle has been found so to comply, and

(*c*) for the refusal of a goods vehicle test certificate for a goods vehicle which is so found not to comply with those requirements and for requiring a written notification to be given—

(i) of any such refusal, and
(ii) of the grounds of the refusal,

and for the refusal of a plating certificate where a goods vehicle test certificate is refused.

(3) References in subsections (1) and (2) above to construction and use requirements shall be construed—

(*a*) in relation to an examination of a vehicle solely for the purpose of ascertaining whether it complies with any such requirements, as references to such of those requirements as are applicable to the vehicle at the time of the test, and

(*b*) in relation to an examination of a vehicle both for that purpose and for the purpose of determining its plated particulars, as references to such of those requirements as will be applicable to the vehicle if a plating certificate is issued for it.

(4) In this Part of this Act—

'examination for plating' means an examination under regulations under this section for the purpose of determining plated particulars for a goods vehicle, and

'goods vehicle test' means an examination under regulations under this section for the purpose of ascertaining whether any prescribed construction and use requirements are complied with in the case of a goods vehicle.

(5) In its application to vehicles in which recording equipment is required by Article 3 of the Community Recording Equipment Regulation to be installed and used, this section shall have effect as if any reference to prescribed construction and use requirements included a reference to prescribed requirements of so much of that Regulation as relates to the installation of recording equipment and the seals to be fixed to such equipment.

[The Goods Vehicles (Plating and Testing) Regulations 1988 (SI 1988 No 1478) (qv) have effect as if made in part under s 49.]

50. Appeals against determinations under section 49 *[Omitted.]*

51. Particular aspects of regulations under section 49

(1) Without prejudice to the generality of subsection (1) of section 49 of this Act, regulations under that section may—

(*a*), (*b*) [*Omitted.*]

(*c*) prescribe the conditions subject to which vehicles will be accepted for such examination and, without prejudice to that—

(i) authorise any person by whom an examination of the vehicle under the regulations or section 50 of this Act is carried out to drive the vehicle, whether on a road or elsewhere, and

(ii) require that a driver of a vehicle examined under those regulations or that section is, except so far as permitted to be absent by the person carrying out the examination, present throughout the whole of the examination and drives the vehicle when directed to do so, and operates the controls in accordance with any directions given to him, by that person,

(*d*)–(*m*) [*Omitted.*]

(2) Regulations under section 49 of this Act may provide that a person who

contravenes or fails to comply with a requirement of regulations imposed by virtue of subsection (1)(*c*)(ii) above is guilty of an offence.

(3) In this section any reference to the driving of a vehicle is, in relation to a trailer, a reference to the driving of the vehicle by which the trailer is drawn.

52. Supplementary provisions about tests, etc, of goods vehicles *[Omitted.]*

53. Obligatory goods vehicle test certificates

(1) If any person at any time on or after the relevant date—

(*a*) uses on a road a goods vehicle of a class required by regulations under section 49 of this Act to have been submitted for examination for plating, or

(*b*) causes or permits to be used on a road a goods vehicle of such a class,

and at that time there is no plating certificate in force for the vehicle, he is guilty of an offence.

In this subsection 'relevant date', in relation to any goods vehicle, means the date by which it is required by the regulations to be submitted for examination for plating.

(2) If any person at any time on or after the relevant date—

(*a*) uses on a road a goods vehicle of a class required by regulations under section 49 of this Act to have been submitted for a goods vehicle test, or

(*b*) causes or permits to be used on a road a goods vehicle of such a class,

and at that time there is no goods vehicle test certificate in force for the vehicle, he is guilty of an offence.

In this subsection 'relevant date', in relation to any goods vehicle, means the date by which it is required by the regulations to be submitted for its goods vehicle test.

(3) Any person who—

(*a*) uses a goods vehicle on a road, or

(*b*) causes or permits a goods vehicle to be so used,

when an alteration has been made to the vehicle or its equipment which is required by regulations under section 49 of this Act to be, but has not been, notified to the Secretary of State [or the prescribed testing authority] is guilty of an offence.

(4) In any proceedings for an offence under subsection (3) above, it shall be a defence to prove that the alteration was not specified in the relevant plating certificate in accordance with regulations under section 49 of this Act.

(5) The Secretary of State may by regulations—

(*a*) exempt from all or any of the preceding provisions of this section the use of goods vehicles for such purposes or in such an area as may be prescribed and

(*b*) make provision for the issue in respect of a vehicle in such circumstances as may be prescribed of a certificate of temporary exemption exempting that vehicle from the provisions of subsection (1) or (2) above for such period as may be specified in the certificate.

[Section 53 is printed as prospectively amended by the Transport Act 1982, s 10(7)(b) (as itself amended by the Road Traffic (Consequential Provisions) Act 1988, s 4 and Sched 2, Part I, para 4(b)). The words printed within square brackets in subs (3) will come into force on a date to be announced; see the Transport Act 1982, s 76(2).

The Goods Vehicles (Plating and Testing) Regulations 1988 (SI 1988 No 1478) qv have effect as if made in part under s 53. As to notifiable alterations, see reg 30; and as to exemptions, see reg 44.]

Approval of design, construction, equipment and marking of vehicles

54. Type approval requirements

(1) Without prejudice to section 41 of this Act, the Secretary of State may by regulations prescribe requirements (in this Part of this Act referred to as 'type approval requirements')—

(*a*) with respect to the design, construction, equipment and marking of vehicles of any class, being requirements which are applicable before, whether or not they are applicable after, vehicles of that class are used on a road,

(*b*) with respect to the design, construction, equipment and marking of vehicle parts of any class, being requirements which are applicable before, whether or not they are applicable after, vehicle parts of that class are fitted to a vehicle used on a road.

(2) Regulations under this section may provide for the determination, according to criteria or by methods prescribed by or determined under the regulations, of weights of any description which in the opinion of the Secretary of State should not be exceeded in the case of vehicles of any class.

(3) In this Part of this Act references to design weights shall be construed as references to weights determined by virtue of subsection (2) above.

(4) Subject to subsection (5) below, the following provisions of this Act to the end of section 60 apply in relation to parts of vehicles as they apply in relation to vehicles and, accordingly, any reference in those provisions to a vehicle, other than a reference to a goods vehicle, is to be read as including a reference to a vehicle part.

(5) Any provision which relates solely to goods vehicles or design weights does not apply in relation to parts of vehicles, but particular exclusions in those provisions do not affect the generality of this exclusion.

(6) In this Part of this Act, 'the relevant aspects of design, construction, equipment and marking', in relation to any vehicle, means those aspects of design, construction, equipment and marking which are subject to the type approval requirements or which were used as criteria in determining design weights for that vehicle.

[The Motor Vehicles (Types Approval for Goods Vehicles) (Great Britain) Regulations 1982 (SI 1982 No 1271) qv and the Motor Vehicles (Type Approval) (Great Britain) Regulations 1984 (SI 1984 No 981) qv have effect as if made in part under s 54.]

55. Type approval certificates

(1) Where the Secretary of State is satisfied on application made to him by the manufacturer of a vehicle of a class to which regulations under section 54 of this Act apply and after examination of the vehicle—

(*a*) that the vehicle complies with the relevant type approval requirements, and

(*b*) that adequate arrangements have been made to secure that other vehicles purporting to conform with that vehicle in the relevant aspects of design, construction, equipment and marking will so conform in all respects or with such variations as may be permitted,

he may approve that vehicle as a type vehicle.

(2) Where the Secretary of State approves a vehicle as a type vehicle he must issue a certificate (in this Part of this Act referred to as a 'type approval certificate') stating that the vehicle complies with the relevant type approval requirements and specifying—

(*a*) the permitted variations from the type vehicle, and

(*b*) the design weights for vehicles so conforming in all respects and for vehicles so conforming with any such variations.

(3) In the following provisions of this section and in sections 56 to 59 of this Act 'conform' means conform in all respects or with any permitted variation.

(4) Subject to subsection (6) below, a type approval certificate may be issued for a type vehicle where the Secretary of State is satisfied that one or more, but not all, of the relevant type approval requirements are complied with in the case of that vehicle.

(5) A further type approval certificate may be issued by virtue of subsection (4) above on the application of any person—

(*a*) who manufactures any part of the vehicle, or

(*b*) by whom the vehicle is finally assembled;

and references in the following provisions of this section and in sections 56 to 59 of this Act to a manufacturer shall be construed accordingly.

(6) The first type approval certificate issued for a type vehicle by virtue of subsection (4) above must specify the design weights for conforming vehicles, and accordingly—

(*a*) so much of subsection (2) above or section 57(1) to (3) of this Act as requires the Secretary of State or a manufacturer to specify in any certificate under this or that section the design weights or plated weights for a vehicle or as requires the Secretary of State [or the prescribed testing authority] or a manufacturer to mark or secure the marking of the plated weights on a vehicle does not apply to a subsequent type approval certificate issued by virtue of subsection (4) above or to the certificates of conformity issued in consequence of such a type approval certificate, and

(*b*) so much of section 58(2) of this Act as requires the Secretary of State to specify in any certificate issued by him the design weights and plated weights for a vehicle or to secure that the plated weights are marked on a vehicle does not apply to a Minister's approval certificate issued by virtue of subsection (4) above.

(7) Subsection (6) above does not apply in relation to vehicle parts.

(8) Where the Secretary of State determines on an application under this section not to issue a type approval certificate in respect of a vehicle, he must give to the applicant a written notification of the determination, stating the grounds on which it is based.

[Section 55 is printed as prospectively amended by the Transport Act 1982, s 17(1)(a) (as itself amended by the Road Traffic (Consequential Provisions) Act 1988, s 4 and Sched 2, Part I, para 6(1)(b)). The words printed within square brackets in subs (6) will come into force on a date to be announced; see the Transport Act 1982, s 76(2).

As to the application of s 55 to parts of vehicles, see s 54(4) and (5) above.]

56. Conditions of, and cancellation or suspension of, type approval certificates *[Omitted.]*

57. Certificates of conformity

(1) The manufacturer of a type vehicle in respect of which a type approval certificate is in force may issue, in respect of each vehicle manufactured by him which conforms with the type vehicle in such of the relevant aspects of design, construction,

equipment and marking as are mentioned in the type approval certificate, a certificate (in this Part of this Act referred to as a 'certificate of conformity')—

(*a*) stating that it does so conform, and

(*b*) specifying the design weights for the vehicle,

and must in the case of goods vehicles of such classes as may be prescribed specify in the certificate one or more of the plated weights for the vehicle.

(2) *[Specification of plated weights in certificate of conformity.]*

(3) *[Marking of plated weights by means of plate.]*

(4) Any certificate of conformity issued in consequence of any type approval certificate issued by virtue of section 55(4) of this Act shall relate only to the requirement or requirements to which that type approval certificate relates.

(5) *[Inapplicability of subss (2) and (3) to vehicle parts.]*

[As to the application of s 57 to parts of vehicles, see s 54(4) and (5) above.
As to the terms 'conform' and 'manufacturer', see s 55(3) and (5) above; as to the term 'goods vehicle', see s 62(3) below.]

58. Minister's approval certificates

(1) Where the Secretary of State is satisfied, on application made to him by any person in respect of a vehicle of a class to which regulations under section 54 of this Act apply and after examination of the vehicle, that—

(*a*) the vehicle complies with the relevant type approval requirements, and

(*b*) in the case of a goods vehicle, the Secretary of State has sufficient information to enable the plated weights to be ascertained for the vehicle,

he may issue a certificate (in this Part of this Act referred to as a 'Minister's approval certificate').

(2) *[Content of Minister's approval certificate.]*

(3) Where by virtue of section 57(4) of this Act a certificate of conformity issued in respect of a vehicle relates to one or more, but not all, of the relevant type approval requirements, the Secretary of State may issue in respect of that vehicle a Minister's approval certificate relating to one or more of the other relevant type approval requirements.

(4)–(6) *[Issue of Minister's approval certificate in respect of another vehicle without examination.]*

(7) *[Notice of refusal of Minister's approval certificate.]*

[As to the application of s 58 to parts of vehicles, see s 54(4) and (5) above.
As to the terms 'goods vehicle', see s 62(3) below.]

59. Supplementary provisions as to certificates of conformity and Minister's approval certificates

(1) The Secretary of State may by regulations require the prescribed alterations—

(*a*) in any of the relevant aspects of design, construction, equipment or marking, or

(*b*) in any such aspect which affects the plated weight,

made to any vehicle for which a certificate of conformity or a Minister's approval certificate is issued shall, subject to any exemption granted under subsection (2) below, be notified to the Secretary of State [or the prescribed testing authority].

(2) The Secretary of State may by notice in writing given to the manufacturer of vehicles or to the owner of a vehicle for which a Minister's approval certificate is issued—

(*a*) direct that any specified alteration in any of the aspects mentioned in subsection (1) above to a vehicle to which the direction relates shall be notified to the Secretary of State [or the prescribed testing authority],

(*b*) exempt a vehicle to which the notice relates from all or any of the requirements of regulations under subsection (1) above, subject to compliance with any conditions specified in the notice.

(3) *[Regulation-making power.]*

(4) A certificate of conformity or a Minister's approval certificate specifying any plated weights shall be treated for the purposes of the provisions of this Part of this Act and any regulations made under them relating to plating certificates (except section 50(1) and (2) of this Act) as a plating certificate.

This subsection does not apply in relation to vehicle parts.

[Section 59 is printed as prospectively amended by the Transport Act 1982, s 10(7) (as itself amended by the Road Traffic (Consequential Provisions) Act 1988, s 4 and Sched 2, Part I, para 4(d)). The words printed within square brackets in subss (1) and (2) will come into force on a date to be announced; see the Transport Act 1982, s 76(2).

As to the application of s 59(1) and (2) to parts of vehicles, see s 54(4) and (5), above.

The Motor Vehicles (Type Approval for Goods Vehicles) (Great Britain) Regulations 1982 (SI 1982 No 1271) qv have effect as if made in part under s 59(1). As to the requirement to notify prescribed alterations, see reg 10.]

60. Appeals against determinations under sections 54 to 59 *[Omitted.]*

61. Regulations for the purposes of sections 54 to 60

(1)–(3) [*Omitted.*]

(4) Where regulations under this section impose the like requirement as may be imposed by regulations made by virtue of section 51(1)(*c*)(ii) of this Act, the regulations may provide that a person who contravenes or fails to comply with a requirement so imposed is guilty of an offence.

(5) *[Definition of 'public service vehicle examiner' for purposes of s 61.]*

[The Motor Vehicles (Type Approval for Goods Vehicles) (Great Britain) Regulations 1982 (SI 1982 No 1271) qv and the Motor Vehicles (Type Approval) (Great Britain) Regulations 1984 (SI 1984 No 981) qv have effect as if made in part under s 61(1).]

62. Other supplementary provisions

(1) *[Provision of stations for examination of vehicles.]*

(2) *[Power to make regulations as to recognition of foreign type approval certificates, etc.]*

(3) Except in the case of vehicles of such class as may be prescribed, in sections 57, 58 and 61 of this Act 'goods vehicle' includes a vehicle which is a chassis for, or will otherwise form part of, a vehicle which when completed will be a goods vehicle.

63. Obligatory type approval certificates, certificates of conformity and Minister's approval certificates

(1) If—

(*a*) any person at any time on or after the day appointed by regulations made by the Secretary of State in relation to vehicles or vehicle parts of a prescribed class, being vehicles or vehicle parts to which type approval requirements prescribed by those regulations apply—

(i) uses on a road, or

(ii) causes or permits to be so used,

a vehicle of that class or a vehicle to which is fitted a vehicle part of that class, and

(*b*) it does not appear from one or more certificates then in force under sections 54 to 58 of this Act that the vehicle or vehicle part complies with those requirements,

he is guilty of an offence.

Different days may be appointed under this subsection in relation to different classes of vehicles or vehicle parts.

(2) If a plating certificate—

(*a*) has been issued for a goods vehicle to which section 53(1) of this Act or subsection (1) above applies, but

(*b*) does not specify a maximum laden weight for the vehicle together with any trailer which may be drawn by it,

any person who on or after the relevant date within the meaning of section 53(1) of this Act or, as the case may be, the day appointed under subsection (1) above uses the vehicle on a road for drawing a trailer, or causes or permits it to be so used, is guilty of an offence.

(3) Any person who—

(*a*) uses a vehicle on a road, or

(*b*) causes or permits a vehicle to be so used,

when an alteration has been made to the vehicle or its equipment which is required by regulations or directions under section 59 of this Act to be, but has not been, notified to the Secretary of State [or the prescribed testing authority] is guilty of an offence.

(4) In any proceedings for an offence under subsection (3) above, it shall be a defence to prove that the regulations were not or, as the case may be, the alteration was not, specified in the relevant certificate of conformity or Minister's approval certificate in accordance with regulations under section 59(3) of this Act.

(5) The Secretary of State may by regulations—

(*a*) exempt from all or any of the preceding provisions of this section the use of vehicles for such purposes or in such an area as may be prescribed,

(*b*) except any class of goods vehicles from the provisions of subsection (2) above, and

(*c*) make provision for the issue in respect of a vehicle or vehicle part in such circumstances as may be prescribed of a certificate of temporary exemption exempting that vehicle or vehicle part from the provisions of subsection (1) above for such period as may be specified in the certificate.

[Section 63 is printed as prospectively amended by the Transport Act 1982, s 10(7)(c) (as itself amended by the Road Traffic (Consequential Provisions) Act 1988, s 4 and Sched 2, Part I, para

4(c)). The words printed within square brackets in subs (3) will come into force on a date to be announced; see the Transport Act 1982, s 76(2).

The Motor Vehicles (Type Approval) (Great Britain) Regulations 1984 (SI 1984 No 981) (qv) have effect as if made in part under s 63(1).]

[[63A]. Alteration of plated weights for goods vehicles without examination

(1) *[Regulation-making power.]*

(2) *[Appeal against determination under regulations under this section.]*

(3) *[Amplification of regulation-making power.]*

(4) In this section 'approval certificate' means a plating certificate and any certificate of conformity or Minister's approval certificate specifying any plated weights.

(5) Any certificate issued in respect of a goods vehicle under regulations made under this section in replacement of an approval certificate of any description mentioned in subsection (4) above—

(*a*) shall be in the form appropriate for an approval certificate of that description;

(*b*) shall be identical in content with the certificate it replaces, save for any alterations in the plated weights authorised by the regulations; and

(*c*) shall be treated for the purposes of this Part of this Act (including this section) and any regulations made under any provision of this Part of this Act as if it were the same certificate as the certificate it replaces;

and any plate so issued in replacement of a plate fixed to the vehicle under [section 57 or 58] of this Act shall, when fixed to the vehicle, be treated as so fixed under that section.]

[Section 63A has been prospectively inserted by the Transport Act 1982, s 18, and is printed as amended by the Road Traffic (Consequential Provisions) Act 1988, s 4 and Sched 2, Part I, para 7. Section 63A will come into force on a date to be announced; see the Transport Act 1982, s 76(2).]

64. Using goods vehicle with unauthorised weights as well as authorised weights marked on it

(1) If there is fixed to a goods vehicle a plate containing plated weights of any description—

(*a*) determined for that vehicle by virtue of sections 49 to 52 of this Act, or

(*b*) specified in a certificate for that vehicle under section 57(1) or (2) or 58(2) or (5) of this Act,

the vehicle shall not, while it is used on a road, be marked with any other weights, except other plated weights, other weights required or authorised to be marked on the vehicle by regulations under section 41 of this Act or weights so authorised for the purposes of this section by regulations made by the Secretary of State and marked in the prescribed manner.

(2) In the event of a contravention of or failure to comply with this section the owner of the vehicle is guilty of an offence.

65. Vehicles and parts not to be sold without required certificate of conformity or Minister's approval certificate

(1) If—

(*a*) any person at any time on or after the day appointed by regulations under section 63(1) of this Act supplies a vehicle or vehicle part of a class to which those regulations apply, and (*b*) it does not appear from one or more certificates in force at that time under sections 54 to 58 of this Act that the vehicle or vehicle part complies with all the relevant type approval requirements prescribed by those regulations,

he is guilty of an offence.

(2) In this section references to supply include—

(*a*) sell,

(*b*) offer to sell or supply, and

(*c*) expose for sale.

(3) A person shall not be convicted of an offence under this section in respect of the supply of a vehicle or vehicle part if he proves—

(*a*) that it was supplied for export from Great Britain,

(*b*) that he had reasonable cause to believe that it would not be used on a road in Great Britain or, in the case of a vehicle part, that it would not be fitted to a vehicle used on a road in Great Britain or would not be so used or fitted until it had been certified under sections 54 to 58 of this Act, or

(*c*) that he had reasonable cause to believe that it would only be used for purposes or in any area prescribed by the Secretary of State under section 63(5) of this Act or, in the case of a goods vehicle, under section 53(5) of this Act.

(4) Nothing in subsection (1) above shall affect the validity of a contract or any rights arising under or in relation to a contract.

Conditions for grant of excise licence

66. Regulations prohibiting the grant of excise licences for certain vehicles except on compliance with certain conditions *[Omitted.]*

Testing vehicles on roads

67. Testing of condition of vehicles on roads

(1) An authorised examiner may test a motor vehicle on a road for the purpose of—

(*a*) ascertaining whether the requirements imposed by law as to—

(i) brakes, silencers, steering gear and tyres,

(ii) the prevention or reduction of noise, smoke, fumes or vapour, and

(iii) lighting equipment and reflectors,

are complied with as respects the vehicle, and

(*b*) bringing to the notice of the driver any failure to comply with those requirements.

(2) The examiner may drive the vehicle for the purpose of testing it.

(3) A vehicle shall not be required to stop for a test except by a constable in uniform.

(4) The following persons may act as authorised examiners for the purposes of this section [and section 67A of this Act]—

(*a*) a certifying officer or public service vehicle examiner appointed under the Public Passenger Vehicles Act 1981,

(*b*) a person appointed as an examiner under section 68(1) of this Act,

(*c*) a person appointed to examine and inspect public carriages for the purposes of the Metropolitan Public Carriage Act 1869, (*d*) a person appointed to act for the purposes of this section by the Secretary of State,

(*e*) a constable authorised so to act by or under instructions of the chief officer of police, and

(*f*) a person appointed by the police authority for a police area to act, under the directions of the chief officer of police, for the purposes of this section.

(5) A person mentioned in subsection (4)(*a*) to (*d*) and (*f*) must produce his authority to act for the purposes of this section if required to do so.

(6) On the examiner proceeding to test a vehicle under this section, the driver may, unless the test is required under subsection (7) or (8) below to be carried out forthwith, elect that the test shall be deferred to a time, and carried out at a place, fixed in accordance with Schedule 2 to this Act, and the provisions of that Schedule shall apply accordingly.

(7) Where it appears to a constable that, by reason of an accident having occurred owing to the presence of the vehicle on a road, it is requisite that a test should be carried out forthwith, he may require it to be so carried out and, if he is not to carry it out himself, may require that the vehicle shall not be taken away until the test has been carried out.

(8) Where in the opinion of a constable the vehicle is apparently so defective that it ought not to be allowed to proceed without a test being carried out, he may require the test to be carried out forthwith.

(9) If a person obstructs an authorised examiner acting under this section, or fails to comply with a requirement of this section or Schedule 2 to this Act, he is guilty of an offence.

(10) In this section and in Schedule 2 to this Act—

(*a*) 'test' includes 'inspect' or 'inspection', as the case may require, and

(*b*) references to a vehicle include references to a trailer drawn by it.

[Section 67 is printed as prospectively amended by the Road Traffic (Consequential Provisions) Act 1988, s 4 and Sched 2, Part III, para 24. The words in subs (4) printed within square brackets will come into force on a date to be announced; see ibid, s 8(3), below.]

[67A. Remedying defects discovered on roadside test

(1) Where on testing a motor vehicle under section 67 of this Act it appears to an authorised examiner that there is a defect in the vehicle by reason that the vehicle does not comply with a construction and use requirement applicable to the vehicle, he may give a notice in writing to the person who is then the owner of the vehicle—

(*a*) specifying the defect and the requirement in question, and

(*b*) requiring him to give to the Secretary of State within the permitted period a certificate complying with subsection (4) below or a declaration complying with subsection (5) below.

(2) The powers conferred by subsection (1) above may be exercised whether or not the requirement is one mentioned in section 67(1) above and whether or not proceedings are instituted for a breach of the requirement.

(3) On testing a motor vehicle under section 67 of this Act an authorised examiner may require the person in charge of the vehicle to state whether he is the owner of the vehicle and, if he is not the owner, the name and address of the owner.

(4) A certificate under this section must contain—

(*a*) a statement signed by the person to whom the notice under this section was given that he has taken steps to secure—

(i) that repairs for the purpose of remedying the defects specified in the notice have been carried out at a vehicle testing station, or

(ii) that the vehicle has been examined at such a station for the purpose of ascertaining whether any such repairs have been carried out, and

(*b*) a statement signed by a person having power to carry out examinations at such a station under section 67 of this Act—

(i) that the signatory has either carried out any such repairs or examined the vehicle for the purpose of ascertaining whether those repairs have been carried out, and

(ii) that in his opinion the vehicle complies with the construction and use requirement specified in the notice.

(5) A declaration under this section—

(*a*) must be signed by the person to whom the notice under this section was given, and

(*b*) must state that he has sold or disposed of his interest in the vehicle to which the notice relates or that he does not intend to use it any further on a road in Great Britain.

(6) A person who, having been given a notice under this section, fails to give a certificate or declaration under this section within the permitted period to the Secretary of State is guilty of an offence.

(7) A person who fails to comply with a requirement imposed on him by an authorised examiner under subsection (3) above is guilty of an offence.

(8) *[Regulation-making power for purposes of subs (4).]*

(9) In this section 'permitted period' means a period of twenty-eight days beginning with the date of the notice under this section or such longer period as the Secretary of State may, on the application of the owner of a motor vehicle, specify in writing.]

[Section 67A has been prospectively inserted by the Road Traffic (Consequential Provisions) Act 1988, s 4 and Sched 2, Part III, para 25. Section 67A will come into force on a date to be announced; see ibid, s 8(3), below.]

[67B. Tests to check whether defects have been remedied

(1) Where a certificate has been given under section 67A of this Act with respect to a motor vehicle, the Secretary of State may, within the period of thirty days beginning with the date on which he receives the certificate, require the person who is the owner of the vehicle at the time of the requirement to make the vehicle available for a further test by an officer of the Secretary of State.

(2) For that purpose the Secretary of State may request that person to specify—

(*a*) a period of seven days within which the examination is to take place, being a period falling within the period of thirty days beginning with the date of the requirement, disregarding any day in which the vehicle is outside Great Britain, and

(*b*) a place, or if that person thinks fit, a local government area, where the test may conveniently be carried out.

In this subsection 'local government area' means, as respects England and Wales, a county district or Greater London and, as respects Scotland, a region or islands area.

(3) Where a vehicle is made available under subsection (1) above for a further test, any officer of the Secretary of State may test and inspect it for the purpose of ascertaining whether any defect specified in the notice relating to it under section 67A of this Act has been remedied.

(4) Section 67A of this Act shall apply in relation to a test under this section as it applies in relation to a test under section 67 of this Act but as if references to an authorised examiner were references to an officer of the Secretary of State.

(5) Paragraphs 3 and 4 of Schedule 2 to this Act shall apply in relation to a test under this section as they apply in relation to a deferred test, but subject to the following modifications—

(*a*) references to the preceding provisions of that Schedule shall be read as references to subsection (1) above,

(*b*) in those paragraphs 'owner' shall have the meaning given by section 192 of this Act and not the meaning given by paragraph 5 of that Schedule, and

(*c*) the references in paragraph 3 to premises shall be read as a reference to a place.

(6) If a person obstructs an officer of the Secretary of State acting under this section, or fails to comply with a requirement of this section or of paragraphs 3 and 4 of Schedule 2 as applied by this section, he is guilty of an offence.

(7) *[Use of premises, etc, for examinations, tests, etc.]*]

[Section 67B has been prospectively inserted by the Road Traffic (Consequential Provisions) Act 1988, s 4 and Sched 2, Part III, para 25. Section 67B will come into force on a date to be announced; see ibid, s 8(3), below.]

Maintenance and loading of goods vehicles

68. Power to inspect goods vehicles to secure proper maintenance

(1) For the purpose of securing that goods vehicles are maintained in a fit and serviceable condition and that, in relation to goods vehicles, the provisions of this Part of this Act (except section 74) and of Part V of the Transport Act 1968 are observed, the Secretary of State must appoint such examiners as he considers necessary.

(2) In this Part of this Act 'goods vehicle examiner' means an examiner appointed under subsection (1) above or a certifying officer appointed under the Public Passenger Vehicles Act 1981.

(3) A goods vehicle examiner—

(*a*) may at any time, on production if so required of his authority, enter and inspect any goods vehicle, and for that purpose detain the vehicle during such time as is required for the inspection and

(*b*) may at any time which is reasonable having regard to the circumstances of the case enter any premises on which he has reason to believe that a goods vehicle is kept.

(4) A person who obstructs a goods vehicle examiner in the performance of his duty under subsection (3) above is guilty of an offence.

(5) A goods vehicle examiner or a constable in uniform may at any time require any person in charge of a stationary goods vehicle on a road to proceed with the

vehicle for the purpose of having it inspected under this section to any place where an inspection can be suitably carried out (not being more than five miles from the place where the requirement is made).

(6) A person in charge of a goods vehicle who refuses or neglects to comply with a requirement made under subsection (5) above is guilty of an offence [and an authorised inspector may exercise the powers given by paragraph (*a*) above in relation to any vehicle brought to the place of inspection in pursuance of a direction under subsection (4) below].

[Section 68 is printed as prospectively amended by the Transport Act 1982, s 10(6) (as itself amended by the Road Traffic (Consequential Provisions) Act 1988, s 4 and Sched 2, Part I, para 4(3)). The words printed inside square brackets in subs (3) will come into force on a date to be announced; see the Transport Act 1982, s 76(2).]

69. Power to prohibit the driving of unfit goods vehicles

(1) If—

(*a*) on any inspection of a goods vehicle under section 68 of this Act, or

(*b*) on an examination of such a vehicle under regulations under section 49 or 61 of this Act,

it appears to a good vehicle examiner [or an authorised inspector] that, owing to any defects in the vehicle, it is, or is likely to become, unfit for service, he may prohibit the driving of the vehicle on a road either absolutely or for a specified purpose.

(2) Where a goods vehicle examiner [or an authorised inspector] prohibits the driving of a vehicle under subsection (1) above, he must forthwith give notice in writing of the prohibition to the person in charge of the vehicle at the time of the inspection—

(*a*) specifying the defects which occasioned the prohibition,

(*b*) stating whether the prohibition is on all driving of the vehicle or driving it for a specified purpose (and if the latter specifying the purpose), and

(*c*) stating whether the prohibition is to come into force immediately or at the end of a specified period.

(3) A prohibition under subsection (1) above with respect to any vehicle shall, subject to any exemption granted under subsection (6) below, come into force as soon as notice of it has been given under subsection (2) above if, in the opinion of the examiner [or authorised inspector], the defects in the vehicle are such that driving it, or driving it for any purpose specified in the notice, will create an immediate risk to public safety, and the prohibition shall afterwards continue in force until it is removed under section 72 of this Act.

(4) In any other case a prohibition under subsection (1) above shall unless previously removed under section 72 and subject to any exemption under subsection (6) below, come into force at such time not later than ten days from the date of the inspection as seems appropriate to the examiner [or authorised inspector] having regard to all the circumstances, and shall afterwards continue in force until it is so removed.

(5) A prohibition under subsection (1) above may be imposed with a direction making it irremovable unless and until the vehicle has been inspected at an official testing station.

(6) Where a notice has been given under subsection (2) above any examiner [or authorised inspector] may grant an exemption in writing for the use of the vehicle in

such manner, subject to such conditions and for such purpose as may be specified in the exemption.

(7) Where any such notice has been given an examiner [or authorised inspector] may by endorsement on the notice vary its terms and, in particular, alter the time at which the prohibition is to come into force or suspend it if it has come into force [or cancel a direction under subsection [(5)] above with which the prohibition was imposed].

[Section 69 is printed as prospectively amended by the Transport Act 1982, ss 10(3)(c), 10(3) in fine and 19(2) (as those provisions are themselves amended by the Road Traffic (Consequential Provisions) Act 1988, s 4 and Sched 2, Part I, paras 4(2)(c),(d) and 8(b). The words printed within square brackets will take effect from a date to be announced; see the Transport Act 1982, s 76(2). Also from a date to be announced in accordance with s 76(2), in s 69(3) above the words 'will create an immediate risk to public safety' will be replaced by the words 'would involve danger to any person'; see the Transport Act 1982, s 19(1), as amended by s 4 of and Sched 2, Part I, para 8(a), to the 1988 Act.]

70. Power to prohibit driving of overloaded goods vehicles

(1) Subsections (2) and (3) below apply where a goods vehicle has been weighed in pursuance of a requirement imposed under section78 of this Act and it appears to—

(*a*) a goods vehicle examiner,

(*b*) a person authorised with the consent of the Secretary of State to act for the purposes of this subsection by—

(i) a highway authority other than the Secretary of State, or

(ii) a local roads authority in Scotland, or

(*c*) a constable authorised to act for those purposes by or on behalf of a chief officer of police,

that the limit imposed by construction and use requirements with respect to any description of weight which is applicable to that vehicle has been exceeded or would be exceeded if it were used on a road.

(2) The person to whom it so appears may, whether or not a notice is given under section 69(2) of this Act, give notice in writing to the person in charge of the vehicle prohibiting the driving of the vehicle on a road until—

(*a*) that weight is reduced to that limit, and

(*b*) official notification has been given to whoever is for the time being in charge of the vehicle that it is permitted to proceed.

(3) The person to whom it so appears may also by direction in writing require the person in charge of the vehicle to remove it (and, if it is a motor vehicle drawing a trailer, also remove the trailer) to such place and subject to such conditions as are specified in the direction; and the prohibition shall not apply to the removal of the vehicle or trailer in accordance with that direction.

(4) Official notification for the purposes of subsection (2) above—

(*a*) must be writing and be given by a goods vehicle examiner, a person authorised as mentioned in subsection (1) above or a constable authorised as so mentioned, and

(*b*) may be withheld until the vehicle has been weighed or reweighed in order to satisfy the person giving the notification that the weight has been sufficiently reduced.

(5) Nothing in this section shall be construed as limiting the power of the Secretary of State to make regulations under section 71(2) of this Act.

71. Offences in connection with unfit or overloaded goods vehicles

(1) A person who—

(*a*) drives a goods vehicle on a road, or causes or permits a goods vehicle to be so driven, in contravention of a prohibition under section 69 or 70 of this Act, or

(*b*) refuses, neglects or otherwise fails to comply within a reasonable time with a direction under section 70(3) of this Act,

is guilty of an offence.

(2) The Secretary of State may by regulations exempt from subsection (1) above the use of vehicles for such purposes as may be prescribed.

[Section 71 has been prospectively amended by the Transport Act 1982, s 19(3) (as itself amended by the Road Traffic (Consequential Provisions) Act 1988, s 4 and Sched 2, Part I, para 8(c)) with effect from a date to be announced; see the Transport Act 1982, s 76(2). When the prospective amendments take effect, the following text will replace s 71(1)(a) above:

[(*a*) knowingly drives a goods vehicle on a road in contravention of a prohibition under this section; or]

[(*aa*) subject to subsection [(1A)] below, causes or permits a goods vehicle to be driven on a road in contravention of such a prohibition; or]

and the following subsection will be inserted into s 71:

[[(1A)] It shall be a defence for a person charged with an offence under subsection [(1) (*aa*)] above to prove that he took all reasonable precautions and exercised all due diligence to avoid the commission of any offence under that provision.]]

72. Removal of prohibitions *[Omitted.]*

73. Provisions supplementary to sections 69 to 72

(1) *[Action on giving notice under s 69(2) or s 70(2).]*

(2) *[Goods vehicle examiner, etc, to act under directions of Secretary of State.]*

(3) Any reference in sections 69 to 72 of this Act to the driving of a vehicle is, in relation to a trailer, a reference to the driving of the vehicle by which the trailer is drawn.

(4) *[Definitions of 'authorised vehicle' and 'operator's licence' for purposes of ss 72, 73.]*

Miscellaneous provisions about vehicles and vehicle parts

74. Operator's duty to inspect, and keep records of inspections of, goods vehicles

(1) The Secretary of State may make regulations requiring the operator for the time being of a goods vehicle to which the regulations apply to secure—

(*a*) the carrying out by a suitably qualified person (including the operator if so qualified) of an inspection of the vehicle for the purpose of ascertaining whether the construction and use requirements with respect to any prescribed matters, being requirements applicable to the vehicle, are complied with, and

(*b*) the making and authentication of records of such matters relating to any such inspection as may be prescribed, including records of the action taken to remedy any defects discovered on the inspection, and providing for the preservation of such records for a prescribed period not exceeding fifteen months and their custody and production during that period.

(2) Regulations under this section may—

(*a*) apply to all goods vehicles or to goods vehicles of such classes as may be prescribed,

(*b*) require the inspection of goods vehicles under the regulations to be carried out at such times, or before the happening of such events, as may be prescribed, and

(*c*) make different provision for different cases.

(3) Any person who contravenes or fails to comply with any provision of regulations under this section is guilty of an offence.

(4) In this section 'the operator', in relation to a goods vehicle, means the person to whom it belongs or the hirer of it under a hire purchase agreement; but, if he has let it on hire (otherwise than by way of hire-purchase) or lent it to any other person, it means a person of a class prescribed by regulations under this section in relation to any particular class of goods vehicles or, subject to any such regulations, that other person.

75. Vehicles not to be sold in unroadworthy condition or altered so as to be unroadworthy

(1) Subject to the provisions of this section no person shall supply a motor vehicle or trailer in an unroadworthy condition.

(2) In this section references to supply include—

(*a*) sell,

(*b*) offer to sell or supply, and

(*c*) expose for sale.

(3) For the purposes of subsection (1) above a motor vehicle or trailer is in an unroadworthy condition if—

(*a*) it is in such a condition that the use of it on a road in that condition would be unlawful by virtue of any provision made by regulations under section 41 of this Act as respects—

(i) brakes, steering gear or tyres, or

(ii) the construction, weight or equipment of vehicles, or

(iii) the maintenance of vehicles, their parts and accessories in such a condition that no danger is or is likely to be caused, or

(*b*) it is in such a condition, as respects lighting equipment or reflectors or their maintenance, that it is not capable of being used on a road during the hours of darkness without contravention of the requirements imposed by law as to obligatory lamps or reflectors.

(4) Subject to the provisions of this section no person shall alter a motor vehicle or trailer so as to render its condition such that the use of it on a road in that condition would be unlawful by virtue of any provision made as respects the construction, weight or equipment of vehicles by regulations under section 41.

(5) A person who supplies or alters a motor vehicle or trailer in contravention of this section, or causes or permits it to be so supplied or altered, is guilty of an offence.

(6) A person shall not be convicted of an offence under this section in respect of the supply or alteration of a motor vehicle or trailer if he proves—

(*a*) that it was supplied or altered, as the case may be, for export from Great Britain, or

(*b*) that he had reasonable cause to believe that the vehicle or trailer would not be used on a road in Great Britain, or would not be so used until it had been put into a condition in which it might lawfully be so used, or

(*c*) in the case of a vehicle or trailer the supply of which is alleged to be unlawful by reason of its condition as respects lighting equipment or reflectors or their maintenance, that he had reasonable cause to believe that the vehicle or trailer would not be used on a road in Great Britain during the hours of darkness until it had been put into a condition in which it might be so used during those hours without contravention of the requirements imposed by law as to obligatory lamps or reflectors.

(7) Nothing in the preceding provisions of this section shall affect the validity of a contract or any rights arising under a contract.

(8) In this section 'obligatory lamps or reflectors' means, in relation to a motor vehicle or trailer, the lamps or reflectors required by law to be carried on it while it is on a road—

(*a*) during the hours of darkness, and

(*b*) when it is neither drawing nor being drawn by another vehicle,

except that the expression does not, in the case of a trailer, include any lamps showing a white light to the front.

76. Fitting and supply of defective or unsuitable vehicle parts

(1) If any person—

(*a*) fits a vehicle part to a vehicle, or

(*b*) causes or permits a vehicle part to be fitted to a vehicle,

in such circumstances that the use of the vehicle on a road would, by reason of that part being fitted to the vehicle, constitute a contravention of or failure to comply with any of the construction and use requirements, he is guilty of an offence.

(2) A person shall not be convicted of an offence under subsection (1) above if he proves—

(*a*) that the vehicle to which the part was fitted was to be exported from Great Britain, or

(*b*) that he had reasonable cause to believe that that vehicle—

(i) would not be used on a road in Great Britain, or

(ii) that it would not be so used until it had been put into a condition in which its use would not constitute a contravention of or a failure to comply with any of the construction and use requirements.

(3) If a person—

(*a*) supplies a vehicle part or causes or permits a vehicle part to be supplied, and

(*b*) has reasonable cause to believe that the part is to be fitted to a motor vehicle, or to a vehicle of a particular class, or to a particular vehicle,

he is guilty of an offence if that part could not be fitted to a motor vehicle or, as the case may require, to a vehicle of that class or of a class to which the particular vehicle belongs, except in such circumstances that the use of the vehicle on a road would, by reason of that part being fitted to the vehicle, constitute a contravention of or failure to comply with any of the construction and use requirements.

(4) In this section references to supply include—

(*a*) sell, and

(*b*) offer to sell or supply.

(5) A person shall not be convicted of an offence under subsection (3) above in respect of the supply of a vehicle part if he proves—

(*a*) that the part was supplied for export from Great Britain, or

(*b*) that he had reasonable cause to believe that—

(i) it would not be fitted to a vehicle used on a road in Great Britain, or

(ii) it would not be so fitted until it had been put into such a condition that it could be fitted otherwise than in such circumstances that the use of the vehicle on a road would, by reason of that part being fitted to the vehicle, constitute a contravention of or failure to comply with any of the construction and use requirements.

(6) An authorised examiner may at any reasonable hour enter premises where, in the course of a business, vehicle parts are fitted to vehicles or are supplied and test and inspect any vehicle or vehicle part found on those premises for the purpose of ascertaining whether—

(*a*) a vehicle part has been fitted to the vehicle in such circumstances that the use of the vehicle on a road would, by reason of that part being fitted to the vehicle, constitute a contravention of or failure to comply with any of the construction and use requirements, or

(*b*) the vehicle part could not be supplied for fitting to a vehicle used on roads in Great Britain without the commission of an offence under subsection (3) above.

(7) For the purpose of testing a motor vehicle and any trailer drawn by it the authorised examiner may drive it and for the purpose of testing a trailer may draw it with a motor vehicle.

(8) Any person who obstructs an authorised examiner acting under subsection (6) or (7) above is guilty of an offence.

(9) In subsections (6) to (8) above 'authorised examiner' means a person who may act as an authorised examiner for the purposes of section 67 of this Act; and any such person, other than a constable in uniform, shall produce his authority to act for the purpose of subsections (6) and (7) above if required to do so.

(10) Nothing in this section shall affect the validity of a contract or of any rights arising under a contract.

77. Testing condition of used vehicles at sale rooms, etc

(1) An authorised examiner may at any reasonable hour enter premises where used motor vehicles or trailers are supplied in the course of a business and test and inspect any used motor vehicle or trailer found on the premises for the purpose of ascertaining whether it is in an unroadworthy condition for the purposes of section 75(1) of this Act.

(2) In this section (except paragraph (*d*) below) references to supply include—

(*a*) sell,

(*b*) offer for sale or supply,

(*c*) expose for sale, and

(*d*) otherwise keep for sale or supply.

(3) An authorised examiner may at any reasonable hour enter premises where vehicles or vehicle parts of a class prescribed for the purposes of section 63 of this Act are supplied in the course of a business and test and inspect any such vehicle or vehicle part for the purpose of ascertaining whether the vehicle or vehicle part complies with the type approval requirements applicable to a vehicle or vehicle part of that class.

(4) For the purpose of testing a motor vehicle and any trailer drawn by it the authorised examiner may drive it and for the purpose of testing a trailer may draw it with a motor vehicle.

(5) A person who obstructs an authorised examiner acting under this section is guilty of an offence.

(6) In this section 'authorised examiner' means a person who may act as an authorised examiner for the purposes of section 67 of this Act; and any such person, other than a constable in uniform, shall produce his authority to act for the purposes of that section if required to do so.

(7) A motor vehicle or trailer shall be treated for the purposes of this section as used if, but only if, it has previously been sold or supplied by retail.

78. Weighing of motor vehicles

(1) Subject to any regulations made by the Secretary of State, an authorised person may, on production of his authority, require the person in charge of a motor vehicle—

(*a*) to allow the vehicle or any trailer drawn by it to be weighed, either laden or unladen, and the weight transmitted to the road by any parts of the vehicle or trailer in contact with the road to be tested, and

(*b*) for that purpose, to proceed to a weighbridge or other machine for weighing vehicles.

(2) For the purpose of enabling a vehicle or a trailer drawn by it to be weighed or a weight to be tested in accordance with regulations under subsection (1) above, an authorised person may require the person in charge of the vehicle to drive the vehicle or to do any other thing in relation to the vehicle or its load or the trailer or its load which is reasonably required to be done for that purpose.

(3) If a person in charge of a motor vehicle—

(*a*) refuses or neglects to comply with any requirement under subsection (1) or (2) above, or

(*b*) obstructs an authorised person in the exercise of his functions under this section,

he is guilty of an offence.

(4) An authorised person may not require the person in charge of the motor vehicle to unload the vehicle or trailer, or to cause or allow it to be unloaded, for the purpose of its being weighed unladen.

(5) *[Regulation-making power.]*

(6) If—

(*a*) at the time when the requirement is made the vehicle is more than five miles from the weighbridge or other machine, and

(*b*) the weight is found to be within the limits authorised by law, the highway authority (in Scotland, roads authority) on whose behalf the requirement is made must pay, in respect of loss occasioned, such amount as in default of agreement may be determined by a single arbitrator (in Scotland, arbiter) agreed upon by the parties or, in default of agreement, appointed by the Secretary of State.

(7) The Secretary of State may by order designate areas in Great Britain where subsection (6) above is to have effect, in such cases as may be specified by the order, with the substitution for five miles of a greater distance so specified.

An order under this subsection shall be made by statutory instrument subject to annulment by a resolution of either House of Parliament.

(8) In this section—

(*a*) 'road' includes any land which forms part of a harbour or which is adjacent to a harbour and is occupied wholly or partly for the purposes of harbour operations,

(*b*) 'authorised person' means a person authorised by a highway authority (in Scotland, a roads authority) or a constable authorised on behalf of such an authority by a police authority or a chief officer of police,

and in this subsection 'harbour' and 'harbour operations' have the meanings given to them by section 57(1) of the Harbours Act 1964 [*qv*].

79. Further provisions relating to weighing of motor vehicles

(1) Where a motor vehicle or trailer is weighed under section 78 of this Act, a certificate of weight must be given to the person in charge of the vehicle, and the certificate so given shall exempt the motor vehicle and the trailer, if any, from being weighed so long as it is during the continuance of the same journey carrying the same load.

(2) On production of his authority—

(*a*) a certifying officer appointed under the Public Passenger Vehicles Act 1981, or

(*b*) an examiner appointed under section 68(1) of this Act, or

(*c*) any of the Secretary of State's officers authorised by him in that behalf,

may at any time exercise with respect to the weighing of vehicles of a class prescribed for the purposes of section 63 of this Act and goods vehicles generally all such powers with respect to the weighing of motor vehicles and trailers as are exercisable under section 78 of this Act by a constable authorised as mentioned in subsection (8) of that section.

(3) The provisions of section 78 of this Act shall apply accordingly in relation to vehicles of a class so prescribed and goods vehicles generally—

(*a*) as if references to a constable so authorised included references to such a certifying officer, examiner or officer of the Secretary of State, and

(*b*) as if the reference in subsection (6) to the authority on whose behalf the requirement is made were a reference to the Secretary of State, and

(*c*) as if the reference in that subsection to the Secretary of State were a reference, in relation to England and Wales, to the Lord Chief Justice of England and, in relation to Scotland, to the Lord President of the Court of Session.

(4) A certificate in the prescribed form which—

(*a*) purports to be signed by an authorised person (within the meaning of section 78 of this Act) or by a person exercising powers by virtue of subsection (2) above, and

(*b*) states, in relation to a vehicle identified in the certificate, any weight determined in relation to that vehicle on the occasion of its being brought to a weighbridge or other machine in pursuance of a requirement under section 78(1) of this Act,

shall be evidence (in Scotland, sufficient evidence) of the matter so stated.

(5) If, for the purposes of or in connection with the determination of any weight in relation to a vehicle which is brought to a weighbridge or other machine as mentioned in section 78(1) of this Act, an authorised person (within the meaning of that section) or a person exercising powers by virtue of subsection (2) above—

(*a*) drives a vehicle or does any other thing in relation to a vehicle or its load or a trailer or its load, or

(*b*) requires the driver of a vehicle to drive it in a particular manner or to a particular place or to do any other thing in relation to a vehicle or its load or a trailer or its load,

neither he nor any person complying with such a requirement shall be liable for any damage to or loss in respect of the vehicle or its load or the trailer or its load unless it is shown that he acted without reasonable care.

80. Approval marks

(1) Where any international agreement to which the United Kingdom is a party or a Community obligation provides—

(*a*) for markings to be applied—

(i) to motor vehicle parts of any description to indicate conformity with a type approved by any country, or

(ii) to a motor vehicle to indicate that the vehicle is fitted with motor vehicle parts of any description and either that the parts conform with a type approved by any country or that the vehicle is such that as so fitted it conforms with a type so approved, and

(*b*) for motor vehicle parts or, as the case may be, motor vehicles, bearing those markings to be recognised as complying with the requirements imposed by the law of another country,

the Secretary of State may by regulations designate the markings as approval marks, and any markings so designated shall be deemed for the purposes of the Trade Descriptions Act 1968 to be a trade description, whether or not the markings fall within the definition of the expression in section 2 of that Act.

(2) Any person who, without being authorised by the competent authority to apply any approval mark, applies that mark or a mark so nearly resembling it as to be calculated to deceive is guilty of an offence under the Trade Descriptions Act 1968, whether or not he would be guilty of such an offence apart from this subsection.

(3) The conditions subject to which approval of any type may be given on behalf of the United Kingdom or the use of approval marks indicating conformity with a type approved by the United Kingdom may be authorised may include such conditions as to testing or inspection and the payment of fees as the Secretary of State may impose.

(4) In this section—

'motor vehicle' means a mechanically propelled vehicle or a vehicle designed or adapted for towing by a mechanically propelled vehicle,

'motor vehicle part' means any article made or adapted for use as part of a mechanically propelled vehicle or a vehicle drawn by a mechanically propelled vehicle, or for use as part of the equipment of any such vehicle, shall be treated as including any equipment for the protection of drivers or passengers in or on a motor vehicle notwithstanding that it does not form part of, or of the equipment of, that vehicle, and

'the competent authority' means—

(*a*) as respects any approval marks indicating conformity with a type approved by the United Kingdom, the Secretary of State, and

(*b*) as respects any approval marks indicating conformity with a type approved by any other country, the authority having power under the law of that country to authorise the use of that mark.

[The Motor Vehicles (Designation of Approval Marks) Regulations 1979 (SI 1979 No 1088) have effect as if made under s 80.

The Trade Descriptions Act 1968, s 1, makes it an offence for any person in the course of a trade or business to (a) apply a false trade description to any goods, or (b) supply, or offer to supply, any goods to which a false trade description is applied. Under ibid, s 18, the penalty, on summary conviction, is a fine up to the prescribed sum and, on conviction on indictment, a fine and/or imprisonment for up to two years (s 18 has been amended by the Magistrates' Courts Act 1980, s 32(2)). For the statutory defences to charges under the Trade Descriptions Act 1968, see ss 24 and 25 of that Act.]

Pedal cycles and horse-drawn vehicles

81. Regulation of brakes, bells etc, on pedal cycles

(1)–(4) *[Regulation-making powers.]*

(5) Regulations under this section as to the use on roads of cycles may prohibit the sale or supply, or the offer of a sale or supply, of a cycle for delivery in such a condition that the use of it on a road in that condition would be a contravention of the regulations, but no provision made by virtue of this subsection shall affect the validity of any contract or any rights arising under a contract.

(6) If a person sells or supplies or offers to sell or supply a cycle in contravention of any prohibition imposed by regulations made by virtue of subsection (5) above, he is guilty of an offence, unless he proves—

(*a*) that it was sold, supplied or offered for export from Great Britain, or

(*b*) that he had reasonable cause to believe that it would not be used on a road in Great Britain, or would not be so used until it had been put into a condition in which it might lawfully be so used.

[The Pedal Cycles (Construction and Use) Regulations 1983 (SI 1983 No 1176) have effect as if made under s 81.]

82. Regulation of brakes on horse-drawn vehicles *[Omitted.]*

Miscellaneous

83. Offences to do with reflectors and tail lamps

A person who sells, or offers or exposes for sale, any appliance adapted for use as a reflector or tail lamp to be carried on a vehicle in accordance with the provisions of this Act or of any regulations made under it, not being an appliance which complies with the construction and use requirements applicable to a class of vehicles for which the appliance is adapted, is guilty of an offence.

84. Appointment of officials and destination of fees *[Omitted.]*

85. Interpretation of Part II

[(1)] In this Part of this Act—

'the Community Recording Equipment Regulation' means Council Regulation (EEC) No 3821/85 of 20th December 1985 on recording equipment in road transport [*qv*], as read with the Community Drivers' Hours and Recording Equipment (Exemptions and Supplementary Provisions) Regulations 1986 *[SI 1986 No 1456, qv]*, the Community Drivers' Hours and Recording Equipment (Exemptions and Supplementary Provisions) (Amendment) Regulations 1986 *[SI 1986 No 1669]* and the Community Drivers' Hours and Recording Equipment (Exemptions and Supplementary Provisions) (Amendment) Regulations 1987 *[SI 1987 No 805]*,

'licensing authority' means a licensing authority for the purposes of Part V of the Transport Act 1968,

'official testing station' means a testing station maintained by the Secretary of State under section 72(8) of this Act [or premises designated by him under section 10(12) of the Transport Act 1982],

'prescribed' means prescribed by regulations made by the Secretary of State,

['prescribed testing authority' means such approved testing authority as may be prescribed,]

'sold or supplied by retail' means sold or supplied otherwise than to a person acquiring solely for the purpose of resale or of re-supply for a valuable consideration,

'tail lamp' means, in relation to a vehicle, any lamp carried attached to the vehicle for the purpose of showing a red light to the rear in accordance with regulations under section 41 of this Act,

'traffic area' has the same meaning as in the Public Passenger Vehicles Act 1981, and

'vehicle part' means any article which is a motor vehicle part, within the meaning of section 80 of this Act, and any other article which is made or adapted for use as part of, or as part of the equipment of, a vehicle which is intended or adapted to be used on roads but which is not a motor vehicle within the meaning of that section.

[(2) References in any provision of this Part of this Act to an authorised inspector are references to a person authorised by the Secretary of State under section 8 of the Transport Act 1982 to exercise the function to which that provision relates.]

[Section 85 is printed as prospectively amended by the Road Traffic (Consequential Provisions) Act 1988, s 4 and Sched 2, Part I, para 17 (a)–(c). The words printed within square brackets will come into force on a date to be announced; see s 8(3), below. The text of s 85 as enacted has prospectively been designated as s 85(1) (although no such textual amendment has been formally effected) following the prospective addition of s 85(2).

Section 8 of the Transport Act 1982 (which has not yet been brought into force) will make provision for private sector plating and testing by 'authorised inspectors'.]

86. Index to Part II

The expressions listed in the left-hand column below are respectively defined or (as the case may be) fall to be construed in accordance with the provisions of this Part of this Act listed in the right-hand column in relation to those expressions.

Expression	*Relevant provision*
Certificate of conformity	Section 57(1)
Community Recording Equipment Regulation	Section 85
Construction and use requirements	Section 41(7)
Design weights	Section 54(3)
Examination for plating	Section 49(4)
Goods vehicle examiner	Section 68(2)
Goods vehicle test	Section 49(4)
Goods vehicle test certificate	Section 49(2)(*b*)
Licensing authority	Section 85
Minister's approval certificate	Section 58(1)
Official testing station	Section 85
Plating certificate	Section 49(2)(*a*)
Plated particulars	Section 41(7)
Plated weights	Section 41(7)
Prescribed	Section 85
Relevant aspects of design, construction, equipment and marking	Section 54(6)
Sold or supplied by retail	Section 85
Tail lamp	Section 85
Test certificate	Section 45(2)
Traffic area	Section 85
Type approval certificate	Section 55(2)
Type approval requirements	Section 54(1)
Vehicle part	Section 85

PART III

Licensing of Drivers of Vehicles

Requirement to hold licence

87. Drivers of motor vehicles to have driving licences

(1) It is an offence for a person to drive on a road a motor vehicle of any class if he is not the holder of a licence authorising him to drive a motor vehicle of that class.

(2) It is an offence for a person to cause or permit another person to drive on a road a motor vehicle of any class if that other person is not the holder of a licence authorising him to drive a motor vehicle of that class.

[The fixed penalty procedure applies to offences under s 87(1); see the Road Traffic Offenders Act 1988, Sched 3, below.]

88. Exceptions

(1) Nothwithstanding section 87 of this Act, a person may drive or cause or permit another person to drive a vehicle of any class if—

(*a*) the driver has held a licence to drive vehicles of that class or an exchangeable licence to drive vehicles of a category corresponding to that class and (in either case) is entitled to obtain a licence to drive vehicles of that class, and (*b*) an application by the driver for the grant of such a licence for a period which includes that time has been received by the Secretary of State or such a licence granted to him has been revoked or surrendered in pursuance of section 99 of this Act, and

(*c*) any conditions which by virtue of section 97(3) or 98(2) of this Act apply to the driving under the authority of the licence of vehicles of that class are complied with.

(2) The benefit of subsection (1) above does not extend—

(*a*) beyond the date when a licence is granted in pursuance of the application mentioned in subsection (1)(*b*) above or (as the case may be) in pursuance of section 99(7) of this Act in consequence of the revocation or surrender so mentioned, or

(*b*) in a case where a licence is not in fact so granted, beyond the expiration of the period of one year or such shorter period as may be prescribed, beginning on the date of the application or (as the case may be) the revocation or surrender mentioned in subsection (1)(*b*) above.

(3) The Secretary of State may by regulations provide that subsection (1) above shall also apply (where the requirements of that subsection are otherwise met) in the case of a person who has not previously held a licence to drive vehicles of the relevant class.

(4) Regulations made by virtue of subsection (3) above shall, if not previously revoked, expire at the end of the period of one year beginning with the day on which they came into operation.

(5) Regulations may provide that a person who becomes resident in Great Britain shall, during the prescribed period after he becomes so resident, be treated for the purposes of section 87 of this Act as the holder of a licence authorising him to drive motor vehicles of the prescribed classes if—

(*a*) he satisfies the prescribed conditions, and

(*b*) he is the holder of a permit of the prescribed description authorising him to drive vehicles under the law of a country outside the United Kingdom.

(6) Regulations made by virtue of subsection (5) above may provide for the application of any enactment relating to licences or licence holders, with or without modifications, in relation to any such permit and its holder respectively.

(7) Notwithstanding section 87 of this Act—

(*a*) a person who is not a holder of a licence may act as steersman of a motor vehicle, being a vehicle on which a speed limit of five miles per hour or less is imposed by or under section 86 of the Road Traffic Regulation Act 1984 [*qv*], under the orders of another person engaged in the driving of the vehicle who is licensed in that behalf in accordance with the requirements of this Part and Part IV of this Act, and

(*b*) a person may cause or permit another person who is not the holder of a licence so to act.

[The Motor Vehicles (Driving Licences) Regulations 1987 (SI 1987 No 1378) qv have effect as if made in part under s 88.

As to the term 'Great Britain' in s 88(5), see the Driving Licences (Community Driving Licences) Regulations 1982 (SI 1982 No 1555), reg 4(1), below.]

Tests

89. Tests of competence to drive

(1) A licence authorising the driving of motor vehicles of any class shall not be granted to any person unless he satisfies the Secretary of State—

(*a*) that at some time during the period of ten years ending on the date of the coming into force of the licence applied for he has passed the test of competence to drive prescribed by virtue of subsection (3) below or a test of competence which under subsection (6) below is a sufficient test, or

(*b*) that within that period of ten years he has held a licence authorising the driving of vehicles of that class, not being a provisional licence, a licence granted by virtue of section 99(4) of the Road Traffic Act 1960 or a licence which has been revoked in pursuance of section 99(3) of this Act, or

(*c*) that, at the time of application for the licence—

(i) he holds an exchangeable licence authorising the driving of vehicles of a category corresponding to that class, and

(ii) he is normally resident in Great Britain or (where the exchangeable licence is a Community licence) the United Kingdom but has not been so resident for more than one year, or

(*d*) that—

(i) within that period of ten years he has held a licence granted under a relevant external law to drive vehicles of that class, not being a licence corresponding to a provisional licence or a licence granted under any provision of that law corresponding to section 99(4) of the Road Traffic Act 1960, and

(ii) he is not, at the time of application for the licence, disqualified under that law for holding or obtaining a licence under it to drive vehicles of any class.

This subsection is subject to the provisions of this Part of this Act as to provisional licences and to the provisions of any regulations made by virtue of section 105(2)(*f*) of this Act.

(2) For the purposes of subsection (1)(*d*) above 'relevant external law' means the law for the time being in force in Northern Ireland, that for the time being in force in the Isle of Man or that for the time being in force in any of the Channel Islands that corresponds to this Part of this Act.

(3)–(5) *[Regulation-making powers.]*

(6) For the purposes of subsection (1)(*a*) above, a test of competence shall be sufficient for the granting of a licence authorising the driving of—

(*a*) vehicles of any class, if at the time the test was passed it authorised the granting of a licence to drive vehicles of that class,

(*b*) vehicles of any classes which are designated by regulations as a group for the purposes of subsection (1)(*a*) above, if at the time the test was passed it authorised the granting of a licence to drive vehicles of any class included in the group.

(7) If vehicles of any classes are designated by regulations as a group for the purposes of subsection (1)(*b*) above, a licence authorising the driving of vehicles of a class included in the group shall be deemed for the purposes of subsection (1)(*b*) to authorise the driving of vehicles of all classes included in the group.

The reference in this subsection to a licence does not include a licence which has been revoked in pursuance of section 99(3) of this Act.

(8) For the purposes of this section and section 88(1) of this Act, an exchangeable licence issued in respect of a member State, country or territory shall not be treated as authorising a person to drive a vehicle of any category if—

(*a*) the licence is not for the time being valid for that purpose, or

(*b*) it was issued in respect of that category for a purpose corresponding to that mentioned in section 97(2) of this Act.

(9) Where an exchangeable licence authorises the driving of vehicles of any category and any vehicle falling within that category falls also within any of the classes designated as a group for the purposes of subsection (1)(*b*) above—

(*a*) that category shall be treated for the purposes of subsection (1)(*c*) above as corresponding to all classes included in the group, and

(*b*) where, by virtue of regulations, a person who passes a test of competence authorising the granting of a licence to drive vehicles of any class included in the group is treated as competent also to drive vehicles of a class included in another group, that category shall be treated for the purposes of subsection (1)(*c*) above as corresponding to all categories included in that other group.

[The Motor Vehicles (Driving Licences) Regulations 1987 (SI 1987 No 1378) qv have effect as if made in part under s 89.

Section 99(4) of the Road Traffic Act 1960 empowered the making of regulations dispensing with requirements corresponding to those contained in s 89(1) in the case of persons not resident in Great Britain.]

90. Review of conduct of test by magistrates' court *[Omitted.]*

91. Repayment of test fees *[Omitted.]*

Physical fitness

92. Requirements as to physical fitness of drivers

(1) An application for the grant of a licence must include a declaration by the applicant, in such form as the Secretary of State may require, stating whether he is suffering or has at any time (or, if a period is prescribed for the purposes of this subsection, has during that period) suffered from any relevant disability or any prospective disability.

(2) In this Part of this Act—

'disability' includes disease,

'relevant disability' in relation to any person means—

(*a*) any prescribed disability, and

(*b*) any other disability likely to cause the driving of a vehicle by him in pursuance of a licence to be a source of danger to the public, and

'prospective disability' in relation to any person means any other disability which—

(*a*) at the time of the application for the grant of a licence or, as the case may be, the material time for the purposes of the provision in which the expression is used, is not of such a kind that it is a relevant disability, but

(*b*) by virtue of the intermittent or progressive nature of the disability or otherwise, may become a relevant disability in course of time.

(3) If it appears from the applicant's declaration, or if on inquiry the Secretary of

State is satisfied from other information, that the applicant is suffering from a relevant disability, the Secretary of State must, subject to the following of this section, refuse to grant the licence.

(4) The Secretary of State must not by virtue of subsection (3) above refuse to grant a licence—

(*a*) on account of any relevant disability which is prescribed for the purposes of this paragraph, if the applicant has at any time passed a relevant test and it does not appear to the Secretary of State that the disability has arisen or become more acute since that time or was, for whatever reason, not disclosed to the Secretary of State at that time,

(*b*) on account of any relevant disability which is prescribed for the purposes of this paragraph, if the applicant satisfies such conditions as may be prescribed with a view to authorising the grant of a licence to a person in whose case the disability is appropriately controlled,

(*c*) on account of any relevant disability which is prescribed for the purposes of this paragraph, if the application is for a provisional licence.

(5) Where as a result of a test of competence to drive the Secretary of State is satisfied that the person who took the test is suffering from a disability such that there is likely to be a danger to the public—

(*a*) if he drives any vehicle, or

(*b*) if he drives a vehicle other than a vehicle of a particular construction or design,

the Secretary of State must serve notice in writing to that effect on that person and must include in the notice a description of the disability.

(6) Where a notice is served in pursuance of subsection (5)(*a*) above, then—

(*a*) if the disability is not prescribed under subsection (2) above, it shall be deemed to be so prescribed in relation to the person who took the test, and

(*b*) if the disability is prescribed for the purposes of subsection (4)(*c*) above it shall be deemed not to be so prescribed in relation to him.

(7) Where a notice is served in pursuance of subsection (5)(*b*) above, any licence granted to the person who took the test shall be limited to vehicles of the particular construction or design specified in the notice.

(8) In this section 'relevant test', in relation to an application for a licence, means any such test of competence as is mentioned in section 89 of this Act or a test as to fitness or ability in pursuance of section 100 of the Road Traffic Act 1960 as originally enacted, being a test authorising the grant of a licence in respect of vehicles of the classes to which the application relates.

(9) Without prejudice to subsection (8) above, for the purposes of subsection (4)(*a*) above—

(*a*) an applicant shall be treated as having passed a relevant test if, and on the day on which, he has passed a test of competence to drive which, under a provision of a relevant external law corresponding to subsections (3) and (4) or (6) and (7) of section 89 of this Act, either is prescribed in relation to vehicles of the classes to which the application relates or is sufficient under that law for granting of a licence authorising the driving of vehicles of those classes, and

(*b*) in the case of an applicant who is treated as having passed a relevant test by virtue of paragraph (*a*) above, disclosure of a disability to the authority having power under the relevant external law to grant a licence to drive a motor vehicle shall be treated as disclosure to the Secretary of State.

In this subsection 'relevant external law' has the meaning given by section 89(2) of this Act.

[The Motor Vehicles (Driving Licences) Regulations 1987 (SI 1987 No 1378) qv have effect as if made in part under s 92.

In relation to s 92(4)(a), see further the Road Traffic (Consequential Provisions) Act 1988, s 5 and Sched 4, para 7(1), below.]

93. Revocation of licence because of disability or prospective disability

[Omitted.]

94. Provision of information, etc relating to disabilities

(1) If at any time during the period for which his licence remains in force, a licence holder becomes aware—

(*a*) that he is suffering from a relevant or prospective disability which he has not previously disclosed to the Secretary of State, or

(*b*) that a relevant or prospective disability from which he has at any time suffered (and which has been previously so disclosed) has become more acute since the licence was granted,

the licence holder must forthwith notify the Secretary of State in writing of the nature and extent of his disability.

(2) The licence holder is not required to notify the Secretary of State under subsection (1) above if—

(*a*) the disability is one from which he has not previously suffered, and

(*b*) he has reasonable grounds for believing that the duration of the disability will not extend beyond the period of three months beginning with the date on which he first becomes aware that he suffers from it.

(3) A person who fails without reasonable excuse to notify the Secretary of State as required by subsection (1) above is guilty of an offence.

(4) If the Secretary of State has reasonable grounds for believing that a person who is an applicant for, or the holder of, a licence may be suffering from a relevant or prospective disability, subsection (5) below applies for the purpose of enabling the Secretary of State to satisfy himself whether or not that is the case.

(5) The Secretary of State may by notice in writing served on the applicant or holder—

(*a*) require him to provide the Secretary of State, within such reasonable time as may be specified in the notice, with such an authorisation as is mentioned in subsection (6) below, or

(*b*) require him, as soon as practicable, to arrange to submit himself for examination—

(i) by such registered medical practitioner or practitioners as may be nominated by the Secretary of State, or

(ii) with respect to a disability of a prescribed description, by such officer of the Secretary of State as may be so nominated,

for the purpose of determining whether or not he suffers or has at any time suffered from a relevant or prospective disability, or

(*c*) except where the application is for, or the licence held is, a provisional licence, require him to submit himself for a test of competence to drive, being a test authorising the grant of a licence in respect of vehicles—

(i) of all or any of the classes to which the application relates, or

(ii) which he is authorised to drive (otherwise than by virtue of section 98(2) of this Act) by the licence which he holds,

as the case may be.

(6) The authorisation referred to in subsection (5)(*a*) above—

(*a*) shall be in such form and contain such particulars as may be specified in the notice by which it is required to be provided, and

(*b*) shall authorise any registered medical practitioner who may at any time have given medical advice or attention to the applicant or licence holder concerned to release to the Secretary of State any information which he may have, or which may be available to him, with respect to the question whether, and if so to what extent, the applicant or licence holder concerned may be suffering, or may at any time have suffered, from a relevant or prospective disability.

(7) If he considers it appropriate to do so in the case of any applicant or licence holder, the Secretary of State—

(*a*) may include in a single notice under subsection (5) above requirements under more than one paragraph of that subsection, and

(*b*) may at any time after the service of a notice under that subsection serve a further notice or notices under that subsection.

(8) If any person on whom a notice is served under subsection (5) above—

(*a*) fails without reasonable excuse to comply with a requirement contained in the notice, or

(*b*) fails any test of competence which he is required to take as mentioned in paragraph (*c*) of that subsection,

the Secretary of State may exercise his powers under sections 92 and 93 of this Act as if he were satisfied that the applicant or licence holder concerned is suffering from a relevant disability which is not prescribed for the purposes of any paragraph of section 92(4) of this Act or, if the Secretary of State so determines, as if he were satisfied that the applicant or licence holder concerned is suffering from a prospective disability.

(9) *[Secretary of State to defray expenses, etc, under subs (5).]*

95. Notification of refusal of insurance on grounds of health

(1) If an authorised insurer refuses to issue to any person such a policy of insurance as complies with the requirements of Part VI of this Act on the ground that the state of health of that person is not satisfactory, or on grounds which include that ground, the insurer shall as soon as practicable notify the Secretary of State of that refusal and of the full name, address, sex and date of birth of that person as disclosed by him to the insurer.

(2) In subsection (1) above 'authorised insurer' means a person or body of persons carrying on insurance business within Group 2 in Part II of Schedule 2 to the Insurance Companies Act 1982 [*qv*] and being a member of the Motor Insurers' Bureau (a company limited by guarantee and incorporated under the Companies Act 1929 on 14th June 1946).

96. Driving with uncorrected defective eyesight

(1) If a person drives a motor vehicle on a road while his eyesight is such (whether through a defect which cannot be or one which is not for the time being sufficiently

corrected) that he cannot comply with any requirement as to eyesight prescribed under this Part of this Act for the purposes of tests of competence to drive, he is guilty of an offence.

(2) A constable having reason to suspect that a person driving a motor vehicle may be guilty of an offence under subsection (1) above may require him to submit to a test for the purpose of ascertaining whether, using no other means of correction than he used at the time of driving, he can comply with the requirement concerned.

(3) If that person refuses to submit to the test he is guilty of an offence.

Granting of licences, their form and duration

97. Grant of licences

(1) Subject to subsection (2) below and section 92 of this Act, the Secretary of State must, on payment of such fee (if any) as may be prescribed, grant a licence to a person who—

(*a*) makes an application for it in such manner and containing such particulars as the Secretary of State may specify,

(*b*) provides the Secretary of State with such evidence or further evidence in support of the application as the Secretary of State may require,

(*c*) surrenders to the Secretary of State any previous licence granted to him after 1st June 1970 or provides the Secretary of State with an explanation for not surrendering it which the Secretary of State considers adequate and, where the application is made by virtue of section 89(1)(*c*) of this Act, surrenders to the Secretary of State his exchangeable licence, and

(*d*) is not disqualified by reason of age or otherwise from obtaining the licence for which he makes the application and is not prevented from obtaining it by the provisions of section 89 of this Act.

(2) If the application for the licence states that it is made for the purpose of enabling the applicant to drive a motor vehicle with a view to passing a test of competence to drive, any licence granted in pursuance of the application shall be a provisional licence for that purpose, and nothing in section 89 of this Act shall apply to such a licence.

(3) A provisional licence—

(*a*) shall be granted subject to prescribed conditions,

(*b*) shall, in any cases prescribed for the purposes of this paragraph, be restricted so as to authorise only the driving of vehicles of the classes so prescribed,

(*c*) may, in the case of a person appearing to the Secretary of State to be suffering from a relevant disability or a prospective disability, be restricted so as to authorise only the driving of vehicles of a particular construction or design specified in the licence, and

(*d*) shall not authorise a person, before he has passed a test of competence to drive, to drive a motor cycle having two wheels only, unless it is a learner motor cycle (as defined in subsection (5) below) or its first use (as defined in regulations) occurred before 1st January 1982 and the cylinder capacity of its engine does not exceed 125 cubic centimetres.

(4) Regulations may authorise or require the Secretary of State to refuse a provisional licence authorising the driving of a motor cycle of a prescribed class if the applicant has held such a provisional licence and the licence applied for would come into force within the prescribed period—

(*a*) beginning at the end of the period for which the previous licence authorised (or would, if not surrendered or revoked, have authorised) the driving of such a motor cycle, or

(*b*) beginning at such other time as may be prescribed.

(5) A learner motor cycle is a motor cycle which either is propelled by electric power or has the following characteristics—

(*a*) the cylinder capacity of its engine does not exceed 125 cubic centimetres,

(*b*) the maximum power output of its engine does not exceed nine kilowatts (as measured in accordance with International Standards Organisation standard 4106–1978.09.01), and

(*c*) its power to weight ratio does not exceed 100 kilowatts per metric tonne, the power being the maximum power output mentioned in paragraph (*b*) above and the weight that mentioned in subsection (6) below.

(6) The weight referred to in subsection (5) above is the weight of the motor vehicle with a full supply of fuel in its tank, an adequate supply of other liquids needed for its propulsion and no load other than its normal equipment, including loose tools.

(7) A person who fails to comply with any condition applicable to him by virtue of subsection (3) above is guilty of an offence.

[The fixed penalty procedure applies to offences under s 97; see the Road Traffic Offenders Act 1988, Sched 3.

The Motor Vehicles (Driving Licences) Regulations 1987 (SI 1987 No 1378) qv have effect as if made in part under s 97.]

98. Form of licence

(1) A licence shall be in such form as the Secretary of State may determine and shall—

(*a*) state whether, apart form subsection (2) below, it authorises its holder to drive motor vehicles of all classes or of certain classes only and, in the latter case, specify those classes,

(*b*) specify the restrictions on the driving of vehicles of any class in pursuance of the licence to which its holder is subject by virtue of the provisions of section 101 of this Act,

(*c*) in the case of a provisional licence, specify the conditions subject to which it is granted, and

(*d*) where, by virtue of subsection (2) below, the licence authorises its holder to drive vehicles of classes other than those specified in the licence in pursuance of paragraph (*a*) above, contain such statements as the Secretary of State considers appropriate for indicating the effect of that subsection.

(2) Subject to subsections (3) and (4) below, a licence which, apart from this subsection, authorises its holder to drive motor vehicles of certain classes only (not being—

(*a*) a licence granted before 1st June 1970,

(*b*) a provisional licence granted after that date, or

(*c*) any other licence of a description prescribed for the purposes of this subsection)

shall also authorise him to drive motor vehicles of all other classes subject to the same conditions as if he were authorised by a provisional licence to drive motor vehicles of those other classes.

(3) A licence shall not by virtue of subsection (2) above authorise a person to drive—

(*a*) a vehicle of a class for the driving of which he could not, by reason of the provisions of section 101 of this Act, lawfully hold a licence, or

(*b*) unless he has passed a test of competence to drive, a motor cycle which, by virtue of section 97(3)(*d*) of this Act, a provisional licence would not authorise him to drive before he had passed that test.

(4) In such cases as the Secretary of State may prescribe, the provisions of subsections (2) and (3) above shall not apply or shall apply subject to such limitations as he may prescribe.

(5) A person who fails to comply with any condition applicable to him by virtue of subsection (2) above is guilty of an offence.

[The Motor Vehicles (Driving Licences) Regulations 1987 (SI 1987 No 1378) qv have effect as if made in part under s 98.]

99. Duration of licences

(1) A licence shall, unless previously revoked or surrendered, remain in force, subject to subsection (2) below—

(*a*) except in a case falling within paragraph (*b*) or (*c*) of this subsection, for the period ending on the seventieth anniversary of the applicant's date of birth or for a period of three years, whichever is the longer,

(*b*) except in a case falling within paragraph (*c*) of this subsection, if the Secretary of State so determines in the case of a licence to be granted to a person appearing to him to be suffering from a relevant or prospective disability, for such period of not more than three years and not less than one year as the Secretary of State may determine, and

(*c*) in the case of a licence granted in exchange for a subsisting licence and in pursuance of an application requesting a licence for the period authorised by this paragraph, for a period equal to the remainder of that for which the subsisting licence was granted,

and any such period shall begin with the date on which the licence in question is expressed to come into force.

(2) To the extent that a provisional licence authorises the driving of a motor cycle of a prescribed class it shall, unless previously surrendered or revoked, remain in force—

(*a*) for such period as may be prescribed, or

(*b*) if the licence is granted to the holder of a previous licence which was surrendered, revoked or treated as being revoked—

(i) for the remainder of the period for which the previous licence would have authorised the driving of such a motor cycle, or

(ii) in such circumstances as may be prescribed, for a period equal to that remainder at the time of surrender or revocation.

(3) Where it appears to the Secretary of State—

(*a*) that a licence granted by him to any person is required to be endorsed in pursuance of any enactment or was granted in error or with an error or omission in the particulars specified in the licence or required to be so endorsed on it, or (*b*) that the particulars specified in a licence granted by him to any person do not comply with any requirement imposed since the licence was granted by any provision made by or having effect under any enactment,

the Secretary of State may serve notice in writing on that person revoking the licence and requiring him to surrender the licence forthwith to the Secretary of State.

(4) Where the name or address of the licence holder as specified in a licence ceases to be correct, its holder must forthwith surrender the licence to the Secretary of State and provide him with particulars of the alterations falling to be made in the name or address and, in the case of a provisional licence as respects which the prescribed conditions are satisfied, with a statement of his sex and date of birth.

(5) A person who fails to comply with the duty under subsection (4) above is guilty of an offence.

(6) Where a person who has a duty under this section to surrender his licence is not in possession of the licence in consequence of the fact that he has surrendered it to a constable or authorised person (within the meaning of Part III of the Road Traffic Offenders Act 1988) on receiving a fixed penalty notice given to him under section 54 of that Act, he does not fail to comply with the duty if he surrenders the licence to the Secretary of State immediately on its return.

(7) On the surrender of a licence by any person in pursuance of subsection (3) or (4) above, the Secretary of State—

(*a*) must, except where the licence was granted in error or is surrendered in pursuance of subsection (3) above in consequence of an error or omission appearing to the Secretary of State to be attributable to that person's fault or in consequence of a current disqualification, and

(*b*) may in such an excepted case which does not involve a current disqualification,

grant to that person free of charge a new licence for such period (subject to subsection (8) below) that it expires on the date on which the surrendered licence would have expired had it not been surrendered.

(8) Where the period for which the surrendered licence was granted was based on an error with respect to the licence holder's date of birth such that, if that error had not been made, that licence would have been expressed to expire on a different date, the period of the new licence shall be such that it expires on that different date.

[The Motor Vehicles (Driving Licences) Regulations 1987 (SI 1987 No 1378) qv have effect as if made in part under s 99.]

Appeals

100. Appeals relating to licences

(1) A person who is aggrieved by the Secretary of State's—

(*a*) refusal to grant or revocation of a licence in pursuance of section 92 or 93 of this Act, or

(*b*) determination under section 99(1)(*b*) of this Act to grant a licence for three years or less, or

(*c*) revocation of a licence in pursuance of section 99(3) of this Act,

or by a notice served on him in pursuance of section 92(5) of this Act may, after giving to the Secretary of State notice of his intention to do so, appeal to a magistrates' court acting for the petty sessions area in which he resides.

(2) On any such appeal the court may make such order as it or he thinks fit and the order shall be binding on the Secretary of State.

(3) It is hereby declared that, without prejudice to section 90 of this Act, in any proceedings under this section the court is not entitled to entertain any question as to whether the appellant passed a test of competence to drive if he was declared by the person who conducted it to have failed it.

[Words relating exclusively and expressly to Scotland have been omitted from s 100.]

Disqualification (otherwise than on conviction)

101. Disqualification of persons under age

(1) A person is disqualified for holding or obtaining a licence to drive a motor vehicle of a class specified in the following Table if he is under the age specified in relation to it in the second column of the Table.

Class of motor vehicle	*Age (in years)*
1. Invalid carriage	16
2. Motor cycle	16
3. Small passenger vehicle or small goods vehicle	17
4. Agricultural tractor	17
5. Medium-sized goods vehicle	18
6. Other motor vehicles	21

(2) The Secretary of State may by regulations provide that subsection (1) above shall have effect as if for the classes of vehicles and the ages specified in the Table in that subsection there were substituted different classes of vehicles and ages or different classes of vehicles or different ages.

(3) Subject to subsection (4) below, the regulations may—

(*a*) apply to persons of a class specified in or under the regulations,

(*b*) apply in circumstances so specified,

(*c*) impose conditions or create exemptions or provide for the imposition of conditions or the creation of exemptions,

(*d*) contain such transitional and supplemental provisions (including provisions amending section 108, 120 or 183(5) of this Act) as the Secretary of State considers necessary or expedient.

(4) For the purpose of defining the class of persons to whom, the class of vehicles to which, the circumstances in which or the conditions subject to which regulations made by virtue of subsection (2) above are to apply where an approved training scheme for drivers is in force, it is sufficient for the regulations to refer to a document which embodies the terms (or any of the terms) of the scheme or to a document which is in force in pursuance of the scheme.

(5) In subsection (1) above—

'approved' means approved for the time being by the Secretary of State for the purpose of the regulations,

'training scheme for drivers' means a scheme for training persons to drive vehicles of a class in relation to which the age which is in force under this section (but apart from any such scheme) is 21 years, but no approved training scheme for drivers shall be amended without the approval of the Secretary of State.

[The Motor Vehicles (Driving Licences) Regulations 1987 (SI 1987 No 1378) qv have effect as if made in part under s 101; see, in particular, reg 4.

As to the application of s 101 to persons who fulfilled certain conditions before 1 January 1976, see the Road Traffic (Consequential Provisions) Act 1988, s 5 and Sched 4, para 4(1), below.]

102. Disqualification to prevent duplication of licences

A person is disqualified for obtaining a licence authorising him to drive a motor vehicle of any class so long as he is the holder of another licence authorising him to drive a motor vehicle of that class, whether the licence is suspended or not.

103. Obtaining licence, or driving, while disqualified

(1) If a person disqualified for holding or obtaining a licence—

(*a*) obtains a licence while he is so disqualified, or

(*b*) while he is so disqualified drives on a road a motor vehicle or, if the disqualification is limited to the driving of a motor vehicle of a particular class, a motor vehicle of that class,

he is guilty of an offence.

(2) A licence obtained by any person who is disqualified is of no effect.

(3) A constable in uniform may arrest without warrant any person driving or attempting to drive a motor vehicle on a road whom he has reasonable cause to suspect of being disqualified.

Miscellaneous

104. Conduct of proceedings in certain courts by or against the Secretary of State. *[Omitted.]*

105. Regulations under this Part and the Road Traffic Offenders Act 1988 *[Omitted.]*

106. Destination of fees for licences, etc *[Omitted.]*

107. Service of notices under ss 92, 93 and 99(3) *[Omitted.]*

108. Interpretation

(1) In this Part of this Act—

'agricultural tractor' means a tractor used primarily for work on land in connection with agriculture,

'articulated goods vehicle' means a motor vehicle which is so constructed that a trailer designed to carry goods may by partial superimposition be attached to it in such manner as to cause a substantial part of the weight of the trailer to be borne by the motor vehicle, and 'articulated goods vehicle combination' means an articulated goods vehicle with a trailer so attached,

'Community licence' means a document issued in respect of a member State other than the United Kingdom by an authority of that or another member State (including the United Kingdom) authorising the holder to drive a motor vehicle, not being—

(*a*) a document containing a statement to the effect that that or a previous document was issued in exchange for a document issued in respect of a State other than a member State, or (*b*) a document in any of the forms for an international driving permit annexed to the Paris Convention on Motor Traffic of 1926 *[Cd 3510]*, the Geneva Convention on Road Traffic of 1949 *[Cmd 578]* or the Vienna Convention on Road Traffic of 1968 *[Cmnd 4032]*,

'disability' has the meaning given by section 92 of this Act,

'disqualified' means disqualified for holding or obtaining a licence, and 'disqualification' is to be interpreted accordingly,

'exchangeable licence' means a Community licence or a document which would be a Community licence if—

(*a*) Gibraltar, and

(*b*) each country or territory within this paragraph by virtue of an order under subsection (2) below,

were or formed part of a member State other than the United Kingdom,

'licence' means a licence to drive a motor vehicle granted under this Part of this Act,

'maximum gross weight', in relation to a motor vehicle or trailer, means the weight of the vehicle laden with the heaviest load which it is constructed or adapted to carry,

'maximum train weight', in relation to an articulated goods vehicle combination, means the weight of the combination laden with the heaviest load which it is constructed or adapted to carry,

'medium-sized goods vehicle' means a motor vehicle which is constructed or adapted to carry or to haul goods and is not adapted to carry more than nine persons inclusive of the driver and the permissible maximum weight of which exceeds 3.5 but not 7.5 tonnes,

'permissible maximum weight', in relation to a goods vehicle (of whatever description), means—

(*a*) in the case of a motor vehicle which neither is an articulated goods vehicle nor is drawing a trailer, the relevant maximum weight of the vehicle,

(*b*) in the case of an articulated goods vehicle—

(i) when drawing only a semi-trailer, the relevant maximum train weight of the articulated goods vehicle combination,

(ii) when drawing a trailer as well as a semi-trailer, the aggregate of the relevant maximum train weight of the articulated goods vehicle combination and the relevant maximum weight of the trailer,

(iii) when drawing a trailer but not a semi-trailer, the aggregate of the relevant maximum weight of the articulated goods vehicle and the relevant maximum weight of the trailer,

(iv) when drawing neither a semi-trailer nor a trailer, the relevant maximum weight of the vehicle,

(*c*) in the case of a motor vehicle (not being an articulated goods vehicle) which is drawing a trailer, the aggregate of the relevant maximum weight of the motor vehicle and the relevant maximum weight of the trailer,

'prescribed' means prescribed by regulations,

'prospective disability' has the meaning given by section 92 of this Act,

'provisional licence' means a licence granted by virtue of section 97(2) of this Act,

'regulations' means regulations made under section 105 of this Act,

'relevant disability' has the meaning given by section 92 of this Act, 'relevant maximum weight', in relation to a motor vehicle or trailer, means—

(*a*) in the case of a vehicle to which regulations under section 49 of this Act apply which is required by regulations under section 41 of this Act to have a maximum gross weight for the vehicle marked on a plate issued by the Secretary of State under regulations under section 41, the maximum gross weight so marked on the vehicle,

(*b*) in the case of a vehicle which is required by regulations under section 41 of this Act to have a maximum gross weight for the vehicle marked on the vehicle and does not also have a maximum gross weight marked on it as mentioned in paragraph (*a*) above, the maximum gross weight marked on the vehicle,

(*c*) in the case of a vehicle on which a maximum gross weight is marked by the same means as would be required by regulations under section 41 of this Act if those regulations applied to the vehicle, the maximum gross weight so marked on the vehicle,

(*d*) in the case of a vehicle on which a maximum gross weight is not marked as mentioned in paragraph (*a*), (*b*) or (*c*) above, the notional maximum gross weight of the vehicle, that is to say, such weight as is produced by multiplying the unladen weight of the vehicle by the number prescribed by the Secretary of State for the class of vehicle into which that vehicle falls,

'relevant maximum train weight', in relation to an articulated goods vehicle combination, means—

(*a*) in the case of an articulated goods vehicle to which regulations under section 49 of this Act apply which is required by regulations under section 41 of this Act to have a maximum train weight for the combination marked on a plate issued by the Secretary of State under regulations under section 41, the maximum train weight so marked on the motor vehicle,

(*b*) in the case of an articulated goods vehicle which is required by regulations under section 41 of this Act to have a maximum train weight for the combination marked on the vehicle and does not also have a maximum train weight marked on it as mentioned in paragraph (*a*) above, the maximum train weight marked on the motor vehicle,

(*c*) in the case of an articulated goods vehicle on which a maximum train weight is marked by the same means as would be required by regulations under section 41 of this Act if those regulations applied to the vehicle, the maximum train weight so marked on the motor vehicle,

(*d*) in the case of an articulated goods vehicle on which a maximum train weight is not marked as mentioned in paragraph (*a*), (*b*) or (*c*) above, the notional maximum gross weight of the combination, that is to say, such weight as is produced by multiplying the sum of the unladen weights of the motor vehicle and the semi-trailer by the number prescribed by the Secretary of State for the class of articulated goods vehicle combination into which that combination falls,

'semi-trailer', in relation to an articulated goods vehicle, means a trailer attached to it in the manner described in the definition of articulated goods vehicle,

'small goods vehicle' means a motor vehicle (other than a motor cycle or invalid carriage) which is constructed or adapted to carry or to haul goods and is not adapted to carry more than nine persons inclusive of the driver and the permissible maximum weight of which does not exceed 3.5 tonnes,

'small passenger vehicle' means a motor vehicle (other than a motor cycle or invalid carriage) which is constructed solely to carry passengers and their effects and is adapted to carry not more than nine persons inclusive of the driver, and

'test of competence to drive' means such a test conducted under section 89 of this Act.

(2), (3) *[Power to make orders designating countries, etc, for purposes of para (b) of the definition of 'exchangeable licences' in subs (1).]*

[The following orders have effect as is made under s 108(2): the Driving Licences (Exchangeable Licences) Order 1984 (SI 1984 No 672), taking effect on 1 June 1984; the Driving Licences (Exchangeable Licences) Order 1985 (SI 1985 No 65), taking effect on 2 February 1985; the Driving Licences (Exchangeable Licences) (No 2) Order 1985 (SI 1985 No 1461), taking effect on 1 November 1985.

As a result of these orders the following countries have been designated for the purposes of s 108(2):

Australia	SI 1984 No 672
Austria	SI 1985 No 1461
Barbados	SI 1985 No 65
British Virgin Islands	SI 1985 No 65
Cyprus	SI 1985 No 65
Finland	SI 1985 No 65
Hong Kong	SI 1984 No 672
Japan	SI 1985 No 1461
Kenya	SI 1984 No 672
Malta	SI 1985 No 65
New Zealand	SI 1984 No 672
Norway	Si 1984 No 672
Singapore	SI 1984 No 672
Sweden	SI 1984 No 672
Switzerland	SI 1984 No 672
Zimbabwe	SI 1985 No 65.]

109. Provisions as to Northern Ireland drivers' licences

(1) The holder of a licence to drive a motor vehicle granted under the law of Northern Ireland may drive, and a person may cause or permit the holder of such a licence to drive, in Great Britain, a motor vehicle of any class which he is authorised by that licence to drive, and which he is not disqualified from driving under this Part of this Act, notwithstanding that he is not the holder of a licence under this Part of this Act.

(2) Any driver holding a licence so granted shall be under the like obligation to produce such a licence as if it had been a licence granted under this Part of this Act, and the provisions—

(*a*) of this Act, and

(*b*) of the Road Traffic Offenders Act 1988, being the provisions connected with the licensing of drivers within the meaning of that Act,

as to the production of licences granted under this Part of this Act shall apply accordingly.

(3) The holder of any such licence who by an order of the court is disqualified for holding or obtaining a licence under this Part of this Act must produce the licence so held by him to the court within such time as the court may determine, and the court must, on production of the licence, forward it to the Secretary of State.

(4) If the holder fails to produce the licence within that time, he is guilty of an offence.

(5) If the holder of any such licence is convicted of an offence and the court orders particulars of the conviction to be endorsed in accordance with section 44 of the Road Traffic Offenders Act 1988, the court shall send those particulars to the Secretary of State.

PART IV

Licensing of Drivers of Heavy Goods Vehicles

Requirement for HGV licence

110. Drivers of heavy goods vehicles to be licensed

(1) It is an offence for a person to drive a heavy goods vehicle of any class on a road if he is not licensed under this Part of this Act to drive a heavy goods vehicle of that class.

(2) It is an offence for a person to cause or permit another person to drive a heavy goods vehicle of any class on a road if that other person is not so licensed to drive a heavy goods vehicle of that class.

(3) Nothing in subsection (1) or (2) above makes it unlawful—

(*a*) for a person who is not so licensed to act, or

(*b*) for a person to cause or permit such a person to act,

as steersman of a heavy goods vehicle (being a vehicle on which a speed limit of five miles per hour or less is imposed by or under section 86 of the Road Traffic Regulation Act 1984 [*qv*]) under the orders of another person engaged in the driving of the vehicle who is licensed in that behalf in accordance with the requirements of Part III of this Act and this section.

(4) Neither subsection (1) nor subsection (2) above applies to the driving of, or the causing or permitting of a person to drive, a vehicle in any case where—

(*a*) the excise duty in respect of the vehicle under the Vehicles (Excise) Act 1971 is chargeable at the rate applicable to vehicles specified in paragraph 2(1) of Schedule 3 to that Act [*qv*], and

(*b*) the vehicle is being driven for one of the purposes for which it must solely be used if the duty is to remain chargeable at that rate.

Grant, duration and revocation of licences

111. Licensing authority, and applications, for HGV drivers' licences

(1) The traffic commissioner for any area constituted for the purposes of the Public Passenger Vehicles Act 1981 shall exercise the function of granting licences under this Part of this Act (in this Part of this Act referred to as 'heavy goods vehicle drivers' licences') and is in this Part of this Act referred to as 'the licensing authority'.

(2) *[Applications for heavy goods vehicle driver's licences.]*

112. Grant of HGV drivers' licences

(1)–(4) *[Grant of licences.]*

(5) For the purpose of enabling an applicant to learn to drive a heavy goods vehicle

with a view to passing the prescribed test of competence to drive, the licensing authority may issue to him a heavy goods vehicle driver's licence as a provisional licence.

(6) A licence issued by virtue of subsection (5) above or a full licence granted to an applicant who is under the age of 21 on the date of the application shall be subject to the prescribed conditions, and if the person to whom it is issued fails to comply with any of the conditions he is guilty of an offence.

(7) It is an offence for a person to cause or permit another person who is under the age of 21 to drive a heavy goods vehicle of any class in contravention of any prescribed conditions subject to which that other person's licence is issued.

(8) *[Definitions of 'Community licence' and 'exchangeable licence' for purposes of s 112.]*

[The Heavy Goods Vehicles (Drivers' Licences) Regulations 1977 (SI 1977 No 1309) have effect as if made in part under s 112.]

113. Duration of HGV drivers' licences

(1) Subject to subsection (4) below, a heavy goods vehicle driver's licence shall, unless previously revoked, continue in force for three years from the date on which it is expressed to take effect.

(2), (3) *[Revocation and suspension of licences by licensing authority.]*

(4) Subject to subsection (5) below, a licence issued by virtue of section 112(5) of this Act shall, unless previously revoked, continue in force for six months from the date on which it is expressed to take effect.

(5) Subsection (4) above does not apply to a licence treated as a provisional licence by virtue of section 117(2)(*e*) of this Act.

(6) Without prejudice to section 116(5) of this Act, if on the date on which an application is made for a heavy goods vehicle driver's licence, the applicant is the holder of such a licence, his existing licence shall not expire in accordance with subsection (1) above before the application is disposed of.

114. Disqualification by licensing authority on revocation of HGV driver's licence *[Omitted.]*

Appeals and review of tests

115. Review of conduct of test *[Omitted.]*

116. Appeals relating to HGV drivers' licences

(1)–(4) *[Appeals against decisions of licensing authority.]*

(5) Where an applicant for a heavy goods vehicle driver's licence who is at the date of his application the holder of such a licence (other than one issued as a provisional licence) appeals under this section on the ground of refusal or failure to grant the licence, the existing licence shall not expire before the appeal is disposed of.

General and supplemental

117. Regulations

(1) The Secretary of State may make regulations for the purpose of carrying the provisions of this Part of this Act into effect.

(2) Without prejudice to the generality of subsection (1) above, the regulations may—

(*a*)–(*d*) *[Omitted.]*

(*e*) provide that a full licence to drive a heavy goods vehicle of a particular class shall also be treated for the purposes of this Part of this Act as a provisional licence to drive heavy goods vehicles of another prescribed class,

(*f*)–(*m*) *[Omitted.]*

and different provision may be made by the regulations for different cases.

(3) *[Definitions of terms used in subs (2)(b).]*

(4) Regulations under this section may provide that a person who contravenes or fails to comply with any specified provision of the regulations is guilty of an offence.

(5) *[Power to exclude application of this Part.]*

[The Heavy Goods Vehicles (Drivers' Licences) Regulations 1977 (SI 1977 No 1309) have effect as if made in part under s 117; as to offences under the regulations, see ibid, reg 28.]

118. Fees and expenses *[Omitted.]*

119. Common test of competence to drive for the purposes of Parts III and IV
[Omitted.]

120. Interpretation

In this Part of this Act—

'full licence' means a heavy goods vehicle driver's licence other than a provisional licence,

'heavy goods vehicle' means—

(*a*) an articulated goods vehicle, or

(*b*) a large goods vehicle, that is to say, a motor vehicle (not being an articulated goods vehicle) which is constructed or adapted to carry or to haul goods and the permissible maximum weight of which exceeds 7.5 tonnes,

'heavy goods vehicle driver's licence' has the meaning given by section 111 of this Act,

'licensing authority' has the meaning given by section 111 of this Act,

'prescribed' means prescribed by regulations under section 117 of this Act,

and in this section 'articulated goods vehicle' and 'permissible maximum weight' have the same meaning as in Part III of this Act.

121. Provisions as to Northern Ireland heavy goods vehicle drivers' licences

(1) The holder of a licence specifically to drive heavy goods vehicles granted under the law of Northern Ireland (in this section referred to as a 'Northern Ireland licence') may drive, and be employed in driving, on a road in Great Britain heavy goods vehicles of any class which he is authorised by that licence to drive, notwithstanding that he is not the holder of a heavy goods vehicle driver's licence.

(2) *[Grant of heavy goods vehicle driver's licence to holder of Northern Ireland licence.]*

(3), (4) *[Suspension and revocation of Northern Ireland licences by prescribed licensing authority.]*

122. Protection of public interests *[Omitted.]*

PART V

Driving Instruction

Instructors to be registered or licensed

123. Driving instruction for payment to be given only by registered or licensed persons

(1) No paid instruction in the driving of a motor car shall be given unless—

(*a*) the name of the person giving the instruction is in the register of approved instructors established in pursuance of section 23 of the Road Traffic Act 1962 (in this Part of this Act referred to as 'the register'), or

(*b*) the person giving the instruction is the holder of a current licence granted under this Part of this Act authorising him to give such instruction.

(2) No paid instruction in the driving of a motor car shall be given unless there is fixed to and exhibited on that motor car in such manner as may be prescribed by regulations either—

(*a*) a certificate in such forms as may be so prescribed that the name of the person giving the instruction is in the register, or

(*b*) a current licence granted under this Part of this Act authorising the person giving the instruction to give such instruction.

(3) For the purposes of subsections (1) and (2) above, instruction is paid instruction if payment of money or money's worth is, or is to be, made by or in respect of the person to whom the instruction is given for the giving of the instruction and for the purposes of this subsection instruction which is given—

(*a*) free of charge to a person who is not the holder of a current licence to drive a motor vehicle granted under Part III of this Act (other than a provisional licence),

(*b*) by, or in pursuance of arrangements made by, a person carrying on business in the supply of motor cars, and

(*c*) in connection with the supply of a motor car in the course of that business,

shall be deemed to be given for payment of money by the person to whom the instruction is given.

(4) Where instruction is given in contravention of subsection (1) above—

(*a*) the person by whom it is given, and

(*b*) if that person is employed by another to give that instruction, that other, as well as that person,

is guilty of an offence.

(5) In proceedings against a person for an offence under subsection (4) above it shall be a defence for him to prove that he did not know, and had no reasonable cause to believe, that his name or, as the case may be, that of the person employed by him, was not in the register at the material time.

(6) If instruction is given in contravention of subsection (2) above, the person by whom it is given is guilty of an offence.

(7) Any reference in this Part of this Act to a current licence is a reference to a licence which has not expired and has not been cancelled, revoked or suspended.

(8) In this section 'provisional licence' has the same meaning as in Part III of this Act.

[The register is now maintained under s 125 of this Act.
See further the Motor Cars (Driving Instruction) Regulations 1977 (SI 1977 No 1043) which have effect as if made under this Act.]

124. Exemption of police instructors from prohibition imposed by section 123

(1) Section 123(1) and (2) of this Act does not apply to the giving of instruction by a police instructor in pursuance of arrangements made by a chief officer of police or, under the authority of a chief officer of police, in pursuance of arrangements made by a local authority.

(2) In this section—

'police instructor' means a person who is—

(*a*) a member of a police force whose duties consist of or include, or have consisted of or included, the giving of instruction in the driving of motor cars to persons being members of a police force, or

(*b*) a civilian employed by a police authority for the purpose of giving such instruction to such persons, and

'local authority' means—

(*a*) in relation to England and Wales, the council of a county, metropolitan district, or London borough or the Common Council of the City of London,

(*b*) *[Applies to Scotland.]*

(3) In the application of subsection (2) above to the metropolitan police, the reference to a civilian employed by a police authority is to be read as a reference to a civilian employed under the Commissioner of Police of the Metropolis or the Receiver for the Metropolitan Police District.

Registration

125. The register of approved instructors *[Omitted.]*

126. Duration of registration *[Omitted.]*

127. Extension of duration of registration *[Omitted.]*

128. Removal of names from register *[Omitted.]*

Licences

129. Licences for giving instruction so as to obtain practical experience

(1) A licence under this section is granted for the purpose of enabling a person to acquire practical experience in giving instruction in driving motor cars with a view to undergoing such part of the examination referred to in section 125(3)(*a*) of this Act as consists of a practical test of ability and fitness to instruct.

(2) *[Application for licence.]*

(3) *[Refusal of licence.]*

(4) *[Notice of decision.]*

(5) *[Form of licence, and conditions.]*

(6) *[Renewal of licence.]*

(7), (8) *[Notice of refusal of licence.]*

130. Revocation of licences *[Omitted.]*

Appeals

131. Appeals against decisions of the Registrar *[Omitted.]*

Examinations and tests

132. Examinations and tests of ability to give driving instruction *[Omitted.]*

133. Review of examinations

(1) On the application of a person who has submitted himself for any part of an examination of ability to give instruction in the driving of motor cars—

(*a*) the magistrates' court acting for the petty sessions area in which he resides, or

(*b*) *[Applies to Scotland.]*,

may determine whether that part of the examination was properly conducted in accordance with regulations.

(2) If it appears to the court that that part of the examination was not so conducted, the court may order that any fee payable by the applicant in respect of that part shall not be paid or, if it has been paid, shall be repaid.

(3) No appeal shall lie under section 131 of this Act in respect of any matter in respect of which an application may be made to a magistrates' court under subsection (1) above.

[Words relating exclusively to Scotland have been omitted from s 133.
The regulations to which reference is made are the Motor Cars (Driving Instruction) Regulations 1977 (SI 1977 No 1043) which have effect as if made in part under s 132 and this section.]

General and supplemental

134. Power to alter conditions for entry or retention in, and removal from, register and for grant or revocation of licences *[Omitted.]*

135. Power to prescribe form of certificate of registration, etc

(1) Regulations may prescribe all or any of the following—

(*a*) a form of certificate for issue to persons whose names are in the register as evidence of their names' being in the register,

(*b*) a form of badge for use by such persons, and

(*c*) an official title for such use.

(2) If a person whose name is not in the register—

(*a*) takes or uses a title prescribed under this section, or

(*b*) wears or displays a badge or certificate so prescribed, or

(*c*) takes or uses any name, title, addition or description implying that his name is in the register, he is guilty of an offence unless he proves that he did not know, and had no reasonable cause to believe, that his name was not in the register at the material time.

(3) If a person carrying on business in the provision of instruction in the driving of motor vehicles—

(*a*) uses a title or description so prescribed in relation to any person employed by him whose name is not in the register, or

(*b*) issues any advertisement or invitation calculated to mislead with respect to the extent to which persons whose names are in the register are employed by him,

he is guilty of an offence unless he proves that he did not know, and had no reasonable cause to believe, that the name or names in question were not in the register at the material time.

[The Motor Cars (Driving Instruction) Regulations 1977 (SI 1977 No 1043) have effect as if made in part under s 135.]

136. Surrender of certificates and licences

Where—

(*a*) the name of a person to whom a certificate prescribed under section 135 of this Act has been issued is removed from the register in pursuance of this Part of this Act, or

(*b*) a licence granted under this Part of this Act to a person expires or is revoked,

that person must, if so required by the Registrar by notice in writing, surrender the certificate or licence, as the case may be, to the Registrar within the period of fourteen days beginning with that on which the notice is given and, if he fails to do so, he is guilty of an offence.

137. Production of certificates and licences to constables and authorised persons

(1) A person to whom a certificate prescribed under section 135 of this Act is issued, or to whom a licence under this Part of this Act is granted, must, on being so required by a constable or any person authorised in writing by the Secretary of State in that behalf, produce the certificate or licence for examination.

(2) Where—

(*a*) the name of a person is removed from the register, or

(*b*) a licence granted under this Part of this Act to a person expires or is revoked,

then, if that person fails to satisfy an obligation imposed on him by section 136 of this Act, a constable or a person authorised in writing by the Secretary of State in that behalf may require him to produce any such certificate issued to him or the licence, and upon its being produced may seize it and deliver it to the Registrar.

(3) A person who is required under subsection (1) or (2) above to produce a document and fails to do so is, subject to subsection (4) below, guilty of an offence.

(4) In proceedings against any person for an offence under subsection (3) above, it shall be a defence for him to show that—

(*a*) within seven days beginning with the day following that on which the production of the document was so required, it was produced—

(i) where the requirement was made by a constable, at a police station specified at the time the production was required by the person required to produce the document,

(ii) where the requirement was made by a person other than a constable, at a place specified at that time by that person, or

(*b*) the document was produced at that police station or, as the case may be, place as soon as was reasonably practicable, or

(*c*) it was not reasonably practicable for it to be produced at that police station or, as the case may be, place before the day on which the proceedings were commenced,

and for the purposes of this subsection the laying of the information shall be treated as the commencement of the proceedings.

[Words relating exclusively and expressly to Scotland have been omitted from s 137.]

138. Offences by corporations

Where a body corporate is guilty of an offence under this Part of this Act and the offence is proved to have been committed with the consent or connivance of, or to be attributable to neglect on the part of, a director, manager, secretary or other similar officer of the body corporate, or a person who was purporting to act in any such capacity, he, as well as the body corporate, is guilty of that offence and liable to be proceeded against and punished accordingly.

139. Service of notices *[Omitted.]*

140. Receipts *[Omitted.]*

141. Regulations *[Omitted.]*

142. Index to Part V

The expressions listed in the left-hand column below are respectively defined or (as the case may be) fall to be construed in accordance with the provisions of this Part of this Act listed in the right-hand column in relation to those expressions.

Expression	*Relevant provision*
Current licence	Section 123(7)
The register	Section 123
The Registrar	Section 125(2)
Regulations	Section 141

[Section 125(2) is not reproduced in this work; in that provision, 'the registrar' is defined as the officer of the Secretary of State by whom, on behalf of the Secretary of State, the register of approved instructors is compiled and maintained.]

PART VI

Third-Party Liabilities

Compulsory insurance or security against third-party risks

143. Users of motor vehicles to be insured or secured against third-party risks

(1) Subject to the provisions of this Part of this Act—

(*a*) a person must not use a motor vehicle on a road unless there is in force in relation to the use of the vehicle by that person such a policy of insurance or such a security in respect of third party risks as complies with the requirements of this Part of this Act, and

(*b*) a person must not cause or permit any other person to use a motor vehicle on a road unless there is in force in relation to the use of the vehicle by that other person such a policy of insurance or such a security in respect of third party risks as complies with the requirements of this Part of this Act.

(2) If a person acts in contravention of subsection (1) above he is guilty of an offence.

(3) A person charged with using a motor vehicle in contravention of this section shall not be convicted if he proves—

(*a*) that the vehicle did not belong to him and was not in his possession under a contract of hiring or of loan,

(*b*) that he was using the vehicle in the course of his employment, and

(*c*) that he neither knew nor had reason to believe that there was not in force in relation to the vehicle such a policy of insurance or security as is mentioned in subsection (1) above.

(4) This Part of this Act does not apply to invalid carriages.

144. Exceptions from requirement of third-party insurance or security

(1) Section 143 of this Act does not apply to a vehicle owned by a person who has deposited and keeps deposited with the Accountant General of the Supreme Court the sum of £15,000, at a time when the vehicle is being driven under the owner's control.

(2) Section 143 does not apply—

(*a*) to a vehicle owned—

(i) by the council of a county or county district in England and Wales, the Common Council of the City of London, the council of a London borough, the Inner London Education Authority, or a joint authority (other than a police authority) established by Part IV of the Local Government Act 1985,

(ii) by a regional, islands or district council in Scotland, or

(iii) by a joint board or committee in England or Wales, or joint committee in Scotland, which is so constituted as to include among its members representatives of any such council,

at a time when the vehicle is being driven under the owner's control,

(*b*) to a vehicle owned by a police authority or the Receiver for the Metropolitan Police district, at a time when it is being driven under the owner's control, or to a vehicle at a time when it is being driven for police purposes by or under the direction of a constable, or by a person employed by a police authority, or employed by the Receiver, or

(*c*) to a vehicle at a time when it is being driven on a journey to or from any place undertaken for salvage purposes pursuant to Part IX of the Merchant Shipping Act 1894,

(*d*) to the use of a vehicle for the purpose of its being provided in pursuance of a direction under section 166(2)(*b*) of the Army Act 1955 or under the corresponding provision of the Air Force Act 1955,

(*e*) to a vehicle which is made available by the Secretary of State to any person, body or local authority in pursuance of section 23 or 26 of the National Health

Service Act 1977 at a time when it is being used in accordance with the terms on which it is so made available,

(*f*) to a vehicle which is made available by the Secretary of State to any local authority, education authority or voluntary organisation in Scotland in pursuance of section 15 or 16 of the National Health Service (Scotland) Act 1978 at a time when it is being used in accordance with the terms on which it is so made available.

145. Requirements in respect of policies of insurance

(1) In order to comply with the requirements of this Part of this Act, a policy of insurance must satisfy the following conditions.

(2) The policy must be issued by an authorised insurer.

(3) Subject to subsection (4) below, the policy—

(*a*) must insure such person, persons or classes of persons as may be specified in the policy in respect of any liability which may be incurred by him or them in respect of the death of or bodily injury to any person or damage to property caused by, or arising out of, the use of the vehicle on a road in Great Britain, and

(*b*) must insure him or them in respect of any liability which may be incurred by him or them in respect of the use of the vehicle and of any trailer, whether or not coupled, in the territory other than Great Britain and Gibraltar of each of the member States of the Communities according to the law on compulsory insurance against civil liability in respect of the use of vehicles of the State where the liability may be incurred, and

(*c*) must also insure him or them in respect of any liability which may be incurred by him or them under the provisions of this Part of this Act relating to payment for emergency treatment.

(4) The policy shall not, by virtue of subsection (3)(*a*) above, be required—

(*a*) to cover liability in respect of the death, arising out of and in the course of his employment, of a person in the employment of a person insured by the policy or of bodily injury sustained by such a person arising out of and in the course of his employment, or

(*b*) to provide insurance of more than £250,000 in respect of all such liabilities as may be incurred in respect of damage to property caused by, or arising out of, any one accident involving the vehicle, or

(*c*) to cover liability in respect of damage to the vehicle, or

(*d*) to cover liability in respect of damage to goods carried for hire or reward in or on the vehicle or in or on any trailer (whether or not coupled) drawn by the vehicle, or

(*e*) to cover any liability of a person in respect of damage to property in his custody or under his control, or

(*f*) to cover any contractual liability.

(5) In this Part of this Act 'authorised insurer' means a person or body of persons carrying on insurance business within Group 2 in Part II of Schedule 2 to the Insurance Companies Act 1982 [*qv*] and being a member of the Motor Insurers' Bureau (a company limited by guarantee and incorporated under the Companies Act 1929 on 14th June 1946).

(6) If any person or body of persons ceases to be a member of the Motor Insurers'

Bureau, that person or body shall not by virtue of that cease to be treated as an authorised insurer for the purposes of this Part of this Act—

(*a*) in relation to any policy issued by the insurer before ceasing to be such a member, or

(*b*) in relation to any obligation (whether arising before or after the insurer ceased to be such a member) which the insurer may be called upon to meet under or in consequence of any such policy or under section 157 of this Act by virtue of making a payment in pursuance of such an obligation.

[As to s 145(2), see the Motor Vehicles (Compulsory Insurance) (No 2) Regulations 1973 (SI 1973 No 2143), reg 8, below.]

146. Requirements in respect of securities *[Omitted.]*

147. Issue and surrender of certificates of insurance and of security

(1) A policy of insurance shall be of no effect for the purposes of this Part of this Act unless and until there is delivered by the insurer to the person by whom the policy is effected a certificate (in this Part of this Act referred to as a 'certificate of insurance') in the prescribed form and containing such particulars of any conditions subject to which the policy is issued and of any other matters as may be prescribed.

(2) *[Certificate of security.]*

(3) Different forms and different particulars may be prescribed for the purposes of subsection (1) or (2) above in relation to different cases or circumstances.

(4) Where a certificate has been delivered under this section and the policy or security to which it relates is cancelled by mutual consent or by virtue of any provision in the policy or security, the person to whom the certificate was delivered must, within seven days from the taking effect of the cancellation—

(*a*) surrender the certificate to the person by whom the policy was issued or the security was given, or

(*b*) if the certificate has been lost or destroyed, make a statutory declaration to that effect.

(5) A person who fails to comply with subsection (4) above is guilty of an offence.

[As to s 147(1), see the Motor Vehicles (Compulsory Insurance) (No 2) Regulations 1973 (SI 1973 No 2143), reg 8, below.
As to the prescribed forms of certificates under s 147(3) and provisions relating to the forms and completion of certificates, see the Motor Vehicles (Third Party Risks) Regulations 1972 (SI 1972 1217), Schedule, below.]

148. Avoidance of certain exceptions to policies or securities

(1) Where a certificate of insurance or certificate of security has been delivered under section 147 of this Act to the person by whom a policy has been effected or to whom a security has been given, so much of the policy or security as purports to restrict—

(*a*) the insurance of the persons insured by the policy, or

(*b*) the operation of the security,

(as the case may be) by reference to any of the matters mentioned in subsection (2) below shall, as respects such liabilities as are required to be covered by a policy under section 145 of this Act, be of no effect.

(2) Those matters are—

(*a*) the age or physical or mental condition of persons driving the vehicle,

(*b*) the condition of the vehicle,

(*c*) the number of persons that the vehicle carries,

(*d*) the weight or physical characteristics of the goods that the vehicle carries,

(*e*) the time at which or the areas within which the vehicle is used,

(*f*) the horsepower or cylinder capacity or value of the vehicle,

(*g*) the carrying on the vehicle of any particular apparatus, or

(*h*) the carrying on the vehicle of any particular means of identification other than any means of identification required to be carried by or under the Vehicles (Excise) Act 1971.

(3) Nothing in subsection (1) above requires an insurer or the giver of a security to pay any sum in respect of the liability of any person otherwise than in or towards the discharge of that liability.

(4) Any sum paid by an insurer or the giver of a security in or towards the discharge of any liability of any person which is covered by the policy or security by virtue only of subsection (1) above is recoverable by the insurer or giver of the security from that person.

(5) A condition in a policy or security issued or given for the purposes of this Part of this Act providing—

(*a*) that no liability shall arise under the policy or security, or

(*b*) that any liability so arising shall cease,

in the event of some specified thing being done or omitted to be done after the happening of the event giving rise to a claim under the policy or security, shall be of no effect in connection with such liabilities as are required to be covered by a policy under section 145 of this Act.

(6) Nothing in subsection (5) above shall be taken to render void any provision in a policy or security requiring the person insured or secured to pay to the insurer or the giver of the security any sums which the latter may have become liable to pay under the policy or security and which have been applied to the satisfaction of the claims of third parties.

(7) Notwithstanding anything in any enactment, a person issuing a policy of insurance under section 145 of this Act shall be liable to indemnify the persons or classes of persons specified in the policy in respect of any liability which the policy purports to cover in the case of those persons or classes of persons.

149. Avoidance of certain agreements as to liability towards passengers

(1) This section applies where a person uses a motor vehicle in circumstances such that under section 143 of this Act there is required to be in force in relation to his use of it such a policy of insurance or such a security in respect of third-party risks as complies with the requirements of this Part of this Act.

(2) If any other person is carried in or upon the vehicle while the user is so using it, any antecedent agreement or understanding between them (whether intended to be legally binding or not) shall be of no effect so far as it purports or might be held—

(*a*) to negative or restrict any such liability of the user in respect of persons carried in or upon the vehicle as is required by section 145 of this Act to be covered by a policy of insurance, or

(*b*) to impose any conditions with respect to the enforcement of any such liability of the user.

(3) The fact that a person so carried has willingly accepted as his the risk of negligence on the part of the user shall not be treated as negativing any such liability of the user.

(4) For the purposes of his section—

(*a*) references to a person being carried in or upon a vehicle include references to a person entering or getting on to, or alighting from, the vehicle, and

(*b*) the reference to an antecedent agreement is to one made at any time before the liability arose.

150. Insurance or security in respect of private use of vehicle to cover use under car-sharing arrangements

(1) To the extent that a policy or security issued or given for the purposes of this Part of this Act—

(*a*) restricts the insurance of the persons insured by the policy or the operation of the security (as the case may be) to use of the vehicle for specified purposes (for example, social, domestic and pleasure purposes) of a non-commerical character, or

(*b*) excludes from that insurance or the operation of the security (as the case may be)—

(i) use of the vehicle for hire or reward, or

(ii) business or commercial use of the vehicle, or

(iii) use of the vehicle for specified purposes of a business or commercial character,

then, for the purposes of that policy or security so far as it relates to such liabilities as are required to be covered by a policy under section 145 of this Act, the use of a vehicle on a journey in the course of which one or more passengers are carried at separate fares shall, if the conditions specified in subsection (2) below are satisfied, be treated as falling within that restriction or as not falling within that exclusion (as the case may be).

(2) The conditions referred to in subsection (1) above are—

(*a*) the vehicle is not adapted to carry more than eight passengers and is not a motor cycle,

(*b*) the fare or aggregate of the fares paid in respect of the journey does not exceed the amount of the running costs of the vehicle for the journey (which for the purposes of this paragraph shall be taken to include an appropriate amount in respect of depreciation and general wear), and

(*c*) the arrangements for the payment of fares by the passenger or passengers carried at separate fares were made before the journey began.

(3) Subsections (1) and (2) above apply however the restrictions or exclusions described in subsection (1) are framed or worded.

(4) In subsections (1) and (2) above 'fare' and 'separate fares' have the same meaning as in section 1(4) of the Public Passenger Vehicles Act 1981 [*qv*].

151. Duty of insurers or persons giving security to satisfy judgment against persons insured or secured against third-party risks *[Omitted.]*

152. Exceptions to section 151 *[Omitted.]*

153. Bankruptcy, etc, of insured or secured persons not to affect claims by third parties *[Omitted.]*

154. Duty to give information as to insurance or security where claim made

(1) A person against whom a claim is made in respect of any such liability as is required to be covered by a policy of insurance under section 145 of this Act must, on demand by or on behalf of the person making the claim—

(*a*) state whether or not, in respect of that liability—

(i) he was insured by a policy having effect for the purposes of this Part of this Act or had in force a security having effect for those purposes, or

(ii) he would have been so insured or would have had in force such a security if the insurer or, as the case may be, the giver of the security had not avoided or cancelled the policy or security, and

(*b*) if he was or would have been so insured, or had or would have had in force such a security—

(i) give such particulars with respect to that policy or security as were specified in any certificate of insurance or security delivered in respect of that policy or security, as the case may be, under section 147 of this Act, or

(ii) where no such certificate was delivered under that section, give the following particulars, that is to say, the registration mark or other identifying particulars of the vehicle concerned, the number or other identifying particulars of the insurance policy issued in respect of the vehicle, the name of the insurer and the period of the insurance cover.

(2) If without reasonable excuse, a person fails to comply with the provisions of subsection (1) above, or wilfully makes a false statement in reply to any such demand as is referred to in that subsection, he is guilty of an offence.

155. Deposits *[Omitted.]*

156. Power to require evidence of insurance or security on application for vehicle excise licence *[Omitted.]*

Payments for treatment of traffic casualties

157. Payment for hospital treatment of traffic casualties

(1) Subject to subsection (2) below, where—

(*a*) a payment, other than a payment under section 158 of this Act, is made (whether or not with an admission of liability) in respect of the death of, or bodily injury to, any person arising out of the use of a motor vehicle on a road or in a place to which the public have a right of access, and

(*b*) the payment is made—

(i) by an authorised insurer, the payment being made under or in consequence of a policy issued under section 145 of this Act, or

(ii) by the owner of a vehicle in relation to the use of which a security under this Part of this Act is in force, or

(iii) by the owner of a vehicle who has made a deposit under this Part of this Act, and

(*c*) the person who has so died or been bodily injured has to the knowledge of the insurer or owner, as the case may be, received treatment at a hospital, whether as an in-patient or as an out-patient, in respect of the injury so arising,

the insurer or owner must pay the expenses reasonably incurred by the hospital in affording the treatment, after deducting from the expenses any moneys actually received in payment of a specific charge for the treatment, not being moneys received under any contributory scheme.

(2) The amount to be paid shall not exceed £2,000.37 for each person treated as an in-patient or £200.04 for each person treated as an out-patient.

(3) For the purposes of this section 'expenses reasonably incurred' means—

(*a*) in relation to a person who receives treatment at a hospital as an in-patient, an amount for each day he is maintained in the hospital representing the average daily cost, for each in-patient, of the maintenance of the hospital and the staff of the hospital and the maintenance and treatment of the in-patients in the hospital, and

(*b*) in relation to a person who receives treatment at a hospital as an out-patient, reasonable expenses actually incurred.

[As to payments under s 157 where the accident occurred before 1 April 1987, see the Road Traffic (Consequential Provisions) Act 1988, s 5 and Sched 4, para 6, below.]

158. Payment for emergency treatment of traffic casualties

(1) Subsection (2) below applies where—

(*a*) medical or surgical treatment or examination is immediately required as a result of bodily injury (including fatal injury) to a person caused by, or arising out of, the use of a motor vehicle on a road, and

(*b*) the treatment or examination so required (in this Part of this Act referred to as 'emergency treatment') is effected by a legally qualified medical practitioner.

(2) The person who was using the vehicle at the time of the event out of which the bodily injury arose must, on a claim being made in accordance with the provisions of section 159 of this Act, pay to the practitioner (or, where emergency treatment is effected by more than one practitioner, to the practitioner by whom it is first effected)—

(*a*) a fee of £15.00 in respect of each person in whose case the emergency treatment is effected by him, and

(*b*) a sum, in respect of any distance in excess of two miles which he must cover in order—

(i) to proceed from the place from which he is summoned to the place where the emergency treatment is carried out by him, and

(ii) to return to the first mentioned place,

equal to 29 pence for every complete mile and additional part of a mile of that distance.

(3) Where emergency treatment is first effected in a hospital, the provisions of subsections (1) and (2) above with respect to payment of a fee shall, so far as applicable, but subject (as regards the recipient of a payment) to the provisions of section 159 of this Act, have effect with the substitution of references to the hospital for references to a legally qualified medical practitioner.

(4) Liability incurred under this section by the person using a vehicle shall, where the event out of which it arose was caused by the wrongful act of another person, be

treated for the purposes of any claim to recover damage by reason of that wrongful act as damage sustained by the person using the vehicle.

[As to claims under s 158 where the accident occurred before 1 April 1987, see the Road Traffic (Consequential Provisions) Act 1988, s 5 and Sched 4, para 6, below.]

159. Supplementary provisions as to payments for treatment

(1) A payment falling to be made under section 157 or 158 of this Act in respect of treatment in a hospital must be made—

(*a*) in England and Wales, in the case of a hospital vested in the Secretary of State for the purposes of the National Health Service Act 1977, to the Area Health Authority, District Health Authority or special health authority responsible for the administration of the hospital or the Secretary of State if no such authority is so responsible,

(*b*) *[Applies to Scotland.]*

(*c*) in the case of any other hospital, to the hospital.

(2) A claim for a payment under section 158 of this Act may be made at the time when the emergency treatment is effected, by oral request to the person who was using the vehicle, and if not so made must be made by request in writing served on him within seven days from the day on which the emergency treatment was effected.

(3) Any such request in writing—

(*a*) must be signed by the claimant or, in the case of a hospital, by an executive officer of the Authority or hospital claiming the payment or by an officer of the Secretary of State,

(*b*) must state the name and address of the claimant, the circumstances in which the emergency treatment was effected, and that it was first effected by the claimant or, in the case of a hospital, in the hospital, and

(*c*) may be served by delivering it to the person who was using the vehicle or by sending it in a prepaid registered letter, or the recorded delivery service, addressed to him at his usual or last known address.

(4) A payment made under section 158 of this Act shall operate as a discharge, to the extent of the amount paid, of any liability of the person who was using the vehicle, or of any other person, to pay any sum in respect of the expenses or remuneration of the practitioner or hospital concerned of or for effecting the emergency treatment.

(5) A chief officer of police must, if so requested by a person who alleges that he is entitled to claim a payment under section 158 of this Act, provide that person with any information at the disposal of the chief officer—

(*a*) as to the identification marks of any motor vehicle which that person alleges to be a vehicle out of the use of which the bodily injury arose, and

(*b*) as to the identity and address of the person who was using the vehicle at the time of the event out of which it arose.

[Words in s 159(3)(a) relating exclusively and expressly to Scotland have been omitted.]

General

160. Regulations *[Omitted.]*

161. Interpretation

(1) In this Part of this Act—

'hospital' means an institution, not being an institution carried on for profit, which provides medical or surgical treatment for in-patients, 'policy of insurance' includes a covering note,

'salvage' means the preservation of a vessel which is wrecked, stranded or in distress, or the lives of persons belonging to, or the cargo or apparel of, such a vessel, and

'under the owner's control' means, in relation to a vehicle, that it is being driven by the owner or by a servant of the owner in the course of his employment or is otherwise subject to the control of the owner.

(2) In any provision of this Part of this Act relating to the surrender, or the loss or destruction, of a certificate of insurance or certificate of security, references to such a certificate—

(*a*) shall, in relation to policies or securities under which more than one certificate is issued, be construed as references to all certificates, and

(*b*) shall, where any copy has been issued of any certificate, be construed as including a reference to that copy.

(3) In this Part of this Act, any reference to an accident includes a reference to two or more causally related accidents.

162. Index to Part VI

The expressions listed in the left-hand column below are respectively defined or (as the case may be) fall to be construed in accordance with the provisions of this Part of this Act listed in the right-hand column in relation to those expressions.

Expression	*Relevant provision*
Accident	Section 161(3)
Authorised insurer	Section 145(2)
Certificate of insurance	Sections 147(1) and 161(2)
Certificate of security	Sections 147(2) and 161(2)
Hospital	Section 161(1)
Policy of insurance	Section 161(1)
Prescribed	Section 160(1)
Regulations	Section 160(1)
Salvage	Section 161(1)
Under the owner's control	Section 161(1)

PART VII

Miscellaneous and General

Powers of constables and other authorised persons

163. Power of police to stop vehicles

(1) A person driving a motor vehicle on a road must stop the vehicle on being required to do so by a constable in uniform.

(2) A person riding a cycle on a road must stop the cycle on being required to do so by a constable in uniform.

(3) If a person fails to comply with this section he is guilty of an offence.

164. Power of constables to require production of driving licence and in certain cases statement of date of birth

(1) Any of the following persons—

(*a*) a person driving a motor vehicle on a road,

(*b*) a person whom a constable has reasonable cause to believe to have been the driver of a motor vehicle at a time when an accident occurred owing to its presence on a road,

(*c*) a person whom a constable has reasonable cause to believe to have committed an offence in relation to the use of a motor vehicle on a road, or

(*d*) a person—

(i) who supervises the holder of a provisional licence while the holder is driving a motor vehicle on a road, or

(ii) whom a constable has reasonable cause to believe was supervising the holder of a provisional licence while driving, at a time when an accident occurred owing to the presence of the vehicle on a road or at a time when an offence is suspected of having been committed by the holder of the provisional licence in relation to the use of the vehicle on a road,

must, on being so required by a constable, produce his licence for examination, so as to enable the constable to ascertain the name and address of the holder of the licence, the date of issue, and the authority by which it was issued.

(2) Such a person must in prescribed circumstances, on being so required by the constable, state his date of birth.

(3) If—

(*a*) a licence has been revoked by the Secretary of State under section 93 or 99 of this Act, and

(*b*) the holder of the licence fails to deliver it to the Secretary of State in pursuance of the section in question,

a constable may require him to produce it, and upon its being produced may seize it and deliver it to the Secretary of State.

(4) Where a constable has reasonable cause to believe that the holder of a licence, or any other person, has knowingly made a false statement for the purpose of obtaining the grant of the licence, the constable may require the holder of the licence to produce it to him.

(5) Where a person has been required under section 27 of the Road Traffic Offenders Act 1988 [*qv*] to produce a licence to the court and fails to do so, a constable may require him to produce it and, upon its being produced, may seize it and deliver it to the court.

(6) If a person required under the preceding provisions of this section to produce a licence or state his date of birth to a constable fails to do so he is, subject to subsections (7) and (8) below, guilty of an offence.

(7) Subsection (6) above does not apply where a person required on any occasion under the preceding provisions of this section to produce a licence—

(*a*) produces on that occasion a current receipt for the licence issued under section 56 of the Road Traffic Offenders Act 1988 [*qv*] and, if required to do so, produces the licence in person immediately on its return at a police station that was specified on that occasion, or

(*b*) within seven days after that occasion produces such a receipt in person at a police station that was specified by him on that occasion and, if required to do so, produces the licence in person immediately on its return at that police station.

(8) In proceedings against any person for the offence of failing to produce a licence it shall be a defence for him to show that—

(*a*) within seven days after the production of his licence was required he produced it in person at a police station that was specified by him at the time its production was required, or

(*b*) he produced it in person there as soon as was reasonably practicable, or

(*c*) it was not reasonably practicable for him to produce it there before the day on which the proceedings were commenced,

and for the purposes of this subsection the laying of the information shall be treated as the commencement of the proceedings.

(9) Where in accordance with this section a person has stated his date of birth to a constable, the Secretary of State may serve on that person a notice in writing requiring him to provide the Secretary of State—

(*a*) with such evidence in that person's possession or obtainable by him as the Secretary of State may specify for the purpose of verifying that date, and

(*b*) if his name differs from his name at the time of his birth, with a statement in writing specifying his name at that time,

and a person who knowingly fails to comply with a notice under this subsection is guilty of an offence.

(10) A notice authorised to be served on any person by subsection (9) above may be served on him by delivering it to him or by leaving it at his proper address or by sending it to him by post; and for the purposes of this subsection and section 7 of the Interpretation Act 1978 in its application to this subsection the proper address of any person shall be his latest address as known to the person giving the notice.

(11) In this section 'licence' and 'provisional licence' have the same meanings as in Part III of this Act.

[Words in s 164(8) relating exclusively and expressly to Scotland have been omitted.

The circumstances in which a police constable may require a person to state his date of birth are prescribed in the Motor Vehicles (Driving Licences) Regulations 1987 (SI 1987 No 1378), reg 26, qv.

As to the application of s 164(1) and (6) to domestic driving permits, Convention driving licences and British Forces (BFG) driving licences, see ibid, reg 25(3)(d) and (4); and see also the Motor Vehicles (International Circulation) Order 1975 (SI 1975 No 1208), Sched 3, para 5, below.]

165. Power of constables to obtain names and addresses of drivers and others, and to require production of evidence of insurance or security and test certificates

(1) Any of the following persons—

(*a*) a person driving a motor vehicle (other than an invalid carriage) on a road, or

(*b*) a person whom a constable has reasonable cause to believe to have been the driver of a motor vehicle (other than an invalid carriage) at a time when an accident occurred owing to its presence on a road, or

(*c*) a person whom a constable has reasonable cause to believe to have committed an offence in relation to the use on a road of a motor vehicle (other than an invalid carriage),

must, on being so required by a constable, give his name and address and the name and address of the owner of the vehicle and produce the following documents for examination.

(2) Those documents are—

(*a*) the relevant certificate of insurance or certificate of security (within the meaning of Part VI of this Act), or such other evidence that the vehicle is not or was not being driven in contravention of section 143 of this Act as may be prescribed by regulations made by the Secretary of State,

(*b*) in relation to a vehicle to which section 47 of this Act applies, a test certificate issued in respect of the vehicle as mentioned in subsection (1) of that section, and

(*c*) in relation to a goods vehicle the use of which on a road without a plating certificate or goods vehicle test certificate is an offence under section 53(1) or (2) of this Act, any such certificate issued in respect of that vehicle or any trailer drawn by it.

(3) Subject to subsection (4) below, a person who fails to comply with a requirement under subsection (1) above is guilty of an offence.

(4) A person shall not be convicted of an offence under subsection (1) above by reason only of failure to produce any certificate or other evidence to a constable if in proceedings against him for the offence he shows that—

(*a*) within seven days after the date on which the production of the certificate or other evidence was required it was produced at a police station that was specified by him at the time when its production was required, or

(*b*) it was produced there as soon as was reasonably practicable, or

(*c*) it was not reasonably practicable for it to be produced there before the day on which the proceedings were commenced,

and for the purposes of this subsection the laying of the information shall be treated as the commencement of the proceedings.

(5) A person—

(*a*) who supervises the holder of a provisional licence granted under Part III of this Act while the holder is driving on a road a motor vehicle (other than an invalid carriage), or

(*b*) whom a constable has reasonable cause to believe was supervising the holder of such a licence while driving, at a time when an accident occurred owing to the presence of the vehicle on a road or at a time when an offence is suspected of having been committed by the holder of the provisional licence in relation to the use of the vehicle on a road,

must, on being so required by a constable, give his name and address and the name and address of the owner of the vehicle.

(6) A person who fails to comply with a requirement under subsection (5) above is guilty of an offence.

(7) In this section 'owner', in relation to a vehicle which is the subject of a hiring agreement, includes each party to the agreement.

[Words in s 165(4) relating exclusively and expressly to Scotland have been omitted.]

166. Powers of certifying officers and examiners as respects goods vehicles

A certifying officer appointed under the Public Passenger Vehicles Act 1981 or an examiner appointed under section 68 of this Act may at any time, on production if so required of his authority, exercise in the case of goods vehicles all such powers as are, under section 164(1) or 165 of this Act, exercisable by a constable.

167. Power of arrest in Scotland for reckless or careless driving or cycling

[Omitted.]

Duty to give name and address

168. Failure to give, or giving false, name and address in case of reckless or careless or inconsiderate driving or cycling

Any of the following persons—

(*a*) the driver of a motor vehicle who is alleged to have committed an offence under section 2 or 3 of this Act, or

(*b*) the rider of a cycle who is alleged to have committed an offence under section 28 or 29 of this Act,

who refuses, on being so required by any person having reasonable ground for so requiring, to give his name or address, or gives a false name or address, is guilty of an offence.

169. Pedestrian contravening constable's direction to stop to give name and address

A constable may require a person committing an offence under section 37 of this Act to give his name and address, and if that person fails to do so he is guilty of an offence.

Duties in case of accident

170. Duty of driver to stop, report accident and give information or documents

(1) This section applies in a case where, owing to the presence of a motor vehicle on a road, an accident occurs by which—

(*a*) personal injury is caused to a person other than the driver of that motor vehicle, or

(*b*) damage is caused—

(i) to a vehicle other than that motor vehicle or a trailer drawn by that motor vehicle, or

(ii) to an animal other than an animal in or on that motor vehicle or a trailer drawn by that motor vehicle, or

(iii) to any other property constructed on, fixed to, growing in or otherwise forming part of the land on which the road in question is situated or land adjacent to such land.

(2) The driver of the motor vehicle must stop and, if required to do so by any person having reasonable grounds for so requiring, give his name and address and also the name and address of the owner and the identification marks of the vehicle.

(3) If for any reason the driver of the motor vehicle does not give his name and address under subsection (2) above, he must report the accident.

(4) A person who fails to comply with subsection (2) or (3) above is guilty of an offence.

(5) If, in a case where this section applies by virtue of subsection (1)(*a*) above, the driver of the vehicle does not at the time of the accident produce such a certificate of insurance or security, or other evidence, as is mentioned in section 165(2)(*a*) of this Act—

(*a*) to a constable, or

(*b*) to some person who, having reasonable grounds for so doing, has required him to produce it,

the driver must report the accident and produce such a certificate or other evidence.

This subsection does not apply to the driver of an invalid carriage.

(6) To comply with a duty under this section to report an accident or to produce such a certificate of insurance or security, or other evidence, as is mentioned in section 165(2)(*a*) of this Act, the driver—

(*a*) must do so at a police station or to a constable, and

(*b*) must do so as soon as is reasonably practicable and, in any case, within twenty-four hours of the occurrence of the accident.

(7) A person who fails to comply with a duty under subsection (5) above is guilty of an offence, but he shall not be convicted by reason only of a failure to produce a certificate or other evidence if, within five days after the occurrence of the accident, the certificate or other evidence is produced at a police station that was specified by him at the time when the accident was reported.

(8) In this section 'animal' means horse, cattle, ass, mule, sheep, pig, goat or dog.

Other duties to give information or documents

171. Duty of owner of motor vehicle to give information for verifying compliance with requirement of compulsory insurance or security

(1) For the purpose of determining whether a motor vehicle was or was not being driven in contravention of section 143 of this Act on any occasion when the driver was required under section 165(1) or 170 of this Act to produce such a certificate of insurance or security, or other evidence, as is mentioned in section 165(2)(*a*) of this Act, the owner of the vehicle must give such information as he may be required, by or on behalf of a chief officer of police, to give.

(2) A person who fails to comply with the requirement of subsection (1) above is guilty of an offence.

(3) In this section 'owner', in relation to a vehicle which is the subject of a hiring agreement, includes each party to the agreement.

172. Duty to give information as to identity of driver, etc, in certain cases

(1) This section applies—

(*a*) to any offence under the preceding provisions of this Act except—

(i) an offence under Part V, or

(ii) an offence under section 13, 16, 51(2), 61(4), 67(9), [67B(6),] 68(4), 96 or 117,

and to an offence under section 178 of this Act,

(*b*) to any offence under sections 25, 26, 27 and 45 of the Road Traffic Offenders Act 1988 [*qv*], and (*c*) to any offence against any other enactment relating to the use of vehicles on roads.

(2) Where the driver of a vehicle is alleged to be guilty of an offence to which this section applies—

(*a*) the person keeping the vehicle shall give such information as to the identity of the driver as he may be required to give by or on behalf of a chief officer of police [or in the case of an offence under section 19 or 19A of this Act, the council of a county, district or London borough or the Common Council of the City of London], and

(*b*) any other person shall if required as stated above give any information which it is in his power to give and may lead to identification of the driver.

In this subsection references to the driver of a vehicle include references to the person riding a cycle.

(3) A person who fails to comply with the requirement of subsection (2)(*a*) above is guilty of an offence unless he shows to the satisfaction of the court that he did not know and could not with reasonable diligence have ascertained who the driver of the vehicle or, as the case may be, the rider of the cycle was.

(4) A person who fails to comply with the requirement of subsection (2)(*b*) above is guilty of an offence.

[Section 172 is printed as prospectively amended by the Road Traffic (Consequential Provisions) Act 1988, s 4 and Sched 2, paras 22(2) and 26. The words printed within square brackets in s 172(1)(a)(ii) and (2)(a) will be brought into force on a date to be announced; see ibid, s 8(3), below.]

Forgery, false statements, etc

173. Forgery of documents, etc

(1) A person who, with intent to deceive—

(*a*) forges, alters or uses a document or other thing to which this section applies, or

(*b*) lends to, or allows to be used by, any other person a document or other thing to which this section applies, or

(*c*) makes or has in his possession any document or other thing so closely resembling a document or other thing to which this section applies as to be calculated to deceive,

is guilty of an offence.

(2) This section applies to the following documents and other things—

(*a*) any licence under any Part of this Act,

(*b*) any test certificate, goods vehicle test certificate, plating certificate, certificate of conformity or Minister's approval certificate (within the meaning of Part II of this Act),

(*c*) any certificate required as a condition of any exception prescribed under section 14 of this Act,

[(*cc*) any notice removing a prohibition under [section 69 or 70] of this Act;]

(*d*) any plate containing plated particulars (within the meaning of Part II of this Act) or containing other particulars required to be marked on a goods vehicle by section 54 to 58 of this Act or regulations under those sections,

(*e*) any records required to be kept by virtue of section 74 of this Act, (*f*) any document which, in pursuance of section 89(3) or 117(2) of this Act, is issued as evidence of the result of a test of competence to drive,

(*g*) any badge or certificate prescribed by regulations made by virtue of section 135 of this Act,

(*h*) any certificate of insurance or certificate of security under Part VI of this Act,

(*j*) any document produced as evidence of insurance in pursuance of Regulation 6 of the Motor Vehicles (Compulsory Insurance) (No 2) Regulations 1973 *[SI 1973 No 2143, qv]*

(*k*) any document issued under regulations made by the Secretary of State in pursuance of his power under section 165(2)(*a*) of this Act to prescribe evidence which may be produced in lieu of a certificate of insurance or a certificate of security, and

(*l*) any international road haulage permit.

(3) In the application of this section to England and Wales 'forges' means makes a false document or other thing in order that it may be used as genuine.

[Section 173 is printed as prospectively amended by the Transport Act 1982, s 23(3) (as itself amended by the Road Traffic (Consequential Provisions) Act 1988, s 4 and Sched 2, para 12). Section 173(2)(cc), which is printed within square brackets, will be brought into force on a date to be announced; see s 76(2) of the 1982 Act.

As to the application of s 173 to domestic driving permits, Convention driving permits and British Forces (BFG) driving licences, see the Motor Vehicles (Driving Licences) Regulations 1987 (SI 1987 No 1378), reg 25(3)(f) and (4), below; see also the Motor Vehicles (International Circulation) Order 1975 (SI 1975 No 1208), Sched 3, para 5, below, and the Motor Vehicles (International Circulation) (Amendment) Order 1980 (SI 1980 No 1095), art 8(1) and (3), below.]

174. False statements and withholding material information

(1) A person who knowingly makes a false statement for the purpose—

(*a*) of obtaining the grant of a licence under any Part of this Act to himself or any other person, or

(*b*) of preventing the grant of any such licence, or

(*c*) of procuring the imposition of a condition or limitation in relation to any such licence, or

(*d*) of securing the entry or retention of the name of any person in the register of approved instructors maintained under Part V of this Act, or

(*e*) of obtaining the grant of an international road haulage permit to himself or any other person,

is guilty of an offence.

(2) A person who, in supplying information or producing documents for the purposes either of sections 53 to 60 and 63 of this Act or of regulations made under section 49 to 51, 61, 62 and 66(3) of this Act—

(*a*) makes a statement which he knows to be false in a material particular or recklessly makes a statement which is false in a material particular, or

(*b*) produces, provides, sends or otherwise makes use of a document which he knows to be false in a material particular or recklessly produces, provides, sends or otherwise makes use of a document which is false in a material particular,

is guilty of an offence.

(3) A person who—

(*a*) knowingly produces false evidence for the purposes of regulations under section 66(1) of this Act, or

(*b*) knowingly makes a false statement in a declaration required to be made by the regulations,

is guilty of an offence.

[(3A) A person who knowingly makes a false statement in a certificate or declaration under section 67A of this Act (including that section as applied by section 67B(4) of this Act) is guilty of an offence.]

(4) A person who—

(*a*) wilfully makes a false entry in any record required to be made or kept by regulations under section 74 of this Act, or

(*b*) with intent to deceive, makes use of any such entry which he knows to be false,

is guilty of an offence.

(5) A person who makes a false statement or withholds any material information for the purpose of obtaining the issue—

(*a*) of a certificate of insurance or certificate of security under Part VI of this Act, or

(*b*) of any document issued under regulations made by the Secretary of State in pursuance of his power under section 165(2)(*a*) of this Act to prescribe evidence which may be produced in lieu of a certificate of insurance or a certificate of security,

is guilty of an offence.

[Section 174 is printed as prospectively amended by the Road Traffic (Consequential Provisions) Act 1988, s 4 and Sched 2, para 27. Section 174(3A), which is printed within square brackets, will be brought into force on a date to be announced; see ibid, s 8(3), below.

As to the application of s 174 to Convention driving permits, see the Motor Vehicles (International Circulation) (Amendment) Order 1980 (SI 1980 No 1095), art 8(1) and (3), below.]

175. Issue of false documents

If a person issues—

(*a*) any such document as is referred to in section 174(5)(*a*) or (*b*) of this Act, or

(*b*) a test certificate or certificate of conformity (within the meaning of Part II of this Act),

and the document or certificate so issued is to his knowledge false in a material particular, he is guilty of an offence.

[With effect from a date to be announced under the Transport Act 1982, s 76(2), the following will be substituted for the text of s 175 by the 1982 Act, s 24 (as amended by the Road Traffic (Consequential Provisions) Act 1988, s 4 and Sched 2, Part I, para 13(1)):

[[175.] Falsification of documents

(1) A person shall be guilty of an offence who issues—

(*a*) any such document as is referred to in paragraph (*a*) or (*b*) of [section 174(5)] of this Act;

(*b*) a test certificate, plating certificate, goods vehicle test certificate or certificate of conformity;

(*c*) a certificate of temporary exemption under regulations made under [section 48(4) or 53(5)(*b*)] of this Act; or

(*d*) a notice removing a prohibition under [section 69 or 70] of this Act;

if the document or certificate so issued is to his knowledge false in a material particular.

(2) A person who amends a certificate of conformity shall be guilty of an offence if the certificate as amended is to his knowledge false in a material particular.

(3) Expressions used in subsection (1)(*b*) and (2) above have the same meanings as they respectively have for the purposes of Part II of this Act.]]

176. Power to seize articles in respect of which offences under sections 173 to 175 may have been committed

(1) If a constable has reasonable cause to believe that a document produced to him—

(*a*) in pursuance of section 137 of this Act, or

(*b*) in pursuance of any of the preceding provisions of this Part of this Act,

is a document in relation to which an offence has been committed under section 173, 174 or 175 of this Act or under section 115 of the Road Traffic Regulation Act 1984 [*qv*], he may seize the document.

(2) When a document is seized under subsection (1) above, the person from whom it was taken shall, unless—

(*a*) the document has been previously returned to him, or

(*b*) he has been previously charged with an offence under any of those sections,

be summoned before a magistrates' court to account for his possession of the document.

(3) The court must make such order respecting the disposal of the document and award such costs as the justice of the case may require.

(4) If a constable, a certifying officer appointed under the Public Passenger Vehicles Act 1981 or an examiner appointed under section 68(1) of this Act has reasonable cause to believe that a document or plate carried on a motor vehicle or by the driver of the vehicle is a document or plate to which this subsection applies, he may seize it.

For the purposes of this subsection the power to seize includes power to detach from a vehicle.

(5) Subsection (4) above applies to a document or plate in relation to which an offence has been committed under sections 173, 174 or 175 of this Act in so far as they apply—

(*a*) to documents evidencing the appointment of examiners for the purposes of sections 68 to 72 of this Act, or

(*b*) to goods vehicle test certificates, plating certificates, certificates of conformity or Minister's approval certificates (within the meaning of Part II of this Act), or

(*c*) to plates containing plated particulars (within the meaning of that Part) or containing other particulars required to be marked on goods vehicles by sections 54 to 58 of this Act or regulations made under them, or

(*d*) to records required to be kept by virtue of section 74 of this Act, or

(*e*) to international road haulage permits.

(6) When a document or plate is seized under subsection (4) above, either the driver or owner of the vehicle shall, if the document or plate is still detained and neither of them has previously been charged with an offence in relation to the document or plate under section 173, 174 or 175 of this Act, be summoned before a magistrates' court to account for his possession of, or the presence on the vehicle of, the document or plate.

(7) The court must make such order respecting the disposal of the document or plate and award such costs as the justice of the case may require.

[With effect from a date to be announced under the Transport Act 1982, s 76(2), two amendments will be made in s 176 by the 1982 Act, s 24(2) (as amended by the Road Traffic (Consequential Provisions) Act 1988, s 4 and Sched 2, para 13(b)). These amendments are (a) the following words will be substituted in s 176(4) for the words from 'a certifying officer' to 'this Act';

[a certifying officer or a public service vehicle examiner appointed under the Public Passenger Vehicles Act 1981, an examiner appointed under [section 68] or this Act or an authorised inspector under section 8 of the Transport Act 1982]

and (b) the following words will be added to s 176(5)(b) after the words 'plating certificates':

[notices removing prohibitions under [section 69 or 70] of this Act].

Words relating exclusively and expressly to Scotland have been omitted from s 176(2), (3), (6) and (7).]

177. Impersonation of, or of person employed by, authorised examiner

If a person, with intent to deceive, falsely represents himself to be, or to be employed by, a person authorised by the Secretary of State for the purposes of section 45 of this Act, he is guilty of an offence.

Offences in Scotland

178. Taking motor vehicle without authority etc *[Omitted.]*

Inquiries

179. General power to hold inquiries *[Omitted.]*

180. General provisions as to inquiries *[Omitted.]*

181. General provisions as to accident inquiries *[Omitted.]*

182. Special provisions as to accident inquiries in Greater London *[Omitted.]*

Application to the Crown

183. Application to the Crown

(1) Subject to the provisions of this section—

(*a*) Part I of this Act,

(*b*) Part II of this Act, except sections 68 to 74 and 77,

(*c*) Part III of this Act, except section 103(3),

(*d*) Part IV of this Act, and

(*e*) in this Part, sections 163, 164, 168, 169, 170(1) to (4), 177, 178, 181 and 182,

apply to vehicles and persons in the public service of the Crown.

(2) Sections 49 to 63 and section 65 of this Act apply—

(*a*) to vehicles in the public service of the Crown only if they are registered or liable to be registered under the Vehicles (Excise) Act 1971, and

(*b*) to trailers in the public service of the Crown only while drawn by vehicles (whether or not in the public service of the Crown) which are required to be so registered.

(3) Where those sections so apply they do so subject to the following modifications—

(*a*) examinations of such vehicles in pursuance of regulations under section 49 or 61(2)(*a*) of this Act may be made by or under the directions of examiners authorised by the Secretary of State for the purpose instead of by or under the directions of examiners appointed under section 68 of this Act or of certifying officers or public service vehicle examiners appointed under the Public Passenger Vehicles Act 1981, and

(*b*) section 50(1) of this Act does not apply to the determination of an examiner so authorised on any such examination, but any person aggrieved by such a determination may appeal to the Secretary of State and on the appeal the Secretary of State shall cause the vehicle to be re-examined by an officer appointed by him for the purpose and may make such determination on the basis of the re-examination as he thinks fit.

(4) Neither section 97(3) nor section 98(3) of this Act, in so far as they prevent such a licence as is there mentioned from authorising a person to drive certain motor cycles, applies—

(*a*) in the case of motor cycles owned by the Secretary of State for Defence and used for naval, military or air force purposes, or

(*b*) in the case of motor cycles so used while being ridden by persons for the time being subject to the orders of a member of the armed forces of the Crown.

(5) Subject to regulations made under subsection (2) of section 101 of this Act, that section (in so far as it prohibits persons under 21 from holding or obtaining a licence to drive motor vehicles or persons under 18 from holding or obtaining a licence to drive medium-sized goods vehicles) does not apply—

(*a*) in the case of motor vehicles owned by the Secretary of State for Defence and used for naval, military or air force purposes, or

(*b*) in the case of vehicles so used while being driven by persons for the time being subject to the orders of a member of the armed forces of the Crown.

(6) The function of issuing licences under Part IV of this Act to persons subject to the Naval Discipline Act 1957, to military law or to air force law to drive goods vehicles in the public service of the Crown and of revoking and suspending such licences shall be exercised by the prescribed licensing authority, and references in that Part to the licensing authority shall be construed accordingly.

(7) Section 165 of this Act, in so far as it provides for the production of test certificates and the giving of names and addresses, applies to a person in connection with a vehicle to which section 47 of this Act applies notwithstanding that he or the driver is or was at any material time in the public service of the Crown.

(8) Subsection (1) of section 165 of this Act, in so far as it provides for the production of any certificate mentioned in subsection (2)(*c*) of that section, applies to a person in connection with a goods vehicle so mentioned notwithstanding that he or the driver is or was at any material time in the public service of the Crown.

[With effect from a date to be announced under the Road Traffic (Consequential Provisions) Act

1988, s 8(3), ibid, s 4 and Sched 2, Part I, para 18, will effect the following amendments to s 183: (a) in s 183(2), for '63' there will be substituted '63A'; (b) the following words will be inserted at the end of s 183(3)(a)—

[or of authorised inspectors under section 8 of the Transport Act 1982]

and (c) s 183(b) will be omitted.]

184. Application of sections 5 to 10 to persons subject to service discipline

(1) Sections 5 to 10 of this Act, in their application to persons subject to service discipline, apply outside as well as within Great Britain and have effect as if—

(*a*) references to proceedings for an offence under any enactment included references to proceedings for the corresponding service offence,

(*b*) references to the court included a reference to any naval, military or air force authority before whom the proceedings take place,

(*c*) references to a constable included refences to a member of the provost staff,

(*d*) references to a police station included references to a naval, military or air force unit or establishment,

(*e*) references to a hospital included references to a naval, military or air force unit or establishment at which medical or surgical treatment is provided for persons subject to service discipline, and

(*f*) in section 6(1) the reference to a traffic offence included a reference to the corresponding service offence.

(2) In relation to persons for the time being subject to service discipline, the power to arrest conferred on a constable by section 4(6) of this Act is also exercisable by a member of the provost staff and is so exercisable outside as well as within Great Britain.

(3) In this section—

'corresponding service offence', in relation to an offence under any enactment, means an offence under section 42 of the Naval Discipline Act 1957 or an offence against section 70 of the Army Act 1955 or section 70 of the Air Force Act 1955 committed by an act or omission which is punishable under that enactment or would be so punishable if committed in Great Britain,

'member of the provost staff' means a provost officer or any person legally exercising authority under or on behalf of a provost officer,

'persons subject to service discipline' means persons subject to that Act of 1957, to military law or to air force law and other persons to whom section 42 of that Act of 1957 or section 70 of either of those Acts of 1955 for the time being applies,

'provost officer' means a person who is a provost officer within the meaning of that Act of 1957 or either of those Acts of 1955.

Interpretation

185. Meaning of 'motor vehicle' and other expressions relating to vehicles

(1) In this Act—

'heavy locomotive' means a mechanically propelled vehicle which is not constructed itself to carry a load other than any of the excepted articles and the weight of which unladen exceeds 11690 kilograms,

'heavy motor car' means a mechanically propelled vehicle, not being a motor car, which is constructed itself to carry a load or passengers and the weight of which unladen exceeds 2540 kilograms,

'invalid carriage' means a mechanically propelled vehicle the weight of which unladen does not exceed 254 kilograms and which is specially designed and constructed, and not merely adapted, for the use of a person suffering from some physical defect or disability and is used solely by such a person,

'light locomotive' means a mechanically propelled vehicle which is not constructed itself to carry a load other than any of the excepted articles and the weight of which unladen does not exceed 11690 kilograms but does exceed 7370 kilograms,

'motor car' means a mechanically propelled vehicle, not being a motor cycle or an invalid carriage, which is constructed itself to carry a load or passengers and the weight of which unladen—

(*a*) if it is constructed solely for the carriage of passengers and their effects, is adapted to carry not more than seven passengers exclusive of the driver and is fitted with tyres of such type as may be specified in regulations made by the Secretary of State, does not exceed 3050 kilograms,

(*b*) if it is constructed or adapted for use for the conveyance of goods or burden of any description, does not exceed 3050 kilograms, or 3500 kilograms if the vehicle carries a container or containers for holding for the purposes of its propulsion any fuel which is wholly gaseous at 17.5 degrees Celsius under a pressure of 1.013 bar or plant and materials for producing such fuel,

(*c*) does not exceed 2540 kilograms in a case not falling within sub-paragraph (*a*) or (*b*) above,

'motor cycle' means a mechanically propelled vehicle, not being an invalid carriage, with less than four wheels and the weight of which unladen does not exceed 410 kilograms,

'motor tractor' means a mechanically propelled vehicle which is not constructed itself to carry a load, other than the excepted articles, and the weight of which unladen does not exceed 7370 kilograms,

'motor vehicle' means, subject to section 20 of the Chronically Sick and Disabled Persons Act 1970 (which makes special provision about invalid carriages, within the meaning of that Act), a mechanically propelled vehicle intended or adapted for use on roads, and

'trailer' means a vehicle drawn by a motor vehicle.

(2) In subsection (1) 'excepted articles' means any of the following: water, fuel, accumulators and other equipment used for the purpose of propulsion, loose tools and loose equipment.

186. Supplementary provisions about those expressions

(1) For the purposes of section 185 of this Act, a side-car attached to a motor vehicle, if it complies with such conditions as may be specified in regulations made by the Secretary of State, is to be regarded as forming part of the vehicle to which it is attached and as not being a trailer.

(2) For the purposes of section 185 of this Act, in a case where a motor vehicle is so constructed that a trailer may by partial super-imposition be attached to the vehicle in such a manner as to cause a substantial part of the weight of the trailer to be borne

by the vehicle, that vehicle is to be deemed to be a vehicle itself constructed to carry a load.

(3) For the purposes of section 185 of this Act, in the case of a motor vehicle fitted with a crane, dynamo, welding plant or other special appliance or apparatus which is a permanent or essentially permanent fixture, that appliance or apparatus is not to be deemed to constitute a load or goods or burden of any description, but is to be deemed to form part of the vehicle.

(4)–(6) *[Power to vary maximum and minimum weights under s 185 by regulations.]*

187. Articulated vehicles

(1) Unless it falls within subsection (2) below, a vehicle so constructed that it can be divided into two parts both of which are vehicles and one of which is a motor vehicle shall (when not so divided) be treated for the purposes of the enactments mentioned in subsection (3) below as that motor vehicle with the other part attached as a trailer.

(2) A passenger vehicle so constructed that—

(*a*) it can be divided into two parts, both of which are vehicles and one of which is a motor vehicle, but cannot be so divided without the use of facilities normally available only at a workshop, and

(*b*) passengers carried by it when not so divided can at all times pass from either part to the other,

shall (when not so divided) be treated for the purposes of the enactments mentioned in subsection (3) below as a single motor vehicle.

(3) The enactments referred to in subsection (1) and (2) above are the Road Traffic Act 1960, Parts I and II of the Public Passenger Vehicles Act 1981, and the Traffic Acts.

(4) In this section 'passenger vehicle' means a vehicle constructed or adapted for use solely or principally for the carriage of passengers.

188. Hover vehicles

(1) For the purposes of the Road Traffic Acts, a hovercraft within the meaning of the Hovercraft Act 1968 (in this section referred to as a hover vehicle)—

(*a*) is a motor vehicle, whether or not it is intended or adapted for use on roads, but

(*b*) apart from that is to be treated, subject to subsection (2) below, as not being a vehicle of any of the classes defined in section 185 of this Act.

(2) *[Regulations as to application of provisions of this Act to hover vehicles.]*

189. Certain vehicles not to be treated as motor vehicles

(1) For the purposes of the Road Traffic Acts—

(*a*) a mechanically propelled vehicle being an implement for cutting grass which is controlled by a pedestrian and is not capable of being used or adapted for any other purpose,

(*b*) any other mechanically propelled vehicle controlled by a pedestrian which may be specified by regulations made by the Secretary of State for the purposes of this section and section 140 of the Road Traffic Regulation Act 1984 [*qv*], and (*c*) an electrically assisted pedal cycle of such a class as may be prescribed by regulations so made,

is to be treated as not being a motor vehicle.

(2) In subsection (1) above 'controlled by a pedestrian' means that the vehicle either—

(*a*) is constructed or adapted for use only under such control, or

(*b*) is constructed or adapted for use either under such control or under the control of a person carried on it, but is not for the time being in use under, or proceeding under, the control of a person carried on it.

[The Electrically Assisted Pedal Cycles Regulations 1983 (SI 1983 No 1168) have effect as if made under s 189(1)(c); see further §1.9 in Vol 1.]

190. Method of calculating weight of motor vehicles and trailers

(1) This section applies for the purposes of the Traffic Acts and of any other enactments relating to the use of motor vehicles or trailers on roads.

(2) The weight unladen of a vehicle or trailer shall be taken to be the weight of the vehicle or trailer—

(*a*) inclusive of the body and all parts (the heavier being taken where alternative bodies or parts are used) which are necessary to or ordinarily used with the vehicle or trailer when working on a road, but

(*b*) exclusive of the weight of water, fuel or accumulators used for the purpose of the supply of power for the propulsion of the vehicle or, as the case may be, of any vehicle by which the trailer is drawn, and of loose tools and loose equipment.

191. Interpretation of statutory references to carriages

A motor vehicle or trailer—

(*a*) is to be deemed to be a carriage within the meaning of any Act of Parliament, whether a public general Act or a local Act, and of any rule, regulation or byelaw made under any Act of Parliament, and

(*b*) if used as a carriage of any particular class shall for the purpose of any enactment relating to carriages of any particular class be deemed to be a carriage of that class.

192. General interpretation of Act

(1) In this Act—

['approved testing authority' means a person authorised by the Secretary of State under section 8 of the Transport Act 1982 to carry on a vehicle testing business within the meaning of Part II of that Act,]

'bridleway' means a way over which the public have the following, but no other, rights of way: a right of way on foot and a right of way on horseback or leading a horse, with or without a right to drive animals of any description along the way,

'carriage of goods' includes the haulage of goods,

'cycle' means a bicycle, a tricycle, or a cycle having four or more wheels, not being in any case a motor vehicle,

'driver', where a separate person acts as a steersman of a motor vehicle, includes (except for the purposes of section 1 of this Act) that person as well as any other person engaged in the driving of the vehicle, and 'drive' is to be interpreted accordingly,

'footpath', in relation to England and Wales, means a way over which the public have a right of way on foot only,

'goods' includes goods or burden of any description,

'goods vehicle' means a motor vehicle constructed or adapted for use for the carriage of goods, or a trailer so constructed or adapted,

'highway authority', in relation to England and Wales, means—

(*a*) in relation to a road other than a trunk road, the authority (being either the council of a county, metropolitan district or London borough or the Common Council of the City of London) which is responsible for the maintenance of the road, and

(*b*) in relation to a trunk road, the Secretary of State,

'international road haulage permit' means a licence, permit, authorisation or other document issued in pursuance of a Community instrument relating to the carriage of goods by road between member States or an international agreement to which the United Kingdom is a party and which relates to the international carriage of goods by road,

'owner', in relation to a vehicle which is the subject of a hiring agreement or hire-purchase agreement, means the person in possession of the vehicle under that agreement,

'petty sessions area' has the same meaning as in the Magistrates' Courts Act 1980,

'prescribed' means prescribed by regulations made by the Secretary of State,

'road', in relation to England and Wales, means any highway and any other road to which the public has access, and includes bridges over which a road passes,

'the Road Traffic Acts' means the Road Traffic Offenders Act 1988 [*qv*], the Road Traffic (Consequential Provisions) Act 1988 [*qv*] (so far as it reproduces the effect of provisions repealed by that Act) and this Act,

'statutory', in relation to any prohibition, restriction, requirement or provision, means contained in, or having effect under, and enactment (including any enactment contained in this Act),

'the Traffic Acts' means the Road Traffic Acts and the Road Traffic Regulation Act 1984 [*qv*],

'traffic sign' has the meaning given by section 64(1) of the Road Traffic Regulation Act 1984 [*qv*],

'tramcar' includes any carriage used on any road by virtue of an order under the Light Railways Act 1896, and

'trolley vehicle' means a mechanically propelled vehicle adapted for use on roads without rails and moved by power transmitted to it from some external source.

(2) *[Applies to Scotland.]*

(3) References in this Act to a class of vehicles are to be interpreted as references to a class defined or described by reference to any characteristics of the vehicles or to any other circumstances whatsoever.

[In s 192(1), the definition of 'approved testing authority' has been prospectively inserted by the Road Traffic (Consequential Provisions) Act 1988, s 4 and Sched 2, Part I, para 19. That definition will be brought into force on a date to be announced; see ibid, s 8(3).

The term 'petty sessions area' in the Magistrates' Courts Act 1980, s 150(1) is defined by reference to the Justices of the Peace Act 1979, s 4, qv.]

193. Exemptions for tramcars, trolley vehicles, railway locomotives, carriages and trucks

Schedule 4 to this Act (which excludes the application of certain provisions of the Road Traffic Acts to tramcars, trolley vehicles, railway locomotives, carriages and trucks) shall have effect.

194. General index

The expressions listed in the left-hand column below are respectively defined or (as the case may be) fall to be construed in accordance with the provisions of this Act listed in the right-hand column in relation to those expressions.

Expression	*Relevant provision*
Bridleway	Section 192
Carriage of goods	Section 192
Carriageway	Section 192
Cycle	Section 192
Drive	Section 192
Driver	Section 192
Footpath	Section 192
Footway	Section 192
Goods	Section 192
Goods vehicle	Section 192
Goods vehicle test certificate	Section 49(2)(*b*)
Heavy locomotive	Section 185
Heavy motor car	Section 185
Highway authority	Section 192
International road haulage permit	Section 192
Invalid carriage	Section 185
Light locomotive	Section 185
Local roads authority	Section 192
Motor car	Section 185
Motor cycle	Section 185
Motor tractor	Section 185
Motor vehicle	Sections 185, 186(1), 187, 188, 189
Owner	Section 192
Plating certificate	Section 49(2)(*a*)
Prescribed	Section 192
Public road	Section 192
Road	Section 192
Roads authority	Section 192
Road Traffic Acts	Section 192
Special road	Section 192
Statutory	Section 192
Test certificate	Section 45(2)
Traffic Acts	Section 192
Traffic sign	Section 192

Expression	Relevant provision
Trailer	Section 185
Tramcar	Section 192
Trolley vehicle	Section 192
Trunk road	Section 192
Unladen weight	Section 190

Supplementary

195. Provisions as to regulations *[Omitted.]*

196. Provision, etc, of weighbridges *[Omitted.]*

197. Short title, commencement and extent

(1) This Act may be cited as the Road Traffic Act 1988.

(2) This Act shall come into force, subject to the transitory provisions in Schedule 5 to the Road Traffic (Consequential Provisions) Act 1988 [*qv*], at the end of the period of six months beginning with the day on which it is passed.

(3) This Act, except section 80 and except as provided by section 184, does not extend to Northern Ireland.

Sections 17 and 18.

SCHEDULE 1

SUPPLEMENTARY PROVISIONS IN CONNECTION WITH PROCEEDINGS FOR OFFENCES UNDER SECTIONS 17 AND 18(4)

Proceedings in England and Wales

1.—(1) A person against whom proceedings are brought in England and Wales for an offence under section 17 or 18(4) of this Act is, upon information duly laid by him and on giving the prosecution not less than three clear days' notice of his intention, entitled to have any person to whose act or default he alleges that the contravention of that section was due brought before the court in the proceedings.

(2) If, after the contravention has been proved, the original accused proves that the contravention was due to the act or default of that other person—

(*a*) that other person may be convicted of the offence, and

(*b*) if the original accused further proves that he has used all due diligence to secure that section 17 or, as the case may be, 18(4) was complied with, he shall be acquitted of the offence.

(3) Where an accused seeks to avail himself of the provisions of sub-paragraphs (1) and (2) above—

(*a*) the prosecution, as well as the person whom the accused charges with the offence, has the right to cross-examine him, if he gives evidence, and any witness called by him in support of his pleas, and to call rebutting evidence, and

(*b*) the court may make such order as it thinks fit for the payment of costs by any party to the proceedings to any other party to the proceedings.

2.—(1) Where—

(*a*) it appears that an offence under section 17 or 18(4) of this Act has been committed in respect of which proceedings might be taken in England and Wales against some person (referred to below in this paragraph as 'the original offender'), and

(*b*) a person proposing to take proceedings in respect of the offence is reasonably satisfied—

(i) that the offence of which complaint is made was due to an act or default of some other person, being an act or default which took place in England and Wales, and

(ii) that the original offender could establish a defence under paragraph 1 of this Schedule,

the proceedings may be taken against that other person without proceedings first being taken against the original offender.

(2) In any such proceedings the accused may be charged with, and on proof that the contravention was due to his act or default be convicted of, the offence with which the original offender might have been charged.

3.—(1) Where proceedings are brought in England and Wales against a person (referred to below in this paragraph as 'the accused') in respect of a contravention of section 17 or 18(4) of this Act and it is proved—

(*a*) that the contravention was due to the act or default of some other person, being an act or default which took place in Scotland, and

(*b*) that the accused used all due diligence to secure compliance with that section,

the accused shall, subject to the provisions of this paragraph, be acquitted of the offence.

(2) The accused is not entitled to be acquitted under this paragraph unless within seven days from the date of the service of the summons on him—

(*a*) he has given notice in writing to the prosecution of his intention to rely upon the provisions of this paragraph, specifying the name and address of the person to whose act or default he alleges that the contravention was due, and

(*b*) he has sent a like notice to that person.

(3) The person specified in a notice served under this paragraph is entitled to appear at the hearing and give evidence and the court may, if it thinks fit, adjourn the hearing to enable him to do so.

(4) Where it is proved that the contravention of section 17 or 18(4) of this Act was due to the act or default of some person other than the accused, being an act or default which took place in Scotland, the court must (whether or not the accused is acquitted) cause notice of the proceedings to be sent to the Secretary of State.

Proceedings in Scotland

4. *[Omitted.]*

Proceedings in Great Britain

5.—(1) Subject to the provisions of this paragraph, in any proceedings (whether in England and Wales or Scotland) for an offence under section 17 or 18(4) of this Act it shall be a defence for the accused to prove—

(*a*) that he purchased the helmet or appliance in question as being of a type which—

(i) in the case of section 17, could be lawfully sold or offered for sale under that section, and

(ii) in the case of section 18(4), could be lawfully sold or offered for sale under section 18 as authorised for use in the manner in question,

and with a written warranty to that effect, and

(*b*) that he had no reason to believe at the time of the commission of the alleged offence that it was not of such a type, and

(*c*) that it was then in the same state as when he purchased it.

(2) A warranty is only a defence in any such proceedings if—

(*a*) the accused—

(i) has, not later than three clear days before the date of the hearing, sent to the prosecutor a copy of the warranty with a notice stating that he intends to rely on it and specifying the name and address of the person from whom he received it, and

(ii) has also sent a like notice of his intention to that person, and

(*b*) in the case of a warranty given by a person outside the United Kingdom, the accused proves that he had taken reasonable steps to ascertain, and did in fact believe in, the accuracy of the statement contained in the warranty.

(3) Where the accused is a servant of the person who purchased the helmet or appliance in question under a warranty, he is entitled to rely on the provisions of this paragraph in the same way as his employer would have been entitled to do if he had been the accused.

(4) The person by whom the warranty is alleged to have been given is entitled to appear at the hearing and to give evidence and the court may, if it thinks fit, adjourn the hearing to enable him to do so.

6.—(1) An accused who in any proceedings for an offence under section 17 or 18(4) of this Act wilfully applies to a helmet or, as the case may be, appliance a warranty not given in relation to that helmet or appliance is guilty of an offence.

(2) A person who, in respect of a helmet or appliance sold by him, being a helmet or appliance in respect of which a warranty might be pleaded under paragraph 5 of this Schedule, gives to the purchaser a false warranty in writing, is guilty of an offence, unless he proves that when he gave the warranty he had reason to believe that the statements or description contained in it were accurate.

(3) Where the accused in a prosecution for an offence under section 17 or 18(4) of this Act relies successfully on a warranty given to him or his employer, any proceedings under sub-paragraph (2) above in respect of the warranty may, at the option of the prosecutor, be taken either—

(*a*) before a court having jurisdiction in the place where the helmet or appliance, or any of the helmets or appliances, to which the warranty relates was procured, or

(*b*) before a court having jurisdiction in the place where the warranty was given.

7. In this Schedule, 'appliance' means an appliance to which section 18 of this Act applies.

Section 67.

SCHEDULE 2

Deferred Tests of Condition of Vehicles

1. Where the driver is the owner of the vehicle, he may at the time of electing that the test shall be deferred—

(*a*) specify a period of seven days within which the deferred test is to take place, being a period falling within the next thirty days, disregarding any day on which the vehicle is outside Great Britain, and

(*b*) require that the deferred test shall take place on premises then specified by him where the test can conveniently be carried out or that it shall take place in such area in England and Wales, being a county district or Greater London, or such area in Scotland, being an islands area or district, as he may specify at that time.

2. When the driver is not the owner of the vehicle he shall inform the examiner of the name and address of the owner of the vehicle and the owner shall be afforded an opportunity of specifying such a period, and such premises or area.

3.—(1) Where under the preceding provisions of this Schedule a period has been specified within which the deferred test is to be carried out, the time for carrying it out shall be such time within that period as may be notified, being a time not earlier than two days after the giving of the notification.

(2) Where no such period has been specified, the time for the carrying out of the deferred test shall be such time as may be notified, being a time not earlier than seven days after the giving of the notification.

(3) Where premises have been specified under the preceding provisions of this Schedule for the carrying out of the deferred test, and the test can conveniently be carried out on those premises, it must be carried out there.

(4) Where sub-paragraph (3) above does not apply, the place for carrying out the deferred test shall be such place as may be notified with the notification of the time for the carrying out of the test, and where an area has been so specified the place shall be a place in that area.

(5) Notwithstanding the preceding provisions of this paragraph, the time and place for the carrying out of the deferred test may be varied by agreement between an authorised examiner and the owner of the vehicle.

(6) In this paragraph—

'notified' means notified in writing to the owner of the vehicle on behalf of the Secretary of State, and

'notification' shall be construed accordingly,

and any notification under this paragraph may be given by post.

4. The owner of the vehicle must produce it, or secure its production, at the time and place fixed for the carrying out of the deferred test.

5.—(1) References in this Schedule to the owner of a vehicle are references to the owner of the vehicle at the time at which the election is made under section 67(6) of this Act that the test should be deferred.

(2) For the purposes of this Schedule—

(*a*) subject to sub-paragraph (*b*) below, if at the time at which that election is made the vehicle is in the possession of a person under a hire-purchase agreement or hiring agreement, that person shall be deemed to be the owner of the vehicle to the exclusion of any other person,

(*b*) if at that time the vehicle is being used under an international circulation permit, the person to whom the permit was issued shall be deemed to be the owner of the vehicle to the exclusion of any other person.

Section 131.

SCHEDULE 3

Appeals under Section 131 Against Decisions of the Registrar

[Omitted.]

Section 193.

SCHEDULE 4

Provisions Not Applicable to Tramcars, etc

1. Sections 12, 25, 26 and 127 of this Act do not apply to tramcars or trolley vehicles operated under statutory powers.

2. Sections 2, 3, 4(1) and 181 of this Act do not apply to tramcars operated under statutory powers.

3. The provisions of sections 41, 42, 47, 48, 66 and 75 of this Act and any order or regulations made under those provisions do not apply to tramcars or trolley vehicles operated under statutory powers.

4. Section 83 of this Act does not apply to railway locomotives, carriages and trucks or to tramcars.

5. Part III of this Act and, in the Road Traffic Offenders Act 1988 [*qv*], the provisions connected with the licensing of drivers (within the meaning of that Act) do not apply to tramcars operated under statutory powers.

6. Sections 101 and 109 of this Act do not apply to trolley vehicles operated under statutory powers.

7. Part VI of this Act does not apply to tramcars or trolley vehicles operated under statutory powers.

8. Sections 78, 79, 163, 168, 170, 171, 178, 190 and 191 of this Act and sections 1 and 2 of the Road Traffic Offenders Act 1988 [*qv*] do not apply to tramcars or trolley vehicles operated under statutory powers.

9. Section 164 of this Act does not apply to tramcars operated under statutory powers.

10. In this Schedule 'operated under statutory powers' means, in relation to tramcars or trolley vehicles, that their use is authorised or regulated by special Act of Parliament or by an order having the force of an Act.

11. Paragraphs 1 to 3 and 5 to 9 above shall have effect subject to any such Act or order as is mentioned in paragraph 10 above, and any such Act or order may apply to the tramcars or trolley vehicles to which it relates any of the provisions excluded by those paragraphs except sections 47, 48 and 66 of this Act.

The Road Traffic (Consequential Provisions) Act 1988

(1988 c 54)

An Act to make provision for repeals (including a repeal to give effect to a recommendation of the Law Commission and the Scottish Law Commission), consequential amendments, transitional and transitory matters and savings in connection with the consolidation of enactments in the Road Traffic Act 1988 and the Road Traffic Offenders Act 1988.

[15th November 1988]

ARRANGEMENT OF SECTIONS

Section

SCHEDULES

1. Meaning of 'the Road Traffic Acts', 'the repealed enactments', etc

(1) In this Act—

'the Road Traffic Acts' means the Road Traffic Act 1988, the Road Traffic Offenders Act 1988 and, so far as it reproduces the effect of the repealed enactments, this Act, and

'the repealed enactments' means the enactments repealed or revoked by this Act.

(2) Expressions used in this Act and in the Road Traffic Act 1988 have the same meaning as in that Act.

2. Continuity, and construction of references to old and new law

(1) The substitution of the Road Traffic Acts for the repealed enactments does not affect the continuity of the law.

(2) Anything done or having effect as if done under or for the purposes of a provision of the repealed enactments has effect, if it could have been done under or for the purposes of the corresponding provision of the Road Traffic Acts, as if done under or for the purposes of that corresponding provision.

(3) Any reference, whether express or implied, in the Road Traffic Acts or any other enactment, instrument or document to a provision of the Road Traffic Acts is to be read, in relation to the times, circumstances or purposes in relation to which the corresponding provision of the repealed enactments had effect and so far as the nature of the reference permits, as including a reference to that corresponding provision.

(4) Any reference, whether express or implied, in any enactment, instrument or document to a provision of the repealed enactments is to be read, in relation to the times, circumstances or purposes in relation to which the corresponding provision of the Road Traffic Acts have effect and so far as the nature of the reference permits, as including a reference to that corresponding provision.

[In the application of s 2 to s 34(3) of the Road Traffic Offenders Act 1988 (qv), see as to previous convictions s 4 of and Sched 2, para 7(4), to this Act, below.]

3. Repeals

(1) The enactments specified in Part I of Schedule 1 to this Act are repealed to the extent specified in the third column.

(2) Those repeals include the repeal, in accordance with Recommendations of the Law Commission and the Scottish Law Commission, of section 34 of the Road Traffic Act 1972 (requirements as to employment of persons to attend to locomotives and trailers) as no longer of practical utility.

(3) The subordinate legislation specified in Part II of that Schedule is revoked to the extent specified in the third column.

[Effect has been given in the texts reproduced in this work to the repeal and revocation of enactments and subordinate legislation specified in Parts I and II of Sched 1 so far as they are relevant. The text of Sched 1 is accordingly not reproduced.]

4. Prospective and consequential amendments

Schedule 2 to this Act (which re-enacts or makes consequential amendments of provisions which made prospective amendments of the repealed and other enactments, so that the re-enacted or amended provisions prospectively amend the Road Traffic Acts and other enactments) and Schedule 3 to this Act (which makes other consequential amendments) shall have effect.

[Effect has been given in the texts reproduced in this work to the amendments effected by Scheds 2 and 3 of this Act so far as these are relevant. The text of Scheds 2 and 3 is accordingly not reproduced.]

5. Transitional provisions and savings

(1) Schedule 4 to this Act (which makes certain transitional provisions and contains savings in connection with the repeals made by this Act) shall have effect.

(2) Nothing in that Schedule affects the general operation of section 16 of the Interpretation Act 1978 (general savings implied on a repeal).

6. Transitory modifications

Schedule 5 to this Act (which makes transitory modifications of the Road Traffic Act 1988) shall have effect.

7. Saving for law of nuisance

Nothing in the Road Traffic Acts authorises a person to use on a road a vehicle so constructed or used as to cause a public or private nuisance or affects the liability, whether under statute or common law, of the driver or owner so using such a vehicle.

[Words relating exclusively and expressly to Scotland have been omitted from s 7.]

8. Short title, commencement and extent

(1) This Act may be cited as to the Road Traffic (Consequential Provisions) Act 1988.

(2) This Act, except those provisions that may be brought into force in accordance with subsection (3) below, shall come into force at the end of the period of six months beginning with the day on which it is passed.

(3) The following provisions of Schedule 2 to this Act—

(*a*) in Part I, paragraphs 1 and 15 to 20,

(*b*) Part II (except paragraph 22 so far as relates to subsections (5) to (8) of the new section inserted by that paragraph, which therefore come into force in accordance with subsection (2) above), and

(*c*) Parts III and IV,

shall come into force on such day as the Secretary of State may by order made by statutory instrument appoint, and different days may be so appointed for different provisions and for different purposes.

(4) An order under subsection (3) above bringing any provision of Part I of Schedule 2 to this Act (wholly or partly) into force may contain such transitional provisions and savings (whether or not involving the modification of any provision contained in an Act or in subordinate legislation within the meaning of the Interpretation Act 1978) as appear to the Secretary of State necessary or expedient in connection with that provision.

(5) This Act does not extend to Northern Ireland except so far as it affects other enactments extending to Northern Ireland.

SCHEDULES

SCHEDULE 1

Section 3.

REPEALS AND REVOCATIONS

[Omitted.]

SCHEDULE 2

Section 4.

RE-ENACTMENT OR AMENDMENT OF CERTAIN ENACTMENTS NOT BROUGHT INTO FORCE

[Omitted.]

SCHEDULE 3

Section 4.

CONSEQUENTIAL AMENDMENTS

[Omitted.]

Section 5.

SCHEDULE 4

Transitional Provisions and Savings

General rules for old savings and transitional provisions

1.—(1) The repeal by this Act an enactment previously repealed subject to saving does not affect the continued operation of those savings.

(2) The repeal by this Act of a saving made on the previous repeal of an enactment does not affect the operation of the saving in so far as it is not specifically reproduced in the Road Traffic Acts but remains capable of having effect.

(3) Where the purpose of a repealed enactment was to secure that the substitution of the provisions of the Act containing that enactment for provisions repealed by that Act did not affect the continuity of the law, the repealed enactment, so far is it is not specifically reproduced in the Road Traffic Acts, shall continue to have effect, so far is it capable of doing so, for the purposes of the Road Traffic Acts.

Old offences

2. The Road Traffic Acts (including this Act so far as not included in that expression) do not affect the operation of the repealed enactments in relation to offences committed before the commencement of those Acts or to appeals against or suspension of disqualification by virtue of convictions for offences so committed or against orders made in consequence of such convictions.

Road Traffic Act 1974

3.—(1) Any provision contained in an enactment passed or instrument made before 31 July 1974 which was not repealed by the Road Traffic Act 1974 and in which any expression was given the same meaning as in, or was otherwise to be construed by reference to, any provision of sections 68 to 82 of the Road Traffic Act 1972 which was repealed by that Act shall continue to be construed as if that provision had not been so repealed.

(2), (3) *[Power to make regulations implementing the Road Traffic Act 1974, s 9 (extension of construction and use regulations to lights).]*

Road Traffic (Drivers' Ages and Hours of Work) Act 1976

4.—(1) Subject to sub-paragraph (2) below, a person who, immediately before 1st January 1976, fulfilled any of the conditions in paragraph 2(1) of Schedule 2 to the Road Traffic (Drivers' Ages and Hours of Work) Act 1976 shall not, by reason only of the provisions of section 101 of the Road Traffic Act 1988, be disqualified for holding or obtaining a licence authorising him to drive motor vehicles falling within the class described in paragraph 5 or 6 of the Table set out in section 101(1) of that Act.

(2) A person shall not be treated, by virtue of sub-paragraph (1) above, as entitled to the grant of a licence authorising him to drive a goods vehicle the permissible maximum weight of which exceeds 10 tonnes or a motor vehicle constructed solely for the carriage of passengers and their effects which is adapted to carry more than fifteen passengers inclusive of the driver.

Road Traffic Regulation Act 1984

5.—(1) Notwithstanding the repeal by this Act of the provisions of section 98 of and Schedule 7 to the Road Traffic Regulation Act 1984 (prosecution of offences), those provisions shall, in relation to the interim period (within the meaning of Schedule 12 to that Act), continue to have effect in relation to offences under Schedule 12 to that Act.

(2) To the extent that section 135 of that Act (application to Isles of Scilly) applied to the repealed enactments, it shall continue to apply to the corresponding provisions of the Road Traffic Acts.

Payments for traffic casualties

6. Where an accident giving rise to death or bodily injury in respect of which a payment is made under section 157 of the Road Traffic Act 1988, or claimed under section 158 of that Act, occurred before 1st April 1987, the amount payable shall not exceed the amount that would have been payable under the corresponding repealed enactment.

Licences, disqualification and endorsement

7.—(1) For the purposes of section 92(4)(*a*) of the Road Traffic Act 1988, a person to whom a licence was granted after the making of a declaration under paragraph (*c*) of the proviso to section 5(2) of the Road Traffic Act 1930 (which contained transitional provisions with respect to certain disabilities) shall be treated as having passed, at the time of the declaration, a relevant test in respect of vehicles of the classes to which the licence related.

(2) The references in sections 125(3)(*d*), 127(3)(*d*), 128(2)(*b*) and 130(2)(*b*) of the Road Traffic Act 1988 to section 34 or 36 of the Road Traffic Offenders Act 1988 and to Part III of the Road Traffic Act 1988 include a reference—

(*a*) to section 93 of the Road Traffic Act 1972 and to Part III of that Act, and

(*b*) to section 5 of the Road Traffic Act 1962 and Part II of the Road Traffic Act 1960, (but not to section 104 of the 1960 Act).

(3) For the purposes of section 29 of the Road Traffic Offenders Act 1988, an order for endorsement which was made before the commencement of section 19 of the Transport Act 1981 counts as an order made in pursuance of section 44 of the Road Traffic Offenders Act 1988 for the endorsement of three penalty points, unless a disqualification was imposed on the offender on that or any subsequent occasion.

(4) For the purposes of section 2 of this Act as it has effect for the purposes of section 34(3) of the Road Traffic Offenders Act 1988—

(*a*) a previous conviction of an offence under section 6(1) of the Road Traffic Act 1972, as it had effect immediately before the substitution of a new section 6(1) by the Transport Act 1981, shall be treated as a conviction of an offence under section 5(1)(*a*) of the Road Traffic Act 1988, and

(*b*) a previous conviction of an offence under section 9(3) of the 1972 Act, as it had effect immediately before the substitution of a new section 8(7) by the 1981 Act, shall be treated as a conviction of an offence under section 7(6) of the Road Traffic Act 1988.

(5) The references in sections 36(4), 37(3) and 42(6) of the Road Traffic Offenders Act 1988 to an order under subsection (1) of section 36 include a reference to an order

under section 93(7) of the Road Traffic Act 1972, section 5(7) of the Road Traffic Act 1962 or section 104(3) of the Road Traffic Act 1960.

(6) Where, in pursuance of section 93(5) of the Road Traffic Act 1972, a period of disqualification was imposed on an offender in addition to any other period or periods then, for the purpose of determining whether an application may be made under section 42 of the Road Traffic Offenders Act 1988 for the removal of either or any of the disqualifications the periods shall be treated as one continuous period of disqualification.

Hovercraft

8. For the purposes of the Hovercraft Act 1968 (under which enactments and instruments relating, amongst other things, to motor vehicles may, if passed before the commencement of that Act, be applied to hovercraft) any enactment contained in the Road Traffic Acts, being an enactment derived from an enactment so passed, and any instrument made or having effect as if made under such an enactment, shall be treated as included among the enactments and instruments which can be so applied.

Section 6.

SCHEDULE 5

Transitory Modifications

1.—(1) Until the appointed day, section 15 of the Road Traffic Act 1988 shall have effect as if—

(*a*) subsections (3), (4) and (6) to (8) were omitted, and

(*b*) in subsection (5), the words 'or (3)' in paragraphs (*a*) and (*c*) and the words 'or as the rear of the vehicle for the purposes of subsection (3) above' in paragraph (*b*) were omitted,

and section 195(3) and (4) shall have effect as if the references to section 15 were omitted.

(2) In sub-paragraph (1) above, 'the appointed day' means such day as the Secretary of State may by order made by statutory instrument appoint and different days may be appointed for different provisions or different purposes.

The Road Traffic (Foreign Vehicles) Act 1972

(1972 c 27)

An Act to make provision, in relation to foreign goods vehicles and foreign public service vehicles, for securing the observance of certain statutory provisions relating to road traffic; and for purposes connected with those matters.

[11th May 1972]

ARRANGEMENT OF SECTIONS

SCHEDULES

1. Power in certain cases to prohibit driving of foreign vehicle

(1) The provisions of this section shall have effect with respect to any foreign goods vehicle or foreign public service vehicle where—

(*a*) an examiner [or an authorised inspector] exercises, in relation to the vehicle or its driver, any functions of the examiner [or authorised inspector] under an enactment [or instrument] specified in the first column of Schedule 1 to this Act, or

(*b*) an authorised person exercises, in relation to the vehicle, any functions of that person under [sections 78 and 79 of the Road Traffic Act 1988] (weighing of motor vehicles).

(2) If in any such a case as is mentioned in subsection (1)(*a*) of this section—

(*a*) the driver obstructs the examiner [or authorised inspector] in the exercise of his functions under the enactment [or instrument] in question, or refuses, neglects or otherwise fails to comply with any requirement made by the examiner [or authorised inspector] under that enactment, or

(*b*) it appears to the examiner [or authorised inspector] that, in relation to the vehicle or its driver, there has been a contravention of any of the enactments or instruments specified in the first column of Schedule 2 to this Act, or that there will be such a contravention if the vehicle is driven on a road,

the examiner [or authorised inspector] may prohibit the driving of the vehicle on a road, either absolutely or for a specified purpose, and either for a specified period or without any limitation of time.

(3) If in any such case as is mentioned in subsection (1)(*b*) of this section—

(*a*) the driver obstructs the authorised person in the exercise of his functions under [the said sections 78 and 79], or refuses, neglects or otherwise fails to comply with any requirement made by the authorised person under [those sections], or

(*b*) it appears to the authorised person that any limit of weight applicable to the vehicle by virtue of regulations made under [section 41 of the Road Traffic Act 1988] has been exceeded, or will be exceeded if the vehicle is driven on a road,

the authorised person may prohibit the driving of the vehicle on a road, either absolutely or for a specified purpose.

(4) Where an examiner [or an authorised inspector] or an authorised person prohibits the driving of a vehicle under this section, he may also direct the driver to remove the vehicle (and, if it is a motor vehicle drawing a trailer, also to remove the trailer) to such place and subject to such conditions as are specified in the direction; and the prohibition shall not apply to the removal of the vehicle in accordance with that direction.

(5) Where a prohibition is imposed under subsection (2) or subsection (3) of this section, the examiner [or authorised inspector] or authorised person shall forthwith give notice in writing of the prohibition to the driver of the vehicle, specifying the circumstances (as mentioned in paragraph (*a*) or paragraph (*b*) of either of those subsections) in consequence of which the prohibition is imposed, and—

(*a*) stating whether the prohibition is on all driving of the vehicle or only on driving it for a specified purpose (and, if the latter, specifying the purpose), and

(*b*) where the prohibition is imposed under subsection (2) of this section, also stating whether it is imposed only for a specified period (and, if so, specifying the period) or without limitation of time;

and any direction under subsection (4) of this section may be given either in that notice or in a separate notice in writing given to the driver of the vehicle.

[(6) In the case of a goods vehicle—

(*a*) a prohibition under subsection (2)(*b*) above, by reference to a supposed contravention of—

(i) [section 41 of the Road Traffic Act 1988] (construction, weight, equipment etc, of motor vehicles and trailers),

(ii) [*Repealed.*]

(iii) regulations under any of the sections of that Act referred to above in this paragraph,

may be imposed with a direction making it irremovable unless and until the vehicle has been inspected at an official testing station;

(*b*) a prohibition imposed under subsection (3) above may be against driving the vehicle on a road until the weight has been reduced and official notification has been given to whoever is for the time being in charge of the vehicle that it is permitted to proceed.]

[(7) Official notification for the purposes of subsection (6)(*b*) above must be in writing and be given by an authorised person and may be withheld until the vehicle has been weighed or re-weighed in order to satisfy the person giving the notification that the weight has been sufficiently reduced.]

[Section 1 is printed as amended by the Transport Act 1978, s 9(1) and Sched 3, para 8; the Transport Act 1982, s 10(4); the Road Transport (International Passenger Services) Regulations 1984 (SI 1984 No 748), reg 22; the Road Traffic (Consequential Provisions) Act 1988, ss 3(1) and 4 and Sched 1, Part I, and 3, para 9(1).

Subsection (6)(a)(ii) has lapsed.

The references to 'authorised inspector' in this section were inserted by the Transport Act 1982, s 10(4), and will take effect from a date to be announced.]

2. Provisions supplementary to section 1

(1) Subject to any exemption granted under subsection (2) of this section, a prohibition under section 1 of this Act shall come into force as soon as notice of it has been given in accordance with subsection (5) of that section, and shall continue in force until it is removed under the following provisions of this section (or, in the case of a prohibition imposed only for a specified period, shall continue in force until either it is removed under this section or that period expires, whichever first occurs).

(2) Where notice of a prohibition has been given under subsection (5) of section 1 of this Act in respect of a vehicle, an exemption in writing for the use of the vehicle in such manner, subject to such conditions and for such purpose as may be specified in the exemption may be granted—

(*a*) in the case of a prohibition under subsection (2) of that section, by any examiner [or authorised inspector], or

(*b*) in the case of a prohibition under subsection (3) of that section, by any authorised person.

(3) A prohibition under subsection (2) of section 1 of this Act may be removed by any examiner [or authorised inspector], and a prohibition under subsection (3) of that section may be removed by any authorised person, if he is satisfied that appropriate action has been taken to remove or remedy the circumstances (as mentioned in paragraph (*a*) or paragraph (*b*) of either of those subsections) in consequence of which the prohibition was imposed; and on doing so the examiner [or authorised inspector] or authorised person shall forthwith give notice in writing of the removal of the prohibition to the driver of the vehicle.

[(3A) If the prohibition under section 1 of this Act has been imposed with a direction under subsection (6)(*a*) of that section, the prohibition shall not then be removed under subsection (3) above unless and until the vehicle has been inspected at an official testing station.]

[(3B) In the case of vehicles brought to an official testing station for inspection with a view to removal of a prohibition, [section 72(9) of the Road Traffic Act 1988] (fees for inspection) applies.]

(4) In the exercise of his functions under section 1 of this Act or under this section an examiner [or an authorised inspector] shall act in accordance with any general directions given by the Secretary of State; and (without prejudice to the preceding provisions of this subsection) an examiner [or an authorised inspector], in exercising his functions under subsection (2) of this section, shall act in accordance with any directions given by the Secretary of State with respect to the exercise of those functions in any particular case.

[Section 2 is printed as amended by the Transport Act 1978, s 9(1) and Sched 3, para 9; the Transport Act 1982, s 10(4); the Road Traffic (Consequential Provisions) Act 1988, s 4 and Sched 3, para 9(2).

The references to 'authorised inspector' were inserted by the Transport Act 1982, s 10(4), and will take effect from a date to be announced. Also from a date to be announced, the reference in s 2(3B) to s 72(9) of the 1988 Act will be replaced by a reference to s 72(6)(c) and (7); see the Road Traffic (Consequential Provisions) Act 1988, s 4 and Sched 2, para 1.]

3. Enforcement provisions

(1) Any person who—

(*a*) drives a vehicle on a road in contravention of a prohibition imposed under section 1 of this Act, or

(*b*) causes or permits a vehicle to be driven on a road in contravention of such a prohibition, or

(*c*) refuses, neglects or otherwise fails to comply within a reasonable time with a direction given under subsection (4) of that section,

shall be guilty of an offence and shall be liable on summary conviction to a fine not exceeding [level 5 on the standard scale].

(2) . . . .

(3) Where a constable in uniform has reasonable cause to suspect the driver of a vehicle of having committed an offence under subsection (1) of this section, the constable may detain the vehicle, and for that purpose may give a direction, specifying an appropriate person and directing the vehicle to be removed by that person to such place and subject to such conditions as are specified in the direction; and the prohibition shall not apply to the removal of the vehicle in accordance with that direction.

(4) Where under subsection (3) of this section a constable—

(*a*) detains a motor vehicle drawing a trailer, or

(*b*) detains a trailer drawn by a motor vehicle,

then, for the purpose of securing the removal of the trailer, he may also (in a case falling within paragraph (*a*) of this subsection) detain the trailer or (in a case falling within paragraph (*b*) of this subsection) detain the motor vehicle; and a direction under subsection (3) of this section may require both the motor vehicle and the trailer to be removed to the place specified in the direction.

(5) A vehicle which, in accordance with a direction given under subsection (3) of this section, is removed to a place specified in the direction shall be detained in that place, or in any other place to which it is removed in accordance with a further direction given under that subsection, until a constable (or, if that place is in the occupation of the Secretary of State, the Secretary of State) authorises the vehicle to be released on being satisfied—

(*a*) that the prohibition (if any) imposed in respect of the vehicle under section 1 of this Act has been removed, or that no such prohibition was imposed, or

(*b*) that appropriate arrangements have been made for removing or remedying the circumstances in consequence of which any such prohibition was imposed, or

(*c*) that the vehicle will be taken forthwith to a place from which it will be taken out of Great Britain, or

(*d*) in the case of a vehicle detained under subsection (4) of this section, that (in the case of a motor vehicle) the purpose for which it was detained has been fulfilled or (in the case of a trailer) it is no longer necessary to detain it for the purpose of safeguarding the trailer or its load.

(6) Any person who—

(*a*) drives a vehicle in accordance with a direction given under this section, or (*b*) is in charge of a place at which a vehicle is detained under subsection (5) of this section,

shall not be liable for any damage to, or loss in respect of, the vehicle or its load unless it is shown that he did not take reasonable care of the vehicle while driving it or, as the case may be, did not, while the vehicle was detained in that place, take reasonable care of the vehicle or (if the vehicle was detained there with its load) did not take reasonable care of its load.

(7) In this section 'appropriate person'—

(*a*) in relation to a direction to remove a motor vehicle, other than a motor vehicle drawing a trailer, means a person licensed to drive vehicles of the class to which the vehicle belongs, and

(*b*) in relation to a direction to remove a trailer, or to remove a motor vehicle drawing a trailer, means a person licensed to drive vehicles of a class which, when the direction is complied with, will include the motor vehicle drawing the trailer in accordance with that direction.

[Section 3 is printed as amended by the Criminal Justice Act 1982, ss 37, 39(2), 46, and Sched 3; the Police and Criminal Evidence Act 1984, s 119(2) and Sched 7.]

4. Production of certain documents

(1) Subsection (3) of this section shall have effect in relation to a vehicle where it appears to an examiner that the vehicle—

(*a*) is a foreign goods vehicle within the meaning of regulations for the time being in force under section 91(4) of the Transport Act 1968 (which enables certain provisions of that Act to be modified in their application to vehicles brought temporarily into Great Britain), and

(*b*) is being used, or has been brought into Great Britain for the purpose of being used, in such circumstances as, by virtue of section 60(1) of that Act as modified by the regulations, to require a document of a description specified in the regulations to be carried on it.

(2) The next following subsection shall also have effect in relation to a vehicle where it appears to an examiner that the vehicle—

(*a*) is a foreign public service vehicle, and

(*b*) is being used, or has been brought into Great Britain for the purpose of being used, in such circumstances as, by virtue of [section 12(1) of the Public Passenger Vehicles Act 1981 as modified by regulations for the time being in force under section 60(1)(*m*) of that Act] (which enables certain provisions of that Act to be modified in their application to public service vehicles [registered outside Great Britain]), to require a document of a description specified in the regulations to be carried on it.

(3) In the circumstances mentioned in subsection (1) or subsection (2) of this section, the examiner, on production if so required of his authority,—

(*a*) may require the driver of the vehicle to produce a document of the description in question and to permit the examiner to inspect and copy it, and

(*b*) may detain the vehicle for such time as is requisite for the purpose of inspecting and copying the document;

and, if the driver refuses or fails to comply with any such requirement (including any case where he does so by reason that no such document is carried on the vehicle), the examiner may prohibit the driving of the vehicle on a road, either absolutely or for a specified purpose, and either for a specified period or without limitation of time.

(4) In subsections (4) and (5) of section 1 and in section 2 and 3 of this Act any reference to a prohibition imposed under section 1, or under subsection (2) of section 1, of this Act shall be construed as including a reference to a prohibition imposed under this section; and, in relation to a prohibition imposed under this section, so much of section 1(5) or of section 2(3) of this Act as relates to the circumstances in consequence of which the prohibition was imposed shall be read subject to the appropriate modifications.

[Section 4 is printed as amended by the Transport Act 1980, s 43(1) and Sched 5, Part II; the Public Passenger Vehicles Act 1981, s 88(2) and Sched 7, para 16.]

5, 6. *[Repealed.]*

7. Interpretation and transitional provisions

(1) In this Act, except in so far as the context otherwise requires, the following expressions have the meanings hereby assigned to them respectively, that is to say—

'authorised person' means a person (whether an examiner or not) authorised to exercise the powers of [section 78 of the Road Traffic Act 1988] with respect to the weighing of motor vehicles and trailers;

'driver'—

(*a*) in relation to a motor vehicle, includes any person who is in charge of the vehicle and, if a separate person acts as steersman, includes that person as well as any other person in charge of the vehicle or engaged in the driving of it, and

(*b*) in relation to a trailer, means any person who (in accordance with the preceding paragraph) is the driver of the motor vehicle by which the trailer is drawn;

'examiner' means [a certifying officer appointed under section 7(1) or an examiner appointed under section 7(2) of the Public Passenger Vehicles Act 1981] or an examiner appointed under [section 68(1) of the Road Traffic Act 1988];

'foreign goods vehicle' (except in section 4 of this Act) means a goods vehicle which has been brought into Great Britain and which, if a motor vehicle, is not registered in the United Kingdom or, if a trailer, is drawn by a motor vehicle not registered in the United Kingdom which has been brought into Great Britain;

'foreign public service vehicle' means a public service vehicle which has been brought into Great Britain and is not registered in the United Kingdom;

'goods vehicle' means a motor vehicle constructed or adapted for use for the carriage or haulage of goods or burden of any description, or a trailer so constructed or adapted;

['official testing station' means a station maintained by the Secretary of State under [section 72(8) of the Road Traffic Act 1988] [or premises designated by him under section 10(12) of the Transport Act 1982];]

'public service vehicle' shall be construed in accordance with [the Public Passenger Vehicles Act 1981];

'road' means any highway and any other road to which the public has access, and includes bridges over which a road passes.

[(1A) References in any provision of this Act to an authorised inspector are references to a person authorised by the Secretary of State under section 8 of the Transport Act 1982 to exercise the function to which that provision relates.]

(2) In this Act any reference to driving a vehicle shall, in relation to a trailer, be construed as a reference to driving the motor vehicle by which the trailer is drawn.

(3) In this Act any reference to a motor vehicle drawing a trailer, or to a motor vehicle by which a trailer is drawn, shall be construed as a reference to a motor vehicle to which a trailer is attached for the purpose of being drawn by it; and where, for the purpose of being drawn by a motor vehicle, two or more trailers (one of which is attached to the motor vehicle) are attached to each other, the motor vehicle shall for the purposes of this Act be treated as drawing each of those trailers.

(4) For the purposes of this Act a motor vehicle which does not for the time being have exhibited on it a licence or trade plates issued—

(*a*) under the Vehicle (Excise) Act 1971 or under an enactment repealed by that Act, or

(*b*) under the Vehicle (Excise) Act (Northern Ireland) 1954 or under any Act of the Parliament of Northern Ireland repealing that Act and re-enacting it with or without modifications,

shall be presumed, unless the contrary is proved, not to be registered in the United Kingdom.

(5) Where, in accordance with subsection (4) of this section, motor vehicle is presumed not to be registered in the United Kingdom, but is subsequently proved to have been so registered, anything which—

(*a*) has been done in relation to the vehicle, or in relation to a trailer drawn by it, by a person relying in good faith on that presumption and purporting to act by virtue of any provision of this Act, and

(*b*) would have been lawfully done by virtue of that provision if the vehicle had not been registered in the United Kingdom,

shall be treated as having been lawfully done by virtue of that provision.

(6) Any reference in any provision of this Act to regulations made under an enactment specified in that provision shall be construed as including a reference to any regulations which, by virtue of that or any other enactment, have effect, or are to be treated, as if made under the enactment so specified.

(7) . . . .

[Section 7 is printed as amended by the Road Traffic Act 1974, s 24(3) and Sched 7; the Transport Act 1978, s 9(1) and Sched 3, para 10; the Transport Act 1980, s 13(1) and Sched 5, Part II; the Public Passenger Vehicles Act 1981, s 88(2) and Sched 7, para 17; the Transport Act 1982, s 74(1) and Sched 5, para 17(2); the Road Traffic (Consequential Provisions) Act 1988, s 4 and Sched 3, para 9(3).

The reference in the definition of 'official testing station' to premises designated under s 10(2) of the Transport Act 1982 and sub-s (1A) above were inserted by s 74(1) and Sched 5, para 17(2), with effect from a date to be announced.]

8. Short title, commencement and extent *[Omitted.]*

SCHEDULE 1

Section 1.

[PROVISIONS] CONFERRING FUNCTIONS ON EXAMINERS

Provisions	*Function conferred*
[Section 128(3) of the Public Passenger Vehicles Act 1981.]	To enter and inspect public service vehicles.
[Section 99 of the Transport Act 1968.]	[To inspect and copy record sheets, books, registers and other documents required to be carried on goods vehicles and public service vehicles, to inspect recording equipment and to inspect and copy record sheets on which records have been produced by such equipment or entries have been made.]
[Section 67 of the Road Traffic Act 1988.]	To test the condition of motor vehicles on roads.
[Section 68 of the Road Traffic Act 1988.]	To inspect goods vehicles to secure proper maintenance.
[Regulation 19 of the Road Transport (International Passenger Services) Regulations 1984.]	[To impose penalties for contravention of certain requirements relating to international passenger services.]

[Schedule 1 is printed as amended by the Passenger and Goods Vehicles (Recording Equipment) Regulations 1979 (SI 1979 No 1746), reg 3; the Transport Act 1980, s 43(1) and Sched 5, Part II; the Public Passenger Vehicles Act 1981, s 88(2) and Sched 7, para 18; the Road Transport (International Passenger Services) Regulations 1984 (SI 1984 No 748), reg 22; the Road Traffic (Consequential Provisions) Act 1988, s 4 and Sched 3, para 9(4).]

SCHEDULE 2

Section 1.

PROVISIONS RELATING TO VEHICLE AND THEIR DRIVERS

Provisions	*Effect*
Section 60 of the Transport Act 1968.	To require users of certain goods vehicles to hold operators' licences unless exempted from doing so.
Regulations under section 91(1)(*c*) of the Transport Act 1968.	To require goods vehicles to be identified by plates, marks etc.
Sections 96 to 98 of the Transport Act 1968 and regulations and orders made under those sections [and [the applicable Community rules] within the meaning of Part VI of that Act].	To limit driving time and periods of duty of drivers of goods and public service vehicles and to require the installation of recording equipment in, and the keeping of records on, such vehicles.
Any order under section 100 of the Transport Act 1968.	To give effect to international agreements relating to vehicles used on international journeys.
[Regulations under section 41 of the Road Traffic Act 1988.]	To regulate the construction, weight, equipment and use of motor vehicles and trailers on roads.

Provisions	*Effect*
Sections 68 to 73 and 76 to 79 of the Road Traffic Act 1972 and regulations made under those sections.	*To require vehicles to carry front and rear lamps, headlamps and reflectors, to regulate their position, character and use and to make special provision for vehicles carrying overhanging or projecting loads and vehicles towing and being towed.*
[Regulation 19 of the Road \Transport (International Passenger Services) Regulations 1984.]	[To impose penalties for contravention of certain requirements relating to international passenger services.]

[Schedule 2 is printed as amended by the European Communities Act 1972, s 4(1) and Sched 4, para 9(4); the Road Traffic (Drivers' Ages and Hours of Work) Act 1976, s 2(3); the Road Transport (International Passenger Services) Regulations 1984 (SI 1984 No 748), reg 22; the Road Traffic (Consequential Provisions) Act 1988, ss 3(1) and 4 and Scheds 1, Part I, and 3, para 9(5).

The words printed in italic have lapsed.]

The Road Traffic Offenders Act 1988

(1988 c 53)

An Act to consolidate certain enactments relating to the prosecution and punishment (including the punishment without conviction) of road traffic offences with amendments to give effect to recommendations of the Law Commission and the Scottish Law Commission.

[15th November 1988]

ARRANGEMENT OF SECTIONS

PART I

TRIAL

Introductory

Verdict

. . . .

24. Alternative verdicts in England and Wales

After conviction

25. Information as to date of birth and sex
26. Interim disqualification on committal for sentence in England and Wales

PART II

SENTENCE

Introductory

27. Production of licence
28. Penalty points to be attributed to an offence
29. Penalty points to be taken into account on conviction
30. Penalty points: modification where fixed penalty also in question
31. Court may take particulars endorsed on licence into consideration

. . . .

Fine and imprisonment

33. Fine and imprisonment

Disqualification

34. Disqualification for certain offences
35. Disqualification for repeated offences
36. Disqualification until test is passed
37. Effect of order of disqualification
38. Appeal against disqualification
39. Suspension of disqualification pending appeal
40. Power of appellate courts in England and Wales to suspend disqualification

. . . .

42. Removal of disqualification
43. Rule for determining end of period of disqualification

Endorsement

44. Endorsement of licences
45. Effect of endorsement

General

46. Combination of disqualification and endorsement with probation orders and orders for discharge
47. Supplementary provisions as to disqualifications and endorsements
48. Exemption from disqualification and endorsement for offences against construction and use regulations
49. Offender escaping consequences of endorseable offence by deception

. . . .

PART III

Fixed Penalties

Introductory

51. Fixed penalty offences
52. Fixed penalty notices
53. Amount of fixed penalty

Giving notices to suspected offenders

54. Notices on-the-spot or at a police station
55. Effect of fixed penalty notice given under section 54
56. Licence receipts
57. Endorsement of licences without hearings
58. Effect of endorsement without hearing
59. Notification of court and date of trial in England and Wales

. . . .

61. Fixed penalty notice mistakenly given: exclusion of fixed penalty procedures

Notices fixed to vehicles

62. Fixing notices to vehicles
63. Service of notice to owner if penalty not paid
64. Enforcement or proceedings against owner
65. Restrictions on proceedings against owner and others
66. Hired vehices
67. False statements in response to notices to owner
68. 'Owner', 'statutory statement' and 'official form'

The fixed penalty procedure

69. Payment of penalty
70. Registration certificates
71. Registration of sums payable in default
72. Notices on-the-spot or at a police station: when registration and endorsement invalid
73. Notices fixed to vehicles: when registration invalid
74. Provisions supplementary to sections 72 and 73

Conditional offer of fixed penalty in Scotland

. . . .

Proceedings in fixed penalty cases

78. General restriction on proceedings
79. Statements by constables
80. Certificates about payment
81. Documents signed by the accused

Miscellaneous

82. Accounting for fixed penalties: England and Wales
83. Powers of court where clerk deceived

. . . .

PART IV

MISCELLANEOUS AND GENERAL

SCHEDULES

PART I

TRIAL

Introductory

1. Requirement of warning etc of prosecutions for certain offences

(1) Subject to section 2 of this Act, where a person is prosecuted for an offence to which this section applies, he is not to be convicted unless—

(*a*) he was warned at the time the offence was committed that the question of prosecuting him for some one or other of the offences to which this section applies would be taken into consideration, or

(*b*) within fourteen days of the commission of the offence a summons for the offence was served on him, or

(*c*) within fourteen days of the commission of the offence a notice of the intended prosecution specifying the nature of the alleged offence and the time and place where it is alleged to have been committed, was—

(i) in the case of an offence under section 28 or 29 of the Road Traffic Act 1988 (cycling offences), served on him,

(ii) in the case of any other offence, served on him or on the person, if any, registered as the keeper of the vehicle at the time of the commission of the offence.

(2) A notice shall be deemed for the purposes of subsection (1)(*c*) above to have been served on a person if it was sent by registered post or recorded delivery service addressed to him at his last known address, notwithstanding that the notice was returned as undelivered or was for any other reason not received by him.

(3) The requirement of subsection (1) above shall in every case be deemed to have been complied with unless and until the contrary is proved.

(4) Schedule 1 to this Act shows the offences to which this section applies.

[Words in s 1(1)(b) relating exclusively and expressly to Scotland have been omitted.]

2. Requirement of warning etc: supplementary

(1) The requirement of section 1(1) of this Act does not apply in relation to an offence if, at the time of the offence or immediately after it, an accident occurs owing to the presence on a road of the vehicle in respect of which the offence was committed.

(2) The requirement of section 1(1) of this Act does not apply in relation to an offence in respect of which—

(*a*) a fixed penalty notice (within the meaning of Part III of this Act) has been given or fixed under any provision of that Part, or

(*b*) a notice has been given under section 54(4) of this Act.

(3) Failure to comply with the requirement of section 1(1) of this Act is not a bar to the conviction of the accused in a case where the court is satisfied—

(*a*) that neither the name and address of the accused nor the name and address of the registered keeper, if any, could with reasonable diligence have been ascertained in time for a summons or, as the case may be, a complaint to be served or for a notice to be served or sent in compliance with the requirement, or

(*b*) that the accused by his own conduct contributed to the failure.

(4) Where a person is prosecuted on indictment in England and Wales—

(*a*) for an offence to which section 1 of this Act does not apply, or

(*b*) for an offence to which that section does apply, but as respects which the requirement of subsection (1) of that section has been satisfied,

that subsection does not prejudice any power of the jury on the charge for that offence, if they find him not guilty of it, to find him guilty of an offence under section 2 or 3 of the Road Traffic Act 1988 (reckless driving or careless or inconsiderate driving).

(5) *[Applies to Scotland.]*

(6) A person may be convicted of an offence under section 3 or 29 of that Act (careless and inconsiderate driving or careless and inconsiderate cycling) notwithstanding that the requirement of section 1(1) of this Act has not been satisfied as respects that offence where—

(*a*) the charge for the offence has been preferred against him by virtue of section 24(3) of this Act, and

(*b*) that requirement has been satisfied as respects the alleged offence under section 2 or, as the case may be, 28 of that Act (reckless driving or reckless cycling).

3. Restriction on institution of proceedings for certain offences

(1) Proceedings for an offence under section 110 or 112(6) of the Road Traffic Act 1988 (driving, or causing or permitting another to drive, an HGV without an HGV driver's licence, or failing to comply with conditions of such a licence) shall not be instituted in England and Wales except—

(*a*) by or on behalf of the Director of Public Prosecutions, or

(*b*) by a person authorised in that behalf by a traffic commissioner (within the meaning of the Public Passenger Vehicles Act 1981), a chief officer of police or the council of a county or county district.

(2) In England and Wales, proceedings for an offence under section 94(3) of the Road Traffic Act 1988 (notice about relevant or prospective disability) shall not be instituted except by the Secretary of State or by a constable acting with the approval of the Secretary of State.

4. Offences for which local authorities in England and Wales may institute proceedings

(1) The council of a county, metropolitan district or London Borough or the Common Council of the City of London may institute proceedings for an offence under section 17 or 18 of the Road Traffic Act 1988 (helmets and other head-worn appliances for motor cyclists).

(2) The council of a county, metropolitan district or London Borough or the Common Council of the City of London may institute proceedings for an offence under section 27 of that Act (dogs on roads) relating to a road in their area.

(3) The council of a county, district or London borough or the Common Council of the City of London may institute proceedings for offences under section 35(4), (5) or (7) of the Road Traffic Regulation Act 1984 which are committed in connection with parking places provided by the council, or provided under any letting arrangements made by the council under section 33(4) of that Act.

(4) The council of a county, metropolitan district or London borough or the Common Council of the City of London may institute proceedings for an offence under section 47 or 52 of the Road Traffic Regulation Act 1984 in connection with a designated parking place controlled by the council.

(5) In England, the council of a county or metropolitan district and, in Wales, the council of a county or district may institute proceedings for an offence under section 53 of the Road Traffic Regulation Act 1984 in connection with a designated parking place in the council's area except, in Wales, any parking place for which another council has responsibility

(6) In this section 'parking place' means a place where vehicles, or vehicles of any class, may wait and 'designated parking place' has the same meaning as in the Road Traffic Regulation Act 1984.

(7) This section extends to England and Wales only.

[*The term 'designated parking place' is defined in the Road Traffic Regulation Act 1984, s 142(1), qv*]

5. Exemption from Licensing Act offence

A person liable to be charged with an offence under section 4, 5, 7 or 30 of the Road Traffic Act 1988 (drink and drugs) is not liable to be charged under section 12 of the Licensing Act 1872 with the offence of being drunk while in charge, on a highway or other public place, of a carriage.

6. Time within which summary proceedings for certain offences must be commenced

(1) Subject to subsection (2) below, summary proceedings for an offence to which this section applies may be brought within a period of six months from the date on which evidence sufficient in the opinion of the prosecutor to warrant the proceedings came to his knowledge.

(2) No such proceedings shall be brought by virtue of this section more than three years after the commission of the offence.

(3) For the purposes of this section, a certificate signed by or on behalf of the prosecutor and stating the date on which evidence sufficient in his opinion to warrant the proceedings came to his knowledge shall be conclusive evidence of that fact.

(4) A certificate stating that matter and purporting to be so signed shall be deemed to be so signed unless the contrary is proved.

(5) *[Applies to Scotland.]*

(6) Schedule 1 to this Act shows the offences to which this section applies.

7. Duty of accused to provide licence

A person who is prosecuted for an offence involving obligatory endorsement and who is the holder of a licence must—

(*a*) cause it to be delivered to the clerk of the court not later than the day before the date appointed for the hearing, or

(*b*) post it, at such a time that in the ordinary course of post it would be delivered not later than that day, in a letter duly addressed to the clerk and either registered or sent by the recorded delivery service, or

(*c*) have it with him at the hearing.

[As to the application of s 7 to domestic driving permits, Convention driving permits and British Forces (BFG) driving licences, see the Motor Vehicles (Driving Licences) Regulations 1987 (SI 1987 No 1378), reg 23(3)(b) and (4), below.]

8. Duty to include date of birth and sex in written plea of guilty

A person who—

(*a*) gives a notification to the clerk of a court in pursuance of section 12(2) of the Magistrates' Courts Act 1980 (written pleas of guilty), or

(*b*) *[Applies to Scotland.]*

in respect of an offence involving obligatory or discretionary disqualification or of such other offence as may be prescribed by regulations under section 105 of the Road Traffic Act 1988, must include in the notification or intimation a statement of the date of birth and sex of the accused.

Trial

9. Mode of trial

An offence against a provision of the Traffic Acts specified in column 1 of Part I of Schedule 2 to this Act or regulations made under such a provision (the general nature of which offence is indicated in column 2) shall be punishable as shown against the offence in column 3 (that is, on summary conviction or on indictment or in either one way or the other).

10. Jurisdiction of district court in Scotland *[Omitted.]*

11. Evidence by certificate as to driver, user or owner

(1) In any proceedings in England and Wales for an offence to which this section applies, a certificate in the prescribed form, purporting to be signed by a constable and certifying that a person specified in the certificate stated to the constable—

(*a*) that a particular motor vehicle was being driven or used by, or belonged to, that person on a particular occasion, or

(*b*) that a particular motor vehicle on a particular occasion was used by, or belonged to, a firm and that he was, at the time of the statement, a partner in that firm, or

(*c*) that a particular motor vehicle on a particular occasion was used by, or belonged to, a corporation and that he was, at the time of the statement, a director, officer or employee of that corporation,

shall be admissible as evidence for the purpose of determining by whom the vehicle was being driven or used, or to whom it belonged, as the case may be, on that occasion.

(2) Nothing in subsection (1) above makes a certificate admissible as evidence in proceedings for an offence except in a case where and to the like extent to which oral evidence to the like effect would have been admissible in those proceedings.

(3) Nothing in subsection (1) above makes a certificate admissible as evidence in proceedings for an offence—

(*a*) unless a copy of it has, not less than seven days before the hearing or trial, been served in the prescribed manner on the person charged with the offence, or

(*b*) if that person, not later than three days before the hearing or trial or within such further time as the court may in special circumstances allow, serves a notice in the prescribed form and manner on the prosecutor requiring attendance at the trial of the person who signed the certificate.

(4) In this section 'prescribed' means prescribed by rules made by the Secretary of State by statutory instrument.

(5) Schedule 1 to this Act shows the offences to which this section applies.

[The Evidence by Certificate Rules 1961 (SI 1962 No 248) have effect as if made under s 11; see further §2.79 in Vol 1.]

12. Proof, in summary proceedings, of identity of driver of vehicle

(1) Where on the summary trial in England and Wales of an information for an offence to which this subsection applies—

(*a*) it is proved to the satisfaction of the court, on oath or in manner prescribed by rules made under section 144 of the Magistrates' Courts Act 1980, that a requirement under section 172(2) of the Road Traffic Act 1988 [*qv*] to give information as to the identity of the driver of a particular vehicle on the particular occasion to which the information relates has been served on the accused by post, and

(*b*) a statement in writing is produced to the court purporting to be signed by the accused that the accused was the driver of that vehicle on that occasion,

the court may accept that statement as evidence that the accused was the driver of that vehicle on that occasion.

(2) Schedule 1 to this Act shows the offences to which subsection (1) above applies.

(3) Where on the summary trial in England and Wales of an information for an offence to which section 112 of the Road Traffic Regulation Act 1984 [*qv*] applies—

(*a*) it is proved to the satisfaction of the court, on oath or in manner prescribed by rules made under section 144 of the Magistrates' Courts Act 1980, that a requirement under section 112(2) of the Road Traffic Regulation Act 1984 to give information as to the identity of the driver of a particular vehicle on the particular occasion to which the information relates has been served on the accused by post, and

(*b*) a statement in writing is produced to the court purporting to be signed by the accused that the accused was the driver of that vehicle on that occasion,

the court may accept that statement as evidence that the accused was the driver of that vehicle on that occasion.

13. Admissibility of records as evidence

(1) This section applies to a statement contained in a document purporting to be—

(*a*) a part of the records maintained by the Secretary of State in connection with any functions exercisable by him by virtue of Part III of the Road Traffic Act 1988 or a part of any other records maintained by the Secretary of State with respect to vehicles [or of any records maintained with respect to vehicles by an approved testing authority in connection with the exercise by that authority of any functions conferred on such authorities, or on that authority as such an authority, by or under any enactment], or

(*b*) a copy of a document forming part of those records, or

(*c*) a note of any information contained in those records,

and to be authenticated by a person authorised in that behalf by the Secretary of State [or (as the case may be) the approved testing authority].

(2) A statement to which this section applies shall be admissible in any proceedings as evidence of any fact stated in it to the same extent as oral evidence of that fact is admissible in those proceedings.

(3) In the preceding subsections—

(*a*) 'document' and 'statement' have the same meanings as in section 10(1) of the Civil Evidence Act 1968 [*qv*], and

(*b*) the reference to a copy of a document shall be construed in accordance with section 10(2) of the Civil Evidence Act 1968 [*qv*].

Nothing in this subsection shall be construed as limiting to civil proceedings the references to proceedings in the preceding provisions of this section.

(4) In any case where—

(*a*) a statement to which this section applies is produced to a magistrates' court in any proceedings for an offence involving obligatory or discretionary disqualification,

(*b*) the statement specifies an alleged previous conviction of an accused person of any such offence or any order made on the conviction,

(*c*) it is proved to the satisfaction of the court, on oath or in such manner as may be prescribed by rules under section 144 of the Magistrates' Courts Act 1980, that not less than seven days before the statement is so produced a notice was served on the accused, in such form and manner as may be so prescribed, specifying the previous conviction or order and stating that it is proposed to bring it to the notice of the court in the event of or, as the case may be, in view of his conviction, and

(*d*) the accused is not present in person before the court when the statement is so produced,

the court may take account of the previous conviction or order as if the accused had appeared and admitted it.

(5) Nothing in the preceding provisions of this section enables evidence to be given in respect of any matter other than a matter of a description prescribed by regulations made by the Secretary of State.

(6) *[Regulation-making power.]*

[Section 13 is printed as prospectively amended by the Road Traffic (Consequential Provisions) Act 1988, s 4 and Sched 2, Part I, para 20. The words printed within square brackets will come into force on a date to be announced; see ibid, s 8(3), above.

Words in s 13(2) and (3) which relate exclusively and expressly to Scotland have been omitted.

As to the application of s 13 to records maintained for the purposes of the Motor Vehicles (International Circulation) Order 1975 (SI 1975 No 1208), art 1 (qv), see the Motor Vehicles (International Circulation) (Amendment) Order 1980 (SI 1980 No 1095), art 8(2), below.]

14. Use of records kept by operators of goods vehicles

In any proceedings for a contravention of or failure to comply with construction and use requirements (within the meaning of Part II of the Road Traffic Act 1988) or regulations under section 74 of that Act [*qv*], any record purporting to be made and authenticated in accordance with regulations under that section shall be evidence of the matters stated in the record and of its due authentication.

[Words in s 14 which relate exclusively and expressly to Scotland have been omitted.

As to the meaning of the term 'construction and use requirements' in Part II of the Road Traffic Act 1988, see ibid, s 41(7), above.]

15. Use of specimens in proceedings for an offence under section 4 or 5 of the Road Traffic Act

(1) This section and section 16 of this Act apply in respect of proceedings for an offence under section 4 or 5 of the Road Traffic Act 1988 (motor vehicles: drink and drugs) [*qv*]; and expressions used in this section and section 16 of this Act have the same meaning as in sections 4 to 10 of that Act.

(2) Evidence of the proportion of alcohol or any drug in a specimen of breath, blood or urine provided by the accused shall, in all cases, be taken into account and, subject to subsection (3) below, it shall be assumed that the proportion of alcohol in the accused's breath, blood or urine at the time of the alleged offence was not less than in the specimen.

(3) If the proceedings are for an offence under section 5 of that Act or, where the accused is alleged to have been unfit through drink, for an offence under section 4 of that Act, that assumption shall not be made if the accused proves—

(*a*) that he consumed alcohol after he had ceased to drive, attempt to drive or be in charge of a motor vehicle on a road or other public place and before he provided the specimen, and

(*b*) that had he not done so the proportion of alcohol in his breath, blood or urine would not have exceeded the prescribed limit and, if the proceedings are for an offence under section 4 of that Act, would not have been such as to impair his ability to drive properly.

(4) A specimen of blood shall be disregarded unless it was taken from the accused with his consent by a medical practitioner.

(5) Where, at the time a specimen of blood or urine was provided by the accused, he asked to be provided with such a specimen, evidence of the proportion of alcohol or any drug found in the specimen is not admissible on behalf of the prosecution unless—

(*a*) the specimen in which the alcohol or drug was found is one of two parts into which the specimen provided by the accused was divided at the time it was provided, and

(*b*) the other part was supplied to the accused.

16. Documentary evidence as to specimens in such proceedings

(1) Evidence of the proportion of alcohol or a drug in a specimen of breath, blood or urine may, subject to subsections (3) and (4) below and to section 15(5) of this Act, be given by the production of a document or documents purporting to be whichever of the following is appropriate, that is to say—

(*a*) a statement automatically produced by the device by which the proportion of alcohol in a specimen of breath was measured and a certificate signed by a constable (which may but need not be contained in the same document as the statement) that the statement relates to a specimen provided by the accused at the date and time shown in the statement, and

(*b*) a certificate signed by an authorised analyst as to the proportion of alcohol or any drug found in a specimen of blood or urine identified in the certificate.

(2) Subject to subsections (3) and (4) below, evidence that a specimen of blood was taken from the accused with his consent by a medical practitioner may be given by the production of a document purporting to certify that fact and to be signed by a medical practitioner.

(3) Subject to subsection (4) below—

(*a*) a document purporting to be such a statement or such a certificate (or both such a statement and such a certificate) as is mentioned in subsection (1)(*a*) above is admissible in evidence on behalf of the prosecution in pursuance of this section only if a copy of it either has been handed to the accused when the document was produced or has been served on him not later than seven days before the hearing, and

(*b*) any other document is so admissible only if a copy of it has been served on the accused not later than seven days before the hearing.

(4) A document purporting to be a certificate (or so much of a document as purports to be a certificate) is not so admissible if the accused, not later than three days

before the hearing or within such further time as the court may in special circumstances allow, has served notice on the prosecutor requiring the attendance at the hearing of the person by whom the document purports to be signed.

(5) *[Applies to Scotland.]*

(6) A copy of a certificate required by this section to be served on the accused or a notice required by this section to be served on the prosecutor may be served personally or sent by registered post or recorded delivery service.

(7) In this section 'authorised analyst' means—

(*a*) any person possessing the qualifications prescribed by regulations made under section 76 of the Food Act 1984 or section 27 of the Food and Drugs (Scotland) Act 1956 as qualifying persons for appointment as public analysts under those Acts, and

(*b*) any other person authorised by the Secretary of State to make analyses for the purposes of this section.

17. Provisions as to proceedings for certain offences in connection with the construction and use of vehicles and equipment

(1) If in any proceedings for an offence under section 42(1) of the Road Traffic Act 1988 (contravention of construction and use regulations) [*qv*]—

(*a*) any question arises as to weight of any description specified in the plating certificate for a goods vehicle, and

(*b*) a weight of that description is marked on the vehicle,

it shall be assumed, unless the contrary is proved, that the weight marked on the vehicle is the weight so specified.

(2) If, in any proceedings for an offence—

(*a*) under Part II of the Road Traffic Act 1988, except sections 47 and 75, or

(*b*) under section 174(2) or (5) (false statement and deception) of that Act,

any question arises as to the date of manufacture of a vehicle, a date purporting to be such a date and marked on the vehicle in pursuance of regulations under that Part of that Act shall be evidence that the vehicle was manufactured on the date so marked.

(3) If in any proceedings for the offence of driving a goods vehicle on a road, or causing or permitting a goods vehicle to be so driven, in contravention of a prohibition under section 70(2) of the Road Traffic Act 1988 any question arises whether a weight of any description has been reduced to a limit imposed by construction and use requirements, the burden of proof shall lie on the accused.

(4) *[Applies to Scotland.]*

[Words in s 17(2) relating exclusively and expressly to Scotland have been omitted.]

18. Evidence by certificate as to registration of driving instructors and licences to give instruction

(1) A certificate signed by the Registrar and stating that, on any date—

(*a*) a person's name was, or was not, in the register,

(*b*) the entry of a person's name was made in the register or a person's name was removed from it,

(*c*) a person was, or was not, the holder of a current licence under section 129 of the Road Traffic Act 1988 [*qv*], or (*d*) a licence under that section granted to a person came into force or ceased to be in force,

shall be evidence of the facts stated in the certificate in pursuance of this section.

(2) A certificate so stating and purporting to be signed by the Registrar shall be deemed to be so signed unless the contrary is proved.

(3) In this section 'current licence', 'Registrar' and 'register' have the same meanings as in Part V of the Road Traffic Act 1988.

19. Evidence of disqualification in Scotland *[Omitted.]*

20. Admissibility of measurement of speed by radar

On the prosecution of a person for any speeding offence, evidence of the measurement of any speed by a device designed or adapted for measuring by radar the speed of motor vehicles shall not be admissible unless the device is of a type approved by the Secretary of State.

[The following radar speed measuring devices have been approved by the Home Secretary (the Radar Speed Devices Approval dated 1 July 1986):

'Kustom HR 4'

'Kustom HR 8'

'MPH K 15'

'Muniquip T 3'

'Gatso Mini Radar MK 3', and

'Gatso Mini Radar MK 4'.*]*

21. Proceedings in which evidence of one witness sufficient in Scotland

[Omitted.]

22. Notification of disability

(1) If in any proceedings for an offence committed in respect of a motor vehicle it appears to the court that the accused may be suffering from any relevant disability or prospective disability (within the meaning of Part III of the Road Traffic Act 1988) the court must notify the Secretary of State.

(2) A notice sent by a court to the Secretary of State in pursuance of this section must be sent in such manner and to such address and contain such particulars as the Secretary of State may determine.

[As to the meaning of the terms 'relevant disability' and 'prospective disability' in Part III of the Road Traffic Act 1988, see ibid, s 92(2), above.]

Verdict

23. Alternative verdicts in Scotland *[Omitted.]*

24. Alternative verdicts in England and Wales

(1) Where on a person's trial on indictment in England and Wales for an offence under section 1 (causing death by reckless driving), 2 (reckless driving) or 28 (reckless cycling) of the Road Traffic Act 1988 [*qv*] the jury find him not guilty of the offence specifically charged in the indictment, they may (without prejudice to section 6(3) of the Criminal Law Act 1967) find him guilty—

(*a*) where the offence so charged is an offence under section 1 or 2 of the Road Traffic Act 1988, of an offence under section 3 (careless and inconsiderate driving) of that Act, or

(*b*) where the offence so charged is an offence under section 28 of that Act, of an offence under section 29 (careless and inconsiderate cycling) of that Act.

(2) The Crown Court has the like powers and duties in the case of a person who is by virtue of subsection (1) above convicted before it of an offence under section 3 or 29 of that Act as a magistrates' court would have had on convicting him of that offence.

(3) Where—

(*a*) a person is charged in England and Wales before a magistrates' court with an offence under section 2 or 28 of that Act, and

(*b*) the court is of the opinion that the offence is not proved,

then, at any time during the hearing or immediately after it the court may (without prejudice to any other powers possessed by the court) direct or allow a charge for an offence under section 3 or, as the case may be, section 29 of that Act to be preferred forthwith against the defendant and may thereupon proceed with that charge.

(4) Where a magistrates' court exercises the power conferred by subsection (3) above—

(*a*) the defendant or his solicitor or counsel must be informed of the new charge and be given an opportunity, whether by way of cross-examining any witness whose evidence has already been given against the defendant or otherwise, of answering the new charge, and

(*b*) the court must, if it considers that the defendant is prejudiced in his defence by reason of the new charge's being so preferred, adjourn the hearing.

After conviction

25. Information as to date of birth and sex

(1) If on convicting a person of an offence involving obligatory or discretionary disqualification or of such other offence as may be prescribed by regulations under section 105 of the Road Traffic Act 1988 the court does not know his date of birth, the court must order him to give that date to the court in writing.

(2) If a court convicting a person of such an offence in a case where—

(*a*) notification has been given to the clerk of a court in pursuance of section 12(2) of the Magistrates' Courts Act 1980 (written pleas of guilty), and

(*b*) the notification or intimation did not include a statement of the person's sex,

does not know the person's sex, the court must order the person to give that information to the court in writing.

(3) A person who knowingly fails to comply with an order under subsection (1) or (2) above is guilty of an offence.

(4) Nothing in section 56(5) of the Criminal Justice Act 1967 (where magistrates' court commits a person to the Crown Court to be dealt with, certain powers and duties transferred to that court) applies to any duty imposed upon a magistrates' court by subsection (1) or (2) above.

(5) Where a person has given his date of birth in accordance with this section or section 8 of this Act, the Secretary of State may serve on that person a notice in writing requiring him to provide the Secretary of State—

(*a*) with such evidence in that person's possession or obtainable by him as the Secretary of State may specify for the purpose of verifying that date, and

(*b*) if his name differs from his name at the time of his birth, with a statement in writing specifying his name at that time.

(6) A person who knowingly fails to comply with a notice under subsection (5) above is guilty of an offence.

(7) A notice to be served on any person under subsection (5) above may be served on him by delivering it to him or by leaving it at his proper address or by sending it to him by post; and for the purposes of this subsection and section 7 of the Interpretation Act 1978 in its application to this subsection the proper address of any person shall be his latest address as known to the person serving the notice.

[Words in s 25(2) relating exclusively and expressly to Scotland have been omitted.]

26. Interim disqualification on committal for sentence in England and Wales

(1) Where a magistrates' court—

(*a*) commits an offender to the Crown Court under subsection (1) of section 56 of the Criminal Justice Act 1967 or any enactment to which that section applies, and

(*b*) by reason of the provisions of that section the magistrates' court does not exercise its power or discharge its duty under section 34, 35 or 36 of this Act of ordering the offender to be disqualified,

it may nevertheless order him to be disqualified until the court to which he is committed has dealt with him in respect of the offence.

(2) Where a court makes an order under subsection (1) above in respect of any person, it must require him to produce to the court any licence held by him and must cause such licence to be sent to the clerk of the court to which he is committed.

(3) A person who fails to comply with a requirement under subsection (2) above is guilty of an offence.

(4) Subsection (3) above does not apply to a person who—

(*a*) surrenders to the court a current receipt for his licence issued under section 56 of this Act, and

(*b*) produces the licence to the court immediately on its return.

(5) Where a court makes an order under subsection (1) above in respect of any person, sections 44(1) and 47(2) of this Act and section 109(3) of the Road Traffic Act 1988 (Northern Ireland drivers' licences) shall not apply in relation to the order, but—

(*a*) the court must send notice of the order to the Secretary of State, and

(*b*) the court to which he is committed must, if it determines not to order him to be disqualified under section 34, 35 or 36 of this Act, send notice of the determination to the Secretary of State.

(6) A period of disqualification imposed on any person by virtue of section 56(5) of the Criminal Justice Act 1967 (exercise by Crown Court on committal for sentence of certain powers of magistrates' courts) shall be treated as reduced by any period during which he was disqualified by reason only of an order made under subsection (1) above; but a period during which he was so disqualified shall not be taken into account under this subsection for the purpose of reducing more than one other period of disqualification.

(7) A notice sent by a court to the Secretary of State in pursuance of subsection (5) above must be sent in such manner and to such address and contain such particulars as the Secretary of State may determine.

PART II

SENTENCE

Introductory

27. Production of licence

(1) Where a person who is the holder of a licence is convicted of an offence involving obligatory endorsement, the court must, before making any order under section 44 of this Act, require the licence to be produced to it.

(2) Where a magistrates' court—

(*a*) commits a person who is the holder of a licence to the Crown Court, under section 56 of the Criminal Justice Act 1967 or any enactment to which that section applies, to be dealt with in respect of an offence involving obligatory endorsement, and

(*b*) does not make an order in his case under section 26(1) of this Act,

the Crown Court must require the licence to be produced to it.

(3) If the holder of the licence has not caused it to be delivered, or posted it, in accordance with section 7 of this Act and does not produce it as required then, unless he satisfies the court that he has applied for a new licence and has not received it—

(*a*) he is guilty of an offence, and

(*b*) the licence shall be suspended from the time when its production was required until it is produced to the court and shall, while suspended, be of no effect.

(4) Subsection (3) above does not apply where the holder of the licence—

(*a*) has caused a current receipt for the licence issued under section 56 of this Act to be delivered to the clerk of the court not later than the day before the date appointed for the hearing, or

(*b*) has posted such a receipt, at such time that in the ordinary course of post it would be delivered not later than that day, in a letter duly addressed to the clerk and either registered or sent by the recorded delivery service, or

(*c*) surrenders such a receipt to the court at the hearing,

and produces the licence to the court immediately on its return.

28. Penalty points to be attributed to an offence

(1) Where a person is convicted of an offence involving obligatory or discretionary disqualification, the number of penalty points to be attributed to the offence, subject to subsection (2) below, is—

(*a*) in the case of an offence under a provision of the Traffic Acts specified in column 1 of Part I of Schedule 2 to this Act or an offence specified in column 1 of Part II of that Schedule, the number shown against the provision or offence in the last column or, where a range of numbers is so shown, a number falling within the range, and

(*b*) in the case of an offence committed by aiding, abetting, counselling or procuring, or inciting to the commission of, an offence involving obligatory disqualification, ten penalty points.

(2) Where a person is convicted of two or more such offences, the number of penalty points to be attributed to those of them that were committed on the same occasion is the number or highest number that would be attributed on a conviction of one of them.

(3) *[Power to vary penalty points by order.]*

29. Penalty points to be taken into account on conviction

(1) Where a person is convicted of an offence involving obligatory or discretionary disqualification, the penalty points to be taken into account on that occasion are (subject to subsection (2) below)—

(*a*) any that are to be attributed to the offence or offences of which he is convicted, and

(*b*) any that were on a previous occasion ordered to be endorsed on any licence held by him, unless the offender has since that occasion and before the conviction been disqualified under section 34 or 35 of this Act.

(2) If any of the offences was committed more than three years before another, the penalty points in respect of that offence shall not be added to those in respect of the other.

[As to orders for endorsement made before 1 November 1982 (the date on which the Transport Act 1981, s 19, was brought into force by the Transport Act 1981 (Commencement No 7) Order 1982 (SI 1982 No 1451)), see the Road Traffic (Consequential Provisions) Act 1988, s 5 and Sched 4, para 7(3), above.]

30. Penalty points: modification where fixed penalty also in question

(1) Sections 28 and 29 of this Act shall have effect subject to this section in any case where—

(*a*) a person is convicted of an offence involving obligatory or discretionary disqualification, and

(*b*) the court is satisfied that his licence has been or is liable to be endorsed under section 57 or 77 of this Act in respect of an offence (referred to in this section as the 'connected offence') committed on the same occasion as the offence of which he is convicted.

(2) Subject to section 28(2) of this Act, the number of penalty points to be attributed to the offence of which he is convicted is—

(*a*) the number of penalty points to be attributed to that offence under section 28(1) of this Act apart from this section, less

(*b*) the number of penalty points required to be endorsed on his licence under section 57 or 77 of this Act in respect of the connected offence.

(3) For the purposes of subsection (2) above, where a range of numbers is shown in the last column of Part I of Schedule 2 to this Act against the provision of the Traffic Acts under which his offence is committed or punishable or in Part II of that Schedule against the offence of which he is convicted, the number of penalty points referred to in subsection (2)(*a*) above shall be taken to be a number falling within that range determined by the court as the number of penalty points to be attributed to the offence under section 28(1) of this Act apart from this section.

31. Court may take particulars endorsed on licence into consideration

(1) Where a person is convicted of an offence involving obligatory endorsement and his licence is produced to the court—

(*a*) any existing endorsement on his licence is prima facie evidence of the matters endorsed, and

(*b*) the court may, in determining what order to make in pursuance of the conviction, take those matters into consideration.

(2) *[Applies to Scotland.]*

32. In Scotland, court may take extract from licensing records into account

[Omitted.]

Fine and imprisonment

33. Fine and imprisonment

(1) Where a person is convicted of an offence against a provision of the Traffic Acts specified in column 1 of Part I of Schedule 2 to this Act or regulations made under any such provision, the maximum punishment by way of fine or imprisonment which may be imposed on him is that shown in column 4 against the offence and (where appropriate) the circumstances or the mode of trial there specified.

(2) Any reference in column 4 of that Part to a period of years or months is to be construed as a reference to a term of imprisonment of that duration.

Disqualification

34. Disqualification for certain offences

(1) Where a person is convicted of an offence involving obligatory disqualification, the court must order him to be disqualified for such period not less than twelve months as the court thinks fit unless the court for special reasons thinks fit to order him to be disqualified for a shorter period or not to order him to be disqualified.

(2) Where a person is convicted of an offence involving discretionary disqualification, the court may order him to be disqualified for such period as the court thinks fit.

(3) Where a person convicted of an offence under any of the following provisions of the Road Traffic Act 1988, that is—

(*a*) section 4(1) [*qv*] (driving or attempting to drive while unfit),

(*b*) section 5(1)(*a*) [*qv*] (driving or attempting to drive with excess alcohol), and

(*c*) section 7(6) [*qv*] (failing to provide a specimen) where that is an offence involving obligatory disqualification,

has within the ten years immediately preceding the commission of the offence been convicted of any such offence, subsection (1) above shall apply in relation to him as if the reference to twelve months were a reference to three years.

(4) Where a person is convicted of an offence under section 1 of the Road Traffic Act 1988 [*qv*] (causing death by reckless driving), subsection (1) above shall apply in relation to him as if the reference to twelve months were a reference to two years.

(5) The preceding provisions of this section shall apply in relation to a conviction of an offence committed by aiding, abetting, counselling or procuring, or inciting to

the commission of, an offence involving obligatory disqualification as if the offence were an offence involving discretionary disqualification.

(6) This section is subject to section 48 of this Act.

35. Disqualification for repeated offences

(1) Where—

(*a*) a person is convicted of an offence involving obligatory or discretionary disqualification, and

(*b*) the penalty points to be taken into account on that occasion number twelve or more,

the court must order him to be disqualified for not less than the minimum period unless the court is satisfied, having regard to all the circumstances, that there are grounds for mitigating the normal consequences of the conviction and thinks fit to order him to be disqualified for a shorter period or not to order him to be disqualified.

(2) The minimum period referred to in subsection (1) above is—

(*a*) six months if no previous disqualification imposed on the offender is to be taken into account, and

(*b*) one year if one, and two years if more than one, such disqualification is to be taken into account;

and a previous disqualification imposed on an offender is to be taken into account if it was imposed within the three years immediately preceding the commission of the latest offence in respect of which penalty points are taken into account under section 29 of this Act.

(3) Where an offender is convicted on the same occasion of more than one offence involving obligatory or discretionary disqualification—

(*a*) not more than one disqualification shall be imposed on him under subsection (1) above,

(*b*) in determining the period of the disqualification the court must taken into account all the offences, and

(*c*) for the purposes of any appeal any disqualification imposed under subsection (1) above shall be treated as an order made on the conviction of each of the offences.

(4) No account is to be taken under subsection (1) above of any of the following circumstances—

(*a*) any circumstances that are alleged to make the offence or any of the offences not a serious one,

(*b*) hardship, other than exceptional hardship, or

(*c*) any circumstances which, within the three years immediately preceding the conviction, have been taken into account under that subsection in ordering the offender to be disqualified for a shorter period or not ordering him to be disqualified.

(5) References in this section to disqualification do not include a disqualification imposed under section 26 of this Act or section 44 of the Powers of Criminal Courts Act 1973 [*qv*] (disqualification by Crown Court where vehicle used for commission of offence).

(6) *[Applies to Scotland.]*

(7) This section is subject to section 48 of this Act.

36. Disqualification until test is passed

(1) Where a person is convicted of an offence involving obligatory or discretionary disqualification, the court may order him to be disqualified until he passes the test of competence to drive prescribed by virtue of section 89(3) of the Road Traffic Act 1988.

(2) That power is exercisable by the court whether or not the person convicted has previously passed that test and whether or not the court makes an order under section 34 or 35 of this Act.

(3) A disqualification by virtue of an order under subsection (1) above shall be deemed to have expired on production to the Secretary of State of evidence, in such form as may be prescribed by regulations under section 105 of the Road Traffic Act 1988, that the person disqualified has passed that test since the order was made.

(4) On the issue of a licence to a person who stands disqualified by an order under subsection (1) above, there shall be added to the endorsed particulars of the disqualification a statement that the person disqualified has passed that test since the order was made.

(5) This section is subject to section 48 of this Act.

[The reference in s 36(4) to an order under s 36(1) includes a reference to an order made under earlier legislation; see the Road Traffic (Consequential Provisions) Act 1988, s 5 and Sched 4, para 7(4), above.]

37. Effect of order of disqualification

(1) Where the holder of a licence is disqualified by an order of a court, the licence shall be treated as being revoked with effect from the beginning of the period of disqualification.

(2) Where the holder of the licence appeals against the order and the disqualification is suspended under section 39 of this Act, the period of disqualification shall be treated for the purpose of subsection (1) above as beginning on the day on which the disqualification ceases to be suspended.

(3) Notwithstanding anything in Part III of the Road Traffic Act 1988, a person disqualified by an order of a court under section 36(1) of this Act is (unless he is also disqualified otherwise than by virtue of such an order) entitled to obtain and to hold a provisional licence and to drive a motor vehicle in accordance with the conditions subject to which the provisional licence is granted.

[The reference in s 37(3) to an order under s 36(1) includes a reference to an order made under earlier legislation; see the Road Traffic (Consequential Provisions) Act 1988, s 5 and Sched 4, para 4(7), above.]

38. Appeal against disqualification

(1) A person disqualified by an order of a magistrates' court under section 34 or 35 of this Act may appeal against the order in the same manner as against a conviction.

(2) *[Applies to Scotland.]*

39. Suspension of disqualification pending appeal

(1) Any court in England and Wales (whether a magistrates' court or another) which makes an order disqualifying a person may, if it thinks fit, suspend the disqualification pending an appeal against the order.

(2) *[Applies to Scotland.]*

(3) Where a court exercises its power under subsection (1) or (2) above, it must send notice of the suspension to the Secretary of State.

(4) The notice must be sent in such manner and to such address and must contain such particulars as the Secretary of State may determine.

40. Power of appellate courts in England and Wales to suspend disqualification

(1) This section applies where a person has been convicted by or before a court in England and Wales of an offence involving obligatory or discretionary disqualification and has been ordered to be disqualified; and in the following provisions of this section—

(*a*) any reference to a person ordered to be disqualified is to be construed as a reference to a person so convicted and so ordered to be disqualified, and

(*b*) any reference to his sentence includes a reference to the order of disqualification and to any other order made on his conviction and, accordingly, any reference to an appeal against his sentence includes a reference to an appeal against any order forming part of his sentence.

(2) Where a person ordered to be disqualified—

(*a*) appeals to the Crown Court, or

(*b*) appeals or applies for leave to appeal to the Court of Appeal,

against his conviction or his sentence, the Crown Court or, as the case may require, the Court of Appeal may, if it thinks fit, suspend the disqualification.

(3) Where a person ordered to be disqualified has appealed or applied for leave to appeal to the House of Lords—

(*a*) under section 1 of the Administration of Justice Act 1960 from any decision of a Divisional Court of the Queen's Bench Division which is material to his conviction or sentence, or

(*b*) under section 33 of the Criminal Appeal Act 1968 from any decision of the Court of Appeal which is material to his conviction or sentence,

the Divisional Court or, as the case may require, the Court of Appeal may, if it thinks fit, suspend the disqualification.

(4) Where a person ordered to be disqualified makes an application in respect of the decision of the court in question under section 111 of the Magistrates' Courts Act 1980 (statement of case by magistrates' court) or section 28 of the Supreme Court Act 1981 (statement of case by Crown Court) the High Court may, if it thinks fit, suspend the disqualification.

(5) Where a person ordered to be disqualified—

(*a*) applies to the High Court for an order of certiorari to remove into the High Court any proceedings of a magistrates' court or of the Crown Court, being proceedings in or in consequence of which he was convicted or his sentence was passed, or

(*b*) applies to the High Court for leave to make such an application,

the High Court may, if it thinks fit, suspend the disqualification.

(6) Any power of a court under the preceding provisions of this section to suspend the disqualification of any person is a power to do so on such terms as the court thinks fit.

(7) Where, by virtue of this section, a court suspends the disqualification of any person, it must send notice of the suspension to the Secretary of State.

(8) The notice must be sent in such manner and to such address and must contain such particulars as the Secretary of State may determine.

41. Power of High Court of Justiciary to suspend disqualification *[Omitted.]*

42. Removal of disqualification

(1) Subject to the provisions of this section, a person who by an order of a court is disqualified may apply to the court by which the order was made to remove the disqualification.

(2) On any such application the court may, as it thinks proper having regard to—

(*a*) the character of the person disqualified and his conduct subsequent to the order,

(*b*) the nature of the offence, and

(*c*) any other circumstances of the case,

either by order remove the disqualification as from such date as may be specified in the order or refuse the application.

(3) No application shall be made under subsection (1) above for the removal of a disqualification before the expiration of whichever is relevant of the following periods from the date of the order by which the disqualification was imposed, that is—

(*a*) two years, if the disqualification is for less than four years,

(*b*) one half of the period of disqualification, if it is for less than ten years but not less than four years,

(*c*) five years in any other case;

and in determining the expiration of the period after which under this subsection a person may apply for the removal of a disqualification, any time after the conviction during which the disqualification was suspended or he was not disqualified shall be disregarded.

(4) Where an application under subsection (1) above is refused, a further application under that subsection shall not be entertained if made within three months after the date of the refusal.

(5) If under this section a court orders a disqualification to be removed, the court—

(*a*) must cause particulars of the order to be endorsed on the licence, if any, previously held by the applicant, and

(*b*) may in any case order the applicant to pay the whole or any part of the costs of the application.

(6) The preceding provisions of this section shall not apply where the disqualification was imposed by order under section 36(1) of this Act.

[As to applications under s 42 where an order was made under s 95(3) of the Road Traffic Act 1972, see the Road Traffic (Consequential Provisions) Act 1988, s 5 and Sched 4, para 7(6), above.

The reference in s 42(6) to an order under s 36(1) includes a reference to an order made under earlier legislation; see the Road Traffic (Consequential Provisions) Act 1988, s 5 and Sched 4, para 7(4), above.]

43. Rule for determining end of period of disqualification

In determining the expiration of the period for which a person is disqualified by an order of a court made in consequence of a conviction, any time after the conviction during which the disqualification was suspended or he was not disqualified shall be disregarded.

Endorsement

44. Endorsement of licences

(1) Where a person is convicted of an offence involving obligatory endorsement, the court must order there to be endorsed on any licence held by him particulars of the conviction and also—

(*a*) if the court orders him to be disqualified, particulars of the disqualification, or

(*b*) if the court does not order him to be disqualified—

(i) particulars of the offence, including the date when it was committed, and

(ii) the penalty points to be attributed to the offence.

(2) Where the court does not order the person convicted to be disqualified, it need not make an order under subsection (1) above if for special reasons it thinks fit not to do so.

(3) *[Applies to Scotland.]*

(4) This section is subject to section 48 of this Act.

45. Effect of endorsement

(1) An order that any particulars or penalty points are to be endorsed on any licence held by the person convicted shall, whether he is at the time the holder of a licence or not, operate as an order that any licence he may then hold or may subsequently obtain is to be so endorsed until he becomes entitled under subsection (4) below to have a licence issued to him free from the particulars or penalty points.

(2) On the issue of a new licence to a person, any particulars or penalty points ordered to be endorsed on any licence held by him shall be entered on the licence unless he has become entitled under subsection (4) below to have a licence issued to him free from those particulars or penalty points.

(3) If a person whose licence has been ordered to be endorsed with any particulars or penalty points applies for or obtains a licence without giving particulars of the order when he has not previously become entitled under subsection (4) below to have a licence issued to him free from those particulars or penalty points, he is guilty of an offence and any licence so obtained shall be of no effect.

(4) A person whose licence has been ordered to be endorsed is entitled to have a new licence issued to him free from the endorsement if, after the end of the period for which the endorsement remains effective, he applies for a new licence in pursuance of section 97(1) of the Road Traffic Act 1988, surrenders any subsisting licence, pays the fee prescribed by regulations under Part III of that Act and satisfies the other requirements of section 97(1).

(5) An endorsement ordered on a person's conviction of an offence remains effective (subject to subsections (6) and (7) below)—

(*a*) if an order is made for the disqualification of the offender, until four years have elapsed since the conviction, and

(*b*) if no such order is made, until either—
(i) four years have elapsed since the commission of the offence, or
(ii) such an order is made.

(6) Where the offence was one under section 1 or 2 of that Act (causing death by reckless driving and reckless driving), the endorsement remains in any case effective until four years have elapsed since the conviction.

(7) Where the offence was one—

(*a*) under section 4(1) or 5(1)(*a*) of that Act (driving when under influence of drink or drugs or driving with alcohol concentration above prescribed limit), or

(*b*) under section 7(6) of that Act (failing to provide specimen) involving obligatory disqualification,

the endorsement remains effective until eleven years have elapsed since the conviction.

General

46. Combination of disqualification and endorsement with probation orders and orders for discharge

(1) Notwithstanding anything in section 13(3) of the Powers of Criminal Courts Act 1973 (conviction of offender placed on probation or discharged to be disregarded for the purposes of enactments relating to disqualification), a court in England and Wales which on convicting a person of an offence involving obligatory or discretionary disqualification makes—

(*a*) a probation order, or

(*b*) an order discharging him absolutely or conditionally,

may on that occasion also exercise any power conferred, and must also discharge any duty imposed, on the court by sections 34, 35, 36 or 44 of this Act.

(2) A conviction—

(*a*) in respect of which a court in England and Wales has ordered a person to be disqualified, or

(*b*) of which particulars have been endorsed on any licence held by him,

is to be taken into account, notwithstanding anything in section 13(1) of the Powers of Criminal Courts Act 1973 (conviction of offender placed on probation or discharged to be disregarded for the purpose of subsequent proceedings), in determining his liability to punishment or disqualification for any offence involving obligatory or discretionary disqualification committed subsequently.

(3) *[Applies to Scotland.]*

47. Supplementary provisions as to disqualifications and endorsements

(1) In any case where a court exercises its power under section 34, 35 or 44 of this Act not to order any disqualification or endorsement or to order disqualification for a shorter period than would otherwise be required, it must state the grounds for doing so in open court and, if it is a magistrates' court, must cause them to be entered in the register of its proceedings.

(2) Where a court orders the endorsement of any licence held by a person it may and, if it orders him to be disqualified, must, send the licence, on its being produced to the court, to the Secretary of State; and if the court orders the endorsement but does not send the licence to the Secretary of State it must send him notice of the endorsement.

(3) Where on an appeal against any such order the appeal is allowed, the court by which the appeal is allowed must send notice of that fact to the Secretary of State.

(4) A notice sent by a court to the Secretary of State in pursuance of this section must be sent in such manner and to such address and contain such particulars as the Secretary of State may determine, and a licence so sent in pursuance of this section must be sent to such address as the Secretary of State may determine.

[Words relating exclusively and expressly to Scotland have been omitted from s 47(1).]

48. Exemption from disqualification and endorsement for offences against construction and use regulations

Where a person is convicted of an offence under section 42(1) of the Road Traffic Act 1988 (contravention of construction and use regulations) committed in a manner described against that section in column 5 of Part I of Schedule 2 to this Act, the court must not—

(*a*) order him to be disqualified, or

(*b*) order any particulars or penalty points to be endorsed on any licence held by him,

if he proves that he did not know, and had no reasonable cause to suspect, that the facts of the case were such that the offence would be committed.

49. Offender escaping consequences of endorseable offence by deception

(1) This section applies where in dealing with a person convicted of an offence involving obligatory endorsement a court was deceived regarding any circumstances that were or might have been taken into account in deciding whether or for how long to disqualify him.

(2) If—

(*a*) the deception constituted or was due to an offence committed by that person, and

(*b*) he is convicted of that offence,

the court by or before which he is convicted shall have the same powers and duties regarding an order for disqualification as had the court which dealt with him for the offence involving obligatory endorsement but must, in dealing with him, take into account any order made on his conviction of the offence involving obligatory endorsement.

50. Powers of district court in Scotland *[Omitted.]*

PART III

Fixed Penalties

Introductory

51. Fixed penalty offences

(1) Any offence in respect of a vehicle under an enactment specified in column 1 of Schedule 3 to this Act is a fixed penalty offence for the purposes of this Part of this Act, but subject to subsection (2) below and to any limitation or exception shown against the enactment in column 2 (where the general nature of the offence is also indicated).

(2) An offence under an enactment so specified is not a fixed penalty offence for those purposes if it is committed by causing or permitting a vehicle to be used by another person in contravention of any provision made or restriction or prohibition imposed by or under any enactment.

(3) *[Power to vary fixed penalty offences by order.]*

52. Fixed penalty notices

(1) In this Part of this Act 'fixed penalty notice' means a notice offering the opportunity of the discharge of any liability to conviction of the offence to which the notice relates by payment of a fixed penalty in accordance with this Part of this Act.

(2) A fixed penalty notice must give such particulars of the circumstances alleged to constitute the offence to which it relates as are necessary for giving reasonable information about the alleged offence.

(3) A fixed penalty notice must state—

(*a*) the period during which, by virtue of section 78(1) of this Act, proceedings cannot be brought against any person for the offence to which the notice relates, being the period of twenty-one days following the date of the notice or such longer period (if any) as may be specified in the notice (referred to in this Part of this Act as the 'suspended enforcement period'),

(*b*) the amount of the fixed penalty, and

(*c*) the justices' clerk to whom and the address at which the fixed penalty may be paid.

(4) *[Applies to Scotland.]*

[Words relating exclusively and expressly to Scotland have been omitted from s 52(3)(c).
When the fixed penalty provisions came into operation, a Home Office circular (circular 92/1985) recommended that 28 days (rather than the 21 days specified in s 52(3)(a)) should be allowed as the suspended enforcement period.]

53. Amount of fixed penalty

(1) The fixed penalty for an offence is—

(*a*) the amount mentioned in subsection (2) below, or

(*b*) one-half of the maximum amount of the fine to which a person committing that offence would be liable on summary conviction,

whichever is the less.

(2) The amount referred to in subsection (1)(*a*) above is—

(*a*) £24 in the case of any offence involving obligatory endorsement, and

(*b*) £12 in any other case.

(3) *[Power to alter amounts specified in s 53(2) by order.]*

Giving notices to suspected offenders

54. Notices on-the-spot or at a police station

(1) This section applies where on any occasion a constable in uniform has reason to believe that a person he finds is committing or has on that occasion committed a fixed penalty offence.

(2) Subject to subsection (3) below, the constable may give him a fixed penalty notice in respect of the offence.

(3) Where the offence appears to the constable to involve obligatory endorsement, the constable may only give him a fixed penalty notice under subsection (2) above in respect of the offence if—

(*a*) he produces his licence for inspection by the constable,

(*b*) the constable is satisfied, on inspecting the licence, that he would not be liable to be disqualified under section 35 of this Act if he were convicted of that offence, and

(*c*) he surrenders his licence to the constable to be retained and dealt with in accordance with this Part of this Act.

(4) Where—

(*a*) the offence appears to the constable to involve obligatory endorsement, and

(*b*) the person concerned does not produce his licence for inspection by the constable,

the constable may give him a notice stating that if, within seven days after the notice is given, he produces the notice together with his licence in person to a constable or authorised person at the police station specified in the notice (being a police station chosen by the person concerned) and the requirements of subsection (5)(*a*) and (*b*) below are met he will then be given a fixed penalty notice in respect of the offence.

(5) If a person to whom a notice has been given under subsection (4) above produces the notice together with his licence in person to a constable or authorised person at the police station specified in the notice within seven days after the notice was so given to him and the following requirements are met, that is—

(*a*) the constable or authorised person is satisfied, on inspecting the licence, that he would not be liable to be disqualified under section 35 of this Act if he were convicted of the offence, and

(*b*) he surrenders his licence to the constable or authorised person to be retained and dealt with in accordance with this Part of this Act,

the constable or authorised person must give him a fixed penalty notice in respect of the offence to which the notice under subsection (4) above relates.

(6) A notice under subsection (4) above shall give such particulars of the circumstances alleged to constitute the offence to which it relates as are necessary for giving reasonable information about the alleged offence.

(7) A licence surrendered in accordance with this section must be sent to the fixed penalty clerk.

(8) Subsection (4) above does not apply in respect of offences committed in Scotland and a notice under that subsection may not specify a police station in Scotland.

(9) In this Part of this Act 'authorised person', in relation to a fixed penalty notice given at a police station, means a person authorised for the purposes of this section by or on behalf of the chief officer of police for the area in which the police station is situated.

55. Effect of fixed penalty notice given under section 54

(1) This section applies where a fixed penalty notice relating to an offence has been given to any person under section 54 of this Act, and references in this section to the recipient are to the person to whom the notice was given.

(2) No proceedings shall be brought against the recipient for the offence to which the fixed penalty notice relates unless before the end of the suspended enforcement

period he has given notice requesting a hearing in respect of that offence in the manner specified in the fixed penalty notice.

(3) Where—

(*a*) the recipient has not given notice requesting a hearing in respect of the offence to which the fixed penalty notice relates in the manner so specified, and

(*b*) the fixed penalty has not been paid in accordance with this Part of this Act before the end of the suspended enforcement period,

a sum equal to the fixed penalty plus one-half of the amount of that penalty may be registered under section 71 of this Act for enforcement against the recipient as a fine.

56. Licence receipts

(1) A constable or authorised person to whom a person surrenders his licence on receiving a fixed penalty notice given to him under section 54 of this Act must issue a receipt for the licence under this section.

(2) The fixed penalty clerk may, on the application of a person who has surrendered his licence in those circumstances, issue a new receipt for the licence.

(3) A receipt issued under this section ceases to have effect—

(*a*) if issued by a constable or authorised person, on the expiration of the period of one month beginning with the date of issue or such longer period as may be prescribed, and

(*b*) if issued by the fixed penalty clerk, on such date as he may specify in the receipt,

or, if earlier, on the return of the licence to the licence holder.

57. Endorsement of licences without hearings

(1) Subject ot subsection (2) below, where a person (referred to in this section as 'the licence holder') has surrendered his licence to a constable or authorised person on the occasion when he was given a fixed penalty notice under section 54 of this Act, his licence may be endorsed in accordance with this section without any order of a court.

(2) A person's licence may not be endorsed under this section if at the end of the suspended enforcement period—

(*a*) he has given notice, in the manner specified in the fixed penalty notice, requesting a hearing in respect of the offence to which the fixed penalty notice relates, and

(*b*) the fixed penalty has not been paid in accordance with this Part of this Act.

(3) On the payment of the fixed penalty before the end of the suspended enforcement period, the fixed penalty clerk must endorse the relevant particulars on the licence and return it to the licence holder.

(4) Where any sum determined by reference to the fixed penalty is registered under section 71 of this Act for enforcement against the licence holder as a fine, the fixed penalty clerk must endorse the relevant particulars on the licence and return it to the licence holder—

(*a*) if he is himself the clerk who registers that sum, on the registration of that sum, and

(*b*) in any other case, on being notified of the registration by the clerk who registers that sum.

(5) References in this section to the relevant particulars are to—

(*a*) particulars of the offence, including the date when it was committed, and

(*b*) the number of penalty points to be attributed to the offence.

(6) On endorsing a person's licence under this section the fixed penalty clerk must send notice of the endorsement and of the particulars endorsed to the Secretary of State.

58. Effect of endorsement without hearing

(1) Where a person's licence is endorsed under section 57 of this Act he shall be treated for the purposes of sections 13(4), 28, 29 and 45 of this Act and of the Rehabilitation of Offenders Act 1974 as if—

(*a*) he had been convicted of the offence,

(*b*) the endorsement had been made in pursuance of an order made on his conviction by a court under section 44 of this Act, and

(*c*) the particulars of the offence endorsed by virtue of section 57(5)(*a*) of this Act were particulars of his conviction of that offence.

(2) In relation to any endorsement of a person's licence under section 57 of this Act—

(*a*) the reference in section 45(4) of this Act to the order for endorsement, and

(*b*) the references in section 13(4) of this Act to any order made on a person's conviction,

are to be read as references to the endorsement itself.

59. Notification of court and date of trial in England and Wales

(1) On an occasion when a person is given a fixed penalty notice under section 54 of this Act in respect of an offence, he may be given written notification specifying the magistrates' court by which and the date on which the offence will be tried if he gives notice requesting a hearing in respect of the offence as permitted by the fixed penalty notice.

(2) Subject to subsections (4) and (5) below, where—

(*a*) a person has been notified in accordance with this section of the court and date of trial of an offence in respect of which he has been given a fixed penalty notice, and

(*b*) he has given notice requesting a hearing in respect of the offence as permitted by the fixed penalty notice,

the provisions of the Magistrates' Courts Act 1980 shall apply as mentioned in subsection (3) below.

(3) Those provisions are to have effect for the purpose of any proceedings in respect of that offence as if—

(*a*) the allegation in the fixed penalty notice with respect to that offence were an information duly laid in accordance with section 1 of that Act, and

(*b*) the notification of the court and date of trial were a summons duly issued on that information by a justice of the peace for the area for which the magistrates' court notified as the court of trial acts, requiring the person notified to appear before that court to answer to that information and duly served on him on the date on which the notification was given.

(4) If, in a case within subsection (2) above, notice is served by or on behalf of the

chief officer of police on the person who gave notice requesting a hearing stating that no proceedings are to be brought in respect of the offence concerned, that subsection does not apply and no such proceedings are to be brought against the person who gave notice requesting a hearing.

(5) Section 14 of that Act (proceedings invalid where accused did not know of them) is not applied by subsection (2) above in a case where a person has been notified in accordance with this section of the court and date of trial of an offence.

(6) This section does not extend to Scotland.

[Section 59 will be brought into force on a date to be announced; see s 99(5), below.]

60. Court procedure in Scotland *[Omitted.]*

61. Fixed penalty notice mistakenly given: exclusion of fixed penalty procedures

(1) This section applies where, on inspection of a licence sent to him under section 54(7) of this Act, it appears to the fixed penalty clerk that the person whose licence it is would be liable to be disqualified under section 35 of this Act if he were convicted of the offence in respect of which the fixed penalty notice was given.

(2) The fixed penalty clerk must not endorse the licence under section 57 of this Act but must instead send it to the chief officer of police.

(3) Nothing in this Part of this Act prevents proceedings being brought in respect of the offence in respect of which the fixed penalty notice was given where those proceedings are commenced before the end of the period of six months beginning with the date on which that notice was given.

(4) Where proceedings in respect of that offence are commenced before the end of that period, the case is from then on to be treated in all respects as if no fixed penalty notice had been given in respect of the offence.

(5) Accordingly, where proceedings in respect of that offence are so commenced, any action taken in pursuance of any provision of this Part of this Act by reference to that fixed penalty notice shall be void (including, but without prejudice to the generality of the preceding provision—

(*a*) the registration under section 71 of this Act of any sum, determined by reference to the fixed penalty for that offence, for enforcement against the person whose licence it is as a fine, and

(*b*) any proceedings for enforcing payment of any such sum within the meaning of sections 73 and 74 of this Act (defined in section 74(5)).

Notices fixed to vehicles

62. Fixing notices to vehicles

(1) Where on any occasion a constable has reason to believe in the case of any stationary vehicle that a fixed penalty offence is being or has on that occasion been committed in respect of it, he may fix a fixed penalty notice in respect of the offence to the vehicle unless the offence appears to him to involve obligatory endorsement.

(2) A person is guilty of an offence if he removes or interferes with any notice fixed to a vehicle under this section, unless he does so by or under the authority of the driver or person in charge of the vehicle or the person liable for the fixed penalty offence in question.

63. Service of notice to owner if penalty not paid

(1) This section applies where a fixed penalty notice relating to an offence has been fixed to a vehicle under section 62 of this Act.

(2) Subject to subsection (3) below, if at the end of the suspended enforcement period the fixed penalty has not been paid in accordance with this Part of this Act, a notice under this section may be served by or on behalf of the chief officer of police on any person who appears to him (or to any person authorised to act on his behalf for the purposes of this section) to be the owner of the vehicle.

Such a notice is referred to in this Part of this Act as a 'notice to owner'.

(3) Subsection (2) above does not apply where before the end of the suspended enforcement period—

(*a*) any person has given notice requesting a hearing in respect of the offence in the manner specified in the fixed penalty notice, and

(*b*) the notice so given contains a statement by that person to the effect that he was the driver of the vehicle at the time when the offence is alleged to have been committed.

That time is referred to in this Part of this Act as the 'time of the alleged offence'.

(4) A notice to owner—

(*a*) must give particulars of the alleged offence and of the fixed penalty concerned,

(*b*) must state the period allowed for response to the notice, and

(*c*) must indicate that, if the fixed penalty is not paid before the end of that period, the person on whom the notice is served is asked to provide before the end of that period to the chief officer of police by or on whose behalf the notice was served a statutory statement of ownership (as defined in Part I of Schedule 4 to this Act).

(5) For the purposes of this Part of this Act, the period allowed for response to a notice to owner is the period of twenty-one days from the date on which the notice is served, or such longer period (if any) as may be specified in the notice.

(6) A notice to owner relating to any offence must indicate that the person on whom it is served may, before the end of the period allowed for response to the notice, either—

(*a*) give notice requesting a hearing in respect of the offence in the manner indicated by the notice, or

(*b*) if—

(i) he was not the driver of the vehicle at the time of the alleged offence, and

(ii) a person purporting to be the driver wishes to give notice requesting a hearing in respect of the offence,

provide, together with a statutory statement of ownership provided as requested in that notice, a statutory statement of facts (as defined by Part II of Schedule 4 to this Act) having the effect referred to in paragraph 3(2) of that Schedule (that is, as a notice requesting a hearing in respect of the offence given by the driver).

(7) In any case where a person on whom a notice to owner relating to any offence has been served provides a statutory statement of facts in pursuance of subsection (6)(*b*) above—

(*a*) any notice requesting a hearing in respect of the offence that he purports to give on his own account shall be of no effect, and

(*b*) no sum may be registered for enforcement against him as a fine in respect of the offence unless, within the period of two months immediately following the period allowed for response to the notice to owner, no summons in respect of the offence in question is served on the person identified in the statement as the driver.

[Words relating exclusively and expressly to Scotland have been omitted from s 63(7).]

64. Enforcement or proceedings against owner

(1) This section applies where—

(*a*) a fixed penalty notice relating to an offence has been fixed to a vehicle under section 62 of this Act,

(*b*) a notice to owner relating to the offence has been served on any person under section 63(2) of this Act before the end of the period of six months beginning with the day on which the fixed penalty notice was fixed to the vehicle, and

(*c*) the fixed penalty has not been paid in accordance with this Part of this Act before the end of the period allowed for response to the notice to owner.

(2) Subject to subsection (4) below and to section 63(7)(*b*) of this Act, a sum equal to the fixed penalty plus one-half of the amount of that penalty may be registered under section 71 of this Act for enforcement against the person on whom the notice to owner was served as a fine.

(3) Subject to subsection (4) below and to section 65 of this Act, proceedings may be brought in respect of the offence against the person on whom the notice to owner was served.

(4) If the person on whom the notice to owner was served—

(*a*) was not the owner of the vehicle at the time of the alleged offence, and

(*b*) provides a statutory statement of ownership to that effect in response to the notice before the end of the period allowed for response to the notice,

he shall not be liable in respect of the offence by virtue of this section nor shall any sum determined by reference to the fixed penalty for the offence be so registered by virtue of this section for enforcement against him as a fine.

(5) Subject to subsection (6) below—

(*a*) for the purposes of the institution of proceedings by virtue of subsection (3) above against any person on whom a notice to owner has been served, and

(*b*) in any proceedings brought by virtue of that subsection against any such person,

it shall be conclusively presumed (notwithstanding that that person may not be an individual) that he was the driver of the vehicle at the time of the alleged offence and, accordingly, that acts or omissions of the driver of the vehicle at that time were his acts or omissions.

(6) That presumption does not apply in any proceedings brought against any person by virtue of subsection (3) above if, in those proceedings, it is proved that at the time of the alleged offence the vehicle was in the possession of some other person without the consent of the accused.

(7) Where—

(*a*) by virtue of subsection (3) above proceedings may be brought in respect of an offence against a person on whom a notice to owner was served, and

(*b*) section 74(1) of this Act does not apply,

section 127(1) of the Magistrates' Courts Act 1980 (information must be laid within six months of time offence committed) shall have effect as if for the reference to six months there were substituted a reference to twelve months.

[Words relating exclusively and expressly to Scotland in s 64(7) have been omitted.]

65. Restrictions on proceedings against owner and others

(1) In any case where a notice to owner relating to an offence may be served under section 63 of this Act, no proceedings shall be brought in respect of the offence against any person other than a person on whom such a notice has been served unless he is identified as the driver of the vehicle at the time of the alleged offence in a statutory statement of facts provided in pursuance of section 63(6)(*b*) of this Act by a person on whom such a notice has been served.

(2) Proceedings in respect of an offence to which a notice to owner relates shall not be brought against the person on whom the notice was served unless, before the end of the period allowed for response to the notice, he has given notice, in the manner indicated by the notice to owner, requesting a hearing in respect of the offence.

(3) Proceedings in respect of an offence to which a notice to owner relates may not be brought against any person identified as the driver of the vehicle in a statutory statement of facts provided in response to the notice if the fixed penalty is paid in accordance with this Part of this Act before the end of the period allowed for response to the notice.

(4) Once any sum determined by reference to the fixed penalty for an offence has been registered by virtue of section 64 of this Act under section 71 for enforcement as a fine against a person on whom a notice to owner relating to that offence has been served, no proceedings shall be brought against any other person in respect of that offence.

66. Hired vehicles

(1) This section applies where—

(*a*) a notice to owner has been served on a vehicle-hire firm,

(*b*) at the time of the alleged offence the vehicle in respect of which the notice was served was let to another person by the vehicle-hire firm under a hiring agreement to which this section applies, and

(*c*) within the period allowed for response to the notice the firm provides the chief officer of police by or on whose behalf the notice was served with the documents mentioned in subsection (2) below.

(2) Those documents are a statement on an official form, signed by or on behalf of the firm, stating that at the time of the alleged offence the vehicle concerned was hired under a hiring agreement to which this section applies, together with—

(*a*) a copy of that hiring agreement, and

(*b*) a copy of a statement of liability signed by the hirer under that hiring agreement.

(3) In this section a 'statement of liability' means a statement made by the hirer under a hiring agreement to which this section applies to the effect that the hirer acknowledges that he will be liable, as the owner of the vehicle, in respect of any fixed

penalty offence which may be committed with respect to the vehicle during the currency of the hiring agreement and giving such information as may be prescribed.

(4) In any case where this section applies, sections 63, 64 and 65 of this Act shall have effect as if—

(*a*) any reference to the owner of the vehicle were a reference to the hirer under the hiring agreement, and

(*b*) any reference to a statutory statement of ownership were a reference to a statutory statement of hiring,

and accordingly references in this Part of this Act (with the exceptions mentioned below) to a notice to owner include references to a notice served under section 63 of this Act as it applies by virtue of this section.

This subsection does not apply to references to a notice to owner in this section or in section 81(2)(*b*) of or Part I of Schedule 4 to this Act.

(5) In any case where this section applies, a person authorised in that behalf by the chief officer of police to whom the documents mentioned in subsection (2) above are provided may, at any reasonable time within six months after service of the notice to owner (and on the production of his authority) require the firm to produce the originals of the hiring agreement and statement of liability in question.

(6) If a vehicle-hire firm fails to produce the original of a document when required to do so under subsection (5) above, this section shall thereupon cease to apply (and section 64 of this Act shall apply accordingly in any such case after that time as it applies in a case where the person on whom the notice to owner was served has failed to provide a statutory statement of ownership in response to the notice within the period allowed).

(7) This section applies to a hiring agreement under the terms of which the vehicle concerned is let to the hirer for a fixed period of less than six months (whether or not that period is capable of extension by agreement between the parties or otherwise); and any reference in this section to the currency of the hiring agreement includes a reference to any period during which, with the consent of the vehicle-hire firm, the hirer continues in possession of the vehicle as hirer, after the expiry of the fixed period specified in the agreement, but otherwise on the terms and conditions so specified.

(8) In this section—

'hiring agreement' refers only to an agreement which contains such particulars as may be prescribed and does not include a hire-purchase agreement within the meaning of the Consumer Credit Act 1974, and

'vehicle-hire firm' means any person engaged in hiring vehicles in the course of a business.

67. False statements in response to notices to owner

A person who, in response to a notice to owner, provides a statement which is false in a material particular and does so recklessly or knowing it to be false in that particular is guilty of an offence.

68. 'Owner', 'statutory statement' and 'official form'

(1) For the purposes of this Part of this Act, the owner of a vehicle shall be taken to be the person by whom the vehicle is kept; and for the purposes of determining, in the course of any proceedings brought by virtue of section 64(3) of this Act, who was the owner of a vehicle at any time, it shall be presumed that the owner was the person who was the registered keeper of the vehicle at that time.

(2) Notwithstanding the presumption in subsection (1) above, it is open to the defence in any proceedings to prove that the person who was the registered keeper of a vehicle at a particular time was not the person by whom the vehicle was kept at that time and to the prosecution to prove that the vehicle was kept by some other person at that time.

(3) References in this Part of this Act to statutory statements of any description are references to the statutory statement of that description defined in Schedule 4 to this Act; and that Schedule shall also have effect for the purpose of requiring certain information to be provided in official forms for the statutory statements so defined to assist persons in completing those forms and generally in determining what action to take in response to a notice to owner.

(4) In this Part of this Act 'official form', in relation to a statutory statement mentioned in Schedule 4 to this Act or a statement under section 66(2) of this Act, means a document supplied by or on behalf of a chief officer of police for use in making that statement.

The fixed penalty procedure

69. Payment of penalty

(1) Payment of a fixed penalty under this Part of this Act must be made to such justices' clerk as may be specified in the fixed penalty notice relating to that penalty.

(2) Without prejudice to payment by any other method, payment of a fixed penalty under this Part of this Act may be made by properly addressing, pre-paying and posting a letter containing the amount of the penalty (in cash or otherwise) and, unless the contrary is proved, shall be regarded as having been made at the time at which that letter would be delivered in the ordinary course of post.

(3) A letter is properly addressed for the purposes of subsection (2) above if it is addressed to the fixed penalty clerk at the address specified in the fixed penalty notice relating to the fixed penalty as the address at which the fixed penalty may be paid.

(4) References in this Part of this Act, in relation to any fixed penalty or fixed penalty notice, to the fixed penalty clerk are references to the clerk specified in accordance with subsection (1) above in the fixed penalty notice relating to that penalty or (as the case may be) in that fixed penalty notice.

[Words relating exclusively and expressly to Scotland in s 69(1) have been omitted.]

70. Registration certificates

(1) This section and section 71 of this Act apply where by virtue of section 55(3) or 64(2) of this Act a sum determined by reference to the fixed penalty for any offence may be registered under section 71 of this Act for enforcement against any person as a fine.

In this section and section 71 of this Act—

(*a*) that sum is referred to as a 'sum payable in default', and

(*b*) the person against whom that sum may be so registered is referred to as the 'defaulter'.

(2) Subject to subsection (3) below, the chief officer of police may in respect of any sum payable in default issue a certificate (referred to in this section and section 71 as a 'registration certificate') stating that the sum is registrable under section 71 for enforcement against the defaulter as a fine.

(3) *[Applies to Scotland.]*

(4) Where the chief officer of police or the fixed penalty clerk issues a registration certificate under this section, he must—

(*a*) if the defaulter appears to him to reside in England and Wales, cause it to be sent to the clerk to the justices for the petty sessions area in which the defaulter appears to him to reside, and

(*b*) *[Applies to Scotland.]*

(5) A registration certificate issued under this section in respect of any sum payable in default must—

(*a*) give particulars of the offence to which the fixed penalty notice relates,

(*b*) indicate whether registration is authorised under section 55(3) or 64(2) of this Act, and

(*c*) state the name and last known address of the defaulter and the amount of the sum payable in default.

71. Registration of sums payable in default

(1) Where the clerk to the justices for a petty sessions area receives a registration certificate issued under section 70 of this Act in respect of any sum payable in default, he must, subject to subsection (4) below, register that sum for enforcement as a fine in that area by entering it in the register of a magistrates' court acting for that area.

(2) Where the clerk of a court of summary jurisdiction receives a registration certificate issued under section 70 of this Act in respect of any sum payable in default, he must, subject to subsection (4) below, register that sum for enforcement as a fine by that court.

(3) Where—

(*a*) the fixed penalty notice in question was given to the defaulter under section 54 of this Act in respect of an offence committed in Scotland, and

(*b*) the defaulter appears to the fixed penalty clerk to reside within the jurisdiction of the court of summary jurisdiction of which he is himself the clerk,

the fixed penalty clerk must register the sum payable in default for enforcement as a fine by that court.

(4) Where it appears to the clerk receiving a registration certificate issued under section 70 of this Act in respect of any sum payable in default that the defaulter does not reside in the petty sessions area or (as the case may be) within the jurisdiction of the court of summary jurisdiction in question—

(*a*) he is not required by subsection (1) or (2) above to register that sum, but

(*b*) he must cause the certificate to be sent to the appropriate clerk,

and subsection (1) or, as the case may be, (2) above shall apply accordingly on receipt by the appropriate clerk of the certificate as it applies on receipt by the clerk to whom it was originally sent.

(5) For the purposes of subsection (4) above, the appropriate clerk—

(*a*) if the defaulter appears to the clerk receiving the registration certificate to reside in England and Wales, is the clerk to the justices for the petty sessions area in which the defaulter appears to him to reside, and

(*b*) if the defaulter appears to the clerk receiving the registration certificate to reside in Scotland, is the clerk of a court of summary jurisdiction for the area in which the defaulter appears to him to reside.

(6) On registering any sum under this section for enforcement as a fine, the clerk to

the justices for a petty sessions area or, as the case may be, the clerk of a court of summary jurisdiction must give to the defaulter notice of registration—

(*a*) specifying the amount of that sum, and

(*b*) giving the information with respect to the offence and the authority for registration included in the registration certificate by virtue of section 70(5)(*a*) and (*b*) of this Act or (in a case within subsection (3) above) the corresponding information.

(7) On the registration of any sum in a magistrates' court or a court of summary jurisdiction by virtue of this section any enactment referring (in whatever terms) to a fine imposed or other sum adjudged to be paid on the conviction of such a court shall have effect in the case in question as if the sum so registered were a fine imposed by that court on the conviction of the defaulter on the date of the registration.

(8) Accordingly, in the application by virtue of this section of the provisions of the Magistrates' Courts Act 1980 relating to the satisfaction and enforcement of sums adjudged to be paid on the conviction of a magistrates' court, section 85 of that Act (power to remit a fine in whole or in part) is not excluded by subsection (2) of that section (references in that section to a fine not to include any other sum adjudged to be paid on a conviction) from applying to a sum registered in a magistrates' court by virtue of this section.

(9) For the purposes of this section, where the defaulter is a body corporate, the place where that body resides and the address of that body are either of the following—

(*a*) the registered or principal office of that body, and

(*b*) the address which, with respect to the vehicle concerned, is the address recorded in the record kept under the Vehicles (Excise) Act 1971 as being that body's address.

72. Notices on-the-spot or at a police station: when registration and endorsement invalid

(1) This section applies where—

(*a*) a person who has received notice of the registration, by virtue of section 55(3) of this Act, of a sum under section 71 of this Act for enforcement against him as a fine makes a statutory declaration to the effect mentioned in subsection (2) below, and

(*b*) that declaration is, within twenty-one days of the date on which the person making it received notice of the registration, served on the clerk of the relevant court.

(2) The statutory declaration must state—

(*a*) that the person making the declaration was not the person to whom the relevant fixed penalty notice was given, or

(*b*) that he gave notice requesting a hearing in respect of the alleged offence as permitted by the fixed penalty notice before the end of the suspended enforcement period.

(3) In any case within subsection (2)(*a*) above, the relevant fixed penalty notice, the registration and any proceedings taken before the declaration was served for enforcing payment of the sum registered shall be void.

(4) Where in any case within subsection (2)(*a*) above the person to whom the relevant fixed penalty notice was given surrendered a licence held by the person making

the declaration, any endorsement of that licence made under section 57 of this Act in respect of the offence in respect of which that notice was given shall be void.

(5) In any case within subsection (2)(*b*) above—

(*a*) the registration, any proceedings taken before the declaration was served for enforcing payment of the sum registered, and any endorsement, in respect of the offence in respect of which the relevant fixed penalty notice was given, made under section 57 of this Act before the declaration was served, shall be void, and

(*b*) the case shall be treated after the declaration is served as if the person making the declaration had given notice requesting a hearing in respect of the alleged offence as stated in the declaration.

(6) The clerk of the relevant court must—

(*a*) cancel an endorsement of a licence under section 57 of this Act that is void by virtue of this section on production of the licence to him for that purpose, and

(*b*) send notice of the cancellation to the Secretary of State.

(7) References in this section to the relevant fixed penalty notice are to the fixed penalty notice relating to the fixed penalty concerned.

73. Notices fixed to vehicles: when registration invalid

(1) This section applies where—

(*a*) a person who has received notice of the registration, by virtue of section 64(2) of this Act, of a sum under section 71 of this Act for enforcement against him as a fine makes a statutory declaration to the effect mentioned in subsection (2) below, and

(*b*) that declaration is, within twenty-one days of the date on which the person making it received notice of the registration, served on the clerk of the relevant court.

(2) The statutory declaration must state either—

(*a*) that the person making the declaration did not know of the fixed penalty concerned or of any fixed penalty notice or notice to owner relating to that penalty until he received notice of the registration, or

(*b*) that he was not the owner of the vehicle at the time of the alleged offence of which particulars are given in the relevant notice to owner and that he has a reasonable excuse for failing to comply with that notice, or

(*c*) that he gave notice requesting a hearing in respect of that offence as permitted by the relevant notice to owner before the end of the period allowed for response to that notice.

(3) In any case within subsection (2)(*a*) or (*b*) above—

(*a*) the relevant notice to owner,

(*b*) the registration, and

(*c*) any proceedings taken before the declaration was served for enforcing payment of the sum registered,

shall be void but without prejudice, in a case within subsection (2)(*a*) above, to the service of a further notice to owner under section 63 of this Act on the person making the declaration.

This subsection applies whether or not the relevant notice to owner was duly served in accordance with that section on the person making the declaration.

(4) In any case within subsection (2)(*c*) above—

(*a*) no proceedings shall be taken, after the statutory declaration is served until the end of the period of twenty-one days following the date of that declaration, for enforcing payment of the sum registered, and

(*b*) where before the end of that period a notice is served by or on behalf of the chief officer of police on the person making the declaration asking him to provide a new statutory statement of ownership to that chief officer of police before the end of the period of twenty-one days from the date on which the notice is served, no such proceedings shall be taken until the end of the period allowed for response to that notice.

(5) Where in any case within subsection (2)(*c*) above—

(*a*) no notice is served by or on behalf of the chief officer of police in accordance with subsection (4) above, or

(*b*) such a notice is so served and the person making the declaration provides a new statutory statement of ownership in accordance with the notice,

then—

(i) the registration and any proceedings taken before the declaration was served for enforcing payment of the sum registered shall be void, and

(ii) the case shall be treated after the time mentioned in subsection (6) below as if the person making the declaration had given notice requesting a hearing in respect of the alleged offence as stated in the declaration.

(6) The time referred to in subsection (5) above is—

(*a*) in a case within paragraph (*a*) of that subsection, the end of the period of twenty-one days following the date of the statutory declaration,

(*b*) in a case within paragraph (*b*) of that subsection, the time when the statement is provided.

(7) In any case where notice is served by or on behalf of the chief officer of police in accordance with subsection (4) above, he must cause the clerk of the relevant court to be notified of that fact immediately on service of the notice.

(8) References in this section to the relevant notice to owner are to the notice to owner relating to the fixed penalty concerned.

74. Provisions supplementary to sections 72 and 73

(1) In any case within section 72(2)(*b*) or 73(2) of this Act—

(*a*) section 127(1) of the Magistrates' Courts Act 1980 (limitation of time), and

(*b*) *[Applies to Scotland.]*

shall have effect as if for the reference to the time when the offence was committed or (as the case may be) the time when the contravention occurred there were substituted a reference to the date of the statutory declaration made for the purposes of section 72(1) or, as the case may be, 73(1).

(2) Where, on the application of a person who has received notice of the registration of a sum under section 71 of this Act for enforcement against him as a fine, it appears to the relevant court (which for this purpose may be composed of a single justice) that it was not reasonable to expect him to serve, within twenty-one days of the date on which he received the notice, a statutory declaration to the effect mentioned in section 72(2) or, as the case may be, 73(2) of this Act, the court may accept service of such a declaration by that person after that period has expired.

(3) A statutory declaration accepted under subsection (2) above shall be taken to have been served as required by section 72(1) or, as the case may be, section 73(1) of this Act.

(4) For the purposes of sections 72(1) and 73(1) of this Act, a statutory declaration shall be taken to be duly served on the clerk of the relevant court if it is delivered to him, left at his office, or sent in a registered letter or by the recorded delivery service addressed to him at his office.

(5) In sections 72, 73 and this section—

(*a*) references to the relevant court are—

(i) in the case of a sum registered under section 71 of this Act for enforcement as a fine in a petty sessions area in England and Wales, references to any magistrates' court acting for that area, and

(ii) *[Applies to Scotland.]*

(*b*) references to the clerk of the relevant court, where that court is a magistrates' court, are references to a clerk to the justices for the petty sessions area for which that court is acting, and

(*c*) references to proceedings for enforcing payment of the sum registered are references to any process issued or other proceedings taken for or in connection with enforcing payment of that sum.

(6) For the purposes of sections 72, 73 and this section, a person shall be taken to receive notice of the registration of a sum under section 71 of this Act for enforcement against him as a fine when he receives notice either of the registration as such or of any proceedings for enforcing payment of the sum registered.

(7) Nothing in the provisions of sections 72 or 73 or this section is to be read as prejudicing any rights a person may have apart from those provisions by virtue of the invalidity of any action purportedly taken in pursuance of this Part of this Act which is not in fact authorised by this Part of this Act in the circumstances of the case; and, accordingly, references in those provisions to the registration of any sum or to any other action taken under or by virtue of any provision of this Part of this Act are not to be read as implying that the registration or action was validly made or taken in accordance with that provision.

Conditional offer of fixed penalty in Scotland

75. Conditional offer by procurator fiscal *[Omitted.]*

76. Effect of offer with s 75 and payment of penalty *[Omitted.]*

77. Endorsement where penalty paid under s 76 *[Omitted.]*

Proceedings in fixed penalty cases

78. General restriction on proceedings

(1) Proceedings shall not be brought against any person for the offence to which a fixed penalty notice relates until the end of the suspended enforcement period.

(2) Proceedings shall not be brought against any person for the offence to which a fixed penalty notice relates if the fixed penalty is paid in accordance with this Part of this Act before the end of the suspended enforcement period.

79. Statements by constables

(1) In any proceedings a certificate that a copy of a statement by a constable with respect to the alleged offence (referred to in this section as a 'constable's witness statement') was included in or given with a fixed penalty notice or a notice under section 54(3) of this Act given to the accused on a date specified in the certificate shall, if the certificate purports to be signed by the constable or authorised person who gave the accused the notice, be evidence of service of a copy of that statement by delivery to the accused on that date.

(2) In any proceedings a certificate that a copy of a constable's witness statement was included in or served with a notice to owner served on the accused in the manner and on a date specified in the certificate shall, if the certificate purports to be signed by any person employed by the police authority for the police area in which the offence to which the proceedings relate is alleged to have been committed, be evidence of service in the manner and on the date so specified both of a copy of that statement and of the notice to owner.

(3) Any address specified in any such certificate as is mentioned in subsection (2) above as being the address at which service of the notice to owner was effected shall be taken for the purposes of any proceedings in which the certificate is tendered in evidence to be the accused's proper address, unless the contrary is proved.

(4) Where a copy of a constable's witness statement is included in or served with a notice to owner served in any manner in which the notice is authorised to be served under this Part of this Act, the statement shall be treated as duly served for the purposes of section 9 of the Criminal Justice Act 1967 (proof by written statement) notwithstanding that the manner of service is not authorised by subsection (8) of that section.

(5) In relation to any proceedings in which service of a constable's witness statement is proved by certificate under this section—

(*a*) that service shall be taken for the purposes of subsection (2)(*c*) of that section (copy of statement to be tendered in evidence to be served before hearing on other parties to the proceedings by or on behalf of the party proposing to tender it) to have been effected by or on behalf of the prosecutor, and

(*b*) subsection (2)(*d*) of that section (time for objection) shall have effect with the substitution, for the reference to seven days from the service of the copy of the statement, of a reference to seven days from the relevant date.

(6) In subsection (5)(*b*) above 'relevant date' means—

(*a*) where the accused gives notice requesting a hearing in respect of the offence in accordance with any provision of this Part of this Act, the date on which he gives that notice, and

(*b*) where a notice in respect of the offence was given to the accused under section 54(4) of this Act but no fixed penalty notice is given in respect of it, the last day for production of the notice under section 54(5) at a police station in accordance with that section.

(7) This section does not extend to Scotland.

80. Certificates about payment

In any proceedings a certificate—

(*a*) that payment of a fixed penalty was or was not received, by a date specified in the certificate, by the fixed penalty clerk, or (*b*) that a letter containing an amount sent by post in payment of a fixed penalty was marked as posted on a date so specified,

shall, if the certificate purports to be signed by the fixed penalty clerk, be evidence of the facts stated.

[Words relating exclusively and expressly to Scotland in s 80 have been omitted.]

81. Documents signed by the accused

(1) Where—

(*a*) any person is charged with a fixed penalty offence, and

(*b*) the prosecutor produces to the court a document to which this subsection applies purporting to have been signed by the accused,

the document shall be presumed, unless the contrary is proved, to have been signed by the accused and shall be evidence in the proceedings of any facts stated in it tending to show that the accused was the owner, the hirer or the driver of the vehicle concerned at a particular time.

(2) Subsection (1) above applies to any document purporting to be—

(*a*) a notice requesting a hearing in respect of the offence charged given in accordance with a fixed penalty notice relating to that offence, or

(*b*) a statutory statement of any description defined in Schedule 4 to this Act or a copy of a statement of liability within the meaning of section 66 of this Act provided in response to a notice to owner.

[Words relating exclusively and expressly to Scotland in s 81(1) have been omitted.]

Miscellaneous

82. Accounting for fixed penalties: England and Wales

(1) In England and Wales, sums paid by way of fixed penalty for an offence shall be treated for the purposes of section 61 (application of fines and fees) of the Justices of the Peace Act 1979 as if they were fines imposed on summary conviction for that offence.

(2) Where, in England and Wales, a justices' clerk for a petty sessions area comprised in the area of one responsible authority (within the meaning of section 59 of that Act) discharges functions in connection with a fixed penalty for an offence alleged to have been committed in a petty sessions area comprised in the area of another such authority—

(*a*) that other authority must make to the first-mentioned authority such payment in connection with the discharge of those functions as may be agreed between them or, in default of such agreement, as may be determined by the Secretary of State, and

(*b*) any such payment between responsible authorities shall be taken into account in determining for the purposes of subsection (4) of that section the net cost to those authorities respectively of the functions referred to in subsection (1) of that section.

(3) Subsection (2) above does not apply to functions discharged in connection with a fixed penalty on or after the registration of a sum determined by reference to the penalty under section 71 of this Act.

83. Powers of court where clerk deceived

(1) This section applies where—

(*a*) in endorsing any person's licence under section 57 of this Act, the fixed penalty clerk is deceived as to whether endorsement under that section is excluded by section 61(2) of this Act by virtue of the fact that the licence holder would be liable to be disqualified under section 35 of this Act if he were convicted of the offence, or

(*b*) in endorsing any person's licence under section 77 of this Act the clerk of court specified in the conditional offer (within the meaning of that section) is deceived as to whether he is required by section 76(5) of this Act to return the licence without endorsing it by virtue of the fact that the licence holder would be liable to be disqualified under section 35 of this Act if he were convicted of the offence.

(2) If—

(*a*) the deception constituted or was due to an offence committed by the licence holder, and

(*b*) the licence holder is convicted of that offence,

the court by or before which he is convicted shall have the same powers and duties as it would have had if he had also been convicted by or before it of the offence of which particulars were endorsed under section 57 or, as the case may be, 77 of this Act.

84. Regulations *[Omitted.]*

85. Service of documents

(1) Subject to any requirement of this Part of this Act with respect to the manner in which a person may be provided with any such document, he may be provided with the following documents by post (but without prejudice to any other method of providing him with them), that is to say—

(*a*) any of the statutory statements mentioned in Schedule 4 to this Act, and

(*b*) any of the documents mentioned in section 66(2) of this Act.

(2) Where a notice requesting a hearing in respect of an offence is permitted by a fixed penalty notice or notice to owner relating to that offence to be given by post, section 7 of the Interpretation Act 1978 (service of documents by post) shall apply as if that notice were permitted to be so given by this Act.

(3) A notice to owner may be served on any person—

(*a*) by delivering it to him or leaving it at his proper address, or

(*b*) by sending it to him by post,

and where the person on whom such a notice is to be served is a body corporate it is duly served if it is served on the secretary or clerk of that body.

(4) For the purposes of this Part of this Act and of section 7 of the Interpretation Act 1978 as it applies for the purposes of subsection (3) above the proper address of any person in relation to the service on him of a notice to owner is—

(*a*) in the case of the secretary or clerk of a body corporate, that of the registered or principal office of that body or the registered address of the person who is or was the registered keeper of the vehicle concerned at the time of service, and

(*b*) in any other case, his last known address at the time of service.

(5) In subsection (4) above, 'registered address', in relation to the registered keeper of a vehicle, means the address recorded in the record kept under the Vehicles (Excise) Act 1971 with respect to that vehicle as being that person's address.

086. Functions of traffic wardens

(1) An order under section 95(5) of the Road Traffic Regulation Act 1984 may not authorise the employment of a traffic warden to discharge any function under this Part of this Act in respect of an offence if the offence appears to the traffic warden to be an offence involving obligatory endorsement.

(2) In so far as an order under that section authorises the employment of traffic wardens for the purposes of this Part of this Act, references in this Part of this Act to a constable or, as the case may be, to a constable in uniform include a traffic warden.

[The Functions of Traffic Wardens Order 1970 (SI 1970 No 1958) qv has effect as if made under the Road Traffic Regulation Act 1984, s 95(5).]

87. Guidance on application of Part III *[Omitted.]*

88. Procedure for regulations and orders *[Omitted.]*

89. Interpretation

(1) In this Part of this Act—

'authorised person' has the meaning given by section 54(9) of this Act,

'chief officer of police' (except in the definition of 'authorised person') means, in relation to any fixed penalty notice or notice to owner, the chief officer of police for the police area in which the fixed penalty offence in question is alleged to have been committed,

'driver' except in section 62 of this Act means, in relation to an alleged fixed penalty offence, the person by whom, assuming the offence to have been committed, it was committed,

'justices' clerk' means the clerk to the justices for a petty sessions area,

'petty sessions area' has the same meaning as in the Magistrates' Courts Act 1980, and

'proceedings', except in relation to proceedings for enforcing payment of a sum registered under section 71 of this Act, means criminal proceedings.

(2) In this Part of this Act—

(*a*) references to a notice requesting a hearing in respect of an offence are references to a notice indicating that the person giving the notice wishes to contest liability for the offence or seeks a determination by a court with respect to the appropriate punishment for the offence,

(*b*) references to an offence include an alleged offence, and

(*c*) references to the person who is or was at any time the registered keeper of a vehicle are references to the person in whose name the vehicle is or was at that time registered under the Vehicles (Excise) Act 1971.

[The term 'petty sessions area' in the Magistrates' Courts Act 1980, s 150(1), is defined by reference to the Justices of the Peace Act 1979, s 4, qv.

A definition ('court of summary jurisdiction') which is applicable exclusively to Scotland has been omitted from s 89(1).]

90. Index to Part III

The expressions listed in the left hand column below are respectively defined or (as the case may be) fall to be construed in accordance with the provisions of this Part of this Act listed in the right-hand column in relation to those expressions.

Expression	*Relevant provision*
Authorised person	Section 54(9)
Conditional offer	Section 75(4)
Fixed penalty	Section 53
Fixed penalty clerk	Section 69(4)
Fixed penalty notice	Section 52
Fixed penalty offence	Section 51
Notice to owner	Sections 63(2) and 66(4)
Notice requesting a hearing in respect of an offence	Section 89(2)
Offence	Section 89(2)
Official form	Section 68(4)
Owner	Section 68(1)
Period allowed for response to a notice to owner	Section 63(5)
Proper address, in relation to the service of a notice to owner	Section 85(4)
Registered keeper	Section 89(2)
Statutory statement of facts	Part II of Schedule 4
Statutory statement of hiring	Part I of Schedule 4
Statutory statement of ownership	Part I of Schedule 4
Suspended enforcement period	Section 52(3)(*a*)
Time of the alleged offence	Section 63(3)

[A 'conditional offer' (which is defined in s 75(4)) is applicable only in Scotland.]

PART IV

MISCELLANEOUS AND GENERAL

91. Penalty for breach of regulations

If a person acts in contravention of or fails to comply with—

(*a*) any regulations made by the Secretary of State under the Road Traffic Act 1988 other than regulations made under section 31, 45 [67A (including that section as applied by section 67B)] or 132,

(*b*) any regulations made by the Secretary of State under the Road Traffic Regulation Act 1984, other than regulations made under section 28, Schedule 4, Part III of Schedule 9 or Schedule 12,

and the contravention of failure to comply is not made an offence under any other provision of the Traffic Acts, he shall for each offence be liable on summary conviction to a fine not exceeding level 3 on the standard scale.

[Section 91 is printed as prospectively amended by the Road Traffic (Consequential Provisions) Act 1988, s 4 and Sched 2, Part III, para 28. The words printed within square brackets in s 91(a) will be brought into force on a date to be announced; see ibid, s 8(3), above.]

92. Application to Crown

The following provisions of this Act apply to vehicles and persons in the public service of the Crown: sections 1, 2, 3, 15, 16 and 49 and the provisions connected with the licensing of drivers.

93. Application of sections 15 and 16 to persons subject to service discipline

(1) Sections 15 and 16, in their application to persons subject to service discipline, apply outside as well as within Great Britain and have effect as if—

(*a*) references to proceedings for an offence under an enactment included references to proceedings for the corresponding service offence,

(*b*) references to the court included a reference to any naval, military, or air force authority before whom the proceedings take place,

(*c*) references to a constable included references to a member of the provost staff, and

(*d*) in section 15, subsection (4) were omitted.

(2) Expressions used in this section have the same meaning as in sections 4 to 10 of the Road Traffic Act 1988 [*qv*].

94. Proceedings in respect of offences in connection with Crown vehicles

(1) Where an offence under the Traffic Acts is alleged to have been committed in connection with a vehicle in the public service of the Crown, proceedings may be brought in respect of the offence against a person nominated for the purpose on behalf of the Crown

(2) Subject to subsection (3) below, where any such offence is committed any person so nominated shall also be guilty of the offence as well as any person actually responsible for the offence (but without prejudice to proceedings against any person so responsible).

(3) Where any person is convicted of an offence by virtue of this section—

(*a*) no order is to be made on his conviction save an order imposing a fine,

(*b*) payment of any fine imposed on him in respect of that offence is not to be enforced against him, and

(*c*) apart from the imposition of any such fine, the conviction is to be disregarded for all purposes other than any appeal (whether by way of case stated or otherwise).

95. Destination of Scottish fines *[Omitted.]*

96. Meaning of 'offence involving obligatory endorsement'

For the purposes of this Act, an offence involves obligatory endorsement if it is an offence under a provision of the Traffic Acts specified in column 1 of Part I of Schedule 2 to this Act or an offence specified in column 1 of Part II of that Schedule and either—

(*a*) the word 'obligatory' (without qualification) appears in column 6 (in the case of Part I) or column 3 (in the case of Part II) against the offence, or

(*b*) that word appears there qualified by conditions relating to the offence which are satisfied.

97. Meaning of 'offence involving obligatory disqualification' and 'offence involving discretionary disqualification'

(1) For the purposes of this Act, an offence involves obligatory disqualification if it is an offence under a provision of the Traffic Acts specified in column 1 of Part I of Schedule 2 to this Act or an offence specified in column 1 of Part II of that Schedule and either—

(*a*) the word 'obligatory' (without qualification) appears in column 5 (in the case of Part I) or column 2 (in the case of Part II) against the offence, or

(*b*) that word appears there qualified by conditions or circumstances relating to the offence which are satisfied or obtain.

(2) For the purposes of this Act, an offence involves discretionary disqualification if it is an offence under a provision of the Traffic Acts specified in column 1 of Part I of Schedule 2 to this Act or an offence specified in column 1 of Part II of that Schedule and either—

(*a*) the word 'discretionary' (without qualification) appears in column 5 (in the case of Part I) or column 2 (in the case of Part II) against the offence, or

(*b*) that word appears there qualified by conditions or circumstances relating to the offence which are satisfied or obtain.

98. General interpretation

(1) In this Act—

'disqualified' means disqualified for holding or obtaining a licence and 'disqualification' is to be construed accordingly,

'drive' has the same meaning as in the Road Traffic Act 1988,

'licence' means a licence to drive a motor vehicle granted under Part III of that Act,

'provisional licence' means a licence granted by virtue of section 97(2) of that Act [*qv*]

'the provisions connected with the licensing of drivers' means sections 7, 8, 22, 25 to 29, 31, 32, 34 to 48, 96 and 97 of this Act,

'road'—

(*a*) in relation to England and Wales, means any highway and any other road to which the public has access, and includes bridges over which a road passes, and

(*b*) *[Applies to Scotland.]*

'the Road Traffic Acts' means the Road Traffic Act 1988, the Road Traffic (Consequential Provisions) Act 1988 (so far as it reproduces the effect of provisions repealed by that Act) and this Act, and

'the Traffic Acts' means the Road Traffic Acts and the Road Traffic Regulation Act 1984.

(2) Sections 185 and 186 of the Road Traffic Act 1988 [*qv*] (meaning of 'motor vehicle' and other expressions relating to vehicles) apply for the purposes of this Act as they apply for the purposes of that.

(3) In the Schedules to this Act—

'RTRA' is used as an abbreviation for the Road Traffic Regulation Act 1984, and

'RTA' is used as an abbreviation for the Road Traffic Act 1988.

(4) Subject to any express exception, references in this Act to any Part of this Act include a reference to any Schedule to this Act so far as relating to that Part.

[As to the meaning of the term 'drive' in the Road Traffic Act 1988, see ibid, s 192, above. As to the meaning of 'licence' in Part III of that Act, see ibid, s 108, above.]

99. Short title, commencement and extent

(1) This Act may be cited as the Road Traffic Offenders Act 1988.

(2) This Act, except so far as it may be brought into force under subsection (3) or (5) below, shall come into force at the end of the period of six months beginning with the day on which it is passed.

(3), (4) *[Apply to Scotland.]*

(5) Section 59 of this Act shall come into force on such day or days as the Secretary of State may by order made by statutory instrument appoint.

(6) An order under subsection (3) or (5) above may contain such transitional provisions and savings (whether or not involving the modification of any provisions contained in an Act or in subordinate legislation (within the meaning of the Interpretation Act 1978)) as appear to the Secretary of State necessary or expedient in connection with the provisions brought (wholly or partly) into force by the order, and different days may be appointed for different purposes.

(7) This Act, except as provided by section 93, does not extend to Northern Ireland.

SCHEDULE 1

Sections 1 etc.

OFFENCES TO WHICH SECTIONS 1, 6, 11 AND 12(1) APPLY

1.—(1) Where section 1, 6, 11 or 12(1) of this Act is shown in column 3 of this Schedule against a provision of the Road Traffic Act 1988 specified in column 1, the section in question applies to an offence under that provision.

(2) The general nature of the offence is indicated in column 2.

2. Section 6 also applies—

(*a*) to an offence under section 67 of this Act, and

(*b*) *[Applies to Scotland.]*

3. Section 11 also applies to—

(*a*) any offence to which section 112 of the Road Traffic Regulation Act 1984 [*qv*] (information as to identity of driver or rider) applies except an offence under section 61(5) of that Act,

(*b*) any offence which is punishable under section 91 of this Act, and

(*c*) any offence against any other enactment relating to the use of vehicles on roads.

4. Section 12(1) also applies to—

(*a*) any offence which is punishable under section 91 of this Act, and

(*b*) any offence against any other enactment relating to the use of vehicles on roads.

(1) *Provision creating offence*	(2) *General nature of offence*	(3) *Applicable provisions of this Act*
RTA section 1	Causing death by reckless driving.	Section 11 of this Act.
RTA section 2	Reckless driving.	Sections 1, 11 and 12(1) of this Act.
RTA section 3	Careless, and inconsiderate driving.	Sections 1, 11 and 12(1) of this Act.
RTA section 4	Driving or attempting to drive, or being in charge of a motor vehicle, when unfit to drive through drink or drugs.	Sections 11 and 12(1) of this Act.
RTA section 5	Driving or attempting to drive, or being in charge of a motor vehicle, with excess alcohol in breath, blood or urine.	Sections 11 and 12(1) of this Act.
RTA section 6	Failing to provide a specimen of breath for a breath test.	Sections 11 and 12(1) of this Act.
RTA section 7	Failing to provide specimen for analysis or laboratory test.	Sections 11 and 12(1) of this Act.
RTA section 12	Motor racing and speed trials.	Sections 11 and 12(1) of this Act.
RTA section 14	Driving or riding in a motor vehicle in contravention of regulations requiring wearing of seat belts.	Sections 11 and 12(1) of this Act.
RTA section 15	Driving motor vehicle with child not wearing seat belt.	Sections 11 and 12(1) of this Act
RTA section 19	Prohibition of parking of heavy commercial vehicles on verges and footways.	Sections 11 and 12(1) of this Act.
[RTA section 19A	Prohibition of parking of vehicles other than heavy commercial vehicles on verges, etc.	Sections 11 and 12 of this Act.]
RTA section 22	Leaving vehicles in dangerous positions.	Sections 1, 11 and 12(1) of this Act.
RTA section 23	Carrying passenger on motor-cycle contrary to section 23.	Sections 11 and 12(1) of this Act.
RTA section 24	Carrying passenger on bicycle contrary to section 24.	Sections 11 and 12(1) of this Act.
RTA section 25	Tampering with motor vehicles.	Section 11 of this Act.
RTA section 26(1)	Holding or getting onto vehicle in order to be carried.	Section 11 of this Act.
RTA section 26(2)	Holding onto vehicle in order to be towed.	Sections 11 and 12(1) of this Act.
RTA section 28	Reckless cycling.	Sections 1, 11 and 12(1) of this Act.
RTA section 29	Careless, and inconsiderate, cycling.	Sections 1, 11 and 12(1) of this Act.

(1) *Provision creating offence*	(2) *General nature of offence*	(3) *Applicable provisions of this Act*
RTA section 30	Cycling when unfit through drink or drugs.	Sections 11 and 12(1) of this Act.
RTA section 31	Unauthorised or irregular cycle racing, or trials of speed.	Sections 11 and 12(1) of this Act.
RTA section 33	Unauthorised motor vehicle trial on footpaths or bridleways.	Sections 11 and 12(1) of this Act.
RTA section 34	Driving motor vehicles elsewhere than on roads.	Sections 11 and 12(1) of this Act.
RTA section 35	Failing to comply with traffic directions.	Sections 1, 11 and 12(1) of this Act.
RTA section 36	Failing to comply with traffic signs.	Sections 1, 11 and 12(1) of this Act.
RTA section 42	Contravention of construction and use regulations.	Sections 11 and 12(1) of this Act.
RTA section 47	Using, etc, vehicle without required test certificate being in force.	Sections 11 and 12(1) of this Act.
RTA section 53	Using, etc, goods vehicle without required plating certificate or goods vehicle test certificate being in force, or where Secretary of State is required by regulations under section 49 to be notified of an alteration to the vehicle or its equipment but has not been notified.	Sections 11 and 12(1) of this Act.
RTA section 63	Using, etc, vehicle without required certificate being in force showing that it, or a part fitted to it, complies with type approval requirements applicable to it, or using, etc, certain goods vehicles for drawing trailer when plating certificate does not specify maximum laden weight for vehicle and trailer, or using, etc, goods vehicle where Secretary of State has not been but is required to be notified under section 48 of alteration to it or its equipment.	Sections 11 and 12(1) of this Act.
RTA section 71	Driving, etc, goods vehicle in contravention of prohibition on driving it as being unfit for service or overloaded, or refusing, neglecting or otherwise failing to comply with a direction to remove a goods vehicle found overloaded.	Sections 11 and 12(1) of this Act.
RTA section 78	Failing to comply with requirement about weighing motor vehicle or obstructing authorised person.	Sections 11 and 12(1) of this Act.
RTA section 87(1)	Driving without a licence.	Sections 11 and 12(1) of this Act.

(1) *Provision creating offence*	(2) *General nature of offence*	(3) *Applicable provisions of this Act*
RTA section 87(2)	Causing or permitting a person to drive without a licence.	Section 11 of this Act.
RTA section 94	Failure to notify the Secretary of State of onset of, or deterioration in, relevant or prospective disability.	Section 6 of this Act.
RTA section 97	Failing to comply with any conditions prescribed for driving under provisional licence.	Sections 11 and 12(1) of this Act.
RTA section 98	Failing to comply with any conditions prescribed for driving under provisional licence where conditions applicable to driving under full licence.	Sections 11 and 12(1) of this Act.
RTA section 99	Driving licence holder failing, when his particulars become incorrect, to surrender licence and give particulars.	Section 6 of this Act.
RTA section 103(1)(*a*)	Obtaining driving licence while disqualified.	Section 6 of this Act.
RTA section 103(1)(*b*)	Driving while disqualified.	Sections 6, 11 and 12(1) of this Act.
RTA section 110(1)	Driving HGV without HGV driver's licence.	Sections 11 and 12(1) of this Act.
RTA section 110(2)	Causing or permitting person to drive HGV without HGV driver's licence.	Section 11 of this Act.
RTA section 112(6)	Failing to comply with conditions of HGV driver's licence.	Sections 11 and 12(1) of this Act.
RTA section 112(7)	Causing or permitting a person under 21 to drive HGV in contravention of conditions of HGV driver's licence.	Section 11 of this Act.
RTA section 143	Using motor vehicle, or causing or permitting it to be used, while uninsured or unsecured against third party risks.	Sections 6, 11 and 12(1) of this Act.
RTA section 163	Failing to stop vehicle when required by constable.	Sections 11 and 12(1) of this Act.
RTA section 164(6)	Failing to produce driving licence to constable or to state date of birth.	Sections 11 and 12(1) of this Act.
RTA section 165(3)	Failing to give constable certain names and addresses or to produce certificate of insurance or certain test and other like certificates.	Sections 11 and 12(1) of this Act.
RTA section 165(6)	Supervisor of learner driver failing to give constable certain names and addresses.	Section 11 of this Act.
RTA section 168	Refusing to give, or giving false, name and address in case of reckless, careless or inconsiderate driving or cycling.	Sections 11 and 12(1) of this Act.
RTA section 170	Failure by driver to stop, report accident or give information or documents.	Sections 11 and 12(1) of this Act.

(1) *Provision creating offence*	(2) *General nature of offence*	(3) *Applicable provisions of this Act*
RTA section 171	Failure by owner of motor vehicle to give police information for verifying compliance with requirement of compulsory insurance or security.	Sections 11 and 12(1) of this Act.
RTA section 174(1) or (6)	Making false statements in connection with licences under this Act and with registration as an approved driving instructor; or making false statement or withholding material information in order to obtain the issue of insurance certificates, etc.	Section 6 of this Act.
RTA section 175	Issuing false documents [falsely amending certificate of conformity].	Section 6 of this Act.

[Schedule 1 is printed as prospectively amended by the Road Traffic (Consequential Provisions) Act 1988, s 4 and Sched 2, Part I, para 13(c)(i) and (iv), and Part II, para 22(3). The entry in the table relating to the Road Traffic Act 1988, s 19A, and the words printed within square brackets in the second column of the table in the entry relating to ibid, s 175, will come into force on dates to be announced; see the Road Traffic (Consequential Provisions) Act 1988, s 8(3), above.]

Section 9 etc.

SCHEDULE 2

Prosecution and Punishment of Offences

Part I

Offences under the Traffic acts

(1) Provision creating offence	(2) General nature of offence	(3) Mode of prosecution	(4) Punishment	(5) Disqualification	(6) Endorsement	(7) Penalty points
		Offences under the Road Traffic Regulation Act 1984				
RTRA section 5	Contravention of traffic regulation order.	Summarily.	Level 3 on the standard scale.			
RTRA section 8	Contravention of order regulating traffic in Greater London.	Summarily.	Level 3 on the standard scale.			
RTRA section 11	Contravention of experimental traffic order.	Summarily.	Level 3 on the standard scale.			
RTRA section 13	Contravention of experimental traffic scheme in Greater London.	Summarily.	Level 3 on the standard scale.			
RTRA section 16(1)	Contravention of temporary prohibition or restriction.	Summarily.	Level 3 on the standard scale.			

RTRA section 17(4)	Use of special road contrary to scheme or regulations.	Summarily.	Level 4 on the standard scale.	Discretionary if committed in respect of a motor vehicle otherwise than by unlawfully stopping or allowing the vehicle to remain at rest on a part of a special road on which vehicles are in certain circumstances permitted to remain at rest.	Obligatory if committed as mentioned in the entry in column 5.	3
RTRA section 18(3)	One-way traffic on trunk road.	Summarily.	Level 3 on the standard scale.			
RTRA section 20(5)	Contravention of prohibition or restriction for roads of certain classes.	Summarily.	Level 3 on the standard scale.			
RTRA section 25(5)	Contravention of pedestrian crossing regulations.	Summarily.	Level 3 on the standard scale.	Discretionary if committed in respect of a motor vehicle.	Obligatory if committed in respect of a motor vehicle.	3
RTRA section 28(3)	Not stopping at school crossing.	Summarily.	Level 3 on the standard scale.	Discretionary if committed in respect of a motor vehicle.	Obligatory if committed in respect of a motor vehicle.	3

(1) Provision creating offence	(2) General nature of offence	(3) Mode of prosecution	(4) Punishment	(5) Disqualification	(6) Endorsement	(7) Penalty points
		Offences under the Road Traffic Regulation Act 1984—contd				
RTRA section 29(3)	Contravention of order relating to street playground.	Summarily.	Level 3 on the standard scale.	Discretionary if committed in respect of a motor vehicle.	Obligatory if committed in respect of a motor vehicle.	2
RTRA section 30(5)	As above (Greater London).	Summarily.	Level 3 on the standard scale.	Discretionary if committed in respect of a motor vehicle.	Obligatory if committed in respect of a motor vehicle.	2
RTRA section 35(4)	Contravention of order as to use of parking place.	Summarily.	(*a*) Level 3 on the standard scale in the case of an offence committed by a person in a street parking place reserved for disabled persons' vehicles or in an off-street parking place reserved for such vehicles, where that person would			

			not have been guilty of that offence if the motor vehicle in respect of which it was committed had been a disabled person's vehicle. (*b*) Level 2 on the standard scale in any other case.			
RTRA section 35(5)	Interference with apparatus for collecting charges.	Summarily.	Level 3 on the standard scale.			
RTRA section 35(7)	Plying for hire in parking place.	Summarily.	Level 2 on the standard scale.			
RTRA section 43(5)	Unauthorised disclosure of information in respect of licensed parking place.	Summarily.	Level 3 on the standard scale.			
RTRA section 43(10)	Failure to comply with term or conditions of licence to operate parking place.	Summarily.	Level 3 on the standard scale.			
RTRA section 43(12)	Operation of public off-street parking place without licence.	Summarily.	Level 5 on the standard scale.			

(1) Provision creating offence	(2) General nature of offence	(3) Mode of prosecution	(4) Punishment	(5) Disqualification	(6) Endorsement	(7) Penalty points
		Offences under the Road Traffic Regulation Act 1984—contd				
RTRA section 47(1)	Contraventions relating to designated parking places.	Summarily.	(*a*) Level 3 on the standard scale in the case of an offence committed by a person in a street parking place reserved for disabled persons' vehicles where that person would not have been guilty of that offence if the motor vehicle in respect of which it was committed had been a disabled person's vehicle. (*b*) Level 2 in any other case.			
RTRA section 47(3)	Tampering with parking meter	Summarily.	Level 3 on the standard scale.			
RTRA section 52(1)	Misuse of parking device.	Summarily.	Level 2 on the standard scale.			

RTRA section 53(5)	Contravention of certain provisions of designation orders.	Summarily.	Level 3 on the standard scale.			
RTRA section 53(6)	Other contraventions of designation orders.	Summarily.	Level 2 on the standard scale.			
RTRA section 61(5)	Unauthorised use of loading area.	Summarily.	Level 3 on the standard scale.			
RTRA section 88(7)	Contravention of minimum speed limit.	Summarily.	Level 3 on the standard scale.			
RTRA section 89(1)	Exceeding speed limit.	Summarily.	Level 3 on the standard scale.	Discretionary.	Obligatory.	3
RTRA section 104(5)	Interference with notice as to immobilisation device.	Summarily.	Level 2 on the standard scale.			
RTRA section 104(6)	Interference with immobilisation device.	Summarily.	Level 3 on the standard scale.			
RTRA section 105(5)	Misuse of disabled person's badge (immobilisation devices).	Summarily.	Level 3 on the standard scale.			
RTRA section 108(2) (or that sub-section as modified by section 109(2), (3)).	Non-compliance with notice (excess charge).	Summarily.	Level 3 on the standard scale.			

(1) Provision creating offence	(2) General nature of offence	(3) Mode of prosecution	(4) Punishment	(5) Disqualification	(6) Endorsement	(7) Penalty points
		Offences under the Road Traffic Regulation Act 1984—contd				
RTRA section 108(3) (or that sub-section as modified by section 109(2) and (3)).	False response to notice (excess charge).	Summarily.	Level 5 on the standard scale.			
RTRA section 112(4)	Failure to give information as to identity of driver.	Summarily.	Level 3 on the standard scale.			
RTRA section 115(1)	Mishandling or faking parking documents.	(*a*) Summarily.	(*a*) The statutory maximum.			
		(*b*) On indictment.	(*b*) 2 years.			
RTRA section 115(2)	False statement for procuring authorisation.	Summarily.	Level 4 on the standard scale.			
RTRA section 116(1)	Non-delivery of suspect document or article.	Summarily.	Level 3 on the standard scale.			
RTRA section 117	Wrongful use of disabled person's badge.	Summarily.	Level 3 on the standard scale.			
RTRA section 129(3)	Failure to give evidence at inquiry.	Summarily.	Level 3 on the standard scale.			

Offences under the Road Traffic Act 1988—contd

RTA section 1	Causing death by reckless driving.	On indictment.	5 years.	Obligatory.	Obligatory.	4
RTA section 2	Reckless driving.	(*a*) Summarily.	(*a*) 6 months or the statutory maximun or both.	(i) Obligatory, if committed within 3 years after a previous conviction of an offence under RTA section 1 or 2. (ii) Discretionary, if committed otherwise than as mentioned in paragraph (i) above.	Obligatory.	(i) 4, if committed as mentioned in column (5)(i). (ii) 10, if committed otherwise than as mentioned in column (5)(i).
		(*b*) On indictment.	(*b*) 2 years or a fine or both.			
RTA section 3	Careless, and inconsiderate, driving.	Summarily.	Level 4 on the standard scale.	Discretionary.	Obligatory.	3–9
RTA section 4(1)	Driving or attempting to drive when unfit to drive through drink or drugs.	Summarily.	6 months or level 5 on the standard scale or both.	Obligatory.	Obligatory.	4

(1) Provision creating offence	(2) General nature of offence	(3) Mode of prosecution	(4) Punishment	(5) Disqualification	(6) Endorsement	(7) Penalty points
Offences under the Road Traffic Act 1988—contd						
RTA section 4(2)	Being in charge of a motor vehicle when unfit to drive through drink or drugs.	Summarily.	3 months or level 4 on the standard scale or both.	Discretionary.	Obligatory.	10
RTA section 5(1)(*a*)	Driving or attempting to drive with excess alcohol in breath, blood or urine.	Summarily.	6 months or level 5 on the standard scale or both.	Obligatory.	Obligatory.	4
RTA section 5(1)(*b*)	Being in charge of a motor vehicle with excess alcohol in breath, blood or urine.	Summarily.	3 months or level 4 on the standard scale or both.	Discretionary.	Obligatory.	10
RTA section 6	Failing to provide a specimen of breath for a breath test.	Summarily.	Level 3 on the standard scale.	Discretionary.	Obligatory.	4
RTA section 7	Failing to provide specimen for analysis or laboratory test.	Summarily.	(*a*) Where the specimen was required to ascertain ability to drive or proportion of alcohol at the time offender	(*a*) Obligatory in case mentioned in column 4(*a*).	Obligatory.	(*a*) 4 in case mentioned in column 4(*a*).

			was driving or attempting to drive, 6 months or level 5 on the standard scale or both. (*b*) In any other case, 3 months or level 4 on the standard scale or both.	(*b*) Discretionary in any other case.		(*b*) 10 in any other case.
RTA section 12	Motor racing and speed trials on public ways.	Summarily.	Level 4 on the standard scale.	Obligatory.	Obligatory.	4
RTA section 13	Other unauthorised or irregular competitions or trials on public ways.	Summarily.	Level 3 on the standard scale.			
RTA section 14	Driving or riding in a motor vehicle in contravention of regulations requiring wearing of seat belts.	Summarily.	Level 2 on the standard scale.			
RTA section 15(2)	Driving motor vehicle with child in front not wearing seat belt.	Summarily.	Level 2 on the standard scale.			
RTA section 15(4)	Driving motor vehicle with child in rear not wearing seat belt.	Summarily.	Level 1 on the standard scale.			

(1) Provision creating offence	(2) General nature of offence	(3) Mode of prosecution	(4) Punishment	(5) Disqualification	(6) Endorsement	(7) Penalty points
		Offences under the Road Traffic Act 1988—contd				
RTA section 16	Driving or riding motor cycles in contravention of regulations requiring wearing of protective headgear.	Summarily.	Level 2 on the standard scale.			
RTA section 17	Selling, etc, helmet not of the prescribed type as helmet for affording protection for motor cyclists.	Summarily.	Level 3 on the standard scale.			
RTA section 18(3)	Contravention of regulations with respect to use of headworn appliances on motor cycles.	Summarily.	Level 2 on the standard scale.			
RTA section 18(4)	Selling, etc, appliance not of prescribed type as approved for use on motor cycles.	Summarily.	Level 3 on the standard scale.			

RTA section 19	Prohibition of parking of heavy commercial vehicles on verges, etc.	Summarily.	Level 3 on the standard scale.			
[RTA section 19A	Prohibition of parking of vehicles other than heavy commercial vehicles on verges, etc.	Summarily.	Level 3 on the standard scale.	—	—	—]
RTA section 21	Driving or parking on cycle track.	Summarily.	Level 3 on the standard scale.			
RTA section 22	Leaving vehicles in dangerous positions.	Summarily.	Level 3 on the standard scale.	Discretionary if committed in respect of a motor vehicle.	Obligatory if committed in respect of a motor vehicle.	3
RTA section 23	Carrying passenger on motor-cycle contrary to section 23.	Summarily.	Level 3 on the standard scale.	Discretionary.	Obligatory.	1
RTA section 24	Carrying passenger on bicycle contrary to section 24.	Summarily	Level 1 on the standard scale.			
RTA section 25	Tampering with motor vehicles.	Summarily.	Level 3 on the standard scale.			
RTA section 26	Holding or getting on to vehicle, etc, in order to be towed or carried.	Summarily.	Level 1 on the standard scale.			

(1) Provision creating offence	(2) General nature of offence	(3) Mode of prosecution	(4) Punishment	(5) Disqualification	(6) Endorsement	(7) Penalty points
		Offences under the Road Traffic Act 1988—contd				
RTA section 27	Dogs on designated roads without being held on lead.	Summarily.	Level 1 on the standard scale.			
RTA section 28	Reckless cycling.	Summarily.	Level 3 on the standard scale.			
RTA section 29	Careless, and inconsiderate, cycling.	Summarily.	Level 1 on the standard scale.			
RTA section 30	Cycling when unfit through drink or drugs.	Summarily.	Level 3 on the standard scale.			
RTA section 31	Unauthorised or irregular cycle racing or trials of speed on public ways.	Summarily.	Level 1 on the standard scale.			
RTA section 32	Contravening prohibition on persons under 14 driving electrically assisted pedal cycles.	Summarily.	Level 2 on the standard scale.			
RTA section 33	Unauthorised motor vehicle trial on footpaths or bridleways.	Summarily.	Level 3 on the standard scale.			

RTA section 34	Driving motor vehicles elsewhere than on roads.	Summarily.	Level 3 on the standard scale.			
RTA section 35	Failing to comply with traffic directions.	Summarily.	Level 3 on the standard scale.	Discretionary, if committed in respect of a motor vehicle by failure to comply with a direction of a constable or traffic warden.	Obligatory if committed as described in column 5.	3
RTA section 36	Failing to comply with traffic signs.	Summarily.	Level 3 on the standard scale.	Discretionary, if committed in respect of a motor vehicle by failure to comply with an indication given by a sign specified for the purposes of this paragraph in regulations under RTA section 36.	Obligatory if committed as described in column 5.	3
RTA section 37	Pedestrian failing to stop when directed by constable regulating traffic.	Summarily.	Level 3 on the standard scale.			

(1) Provision creating offence	(2) General nature of offence	(3) Mode of prosecution	(4) Punishment	(5) Disqualification	(6) Endorsement	(7) Penalty points
		Offences under the Road Traffic Act 1988—contd				
RTA section 42	Contravention of construction and use regulations.	Summarily.	(*a*) Level 5 on the standard scale in the case of an offence of using, or causing or permitting the use of, a goods vehicle or a vehicle adapted to carry more than eight passengers — (i) so as to cause, or to be likely to cause, danger by the condition of the vehicle or its parts or accessories, the number of passengers carried by it, or the weight, distribution, packing or	(*a*) Discretionary if committed by using, or causing or permitting the use of, any motor vehicle or trailer— (i) as described in paragraph (*a*)(i) or (iii) in the entry in column 4, or (ii) in breach of a construction and use requirement (within the meaning of Part II of that Act) as to brakes, steering-gear, or tyres. (*b*) Discretionary if committed by	Obligatory if committed as described in the entry in column 5.	3

			adjustment of its load, or (ii) in breach of a construction and use requirement (within the meaning of Part II of the Road Traffic Act 1988) as to brakes, steering-gear, tyres or any description of weight, or (iii) for any purpose for which it is so unsuitable as to cause or to be likely to cause danger. (*b*) Level 5 on the standard scale in the case of an offence of carrying on a goods vehicle a load which, by reason of its insecurity or	carrying on a motor vehicle or trailer a load which, by reason of its insecurity or position, is likely to cause danger.			

(1) Provision creating offence	(2) General nature of offence	(3) Mode of prosecution	(4) Punishment	(5) Disqualification	(6) Endorsement	(7) Penalty points
		Offences under the Road Traffic Act 1988—contd				
			position, is likely to cause danger. (*c*) Level 4 on the standard scale in any other case.			
RTA section 47	Using, etc, vehicle without required test certificate being in force.	Summarily.	(*a*) Level 4 on the standard scale in the case of a vehicle adapted to carry more than eight passengers. (*b*) Level 3 on the standard scale in any other case.			
Regulations under RTA section 49 made by virtue of section 51(2)	Contravention of requirement of regulations (which is declared by regulations to be an offence) that driver of goods vehicle being	Summarily.	Level 3 on the standard scale.			

	tested be present throughout test or drive, etc, vehicle as and when directed.					
RTA section 53(1)	Using, etc, goods vehicle without required plating certificate being in force.	Summarily.	Level 3 on the standard scale.			
RTA section 53(2)	Using, etc, goods vehicle without required goods vehicle test certificate being in force.	Summarily.	Level 4 on the standard scale.			
RTA section 53(3)	Using, etc, goods vehicle where Secretary of State is required by regulations under section 49 to be notified of an alteration to the vehicle or its equipment but has not been notified.	Summarily.	Level 3 on the standard scale.			
Regulations under RTA section 61 made by virtue of	Contravention of requirement of regulations (which is declared by	Summarily.	Level 3 on the standard scale.			

(1) Provision creating offence	(2) General nature of offence	(3) Mode of prosecution	(4) Punishment	(5) Disqualification	(6) Endorsement	(7) Penalty points
		Offences under the Road Traffic Act 1988—contd				
subsection (4).	regulations to be an offence) that driver of goods vehicle being tested after notifiable alteration be present throughout test and drive, etc, vehicle as and when directed.					
RTA section 63(1)	Using, etc, goods vehicle without required certificate being in force showing that it complies with type approval requirements applicable to it.	Summarily.	Level 4 on the standard scale.			
RTA section 63(2)	Using, etc, certain goods vehicles for drawing trailer when plating certificate does	Summarily.	Level 3 on the standard scale.			

	not specify maximum laden weight for vehicle and trailer.					
RTA section 63(3)	Using, etc, goods vehicle where Secretary of State is required to be notified under section 59 of alteration to it or its equipment but has not been notified.	Summarily.	Level 3 on the standard scale.			
RTA section 64	Using goods vehicles with unauthorised weights as well as authorised weights marked on it.	Summarily.	Level 3 on the standard scale.			
RTA section 65	Supplying vehicle or vehicle part without required certificate being in force showing that it complies with type approval requirements applicable to it.	Summarily.	Level 5 on the standard scale.			
RTA section 67	Obstructing testing of vehicle by	Summarily.	Level 3 on the standard scale.			

(1) Provision creating offence	(2) General nature of offence	(3) Mode of prosecution	(4) Punishment	(5) Disqualification	(6) Endorsement	(7) Penalty points
		Offences under the Road Traffic Act 1988—contd				
	examiner on road or failing to comply with requirements of RTA section 67 or Schedule 2.					
[RTA section 67A (including application by section 67B(4))	Failure of owner of apparently defective vehicle to give required certificate or declaration, or failure of person in charge of vehicle being tested to give information.	Summarily.	Level 3 on the standard scale.	—	—	—]
[RTA section 67B	Obstructing further testing of vehicle by Secretary of State's officer or failing to comply with requirements of RTA section 67B or paragraph 3 or 4 of Schedule 2.	Summarily.	Level 3 on the standard scale.	—	—	—]

RTA section 68	Obstructing inspection, etc, of goods vehicle by examiner or failing to comply with requirement to take goods vehicle for inspection.	Summarily.	Level 3 on the standard scale.			
RTA section 71	Driving, etc, goods vehicle in contravention of prohibition on driving it as being unfit for service, or refusing, neglecting or otherwise failing to comply with direction to remove a goods vehicle found overloaded.	Summarily.	Level 5 on the standard scale.			
RTA section 74	Contravention of regulations requiring goods vehicle operator to inspect, and keep records of inspection of, goods vehicles.	Summarily.	Level 3 on the standard scale.			
RTA section 75	Selling, etc, unroadworthy	Summarily.	Level 5 on the standard scale.			

(1) Provision creating offence	(2) General nature of offence	(3) Mode of prosecution	(4) Punishment	(5) Disqualification	(6) Endorsement	(7) Penalty points
Offences under the Road Traffic Act 1988—contd						
	vehicle or trailer or altering vehicle or trailer so as to make it unroadworthy.					
RTA section 76(1)	Fitting of defective or unsuitable vehicle parts.	Summarily.	Level 5 on the standard scale.			
RTA section 76(3)	Supplying defective or unsuitable vehicle parts.	Summarily.	Level 4 on the standard scale.			
RTA section 76(8)	Obstructing examiner testing vehicles to ascertain whether defective or unsuitable part has been fitted, etc.	Summarily.	Level 3 on the standard scale.			
RTA section 77	Obstructing examiner testing condition of used vehicles at sale rooms, etc.	Summarily.	Level 3 on the standard scale.			
RTA section 78	Failing to comply with requirement about weighing	Summarily.	Level 5 on the standard scale.			

	motor vehicle or obstructing authorised person.					
RTA section 81	Selling, etc, pedal cycle in contravention of regulations as to brakes, bells, etc.	Summarily.	Level 3 on the standard scale.			
RTA section 83	Selling, etc, wrongly made tail lamps or reflectors.	Summarily.	Level 5 on the standard scale.			
RTA section 87(1)	Driving without a licence.	Summarily.	Level 3 on the standard scale.	Discretionary if committed by driving a motor vehicle in a case where either no licence authorising the driving of that vehicle could have been granted to the offender or, if a provisional (but no other) licence to drive it could have been granted to him, the driving would not have complied with the conditions of the licence.	Obligatory if committed as described in the entry in column 5.	2

(1) Provision creating offence	(2) General nature of offence	(3) Mode of prosecution	(4) Punishment	(5) Disqualification	(6) Endorsement	(7) Penalty points
		Offences under the Road Traffic Act 1988—contd				
RTA section 87(2)	Causing or permitting a person to drive without a licence.	Summarily.	Level 3 on the standard scale.			
RTA section 94	Failure to notify Secretary of State of onset of, or deterioration in, relevant or prospective disability.	Summarily.	Level 3 on the standard scale.			
RTA section 96	Driving with uncorrected defective eyesight, or refusing to submit to test of eyesight.	Summarily.	Level 3 on the standard scale.	Discretionary.	Obligatory.	2
RTA section 97	Failing to comply with any conditions prescribed for driving under provisional licence.	Summarily.	Level 3 on the standard scale.	Discretionary.	Obligatory.	2
RTA section 98	Failing to comply with any	Summarily.	Level 3 on the standard scale.	Discretionary.	Obligatory.	2

	conditions prescribed for driving under provisional licence where conditions applicable to driving under full licence.					
RTA section 99	Driving licence holder failing, when his particulars become incorrect, to surrender licence and give particulars.	Summarily.	Level 3 on the standard scale.			
RTA section 103(1)(*a*)	Obtaining driving licence while disqualified.	Summarily.	Level 3 on the standard scale.			
RTA section 103(1)(*b*)	Driving while disqualified.	(*a*) Summarily, in England and Wales.	(*a*) 6 months or level 5 on the standard scale or both.	Discretionary.	Obligatory.	2 where offender was disqualified as under age, 6 where offender was disqualified by order of court.

(1) Provision creating offence	(2) General nature of offence	(3) Mode of prosecution	(4) Punishment	(5) Disqualification	(6) Endorsement	(7) Penalty points
		Offences under the Road Traffic Act 1988—contd				
		(*b*) Summarily, in Scotland.	(*b*) 6 months or the statutory maximum or both.			
		(*c*) On indictment, in Scotland.	(*c*) 12 months or a fine or both.			
RTA section 109	Failing to produce to court Northern Ireland driving licence.	Summarily.	Level 3 on the standard scale.			
RTA section 110	Driving, or causing or permitting person to drive, HGV without HGV driver's licence.	Summarily.	Level 4 on the standard scale.			
RTA section 112	Failing to comply with conditions of HGV driver's licence, or causing or permitting person under 21 to drive HGV in contravention of such conditions.	Summarily.	Level 3 on the standard scale.			

Regulations made by virtue of RTA section 117(4)	Contravention of provisions of regulations (which is declared by regulations to be an offence) about HGV drivers' licences.	Summarily.	Level 3 on the standard scale.			
RTA section 123(4)	Giving of paid driving instruction by unregistered and unlicensed persons or their employers.	Summarily.	Level 4 on the standard scale.			
RTA section 123(6)	Giving paid instruction without there being exhibited on the motor car a certificate of registration or a licence under RTA Part V.	Summarily.	Level 3 on the standard scale.			
RTA section 135	Unregistered instructor using title or displaying badge, etc, prescribed for registered instructor, or employer using	Summarily.	Level 4 on the standard scale.			

(1) Provision creating offence	(2) General nature of offence	(3) Mode of prosecution	(4) Punishment	(5) Disqualification	(6) Endorsement	(7) Penalty points
		Offences under the Road Traffic Act 1988—contd				
	such title, etc, in relation to his unregistered instructor or issuing misleading advertisement, etc.					
RTA section 136	Failure of instructor to surrender to Registrar certificate or licence.	Summarily.	Level 3 on the standard scale.			
RTA section 137	Failing to produce certificate of registration or licence as driving instructor.	Summarily.	Level 3 on the standard scale.			
RTA section 143	Using motor vehicle while uninsured or unsecured against third-party risks.	Summarily.	Level 4 on the standard scale.	Discretionary.	Obligatory.	6–8
RTA section 147	Failing to surrender certificate of insurance or security to insurer	Summarily.	Level 3 on the standard scale.			

	on cancellation or to make statutory declaration of loss or destruction.					
RTA section 154	Failing to give information, or wilfully making a false statement, as to insurance or security when claim made.	Summarily.	Level 4 on the standard scale.			
RTA section 163	Failing to stop motor vehicle or cycle when required by constable.	Summarily.	Level 3 on the standard scale.			
RTA section 164	Failing to produce driving licence to constable or to state date of birth, or failing to provide the Secretary of State with evidence of date of birth, etc.	Summarily.	Level 3 on the standard scale.			
RTA section 165	Failing to give constable certain names and addresses or to produce certain documents.	Summarily.	Level 3 on the standard scale.			
RTA section 168	Refusing to give, or giving false, name	Summarily.	Level 3 on the standard scale.			

(1) Provision creating offence	(2) General nature of offence	(3) Mode of prosecution	(4) Punishment	(5) Disqualification	(6) Endorsement	(7) Penalty points
	Offences under the Road Traffic Act 1988—contd					
	and address in case of reckless, careless or inconsiderate driving or cycling.					
RTA section 169	Pedestrian failing to give constable his name and address after failing to stop when directed by constable controlling traffic.	Summarily.	Level 1 on the standard scale.			
RTA section 170(4)	Failing to stop after accident and give particulars or report accident.	Summarily.	Level 5 on the standard scale.	Discretionary.	Obligatory.	8–10
RTA section 107(7)	Failure by driver, in case of accident involving injury to another, to produce evidence of insurance or security or to report accident.	Summarily.	Level 3 on the standard scale.			
RTA section 171	Failure by owner of motor vehicle to	Summarily.	Level 4 on the standard scale.			

	give police information for verifying compliance with requirement of compulsory insurance or security.					
RTA section 172	Failure of person keeping vehicle and others to give police information as to identity of driver, etc, in the case of certain offences.	Summarily.	Level 3 on the standard scale.			
RTA section 173	Forgery, etc, of licences, test certificates, certificates of insurance and other documents and things.	(*a*) Summarily. (*b*) On indictment	(*a*) The statutory maximum. (*b*) 2 years.			
RTA section 174	Making certain false statements, etc, and withholding certain material information.	Summarily.	Level 4 on the standard scale.			
RTA section [175(1)]	Issuing false documents.	Summarily.	Level 4 on the standard scale.			

(1) Provision creating offence	(2) General nature of offence	(3) Mode of prosecution	(4) Punishment	(5) Disqualification	(6) Endorsement	(7) Penalty points
		Offences under the Road Traffic Act 1988—contd				
[[RTA section] [175(2)]	Falsely amending certificate of conformity.	Summarily.	[Level 4 on the standard scale.]	—	—	. . .]
RTA section 177	Impersonation of, or of person employed by, authorised examiner.	Summarily.	Level 3 on the standard scale.			
RTA section 178	Taking, etc, in Scotland a motor vehicle without authority or, knowing that it has been so taken, driving it or allowing oneself to be carried in it without authority.	(*a*) Summarily. (*b*) On indictment.	(*a*) 3 months or the statutory maximum or both. (*b*) 12 months or a fine or both.	Discretionary.	Obligatory.	8
RTA section 180	Failing to attend, give evidence or produce documents to, inquiry held by Secretary of State, etc.	Summarily.	Level 3 on the standard scale.			

RTA section 181	Obstructing inspection of vehicles after accident.	Summarily.	Level 3 on the standard scale.			
RTA Schedule 1 paragraph 6	Applying warranty to protective helmet or appliance in defending proceedings under RTA section 17 or 18(4) where no warranty given, or applying false warranty.	Summarily.	Level 3 on the standard scale.			
			Offences under this Act			
Section 25 of this Act	Failing to give information as to date of birth or sex to court or to provide Secretary of State with evidence of date of birth, etc.	Summarily.	Level 3 on the standard scale.			
Section 26 of this Act	Failing to produce driving licence to court making order for interim disqualification on committal for sentence, etc.	Summarily.	Level 3 on the standard scale.			

(1) Provision creating offence	(2) General nature of offence	(3) Mode of prosecution	(4) Punishment	(5) Disqualification	(6) Endorsement	(7) Penalty points
		Offences under this Act—contd				
Section 27 of this Act	Failing to produce licence to court for endorsement on conviction of offence involving obligatory endorsement or on committal for sentence, etc, for offence involving obligatory or discretionary disqualification when no interim disqualification ordered.	Summarily.	Level 3 on the standard scale.			
Section 45 of this Act	Applying for or obtaining licence without giving particulars of current endorsement.	Summarily.	Level 3 on the standard scale.			
Section 62 of this Act	Removing fixed penalty notice fixed to vehicle.	Summarily.	Level 2 on the standard scale.			
Section 67 of this Act	False statement in response to notice to owner.	Summarily.	Level 5 on the standard scale.			

[The entries in Part I of Sched 2 are printed as prospectively amended by the Transport Act 1982, s 24(3) (as itself amended by the Criminal Justice Act 1982, s 46(1) and (3)(c), and the Road Traffic (Consequential Provisions) Act 1988, s 4 and Sched 2, Part I, para 13(c)) [as to the entries relating to the Road Traffic Act 1988, s 175(1) and (2)], and the Road Traffic (Consequential Provisions) Act 1988, s 4 and Sched 2, Part II, para 22(4) [as to the entry relating to the Road Traffic Act 1988, s 19A] and para 30 [as to the entries relating to ibid, ss 67A and 67B].

The entries relating to the Road Traffic Act 1988, ss 19A, 67A and 67B, will be brought into force on dates to be announced under the Road Traffic (Consequential Provisions) Act 1988, s 8(3), above. The entry relating to the Road Traffic Act 1988, s 175(2), will be brought into force on a date to be announced under the Transport Act 1982, s 76(2); until that date, in the entry relating to the Road Traffic Act 1988, s 175(1), the reference to 'section 175(1)' should read 'section 175'.

The effect of the Penalty Points (Alteration) Order 1988 (SI 1988 No 1906) has been incorporated into Part I of this Schedule. That order amended the corresponding earlier provisions (the Transport Act 1981, Sched 7, Part II) with effect from 1 March 1989, subject to certain savings. Articles 2 and 3 of that order are set out below for reference in relation to offences committed and accidents which occurred before that date. (As to ss 3, 25(4) and 143 of the Road Traffic Act 1972, see now ss 3, 170(4) and 143 of the Road Traffic Act 1988.)

2. In Part II of Schedule 7 to the Transport Act 1981 (Penalty Points) the following alterations shall be made—

(*a*) in the entry relating to section 3 of the 1972 Act (careless or inconsiderate driving), for '2–5' there shall be substituted '3–9';

(*b*) in the first entry relating to section 25(4) of the 1972 Act (failing to stop after accident), for '5–9' there shall be substituted '8–10';

(*c*) in the second entry relating to section 25(4) of the 1972 Act (failing to give particulars or report accident), for '4–9' there shall be substituted '8–10'; and

(*d*) in the entry relating to section 143 of the 1972 Act (using, or causing or permitting use of, motor vehicle uninsured or unsecured against third party risks), for '4–8' there shall be substituted '6–8'.

3. This Order shall not apply to—

(*a*) an offence committed before 1st March 1989, or

(*b*) an offence under section 25(4) of the 1972 Act relating to an accident occurring before that date.]

Part II

Other Offences

(1) Offence	(2) Disqualification	(3) Endorsement	(4) Penalty points
Manslaughter or, in Scotland, culpable homicide by the driver of a motor vehicle.	Obligatory.	Obligatory.	4
Stealing or attempting to steal a motor vehicle.	Discretionary.	Obligatory.	8
An offence or attempt to commit an offence in respect of a motor vehicle under section 12 of the Theft Act 1968 (taking conveyance without consent of owner etc or, knowing it has been so taken, driving it or allowing oneself to be carried in it).	Discretionary.	Obligatory.	8
An offence under section 25 of the Theft Act 1968 (going equipped for stealing, etc) committed with reference to the theft or taking of motor vehicles.	Discretionary.	Obligatory.	8

SCHEDULE 3

Fixed Penalty Offences

(1) Provision creating offence	(2) General nature of offence
Offences under the Vehicles (Excise) Act 1971	
Section 12(4) of the Vehicles (Excise) Act 1971.	Using or keeping a vehicle on a public road without licence being exhibited in the prescribed manner.
Section 22(1) of that Act.	Driving or keeping a vehicle without required registration mark or hackney carriage sign.
Section 22(2) of that Act.	Driving or keeping a vehicle with registration mark or hackney carriage sign obscured, etc.
Offence under the Greater London Council (General Powers) Act 1974	
Section 15 of the Greater London Council (General Powers) Act 1974.	Parking vehicles on footways, verges, etc.
Offence under the Highways Act 1980	
Section 137 of the Highways Act 1980.	Obstructing a highway, but only where the offence is committed in respect of a vehicle.
Offences under the Road Traffic Regulation Act 1984	
RTRA section 5(1)	Using a vehicle in contravention of a traffic regulation order outside Greater London.
RTRA section 8(1)	Breach of traffic regulation order in Greater London.
RTRA section 11	Breach of experimental traffic order.
RTRA section 13	Breach of experimental traffic scheme regulations in Greater London.
RTRA section 16(1)	Using a vehicle in contravention of temporary prohibition or restriction of traffic in case of execution of works, etc.
RTRA section 17(4)	Wrongful use of special road.
RTRA section 18(3)	Using a vehicle in contravention of provision for one-way traffic on trunk road.
RTRA section 20(5)	Driving a vehicle in contravention of order prohibiting or restricting driving vehicles on certain classes of roads.
RTRA section 25(5)	Breach of pedestrian crossing regulations, except an offence in respect of a moving motor vehicle.

(1) Provision creating offence	(2) General nature of offence
RTRA section 29(3)	Using a vehicle in contravention of a street playground order outside Greater London.
RTRA section 30(5)	Using a vehicle in contravention of a street playground order in Greater London.
RTRA section 35(4)	Breach of an order regulating the use, etc, of a parking place provided by a local authority, but only where the offence is committed in relation to a parking place provided on a road.
RTRA section 47(1)	Breach of a provision of a parking place designation order and other offences committed in relation to a parking place designated by such an order, except any offence of failing to pay an excess charge within the meaning of section 46.
RTRA section 53(5)	Using vehicle in contravention of any provision of a parking place designation order having effect by virtue of section 53(1)(*a*) (inclusion of certain traffic regulation provisions).
RTRA section 53(6)	Breach of a provision of a parking place designation order having effect by virtue of section 53(1)(*b*) (use of any part of a road for parking without charge).
RTRA section 88(7)	Driving a motor vehicle in contravention of an order imposing a minimum speed limit under section 88(1)(*b*).
RTRA section 89(1)	Speeding offences under RTRA and other Acts.

Offences under the Road Traffic Act 1988

RTA section 14	Breach of regulations requiring wearing of seat belts.
RTA section 15(2)	Breach of restriction on carrying children in the front of vehicles.
RTA section 16	Breach of regulations relating to protective headgear for motor cycle drivers and passengers.
RTA section 19	Parking a heavy commercial vehicle on verge or footway.
[RTA section 19A	Parking a vehicle other than a heavy commercial vehicle on verge, etc.]
RTA section 22	Leaving vehicle in dangerous position.
RTA section 23	Unlawful carrying of passengers on motor cycles.

(1) Provision creating offence	(2) General nature of offence
RTA section 34	Driving motor vehicles elsewhere than on a road.
RTA section 35	Failure to comply with traffic directions.
RTA section 36	Failure to comply with traffic signs.
RTA section 42	Breach of construction and use regulations; or the use on a road of a motor vehicle or trailer which does not comply with construction and use regulations.
RTA section 87(1)	Driving vehicle without requisite licence.
RTA section 97	Breach of provisional licence conditions.
RTA section 163	Failure to stop vehicle on being so required by constable in uniform.

[The entries in Sched 3 are printed as prospectively amended by the Road Traffic (Consequential Provisions) Act 1988, s 4 and Sched 2, Part II, para 22(5). The entries relating to s 19A of the Road Traffic Act 1988 will be brought into force on a date to be announced; see the Road Traffic (Consequential Provisions) Act 1988, s 8(3), above.]

SCHEDULE 4

Section 68.

STATUTORY STATEMENTS

PART I

STATUTORY STATEMENT OF OWNERSHIP OR HIRING

1.—(1) For the purposes of Part III of this Act, a statutory statement of ownership is a statement on an official form signed by the person providing it and stating whether he was the owner of the vehicle at the time of the alleged offence and, if he was not the owner of the vehicle at that time, whether—

(*a*) he was never the owner, or

(*b*) he ceased to be the owner before, or became the owner after, that time,

and in a case within paragraph (*b*) above, stating, if the information is in his possession, the name and address of the person to whom, and the date on which, he disposed of the vehicle or (as the case may be) the name and address of the person from whom, and the date on which, he acquired it.

(2) An official form for a statutory statement of ownership shall—

(*a*) indicate that the person providing the statement in response to a notice to owner relating to an offence may give notice requesting a hearing in respect of the offence in the manner specified in the form, and

(*b*) direct the attention of any person proposing to complete the form to the information provided in accordance with paragraph 3(3) below in any official form for a statutory statement of facts.

2.—(1) For the purposes of Part III of this Act, a statutory statement of hiring is a statement on an official form, signed by the person providing it, being a person by whom a statement of liability was signed, and stating—

(*a*) whether at the time of the alleged offence the vehicle was let to him under the hiring agreement to which the statement of liability refers, and

(*b*) if it was not, the date on which he returned the vehicle to the possession of the vehicle-hire firm concerned.

(2) An official form for a statutory statement of hiring shall—

(*a*) indicate that the person providing the statement in pursuance of a notice relating to an offence served under section 63 of this Act by virtue of section 66 of this Act may give notice requesting a hearing in respect of the offence in the manner specified in the form, and

(*b*) direct the attention of any person proposing to complete the form to the information provided in accordance with paragraph 3(3) below in any official form for a statutory statement of facts.

(3) In sub-paragraph (1) above 'statement of liability', 'hiring agreement' and 'vehicle-hire firm' have the same meanings as in section 66 of this Act.

PART II

Statutory Statement of Facts

3.—(1) For the purposes of Part III of this Act, a statutory statement of facts is a statement on an official form, signed by the person providing it, which—

(*a*) states that the person providing it was not the driver of the vehicle at the time of the alleged offence, and

(*b*) states the name and address at the time when the statement is provided of the person who was the driver of the vehicle at the time of the alleged offence.

(2) A statutory statement of facts has effect as a notice given by the driver requesting a hearing in respect of the offence if it is signed by the person identified in the statement as the driver of the vehicle at the time of the alleged offence.

(3) An official form for a statutory statement of facts shall indicate—

(*a*) that if a person identified in the statement as the driver of the vehicle at the time of the alleged offence signs the statement he will be regarded as having given notice requesting a hearing in respect of the offence,

(*b*) that the person on whom the notice to owner relating to the offence is served may not give notice requesting a hearing in respect of the offence on his own account if he provides a statutory statement of facts signed by a person so identified, and

(*c*) that if the fixed penalty is not paid before the end of the period stated in the notice to owner as the period for response to the notice, a sum determined by reference to that fixed penalty may be registered without any court hearing for enforcement as a fine against the person on whom the notice to owner is served, unless he has given notice requesting a hearing in respect of the offence,

but that, in a case within paragraph (*c*) above, the sum in question may not be so registered if the person on whom the notice to owner is served provides a statutory statement of facts as mentioned in paragraph (*b*) above until two months have elapsed from the end of the period so stated without service of a summons or, in Scotland, complaint in respect of the offence on the person identified in that statement as the driver of the vehicle.

SCHEDULE 5

Section 75.

Scotland; Additional Offences Open to Conditional Offer

[Omitted.]

The Road Traffic Regulation Act 1984

(1984 c 27)

An Act to consolidate the Road Traffic Regulation Act 1967 and certain related enactments, with amendments to give effect to recommendations of the Law Commission and the Scottish Law Commission.

[26th June 1984]

ARRANGEMENT OF SECTIONS

* * *

PART II

TRAFFIC REGULATION IN SPECIAL CASES

* * *

PART III

CROSSINGS AND PLAYGROUNDS

* * *

PART IV

PARKING PLACES

* * *

Parking on highways for payment

* * *

* * *

Special parking provisions

61. Loading areas

* * *

PART V

Traffic Signs

64. General provisions as to traffic signs

* * *

PART VI

Speed Limits

81. General speed limit for restricted roads
82. What roads are restricted roads
83. Provisions as to directions under s 82(2)
84. Speed limits on roads other than restricted roads
85. Traffic signs for indicating speed restrictions
86. Speed limits for particular classes of vehicles
87. Exemption of fire brigade, ambulance and police vehicles from speed limits
88. Temporary speed limits
89. Speeding offences generally

. . . .

91. Interpretation of Part VI

* * *

PART VIII

Control and Enforcement

Removal or immobilisation of vehicles

99. Removal of vehicles illegally, obstructively or dangerously parked, or abandoned or broken down

. . . .

104. Immobilisation of vehicles illegally parked
105. Exemptions from s 104

Enforcement of excess parking charges

107. Liability of vehicle owner in respect of excess parking charge
108. Notice in respect of excess parking charge
109. Modifications of ss 107 and 108 in relation to hired vehicles

110. Time for bringing, and evidence in, proceedings for certain offences
111. Supplementary provisions as to excess charges

PART IX

Further Provisions as to Enforcement

General provisions

112. Information as to identity of driver or rider

. . . .

115. Mishandling of parking documents and related offences
116. Provisions supplementary to s 115
117. Wrongful use of disabled person's badge

* * *

PART X

General and Supplementary Provisions

* * *

i30. Application of Act to Crown

. . . .

136. Meaning of 'motor vehicle' and other expressions relating to vehicles
137. Supplementary provisions relating to s 136
138. Meaning of 'heavy commercial vehicle'

. . . .

140. Certain vehicles not to be treated as motor vehicles
141. Tramcars and trolley vehicles
142. General interpretation of Act

. . . .

144. Transitional provisions and savings

* * *

SCHEDULES

. . . .

Schedule 6—Speed limits for vehicles of certain classes

. . . .

Schedule 8—Statutory statements (excess charges)

. . . .

Schedule 10—Transitional provisions and savings
Schedule 11—Provisions of this Act and instruments referred to in section 144(2)

* * *

PART II

TRAFFIC REGULATION IN SPECIAL CASES

* * *

17. Traffic regulation on special roads

(1) A special road shall not, except as provided by or under regulations made under subsection (2) below, be used—

(*a*) by any traffic other than traffic of a class authorised in that behalf by a scheme made, or having effect as if made, under section 16 of the Highways Act 1980, or

(*b*) if the road is one to which certain provisions of the Highways Act 1980 apply by virtue of paragraph 3 of Schedule 23 to that Act, by any traffic other than traffic of a class for the time being authorised by virtue of that paragraph.

(2) The Secretary of State may make regulations with respect to the use of special roads, and such regulations may in particular—

(*a*) regulate the manner in which and the conditions subject to which special roads may be used by traffic of the class authorised in that behalf by such a scheme as is mentioned in subsection (1)(*a*) above or, as the case may be, by virtue of the said paragraph 3;

(*b*) authorise, or enable such authority as may be specified in the regulations to authorise, the use of special roads on occasion or in an emergency or for the purpose of crossing, or for the purpose of securing access to premises abutting on or adjacent to the roads, by traffic other than that described in paragraph (*a*) above; or

(*c*) relax, or enable any authority so specified to relax, any prohibition or restriction imposed by the regulations.

(3) Regulations made under subsection (2) above may make provision with respect to special roads generally, or may make different provision with respect to special roads provided for the use of different classes of traffic, or may make provision with respect to any particular special road.

(4) If a person uses a special road in contravention of this section or of regulations under subsection (2) above, he shall be guilty of an offence.

(5) Where, in the case of any part of a special road, the date of opening is a date after the commencement of this Act, the provisions of this section and of any regulations made under subsection (2) above shall not apply to that part of the road until the date of opening; but nothing in this subsection shall be construed as preventing the making of regulations under subsection (2) above so as to come into force, in relation to that part of the road, on the date of opening.

(6) In the section 'use', in relation to a road, includes crossing, and 'the date of opening', in relation to a part of a special road, means the date declared, by a notice published as mentioned in section 1(4) of this Act, to be the date on which it is open for use as a special road.

[Words in s 17(1) relating expressly and exclusively to Scotland have been omitted.

The Motorways Traffic (England and Wales) Regulations 1982 (SI 1982 No 1163) (qv) have effect as if made under this section.

For the application of the fixed penalty procedure to offences under subs (4), see the Road Traffic Offenders Act 1988, Part III and Sched 3, above.]

* * *

PART III

Crossings and Playgrounds

* * *

25. Pedestrian crossing regulations

(1) The Secretary of State may make regulations with respect to the precedence of vehicles and pedestrians respectively, and generally with respect to the movement of traffic (including pedestrians), at and in the vicinity of crossings.

(2)–(4) *[Omitted.]*

(5) A person who contravenes any regulations made under this section shall be guilty of an offence.

(6) In this section 'crossing' means a crossing for pedestrians established—

(*a*) by a local authority under section 23 of this Act, or

(*b*) by the Secretary of State in the discharge of the duty imposed on him by section 24 of this Act,

and (in either case) indicated in accordance with the regulations having effect as respects that crossing; and, for the purposes of a prosecution for a contravention of the provisions of a regulation having effect as respects a crossing, the crossing shall be deemed to be so established and indicated unless the contrary is proved.

[Section 23 and 24 of this Act provide for the establishment of pedestrian crossings by local authorities on roads in their areas (other than trunk roads) and the establishment of pedestrian crossings by the Secretary of State on trunk roads, respectively.

The 'Pelican' Pedestrian Crossings Regulations and General Directions 1987 (SI 1987 No 16) and the 'Zebra' Pedestrian Crossings Regulations 1971 (SI 1971 No 1524) (qv) have effect in part as if made under this section.

See also para 9(2) of Sched 10 to this Act, below.

For the application of the fixed penalty procedure to offences under subs (5) (except offences in respect of moving motor vehicles), see the Road Traffic Offenders Act 1988, Part III, and Sched 3, above.]

* * *

28. Stopping of vehicles at school crossings

(1) When between the hours of eight in the morning and half-past five in the afternoon a vehicle is approaching a place in a road where children on their way to or from school, or from one part of a school to another, are crossing or seeking to cross the road, a school crossing patrol wearing a uniform approved by the Secretary of State shall have power, by exhibiting a prescribed sign, to require the person driving or propelling the vehicle to stop it.

(2) When a person has been required under subsection (1) above to stop a vehicle—

(*a*) he shall cause the vehicle to stop before reaching the place where the children are crossing or seeking to cross and so as not to stop or impede their crossing, and

(*b*) the vehicle shall not be put in motion again so as to reach the place in question so long as the sign continues to be exhibited.

(3) A person who fails to comply with paragraph (*a*) of subsection (2) above, or who causes a vehicle to be put in motion in contravention of paragraph (*b*) of that subsection, shall be guilty of an offence.

(4) In this section—

(*a*) 'prescribed sign' means a sign of a size, colour and type prescribed by regulations made by the Secretary of State or, if authorisation is given by the Secretary of State for the use of signs of a description not so prescribed, a sign of that description;

(*b*) 'school crossing patrol' means a person authorised to patrol in accordance with arrangements under section 26 of this Act;

and regulations under paragraph (*a*) above may provide for the attachment of reflectors to signs or for the illumination of signs.

(5) For the purposes of this section—

(*a*) where it is proved that a sign was exhibited by a school crossing patrol, it shall be presumed, unless the contrary is proved, to be of a size, colour and type prescribed, or of a description authorised, under subsection (4)(*b*) above, and, if it was exhibited in circumstances in which it was required by the regulations to be illuminated, to have been illuminated in the prescribed manner;

(*b*) where it is proved that a school crossing patrol was wearing a uniform, the uniform shall be presumed, unless the contrary is proved, to be a uniform approved by the Secretary of State; and

(*c*) where it is proved that a prescribed sign was exhibited by a school crossing patrol at a place in a road where children were crossing or seeking to cross the road, it shall be presumed, unless the contrary is proved, that those children were on their way to or from school or from one part of a school to another.

[The Traffic Signs Regulations and General Directions 1981 (SI 1981 No 859) and the Traffic Signs (Welsh and English Language Provisions) Regulations and General Directions 1985 (SI 1985 No 713), below, have effect in part as if made under this section.]

* * *

PART IV

PARKING PLACES

* * *

Parking on highways for payment

* * *

46. Charges at, and regulation of, designated parking places

(1) Subject to Parts I to III of Schedule 9 to this Act the authority by whom a designation order is made shall by order prescribe any charges to be paid for vehicles

left in a parking place designated by the order; and any such charge may be prescribed either—

(*a*) as an amount (in this Act referred to as an 'initial charge') payable in respect of an initial period and an amount (in this Act referred to as an 'excess charge') payable, in addition to an initial charge, in respect of any excess over an initial period, or

(*b*) as an amount payable regardless of the period for which a vehicle is left.

(2) The authority by whom a designation order is made may, subject to Parts I to III of Schedule 9 to this Act, by order make such provision as may appear to that authority to be necessary or expedient for regulating or restricting the use of any parking place designated by the order, or otherwise for or in connection with the operation of such a parking place, and in particular (but without prejudice to the generality of the foregoing words) provision—

(*a*) for regulating the time at which and the method by which any charge is to be paid and for requiring the use of apparatus (in this Act referred to as a 'parking meter') of such type or design as may be approved either generally or specially by the Secretary of State, being apparatus designed either—

(i) to indicate whether any charge has been paid and whether the period for which it has been paid or any further period has elapsed, or

(ii) to indicate the time and to issue tickets indicating the payment of a charge and the period in respect of which it has been paid;

(*b*) for treating the indications given by a parking meter or any ticket issued by it, or the absence of any such ticket from a vehicle left in a parking place, as evidence (and, in Scotland, sufficient evidence) of such facts as may be provided by the order;

(*c*) for prohibiting the insertion in a parking meter of coins additional to those inserted by way of payment of any charge;

(*d*)–(*k*) [*Omitted.*]

(3) [*Periodical inspection of parking meters.*]

(4) [*Periodical inspection of apparatus.*]

* * *

Special parking provisions

61. Loading areas

(1) If it appears to [the council of a county, metropolitan district or London borough or the Common Council of the City of London] that any land in their area which is not part of a highway has been set apart by the occupier of the land for use as a place where vehicles may be driven and parked for the purpose of being loaded or unloaded in connection with a trade or business carried on or in the vicinity of the land, the council may, subject to Part III of Schedule 9 to this Act, by an order made with the consent of the owner and the occupier of the land—

(*a*) designate the land as an area to which the following provisions of this section apply (in this section referred to as a 'loading area'), and

(*b*) specify the trade or business in question.

(2) A council which has made an order in pursuance of subsection (1) above—

(*a*) may vary the order by a subsequent order made with the consent of the owner and the occupier of the land to which the order relates;

(*b*) may revoke the order by a subsequent order made with the consent of the owner and the occupier of the loading area in question; and

(*c*) shall revoke the order by a subsequent order if requested in writing to do so by the owner and the occupier of the loading area in question.

(3) An order in pursuance of subsection (1) or (2)(*a*) above may contain provisions prohibiting the parking, in the loading area to which the order relates, of vehicles of such kinds as are specified in the order, except authorised vehicles, at all times or at times so specified, and may make different provision in pursuance of the preceding provisions of this subsection for different parts of the area; and in this subsection 'authorised vehicle', in relation to a loading area, means a goods vehicle (as defined by [section 192(1) of the Road Traffic Act 1988]) which is in the area for the purpose of being loaded or unloaded in connection with the trade or business specified in the order designating the area.

(4) Where an order has been made by a council in pursuance of subsection (1) above and, by virtue of paragraph 22(1)(*e*) of Schedule 9 to this Act, traffic signs are required to be placed on the loading area to which the order relates, a person authorised in that behalf by the council may enter on the loading area for the purpose of placing any such traffic signs and for the purpose of maintaining or removing the signs.

(5) A person who, without reasonable excuse, causes a vehicle to be in any part of a loading area at a time when the parking of it there is prohibited by an order made in pursuance of subsection (1) above shall be guilty of an offence.

(6) References in subsections (2) to (5) above to an order made in pursuance of subsection (1) above include, in the case of such an order which has been varied in pursuance of subsection (2)(*a*) of this section, references to the order as so varied.

(7) Subsections (3) to (5) of section 44 of the Local Government (Miscellaneous Provisions) Act 1976 (which contain ancillary provisions for the purposes of Part I of that Act) shall have effect as if this section were included in that Part of that Act.

(8) In this section 'owner', in relation to any land, means a person who, either on his own account or as agent or trustee for another person, is receiving the rackrent of the land or would be entitled to receive it if the land were let at a rackrent; and any reference to a traffic sign, in relation to any land which is not a road, includes a reference to any object, device, line or mark which would be a traffic sign (as defined by section 64 of this Act) if the land were a road.

[Section 61 is printed as amended by the Local Government Act 1985, s 8(1) and Sched 5, Part I, para 4(25); the Road Traffic (Consequential Provisions) Act 1988, s 4 and Sched 3, para 25(2).]

* * *

PART V

TRAFFIC SIGNS

64. General provisions as to traffic signs

(1) In this Act 'traffic sign' means any object or device (whether fixed or portable) for conveying, to traffic on roads or any specified class of traffic, warnings, information, requirements, restrictions or prohibitions of any description—

(*a*) specified by regulations made by the Ministers acting jointly, or

(*b*) authorised by the Secretary of State,

and any line or mark on a road for so conveying such warnings, information, requirements, restrictions or prohibitions.

(2) Traffic signs shall be of the size, colour and type prescribed by regulations made as mentioned in subsection (1)(*a*) above except where the Secretary of State authorises the erection or retention of a sign of another character; and for the purposes of this subsection illumination, whether by lighting or by the use of reflectors or reflecting material, or the absence of such illumination, shall be part of the type or character of a sign.

(3) Regulations under this section may be made so as to apply either generally or in such circumstances only as may be specified in the regulations.

(4) Except as provided by this Act, no traffic sign shall be placed on or near a road except—

(*a*) a notice in respect of the use of a bridge;

(*b*) a traffic sign placed, in pursuance of powers conferred by a special Act of Parliament or order having the force of an Act, by the owners or operators of a tramway, light railway or trolley vehicle undertaking, a dock undertaking or a harbour undertaking; or

(*c*) a traffic sign placed on any land—

(i) by a person authorised under the following provisions of this Act to place the sign on a highway, and

(ii) for a purpose for which he is authorised to place it on a highway.

(5) Regulations under this section, or any authorisation under subsection (2) above, may provide that [section 36 of the Road Traffic Act 1988] (drivers to comply with traffic directions) shall apply to signs of a type specified in that behalf by the regulations or, as the case may be, to the sign to which the authorisation relates.

(6) References in any enactment (including any enactment contained in this Act) to the erection or placing of traffic signs shall include references to the display of traffic signs in any manner, whether or not involving fixing or placing.

[Section 64 is printed as amended by the Road Traffic (Consequential Provisions) Act 1988, s 4 and Sched 3, para 25(3).

The Traffic Signs Regulations and General Directions 1981 (SI 1981 No 859), the Traffic Signs (Welsh and English Language Provisions) Regulations and General Directions 1985 (SI 1985 No 713), and the 'Pelican' Pedestrian Crossings Regulations and General Directions 1987 (SI 1987 No 16) (qv) were made in part or have effect in part as if made under this section.]

* * *

PART VI

Speed Limits

81. General speed limit for restricted roads

(1) It shall not be lawful for a person to drive a motor vehicle on a restricted road at a speed exceeding 30 miles per hour.

(2) The Ministers acting jointly may by order made by statutory instrument and

approved by a resolution of each House of Parliament increase or reduce the rate of speed fixed by subsection (1) above, either as originally enacted or as varied under this subsection.

[Paragraph 14 of Sched 10 to this Act provides as follows:

(1) A direction in an order made under section 1 of the Road Traffic Act 1934 that a length of road is to be deemed to be, or not to be, a road in a built-up area, if—

(*a*) by virtue of paragraph 10 of Schedule 8 to the 1967 Act it had effect as a direction that that length of road was to become, or (as the case may be) was to cease to be, a restricted road for the purposes of section 71 of that Act, and

(*b*) the direction continues so to have effect immediately before the commencement of this Act,

shall have the like effect for the purposes of section 81 of this Act.

(2) Any reference in any provision of an Act, or of any instrument (other than such an order as is mentioned in sub paragraph (1) above) made under an enactment repealed by the Road Traffic Act 1960, to a road in a built-up area, if the provision is in force immediately before the commencement of this Act, shall be construed as a reference to a restricted road for the purposes of section 81 of this Act.*]*

82. What roads are restricted roads

(1) Subject to the provisions of this section and of section 84(3) of this Act, a road is a restricted road for the purposes of section 81 of this Act if there is provided on it a system of street lighting furnished by means of lamps placed not more than 200 yards apart.

(2) A direction may be given—

(*a*) that a specified road which is a restricted road for the purposes of section 81 of this Act shall cease to be a restricted road for those purposes, or

(*b*) that a specified road which is not a restricted road for those purposes shall become a restricted road for those purposes.

(3) Where, by a notice published as mentioned in section 1(4) of this Act, a date has been or is declared to be the date on which a part of a special road is open for use as a special road, that part of the road shall not be a restricted road for the purposes of section 81 of this Act or (if the date so declared is a date after the commencement of this section) shall not be a restricted road for those purposes on or after that date.

[Paragraph 16 of Sched 10 to this Act provides as follows:

(1) This paragraph applies to any road which—

(*a*) would have become a restricted road for the purposes of section 71 of the 1967 Act on 1st November 1982 as a result of the repeal of section 72(2) of the 1967 Act by section 61 of the Transport Act 1982; but

(*b*) by reason of section 61(2) of that Act was taken to have ceased to be a restricted road before that day by virtue of a direction duly given under section 72(3) of the 1967 Act and still in force at the beginning of that day; and

(*c*) did not become a restricted road at any time between the beginning of that day and the commencement of this Act.

(2) At the commencement of this Act, any road to which this paragraph applies

shall be treated as if it were the subject of a direction duly given under section 82(2)(*a*) of this Act.

(3) Nothing in sub-paragraph (2) above prevents a direction under section 82(2)(*b*) of this Act being given in respect of any road to which this paragraph applies.]

83. Provisions as to directions under s 82(2)

(1) Any direction under section 82(2) of this Act in respect of a trunk road shall be given by means of an order made by the Secretary of State after giving public notice of his intention to make an order.

(2) Any such direction in respect of a road which is not a trunk road shall, subject to Parts I to III of Schedule 9 to this Act, be given by means of an order made by the local authority.

(3) Section 68(1)(*c*) of this Act shall apply to any order made under subsection (2) above.

[In anticipation of the abolition of the Greater London Council, art 2 of the London Traffic Orders (Anticipatory Exercise of Powers) Order 1985 (SI 1985 No 1320) (made under the Local Government Act 1985, s 101), provided as follows:

> The councils of London boroughs and the Common Council of the City of London may, at any time before 1 April 1986, take steps which are required to be taken as a preliminary to the exercise of the powers conferred by sections 6, 9, 45, 46, 61, 83(2) and 84 of the Road Traffic Regulation Act 1984 (which powers will become exercisable by those authorities on that date).]

84. Speed limits on roads other than restricted roads

(1) An order made under this subsection as respects any road may prohibit, either generally or during periods specified in the order, the driving of motor vehicles on that road at a speed exceeding that specified in the order.

(2) The power to make an order under subsection (1) above shall be exercisable by an authority after giving public notice of their intention to make an order under that subsection; and the authority having that power—

(*a*) as respects a trunk road, shall be the Secretary of State, and

(*b*) as respects any other road, subject to Parts I to III of Schedule 9 to this Act, shall be the local authority.

(3) While an order under subsection (1) above is in force as respects a road, that road shall not be a restricted road for the purposes of section 81 of this Act.

(4) This section does not apply to any part of a special road which is open for use as a special road.

(5) Section 68(1)(*c*) of this Act shall apply to any order made under subsection (1) above.

[See the note to s 83, above.]

85. Traffic signs for indicating speed restrictions

(1) For the purpose of securing that adequate guidance is given to drivers of motor vehicles as to whether any, and if so what, limit of speed is to be observed on any road, it shall be the duty of the Secretary of State, in the case of a trunk road, to erect

and maintain the prescribed traffic signs in such positions as may be requisite for that purpose.

(2) In the case of any road which is not a trunk road, it shall be the duty of the local authority—

(*a*) to erect and maintain the prescribed traffic signs in such positions as may be requisite in order to give effect to general or other directions given by the Secretary of State for the purpose mentioned in subsection (1) above, and

(*b*) to alter or remove traffic signs as may be requisite in order to give effect to such directions, either in consequence of the making of an order by the Secretary of State or otherwise.

(3) If a local authority makes default in executing any works required for the performance of the duty imposed on them by subsection (2) above, the Secretary of State may himself execute the works; and the expense incurred by him in doing so shall be recoverable by him from the local authority and, in England or Wales, shall be so recoverable summarily as a civil debt.

(4) Where no system of street lighting furnished by means of lamps placed not more than 200 yards apart is provided on a road, but a limit of speed is to be observed on the road, a person shall not be convicted of driving a motor vehicle on the road at a speed exceeding the limit unless the limit is indicated by means of such traffic signs as are mentioned in subsection (1) or subsection (2) above.

(5) In any proceedings for a contravention of section 81 of this Act, where the proceedings relate to driving on a road provided with such a system of street lighting as is specified in subsection (4) above, evidence of the absence of traffic signs displayed in pursuance of this section to indicate that the road is not a restricted road for the purposes of that section shall be evidence that the road is a restricted road for those purposes.

(6) Where by regulations made under section 17(2) of this Act a limit of speed is to be observed then, if it is to be observed—

(*a*) on all special roads, or

(*b*) on all special roads provided for the use of particular classes of traffic, or

(*c*) on all special roads other than special roads of such description as may be specified in the regulations, or

(*d*) as mentioned in paragraph (*a*), (*b*) or (*c*) above except for such lengths of special road as may be so specified,

this section shall not apply in relation to that limit (but without prejudice to its application in relation to any lower limit of maximum speed or, as the case may be, any higher limit of minimum speed, required by any such regulations to be observed on any specified length of any specified special road).

(7) The power to give general directions under subsection (2) above shall be exercisable by statutory instrument.

86. Speed limits for particular classes of vehicles

(1) It shall not be lawful for a person to drive a motor vehicle of any class on a road at a speed greater than the speed specified in Schedule 6 to this Act as the maximum speed in relation to a vehicle of that class.

(2)–(6) *[Omitted.]*

87. Exemption of fire brigade, ambulance and police vehicles for speed limits

No statutory provisions imposing a speed limit on motor vehicles shall apply to any vehicle on an occasion when it is being used for fire brigade, ambulance or police purposes, if the observance of that provision would be likely to hinder the use of the vehicle for the purpose for which it is being used on that occasion.

88. Temporary speed limits

(1) Where it appears to the Secretary of State desirable to do so in the interests of safety or for the purpose of facilitating the movement of traffic, he may, after giving public notice of his intention to do so, by order prohibit, for a period not exceeding 18 months, the driving of motor vehicles—

(*a*) on all roads, or on all roads in any area specified in the order, or on all roads of any class so specified, or on all roads other than roads of any class so specified, or on any road so specified, at a speed greater than that specified in the order, or

(*b*) on any road specified in the order, at a speed less than the speed specified in the order, subject to such exceptions as may be so specified.

(2) Any prohibition imposed by an order under subsection (1) above may be so imposed either generally, or at times, on days or during periods specified in the order; but the provisions of any such order shall not, except in so far as may be provided by the order, affect the provisions of sections 81 to 84 of this Act.

(3) For the purposes of an order under subsection (1)(*a*) above, roads may be classified by reference to any circumstances appearing to the Secretary of State to be suitable for the purpose, including their character, the nature of the traffic to which they are suited or the traffic signs provided on them.

(4) The provisions of any order under subsection (1) above may be continued, either indefinitely or for a specified period, by an order of the Secretary of State made by statutory instrument, which shall be subject to annulment in pursuance of a resolution of either House of Parliament.

(5) Where by virtue of an order under this section a speed limit is to be observed, then—

(*a*) if it is to be observed on all roads, on all roads of any class specified in the order or on all roads other than roads of any class so specified, section 85 of this Act shall not apply in relation to that limit;

(*b*) if it is to be observed on all roads in any area and, at all points where roads lead into the area, is indicated as respects the area as a whole by means of such traffic signs as are mentioned in subsection (1) or subsection (2) of section 85 of this Act, the limit shall, for the purposes of subsection (4) of that section, be taken as so indicated with respect to all roads in the area.

(6) This section does not apply to any part of a special road which is open for use as a special road.

(7) If a person drives a motor vehicle on a road in contravention of an order under subsection (1)(*b*) above, he shall be guilty of an offence; but a person shall not be liable to be convicted of so driving solely on the evidence of one witness to the effect that, in the opinion of the witness, he was driving the vehicle at a speed less than that specified in the order.

[For the application of the fixed penalty procedure to offences under subs (7), see the Road Traffic Offenders Act 1988, Part III, and Sched 3, above.]

89. Speeding offences generally

(1) A person who drives a motor vehicle on a road at a speed exceeding a limit imposed by or under any enactment to which this section applies shall be guilty of an offence.

(2) A person prosecuted for such an offence shall not be liable to be convicted solely on the evidence of one witness to the effect that, in the opinion of the witness, the person prosecuted was driving the vehicle at a speed exceeding a specified limit.

(3) The enactments to which this section applies are—

(*a*) any enactment contained in this Act except section 17(2);

(*b*) section 2 of the Parks Regulation (Amendment) Act 1926; and

(*c*) any enactment not contained in this Act, but passed after 1st September 1960, whether before or after the passing of this Act.

(4) If a person who employs other persons to drive motor vehicles on roads publishes or issues any time-table or schedule, or gives any directions, under which any journey, or any stage or part of any journey, is to be completed within some specified time, and it is not practicable in the circumstances of the case for that journey (or that stage or part of it) to be completed in the specified time without the commission of such an offence as is mentioned in subsection (1) above, the publication or issue of the time-table or schedule, or the giving of the directions, may be produced as prima facie evidence that the employer procured or (as the case may be) incited the persons employed by him to drive the vehicles to commit such an offence.

[For the application of the fixed penalty procedure to offences under subs (1), see the Road Traffic Offenders Act 1988, Part III, and Sched 3, below.]

90. *[Repealed.]*

91. Interpretation of Part VI

In section 83 to 85 of this Act 'local authority'—

(*a*) in relation to a road in Greater London, means [the council of the London borough or the Common Council of the City of London];

(*b*) in relation to a road elsewhere in England and Wales, means the council of the county [or metropolitan district]; and

(*c*) *[Applies to Scotland.]*

[Section 91 is printed as amended by the Local Government Act 1985, s 8(1) and Sched 5, para 4(29).]

* * *

PART VIII

CONTROL AND ENFORCEMENT

* * *

98. *[Repealed.]*

Removal or immobilisation of vehicles

99. Removal of vehicles illegally, obstructively or dangerously parked, or abandoned or broken down

(1), (2) *[Power to make regulations for removal of vehicles.]*

(3) *[Notice to occupier of land where vehicle is.]*

(4) *[Notice of intention to remove vehicle for destruction.]*

(5) In this section 'vehicle' means any vehicle, whether or not it is in a fit state for use on roads, and includes any chassis or body, with or without wheels, appearing to have formed part of such a vehicle, and any load carried by, and anything attached to, such a vehicle.

[The definition in s 99(5) has been incorporated by reference into the Removal and Disposal of Vehicles (Loading Areas) Regulations 1986 (SI 1986 No 184), reg 2 (qv), and the Removal and Disposal of Vehicles Regulations 1986 (SI 1986 No 183), reg 2 (qv).]

100. Interim disposal of vehicles removed under s 99 *[Omitted.]*

101. Ultimate disposal of vehicles abandoned and removable under this Act *[Omitted.]*

102. Charges for removal, storage and disposal of vehicles *[Omitted.]*

103. Supplementary provisions as to removal of vehicles *[Omitted.]*

104. Immobilisation of vehicles illegally parked

(1) Subject to sections 105 and 106 of this Act, where a constable finds on a road a vehicle which has been permitted to remain at rest there in contravention of any prohibition or restriction imposed by or under any enactment, he may—

(*a*) fix an immobilisation device to the vehicle while it remains in the place in which he finds it; or

(*b*) move it from that place to another place on the same or another road and fix an immobilisation device to it in that other place;

or authorise another person to take under his direction any action he could himself take by virtue of paragraph (*a*) or (*b*) above.

(2) On any occasion when an immobilisation device is fixed to a vehicle in accordance with this section the constable or other person fixing the device shall also affix to the vehicle a notice—

(*a*) indicating that such a device has been fixed to the vehicle and warning that no attempt should be made to drive it or otherwise put it in motion until it has been released from that device;

(*b*) specifying the steps to be taken in order to secure its release; and

(*c*) giving such other information as may be prescribed.

(3) A vehicle to which an immobilisation device has been fixed in accordance with this section may only be released from that device by or under the direction of a constable.

(4) Subject to subsection (3) above, a vehicle to which an immobilisation device has been fixed in accordance with this section shall be released from that device on payment in any manner specified in the notice affixed to the vehicle under subsection (2) above of such charge in respect of the release as may be prescribed.

(5) A notice affixed to a vehicle under this section shall not be removed or interfered with except by or under the authority of the person in charge of the vehicle or the person by whom it was put in the place where it was found by the constable; and any person contravening this subsection shall be guilty of an offence.

(6) Any person with, without being authorised to do so in accordance with this section, removes or attempts to remove an immobilisation device fixed to a vehicle in accordance with this section shall be guilty of an offence.

(7) Where a vehicle is moved in accordance with this section before an immobilisation device is fixed to it, any power of removal under regulations for the time being in force under section 99 of this Act which was exercisable in relation to that vehicle immediately before it was so moved shall continue to be exercisable in relation to that vehicle while it remains in the place to which it was so moved.

(8) In relation to any vehicle which is removed in pursuance of any such regulations or under section 3 of the Refuse Disposal (Amenity) Act 1978 [*qv*] (duty of local authority to remove abandoned vehicles) from a place to which it was moved in accordance with this section, references in the definition of 'person responsible' in section 102(8) of this Act and section 5 of the said Act of 1978 mentioned above (recovery from person responsible of charges and expenses in respect of vehicles removed) to the place from which the vehicle was removed shall be read as references to the place in which it was immediately before it was moved in accordance with this section.

(9) In this section 'immobilisation device' means any device or appliance designed or adapted to be fixed to a vehicle for the purpose of preventing it from being driven or otherwise put in motion, being a device or appliance of a type approved by the Secretary of State for use for that purpose in accordance with this section.

(10)–(12) *[Omitted.]*

[Section 106 (to which this section is subject) states that ss 104 and 105 only extend to such areas as the Secretary of State specifies. At 1 January 1987, the only order having effect under s 106 was the Immobilisation of Vehicles Illegally Parked (London Boroughs of Camden, Kensington and Chelsea, and Westminster, and the City of London) Order 1986 (SI 1986 No 1225). However, ss 104 to 106 of this Act have been applied to Crown roads in the royal parks (Hyde Park, Kensington Gardens, Regent's Park, St. James's Park and Green Park in Greater London) as they apply in relation to other roads to which the public has access; Crown Roads (Royal Parks) (Application of Road Traffic Enactments) Order 1987 (SI 1987 No 363), art 5.

The following immobilisation devices have been approved:

the 'Wheelok "P"'	*Immobilisation Devices (Approval) Order 1983*
the 'Bulldog Model 11 T'	*Immobilisation Devices (Approval) Order 1983*
the 'Wheelok Model P II'	*Immobilisation Device (Approval) Order 1986*
the 'Claw'	*Immobilisation Device (Approval) Order 1987.*

These orders are not published as statutory instruments. The 1983 Order was dated 22 April 1983, the 1986 Order was dated 30 June 1986 and the 1987 Order was dated 2 November 1987.]

105. Exemptions from s 104

(1) Subject to the following provisions of this section, section 104(1) of this Act shall not apply in relation to a vehicle found by a constable in the circumstances mentioned in that subsection if either—

(*a*) a current disabled person's badge is displayed on the vehicle; or

(*b*) the vehicle is in a meter bay within a parking place designated by a designation order.

(2) The exemption under subsection (1)(*b*) above shall not apply in the case of any vehicle if—

(*a*) the meter bay in which it was found was not authorised for use as such at the time when it was left there (referred to below in this section as the time of parking); or

(*b*) an initial charge was not duly paid at the time of parking; or

(*c*) there has been since that time any contravention in relation to the relevant parking meter of any provision made by virtue of section 46(2)(*c*) of this Act; or

(*d*) more than two hours have elapsed since the end of any period for which an initial charge was duly paid at the time of parking or (as the case may be) since the end of any unexpired time in respect of another vehicle available on the relevant parking meter at the time of parking.

(3) For the purposes of subsection (2)(*a*) above, a meter bay in a parking place designated by a designation order is not authorised for use as such at any time when—

(*a*) by virtue of section 49(1)(*a*) of this Act the parking place is treated for the purposes of sections 46 and 47 of this Act as if it were not designated by that order; or

(*b*) the use of the parking place or of any part of it that consists of or includes that particular meter bay is suspended under section 49(4) of this Act.

(4) In relation to any vehicle found in a meter bay within a parking place designated by a designation order, references in subsection (2) above to an initial charge are references to an initial charge payable in respect of that vehicle under section 45 or 50 of this Act.

(5) In any case where section 104(1) of this Act would apply in relation to a vehicle but for subsection (1)(*a*) above, the person guilty of contravening the prohibition or restriction mentioned in section 104(1) is also guilty of an offence under this subsection if the conditions mentioned in subsection (6) below are met.

(6) Those conditions are that at the time when the contravention occurred—

(*a*) the vehicle was not being used either by the person to whom the disabled person's badge was issued or under subsection (4) (institutional use) of section 21 of the Chronically Sick and Disabled Persons Act 1970 (badges for display on motor vehicles used by disabled persons); and

(*b*) he was not using the vehicle in circumstances falling within section 117(2)(*b*) of this Act.

(7) In this section, 'meter bay' means a parking space equipped with a parking meter; and the references in subsection (2) above to the relevant parking meter are

references to the parking meter relating to the meter bay in which the vehicle in question was found.

* * *

Enforcement of excess parking charges

107. Liability of vehicle owner in respect of excess parking charge

(1) This section applies where—

(*a*) an excess charge has been incurred in pursuance of an order under sections 45 and 46 of this Act;

(*b*) notice of the incurring of the excess charge has been given or affixed as provided in the order; and

(*c*) the excess charge has not been duly paid in accordance with the order;

and in the following provisions of this Part of this Act 'the excess charge offence' means the offence under section 47 of this Act of failing duly to pay the excess charge.

(2) Subject to the following provisions of this section

(*a*) for the purposes of the institution of proceedings in respect of the excess charge offence against any person as being the owner of the vehicle at the relevant time, and

(*b*) in any proceedings in respect of the excess charge offence brought against any person as being the owner of the vehicle at the relevant time,

it shall be conclusively presumed (notwithstanding that that person may not be an individual) that he was the driver of the vehicle at the time and, accordingly, that acts or omissions of the driver of the vehicle at that time were his acts or omissions.

(3) Subsection (2) above shall not apply in relation to any person unless, within the period of 6 months beginning on the day on which the notice of the incurring of the excess charge was given or affixed as mentioned in subsection (1)(*b*) above, a notice under section 108 of this Act has been served on him—

(*a*) by or on behalf of the authority which is the local authority for the purposes of sections 45 and 46 of this Act in relation to the parking place concerned, or

(*b*) by or on behalf of the chief officer of police.

(4) If the person on whom a notice under section 108 of this Act is served in accordance with subsection (3) above was not the owner of the vehicle at the relevant time, subsection (2) above shall not apply in relation to him if he furnishes a statutory statement of ownership to that effect in compliance with the notice.

(5) The presumption in subsection (2) above shall not apply in any proceedings brought against any person as being the owner of the vehicle at the relevant time if, in those proceedings, it is proved—

(*a*) that at the relevant time the vehicle was in the possession of some other person without the consent of the accused, or

(*b*) that the accused was not the owner of the vehicle at the relevant time and that he has a reasonable excuse for failing to comply with the notice under section 108 of this Act served on him in accordance with subsection (3) above.

108. Notice in respect of excess parking

(1) A notice under this section shall be in the prescribed form, shall give particulars of the excess charge and shall provide that, unless the excess charge is paid before the expiry of the appropriate period, the person on whom the notice is served—

(*a*) is required, before the expiry of that period, to furnish to the authority or chief officer of police by or on behalf of whom the notice was served a statutory statement of ownership (as defined in Part I of Schedule 8 to this Act), and

(*b*) is invited, before the expiry of that period, to furnish to that authority or chief officer of police a statutory statement of facts (as defined in Part II of that Schedule).

(2) If, in any case where—

(*a*) a notice under this section has been served on any person, and

(*b*) the excess charge specified in the notice is not paid within the appropriate period,

the person so served fails without reasonable excuse to comply with the notice by furnishing a statutory statement of ownership he shall be guilty of an offence.

(3) If, in compliance with or in response to a notice under this section any person furnishes a statement which is false in a material particular, and does so recklessly or knowing it to be false in that particular, he shall be guilty of an offence.

(4) Where a notice under this section has been served on any person in respect of any excess charge—

(*a*) payment of the charge by any person before the date on which proceedings are begun for the excess charge offence, or, as the case may be, for an offence under subsection (2) above in respect of a failure to comply with the notice, shall discharge the liability of that or any other person (under this or any other enactment) for the excess charge offence or, as the case may be, for the offence under subsection (2) above;

(*b*) conviction of any person of the excess charge offence shall discharge the liability of any other person (under this or any other enactment) for that offence and the liability of any person for an offence under subsection (2) above in respect of a failure to comply with the notice; and

(*c*) conviction of the person so served of an offence under subsection (2) above in respect of a failure to comply with the notice shall discharge the liability of any person for the excess charge offence;

but, except as provided by this subsection, nothing in section 107 of this Act or this section shall affect the liability of any person for the excess charge offence.

109. Modifications of ss 107 and 108 in relation to hired vehicles

(1) This section shall apply where—

(*a*) a notice under section 108 of this Act has been served on a vehicle-hire firm, and

(*b*) at the relevant time the vehicle in respect of which the notice was served was let to another person by the vehicle-hire firm under a hiring agreement to which this section applies.

(2) Where this section applies, it shall be a sufficient compliance with the notice served on the vehicle-hire firm if the firm furnishes to the chief officer of police or local authority by or on behalf of whom the notice was served a statement in the prescribed form, signed by or on behalf of the vehicle-hire firm, stating that at the relevant time the vehicle concerned was hired under a hiring agreement to which this section applies, together with—

(*a*) a copy of that hiring agreement, and

(*b*) a copy of a statement of liability in the prescribed form, signed by the hirer under that hiring agreement;

and accordingly, in relation to the vehicle-hire firm on whom the notice was served, the reference in section 108(2) of this Act to a statutory statement of ownership shall be construed as a reference to a statement under this subsection together with the documents specified in paragraphs (*a*) and (*b*) above.

(3) If, in a case where this section applies, the vehicle-hire firm has complied with the notice served on the firm by furnishing the statement and copies of the documents specified in subsection (2) above, then sections 107 and 108 of this Act shall have effect as if in those provisions—

(*a*) any reference to the owner of the vehicle were a reference to the hirer under the hiring agreement, and

(*b*) any reference to a statutory statement of ownership were a reference to a statutory statement of hiring.

(4) Where, in compliance with a notice under section 108 of this Act, a vehicle-hire firm has furnished copies of a hiring agreement and statement of liability as mentioned in subsection (2) above, a person authorised in that behalf by the chief officer of police or local authority to whom the documents are furnished may, at any reasonable time within 6 months after service of that notice, and on production of his authority, require the production by the firm of the originals of those documents; and if, without reasonable excuse, a vehicle-hire firm fails to produce the original of a document when required to do so under this subsection, the firm shall be treated as not having complied with the notice under section 108 of this Act.

(5) This section applies to a hiring agreement, under the terms of which the vehicle concerned is let to the hirer for a fixed period of less than 6 months (whether or not that period is capable of extension by agreement between the parties or otherwise); and any reference in this section to the currency of the hiring agreement includes a reference to any period during which, with the consent of the vehicle-hire firm, the hirer continues in possession of the vehicle as hirer, after the expiry of the fixed period specified in the agreement, but otherwise on terms and conditions specified in it.

(6) In this section 'statement of liability' means a statement made by the hirer under a hiring agreement to which this section applies to the effect that the hirer acknowledges that he will be liable, as the owner of the vehicle, in respect of any excess charge which, during the currency of the hiring agreement, may be incurred with respect to the vehicle in pursuance of an order under section 45 and 46 of this Act.

(7) In this section—

'hiring agreement' refers only to an agreement which contains such particulars as may be prescribed and does not include a hire-purchase agreement within the meaning of the Consumer Credit Act 1974, and

'vehicle-hire firm' means any person engaged in hiring vehicles in the course of a business.

[Orders under ss 45 and 46 of this Act provide for the designation of parking places on the highway (s 45) and for the payment of charges and the regulation and restriction of the use of parking places (s 46).]

110. Time for bringing, and evidence in, proceedings for certain offences

(1) Proceedings in England and Wales for an offence under section 108(3) of this Act may be brought within a period of six months from the date on which evidence

sufficient in the opinion of the prosecutor to warrant the proceedings came to his knowledge; but no such proceedings shall be brought by virtue of this section more than 3 years after the commission of the offence.

(2) *[Omitted.]*

(3) For the purposes of subsections (1) and (2) above a certificate signed by or on behalf of the prosecutor or, as the case may be, the Lord Advocate or the local authority, and stating the date on which evidence such as is mentioned in the subsection in question came to his or their knowledge, shall be conclusive evidence of that fact; and a certificate stating that matter and purporting to be so signed shall be deemed to be so signed unless the contrary is proved.

(4) Where any person is charged with the offence of failing to pay an excess charge, and the prosecutor produces to the court any of the statutory statements in Schedule 8 to this Act or a copy of a statement of liability (within the meaning of section 109 of this Act) purporting—

(*a*) to have been furnished in compliance with or in response to a notice under section 108 of this Act, and

(*b*) to have been signed by the accused,

the statement shall be presumed, unless the contrary is proved, to have been signed by the accused and shall be evidence (and, in Scotland, sufficient evidence) in the proceedings of any facts stated in it tending to show that the accused was the owner, the hirer or the driver of the vehicle concerned at a particular time.

111. Supplementary provisions as to excess charges

(1) The provisions of Schedule 8 to this Act shall have effect for the purposes of sections 107 to 109 of this Act (in this section referred to as 'the specified sections').

(2) In the specified sections—

'appropriate period', in relation to a notice under section 108 of this Act, means the period of 14 days from the date on which the notice is served, or such longer period as may be specified in the notice or as may be allowed by the chief officer of police or authority by or on behalf of whom the notice is served;

'driver', in relation to an excess charge and in relation to an offence of failing duly to pay such a charge, means the person driving the vehicle at the time when it is alleged to have been left in the parking place concerned;

'relevant time', in relation to an excess charge, means the time when the vehicle was left in the parking place concerned, notwithstanding that the period in respect of which the excess charge was incurred did not begin at that time.

(3) For the purposes of the specified sections the owner of a vehicle shall be taken to be the person by whom the vehicle is kept; and for the purpose of determining, in the course of any proceedings brought by virtue of the specified sections, who was the owner of the vehicle at any time, it shall be presumed that the owner was the person who was the registered keeper of the vehicle at that time.

(4) Notwithstanding the presumption in subsection (3) above, it shall be open to the defence in any proceedings to prove that the person who was the registered keeper of a vehicle at a particular time was not the person by whom the vehicle was kept at that time, and it shall be open to the prosecution to prove that the vehicle was kept by some other person at that time.

(5) A notice under section 108 of this Act may be served on any person—

(*a*) by delivering it to him or by leaving it at his proper address, or (*b*) by sending it to him by post;

and, where the person on whom such a notice is to be served is a body corporate, it shall be duly served if it is served on the secretary or clerk of that body.

(6) For the purposes of subsection (5) above and of section 7 of the Interpretation Act 1978 (references to service by post) in its application to that subsection, the proper address of any person on whom such a notice is to be served—

(*a*) shall, in the case of the secretary or clerk of a body corporate, be that of the registered or principal office of that body or the registered address of the person who is the registered keeper of the vehicle concerned at the time of service, and

(*b*) shall in any other case be the last known address of the person to be served.

(7) References in this section to the person who was or is the registered keeper of a vehicle at any time are references to the person in whose name the vehicle was or is at that time registered under the Vehicles (Excise) Act 1971; and, in relation to any such person, the reference in subsection (6)(*a*) above to that person's registered address is a reference to the address recorded in the record kept under that Act with respect to that vehicle as being that person's address.

(8) For the purposes of sections 1(2) and 2(1) of the Magistrates' Courts Act 1980 (power to issue summons or warrant and jurisdiction to try offences), any offence under subsection (2) of section 108 of this Act shall be treated as committed at any address which at the time of service of the notice under that section to which the offence relates was the accused's proper address (in accordance with subsection (6) above) for the service of any such notice as well as at the address to which any statutory statement furnished in response to that notice is required to be returned in accordance with the notice.

PART IX

Further Provisions as to Enforcement

General provisions

112. Information as to identity of driver or rider

(1) This section applies to any offence under any of the foregoing provisions of this Act except—

(*a*) sections 43, 52, 88(7), 104, 105 and 108;

(*b*) the provisions of subsection (2) or (3) of section 108 as modified by subsections (2) and (3) of section 109; and

(*c*) section 35(7) in its application to England and Wales.

(2) Where the driver of a vehicle is alleged to be guilty of an offence to which this section applies—

(*a*) the person keeping the vehicle shall give such information as to the identity of the driver as he may be required to give—

(i) by or on behalf of a chief officer of police, or

(ii) in the case of an offence under section 35(4) or against section 47 of this Act, by or on behalf of a chief officer of police or, in writing, by or on behalf of the local authority for the parking place in question; and

(*b*) any other person shall, if required as mentioned in paragraph (*a*) above, give any information which it is in his power to give and which may lead to the identification of the driver.

(3) In subsection (2) above, references to the driver of a vehicle include references to the person riding a bicycle or tricycle (not being a motor vehicle); and—

(*a*) *[Repealed.]*

(*b*) in relation to an offence under section 61(5) of this Act, subsection (2)(*a*) above shall have effect as if, for subparagraphs (i) and (ii), there were substituted the words 'by a notice in writing given to him by a local authority in whose area the loading area in question is situated',

and in subsection (2)(*a*) above, as modified by paragraph (*b*) of this subsection, 'local authority' means any of the following, that is to say, a county council, . . . a district council, a London borough council and the Common Council of the City of London.

(4) Except as provided by subsection (5) below, a person who fails to comply with the requirements of subsection (2)(*a*) above shall be guilty of an offence unless he shows to the satisfaction of the court that he did not know, and could not with reasonable diligence have ascertained, who was the driver of the vehicle or, as the case may be, the rider of the bicycle or tricycle; and a person who fails to comply with the requirements of subsection (2)(*b*) above shall be guilty of an offence.

(5) *[Applies to Scotland.]*

[Section 112 is printed as amended by the Local Government Act 1985, s 102(2) and Sched 17.]

113. *[Repealed.]*

114. *[Repealed.]*

115. Mishandling of parking documents and related offences

[(1) A person shall be guilty of an offence who, with intent to deceive—

(*a*) uses, or lends to, or allows to be used by, any other person,—

(i) any parking device or apparatus designed to be used in connection with parking devices;

(ii) any ticket issued by a parking meter, parking device or apparatus designed to be used in connection with parking devices;

(iii) any authorisation by way of such a certificate, other means of identification or device as is referred to in any of sections 4(2), 4(3), 7(2) and 7(3) of this Act; or

(iv) any such permit or token as is referred to in section 46(2)(*i*) of this Act;

(*b*) makes or has in his possession anything so closely resembling any such thing as is mentioned in paragraph (*a*) above as to be calculated to deceive; or

(*c*) *[Applies to Scotland.]*]

(2) A person who knowingly makes a false statement for the purpose of procuring the grant or issue to himself or any other person of any such authorisation as is mentioned in subsection (1) above shall be guilty of an offence.

(3) *[Applies to Scotland.]*

[Section 115 is printed as amended by the Road Traffic Regulation (Parking) Act 1986, s 2(2).]

116. Provisions supplementary to s 115

(1) If any person authorised in that behalf by or under a designation order has reasonable cause to believe that a document or article carried on a vehicle, or by the driver or person in charge of a vehicle, is a document or article in relation to which an offence has been committed under subsection (1) of section 115 of this Act (so far as that subsection relates to such authorisations as are referred to in it) or under subsection (2) of that section, he may detain that document or article, and may for that purpose require the driver or person in charge of the vehicle to deliver up the document or article; and if the driver or person in charge of the vehicle fails to comply with that requirement, he shall be guilty of an offence.

(2) When a document or article has been detained under subsection (1) above and—

(*a*) at any time after the expiry of 6 months from the date when that detention began no person has been charged since that date with an offence in relation to the document or article under subsection (1) or (2) of section 115 of this Act, and

(*b*) the document or article has not been returned to the person to whom the authorisation in question was issued or to the person who at that date was the driver or person in charge of the vehicle,

then, on an application made for the purpose to a magistrates' court (or, in Scotland, on a summary application made for the purpose to the sheriff court), the court shall make such order respecting disposal of the document or article and award such costs (or, in Scotland, expenses) as the justice of the case may require.

(3) Any of the following, but no other, persons shall be entitled to make an application under subsection (2) above with respect to a document or article, that is to say—

(*a*) the person to whom the authorisation was issued;

(*b*) the person who, at the date when the detention of the document or article began, was the driver or person in charge of the vehicle; and

(*c*) the person for the time being having possession of the document or article.

117. Wrongful use of disabled person's badge

(1) A person who is guilty of an offence in relation to a motor vehicle under a provision of this Act other than this section ('the first offence') is also guilty of an offence under this section if the conditions specified in subsection (2) below are satisfied.

(2) The conditions mentioned in subsection (1) above are that at the time of the commission of the first offence—

(*a*) a disabled person's badge was displayed on the motor vehicle;

(*b*) he was using the motor vehicle in circumstances where a disabled person's concession would be available to a disabled person's vehicle; and

(*c*) the vehicle was not being used either by the person to whom the badge was issued or under section 21(4) (institutional use) of the Chronically Sick and Disabled Persons Act 1970.

(3) In this section—

'disabled person's badge' means a badge of a form prescribed under section 21(2) of the Chronically Sick and Disabled Persons Act 1970; and

'disabled person's concession' means—

(*a*) an exemption from an order under this Act given by reference to disabled persons' vehicles; or

(*b*) a provision made in any order under this Act for the use of a parking place by disabled persons' vehicles.

[Disabled persons' badges are in the form prescribed in the Schedule to the Disabled Persons (Badges for Motor Vehicles) Regulations 1982 (SI 1982 No 1740) which were made under the Chronically Sick and Disabled Persons Act 1970, s 21.]

118. *[Repealed.]*

* * *

PART X

General and Supplementary Provisions

* * *

130. Application of Act to Crown

(1) Subject to the provisions of this section and section 132 of this Act, the provisions of this Act specified in subsection (2) below shall apply to vehicles and persons in the public service of the Crown.

(2) The provisions referred to in subsection (1) above are—

(*a*) sections 1 to 5, 9 to 16, 21 to 26, 38, 42, 45 to 51, 52(2) and (3), 58 to 60, 62 to 67, 69 to 71, 76 to 91, 99, 100, 104, 105, 125 and 126;

(*b*) except in relation to vehicles and persons in the armed forces of the Crown when on duty, sections 6 to 8; and

(*c*) . . .

(3) In relation to vehicles used for naval, military or air force purposes, while being driven by persons for the time being subject to the orders of a member of the armed forces of the Crown, the Secretary of State may by regulations vary the provisions of any statutory provision imposing a speed limit on motor vehicles; but regulations under this subsection may provide that any variation made by the regulations shall have effect subject to such conditions as may be specified in the regulations.

(4) *[Repealed.]*

(5) *[Repealed.]*

[Section 130 is printed as amended by the Road Traffic (Consequential Provisions) Act 1988, s 3(1) and Sched 1, Part I.

Section 132 of this Act (to which this section is subject) makes special provision regarding certain Crown roads.]

* * *

136. Meaning of 'motor vehicle' and other expressions relating to vehicles

(1) In this Act, subject to section 20 of the Chronically Sick and Disabled Persons Act 1970 (which makes special provision with respect to invalid carriages), 'motor vehicle' means a mechanically propelled vehicle intended or adapted for use on roads and 'trailer' means a vehicle drawn by a motor vehicle.

(2) In this Act 'motor car' means a mechanically propelled vehicle, not being a motor cycle or an invalid carriage, which is constructed itself to carry a load or passengers and of which the weight unladen—

(*a*) if it is constructed solely for the carriage of passengers and their effects, is adapted to carry not more than 7 passengers exclusive of the driver, and is fitted with tyres of such type as may be specified in regulations made by the Secretary of State, does not exceed 3050 kilograms;

(*b*) if it is constructed or adapted for use for the conveyance of goods or burden of any description, does not exceed 3050 kilograms (or 3500 kilograms if the vehicle carries a container or containers for holding, for the purposes of its propulsion, any fuel which is wholly gaseous at 17.5 degrees Celsius under a pressure of 1.013 bar or plant and materials for producing such fuel); or

(*c*) in a case falling within neither of the foregoing paragraphs, does not exceed 2540 kilograms.

(3) In this Act 'heavy motor car' means a mechanically propelled vehicle, not being a motor car, which is constructed itself to carry a load or passengers and of which the weight unladen exceeds 2540 kilograms.

(4) In this Act (except for the purposes of section 57) 'motor cycle' means a mechanically propelled vehicle (not being an invalid carriage) with fewer than 4 wheels, of which the weight unladen does not exceed 410 kilograms.

(5) In this Act 'invalid carriage' means a mechanically propelled vehicle of which the weight unladen does not exceed 254 kilograms and which is specially designed and constructed, and not merely adapted, for the use of a person suffering from some physical default or disability and is used solely by such a person.

(6) In this Act 'motor tractor' means a mechanically propelled vehicle which is not constructed itself to carry a load, other than excepted articles, and of which the weight unladen does not exceed 7370 kilograms.

(7) In this Act 'light locomotive' and 'heavy locomotive' mean a mechanically propelled vehicle which is not constructed itself to carry a load, other than excepted articles, and of which the weight unladen—

(*a*) in the case of a light locomotive, exceeds 7370 but does not exceed 11690 kilograms, and

(*b*) in the case of a heavy locomotive, exceeds 11690 kilograms.

(8) In subsections (6) and (7) above 'excepted articles' means any of the following, that is to say, water, fuel, accumulators and other equipment used for the purpose of propulsion, loose tools and loose equipment.

137. Supplementary provisions relating to s 136

(1) A sidecar attached to a motor vehicle shall, if it complies with such conditions as may be specified in regulations made by the Secretary of State, be regarded as forming part of the vehicle to which it is attached and not as being a trailer.

(2) For the purposes of section 136 of this Act, in a case where a motor vehicle is so constructed that a trailer may by partial superimposition be attached to the vehicle in such a manner as to cause a substantial part of the weight of the trailer to be borne by the vehicle, that vehicle shall be deemed to be a vehicle itself constructed to carry a load.

(3) For the purposes of that section, in the case of a motor vehicle fitted with a

crane, dynamo, welding plant or other special appliance or apparatus which is a permanent or essentially permanent fixture, the appliance of apparatus shall not be deemed to constitute a load or goods or burden of any description, but shall be deemed to form part of the vehicle.

(4) The Secretary of State may by regulations vary any of the maximum or minimum weights specified in section 136 of this Act; and such regulations may have effect—

(*a*) either generally or in the case of vehicles of any class specified in the regulations, and

(*b*) either for the purposes of this Act and of all regulations made under it or for such of those purposes as may be so specified.

(5) Nothing in section 86 of this Act shall be construed as limiting the powers conferred by subsection (4) above.

138. Meaning of 'heavy commercial vehicle'

(1) Subject to subsections (4) to (7) below, in this Act 'heavy commercial vehicle' means any goods vehicle which has an operating weight exceeding 7.5 tonnes.

(2) The operating weight of a goods vehicle for the purposes of this section is—

(*a*) in the case of a motor vehicle not drawing a trailer, or in the case of a trailer, its maximum laden weight;

(*b*) in the case of an articulated vehicle, its maximum laden weight (if it has one) and otherwise the aggregate maximum laden weight of all the individual vehicles forming part of that articulated vehicle; and

(*c*) in the case of a motor vehicle (other than an articulated vehicle) drawing one or more trailers, the aggregate maximum laden weight of the motor vehicle and the trailer or trailers attached to it.

(3) In this section—

'articulated vehicle' means a motor vehicle with a trailer so attached to it as to be partially superimposed upon it;

'goods vehicle' means a motor vehicle constructed or adapted for use for the carriage of goods or burden of any description, or a trailer so constructed or adapted;

'trailer' means any vehicle other than a motor vehicle;

and references to the maximum laden weight of a vehicle are references to the total laden weight which must not be exceeded in the case of that vehicle if it is to be used in Great Britain without contravening any regulations for the time being in force under [section 41 of the Road Traffic Act 1988] (construction and use regulations).

(4) The Secretary of State may by regulations amend subsections (1) and (2) above (whether as originally enacted or as previously amended under this subsection)—

(*a*) by substituting weights of a different description for any of the weights there mentioned, or

(*b*) in the case of subsection (1) above, by substituting a weight of a different description or amount, or a weight different both in description and amount, for the weight there mentioned.

(5) Different regulations may be made under subsection (4) above for the purposes of different provisions of this Act and as respects different classes of vehicles or as

respects the same class of vehicles in different circumstances and as respects different times of the day or night and as respects roads in different localities.

(6) Regulations made under subsection (4) above shall not so amend subsection (1) above that there is any case in which a goods vehicle whose operating weight (ascertained in accordance with subsection (2) above as originally enacted) does not exceed 7.5 tonnes is a heavy commercial vehicle for any of the purposes of this Act.

(7) For the purpose of determining whether or not any vehicle is a heavy commercial vehicle for the purposes of a traffic regulation order or experimental traffic order—

(*a*) made before 13th August 1981 (whether or not varied or, in the case of an experimental traffic order, continued after that date); and

(*b*) including any such provision as is referred to in section 2(4) of this Act;

the provisions contained in paragraph 8 of Schedule 10 to this Act shall, during the transitional period specified in that paragraph, have effect in substitution for the provisions of subsections (1) to (6) above.

(8) In subsection (7) above, 'experimental traffic order' does not include an order made in respect of traffic on roads in Greater London.

[Section 138 is printed as amended by the Road Traffic (Consequential Provisions) Act 1988, s 4 and Sched 3, para 25(8).]

139. Hovercraft *[Omitted.]*

140. Certain vehicles not to be treated as motor vehicles

(1) For the purposes of this Act—

(*a*) a mechanically propelled vehicle which is an implement for cutting grass, is controlled by a pedestrian and is not capable of being used or adapted for any other purpose;

(*b*) any other mechanically propelled vehicle controlled by a pedestrian which may be specified by regulations made by the Secretary of State for the purposes of this section and of [section 189 of the Road Traffic Act 1988]; and

(*c*) an electrically assisted pedal cycle of such class as may be prescribed by regulations so made,

shall be treated as not being a motor vehicle.

(2) In this section 'controlled by a pedestrian' means that the vehicle either—

(*a*) is constructed or adapted for use only under such control, or

(*b*) is constructed or adapted for use either under such control or under the control of a person carried on it, but is not for the time being in use under, or proceeding under, the control of a person carried on it.

[Section 140 is printed as amended by the Road Traffic (Consequential Provisions) Act 1988, s 4 and Sched 3, para 25(9).]

141. Tramcars and trolley vehicles

(1) Subject to subsection (4) of this section, none of the provisions of this Act specified in subsection (2) below, nor any orders or regulations made under those provisions, shall apply to tramcars or trolley vehicles operated under statutory powers.

(2) The provisions of this Act referred to in subsection (1) above are sections 1 to 5, 14, 18 and 81 to 89.

(3) In this section 'operated under statutory powers', in relation to tramcars and trolley vehicles, means that their use is authorised or regulated by a special Act of Parliament or by an order having the force of an Act.

(4) Subsection (1) above shall have effect subject to any such Act or order as is mentioned in subsection (3) above; and any such Act or order may apply any of the following provisions of this Act, namely, sections 81 to 89, to tramcars or trolley vehicles to which the Act or order relates.

(5) In this section 'tramcar' includes any carriage used on any road by virtue of an order under the Light Railways Act 1896, and 'trolley vehicle' means a mechanically propelled vehicle adapted for use on roads without rails and moved by power transmitted to it from some external source.

142. General interpretation of Act

(1) In this Act, except where the context otherwise requires, the following expressions have the meanings hereby assigned to them respectively, that is to say—

'bridge authority' means the authority or person responsible for the maintenance of a bridge;

'bridleway' means a way over which the public have the following, but no other, rights of way, that is to say, a right of way on foot and a right of way on horseback or leading a horse, with or without a right to drive animals of any description along the way;

'designation order' means an order under section 45 of this Act (including any order so made by virtue of section 50(1) of this Act) and 'designated parking place' means a parking place designated by a designation order;

'disabled person's badge' means any badge issued, or having effect as if issued, under any regulations for the time being in force under section 21 of the Chronically Sick and Disabled Persons Act 1970;

'disabled person's vehicle' means a vehicle lawfully displaying a disabled person's badge;

'driver' where a separate person acts as steersman of a motor vehicle, includes that person as well as any other person engaged in the driving of the vehicle, and 'drive' and 'driving' shall be construed accordingly;

'excess charge' has the meaning assigned to it by section 46(1) of this Act [*qv*];

'experimental traffic order' has the meaning assigned to it by section 9(1) of this Act;

except in section 71(2) of this Act, 'footpath' means a way over which the public has a right of way on foot only;

'highway authority'—

(*a*) for the purposes of the application of this Act to England and Wales, means the Secretary of State in relation to a trunk road and, in relation to a road other than a trunk road, means . . . the authority being either the council of a county, [metropolitan district or London borough or the Common Council of the City of London] which is responsible for the maintenance of the road, . . .

'initial charge' has the meaning assigned to it by section 46(1) of this Act [*qv*];

'local highway authority' means a regional or islands council;

'magistrates' court' and 'petty sessions area' have the same meanings as in the Magistrates' Courts Act 1980 [*qv*];

'the Ministers' means the Secretaries of State charged with general responsibility under this Act in relation to England, Wales and Scotland respectively;

subject to section 111(3) and (4) of, and paragraph 11(2) and (3) of Schedule 12 to, this Act, 'owner', in relation to a vehicle which is subject to a hiring agreement or hire-purchase agreement, means the person in possession of the vehicle under that agreement;

'parking device' has the meaning assigned to it by section 51(4) of this Act;

'parking meter' has the meaning assigned to it by section 46(2)(*a*) of this Act [*qv*];

'prescribed' means prescribed by regulations made by the Secretary of State;

'public service vehicle' [has the same meaning] as in the Public Passenger Vehicles Act 1981 [*qv*];

'road' means any length of highway or of any other road to which the public has access, and includes bridges over which a road passes;

'special road' means a road provided or to be provided in pursuance of a scheme under section 1 of the Special Roads Act 1949, section 11 of the Highways Act 1959 or section 16 of the Highways Act 1980, or a road to which, by virtue of paragraph 3 of Schedule 23 to the Highways Act 1980, certain provisions of that Act apply as if it were a special road provided in pursuance of a scheme made under section 16 of that Act, and includes any part of a special road;

'statutory', in relation to any prohibition, restriction, requirement or provision, means contained in, or having effect under, any enactment (including any enactment contained in this Act);

'street parking place' and 'off-street parking place' refer respectively to parking places on land which does, and on land which does not, form part of a road;

'traffic sign' has the meaning assigned to it by section 64(1) of this Act [*qv*]; and

'traffic regulation order' has the meaning assigned to it by section 1 of this Act.

(2) Any reference in this Act to a tricycle shall be construed as including a reference to a cycle which is not a motor vehicle and has 4 or more wheels.

(3) References in this Act to a class of vehicles or traffic (other than the references in section 17) shall be construed as references to a class defined or described by reference to any characteristics of the vehicles or traffic or to any other circumstances whatsoever.

[Section 142 is printed as amended by the Roads (Scotland) Act 1984, s 156(1) and (3), Sched 9, para 93(44), and Sched 11; the Local Government Act 1985, ss 8(1) and 102(2), Sched 5, para 4(37), and Sched 17; the Transport Act 1985, s 1(3) and Sched 1, para 15(4).]

143. Saving for law of nuisance *[Omitted.]*

144. Transitional provisions and savings

(1) The transitional provisions and savings in Schedule 10 to this Act shall have effect.

(2) The enactment in this Act of the provisions specified in the first column of Schedule 11 to this Act (being re-enactments, with or without modifications, of provisions contained in the instruments specified in the corresponding entries in the second column of that Schedule, which were instruments made in the exercise of powers conferred by Acts of Parliament) shall be without prejudice to the validity of those re-enacted provisions; and any question as to their validity shall be determined

as if the re-enacted provisions were contained in instruments made in the exercise of those powers.

* * *

SCHEDULE 6

Section 86.

Speed Limits for Vehicles of Certain Classes

PART I

Vehicles Fitted with Pneumatic Tyres on all Wheels
(see application provisions below the following Table)

Table

1	2	3		
Item No	Class of Vehicle	Maximum speed (in miles per hour) while vehicle is being driven on:		
		(a) Motorway	(b) Dual carriage-way road not being a motorway	(c) Other road
1	A passenger vehicle, motor caravan or dual-purpose vehicle not drawing a trailer being a vehicle with an unladen weight exceeding 3·05 tonnes or adapted to carry more than 8 passengers: (i) if not exceeding 12 metres in overall length (ii) if exceeding 12 metres in overall length	 70 60	 60 60	 50 50
2	An invalid carriage	not applicable	20	20
3	A passenger vehicle, motor caravan, car-derived van or dual-purpose vehicle drawing one trailer	[60]	[60]	50
4	A passenger vehicle, motor caravan, car-derived van or dual-purpose vehicle drawing more than one trailer	40	20	20
5	(1) A goods vehicle having a maximum laden weight not exceeding 7·5 tonnes and which is not— (a) an articulated vehicle, or (b) drawing a trailer, or (c) a car-derived van	70	60	50

1	2	3		
Item No	Class of Vehicle	Maximum speed (in miles per hour) while vehicle is being driven on:		
		(a) Motorway	(b) Dual carriage-way road not being a motorway	(c) Other road
	(2) A goods vehicle which is—			
	(a) (i) an articulated vehicle having a maximum laden weight not exceeding 7·5 tonnes, or (ii) a motor vehicle, other than a car-derived van, which is drawing one trailer where the aggregate maximum laden weight of the motor vehicle and the trailer does not exceed 7·5 tonnes	60	[60]	50
	(b) (i) an articulated vehicle having a maximum laden weight exceeding 7·5 tonnes, (ii) a motor vehicle having a maximum laden weight exceeding 7·5 tonnes and not drawing a trailer, or (iii) a motor vehicle drawing one trailer where the aggregate maximum laden weight of the motor vehicle and the trailer exceeds 7·5 tonnes	60	50	40
	(c) a motor vehicle, other than a car-derived van, drawing more than one trailer	40	20	20
6	A motor tractor (other than an industrial tractor), a light locomotive or a heavy locomotive—			
	(a) if the provisions about springs and wings as specified in paragraph 3 of Part IV of this Schedule are complied with and the vehicle is not drawing a trailer, or if those provisions are complied with and the vehicle is drawing one trailer which also complies with those provisions	40	30	30
	(b) in any other case	20	20	20
7	A works truck	18	18	18
8	An industrial tractor	not applicable	18	18
[9	An agricultural motor vehicle	40	40	40]

Application

This Part applies only to motor vehicles, not being track-laying vehicles, every wheel of which is fitted with a pneumatic tyre and to such vehicles drawing one or more trailers, not being track-laying vehicles, every wheel of which is fitted with a pneumatic tyre.

[Schedule 6, Part I, is printed as amended by the Motor Vehicles (Variation of Speed Limits) Regulations 1986 (SI 1986 No 1175).]

PART II

Vehicles (Other than Track-Laying Vehicles) not Fitted with Pneumatic Tyres on all Wheels
(see application provisions below the following Table)

Table

1	2	3
Item No	Class of Vehicle	Maximum speed (in miles per hour) while vehicle is being driven on a road
1	A motor vehicle, or in the case of a motor vehicle drawing one or more trailers, the combination, where— (a) every wheel is fitted with a resilient tyre, or (b) at least one wheel is fitted with a resilient tyre and every wheel which is not fitted with a resilient tyre is fitted with a pneumatic tyre	20
2	A motor vehicle, or in the case of a motor vehicle drawing one or more trailers, the combination, where any wheel is not fitted with either a pneumatic tyre or a resilient tyre	5

Application

This Part does not apply to—

(*a*) a motor vehicle which is a track-laying vehicle; or

(*b*) a motor vehicle which is not a track-laying vehicle but which is drawing one or more trailers any one of which is a track-laying vehicle.

PART III

Track-Laying Vehicles
(see application provisions below the following Table)

Table

1	2	3
Item No	Class of Vehicle	Maximum speed (in miles per hour) while vehicle is being driven on a road
1	A motor vehicle, being a track-laying vehicle which is fitted with— (a) springs between its frame and its weight-carrying rollers, and (b) resilient material between the rim of its weight-carrying rollers and the surface of the road, and which is not drawing a trailer	20

1	2	3
Item No	Class of Vehicle	Maximum speed (in miles per hour) while vehicle is being driven on a road
2	A vehicle specified in item 1 above drawing one or more trailers each one of which is either— (a) a track-laying vehicle fitted with springs and resilient material as mentioned in that item, or (b) not a track-laying vehicle and each wheel of which is fitted with either a pneumatic tyre or a resilient tyre	20
3	A vehicle specified in item 1 above drawing one or more trailers any one of which is either— (a) a track-laying vehicle not fitted with springs and resilient material as mentioned in that item, or (b) not a track-laying vehicle and at least one wheel of which is not fitted with either a pneumatic tyre or a resilient tyre	5
4	A motor vehicle being a track-laying vehicle which is not fitted with springs and resilient material as mentioned in item 1 above, whether drawing a trailer or not	5
5	A motor vehicle not being a track-laying vehicle, which is drawing one or more trailers any one or more of which is a track-laying vehicle— (a) if every wheel of the motor vehicle and of any non-track-laying trailer is fitted with a pneumatic tyre or with a resilient tyre, and every trailer which is a track-laying vehicle is fitted with springs and resilient material as mentioned in item 1 (b) in any other case	20 5

Application

This Part applies to—

(*a*) a motor vehicle which is a track-laying vehicle, and

(*b*) a motor vehicle of any description which is drawing one or more trailers any one or more of which is a track-laying vehicle.

PART IV

Application and Interpretation

1. This Schedule does not apply to a vehicle which is being used for the purpose of experiments or trials under section 6 of the Road Improvements Act 1925 or section 283 of the Highways Act 1980.

2. In this Schedule—

['agricultural motor vehicle',] 'articulated vehicle', 'dual-purpose vehicle', 'industrial tractor', 'passenger vehicle', 'pneumatic tyre', 'track-laying', 'wheel' and 'works truck' have the same meanings as are respectively given to those expressions in [Regulation 3(2) of the Road Vehicles (Construction and Use) Regulations 1986] [*SI 1986 No 1078* [*qv*]];

'car-derived van' means a goods vehicle which is constructed or adapted as a derivative of a passenger vehicle and which has a maximum laden weight not exceeding 2 tonnes;

'construction and use requirements' has the same meaning as in [section 41(7) of the Road Traffic Act 1988];

'dual-carriageway road' means a road part of which consists of a central reservation to separate a carriageway to be used by vehicles proceeding in one direction from a carriageway to be used by vehicles proceeding in the opposite direction;

'goods vehicle' has the same meaning as in [section 192(1) of the Road Traffic Act 1988];

'maximum laden weight' in relation to a vehicle or a combination of vehicles means—

(*a*) in the case of a vehicle, or combination of vehicles, in respect of which a gross weight not to be exceeded in Great Britain is specified in construction and use requirements, that weight;

(*b*) in the case of any vehicle, or combination of vehicles, in respect of which no such weight is specified in construction and use requirements, the weight which the vehicle, or combination of vehicles, is designed or adapted not to exceed when in normal use and travelling on a road laden;

'motor caravan' has the same meaning as in [Regulation 2(1) of the Motor Vehicles (Type Approval) (Great Britain) Regulations 1984] [*SI 1984 No 981* [*qv*]];

'motorway' has the same meaning as in Regulation 3(1) of the Motorways Traffic (England and Wales) Regulations 1982 [*SI 1982 No 1163* [*qv*]], as regards England and Wales; and

'resilient tyre' means a tyre, not being a pneumatic tyre, which is soft or elastic.

3. The specification as regards springs and wings mentioned in item 6 of Part I of this Schedule is that the vehicle—

(i) is equipped with suitable and sufficient springs between each wheel and the frame of the vehicle, and

(ii) unless adequate protection is afforded by the body of the vehicle, is provided with wings or other similar fittings to catch, so far as practicable, mud or water thrown up by the rotation of the wheels.

4. A vehicle falling in two or more classes specified in Part I, II or III of this Schedule shall be treated as falling within the class for which the lower or lowest speed limit is specified.

[Schedule 6, Part IV, is printed as amended by the Interpretation Act 1978, ss 17(2)(a) and 23; the Motor Vehicles (Variation of Speed Limits) Regulations 1986 (SI 1986 No 1175); the Road Traffic (Consequential Provisions) Act 1988, s 4 and Sched 3, para 25(10).

Words in the definition of 'motorway' relating expressly and exclusively to Scotland have been omitted.

See also s 144(2), above.]

SCHEDULE 7

[*Repealed.*]

SCHEDULE 8

Section 111.

STATUTORY STATEMENTS (EXCESS CHARGES)

PART I

STATUTORY STATEMENT OF OWNERSHIP OR HIRING

1. For the purposes of the specified sections, a statutory statement of ownership is a statement in the prescribed form, signed by the person furnishing it and stating—

(*a*) whether he was the owner of the vehicle at the relevant time; and

(*b*) if he was not the owner of the vehicle at the relevant time, whether he ceased to be the owner before, or became the owner after, the relevant time, and, if the information is in his possession, the name and address of the person to whom, and the date on which, he disposed of the vehicle or, as the case may be, the name and address of the person from whom, and the date on which, he acquired it.

2. For the purposes of the specified sections, a statutory statement of hiring is a statement in the prescribed form, signed by the person furnishing it, being the person by whom a statement of liability was signed and stating—

(*a*) where at the relevant time the vehicle was let to him under the hiring agreement to which the statement of liability refers; and

(*b*) if it was not, the date on which he returned the vehicle to the possession of the vehicle-hire firm concerned.

PART II

STATUTORY STATEMENT OF FACTS

3. For the purposes of the specified sections, a statutory statement of facts is a statement which is in the prescribed form and which—

(*a*) states that the person furnishing it was not the driver of the vehicle at the relevant time;

(*b*) states the name and address at the time when the statement is furnished of the person who was the driver of the vehicle at the relevant time; and

(*c*) is signed both by the person furnishing it and by the person stated to be the driver of the vehicle at the relevant time.

PART III

INTERPRETATION

4. In this Schedule 'the specified sections' has the meaning assigned to it by subsection (1) of section 111 of this Act.

5. Subsections (2) to (4) of that section shall have effect for the purposes of Parts I and II of this Schedule as they have effect for the purposes of the specified sections.

6. In paragraph 2 above 'statement of liability', 'hiring agreement' and 'vehicle-hire firm' have the same meanings as in section 109 of this Act.

[Paragraph 3 of Sched 8 will come into operation on a date to be appointed under s 145(2). Until such date, para 20(2) of Sched 10 has effect: see below.]

SCHEDULE 9

Special Provisions as to Certain Orders

[Omitted.]

SCHEDULE 10

Transitional Provisions and Savings

* * *

Meaning of 'heavy commercial vehicle'

8.—(1) The following are the provisions referred to in subsection (7) of section 138 of this Act which, by virtue of that subsection, are to have effect for the purpose specified in that subsection during a transitional period; and the transitional period referred to in that section is the period beginning 28th October 1982 and ending with 31st December 1989.

(2) Subject to sub-paragraphs (3) to (6) below, for the purpose and during the transitional period referred to in sub-paragraph (1) above, 'heavy commercial vehicle' means any vehicle, whether mechanically propelled or not, which is constructed or adapted for the carriage of goods and has an unladen weight exceeding 3 tons.

(3) The Secretary of State may by regulations amend sub-paragraph (2) above in either or both of the following ways, that is to say—

(*a*) by substituting, for the reference to unladen weight, a reference to such other description of weight as may be specified in the regulations;

(*b*) by substituting, for the reference to 3 tons, a reference to such other weight as may be so specified.

(4) Different regulations may be made under sub-paragraph (3) above for the purposes of different provisions of this Act and as respects different classes of vehicles or as respects the same class of vehicles in different circumstances and as regards different times of the day or night and as respects roads in different localities.

(5) Regulations under sub-paragraph (3) above shall not so amend sub-paragraph (2) above that there is any case in which a vehicle whose unladen weight does not exceed 3 tons is, by virtue of this paragraph, a heavy commercial vehicle for the purposes of any of the provisions of this Act.

(6) In the application of sub-paragraphs (2) to (5) above to a vehicle drawing one or more trailers, the drawing vehicle and the trailer or trailers shall be treated as one vehicle.

Pedestrian crossings

9.—(1) *[Omitted.]*

(2) Section 25(6) of this Act shall apply in relation to a crossing established, or having effect as if established—

(*a*) by a local authority under section 21 of the 1967 Act (whether as that section had effect at any time before the commencement of the said Act of 1980 or as it had effect by virtue of that Act), or

(*b*) by a Minister under section 22 of the 1967 Act,

as it applies in relation to a crossing established by a local authority under section 23 or by the Secretary of State under section 24 of this Act.

* * *

Speed limits

* * *

15. Any limit of speed which was in force on 1st November 1962 by virtue of any direction, order or regulation given or made by an authority under section 19(2), 26 or 34 of the Road Traffic Act 1960, if—

(*a*) by virtue of paragraph 12 of Schedule 8 to the 1967 Act it was deemed to have been imposed by an order made by that authority under section 74(1) of the 1967 Act, and

(*b*) it continues to be in force immediately before the commencement of this Act

shall be deemed to have been imposed by an order made by that authority under section 84(1) of this Act and may be revoked or varied accordingly.

* * *

Statutory statement of facts

20.—(1) Sub-paragraph (2) below shall have effect until the coming into operation of paragraph 3 of Schedule 8 to this Act as if that sub-paragraph were contained in Part II of Schedule 8.

(2) For the purposes of sections 107 to 109 of this Act, a statutory statement of facts is a statement which is in the prescribed form and which either—

(*a*) states that the person furnishing it was the driver of the vehicle at the relevant time and is signed by him; or

(*b*) states that that person was not the driver of the vehicle at the relevant time, states the name and address at the time the statement is furnished of the person who was the driver of the vehicle at the relevant time and is signed both by the person furnishing it and by the person stated to be the driver of the vehicle at the relevant time.

SCHEDULE 11

PROVISIONS OF THIS ACT AND INSTRUMENTS REFERRED TO IN SECTION 144(2)

Provisions of Act	*Instruments*
1. Sections 99 to 102 and 103(3).	The Removal and Disposal of Vehicles (Alteration of Enactments) Order 1967 (SI 1967 No 1900).
2. Schedule 6.	The Motor Vehicles (Variation of Speed Limits) Regulations 1984 (SI 1984 No 325).

* * *

The Telecommunications Act 1984

(1984 c 12)

An Act . . . to amend the Wireless Telegraphy Acts 1949 to 1967, to make further provision for enforcing those Acts and otherwise to make provision with respect to wireless telegraphy apparatus and certain related apparatus . . . and for connected purposes.

[12th April 1984]

* * *

4. Meaning of 'telecommunication system' and related expressions

(1) In this Act 'telecommunication system' means a system for the conveyance, through the agency of electric, magnetic, electro-magnetic, electro-chemical or electro-mechanical energy, of—

(*a*) speech, music and other sounds;

(*b*) visual images;

(*c*) signals serving for the impartation (whether as between persons and persons, things and things or persons and things) of any matter otherwise than in the form of sounds or visual images; or

(*d*) signals serving for the actuation or control of machinery or apparatus.

(2) *[Omitted.]*

(3) In this Act—

. . .

'telecommunication apparatus' means (except where the extended definition in Schedule 2 to this Act applies) apparatus construed or adapted for use—

(*a*) in transmitting or receiving anything falling within paragraphs (*a*) to (*d*) of subsection (1) above which is to be or has been conveyed by means of a telecommunication system; or

(*b*) in conveying, for the purposes of such a system, anything falling within those paragraphs;

. . .

(4)–(7) *[Omitted.]*

* * *

10. The telecommunications code

(1) Subject to the following provisions of this section, the code (to be known as 'the telecommunications code') which is contained in Schedule 2 to this Act shall have effect—

(*a*) where it is applied to a particular person by a licence granted by the Secretary of State under section 7 above authorising that person to run a telecommunication system; and (*b*) where the Secretary of State or a Northern Ireland department is running or is proposing to run a telecommunication system.

(2)–(11) *[Omitted.]*

* * *

SCHEDULE 2

The Telecommunications Code

Interpretation of code

1.—(1) In this code, except so far as the context otherwise requires—

. . .

'telecommunications apparatus' includes any apparatus falling within the definition in section 4(3) of this Act and any apparatus not so falling which is designed or adapted for use in connection with the running of a telecommunication system and, in particular—

(*a*) any line, that is to say, any wire, cable, tube, pipe or other similar thing (including its casing or coating) which is so designed or adapted; and

(*b*) any structure, pole or other thing in, on, by or from which any telecommunication apparatus is or may be installed, supported, carried or suspended;

and references to the installation of telecommunication apparatus shall be construed accordingly.

(2)–(5) *[Omitted.]*

[The definition of 'telecommunications apparatus' in this Schedule is incorporated by reference into reg 101 of the Road Vehicles (Construction and Use) Regulations 1986 (SI 1986 No 1078) (qv).]

* * *

Section 109

SCHEDULE 4

Minor and Consequential Amendments

Interpretation

1.—(1) In this Schedule and in any enactment amended by this Schedule—

* * *

'telecommunication system' has the meaning given by subsection (1) of section 4 above (read with subsection (2) of that section);

'the telecommunications code' means the code contained in Schedule 2 to this Act;

'telecommunications code system' means—

(*a*) a telecommunication system the running of which is authorised by a licence under section 7 of this Act applying the telecommunications code to any person; or

(*b*) a telecommunication system which the Secretary of State or a Northern Ireland department is running or proposing to run and in relation to which the telecommunications code has effect by virtue of section 10(1)(*b*) of this Act.

(2) *[Omitted.]*

[The definition of 'telecommunications code system' is incorporated by reference into s 21(3) of the Road Traffic Act 1988 (qv).]

* * *

The Theft Act 1968

(1968 c 60)

An Act to revise the law of England and Wales as to theft and similar or associated offences . . .

[26th July 1968]

* * *

12. Taking motor vehicle or other conveyance without authority

(1) Subject to subsections (5) and (6) below, a person shall be guilty of an offence if, without having the consent of the owner or other lawful authority, he takes any conveyance for his own or another's use or, knowing that any conveyance has been taken without such authority, drives it or allows himself to be carried in or on it.

(2) A person guilty of an offence under subsection (1) above shall [be liable on summary conviction to a fine not exceeding level 5 on the standard scale, to imprisonment for a term not exceeding six months, or to both].

(3) *[Repealed.]*

(4) If on the trial of an indictment for theft the jury are not satisfied that the accused committed theft, but it is proved that the accused committed an offence under subsection (1) above, the jury may find him guilty of the offence under subsection (1) [and if he is found guilty of it, he shall be liable as he would have been liable under subsection (2) above on summary conviction].

(5) Subsection (1) above shall not apply in relation to pedal cycles; but, subject to subsection (6) below, a person who, without having the consent of the owner or other lawful authority, takes a pedal cycle for his own or another's use, or rides a pedal cycle knowing it to have been taken without such authority, shall on summary conviction be liable to a fine not exceeding [level 3 on the standard scale].

(6) A person does not commit an offence under this section by anything done in the belief that he has lawful authority to do it or that he would have the owner's consent if the owner knew of his doing it and the circumstances of it.

(7) For the purposes of this section—

(*a*) 'conveyance' means any conveyance constructed or adapted for the carriage of a person or persons whether by land, water or air, except that it does not include a conveyance constructed or adapted for use only under the control of a person not carried in or on it, and 'drive' shall be construed accordingly; and

(*b*) 'owner', in relation to a conveyance which is the subject of a hiring agreement or hire-purchase agreement, means the person in possession of the conveyance under that agreement.

[Section 12 is printed as amended by the Criminal Justice Act 1982, ss 38, 46; the Police and Criminal Evidence Act 1984, s 119(2) and Sched 7, Part I; and (with effect from 12 October 1988) the Criminal Justice Act 1988, ss 37(1) and 171(1) (see the Criminal Justice Act 1988 (Commencement No 2) Order 1988 (SI 1988 No 1676)).]

* * *

25. Going equipped for stealing, etc

(1) A person shall be guilty of an offence if, when not at his place of abode, he has with him any article for use in the course of or in connection with any burglary, theft or cheat.

(2) A person guilty of an offence under this section shall on conviction on indictment be liable to a term of imprisonment for a term not exceeding three years.

(3) Where a person is charged with an offence under this section, proof that he had with him any article made or adapted for use in committing a burglary, theft or cheat shall be evidence that he had it with him for such use.

(4) Any person may arrest without warrant anyone who is or whom he, with reasonable cause, suspects to be, committing an offence under this section.

(5) For the purposes of this section an offence under section 12(1) of this Act of taking a conveyance shall be treated as theft and 'cheat' means an offence under section 15 of this Act.

* * *

The Town Police Clauses Act 1847

(10 & 11 Vict c 89)

An Act for consolidating in one Act certain provisions usually contained in Acts for regulating the police of towns.

[22nd July 1847]

* * *

38. What vehicles to be deemed hackney carriages

Every wheeled carriage, whatever may be its form or construction, used in standing or plying for hire in any street within the prescribed distance, and every carriage standing upon any street within the prescribed distance, having thereon any numbered plate required by this or the special Act to be fixed upon a hackney carriage, or having thereon any plate resembling or intended to resemble any such plate as aforesaid, shall be deemed to be a hackney carriage within the meaning of this Act; and in all proceedings at law or otherwise the term 'hackney carriage' shall be sufficient to describe any such carriage: Provided always, that no stage coach used for the purpose of standing or plying for passengers to be carried for hire at separate fares, and duly licensed for that purpose, and having thereon the proper numbered plates required by law to be placed on such stage coaches, shall be deemed to be a hackney carriage within the meaning of this Act.

[The definition of 'hackney carriage' in this Act is incorporated by reference into s 80 of the Local Government (Miscellaneous Provisions) Act 1976 (qv).]

* * *

The Trade Marks Act 1938

(1 & 2 Geo 6 c 22)

An Act to consolidate the Trade Marks Act 1905, the Trade Marks Act 1919 and the Trade Marks (Amendment) Act 1937.

[13th April 1938]

* * *

37. Certification trade marks

(1) A mark adapted in relation to any goods to distinguish in the course of trade goods certified by any person in respect of origin, material, mode of manufacture, quality, accuracy or other characteristic, from goods not so certified shall be registrable as a certification trade mark in Part A of the register in respect of those goods in the name, as proprietor thereof, of that person:

Provided that a mark shall not be so registrable in the name of a person who carries on a trade in goods of the kind certified.

(2)–(9) *[Omitted.]*

* * *

68. Interpretation

(1) In this Act, unless the context otherwise requires, the following expressions have the meanings hereby assigned to them respectively, that is to say:–

. . .

'trade mark' means, except in relation to a certification trade mark, a mark used or proposed to be used in relation to goods for the purpose of indicating, or so as to indicate, a connection in the course of trade between the goods and some person having the right either as proprietor or as registered user to use the mark, whether with or without any indication of the identity of that person, and means, in relation to a certification trade mark, a mark registered or deemed to have been registered under section thirty-seven of this Act;

. . .

(2), (3) *[Omitted.]*

[The definition of 'trade mark' is incorporated by reference into reg 70A of the Road Vehicles (Construction and Use) Regulations 1986 (SI 1986 No 1078) (qv).]

The Transport Act 1968

(1968 c 73)

An Act to make further provision with respect to transport and related matters.

[25th October 1968]

ARRANGEMENT OF SECTIONS

* * *

PART V

REGULATION OF CARRIAGE OF GOODS BY ROAD

* * *

Operators' licences

* * *

Control of operating centres for goods vehicles on environmental grounds

* * *

Supplementary

* * *

PART VI

DRIVERS' HOURS

* * *

PART V

Regulation of Carriage of Goods by Road

* * *

Operators' licences

60. Users of certain goods vehicles to hold operators' licences

(1) Subject to subsection (2) of this section and to the other provisions of this Part of this Act, no person shall, after the appointed day for the purposes of this section, use a goods vehicle on a road for the carriage of goods—

(*a*) for hire or reward; or

(*b*) for or in connection with any trade or business carried on by him,

except under a licence granted under this Part of this Act (hereafter in this Part of this Act referred to as an 'operator's licence').

(2) Subsection (1) of this section shall not apply—

(*a*) to the use of a small goods vehicle as defined in subsection (4) of this section; or

(*b*) to the use of a vehicle of any class specified in regulations.

(3) It is hereby declared that, for the purposes of this Part of this Act, the performance by a local or public authority of their functions constitutes the carrying on of a business.

(4) For the purposes of subsection (2)(*a*) of this section a small goods vehicle is a goods vehicle which—

(*a*) does not form part of a vehicle combination and has a relevant plated weight not exceeding [3.5 tonnes] or (not having a relevant plated weight) has an unladen weight not exceeding [1525 kilograms]; or

(*b*) forms part of a vehicle combination (not being an articulated combination) which is such that—

(i) if all the vehicles comprised in the combination (or all of them except any small trailer) have relevant plated weights, the aggregate of the relevant plated weights of the vehicles comprised in the combination (exclusive of any such trailer) does not exceed [3.5 tonnes];

(ii) in any other case, the aggregate of the unladen weights of those vehicles (exclusive of any such trailer) does not exceed [1525 kilograms]; or

(*c*) forms part of an articulated combination which is such that—

(i) if the trailer comprised in the combination has a relevant plated weight, the aggregate of the unladen weight of the motor vehicle comprised in the combination and the relevant plated weight of that trailer does not exceed [3.5 tonnes];

(ii) in any other case, the aggregate of the unladen weights of the motor vehicle and the trailer comprised in the combination does not exceed [1525 kilograms].

In any provision of this subsection 'relevant plated weights' means a plated weight of the description specified in relation to that provision by regulations; and in paragraph (*b*) of this subsection 'small trailer' means a trailer having an unladen weight not exceeding [1020 kilograms].

(5) A person who uses a vehicle in contravention of this section shall be liable on summary conviction to a fine not exceeding [level 4 on the standard scale].

[Section 60 is printed as amended by the Road Traffic Acts 1960 and 1972, Road Traffic Regulation Act 1967, Transport Act 1968 (Metrication) (Regulations) 1981 (SI 1981 No 1373), Transport Act 1968 (Metrication) (Amendment) Regulations 1984 (SI 1984 No 177), and the Criminal Justice Act 1982, ss 38 and 46(1).

The reference in s 60(2)(b) to any class specified in regulations is a reference to any class specified in Sched 5 to the Goods Vehicles (Operators' Licences, Qualifications and Fees) Regulations 1984 (SI 1984 No 176); see reg 34 of those regulations, below.]

61. Authorised vehicles

(1) Subject to subsection (2) of this section, the vehicles authorised to be used under an operator's licence shall be—

(*a*) such motor vehicles, being vehicles belonging to the holder of the licence or in his possession under an agreement for hire-purchase, hire or loan, as are specified in the licence;

(*b*) trailers from time to time belonging to the holder of the licence or in his possession under an agreement for hire-purchase, hire or loan, not exceeding at any time such maximum number as is specified in the licence;

(*c*) unless the licence does not permit the addition of authorised vehicles under this paragraph and subject to subsection (3) of this section, motor vehicles not exceeding such maximum number as is specified in the licence, being vehicles belonging to the holder of the licence or in his possession under an agreement for hire-purchase, hire or loan, but acquired by him, or coming into his possession under such an agreement, only after the grant of the licence.

For the purposes of paragraphs (*b*) and (*c*) of this subsection different types of trailers or different types of motor vehicles, as the case may be, may be distinguished in a licence and a maximum number may be specified in the licence for trailers or vehicles of each type.

(2) An operator's licence shall not authorise the use of any vehicle unless the place which is for the time being its operating centre—

(*a*) is in the area of the licensing authority by whom the licence was granted; or

(*b*) is outside that area and has not been the operating centre of that vehicle for a period of more than three months.

For the purposes of paragraph (*b*) of this subsection, two or more successive periods which are not separated from each other by an interval of at least three months shall be treated as a single period having a duration equal to the total duration of those periods.

(3) A motor vehicle which, after the grant of an operator's licence, is acquired by the holder of the licence, or comes into his possession under an agreement for hire-purchase, hire or loan, and thereupon becomes an authorised vehicle by virtue of subsection (1)(*c*) of this section, shall cease to be an authorised vehicle on the expiration

of one month from the date on which it was acquired by him or came into his possession unless before the expiration of that period he delivers to the licensing authority a notice in such form as the authority may require to the effect that the vehicle has been acquired by him, or has come into his possession, as the case may be.

(4) *[Licensing authority to vary licence on receipt of such notice.]*

(5) A motor vehicle specified in an operator's licence shall not, while it remains so specified, be capable of being effectively specified in any other operator's licence.

(6) *[Power to vary licence by removing vehicle therefrom.]*

* * *

Control of operating centres for goods vehicles on environmental grounds

[69A. Operating centres for authorised vehicles to be specified in operators' licences

(1) A person may not use a place in the area of any licensing authority as an operating centre for authorised vehicles under any operator's licence granted to him by that authority unless it is specified in that licence.

(2) *[Applicant for operator's licence to provide particulars.]*

(3) *[Licensing authority may require additional particulars.]*

(4) Any person who contravenes subsection (1) of this section shall be liable on summary conviction to a fine not exceeding [level 4 on the standard scale]].

[Section 69A was added by the Transport Act 1982, s 52(2) and Sched 4, Part I, and is printed as amended by the Criminal Justice Act 1982, s 46(1).]

* * *

[69C. Conditions as to the use of operating centres

(1) Subject to the following provisions of this section, a licensing authority may attach such conditions to an operator's licence as appear to him to be appropriate for the purpose of preventing or minimising any adverse effects on environmental conditions arising from the use for authorised vehicles under the licence of any operating centre of the holder of the licence in the area of the authority.

(2) The conditions which may be attached to a licence under this section shall be of such description as may be prescribed; and, without prejudice to the generality of the preceding provision, the descriptions which may be prescribed include conditions regulating—

(*a*) the number, type and size of motor vehicles or trailers which may at any one time be at any operating centre of the holder of the licence in the area of the authority for any prescribed purpose;

(*b*) the parking arrangements to be provided at or in the vicinity of any such centre; and

(*c*) the hours at which operations of any prescribed description may be carried on at any such centre.

(3) *[Power to vary or remove conditions.]*

(4) *[Time when conditions may be granted, etc.]*

(5) *[When condition may not be attached unless applicant first given opportunity to make representations.]*

(6) Any person who contravenes any condition attached under this section to a licence of which he is the holder shall be liable on summary conviction to a fine not exceeding [level 4 on the standard scale]].

[Section 69C was added by the Transport Act 1982, s 52(2) and Sched 4, Part I and is printed as amended by the Criminal Justice Act 1982, s 46(1).]

Supplementary

* * *

91. Regulations and orders for purposes of Part V

(1)–(5) *[Omitted.]*

(6) Any person who contravenes a provision of regulations under this section, a contravention of which is declared by the regulations to be an offence, shall be liable on summary conviction to a fine not exceeding [level 1 on the standard scale].

(7), (8) *[Omitted.]*

[Section 91(6) is printed as amended by the Criminal Justice Act 1982, s 38.
The Goods Vehicles (Operators' Licences, Qualifications and Fees) Regulations 1984 (SI 1984 No 176) (qv) were made in part under this section.]

92. Interpretation of Part V

(1) In this Part of this Act . . . , unless the context otherwise requires—

'articulated combination' means a combination made up of—

(*a*) a motor vehicle which is so constructed that a trailer may by partial superimposition be attached to the vehicle in such a manner as to cause a substantial part of the weight of the trailer to be borne by the vehicle, and

(*b*) a trailer attached to it as aforesaid;

'authorised vehicle' means, in relation to an operator's licence, a vehicle authorised to be used thereunder, whether or not it is for the time being in use for a purpose for which an operator's licence is required and whether it is specified therein as so authorised or, being of a type so authorised subject to a maximum number, belongs to the holder of the licence or is in his possession under an agreement for hire purchase, hire or loan;

'carriage of goods' includes haulage of goods;

'carrier's licence' means a licence granted under Part IV of the Act of 1960;

'contravention', in relation to any condition or provision, includes a failure to comply with the condition or provision, and 'contravenes' shall be constructed accordingly;

'driver' means, in relation to a trailer, the driver of the vehicle by which the trailer is drawn and 'drive' shall be construed accordingly;

'goods' includes goods or burden of any description;

'goods vehicle' means, subject to subsection (5) of this section, a motor vehicle constructed or adapted for use for the carriage of goods, or a trailer so construed or adapted;

'large goods vehicle' shall be construed in accordance with section 71 of this Act;

['operating centre', in relation to any vehicles, means the base or centre at which the vehicle is normally kept, and references to an operating centre of the holder of an operator's licence are references to any place which is an operating centre for authorised vehicles under the licence;]

['owner', in relation to any land in England and Wales, means a person, other than a mortgagee not in possession, who, whether in his own right or as trustee for any other person, is entitled to receive the rack rent of the land or, where the land is not let at a rack rent, would be so entitled if it were so let;]

'prescribed' means prescribed by regulations;

'regulations' means regulations made by the [Secretary of State for Transport] under this Part of this Act;

'subsidiary' means a subsidiary as defined by [section 736 of the Companies Act 1985 [*qv*]];

'vehicle combination' means a combination of goods vehicles made up of one or more motor vehicles and one or more trailers all of which are linked together when travelling;

and any expression not defined above which is also used in the Act of 1960 has the same meaning as in that Act.

(2) For the purposes of this Part of this Act, the driver of a vehicle, if it belongs to him or is in his possession under an agreement for hire, hire-purchase or loan, and in any other case the person whose servant or agent the driver is, shall be deemed to be the person using the vehicle; and references to using a vehicle shall be construed accordingly.

(3) In this Part of this Act references to directing that an operator's licence be curtailed are references to directing (with effect for the remainder of the duration of the licence or for any shorter period) all or any of the following, that is to say—

(*a*) that any one or more of the vehicles specified in the licence be removed therefrom;

(*b*) that the maximum number of trailers or of motor vehicles specified in the licence in pursuance of section 61(1)(*b*) or (*c*) of this Act be reduced;

(*c*) that the addition of authorised vehicles under the said section 61(1)(*c*) be no longer permitted.

[(*d*) that any one or more of the places specified in the licence as operating centres be removed therefrom.]

(4) *[Bankruptcy includes sequestration in Scotland.]*

(5) In this Part of this Act . . . , references to goods vehicles do not include references to tramcars or trolley vehicles operated under statutory powers within the meaning of [Schedule 4 to the Road Traffic Act 1988].

(6) Anything required or authorised by this Part of this Act to be done to or by a licensing authority by whom a licence . . . was granted may be done to or by any person for the time being acting as licensing authority for the area for which the first mentioned authority was acting at the time of the granting of the licence . . .

[Section 92 is printed as amended by the Secretary of State for the Environment Order 1970 (SI 1970 No 1681); the Road Traffic Act 1972, s 203(1) and Sched 7; the Secretary of State for Transport Order 1976 (SI 1976 No 1775); the Minister of Transport Order 1979 (SI 1979 No 571); the Transport Act 1980, s 69 and Sched 12, Part II; the Transfer of Functions (Trans-

port) Order 1981 (SI 1981 No 238); the Transport Act 1982, ss 52(1), (3), 74(2), Sched 4, Part II, and Sched 6; the Companies Consolidation (Consequential Provisions) Act 1985, ss 30 and 34 and Sched 2; the Road Traffic (Consequential Provisions) Act 1988, s 4 and Sched 3, para 6(4).

Part V of this Act and regulations under that part have effect in relation to standard licences subject to the provisions of the Goods Vehicles (Operators' Licences, Qualifications and Fees) Regulations 1984 (SI 1984 No 176); see ibid, reg 36(7). But, except as provided in reg 36, those regulations do not affect the application of Part V or of any regulations under that part to restricted licences; see reg 36(8).]

* * *

PART VI

Drivers' Hours

95. Vehicles and drivers subject to control under Part VI

(1), (1A) *[Omitted.]*

(2) This Part of this Act applies to—

(*a*) passenger vehicles, that is to say—

(i) public service vehicles; and

(ii) motor vehicles (other than public service vehicles) constructed or adapted to carry more than twelve passengers;

(*b*) goods vehicles, that is to say—

(i) heavy locomotives, light locomotives, motor tractors and any motor vehicle so constructed that a trailer may by partial superimposition be attached to the vehicle in such a manner as to cause a substantial part of the weight of the trailer to be borne by the vehicle; and

(ii) motor vehicles (except those mentioned in paragraph (*a*) of this sub-section) constructed or adapted to carry goods other than the effects of passengers.

(3) This Part of this Act applies to any such person as follows (in this Part of this Act referred to as 'a driver'), that is to say—

(*a*) a person who drives a vehicle to which this Part of this Act applies in the course of his employment (in this Part of this Act referred to as 'an employee-driver'); and

(*b*) a person who drives such a vehicle for the purposes of a trade or business carried on by him (in this Part of this Act referred to as 'an owner-driver');

and in this Part of this Act references to driving by any person are references to his driving as aforesaid.

96. Permitted driving time and periods of duty

(1) Subject to the provisions of this section, a driver shall not on any working day drive a vehicle or vehicles to which this Part of this Act applies for periods amounting in the aggregate to more than ten hours.

(2) Subject to the provisions of this section, if on any working day a driver has been on duty for a period of, or for periods amounting in the aggregate to, five and a half hours and—

(*a*) there has not been during that period, or during or between any of those periods, an interval of not less than half an hour which he was able to obtain rest and refreshment; and

(*b*) the end of that period, or of the last of those periods, does not mark the end of that working day,

there shall at the end of that period, or of the last of those periods, be such an interval as aforesaid.

(3) Subject to the provisions of this section, the working day of a driver—

(*a*) except where paragraph (*b*) or (*c*) of this subsection applies, shall not exceed eleven hours;

(*b*) if during that day he is off duty for a period which is, or periods which taken together are, not less than the time by which his working day exceeds eleven hours, shall not exceed twelve and a half hours;

(*c*) if during that day—

(i) all the time when he is driving vehicles to which this Part of this Act applies is spent in driving one or more express carriages or contract carriages, and

(ii) he is able for a period of not less than four hours to obtain rest and refreshment,

shall not exceed fourteen hours.

(4) Subject to the provisions of this section, there shall be, between any two successive working days of a driver, an interval for rest which—

(*a*) subject to paragraph (*b*) of this subsection, shall not be of less than eleven hours;

(*b*) if during both those days all or the greater part of the time when he is driving vehicles to which this Part of this Act applies is spent in driving one or more passenger vehicles, may, on one occasion in each working week, be of less than eleven hours but not of less than nine and a half hours;

and for the purposes of this Part of this Act a period of time shall not be treated, in the case of an employee-driver, as not being an interval for rest by reason only that he may be called upon to report for duty if required.

(5) Subject to the provisions of this section a driver shall not be on duty in any working week for periods amounting in the aggregate to more than sixty hours.

(6) Subject to the provisions of this section, there shall be, in the case of each working week of a driver, a period of not less than twenty-four hours for which he is off duty, being a period either falling wholly in that week or beginning in that week and ending in the next week; but—

(*a*) where the requirements of the foregoing provisions of this subsection have been satisfied in the case of any week by reference to a period ending in the next week, no part of that period (except any part after the expiration of the first twenty-four hours of it) shall be taken into account for the purpose of satisfying those requirements in the case of the next week; and

(*b*) those requirements need not be satisfied in the case of any working week of a driver who on each working day falling wholly or partly in that week drives one or more stage carriages if that week is immediately preceded by a week in the case of which those requirements have been satisfied as respects that driver or during which he has not at any time been on duty.

(7) If in the case of the working week of any driver the following requirement is

satisfied, that is to say, that, in each of the periods of twenty-four hours beginning at midnight which make up that week, the driver does not drive a vehicle to which this Part of this Act applies for a period of, or periods amounting in the aggregate to, more than four hours, the foregoing provisions of this section shall not apply to him in that week, except that the provisions of subsections (1), (2) and (3) shall nevertheless have effect in relation to the whole of any working day falling partly in that week and partly in a working week in the case of which that requirement is not satisfied.

(8) If on any working day a driver does not drive any vehicle to which this Part of this Act applies—

(*a*) subsections (2) and (3) of this section shall not apply to that day, and

(*b*) the period or periods of duty attributable to that day for the purposes of subsection (5) of this section shall, if amounting to more than eleven hours, be treated as amounting to eleven hours only.

(9) For the purposes of subsections (1) and (7) of this section no account shall be taken of any time spent driving a vehicle elsewhere than on a road if the vehicle is being so driven in the course of operations of agriculture or forestry.

(10) For the purposes of enabling drivers to deal with cases of emergency or otherwise to meet a special need, the [Secretary of State for Transport] may by regulations—

(*a*) create exemptions from all or any of the requirements of subsections (1) to (6) of this section in such cases and subject to such conditions as may be specified in the regulations;

(*b*) empower the traffic [commissioner] for any area, subject to the provisions of the regulations—

(i) to dispense with the observance of all or any of those requirements (either generally or in such circumstances or to such extent as the [commissioner] thinks fit) in any particular case for which provision is not made under paragraph (*a*) of this subsection;

(ii) to grant a certificate (which, for the purposes of any proceedings under this Part of this Act, shall be conclusive evidence of the facts therein stated) that any particular case falls or fell within any exemption created under the said paragraph (*a*);

and regulations under this subsection may enable any dispensation under paragraph (*b*)(i) of this subsection to be granted retrospectively and provide for a document purporting to be a certificate granted by virtue of paragraph (*b*)(ii) of this subsection to be accepted in evidence without further proof.

(11) If any of the requirements of [the domestic drivers' hours code] is contravened in the case of any driver—

(*a*) that driver; and

(*b*) any other person (being that driver's employer or a person to whose orders that driver was subject) who caused or permitted the contravention.

shall be liable on summary conviction to a fine not exceeding [level 4 on the standard scale]; but a person shall not be liable to be convicted under this subsection if he proves to the court—

(i) that the contravention was due to unavoidable delay in the completion of a journey arising out of circumstances which he could not reasonably have foreseen; or

(ii) in the case of a person charged under paragraph (*b*) of this subsection, that the contravention was due to the fact that the driver had for any particular period or periods driven or been on duty otherwise than in the employment of that person or, as the case may be, otherwise than in the employment in which he is subject to the orders of that person, and that the person charged was not, and could not reasonably have become, aware of that fact.

[(11A) Where, in the case of a driver . . . of a motor vehicle, there is in Great Britain a contravention of any requirement of [the applicable Community rules] as to period of driving, or distance driven, or periods on or off duty, then the offender and any other person (being the offender's employer or a person to whose orders the offender was subject) who caused or permitted the contravention shall be liable on summary conviction to a fine not exceeding [level 4 on the standard scale].]

[(11B) But a person shall not be liable to be convicted under subsection (11A) if—

(*a*) he proves the matters specified in paragraph (i) of subsection (11); or

(*b*) being charged as the offender's employer or a person to whose orders the offender was subject, he proves the matters specified in paragraph (ii) of that subsection.]

(12) The [Secretary of State for Transport] may by order—

(*a*) direct that subsection (1) of this section shall have effect with the substitution for the reference to ten hours of a reference to nine hours, either generally or with such exceptions as may be specified in the order;

(*b*) direct that paragraph (*a*) of subsection (3) of this section shall have effect with the substitution for the reference to eleven hours of a reference to any shorter period, or remove, modify or add to the provisions of that subsection containing exceptions to the said paragraph (*a*);

(*c*) remove, modify or add to any of the requirements of subsections (1), (4), (5) or (6) of this section or any of the exemptions provided for by subsections (7), (8) and (9) thereof;

and any order under this subsection may contain such transitional and supplementary provisions as the [Secretary of State for Transport] thinks necessary or expedient, including provisions amending any definition in section 103 of this Act which is relevant to any of the provisions affected by the order.

[(13) In the Part of this Act 'the domestic drivers' hours code' means the provisions of subsection (1) to (6) of this section as for the time being in force (and, in particular, as modified, added to or substituted by or under any instrument in force under section 95(1) of this Act or subsection (10) or (12) of this section).]

[Section 96 is printed as amended by the Secretary of State for the Environment Order 1970 (SI 1970 No 1681); the European Communities Act 1972, s 4, and Sched 4, para 9(2); the Road Traffic (Drivers' Ages and Hours of Work) Act 1976, s 2(1); the Secretary of State for Transport Order 1976 (SI 1976 No 1775); the Transport Act 1978, s 10; the Minister of Transport Order 1979 (SI 1979 No 571); the Transfer of Functions (Transport) Order 1981 (SI 1981 No 238); the Criminal Justice Act 1982, ss 38 and 46(1); the Transport Act 1985, s 3 and Sched 2, Part II, para 1(2); the Community Drivers' Hours and Recording Equipment Regulations 1986 (SI 1986 No 1457), reg 2.

For modifications of subs (9), above, in relation to drivers engaged in quarrying operations or on building construction and civil engineering work, see the Drivers' Hours (Goods Vehicles) (Modifications) Order 1970 (SI 1970 No 257), below.

The text of s 96 as it applies to the drivers of passenger vehicles is modified by the Drivers' Hours (Passenger and Goods Vehicles) (Modifications) Order 1971 (SI 1971 No 818); and the text as so modified is set out as an appendix to SI 1971 No 818, below. The text of s 96 as it applies to the drivers of goods vehicles is modified by the Drivers' Hours (Goods Vehicles) (Modifications) Order 1986 (SI 1986 No 1459); and the text as so modified is set out as an appendix to SI 1986 No 1459 (qv).

Exemptions from certain provisions of s 96 are granted in the case of emergencies, etc; see the Drivers' Hours (Passenger Vehicles) (Exemptions) Regulations 1970 (SI 1970 No 145) and the Drivers' Hours (Goods Vehicles) (Exemptions) Regulations 1986 (SI 1986 No 1492).

Temporary exemption from the domestic drivers' code was provided by the Drivers' Hours (Passenger and Goods Vehicles) (Exemption) Regulations 1987 (SI 1987 No 28) in severe weather conditions from 17 January 1987 until 2 February 1987, when those regulations were revoked by the Drivers' Hours (Passenger and Goods Vehicles) (Exemption) (Revocation) Regulations 1987 (SI 1987 No 98).

Section 95(1) of this Act, as amended, inter alia, empowers the Secretary of State for Transport to make regulations substituting, adapting, etc, the provisions of this Part of this Act to take account of the operation of any Community provision.]

[97. Installation and use of recording equipment

[(1) No person shall use, or cause or permit to be used, a vehicle to which this section applies unless there is in the vehicle recording equipment which—

(*a*) has been installed in accordance with the Community Recording Equipment Regulations;

(*b*) complies with Annexes I and II to that Regulation; and

(*c*) is being used as provided by [Articles 13 to 15] of that Regulation

and any person who contravenes this subsection shall be liable on summary conviction to a fine not exceeding level 4 on the standard scale.]

(2) A person shall not be liable to be convicted under subsection (1) of this section if he proves to the court that the vehicle in question was proceeding to a place where recording equipment which would comply with the requirements of Annexes I and II of the Community Recording Equipment Regulation was to be installed in the vehicle in accordance with that Regulation.

(3) A person shall not be liable to be convicted under subsection (1) of this section by reason of the recording equipment installed in the vehicle in question not being in working order if he proves to the court that—

(*a*) it had not become reasonably practicable for the equipment to be repaired by an approved fitter or workshop; and

(*b*) the requirements of [Articles 18(2), 16(2)] of the Community Recording Equipment Regulation were being complied with.

(4) A person shall not be liable to be convicted under subsection (1) of this section by reason of any seal on the recording equipment installed in the vehicle in question not being intact if he proves to the court that—

(*a*) the breaking or removal of the seal could not have been avoided;

(*b*) it had not become reasonably practicable for the seal to be replaced by an approved fitter or workshop; and

(*c*) in all other respects the equipment was being used as provided by [Articles 13 to 15] of the Community Recording Equipment Regulations.

(5) For the purposes of this section recording equipment is used as provided by [Articles 13 to 15] of the Community Recording Equipment Regulation if, and only if, the circumstances of its use are such that each requirement of those Articles is complied with.

(6) This section applies at any time to any vehicle to which this Part of this Act applies if, at that time, Article 3 of the Community Recording Equipment Regulation requires recording equipment to be installed and used in that vehicle; and in this section and sections 97A and 97B of the Act any expression which is also used in that Regulation has the same meaning as in that Regulation.

(7) In this Part of this Act—

['the Community Recording Equipment Regulation' means Council Regulation (EEC) No 3821/85 of 20th December 1985 on recording equipment in road transport [*qv*] as read with the Community Drivers' Hours and Recording Equipment (Exemptions and Supplementary Provisions) Regulations 1986 *[SI 1986 No 1456 [qv]*;]

'recording equipment' means equipment for recording information as to the use of a vehicle.]

[Section 97 was substituted by the Passenger and Goods Vehicles (Recording Equipment) Regulations 1979 (SI 1979 No 1746) and was subsequently amended by the Passenger and Goods Vehicles (Recording Equipment) (Amendment) Regulations 1984 (SI 1984 No 144), reg 2(2); the Criminal Justice Act 1982, ss 39(2), 46(1) and Sched 3; the Community Drivers' Hours and Recording Equipment Regulations 1986 (SI 1986 No 1457), reg 3.]

[97A. Provisions supplementary to section 97

(1) If an employed [driver] of a vehicle to which section 97 of this Act applies fails—

(*a*) without reasonable excuse to return any record sheet which relates to him to his employer within twenty-one days of completing it; or

(*b*) where he has two or more employers by whom he is employed as a [driver] of such a vehicle, to notify each of them of the name and address of the other or others of them,

he shall be liable on summary conviction to a fine not exceeding [level 4 on the standard scale].

(2) If the employer of [drivers] of a vehicle to which section 97 of this Act applies fails without reasonable excuse to secure that they comply with subsection (1)(*a*) of this section, he shall be liable on summary conviction to a fine not exceeding [level 4 on the standard scale].

(3) Where a [driver] of a vehicle to which section 97 of this Act applies has two or more employers by whom he is employed as a [driver] of such a vehicle, subsection (1)(*a*) and subsection (2) of this section shall apply as if any reference to his employer, or any reference which is to be construed as such a reference, were a reference to such of those employers as was the first to employ him in that capacity.]

[Section 97A was inserted by the Passenger and Goods Vehicles (Recording Equipment) Regulations 1979 (SI 1979 No 1746) and was subsequently amended by the Criminal Justice Act 1982, ss 39(2), 46(1), and Sched 3; the Community Drivers' Hours and Recording Equipment Regulations 1986 (SI 1986 No 1457), reg 3.]

[97B. Records etc produced by equipment may be used in evidence

(1) Where recording equipment is installed in a vehicle to which this Part of this Act applies, any record produced by means of the equipment shall, in any proceedings under this Part of this Act, be evidence, and in Scotland sufficient evidence, of the matters appearing from the record.

(2) Any entry made on a record sheet by a [driver] for the purposes of [Article 1(2) or (5) or 16(2)] of the Community Recording Equipment Regulation shall, in any proceedings under this Part of this Act, be evidence, and in Scotland sufficient evidence, of the matters appearing from that entry.]

[Section 97B was inserted by the Passenger and Goods Vehicles (Recording Equipment) Regulations 1979 (SI 1979 No 1746) and was subsequently amended by the Community Drivers' Hours and Recording Equipment Regulations 1986 (SI 1986 No 1457), reg 3.]

98. Written records

(1) *[Power to make regulations regarding keeping records and maintaining registers.]*

(2) *[Power to include supplementary and incidental provisions in regulations.]*

[(2A) The requirements of regulations made under this section shall not apply as respects the driving of a vehicle to which section 97 of this Act applies and in relation to which subsection (1)(*b*) of that section has come into force.]

(3) *[Dispensations from requirements imposed by this section.]*

(4) Any person who contravenes any regulations made under this section [or any requirement as to books, records or documents] of [the applicable Community rules] shall be liable on summary conviction to a fine not exceeding [level 4 on the standard scale]; but the employer of an employee-driver shall not be liable to be convicted under this subsection by reason of contravening any such regulation whereby he is required to cause any records to be kept if he proves to the court that he has given proper instructions to his employees with respect to the keeping of the records and has from time to time taken reasonable steps to secure that those instructions are being carried out.

[(4A) A person shall not be liable to be convicted under subsection (4) of this section by reason of contravening any regulation made under this section if he proves to the court that, if the vehicle in question had been such a vehicle as is mentioned in subsection (2A) of this section, there would have been no contravention of the provisions of this Part of this Act so far as they relate to the use of such vehicles.]

(5) Any entry made by an employee-driver for the purposes of regulations under this section [or of [the applicable Community rules]] shall, in any proceedings under this Part of this Act, be admissible in evidence against his employer.

[Section 98 is printed as amended by the European Communities Act 1972, s 4, and Sched 4, para 9, the Road Traffic (Drivers' Ages and Hours of Work) Act 1976, s 2(1), the Passenger and Goods Vehicles (Recording Equipment) Regulations 1970 (SI 1979 No 1746), and the Criminal Justice Act 1982, ss 38, 46(1).

The Drivers' Hours (Goods Vehicles) (Keeping of Records) Regulations 1987 (SI 1987 No 1421) (qv) were made under s 98.]

99. Inspection of records and other documents

(1) An officer may, on production if so required of his authority, require any person to produce, and permit him to inspect and copy—

(*a*) any book or register which that person is required by regulations under section 98 of this Act to carry or have in his possession for the purpose of making in it any entry required by those regulations or which is required under those regulations to be carried on any vehicle of which that person is the driver;

(*b*) any . . . , book or register which that person is required by regulations under section . . . 98 of this Act to preserve;

[(*bb*) any record sheet which that person is required by [Article 14(2)] of the Community Recording Equipment Regulation to retain or by [Article 15(7)] of that Regulation to be able to produce;]

(*c*) if that person is the owner of a vehicle to which this Part of this Act applies, any other document of that person which the officer may reasonably require to inspect for the purpose of ascertaining whether the provisions of this Part of this Act or of regulations made thereunder have been complied with;

[(*d*) any . . . book, register or document required by [the applicable Community rules] or which the officer may reasonably require to inspect for the purpose of ascertaining whether the requirements of [the applicable Community rules] have been complied with;]

and that record [sheet], book, register or document shall, if the officer so requires by notice in writing served on that person, be produced at the office of the traffic [commissioner] specified in the notice within such time (not being less than ten days) from the service of the notice as may be so specified.

(2) An officer may, on production if so required of his authority—

[(*a*) at any time, enter any vehicle to which this Part of this Act applies and inspect that vehicle and any recording equipment installed in it and inspect and copy any record sheet on the vehicle on which a record has been produced by means of the equipment or an entry has been made;]

(*b*) at any time which is reasonable having regard to the circumstances of the case, enter any premises on which he has reason to believe that such a vehicle is kept or that any such [record sheets], books, registers or other documents as are mentioned in subsection (1) of this section are to be found, and inspect any such vehicle, and inspect and copy any such record [sheet], book, register, or document which he finds there.

(3) For the purpose of exercising his powers under subsection (2)(*a*) and, in respect of a document carried on, or by the driver of, a vehicle, under subsection (1)(*a*) [or (*d*)] of this section, an officer may detain the vehicle in question during such time as is required for the exercise of that power.

(4) Any person who—

(*a*) fails to comply with any requirement under subsection (1) of this section; or

(*b*) obstructs an officer in the exercise of his powers under subsection (2) or (3) of this section,

shall be liable on summary conviction to a fine not exceeding [level 3 on the standard scale].

[(4A) A person shall not be liable to be convicted under subsection (4) of this section by reason of failing to comply with any requirement under subsection 6(1)(*a*) or (*b*) of this section if he proves to the court that, if the vehicle in question had been such a vehicle as is mentioned in section 98(2A) of this Act, there would have been no contravention of the provisions of this Part of this Act so far as they relate to the use of such vehicles.]

(5) Any person who makes, or causes to be made, [any record or entry on a record sheet kept or carried for the purposes of the Community Recording Equipment Regulation or] section 97 of this Act or any entry in a [book, register or document kept or carried] for the purposes of regulations under section 98 thereof [or the applicable Community rules] which he knows to be false or, with intent to deceive, alters or causes to be altered any such record or entry shall be liable—

(*a*) on summary conviction, to a fine not exceeding [the prescribed sum];

(*b*) on conviction on indictment, to imprisonment for a term not exceeding two years.

(6) If an officer has reason to believe that an offence under subsection (5) of this section has been committed in respect of any record or document inspected by him under this section, he may seize that record or document; and where a record or document is seized as aforesaid and within six months of the date on which it was seized no person has been charged since that date with an offence in relation to that record or document under that subsection and the record or document has not been returned to the person from whom it was taken, a magistrates' court shall, on an application made for the purpose by that person or by an officer, make such order respecting the disposal of the record or document and award such costs as the justice of the case may require.

(7) *[Applies to Scotland.]*

(8) In this section 'officer' means a certifying officer appointed under [section 68 of the Road Traffic Act 1988], a public service vehicle examiner, an examiner appointed under Part IV of that Act and any person authorised for the purposes of this section by the traffic [commissioner] for any area.

(9) The powers conferred by this section on an officer as defined in subsection (8) of this section shall be exercisable also by a police constable, who shall not, if wearing uniform, be required to produce any authority.

(10) In this section references to the inspection and copying of any record produced by means of equipment installed for the purposes of section 97 of this Act in a vehicle include references to the application to the record of any process for eliciting the information recorded thereby and to taking down the information elicited from it.

[Section 99 is printed as amended by the European Communities Act 1972, s 4, and Sched 4, para 9; the Road Traffic Act 1972, s 203(1), and Sched 7; the Road Traffic (Drivers' Ages and Hours of Work) Act 1976, s 2(1); the Passenger and Goods Vehicles (Recording Equipment) Regulations 1979 (SI 1979 No 1746); the Magistrates' Courts Act 1980, s 32(2); the Criminal Justice Act 1982, ss 38, 46(1); the Transport Act 1985, s 3(5) and Sched 2, Part II, para 1(4); the Community Drivers' Hours and Recording Equipment Regulations 1986 (SI 1986 No 1457), reg 3; the Road Traffic (Consequential Provisions) Act 1988, s 4 and Sched 3, para 6(5).

Officers are appointed under the Road Traffic Act 1988, s 68, to inspect goods vehicles. Part IV of that Act (ss 110–122) relates to the licensing of drivers of heavy goods vehicles.

As to the 'prescribed sum', see the Magistrates' Courts Act 1980, s 32(9), above.]

* * *

102. Application to the Crown and exemption for police and fire brigade

(1) Subject to subsection (2) of this section, this Part of this Act shall apply to vehicles and persons in the public service of the Crown.

(2) This Part of this Act shall not apply in the case of motor vehicles owned by the Secretary of State for Defence and used for naval, military or air force purposes or in the case of vehicles so used while being driven by persons for the time being subject to the orders of a member of the armed forces of the Crown.

[(3) Where an offence under this Part of this Act is alleged to have been committed in connection with a vehicle in the public service of the Crown, proceedings may be brought in respect of the offence against a person nominated for the purpose on behalf of the Crown; and, subject to subsection (3A) below, where any such offence is committed any person so nominated shall also be guilty of the offence as well as any person actually responsible for the offence (but without prejudice to proceedings against any person so responsible).]

[(3A) Where a person is convicted of an offence by virtue of subsection (3) above—

(*a*) no order may be made on his conviction save an order imposing a fine,

(*b*) payment of any fine imposed on him in respect of that offence may not be enforced against him, and

(*c*) apart from the imposition of any such fine, the conviction shall be disregarded for all purposes other than any appeal (whether by way of case stated or otherwise).]

(4) This Part of this Act shall not apply in the case of motor vehicles while being used for police or fire brigade purposes.

[Section 102 is printed as amended by the Road Traffic (Consequential Provisions) Act 1988, s 4 and Sched 3, para 6(6).]

[102A. Exclusion of application to tramcars and trolley vehicles

(1) This Part of this Act and section 255 of the Road Traffic Act 1960 in its application thereto shall not apply to tramcars or trolley vehicles operated under statutory powers.

(2) In this section 'operated under statutory powers' means, in relation to tramcars or trolley vehicles, that their use is authorised or regulated by special Act of Parliament or by an order having the force of an Act.

(3) Subsection (1) above shall have effect subject to any such Act or order as is mentioned in subsection (2) above, and any such Act or order may apply to tramcars or trolley vehicles to which it relates any of the provisions excluded by the said subsection (1).]

[Section 102A was inserted by the Road Traffic (Consequential Provisions) Act 1988, s 4 and Sched 3, para 6(7).]

103. Interpretation, supplementary provisions, etc, for Part VI

(1) In this Part of this Act—

'agriculture' has the meaning assigned by section 109(3) of the Agriculture Act 1947;

['the applicable Community rules' means any directly applicable Community provision for the time being in force about the driving of road vehicles;]

['the Community Recording Equipment Regulation' has the meaning given by section 97(7) of this Act;]

['the domestic drivers' hours code' has the meaning given by section 96(13) of this Act;]

'driver', 'employee-driver' and 'owner-driver' have the meaning assigned by section 95(3) of this Act;

'employer', in relation to an employee-driver, means the employer of that driver in the employment by virtue of which that driver is an employee-driver;

. . .

'prescribed' means prescribed by regulations made by the [Secretary of State for Transport];

['recording equipment' has the meaning given by section 97(7) of this Act;]

['record sheet" includes a temporary sheet attached to a record sheet in accordance with [Article 16(2), of the Community Recording Equipment Regulation;]

['relevant Community provision' means any Community provision for the time being in force about the driving of road vehicles, whether directly applicable or not;]

'working day' in relation to any driver, means—

(*a*) any period during which he is on duty and which does not fall to be aggregated with any other such period by virtue of paragraph (*b*) of this definition; and

(*b*) where a period during which he is on duty is not followed by an interval for rest of not less than eleven hours or (where permitted by virtue of section 96(4)(*b*) of this Act) of not less than nine and a half hours, the aggregate of that period and each successive such period until there is such an interval as aforesaid, together with any interval or intervals between periods so aggregated;

['working week' means, subject to subsection (5) of this section, a week beginning at midnight between Sunday and Monday;]

and any expression not defined above which is also used in the [Act of 1972] has the same meaning as in that Act.

(2) For the purposes of this Part of this Act a director of a company shall be deemed to be employed by it.

(3) In this Part of this Act references to a person driving a vehicle are references to his being at the driving controls of the vehicle for the purpose of controlling its movement, whether it is in motion or is stationary with the engine running.

(4) In this Part of this Act references to a driver on duty are references—

(*a*) in the case of an employee-driver, to his being on duty (whether for the purpose of driving a vehicle to which this Part of this Act applies or for other purposes) in the employment by virtue of which he is an employee-driver, or in any other employment under the person who is his employer in the first-mentioned employment; and

(*b*) in the case of an owner-driver, to his driving a vehicle to which this Part of this Act applies for the purposes of a trade or business carried on by him or being otherwise engaged in work for the purposes of that trade or business, being work in connection with such a vehicle or the load carried thereby.

(5) The traffic [commissioner] for any area may, on the application of an owner-driver or of the employer of an employee-driver, from time to time direct that a week beginning at midnight between two days other than [Sunday and Monday] shall be, or be deemed to have been, a working week in relation to that owner-driver or employee-driver; but where by virtue of any such direction a new working week begins before the expiration of a previous working week then, without prejudice to the application of the provisions of this Part of this Act in relation to the new working week, those provisions shall continue to apply in relation to the previous working week until its expiration.

(6) In [section] 98(2)(*e*) of this Act 'a small goods vehicle' means a goods vehicle which has a plated weight of the prescribed description not exceeding [3500 kilograms] or (not having a plated weight) had an unladen weight not exceeding [1525 kilograms]; but the [Secretary of State for Transport] may by regulations direct that the foregoing provisions of this subsection shall have effect, in relation to either or both of those sections—

(*a*) with the substitution for either of the weights there specified of such other weight as may be specified in the regulations;

(*b*) with the substitution for either of those weights or for any other weight for the time being specified as aforesaid of a weight expressed in terms of the metric system, being a weight which is equivalent to that for which it is substituted or does not differ from it by more than 5 per cent thereof.

[(7) An offence under this Part of this Act may be treated for the purpose of conferring jurisdiction on a court (but without prejudice to any jurisdiction it may have apart from this subsection) as having been committed in any of the following places, that is to say—

(*a*) the place where the person charged with the offence was driving when evidence of the offence first came to the attention of a constable or vehicle examiner;

(*b*) the place where that person resides or is believed to reside or be at the time when the proceedings are commenced; or

(*c*) the place where at that time that person or, in the case of an employee-driver, that person's employer or, in the case of an owner-driver, the person for whom he was driving, has his place or principal place of business or his operating centre for the vehicle in question.

In this subsection 'vehicle examiner' means an officer within the meaning of section 99 of this Act.]

(8) The enactments specified in Schedule 11 to this Act shall have effect subject to the amendments there specified.

(9) Any order made under section 166(2) of this Act appointing a day for the purposes of any of the provisions of this Part of this Act may contain such transitional provisions as the [Secretary of State for Transport] thinks necessary or expedient as respects the application of any particular provision of this Part of this Act to a working week or working day falling partly before and partly after the date on which that provision comes into operation.

[Section 103 is printed as amended by the Road Traffic (Drivers' Ages and Hours of Work) Act 1976, ss 2(1) and 3; the Minister of Transport Order 1979 (SI 1979 No 571); the Passenger and Goods Vehicles (Recording Equipment) Regulations 1979 (SI 1979 No 1746); the Transfer of Functions (Transport) Order 1981 (SI 1981 No 238); the Road Traffic Acts 1960 and 1972, Road Traffic Regulation Act 1967, and Transport Act 1968 (Metrication) Regulations 1981 (SI 1981 No 1373); the Transport Act 1985, ss 3(5) and 139(3), Sched 2, Part II, para 1(5), Sched 8; the Community Drivers' Hours and Recording Equipment Regulations 1986 (SI 1986 No 1457), reg 3; the Drivers' Hours (Harmonisation with Community Rules) Regulations 1986 (SI 1986 No 1458), reg 3.

In the definition of 'agriculture', words relating expressly and exclusively to Scotland have been omitted.

The definition of 'working day' has been modified in its application to the drivers of passenger vehicles and goods vehicles; see further the Drivers' Hours (Passenger and Goods Vehicles) (Modifications) Order 1971 (SI 1971 No 818) and the Drivers' Hours (Goods Vehicles) (Modifications) Order 1986 (SI 1986 No 1459), below.

The amendments to subs (6) effected by the Road Traffic Acts 1960 and 1972, Road Traffic Regulation Act 1967, and Transport Act 1968 (Metrication) Regulations (SI 1981 No 1373) (namely '3500 kilograms' for '3½ tons' and '1525 kilograms' for '30 hundredweight') were expressed specifically to apply to s 98(2) of this Act.]

* * *

The Transport Act 1980

(1980 c 34)

An Act to . . . prohibit the display of certain roof-signs on vehicles other than taxis; . . . and for connected purposes.

[30th June 1980]

*   *   *

64. Roof-signs on vehicles other than taxis

(1) There shall not, in any part of England and Wales outside the metropolitan police district and the City of London, be displayed on or above the roof of any vehicle which is used for carrying passengers for hire or reward but which is not a taxi—

(*a*) any sign which consists of or includes the word 'taxi' or 'cab', whether in the singular or plural, or 'hire', or any word of similar meaning or appearance to any of those words, whether alone or as part of another word; or

(*b*) any sign, notice, mark, illumination or other feature which may suggest that the vehicle is a taxi.

(2) Any person who knowingly—

(*a*) drives a vehicle in respect of which subsection (1) is contravened; or

(*b*) causes or permits that subsection to be contravened in respect of any vehicle,

shall be liable on summary conviction to a fine not exceeding [level 3 on the standard scale].

(3) In this section 'taxi' means a vehicle licensed under section 37 of the Town Police Clauses Act 1847, section 6 of the Metropolitan Carriage Act 1869, [section 10 of the Civic Government (Scotland) Act 1982] or any similar local enactment.

[Section 64 is printed as amended by the Criminal Justice Act 1982, s 46(1); the Transport Act 1985, s 139(2) and Sched 7, para 20.

The definition of 'taxi' is incorporated by reference into the Motor Vehicles (Wearing of Seat Belts) Regulations 1982 (SI 1982 No 1203), reg 3(1) (qv), and the Road Traffic Act 1988, s 47(3) (qv).]

*   *   *

The Transport Act 1985

(1985 c 67)

An Act to amend the law relating to road passenger transport . . .

[30th October 1985]

ARRANGEMENT OF SECTIONS

PART I

General Provisions relating to Road Passenger Transport

* * *

Meaning of 'local service'

* * *

Taxis and hire cars

* * *

Modification of PSV requirements in relation to vehicles used for certain purposes

Further amendments with respect to PSV operators' licences

PART II

Regulation of Road Passenger Transport in London

London local service licences

* * *

PART VI

Miscellaneous and General

Provisions supplementary to Parts I and II

General supplementary provisions

SCHEDULES

* * *

PART I

General Provisions relating to Road Passenger Transport

* * *

Meaning of 'local service'

2. Local services

(1) In this Act 'local service' means a service, using one or more public service vehicles, for the carriage of passengers by road at separate fares other than one—

(*a*) which is excluded by subsection (4) below; or

(*b*) in relation to which (except in an emergency) one or both of the conditions mentioned in subsection (2) below are met with respect to every passenger using the service.

(2) The conditions are that—

(*a*) the place where he is set down is fifteen miles or more, measured in a straight line, from the place where he was taken up;

(*b*) some point on the route between those places is fifteen miles or more, measured in a straight line, from either of those places.

(3) Where a service consists of one or more parts with respect to which one or both of the conditions are met, and one or more parts with respect to which neither of them is met, each of those parts shall be treated as a separate service for the purposes of subsection (1) above.

(4) A service shall not be regarded for the purposes of this Act as a local service if—

(*a*) the conditions set out in Part III of Schedule 1 to the 1981 Act (trips organised privately by persons acting independently of vehicle operators, etc) are met in respect of each journey made by the vehicles used in providing the service; or

(*b*) every vehicle used in providing the service is so used under a permit granted under section 19 of this Act.

(5) Subsections (5)(*b*), (*c*) and (6) of section 1 of the 1981 Act (meaning of 'fares') shall apply for the purposes of this section.

* * *

Taxis and hire cars

* * *

11. Advance booking of taxis and hire cars at separate fares

(1) Where the conditions mentioned in subsection (2) below are met, a licensed taxi or licensed hire car may be used for the carriage of passengers for hire or reward at separate fares without thereby—

(*a*) becoming a public service vehicle for the purposes of the 1981 Act or any related enactment; or

(*b*) ceasing (otherwise than by virtue of any provision made under section 13 of this Act) to be subject to the taxi code or (as the case may be) the hire car code.

(2) The conditions are that—

(*a*) all the passengers carried on the occasion in question booked their journeys in advance; and

(*b*) each of them consented, when booking his journey, to sharing the use of the vehicle on that occasion with others on the basis that a separate fare would be payable by each passenger for his own journey on that occasion.

12. Use of taxis in providing local services

(1) Where the holder of a taxi licence—

(*a*) applies to the appropriate traffic commissioner for a restricted PSV operator's licence to be granted to him under Part II of the 1981 Act; and (*b*) states in his application that he proposes to use one or more licensed taxis to provide a local service;

section 14 of the 1981 Act (conditions to be met before grant of PSV operator's licence) shall not apply and the commissioner shall grant the application.

(2) In this section 'special licence' means a restricted PSV operator's licence granted by virtue of this section.

(3) Section 15 of the 1981 Act (duration of licences) shall apply in relation to any special licence as if it required the duration of the licence to be—

(*a*) five years; or

(*b*) where the application for the licence specifies a shorter period, that shorter period.

(4) Without prejudice to his powers to attach other conditions under section 16 of the 1981 Act, any traffic commissioner granting a special licence shall attach to it, under that section, the conditions mentioned in subsection (5) below.

(5) The conditions are—

(*a*) that every vehicle used under the licence shall be one for which the holder of the licence has a taxi licence; and

(*b*) that no vehicle shall be used under the licence otherwise than for the purpose of providing a local service with one or more stopping places within the area of the authority which granted the taxi licence of the vehicle in question.

(6) In subsection (5)(*b*) above 'local service' does not include an excursion or tour.

(7) The maximum number of vehicles which the holder of a special licence may at any one time use under the licence shall be the number of vehicles for which (for the time being) he holds taxi licences; and a condition to that effect shall be attached to every special licence under section 16(1) of the 1981 Act.

(8) Section 1(2) of the 1981 Act (vehicle used as public service vehicle to be treated as such until that use is permanently discontinued) shall not apply to any use of a licensed taxi for the provision of a local service under a special licence.

(9) At any time when a licensed taxi is being so used it shall carry such documents, plates and marks, in such manner, as may be prescribed.

(10) Such provisions in the taxi code as may be prescribed shall apply in relation to a licensed taxi at any time when it is being so used; and any such provision may be so applied subject to such modifications as may be prescribed.

(11) For the purposes of section 12(3) of the 1981 Act (which provides that where two or more PSV operators' licences are held they must be granted by traffic commissioners for different traffic areas), special licences shall be disregarded.

(12) A person may hold more than one special licence but shall not at the same time hold more than one such licence granted by the traffic commissioner for a particular traffic area.

(13) The following provisions shall not apply in relation to special licences or (as the case may be) the use of vehicles under such licences—

(*a*) sections 16(1A) and (2), 17(3)(*d*), 18 to 20, 22 and 26 of the 1981 Act; and

(*b*) section 26(5) and (6) of this Act;

and for the purposes of section 12 of that Act this section shall be treated as if it were in Part II of that Act.

13. Provisions supplementary to sections 10 to 12

(1), (2) *[Power to make orders modifying taxi code and hire car code.]*

(3) In this section, and in sections 10 to 12 of this Act—

'licensed taxi' means—

(*a*) in England and Wales, a vehicle licensed under—

(i) section 37 of the Town Police Clauses Act 1847; or

(ii) section 6 of the Metropolitan Public Carriage Act 1869;

or under any similar enactment; and

(*b*) *[Applies to Scotland.]*

'London taxi area' means the area to which the Metropolitan Public Carriage Act 1869 applies;

'licensed hire car' means a vehicle which is licensed under section 48 of the Local Government (Miscellaneous Provisions) Act 1976;

'hire car code'; in relation to a licensed hire car used as mentioned in section 11 of this Act, means those provisions made by or under any enactment which would apply if it were hired by a single passenger for his exclusive use;

'related enactment', in relation to the 1981 Act, means any statutory provision (whenever passed or made) relating to public service vehicles in which public service vehicle is defined directly or indirectly by reference to the provisions of the 1981 Act;

'taxi code', in relation to any licensed taxi used as mentioned in section 10, 11 or 12 of this Act, means—

(*a*) in England and Wales, those provisions made by or under any enactment which would apply if the vehicle were plying for hire and were hired by a single passenger for his exclusive use; and

(*b*) *[Applies to Scotland.]*

'taxi licence' means a licence under section 6 of the Metropolitan Public Carriage Act 1869, section 37 of the Town Police Clauses Act 1847 or any similar enactment, or a taxi licence under section 10 of the Civic Government (Scotland) Act 1982.

(4) *[Scope of orders under s 13(1).]*

* * *

Modification of PSV requirements in relation to vehicles used for certain purposes

18. Exemption from PSV operator and driver licensing requirements of vehicles used under permits

Sections 12(1) and 22 of the 1981 Act (licensing of operators and drivers in relation to the use of public service vehicles for the carriage of passengers) shall not apply

(*a*) to the use of any vehicle under a permit granted under section 19 of this Act, if and so long as the requirements under subsection (2) of that section are met;

(*b*) to the use of any vehicle under a permit granted under section 22 of this Act; or

(*c*) in relation to the driving of any vehicle at a time when it is being used as mentioned in paragraph (*a*) or (*b*) above.

19. Permits in relation to use of buses by educational and other bodies

(1) In this section and sections 20 and 21 of this Act—

'bus' means a vehicle which is adapted to carry more than eight passengers;

'large bus' means a vehicle which is adapted to carry more than sixteen passengers;

'small bus' means a vehicle which is adapted to carry more than eight but not more than sixteen passengers; and

'permit' means a permit granted under this section in relation to the use of a bus for carrying passengers for hire or reward.

(2) The requirements that must be met in relation to the use of a bus under a permit for the exemption under section 8(*a*) of this Act to apply are that the bus—

(*a*) is being used by a body to whom a permit has been granted under this section;

(*b*) is not being used for the carriage of members of the general public nor with a view to profit nor incidentally to an activity which is itself carried on with a view to profit;

(*c*) is being used in every respect in accordance with any conditions attached to the permit; and

(*d*) is not being used in contravention of any provision of regulations made under section 21 of this Act.

(3) A permit in relation to the use of a small bus may be granted by a body designated by an order under subsection (7) below either to itself or to any other body to whom, in accordance with the order, it is entitled to grant a permit.

(4) A permit in relation to the use of a small bus may be granted by a traffic commissioner to any body appearing to him to be eligible in accordance with subsection (8) below and to be carrying on in his area an activity which makes it so eligible.

(5) A permit in relation to the use of a large bus may be granted by a traffic commissioner to any body which assists and co-ordinates the activities of bodies within his area which appear to him to be concerned with

(*a*) education;

(*b*) religion;

(*c*) social welfare; or

(*d*) other activities of benefit to the community.

(6) A traffic commissioner shall not grant a permit in relation to the use of a large bus unless satisfied that there will be adequate facilities or arrangements for maintaining any bus used under the permit in a fit and serviceable condition.

(7) The Secretary of State may by order designate for the purpose of this section bodies appearing to him to be eligible in accordance with subsection (8) below and, with respect to any body designated by it, any such order—

(*a*) shall specify the classes of body to whom the designated body may grant permits;

(*b*) may impose restrictions with respect to the grant of permits by the designated body and, in particular, may provide that no permit may be granted, either generally or in such cases as may be specified in the order, unless there are attached to the permit such conditions as may be so specified; and

(*c*) may require the body to make returns with regard to the permits granted by it.

(8) A body is eligible in accordance with this subsection if it is concerned with—

(*a*) education;

(*b*) religion;

(*c*) social welfare;

(*d*) recreation; or

(*e*) other activities of benefit to the community.

(9) A body may hold more than one permit but may not use more than one bus at any one time under the same permit.

[For the bodies designated for the purposes of s 19(7), see the Section 19 Minibus (Designated Bodies) Order 1987 (SI 1987 No 1229) (not reproduced in this work).]

* * *

21. Permits under section 19: regulations

(1) Regulations may prescribe—

(*a*) the conditions to be fulfilled by any person driving a bus while it is being used under a permit;

(*b*) the conditions as to fitness which are to be fulfilled by any small bus used under a permit;

(*c*) the form of permits; and

(*d*) the documents, plates and marks to be carried by any bus while it is being used under a permit and the manner and position in which they are to be carried.

(2) Where regulations are made by virtue of subsection (1)(*b*) above, section 6 of the 1981 Act (certificate of initial fitness for public service vehicles) shall not apply in relation to any small bus subject to the regulations.

(3) Regulations under this section may contain such transitional provisions as the Secretary of State thinks fit.

22. Community bus permits

(1) In this section and section 23 of this Act—

'community bus service' means a local service provided—

(*a*) by a body concerned for the social and welfare needs of one or more communities;

(*b*) without a view to profit, either on the part of that body or of anyone else; and

(*c*) by means of a vehicle adapted to carry more than eight but not more than sixteen passengers; and

'community bus permit' means a permit granted under this section in relation to the use of a public service vehicle—

(*a*) in providing a community bus service; or

(*b*) in providing a community bus service and (other than in the course of a local service) carrying passengers for hire or reward where the carriage of those passengers will directly assist the provision of the community bus service by providing financial support for it.

(2)–(4) *[Omitted.]*

23. Further provisions with respect to community bus permits

(1)–(4) *[Omitted.]*

(5) Subject to section 68(3) of the 1981 Act (as applied by section 127(4) of this

Act), if a condition attached to a community bus permit is contravened, the holder of the permit shall be liable on summary conviction to a fine not exceeding level 3 on the standard scale.

(6), (7) *[Omitted.]*

Further amendments with respect to PSV operators' licences

* * *

30. Plying for hire by large public service vehicles

(1) A public service vehicle which is adapted to carry more than eight passengers shall not be used on a road in plying for hire as a whole.

(2) Subject to section 68(3) of the 1981 Act (as applied by section 127(4) of this Act), if a vehicle is used in contravention of subsection (1) above, the operator of the vehicle shall be liable on summary conviction to a fine not exceeding level 3 on the standard scale.

* * *

PART II

Regulation of Road Passenger Transport in London

London local service licences

34. London local services

(1) In this Act 'London local service' means (subject to subsection (3) below) a local service with one or more stopping places in London.

(2) In this Part of this Act—

(*a*) 'bus service' means a local service other than an excursion or tour; and

(*b*) 'London bus service' means a London local service other than an excursion or tour.

(3) Where a local service is or is to be provided both inside and outside London, any part of the service which is or is to be provided outside London shall be treated as a separate service for the purposes of this Act if there is any stopping place for that part of the service outside London.

35. London local service licences

(1) Subject to subsection (2) below and to section 36 of this Act, a London local service shall not be provided except under a London local service licence granted in accordance with the following provisions of this Part of this Act.

(2) A London local service licence is not required for the provision by any person under an agreement with the Railways Board of any service secured by the Board under section 4A of the 1962 Act (Board's power to secure the provision of bus service where a railway service has been temporarily interrupted or discontinued).

(3) The traffic commissioner for the Metropolitan Traffic Area (referred to below in this Part of this Act as the metropolitan traffic commissioner) shall be responsible for granting London local service licences.

(4) Subject to subsection (5) below and to section 38(4) of this Act, a London local service licence shall be of no effect at any time at which the holder does not also hold—

(*a*) a PSV operator's licence granted by the metropolitan traffic commissioner or by the traffic commissioner for any other traffic area, not being a licence which is at that time of no effect by reason of its suspension; or

(*b*) a permit under section 22 of this Act.

(5) Subsection (4) above does not apply to a London local service licence held by a local education authority.

(6) Subject to section 68(3) of the 1981 Act (as applied by section 127(4) of this Act), if a London local service is provided in contravention of subsection (1) above, the operator of the service shall be liable on summary conviction to a fine not exceeding level 3 on the standard scale.

[See further s 39(4) of this Act, below.]

36. London bus services under the control of London Regional Transport

(1) A London local service licence is not required for the provision of a London bus service—

(*a*) by London Regional Transport or any subsidiary of theirs; or

(*b*) by any other person in pursuance of any agreement entered into by London Regional Transport by virtue of section 3(2) of the London Regional Transport Act 1984 (referred to below in this section as the 1984 Act).

(2)–(7) *[Omitted.]*

* * *

38. Conditions attached to licences

(1)–(6) *[Omitted.]*

(7) Subject to section 68(3) of the 1981 Act (as applied by section 127(4) of this Act), if a condition attached under this section to a London local service licence is contravened, the holder of the licence shall be liable on summary conviction to a fine not exceeding level 3 on the standard scale.

39. Grant of licences for certain excursions or tours

(1) This section applies where, in the case of any application for a London local service licence, the metropolitan traffic commissioner is satisfied that the service which the applicant proposes to provide under the licence ('the proposed service') would be an excursion or tour and is also satisfied either—

(*a*) that the proposed service would not compete directly with any authorised London bus service; or

(*b*) that the proposed service would operate only to enable passengers to attend special events.

(2) In subsection (1)(*a*) above, 'authorised London bus service' means—

(*a*) any London bus service for which a London local service licence has been granted; and

(*b*) any London bus service which, by virtue of section 36(1) of this Act, does not require a London local service licence.

(3) In any case to which this section applies, sections 35, 37 and 38 of this Act shall apply subject to the modifications provided by the following provisions of this section.

(4) Section 35(4) of this Act shall not prevent a London local service licence granted in pursuance of this section from having effect for the purposes of the provision of a service by means of a vehicle whose operator holds any such licence or permit as is there mentioned (not being, in the case of a PSV operator's licence, a licence which is for the time being of no effect by reason of its suspension).

(5)–(10) *[Omitted.]*

* * *

PART VI

Miscellaneous and General

* * *

Provisions supplementary to Parts I and II

* * *

127. Offences and legal proceedings

(1) Section 65 of the 1981 Act (forgery and misuse of documents) shall apply to the following documents, namely—

(*a*) a permit under section 19 or 22 of this Act; and

(*b*) a London local service licence.

(2) Section 66 of that Act (false statements to obtain licence, etc) shall apply in relation to a false statement for the purpose of obtaining the grant of any such permit or licence as it applies in relation to a false statement for the purposes there mentioned.

(3) Section 67 of that Act (penalty for breach of regulations under that Act) shall have effect as if Parts I and II of this Act were contained in that Act.

(4) The defence provided by section 68(3) of that Act (that the person charged took all reasonable precautions and exercised all due diligence to avoid the commission of an offence under certain provisions of that Act) shall apply in relation to an offence under any of the following provisions of this Act, that is to say, sections 23(5), 30(2), 35(6) and 37(7).

(5) The provisions of that Act mentioned in subsection (6) below shall apply in relation to an offence, or (as the case may be) in relation to proceedings for an offence, under Part I or II of this Act as they apply in relation to an offence, or in relation to proceedings for an offence, under Part II of that Act.

(6) Those provisions are—

section 69 (restrictions on institution in England or Wales of proceedings for an offence under Part II);

section 70 (duty to give information as to identity of driver in certain cases);

section 71 (evidence of certificate in proceedings in England or Wales for an offence under Part II);

section 72 (proof in summary proceedings in England and Wales of identity of driver of vehicle); and

section 74 (offences under Part II committed by companies).

(7) *[Applies to Scotland.]*

General supplementary provisions

* * *

137. Interpretation

(1) In this Act, unless the context otherwise requires—

'the 1962 Act' means the Transport Act 1962;

'the 1972 Act' means the Local Government Act 1972;

'the 1968 Act' means the Transport Act 1968;

'the 1981 Act' means the Public Passenger Vehicles Act 1981;

'body' means a body of persons, whether corporate or unincorporate;

. . .

'excursion or tour' means a service for the carriage of passengers by road at separate fares on which the passengers travel together on a journey, with or without breaks, from one or more places to one or more other places and back;

. . .

'local service' has the meaning given by section 2 of this Act;

'London' means the administrative area of Greater London as for the time being constituted;

'London local service' has the meaning given by section 34(1) of this Act;

. . .

'prescribed' means prescribed by regulations;

. . .

'regulations' means regulations made by the Secretary of State;

. . .

'social services functions' means functions which are social services functions for the purposes of the Local Authority Social Services Act 1970;

. . .

'the standard scale' has the meaning given by *section 75 of the Criminal Justice Act 1982*;

'stopping place' means, in relation to any service or part of a service, a point at which passengers are (or, in the case of a proposed service, are proposed to be) taken up or set down in the course of that service or part;

. . .

'traffic area' means a traffic area constituted for the purposes of the 1981 Act, and section 80 of that Act shall apply to references in this Act to the Metropolitan Traffic Area;

'trunk road' has the meaning given by section 329 of the Highways Act 1980 [*qv*];

. . .

and the expressions listed in subsection (2) below have the same meaning as in the 1981 Act.

(2) Those expressions are—

'company';
'contravention';
'fares';
'modification';
'operator' (in references to the operator of a vehicle);
'operating centre';
'PSV operator's licence';
'public service vehicle';
'road';
'statutory provision'; and
'traffic commissioner'.

(3) References in this Act to a vehicle's being used for carrying passengers for hire or reward shall be read in accordance with section 1(5) of the 1981 Act.

(4)–(6) *[Omitted.]*

(7) For the purposes of this Act the operator of a passenger transport service of any description is the person, or each of the persons, providing the service; and for those purposes the operator of a vehicle being used on a road for the carriage of passengers for hire or reward at separate fares shall be taken to be providing the service by means of the vehicle unless he proves that the service is or forms part of a service provided not by himself but by one or more other persons.

(8) *[Omitted.]*

[Only selected definitions in s 137(1) are reproduced. Reference to the meaning of 'trunk road' in Scotland has been omitted.

The Local Authority Social Services Act 1970 prescribes (s 2 and Sched 1) certain functions which are to be referred to local authorities' social services committees.

The Criminal Justice Act 1982, s 75 (to which reference is made in the definition of 'the standard scale') was repealed by the Criminal Justice Act 1988, s 170(2) and Sched 16. The term is now defined in the Interpretation Act 1978, Sched 1 (qv).]

* * *

SCHEDULE 1

Amendments Consequential on the Abolition of Road Service Licensing

* * *

16.—(1) Subject to any provision made by or under this Act, in any enactment or instrument passed or made before the commencement of section 1 of this Act—

(*a*) any reference to a stage carriage service shall be construed as a reference to a local service;

(*b*) any reference to an express carriage service shall be construed as a reference to any service for the carriage of passengers for hire or reward at separate fares which is neither a local service nor one provided by a vehicle to which sub-paragraph (2) below applies;

(*c*) any reference to a stage carriage shall be construed as a reference to a public service vehicle being used in the provision of a local service;

(*d*) any reference to any express carriage shall be construed as a reference to a public service vehicle being used to carry passengers for hire or reward at separate fares other than one being used in the provision of a local service; and

(*e*) any reference to a contract shall be construed as a reference to a public service vehicle being used to carry passengers for hire or reward otherwise than at separate fares.

(2) When used in circumstances in which the conditions set out in Part III of Schedule I to the 1981 Act are fulfilled, a public service vehicle carrying passengers at separate fares shall be treated, for the purposes of any enactment or instrument to which paragraph (*d*) or (*e*) of sub-paragraph (1) above applies, as being used to carry passengers otherwise than at separate fares.

[Although s 1(3) of the Act was brought into operation on 6 January 1986 (see the Transport Act 1985 (Commencement No 1) Order 1985 (SI 1985 No 1887), art 3(1) and Schedule) for limited purposes ('to the extent necessary for the bringing into force of the provisions of Schedule 1 brought into force by this Order'), it is thought that 'commencement' of s 1 (see para 16(1) above) is the date when that section was brought fully into operation (ie 26 October 1986) (see the Transport Act 1985 (Commencement) (No 6) Order 1986 (SI 1986 No 1794)).]

* * *

SCHEDULE 7

Minor and Consequential Amendments

General

1. In England and Wales, the provisions made by or under any enactment which apply to motor vehicles used—

(*a*) to carry passengers under a contract express or implied for the use of the vehicle as a whole at or for a fixed or agreed rate or sum; and

(*b*) to ply for hire for such use;

shall apply to motor vehicles adapted to carry less than nine passengers as they apply to motor vehicles adapted to carry less than eight passengers.

* * *

The Value Added Tax Act 1983

(1983 c 55)

An Act to consolidate the enactments relating to value added tax.

[26th July 1983]

*   *   *

2. Scope of tax

(1) *[Omitted.]*

(2) A person who makes or intends to make taxable supplies is a taxable person while he is or is required to be registered under this Act; and a taxable supply is a supply of goods or services made in the United Kingdom other than an exempt supply.

(3)–(5) *[Omitted.]*

[The meaning of 'taxable person' is incorporated by reference into the Vehicles (Excise) Act 1971, s 6 (qv).

Exempt supplies for value added tax purposes are listed in Sched 6 to this Act.]

*   *   *

The Vehicles (Excise) Act 1971

(1971 c 10)

An Act to consolidate certain enactments relating to excise duties on mechanically propelled vehicles, and to the licensing and registration of such vehicles with amendments to give effect to recommendations of the Law Commission and the Scottish Law Commission.

[16th March 1971]

ARRANGEMENT OF SECTIONS

* * *

Exemptions from duty

* * *

Exemptions from duty

4. Exemptions from duty of certain descriptions of vehicle

(1) No duty shall be chargeable under this Act in respect of mechanically propelled vehicles of any of the following descriptions, that is to say—

[(*aa*) electrically propelled vehicles;]

(*a*) fire engines;

(*b*) vehicles kept by a local authority while they are used or kept on a road for the purposes of their fire brigade service;

(*c*) ambulances;

(*d*) road rollers;

(*e*) vehicles used on tram lines . . . ;

(*f*) vehicles used or kept on a road for no purpose other than the haulage of lifeboats and the conveyance of the necessary gear of the lifeboats which are being hauled;

(*g*) vehicles (including cycles with an attachment for propelling them by mechanical power) which do not exceed [ten] hundredweight in weight unladen and are adapted, and used or kept on a road, for invalids;

(*h*) road construction vehicles used or kept on a road solely for the conveyance of built-in road construction machinery (with or without articles or material used for the purposes of that machinery);

(*i*) vehicles constructed or adapted, and used, solely for the conveyance of machinery for spreading material on roads to deal with frost, ice or snow or for the conveyance of such machinery and articles and material used for the purposes of that machinery;

(*j*) local authority's watering vehicles;

(*k*) tower wagons used solely by a street lighting authority, or by any person acting in pursuance of a contract with such an authority, for the purpose of installing or maintaining materials or apparatus for lighting streets, roads or public places;

[(*l*) vehicles which are made available by the Secretary of State to any person, body or local authority in pursuance of [section 23 or section 26 of the National Health Service Act 1977] and which are used in accordance with the terms on which they are so made available].

(2) In this section—

'road construction vehicle' means a vehicle constructed or adapted for use for the conveyance of built-in road construction machinery and not constructed or adapted for the conveyance of any other load except articles and material used for the purposes of that machinery;

'road construction machinery' means a machine or contrivance suitable for use for the construction or repair of roads and used for no purpose other than the construction or repair of roads at the public expense;

'built-in road construction machinery', in relation to a vehicle, means road construction machinery built in as part of the vehicle or permanently attached thereto;

'local authority's watering vehicle' means a vehicle used solely within the area of a local authority by that local authority, or by any person acting in pursuance of a contract with that local authority, for the purpose of cleansing or watering roads or cleansing gulleys;

['tower wagon' means a good vehicle—

(*a*) into which there is built, as part of the vehicle, any expanding or extensible contrivance designed for facilitating the erection, inspection, repair or maintenance of overhead structures or equipment, and

(*b*) which is neither constructed nor adapted for use nor used for the conveyance of any load other than—

(i) such a contrivance and articles used in connection therewith; and

(ii) articles in connection with the installation or maintenance, by means of such a contrivance, of materials or apparatus for lighting streets, roads or public places];

'street lighting authority' means any local authority or Minister having power under any enactment to provide or maintain materials or apparatus for lighting streets, roads or public places.

[Section 4 is printed as amended by the Finance Act 1972, s 128(3); the National Health Service (Vehicles) Order 1974 (SI 1974 No 168); the Finance Act 1975, ss 5(5), 75(5), and Sched 14, Part II; the National Health Service Act 1977, Sched 14, para 2; the Finance Act 1980, s 4; the Finance Act 1986, s 3(7) and Sched 2, Part I, para 2.]

5. Exemptions from duty in connection with vehicle testing, etc

(1) A mechanically propelled vehicle shall not be chargeable with any duty under this Act by reason of its use on public roads—

(*a*) solely for the purpose of submitting it by previous arrangement for a specified time on a specified date for, or bringing it away from, a compulsory test; or (*b*) in the course of a compulsory test, soley for the purpose of taking it to, or bringing it away from, any place where a part of the test is to be or, as the case may be, has been carried out, or of carrying out any part of the test, the person so using it being an authorised person; or

(*c*) where the relevant certificate is refused on a compulsory test, solely for the purpose of delivering it by previous arrangement for a specified time on a specified date at a place where work is to be done on it to remedy the defects on the ground of which the certificate was refused, or bringing it away from a place where work has been done on it to remedy such defects.

(2) In paragraph (*c*) above the reference to work done or to be done on the vehicle to remedy the defects there mentioned is, in a case where the relevant certificate which is refused is a test certificate, a reference to work done or to be done to remedy those defects for a further compulsory test and includes, in a case where the relevant certificate which is refused is a goods vehicle test certificate, type approval certificate or Minister's approval certificate, a reference to work done or to be done to alter the vehicle in some aspect of design, construction, equipment or marking on account of which the certificate was refused.

(3) In this section—

'compulsory test' means an examination under [section 45 of the Road Traffic Act 1988] with a view to obtaining a test certificate without which a vehicle licence cannot be granted for the vehicle under this Act or, in the case of a goods vehicle for which by virtue of [section 66(3) of that Act] a vehicle licence cannot be so granted an examination under regulations under [section 49 or for the purposes of sections 54 to 58] of that Act (examinations as to a goods vehicle's compliance with construction and use or type approval requirements respectively) or an examination under regulations under [section 61(2)(*a*)] of that Act (in connection with alterations to goods vehicles subject to type appproval requirements) or for the purposes of [section 60] of that Act (appeals);

'the relevant certificate' means a test certificate as defined in subsection (2) of the said [section 45], a goods vehicle test certificate as defined in the said [section 49], a type approval certificate or a Minister's approval certificate as defined in the said [sections 54 to 58];

'authorised person' in the case of a compulsory test under the said [section 45] means a person authorised as an examiner or appointed as an inspector under that section or acting on behalf of a person so authorised, or a person acting under the personal direction of such a person as aforesaid; and in the case of any other compulsory test means a goods vehicle examiner or a person carrying out the test under his direction or a person driving the vehicle in pursuance of a requirement to do so under regulations under which the compulsory test is carried out;

'goods vehicle examiner' means an examiner appointed under [section 68 of the Road Traffic Act 1988] or a certifying officer appointed under [the Public Passengers Vehicles Act 1981].

[Section 5 is printed as amended by the Road Traffic Act 1972, s 203(1) and Sched 7; the Interpretation Act 1978, s 17(2)(a); the Road Traffic (Consequential Provisions) Act 1988, s 4 and Sched 3, para 8(2).]

6. Exemptions from duty in respect of vehicles acquired by overseas residents

[(1) A mechanically propelled vehicle shall not be chargeable with any duty under this Act if it has been supplied to the person keeping it by a taxable person within the meaning of [section 2(2) of the Value Added Tax Act 1983 [*qv*]] and the supply has been zero-rated in pursuance of [subsection (7) of section 16] of that Act; but if, at any time, the value added tax that would have been chargeable on the supply but for the zero-rating becomes payable under [subsection (9)] of that section, or would have become so payable but for any authorisation or waiver under that subsection, then the provisions of subsection (3) below shall apply in relation to that vehicle.]

(2) *[Repealed.]*

(3) Where under subsection (1) . . . above the provisions of this subsection are to apply in relation to a vehicle, the vehicle shall be deemed to have been exempted from duty under the said subsection (1) . . . and, without prejudice to the provisions of section 9 of this Act, unless, or except to the extent that, the [Secretary of State for Transport] sees fit to waive payment of the whole or part of the duty, there shall be recoverable by the [Secretary of State for Transport] as a debt due to him—

(*a*) from the person by whom the vehicle was acquired from its manufacturer, the duty in respect of the whole period since the registration of the vehicle; or

(*b*) from any other person who is for the time being the keeper of the vehicle, the duty in respect of the period since the vehicle was first kept by that other person,

other than any part of that period by reference to which there was calculated an amount ordered to be paid by the person in question in respect of the vehicle in pursuance of section 9(1) of this Act.

[Section 6 is printed as amended by the Finance Act 1972, ss 54(8), 55(6), 134, and Sched 28, Part II; the Secretary of State for Transport Order 1976 (SI 1976 No 1775); the Minister of Transport Order 1979 (SI 1979 No 571); the Transfer of Functions (Transport) Order 1981 (SI 1981 No 238); and the Value Added Tax 1983, ss 50(1), 51(2), and Sched 9, para 2.]

7. Miscellaneous exemptions from duty

(1) If an applicant for a vehicle licence satisfies the [Secretary of State for Transport] that the vehicle is intended to be used on public roads—

(*a*) only in passing from land in his occupation to other land in his occupation, and

(*b*) for distances not exceeding in the aggregate six miles in any calendar week,

then, with the consent of the Treasury, the [Secretary of State for Transport] may exempt the vehicle from the duty chargeable under this Act in respect of the use of the vehicle on roads; but if a vehicle so exempted is used on public roads otherwise than for the purpose or to the extent specified above, the vehicle shall cease to be exempted.

[(2) A mechanically propelled vehicle shall not be chargeable with any duty under this Act by reason of its use by or for the purposes of a person ('a disabled person') suffering from a physical defect or disability by reason of its being kept for such use if—

(*a*) it is registered under this Act in the name of that person; and

(*b*) he has obtained, or is eligible for, a grant under paragraph 2 of Schedule 2 to the National Health Service Act 1977 [or section 46(3) of the National Health Service (Scotland) Act 1978] in relation to that vehicle or is in receipt of a mobility allowance [or a mobility supplement]; and

(*c*) no other vehicle registered in his name under this Act is exempted from duty under this subsection of section 7 of the Finance Act 1971;

and for the purposes of this subsection this vehicle shall be deemed to be registered in the name of a disabled person in receipt of a mobility allowance [or a mobility supplement] if it is registered in the name of [an appointee] or in the name of a person nominated for the purposes of this subsection by the disabled person or by [an appointee].]

[(2A) In subsection (2) above—

'mobility supplement' means a mobility supplement under—

(*a*) a scheme under the Personal Injuries (Emergency Provisions) Act 1939, or

(*b*) an Order in Council made under section 12 of the Social Security (Miscellaneous Provisions) Act 1977,

or any payment appearing to the Secretary of State to be of a similar kind and specified by him by order made by statutory instrument; and

'appointee' means—

(i) a person appointed pursuant to regulations under the Social Security Act 1975 to exercise any of the rights or powers of a person in receipt of a mobility allowance, or

(ii) a person to whom a mobility supplement is paid for application for the benefit of another person in receipt of the supplement.]

[(2B) An order under subsection (2A) above may provide that it shall be deemed to have come into force on any date after 20th November 1983.]

(3) A mechanically propelled vehicle shall not be chargeable with any duty under this Act by reason of its use for clearing snow from public roads by means of a snow plough or similar contrivance, whether forming part of the vehicle or not, or by reason of its being kept for such use or by reason of its use for the purpose of going to or from the place where it is to be used for clearing snow from public roads by those means.

[(3A) Regulations under this Act may provide that, in such cases, subject to such conditions and for such period as may be prescribed, a mechanically propelled vehicle shall not be chargeable with any duty under this Act if it has been imported by—

(*a*) a person for the time being appointed to serve with any body, contingent or detachment of the forces of any prescribed country, being a body, contingent or detachment which is for the time being present in the United Kingdom on the invitation of Her Majesty's Government in the United Kingdom, or

(*b*) a member of any country's military forces, except Her Majesty's United Kingdom forces, who is for the time being appointed to serve in the United Kingdom under the orders of any prescribed organisation, or

(*c*) a person for the time being recognised by the Secretary of State as a member of a civilian component of such a force as is mentioned in paragraph (*a*) above or as a civilian member of such an organisation as is mentioned in paragraph (*b*) above, or

(*d*) any prescribed dependant of a person falling within paragraph (*a*), paragraph (*b*) or paragraph (*c*) above.]

(4) Regulations under this Act may provide that, in such cases and subject to such conditions as may be prescribed, a mechanically propelled vehicle shall not be chargeable with any duty under this Act by reason of any use made of it for the purpose of a public or local authority's functions in connection with civil defence as defined in the Civil Defence Act 1948, or by reason of its being kept on a road for any such use, or both.

(5) Regulations under this Act may provide for the total or partial exemption for a limited period from the duty chargeable under this Act of any mechanically propelled vehicles for the time being licensed under section 1 or 10 of the Vehicles (Excise) Act

(Northern Ireland) 1954; and, without prejudice to section 37(1) of this Act, regulations made under this subsection may—

(*a*) make different provision in relation to vehicles of different descriptions;

(*b*) provide that any exemption conferred by the regulations in respect of any vehicle shall have effect subject to such conditions as may be prescribed.

[Section 7 is printed as amended by the Secretary of State for Transport Order 1976 (SI 1976 No 1775); the Finance Act 1978, s 8(1); the Minister of Transport Order 1979 (SI 1979 No 571); the Finance Act 1980, s 4(6); the Transfer of Functions (Transport) Order 1981 (SI 1981 No 238); the Finance Act 1984, s 5; the Finance Act 1986, s 3(7) and Sched 2, para 3.

The Motor Vehicles (Exemption from Vehicles Excise Duty) Order 1985 (SI 1985 No 722) (qv) has been made under subss (2A) and (2B) above.]

Liability to pay duty and consequences of non-payment thereof

8. Using and keeping vehicles without a licence

(1) If any person uses or keeps on a public road any mechanically propelled vehicle for which a licence is not in force, not being a vehicle exempted from duty under this Act by virtue of any enactment (including any provision of this Act), he shall be liable to the greater of the following penalties, namely—

(*a*) an excise penalty of [level 3 on the standard scale]; or

(*b*) an excise penalty equal to five times the amount of the duty chargeable in respect of the vehicle.

(2) . . .

(3) For the purposes of this section—

(*a*) where a vehicle for which a licence is in force is transferred by the holder of the licence to another person, the licence shall be treated as no longer in force unless it is delivered to that other person with the vehicle;

(*b*) the amount of the duty chargeable in respect of a vehicle shall be taken to be an amount equal to the annual rate of duty applicable to the vehicle at the date on which the offence was committed or, where in the case of a vehicle kept on a public road that rate differs from the annual rate by reference to which the vehicle was at that date chargeable under section 1 of this Act in respect of the keeping thereof, equal to the last mentioned rate.

For the purposes of paragraph (*b*) above the offence shall, in the case of a conviction for a continuing offence, be taken to have been committed on the date or latest date to which the conviction relates.

[Section 8 is printed as amended by s 39 and Sched 7, para 6. Subsection (2) is accordingly omitted until such date as the Secretary of State for Transport may order. Section 8 is printed as further amended by the Criminal Justice Act 1982, ss 38, 46(1).

Section 1 of this Act relates to the charge to excise duty.]

9. Additional liability for keeping unlicensed vehicle

(1) Where a person convicted of an offence under section 8 of this Act is the person by whom the vehicle in respect of which the offence was committed was kept at the time it was committed, the court shall, in addition to any penalty which it may impose under that section, order him to pay an amount calculated in accordance with subsections (2) to (4) below.

(2) The said amount shall, subject to subsection (3) below, be an amount equal to [one-twelfth] of the annual rate of duty appropriate to the vehicle in question for each

[calendar month or part of a calendar month in the relevant period], and the relevant period shall be one ending with the date of the offence and beginning—

(*a*) if the person convicted has before that date notified the [Secretary of State for Transport] of his acquisition of the vehicle in accordance with regulations under this Act, with the date on which the notification was received by the [Secretary of State for Transport] or, if later, with the expiry of the vehicle licence last in force for the vehicle, or

(*b*) in any other case, with the expiry of the vehicle licence last in force for the vehicle before the date of the offence or, if there has not at any time before that date been a vehicle licence in force for the vehicle, with the date on which the vehicle was first kept by that person:

Provided that, where the person convicted has been ordered to pay an amount under this section on the occasion of a previous conviction in respect of the same vehicle, and the offence then charged was committed after the date specified above for the beginning of the relevant period, that period shall begin instead with the [calendar month immediately following that in which] the former offence was committed.

(3) Where the person convicted proves—

(*a*) that throughout any [month or part of a month] comprised in the relevant period the vehicle in question was not kept by him, or

(*b*) *[Repealed.]*

(*c*) *[Repealed.]*

(*d*) that he has paid duty in respect of the vehicle for any such [month or part], whether or not on a licence,

the said amount shall be calculated as if that [month or part] were not comprised in the relevant period.

(4) [In relation to any month or part of a month] comprised in the relevant period, the reference in subsection (2) above to the annual rate of duty appropriate to the vehicle in question is a reference to the annual rate applicable to it [at the beginning of that month or part]; and, except so far as it is proved to have fallen within some other description for the whole of any [such month or part], a vehicle shall be taken for the purposes of this section to have belonged throughout the relevant period to that description of vehicle to which it belonged for the purposes of duty at the date of the offence or, if the prosecution so elect, the date when a vehicle licence for it was last issued.

(5) Where, on a person's conviction of an offence under section 8 of this Act, an order is made under Part I of the Criminal Justice Act 1948 placing him on probation or discharging him absolutely or conditionally, the foregoing provisions of this section shall apply as if the conviction were deemed to be a conviction for all purposes.

(6) In the foregoing provisions of this section any reference to the expiry of a vehicle licence includes a reference to its surrender, and to its being treated as no longer in force for the purposes of section 8 of this Act by virtue of subsection (3)(*a*) of that section; and in the case of a conviction for a continuing offence, the offence shall be taken for the purposes of those provisions to have been committed on the date or latest date to which the conviction relates.

(7) The foregoing provisions of this section shall have effect subject to the provisions (applying with the necessary modifications) of any enactment relating to the imposition of fines by magistrates' courts, other than one conferring a discretion as to their amount; and any sum payable by virtue of an order under this section shall be

treated as a fine, and the order as a conviction, for the purposes of [Part III of the Magistrates' Courts Act 1980] (including any enactment having effect as if contained in that Part) and of any other enactment relating to the recovery or application of sums ordered to be paid by magistrates' courts.

(8) *[Application to Scotland.]*

[Section 9 is printed as amended by s 39 and Sched 7, para 7; the Secretary of State for Transport Order 1976 (SI 1976 No 1775); the Minister of Transport Order 1979 (SI 1979 No 571); the Magistrates' Courts Act 1980, s 154, and Sched 8, para 5; the Transfer of Functions (Transport) Order 1981 (SI 1981 No 238); the Finance Act 1987, s 2(6) and (8)(a) and Sched 1, Part III, para 8.

Several of the provisions in Part I of the Criminal Justice Act 1948 have been repealed by the Powers of Criminal Courts Act 1973. As to orders of probation and discharge under the 1973 Act, see (by virtue of Sched 4, para 1(b), to that Act) ss 2 to 13.]

10. Continuous liability for duty *[Omitted.]*

11. Provisions supplementary to s 10 *[Omitted.]*

Issue, exhibition, exchange, surrender etc of licences

12. Issue and exhibition of licences

(1)–(3) *[Omitted.]*

(4) Subject to the provisions of regulations under this Act, and without prejudice to section 8 thereof, any person who uses or keeps on a public road any mechanically propelled vehicle on which duty under this Act is chargeable without there being fixed to and exhibited on that vehicle in the prescribed manner a licence for, or in respect of the use of, that vehicle issued under this Act and for the time being in force shall be liable on summary conviction to a fine not exceeding [level 1 on the standard scale].

(5) . . .

(6), (7) *[Omitted.]*

[Section 12 is printed as amended by s 39 and Sched 7, para 9. Subsection (5) is accordingly omitted until such date as the Secretary of State for Transport may order. Section 12 is printed as further amended by the Criminal Justice Act 1982, ss 38, 46(1).

The amending provisions of the Criminal Justice Act 1982 referred to above would not have been applicable to s 12(4) if the penalty had been amended by the Criminal Law Act 1977, s 30 or s 31. (Section 30 of that Act relates to specified provisions of which s 12(4) is not one.) Section 31 of the 1977 Act provides (inter alia) for an increase in the penalty for any summary offence created under a pre-1949 enactment (which is defined as including enactments passed after 1 January 1949 which re-enact with or without modification pre-1949 enactments) in respect of which no 'alteration' had otherwise been made since the end of 1948. It is believed that s 31 of the 1977 Act did not affect the penalty enacted in s 12(4) of the Vehicles (Excise) Act 1971, since s 12(4) of the 1971 Act (notwithstanding the fact that it is a consolidation Act) does not re-enact with modification an enactment passed before 1 January 1949.

For the application of the fixed penalty procedure to offences under s 12(4), see the Road Traffic Offenders Act 1988, Part III, and Sched 3, above.]

* * *

16. Trade licences

(1) If a motor trader or a vehicle tester applies in the prescribed manner to the [Secretary of State for Transport] to take out a licence under this section (in this Act referred to as a 'trade licence')—

(i) in the case of a motor trader, for all mechanically propelled vehicles which are from time to time temporarily in his possession in the course of his business as a motor trader . . . ; or

(ii) in the case of a vehicle tester, for all mechanically propelled vehicles which are from time to time submitted to him for testing in the course of his business as a vehicle tester; or

(iii) in the case of a motor trader who is a manufacturer of mechanically propelled vehicles, for all vehicles kept and used by him solely for purposes of conducting research and development in the course of his business as such a manufacturer [and all vehicles which are from time to time submitted to him by other manufacturers for testing on roads in the course of that business],

the [Secretary of State for Transport] may, subject to the prescribed conditions, issue to him a trade licence on payment of duty at the rate applicable to the licence in accordance with the following provisions of this section:

Provided that the holder of a trade licence shall not be entitled by virtue of that licence—

(*a*) to use more than one mechanically propelled vehicle at any one time . . . ; or

(*b*) *[Repealed.]*

(*c*) [except in such circumstances as may be prescribed] to keep any vehicle on a road if it is not being used thereon.

[(1A) Subsection (1) above has effect in relation to an application made by a person who satisfies the Secretary of State that he intends to commence business as a motor trader or vehicle tester as it has effect in relation to an application made by the motor trader or vehicle tester.]

(2) Regulations shall be made under this section prescribing the conditions subject to which trade licences are to be issued and the purposes for which the holder of a trade licence may use a vehicle under the licence.

(3) The purposes which may be prescribed as those for which the holder of a trade licence may use a vehicle under the licence shall not include the conveyance of goods or burden of any description other than—

(*a*) a load which is carried solely for the purpose of testing or demonstrating the vehicle or any of its accessories or equipment and which is returned to the place of loading without having been removed from the vehicle except for such purpose or in the case of accident; or

(*b*) in the case of a recovery vehicle, any such load as is referred to in the definition of such a vehicle contained in subsection (8) below or a load consisting of a disabled vehicle; or

[(*bb*) in the case of a vehicle which is being delivered or collected, a load consisting of another vehicle used or to be used for travel from or to the place of delivery or collection or]

(*c*) any load built in as part of the vehicle or permanently attached thereto; or

(*d*) a load consisting of parts, accessories or equipment designed to be fitted to the vehicle and of tools for so fitting them; or (*e*) a load consisting of a trailer [other than a trailer which is for the time being a disabled vehicle];

and, for the purposes of this subsection, where a vehicle is so constructed that a trailer may by partial superimposition be attached to the vehicle in such a manner as to cause a substantial part of the weight of the trailer to be borne by the vehicle, the vehicle and the trailer shall be deemed to constitute a single vehicle.

[(4) [Subject to subsections (4A) and (4B) below, a trade licence may be taken out either for one calendar year or [for a period of six months beginning with the first day of January or of July].]

[(4A) A trade licence taken out by a person who is not a motor trader or vehicle tester (having satisfied the Secretary of State as mentioned in subsection (1A) above) shall be for a period of six months only.]

[(4B) The Secretary of State may require that a trade licence taken out by a motor trader or vehicle tester who does not hold any existing trade licence shall be for a period of six months only.]

[(5) The rate of duty applicable to a trade licence taken out for a calendar year shall be [£85] or, if the licence is to be used only for vehicles to which Schedule 1 to this Act relates, [£17]; and the rate of duty applicable to a licence taken out of a period of [six months] shall be [eleven twentieths] of the rate applicable to the corresponding trade licence taken out for a calendar year, any fraction of 5p being treated as 5p if it exceeds 2.5p but otherwise being disregarded.]

(6) Nothing in this section shall operate to prevent a person entitled to take out a trade licence from holding two or more trade licences.

(7) If any person holding a trade licence or trade licences issued under this section uses on a public road by virtue of that licence or those licences—

(i) a greater number of vehicles at any one time than he is authorised to use by virtue of that licence or those licences; or

(ii) any vehicle for any purpose other than such purposes as may have been prescribed under subsection (2) above;

or if that person uses that licence or any of those licences for the purpose of keeping on a road [in any circumstances other than such circumstances as may have been prescribed under paragraph (*c*) of the proviso to subsection (1) above] a vehicle which is not being used on that road, he shall be liable to the greater of the following penalties, namely—

(*a*) an excise of [level 3 on the standard scale]; or

(*b*) an excise penalty equal to five times the amount of the duty chargeable in respect of the vehicles or vehicles.

The amount of the duty chargeable in respect of a vehicle shall be calculated for the purposes of this subsection in the same manner as it is calculated for the purposes of section 8 of this Act by virtue of subsection (3) thereof.

(8) In this section—

['disabled vehicle' includes a vehicle which has been abandoned or is scrap;]

'motor trader' [means—

(*a*) a manufacturer or repairer of, or dealer in, mechanically propelled vehicles, or

(*b*) any person not falling within paragraph (*a*) above who carries on a business of such description as may be prescribed;

and a person shall be treated for the purposes of paragraph (*a*) above] as a dealer in such vehicles if he carries on a business consisting wholly or mainly of collecting and delivering mechanically propelled vehicles, and not including any other activities except activities as a manufacturer or repairer of, or dealer in, such vehicles;

'vehicle tester' means a person, other than a motor trader, who regularly in the course of his business engages in the testing on roads of mechanically propelled vehicles belonging to other persons; and

. . .

[Section 16 is printed as amended by s 39 and Sched 7, para 12; the Secretary of State for Transport Order 1976 (SI 1976 No 1775); the Finance Act 1977, s 5(3); the Minister of Transport Order 1979 (SI 1979 No 571); the Finance Act 1980, s 4(3); the Transfer of Functions (Transport) Order 1981 (SI 1981 No 238); the Criminal Justice Act 1982, ss 38, 46(1), 47(1); the Finance Act 1984; s 4(4); the Finance Act 1986, s 3(4), (6)–(8), and Sched 2, para 4; the Finance Act 1987, s 2(3) and (5)–(8) and Sched 1, Part II, para 5, and Part III, para 14.]

17. Surrender of licences *[Omitted.]*

18. Alteration of vehicle or of its use

(1) Subject to the provisions of this section, where a vehicle licence has been taken out for a vehicle at any rate under this Act and the vehicle is at any time while the licence is in force used in an altered condition or in a manner or for a purpose which brings it within, or which if it was used solely in that condition or in that manner or for that purpose would bring it within, a description of vehicle to which a higher rate of duty is applicable under this Act, duty at that higher rate shall become chargeable in respect of the licence for the vehicle.

(2), (3) *[Omitted.]*

(4) Where a vehicle licence has been taken out for a vehicle, and by reason of the vehicle being used as mentioned in subsection (1) above, a higher rate of duty becomes chargeable and duty at the higher rate was not paid before the vehicle was so used, the person so using the vehicle shall be liable to the greater of the following penalties, namely—

(*a*) an excise penalty of [level 3 on the standard scale]; or

(*b*) an excise penalty of an amount equal to five times the difference between the duty actually paid on the licence and the amount of the duty at that higher rate.

(5)–(9) *[Omitted.]*

[Section 18 is printed as amended by the Criminal Justice Act 1982, ss 38, 46(1), 47(1).]

[18A. Additional liability in relation to alteration of vehicle or its use

(1) Where a person convicted of an offence under section 18 of this Act is the person by whom the vehicle in respect of which the offence was committed was kept at the time it was committed, the court shall, in addition to any penalty which it may impose under that section, order him to pay an amount (the 'additional duty') calculated in accordance with this section.

(2) The additional duty shall, subject to subsections (7) and (8) below, be an

amount equal to [one-twelfth] of the appropriate annual rate of duty for each [calendar month or part of a calendar month in the relevant period].

(3) The following Cases are referred to in subsections (5) and (6) below—

CASE A

Where—

(*a*) at the time of the offence the vehicle in question had a plated weight (the 'higher plated weight') which exceeds the plated weight (the 'previous plated weight') which it had when the current licence was taken out; and

(*b*) the current licence was taken out at the rate of duty applicable to the previous plated weight.

CASE B

Where—

(*a*) the vehicle in question is a tractor unit (within the meaning of paragraph 15 of Schedule 4 to this Act);

(*b*) the current licence was taken out at a rate of duty applicable to the use of the vehicle only with semi-trailers having not less than two axles or, as the case may be, only with semi-trailers having not less than three axles; and

(*c*) the offence consisted in using the vehicle with a semi-trailer with a smaller number of axles than that mentioned in paragraph (*b*) above, in circumstances in which it was not treated by virtue of paragraph 14(2) of Schedule 4 to this Act as being licensed in accordance with the requirements of this Act.

CASE C

Where—

(*a*) the current licence was taken out at the rate of duty applicable, by virtue of paragraph 8 of Schedule 4 to this Act, to a weight lower than the plated weight of the vehicle in question; and

(*b*) the offence consisted in using the vehicle in contravention of a condition imposed by virtue of paragraph 8(3) of Schedule 4.

CASE D

Where the current licence was taken out at a rate of duty lower than that applicable to the vehicle in question by reference to its plated weight and the circumstances of the case do not bring it within Case A, B or C.

CASE E

Where the current licence was taken out at a rate of duty lower than that at which duty was chargeable in respect of that condition or manner of use of the vehicle which constituted the offence and the circumstances of the case do not bring it within Case A, B, C or D.

(4) In this section 'current licence' means the licence in relation to which the offence was committed.

(5) In this section 'appropriate annual rate of duty' means the difference between the rate of duty at which the current licence was taken out and—

(*a*) in Case A, the rate which would have been applicable had the current licence been taken out by reference to the higher plated weight;

(*b*) in Case B, the rate which would have been applicable had the current licence been taken out by reference to that use of the vehicle which constituted the offence;

(*c*) in Case C, the rate which would have been applicable had the current licence been taken out by reference to the plated weight of the vehicle;

(*d*) in Case D, the rate which would have been applicable had the current licence been taken out by reference to the plated weight of the vehicle; and

(*e*) in Case E, the rate which would have been applicable had the current licence been taken out by reference to that condition or use of the vehicle which constituted the offence.

(6) In this section 'relevant period' means the period ending with the day on which the offence was committed and beginning—

(*a*) in relation to Case A, with the day on which the vehicle in question was plated with the higher plated weight; and

(*b*) in relation to each of the other Cases, with the day on which the current licence first took effect.

(7) Where the person convicted proves—

(*a*) that throughout any [month or part of a month] comprised in the relevant period he was not the keeper of the vehicle in question; [or]

(*b*) *[Repealed.]*

(*c*) that he had, before his conviction, paid the higher of the two rates of duty referred to in the relevant paragraph of subsection (5) above in respect of the vehicle for any such [month or part], whether or not on a licence; . . .

(*d*) *[Repealed.]*

the additional duty shall be calculated as if that [month or part] were not comprised in the relevant period.

(8) Where a person is convicted of more than one contravention of section 18 of this Act in respect of the same vehicle (whether or not in the same proceedings) the court shall, in calculating the additional duty payable in respect of any one of those offences, reduce the amount calculated in accordance with the preceding provisions of this section in relation to a particular period by the amount of the additional duty ordered to be paid under this section in relation to that period in respect of the other offence or, as that case may be, offences.

(9) Except so far as it is proved to have fallen within some other description for the whole of [any month or part of a month comprised in the relevant period], the vehicle in question shall be taken for the purposes of this section to have belonged throughout the relevant period to that description of vehicle to which it belonged for the purposes of duty at the date of the offence.

(10) Where, on a person's conviction of an offence under section 18 of this Act, an order is made under Part I of the Powers of Criminal Courts Act 1973 placing him on probation or discharging him absolutely or conditionally, this section shall apply as if the conviction were deemed to be a conviction for all purposes.

(11) This section shall have effect subject to the provisions (applying with the necessary modifications) of any enactment relating to the imposition of fines by magistrates' courts, other than one conferring a discretion as to their amount; and any sum payable by virtue of an order under this section shall be treated as a fine, and the order as a conviction, for the purposes of Part III of the Magistrates' Courts Act 1980 (including any enactment having effect as if contained in that Part) and of any

other enactment relating to the recovery or application of sums ordered to be paid by magistrates' courts.

(12) *[Applies to Scotland.]*

(13) This section is subject to Schedule 7 to this Act.]

[Section 18A was inserted by the Finance Act 1982, s 7(1), and is printed as amended by Sched 7, para 17A, to the Vehicles (Excise) Act 1971 (para 17A having been inserted into Sched 7 by the Finance Act 1982, s 7(3)) and as subsequently amended by the Finance Act 1987, s 2(6) and (8) and Sched 1, Part III, para 10.]

Registration and registration marks, etc

19. Registration and registration marks *[Omitted.]*

20. Issue etc of vehicle registration marks by motor dealers *[Omitted.]*

21. Distinctive signs for hackney carriages *[Omitted.]*

22. Failure to fix, and obstruction of, marks and signs

(1) If any mark to be fixed or sign to be exhibited on a vehicle in accordance with section 19 or 21 of this Act is not so fixed or exhibited, the person driving the vehicle, or, where the vehicle is not being driven, the person keeping the vehicle, shall be guilty of an offence:

Provided that it shall be a defence for a person charged under this subsection with failing to fix a mark on a vehicle to prove—

(*a*) that he had no reasonable opportunity of registering the vehicle under this Act and that the vehicle was being driven on a public road for the purpose of being so registered; or

(*b*) in a case where the charge relates to a vehicle to which [section 47 of the Road Traffic Act 1988 applies by virtue of subsection (2)(*b*) thereof (vehicles manufactured before the prescribed period and used before registration)], that he had no reasonable opportunity of so registering the vehicle and that the vehicle was being driven on a road for the purposes of or in connection with its examination under [section 45 of the said Act of 1988 (examinations for test certificates) in circumstances in which its use is exempted from the said section 47(1) by regulations under section 47(6) thereof].

(2) If any mark fixed or sign exhibited on a vehicle as aforesaid is in any way obscured or rendered or allowed to become not easily distinguishable, the person driving the vehicle, or, where the vehicle is not being driven, the person keeping the vehicle, shall be guilty of an offence:

Provided that it shall be a defence for a person charged with such an offence to prove that he took all steps reasonably practicable to prevent the mark or sign being obscured or rendered not easily distinguishable.

(3) Any person guilty of an offence under this section shall be liable on summary conviction . . . to a fine not exceeding [level 3 on the standard scale].

[Section 22 is printed as amended by the Road Traffic Act 1972, s 203(1) and Sched 7; the Criminal Justice Act 1982, ss 38(4), 46(1) (this section fell within the term 'pre-1949 enactment' in the Criminal Law Act 1977, s 31(9), its pedigree being traceable back to the Roads Act 1920, ss 6(2), 11(1); accordingly, the '£20' in subs (3)(a) was increased to '£50' under s 31(5)(a), (6)(a) and (7) of the 1977 Act, notwithstanding the fact that this resulted in the same penalty being

applicable under subs (3)(a) (first conviction) and (3)(b) (subsequent conviction)); the Road Traffic (Consequential Provisions) Act 1988, s 4 and Sched 3, para 8(3).

For the application of the fixed penalty procedure to offences under subss (1) and (2), see the Road Traffic Offenders Act 1988, Part III, and Sched 3, above.]

* * *

Miscellaneous

* * *

26. Forgery and false information

(1) If any person forges or fraudulently alters or uses, or fraudulently lends or allows to be used by any other person—

(*a*) any mark to be fixed or sign to be exhibited on a mechanically propelled vehicle in accordance with section 19 or 21 of this Act; or

(*b*) any trade plates or replacements such as are mentioned in [section 23(2)(*c*)] of this Act; or

(*c*) any licence or registration document under this Act,

he shall be liable on summary conviction to a fine not exceeding [the prescribed sum] or on conviction on indictment to imprisonment for a term not exceeding two years.

(2) Any person who—

(*a*) in connection with an application for a licence . . . makes a declaration which to his knowledge is false or in any material respect misleading; or

(*b*) being required by virtue of this Act to furnish particulars relating to, or to the keeper of, any vehicle, furnishes any particulars which to his knowledge are false or in any material respect misleading,

shall be liable on summary conviction to a fine not exceeding [the prescribed sum] or on conviction on indictment to imprisonment for a term not exceeding two years.

[Section 26 is printed as amended by s 39 and Sched 7, para 23, and the Criminal Law Act 1977, s 28(2).

As to the 'prescribed sum', see the Magistrates' Courts Act 1980, s 32(9), above.]

27. Duty to give information

(1) Where it is alleged that a mechanically propelled vehicle has been used or kept in contravention of section 8, 16(7) or 18(4) of this Act—

(*a*) the person keeping the vehicle shall give such information as he may be required by or on behalf of a chief officer of police or the [Secretary of State for Transport] to give as to the identity of the person or persons concerned and, if he fails to do so, shall be guilty of an offence unless he shows to the satisfaction of the court that he did not know and could not with reasonable diligence have ascertained the identity of the person or persons concerned;

(*b*) any other person shall, if required as aforesaid, give such information as it is in his power to give and which may lead to the identification of any of the persons concerned and, if he fails to do so, shall be guilty of an offence; and

(*c*) in a case where it is alleged that the vehicle has been used at any time in contravention of the said section 8, the person who is alleged to have so used the vehicle shall, if required as aforesaid, give such information as it is in his power to give as to the identity of the person by whom the vehicle was kept at that time and, if he fails to do so, shall be guilty of an offence.

(2) The following persons shall be treated for the purposes of subsection (1)(*a*) and (*b*) above as persons concerned, that is to say—

(*a*) in relation to an alleged offence of using a vehicle in contravention of section 8, 16(7) or 18(4) of this Act, both the driver and any person using the vehicle;

(*b*) in relation to an alleged offence of keeping the vehicle in contravention of the said section 8, the person keeping the vehicle.

(3) A person guilty of an offence under subsection (1) of this section shall be liable on summary conviction to a fine not exceeding [level 3 on the standard scale].

[Section 27 is printed as amended by the Secretary of State for Transport Order 1976 (SI 1976 No 1775); the Minister of Transport Order 1979 (SI 1979 No 571); the Transfer of Functions (Transport) Order 1981 (SI 1981 No 238); and the Criminal Justice Act 1982, ss 38, 46(1).]

Legal proceedings, etc

28. Institution and conduct of proceedings in England and Wales

(1) Subject to the provisions of this section, summary proceedings for an offence under section 8, 11(2), 16(7), 18(4) or 26(1) or (2) of this Act or under regulations made in pursuance of this Act may be instituted in England and Wales by the [Secretary of State for Transport] or a constable (in this section severally referred to as 'the authorised prosecutor') at any time within six months from the date on which evidence sufficient in the opinion of the authorised prosecutor to warrant the proceedings came to his knowledge; but no proceedings for any offence shall be instituted by virtue of this subsection more than three years after the commission of the offence.

(2) No proceedings for an offence under section 8, 16(7) or 18(4) of this Act shall be instituted in England and Wales except by the authorised prosecutor; and no proceedings for such an offence shall be so instituted by a constable except with the approval of the [Secretary of State for Transport].

(3) A certificate stating—

(*a*) the date on which such evidence as is mentioned in subsection (1) above came to the knowledge of the authorised prosecutor; or

(*b*) that the [Secretary of State for Transport's] approval is given for the institution by a constable of any proceedings specified in the certificate,

and signed by or on behalf of the authorised prosecutor or, as the case may be, the [Secretary of State for Transport] shall for the purposes of this section be conclusive evidence of the date or approval in question; and a certificate purporting to be given in pursuance of this subsection and to be signed as aforesaid shall be deemed to be so signed unless the contrary is proved.

(4) In a magistrates' court or before the registrar of a county court any proceedings by or against the [Secretary of State for Transport] under this Act may be conducted on behalf of the [Secretary of State for Transport] by a person authorised by him for the purposes of this subsection.

(5) [Section 115 of the Customs and Excise Management Act 1979] (which restricts the bringing of proceedings under that Act) and [section 147(1)] of that Act (which extends the time for bringing such proceedings) shall not apply to proceedings in England and Wales for offences under this Act.

[Section 28 is printed as amended by the Secretary of State for Transport Order 1976 (SI 1976

No 1775); the Customs and Excise Management Act 1979, s 177(1) and Sched 4, para 12; the Minister of Transport Order 1979 (SI 1979 No 571); and the Transfer of Functions (Transport) Order 1981 (SI 1981 No 238).]

* * *

31. Admissibility of records as evidence

(1) A statement contained in a document purporting to be—

(*a*) a part of the records maintained by the [Secretary of State for Transport] in connection with any functions exercisable by the [Secretary of State for Transport] by virtue of this Act; or

(*b*) a copy of a document forming part of those records; or

(*c*) a note of any information contained in those records,

and to be authenticated by a person authorised in that behalf by the [Secretary of State for Transport] shall be admissible in any proceedings as evidence of any fact stated therein to the same extent as oral evidence of that fact is admissible in those proceedings.

(2) In subsection (1) above 'document' and 'statement' have the same meanings as in subsection (1) of section 10 of the Civil Evidence Act 1968 [*qv*], and the reference to a copy of a document shall be construed in accordance with subsection (2) of that section; but nothing in this subsection shall be construed as limiting to civil proceedings the references to proceedings in subsection (1) above.

(3) Nothing in the foregoing provisions of this section shall enable evidence to be given with respect to any matter other than a matter of the prescribed description.

(4) *[Applies to Scotland.]*

[Section 31 is printed as amended by the Secretary of State for Transport Order 1976 (SI 1976 No 1775); the Minister of Transport Order 1979 (SI 1979 No 571); and the Transfer of Functions (Transport) Order 1981 (SI 1981 No 238).]

32. Evidence of admissions in certain proceedings

Where in any proceedings in England and Wales for an offence under section 8 or section 16(7) of this Act—

(*a*) it is proved to the satisfaction to the court, on oath or in manner prescribed by rules made under section 15 of the Justices of the Peace Act 1949, that a requirement under section 27(1)(*a*) or (*b*) of this Act to give information as to the identity of the driver of, or the person using or keeping, a particular vehicle on the particular occasion on which the offence is alleged to have been committed has been served on the accused by post; and

(*b*) a statement in writing is produced to the court purporting to be signed by the accused that the accused was the driver of, or the person using or keeping, that vehicle on that occasion,

the court may accept the statement as evidence that the accused was the driver of, or the person using or keeping, that vehicle on that occasion.

33. Burden of proof in certain proceedings

If in any proceedings under section 8, 16(7) or 26(2) of this Act any question arises—

(*a*) as to the number of mechanically propelled vehicles used, or (*b*) as to the character, weight, horse-power or cylinder capacity of any mechanically propelled vehicle, or

(*c*) as to the number of persons for which a mechanically propelled vehicle has seating capacity, or

(*d*) as to the purpose for which any mechanically propelled vehicle has been used,

the burden of proof in respect of the matter in question shall lie on the defendant.

34. Fixing of amount payable under s 9 on plea of guilty by absent accused

Where in pursuance of [section 12(2) of the Magistrates' Courts Act 1980] a person is convicted in his absence of an offence under section 8 of this Act and it is proved to the satisfaction of the court, on oath or in the manner prescribed by rules made under [section 44 of the Magistrates' Courts Act 1980], that there was served on the accused with the summons a notice stating that, in the event of his being convicted of the offence, it will be alleged that an order requiring him to pay an amount specified in the notice falls to be made by the court in pursuance of section 9(1) of this Act then, unless in the notification purporting to be given by or on behalf of the accused in pursuance of [the said section 12(2)] it is stated that the amount so specified is inappropriate, the court shall proceed in pursuance of the said section 9(1) as if that amount had been calculated as required by that subsection.

[Section 34 is printed as amended by the Magistrates' Courts Act 1980, s 154(1), and Sched 7, para 93.]

* * *

37. Regulations

(1), (2) *[Omitted.]*

[(3) Any person who contravenes or fails to comply with any regulations under this Act (other than regulations under section 2(5), 11(3), 14, 20 or 24) shall be guilty of an offence and liable on summary conviction—

(*a*) in the case of regulations prescribed for the purposes of this paragraph, to a fine not exceeding level 3 on the standard scale; and

(*b*) in any other case, to a fine not exceeding level 2 on the standard scale.]

[(3A) Regulations under section 14, 20 or 24 above may provide that a person who contravenes or fails to comply with any specified provision of the regulations shall be guilty of an offence and a person guilty of such an offence shall be liable on summary conviction—

(*a*) in the case of regulations under section 14 or 20, to a fine not exceeding level 1 on the standard scale; and

(*b*) in the case of regulations under section 24, to a fine not exceeding level 3 on the standard scale.]

[(3B) The prescribing of regulations for the purposes of subsection (3)(*a*) above shall not affect the punishment for a contravention of or failure to comply with those regulations before they were so prescribed.]

(4), (5) *[Omitted.]*

[Section 37 is printed as amended by s 39 of and Sched 7, Part I, para 24, to this Act, and as subsequently amended by the Finance Act 1987, s 2(6) and (8) and Sched 1, Part III, para 18(4).

Sections 2(5), 11(3), 14, 20 and 24 of this Act (to which reference is made in s 37(3) above) are not currently in force; see s 39 and Sched 7, Part I.

The Road Vehicles (Prescribed Regulations for the Purposes of Increased Penalties) Regulations 1987 (SI 1987 No 2085) (qv) were made under s 37(3)(a) above.]

38. Interpretation

(1) In this Act, unless the context otherwise requires—

['conditional sale agreement' means an agreement for the sale of a vehicle under which the purchase price or part of it is payable by instalments, and the property in the vehicle is to remain in the seller (notwithstanding that the buyer is to be in possession of the vehicle) until such conditions as may be specified in the agreement are fulfilled;]

'gas' means any fuel which is wholly gaseous at a temperature of 60 degrees Fahrenheit under a pressure of 30 inches of mercury;

['hackney carriage' means a mechanically propelled vehicle standing or plying for hire and includes any mechanically propelled vehicle bailed or (in Scotland) hired under a hire agreement by a person whose trade it is to sell such vehicles or bail or hire them under hire agreements;]

['hire agreement' means an agreement for the bailment or (in Scotland) the hiring of a vehicle which is not a hire-purchase agreement;]

['hire-purchase agreement' means an agreement, other than a conditional sale agreement, under which—

(*a*) a vehicle is bailed or (in Scotland) hired in return for periodical payments by the person to whom it is bailed or hired, and

(*b*) the property in the vehicle will pass to that person if the terms of the agreement are complied with and one or more of the following occurs—

(i) the exercise of an option to purchase by that person,

(ii) the doing of any other specified act by any party to the agreement,

(iii) the happening of any other specified event;]

'licence' means a vehicle licence or a trade licence;

'motor dealer' means a person carrying on the business of selling or supplying mechanically propelled vehicles;

'prescribed' means prescribed by regulations made by the Secretary of State;

'public road' means a road which is repairable at the public expense;

. . .

'temporary licence' has the meaning assigned to it by section 13(1) of this Act;

'trade licence' means a licence issued under section 16(1) of this Act; and

'transfer date' has the same meaning as in the Vehicle and Driving Licences Act 1969, that is to say, such date as the Secretary of State may by order appoint for the purposes of section 1(1) of that Act;

'vehicle licence' means a licence under this Act for a mechanically propelled vehicle.

(2) For the purposes of any provision of this Act and any subsequent enactment relating to the keeping of mechanically propelled vehicles on public roads, a person keeps such a vehicle on a public road if he causes it to be on such a road for any period, however short, when it is not in use there.

(3) A mechanically propelled vehicle shall not be treated as an electrically propelled vehicle for the purposes of this Act unless the electrical motive power is derived either from a source external to the vehicle or from any electrical storage battery which is not connected to any source of power when the vehicle is in motion.

(4) References in this Act [, except in Schedule 4,] to the unladen weight of any mechanically propelled vehicle shall be construed in accordance with the provisions of Schedule 6 to this Act.

(5) The unit of horse-power or cylinder capacity for the purposes of any rate of duty under this Act shall be calculated in accordance with regulations under this Act.

(6) References in this Act to any enactment shall be construed, unless the context otherwise requires, as references to that enactment as amended by or under any other enactment.

[Section 38 is printed as amended by the Consumer Credit Act 1974, s 192(3) and Sched 4, para 32; the Finance Act 1982, s 5(6); the Finance Act 1988, s 145 and Sched 2, Part II.]

* * *

SCHEDULE 1

Annual Rates of Duty on Certain Vehicles not Exceeding [425 kg] in Weight Unladen

[Omitted.]

SCHEDULE 2

Annual Rates of Duty on Hackney Carriages

[Omitted.]

SCHEDULE 3

Annual Rates of Duty on Tractors, etc

PART I

1. The annual rate of duty applicable to a mechanically propelled vehicle of a description specified in the first column of Part II of this Schedule shall, according to the unladen weight of the vehicle as set out in the second and third columns of that Table, be the initial rate specified in relation to vehicles of that description and that weight in the fourth column of that Table together with any additional rate so specified in the fifth column of that Table.

2.—(1) In this Schedule 'agricultural machine' means a locomotive ploughing engine, tractor, agricultural tractor or other agricultural engine which is not used on public roads for hauling any objects, except as follows, that is to say—

(*a*) for hauling its own necessary gear, threshing appliances, farming implements, a living van for the accommodation of persons employed in connection with the vehicle, or supplies of water or fuel required for the purposes of the vehicle or for agricultural purposes;

(*b*) for hauling, from one part of a farm to another part of that farm, agricultural or woodland produce of, or articles required for, the farm;

(*c*) for hauling, within 15 miles of a farm in the occupation of the person in whose name the vehicle is registered under this Act, agricultural or woodland produce of that farm, or agricultural or woodland produce of land occupied with that farm, or fuel required for any purpose on that farm or for domestic purposes by persons employed on that farm by the occupier of the farm;

(*d*) for hauling articles required for a farm by the person in whose name the vehicle is registered as aforesaid, being either the owner or occupier of the farm or a contractor engaged to do agricultural work on the farm by the owner or occupier of the farm, or for hauling articles required by that person for land occupied by him with a farm;

(*e*) for hauling, within 15 miles of a forestry estate in the occupation of the person in whose name the vehicle is registered as aforesaid, agricultural or woodland produce of that estate or fuel required for any purpose on that estate or for domestic purposes by persons employed on that estate by the occupier of the estate, or for hauling articles required for such a forestry estate by the occupier of the estate:

(*f*) for hauling, within 15 miles of a farm in the occupation of the person in whose name the vehicle is registered as aforesaid, material to be spread on roads to deal with frost, ice or snow;

(*g*) for hauling, for the purpose of clearing snow, a snow plough or similar contrivance.

(2) In this paragraph—

(*a*) any reference to a farm includes a market garden;

(*b*) any reference to woodland produce includes the wood and other produce of trees which are not woodland trees;

(*c*) any reference to articles required for a farm, forestry estate or other land includes articles which are or have been required for doing work on and for the purposes of the farm, forestry estate or other land, except that—

(i) the reference to articles required for a farm by a contractor engaged to do agricultural work on the farm shall include only articles required for the farm in connection with that work, and

(ii) the reference to articles required for land occupied with a farm shall include only articles required for the land in connection with the doing on the land of any agricultural or forestry work (including the getting and carrying away of any woodland produce);

(*d*) any reference to the owner of a farm includes any person having any estate or interest in land comprised in the farm.

3. In this Schedule 'digging machine' means a vehicle designed, constructed and used for the purpose of trench digging or any kind of excavating or shovelling work which—

(*a*) is used on public roads only for that purpose or for the purpose of proceeding to and from the place where it is to be used for that purpose; and

(*b*) when so proceeding, neither carries nor hauls any load than such as is necessary for its propulsion or equipment.

4. In this Schedule 'mobile crane' means a vehicle designed and constructed as a mobile crane which—

(*a*) is used on public roads only either as a crane in connection with work being carried on on a site in the immediate vicinity or for the purpose of proceeding to and from a place where it is to be used as a crane; and

(*b*) when so proceeding neither carries nor hauls any load than such as is necessary for its propulsion or equipment.

5. In this Schedule 'works truck' means a goods vehicle (within the meaning of Schedule 4 to this Act) designed for use in private premises and used on public roads only for carrying goods between such premises and a vehicle on a road in the immediate vicinity, or in passing from one part of any such premises to another or to other private premises in the immediate vicinity, or in connection with road works while at or in the immediate vicinity of the site of such works.

[5A. In this Schedule 'fisherman's tractor' means a tractor registered under this Act in the name of a person engaged in the business of sea fishing for food and not used on public roads for hauling anything except—

(*a*) a fishing boat and anything (including the catch) carried in it, which belongs to that person or to him and other persons engaged in that business in the same locality;

(*b*) fishing tackle or other equipment required by the crew, or for the operation, of any such boat;

(*c*) fishing tackle or other equipment required for and the catch from, fishing operations carried out with the tractor.]

[Paragraph 5A was inserted by the Finance Act 1976, s 11(2).]

6. In this Schedule 'haulage vehicle' means a vehicle (other than one [to which Schedule 4A to this Act applies or which is] described in any of the foregoing paragraphs [or paragraph 8 below]) which is constructed and used on public roads for haulage solely and not for the purpose of carrying or having superimposed upon it any load except such as is necessary for its propulsion or equipment.

[Paragraph 6 is printed as amended by the Finance Act 1988, s 4(3)(a), (7) and (9) and Sched 2, Part II, para 3.]

7. In this Schedule 'showman's vehicle' means a vehicle registered under this Act in the name of a person following the business of a travelling showman and used solely by him for the purposes of his business and for no other purpose.

[8.—(1) In this Schedule 'recovery vehicle' means, subject to the provisions of this paragraph, a vehicle which is either constructed or permanently adapted primarily for the purposes of lifting, towing and transporting a disabled vehicle or for any one or more of those purposes.

(2) Subject to sub-paragraph (3) below, a vehicle which is constructed or permanently adapted as mentioned in sub-paragraph (1) above shall not be a recovery vehicle if at any time it is used for any purpose other than—

(*a*) the recovery of a disabled vehicle;

(*b*) the removal of a disabled vehicle from the place where it became disabled to premises at which it is to be repaired or scrapped;

(*c*) the removal of a disabled vehicle from premises to which it was taken for repair to other premises at which it is to be repaired or scrapped;

(*d*) carrying any load other than fuel and other liquids required for its propulsion and tools and other articles required for the operation of or in connection with apparatus designed to lift, tow or transport a disabled vehicle; [and]

[(*e*) any purpose prescribed for the purposes of this sub-paragraph].

(3) At any time when a vehicle is being used for purposes specified in paragraphs (*a*) and (*b*) of sub-paragraph (2) above, the following uses shall be disregarded in determining whether the vehicle is a recovery vehicle—

(*a*) use for the carriage of any person who immediately before a vehicle became disabled, was the driver of or a passenger in that vehicle;

(*b*) use for the carriage of any goods which, immediately before a vehicle became disabled, were being carried in the disabled vehicle; and

(*c*) use for any purpose prescribed for the purposes of this [sub-paragraph].]

[(4) A vehicle which is constructed or permanently adapted as mentioned in sub-paragraph (1) above shall not be a recovery vehicle if at any time the number of vehicles which it is used to recover exceeds a number specified by an order of the Secretary of State made for the purposes of this sub-paragraph.]

[(5) *[Omitted.]*]

[Paragraph 8 was inserted by the Finance Act 1987, s 2(5) and (7) and Sched 1, Part II, para 2, and is printed as subsequently amended by the Finance Act 1988, s 4(3)(b) to (d).

The definition of 'recovery vehicle' in para 8 above has been incorporated by reference into the Goods Vehicles (Operators' Licences, Qualifications and Fees) Regulations 1984 (SI 1984 No 176), reg 3(1) (qv).

The Recovery Vehicles (Prescribed Purposes) Regulations 1987 (SI 1987 No 2120) (qv) were made under para 8(3)(c).]

PART II

	Weight unladen of vehicle		Rate of duty	
1. Description of vehicle	2. Exceeding	3. Not exceeding	4. Initial	5. Additional for each ton or part of a ton in excess of the weight in column 2
			£	£
1. Agricultural machines; digging machines; mobile cranes; works trucks; mowing machines; fishermen's tractors.	—	—	16.00	—
2. Haulage vehicles, being showmen's vehicles.	—	$7\frac{1}{4}$ tons	151.00	—
	$7\frac{1}{4}$ tons	8 tons	180.00	—
	8 tons	10 tons	212.00	—
	10 tons	—	212.00	32.50
3. Haulage vehicles, not being showmen's vehicles.	—	2 tons	179.00	—
	2 tons	4 tons	322.00	—
	4 tons	6 tons	465.00	—
	6 tons	$7\frac{1}{4}$ tons	608.00	
	$7\frac{1}{4}$ tons	8 tons	743.00	—
	8 tons	9 tons	869.00	—
	9 tons	10 tons	995.00	—
	10 tons	11 tons	1138.00	—
	11 tons	—	1138.00	—]
[4. Recovery vehicles	—	—	50	—]

[Part II of Sched 3 is printed as substituted by the Finance Act 1985, s 4(2), (8) and Sched 2, Part I and as subsequently amended by the Finance Act 1987, s 2(5) and (7) and Sched 1, Part II, para 3.]

[SCHEDULE 4

Annual Rates of Duty on Goods Vehicles

PART I

* * *

Special types of vehicles

5.—(1) This paragraph applies to a goods [vehicle (other than, in the case of a vehicle falling within paragraph (*a*) below, one of a prescribed class) which has an unladen weight exceeding 1,525 kilograms; and

(*a*) which has, for the purposes of this Schedule, a plated gross weight or plated train weight by virtue only of paragraph 9(2A)(*c*) below; or

(*b*)] which is for the time being authorised for use on roads by virtue of an order under section 42 of that Act (authorisation of special vehicles).

(2)–(5) [*Provide the annual rates of duty.*]

[Paragraph 5 is printed as substituted by the Finance Act 1982, s 5(4) and Sched 5, Part A, and as subsequently amended by the Finance Act 1983, s 4(3) and Sched 3, Part II, para 9.
This paragraph is incorporated by reference into Sched 4A, para 3, to this Act.]

* * *

Plated and unladen weights

9.—(1) Any reference in this Schedule to the plated gross weight of a goods vehicle or trailer is a reference—

(*a*) to that [weight], which is the maximum gross weight which may not be exceeded in Great Britain for the vehicle or trailer in question [as indicated on the appropriate plate]; or

(*b*) in the case of any trailer which may lawfully be used in Great Britain without [such a plate], to the maximum laden weight at which the trailer may lawfully be used in Great Britain.

(2) Any reference in this Schedule to the plated train weight of a vehicle is a reference to that [weight], which is the maximum gross weight which may not be exceeded in Great Britain for an articulated vehicle consisting of the vehicle in question and any semi-trailer which may be drawn by it [as indicated on the appropriate plate].

[(2A) In this paragraph 'appropriate plate', in relation to a vehicle or trailer, means—

(*a*) where a Ministry plate (within the meaning of regulations made under [section 41 or 49 of the Road Traffic Act 1988]) has been issued, or has effect as if issued, for the vehicle or trailer following the issue or amendment of a plating certificate (within the meaning of Part II of that Act), that plate;

(*b*) where paragraph (*a*) does not apply, but such a certificate is in force for the vehicle or trailer, that certificate; and

(*c*) where neither paragraph (*a*) nor paragraph (*b*) above applies but the vehicle or trailer has been equipped with a plate in accordancce with regulations made under [section 41 of the Act of 1988], that plate.]

(3) A mechanically propelled vehicle which—

(*a*) is constructed or adapted for use and used for the conveyance of a machine or contrivance and no other load except articles used in connection with the machine or contrivance; and

(*b*) is not a vehicle for which an annual rate of duty is specified in Schedule 3 to this Act; and

(*c*) has neither a plated gross weight nor a plated train weight,

shall, notwithstanding that the machine or contrivance is built in as part of the vehicle, be chargeable with duty at the rate which would be applicable if the machine or contrivance were burden.

[Paragraph 9 is printed as substituted by the Finance Act 1982, s 5(4) and Sched 5, Part A, and as subsequently amended by the Finance Act 1983, s 4(3) and Sched 3, Part II, paras 10 and 11; the Road Traffic (Consequential Provisions) Act 1988, s 4 and Sched 3, para 8(4)(a).]

* * *

Interpretation

15.—(1) In this Schedule, unless the context otherwise requires—

. . .

'goods vehicle' means [subject to sub-paragraph (1A) below] a mechanically propelled vehicle (including a tricycle as defined in Schedule 1 to this Act and weighing more than 425 kilograms unladen) constructed or adapted for use and used for the conveyance of goods or burden of any description whether in the course of trade or otherwise;

. . .

'showman's goods vehicle' means a showman's vehicle which is a goods vehicle and is permanently fitted with a living van or some other special type of body or superstructure, forming part of the equipment of the show of the person in whose name the vehicle is registered under this Act;

'showman's vehicle' has the name meaning as in Schedule 3 to this Act;

. . .

'tower wagon' means a goods vehicle—

(*a*) into which there is built, as part of the vehicle, any expanding or extensible contrivance designed for facilitating the erection, inspection, repair or maintenance of overhead structures or equipment; and

(*b*) which is neither constructed nor adapted for use nor used for the conveyance of any load, except such a contrivance and article used in connection therewith;

. . .

[(1A) In this Schedule 'goods vehicle' does not include a vehicle to which Schedule 4A to this Act applies.]

(2) *[Omitted.]]*

* * *

[The provisions of para 15 which are set out above are printed as substituted by the Finance Act 1982, s 5(4) and Sched 5, Part A (which substituted the whole of Sched 4), and as subsequently amended by the Finance Act 1988, s 4(7) and (9) and Sched 2, Part II, para 4.

The definition of 'showman's goods vehicle' is incorporated by reference into the Goods Vehicles

(Operators' Licences, Qualifications and Fees) Regulations 1984 (SI 1984 No 176) (qv) and the Goods Vehicles (Plating and Testing) Regulations 1988 (SI 1988 No 1478), (qv).]

[SCHEDULE 4A

ANNUAL RATES OF DUTY ON VEHICLES USED FOR CARRYING OR DRAWING EXCEPTIONAL LOADS

1. This Schedule applies to a vehicle—

(*a*) which is a heavy motor car used for the carriage of exceptional loads; or

(*b*) which is a heavy locomotive, light locomotive or motor tractor used to draw trailers carrying such loads,

and which, when so used, is authorised for use on roads by virtue of an order under [section 44 of the Road Traffic Act 1988].

2. *[Annual rate of duty.]*

3. Where a vehicle—

(*a*) to which this Schedule applies; and

(*b*) which would, but for paragraphs 5 and 15(1A) of Schedule 4 to this Act, be a goods vehicle of a description to which a highter rate of duty is applicable under this act,

is at any time used on roads otherwise than as mentioned in paragraph 1 above, section 18 of this Act shall apply as if that vehicle were then being used in a manner or for a purpose which brings it within that description of vehicle.

4. In this Schedule—

'exceptional load' means a load which—

(*a*) by reason of its dimensions, cannot be carried by a heavy motor car or trailer, or a combination of a heavy motor car and trailer, which (in either case) complies in all respects with requirements of regulations under [section 41 of the Road Traffic Act 1988]; or

(*b*) by reason of its weight, cannot be carried by a heavy motor car or trailer, or a combination of a heavy motor car and trailer, which (in either case) has a total laden weight of not more than the specified amount and complies in all respects with such requirements;

'specified amount' means—

(*a*) in relation to any time before 1st October 1989, 32,520 kilograms;

(*b*) in relation to any time on or after that date, 38,000 kilograms;

and other expressions which are also used in [the Road Traffic Act 1988] have the same meanings as in that Act.]

[Schedule 4A was inserted by the Finance Act 1988, s 4(7) and (9) and Sched 2, Part II, para 5, and is printed as amended by the Interpretation Act 1978, s 17(2)(a).]

SCHEDULE 5

ANNUAL RATES OF DUTY ON VEHICLES NOT FALLING WITHIN SCHEDULES 1 TO 4 TO THIS ACT

[Omitted.]

SCHEDULE 6

Provisions as to the Computation of the Unladen Weight of Vehicles

[Omitted.]

SCHEDULE 7

Transitional Provisions

[Omitted.]

SCHEDULE 8

Repeals and Revocation

[Omitted.]

The Wireless Telegraphy Act 1949

(12, 13 & 14 Geo 6 c 54)

An Act to amend the Law relating to wireless telegraphy.

[30 July 1949]

*   *   *

19. Interpretation

(1) In this Act, except where the context otherwise requires, the expression 'wireless telegraphy' means the emitting or receiving, over paths which are not provided by any material substance constructed or arranged for that purpose, of electromagnetic energy of a frequency not exceeding three million megacycles a second, being energy which either—

(*a*) serves for the conveying of messages, sound or visual images (whether the messages, sound or images are actually received by any person or not), or for the actuation or control of machinery of apparatus; or

(*b*) is used in connection with the determination of position, bearing, or distance, or for the gaining of information as to the presence, absence, position or motion of any object or of any objects of any class.

and references to stations for wireless telegraphy and apparatus for wireless telegraphy or wireless telegraphy apparatus shall be construed as references to stations and apparatus for the emitting or receiving as aforesaid of such electromagnetic energy as aforesaid: . . .

(2)–(10) *[Omitted.]*

[Section 19 is printed as amended by the Cable and Broadcasting Act 1984, s 57(2) and Sched 6.

The definition of 'wireless telegraphy' is incorporated by reference into the Public Service Vehicles (Conduct of Drivers, Conductors and Passengers) Regulations 1936 (S R & O 1936 No 619), reg 2.]

*   *   *

Section B

Statutory Instruments

The Community Drivers' Hours and Recording Equipment (Exemptions and Supplementary Provisions) Regulations 1986

(SI 1986 No 1456)

[The text of these regulations is printed as amended by:
the Community Drivers' Hours and Recording Equipment (Exemptions and Supplementary Provisions) (Amendment) Regulations 1986 (SI 1986 No 1669) (26 October 1986);
the Community Drivers' Hours and Recording Equipment (Exemptions and Supplementary Provisions) (Amendment) Regulations 1987 (SI 1987 No 805) (1 June 1987); and
the Community Drivers' Hours and Recording Equipment (Exemptions and Supplementary Provisions) (Amendment) Regulations 1988 (SI 1988 No 760) (20 May 1988).
The amending regulations are referred to in the notes to the main regulations by their years and numbers. The dates referred to above are the dates on which the regulations came into force.]

1. Citation, commencement, interpretation and revocation

(1) *[Omitted.]*

(2) In these Regulations—

'the Community Drivers' Hours Regulations' means Council Regulation (EEC) No 3820/85 of 20th December 1985 on the harmonisation of certain social legislation relating to road transport [*qv*];

'the Community Recording Equipment Regulation' means Council Regulation (EEC) No 3821/85 of 20th December 1985 on recording equipment in road transport [*qv*];

'permissible maximum weight' has the same meaning as in [section 108 of the Road Traffic Act 1988].

(3) Subject to paragraph (2) above, any expression used in these Regulations which is used in the Community Drivers' Hours Regulation has the same meaning as in that Regulation.

(4) *[Revocations.]*

[Regulation 1 is printed as amended by the Interpretation Act 1978, ss 17(2)(a) and 23(1).]

2. Exemption from the Community Drivers' Hours Regulation

[(1) Pursuant to Article 13(1) of the Community Drivers' Hours Regulation, exemption is granted from all the provisions of that Regulation, except Article 5 (minimum ages for drivers) in respect of any vehicle falling within a description specified in Part I of the Schedule to these Regulations.

(2) Pursuant to Article 13(2) of the Community Drivers' Hours Regulation, exemption is granted from all the provision of that Regulation, except Article 5, in respect of any vehicle falling within a description specified in Part II of the Schedule to these Regulations.]

[Regulation 2 is printed as substituted by SI 1987 No 805.]

3. Supplementary provisions relating to the Community Drivers' Hours Regulation

(1) Pursuant to Article 6(1) of the Community Drivers' Hours Regulation, the application of the fourth sub-paragraph of that Article shall be extended to national passenger services other than regular passenger services.

(2) Pursuant to Article 7(3) of the Community Drivers' Hours Regulation, if—

(*a*) the driver of a vehicle which is engaged in the national carriage of passengers on a regular service observes in a relevant area, immediately after any period of driving not exceeding four hours, a break of a least 30 minutes; and

(*b*) it was not possible for him to observe, at any time during that period of driving, a break of at least 15 minutes,

that period of driving shall be disregarded for the purposes of Article 7(1) of that Regulation.

(3) In paragraph (2) above 'relevant area', in relation to the driver of a vehicle which is engaged in the national carriage of passengers on a regular service, means any of the following areas, namely—

(*a*) The London Borough of Camden;

(*b*) the Royal Borough of Kensington and Chelsea;

(*c*) the London Borough of Islington;

(*d*) the City of Westminister,

[(*e*) in the City of Birmingham, an area comprising Digbeth Coach Station, Rea Street, Bradford Street, Barford Street, Cheapside and Birchall Street;]

[(*f*) in the City of Bristol an area comprising Marlborough Street Coach Station, Marlborough Street, Maudlin Street, Lower Maudlin Street, Earl Street and Whitson Street;]

[(*g*) in the City of Leeds an area comprising Wellington Street Coach Station, Wellington Street, York Place, Queen Street, Little Queen Street and King Street;]

[(*h*) in the City of Leicester, an area comprising St Margaret's Bus Station, Abbey Street, Gravel Street, Church Gate, Mansfield Street, Sandacre Street, New Road, Burleys Way and St Margaret's Way;]

[(*i*) in the City of Nottingham, an area comprising Victoria Bus Station, Glasshouse Street, Huntingdon Street, York Street, Cairns Street, Woodborough Road, Mansfield Road, Milton Street, Lower Parliament Street and Union Road; and]

[(*j*) in the City of Oxford an area comprising Oxpens Coach Park, Oxpens Road, Thames Street and Holybush Hill,]

in which passengers are taken up or set down in the course of the service.

[Regulation 3 is printed as amended by SI 1986 No 1669.]

4. Exemption from the Community Recording Equipment Regulation

[(1) Pursuant to Article 3(2) of the Community Recording Equipment Regulation, exemption is granted from the provisions of that Regulation in respect of any vehicle falling within a description specified in Part I of the Schedule to these Regulations.

(2) Pursuant to Article 3(3) of the Community Recording Equipment Regulation, exemption is granted from the provisions of that Regulation in respect of:

(*a*) any vehicle falling within a description specified in Part II of the Schedule to these Regulations; and

(*b*) any vehicle which is being used for collecting sea coal.]

[Regulation 4 is printed as substituted by SI 1987 No 805.]

5. Application of the Community Recording Equipment Regulation

(1) Pursuant to Article 3(4) of the Community Recording Equipment Regulation, that Regulation shall apply (notwithstanding the exception in Article 3(1)) to vehicles used for the carriage of postal articles on national transport operations except—

(*a*) vehicles which have a permissible maximum weight which does not exceed 3.5 tonnes; and

(*b*) vehicles which are being used by the Post Office in connection with the carriage of letters.

(2) In paragraph (1) above 'letter' has the same meaning as in the Post Office Inland Post Scheme 1979.

(3) This Regulation shall not have effect—

(*a*) before 1st April 1988 in relation to vehicles which have a permissible maximum weight of 7.5 tonnes or more; or

(*b*) before 1st January 1990 in relation to vehicles which have a permissible maximum weight which exceeds 3.5 tonnes but which is less than 7.5 tonnes.

SCHEDULE

EXEMPTED VEHICLES

[PART I

VEHICLES EXEMPTED BY REGULATIONS 2(1) AND 4(1)]

[The text of the original Schedule was designated as Part I (and Part II of the Schedule was added) by SI 1987 No 805, which also substituted the heading to what is now Part I.]

1. Any vehicle used for the carriage of passengers which is by virtue of its construction and equipment suitable for carrying not more than 17 persons including the driver and is intended for that purpose.

2.—(1) Any vehicle which, on or after 1st January 1990, is being used by a public authority to provide public services otherwise than in competition with professional road hauliers.

(2) A vehicle does not fall within the description specified in this paragraph unless the vehicle—

(*a*) is being used by a health authority in England and Wales or a Health Board in Scotland or the Common Services Agency for the Scottish Health Service—

(i) to provide ambulance services in pursuance of its duty under the National Health Service Act 1977 or the National Health Service (Scotland) Act 1978; or

(ii) to carry staff, patients, medical supplies or equipment in pursuance of its general duties under that Act;

(*b*) is being used by a local authority for the purposes of the Local Authority Social

Services Act 1970 or the Social Work (Scotland) Act 1968 to provide, in the exercise of social services functions—

(i) services for old persons; or

(ii) services for persons to whom section 29 of the National Assistance Act 1948 (welfare arrangements for physically and mentally handicapped persons) applies;

(*c*) is being used by Her Majesty's Coastguard, a general lighthouse authority or a local lighthouse authority;

(*d*) is being used by a harbour authority within the limits of a harbour for the improvement, maintenance or management of which the authority is responsible;

(*e*) is being used by an airports authority within the perimeter of an airport owned or managed by the authority;

(*f*) is being used by the British Railways Board, London Regional Transport, any wholly owned subsidiary of London Regional Transport, a Passenger Transport Executive or a local authority for the purpose of maintaining railways; or

(*g*) is being used by the British Waterways Board for the purpose of maintaining navigable waterways.

(3) In this paragraph—

'airport' means an aerodrome within the meaning given by section 105(1) of the Civil Aviation Act 1982 [*qv*];

'airports authority' means the British Airports Authority or a local authority which owns or manages an airport;

'general lighthouse authority' and 'local lighthouse authority' have the meanings given by section 634 of the Merchant Shipping Act 1894;

'harbour' and 'harbour authority' have the meanings given by section 57(1) of the Harbours Act 1964;

'local authority', unless the contrary intention appears, means—

(*a*) in relation to England and Wales, a county or district council, a London borough council or the Common Council of the City of London; and

(*b*) *[Applies to Scotland.]*

'social services functions'—

(*a*) in relation to England and Wales, has the meaning given by section 3(1) of the Local Authority Social Services Act 1970; and

(*b*) *[Applies to Scotland.]*

'wholly owned subsidiary', in relation to London Regional Transport, has the meaning given by section 68 of the London Regional Transport Act 1984.

[The Merchant Shipping Act 1894, s 634, designates 'any person or body of persons having by law or usage authority over local lighthouses, buoys or beacons' as 'local lighthouse authorities'; it also designates Trinity House, the Commissioners of Northern Lighthouses and the Commissioners of Irish Lights as 'general lighthouse authorities'.

The Local Authority Social Services Act 1970, s 3(1) (as substituted by the Local Government, Planning and Land Act 1980, s 183(1)), designates as 'social service functions' those local authority functions matters relating to which stand referred to the authority's social services committee by virtue of s 2 of that Act (ie functions conferred by enactments listed in Sched 1 to the 1970 Act or designated by the Secretary of State).]

3.—(1) Any vehicle which is being used by an agricultural, horticultural, forestry or fishery undertaking to carry goods within a 50 kilometre radius of the place where the vehicle is normally based, including local administrative areas the centres of which are situated within that radius.

(2) A vehicle which is being used by a fishery undertaking does not fall within the description specified in this paragraph unless the vehicle is being used—

(*a*) to carry live fish; or

(*b*) to carry a catch of fish from the place of landing to a place where it is to be processed.

4. Any vehicle which is being used to carry animal waste or carcases which are not intended for human consumption.

5. Any vehicle which is being used to carry live animals between a farm and a local market or from a market to a local slaughterhouse.

6. Any vehicle which is being used—

(*a*) as a shop at a local market;

(*b*) for door-to-door selling;

(*c*) for mobile banking, exchange or saving transactions;

(*d*) for worship;

(*e*) for the lending of books, records or cassettes; or

(*f*) for cultural events or exhibitions,

and is specially fitted for that use.

7.—(1) Any vehicle used for the carriage of goods which has a permissible maximum weight not exceeding 7.5 tonnes and is carrying material or equipment for the driver's use in the course of his work within a 50 kilometre radius of the place where the vehicle is normally based.

(2) A vehicle does not fall within the description specified in this paragraph if driving the vehicle constitutes the driver's main activity.

8. Any vehicle which operates exclusively on an island which does not exceed 2300 square kilometres in area and is not linked to the rest of Great Britain by a bridge, ford or tunnel open for use by motor vehicles.

9. Any vehicle used for the carriage of goods which has a permissible maximum weight not exceeding 7.5 tonnes and is propelled by means of gas produced on the vehicle or by means of electricity.

10.—(1) Any vehicle which is being used for driving instruction with a view to obtaining a driving licence.

(2) A vehicle does not fall within the description specified in this paragraph if the vehicle or any trailer or semi-trailer drawn by it is being used for the carriage of goods—

(*a*) for hire or reward; or

(*b*) for or in connection with any trade or business.

11. Any tractor which, on or after 1st January 1990, is used exclusively for agricultural and forestry work.

[PART II

VEHICLES EXEMPTED BY REGULATIONS 2(2) AND 4(2)

12. Any vehicle which is being used by the Royal National Lifeboat Institution for the purpose of hauling lifeboats.

13. Any vehicle which was manufactured before 1st January 1947.

14. Any vehicle which is propelled by steam.]

[15.—(1) Any vehicle which is by virtue of its construction and equipment suitable for carrying passengers and which on the occasion on which it is being driven—

(*a*) is a vintage vehicle;

(*b*) is not carrying more than 9 persons including the driver;

(*c*) is not used for carrying passengers with a view to profit; and

(*d*) is being driven—

(i) in a vintage vehicle rally or to or from such a rally, or

(ii) to or from a museum, or other place where the vehicle is to be or has been displayed to members of the public, or

(iii) to or from a place where the vehicle is to be or has been repaired, maintained or tested.

(2) For the purposes of this paragraph:—

(*a*) a vehicle is a vintage vehicle on any occasion on which it is being driven if it was manufactured more than 25 years before that occasion; and

(*b*) 'vintage vehicle rally' means an event in which a collection of historic vehicles are driven on a road open to the public along a pre-determined route.]

[Part II of this Schedule was added by SI 1987 No 805 (which at the same time designated the original text of the Schedule as Part I) and is printed as subsequently amended by SI 1988 No 760.]

The Disabled Persons (Badges for Motor Vehicles) Regulations 1982

(SI 1982 No 1740)

ARRANGEMENT OF REGULATIONS

1. Commencement and citation *[Omitted.]*

2. Revocation

(1) The Disabled Persons (Badges for Motor Vehicles) Regulations 1975 *[SI 1975 No 266]* are hereby revoked.

(2) Any application made, any badge issued or anything else done under and in accordance with the Regulations hereby revoked or having effect as if so made, issued or done shall not be invalidated by the revocation thereof but shall have effect as if made, issued or done under and in accordance with the corresponding provision of these Regulations.

3. Interpretation

(1) In these Regulations—

'the Act' means the [Road Traffic Regulation Act 1984];

'disabled person' means a person who is over two years of age and who is of a description prescribed by Regulation 5;

'disabled person's badge' means a badge in the form prescribed by Regulation 4 issued by a local authority for display on a motor vehicle driven by a disabled person, or used for the carriage of a disabled person or of several disabled persons, and includes a duplicate badge issued pursuant to Regulation 8;

'holder', in relation to a disabled person's badge, means the person to whom the badge was issued;

'institution' means an institution concerned with the care of the disabled;

'local authority' means an authority referred to in section 21(8) of the Chronically Sick and Disabled Persons Act 1970 [*qv*];

'relevant conviction' means

(*a*) the conviction of either—

(i) the holder of a disabled person's badge; or

(ii) any other person using a disabled person's badge with holder's consent,

of an offence of using or causing or permitting a vehicle to be used arising—

(A) under section 1(8), 6(9), 9(9) or 12(9) of the Act if the offence consisted of the unlawful parking of the vehicle, or

(B) under section 31(3), 31(3A), 42(1) or 42(1A) of the Act; and

(*b*) the conviction of any person other than the holder of a disabled person's badge of an offence under [section 117] of the Act where the badge was displayed on the vehicle with the consent of the holder at any time during which the offence was being committed;

and the expression 'relevant conviction' includes the liability of any person who would be liable to the conviction of an offence as mentioned above but who is liable, instead, to pay a fixed penalty pursuant to [sections 107 to 111 of and Schedule 12 to the Act].

(2) *[Omitted.]*

[Regulation 3 is printed as amended by the Road Traffic Regulation Act 1984, s 144(1) and Sched 10, para 2.]

4. Form of badge *[Omitted.]*

5. Descriptions of disabled persons

The prescribed descriptions of disabled person to whom a local authority may issue a disabled person's badge are a person who—

(*a*) receives a mobility allowance pursuant to section 37A of the Social Security Act 1975;

(*b*) uses a motor vehicle supplied by the Department of Health and Social Security, the Scottish Home and Health Department or the Welsh Office or is in receipt of a grant pursuant to section 5(2)(*a*) of the National Health Service Act 1977 or section 46 of the National Health Service (Scotland) Act 1978;

(*c*) is registered as blind under section 29 of the National Assistance Act 1948, or, in Scotland, is a blind person within the meaning of section 64(1) of that Act; or

(*d*) has a permanent and substantial disability which causes inability to walk or very considerable difficulty in walking.

[Section 37A was inserted into the Social Security Act 1975 by the Social Security Pensions Act 1975, s 22(1). A footnote in the regulations draws attention, in the context of s 37A, to the Social Security (Miscellaneous Provisions) Act 1977, s 13.]

6. Badges for institutions

An institution is eligible to apply for the issue to it of a disabled person's badge for any motor vehicle or, as the case may be, for each motor vehicle used by or on behalf of the institution to carry disabled persons.

7. Period of issue of badge

Subject to the provisions of Regulation 11, a disabled person's badge shall be issued for a period of three years beginning with the date upon which it is issued.

8. Duplicate badge *[Omitted.]*

9. Fee for badge *[Omitted.]*

10. Grounds for refusing to issue badge

(1) The cases in which a local authority may refuse to issue a disabled person's badge are cases where—

(*a*) the applicant for the badge holds or has held a disabled person's badge, either under the provisions of these Regulations or under any of the provisions mentioned in Regulation 13, and in respect of that badge there has occurred on at least three occasions misuse which has led to a relevant conviction or which would give grounds for a relevant conviction; or

(*b*) the applicant fails to provide the authority with adequate evidence that he is a person to whom one or more of the descriptions of disabled person prescribed in Regulation 5 applies; or

(*c*) the applicant fails to pay the fee (if any) chargeable for the issue of the badge.

(2) In a case where a local authority refuses to issue a disabled person's badge in response to an application for one, it shall issue to the applicant a notice stating the grounds for refusal.

11. Return of badge to issuing authority

(1) A disabled person's badge shall be returned to the local authority by whom it was issued immediately on the occurrence of any of the following events, namely—

(*a*) if the badge ceases to be required for the motor vehicle or all the motor vehicles in respect of which it was issued;

(*b*) on the expiry of the period for which the badge was issued;

(*c*) on the death of the person to whom the badge was issued or, where the badge was issued to an institution, on the institution ceasing to exist;

(*d*) if the holder of the badge ceases to be a disabled person or, in the case of an institution, ceases to be eligible under Regulation 6;

(*e*) if the badge has been obtained by false representation;

(*f*) where a duplicate badge has been issued to replace a badge lost or stolen, and the duplicated badge is subsequently found or recovered.

(2) Subject to the provisions of Regulation 12, a disabled person's badge shall, within the time prescribed in paragraph (3), be returned to the local authority by whom it was issued in the event of that authority issuing a notice stating—

(*a*) that the authority refuses to allow the issue of the badge to continue in consequence of the misuse on at least three occasions of the badge which has either led to a relevant conviction or would give grounds for a relevant conviction; and

(*b*) particulars of that misuse.

(3) The prescribed time for the return of a disabled person's badge in a case where a notice is issued as mentioned in paragraph (2) is—

(*a*) where no appeal is made as mentioned in Regulation 12, 28 days from the date of the issue of the notice;

(*b*) where an appeal is made as mentioned in Regulation 12, and the appeal is not allowed, 28 days from the date on which the Secretary of State issues a notice of his determination of the appeal.

(4) A local authority by whom a disabled person's badge is issued may take such action as may be appropriate to recover a badge which the holder is liable to return in accordance with paragraph (1) or (2).

12. Appeals

(1) A person to whom a notice has been issued as provided in Regulation 10(2) stating as the grounds for refusal the grounds mentioned in Regulation 10(1)(*a*) or as provided in Regulation 11(2) may appeal, against the decision in respect of which the notice is issued, to the Secretary of State within 28 days of the date on which the notice is issued, and in relation to any such appeal the procedure specified in paragraph (2) shall, subject to paragraph (3), be followed.

(2) The procedure mentioned in paragraph (1) is as follows:—

(*a*) every appeal shall be written, dated, signed by the appellant or by another person authorised to sign on the appellant's behalf, and shall state the ground on which the appeal is made;

(*b*) the appellant shall serve the appeal on the Secretary of State either by post or otherwise by delivery—

(i) if the local authority against whose decision the appeal is made is in England, to the Department of Transport, 2 Marsham Street, London SW1P 3EB,

(ii) if the local authority against whose decision the appeal is made is in Scotland, to the Scottish Development Department, New St. Andrew's House, Edinburgh EH1 3SZ,

(iii) if the local authority against whose decision the appeal is made is in Wales, to the Welsh Office, Cathays Park, Cardiff CP1 3NQ;

(*c*) on receipt of an appeal made as provided above, the Secretary of State shall send a copy of it to the local authority against whose decision the appeal is made,

(*d*) within 28 days of the date on which a local authority receives a copy of an appeal as mentioned in sub-paragraph (*c*), it shall send to the Secretary of State—

(i) a copy of the notice mentioned in Regulation 10(2) or, as the case may be, Regulation 11(2), and

(ii) any comments it may wish the Secretary of State to take into account in determining the appeal;

(*e*) when the Secretary of State determines an appeal made as mentioned in paragraph (1) he shall issue a notice to the appellant stating whether he confirms or reverses the decision of the local authority, and such notice shall state the reasons for the determination; and

(*f*) the Secretary of State shall send a copy of the notice mentioned in sub-paragraph (*e*) to the local authority against whose decision the appeal was made.

(3) The Secretary of State may in his discretion determine an appeal made under

paragraph (1) even if the provisions specified in paragraph (2)(*a*) to (*d*) have not been fully complied with.

(4) If the Secretary of State confirms the decision of the local authority the appellant shall return the disabled person's badge in question to the local authority within the time prescribed in Regulation 11(3).

13. Transitional provisions

(1) Any order made before the coming into operation of these Regulations, being an order made or having effect as if made under [section 1, 6, 9, 35, 45 or 46] of the Act and containing a provision operating with reference to—

(*a*) badges issued by a local authority in pursuance of any scheme having effect under section 29 of the National Assistance Act 1948, or any similar scheme having effect in Scotland, and borne by vehicles or a class of vehicle; or

(*b*) badges issued under and in accordance with Regulations revoked by Regulation 2 and borne by vehicles or a class of vehicle,

shall, on and after the coming into operation of these Regulations, apply and operate as if the reference in that provision to any such badge as is mentioned in (*a*) or (*b*) above were a reference to a disabled person's badge issued, or having effect as if issued, under and in accordance with these Regulations, borne by vehicles or, as the case may require, by the same class of vehicles, and displayed on a vehicle in the relevant position.

(2) For the purposes of paragraph (1) and any order referred to therein, a vehicle shall be regarded as displaying a disabled person's badge in the relevant position when—

(*a*) in the case of a vehicle fitted with a front windscreen, the badge is exhibited thereon with the front facing forwards on the near side of and immediately behind the windscreen; and

(*b*) in the case of a vehicle not fitted with a front windscreen, the badge is exhibited in a conspicuous position on the front or near side of the vehicle.

[Regulation 13 is printed as amended by the Road Traffic Regulation Act 1984, s 144(1) and Sched 10, para 2.]

* * *

The Drivers' Hours (Goods Vehicles) (Exemptions) Regulations 1986

(SI 1986 No 1492)

1. Citation, commencement and revocation *[Omitted.]*

2. Exemptions from requirements as to drivers' hours

(1) A driver who during any working day spends all or the greater part of the time when he is driving vehicles to which Part VI of the Transport Act 1968 applies in driving goods vehicles and who spends time on duty during that working day to deal with any of the cases of emergency specified in paragraph (2) below is exempted from the requirements of section 96(1) and (3)(*a*) of that Act in respect of that working day subject to the condition that he does not spend time on such duty (otherwise than to deal with the emergency) for a period of or periods amounting in the aggregate to more than 11 hours.

(2) The cases of emergency referred to in paragraph (1) above are—

(*a*) events which cause or are likely to cause such—

(i) danger to life or health of one or more individuals or animals or

(ii) a serious interruption in the maintenance of public services for the supply of water, gas, electricity or drainage or of telecommunication or postal services, or

(iii) a serious interruption in the use of roads, railways, ports or airports,

as to necessitate the taking of immediate action to prevent the occurrence or continuance of such danger or interruption and

(*b*) events which are likely to cause such serious damage to property as to necessitate the taking of immediate action to prevent the occurrence of such damage.

The Drivers' Hours (Goods Vehicles) (Keeping of Records) Regulations 1987

(SI 1987 No 1421)

ARRANGEMENT OF REGULATIONS

SCHEDULE

MODEL FOR DRIVER'S RECORD BOOK

1. Commencement and citation *[Omitted.]*

2. Revocation *[Omitted.]*

3. Interpretation

In these Regulations, unless the context otherwise requires—

'the Act' means the Transport Act 1968;

'driver's record book' means a book which complies with regulation 5, and any reference in relation to a driver's record book to a front sheet, instructions to drivers for completion of sheets, and weekly record sheets is a reference to those components of a driver's record book referred to in regulation 5.

'operator's licence' has the same meaning as in section 60(1) of the Act [*qv*]; and

'passenger vehicles' and 'goods vehicles' have the same meaning as in section 95(2) of the Act [*qv*].

4. Application of Regulations

Subject to the provisions of regulations 12 and 13 these Regulations apply to drivers of goods vehicles and to employers of employee-drivers of such vehicles but they do not so apply in relation to a journey made or work done by a driver in a case where the journey or, as the case may be, the work is a journey or work to which the applicable Community rules apply.

5. Form of driver's record book

A driver's record book shall contain—

(*a*) a front sheet;

(*b*) instructions to drivers for completion of sheets;

(*c*) notes for guidance on use of the book; and

(*d*) weekly record sheets divided up into boxes for entry of information relating to each day of the week and a duplicate of each weekly record sheet together with one sheet of carbon paper or other means whereby an entry on a weekly record sheet may be simultaneously reproduced on the duplicate of that sheet

each of which shall conform to the model in the Schedule to these Regulations and shall have the standard A6 format (105 × 148mm) or a larger format.

6. Issue of driver's record books

(1) Where an employee-driver is required by these Regulations to enter information in a driver's record book the employer shall issue to him and from time to time as may be necessary while the employee-driver remains in the employment of that employer supply him with a new driver's record book.

(2) If on the date of the coming into operation of these Regulations or at any time thereafter an employee-driver has more than one employer in relation to whom he is an employee-driver of a vehicle, the employer who is to issue a new driver's record book to him shall be the employer for whom the employee-driver first acts in the course of his employment on or after the said date or time.

(3) Where during the currency of a driver's record book an employee-driver ceases to be employed by an employer who has issued that book to him he shall return that book, (including all unused weekly record sheets), to that employer and, if he is at that time employed by some other person or persons in relation to whom he is an employee-driver of a vehicle, that other person, or if there is more than one such other person, that one of them for whom he first acts in the course of his employment after ceasing to be so employed as aforesaid, shall issue a new driver's record book to him in accordance with the provisions of paragraph (1) above.

7. Entries in driver's record books

(1) An employer of an employee-driver or an owner-driver shall enter or secure that there is entered on the front sheet the information specified in items 4 and 6 of that sheet.

(2) The entries referred to in paragraph (1) shall be made—

(*a*) in the case of an employer, before the driver's record book is issued to the driver pursuant to regulation 6, and

(*b*) in the case of an owner-driver before the book is used.

(3)(*a*) For the purpose of entering the information specified in item 4, the address shall, in the case of an owner-driver, be the address of the driver's place of business.

(*b*) For the purpose of entering the information specified in item 6 the Operator's Licence No shall be the serial number of the operator's licence granted under Part V of the Act by virtue of which each goods vehicle used by the driver during the currency of the record book is an authorised vehicle for the purposes of the said Part V.

(4) A driver shall enter, and where he is an employee-driver, his employer shall cause him to enter, in accordance with the instructions to drivers for the completion of sheets—

(*a*) on the front sheet the information specified in relation to the front sheet in those instructions; and

(*b*) in the appropriate boxes in the weekly record sheet the information specified in relation to weekly record sheets in those instructions.

(5) A driver when making an entry in a weekly record sheet (including signing such a sheet) shall ensure by the use of the carbon paper or otherwise, that the entry is simultaneously reproduced on the duplicate of that sheet.

8. Manner of keeping driver's record books—supplementary

(1) Where a weekly record sheet has been completed by an employee-driver he shall deliver the driver's record book (including the duplicate of the weekly record sheet which has been completed) to the employer who issued or should have issued the record book to him within a period of seven days from the date when the weekly record sheet was completed or earlier if so required by the employer.

(2) An employer to whom a driver's record book has been delivered pursuant to paragraph 1 above shall—

(*a*) examine the weekly record sheeet which has been completed and sign it and its duplicate;

(*b*) detach the duplicate sheet; and

(*c*) return the book to the driver before he is next on duty.

(3) When all the weekly record sheets in a driver's record book have been used, the driver shall retain the book for a period of fourteen days from the date on which the book was last returned to him pursuant to paragraph (2)(*c*) above and shall then return the book to the employer as soon as is reasonably practicable.

(4) When a weekly record sheet has been completed by an owner-driver he shall, within a period of seven days from the date of its being completed, detach the duplicate sheet and deliver it to the address which is required to be entered in item 4 on the front sheet.

(5) An employee-driver or an owner-driver shall not be treated as having failed to comply with any of the requirements of paragraphs (1) and (4) above with respect to the period within which the duplicate of a weekly record sheet shall be delivered if he can show that it was not reasonably practicable to comply with that requirement and that the duplicate of the weekly record sheet was delivered as soon as it was reasonably practicable to do so.

(6) A driver who is in possession of a driver's record book in which he has made any entry pursuant to regulation 7 shall not, until all the weekly record sheets in that book have been completed, make any entry in any other record book.

(7) An employee-driver shall not make any entry in a driver's record book

pursuant to regulation 7 if the book was not supplied to him by his employer unless a driver's record book so supplied was not available to him.

(8) No person shall erase or obliterate any entry once made in a driver's record book, and if a correction is required it shall be made by striking the original entry through in such a way that it may still be read and by writing the appropriate correction near to the entry so struck through, and any person making such a correction shall initial it.

9. Production of driver's record book by employee-drivers

(1) Where an employee-driver has or has had during any period more than one employer in relation to whom he is an employee-driver each employer, who is not the employer who is required by these Regulations to issue a driver's record book to that employee-driver, shall require that driver to produce his current driver's record book and shall enter on the front sheet the information contained in item 5.

(2) An employee-driver shall produce his current driver's record book for inspection by the employer who issued it to him, or by any other person in relation to whom he is at any time during the period of the currency of that book and employee-driver, whenever required to do so by that employer or that other person.

10. Driver's record books to be carried by drivers

A driver shall have his current driver's record book (including all unused record sheets) in his possession at all times when he is on duty.

11. Preservation of driver's record books

(1) An owner-driver shall preserve his driver's record book intact when it has been completed or he has ceased to use it, and the employer of an employee-driver to whom any driver's record book relating to that employee-driver has been returned shall preserve that book intact, for the period specified in paragraph (3) below.

(2) An employer of an employee-driver or an owner-driver who has detached duplicates of weekly sheets pursuant to regulation 8(2)(*b*) or as the case may be regulation 8(4) shall preserve those sheets for the period specified in paragraph (3) below.

(3) The period for which driver's record books and duplicates of weekly record sheets must be preserved as required by this regulation shall be one year reckoned, in the case of an owner-driver, from the day on which that book was completed or ceased to be used by him, or in the case of an employee-driver, from the day on which that book was returned to his employer pursuant to regulation 8(3).

12. Exemptions

(1) Where a driver does not during any working day drive any goods vehicle other than a vehicle the use of which is exempted from any requirement to have an operator's licence or, in the case of a vehicle in the public service of the Crown, would be so exempted by virtue of section 60(2) of the Act, were it not such a vehicle, that driver and, if he is an employee-driver, his employer, shall be exempted for that period from the specified requirements.

(2)(*a*) Where in any working day a driver does not drive a goods vehicle for more than four hours and does not drive any such vehicle outside a radius of 50 kilometres from the operating centre of the vehicle, then he and, if he is an employee-driver, his employer shall be exempted for that period from the specified requirements.

(*b*) For the purposes of computing the period of four hours mentioned in sub-paragraph (*a*) above no account shall be taken of any time spent in driving a vehicle elsewhere than on a road if the vehicle is being so driven in the course of operations of agriculture, forestry or quarrying or in the course of carrying out work in the construction, reconstruction, alteration or extension or maintenance of, or of a part of, a building, or of any other fixed works of construction of [*sic*] civil engineering (including works for the construction, improvement or maintenance of a road) and, for the purposes of this sub-paragraph, where the vehicle is being driven on, or on a part of, a road in the course of carrying out of any work for the improvement or maintenance of, or that part of, that road, it shall be treated as being driven elsewhere than on a road.

(3) Where during any working day a driver does not spend all or the greater part of the time when he is driving vehicles to which Part VI of the Act applies in driving goods vehicles, then he and, if he is an employee-driver, his employer shall be exempted for that working day from the specified requirements.

(4) Where a vehicle is used in such circumstances that by virtue of regulation 5 of the Community Drivers' Hours and Recording Equipment (Exemptions and Supplementary Provisions) Regulations 1986 [*SI 1986 No 1456, qv*] Council Regulation (EEC) No 3821/85 of 20th December 1985 on recording equipment in road transport [*qv*] applies to the vehicle, the driver of the vehicle and, if he is an employee-driver, his employer shall be exempted from the specified requirements in relation to the use of the vehicle in those circumstances.

(5)(*a*) In this regulation 'the specified requirements' means the provisions of regulations 7 and 10.

(*b*) In paragraph (2)(*a*) above 'operating centre' has the same meaning as in section 92 of the Act [*as amended*].

13. Drivers of goods vehicles and passenger vehicles

(1) Subject to the provisions of regulation 12(3), regulations 7 and 10 apply to a driver who in any working week drives goods and passenger vehicles as they apply to a driver who only drives a goods vehicle and the information to be entered in the driver's record book pursuant to regulation 7 shall be information in relation to his employment in connection with both goods and passenger vehicles.

(2) If a driver of both goods vehicles and passenger vehicles has a different employer in relation to his employment in connection with goods vehicles from his employer in relation to his employment in connection with passenger vehicles his employer for the purpose of regulation 6 shall be his employer in relation to his employment in connection with goods vehicles notwithstanding the provisions of regulation 6(2).

[*The Schedule is set out on pp 2/470–73.*]

SCHEDULE

Model for Driver's Record Book

(a) *Front sheet*

RECORD BOOK FOR DRIVERS IN ROAD TRANSPORT

1. Date book first used ....

2. Date book last used ....

3. Surname, first name(s), and address of holder of book ....
....
....

4. Name, address, telephone number and stamp (if any) of employer/undertaking.
....
....

5. Name, address, telephone number and stamp (if any) of any other employer(s) .
....
....

6. Operator's Licence No. (Nos.) ....

(b) *Instructions to drivers for completion of sheets*

INSTRUCTIONS TO DRIVERS FOR COMPLETION OF SHEETS

FRONT SHEET

1. Enter your surname, first name(s) and address (item 3). Owner-drivers need not make any entry in item 3 unless their personal address is different from the address of their place of business.

2. Enter the date on which you first use the book (item 1).

3. Immediately after you have completed all the weekly sheets enter in item 2 the date on which you last made an entry in a weekly sheet. If you cease to be employed by the employer who issued you with a record book enter the last date on which you were employed in item 2.

WEEKLY RECORD SHEET

4. Use a new sheet each week. A week runs from midnight on Sunday/Monday to midnight the next Sunday/Monday.

5. Complete boxes 1 and 2 at the beginning of each week in which you work as a driver.

6. Each day on which you do not work as a driver complete boxes 3–9 in accordance with the instructions below.

7. Enter in box 3 for the day in question the registration number of any vehicle used during that day.

8. Complete boxes 4 and 5 at the beginning of each day on which you do work as a driver.

9. Complete boxes 6, 7 and 8 and 9 at the end of the day's work.

(c) *Notes for guidance on the use of book*

NOTES FOR GUIDANCE ON THE USE OF RECORD BOOKS

FOR EMPLOYERS

1. After completing items 4 and 6 on the front sheet, issue a record book to the drivers employed by you.

2. Give the holder the necessary instructions for correct use of the book.

3. When the record book is handed in to you by the drivers employed by you within seven days of the end of each week of driving, examine and sign the weekly record sheet (including the duplicate sheet) for the week to which it relates. Tear out and keep the duplicate sheets, leaving the top sheets in the book and return the book to the driver before he is next on duty.

4. When the used books have been handed back to you by the drivers employed by you preserve them together with the duplicate sheets for not less than one year.

FOR EMPLOYEE-DRIVERS

5. Ensure that items 1 and 3 on the front sheet are completed before you use the book.

6. This record book is personal. Carry it with you when on duty and produce it to any authorised inspecting officer on request. Hand it over to your employer when you leave the undertaking.

7. Produce this record book to your employer within 7 days of the end of each week of driving, so that he can check and countersign your entries. Keep the top sheets in the book.

8. When the book is completed, complete item 2 on the front sheet and keep the book for 2 weeks so that it can be produced at any time to an authorised inspecting officer and then hand it to your employer.

FOR OWNER-DRIVERS

9. Ensure that items 1, 3 (if applicable) 4 and 6 on the front sheet are completed before you use the record book. Enter your business address in item 4.

10. This record book is personal. Carry it with you when on duty and produce it to any authorised inspecting officer on request.

11. Tear out and keep the duplicate of each weekly record sheet at the end of the week to which it relates.

12. When the book is completed, complete item 2 on the front sheet. Preserve the used books and the duplicate sheets for not less than a year.

GENERAL

13. All entries must be made in ink or with a ball-point pen.

14. If you have to correct an entry, strike the incorrect entry through, write the correct entry near it and initial the correction.

(These notes are for guidance only and reference should be made to Part VI of the Transport Act 1968 and, the Drivers' Hours (Keeping of Records) Regulations 1987 for particulars of the statutory provisions).

[The weekly sheet is set out on the next page.]

(d) *Weekly record sheets*

WEEKLY SHEET							
1. DRIVER'S NAME			2. PERIOD COVERED BY SHEET WEEK COMMENCING (DATE) .... TO WEEK ENDING (DATE)				
DAY ON WHICH DUTY COMMENCED	*REGISTRATION NO OF VEHICLE(S)* 3	*PLACE WHERE VEHICLE(S) BASED* 4	*TIME OF GOING ON DUTY* 5	*TIME OF GOING OFF DUTY* 6	*TIME SPENT DRIVING* 7	*TIME SPENT ON DUTY* 8	*SIGNATURE OF DRIVER* 9
MONDAY							
TUESDAY							
WEDNESDAY							
THURSDAY							
FRIDAY							
SATURDAY							
SUNDAY							
10. CERTIFICATION BY EMPLOYER				I HAVE EXAMINED THE ENTRIES IN THIS SHEET SIGNATURE .... POSITION HELD			

The Drivers' Hours (Goods Vehicles) (Modifications) Order 1970

(SI 1970 No 257)

[The text of this order is printed as amended by:

the Drivers' Hours (Passenger and Goods Vehicles) (Modifications) Order 1971 (SI 1971 No 818) (29 May 1971);

the Drivers' Hours (Goods Vehicles) (Modifications) Order 1986 (SI 1986 No 1459) (29 September 1986).

The amending orders are referred to in the notes to the main order by their years and numbers. The dates referred to above are the dates on which the orders came into force.]

1. Commencement and citation *[Omitted.]*

2. Interpretation

(1) In this Order, unless the context otherwise requires, 'the Act' means the Transport Act 1968 and any other expression which is also used in Part VI of the Act has the same meaning as in that Part of the Act.

(2) Any reference in this Order to a numbered section is a reference to the section bearing that number in the Act except where otherwise expressly provided.

(3) Any reference in this Order to any enactment or instrument shall be construed, unless the context otherwise requires, as a reference to that enactment or instrument as amended by any subsequent enactment or instrument.

(4) The [Interpretation Act 1978] shall apply for the interpretation of this Order as it applies for the interpretation of an Act of Parliament.

3. *[Revoked by SI 1986 No 1459.]*

4. Exemptions for drivers engaged [in quarrying operations or] on building, construction and civil engineering work

There shall be added to the exemption provided for by section 96(9) (which provides that for the purposes of subsections (1) and (7) of section 96 no account is to be taken of any time spent in driving a vehicle elsewhere than on a road if the vehicle is being so driven in the course of operations of agriculture or forestry) the following exemption, that is to say—

'For the purposes of subsections (1) and (7) of section 96 no account shall be taken of any time spent in driving a goods vehicle elsewhere than on a road if the vehicle is being so driven in the course of [operations of quarrying or of] carrying out any work in the construction, reconstruction, alteration, extension or maintenance of, or of a part of, a building, or of any other fixed works of construction or civil engineering (including works for the construction, improvement or maintenance of a road) and, for the purposes of this exemption, where the vehicle is being driven on, or on a part of, a road in the course of carrying out any work for the improvement or maintenance of, or of that part of, that road, it shall be treated as if it were being driven elsewhere than on a road.'

[Article 4 is printed as amended by SI 1971 No 818.]

The Drivers' Hours (Goods Vehicles) (Modifications) Order 1986

(SI 1986 No 1459)

[Note. The text of s 96 of the Transport Act 1968 as modified by this order is set out as an appendix to this order.]

1. Citation, commencement, interpretation and revocation

(1) *[Omitted.]*

(2) In this Order 'the 1968 Act' means the Transport Act 1968.

(3) *[Revokes SI 1970 No 257, art 3, and SI 1971 No 818, art 5(a).]*

2. Goods vehicles generally

Where during any working day a driver spends all or the greater part of the time when he is driving vehicles to which Part VI of the 1968 Act applies in driving goods vehicles, that Part of that Act shall have effect, as respects that driver and that working day, as if—

(*a*) subsections (2), (3)(*b*), (4) to (6) and (8)(*b*) of section 96 were omitted;

(*b*) for the words 'subsections (1), (2) and (3)' in subsection (7) of that section there were substituted the words 'subsections (1) and (3)(*a*)';

(*c*) for the words 'subsections (2) and (3)' in subsection (8)(*a*) of that section there were substituted the words 'subsection (3)(*a*)'; and

(*d*) for the definition of 'working day' in section 103(1) there were substituted the following definition—

' "working day", in relation to any driver, means—

(*a*) any working period (that is to say, any period during which he is on duty) which does not fall to be aggregated with the whole or part of any other such period or periods by virtue of paragraph (*b*) of this definition; and

(*b*) where a working period is followed by one or more other such periods beginning within the 24 hours next after the beginning of that working period, the aggregate of that working period and so much of the other such period or periods as fall within those 24 hours;'.

3. Light goods vehicles

(1) Where during any working week a driver spends all of the time when he is driving vehicles to which Part VI of the 1968 Act applies in driving light goods vehicles and, in so far as he drives such a vehicle during that week otherwise than for social, domestic or pleasure purposes, he does so—

(*a*) solely in connection with the carrying on by him or by his employer of the profession of medical practitioner, nurse, midwife, dentist or veterinary surgeon;

(*b*) wholly or mainly in connection with the carrying out of any service of inspection, cleaning, maintenance, repair, installation or fitting;

(*c*) solely while he is acting as a commercial traveller and is carrying in the vehicle (apart from the effects of any person carried in it) no goods other than goods carried for the purpose of soliciting orders;

(*d*) solely while he is acting in the course of his employment by the Automobile Association, the Royal Automobile Club or Royal Scottish Automobile Club; or

(*e*) solely in connection with the carrying on by him or by his employer of the business of cinematography or of radio or television broadcasting,

that Part of that Act shall have effect, as respects that driver and any working day falling wholly within that working week, not only with the modifications made by article 2 above but also as if subsections (3)(*a*) and (8)(*a*) of section 96 were omitted.

(2) In this article 'light goods vehicle' means a vehicle which—

(*a*) is a goods vehicle which has a permissible maximum weight within the meaning of [section 108 of the Road Traffic Act 1988] not exceeding 3.5 tonnes; or

(*b*) is a dual purpose vehicle within the meaning of [Regulation 3(2) of the Road Vehicles (Construction and Use) Regulations 1986] [*SI 1986 No 1078, qv*],

and (in either case) is a vehicle to which Part VI of the 1968 Act applies.

[Article 3 is printed as amended by the Interpretation Act 1978, ss 17(2)(a) and 23.]

APPENDIX (Transport Act 1986, s 96, as applied to drivers of goods vehicles)

96. Permitted driving time and periods of duty

(1) Subject to the provisions of this section, a driver shall not on any working day drive a vehicle or vehicles to which this Part of this Act applies amounting in the aggregate to more than ten hours.

(2) *[Inapplicable.]*

(3) Subject to the provisions of this section, the working day of a driver—

(*a*) except where paragraph (*b*) or (*c*) of this subsection applies, shall not exceed eleven hours;

(*b*) *[Inapplicable.]*

(4)–(6) *[Inapplicable.]*

(7) If in the case of the working week of any driver the following requirement is satisfied, that is to say, that, in each of the periods of twenty-four hours beginning at midnight which make up that week, the driver does not drive a vehicle to which this Part of this Act applies for a period of, or periods amounting in the aggregate to, more than four hours, the foregoing provisions of this section shall not apply to him in that week, except that the provisions of subsections (1) and (3)(*a*) shall nevertheless have effect in relation to the whole of any working day falling partly in that week and partly in a working week in the case of which that requirement is not satisfied.

(8) If on any working day a driver does not drive any vehicle to which this Part of this Act applies—

(*a*) subsection (3)(*a*) of this section shall not apply to that day, and

(*b*) *[Inapplicable.]*

(9) For the purposes of subsections (1) and (7) of this section no account shall be taken of any time spent driving a vehicle elsewhere than on a road if the vehicle is being so driven in the course of operations of agriculture or forestry.

(10) For the purpose of enabling drivers to deal with cases of emergency or otherwise to meet a special need, the Secretary of State for Transport may by regulations—

(*a*) create examinations from all or any of the requirements of subsections (1) to (6) of this section in such cases and subject to such conditions as may be specified in the regulations;

(*b*) empower the traffic commissioner for any area, subject to the provisions of the regulations—

(i) to dispense with the observance of all or any of those requirements (either generally or in such circumstances or to such extent as the commissioner thinks fit) in any particular case for which provision is not made under paragraph (*a*) of this subsection;

(ii) to grant a certificate (which, for the purposes of any proceedings under this Part of this Act, shall be conclusive evidence of the facts therein stated) that any particular case falls or fell within any exemption created under the said paragraph (*a*)

and regulations under this subsection may enable any dispensation under paragraph (*b*)(i) of this subsection to be granted retrospectively and provide for a document purporting to be a certificate granted by virtue of paragraph (*b*)(ii) of this subsection to be accepted in evidence without further proof.

(11) If any of the requirements of the domestic drivers' hours code is contravened in the case of any driver—

(*a*) that driver; and

(*b*) any other person (being that driver's employer or a person to whose orders that driver was subject) who caused or permitted the contravention,

shall be liable on summary conviction to a fine not exceeding level 4 on the standard scale; but a person shall not be liable to be convicted under this subsection if he proves to the court—

(i) that the contravention was due to unavoidable delay in the completion of a journey arising out of circumstances which he could not reasonably have foreseen; or

(ii) in the case of a person charged under paragraph (*b*) of this subsection, that the contravention was due to the fact that the driver had for any particular period or periods driven or been on duty otherwise than in the employment of that person or, as the case may be, otherwise than in the employment in which he is subject to the orders of that person, and that the person charged was not, and could not reasonably have become, aware of that fact.

(11A) Where, in the case of a driver of a motor vehicle, there is in Great Britain a contravention of any requirement of the applicable Community rules as to period of driving, or distance driven, or periods on or off duty, then the offender and any other person (being the offender's employer or a person to whose orders the offender was subject) who caused or permitted the contravention shall be liable on summary conviction to a fine not exceeding level 4 on the standard scale.

(11B) But a person shall not be liable to be convicted under subsection (11A) if—

(*a*) he proves the matters specified in paragraph (i) of subsection (11); or

(*b*) being charged as the offender's employer or a person to whose orders the offender was subject, he proves the matters specified in paragraph (ii) of that subsection.

(12) The Secretary of State for Transport may by order—

(*a*) direct that subsection (1) of this section shall have effect with the substitution for the reference to ten hours of a reference to nine hours, either generally or with such exceptions as may be specified in the order;

(*b*) direct that paragraph (*a*) of subsection (3) of this section shall have effect with the substitution for the reference to eleven hours of a reference to any shorter period, or remove, modify or add to the provisions of that subsection containing exceptions to the said paragraph (*a*);

(*c*) remove, modify or add to any of the requirements of subsections (2), (4), (5) or (6) of this section or any of the exemptions provided for by subsections (7), (8) and (9) thereof;

and any order under this subsection may contain such transitional and supplementary provisions as the Secretary of State for Transport thinks necessary or expedient, including provisions amending any definition in section 103 of this Act which is relevant to any of the provisions affected by the order.

(13) In this Part of this Act 'the domestic drivers' hours code' means the provisions of subsection (1) to (6) of this section as for the time being in force (and, in particular, as modified, added to or substituted by or under any instrument in force under section 95(1) of this Act or subsection (10) or (12) of this section).

[This version of the Transport Act 1968, s 96, is the text of s 96 as modified by the Drivers' Hours (Goods Vehicles) (Modifications) Order 1986 (SI 1986 No 1459), art 2 (goods vehicles generally); in relation to light goods vehicles, subss (3)(a) and (8)(a) are also inapplicable (see SI 1986 No 1459, art 3).

This version of s 96 is printed as further amended by the Secretary of State for the Environment Order 1970 (SI 1970 No 1681); the European Communities Act 1972, s 4, and Sched 4, para 9(2); the Road Traffic (Drivers' Ages and Hours of Work) Act 1976, s 2(1); the Secretary of State for Transport Order 1976 (SI 1976 No 1775); the Transport Act 1978, s 10; the Minister of Transport Order 1979 (SI 1979 No 571); the Transfer of Functions (Transport) Order 1981 (SI 1981 No 238); the Criminal Justice Act 1982, ss 38 and 46(1); the Transport Act 1985, s 3 and Sched 2, Part II, para 1(2); the Community Drivers' Hours and Recording Equipment Regulations 1986 (SI 1986 No 1457), reg 2.]

The Drivers' Hours (Harmonisation with Community Rules) Regulations 1986

(SI 1986 No 1458)

1. Citation, commencement, interpretation and revocation

(1) *[Omitted.]*

(2) In these Regulations 'the 1968 Act' means the Transport Act 1968.

(3) *[Revocation.]*

2. Domestic drivers' hours code, etc

(1) Subject to the provisions of this Regulation, the domestic drivers' hours code shall not apply in relation to any Community driving or work of a driver of a vehicle to which Part VI of the 1968 Act applies.

(2) Paragraphs (3) and (4) below apply where during any working day a driver of a vehicle to which Part VI of the 1968 Act applies spends time both on Community driving or work and on domestic driving or work.

(3) Any time spent on Community driving or work shall be regarded for the purpose of—

(*a*) applying the limits in the domestic drivers' hours code on periods of driving or length of working day; or

(*b*) calculating periods of driving for the purposes of section 96(7) of the 1968 Act,

as time spent on domestic driving, or as the case may be, domestic work.

(4) Without prejudice to paragraph (3) above, any time spent on Community driving or work shall not be regarded for the purposes of any of the provisions of the domestic drivers' hours code as constituting or forming part of an interval for rest or an interval for rest and refreshment.

(5) In this Regulation 'the domestic drivers' hours code' has the meaning given by section 96(13) of the 1968 Act.

(6) In this Regulation—

(*a*) any reference to Community driving or work is a reference to driving or, as the case may be, work to which the applicable Community Rules apply; and

(*b*) any reference to domestic driving or work is a reference to driving or, as the case may be, work to which Part VI of the 1968 Act applies and those Rules do not apply.

3. Meaning of 'working week'

[Amends s 103(1) and (5) of the 1968 Act, qv.]

The Drivers' Hours (Passenger and Goods Vehicles) (Modifications) Order 1971

(SI 1971 No 818)

[Note: The text of s 96 of the Transport Act 1968 as modified by this order is set out as an appendix to this order.]

PART I

General

* * *

2.—(1) In this Order, 'the Act' means the Transport Act 1968 and any other expression which is also used in Part VI of the Act has the same meaning as in that Part.

(2) The [Interpretation Act 1978] shall apply for the interpretation of this Order as it applies for the interpretation of an Act of Parliament, and as if for the purposes of [sections 16(1) and 17(2)(*a*)] of that Act this Order were an Act of Parliament and the Order revoked by Article 3 below were an Act of Parliament thereby repealed.

[Article 2 is printed as amended by the Interpretation Act 1978, s 17(2)(a).]

PART II

Drivers of Passenger Vehicles

3. *[Revokes SI 1970 No 356.]*

4.—(1) Where during any working day, or during each working day which falls wholly or partly within any working week, a driver spends all or the greater part of the time when he is driving vehicles to which Part VI of the Act applies in driving one or more passenger vehicles, then, as respects that driver and that working day or working week (as the case may be), the provisions of section 96 of the Act (permitted driving time and periods of duty of drivers of certain vehicles) and of section 103 thereof (interpretation of Part VI of the Act) mentioned in paragraphs (2) to (8) below shall have effect with the modifications or amendments respectively specified in those paragraphs.

(2) Section 96(2) (interval for rest between periods of duty) shall have effect as if for the words from 'if on any working day' onwards there were substituted the following words:—

'if on any working day a driver has been driving a vehicle or vehicles to which this Part of this Act applies—

(*a*) for a period of five and a half hours and the end of that period does not mark the end of the working day; or

(*b*) for periods amounting in the aggregate to five and a half hours and there has not been between any of those periods an interval of not less than half an hour in which the driver was able to obtain rest and refreshment and the end of the last of those periods does not mark the end of the working day,

there shall, as respects the period mentioned in paragraph (*a*) above, at the end of that period or, in the case of the periods mentioned in paragraph (*b*) above, at the end of the last of those periods, be such an interval as aforesaid; but the requirements of the foregoing provisions of this subsection need not be satisfied in relation to a driver who, within any continuous period of eight and a half hours in the working day, drives for periods amounting in the aggregate to not more than seven and three-quarter hours, being periods of driving between which there is a period of, or there are periods amounting in the aggregate to, not less than forty-five minutes driving which the driver has not been driving, if—

(i) the end of the last of those periods of driving marks the end of the working day, or

(ii) at the end of the last of those periods, there is such an interval as is mentioned in paragraph (*b*) above.'.

(3) Section 96(3) (the working day of a driver) shall have effect as if for paragraph (*c*) there were substituted the following paragraph:—

'(*c*) if during that day all or the greater part of the time when he is driving vehicles to which this Part of this Act applies is spent in driving one or more passenger vehicles, shall not exceed sixteen hours.'.

(4) Section 96(4) (interval for rest between working days) shall have effect as if for paragraphs (*a*) and (*b*) there were substituted the words 'shall not be of less than ten hours except that on not more than three occasions in any working week the said interval may be of less than ten hours but not of less than eight and a half hours;'.

(5) Section 96(5) and (8)(*b*) (maximum duty periods in a working week) shall not apply.

(6) Section 96(6) (off-duty periods in a working week) shall have effect as if for the words from 'in the case of each working week of a driver' onwards there were substituted the following words:—

'in the case of every two successive working weeks of a driver, a period of not less than twenty-four hours for which he is off duty, being a period either falling wholly in those weeks or beginning in the second of those weeks and ending in the first of the next two successive weeks; but where the requirements of the foregoing provisions of this subsection have been satisfied in the case of any two successive working weeks by reference to a period ending in the first of the next two successive weeks, no part of that period (except any part after the expiration of the first twenty-four hours of it) shall be taken into account for the purpose of satisfying those requirements in the case of the said next two successive weeks.'.

(7) For section 96(7) there shall be substituted the following subsections:—

'(7) If in the case of the working week of any driver the following requirements are satisfied, that is to say, that—

(*a*) the driver does not drive any vehicle to which this Part of this Act applies for a period of, or for periods amounting in the aggregate to, more than four hours in more than two of the periods of twenty-four hours beginning at midnight which make up that working week (any such period of twenty-four hours in which the driver does drive for a period of, or for periods amounting in the aggregate to, more than four hours being in this subsection, and in subsection (7B) below, referred to as "a full time day"); and (*b*) the provisions of subsection (7B) of this section are complied with in relation to him as respects each full time day in that week,

then, subject to subsection (7A) of this section, the provisions of subsections (1) to (4) of this section shall not apply to that driver in that week, and where the said requirements are satisfied in the case of two successive working weeks of that driver the provisions of subsection (6) of this section shall not apply to him as respects those working weeks.

(7A) Where in the case of the working week of a driver the requirements mentioned in subsection (7) above are satisfied but there is a working day of the driver which falls partly in that working week and partly in a working week in the case of which the said requirements are not satisfied, then the provisions of subsections (1), (2) and (3) of this section shall nevertheless have effect in relation to the whole of that working day.

(7B) The following provisions shall apply as respects each full time day in a working week of a driver in the case of which the requirement mentioned in subsection (7)(*a*) above is satisfied, that is to say—

(*a*) each period of duty of that driver shall fall wholly within the full time day;

(*b*) there shall be an interval for rest of not less than ten hours immediately before his first period of duty and immediately after his last period of duty in the full time day or, if there is only one such period of duty therein, immediately before and after that period of duty;

(*c*) the driver shall not in the full time day drive a vehicle or vehicles to which this Part of this Act applies for periods amounting in the aggregate to more than ten hours;

(*d*) if in the full time day the driver has been driving a vehicle or vehicles to which this Part of this Act applies—

(i) for a period of five and a half hours and the end of that period of driving does not mark the end of his period of duty, or of the last of his periods of duty, in that day, or

(ii) for periods amounting in the aggregate to five and a half hours and there has not been between any of those periods of driving an interval of not less than half an hour in which the driver was able to obtain rest and refreshment and the end of the last of those periods of driving does not mark the end of his period of duty, or of the last of his periods of duty, in that day,

there shall be such an interval as aforesaid at the end of the period of driving mentioned in sub-paragraph (i) above or of the last of the periods of driving mentioned in sub-paragraph (ii) above: provided however that the foregoing requirements of this paragraph need not be satisfied in relation to a driver who, within any continuous period of eight and a half hours falling wholly within the full time day, drives for periods amounting in the aggregate to not more than seven and three-quarter hours, being periods of driving between which there is a period of, or there are periods amounting in the aggregate to, not less than forty-five minutes during which the driver has not been driving, if the end of the last of those periods of driving marks the end of his period, or of the last of his periods, of duty in that day, or at the end of the last of those periods of driving there is such an interval as is mentioned in sub-paragraph (ii) above; and

(*e*) the period during which the driver is on duty in the full time day or, if there is more than one such period, the period between the beginning of his first period of duty in that day and the end of his last period of duty therein, shall not exceed 16 hours.'.

(8) The definition of 'working day' in section 103 shall have effect for the purposes of subsections (1) to (4) and (6) to (8) of section 96 as if for the words from 'eleven hours' to the words 'nine and a half hours' there were substituted the words 'ten hours or (where permitted by virtue of section 96(4) of this Act) of not less than eight and a half hours'.'

PART III

DRIVERS OF GOODS VEHICLES

5. *[Amends the Drivers' Hours (Goods Vehicles) (Modification) Order 1970 (SI 1970 No 257), qv.]*

APPENDIX (Transport Act 1968, s 96, as applied to drivers of passenger vehicles)

96. Permitted driving time and periods of duty

(1) Subject to the provisions of this section, a driver shall not on any working day drive a vehicle or vehicles to which this Part of this Act applies for periods amounting in the aggregate to more than ten hours.

(2) Subject to the provisions of this section, if on any working day a driver has been driving a vehicle or vehicles to which this Part of this Act applies—

(*a*) for a period of five and a half hours and the end of that period does not mark the end of the working day; or

(*b*) for periods amounting in the aggregate to five and a half hours and there has not been between any of those periods an interval of not less than half an hour in which the driver was able to obtain rest and refreshment and the end of the last of those periods does not mark the end of the working day,

there shall, as respects the period mentioned in paragraph (*a*) above, at the end of that period or, in the case of the periods mentioned in paragraph (*b*) above, at the end of the last of those periods, be such an interval as aforesaid; but the requirements of the foregoing provisions of this subsection need not be satisfied in relation to a driver who, within any continuous period of eight and a half hours in the working day, drives for periods amounting in the aggregate to not more than seven and three-quarter hours, being periods of driving between which there is a period of, or there are periods amounting in the aggregate to, not less than forty-five minutes during which the driver has not been driving, if—

(i) the end of the last of those periods of driving marks the end of the working day, or

(ii) at the end of the last of those periods there is such an interval as is mentioned in paragraph (*b*) above.

(3) Subject to the provisions of this section, the working day of a driver—

(*a*) except where paragraph (*b*) or (*c*) of this subsection applies, shall not exceed eleven hours;

(*b*) if during that day he is off duty for a period which is, or periods which taken together are, not less than the time by which his working day exceeds eleven hours, shall not exceed twelve and a half hours;

(*c*) if during that day all or the greater part of the time when he is driving vehicles to which this Part of this Act applies is spent in driving one or more passenger vehicles, shall not exceed sixteen hours.

(4) Subject to the provisions of this section, there shall be, between any two successive working days of a driver, an interval for rest which shall not be of less than ten hours except that on not more than three occasions in any working week the said interval may be of less than ten hours but not of less than eight and a half hours, and for the purposes of this Part of this Act a period of time shall not be treated, in the case of an employee-driver, as not being an interval for rest by reason only that he may be called upon to report for duty if required.

(5) *[Inapplicable.]*

(6) Subject to the provisions of this section, there shall be, in the case of every two successive working weeks of a driver, a period of not less than twenty-four hours for which he is off duty, being a period either falling wholly in those weeks or beginning in the second of those weeks and ending in the first of the next two successive weeks; but where the requirements of the foregoing provisions of this subsection have been satisfied in the case of any two successive working weeks by reference to a period ending in the first of the next two successive weeks, no part of that period (except any part after the expiration of the first twenty-four hours of it) shall be taken into account for the purpose of satisfying those requirements in the case of the said next two successive weeks.

(7) If in the case of the working week of any driver the following requirements are satisfied, that is to say, that—

(*a*) the driver does not drive any vehicle to which this Part of this Act applies for a period of, or for periods amounting in the aggregate to, more than four hours in more than two of the periods of twenty-four hours beginning at midnight which make up that working week (any such period of twenty-four hours in which the driver does drive for a period of, or for periods amounting in the aggregate to, more than four hours being in this subsection, and in subsection (7B) below, referred to as 'a full time day'); and

(*b*) the provisions of subsection (7B) of this section are complied with in relation to him as respects each full time day in that week,

then, subject to subsection (7A) of this section, the provisions of subsections (1) to (4) of this section shall not apply to that driver in that week, and where the said requirements are satisfied in the case of two successive working weeks of that driver the provisions of subsection (6) of this section shall not apply to him as respects those working weeks.

(7A) Where in the case of the working week of a driver the requirements mentioned in subsection (7) above are satisfied but there is a working day of the driver which falls partly in that working week and partly in a working week in the case of which the said requirements are not satisfied, then the provisions of subsections (1), (2) and (3) of this section shall nevertheless have effect in relation to the whole of that working day.

(7B) The following provisions shall apply as respects each full time day in a working week of a driver in the case of which the requirement mentioned in subsection (7)(*a*) above is satisfied, that is to say—

(*a*) each period of duty of that driver shall fall wholly within the full time day;

(*b*) there shall be an interval for rest of not less than ten hours immediately before his first period of duty and immediately after his last period of duty in the full time day or, if there is only one such period of duty therein, immediately before and after that period of duty;

(*c*) the driver shall not in the full time day drive a vehicle or vehicles to which this Part of this Act applies for periods amounting in the aggregate to more than ten hours;

(*d*) if in the full time day the driver has been driving a vehicle or vehicles to which this Part of this Act applies—

(i) for a period of five and a half hours and the end of that period of driving does not mark the end of his period of duty, or of the last of his periods of duty, in that day, or

(ii) for periods amounting in the aggregate to five and a half hours and there has not been between any of those periods of driving an interval of not less than half an hour in which the driver was able to obtain rest and refreshment and the end of the last of those periods of driving does not mark the end of his period of duty, or of the last of his periods of duty, in that day,

there shall be such an interval as aforesaid at the end of the period of driving mentioned in sub-paragraph (i) above or of the last of the periods of driving mentioned in sub-paragraph (ii) above: provided however that the foregoing requirements of this paragraph need not be satisfied in relation to a driver who, within any continuous period of eight and a half hours falling wholly within the full time day, drives for periods amounting in the aggregate to not more than seven and three-quarter hours, being periods of driving between which there is a period of, or there are periods amounting in the aggregate to, not less than forty-five minutes during which the driver has not been driving, if the end of the last of those periods of driving marks the end of his period, or of the last of his periods, of duty in that day, or at the end of the last of those periods of driving there is such an interval as is mentioned in sub-paragraph (ii) above; and

(*e*) the period during which the driver is on duty in the full time day or, if there is more than one such period, the period between the beginning of his first period of duty in that day and the end of his last period of duty therein, shall not exceed sixteen hours.

(8) If on any working day a driver does not drive any vehicle to which this Part of this Act applies—

(*a*) subsections (2) and (3) of this section shall not apply to that day, and

(*b*) *[Inapplicable.]*

(9) For the purposes of subsections (1) and (7) of this section no account shall be taken of any time spent driving a vehicle elsewhere than on a road if the vehicle is being so driven in the course of operations of agriculture or forestry.

(10) For the purposes of enabling drivers to deal with cases of emergency or otherwise to meet a special need, the Secretary of State for Transport may by regulations—

(*a*) create exemptions from all or any of the requirements of subsections (1) to (6) of this section in such cases and subject to such conditions as may be specified in the regulations;

(*b*) empower the traffic commissioner for any area, subject to the provisions of the regulations—

(i) to dispense with the observance of all or any of those requirements (either generally or in such circumstances or to such extent as the commissioner thinks fit) in any particular case for which provision is not made under paragraph (*a*) of this subsection;

(ii) to grant a certificate (which, for the purposes of any proceedings under this Part of this Act, shall be conclusive evidence of the facts therein stated) that any particular case falls or fell within any exemption created under the said paragraph (*a*)

and regulations under this subsection may enable any dispensation under paragraph (*b*)(i) of this subsection to be granted retrospectively and provide for a document purporting to be a certificate granted by virtue of paragraph (*b*)(ii) of this subsection to be accepted in evidence without further proof.

(11) If any of the requirements of the domestic drivers' hours code is contravened in the case of any driver—

(*a*) that driver; and

(*b*) any other person (being that driver's employer or a person to whose orders that driver was subject) who caused or permitted the contravention,

shall be liable on summary conviction to a fine not exceeding level 4 on the standard scale; but a person shall not be liable to be convicted under this subsection if he proves to the court—

(i) that the contravention was due to unavoidable delay in the completion of a journey arising out of circumstances which he could not reasonably have foreseen; or

(ii) in the case of a person charged under paragraph (*b*) of this subsection, that the contravention was due to the fact that the driver had for any particular period or periods driven or been on duty otherwise than in the employment of that person or, as the case may be, otherwise than in the employment in which he is subject to the orders of that person, and that the person charged was not, and could not reasonably have become, aware of that fact.

(11A) Where, in the case of a driver of a motor vehicle, there is in Great Britain a contravention of any requirement of the applicable Community rules as to period of driving, or distance driven, or periods on or off duty, then the offender and any other person (being the offender's employer or a person to whose orders the offender was subject) who caused or permitted the contravention shall be liable on summary conviction to a fine not exceeding level 4 on the standard scale.

(11B) But a person shall not be liable to be convicted under subsection (11A) if—

(*a*) he proves the matters specified in paragraph (i) of subsection (11); or

(*b*) being charged as the offender's employer or a person to whose orders the offender was subject, he proves the matters specified in paragraph (ii) of that subsection.

(12) The Secretary of State for Transport may by order—

(*a*) direct that subsection (1) of this section shall have effect with the substitution for the reference to ten hours of a reference to nine hours, either generally or with such exceptions as may be specified in the order;

(*b*) direct that paragraph (*a*) of subsection (3) of this section shall have effect with the substitution for the reference to eleven hours of a reference to any shorter period, or remove, modify or add to the provisions of that subsection containing exceptions to the said paragraph (*a*);

(*c*) remove, modify or add to any of the requirements of subsections (2), (4), (5) or

(6) of this section or any of the exemptions provided for by subsections (7), (8) and (9) thereof;

and any order under this subsection may contain such transitional and supplementary provisions as the Secretary of State for Transport thinks necessary or expedient, including provisions amending any definition in section 103 of this Act which is relevant to any of the provisions affected by the order.

(13) In this Part of this Act 'the domestic drivers' hours code' means the provisions of subsection (1) to (6) of this section as for the time being in force (and, in particular, as modified, added to or substituted by or under any instrument in force under section 95(1) of this Act or subsection (10) or (12) of this section).

[This version of the Transport Act 1968, s 96, is the text of s 96 as modified by the Drivers' Hours (Passenger and Goods Vehicles) (Modifications) Order 1971 (SI 1971 No 818) above.

This version of s 96 is printed as further amended by the Secretary of State for the Environment Order 1970 (SI 1970 No 1681); the European Communities Act 1972, s 4, and Sched 4, para 9(2); the Road Traffic (Drivers' Ages and Hours of Work) Act 1976, s 2(1); the Secretary of State for Transport Order 1976 (SI 1976 No 1775); the Transport Act 1978, s 10; the Minister of Transport Order 1979 (SI 1979 No 571); the Transfer of Functions (Transport) Order 1981 (SI 1981 No 238); the Criminal Justice Act 1982, ss 38 and 46(1); the Transport Act 1985, s 3 and Sched 2, Part II, para 1(2); the Community Drivers' Hours and Recording Equipment Regulations 1986 (SI 1986 No 1457), reg 2.]

The Drivers' Hours (Passenger Vehicles) (Exemptions) Regulations 1970

(SI 1970 No 145)

[The text of these regulations is printed as amended by:

the Drivers' Hours (Passenger Vehicles) (Exemptions) (Amendment) Regulations 1970 (SI 1970 No 649) (12 May 1970).

The amending regulations are referred to in the notes to the main regulation by year and number. The date referred to above is the date on which the regulations came into force.]

1. Commencement and citation *[Omitted.]*

2. Interpretation

(1) In these Regulations, unless the context otherwise requires,—

'the Act' means the Transport Act 1968,

'emergency' means an event which—

(*a*) causes or is likely to cause such—

(i) danger to the life or health of one or more individuals, or

(ii) a serious interruption in the maintenance of public services for the supply of water, gas, electricity or drainage or of telecommunication or postal services, or

(iii) a serious interruption in the use of roads, or

(iv) a serious interruption in private transport or in public transport (not being an interruption caused by a trade dispute (within the meaning of the Trade Disputes Act 1906) involving persons who carry passengers for hire or reward), or

(*b*) is likely to cause such serious damage to property,

as to necessitate the taking of immediate action to prevent the occurrence or continuance of such danger or interruption or the occurrence of such damage;

and any other expression which is also used in Part VI of the Act has the same meaning as in that Part of that Act.

(2) Any reference in these Regulations to an enactment or instrument shall be construed, unless the context otherwise requires, as a reference to that enactment or instrument as amended by any subsequent enactment or instrument.

(3) The [Interpretation Act 1978] shall apply for the interpretation of these Regulations as it applies for the interpretation of an Act of Parliament.

[The Trade Disputes Act 1906 was repealed by the Industrial Relations Act 1971, s 169 and Sched 9. Cf the Trade Union and Labour Relations Act 1974, s 29.]

3. Exemptions from requirements as to drivers' hours

(1) Any driver of a passenger vehicle who spends time on duty to deal with an emergency is, in accordance with paragraphs (2) and (3) of this Regulation, hereby exempted from the requirements of subsections (1) to (6) of section 96 of the Act in respect of the time so spent.

(2) Any time so spent by such a driver for the purposes of—

(*a*) subsection (1) of the said section 96 be deemed not to have been spent in driving vehicles to which Part VI of the Act applies, and

(*b*) subsections (1) to (6) of the said section 96 (including the expression 'working day' used therein)—

(i) be deemed to have been spent by him off duty, and

(ii) if it would apart from the emergency have been spent in taking an interval for rest or an interval for rest and refreshment be deemed to have been so spent by him.

(3) The requirements of subsection (6) of the said section 96 shall, in relation to such a driver, be deemed to be satisfied in respect of a working week in which he spends time on such duty if he is off duty for a period of twenty-four hours in accordance with that subsection less a period equal to the total time which he spends on such duty in that week.

4. Any driver of a passenger vehicle who spends time on duty during a working day to meet a special need, that is to say work done solely in connection with the collection and delivery of blood for the purposes of transfusion, is hereby exempted from the requirements of section 96(3) in relation to that day, subject to the conditions that—

(*a*) he is able to obtain rest and refreshment during that day for a period which is, or for periods which taken together are, not less than the time by which the working day exceeds 10 hours,

(*b*) that day does not exceed 14 hours, and

(*c*) he has not taken advantage of this exemption from the requirements of section 96(3) on more than one previous working day which forms part of the working week of which that day forms part.

[**5.** Any driver of a passenger vehicle who spends time on duty during a working day to meet a special need, that is to say work done in connection with the carriage of persons suffering from physical or mental disability to or from any place at which social or recreational facilities for them are specially provided, is hereby exempted from the requirements of section 96(3) in relation to that day, subject to the conditions that—

(*a*) he is able to obtain rest and refreshment during that day for a period which is, or for periods which taken together are, not less than the time by which the working day exceeds 10 hours,

(*b*) that day does not exceed 14 hours, and

(*c*) he has not taken advantage of this exemption from the requirements of section 96(3) on more than one previous working day which forms part of the working week of which that day forms part.]

[Regulation 5 was added by SI 1970 No 649.]

The Driving Licences (Community Driving Licences) Regulations 1982

(SI 1982 No 1555)

* * *

4. Temporary validity for Community licences

(1) In relation to a person who becomes normally resident in the United Kingdom and who holds a Community licence—

(*a*) [section 88(5) of the 1988 Act] (regulations may provide that holders of foreign permits who become resident in Great Britain may be treated temporarily as holding Part III licences); and

(*b*) [regulation 25(1) of the Motor Vehicles (Driving Licences) Regulations 1987 *[1987 No 1378, qv]* (which makes such provision);

shall have effect as if the references to Great Britain were references to Great Britain, Northern Ireland or Gibraltar.

(2) In this Regulation 'Community licence' has the same meaning as in [Part III of the Road Traffic Act 1988].

[Regulation 4 is printed as amended by the Interpretation Act 1978, ss 17(2)(a) and 23(1).]

* * *

The Fixed Penalty (Procedure) Regulations 1986

(SI 1986 No 1330)

1.—(1) *[Omitted.]*

(2) In these Regulations any reference to a section is a reference to a section of [the Road Traffic Offenders Act 1988].

(3) These Regulations do not extend to Scotland.

[Regulation 1 is printed as amended by the Interpretation Act 1978, ss 17(2)(a) and 23(1).]

2.—(1) Subject to paragraph (2) below, in the documents described in column 1 of the Schedule to these Regulations and referred to in the provisions of the Act specified in column 2 of the Schedule there shall be provided the information or, as the case may be, further information prescribed in column 3 of the Schedule.

(2) The information prescribed in the Schedule in relation to a fixed penalty notice need not be provided if the offender's driving licence would not be subject to endorsement on conviction of the offence in respect of which the notice was given.

3.—(1) A copy of any fixed penalty notice given or affixed under [section 54 or section 62] shall be forwarded by or on behalf of the constable or traffic warden giving or affixing the notice to the fixed penalty clerk unless the fixed penalty clerk has notified the chief officer of police that he does not wish to receive a copy of any such notice.

(2) Where a fixed penalty notice has been given to a person under [section 54] and that person has surrendered his driving licence in accordance with that section the driving licence shall be forwarded by or on behalf of the constable to the fixed penalty clerk.

[Regulation 3 is printed as amended by the Interpretation Act 1978, ss 17(2)(a) and 23(1).]

4.—(1) Where a constable has issued a fixed penalty notice to a person under [section 54(5)], he shall send a notice indicating that fact to the chief officer of police together with that person's driving licence.

(2) Subject to paragraph (3) below, on receipt of the documents referred to in paragraph (1) above the chief officer of police shall send the driving licence and a copy of the notice issued under [section 54(4)] to the fixed penalty clerk and notify him that a fixed penalty notice has been issued under [section 54(5)].

(3) The chief officer of police shall not send a copy of the notice issued under [section 54(4)] to the fixed penalty clerk under paragraph (2) above if the fixed penalty clerk has notified the chief officer of police that he does not wish to receive a copy of any such notice.

[Regulation 4 is printed as amended by the Interpretation Act 1978, ss 17(2)(a) and 23(1).]

5.—(1) On receipt of the remittance in respect of a fixed penalty the fixed penalty clerk shall notify the chief officer of police that the remittance has been received.

(2) If payment of the fixed penalty is made by a person otherwise than as required by the fixed penalty notice the fixed penalty clerk shall return the remittance to that person.

(3) Where a remittance in respect of a fixed penalty is sent by a person to a justices' clerk who is not the fixed penalty clerk specified in the fixed penalty notice, the justices' clerk shall return the remittance to that person.

6. Where—

(*a*) the suspended enforcement period has expired; and

(*b*) the fixed penalty has not been paid; and

(*c*) either the person to whom the fixed penalty notice was given has requested a hearing under [section 55(2)] or [63(3)] or no registration certificate has been issued under [section 70(2)],

the chief officer of police shall notify the fixed penalty clerk accordingly and the fixed penalty clerk shall, where an endorsable offence is involved, return the driving licence to the person to whom the fixed penalty notice was given.

[Regulation 6 is printed as amended by the Interpretation Act 1978, ss 17(2)(a) and 23(1).]

7. Where—

(*a*) the suspended enforcement period has expired; and

(*b*) the fixed penalty has not been paid; and

(*c*) a registration certificate has been issued under [section 70(2)],

the chief officer of police shall notify the fixed penalty clerk accordingly.

[Regulation 7 is printed as amended by the Interpretation Act 1978, ss 17(2)(a) and 23(1).]

8. Where in a case involving an endorsable offence any sum determined by reference to the fixed penalty is registered under [section 71] for enforcement against the licence holder as a fine the justices' clerk at the court where the sum is registered shall notify the fixed penalty clerk to whom the driving licence was sent that the sum has been registered.

[Regulation 8 is printed as amended by the Interpretation Act 1978, ss 17(2)(a) and 23(1).]

9. Where a fixed penalty notice is issued under [section 54(2)] or [(5)] the fixed penalty clerk shall not accept payment of the fixed penalty after the expiry of the suspended enforcement period.

[Regulation 9 is printed as amended by the Interpretation Act 1978, ss 17(2)(a) and 23(1).]

10. Where a fixed penalty is paid within the suspended enforcement period the fixed penalty clerk shall send a receipt for the payment, if requested, to the payer.

11. For the purposes of [section 56(3)(*a*)] (which provides that a licence receipt issued by a constable is to cease to have effect on the expiration of the period of one month beginning with the date of issue) there shall be prescribed a longer period of two months beginning with the same date.

[Regulation 11 is printed as amended by the Interpretation Act 1978, ss 17(2)(a) and 23(1).]

Regulation 2

SCHEDULE

INFORMATION OR FURTHER INFORMATION TO BE PROVIDED IN CERTAIN DOCUMENTS MENTIONED IN [PART III OF THE ROAD TRAFFIC OFFENDERS ACT 1988]

Document	Provision of Act	Information or further information to be provided
1. Fixed penalty notice	[Section 52(1)]	(i) The name of the police force of which the constable giving the notice is a member. (ii) The serial number of the fixed penalty notice. (iii) Whether the notice relates to an endorsable offence. (iv) The name, date of birth and address of the person to whom the notice is given. (v) The date, time and place of the alleged offence. (vi) The details of the vehicle including the registration number. (vii) The documents, if any, to be produced at a police station and the period within which they must be produced. (viii) An explanation of the action to be taken by the driver where (*a*) he has not or (*b*) he has surrendered the licence. (ix) The fact that the person to whom the notice is given may opt for trial. (x) The method of paying the fixed penalty. (xi) The name, rank and number of the constable issuing the fixed penalty notice. (xii) Guidance to the driver as to the legal consequences of a fixed penalty notice.
2. Receipt for driving licence	[Section 56(1)]	(i) Whether the driving licence is full or provisional. (ii) The driver number as shown on the licence. (iii) The groups of vehicles which the driver is entitled to drive. (iv) The expiry date of the licence. (v) The duration of the validity of the licence receipt. (vi) The method of obtaining a new receipt on the expiry of an old receipt.

Document	Provision of Act	Information or further information to be provided
		(vii) The name, rank and number of the constable issuing the fixed penalty notice.
3. Receipt for driving licence	[Section 56(2)]	(i) The date of issue of receipt. (ii) The code of the magistrates' court issuing receipt. (iii) The name, address and date of birth of driver. (iv) Whether the driving licence is full or provisional. (v) The driver number as shown on the licence. (vi) The groups of vehicles which the driver is entitled to drive. (vii) The expiry date of the licence. (viii) The duration of the validity of the licence receipt.
4. Registration certificate	[Section 70]	(i) The serial number and date, time and place of issue of the notice to owner, notice to hirer or fixed penalty notice (as case may be). (ii) The vehicle registration number. (iii) The driver number. (iv) The amount of the appropriate fixed penalty. (v) The sum to be registered in default of payment of the fixed penalty.
5. Notice requesting new statutory statement	[Section 73(4)]	(i) The particulars of the statutory declaration. (ii) The details of the alleged fixed penalty offence. (iii) A request to furnish a statutory statement of ownership. (iv) The period allowed for a response to the notice. (v) The consequences of providing, or, as the case may be, not providing the statutory statement of ownership.
6. Statement of liability	[Section 66(2)]	(i) The name, date of birth and address of hirer. (ii) The duration of the hiring agreement.

[The Schedule is printed as amended by the Interpretation Act 1978, ss 17(2)(a) and 23(1).]

The Functions of Traffic Wardens Order 1970

(SI 1970 No 1958)

* * *

2. In this Order—

'[the Act of 1988]' and '[the Act of 1984]' mean respectively [the Road Traffic Act 1988] and [the Road Traffic Regulation Act 1984];

'street parking place order' means an order made under [the Act of 1984] relating to a street parking place;

'traffic order' means an order made under [section 1, 6, 9, 12 or 37 of or Sched 9 to the Act of 1984].

[Article 2 is printed as amended by the Road Traffic Act 1972, s 205(2) and Sched 10, para 3; the Road Traffic Regulation Act 1984, s 144(1) and Sched 10, para 2.]

3.—(1) The functions set out in the Schedule to this Order are hereby prescribed as appropriate for discharge by traffic wardens.

(2) For the purposes of the discharge by traffic wardens of such functions, references to a constable or police constable in the following enactments shall include references to a traffic warden—

(*a*) section 52 of the Metropolitan Police Act 1839 so far as it relates to the giving by the commissioner of directions to constables for preventing obstruction;

(*b*) section 22 of the local Act of the second and third year of the reign of Queen Victoria, chapter 94, so far as it makes similar provision with respect to the City of London;

(*c*) [sections 35 and 37 of the Act of 1988] (drivers and pedestrians to comply with traffic directions given by police constables);

(*d*) [section 169 of the Act of 1988] (the power of constables to obtain the names and addresses of pedestrians failing to comply with traffic directions);

(*e*) [section 11 of the Road Traffic Offenders Act 1988] (the giving of evidence of an admission by certificate).

(3) For the purposes of the discharge by traffic wardens of the functions set out in the Schedule to this Order, references in section [165(1) of the Act of 1988] to a police constable shall, in so far as it applies to the furnishing of names and addresses, include references to a traffic warden if the traffic warden has reasonable cause to believe that there has been committed an offence—

(*a*) in respect of a vehicle by its being left or parked on a road during the hours of darkness (as defined by the [Act of 1988]) without the lights or reflectors required by law;

(*b*) in respect of a vehicle by its obstructing a road, or waiting, or being left or parked, or being loaded or unloaded, in a road;

(*c*) in contravention of [section 35 of the Act of 1988];

(*d*) in contravention of a provision of the Vehicles (Excise) Act [1971];

(*e*) created by [section 47 of the Act of 1984] (offences relating to parking places on highways where charges made).

(4) References in [section 164(1) and (6) of the Act of 1988] to a constable or police constable shall include references to a traffic warden only where—

(*a*) the traffic warden is employed to perform functions in connection with the custody of vehicles removed from a road or land in the open air in pursuance of regulations made under [section 99 of the Act of 1984] or from a parking place in pursuance of a street parking place order, and

(*b*) he has reasonable cause to believe that there has been committed an offence in respect of a vehicle by its obstructing a road, or waiting, or being left or parked, or being loaded or unloaded, in a road.

[Article 3 is printed as amended by the Vehicles (Excise) Act 1971, s 39(4) and Sched 7, Part II, para 11; the Road Traffic Act 1972, s 205(2) and Sched 10, para 3; the Road Traffic Regulation Act 1984, s 144(1) and Sched 10, para 2.

The definition of 'hours of darkness' (to which reference is made in art 3(3)(a) above) had been included in earlier legislation and was re-enacted in the Road Traffic Act 1972, s 82. The definition was repealed, however, by the Road Traffic Act 1974. The term is now defined in the Road Vehicles Lighting Regulations 1984 (SI 1984 No 812) (qv).]

SCHEDULE

Article 3

Functions of Traffic Wardens

1.—(1) Traffic wardens may be employed to enforce the law with respect to an offence—

(*a*) committed in respect of a vehicle by its being left or parked on a road during the hours of darkness (as defined by [the Act of 1988]) without the lights or reflectors required by law; or

(*b*) committed in respect of a vehicle by its obstructing a road, or waiting, or being left or parked, or being loaded or unloaded, in a road or other public place; or

(*c*) committed in contravention of a provision of the Vehicles (Excise) Act [1971];

(*d*) created by [section 47 of the Act of 1984] (offences relating to parking places on highways where charges made).

[(2) For the purposes of the enforcement of the law with respect to such of the offences described in sub-paragraph (1) of this paragraph as are fixed penalty offences within the meaning of [section 51(1) of the Road Traffic Offenders Act 1988], other than an offence committed in respect of a vehicle by its obstructing a road or the offence created by [section 22 of the Act of 1988] (which relates to leaving vehicles in dangerous positions), traffic wardens may exercise the functions conferred on constables by [Part III of the Road Traffic Offenders Act 1988].]

2.—(1) Traffic wardens may, under arrangements made with the Secretary of State or a local authority, be employed to act as parking attendants at street parking places provided or controlled by the Secretary of State or local authority.

(2) A traffic warden may exercise functions conferred on a traffic warden by a traffic order or a street parking place order.

3. Without prejudice to the generality of paragraph 1 above, traffic wardens may be employed in connection with obtaining information under [section 172 of the Act

of 1988] or [section 112 of the Act of 1984] (duty to give information as to identity of driver, etc in certain cases).

4. Traffic wardens may be employed to perform functions in connection with the custody of vehicles removed from a road or land in the open air in pursuance of regulations under [section 99 of the Act of 1984] or from a parking place in pursuance of a street parking place order.

5. Where a police authority provides school crossing patrols under [section 26 of the Act of 1984], whether as the appropriate authority or by agreement with the appropriate authority, traffic wardens appointed by that police authority may be employed to act as school crossing patrols.

6.—(1) Subject to the foregoing paragraphs, traffic wardens may be employed in the control and regulation of traffic (including foot passengers) or vehicles whether on a highway or not and to discharge any other functions normally undertaken by the police in connection with the control and regulation of traffic (including foot passengers) or vehicles.

(2) Nothing in this paragraph shall permit the functions described in sub-paragraph (1) to be exercised by a traffic warden who is in a moving vehicle.

[The Schedule is printed as amended by the Vehicles (Excise) Act 1971, s 39(4) and Sched 7, Part II, para 11; the Road Traffic Act 1972, s 205(2) and Sched 10, para 3; the Road Traffic Regulation Act 1984, s 144(1) and Sched 10, para 2; the Functions of Traffic Wardens (Amendment) Order 1986 (SI 1986 No 1328).

As to the definition of 'hours of darkness' (to which reference is made in para 1(1)(a) above), see the note to art 3 of this order.]

The Goods Vehicles (Operators' Licences, Qualifications and Fees) Regulations 1984

(SI 1984 No 176)

[The text of these regulations is printed as amended by:

the Goods Vehicles (Operators' Licences, Qualifications and Fees) (Amendment) Regulations 1986 (SI 1986 No 666) (1 May 1986);

the Goods Vehicles (Operators' Licences, Qualifications and Fees) (Amendment) (No 2) Regulations 1986 (SI 1986 No 1391) (12 September 1986);

the Goods Vehicles (Operators' Licences, Qualifications and Fees) (Amendment) Regulations 1987 (SI 1987 No 841) (1 July 1987); and

the Goods Vehicles (Operators' Licences, Qualifications and Fees) (Amendment) (No 2) Regulations 1987 (SI 1987 No 2170) (18 January 1988).

The amending regulations are referred to in the notes to the main regulations only by their years and numbers. The dates referred to above are the dates on which the regulations came into force.

The main regulations have also been amended by the Goods Vehicles (Operators' Licences, Qualifications and Fees) (Amendment) Regulations 1988 (SI 1988 No 2128), but these do not affect the text of any regulation printed in this publication.]

ARRANGEMENT OF REGULATIONS

PART I

GENERAL

PART II

PROVISIONS AS TO LICENCES RELATIVE TO THE COUNCIL DIRECTIVES

* * *

PART VIII

OTHER MATTERS

SCHEDULES

PART I

GENERAL

1. Commencement and citation *[Omitted.]*

2. Revocation *[Omitted.]*

3. Interpretation

(1) In these Regulations, unless the context otherwise requires, any reference to—

(*a*) a numbered section is a reference to the section bearing that number in the Transport Act 1968;

(*b*) a numbered Part is a reference to the Part bearing that number in the Transport Act 1968;

(*c*) a numbered Regulation or Schedule is a reference to the Regulation or, as the case may be, the Schedule bearing that number in these Regulations; and

(*d*) a numbered paragraph is a reference to the paragraph bearing that number in the Regulation in which the reference appears.

(2) In these Regulations, unless the context otherwise requires—

'application' means an application for an operator's licence of which publication is required by section 63(1) or an application for the variation of an operator's licence for which publication is required by section 68(4) or 69D(3);

'Applications and Decisions' means the statement issued by a licensing authority under Regulation 24;

'company', 'holding company' and 'subsidiary' shall be construed as provided in [respectively sections 735 and 736 of the Companies Act 1985 [*qv*]];

'disc' means a disc issued in accordance with Regulation 25(1) and (2) or 29(2);

'dual purpose vehicle' has the same meaning as in [column 2 of the Table in regulation 3(2) of the Road Vehicles (Construction and Use) Regulations 1986 *[SI 1986 No 1078, qv]*;

'goods vehicle' has the same meaning as in section 92(1) but excludes a small goods vehicle as described in section 60(4);

'goods vehicle examiner' has the same meaning as in [section 68(2) of the Road Traffic Act 1988];

. . .

'holder' in relation to a licence means the person to whom the licence was granted;

['international transport operation' has the same meaning as in the 1974 Council Directive, and the expression 'national transport operation' shall be construed accordingly;]

'licence' means an operator's licence (whether standard or restricted) as defined in section 60(1);

'licensing authority' has the meaning given by section 59(1);

'motor vehicle' means a mechanically propelled vehicle intended or adapted for use on roads;

'maintenance' in relation to a vehicle includes inspection, repair and fuelling;

. . .

['recovery vehicle' has the same meaning as in Part I of Schedule 3 to the Vehicles (Excise) Act 1971 [*qv*];]

'relevant conviction' means—

(i) any conviction mentioned in section 69(4), or

(ii) any conviction of contravening any provision of the law of Northern Ireland or of a country or territory outside the United Kingdom corresponding to any of the said convictions,

not in either case being a spent conviction within the meaning of the Rehabilitation of Offenders Act 1974;

'restricted licence' means a licence under which goods vehicles may be used on a road for the carriage of goods for or in connection with any trade or business carried on by the holder of the licence, not being the trade or business of carrying goods for hire or reward;

'road transport undertaking' means an undertaking which involves the use of goods vehicles under an operator's licence, or in accordance with the law of Northern Ireland or of any Member State of the European Economic Community other than the United Kingdom;

'showman's goods vehicle' has the same meaning as in Schedule 4 to the Vehicles (Excise) Act 1971 [*qv*]; and

'standard licence' means a licence under which goods vehicles may be used on a road for the carriage of goods—

(i) for hire or reward, or

(ii) for or in connection with any trade or business carried on by the holder of the licence;

'the 1974 Council Directive' means Council Directive (EEC) 74/561 of 12th November 1974 *[OJ L308/18, 19 November 1974]* on admission to the occupation of road haulage operator in national and international transport operations;

'the 1977 Council Directive' means Council Directive (EEC) 77/796 of 12th December 1977 *[OJ L334/37, 24 December 1977]* aiming at the mutual recognition of diplomas, certificates and other evidence of formal qualifications for goods haulage operators and road passenger transport operators, including measures intending to encourage these operators effectively to exercise their right to freedom of establishment;

'tower wagon' has the same meaning as in [section 4(2) of] the Vehicles (Excise) Act 1971 [*qv*];

'trade licence' has the same meaning as in section 38(1) of the Vehicles (Excise) Act 1971 [*qv*];

'traffic area' means a traffic area constituted for the purposes of the Public Passenger Vehicles Act 1981;

'transport manager', in relation to a business, means an individual who is in, or who is engaged to enter into, the full time employment of the holder of a standard licence and who, either alone or jointly with one or more other persons, has continuous and effective responsibility for the management of the transport operations of the business in so far as they relate to the carriage of goods; and

'visiting force', 'headquarters' and 'vehicle in the service of a visiting force or a headquarters' have the same meanings as in the Visiting Forces and International Headquarters (Application of Law) Order 1965 *[SI 1965 No 1536]*.

(3) For the purposes of these Regulations a person who is an applicant for, or a holder of, a standard licence, or who is a transport manager, shall be regarded as being engaged in a road transport undertaking if the person in question is—

(*a*) the holder or, if an individual, one of the joint holders, of a licence, or

(*b*) the subsidiary of the holder of a licence being a subsidiary to which goods vehicles used under the licence belong or in whose possession they are, or

(*c*) if an individual, in the employment of a person who carries on a road transport undertaking and which gives the individual responsibility for the operation of goods vehicles used under a licence.

(4) For the purposes of these Regulations, the driver of a vehicle, if it belongs to him or is in his possession under an agreement for hire, hire-purchase or loan, and in any other case the person whose servant or agent the driver is, shall be regarded as the person using the vehicle; and references to using the vehicle shall be construed accordingly.

(5) The relevant plated weight of a vehicle, for the purposes of section 60(4) (definition of small goods vehicle) and section 71(6) (definition of large goods vehicle) is the gross weight not to be exceeded in Great Britain of the vehicle as shown on a Ministry plate as defined in [column 2 in the Table in regulation 3(2) of the Road Vehicles (Construction and Use) Regulations 1986], or if no such plate has been issued in respect of that vehicle, the maximum gross weight of the vehicle as shown on a plate affixed to the vehicle by virtue of [regulation 66 of those Regulations].

[Regulation 3 is printed as amended by the Interpretation Act 1978, ss 17(2)(a) and 23(1); SI 1986 No 1391; SI 1987 Nos 841 and 2170.]

PART II

Provisions as to Licences Relative to the Council Directives

4. Classification of licences

(1) For the purposes of enabling the 1974 Council Directive to be implemented in Great Britain licences granted under Part V are divided into two classes, namely—

(*a*) standard licences; and

(*b*) restricted licences.

[(2) Where a company ('the first company') carries goods for hire or reward it shall hold a standard licence unless it is carrying goods the property of another company ('the second company') where the second company is either—

(*a*) a subsidiary of the first company; or

(*b*) a holding company for the first company; or

(*c*) a subsidiary of a company which is a holding company for that subsidiary and for the first company.

In any case specified in sub-paragraph (*a*), (*b*) or (*c*) of this paragraph the first company may hold a restricted licence instead of a standard licence.]

(3) Standard licences may authorise goods vehicles to be used for the carriage of goods—

(*a*) on both international and national transport operations, or

(*b*) on national transport operations only.

(4) A statement shall appear—

(*a*) on the face of each licence, indicating whether it is a standard licence or a restricted licence, and

(*b*) on the face of each standard licence, indicating whether it covers both international and national transport operations or national transport operations only.

[Regulation 4 is printed as amended by SI 1984 No 666.]

* * *

PART VIII

OTHER MATTERS

25. Identification of vehicles

(1) The licensing authority shall, when any motor vehicle to be used under a licence is specified in the licence, issue to the holder of the licence a disc in respect of the vehicle.

(2) Those discs shall distinguish—

(*a*) between a vehicle specified in a standard licence and a vehicle specified in a restricted licence, and

(*b*) in the case of a vehicle specified in a standard licence, between one specified in a licence which covers both international and national transport operations and one specified in a licence which covers national operations only.

(3) The holder of a licence shall, during such time as any motor vehicle is specified in the licence and whether or not for the time being the vehicle is being used for the purpose for which a licence is required, cause a disc appropriate to the vehicle to be affixed to that vehicle in a waterproof container—

(*a*) in the case of a vehicle fitted with a front windscreen, on the near side and near the lower edge of the windscreen with the obverse side facing forwards;

(*b*) in the case of a vehicle not fitted with a front windscreen, in a conspicuous position on the front or near side of the vehicle.

(4) At all times while a disc is affixed to a vehicle in accordance with the requirements of paragraph (3) the person for the time being in control of that vehicle shall keep that disc readily legible, and at no time shall any person except the licensing authority, or a person authorised to do so on his behalf, write on or make any other alteration to a disc.

26. Temporary addition of a vehicle

Where—

(*a*) a motor vehicle specified in an operator's licence ('the specified vehicle') has been rendered unfit for service, or withdrawn from service for overhaul or repair, and the holder of the licence informs the licensing authority of his desire to have a variation of the licence specifying, until it is rendered fit for service again, a motor vehicle in his possession or to be hired without a driver ('the additional vehicle') or

(*b*) the specified vehicle has been rendered fit for service again, and the holder of the licence informs the licensing authority of his desire to have a variation of the licence whereby the additional vehicle will cease to be specified in the licence,

the provisions of Regulations 11 and 12 shall not apply and the holder of the licence shall return to the licensing authority the disc for the specified vehicle, or the additional vehicle, as the case may be.

27. Notification of change of address

If during the currency of a licence its holder changes his address for the service of notice as notified in his application or as subsequently notified under this Regulation he shall within 21 days from the date of such change notify such change to the licensing authority by whom the licence was granted.

28. Production of licence for examination

(1) The holder of a licence shall produce the licence for inspection by—

(*a*) a constable,

(*b*) goods vehicle examiner, or

(*c*) a person authorised in that behalf by the licensing authority

on being required by such a person to do so, and the holder may do so at any operating centre covered by the licence or at his head or principal place of business within the traffic area in which any such operating centre lies or, if the requirement is made by a constable, at a police station chosen by the holder.

(2) The holder of a licence shall comply with any requirement mentioned in paragraph (1) within 14 days of the day on which the requirement is made.

29. Issue of copies of licences and discs

(1) If a licence or disc has been lost, destroyed or defaced, the person to whom it was issued shall forthwith notify in writing the licensing authority by whom the licence or disc was granted or issued.

(2) If—

(*a*) the licensing authority is satisfied that a licence or disc has been lost, destroyed or defaced, and

(*b*) in the case of a licence or disc which has been defaced, it is surrendered to the licensing authority,

the licensing authority shall issue a copy (so marked) which shall have effect as the original licence or disc.

(3) Where a licence or disc has been lost and after a copy has been issued the lost licence or disc is found by or comes into the possession of the holder of the licence he shall forthwith return the original licence or disc to the licensing authority.

30. Return of licences and discs

(1) If the holder of a licence ceases to use under the licence any vehicle specified in the licence he shall within 21 days notify the licensing authority by whom the licence was granted and return to that licensing authority the licence for variation and the disc relating to the vehicle.

(2) If a licence is varied under section 68 or 69D its holder shall, when required by the licensing authority so to do, return to the licensing authority—

(*a*) the licence, and

(*b*) if the number of vehicles specified in the licence has been reduced, the disc relating to any vehicle no longer specified in the licence.

(3) If a licence is revoked, [surrendered,] suspended, terminated prematurely or curtailed, or if a licensing authority has given a direction in respect of a licence under section 69(2), the holder of the licence shall [on or before the date specified in a notice to the effect] delivered to him personally or sent to him by the recorded delivery service at the address shown in his application or last notified in accordance with Regulation 27 send or deliver to the licensing authority by whom the licence was granted—

(*a*) the licence, and

(*b*) the disc relating to any vehicle which the licensing authority may specify

for cancellation, retention during the time of suspension, or alteration as the case may be.

[Regulation 30 is printed as amended by SI 1987 No 841.]

31. Expiry of licences

The dates for the expiry of operators' licences for the purposes of section 67(2) are the last day of every month.

32. Holding companies and subsidiaries

(1) A holding company may apply to the licensing authority for any traffic area—

(*a*) if it does not already hold a licence in respect of that area, or if it desires to replace its existing licence in respect of that area with a new licence, for the grant [of] a licence, or

(*b*) if it already holds a licence in respect of that area and does not desire to replace such licence with a new licence, for a variation of its licence by a direction under section 68(1)(*a*)

which would have the effect, if the application were granted, of including in the licence to be issued to, or already held by, the holding company, vehicles belonging to or in the possession of a subsidiary of that company specified in the application.

(2) An application by a holding company under paragraph (1) shall, unless the subsidiary is not the holder of a licence, or the licence or variation applied for by the holding company will not take effect until any licence held by the subsidiary has expired by effluxion of time, be accompanied by an application by the subsidiary for the variation of the licence held by the subsidiary by a direction under section 68(1)(*b*) for the removal therefrom of all or some of the vehicles authorised to be used thereunder, being the vehicles to which the application of the holding company relates.

(3) Where a holding company, on an application under paragraph (1), signifies to the licensing authority its desire that the provisions of this Regulation should have

effect as respects a subsidiary of that company, then, in relation to the application and to any licence granted to the holding company, or held by the holding company and varied, on that application, and to the use of any vehicle authorised to be used under any such licence, Part V of the Transport Act 1968 and these Regulations shall have effect subject to the modifications specified in Schedule 4.

(4) The provisions of this Regulation shall cease to have effect as respects a holding company and its subsidiary—

(*a*) if the holding company gives notice to the licensing authority who granted or varied its licence that it desires that this Regulation should, as from any date, cease to apply to the holding company and that subsidiary, as from that date; or

(*b*) as from the date on which that subsidiary ceases to be a subsidiary of that holding company.

(5) Where by virtue of the provisions of paragraphs (1) to (3) a holding company holds a licence which includes goods vehicles belonging to or in the possession of a subsidiary of that company, and the holding company gives notice under paragraph (4)(*a*) then in relation to any application by the subsidiary for the grant of a licence in respect of all or any of those vehicles, section 63 shall have effect as if for sub-section (1) there were substituted the following sub-section—

'(1) The licensing authority may publish in the prescribed manner notice of any application to the authority for an operator's licence made by a company or other body corporate in pursuance of regulations made under section 85 of this Act.'

(6) Where the provisions of this Regulation cease to have effect as respects a holding company and its subsidiary by virtue of paragraph 4(*b*) the company which was the holding company shall within 21 days of the event which caused the subsidiary to cease to be a subsidiary of that company notify the licensing authority by whom the licence was granted, supply all material details of the event, and return to the licensing authority the licence and the discs relating to the vehicles authorised to be used thereunder, and in so far as the holding company fails to satisfy that requirement the company which was the subsidiary company shall, on being so directed by the licensing authority, within 7 days of that direction supply the details, or return the licence and the discs, as the case may require.

(7) In a case where the applicant for, or the holder of, a standard licence is a holding company and the goods vehicles used, or to be used, under the licence belong to, or are in the possession of, a subsidiary of that holding company, the provisions of these Regulations apply as if—

(*a*) the road transport undertaking and any operating centre of the subsidiary were the road transport undertaking and an operating centre of the holding company,

(*b*) for purposes of, or relating to, the reputation and financial standing of the holding company, the activities, relevant convictions and financial resources of the subsidiary were activities, convictions and resources of the holding company, and

(*c*) in relation to a transport manager, his employment by the subsidiary were employment by the holding company.

[Regulation 32 is printed as amended by SI 1987 No 841.]

33. Offences

(1) Any contravention of, or failure to comply with, a provision in Regulations 25(3), 25(4), 27, 28, 29(1), 29(3), 30(1), 30(2), 30(3) or 32(6) is, by virtue of section 91(6), hereby declared to be an offence and subject to a fine as provided in section 91(6).

(2) A person who uses a goods vehicle under a restricted licence for carrying goods for hire or reward shall be guilty of an offence and shall be liable on summary conviction to a fine not exceeding £500.

(3) A person who uses a goods vehicle under a standard licence, which covers carrying goods for hire or reward on national transport operations only, for carrying goods for hire or reward on international transport operations shall be guilty of an offence and shall be liable on summary conviction to a fine not exceeding £500.

(4) The above provisions of this Regulation do not apply in relation to offences committed before the date on which these Regulations come into operation.

[These regulations came into operation on 1 June 1984; reg 1.]

34. Classes of vehicle for which a licence is not required

The classes of vehicle specified under section 60(2)(*b*) as those to which section 60(1) does not apply are the classes mentioned in Schedule 5.

* * *

SCHEDULE 5 (see regulation 34)

CASES IN WHICH A LICENCE IS NOT REQUIRED

1. Any vehicle (including a trailer drawn by it) mentioned in paragraph 2(1) of Part I of Schedule 3 to the Vehicles (Excise) Act 1971 whilst being used solely for the haulage of such objects as are referred to in that paragraph.

2. A dual-purpose vehicle and any trailer drawn by it.

3. A vehicle used on a road only in passing from private premises to other private premises in the immediate neighbourhood belonging (except in the case of a vehicle so used only in connection with excavation or demolition) to the same person, provided that the distance travelled on a road by any such vehicle does not exceed in the aggregate six miles in any one week.

[4. A motor vehicle constructed or adapted primarily for the carriage of passengers and their effects, and any trailer drawn by it, while being so used.]

5. *[Revoked.]*

6. *[Revoked.]*

7. A vehicle which is being used for funerals.

8. A vehicle which is being used for police, fire brigade or ambulance purposes.

9. A vehicle which is being used for fire-fighting or rescue operations at mines.

10. A vehicle on which no permanent body has been constructed, which is being used only for carrying burden which either is carried solely for the purpose of test or

trial, or consists of articles and equipment which will form part of the completed vehicle when the body is constructed.

11. A vehicle which is being used under a trade licence.

12. A vehicle in the service of a visiting force or of a headquarters.

[13. A vehicle used by or under the control of Her Majesty's United Kingdom forces.]

14. A trailer not constructed primarily for the carriage of goods but which is being used incidentally for that purpose in connection with the construction, maintenance or repair of roads.

15. A road roller and any trailer drawn by it.

16. A vehicle while being used under the direction of HM Coastguard or of the Royal National Lifeboat Institution for the carriage of life-boats, life-saving appliances or crew.

17. A vehicle fitted with a machine, appliance, apparatus or other contrivance which is a permanent or essentially permanent fixture, provided that the only goods carried on the vehicle are—

(*a*) required for use in connection with the machine, appliance, apparatus or contrivance or the running of the vehicle,

[(*aa*) to be mixed by the machine, appliance, apparatus or contrivance with other goods not carried on the vehicle on a road in order to thrash, grade, clean or chemically treat grain;]

(*b*) to be mixed by the machine, appliance, apparatus or contrivance with other goods not carried on the vehicle in order to make fodder for animals, or

(*c*) mud or other matter swept up from the surface of a road by the use of the machine, appliance, apparatus or other contrivance.

18. A vehicle while being used by a local authority—

(*a*) for road cleansing, road watering, snow-clearing or the collection or disposal of refuse, night-soil or the contents of cess-pools, septic tanks, or for the purposes of the enactments relating to weights and measures or the sale of food and drugs; or

(*b*) for the distribution of grit, salt or other materials on frosted, icebound or snow-covered roads or for going to or from the place where it is to be used for the said purposes or for any other purpose directly connected with those purposes.

19. A vehicle while being used by a local authority in the discharge of any function conferred on or exercisable by that authority under Regulations made under the Civil Defence Act 1948.

20. A steam-propelled vehicle.

[21. A tower wagon or trailer drawn thereby, provided that the only goods carried on the trailer are goods required for use in connection with the work on which the tower wagon is ordinarily used as such.]

22. A vehicle while being used for the carriage of goods within an aerodrome within the meaning of section 23(1) of the Airports Authority Act 1975.

23. An electrically propelled vehicle.

24. A showman's goods vehicle and any trailer drawn thereby.

25. A vehicle first used before 1 January 1977 which has an unladen weight not exceeding 1525 kilograms and for which the maximum gross weight, as shown on a plate affixed to the vehicle by virtue of [Regulation 66 of the Road Vehicles (Construction and Use) Regulations 1986] or any provision which that Regulation replaced, exceeds 3.5 tonnes but does not exceed $3\frac{1}{2}$ tons.

26. A vehicle while being used by a highway authority for the purposes of section 160 or 200 of the Road Traffic Act 1972.

27. A vehicle being held ready for use in an emergency by an undertaking for the supply of water, electricity, gas or telephone services.

[28. A recovery vehicle.]

[Schedule 5 is printed as amended by the Interpretation Act 1978, ss 17(2)(a) and 23(1); SI 1986 No 666; SI 1987 Nos 841 and 2170.]

* * *

The Goods Vehicles (Plating and Testing) Regulations 1988

(SI 1988 No 1478)

PART I

General

1. Commencement and citation *[Omitted.]*

2. Revocation *[Omitted.]*

3. Interpretation

(1) In these Regulations, except where the context otherwise requires, the following expressions have the meanings hereby respectively assigned to them:—

'the 1971 Act' means the Vehicles (Excise) Act 1971 [*qv*];

'[the 1988 Act]' means [the Road Traffic Act 1988] [*qv*];

'the Construction and Use Regulations' means the Road Vehicles (Construction and Use) Regulations 1986 *[SI 1986 No 1078, as amended; qv]*;

'the National Type Approval for Goods Vehicles Regulations' means the Motor Vehicles (Type Approval for Goods Vehicles) (Great Britain) Regulations 1982 *[SI 1982 No 1271, as amended; qv]*;

'agricultural motor vehicle', 'agricultural trailer', 'agricultural trailed appliance', 'agricultural trailed appliance conveyor', 'articulated vehicle', 'converter dolly', 'dual-purpose vehicle', 'engineering plant', 'Ministry plate', 'registered', 'semi-trailer', 'straddle carrier', 'track-laying', 'works trailer', and 'works truck' have the same meanings respectively as in the Construction and Use Regulations;

'appeal officer' means the person appointed by the Secretary of State for the purposes of appeals to the Secretary of State;

'area engineer' means the area mechanical engineer appointed by the Secretary of State for the purposes of appeals other than appeals to the Secretary of State;

'auxiliary station' means a vehicle testing station which is regularly not open for the carrying out of re-tests on certain normal working days;

'break-down vehicle' means a motor vehicle—

(*a*) on which is permanently mounted apparatus designed for raising one disabled vehicle partly from the ground and for drawing that vehicle when so raised; and

(*b*) which is not equipped to carry any load other than articles required for the operation of, or in connection with, that apparatus or for repairing disabled vehicles;

'examination' means any operation being—

(*a*) a first examination;

(*b*) a re-test;

(*c*) a periodical test;

(*d*) a re-examination under regulation 33; or

(*e*) a re-examination on an appeal under regulation 25, 29 or 37;

'first examination', in relation to a vehicle, means an examination being both an examination for plating and a first goods vehicle test;

'Goods Vehicle Centre' means the Goods Vehicle Centre at Welcombe House, 91–92 The Strand, Swansea, SA1 2DH.

'living van' means a vehicle whether mechanically propelled or not which is used as living accommodation by one or more persons, and which is also used for the carriage of goods or burden which are not needed by such one or more persons for the purpose of their residence in the vehicle;

'Ministry test date disc' means a plate issued by the Secretary of State for a goods vehicle being a trailer, following the issue of a goods vehicle test certificate for that trailer under these Regulations and containing—

(*a*) the identification mark allotted to that trailer and shown in that certificate;

(*b*) the date until which that certificate is valid; and

(*c*) the number of the vehicle testing station shown in the said certificate;

'notifiable alteration', in relation to a vehicle, means—

(*a*) an alteration made in the structure or fixed equipment of the vehicle which varies the carrying capacity or towing capacity of the vehicle;

(*b*) an alteration, affecting any part of a braking system or the steering system with which the vehicle is equipped or of the means of operation of either of those systems; or

(*c*) any other alteration made in the structure or fixed equipment of the vehicle which renders or is likely to render the vehicle unsafe to travel on roads at any weight equal to any plated weight shown in the plating certificate for that vehicle.

'periodical test', in relation to a vehicle, means a goods vehicle test carried out under Part IV of these Regulations on a vehicle in respect of which a goods vehicle test certificate has been issued on a first examination of it or as a result of a re-test following that examination or as a result of an appeal under any provision in these Regulations;

'plated particulars' means those particulars which are required to be shown in a Ministry plate under Schedule 10 to the Construction and Use Regulations;

'plated weights' means such of the plated particulars related to gross weight, axle weight for each axle and train weight as are required to be shown in column (2) on the Ministry plate;

'play bus' means a motor vehicle which was originally constructed to carry more than 12 passengers but which has been adapted primarily for the carriage of play things for children (including articles required in connection with the use of those things);

'the prescribed construction and use requirements', in relation to a vehicle, means those of the requirements specified in Schedule 3 which apply to the vehicle;

're-test', in relation to a vehicle, means an examination which is

(*a*) an examination for plating and a goods vehicle test carried out on a vehicle under Part III of these Regulations subsequent to a first examination of that vehicle as a result of which a notice of refusal was issued; or

(*b*) a goods vehicle test carried out on a vehicle under Part IV of these Regulations subsequent to a periodical test of that vehicle as a result of which a notice of refusal was issued;

'Secretary of State' means the Secretary of State for Transport;

'sender' means a person who informs the Secretary of State of a notifiable alteration under regulation 30;

'sold or supplied by retail', in relation to a trailer, means sold or supplied otherwise than to a person acquiring solely for the purpose of resale or of resupply for a valuable consideration;

'the standard lists' means lists—

(*a*) prepared by the Secretary of State after consultation with representative organisations of the motor manufacturing and road transport industries and other connected organisations and published by the Goods Vehicle Centre; and

(*b*) showing, as respects goods vehicles of a make, model and type specified in the lists and complying in the case of motor vehicles with certain particulars relating to the engine, transmission, brakes and dimensions so specified and in the case of trailers with certain particulars relating to type of coupling, dimensions, brakes and tyres so specified (hereinafter referred to as 'the constructional particulars') the gross weight for, and the axle weight for each axle of, vehicles of that make, model and type and, in the case of motor vehicles, the train weight for vehicles of that make, model and type, the said weights being weights at or below which the Secretary of State considers vehicles of that make, model and type could safely be driven on roads having regard to—

(i) the weights at which vehicles of that make, model and type were originally designed to operate;

(ii) in the case of motor vehicles, the requirements as to brakes of regulations 15, 16 and 18 of the Construction and Use Regulations;

(iii) in the case of trailers, the requirements of regulations 15 and 16 of the Construction and Use Regulations and the provisions of Schedule 1 as respects braking force; and

'vehicle testing station' means a station provided by the Secretary of State under [section 52(2) of the 1988 Act].

(2) Any reference in these Regulations to—

(*a*) an examination for plating includes, in relation to a vehicle to which regulation 18 applies, an examination provided for in that regulation; and

(*b*) a vehicle of a make, model and type shall in relation to a trailer, include a reference to a vehicle of a make and bearing a serial number.

(3) For the purpose of these Regulations, in counting the number of axles of a vehicle, where the centres of the areas of contact between all the wheels and the road surface can be included between any two vertical planes at right angles to the longitudinal axis of the vehicle less than 1.02 metres apart, those wheels shall be treated as constituting one axle.

(4) For the purpose of these Regulations, in determining when a trailer is first sold or supplied by retail the date of such first sale or supply by retail shall in the case of a trailer which is constructed with a chassis be taken to be the date on which that chassis (with or without a body mounted on it) is first sold or supplied by retail and in the case of any other trailer be taken to be the date the trailer is first sold or supplied by retail.

(5) Unless the context otherwise requires, any reference in these Regulations to—

(*a*) a numbered regulation or Schedule is a reference to the regulation or Schedule bearing that number in these Regulations;

(*b*) a numbered paragraph is a reference to the paragraph bearing that number in the regulation or Schedule in which the reference appears;

(*c*) a vehicle is a reference to a vehicle to which these Regulations apply.

[Regulation 3 is printed as amended by the Interpretation Act 1978, ss 17(2)(a) and 23(1).]

4. Application

(1) Subject to paragraph (2), these Regulations apply to goods vehicles being—

(*a*) heavy motor cars and motor cars constructed or adapted for the purpose of forming part of an articulated vehicle;

(*b*) other heavy motor cars;

(*c*) other motor cars, the weight of which unladen exceeds 1525 kilograms;

(*d*) semi-trailers;

(*e*) converter dollies of any unladen weight manufactured on or after 1st January 1979; or

(*f*) trailers, not being converter dollies or semi-trailers, the unladen weight of which exceeds 1020 kilograms.

(2) Nothing in these Regulations applies to goods vehicles of any of the classes of vehicle specified in Schedule 2.

5. Prescribed requirements for tests *[Omitted.]*

6. Supervision of tests *[Omitted.]*

7. Authority to drive and duties of driver

(1) The person who drove the vehicle to an examination shall, except so far as he is permitted to be absent by the person who is carrying out the examination, be present throughout the whole of the examination, and shall drive the vehicle and operate its controls when and in such a manner as he may be directed by the person who is carrying out the examination to do so.

(2) The person who is carrying out an examination is authorised to drive the vehicle on a road or elsewhere.

(3) A contravention of this regulation is hereby declared to be an offence.

* * *

PART V

Regulations Governing Notifiable Alterations, Amendments of Plating Certificates and Re-examinations in Connection Therewith

30. Secretary of State to be informed of notifiable alterations

In the event of a notifiable alteration being made to a vehicle in respect of which a plating certificate has been issued, and before the vehicle to which the alteration has been made is used on roads, particulars of that alteration on a form approved by the Secretary of State shall be sent to him at the Goods Vehicle Centre, and any such form may contain a request by the sender for an amendment to be made as respects a plated weight shown on the plating certificate for the vehicle.

[As to the consequences of failure to notify the Secretary of State, see the Road Traffic Act 1988, s 53(3), above.]

* * *

PART VI

MISCELLANEOUS MATTERS

* * *

39. General provisions as to fees

(1) In this Regulation 'exceptional circumstances' means an accident, a fire, an epidemic, severe weather, a failure in the supply of essential services or other unexpected happening (excluding a breakdown or mechanical defect in a vehicle or non-delivery of spare parts therefor).

(2), (3) *[Omitted.]*

[The definition of 'exceptional circumstances' in reg 39(1) is applied by reg 46.]

PART VIII

EXEMPTIONS

44. Exemptions from [section 53(1) and (2) of the 1988 Act]

(1) The provisions of [section 53(1) and (2) of the 1988 Act] do not apply to the use of a vehicle for any of the following purposes—

(*a*) the purpose of submitting it by previous arrangement for, or of bringing it away from, or being used in the course of or in connection with any examination;

(*b*) where a goods vehicle test certificate is refused on an examination—

(i) the purpose of delivering it by previous arrangement at, or bringing it away from, a place where work is to be or has been done on it to remedy the defects on the grounds of which the certificate was refused; or

(ii) the purpose of delivering it, by towing it, to a place where it is to be broken up;

(*c*) when unladen, the purpose of being driven or drawn by a vehicle driven under a trade licence issued under section 16 of the 1971 Act;

(*d*) the purpose of being driven or drawn where it has been imported into Great Britain after arrival in Great Britain on the journey from the place where it has arrived in Great Britain to a place where it is to be kept by the person importing the vehicle or by any other person on whose behalf the vehicle has been imported, and in this sub-paragraph the reference to a vehicle being imported into Great Britain is a reference, in the case of a vehicle which has been so imported more than once, to the first such importation, and in determining for the purposes of this sub-paragraph when a vehicle was first so imported any such importation as is referred to in paragraph 24 of Schedule 2 shall be disregarded.

(*e*) any purpose for which it is authorised to be used on roads by an order under [section 44 of the 1988 Act];

(*f*) any purpose connected with its seizure or detention by a police constable;

(*g*) any purpose connected with its removal, detention, seizure, condemnation or forfeiture under any provision in the Customs and Excise Management Act 1979; and

(*h*) the purpose of removing it under section 3 of the Refuse Disposal (Amenity) Act 1978 [*qv*], or under section 99 of the Road Traffic Regulation Act 1984 or of removing it from a parking place in pursuance of an order under section 35(1) of the Road Traffic Regulation Act 1984, an order relating to a parking place designated under section 45 thereof, or a provision of a designation order having effect by virtue of section 53(3) thereof.

(2) The provisions of [section 53(1) and (2) of the 1988 Act] shall not apply to the use of a vehicle in so far as such use occurs in any place (excluding the Isle of Wight, the islands of Lewis, Mainland (Orkney), Mainland (Shetland) and Skye) being an island or to any area mainly surrounded by water, being an island or area from which motor vehicles not constructed for special purposes can at no time be conveniently driven to a road in any other part of Great Britain by reason of the absence of any bridge, tunnel, ford or other way suitable for the passage of such motor vehicles.

[Regulation 44 is printed as amended by the Interpretation Act 1978, ss 17(2)(a) and 23(1).]

45. Exemption from [section 63(2) of the 1988 Act]

Motor vehicles other than those manufactured on or after 1st October 1982 and first used on or after 1st April 1983, not constructed or adapted to form part of an articulated vehicle are hereby exempted from the provisions of [section 63(2) of the 1988 Act].

[Regulation 45 is printed as amended by the Interpretation Act 1978, ss 17(2)(a) and 23(1).]

46. Certificates of temporary exemption

(1) The person in charge of the Goods Vehicle Centre or a vehicle testing station may issue in respect of a vehicle a certificate of temporary exemption, by virtue of which that vehicle shall not, during the period specified in paragraph (2)(*d*), be subject to the provisions of [section 53(1) or (2) of the 1988 Act], where—

(*a*) he is satisfied that by reason of exceptional circumstances, as defined in regulation 39(1) affecting either a vehicle testing station or the vehicle, an examination cannot be completed by a date fixed under these Regulations for carrying out the examination; and

(*b*) the use of the vehicle on or after that date would be unlawful by virtue of the said provisions.

(2) Every certificate of temporary exemption shall be on a form approved by the Secretary of State and shall be signed by a person duly authorised on his behalf and shall contain—

(*a*) in the case of a certificate issued for a motor vehicle, the registration mark (if any) exhibited on the vehicle or, if no such mark is so exhibited, the chassis or serial number marked on the vehicle or, if no such number is so marked, the identification mark which shall have been allotted to the vehicle by the Secretary of State in the notice of appointment relating to the first examination of the vehicle;

(*b*) in the case of a certificate issued for a trailer, the identification mark which shall have been allotted to the trailer by the Secretary of State in the notice of appointment (if any) relating to the first examination of the trailer or shall have otherwise been allotted to the trailer by the Secretary of State under these Regulations;

(*c*) the date on which the certificate is issued; and

(*d*) the period during which the vehicle is exempted from the provisions of [section 53(1) or (2) of the 1988 Act] so, however, that no such period shall exceed three months in duration.

[Regulation 46 is printed as amended by the Interpretation Act 1978, ss 17(2)(a) and 23(1).]

* * *

Regulation 4

SCHEDULE 2

CLASSES OF VEHICLE TO WHICH THESE REGULATIONS DO NOT APPLY

1. Dual-purpose vehicles not constructed or adapted to form part of an articulated vehicle.

2. Mobile cranes as defined in Schedule 3 to the 1971 Act.

3. Break-down vehicles.

4. Engineering plant and plant, not being engineering plant, which is movable plant or equipment being a motor vehicle or trailer (not constructed primarily to carry a load) especially designed and constructed for the special purposes of engineering operations.

5. Trailers being drying or mixing plant designed for the production of asphalt or of bituminous or tar macadam.

6. Tower wagons as defined in—

(*a*) section 4(2) of the 1971 Act [*qv*]; or

(*b*) Schedule 4 to that Act [*qv*].

7. Road construction vehicles as defined in section 4(2) of the 1971 Act [*qv*] and road rollers.

8. Vehicles designed for fire fighting or fire salvage purposes.

9. Works trucks, straddle carriers used solely as works trucks, and works trailers.

10. Electrically-propelled motor vehicles.

11. Vehicles used solely for one or both of the following purposes—

(*a*) clearing frost, ice or snow from roads by means of a snow plough or similar contrivance, whether forming part of the vehicle or not, and

(*b*) spreading material on roads to deal with frost, ice or snow.

12. Motor vehicles used for no other purpose than the haulage of lifeboats and the conveyance of the necessary gear of the lifeboats which are being hauled.

13. Living vans the unladen weight of which does not exceed 1525 kilograms.

14. Vehicles constructed or adapted for, and used primarily for the purpose of, carrying equipment permanently fixed to the vehicle which equipment is used for medical, dental, veterinary, health, educational, display, clerical or experimental laboratory purposes, such use—

(*a*) not directly involving the sale, hire or loan of goods from the vehicle; and

(*b*) not directly or indirectly involving drain cleaning or sewage or refuse collection.

15. Trailers which have no other brakes than a parking brake and brakes which automatically come into operation on the over-run of the trailer.

16. Vehicles exempted from duty under the 1971 Act by virtue of section 7(1) of that Act [*qv*] and any trailer drawn by such a vehicle.

17. Agricultural motor vehicles and agricultural trailed appliances.

18. Agricultural trailers and agricultural trailed appliance conveyors drawn on roads only by an agricultural motor vehicle.

19. Public service vehicles (as defined in section 1 of the Public Passenger Vehicles Act 1981 [*qv*]).

20. Licensed taxis (as defined in section 13(3) of the Transport Act 1985 [*qv*]).

21. Vehicles used solely for the purposes of funerals.

22. Goods vehicles to which any of the prescribed construction and use requirements do not apply by virtue of either of the following items in the Table in regulation 4(4) of the Construction and Use Regulations [*qv*] namely—

(*a*) item 1 (which relates to vehicles proceeding to a port for export);

(*b*) item 4 (which relates to vehicles in the service of a visiting force or of a headquarters).

23. Vehicles equipped with a new or improved equipment or types of equipment and used, solely by a manufacturer of vehicles or their equipment or by an importer of vehicles, for or in connection with the test or trial of any such equipment.

24. Motor vehicles brought into Great Britain and displaying a registration mark mentioned in regulation 5 of the Motor Vehicles (International Circulation) Regulations 1971 [*SI 1971 No 937*], a period of twelve months not having elapsed since the vehicle in question was last brought into Great Britain.

25. Motor vehicles for the time being licensed under the Vehicles (Excise) Act (Northern Ireland) 1972.

26. Vehicles having a base or centre in any of the following islands, namely, Arran, Bute, Great Cumbrae, Islay, Mull, Tiree or North Uist from which the use of the vehicle on a journey is normally commenced.

27. Trailers brought into Great Britain and having a base or centre in a country outside Great Britain from which the use of the vehicle on a journey is normally commenced, a period of twelve months not having elapsed since the vehicle in question was last brought into Great Britain.

28. Track-laying vehicles.

29. Steam propelled vehicles.

30. Motor vehicles first used before 1st January 1960, used unladen and not drawing a laden trailer, and trailers manufactured before 1st January 1960 and used unladen.

For the purposes of this paragraph any determination as to when a motor vehicle is first used shall be made as provided in regulation 3(3) of the Construction and Use Regulations [*qv*].

31. Motor vehicles constructed, and not merely adapted, for the purpose of street cleansing, or the collection or disposal of refuse or the collection or disposal of the contents of gullies and which are either—

(*a*) three-wheeled vehicles, or

(*b*) vehicles which—

(i) are incapable by reason of their construction of exceeding a speed of 20 miles per hour on the level under their own power, or

(ii) have an inside track width of less than 810 millimetres.

32. Vehicles designed and used for the purpose of servicing or controlling or loading or unloading aircraft while so used—

(*a*) on an aerodrome as defined in section 105(1) of the Civil Aviation Act 1982 [*qv*];

(*b*) on roads outside such an aerodrome if, except when proceeding directly from one part of such an aerodrome to another part thereof, the vehicles are unladen and are not drawing a laden trailer.

33. Vehicles designed for use, and used on an aerodrome mentioned in paragraph 32, solely for the purpose of road cleansing, the collection or disposal of refuse or the collection or disposal of the contents of gullies or cesspools.

34. Vehicles provided for police purposes and maintained in workshops approved by the Secretary of State as suitable for such maintenance, being vehicles provided in England and Wales by a police authority or the Receiver for the metropolitan police district, or, in Scotland, by a police authority or a joint police committee.

35. Heavy motor cars or motor cars constructed or adapted for the purpose of forming part of an articulated vehicle and which are used for drawing only a trailer falling within a class of vehicle specified in paragraph 13, 14 or 15 of this Schedule or a trailer being used for or in connection with any purpose for which it is authorised to be used on roads by an order under [section 44(1) of the 1988 Act] being an order authorising that trailer or any class or description of trailers comprising that trailer to be used on roads.

36. Play buses.

[Schedule 2 is printed as amended by the Interpretation Act 1978, ss 17(2)(a) and 23(1).]

* * *

The Goods Vehicles (Prohibitions) (Exemptions and Appeals) Regulations 1987

(SI 1987 No 1149)

1. Citation and commencement *[Omitted.]*

2. Interpretation

In these regulations—

'[the 1988 Act]' means [the Road Traffic Act 1988];

'certifying officer' has the same meaning as in the Public Passenger Vehicles Act 1981;

'prohibition' means a prohibition under [section 69 or 70 of the 1988 Act];

'vehicle testing station' means a station provided by the Secretary of State under [section 52(2), 62(1) or 72(8) of the 1988 Act].

[Regulation 2 is printed as amended by the Interpretation Act 1978, ss 17(2)(a) and 23(1).]

3. Exemptions from [section 71(1)(*a*) of the 1988 Act]

The use of a goods vehicle on a road—

(*a*) solely for the purpose of submitting it by previous arrangement at a specified time on a specified date for an inspection at a vehicle testing station or such other place as shall have been agreed between the person proposing to carry out, and the person submitting the vehicle for, the inspection;

(*b*) in the course of an inspection for the purpose of—

(i) taking it to, or bringing it away from, any place where a part of the inspection is to be, or (as the case may be) has been, carried out; or

(ii) carrying out any part of the inspection, the person so using it being (in either case) a person carrying out the inspection; or

(*c*) within three miles measured in a straight line from the place where it is being, or has been, repaired solely for the purpose of its test or trial with a view to the removal of a prohibition,

is exempted from [section 71(1)(*a*) of the 1988 Act] (which makes it an offence to drive, or cause or permit to be driven, a goods vehicle on a road in contravention of a prohibition).

[Regulation 3 is printed as amended by the Interpretation Act 1978, ss 17(2)(a) and 23(1).]

4. Prescribed time and manner of appeals relating to prohibitions *[Omitted.]*

5. Revocation *[Omitted.]*

The Local Authorities' Traffic Orders (Exemptions for Disabled Persons) (England and Wales) Regulations 1986

(SI 1986 No 178)

1. Citation, commencement and revocation *[Omitted.]*

2. Interpretation

(1) In these Regulations the following expressions have the meanings hereby assigned to them:—

'the 1984 Act' means the Road Traffic Regulation Act 1984 as read with section 21(1)(*b*) of the Chronically Sick and Disabled Persons Act 1970;

'the bus lane' means a road, or a part of the width of a road, the use of which by vehicles is restricted by or under any enactment, either in both directions or in one direction only and either at all times or at particular times only, to any one or more of the following categories of vehicles—

(i) public service vehicles (as defined in section 1 of the Public Passenger Vehicles Act 1981) or particular classes of such vehicles,

(ii) vehicles (not being motor cars) which are similar in construction to public service vehicles and are being used for the carriage of passengers, or particular classes of such vehicles,

(iii) taxis,

(iv) cycles,

and 'bus lane restriction', in relation to a bus lane, means the restriction by virtue of which the particular road, or the particular part of the width of a road, is a bus lane;

'disabled person' means a disabled person of a description prescribed by regulation 5 of the Disabled Persons (Badges for Motor Vehicles) Regulations 1982 [*SI 1982 No 1740, qv*];

'disabled person's badge' has the same meaning as in regulation 3(1) of the Disabled Persons (Badge for Motor Vehicles) Regulations 1982;

'disabled person's vehicle' means a vehicle lawfully displaying a disabled person's badge and which is a vehicle which, immediately before or after any period of waiting allowed by virtue of a provision of a kind required by regulation 3 of these Regulations to be included in an order under the 1984 Act, has been or is to be driven by a disabled person or, as the case may be, has been or is to be used for carrying disabled persons as passengers;

'London local authority' means the council of a London borough or the Common Council of the City of London;

'road', in relation to an order under section 6 or 9 of the 1984 Act, includes a street as defined in section 6(6) of that Act.

(2) Any reference in these Regulations to an order under any particular section of the 1984 Act includes a reference to an order varying an order made, or having effect as if made, under that section.

3. Application of Regulations

These Regulations apply—

(*a*) to orders made by a local authority (other than a London local authority) under any of the following provisions of the 1984 Act, that is to say, sections 1, 9, 35, 45 and 46: and

(*b*) to orders made by a London local authority under any of the following provisions of the 1984 Act, that is to say, sections 6, 9, 45 and 46 except that they do not apply to an order made by such an authority under any of the said sections in so far as the order applies in the City of London, the City of Westminster or the Royal Borough of Kensington and Chelsea, or any part of the London Borough of Camden south of, and including, Euston Road.

4. Exemptions in orders for vehicles displaying disabled persons' badges

(1) Where an order under section 1, 6, 9, 45 or 46 of the 1984 Act—

(*a*) includes a provision; or

(*b*) applies a provision of an existing order under any such section,

which provision prohibits the waiting of vehicles, or of any class of vehicles, in a road or part of a road and the provision is one which in relation to any particular vehicle prohibits that vehicle from waiting in that road or that part of a road either—

(i) beyond a specified period of waiting by that vehicle permitted by that provision, or

(ii) if less than a specified period has elapsed since a previous period of waiting by that vehicle in that road or that part of a road, as the case may be,

then in the case mentioned in (*a*) above, the order shall also include a provision for exempting from any such prohibition contained therein any disabled person's vehicle which displays in the relevant position a disabled person's badge issued by any local authority, and in the case mentioned at (*b*) above, the order shall also include a provision for exempting from any prohibition as applied and as originally enacted and subsequently extended (where this is the case) any disabled person's vehicle which displays in the relevant position a disabled person's badge issued by any local authority.

(2) Where an order under section 1, 6, 9, 45 or 46 of the 1984 Act—

(*a*) includes a provision, or

(*b*) applies a provision of an existing order under any such section, and the provision is one which—

(i) prohibits the waiting of vehicles, or any class of vehicles, in a road or part of a road, except for the purpose of loading or unloading, and

(ii) in relation to a particular vehicle would have the effect of prohibiting that vehicle from waiting in that road or part of a road at all times in the day or during one or more specified periods in any day, and

(iii) is not a provision applying to a bus lane at a time when the bus lane restriction is in operation, and

(iv) is not a provision to which paragraph (1) of this regulation refers,

then the order shall include the exemption provision described in paragraph (3) of this regulation.

(3) The exemption provision referred to in paragraph (2) above is a provision for exempting from the prohibition included in or applied by the order—

(*a*) in a case where the period of the prohibition is of 2 hours' duration or less, for the whole of that period, and

(*b*) in a case where the period of the prohibition is of more than 2 hours' duration, for a period of 2 hours (not being a period separated by an interval of less than 1 hour from a previous period of waiting by the same vehicle in the same road or part of a road on the same day),

any disabled person's vehicle in relation to which the following requirements are satisfied, namely, that—

(i) in all cases a disabled person's badge is displayed in the relevant position on the vehicle, and

(ii) in the case mentioned at (*b*) above, a parking disc, issued by a local authority, complying with the requirements of the British Standard Specification for Parking Discs (BS 4613: 1970), coloured orange, and capable of showing the quarter hour period during which a period of waiting begins, is displayed in a relevant position on the vehicle, and the driver, or other person in charge of the vehicle, marks on the parking disc the time at which the period of waiting has begun.

(4) Where an order under section 6, 35, 45 or 46 of the 1984 Act—

(*a*) includes a provision; or

(*b*) applies a provision of an existing order under any such section, which provision prohibits the waiting of vehicles, or of any class of vehicles in a street parking place or part of such a parking place and the provision is one which in relation to any particular vehicle prohibits that vehicle from waiting in that parking place or that part of a parking place either—

(i) beyond a specified period of waiting by that vehicle permitted by that provision, or

(ii) if less than a specified period has elapsed since a previous period of waiting by that vehicle in that parking place or that part of a parking place, as the case may be,

then in the case mentioned in (*a*) above, the order shall also include a provision for exempting from any such prohibition contained therein any disabled person's vehicle which displays in the relevant position a disabled person's badge issued by any local authority, and in the case mentioned at (*b*) above, the order shall also include a provision for exempting from any prohibition as applied and as originally enacted and subsequently extended (where this is the case) any disabled person's vehicle which displays in the relevant position a disabled person's badge issued by any local authority.

(5) Where an order under section 45 or 46 of the 1984 Act—

(*a*) includes a provision; or

(*b*) applies a provision of an existing order under either such section, which provision prescribes—

(i) a charge for a vehicle, or a vehicle of any class, left in a parking place,

(ii) a time limit in relation to the leaving of, or waiting by, vehicles, or vehicles of any class, in a parking place, or

(iii) a period which must elapse before a vehicle which has been taken away from a parking place may again be left therein,

then in the case mentioned in (*a*) above, the order shall also include a provision for exempting from any such matter prescribed therein any disabled person's vehicle which displays in the relevant position a disabled person's badge issued by any local authority, and in the case mentioned at (*b*) above, the order shall also include a provision for exempting from any matter prescribed and as applied and as originally and subsequently extended (where this is the case) any disabled person's vehicle which displays in the relevant position a disabled person's badge issued by any local authority.

(6) Any provision for exemption required by this regulation to be contained in any order referred to therein may be limited to the same class of vehicle as that to which the provision, from which exemption is required to be given by this regulation, applies.

(7) For the purposes of this regulation and any order referred to therein, a vehicle shall be regarded as displaying a disabled person's badge in the relevant position when—

(*a*) in the case of a vehicle fitted with a front windscreen, the badge is exhibited thereon with the obverse side facing forwards on the near side of and immediately behind the windscreen; and

(*b*) in the case of a vehicle not fitted with a front windscreen, the badge is exhibited in a conspicuous position on the vehicle.

The Motor Cycles (Eye Protectors) Regulations 1985

(SI 1985 No 1593)

[The text of these regulations is printed as amended by:

the Motor Cycles (Eye Protectors) (Amendment) Regulations 1987 (SI 1987 No 675) (1 July 1987); and

the Motor Cycles (Eye Protectors) (Amendment) Regulations 1988 (SI 1988 No 1031) (11 July 1988).

The amending regulations are referred to in the notes to the main regulations only by their years and numbers. The dates referred to above are the dates on which the amending regulations came into force.]

1. These Regulations may be cited as the Motor Cycles (Eye Protectors) Regulations 1985 and shall come into operation on 1st July 1987.

2. In these Regulations:—

'motor bicycle' means a two wheeled motor cycle, whether having a side-car attached thereto or not, and for the purposes of this definition any wheels of a motor cycle shall, if the distance between the centres of the areas of contact between such wheels and the road surface is less than 460 millimetres, be counted as one wheel;

'eye protector' means an appliance designed or adapted for use with any headgear or by being attached to or placed upon the head by a person driving or riding on a motor bicycle and intended for the protection of the eyes.

[**3.** The types of eye protector hereby prescribed as authorised for use by persons driving or riding (otherwise than in a sidecar) on a motor bicycle are—

(*a*) those which conform to either—

(i) the requirements relating to Grade X in British Standard BS 4110: 1979, or

(ii) the requirements relating to Grades XA, YA or ZA in British Standard BS 4110: 1979 as amended by Amendment No 1 (AMD 3368), Amendment No 2 (AMD 4060) and Amendment No 3 (AMD 4630),

and in either case are marked with the number of the said British Standard, the Grade and the certification mark of the British Standards Institution (whether or not they are required to be so marked by the said British Standard); and

(*b*) until 1st April 1989, those which fulfil both of the following requirements, that is to say—

(i) they are fitted with lenses that are designed to correct a defect in sight and that do not fly into fragments if fractured, and

(ii) they transmit 50 per cent or more of the light with those lenses fitted; and

(*c*) on or after 1st April 1989, those which were first used before that date and fulfil the two requirements mentioned in sub-paragraph (*b*) above.]

[Regulation 3 is printed as substituted by SI 1988 No 1031.]

4. Nothing in Regulation 3 above shall apply to any person driving or riding on a motor bicycle if:

(*a*) it is a mowing machine;

(*b*) it is for the time being propelled by a person on foot; . . .

(*c*) it is a vehicle brought temporarily into Great Britain by a person resident outside the United Kingdom which has not remained in the United Kingdom for a period of more than one year from the date it was last brought into the United Kingdom; or

[(*d*) he is in the armed forces of the Crown, on duty and wearing an eye protector supplied to him as part of his service equipment.]

[Regulation 4 is printed as amended by SI 1987 No 675.]

The Motor Cycles (Protective Helmets) Regulations 1980

(SI 1980 No 1279)

[The text of these regulations is printed as amended by:

the Motor Cycles (Protective Helmets) (Amendment) Regulations 1981 (SI 1981 No 374) (1 April 1981);

the Motor Cycles (Protective Helmets) (Amendment) Regulations 1986 (SI 1986 No 472) (11 April 1986).

The amending regulations are referred to in the notes to the main regulations only by their years and numbers. The dates referred to above are the dates on which the regulations came into force.]

* * *

4.—(1) Save as provided in paragraph (2) below, every person driving or riding (otherwise than in a side-car) on a motor bicycle when on a road shall wear protective headgear.

(2) Nothing in paragraph (1) above shall apply to any person driving or riding on a motor bicycle if—

(*a*) it is a mowing machine;

(*b*) it is for the time being propelled by a person on foot; or

(*c*) he is a follower of the Sikh religion while he is wearing a turban.

(3) Regulation:—

'motor bicycle' means a two wheeled motor cycle, whether having a side-car attached thereto or not, and for the purposes of this definition any wheels of a motor cycle shall, if the distance between the centres of the areas of contact between such wheels and the road surface is less than 460 millimetres, be counted as one wheel; and

'protective headgear' means headgear which—

(*a*) is either—

(i) a helmet bearing a marking applied by its manufacturer indicating compliance with the specifications contained in one of the British Standards mentioned in Schedule 2 (whether or not as modified by any amendment), or

(ii) a helmet of a type manufactured for use by persons on motor cycles which by virtue of its shape, material and construction could reasonably be expected to afford to persons on motor bicycles a degree of protection from injury in the event of an accident similar to or greater than that provided by a helmet of a type prescribed by Regulation 5; and

(*b*) if worn with a chin cup attached to or held in position by a strap or other fastening provided on the helmet, is provided with an additional strap or other fastening (to be fastened under the wearer's jaw) for securing the helmet firmly to the head of the wearer; and

(*c*) is securely fastened to the head of the wearer by means of the straps or other fastening provided on the headgear for that purpose.

5.—[(1) The types of helmet hereby prescribed as types of helmet recommended as affording protection to persons on or in motor cycles from injury in the event of an accident are helmets which as regards their shape, construction and other qualities conform—

(*a*) until 1st September 1986, with any one of the British Standards mentioned in items 5, 6, 7, 8, 9, 10 and 11 in Schedule 2;

(*b*) on and after 1st September 1986 until 1st April 1989, with any one of the British Standards mentioned in items 9, 10 and 11 in Schedule 2;

(*c*) on and after 1st April 1989, with the British Standard mentioned in item 11 in Schedule 2;

and which in the case of any helmet is marked with the number of the British Standard with which it conforms and the certification mark of the British Standards Institution (whether or not it is required to be so marked by the British Standard in point).]

(2) A reference in paragraph (1) above to a helmet which, as respects its shape, construction and other qualities, conforms with one of the British Standards mentioned in an item in Schedule 2 is a reference to a helmet which so conforms with one of those British Standards subject to such (if any) of the amendments to the relevant Standard mentioned in the relevant item as had effect at the time of the manufacture of the helmet.

[Regulation 5 is printed as amended by SI 1986 No 472.]

6. Nothing in Regulation 5(1) shall be taken to authorise any person to apply any number or mark referred to therein in contravention of the Trade Descriptions Act 1968.

* * *

SCHEDULE 2

BRITISH STANDARDS

1. British Standard 2001: 1956 as amended by the following Amendment Slips:—

Number	*Date of Publication*
1	11th January 1957
2	23rd November 1959
3	27th February 1962
4	11th June 1964
5	13th March 1968
6	18th February 1972

2. British Standard 1869: 1960 as amended by the following Amendment Slips:—

Number	*Date of Publication*
1	29th May 1963
4	3rd December 1965
5	13th March 1968
6	10th August 1971
7	3rd January 1972
8	15th May 1973
9	1st February 1974
10	2nd September 1974
11	1st March 1975

3. British Standard 2495: 1960 as amended by the following Amendment Slips:—

Number	*Date of Publication*
1	29th May 1963
2	22nd February 1965
3	7th December 1965
4	22nd July 1966
5	10th August 1971
6	3rd January 1972
7	1st February 1974
8	1st March 1975

4. British Standard 2001: 1972 as amended by the following Amendment Slips:—

Number	*Date of Publication*
1	12th December 1972
2	26th January 1973
3	1st February 1974
4	2nd September 1974
5	1st March 1975

5. British Standard 5361: 1976

6. British Standard 2495: 1977

7. British Standard 5361: 1976 as amended by the following Amendment Slips:—

Number	*Date of Publication*
1	30th September 1977
2	31st August 1978
3	31st August 1979
4	29th February 1980

8. British Standard 2495: 1977 as amended by the following Amendment Slips:—

Number	*Date of Publication*
1	30th September 1977
2	31st August 1978
3	31st August 1979
4	29th February 1980

[9. British Standard 5361: 1976 as amended by the following Amendment Slips:—

Number	*Date of Publication*
1	30th September 1977
2	31st August 1978
3	31st August 1979
4	29th February 1980
5	27th February 1981]

[10. British Standard 2495: 1977 as amended by the following Amendment Slips:—

Number	*Date of Publication*
1	30th September 1977
2	31st August 1978
3	31st August 1979
4	29th February 1980
5	27th February 1981]

[11. British Standard 6658/1985 as amended by the following Amendment Slip:

Number	*Date of Publication*
1	28th February 1986]

[Schedule 2 is printed as amended by SI 1981 No 374; SI 1986 No 472.]

The Motor Vehicles (Authorisation of Special Types) General Order 1979

(SI 1979 No 1198)

[The text of this order is printed as amended by:
correction slip (October 1979);
the Motor Vehicles (Authorisation of Special Types) (Amendment) Order 1981 (SI 1981 No 1664) (29 December 1981);
the Motor Vehicles (Authorisation of Special Types) (Amendment) Order 1984 (SI 1984 No 1810) (1 March 1984);
the Motor Vehicles (Authorisation of Special Types) (Amendment) Order 1985 (SI 1985 No 745) (31 May 1985);
the Motor Vehicles (Authorisation of Special Types) (Amendment) Order 1986 (SI 1986 No 313) (1 April 1986);
the Motor Vehicles (Authorisation of Special Types) (Amendment) Order 1987 (SI 1987 No 1327) (1 January 1988); and
the Motor Vehicles (Authorisation of Special Types) (Amendment) (No 2) Order 1987 (SI 1987 No 2161) (1 January 1988).

As to the application of SI 1987 Nos 1327 and 2161, reference should be made to the Motor Vehicles (Authorisation of Special Types) (Amendment) (No 2) Order 1987 (SI 1987 No 2161), art 6, qv.

The amending orders are referred to in the notes to the main order only by their years and numbers. The dates referred to above are the dates on which the orders came into force.]

[EDITORIAL NOTE

This order sets out the authorisation to use vehicles in specified circumstances which do not comply with all the requirements of the Construction and Use Regulations. The order was made when the Motor Vehicles (Construction and Use) (Track Laying Vehicles) Regulations 1955 (SI 1955 No 990) and the Motor Vehicles (Construction and Use) Regulations 1978 (SI 1978 No 1017) were in force and the order refers expressly to provisions of both sets of regulations. The Road Vehicles (Construction and Use) Regulations 1986 (SI 1986 No 1078), below, have consolidated both the 1955 and the 1978 Regulations and many amending regulations. The 1986 Regulations have a new presentation with more extensive use of tabulations, a more logical arrangement of material and simplified language. In consequence, it is not always possible to correlate references in this order precisely with provisions in the 1986 Regulations. Until the order is further and formally amended, therefore, care should be exercised in relating any provision of the order (other than art 18, *qv*) to any specific provision in the 1986 Regulations; whilst every care has been taken to indicate the latter provisions with such precision as is possible, in any case of doubt reference should be made to the original provisions referred to in the order.]

ARRANGEMENT OF THE ORDER

PART I

Preliminary

Article

PART II

Miscellaneous Vehicles

PART III

Abnormal Indivisible Loads, Engineering Plant and other Vehicles carrying Wide Loads

SCHEDULES

PART I

Preliminary

1. Commencement and citation *[Omitted.]*

2. Revocation *[Omitted.]*

3. Interpretation

(1) In this Order, unless the context otherwise requires, the following expressions have the following meanings—

'abnormal indivisible load' means a load—

(*a*) which cannot without undue expense or risk of damage be divided into two or more loads for the purpose of carriage on roads, and

(*b*) which—

(i) owing to its dimensions, cannot be carried by a heavy motor car or trailer or a combination of a heavy motor car and trailer complying in all respects with the requirements of the Construction and Use Regulations, or

[(ii) owing to its weight, cannot be carried by a heavy motor car or trailer or a combination of a heavy motor car and trailer having a total laden weight of not more than—

(A) prior to 1st October 1989, 32,520 kilograms, and

(B) on or after 1st October 1989, 38,000 kilograms,

and complying in all respects with the requirements of the Construction and Use Regulations;]

['agricultural motor vehicle', 'agricultural trailer' and 'agricultural trailed appliance' have the meanings respectively given to those expressions in [Regulation 3(2)] of the Construction and Use Regulations;]

'articulated vehicle', . . . 'locomotive', 'overall length', 'overall width', 'overhang', 'registered', 'straddle carrier', 'track laying', and 'wheeled' have the same meanings respectively as in the Construction and Use Regulations;

'bank holiday' means a day which is a bank holiday under the Banking and Financial Dealings Act 1971 [*qv*];

'chief officer of police' and 'police area', in relation to England and Wales, have respectively the same meanings as in the Police Act 1964 [*qv*];

'controlled by a pedestrian' has the same meaning as in [section 189(2) of the Road Traffic Act 1988];

'Construction and Use Regulations' means the [Road Vehicles (Construction and Use) Regulations 1986] [*SI 1986 No 1078, qv*];

'day' means any day except a bank holiday, Christmas Day, Good Friday, Sunday or Saturday;

['dual carriageway road' has the same meaning as in Schedule 6 to the Road Traffic Regulation Act 1984 [*qv*];]

'engineering plant' means—

(*a*) moveable plant or equipment which consists of a motor vehicle or trailer specially designed and constructed for the special purposes of engineering operations, and which cannot, owing to the requirements of those purposes, comply in all respects with the requirements of the Construction and Use Regulations . . . and which is not constructed primarily to carry a load other than excavated material raised from the ground by apparatus on the motor vehicle or trailer or materials which the vehicle or trailer is specially designed to treat while carried thereon, or

(*b*) a mobile crane which does not comply in all respects with the requirements of the Construction and Use Regulations . . . ;

['hours of darkness' means the time between half an hour after sunset and half an hour before sunrise;]

'lateral projection', 'forward projection' and 'rearward projection' have the same meanings respectively as in [Regulation 81] of the Construction and Use Regulations and references in this Order to a special appliance or apparatus in relation to a vehicle, to a forward projection or a rearward projection in relation to a vehicle, to the distance between vehicles in relation to vehicles carrying a load, and to a combination of vehicles in relation to a motor vehicle which is drawing one or more trailers, shall be construed respectively in the same manner as is provided in the said [Regulation 81] for the purposes of [Regulation 82] of the said Regulations, and the provisions of sub-paragraphs [(*b*), (*e*), (*h*), (*i*) and (*j*)] of the said [Regulation 81] shall apply for the purposes of this Order as they apply for the purposes of the said [Regulations 81 and 82];

['motorway' has the same meaning as in regulation 3(1) of the Motorways Traffic (England and Wales) Regulations 1982 [*qv*], as regards England and Wales;]

'the Minister' means the Minister of Transport;

. . .

'tractor' means a motor tractor.

(2) Any reference in this Order to a numbered Article or Schedule is a reference to the Article or Schedule bearing that number in this Order except where otherwise expressly provided.

[Article 3 is printed as amended by the Interpretation Act 1978, ss 17(2)(a) and 23(1); SI 1984 No 1810; SI 1987 Nos 1327 and 2161.

In the definitions of 'chief officer of police' and 'motorway' words relating expressly and exclusively to Scotland have been omitted.

References to the Minister of Transport refer to the Secretary of State for Transport; Transfer of Functions (Transport) Order 1981 (SI 1981 No 238).]

4. Speed limits

Nothing in this Order relating to the speed of vehicles shall be taken to authorise any speed which is in excess of any other speed limit imposed by or under any enactment.

PART II

Miscellaneous Vehicles

5. Track laying vehicles (including those used for launching lifeboats)

The Minister authorises the use on roads of track laying motor vehicles and track laying trailers notwithstanding that such vehicles do not comply in all respects with the requirements of the Construction and Use Regulations . . . subject to the following conditions:—

(1)(*a*) the vehicle shall be used only for the purpose of

(i) demonstration, or

(ii) enabling it to proceed to the nearest suitable railway station for conveyance to a port for shipment or to proceed to a port for shipment from a place in the immediate vicinity of that port where suitable railway facilities are not available,

(*b*) before the vehicle is so used the consent of every highway authority or every person responsible for the maintenance and repair of any road on which it is proposed that the vehicle shall be used shall in each case be obtained in writing, and

(*c*) the vehicle shall not be used for the carriage of goods or burden for hire or reward; or

[In condition (*b*) above, the expression 'person responsible for the maintenance and repair of any road' includes any person who is so responsible to a highway authority pursuant to an agreement with that authority.]

(2) the vehicle shall be used only for drawing or in connection with the launching of lifeboats which are the property of the Royal National Lifeboat Institution.

[Article 5 is printed as amended by the Interpretation Act 1978, ss 17(2)(a) and 23(1); SI 1986 No 313.]

6. Naval, military, air force and aviation vehicles

The Minister authorises the use on roads of the vehicles specified in Column 1 of Schedule 1 notwithstanding that such vehicles do not comply in all respects with the requirements of the Regulations of the Construction and Use Regulations . . . specified opposite thereto in Column 2 of Schedule 1, subject to the vehicles being the property of, or for the time being under the control of, the persons respectively specified opposite thereto in Column 3 of Schedule 1.

[Article 6 is printed as amended by the Interpretation Act 1978, ss 17(2)(a) and 23(1).]

7. Grass cutting machines and hedge trimmers

The Minister authorises the use on roads of [motor vehicles] constructed or adapted for use as grass cutters or hedge trimmers (not, in either case, being vehicles controlled by a pedestrian) notwithstanding that such vehicles do not comply with [Regulation 8 or 82] of the Construction and Use Regulations subject to the following conditions:—

(*a*) all other relevant requirements of the Construction and Use Regulations shall be complied with;

(*b*) the overall width of the vehicle [together with any equipment mounted on it], except when it is actually cutting grass or trimming hedges, shall not exceed 2.5 metres; and

(*c*) except where the vehicle is actually engaged in such operations, all cutting and trimming blades which form part of the machinery fitted to [or mounted on] the vehicle shall be effectively guarded so that no danger is caused or is likely to be caused to any person.

[Article 7 is printed as amended by the Interpretation Act 1972, ss 17(2)(a) and 23(1); SI 1984 No 1810.]

8. *[Revoked by SI 1984 No 1810.]*

9. The Minister authorises the use on roads of trailers constructed or adapted for use as grass cutters or hedge trimmers notwithstanding that such trailers do not comply in all respects with such of the requirements of the Construction and Use Regulations as apply to trailers, subject to the following conditions:—

(*a*) the requirements of [Regulation 27] of the Construction and Use Regulations, so far as they apply to trailers, shall be complied with;

(*b*) the unladen weight of the trailer shall not exceed—
  (i) 1020 kilograms if drawn by a locomotive, a motor tractor or a heavy motor car, or
  (ii) 815 kilograms in any other case;

(*c*) the overall width of the motor vehicle by which the trailer is drawn and, except when it is actually cutting grass or trimming hedges, the overall width of the trailer shall not exceed 2.6 metres;

(*d*) except when the trailer is actually engaged in such operations, where it is being drawn in such a manner that its longitudinal axis and that of the drawing vehicle are parallel but lie in different vertical planes, the width of road occupied by both vehicles shall not exceed 2.6 metres.

For the purposes of this paragraph, the said width shall be taken as a distance equivalent to the distance which, if both vehicles were treated as if they were one vehicle at a time when the one is drawing the other in the said manner, would fall to be measured as its overall width;

(*e*) except when the trailer is actually engaged in such operations, all cutting and trimming blades which form part of the machinery fitted to the trailer shall be effectively guarded so that no danger is caused or is likely to be caused to any person; and

(*f*) the trailer shall not be driven at a speed exceeding 20 miles per hour.

[Article 9 is printed as amended by the Interpretation Act 1978, ss 17(2)(a) and 23(1).]

10. Pedestrian controlled road maintenance vehicles

The Minister authorises the use on roads of motor vehicles constructed or adapted for the gritting of roads, the laying of road markings, the clearing of frost, snow or ice from roads or any other work of maintaining roads, being vehicles controlled by a pedestrian and not constructed or adapted for use or used for the carriage of a driver or passenger, notwithstanding that such vehicles do not comply in all respects with the requirements of [Regulations 16, 18, 23, and 61 of and Schedule 3 to] the Construction and Use Regulations subject to the following conditions:—

(*a*) all other relevant requirements of the Construction and Use Regulations shall be complied with;

(*b*) the weight of the vehicle whether laden or unladen, shall not exceed 410 kilograms; and

(*c*) the vehicle shall be equipped with an efficient braking system capable of being set or with sufficient other means, not being a breaking system, whereby it can be brought to a standstill and held stationary.

[Article 10 is printed as amended by the Interpretation Act 1978, ss 17(2)(a) and 23(1).]

11. Vehicles used for experiments or trials

The Minister authorises the use on roads of vehicles in or in connection with the conduct of experiments or trials under [section 283 of the Highways Act 1980] notwithstanding that such vehicles do not comply in all respects with the requirements of the Construction and Use Regulations . . .

[Article 11 is printed as amended by the Interpretation Act 1978, ss 17(2)(a) and 23(1).]

12. Straddle carriers

The Minister authorises the use on roads of straddle carriers notwithstanding that such vehicles do not comply in all respects with the requirements of [Regulations 8, 11, 18(2) and (3), 22, 45 and 66 of and Schedule 3 to] the Construction and Use Regulations, subject to the following conditions:—

(*a*) the vehicle shall not be used otherwise than for the purpose of demonstration or in the course of delivery on sale or when proceeding to or returning from a manufacturer or repairer for the purpose of repair or overhaul and, when so used, shall carry no load other than its necessary gear or equipment:

Provided that a vehicle which does not comply with the said [Regulation 11] may, if it complies with the said [Regulations 8 and 22], be used whether laden or unladen in passing from one part of any private premises to any other part thereof or to other private premises in the immediate neighbourhood;

(*b*) the vehicle shall not travel at a speed exceeding 12 miles per hour;

(*c*) the overall width of the vehicle shall not exceed 2.9 metres;

(*d*) the vehicle shall not be used if the overall length of the vehicle or, where the vehicle is carrying a load, if the overall length of the vehicle together with the length of any forward projection and of any rearward projection of its load exceeds 9.2 metres except with the consent of the chief officer of police of every police area in which it is proposed that the vehicle will be used;

(*e*) save in so far as the chief officer of police of any police area in which it is proposed that the vehicle will be used dispenses, as respects the use of the vehicle in that area, with any of the requirements contained in this paragraph, the [user] of the vehicle shall, not less than two clear days before such use, apply to the chief officer of police of any such area for his consent to the use of the vehicle, and shall, when making the application, furnish to him particulars of the vehicle concerned, of its overall length, of the length of any forward projection or rearward projection of any load proposed to be carried, and of the roads on which it is proposed that the vehicle will be used; and

(*f*) all the relevant requirements of the Construction and Use Regulations other than those specified above shall be complied with.

[Article 12 is printed as amended by the Interpretation Act 1978, ss 17(2)(a) and 23(1); SI 1987 No 1327.]

[13. Agricultural motor vehicles, agricultural trailers and agricultural trailed appliances

(1) Subject to the provisions of paragraph (2), the Secretary of State authorises the use on roads of—

(*a*) an agricultural motor vehicle,

(*b*) an agricultural trailer designed to perform functions, other than the carriage of goods, that necessitate an overall width of 2.5 metres being exceeded, or

(*c*) an agricultural trailed appliance,

notwithstanding that the overall width of the vehicle exceeds 2.5 metres if the relevant conditions specified in Schedule 4 are complied with.

(2) The authorisation specified in paragraph (1) applies only in so far as the width of a vehicle (including an agricultural implement which by virtue of Article 13B is treated as part of the vehicle) cannot, without undue expense or risk of damage, be reduced.]

[Article 13 (together with arts 13A to 13C, below) was substituted for the original text of art 13 by SI 1984 No 1810.]

[13A. Agricultural motor vehicle towing an off-set agricultural trailer or trailed appliance

(1) The Secretary of State authorises the use on roads of an agricultural motor vehicle towing an agricultural trailer or agricultural trailed appliance in such a manner that the longitudinal axis of the motor vehicle and the longitudinal axis of the trailer are parallel but lie in different vertical planes and the width specified in paragraph (2) below exceeds 2.5 metres provided the relevant conditions specified in Schedule 4 are complied with.

(2) The width referred to in paragraph (1) above is the distance equivalent to the distance which, if both the agricultural motor vehicle and the agricultural trailer or agricultural trailed appliance (when being drawn by the agricultural motor vehicle) are treated as one vehicle, would fall to be measured as its overall width.]

[Article 13A (together with art 13, above, and arts 13B and 13C, below) was substituted for the original text of art 13 by SI 1984 No 1810.]

[13B. Provisions supplementary to Articles 13 and 13A

For the purposes of Articles 13 and 13A and Schedule 4, an agricultural implement rigidly mounted on an agricultural motor vehicle, an agricultural trailer or an agricultural trailed appliance shall be treated as part of that vehicle, trailer or appliance whether or not—

(*a*) the implement is permanently attached thereto, and

(*b*) part of the weight of the implement is transmitted to the surface of the road, otherwise than by the wheels or tracks of the motor vehicle, trailer or appliance.]

[Article 13B (together with arts 13 and 13A, above, and art 13C, below) was substituted for the original text of art 13 by SI 1984 No 1810.]

[13C. Agricultural motor vehicles, agricultural trailers and agricultural trailed appliances with implements projecting rearwards or forwards

(1) The Secretary of State authorises the use on roads of—

(*a*) an agricultural motor vehicle,

(*b*) an agricultural trailer, and

(*c*) an agricultural trailed appliance,

with an agricultural implement rigidly mounted thereon whether or not—

(i) the implement is permanently attached thereto, and

(ii) part of the weight of the implement is transmitted to the surface of the road otherwise that by the wheels or tracks of the motor vehicle, trailer or appliance

provided that the requirements mentioned in paragraph (2) are complied with.

(2) Those requirements are that:—

(*a*) if any part of the implement projects rearwards of the rearmost part of the motor vehicle, trailer or appliance by more than a distance specified in an item in column 2 of Part I of Schedule 5 the conditions specified in that item in column 3 are complied with; and

(*b*) if any part of the implement projects forwards of the foremost part of the motor vehicle, trailer or appliance by more than a distance specified in an item in column 2 of Part 1 of Schedule 5 the conditions specified in that item in column 3 are complied with.]

[Article 13C (together with arts 13, 13A and 13B, above) was substituted for the original text of art 13 by SI 1984 No 1810.]

14. *[Revoked by SI 1984 No 1810.]*

15. Vehicles for moving excavated material

The Minister authorises the use on roads of moveable plant or equipment (other than engineering plant) being a heavy motor car, trailer or articulated vehicle specially designed and constructed for use in private premises for the primary purpose of moving excavated material and fitted with a tipping body, moving platform or other similar device for discharging its load, and which cannot, owing to the requirements of that purpose, comply in all respects with the requirements of the Construction and Use Regulations, subject to the following conditions:—

(*a*) the vehicle shall only be used in proceeding to and from private premises or between private premises and a port in either direction and shall carry no load other than its necessary gear or equipment;

(*b*) a heavy motor car not forming part of an articulated vehicle shall not draw any trailer;

(*c*) where a trailer is drawn by a motor vehicle the motor vehicle shall not draw any other trailer;

(*d*) in a case where the overall width of the vehicle exceeds [5 metres] the conditions specified in Article 24 shall be complied with;

(*e*) in the case of a heavy motor car not forming part of an articulated vehicle, and in the case of an articulated vehicle, the sum of the weights transmitted to the road surface by any two wheels in line transversely shall not exceed 22,860 kilograms and the sum of the weights so transmitted by all the wheels shall not exceed 50,800 kilograms;

(*f*) in the case of a trailer, whether or not forming part of an articulated vehicle, the provisions of [Regulation 16(4), items 25 to 27 in the table, of and Schedule 3, paragraph 1, items 4(c), 11 and 14 in the table, to] the Construction and Use Regulations shall not apply if the trailer is equipped with an efficient brake or with suitable scotches or similar devices to hold it stationary when necessary;

(*g*) the overall length of a trailer shall not exceed 8.54 metres and the overall length of an articulated vehicle shall not exceed 13.4 metres;

(*h*) the vehicle shall not travel on any road, other than a [motorway], at a speed exceeding 12 miles per hour;

(*i*) every wheel of the vehicle shall be equipped with a pneumatic tyre;

(*j*) where the overall width of the vehicle exceeds 3.5 metres, at least one person, in addition to the person or persons employed as respects a motor vehicle in driving that vehicle, shall be employed in attending to that vehicle and any load carried thereby and any trailer drawn by that vehicle and any load carried on the trailer and to give warning to the driver of the said motor vehicle and to any other person of any danger likely to be caused to any such other person by reason of the presence of the vehicle or the vehicle and trailer on the road:

Provided that, where three or more vehicles authorised by this Article are travelling together in convoy, it shall be a sufficient compliance with this paragraph if only the foremost and rearmost vehicles in the convoy are attended in the manner prescribed in this paragraph;

(*k*) save in so far as the chief officer of police of any police area in which it is proposed that the vehicle will be used dispenses, as respects the use of the vehicle in that area, with any of the requirements contained in this paragraph as to length of notice or particulars to be given, the [user] of the vehicle, if its overall width exceeds 2.9 metres, before using it on a road, shall give at least two clear days' notice to the chief officer of police of any such area and such notice shall contain particulars of the vehicle concerned, of its overall width, and of the time, date and route of the proposed journey;

(*l*) subject to any variation in the time, date or route of the journey which may be directed by any such chief officer of police, the vehicle shall be used only in circumstances which accord with the particulars given in compliance with the foregoing paragraph as to the time, date and route of the journey and only if the overall width of the vehicle does not exceed the width of which particulars have been given as aforesaid;

(*m*) in the case of the use of a vehicle in respect of which any of the requirements of the Construction and Use Regulations as to the weights of vehicles, whether laden or unladen, or the weights transmitted to the road surface by all or any of the wheels is not complied with, or, where a combination of vehicles is used, if any of the said requirements as to any or all of the vehicles in the combination is not complied with—

(i) save in so far as the highway authority for any road or the bridge authority for any bridge on which it is proposed that the vehicle or, as the case may be, the vehicles will be used dispenses, as respects the use of the vehicle or vehicles on that road or, as the case may be, on that bridge, with the requirements contained in this sub-paragraph as to length of notice or as to the form of notice or the particulars to be given, the [user] of the vehicle or, as the case may be, of the vehicles, before using the vehicle or vehicles on that road or that bridge, shall give to the highway authority for the road and the bridge authority for the bridge at least two clear days' notice in the form and containing the particulars specified in Part I of Schedule 2, and the provisions of Article 26(6) and (7) shall apply as respects any such notice, and

(ii) before using the vehicle or, as the case may be, the vehicles on any road or bridge the [user] of the vehicle or vehicles shall give to the highway authority for the road and to the bridge authority for the bridge an indemnity in the form specified in Part II of Schedule 2, and the provisions of Article 26(6) and (7) shall apply as respects any such indemnity,

and for the purposes of this sub-paragraph references to a combination of vehicles shall be construed in the same manner as is provided in [Regulation 81(*g*)] of the Construction and Use Regulations [and references to the highway authority for any road and to the bridge authority for any bridge shall be read as including references to any other person responsible for the maintenance and repair of the road or bridge in question pursuant to an agreement with the authority]; and

(*n*) in a case specified in an item in column 2 of the Table below, all the Construction and Use Regulations shall apply with the exception of the Regulations which are specified opposite to that item in column 3 of that table and, in relation to items 2 and 3, save as provided in paragraph (*f*) above.

TABLE

1	2	3
Item	Case	Construction and Use Regulations not applicable
1	A heavy motor car not forming part of an articulated vehicle.	[Regulations 8, 16(4), 18(2) and (3), 22, 45, 63, 66, 75, 76, 78 to 80, and Schedule 3].
2	A trailer not forming part of an articulated vehicle.	[Regulations 8, 18(2) and (3), 22, 63 and 66].
3	An articulated vehicle.	[Regulations 7(1), 8, 16(4), 18(2) and (3), 22, 45, 63, 66, 75, 77 to 80, and Schedule 3].

[Article 15 is printed as amended by the Interpretation Act 1978, ss 17(2)(a) and 23(1); SI 1986 No 313; SI 1987 No 1327. See the editorial note on p 530.]

16. Motor vehicles and trailers constructed for use outside the United Kingdom or which are new or improved types constructed for tests or trials or are equipped with new or improved equipment or types of equipment

(1) This Article applies to wheeled motor vehicles and trailers not falling within any description of motor vehicle or trailer specified in Article 18 or 19 and references in this Article to motor vehicles and trailers shall be construed accordingly.

(2) The Minister authorises the use on roads—

(A) of motor vehicles and trailers, or types of motor vehicles and trailers, constructed for use outside the United Kingdom and of new or improved types of motor vehicles and trailers constructed for tests or trials notwithstanding that such vehicles do not comply in all respects with the requirements of the Construction and Use Regulations, and

(B) of motor vehicles and trailers equipped with new or improved equipment or types of equipment notwithstanding that such vehicles do not comply in all respects with such of the requirements of the Construction and Use Regulations as cannot, by reason only of the said equipment, be complied with,

subject, in all cases, to the following conditions:—

(*a*) the vehicle shall not be used otherwise than—

(i) for or in connection with the testing or demonstration of the vehicle, or
(ii) in the course of delivery on sale, or
(iii) for proceeding to or returning from a manufacturer or repairer for the purpose of construction, repair or overhaul;

(*b*) the vehicle shall comply with [Regulations 10, 16, 18(1), 20, 26, 27, 29, 30, 34, 37, 40, 61, 62 and 100 of and Schedule 3 to] the Construction and Use Regulations, and [Regulations 53, 54, 57, 81 to 84, 86, 88 to 90, 92 to 99, and 101 to 108] of the said Regulations shall apply thereto;

(*c*) the vehicle shall not be used for the carriage of any load other than its necessary gear or equipment or such apparatus or ballast as may be necessary for the purpose of carrying out a test or trial of the vehicle;

(*d*) save in so far as the chief officer of police of any police area in which it is proposed that the vehicle will be used dispenses, as respects the use of the vehicle in that area, with any of the requirements contained in this sub-paragraph as to length of notice or particulars to be given, the [user] of the vehicle, if its overall width exceeds 2.9 metres or if its overall length exceeds that specified by any provision in [Regulation 7] of the Construction and Use Regulations, before using it on a road, shall give at least two clear days' notice to the chief officer of police of any such area and such notice shall contain particulars of the vehicle concerned, of its overall width and overall length, and of the width and length of any load proposed to be carried, and of the time, date and route of the proposed journey;

(*e*) subject to any variation in the time, date or route of the journey which may be directed by any such chief officer of police, the vehicle shall be used only in circumstances which accord with the particulars given in compliance with the foregoing sub-paragraph as to the time, date and route of the journey and only if the overall width and overall length of the vehicle and the width and length of any load carried thereon do not exceed the width and length of which particulars have been given as aforesaid;

(*f*) in the case of the use of a vehicle in respect of which any of the Construction and Use Regulations as to the weights of vehicles, whether laden or unladen, or the weights transmitted to the road surface by all or any of the wheels is not complied with, or, where a combination of vehicles is used, if any of the said requirements as to any or all of the vehicles in the combination is not complied with—

(i) save in so far as the highway authority for any road or the bridge authority for any bridge on which it is proposed that the vehicle or, as the case may be, the vehicles will be used dispenses, as respects the use of the vehicle or vehicles on that road or, as the case may be, on that bridge, with the requirements contained in this sub-paragraph as to the length of notice or to the form of notice or the particulars to be given, the [user] of the vehicle or, as the case may be, of the vehicles, before using the vehicle or the vehicles on that road or that bridge shall give to the highway authority for the road and to the bridge authority for the bridge at least two clear days' notice in the form and containing the particulars specified in Part I of Schedule 2, and the provisions of Article 26(6) and (7) shall apply as respects any such notice, and

(ii) before using the vehicle or, as the case may be, the vehicles on any road or bridge the [user] of the vehicle or vehicles shall give to the highway authority for the road and to the bridge authority for the bridge an indemnity in the form specified in Part II of Schedule 2, and the provisions of Article 26(6) and (7) shall apply as respects any such indemnity,

and for the purposes of this sub-paragraph references to a combination of vehicles shall be construed in the same manner as is provided in [Regulation 81(*g*)] of the Construction and Use Regulations [and references to the highway authority for any road and to the bridge authority for any bridge shall be read as including references to any other person responsible for the maintenance and repair of the road or bridge in question pursuant to an agreement with the authority].

[Article 16 is printed as amended by the Interpretation Act 1978, ss 17(2)(a) and 23(1); SI 1981 No 1664; SI 1986 No 313; SI 1987 No 1327.]

17. Vehicles fitted with moveable platforms

(1) The Minister authorises the use on roads of a vehicle fitted with a moveable platform notwithstanding that the vehicle does not comply in all respects with the requirements of [Regulations 7, 8, 11, 20, 23 or 82] of the Construction and Use Regulations subject to the following conditions:—

(*a*) all the relevant requirements of the Construction and Use Regulations other than those specified above shall be complied with;

(*b*) the vehicle shall not be used on a road unless its special equipment is fully retracted except when the vehicle is at a place where it is being used to facilitate overhead working;

(*c*) any jacks with which the vehicle is fitted for stabilising it while the moveable platform is in use and which project from the sides of the vehicle shall be clearly visible to persons using the road within a reasonable distance of the vehicle; and

(*d*) the vehicle, except in respect of its special equipment when the vehicle is at a place where it is being used to facilitate overhead working, shall—

(i) as respects its overall length, comply with [Regulation 7] of the said Regulations,

(ii) as respects its overall width, comply with [Regulation 8] of the said Regulations,

(iii) in the case of a vehicle other than a locomotive, as respects its overhang, comply with [Regulation 11] of the said Regulations.

(2) In this Article—

'moveable platform' means a platform which is attached to, and may be moved by means of, an extensible boom, and

'special equipment' means a moveable platform, the apparatus for moving the platform and any jacks fitted to the vehicle for stabilising it while the moveable platform is in use.

[Article 17 is printed as amended by the Interpretation Act 1978, ss 17(2)(a) and 23(1).]

PART III

ABNORMAL INDIVISIBLE LOADS, ENGINEERING PLANT AND OTHER VEHICLES CARRYING WIDE LOADS

18. Vehicles for carrying or drawing abnormal indivisible loads

(1) The Minister authorises the use on roads of heavy motor cars and trailers specially designed and constructed for the carriage of abnormal indivisible loads and

of locomotives and tractors specially designed and constructed to draw trailers specially so designed and constructed notwithstanding that such vehicles do not comply in all respects with the requirements of the Construction and Use Regulations, subject—

(*a*) in a case where Article 22, 23, 25 or 26 applies to the conditions contained in such of those Articles as are applicable to that case;

(*b*) in a case where the overall width of the vehicle or of the vehicle together with the width of any lateral projection or projections of its load exceeds [5 metres], to the conditions contained in Article 24; and

(*c*) in all cases to the further conditions specified in paragraph (2) below.

[(1A) (*a*) In this article, 'the Construction and Use Regulations' means the Road Vehicles (Construction and Use) Regulations 1986 *[SI 1986 No 1078]*.

(*b*) For the purposes of paragraph (2) below:

(i) 'Category 1' shall consist of any vehicle or combination of vehicles where the total weight of the vehicle or vehicles carrying the load is not more than 46,000 kilograms;

'Category 2' shall consist of any motor vehicle or combination of vehicles where the total weight of the vehicle or vehicles carrying the load is not more than 80,000 kilograms;

'Category 3' shall consist of any motor vehicle or combination of vehicles where the total weight of the vehicle or vehicles carrying the load is not more than 150,000 kilograms;

(ii) a vehicle shall comply with the conditions of an appropriate category, and the category under the conditions of which a vehicle is being used shall be that indicated on the sign mentioned in paragraph (2)(*t*) below.]

(2) The conditions referred to in paragraph 1(*c*) above are as follows:—

(*a*) a heavy motor car or trailer which does not comply with Part II of the Construction and Use Regulations shall be used only, save as provided in paragraphs (*i*) and (*m*) of this Article, for or in connection with the carriage of an abnormal indivisible load;

(*b*) a locomotive or tractor which does not comply with Part II of the Construction and Use Regulations shall be used only for or in connection with the drawing of trailers the use of which on roads is authorised by this Article;

(*c*) the overall width of a heavy motor car [or a trailer] shall not exceed 2.9 metres unless it is used for or in connection with the carriage of a load which can only safely be carried on a heavy motor car which exceeds that overall width;

(*d*) the overall width of a locomotive or tractor shall not exceed 2.9 metres unless it is used for or in connection with the carriage of a load on a trailer which exceeds that overall width, being a load which can only be safely carried on such a trailer;

(*e*) *[Revoked.]*

(*f*) notwithstanding anything in sub-paragraphs (*c*), (*d*) . . . above, the overall width of a heavy motor car, locomotive, tractor or trailer shall not exceed 6.1 metres;

(*g*) where, in relation to the load carried by a vehicle, there is a lateral projection on one or both sides of the vehicle the overall width of the vehicle together with the width of the projection, or, as the case may be, of both projections shall not exceed 6.1 metres;

(*h*) where a load is carried in such a manner that its weight rests—

(i) on one vehicle being a heavy motor car or a trailer, the overall length of the heavy motor car or, as the case may be, of the trailer together with the length of any forward and of any rearward projection of its load shall not exceed 27.4 metres; or

(ii) on more than one vehicle and the vehicles consist of—

(*a*) a motor vehicle drawing one trailer whether constituting an articulated vehicle or not, or

(*b*) any other combination of vehicles,

then, in the case at (*a*) above, the overall length of the trailer together with the length of any forward projection of the load extending beyond the foremost point of the trailer and of any rearward projection of the load shall not exceed 27.4 metres and, in the case at (*b*) above, the overall length of the vehicles together with the distance between vehicles and the length of any forward and of any rearward projection of the load shall not exceed 27.4 metres;

(*i*) the vehicle shall be so constructed that it is a wheeled vehicle;

(*j*) every wheel of the vehicle shall be equipped with a pneumatic tyre or a tyre of soft or elastic material;

[(*k*) The following restrictions on weight shall apply:

(i) for any vehicle or combination of vehicles carrying the load in Category 1:

(*a*) regulations 75, 76, 78 and 79 of the Construction and Use Regulations shall apply, and in respect of an articulated vehicle, regulation 77 shall apply save for a vehicle to which (*b*) below is applicable;

(*b*) for an articulated vehicle with a total of 5 or more axles and with a relevant axle spacing specified in column 2 of the Table below, the total weight shall not exceed the weight specified for that item in column 3 of the Table.

TABLE

1	*2*	*3*
Item	*Relevant axle spacing (in metres)*	*Weight (in kilograms)*
1	at least 6.5	40,000
2	at least 7.0	42,000
3	at least 7.5	44,000
4	at least 8.0	46,000

(ii) [save as provided in sub-paragraph (ii*a*) below] for any vehicle or combination of vehicles carrying the load in Category 2:

(*a*) the total weight shall be transmitted to the road through at least 5 axles;

(*b*) the total weight imposed on the road by all the wheels of any one axle shall not exceed 12,500 kilograms, and by any one wheel, 6,250 kilograms;

(*c*) if the distance between any two adjacent axles is at least 1.1 metres but less than 1.35 metres, the total weight imposed on the road by all the wheels of any one of those axles shall not exceed 12,000 kilograms, and by any one wheel, 6,000 kilograms;

(*d*) the distance between any two adjacent axles shall not be less than 1.1 metres;

(*e*) where the distance between the foremost and rearmost axles of the vehicle or vehicles carrying the load is at least as specified in an item in column 2 of the Table below, the total weight of the vehicle or combination of vehicles shall not exceed the weight given for that item in column 3 of the Table:

TABLE

1	*2*	*3*
Item	*Distance between foremost and rearmost axles (in metres)*	*Weight (in kilograms)*
1	5.07	38,000
2	5.33	40,000
3	6.0	45,000
4	6.67	50,000
5	7.33	55,000
6	8.0	60,000
7	8.67	65,000
8	9.33	70,000
9	10.0	75,000
10	10.67	80,000

(*f*) where the axles are in two or more groups (so that adjacent axles in each group are less than 2 metres apart and adjacent axles of different groups are more than 2 metres apart), then the total weight imposed on the road by all the wheels of any one group of axles shall not exceed 50,000 kilograms;

(ii*a*) until 1st October 1989 an articulated vehicle in Category 2 need not meet the requirements of sub-paragraph (ii) above, but—

(*a*) the total weight shall be transmitted to the road through at least 4 axles;

(*b*) the total weight imposed on the road by all the wheels of any one axle shall not exceed 13,500 kilograms, and by any one wheel 6,750 kilograms;

(*c*) if the total number of axles does not exceed 4, the total weight of the vehicle shall not exceed 46,000 kilograms;]

(iii) [save as provided in sub-paragraph (iii*a*) below] for any [vehicle] or combination of vehicles carrying the load in Category 3:

(*a*) the total weight shall be transmitted to the road through at least 6 axles;

(*b*) the total weight imposed on the road by all the wheels of any one axle shall not exceed 16,500 kilograms, and by any one wheel, 8,250 kilograms;

(*c*) if the distance between any two adjacent axles is at least 1.1 metres but less than 1.35 metres, the total weight imposed on the road by all the wheels of any one of those axles shall not exceed 15,000 kilograms, and by any one wheel 7,500 kilograms;

(*d*) the distance between any two adjacent axles shall not be less than 1.1 metres;

(*e*) where the distance between the foremost and rearmost axles of the vehicle or vehicles carrying the load is at least as specified in an item in column 2 of the Table below the total weight of the vehicle or combination of vehicles shall not exceed the weight given for that item in column 3 of the Table:

TABLE

1	*2*	*3*
Item	*Distance between foremost and rearmost axles (in metres)*	*Weight (in kilograms)*
1	5.77	80,000
2	6.23	85,000
3	6.68	90,000
4	7.14	95,000
5	7.59	100,000
6	8.05	105,000
7	8.50	110,000
8	8.95	115,000
9	9.41	120,000
10	9.86	125,000
11	10.32	130,000
12	10.77	135,000
13	11.23	140,000
14	11.68	145,000
15	12.14	150,000

(*f*) where the axles are in two or more groups (so that adjacent axles in each group are less than 1.5 metres apart and adjacent axles of different groups are more than 1.5 metres aprart) then the total weight imposed on the road by all the wheels of any one group of axles shall not exceed 100,000 kilograms, or 90,000 kilograms for a group where the distance between any two adjacent axles of that group is less than 1.35 metres;

[(iii*a*) until 1st October 1989 a vehicle or combination of vehicles carrying the load in Category 3 need not meet the requirements of sub-paragraphs (*c*) to (*f*) of sub-paragraph (iii) above;]

(iv) for the purpose of this sub-paragraph (*k*):

'axle' shall mean any number of wheels in line transversely;

'relevant axle spacing' shall have the same meaning as in regulation 77(1) of the Construction and Use Regulations;

(v) regulation 3(7) and (8) of the Construction and Use Regulations shall apply to determine the number of wheels and axles for the purpose of this sub-paragraph and regulation 3(10) to determine the distance between axles.]

(*l*) the vehicle or combination of vehicles shall not carry more than one abnormal indivisible load at any one time:

Provided that—

(i) subject to compliance with all the requirements of the Construction and Use Regulations with respect to the laden weights of vehicles and the weights transmitted to the road surface by all or any of the wheels, it shall be permissible for a vehicle or any vehicles comprised in a combination of vehicles to carry more than one abnormal indivisible load of the same character and, where any abnormal indivisible load is carried, to carry any articles of a similar character;

(ii) in the case of vehicles not falling within the foregoing proviso, it shall be permissible for a vehicle or any vehicles comprised in a combination of vehicles to carry more than one abnormal indivisible load each of the same character if—

[(*a*) the vehicle or combination of vehicles is in Category 1 or Category 2;]

(*b*) the overall length in relation to the vehicle or vehicles carrying the loads is such that the provisions of sub-paragraph (i) or (ii) of paragraph (*h*) above would be complied with were '18.3 metres' substituted for '27.4 metres' except that, where such compliance would be impossible by reason of the length of one of the loads if that were the only one carried, the aforesaid distance of 18.3 metres may be increased to such greater distance not exceeding 27.4 metres as may be necessary to permit the carriage of that load;

(*c*) the overall width of any vehicle together with the width of any lateral projection of its load does not exceed 2.9 metres or, where it would be impossible for the aforesaid distance to be complied with by reason of the width of one of the loads if that were the only one carried, such greater distance not exceeding 6.1 metres as may be necessary to permit the carriage of that load; and

(*d*) all the loads carried are loaded at the same place and conveyed to the same destination;

(*m*) where an abnormal indivisible load consists of engineering plant from which one or more constituent parts have been detached, such abnormal indivisible load and such constituent parts may be carried;

Provided that—

(i) no dimension of such constituent parts protrudes beyond any dimension of the vehicle or combination of vehicles on which such abnormal indivisible load and such constituent parts are being carried to an extent greater than such abnormal indivisible load would protrude if it were being carried without such constituent parts;

(ii) such abnormal indivisible load and such constituent parts are loaded at the same place and have the same destination; and

[(iii) the vehicle or combination of vehicles is in Category 1 or Category 2;]

[(*n*) in the case of a trailer whether manufactured before 1st January 1968 or on or after that date, [regulation 16] of the Construction and Use Regulations shall apply as it applies to trailers manufactured before 1st January 1968;]

(*o*) the conditions specified in Articles 21(1) and 27; and

(*p*) [for vehicles manufactured before 1st October 1989 and] in a case specified in column 2 of the Table below, all the Construction and Use Regulations shall apply with the exception of the Regulations which are specified opposite to that item in column 3 of that table, and, in relation to [item 3], save as provided in paragraph (*n*) above.

[TABLE

1	*2*	*3*
Item	*Case*	*Regulations that do not apply*
1	A heavy motor car	8, 16 in so far as it relates to the requirement in item 18(c) of Schedule 3 to the Regulations, 15, 18 (except paragraph (1)), 22, 24, [25,] 45, 63, 75–80, 82, and 83(1)
2	A locomotive or tractor	8, 22, [25,] 45, 75(3), and 76.
3	A trailer	7, 8, 16 in so far as it relates to the requirements in items 3, 4, 11, 15 and 18 of Schedule 3 to the Regulations, 15, 18 (except paragraph (1)), 21, 22, 24, [25,] 63, 64, 75–80, 82 and 83(1)]

[(*q*) in relation to any vehicle or combination of vehicles in a Category specified in column 2 of the Table below and manufactured [on or after 1st October 1989] and any vehicle in Category 1 whenever manufactured, all the Construction and Use Regulations shall apply with the exception of the Regulations which are specified opposite to that item in column 3 of the Table:

TABLE

1	*2*	*3*
Item	*Category*	*Regulations that do not apply*
1	1	7, 8, 80 and 82.
2	2 and 3	7, 8, 15, 16, 18 (except paragraph (1)), [25,] 45, 64, 65, [75 in so far as it relates to items 1–4, 6–11, 15 and 16 of the Table, 76–80], 82 and 83(1).

(*r*) a vehicle or combination of vehicles in Category 2 or Category 3, if manufactured [on or after 1st October 1989] shall have a braking system complying with the construction, fitting, and performance requirements set out in relation to category N3 motor vehicles and O4 trailers in Annexes I, II and VII to

Council Directive 71/320/EEC *[OJ L202, 6.9.71, p 37]* as amended by 74/132/EEC *[OJ L74, 19.3.74, p 7]*, 75/524/EEC *[OJ L326, 8.9.75, p 3]* and 79/489/EEC *[OJ L128, 26.5.79, p 2]* and, if appropriate, Annexes III, IV, V, and VI to the amended Directive, provided that:

(i) for the purposes of tests conducted in accordance with Annex II the laden weight of a vehicle shall be the maximum technically permissible weight specified by the manufacturer for the vehicle speed specified for the test,

(ii) the requirements of paragraphs 1.1.4.2, 1.4 and 2.1.3.2 of Annex II shall not apply;

(*s*) (i) a vehicle in Category 2 or Category 3, if manufactured [on or after 1st October 1988], shall have a plate complying with the specification prescribed in the Road Vehicles (Marking of Special Weights) Regulations 1983 [*SI 1983 No 910, as amended*] except that there need be no indication of any weight in respect of a speed not exceeding 12 miles per hour;

(ii) the plate fitted in accordance with paragraph (i) above shall be marked clearly with the words:

'SPECIAL TYPES USE';

(iii) if a vehicle is made up of several modules, each module may be fitted individually with a plate in accordance with paragraph (i) above, provided that the information required from the plate in relation to the vehicle as a whole can be readily determined from those individual plates;

(iv) a vehicle fitted with any plate in accordance with paragraph (i) above shall not be used at a weight in excess of any weight specified on that plate in relation to the speed at which the vehicle is travelling;

(v) a vehicle in Category 1 shall not be used at a weight in excess of any weight specified on a plate fitted in accordance with regulation 66 of the Construction and Use Regulations in relation to items 6, 7 and 8 in Part I or items 4, 5, and 6 in Part II of Schedule 8 to those Regulations;

(*t*) the vehicle or the drawing vehicle in a combination of vehicles shall be fitted with a sign indicating the relevant category and complying with the requirements specified in Schedule 6;

(*u*) notwithstanding sub-paragraph (*p*) above, regulation 7 of the Construction and Use Regulations shall not apply in the case of:

(i) an articulated vehicle, or a motor vehicle and a trailer, where the semi-trailer is constructed such that the major part of the load platform does not extend over or between the wheels and is at a height that is below the height of the top most point of the tyres of those wheels, measured on level ground and with any adjustable suspension at the normal travelling height, and where the height or stability of the load being carried necessitates the use of such a trailer;

(ii) a vehicle or combination of vehicles unable to comply with that regulation because of the requirements of sub-paragraphs (*k*)(ii)(*e*) or (*k*)(iii)(*e*) above;

(*v*) notwithstanding sub-paragraph (*u*) above, a vehicle consisting of two or more modules may, when being used in connection with the carriage of but not at the time carrying an abnormal indivisible load, be disassembled into two or more parts and arranged such that one part carries the others.]

[Article 18 is printed as amended by SI 1985 No 745; SI 1987 Nos 1327 and 2161.]

19. Engineering plant

The Minister authorises the use on roads of engineering plant notwithstanding that such vehicles do not comply in all respects with the requirements of the Construction and Use Regulations . . . , subject to—

(1) the restriction specified in Article 21(2) [save as provided in paragraph (2A) below],

(2) in a case where Article 22, 23, 25 or 26 applies, the conditions specified in such of those Articles as are applicable [save as provided in paragraph (2A) below],

[(2A) in a case where a vehicle or combination of vehicles disregarding the date of its manufacture complies with the conditions specified in article 18(2)(*k*), (*q*), (*r*), (*s*) and (*t*), the conditions specified in article 21(1) shall apply as if the use of the vehicle or combination of vehicles was authorised by article 18.]

(3) in a case where the overall width of the vehicle, or of the vehicle together with the width of any lateral projection or projections of its load exceeds [5 metres], the conditions specified in Article 24, and

(4) in any case, the following conditions:—

[(*a*) engineering plant shall be used on a road only:
- (i) for testing or demonstration purposes or delivery on sale;
- (ii) for proceeding to or returning from a manufacturer or repairer for repair or maintenance;
- (iii) for proceeding to or from the site of engineering operations or when actually engaged in such operations;

(*b*) engineering plant may carry its own necessary gear and equipment but no other load except;
- (i) engineering plant other than a mobile crane when actually engaged on the construction, maintenance or repair of roads may carry materials which it is specifically designed to treat while being carried on the vehicle or materials which have been excavated and raised from the ground by apparatus on the motor vehicle or trailer, and
- (ii) a mobile crane when actually engaged in engineering operations may lift or transport a load;]

(*c*) engineering plant other than a mobile crane shall only draw a trailer which is engineering plant or a living van or office hut used in connection with the construction, maintenance and repair of roads;

(*d*) no mobile crane shall draw a trailer;

(*e*) the vehicle shall be so constructed that it is either a wheeled vehicle or a track laying vehicle;

(*f*) in the case of a wheeled motor vehicle [Regulations 4, 10, 18(2) and (3), 23, 27, 29 to 32, 34, 37, 39, 40, 48, 50, 52, 54 to 61, 65, 83, 86, 89, 94 to 101, 103 to 105 and 107] of the Construction and Use Regulations shall apply:

Provided that—
- (i) *[Revoked.]*
- (ii) in the case of a machine designed for use and used solely for the purpose of laying materials for the repair or construction of road surfaces, if the weight transmitted to the road surface by any two wheels in line transversely does not exceed 11,180 kilograms, the said [Regulation 23] shall not apply;
- (iii) in the case of a motor vehicle designed for use in work of construction or repair of road surfaces, the wheels of which are equipped with pneu-

matic tyres specially provided with smooth treads for such use and which is incapable by reason of its construction of exceeding a speed of 20 miles per hour on the level under its own power, [Regulation 27(1)(*g*)] of the said Regulations shall not apply;

(*g*) in the case of a wheeled trailer, [Regulations 4, 10, 18(2) and (3), 23, 27, 29, 34, 89, 95, 96, 100 and 103] of the Construction and Use Regulations shall apply:

Provided that in the case of a trailer designed for use in work of construction or repair of road surfaces and the wheels of which are equipped with pneumatic tyres specially provided with smooth treads for such use, [Regulation 27(1)(*b*)] of the said Regulations shall not apply;

(*h*) in the case of a track laying motor vehicle [Regulations 4, 18, 23, 27 to 31, 34, 37, 40, 54, 61, 86, 89, 91, 97 to 101, 103, 104, 106 and 107] of the Construction and Use Regulations shall apply:

Provided that—

(i) in the case of a motor vehicle registered on or before 31st December 1951 [Regulations 31 and 34] of the said Regulations shall not apply, and

(ii) in the case of a motor vehicle which is a road roller the said [Regulation 28] shall not apply;

(*i*) in the case of a track laying trailer [Regulations 4, 18, 23, 27 to 29, 34, 89, 100 and 103] of the Construction and Use Regulations shall apply:

Provided that in the case of a trailer which is a road roller the said [Regulation 28] shall not apply;

(*j*) all the wheels of a vehicle which are not equipped with pneumatic tyres or tyres of soft or elastic material shall be equipped with smooth tyres and have the edges rounded to a radius of not less than 12 millimetres and not more than 25 millimetres:

Provided that in the case of gritting machines designed for use and used for gritting frosted and icebound roads all or any of the tyres may be shod with diagonal cross bars of equal width of not less than 25 millimetres, extending the full breadth of the tyre and so arranged that the distance between adjacent cross bars is not greater than the width of the cross bars;

(*k*) in the case of any vehicle the weight transmitted to the road surface by any one wheel not equipped with pneumatic tyres where no other wheel is in the same line transversely or by all the wheels not equipped with pneumatic tyres in line transversely shall be such that the average weight per 25 millimetres width of tyre in contact with such surface does not exceed 765 kilograms;

(*l*) a motor vehicle shall be equipped with an efficient brake:

Provided that—

(i) in the case of a motor vehicle propelled by steam the engine shall be deemed to be an efficient brake if the engine is capable of being reversed, and

(ii) in the case of a motor vehicle registered on or after 1st January 1952 any brake required by this paragraph shall be capable of being set so as to hold the vehicle when stationary unless another brake fitted to the vehicle is capable of being so set;

(*m*) a trailer shall be equipped with an efficient brake or with suitable scotches or other similar devices to hold the vehicle stationary when necessary;

(*n*) no motor vehicle which exceeds 7.93 metres in overall length shall draw a trailer:

Provided that this paragraph shall not apply to a motor vehicle which is drawing a broken down vehicle in consequence of the breakdown;

(*o*) the sum of weights transmitted to the road surface by all the wheels and tracks of a vehicle shall not exceed 152,400 kilograms;

(*p*) the overall length of a vehicle shall not exceed 27.4 metres;

(*q*) the overall width of a vehicle shall not exceed 6.1 metres;

(*r*) as respects weight—

(i) the weight transmitted to the road surface by any one wheel of a vehicle, other than a heavy motor car registered on or before 31st December 1951 or a trailer manufactured before 1st January 1952, shall not exceed 11,430 kilograms, and for the purposes of this part of this sub-paragraph any two wheels shall be treated as one wheel if the distance between the centres of the areas of contact between such wheels and the road surface is less than 610 millimetres,

(ii) the weight transmitted to any strip of road surface upon which the wheels of a vehicle rest contained between any two parallel lines drawn on that surface at right angles to the longitudinal axis of the vehicle shall not exceed, if the parallel lines are not more than 610 millimetres apart, 45,720 kilograms and, thereafter, additional weight shall be permitted, for any distance apart of the parallel lines in excess of 610 millimetres but not exceeding a total distance apart of 2.13 metres, at a rate of 30,000 kilograms per metre and thereafter, additional weight shall be permitted, for any distance apart of the parallel lines in excess of 2.13 metres, at a rate of 10,000 kilograms per metre,

(iii) the total weight transmitted to the road surface by any wheels of a vehicle in line transversely not fitted with pneumatic tyres shall be such that the average weight per 25 millimetre width of tyre in contact with the road surface shall not exceed 765 kilograms, and

(iv) in the case of a track laying vehicle, in addition to the foregoing restrictions, the weight transmitted by each track thereof to any strip of road surface contained between any two parallel lines drawn on that surface at right angles to the longitudinal axis of the vehicle shall not exceed, if the parallel lines are not more than 610 millimetres apart, 11,430 kilograms, and, thereafter, additional weight shall be permitted, for any distance apart of the parallel lines in excess of 610 millimetres but not exceeding a total distance apart of 2.13 metres, at a rate of 7,500 kilograms per metre and, thereafter, additional weight shall be permitted, for any distance apart of the parallel lines in excess of 2.13 metres, at a rate of 2,500 kilograms per metre.

[Article 19 is printed as amended by the Interpretation Act 1978, ss 17(2)(a) and 23(1); SI 1981 No 1664; SI 1987 No 1327. See the editorial note on p 530.

SI 1987 No 1327 substituted the text of art 19(4)(a) and (b) above for the existing text of art 19(4)(a), ie without formally revoking existing art 19(4)(b) (which read '(b) a mobile crane shall not be used on a road to lift or transport goods or burden except when actually engaged in engineering operations;'). It would appear that the failure to revoke the existing reg 19(4)(b) may have been an oversight; cf the text of reg 19(4)(ii) above.]

20. Other vehicles carrying loads exceeding 4.3 metres in width

The Minister authorises the use on roads of motor vehicles and trailers carrying loads where the overall width of the vehicle on which the load is carried together with the width of any lateral projection or projections of the load exceeds 4.3 metres but does not exceed 6.1 metres, subject to the restrictions and conditions contained in [articles 21(1)], 22, 24 and 25 and also to the condition that the vehicle complies in all respects with the requirements of the Construction and Use Regulations (other than [Regulation 82(1) and (2)]).

[Article 20 is printed as amended by the Interpretation Act 1978, ss 17(2)(a) and 23(1); SI 1987 No 1327.]

21. Speed limits for vehicles authorised by Article 18, 19 or 20

[(1) A vehicle or combination of vehicles the use of which on roads is authorised by article 18, if of Category 2 or Category 3 as defined in that article, or by article 20, as indicated by an item in column 2 of the Table below, shall not travel at a speed exceeding that specified in column 3 for that item in relation to the type of road used:

TABLE

1	*2*	*3*		
Item	*Authorisation*	*Speed (mph)* *Motorway*	*Dual Carriageway*	*Other road*
1	Article 18 Category 2	40	35	30
2	Article 18 Category 3	30	25	20
3	Article 20	30	25	20]

(2) A vehicle the use of which on roads is authorised by Article 19 shall not travel on any road other than a [motorway] at a speed exceeding 12 miles per hour.

(3) *[Revoked.]*

[Article 21 is printed as amended by SI 1987 No 1327.]

22. Attendants

(1) This Article applies in the case of a vehicle the use of which on roads is authorised by Article 20 and in a case where—

(*a*) the overall width of the vehicle the use of which on roads is authorised by Article 18 or 19 or of the vehicle together with the width of any lateral projection or projections of its load exceeds 3.5 metres, or

(*b*) the overall length of the vehicle the use of which on roads is authorised by Article 18 or 19 or of the vehicle together with the length of any forward projection and of any rearward projection of its load exceeds 18.3 metres, or

(*c*) as respects a motor vehicle (whether or not its use is authorised by Article 18 or 19) which is drawing a trailer or trailers the use of which is so authorised, a load is carried in such a manner that its weight rests on more than one of the vehicles being—

(i) the motor vehicle and one trailer whether forming part of an articulated vehicle or not, or

(ii) any other combination of vehicles,

and, in the case at (i) above, the overall length of the trailer together with the length of any forward projection of the load extending beyond the foremost point of the trailer and of any rearward projection of the load exceeds 18.3 metres and, in the case at (ii) above, the overall length of the vehicles together with the distance between vehicles and the length of any forward and of any rearward projection of the load exceeds 18.3 metres, or

(*d*) a motor vehicle (whether or not its use is authorised by Article 18 or 19) is drawing a trailer or trailers the use of which is so authorised and the overall length of the combination of vehicles together with the length of any forward projection of any load extending beyond the foremost point of the drawing vehicle comprised in the combination and the length of any rearward projection of any load extending beyond the rearmost point of the rearmost vehicle comprised therein exceeds 25.9 metres, or

(*e*) a vehicle the use of which is authorised by Article 18 or 19 is carrying a load having a forward projection exceeding 1.83 metres in length or a rearward projection exceeding 3.05 metres in length or is fitted with any special appliance or apparatus having such a projection.

(2) As respects a vehicle to which this Article applies at least one person, in addition to the person or persons employed in driving any motor vehicle to which this Article applies, shall be employed—

(*a*) to warn such driver or drivers, and any other person, of any danger likely to be caused to such other person by the presence of such vehicle, and any vehicle or vehicles being drawn by such vehicle on the road, and

(*b*) to attend to—

(i) such vehicle and its load,

(ii) any vehicle or vehicles drawn by such vehicle, and

(iii) the load carried on any vehicle or vehicles so drawn.

(3) For the purposes of paragraph (2) above—

(*a*) in a case where a motor vehicle is drawing a trailer or trailers any person employed in pursuance of section 34 of the Road Traffic Act 1972 in attending that vehicle or any such trailer shall be treated as being an attendant required by that paragraph so long as he is also employed to discharge the duties mentioned in that paragraph,

(*b*) in a case where a motor vehicle is drawing a trailer or trailers and another motor vehicle is used for the purpose of assisting in their propulsion on the road, the person or persons employed in driving that other motor vehicle shall not be treated as a person or persons employed in attending to the first-mentioned vehicle or any vehicle or vehicles drawn thereby, and

(*c*) in a case where three or more vehicles to which that paragraph applies are travelling together in convoy, it shall be a sufficient compliance with the requirements of that paragraph if only the first and the last vehicles in the convoy are attended in the manner specified in that paragraph.

[Section 34 of the Road Traffic Act 1972 was repealed by the Road Traffic (Consequential Provisions) Act 1988, but (on the recommendation of the Law Commission; see Cm 390) not re-enacted. It is assumed therefore that art 22(3)(a) above has now lapsed.]

23. Marking of projecting loads and fixed appliances or apparatus which project

(1) This Article applies in a case where a vehicle the use of which is authorised by Article 18 or 19—

(*a*) carries a load which—

(i) has a forward or a rearward projection exceeding 1.83 metres in length, or

(ii) has a rearward projection exceeding 1.07 metres in length but not exceeding 1.83 metres in length, or

(*b*) is fitted with a special appliance or apparatus which—

(i) has a forward or a rearward projection exceeding 1.83 metres in length, or

(ii) has a rearward projection exceeding 1.07 metres in length but not exceeding 1.83 metres in length.

(2) Subject to the provisions of paragraphs (3), (4) and (5) of this Article—

(*a*) as respects a projection mentioned in sub-paragraph (*a*)(i) or in sub-paragraph (*b*)(i) of the foregoing paragraph the conditions specified in [paragraph 3 of Schedule 12] to the Construction and Use Regulations shall be complied with, and accordingly the provisions of the said [paragraph 3] shall apply in relation to that projection as they apply in relation to a relevant projection as mentioned in that paragraph, and

(*b*) as respects a projection mentioned in sub-paragraph (*a*)(ii) or in sub-paragraph (*b*)(ii) of the foregoing paragraph the conditions specified in [paragraph 4 of the said Schedule 12] shall be complied with, and accordingly the provisions of the said [paragraph 4] shall apply in relation to that projection as they apply in relation to a relevant projection as mentioned in that paragraph.

(3) Where, in any of the cases mentioned in paragraph (1) of this Article, a vehicle is carrying a load or is fitted with a special appliance or apparatus and the load or the appliance or apparatus has, in relation to the vehicle, a forward projection or a rearward projection, and another vehicle is attached to that end of the vehicle from which the load or, as the case may be, the appliance or apparatus projects and is attached to that vehicle in such a manner that—

(*a*) in the case where there is a forward projection, the foremost point of that other vehicle extends beyond the foremost part of the projection or, in the case where there is a rearward projection, the rearmost point of that other vehicle extends beyond the rearmost part of the projection, or

(*b*) in the case where there is a forward projection, the foremost part of the projection extends beyond the foremost point of that other vehicle or, in the case where there is a rearward projection the rearmost part of the projection extends beyond the rearmost point of that other vehicle, then—

(i) in either of the cases mentioned in sub-paragraph (*a*) of this paragraph, the provisions of paragraph (2) of this Article shall not apply as respects any such projection, and

(ii) in either of the cases mentioned in sub-paragraph (*b*) of this paragraph, the provisions of the said paragraph (2) shall apply as if each of the references in paragraph (1) of this Article to a rearward projection were treated as a reference to so much of a rearward projection as extends beyond the rearmost point of that other vehicle and as if the reference in the said paragraph (1) to a forward projection were treated as a reference to so much of a forward projection as extends beyond the foremost point of that other vehicle measured, in either case, when the longitudinal axis of each vehicle lies in the same vertical plane between vertical planes at right angles to the said longitudinal axis and passing, in the case of a rearward projection, through the rearmost point of the said other vehicle and that part of the projection furthest from that point or, in the case of a forward projection, through the foremost point of the said other vehicle and that part of the projection furthest from that point.

(4) This Article shall not apply to any motor vehicle or trailer being used—

(*a*) for fire brigade, ambulance or police purposes or for defence purposes (including civil defence purposes), or

(*b*) in connection with the removal of any obstruction to traffic

if, in any such case, compliance with any provision of this Article would hinder or be likely to hinder the use of the vehicle for the purpose for which it is being used on that occasion.

(5) Notwithstanding that paragraph (2)(*a*) provides for the conditions specified in [paragraph 3 of Schedule 12] to the Construction and Use Regulations to be complied with as respects a load which has a projection to which sub-paragraph (*a*)(i) of paragraph (1) of this Article applies, those conditions in relation to the exhibition of the end projection surface on that projection need not be complied with in the case of such a load which carries a rear marking in accordance with the [Road Vehicles Lighting Regulations 1984 [*SI 1984 No 812, qv*]].

[Article 23 is printed as amended by the Interpretation Act 1978, ss 17(2)(a) and 23(1).]

24. Approval of the Minister as to the time, date and route of a journey by a vehicle or a vehicle and its load exceeding 4.3 metres in width

[(1) This Article applies in the case of a vehicle the use of which on roads otherwise would be authorised by article 15, 18, 19 or 20 where the overall width of the vehicle or, if it is used for carrying a load, where the overall width of the vehicle together with the width of any lateral projection of its load, exceeds 5 metres.]

(2) Subject to the provisions of paragraph (3) of this Article, a vehicle mentioned in the foregoing paragraph shall be used only—

(*a*) for the purpose of making such a journey between specified places as the Minister may have approved by notice in writing given to the owner of the vehicle and only at such times (if any), on such a date or dates (if any) and on such a route (if any) as the Minister may have specified in the said notice, or as the chief officer of police of any police area in which it is proposed that the vehicle shall be used may have specified, in relation to the use of the vehicle in that area, in a direction given to the [user] of the vehicle, and

(*b*) if the notice referred to in the foregoing sub-paragraph is carried on the vehicle at all times while it is being used for the purpose of making the journey for which the Minister's approval has been given.

(3) Where the effect of any such direction as is mentioned in sub-paragraph (*a*) of the foregoing paragraph is to vary, in relation to a time, a date or a route of the journey approved by the Minister under that sub-paragraph, the time, the date or dates or the route of the said journey, the vehicle shall not be used in accordance with that direction unless the Minister has given his further approval that the vehicle shall be so used.

[Article 24 is printed as amended by SI 1987 No 1327.]

25. Notice to police

(1) This Article applies in a case where:—

(*a*) the overall width of a vehicle the use of which on roads is authorised by Article

18 or 19 or of the vehicle together with the width of any lateral projection or projections of its load exceeds 2.9 metres, or

(*b*) the overall length of a vehicle the use of which on roads is authorised by Article 18 or 19 or of the vehicle together with the length of any forward projection and of any rearward projection of its load exceeds 18.3 metres, or

(*c*) as respects a motor vehicle (whether or not its use is authorised by Article 18 or 19) which is drawing a trailer or trailers the use of which is so authorised, a load is carried in such a manner that its weight rests on more than one of the vehicles being—

(i) the motor vehicle and one trailer whether constituting an articulated vehicle or not, or

(ii) any other combination of vehicles,

and, in the case at (i) above, the overall length of the trailer together with the length of any forward projection of the load extending beyond the foremost point of the trailer and of any rearward projection of the load exceeds 18.3 metres and, in the case at (ii) above, the overall length of the vehicles together with the distance between vehicles and the length of any forward and of any rearward projection of the load exceeds 18.3 metres, or

(*d*) a motor vehicle (whether or not its use on roads is authorised by Article 18 or 19) is drawing a trailer or trailers the use of which is so authorised and the overall length of the combination of vehicles together with the length of any forward projection of any load extending beyond the foremost point of the drawing vehicle comprised in the combination and the length of any rearward projection of any load extending beyond the rearmost point of the rearmost vehicle comprised therein exceeds 25.9 metres, or

(*e*) a vehicle the use of which on roads is authorised by Article 18 or 19 is carrying a load having a forward projection or a rearward projection exceeding 3.05 metres in length or is fitted with any special appliance or apparatus having such a projection as aforesaid, or

(*f*) the total weight of a vehicle the use of which on roads is authorised by Article 18 or 19 or of such a vehicle and its load or, in a case where a motor vehicle (whether or not its use is so authorised), is drawing a trailer or trailers the use of which is so authorised, the total weight of the combination of vehicles or of the said combination and of any load carried by any vehicle or vehicles comprised therein exceeds [80,000 kilograms], or

(*g*) the use of a vehicle on roads is authorised by Article 20.

(2) Save in so far as the chief officer of police of any police area in which it is proposed that the vehicle or, as the case may be, the vehicles, will be used dispenses, as respects the use of the vehicle or vehicles in that area, with the requirements contained in this paragraph as to the length or the form or notice or the particulars to be given, the [user] of the vehicle, or, as the case may be, of the vehicles, before using the vehicle or vehicles on a road, shall give at least two clear days' notice to the chief officer of police of any such area and such notice shall, subject to any necessary modification, be in the form and contain the particulars specified in Part I of Schedule 2 [*not reproduced*].

(3) Subject to any variation in the time, date or route of the journey which may be directed by any such chief officer of police, and subject to any delay which may be occasioned by reason of a direction given by a police constable, in the interests of road safety or to avoid undue traffic congestion, to the driver of a vehicle to halt it in a place on or adjacent to the road on which the vehicle is travelling, the vehicle or

vehicles shall be used only in circumstances which accord with the particulars given in compliance with paragraph (2) above as to the time, date and route of the journey and only if any dimension or measurement relating to the vehicle or the vehicles (including one relating to a combination of vehicles) or to a special appliance or apparatus or to a load to be carried, being a dimension or measurement of which particulars have been given as aforesaid, is not exceeded.

[Article 25 is printed as amended by SI 1987 No 1327.]

26. Notice and indemnity to highway and bridge authorities

(1) This Article applies to—

(*a*) a vehicle the use of which on roads is authorised by Article 18 or 19, whether such vehicle is laden or unladen, or

(*b*) a combination of a motor vehicle (whether or not its use on roads is authorised under Article 18 or 19) and any trailer or trailers the use of which on roads is authorised under the said Articles, whether all or any part of such combination is laden or unladen,

and which, in either case, either—

(i) has a total weight exceeding [80,000 kilograms] or

(ii) does not comply in all respects with the requirements of the Construction and Use Regulations . . . with respect to

(*a*) the weights of vehicles, whether laden or unladen;

(*b*) the weights transmitted to the surface of the road by all or any of the wheels or tracks.

(2) In any case where this Article applies, the [user] of the vehicle or, as the case may be, of the combination of vehicles, shall give to the highway authority for any road and the bridge authority for any bridge on which it is proposed that the vehicle or, as the case may be, the combination of vehicles shall be used—

(*a*) at any time before such use an indemnity in the form specified in Part II of Schedule 2 [*not reproduced*]; and

(*b*) in any case to which sub-paragraph (i) of paragraph (1) above applies, at least [five clear days] (or such less period as the said highway authority or the said bridge authority, as the case may be, may agree) before such use, and in a case to which sub-paragraph (ii) of paragraph (1) above applies at least two clear days (or such less period as the said highway authority or the said bridge authority, as the case may be, may agree) before such a use, a notice in the form and containing the particulars specified in Part I of Schedule 2 [*not reproduced*].

[(2A) In any case where a London council or a metropolitan district council which is a highway authority or a bridge authority has—

(*a*) delegated all or any of its functions with respect to a road or bridge to another London council or (in the case of a metropolitan district council) another metropolitan district council; or

(*b*) entered into an agreement for the discharge of all or any of its functions with respect to a road or bridge by some other person,

the notice and indemnity which are required by the provisions of paragraph (2) above shall be treated as given in accordance with that paragraph if they are given to the other council or (as the case may be) to the other person.]

[(2B) In paragraph (2A) above 'London council' means the council of a London borough or the Common Council of the City of London.]

(3) Where, in accordance with requirements specified in paragraph (2) above, notice is required to be given at least [five clear days] before a journey is proposed to be made by a combination of vehicles which include a trailer the use of which on roads is authorised by Article 18 and it is found impracticable to use any vehicle specified in the said notice (not being a vehicle the use of which on roads is authorised by Article 18 or 19) as a vehicle intended to draw the trailer, then any other vehicle of a similar type may be substituted therefor if at least two clear days' notice of the substitution is given to every authority to whom the notice was given, and thereupon the said notice shall have effect as if the substituted vehicle had always been specified therein as the vehicle intended to draw the trailer.

(4) If, by virtue of Article 18, a vehicle is to be used on roads to carry a vehicle specified in either item 1 or item 2 in column 1 of Schedule 1, being the property of, or for the time being under the control of, the persons respectively specified opposite thereto in column 3 of that Schedule, the requirement specified in paragraph (2) above that before such use an indemnity and at least [five clear days'] notice or at least two clear days' notice, as the case may be, shall be given to the authorities specified in that paragraph shall not apply provided that before the vehicle is used on a road—

(*a*) the notice and indemnity which are required by the provisions of paragraph (2) above are received by or posted to all the said authorities,

(*b*) the [user] of the carrying vehicle has consulted the Minister on the route proposed to be followed, and

(*c*) the proper naval, military or air force authority has certified in writing that the journey is urgent and in the national interest.

(5) The provisions of this Article shall not apply to the use on roads of any vehicle which is the property of, or for the time being under the control of, the Secretary of State for Defence.

(6) In the case of a trunk road—

(i) where by virtue of the provisons of [section 6 of the Highways Act 1980], the functions of the Minister with respect to maintenance are exercised in England by the council of a county [or of a metropolitan district] or of a London Borough [or by any other person acting pursuant to an agreement with the Minister] or the functions of the Secretary of State with respect to maintenance are exercised in Wales by the council of a county, or

(ii) where by virtue of an agreement between, or having effect under paragraph 2 of Schedule 6 to the Transport Act 1962 as if between, the Secretary of State or, as the case may be, the Minister, and either the British Railways Board, the London Transport Executive, the British Transport Docks Board, or the British Waterways Board, the maintenance or, as the case may be, the maintenance and repair of that part are carried out by such Executive or by any such Board,

the notice and indemnity required to be given to the Minister by paragraph (2) of this Article shall be treated as given in accordance with that paragraph only if addressed to, or included in any notice and indemnity given to, such council, Executive or Board [or person] as the case may be.

(7) Any notice and indemnity in respect of any part of a trunk road required by the foregoing paragraph to be addressed to, or included in any notice and indemnity given to, the British Railways Board shall be addressed to, or included in a notice and indemnity given to, the Board at the Headquarters of the Regional Railways Board

responsible for the part of the railway system which is affected by any such agreement as is mentioned in that paragraph by virtue of the agreement applying to that part of the trunk road.

[Article 26 is printed as amended by the Interpretation Act 1978, ss 17(2)(a) and 23(1); SI 1986 No 313; SI 1987 No 1327.

Words relating expressly and exclusively to Scotland have been omitted from para (6)(i) above.

London Transport Executive is now known as 'London Regional Transport'; see the London Regional Transport Act 1984, s 1(2).]

27. Restriction on the passage over bridges of vehicles carrying abnormal indivisible loads

Where a motor vehicle the use of which on roads is authorised by Article 18 is so used or where a motor vehicle (whether or not its use is so authorised) is drawing a trailer or trailers the use of which is so authorised and an abnormal indivisible load is being carried by any such vehicle, the driver of the motor vehicle shall not cause or permit either that vehicle or, in the case of a combination of vehicles, any vehicle comprised in the combination—

(*a*) to enter on any bridge whilst there is on that bridge any other vehicle which is either carrying an abnormal indivisible load or is being used to draw a trailer carrying such a load the presence of which is known to or could reasonably be ascertained by him, or

(*b*) to remain stationary on any bridge except in circumstances beyond his control.

28. Breakdown on bridges of vehicles of excessive weight or carrying excessive loads

(1) This Article applies where—

[(*a*) a vehicle (including an articulated vehicle) laden or unladen has a gross weight of more than:

(i) prior to [1st October 1989], 32,520 kilograms;

(ii) on or after [1st October 1989], 38,000 kilograms, and]

(*b*) the use on roads of a vehicle or of a trailer forming part of an articulated vehicle is authorised by Article 5(2), 6, 11, 15, 16, 18 or 19.

(2) Subject to the provisions of paragraph (3) below, where a vehicle or trailer is caused to stop for any reason while it is on a bridge, it shall, as soon as practicable, be moved clear of the bridge by appropriate action by the person in charge of the vehicle, without applying any concentrated load to the surface of that part of the road carried by the bridge.

(3) If the action described in paragraph (2) above is not practicable and it becomes necessary to apply any concentrated load to the said surface by means of jacks, rollers or other similar means, then the person in charge of the vehicle shall—

(*a*) before any such load is applied to that surface, seek the advice of the bridge authority for that bridge [or any other person responsible for the maintenance and repair of the bridge pursuant to an agreement with that authority] about the use of spreader plates to reduce the possibility of any damage caused by the application of such a load, and

(*b*) arrange that no such load shall be applied without using such spreader plates as the bridge authority [or such other person] may have advised.

[Article 28 is printed as amended by SI 1986 No 313; SI 1987 Nos 1327 and 2161.]

SCHEDULE 1
(see Article 6)

Service and Aviation Vehicles

Column 1	Column 2	Column 3
1 Motor vehicles or trailers constructed either for actual combative purposes or for naval, military or air force training in connection therewith or for use with, or for the carriage or drawing of, instruments of war, including guns and machine guns.	Construction and Use Regulations—All . . .	The Secretary of State for Defence or the Secretary of State for [Trade and Industry], or any contractor making such vehicles for the said Secretaries of State or any sub-contractor of such contractor.
2 Track laying motor vehicles or track laying trailers constructed either for actual combative purposes or for use with, or for the carriage or drawing of, instruments of war, including guns and machine guns, ammunition, equipment or stores in connection therewith.	Construction and Use Regulations—All . . .	The Secretary of State for Defence or the Secretary of State for [Trade and Industry], or any contractor making such vehicles for the said Secretaries of State, or any sub-contractor of such contractor.
3 Motor vehicles or trailers constructed for the carriage of tanks	Construction and Use Regulations—All . . .	The Secretary of State for Defence or the Secretary of State for [Trade and Industry] or any contractor making such vehicles for the said Secretaries of State, or any sub-contractor of such contractor.
4 Motor vehicles or trailers constructed for the carriage of searchlights or the necessary equipment therefor.	Construction and Use [Regulation 22].	The Secretary of State for Defence or the Secretary of State for [Trade and Industry], or any contractor making such vehicles for the said Secretaries of State, or any sub-contractor of such contractor.

Column 1	Column 2	Column 3
5 Motor vehicles or trailers constructed for the carriage of aircraft or aircraft parts.	Construction and Use [Regulations 7, 8, 11, 81 and 82].	The Secretary of State for Defence or the Secretary of State for [Trade and Industry], or any contractor making such vehicles for the said Secretaries of State, or any sub-contractor of such contractor.
6 Motor tractors, heavy motor cars and trailers constructed for naval, military, air force or aviation purposes before 1st January 1949.	Construction and Use [Regulations 8, 11, 16, 18 and Schedule 3].	The Secretary of State for Defence or the Secretary of State for [Trade and Industry].
7 Heavy motor cars or trailers constructed for use and used only in connection with flying operations where the additional width is made necessary by the design of the equipment or its installation on the vehicle.	Construction and Use [Regulation 8].	The Secretary of State for Defence or the Secretary of State for [Trade and Industry], or any contractor making such vehicles for the said Secretaries of State, or any sub-contractor of such contractor.
8 Aircraft drawn by motor vehicles.	Construction and Use [Regulations 8, 16, 18 and 22 and Schedule 3].	The Secretary of State for Defence.
9 Motor vehicles or trailers used for the carriage of generating equipment, being equipment used for naval, military or air force purposes.	Construction and Use [Regulations 8, 75, 76 and 80].	The Minister of Transport.

[Schedule 1 is printed as amended by the Interpretation Act 1978, ss 17(2)(a) and 23(1); the Transfer of Functions (Trade and Industry) Order 1983 (SI 1983 No 1127). See the editorial note on p 530.]

SCHEDULE 2

PART I

FORM OF NOTICE TO POLICE AND TO HIGHWAY AND BRIDGE AUTHORITIES

[Omitted.]

PART II

FORM OF INDEMNITY

[Omitted.]

SCHEDULE 3

ORDERS REVOKED BY ARTICLE 2

[Omitted.]

[SCHEDULE 4
(see Articles 13 and 13A)

CONDITIONS RELATING TO THE WIDTH OF AGRICULTURAL VEHICLES

1. If the overall width of the vehicle, or in the case of a combination of vehicles mentioned in Article 13A(1), the overall width of the combination exceeds the width specified in an item in column 2 of the Table below, the vehicle, or in the case of a combination of vehicles, the drawing vehicle, shall not be driven at a speed exceeding that specified in column 3 of that item.

1 Item No.	2 Overall width	3 Maximum speed
1	3.5 metres	12 miles per hour
2	2.5 metres	20 miles per hour

2. If—

(*a*) the overall width of—

(i) an agricultural motor vehicle,

(ii) an agricultural trailer,

(iii) an agricultural trailed appliance, or

(*b*) the width specified in Article 13A(2) of a combination of vehicles—

exceeds 3 metres and the whole or part of the journey to be made by the vehicle or combination will be on a road on which there is a speed limit of 40 miles per hour or less or will cover a distance exceeding 5 miles, the operator of the vehicle shall—

(A) before using the vehicle or combination on a road, give at least 24 hours notice of the intended use to the chief officer of police for any police area in which the operator proposes to use the vehicle or combination of vehicles and the notice shall contain the following particulars:—
   (i) the time, date and route of the proposed journey,
   (ii) information about the vehicle or combination of vehicles including the overall width; and

(B) use the vehicle or combination only in accordance with the particulars given in the notice mentioned above, subject to any variation in the time, date or route as may be directed by any chief officer of police as regards his police area,

so, however that a chief officer of police may dispense, within his area, with the said requirements as to length of notice and information about the vehicle or combination.

3. In a case where—

(*a*) the width of an agricultural motor vehicle exceeds 3 metres, or

(*b*) an agricultural motor vehicle is towing an agricultural trailer or agricultural trailed appliance in the manner described in Article 13A(1) and the width specified in Article 13A(2) exceeds 3 metres, or

(*c*) an agricultural motor vehicle is towing an agricultural trailer or an agricultural trailed appliance in a manner not described in Article 13A(1) and the overall width of either the motor vehicle or the trailer or trailed appliance, or both, exceeds 3 metres,

the vehicle or the combination of vehicles shall not draw any trailer or, as the case may be, any other trailer, except
   (i) a two-wheeled trailer used solely for the carriage of equipment for use on the drawing vehicle,
   (ii) an agricultural trailed appliance, or
   (iii) an unladen trailer specially designed for use with the drawing vehicle when it is harvesting.

4. If the overall width of an agricultural motor vehicle, an agricultural trailer on which an implement is mounted as mentioned in Article 13B, or an agricultural trailed appliance, or the width specified in Article 13A(2) of a combination of vehicles, exceeds 3.5 metres—

(*a*) at least one person, other than the driver of the vehicle or, in the case of a combination of vehicles, the driver of the drawing vehicle, shall be employed to warn any other person (including the driver of the vehicle or the drawing vehicle) of any danger likely to be caused to that other person by the presence of the vehicle or the combination of vehicles on the road; and

(*b*) the extremities of the vehicle or implement (including any blade or spike) shall be clearly visible at a reasonable distance to any person on the road (other than the driver of the vehicle or, in the case of a combination of vehicles, the driver of the drawing vehicle) and during the hours of darkness or in seriously reduced visibility this condition shall be satisfied by such means as may be required by the Road Vehicles Lighting Regulations 1984 [*SI 1984 No 812, qv*].

5. The overall width of a vehicle, or the width specified in Article 13A(2) of a combination of vehicles, shall not exceed 4.3 metres.]

[Schedule 4 was inserted by SI 1984 No 1810.]

[SCHEDULE 5
(see Article 13C)

PART I

1 Item No.	2 Distance of rearward or forward projection	3 Conditions to be complied with
1	1 metre	A
2	2 metres	B
3	4 metres	B C
4	6 metres	B C D

PART II

1. In this Schedule:—

'Condition A' is the condition that the end of each projection is clearly visible at a reasonable distance to any person using the road other than the driver of the vehicle, or in the case of a combination of vehicles, the driver of the drawing vehicle, and during the hours of darkness or in seriously reduced visibility this condition shall be satisfied by such means as may be required by the Road Vehicles Lighting Regulations 1984.

'Condition B' is the condition that—

(*a*) the end of each projection is marked with a projection marker of a kind specified in relation to an end projection surface in [Part II of Schedule 12] to the Construction and Use Regulations and in respect of which the provisions specified, for the purposes of those Regulations, in [paragraph 3(*b*) of Part I] of that Schedule are complied with,

(*b*) each side of each projection is marked with a projection marker of a kind specified in relation to a side projection surface in [Part II] of that Schedule and in respect of which the provisions specified, for the purposes of the said Regulations, in [paragraph 3(*c*) of Part I] of that Schedule are complied with, and

(*c*) during the hours of darkness or in seriously reduced visibility the markers referred to in paragraphs (*a*) and (*b*) shall be illuminated in the manner described, in relation to the extremities of an appliance, in [paragraph 3(*f*) of Schedule 12] to the Construction and Use Regulations, and kept clean and unobstructed.

'Condition C' is the same condition as is specified, in relation to Articles 13 and 13A, in paragraph 2 of Schedule 4; and

'Condition D' is the same condition as is specified, in relation to Articles 13 and 13A, in paragraph 4(*a*) of Schedule 4.]

[Schedule 5 was inserted by SI 1984 No 1810 and is printed as amended by the Interpretation Act 1978, ss 17(2)(a) and 23(1).]

[SCHEDULE 6

Form of Identification Sign

(See Article 18(2)(*t*))

PART I

1. The sign shall be mounted in a clearly visible position on the front of the vehicle, facing forwards, and as near to the vertical plane as practicable.

2. The sign shall be kept clean and unobscured at all times.

3. The sign shall consist of white letters on a black background.

4. The sign shall take the form shown in Part II. Any variation in a dimension specified in Part II shall be treated as permitted for the purposes of this Order if the variation does not exceed 5 per cent of that dimension.

PART II

400 mm

250 mm

105 mm

70 mm

Note: the category number 3 is shown as an example; the number could be 1, 2 or 3 depending upon the category of the vehicle or combination of vehicles.]

[Schedule 6 was inserted by SI 1987 No 1327.]

The Motor Vehicles (Authorisation of Special Types) (Amendment) (No 2) Order 1987

(SI 1987 No 2161)

1. *[Citation.]*

2–5. *[Amend the Motor Vehicles (Authorisation of Special Types) General Order 1979 (referred to as the 'Principal Order').]*

6.—(1) This article applies to an order made before 1st January 1988 under section 42 of the Road Traffic Act 1972 otherwise than by statutory instrument.

(2) Nothing in the Motor Vehicles (Authorisation of Special Types) (Amendment) Order 1987 *[SI 1987 No 1327]* or this order shall affect the Principal Order as applied by an order such as is mentioned in paragraph (1) above.

The Motor Vehicles (Compulsory Insurance) (No 2) Regulations 1973

(SI 1973 No 2143)

[The text of these regulations is printed as amended by:

the Motor Vehicles (Compulsory Insurance) (No 2) (Amendment) Regulations 1974 (SI 1974 No 791) (27 May 1974);

the Motor Vehicles (Compulsory Insurance) (No 2) (Amendment) (No 2) Regulations 1974 (SI 1974 No 2186); and

the Motor Vehicles (Compulsory Insurance) Regulations 1987 (SI 1987 No 2171) (31 December 1988).

The amending regulations are referred to in the notes to the main regulations only by their years and numbers. The dates referred to above are the dates on which the regulations came into force.]

* * *

2.—(1) In these Regulations 'vehicle' means any motor vehicle intended for travel on land and propelled by mechanical power, but not running on rails, and any trailer, whether or not coupled [and references to a relevant foreign state are references to [Austria, Czechoslovakia, Finland, the German Democratic Republic, Hungary, Norway, Sweden or Switzerland]].

(2) For the purposes of these Regulations the territory in which a vehicle is normally based is—

(*a*) the territory of the state [of which the vehicle bears a registration plate], or

(*b*) in cases where no registration is required for the type of vehicle, but the vehicle bears an insurance plate or distinguishing sign analogous to a registration plate, the territory of the state in which the insurance plate or the sign is issued, or

(*c*) in cases where neither registration plate nor insurance plate nor distinguishing sign is required for the type of vehicle, the territory of the state in which the keeper of the vehicle is permanently resident.

(3) The [Interpretation Act 1978] shall apply for the interpretation of these Regulations as it applies for the interpretation of an Act of Parliament.

[Regulation 2 is printed as amended by SI 1974 No 791; SI 1974 No 2186; SI 1987 No 2171.]

3, 4. *[Revoked by the Road Traffic (Consequential Provisions) Act 1988.]*

5.—(1) It shall be an offence for a person to use a specified motor vehicle registered in Great Britain, or any trailer kept by a person permanently resident in Great Britain, whether or not coupled, in the territory other than Great Britain and Gibraltar of any of the member states of the Communities, unless a policy of insurance is in force in relation to the person using that vehicle which insures him in respect of any liability which may be incurred by him in respect of the use of the vehicle in such territory according to the law on compulsory insurance against civil liability in respect of the use of vehicles of the state where the liability may be incurred.

(2) In this Regulation 'specified motor vehicle' means a motor vehicle which is exempted from the provisions of [section 143 of the Road Traffic Act 1988] (users of motor vehicles to be insured or secured against third-party risks) by virtue of [section 144] of that Act.

(3) A person guilty of an offence under this Regulation shall be liable on summary conviction to a fine not exceeding £50 or to imprisonment for a term not exceeding three months, or to both such fine and such imprisonment.

(4) Proceedings for an offence under this Regulation may be taken, and the offence may for all incidental purposes be treated as having been committed in any place in Great Britain.

(5) [Sections 6 (time within which summary proceedings for certain offences must be commenced) and 11 (evidence by certificate) of the Road Traffic Offenders Act 1988] shall apply for the purposes of an offence under this Regulation as if such an offence were an offence under that Act to which those sections had been applied by [column (3) of Schedule 1 to that Act].

6.—(1) Any person appointed by the [Secretary of State for Transport] for the purpose (in this Regulation referred to as an 'appointed person') may require a person having custody of any vehicle, being a vehicle which is normally based in the territory of a state [(other than a relevant foreign state)] which is not a member of the Communities or in the non-European territory of a member state or in Gibraltar, when entering Great Britain to produce evidence that any loss or injury which may be caused by such a vehicle is covered throughout the territory in which the treaty establishing the European Economic Community is in force, in accordance with the requirements of the laws of the various member states on compulsory insurance against civil liability in respect of the use of vehicles.

(2) An appointed person may, if no such evidence is produced or if he is not satisfied by such evidence, prohibit the use of the vehicle in Great Britain.

(3) Where an appointed person prohibits the use of a vehicle under this Regulation, he may also direct the driver to remove the vehicle to such place and subject to such conditions as are specified in the direction; and the prohibition shall not apply to the removal of the vehicle in accordance with the direction.

(4) Any person who—

(*a*) uses a vehicle or causes or permits a vehicle to be used in contravention of a prohibition imposed under paragraph (2) of this Regulation, or

(*b*) refuses, neglects or otherwise fails to comply in a reasonable time with a direction given under paragraph (3) of this Regulation,

shall be guilty of an offence and shall be liable on summary conviction to a fine not exceeding £50.

(5) [Section 11 of the Road Traffic Offenders Act 1988] shall apply for the purposes of an offence under this Regulation as if such an offence were an offence under that Act to which that section had been applied by [column (3) of Schedule 1 to that Act].

(6) A prohibition under paragraph (2) of this Regulation may be removed by an appointed person if he is satisfied that appropriate action has been taken to remove or remedy the circumstances in consequence of which the prohibition was imposed.

[Regulation 6 is printed as amended by SI 1974 No 791; the Secretary of State for Transport

Order 1976 (SI 1976 No 1775); the Minister of Transport Order 1979 (SI 1979 No 571); the Transfer of Functions (Transport) Order 1981 (SI 1981 No 238).]

7.—(1) Where a constable in uniform has reasonable cause to suspect the driver of a vehicle of having committed an offence under the preceding Regulation, the constable may detain the vehicle, and for that purpose may give a direction, specifying an appropriate person and directing the vehicle to be removed by that person to such place and subject to such conditions as are specified in the direction; and the prohibition shall not apply to the removal of the vehicle in accordance with that direction.

(2) Where under paragraph (1) of this Regulation a constable—

(*a*) detains a motor vehicle drawing a trailer, or

(*b*) detains a trailer drawn by a motor vehicle,

then, for the purpose of securing the removal of the trailer, he may also (in a case falling within sub-paragraph (*a*) above) detain the trailer or (in a case falling within sub-paragraph (*b*) above) detain the motor vehicle; and a direction under paragraph (1) of this Regulation may require both the motor vehicle and the trailer to be removed to the place specified in the direction.

(3) A vehicle which, in accordance with a direction given under paragraph (1) of this Regulation, is removed to a place specified in the direction shall be detained in that place, or in any other place to which it is removed in accordance with a further direction given under that paragraph, until a constable (or, if that place is in the occupation of the [Secretary of State for Transport], the [Secretary of State for Transport]) authorises the vehicle to be released on being satisfied—

(*a*) that the prohibition (if any) imposed in respect of the vehicle under the preceding Regulation has been removed, or that no such prohibition was imposed, or

(*b*) that appropriate arrangements have been made for removing or remedying the circumstances in consequence of which any such prohibition was imposed, or

(*c*) that the vehicle will be taken forthwith to a place from which it will be taken out of Great Britain to a place not in the European territory other than Gibraltar of a member state of the Communities [and not in the territory of a relevant foreign state].

(4) Any person who—

(*a*) drives a vehicle in accordance with a direction given under this Regulation, or

(*b*) is in charge of a place at which a vehicle is detained under this Regulation,

shall not be liable for any damage to, or loss in respect of, the vehicle or its load unless it is shown that he did not take reasonable care of the vehicle while driving it or, as the case may be, did not, while the vehicle was detained in that place, take reasonable care of the vehicle or (if the vehicle was detained there with its load) did not take reasonable care of its load.

(5) In this Regulation 'appropriate person'—

(*a*) in relation to a direction to remove a motor vehicle, other than a motor vehicle drawing a trailer, means a person licensed to drive vehicles of the class to which the vehicle belongs, and

(*b*) in relation to a direction to remove a trailer, or to remove a motor vehicle drawing a trailer, means a person licensed to drive vehicles of a class which, when the direction is complied with, will include the motor vehicle drawing the trailer in accordance with that direction.

[Regulation 7 is printed as amended by SI 1974 No 791; the Secretary of State for Transport

Order 1976 (SI 1976 No 1775); the Minister of Transport Order 1979 (SI 1979 No 571); the Transfer of Functions (Transport) Order 1981 (SI 1981 No 238).]

8. Nothing in [section 145(2) (policies to be issued by authorised insurers) and section 147(1) (policies to be of no effect unless certificates issued) of the Road Traffic Act 1988] shall apply in the case of an insurance policy which is issued elsewhere than in the United Kingdom in respect of a vehicle normally based [in the territory other than the United Kingdom and Gibraltar of a member State of the Communities or of a relevant foreign state].

[Regulation 8 is printed as amended by SI 1974 No 791.]

9. *[Revoked by the Road Traffic (Consequential Provisions) Act 1988.]*

The Motor Vehicles (Driving Licences) Regulations 1987

(SI 1987 No 1378)

[The main regulations have been amended by the Motor Vehicles (Driving Licences) (Amendment) Regulations 1988 (SI 1988 No 965) and by the Motor Vehicles (Driving Licences) (Amendment) (No 2) Regulations 1988 (SI 1988 No 1062), but these do not affect the text of any regulation printed.]

ARRANGEMENT OF REGULATIONS

PART I

PRELIMINARY

PART II

LICENCES

*   *   *

PART IV

SUPPLEMENTARY

SCHEDULES

PART I

PRELIMINARY

1. Citation and commencement *[Omitted.]*

2. Revocation and saving *[Omitted.]*

3. Interpretation

(1) In these Regulations, unless the context otherwise requires, the following expressions have the meanings hereby assigned to them, that is to say—

'[1988 Act]' means the [Road Traffic Act 1988];

'1981 Act' means the Public Passenger Vehicles Act 1981;

'1985 Act' means the Transport Act 1985;

'clerk to the traffic commissioner' means the clerk to the traffic commissioner for any traffic area constituted for the purposes of the 1981 Act;

'controlled by a pedestrian' in relation to a vehicle means that the vehicle either—

(*a*) is constructed or adapted for use under such control; or

(*b*) is constructed or adapted for use either under such control or under the control of a person carried on it but is not for the time being in use under, or proceeding under, the control of a person carried on it;

'disability' includes disease;

'full licence' means a licence other than a provisional licence;

'group' in relation to a class of motor vehicles means a group of motor vehicles of the classes specified in the second column of Schedule 3, and a group identified by a letter means the group corresponding to the letter in the first column of that Schedule;

'kerbside weight' means the weight of a vehicle when it carries—

(*a*) in the case of a motor vehicle—

(i) no person; and

(ii) a full supply of fuel in its tank, an adequate supply of other liquids incidental to its propulsion and no load other than the tools and equipment with which it is normally equipped; or

(*b*) in the case of a trailer, no person and is otherwise unladen;

'licence' means a licence to drive a motor vehicle granted under [Part III of the 1988 Act];

'licensing authority' means the Secretary of State;

'maximum speed' means the speed which a vehicle is incapable, by reason of its construction, of exceeding on the level under its own power when fully laden;

'moped' means—

(*a*) in the case only of motor cycles which are first used on or after 1st August 1977, a motor cycle (not being a motor vehicle of group K) which has a maximum speed which does not exceed 30 miles per hour, a kerbside weight which does not exceed 250 kilograms, and, if propelled by an internal combustion engine, an engine the cylinder capacity of which does not exceed 50 cubic centimetres, or

(*b*) in the case only of motor cycles which are first used before 1st August 1977, a motor cycle which has an engine with a cylinder capacity not exceeding 50 cubic centimetres and is equipped with pedals by means of which the cycle is capable of being propelled;

'part of a test' means Part I or Part II, as the case may require, of the test for motor bicycles prescribed by regulation 20;

'provisional licence' means a licence granted by virtue of [section 97(2) of the 1988 Act];

'test' means a test of competence to drive conducted under [section 89 of the 1988 Act] and includes a reference to a part of a test;

'vehicle propelled by electrical power' means a vehicle of which the motive power is solely derived from any electrical storage battery carried on the vehicle and not connected to any source of power when the vehicle is in motion;

'vehicle with automatic transmission' means a vehicle in which the driver is not provided with any means whereby he may, independently of the use of the accelerator or the brakes, vary gradually the proportion of the power being produced by the engine which is transmitted to the road wheels of the vehicle.

(2) In determining for the purpose of these Regulations when a motor cycle is first used, the date of such first use shall be taken to be such date as is the earliest of the undermentioned relevant dates applicable to that cycle—

(*a*) in the case of a motor cycle registered under the Roads Act 1920, the Vehicles (Excise) Act 1949, the Vehicles (Excise) Act 1962 or the Vehicles (Excise) Act 1971, the relevant date is the date on which it was first so registered; and

(*b*) in each of the following cases—

(i) in the case of a motor cycle which is being or has been used under a trade licence as defined in section 16 of the Vehicles (Excise) Act 1971 [*qv*] (otherwise than for the purposes of demonstration or testing or of being delivered from premises of the manufacturer by whom it was made, or of a distributor of vehicles or dealer in vehicles to premises of a distributor of vehicles, dealer in vehicles or purchaser thereof, or to premises of a person obtaining possession thereof under a hiring agreement or hire purchase agreement);

(ii) in the case of a motor cycle which belongs or has belonged to the Crown and which is or was used or appropriated for use for naval, military or air force purposes;

(iii) in the case of a motor cycle which belongs or has belonged to a visiting force or a headquarters or defence organisation to which in each case the Visiting Forces and International Headquarters (Application of Law) Order 1965 *[SI 1965 No 1536]* applies;

(iv) in the case of a motor cycle which has been used on roads outside Great Britain and has been imported into Great Britain;

(v) in the case of a motor cycle which has been used otherwise than on roads after being sold or supplied by retail and before being registered,

the relevant date is the date of manufacture of the cycle.

In this paragraph 'sold or supplied by retail' means sold or supplied otherwise than to a person acquiring solely for the purpose of re-sale or re-supply for a valuable consideration.

(3) The provisions of paragraph 6 of Schedule 9 to the Road Vehicles (Construction and Use) Regulations 1986 *[SI 1986 No 1078, qv]* shall apply for determining for the purposes of the definition of 'moped' in paragraph (1), whether the maximum speed of a motor cycle does not exceed 30 mph.

(4) Except where otherwise expressly provided, any reference in these Regulations to a numbered regulation or Schedule is a reference to the regulation or Schedule bearing that number in these Regulations, and any reference to a numbered paragraph is a reference to the paragraph bearing that number in the regulation in which the reference occurs.

[Regulation 3 is printed as amended by the Interpretation Act 1978, ss 17(2)(a) and 23(1).]

PART II

Licences

4. Minimum ages for holding or obtaining licences

(1) [Subsection (1) of section 101 of the 1988 Act] (which specifies the minimum age for holding or obtaining a licence to drive certain classes of motor vehicles) shall have effect as if in the Table in that subsection—

(*a*) in item 2, the age of 17 were substituted for the age of 16 in relation to all motor cycles other than—

(i) mopeds;

(ii) motor cycles which are mowing machines; or

(iii) motor cycles which are vehicles controlled by a pedestrian;

(*b*) in item 3, the age of 16 were substituted for the age of 17 in the case of a person to whom an award of a mobility allowance has been made in pursuance of section 37A of the Social Security Act 1975 *[section 37A was inserted by section 22(1) of the Social Security Pensions Act 1975]* provided that where the award was made before he attained the age of 16 it is in force when he attains that age;

(*c*) in item 4, in relation to an agricultural tractor which—

(i) is so constructed that the whole of its weight is transmitted to the road surface by means of wheels;

(ii) has an overall width not exceeding 2.45 metres;

(iii) is chargeable with duty under section 1 of the Vehicles (Excise) Act 1971 by reference to paragraph 1 of Schedule 3 to that Act as being an agricultural machine or, by virtue of the provisions of section 7(1) of that Act, is not chargeable with duty thereunder; and

(iv) is driven without a trailer attached to it, other than a trailer which has an overall width not exceeding 2.45 metres and which is either a two-wheeled or close-coupled four-wheeled trailer,

the age of 16 were substituted for the age of 17, but in the case of a person who has not passed the test of competence prescribed under [section 89(3) of the 1988 Act] to drive such a tractor, only while taking, proceeding to or returning from, such a test;

(*d*) in item 6, the age of 17 were substituted for the age of 21 in relation to a road roller falling within that item if the roller—

(i) is propelled otherwise than by steam;

(ii) has an unladen weight not exceeding 11,690 kilograms; and

(iii) is not constructed or adapted for the conveyance of a load other than the following articles, that is to say, water, fuel, accumulators and other equipment used for the purpose of propulsion, loose tools, loose equipment and objects such as are mentioned in paragraph (3) below,

and if no wheel of the roller is fitted with a pneumatic, soft or elastic tyre;

(*e*) in item 6, the age of 18 were substituted for the age of 21 in the case of a person employed by a Health Authority or, in Scotland, the Common Services Agency *[the Common Services Agency is constituted under the National Health Service (Scotland) Act 1978, section 10]* when driving a vehicle for the purposes of an ambulance service of such an Authority or of that Agency;

(*f*) in item 6, the age of 18 were substituted for the age of 21 in the case of a person who fulfils the conditions—

(i) that he is employed by a registered employer; and

(ii) that he is a registered employee of such an employer,

in relation to any vehicle (other than a road roller) which is a heavy goods vehicle (hgv) of a class to which his training agreement applies and is owned by his employer or by a registered hgv driver training establishment;

(*g*) in item 6, the age of 18 were substituted for the age of 21 in relation to a large passenger vehicle where—

(i) the driver of the vehicle is not engaged in the carriage of passengers and either holds a licence to drive a public service vehicle granted under section 22 of the 1981 Act, is undergoing a test of his ability to drive a public service vehicle in pursuance of regulations for the time being in force under that section, or is acting under the supervision of a person who holds such a licence; or

(ii) the driver is engaged in the carriage of passengers—

(*a*) on a regular service over a route which does not exceed 50 kilometres; or

(*b*) on a national transport operation when the vehicle used is constructed and equipped to carry not more than 17 persons including the driver,

and the vehicle is operated under a PSV operator's licence granted under section 12 of the 1981 Act, a permit granted under section 19 of the 1985 Act or a community bus permit granted under section 22 of that Act, and in each case the driver holds a licence to drive the vehicle granted under section 22 of the 1981 Act;

(*h*) in items 5 and 6, the age of 17 were substituted for the ages of 18 and 21 respectively in the case of members of the armed forces of the Crown in relation to any vehicle when being used in the course of urgent work of national importance in accordance with an order of the Defence Council in pursuance of the Defence (Armed Forces) Regulations 1939 which were continued permanently in force in the form set out in Part C of Schedule 2 to the Emergency Laws (Repeal) Act 1959 by section 2 of the Emergency Powers Act 1964;

(*i*) in items 5 and 6, the age of 17 were substituted for the ages of 18 and 21 respectively in the case of a member of the armed forces of the Crown when receiving instruction in the driving of heavy goods vehicles of any class in preparation for a test of competence prescribed under [section 117 of the 1988 Act] to drive vehicles of that class, or when taking, proceeding to, or returning from any such test.

(2) For the purposes of paragraph (1)(*c*) any implement fitted to a tractor shall be

deemed to form part of the tractor notwithstanding that it is not a permanent or essentially permanent fixture, and in that paragraph—

(i) 'overall width', in relation to a vehicle, means the width of the vehicle measured between vertical planes parallel to the longitudinal axis of the vehicle and passing through the extreme projecting points thereof exclusive of any driving mirror and so much of the distortion of any tyre as is caused by the weight of the vehicle; and

(ii) 'close-coupled', in relation to wheels on the same side of a trailer, means fitted so that at all times while the trailer is in motion they remain parallel to the longitudinal axis of the trailer and that the distance between the centres of their respective areas of contact with the road surface does not exceed 840 millimetres.

(3) For the purposes of paragraph 1(*d*) the unladen weight of a vehicle shall be treated as including the weight of any object for the time being attached to the vehicle, being an object specially designed to be so attached for the purpose of temporarily increasing the vehicle's gross weight.

(4) In paragraph 1(*f*) and in this paragraph—

'heavy goods vehicle' has the same meaning as in [section 120 of the 1988 Act];

'registered' means registered for the time being by the Training Committee in accordance with the relevant provisions of the training scheme;

'the Training Committee' means the committee which has been established by the employers' associations and the trade unions in the road goods transport industry with a constitution approved by the Secretary of State and which is known as the National Joint Training Committee for Young HGV Drivers in the Road Goods Transport Industry;

'the training scheme' means the scheme which has been established by the Training Committee with the approval of the Secretary of State for training young drivers of hgvs and which provides for—

(*a*) the registration by the Training Committee of employers who are willing and able to provide hgv driver training for persons employed by them;

(*b*) the registration by the Training Committee of persons operating establishments for providing hgv driver training;

(*c*) a syllabus for hgv driver training; and

(*d*) the registration by the Training Committee of individual employees who are undergoing, or are to undergo, hgv driver training in the service of registered employer in accordance with a form of agreement approved by the Training Committee;

and 'training agreement', in relation to an individual who is undergoing, or is to undergo, such training as aforesaid, means his agreement therefor with his registered employer in pursuance of the training scheme.

(5) In paragraph (1)(*g*), 'large passenger vehicle' means a motor vehicle which is constructed solely to carry passengers and their effects and is adapted to carry more than nine persons inclusive of the driver and expressions used which are also used in the Community Drivers' Ages and Hours of Work Regulation have the same meaning as in that instrument.

(6) In paragraph (5), 'the Community Drivers' Ages and Hours of Work Regulation' means Council Regulation (EEC) 3820/85 [*qv*] as read with regulation 4 of the

Community Drivers Hours and Recording Equipment (Exemptions and Supplementary Provisions) Regulations 1986 *[SI 1986 No 1456, qv]*.

[Regulation 4 is printed as amended by the Interpretation Act 1978, ss 17(2)(a) and 23(1).]

* * *

8. Duration of provisional licences

(1) Subject to paragraph (2), for the purposes of [subsection (2) of section 99 of the 1988 Act] there is hereby prescribed—

(*a*) a motor cycle of a class falling within group D;

(*b*) a period of two years; and

(*c*) in relation to a licence granted to the holder of a previous licence which was surrendered, revoked or treated as being revoked, the circumstances—

(i) that the licence would come into force within the period of one year beginning on the date the previous licence was surrendered, revoked, or treated as being revoked; and

(ii) that the licence when granted would be for a period of one month or more.

(2) Paragraph (1) shall not apply in the case of a licence granted in pursuance of [section 99(1)(*b*) or (7) of the 1988 Act].

[Regulation 8 is printed as amended by the Interpretation Act 1978, ss 17(2)(a) and 23(1).]

9. Conditions attached to provisional licences

(1) Subject to paragraphs (2), (3), (4) and (5), the holder of a provisional licence shall comply with the following conditions in relation to motor vehicles of a class which he is authorised to drive by virtue of the provisional licence, that is to say he shall not drive or ride such a motor vehicle—

(*a*) otherwise than under the supervision of a qualified driver who is present with him in or on the vehicle;

(*b*) unless a distinguishing mark in the form set out in Schedule 2 is displayed on the vehicle in such manner as to be clearly visible to other persons using the road from within a reasonable distance from the front and from the back of the vehicle;

(*c*) while it is being used to draw a trailer; and

(*d*) in the case of a motor bicycle not having attached thereto a side-car, while carrying on it a person who is not a qualified driver:

Provided that where the holder of a provisional licence has passed a test which authorises him to be granted a full licence to drive or ride a particular class of vehicles the above-mentioned conditions shall cease to apply in relation to the driving or riding (as the case may be) by him of motor vehicles of that class.

(2) The condition specified in paragraph (1)(*a*) shall not apply when the holder of the provisional licence—

(*a*) is undergoing a test or a test of competence to drive heavy goods vehicles under [Part IV of the 1988 Act];

(*b*) is driving a vehicle (not being a motor car) constructed to carry only one person and not adapted to carry more than one person;

(*c*) is driving a vehicle the unladen weight of which does not exceed 815 kilograms, being a vehicle propelled by electrical power, constructed or adapted to carry only one person and constructed or adapted for the carriage of goods or burden of any description;

(*d*) is driving a road roller the unladen weight of which does not exceed 3050 kilograms, being a vehicle constructed or adapted for the carriage of goods or burden of any description;

(*e*) is riding a motor bicycle, whether or not having attached thereto a sidecar; or

(*f*) is driving a motor vehicle on a road in an exempted island.

(3) The condition specified in paragraph (1)(*c*) shall not apply when the holder of the provisional licence is driving an agricultural tractor, nor shall it prevent the holder of a provisional licence from driving an articulated vehicle.

(4) The condition specified in paragraph (1)(*d*) shall not apply when the holder of the provisional licence is riding a pedal cycle of the tandem type to which additional means of propulsion by mechanical power are attached.

(5) Any holder of a provisional licence need not comply with this regulation during any period in which—

(*a*) he is treated, by virtue of regulation 25, for the purposes of [section 87(1) and (2) of the 1988 Act] as the holder of a licence; or

(*b*) he is entitled, by virtue of article 2(1) of the Motor Vehicles (International Circulation) Order 1975 *[SI 1975 No 1208, as amended]*,

to drive motor vehicles of a class which he is authorised to drive by virtue of the provisional licence.

(6) In this regulation—

'exempted island' means any island outside the mainland of Great Britain from which motor vehicles, unless constructed for special purposes, can at no time be conveniently driven to a road in any other part of Great Britain by reason of the absence of any bridge, tunnel, ford or other way suitable for the passage of such motor vehicles but this expression 'exempted island' does not include any of the following islands, namely, the Isle of Wight, St Mary's (Isles of Scilly), the islands of Arran, Barra, Bute, Great Cumbrae, Islay, the island which comprises Lewis and Harris, Mainland (Orkney), Mainland (Shetland), Mull, the island which comprises North Uist, Benbecula and South Uist, Skye and Tiree;

'leg disability' means a disability which consists solely of any one or more of the following—

(*a*) the absence of a leg or legs;
(*b*) the deformity of a leg or legs; or
(*c*) the loss of use of a leg or legs,

and references to a leg include references to a foot or part of a leg or foot, and the reference to loss of use, in relation to a leg, includes a reference to a deficiency of movement or power in the leg;

'qualified driver' means a person who holds—

(i) a full licence authorising him to drive as a full licence holder a motor vehicle of the same class as the vehicle being driven by the holder of the provisional licence; or

(ii) in the case only of the supervision of the driver of a motor car by a person whose licence is limited, in pursuance of an application in that behalf by him or under [section 92(7) of the 1988 Act] solely on account of a leg disability to motor vehicles of a particular construction or design, a full licence authorising him so to drive motor cars of a class falling within the same group as the motor car being driven by the holder of the provisional licence.

[Regulation 9 is printed as amended by the Interpretation Act 1978, ss 17(2)(a) and 23(1).]

10. Restricted provisional licences

A provisional licence shall be restricted so as to authorise only the driving of motor vehicles of a class included in group K in any case where the applicant is unable to read in good daylight at a distance of 20.5 metres (with the aid of glasses or contact lenses if worn) a registration mark which is fixed to a motor vehicle and comprises letters and figures 79.4 millimetres high.

11. Full licences not carrying provisional entitlement

(1) [Section 98(2) and (3) of the 1988 Act] shall not apply in the case of a licence which—

(*a*) is limited to vehicles of a particular construction or design whether pursuant to an application in that behalf by the holder of the licence or pursuant to [section 92(7) of the 1988 Act]; or

(*b*) authorises its holder to drive vehicles of a class included in group K only.

(2) [Section 98(2) and (3) of the 1988 Act] in its application to a full licence granted on or after 1st October 1982 which does not authorise the driving of a vehicle of a class included in group A, B, C, or E shall have effect subject to the limitation that it shall not authorise the holder of such a licence to drive any motor cycle of a class included in group D subject to the same conditions as if he were authorised by a provisional licence to drive the last mentioned vehicles.

[Regulation 11 is printed as amended by the Interpretation Act 1978, ss 17(2)(a) and 23(1).]

12. Signature of licences

Every person to whom a licence is granted shall forthwith sign it in ink with his usual signature.

13. Lost or defaced licences

(1) If the holder of a licence—

(*a*) satisfies the licensing authority that—

(i) the licence has been lost or defaced; and

(ii) the holder is entitled to continue to hold the licence; and

(*b*) pays the fee prescribed by regulation 7,

the licensing authority shall issue to him a duplicate licence and shall endorse thereon any particulars endorsed upon the original licence and the duplicate so issued shall have the same effect as the original.

(2) If at any time while a duplicate licence is in force the original licence is found, the person to whom the original licence was issued, if it is in his possession, shall return it to the licensing authority, or if it is not in his possession, but he becomes aware that it is found, shall take all reasonable steps to obtain possession of it and if successful shall return it as soon as may be to the licensing authority.

PART III

TESTS OF COMPETENCE TO DRIVE

* * *

PART IV

SUPPLEMENTARY

24. Disabilities

(1) The following disabilities are prescribed for the purposes of [section 92(2) of the 1988 Act]—

(*a*) epilepsy;

(*b*) severe mental handicap;

(*c*) liability to sudden attacks of disabling giddiness or fainting, other than such attacks falling within paragraph (1)(*d*);

(*d*) liability to sudden attacks of disabling giddiness or fainting, which are caused by any disorder or defect of the heart as a result of which the applicant for the licence or, as the case may be, the holder of the licence has a device implanted in his body, being a device which, by operating on the heart so as to regulate its action, is designed to correct the disorder or defect; and

(*e*) inability to read in good daylight (with the aid of glasses or contact lenses if worn) a registration mark fixed to a motor vehicle and containing letters and figures 79.4 millimetres high at a distance of—

(i) 20.5 metres, in any case except that mentioned below; or

(ii) 12.3 metres, in the case of an applicant for a licence authorising the driving of vehicles of a class included in group K only.

(2) Epilepsy is prescribed for the purposes of [section 92(4)(*b*) of the 1988 Act] and an applicant for a licence suffering from epilepsy shall satisfy the conditions that—

(*a*) he shall have been free from any epileptic attack during the period of two years immediately preceding the date when the licence is to have effect; or

(*b*) in the case of an applicant who has had such attacks whilst asleep during that period, he shall have had such attacks only whilst asleep during a period of at least three years immediately preceding the date when the licence is to have effect; and

(*c*) the driving of a vehicle by him in pursuance of the licence is not likely to be a source of danger to the public.

(3) The disability prescribed in paragraph (1)(*d*) is prescribed for the purpose of [section 92(4)(*b*) of the 1988 Act] and an applicant for a licence suffering from that disability shall satisfy the conditions that—

(*a*) the driving of a vehicle by him in pursuance of the licence is likely to be a source of danger to the public, and

(*b*) he has made adequate arrangements to receive regular medical supervision by a cardiologist (being a supervision to be continued throughout the period of the licence) and is conforming to those arrangements.

(4) The following disability is prescribed for the purposes of [paragraphs (*a*) and

(*c*) of section 92(4) of the 1988 Act] namely, a disability which is not progressive in nature and which consists solely of any one or more of the following:—

(*a*) the absence of one or more limbs;

(*b*) the deformity of one or more limbs; and

(*c*) the loss of use of one or more limbs.

(5) The disability prescribed in paragraph (1)(*e*) is prescribed for the purposes of [section 91(5)(*b*) of the 1988 Act].

(6) (*a*) In paragraph 1(*b*), the expression 'severe mental handicap' means a state of arrested or incomplete development of mind which includes severe impairment of intelligence and social functioning.

(*b*) In paragraph (3)(*b*), the expression 'cardiologist' means a registered medical practitioner who specialises in disorders or defects of the heart and who, in that connection, holds a hospital appointment.

(*c*) In paragraph (4), references to a limb include references to a part of a limb, and the reference to loss of use, in relation to a limb, includes a reference to a deficiency of limb movement or power.

[Regulation 24 is printed as amended by the Interpretation Act 1978, ss 27(2)(a) and 23(1).]

25. Persons who become resident in Great Britain

(1) A person who becomes resident in Great Britain shall during the period of one year after he becomes so resident be treated for the purposes of [section 87(1) and (2) of the 1988 Act] as the holder of a licence authorising him to drive motor vehicles of the classes which he is authorised to drive by any permit of which he is a holder, if he satisfies the conditions specified in paragraph (2).

(2) The conditions mentioned in paragraph (1) are that:—

(*a*) the person who becomes resident shall be the holder of a permit which is for the time being valid; and

(*b*) he is not disqualified for holding or obtaining a licence in Great Britain.

(3) The following enactments relating to licences or licence holders shall apply in relation to permits or the holders of permits (as the case may be) subject to modifications in accordance with the following provisions:—

(*a*) [section 47(2) of the Road Traffic Offenders Act 1988] (which relates to the duties of a court when they order a disqualification or an endorsement) shall apply as if for the words 'shall also on the production of the licence' onwards there were substituted the words 'shall also on the production of the permit retain it and forward it to the licensing authority who shall keep the permit until the disqualification has expired or been removed or the person entitled to the permit leaves Great Britain and in any case has made a demand in writing for its return to him';

(*b*) [sections 7 and 27 of the Road Traffic Offenders Act 1988] (which relate to the duty of a licence holder to produce it to a court) shall apply as if the references to a licence included a reference to a permit, but with the omission of the words, 'before making any order under section 44 of this Act' in section 27(1) and the words 'then, unless he satisfies the court that he has applied for a new licence and has not received it' in section 27(3);

(*c*) [section 42(5) of the Road Traffic Offenders Act 1988] (which relates to the duty of a court when they order a disqualification to be removed) shall apply in relation to the holder of a permit as if for the words 'endorsed on the licence' onwards there were substituted the words 'notified to the licensing authority';

(*d*) [section 164(1) and (6) of the Road Traffic Act 1988] (which authorises a police constable to require the production of a licence) shall apply as if the references to a licence included a reference to a permit;

(*e*) [section 167 of the Road Traffic Act 1988] (which authorises a police constable to arrest a driver committing certain offences unless the driver gives his name and address or produces his driving licence) shall apply as if the references to a licence included a reference to a permit; and

(*f*) [section 173(1) of the Road Traffic Act 1988] (which relates to the forgery and misuse of licences) shall apply as if the reference in [paragraph (*a*) of sub-section (2) of that section] to a licence included a reference to a permit.

(4) In this regulation 'permit' means a 'domestic driving permit' a 'Convention driving permit' or a 'British Forces (BFG) driving licence' as defined in article 2(6) of the Motor Vehicles (International Circulation) Order 1975 *[SI 1975 No 1208, as amended, qv]* not being a domestic driving permit or a British Forces (BFG) driving licence in the case of which any order made, or having effect as if made, by the Secretary of State is for the time being in force under article 2(5) of that Order.

[Regulation 25 is printed as amended by the Interpretation Act 1978, ss 17(2)(a) and 23(1).

As to the reference to 'Great Britain' in reg 25(1), see the Driving Licences (Community Driving Licences) Regulations 1982 (SI 1982 No 1555), reg 4(1), above.

Section 167 of the Road Traffic Act 1988 (to which reference is made in reg 25(3)(e) above) applies only to Scotland.]

26. Statement of date of birth

The circumstances in which a person specified in [section 164(2) of the 1988 Act] shall, on being required by a police constable, state his date of birth are as follows:—

(1) where that person fails to produce forthwith for examination his licence on being required to do so by a police constable under that section; or

(2) where, on being so required, that person produces a licence—

(*a*) which the police constable in question has reason to suspect—

(i) was not granted to that person;

(ii) was granted to that person in error; or

(iii) contains an alteration in particulars entered on the licence (other than as described in paragraph (*b*) below) made with intent to deceive; or

(*b*) in which the driver number has been altered, removed or defaced.

(3) In paragraph (2), 'driver number' means the number described as the driver number in the licence.

[Regulation 26 is printed as amended by the Interpretation Act 1978, ss 17(2)(a) and 23(1).]

27. Learner motor cycles

For the purposes of [section 97(3)(*d*) of the 1988 Act] (provisional licence not to authorise the driving of certain motor cycles) the first use of a motor cycle shall be taken to have occurred on the date of first use as determined in accordance with paragraph (2) of regulation 3.

[Regulation 27 is printed as amended by the Interpretation Act 1978, ss 17(2)(a) and 23(1).]

28. Invalid carriages

For the purposes of [Part III of the 1988 Act] and all regulations made thereunder the maximum weight specified in [the definition of 'invalid carriage' in section 185(1) of the 1988 Act] shall be varied from 254 kilograms to 510 kilograms.

[Regulation 28 is printed as amended by the Interpretation Act 1978, ss 17(2)(a) and 23(1).]

29. Entitlement to groups

The groups of vehicles specified in column 2 of the table in Schedule 3 are hereby designated as groups for the purposes of [paragraphs (*a*) and (*b*) of section 89(1) of the 1988 Act].

[Regulation 29 is printed as amended by the Interpretation Act 1978, ss 17(2)(a) and 23(1).]

30. Effect of changes in classification of vehicles by reason of changed definition of 'moped'

(1) In licences (whether full or provisional) issued before 1st August 1977—

(*a*) any reference to motor vehicles of group E shall be construed as a reference to motor vehicles of new group E;

(*b*) any reference to motor vehicles of group L shall be construed as a reference to motor vehicles of new group L;

(*c*) any reference to motor vehicles of any other group the constitution of which was affected by the amendments made by the Motor Vehicles (Driving Licences) (Amendment) Regulations 1976 *[SI 1976 No 1764]* shall be construed as references to motor vehicles of the group in question as so amended in constitution; and

(*d*) any reference to a moped shall be construed by reference to the revised definition of 'moped'.

(2) In relation to an application for the grant of a licence by a person who—

(*a*) before 1st August 1977 held a licence granted under [Part III of the 1988 Act], or under any enactment which that Part replaced, or under a relevant external law (as defined in [section 89(2) of the 1988 Act]) to drive motor vehicles of a class included in old group E, or

(*b*) before that date passed a test to drive motor vehicles of a class included in old group E or a test which by virtue of regulation 20(6) is regarded as a test to drive such motor vehicles,

and in relation to any licence issued in pursuance of such applications, the licence which he held, or the test which he passed, before that date shall for the purposes of [section 89(1), (6) and (7) of the 1988 Act] (restrictions on grant of licences etc.) be regarded a licence or test (as the case may be) to drive vehicles of a class included in new group E.

(3) A person whose entitlement to the grant of a licence to drive vehicles of new group E is preserved by this regulation may, notwithstanding anything in [section 87(1) and (2) of the 1988 Act] (drivers of motor vehicles to have driving licences), at any time pending the grant of such a licence to him drive, and be employed in driving, such vehicles if—

(*a*) his application in accordance with [section 97(1)(*a*) of the 1988 Act] (provisions as to grant of licences), together with the fee prescribed under that section, for the grant of such a licence has been received by the Secretary of State;

(*b*) he satisfies the requirements of [subsection (1)(*b*) and (*c*) of that section];

(*c*) he is not disqualified by reason of age or otherwise for obtaining the licence;

(*d*) he is not a person to whom the Secretary of State is required by [section 92(3) of the 1988 Act] (requirements as to physical fitness of drivers) to refuse to grant the licence;

(*e*) in the case of a person on whom notice under [subsection (5) of that section], or any enactment which that provision replaced, has been served, the vehicles are of the particular construction and design specified in the notice; and

(*f*) he complies, in relation to that driving, with such of the conditions specified in regulation 8(1) as will apply to the driving of those vehicles by him under the authority of that licence, when granted.

(4) In this regulation, references to 'old group' and 'new group' followed by a letter are references respectively to the group in question as constituted before and after the coming into operation of the Motor Vehicles (Driving Licences) (Amendment) Regulations 1976, and the reference to the revised definition of 'moped' is a reference to the definition of that word in regulation 3(1), which was inserted in regulation 3(1) of the Motor Vehicles (Driving Licences) Regulations 1976 *[SI 1976 No 1076]* by the said amendment Regulations.

[Regulation 30 is printed as amended by the Interpretation Act 1978, ss 17(2)(a) and 23(1).

The definition of 'moped' inserted by the Motor Vehicles (Driving Licences) (Amendment) Regulations 1976 (SI 1976 No 1764) into the principal regulations is substantially the same as the definition currently included in reg 3 of these regulations, except that the 1976 definition used the term 'maximum design speed' in place of the term 'maximum speed' which is now used.]

31. Effect of changes in classification of vehicles by reason of changed weight limit for motor tricycles

(1) In licences (whether full or provisional) issued before the date of re-classification any reference to motor vehicles of a group identified by a letter shall be construed for all purposes on and after that date as a reference to motor vehicles of the new group as well as the old group identified by that letter.

(2) In relation to an application for the grant of a licence coming into force on or after the date or re-classification by a person who—

(*a*) before that date held a licence granted under [Part III of the 1988 Act], or under any enactment which that [Part III] replaced, or under a relevant external law (as defined in [section 89(2) of the 1988 Act]) to drive motor vehicles of a class included in an old group, or

(*b*) before that date passed a test to drive motor vehicles of a class included in an old group or a test which by virtue of regulation 20(6) is regarded as a test to drive such vehicles,

and in relation to any licence issued in pursuance of such an application, the licence which he held, or the test which he passed, before that date shall, for the purposes of [section 89(1), (6) and (7) of the 1988 Act] (restrictions on the grant of licences etc.), be regarded as a licence or test, as the case may be, to drive vehicles of a class included in the new group as well as the old group identified by the same letter.

(3) In this regulation references to 'old group' and 'new group' are references respectively to the group in question as constituted before and after the date of re-classification and 'the date of re-classification' refers respectively to 12th August 1981 when the weight limit for motor tricycles in group C was increased to 425 kilograms

unladen and 2nd September 1985 when that weight limit was increased to 450 kilograms unladen.

[Regulation 31 is printed as amended by the Interpretation Act 1978, ss 17(2)(a) and 23(1).]

32. Effect of changes in classification of vehicles by reason of deletion of group M

(1) The deletion of group M in Schedule 3 by regulation 9(*e*) of the Motor Vehicles (Driving Licences) (Amendment) (No 4) Regulations 1982 *[SI 1982 No 937]* shall not affect—

(*a*) any entitlement of a holder of a licence for vehicles of a class included in that group granted before the date of coming into operation of the said regulation 9(*e*) to drive vehicles of that class, and vehicles of any other class included in that group, in pursuance of the licence; or

(*b*) any such licence ceasing to be in force whether before or after that date, or any right that the person who held the licence would have had to the grant of a further licence on or after that date authorising him to drive such vehicles.

(2) In licences (whether full or provisional) issued before the date of coming into operation of regulation 9(*e*) of the Motor Vehicles (Driving Licences) (Amendment) (No 4) Regulations 1982 any reference to groups A or B shall be construed for all purposes on and after that date as a reference to the groups as prescribed in these Regulations on and after that date.

* * *

Regulation 9(1)

SCHEDULE 2

DIAGRAM OF DISTINGUISHING MARK TO BE DISPLAYED ON A MOTOR VEHICLE BEING DRIVEN UNDER A PROVISIONAL LICENCE

[Diagram not reproduced]

Regulations 20 and 29

SCHEDULE 3

GROUPS OF MOTOR VEHICLES FOR DRIVING TEST PURPOSES

Group	*Class of vehicle included in the group*	*Additional requirements*	*Additional groups covered*
A	A vehicle without automatic transmission, of any class not included in any other group.	1, 2, 3, 4, 5, 6, 7, 8, 9 and 10	B, C, E, F, K, L and N
B	A vehicle with automatic transmission, of any class not included in any other group.	1, 2, 3, 4, 5, 6, 7, 8, 9 and 10	E, F, K, L and N
C	Motor tricycle weighing not more than 450 kg. unladen, but excluding any vehicle included in group E, J, K or L.	1, 2, 3, 4, 5, 6, 9 and 10 and, if fitted with a means for reversing, 7 and 8	E, K and L

[*continued on next page*

Group	*Class of vehicle included in the group*	*Additional requirements*	*Additional groups covered*
D	Motor bicycle (with or without side-car) but excluding any vehicle included in group E or K.	1, 2, 3, 4, 5, 6, 9 and 10	C and E
E	Moped.	1, 2, 3, 4, 5, 6, 9 and 10	—
F	Agricultural tractor, but excluding any vehicle included in group H.	1, 2, 3, 4, 5, 6, 7, 9 and 10	K
G	Road roller.	1, 2, 3, 4, 5, 6, 7, 9 and 10	—
H	Track-laying vehicle steered by its tracks.	1, 2, 3, 4, 5, 6, 9, 10 and 11	—
J	Invalid carriage.	1, 2, 3, 4, 5, 6, 9 and 10	—
K	Mowing machine or pedestrian controlled vehicle.	1, 2, 3, 4, 5 and 6	—
L	Vehicle propelled by electrical power but excluding any vehicle included in group D, E, J or K.	1, 2, 3, 4, 5, 6, 9 and 10 and, if fitted with a means of reversing, 7 and 8	K
N	Vehicle exempted from duty under section 7(1) of the Vehicles (Excise) Act 1971.	1, 2, 3, 4, 5 and 6	—

The Motor Vehicles (Exemption from Vehicles Excise Duty) Order 1985

(SI 1985 No 722)

* * *

2. In this Order—

'army inter-war pensioners' means former members of Her Majesty's military forces in receipt of a disability pension paid by the Secretary of State for Defence on account of disability attributable to injury sustained after 30 September 1921 but before 3 September 1939.

3. The following payments are hereby specified pursuant to section 7(2A) of the Vehicles (Excise) Act 1971 as payments included within the meaning of the expression 'mobility supplement' for the purposes of section 7(2) of the Vehicles (Excise) Act 1971, being payments appearing to the Secretary of State to be of a similar kind to those specified in paragraphs (*a*) and (*b*) of the said section 7(2A):

(1) mobility supplement paid under the Naval and Marine Pay and Pensions (Disablement Awards) Order 1984 or under the Naval and Marine Pay and Pensions (Disablement Awards) (No 2) Order 1984;

(2) mobility supplement paid under Queen's Regulations for the Royal Air Force; and

(3) supplementary allowance paid under Royal Warrant dated 30th December 1949 to army inter-war pensioners equivalent to the mobility supplement provided for by Article 26A of the Naval Military and Air Forces etc. (Disablement and Death) Service Pensions Order 1983 *[SI 1983 No 883, as amended]*.

[The Naval and Marine Pay and Pensions (Disablement Awards) Order 1984, its amending instrument the Naval and Marine Pay and Pensions (Disablement Awards) (Amendment) Order 1984 and the Naval and Marine Pay and Pensions (Disablement Awards) (No 2) Order 1984 are Orders in Council made under section 11 of the Naval and Marine Pay and Pensions Act 1865; they are not published. Queen's Regulations for the Royal Air Force (4th Edn, 1971) is published by HMSO. The royal warrant dated 30 December 1949 (as amended) is not published.]

4. This Order is deemed to have come into force on 21 December 1983.

The Motor Vehicles (International Circulation) Order 1975

(SI 1975 No 1208)

[The text of this order is printed as amended by:

the Motor Vehicles (International Circulation) (Amendment) Order 1985 (SI 1985 No 459) (21 March 1985 (art 5) and 29 April 1985 (arts 3, 4).

The amending order is referred to in the notes to the main order only by its year and number. The dates referred to above are the dates on which the amendments came into force.

The Motor Vehicles (International Circulation) (Amendment) Order 1980 (SI 1980 No 1095), below, also effects amendments to the main order; but (apart from an amendment to Sched 2 which is not reproduced) these are not yet in operation.]

1. Documents for drivers and vehicles going abroad

(1) The Secretary of State may issue for use outside the United Kingdom a driving permit in each or either of the forms A and B in Schedule 1 to this Order to a person who has attained the age of eighteen years and satisfies the Secretary of State—

(*a*) that he is competent to drive motor vehicles of the classes for which the permit is to be issued, and

(*b*) that he is resident in the United Kingdom:

Provided that a permit in form A which is restricted to motor cycles or invalid carriages may be issued to a person who is under eighteen years of age.

(2) The Secretary of State may issue for use outside the United Kingdom a document in the form D in Schedule 1 to this Order for any motor vehicle registered under the Vehicles (Excise) Act 1971, or in Northern Ireland under the Vehicles (Excise) Act (Northern Ireland) 1972.

(3) The Secretary of State may issue for use outside the United Kingdom with any such motor vehicle or any trailer a document certifying—

(*a*) the weight of the maximum load which it is to be permitted to carry, and

(*b*) the permissible maximum weight, that is to say, the weight of the vehicle when ready for the road and carrying the maximum load so specified.

(4) The Secretary of State may assign to any trailer an identification mark to be carried on the trailer outside the United Kingdom.

(5) The Secretary of State may assign to a motor vehicle to which the Decision of 1957 of the Council of the Organisation for European Economic Co-operation applies, an identification mark in the form of such a trade plate as may be required to be carried on such a vehicle under the provisions of section 1 of the Regulation attached to that Decision.

In this paragraph, 'the Decision of 1957 of the Council of the Organisation for European Economic Co-Operation' means the decision of the Council of the Organisation for European Economic Co-operation concerning the International Circulation of Hired Private Road Motor Vehicles adopted by that Council at its 369th Meeting, in June 1957.

(6) The Secretary of State may charge a fee for any document issued under this

Article or for the assignment of any identification mark under this Article, and the fee shall be of the amount specified in relation thereto in Schedule 2 to this Order [*not reproduced*].

(7) The Secretary of State may for the purpose of his functions under this Article carry out tests of the competency of applicants for driving permits and examination of vehicles.

(8) The Secretary of State may delegate any of his functions under this Article (including any power of charging fees and the carrying out of tests or examinations) to any body concerned with motor vehicles or to any Northern Ireland department.

2. Visitors' driving permits

(1) Subject to the provisions of this Article, it shall be lawful for a person resident outside the United Kingdom who is temporarily in Great Britain and holds—

(*a*) a Convention driving permit, or

(*b*) a domestic driving permit issued in a country outside the United Kingdom, or

(*c*) a British Forces (BFG) driving licence;

during a period of twelve months from the date of his last entry into the United Kingdom to drive, and, except in the case of a holder of a British Forces (BFG) driving licence, be employed in driving, in Great Britain, a motor vehicle of any class which he is authorised by that permit or that licence to drive, notwithstanding that he is not the holder of a driving licence under [Part III of the Road Traffic Act 1988].

(2) Subject to the provisions of this Article, it shall be lawful for a person resident outside the United Kingdom who is temporarily in Great Britain and holds—

(*a*) a Convention driving permit, or

(*b*) a domestic driving permit issued in a country outside the United Kingdom,

during a period of twelve months from the date of his last entry into the United Kingdom to drive, and be employed in driving, in Great Britain a public service or heavy goods vehicle brought temporarily into Great Britain which he is authorised by that permit to drive, notwithstanding that he is not the holder either of such a licence as is required by [section 22 of the Public Passenger Vehicles Act 1981], or of such a licence as may be required by [section 110 of the said Act of 1988].

[(2A) Subject to the provisions of this Article, it shall be lawful for a person resident outside the United Kingdom who is temporarily in Great Britain and holds a British Forces (BFG) public service vehicle driving licence during a period of twelve months from the date of his last entry into the United Kingdom to drive, and be employed in driving, in Great Britain a public service vehicle brought temporarily into Great Britain which he is authorised by that permit to drive, notwithstanding that he is not the holder of such a licence as is required by section 22 of the Public Passenger Vehicles Act 1981.]

(3) The foregoing provisions of this Article shall be without prejudice to [section 4(1) of the said Act of 1988] (which imposes minimum age limits for persons driving motor vehicles of various classes therein specified) except that [paragraph 6 of the Table in that subsection (which makes it unlawful for a person under the age of twenty-one years to drive certain motor vehicles)] shall not apply in relation to a person driving in pursuance of this Article a motor vehicle brought temporarily into Great Britain if he has attained the age of eighteen years.

(4) This Article shall not authorise a person to drive a motor vehicle of any class if,

in consequence of a conviction or of the order of a court, he is disqualified for holding or obtaining a driving licence under [Part III of the said Act of 1988].

(5) The Secretary of State may by order contained in a statutory instrument withdraw the right conferred by paragraph (1)(*b*), (1)(*c*) or (2)(*b*) of this Article, or any two or more of those rights, either in the case of all domestic driving permits or British Forces (BFG) driving licences, or in the case of domestic driving permits or British Forces (BFG) driving licences of a description specified in the order or held by persons of a description so specified.

The power to make orders under this paragraph shall include power to vary or revoke an order so made.

(6) In this Article—

'Convention driving permit' means a driving permit in the form A in Schedule 1 to this Order issued under the authority of a country outside the United Kingdom, whether or not that country is a party to the Convention on Road Traffic concluded at Geneva in the year 1949, or a driving permit in the form B in the said Schedule issued under the authority of a country outside the United Kingdom which is a party to the International Convention relative to Motor Traffic concluded at Paris in the year 1926 but not to the Convention of 1949;

'domestic driving permit' in relation to a country outside the United Kingdom means a document issued under the law of that country and authorising the holder to drive motor vehicles, or a specified class of motor vehicles, in that country, and includes a driving permit issued by the armed forces of any country outside the United Kingdom for use in some other country outside the United Kingdom;

'British Forces (BFG) driving licence' means a driving licence issued in Germany to members of the British Forces or of the civilian component thereof or to the dependants of such members by the British authorities in that country in such a form and in accordance with such licensing system as may from time to time be approved by those authorities [and 'British Forces (BFG) public service vehicle driving licence' means any such driving licence authorising the driving of public service vehicles of any class]; and

'dependants', in relation to such a member of the British Forces or of the civilian component thereof, means any of the following persons, namely:—

(*a*) the wife or husband of that member; and

(*b*) any other person wholly or mainly maintained by him or in his custody, charge or care; [and]

['public service vehicle' has the same meaning as in the Public Passenger Vehicles Act 1981].

(7) The provisions of this Article which authorise the holder of a permit or a licence to drive a vehicle during a specified period shall not be construed as authorising the driving of a vehicle at a time when the permit or licence has ceased to be valid.

[Article 2 is printed as amended by the Interpretation Act 1978, s 17(2)(a) (cf art 7(2) below); SI 1985 No 459, art 3.]

3.—(1) It shall be lawful—

(*a*) for a member of a visiting force of a country to which Part I of the Visiting Forces Act 1952 for the time being applies who holds a driving permit issued under the law of any part of the sending country or issued by the service authorities of the visiting force, or (*b*) for a member of a civilian component of such a visiting force who holds such a driving permit, [or]

[(*c*) for a dependant of any such member of a visiting force or of a civilian component thereof who holds such a driving permit].

to drive, and be employed in driving, in Great Britain a motor vehicle of any class which he is authorised by that permit to drive, notwithstanding that he is not the holder of a driving licence under [Part III of the Road Traffic Act 1988].

(2) This Article shall not authorise a person to drive a motor vehicle of any class if, in consequence of a conviction or of the order of a court, he is disqualified for holding or obtaining a driving licence under [Part III of the said Act of 1988].

(3) This Article shall be without prejudice to [section 101 of the said Act of 1988] (which imposes age limits on young persons driving motor vehicles).

(4) The interpretative provisions of the Visiting Forces Act 1952 shall apply for the interpretation of this Article [and 'dependant', in relation to a member of any such visiting force or a civilian component thereof, means any of the following persons, namely:—

(*a*) the wife or husband of that member; and

(*b*) any other person wholly or mainly maintained by him or in his custody, charge or care].

[Article 3 is printed as amended by the Interpretation Act 1978, s 17(2)(a) (cf art 7(2) below); SI 1985 No 459, art 4.]

4. Schedule 3 to this Order shall have effect as respects the driving permits referred to in Articles 2 and 3 of this Order.

5. Excise exemption and documents for vehicles brought temporarily into Great Britain

(1) The next following paragraph shall apply to a vehicle brought temporarily into Great Britain by a person resident outside the United Kingdom if the person bringing that vehicle into Great Britain—

(*a*) satisfies a registration authority that he is resident outside the United Kingdom and that the vehicle is only temporarily in Great Britain, and

(*b*) complies with any regulations made under paragraph (4) of this Article.

(2) A vehicle to which this paragraph applies shall be exempt from any duty of excise under the Excise Act to the following extent:—

[(*a*) a vehicle which would, but for this Order, be chargeable with excise duty under section 1 of the Excise Act and Schedule 1, 2 or 5 thereto, and in respect of which relief from customs duty has been afforded by virtue of Parts IV or V of the Customs and Excise Duties (Personal Reliefs for Goods Temporarily Imported) Order 1983 *[SI 1983 No 1829]*, shall be exempted from excise duty for such period as relief from customs duty shall continue to be afforded in respect of that vehicle;]

(*b*) a vehicle which would, but for this Order, be chargeable with excise duty under section 1 of the Excise Act and Schedule 2 thereto, and which is exempt from customs duty by virtue of the Temporary Importation (Commercial Vehicles and Aircraft) Regulations 1961 *[SI 1961 No 1523]* shall be exempt from excise duty for such period from the date of importation as that vehicle may remain so exempt from customs duty;

(*c*) a vehicle which, if used for the conveyance of goods or burden, would, but for this Order, be chargeable with excise duty under section 1 of the Excise Act and Schedule 3 or 4 thereto, and which is exempt from customs duty by virtue of the Temporary Importation (Commercial Vehicles and Aircraft) Regulations 1961 shall be exempt from excise duty for such period as that vehicle may remain so exempt from customs duty.

(3) A vehicle registered in the Isle of Man and brought temporarily into Great Britain by a person resident outside the United Kingdom shall be exempt from any duty of excise under the Excise Act for a period not exceeding one year from the date of importation, if the person bringing that vehicle into Great Britain—

(*a*) satisfies a registration authority that he is resident outside the United Kingdom and that the vehicle is only temporarily in Great Britain, and

(*b*) complies with any regulations made under paragraph (4) of this Article.

(4) The Secretary of State may by regulations provide—

(*a*) for the furnishing to a registration authority by a person who imports a vehicle to which either of the two last preceding paragraphs applies of such particulars as may be prescribed, and

[(*b*) for the recording by a registration authority of any particulars which the Secretary of State may by the regulations direct to be recorded, and for the manner of such recording, and for the making of any such particulars available for use by such persons as may be specified in the regulations on payment, in such cases as may be so specified, of such fee as may be prescribed, and]

(*c*) for the production to a registration authority of prescribed documents, and

(*d*) for the registration of vehicles which by virtue of this Article are exempt from excise duty and for the assignment of registration marks to, and for the issue of registration cards for, such vehicles.

(5) The following provisions of the Excise Act, that is to say:—

(*a*) paragraphs (*d*) and (*e*) of section 23(1) as substituted by virtue of section 39(1) of, and paragraph 20 of Part I of Schedule 7 to, the Excise Act (which enable the Secretary of State to make regulations as respects registration books for vehicles in respect of which excise licences are issued), and

(*b*) paragraph (*f*) of the said section 23(1) (which enables the Secretary of State to make regulations as to the display on a vehicle of the registration mark assigned to it), and

(*c*) section 26(1) (which relates to forgery of licences, registration marks or registration documents),

shall apply in relation to a registration card issued, or a registration mark assigned, in pursuance of this Article as they apply in relation to a registration book or registration document issued, or a registration mark assigned, under the Excise Act.

(6) If regulations under this Article provide for the assignment of a registration mark on production of some document relating to a vehicle which is exempt from excise duty by virtue of this Article, then paragraph (*d*) of the said section 23(1) shall apply in relation to that document so as to authorise the Secretary of State to make regulations under that section requiring the production of that document for inspection by persons of classes prescribed by regulations made under that section.

(7) Paragraphs (*d*) and (*f*) of the said section 23(1), and section 26(1) of the Excise Act shall, in Great Britain, apply in like manner in relation to a registration card

issued, or a registration mark assigned, in pursuance of provisions corresponding to paragraph (4) of this Article in Northern Ireland.

(8) In relation to a motor vehicle brought temporarily into Great Britain by a person resident outside the United Kingdom, references in section 19 of the Excise Act and in the said section 23(1) thereof to registration marks shall, where appropriate, include references to nationality signs.

(9) In this Article—

'the Excise Act' means the Vehicles (Excise) Act 1971;

'the date of importation', in relation to a vehicle, means the date on which that vehicle was last brought into the United Kingdom;

['registration authority' means the Automobile Association, the Royal Automobile Club, the Royal Scottish Automobile Club, or the Secretary of State;]

and references to registration marks shall, where appropriate, include references to nationality signs.

[Article 5 is printed as amended by SI 1985 No 459, art 5.]

5A. *[Applies to vehicles brought temporarily into Northern Ireland.]*

6.—(1) An application under Part V of the Transport Act 1968 for an operator's licence for a motor vehicle or trailer brought temporarily into Great Britain by a person resident outside the United Kingdom shall be made to the licensing authority for the purpose of the said Part V for the area where the vehicle is landed.

(2) Regulations made or having effect as if made, under sections 68–82 (provisions as to lighting of vehicles) of the Road Traffic Act 1972, may, either wholly or partially, and subject to any conditions, vary or grant exemptions from, the requirements of those sections in the case of motor vehicles or trailers brought temporarily into Great Britain by persons resident outside the United Kingdom or in the case of any class of such vehicles.

[Sections 68 to 80 and 81(1) of the Road Traffic Act 1972 were repealed by the Road Traffic Act 1974, s 24(3) and Sched 7. Regulations relating to vehicle lighting are now principally made under s 41 of the Road Traffic Act 1988.]

7. Interpretation, repeals, citation and commencement

(1) In this Order—

'the Secretary of State' means the Secretary of State for [Transport];

'prescribed' means prescribed by regulations made by the Secretary of State.

(2) The Interpretation Act [1978] shall apply for the interpretation of this Order (except as provided by the next following paragraph of this Article) as it applies for the interpretation of an Act of Parliament and as if for the purposes of [sections 16(1) and 17(2)(*a*)] of that Act this Order (except as aforesaid) was an Act of Parliament and the Orders revoked by Article 8(1) of this Order were Acts of Parliament thereby repealed.

(3) *[Applies to Northern Ireland.]*

(4) Any reference in this Order to any enactment shall be taken as a reference to that enactment as amended by or under any other enactment; and any reference to an enactment which has effect subject to modifications specified in an enactment shall,

when those modifications cease to have effect, then be construed as a reference to the first mentioned enactment as having effect without those modifications.

[Article 7 is printed as amended by the Secretary of State for Transport Order 1976 (SI 1976 No 1775); the Interpretation Act 1978, s 17(2)(a); the Minister of Transport Order 1979 (SI 1979 No 571); the Transfer of Functions (Transport) Order 1981 (SI 1981 No 238).]

* * *

SCHEDULE 1

Article 1

A
FORM OF INTERNATIONAL DRIVING PERMIT UNDER CONVENTION OF 1949

Page 1

United Kingdom of Great Britain and Northern Ireland*
International Motor Traffic

INTERNATIONAL DRIVING PERMIT
Convention on International Road Traffic of 1949.

** In a permit issued by some other country the name of that country will appear instead and pages 1 and 2 will be drawn up in the language of that country.*

Issued at ....

Date ....

Signature or seal of issuing authority.

Seal or stamp of authority

Page 2

This permit is valid in the territory of all the Contracting States, with the exception of the territory of the Contracting State where issued, for the period of one year from the date of issue, for the driving of vehicles included in the category or categories mentioned on the last page of this permit.

List of Contracting States (optional)

It is understood that this permit shall in no way affect the obligation of the holder to conform strictly to the laws and regulations relating to residence or to the exercise of a profession which are in force in each country through which he travels.

Form of International Driving Permit under Convention of 1949

PART I

Last

Particulars concerning the Driver:	Surname Other names* Place of birth** Date of birth*** Permanent place of residence	1 2 3 4 5
Vehicles for which the permit is valid:		
Motor cycles, with or without a sidecar, invalid carriages and three-wheeled motor vehicles with an unladen weight not exceeding 400 kg (900 lbs).		A
Motor vehicles used for the transport of passengers and comprising, in addition to the driver's seat, at most eight seats, or those used for the transport of goods and having a permissible maximum weight not exceeding 3,500 kg (7,700 lbs.). Vehicles in this category may be coupled with a light trailer.		B
Motor vehicles used for the transport of goods and of which the permissible maximum weight exceeds 3,500 kg (7,700 lbs.). Vehicles in this category may be coupled with a light trailer.		C
Motor vehicles used for the transport of passengers and comprising, in addition to the driver's seat, more than eight seats. Vehicles in this category may be coupled with a light trailer.		D
Motor vehicles of categories B, C or D, as authorised above, with other than a light trailer.		E

'Permissible maximum weight' of a vehicle means the weight of the vehicle and its maximum load when the vehicle is ready for the road.

'Maximum load' means the weight of the load declared permissible by the competent authority of the country of registration of the vehicle.

'Light trailers' shall be those of a permissible maximum weight not exceeding 750 kg (1,650 lbs.).

EXCLUSION	
Holder of this permit is deprived of the right to drive in (country) .... by reason .... Seal or stamp of authority Place .... Date .... Signature	Exclusions: (countries I—VIII)
Should the above space be already filled, use any other space provided for 'Exclusion'.	

The entire last page (Parts I and II) shall be drawn up in French.

Additional pages shall repeat in other languages the text of Part I of the last page. They shall be drawn up in English, Russian, Chinese and Spanish, and other languages may be added.

Form of International Driving Permit under Convention of 1949

Page

PART II

1 ....
2 ....
3 ....
4 ....
5 ....

A	Seal or stamp of authority
B	Seal or stamp of authority
C	Seal or stamp of authority
D	Seal or stamp of authority
E	Seal or stamp of authority

Photograph

Seal or stamp of authority

....
Signature of holder****

EXCLUSIONS
(countries)

I	....	V	....
II	....	VI	....
III	....	VII	....
IV	....	VIII	....

* Father's or husband's name may be inserted.
** If known.
*** Or approximate age on date of issue.
**** Or thumb impression.

B
FORM OF INTERNATIONAL DRIVING PERMIT UNDER CONVENTION OF 1926

Page 1

** In a permit issued by some other country the name of that country will appear instead and the permit will be drawn up in the language of that country.*

United Kingdom of Great Britain and Northern Ireland*

International Motor Traffic

INTERNATIONAL DRIVING PERMIT

International Convention of April 24th, 1926

ISSUE OF PERMIT

Issued at ....

Date ....

Seal of authority

(*Signature of issuing authority*)

Page 2

** This should be a reference to the last page of the permit.

The present permit is valid in the territory of all the undermentioned contracting States for the period of one year from the date of issue for the driving of vehicles included in the category or categories mentioned on p. **

Here insert list of Contracting States

It is understood that this permit in no way diminishes the obligation of the holder to conform strictly to the laws and regulations relating to residence or to the exercise of a profession which are in force in each country through which he travels.

Page 3

PARTICULARS CONCERNING THE DRIVER

Photograph

Seal of authority

Surname .... (1)
Other names .... (2)
Place of birth .... (3)
Date of birth .... (4)
Home address .... (5)

Form of International Driving Permit under Convention of 1926

Page 4

(Name of country)

EXCLUSION

M. (surname and other names) ....
authorised as above by the authority of (country) ....
is deprived of the right to drive in (country) ....
by reason of ....
....
....

Seal of authority

Place ....

Date ....

Signature ....

Page 5 and the following pages should repeat the particulars given on page 3 translated into as many languages as may be necessary to enable the International Permit to be used in all the Contracting States mentioned on page 2.

Here begin last page

A(1)	B(2)	C(3)
Seal of authority	Seal of authority	Seal of authority

(1) A.—Motor vehicles of which the laden weight does not exceed—
3,500 kilog.
(*In all languages.*)

(2) B.—Motor vehicles of which the laden weight exceeds—
3,500 kilog.
(*In all languages.*)

(3) C.—Motor cycles, with or without side-car.
(*In all languages.*)

(1) ....

(2) ....

(3) ....

(4) ....

(5) ....

D

FORM OF INTERNATIONAL CERTIFICATE FOR MOTOR VEHICLES UNDER CONVENTION OF 1926

Page 1

United Kingdom of Great Britain and Northern Ireland*

International Motor Traffic
INTERNATIONAL CERTIFICATE FOR MOTOR VEHICLES
International Convention of April 24th, 1926

ISSUE OF CERTIFICATE

Place ....

Date ....

Seal of authority

Signature of issuing authority.

* *In a permit issued by some other country the name of that country will appear instead and the permit will be drawn up in the language of that country.*

Page 2

This certificate is valid, in the territory of all the undermentioned contracting States, for the period of one year from the date of issue.

Here insert list of contracting States

Page 3

Owner or Holder	Surname	1
	Other names	2
	Home address	3
Class of vchiclc		4
Name of maker of chassis		5
Type of chassis		6
Serial number of type or maker's number of chassis		7
Engine	Number of cylinders	8
	Engine number	9
	Stroke	10
	Bore	11
	Horse-power	12
Body	Shape	13
	Colour	14
	Number of seats	15
Weight of car unladen (in kilos)		16
Weight of car fully laden (in kilos) if exceeding 3,500 kilos		17
Identification mark on the plates		18

Additional pages should repeat the particulars on page 3 translated into as many languages as may be necessary to enable the certificate to be used in all the contracting States mentioned on page 2 and these should be followed by pages for entrance and exit visas.

SCHEDULE 2

Article 1(6)

Fees Chargeable for Documents and Identification Marks

[Omitted.]

SCHEDULE 3

Article 4

Visitors' Driving Permits

1. In this Schedule 'driving permit' means a driving permit which by virtue of this Order authorises a person to drive a motor vehicle without holding a driving licence under [Part III of the Road Traffic Act 1988] and 'driving licence' means a driving licence under the said [Part III].

2.—(1) A court by whom the holder of a driving permit is convicted shall—

(*a*) if in consequence of the conviction or of the order of the court he is disqualified for holding or obtaining a driving licence, or

(*b*) if the court orders particulars of the conviction to be endorsed on any driving licence held by him,

send particulars of the conviction to the Secretary of State.

(2) A court shall in no circumstances enter any particulars in a driving permit.

3.—(1) The holder of a driving permit disqualified in consequence of a conviction or of the order of a court for holding or obtaining a driving licence shall, if so required by the court, produce his driving permit within five days, or such longer time as the court may determine, and the court shall forward it to the Secretary of State.

(2) The Secretary of State on receiving a permit forwarded under the foregoing sub-paragraph—

(*a*) shall record particulars of the disqualification on the permit, and

(*b*) send the holder's name and address, together with the said particulars, to the authority by whom the driving permit was issued, and

(*c*) shall retain the permit until the holder leaves Great Britain or until the disqualification ceases to have effect, whichever is the earlier.

(3) A person failing to produce a driving permit in compliance with this paragraph shall be guilty of an offence which shall be treated for the purposes of [section 9 of the Road Traffic Offenders Act 1988] and of [Part I of Schedule 2 thereto as an offence against the provision specified in column 1 of that Part as section 27] and he shall be liable to be prosecuted and punished accordingly.

4.—(1) A court, on ordering the removal under [section 42(2) of the Road Traffic Offenders Act 1988] of a disqualification for holding or obtaining a driving licence, shall, if it appears that particulars of the disqualification have been forwarded to the Secretary of State under paragraph 2 of this Schedule, cause particulars of the order also to be forwarded to him, and the Secretary of State shall transmit the particulars to the authority who issued the driving permit which the person whose disqualification is removed is shown as holding in the Secretary of State's records.

(2) The Secretary of State shall, where appropriate, enter any particulars so forwarded to him in any driving permit held by him in pursuance of paragraph 3 of this Schedule and shall then return the driving permit to the applicant.

5.—(1) In the following provisions of [the Road Traffic Act 1988], references to a driving licence shall include references to a driving permit.

(2) The said provisions are—

(*a*) [subsections (1) and (6) of section 164 (which authorises a police constable to require the production of a driving licence and in certain cases statement of date of birth by a person who is, or in certain circumstances has been, driving a vehicle),

(*b*) *[Lapsed.]*

(*c*) subsections (1) and (2) of section [173] (which relate to the use of a driving licence by a person other than the holder and to forgery of such a licence).

[Schedule 3 is printed as amended by the Interpretation Act 1978, s 17(2)(a) (cf art 7(2) above).]

SCHEDULE 4

REVOCATIONS

[Omitted.]

The Motor Vehicles (International Circulation) (Amendment) Order 1980

(SI 1980 No 1095)

1. Citation and commencement

This Order may be cited as the Motor Vehicles (International Circulation) (Amendment) Order 1980 and shall come into operation—

(*a*) for all purposes of paragraph (1) of Article 10 on the first day of the month following that in which the Order is made,
and

(*b*) for all other purposes, on the date on which the Convention on Road Traffic concluded at Vienna in 1968 [*Cmnd 4032*] is first in force in respect of the United Kingdom, which date shall be notified in the London, Edinburgh and Belfast Gazettes.

[At 1 January 1989 no date had been notified for the purpose of para (b) above.]

2. Interpretation

In this Order 'the principal Order' means the Motor Vehicles (International Circulation) Order 1975 *[SI 1975 No 1208, qv]*.

3. Documents for drivers going abroad

For paragraph (1) of Article 1 of the principal Order there shall be substituted the following paragraphs:—

'(1) Subject to the following provisions of this Article, the Minister of Transport may issue to a person resident in the United Kingdom a driving permit in any of the forms A, B and C in Schedule 1 to this Order for use outside the United Kingdom.

(1A) A permit shall be issued to a person only for vehicles of a class or classes in respect of which that person either—

(*a*) holds a full licence, or has held and is entitled to obtain such a licence and is authorised to drive by virtue of [section 88(1) of the Road Traffic Act 1988] or any corresponding Northern Ireland provision (licence applied for or surrendered for correction of particulars, etc.); or

(*b*) holds a provisional licence, or has held and is entitled to obtain such a licence and is authorised to drive as mentioned in paragraph (*a*) above, and has passed the test of competence to drive or a test which is a sufficient test;

and in this paragraph "full licence" means a licence (granted under [Part III of the Road Traffic Act 1988] or Part I of the Road Traffic Act (Northern Ireland) 1970) other than a provisional licence, and "provisional licence" and "test of competence to drive" have the same meaning as in the said [Part III] or the said Part I, and "test of competence which is a sufficient test" has the same meaning as in the said [Part III].

(1B) A permit in form A shall not be issued to any person who is under 18 years of age unless the permit is restricted to the driving of motor cycles or invalid carriages, or both.

(1C) A permit in form B shall not be issued to any person who is under 18 years of age.

(1D) A permit in form C shall be limited in its period of validity to three years, or, if shorter—

(*a*) the unexpired period of the permit holder's current United Kingdom driving licence; or

(*b*) where the permit holder is authorised to drive by virtue of [section 88(1) of the Road Traffic Act 1988] or any corresponding Northern Ireland provision (licence applied for or surrendered for correction of particulars, etc.) the remainder of the period for which he is so authorised together with the period of validity of any licence granted while he is so authorised.'.

[Article 3 has not yet been brought into operation; see art 1(b), above.
Article 3 is printed as amended by the Interpretation Act 1978, ss 17(2)(a) and 23(1).]

4. The following words shall be omitted from Article 1 of the principal Order:—

(*a*) in paragraph (7) the words 'tests of the competency of applicants for driving permits and', and

(*b*) in paragraph (8) the words 'tests or'.

[Article 4 has not yet been brought into operation; see art 1(b), above.]

5. Visitors' driving permits

(1) For paragraph (3) of Article 2 of the principal Order there shall be substituted the following paragraph:—

'(3) Nothing in the preceding provisions of this Article shall authorise any person to drive, or to be employed in driving, a vehicle of any class at a time when he is disqualified by virtue of [section 101 of the Road Traffic Act 1988] (persons under age) for holding or obtaining a driving licence authorising him to drive vehicles of that class, but in the case of any such person as is mentioned in paragraphs (1) or (2) of this Article, who is driving a vehicle which—

(*a*) is brought temporarily into Great Britain, and

(*b*) is within the class specified in the first column of paragraph 6 of the Table in subsection (1) of that section, and

(*c*) is either a vehicle registered in a Convention country or a goods vehicle in respect of which that person holds a certificate of competence which satisfies the international requirements,

the second column of that paragraph, in its application for the purposes of this paragraph, shall have effect as if for "21" there were substituted "18".

In this paragraph the following expressions have the meanings respectively assigned to them:—

"the international requirements" means—

(i) in relation to a person who is driving a goods vehicle on a journey to which [Council Regulation (EEC) No. 3820/85 of 20 December 1985] on the harmonisation of certain social legislation relating to road transport [*qv*] applies, the requirements of [Article 5(1)(*b*)] (minimum ages for goods vehicle drivers) of that Regulation;

(ii) in relation to a person who is driving a goods vehicle on a journey to which the European Agreement concerning the work of crews engaged in International Road Transport (AETR) signed at Geneva on 25th March 1971 [*Cmnd 4858, qv*] applies, the requirements of Article 5(1)(*b*) (conditions to be fulfilled by drivers) of that Agreement;

"Convention country" means a country which is not a Member State of the European Economic Community nor a party to the aforementioned European Agreement nor to the Convention on Road Traffic concluded at Vienna in the year 1968 but is a party to the Convention on Road Traffic concluded at Geneva in the year 1949 [*Cmnd 7997*] or the International Convention relative to Motor Traffic concluded at Paris in the year 1926 [*Cmnd 3510*].'.

(2) In paragraph (6) of Article 2 of the principal Order for the definition of 'Convention driving permit' there shall be substituted the following definition:—

' "Convention driving permit" means either—

(i) a driving permit in the form A in Schedule 1 to this Order issued under the authority of a country outside the United Kingdom, whether or not that country is a party to the Convention on Road Traffic concluded at Geneva in the year 1949 but not so issued as aforesaid after the expiry of a period of five years from the date of the entry into force of the Convention on Road Traffic concluded at Vienna in the year 1968 in accordance with Article 47(1) thereof, if that country is a party to that Convention, or

(ii) a driving permit in the form B in that Schedule issued under the authority of a country outside the United Kingdom which is a party to the International Convention relative to Motor Traffic concluded at Paris in the year 1926, but not to the Convention of 1949 nor to the Convention of 1968, or

(iii) a driving permit in the form C in that Schedule issued under the authority of a country outside the United Kingdom which is a party to the Convention of 1968;'.

[Article 5 has not yet been brought into operation; see art 1(b), above.
Article 5 is printed as amended by the Interpretation Act 1978, ss 17(2)(a) and 23(1); Council Regulation (EEC) 3820/85, art 18(2).]

6. At the end of paragraph (7) of Article 2 of the principal Order there shall be added the following words 'and, without prejudice to the provisions of paragraph (3) above, a Convention driving permit in the form C in Schedule 1 to this Order shall, if the validity of the permit is by special endorsement thereon made conditional upon the holder wearing certain devices or upon the vehicle being equipped in a certain manner to take account of his disability, not be valid at a time when any such condition is not satisfied'.

[Article 6 has not yet been brought into operation; see art 1(b), above.]

7. For paragraph (3) of Article 3 of the principal Order there shall be substituted the following paragraph:—

'(3) Nothing in this Article shall authorise any person to drive, or to be employed in driving, a vehicle of any class at a time when he is disqualified by virtue of [section 101 of the Road Traffic Act 1988] (persons under age) for holding or obtaining a driving licence authorising him to drive vehicles of that class.'.

[Article 7 has not yet been brought into operation; see art 1(b), above.
Article 7 is printed as amended by the Interpretation Act 1978, ss 17(2)(a) and 23(1).]

8. Supplementary provisions

(1) [Sections 173 and 174 of the Road Traffic Act 1988] (forgery of documents, etc, false statements and withholding material information) and section 150 of the Road Traffic Act (Northern Ireland) 1970 (false statements in connection with, forgery of and fraudulent use of documents, etc) shall apply to a Convention driving permit as they apply to licences under those Acts.

(2) [Section 13 of the Road Traffic Offenders Act 1988] and section 163C of the said Act of 1970 (admissibility of records as evidence) shall apply to records maintained by the [Secretary of State for Transport] in connection with his functions under Article 1 of the principal Order, or by a body or Northern Ireland department to which in accordance with Article 1(8) of the principal Order he has delegated the function in connection with which the records are maintained, as those sections apply to records maintained in connection with functions under those Acts, and the powers conferred by [section 13(5) of the Road Traffic Offenders Act 1988] and section 163C(4) of the Act of 1970 to prescribe a description of matter which may be admitted as evidence under those sections shall have effect in relation to the application of those sections by this Article.

(3) In this Article 'Convention driving permit' means a permit to drive a vehicle or class of vehicle which is issued under Article 1 of the principal Order in pursuance of, and in the form prescribed by, the International Convention relative to Motor Traffic concluded at Paris in the year 1926, the Convention on Road Traffic concluded at Geneva in the year 1949 or the Convention on Road Traffic concluded at Vienna in the year 1968.

[Article 8 has not yet been brought into operation; see art 1(b), above.
Article 8 is printed as amended by the Interpretation Act 1978, ss 17(2)(a) and 23(1); the Transfer of Functions (Transport) Order 1981 (SI 1981 No 238).]

9. Schedules

In Schedule 1 to the principal Order after form B and before form D there shall be inserted as form C the form set out in the Schedule to this Order.

[Article 9 has not yet been brought into operation; see art 1(b), above.]

10.—(1) *[Amends Sched 2 (Fees) to principal order.]*

(2) In Schedule 3 to the principal Order (Visitors' Driving Permits), in paragraph 1 after the words '[Road Traffic Act 1988]' there shall be inserted the words ' "Convention driving permit" has the meaning assigned to it by Article 2(6) of this Order'.

(3) In the said Schedule 3, in paragraph 3, for sub-paragraph (2) there shall be substituted the following sub-paragraph:—

'(2) The [Secretary of State for Transport] on receiving a permit forwarded under the foregoing sub-paragraph, shall—

(*a*) retain the permit until the disqualification ceases to have effect or until the holder leaves Great Britain, whichever is the earlier; and

(*b*) send the holder's name and address, together with the particulars of the disqualification, to the authority by whom the permit was issued; and (*c*) if the permit is a Convention driving permit, record the particulars of the disqualification on the permit.'.

(4) In the said Schedule 3, in paragraph 4, in sub-paragraph (1) the words from 'and the Secretary of State shall transmit' to the end shall be omitted and the following sub-paragraph shall be substituted for sub-paragraph (2):—

'(2) The [Secretary of State for Transport], on receiving particulars of a court order removing such a disqualification, shall—

(*a*) in the case of a permit on which particulars of a disqualification were entered in accordance with paragraph 3(2)(*c*) of this Schedule, enter on the permit particulars of the order removing the disqualification;

(*b*) send the particulars of the order to the authority by whom the permit was issued; and

(*c*) return the permit to the holder.'.

[Apart from art 10(1), this article has not yet been brought into operation.

Article 10 is printed as amended by the Interpretation Act 1978, s 17(2)(a) and 23(1); the Transfer of Functions (Transport) Order 1981 (SI 1981 No 238).]

[*The Schedule is set out on pp 2/608–10.*]

Article 9

SCHEDULE

[C

FORM OF INTERNATIONAL DRIVING PERMIT UNDER CONVENTION OF 1968

Page No. 1 *(outside of front cover, coloured grey)*

United Kingdom of Great Britain and Northern Ireland GB*

** In a permit issued by some other country the name of that country and its distinguishing sign will appear instead and pages 1 and 2 will be drawn up in the language of that country.*

International Motor Traffic

INTERNATIONAL DRIVING PERMIT

No. ....

Convention on Road Traffic of 8 November, 1968

Valid until ....

Issued by ....

At ....

Date ....

Number of domestic
driving permit ....

Signature of issuing authority or association.

Page No. 2 (*inside front cover, coloured grey*)

This permit is not valid for the territory of the United Kingdom. It is valid for the territories of all the other Contracting Parties. The categories of vehicles for the driving of which it is valid are stated at the end of the booklet.

List of Contracting States (optional)

This permit shall in no way affect the obligation of the holder to conform to the laws and regulations relating to residence and to the exercise of a profession in each State through which he travels. In particular, it shall cease to be valid in a State if its holder establishes his normal residence there.

Form of International Driving Permit under Convention of 1968

Last left-hand page

The last two inside pages shall be facing pages printed in French, and the preceding inside pages shall consist of pages repeating the last left-hand page in several other languages which must include English, Russian and Spanish. All inside pages shall be white.

PARTICULARS CONCERNING THE DRIVER	
Surname	1
Other names(1)	2
Place of birth(2)	3
Date of birth(3)	4
Home address	5
CATEGORIES OF VEHICLES FOR WHICH THE PERMIT IS VALID	
Motor cycles	A
Motor vehicles, other than those in category A, having a permissible maximum weight not exceeding 3,500 kg. (7,700 lb.) and not more than eight seats in addition to the driver's seat	B
Motor vehicles used for the carriage of goods and whose permissible maximum weight exceeds 3,500 kg. (7,700 lb.)	C
Motor vehicles used for the carriage of passengers and having more than eight seats in addition to the driver's seat	D
Combinations of vehicles of which the drawing vehicle is in a category or categories for which the driver is licensed (B and/or C and/or D), but which are not themselves in that category or categories	E
RESTRICTIVE CONDITIONS OF USE(4)	

(1) Father's or husband's name may be inserted here.

(2) If the place of birth is unknown, leave blank.

(3) If date of birth is unknown, state approximate age on date of issue of permit.

(4) For example, 'Must wear corrective lenses', 'Valid only for driving vehicle No. ....', 'Vehicle must be equipped to be driven by a one-legged person'.

Form of International Driving Permit under Convention of 1968

Last right-hand page

The last two inside pages shall be facing pages printed in French. All inside pages shall be white.

1 ....

2 ....

3 ....

4 ....

5 ....

A (5)

B (5)

C (5)

D (5)

E (5)

Photograph

(5)

Signature of holder(6) ....

DISQUALIFICATIONS:

The holder is deprived of the right to drive in the territory of ....(7) until ....
At .... on ....
......................(8)

(8)

The holder is deprived of the right to drive in the territory of ....(7) until ....
At .... on ....
..........................(8) (8)

(5) Seal or stamp of the authority or association issuing the permit. This seal or stamp shall be affixed against categories A, B, C, D and E only if the holder is licensed to drive vehicles in the category in question.

(6) Or thumbprint.

(7) Name of State.

(8) Signature and seal or stamp of the authority which has invalidated the permit in its territory. If the spaces provided for disqualifications on this page have already been used, any further disqualifications should be entered overleaf.]

The Motor Vehicles (Tests) Regulations 1981

(SI 1981 No 1694)

* * *

3. Interpretation

(1) In these Regulations, except where the context otherwise requires, the following expressions have the meanings hereby respectively assigned to them—

'[the 1988 Act]' means [the Road Traffic Act 1988];

. . .

'the Construction and Use Regulations' means the [Road Vehicles (Construction and Use) Regulations 1986] *[SI 1986 No 1078, qv]*;

. . .

['agricultural motor vehicle'], 'articulated bus', 'articulated vehicle', 'dual-purpose vehicle', 'pedestrian controlled vehicle', 'track laying' and 'works truck' have the meanings given by [Regulation 3(2)] of the Construction and Use Regulations;

. . .

'goods vehicle' means a motor vehicle constructed or adapted for use for the carriage of goods or burden of any description, including a living van but excluding—

[(i) a dual-purpose vehicle,

(ii) a motor caravan, and

(iii) a play bus].

. . .

'living van' means a vehicle, whether mechanically propelled or not, which is used as living accommodation by one or more persons, and which is also used for the carriage of goods or burden which are not needed by such one or more persons for the purpose of their residence in the vehicle;

. . .

'motor bicycle' means a two-wheeled motor cycle, whether having a sidecar attached to it or not;

'motor caravan' means a motor vehicle (not being a living van) which is constructed or adapted for the carriage of passengers and their effects and which contains, as permanently installed equipment, the facilities which are reasonably necessary for enabling the vehicle to provide mobile living accommodation for its users;

'play bus' means a motor vehicle which was originally constructed to carry more than 12 passengers but which has been adapted primarily for the carriage of playthings for children (including articles required in connection with the use of those things);]

. . .

(2) Unless the context otherwise requires, any reference in these Regulations to—

(*a*) a numbered section is a reference to the section bearing that number in [the 1988 Act];

(*b*) a numbered Regulation or Schedule is a reference to the Regulation or Schedule bearing that number in these Regulations, and

(*c*) a numbered paragraph is a reference to the paragraph bearing that number in the Regulation in which the reference appears.

(3) For the purposes of these Regulations the unladen weight of a vehicle shall be computed in accordance with Schedule 6 to the Vehicles (Excise) Act 1971.

(4), (5) *[Omitted.]*

[Regulation 3(1) as printed above contains only selected definitions.
Regulation 3 is printed as amended by the Interpretation Act 1978, ss 17(2)(a) and 23(1); the Motor Vehicles (Tests) (Amendment) (No 3) Regulations 1982 (SI 1982 No 1477); the Motor Vehicle (Tests) (Amendment) (No 2) Regulations 1983 (SI 1983 No 1434); the Motor Vehicles (Tests) (Amendment) Regulations 1985 (SI 1985 No 45).]

* * *

6. Exemptions

(1) Pursuant to [section 47(5)] the Secretary of State hereby prescribes the following vehicles as those to which [section 47] does not apply:—

(i) a heavy locomotive;

(ii) a light locomotive;

(iii) a motor tractor;

(iv) a track laying vehicle;

(v) a goods vehicle, the unladen weight of which exceeds 1,525 kilograms;

(vi) an articulated vehicle not being an articulated bus;

(vii) a vehicle exempt from duty under section 7(1) of the Vehicles (Excise) Act 1971;

(viii) a works truck;

(ix) a pedestrian controlled vehicle;

(x) a vehicle (including a cycle with an attachment for propelling it by mechanical power) which is adapted, and used or kept on a road, for invalids, and which—

(i) does not exceed 306 kilograms in weight unladen, or

(ii) exceeds 306 kilograms but does not exceed 510 kilograms in weight unladen, and are supplied and maintained by or on behalf of the Department of Health and Social Security, the Scottish Office or the Welsh Office;

(xi) a vehicle temporarily in Great Britain displaying a registration mark mentioned in [Regulation 5 of the Motor Vehicles (International Circulation) Regulations 1985] *[SI 1985 No 610]*, a period of twelve months not having elapsed since the vehicle was last brought into Great Britain;

(xii) a vehicle proceeding to a port for export;

(xiii) a vehicle in the service of a visiting force or of a headquarters (within the meaning given by Article 8(6) of the Visiting Forces and International Headquarters (Application of Law) Order 1965 *[SI 1965 No 1536]*);

(xiv) a vehicle provided for police purposes and maintained in workshops approved by the Secretary of State as suitable for such maintenance, being a vehicle provided in England and Wales by a police authority or the Receiver for the Metropolitan Police District, or, in Scotland, by a police authority or a joint police committee;

(xv) a vehicle which has been imported into Great Britain and to which [section 47(2)(*b*)] applies, being a vehicle owned by or in the service of the naval, military or air forces of Her Majesty raised in the United Kingdom and used for naval, military or air force purposes;

(xvi) a vehicle in respect of which a test certificate issued in accordance with Article 34 of the Road Traffic (Northern Ireland) Order 1981 *[SI 1981 No 154]* is in force or which are licensed under the Vehicles (Excise) Act (Northern Ireland) 1972;

(xvii) an electrically propelled goods vehicle the unladen weight of which does not exceed 1,525 kilograms; and

(xviii) subject to the provisions of paragraph (4), a hackney carriage or a cab in respect of which there is in force a licence under—

(*a*) section 6 of the Metropolitan Public Carriage Act 1869, or

(*b*) the Town Police Clauses Act 1847, or any similar local statutory provision,

to ply for hire;

(xix) subject to the provisions of paragraph (4), a private hire car in respect of which there is in force a licence granted by a local authority, or, in Scotland, by a local authority or a police authority;

[(xx) an agricultural motor vehicle].

[(1A) [Added by SI 1982 No 814; lapsed.]]

(2) Pursuant to [section 47(6)] the Secretary of State hereby exempts from [section 47(1)] the use of a vehicle—

(*a*) (i) for the purpose of submitting it by previous arrangement for, or bringing it away from, an examination, or

(ii) in the course of an examination, for the purpose of taking it to, or bringing it away from, any place where a part of the examination is to be or, as the case may be, has been, carried out, or of carrying out any part of the examination, the person so using it being either—

(A) an examiner, or a Ministry Inspector or an inspector appointed by a designated council, or

(B) a person acting under the personal direction of an examiner, a Ministry Inspector or a designated Council, or

(iii) where a test certificate is refused on an examination—

(A) for the purpose of delivering it by previous arrangement at, or bringing it away from, a place where work is to be or has been done on it to remedy for a further examination the defects on the ground of which the test certificate was refused; or

(B) for the purpose of delivering it, by towing it, to a place where the vehicle is to be broken up;

(*b*) for any purpose for which the vehicle is authorised to be used on roads by an order under [section 44];

(*c*) where the vehicle has been imported into Great Britain, for the purpose of its being driven after arrival in Great Britain on the journey from the place where it has arrived in Great Britain to a place of residence of the owner or driver of the vehicle;

(*d*) for the purpose of removing it in pursuance of section 3 of the Refuse Disposal

(Amenity) Act 1978 [*qv*], of moving or removing it in pursuance of regulations under [section 99 of the Road Traffic Regulation Act 1984], or of removing it from a parking place in pursuance of an order under [section 35(1) of the Road Traffic Regulation Act 1984], an order relating to a parking place designated under [section 45] thereof, or a provision of a designation order having effect by virtue of [section 53(3)] thereof;

(*e*) where the vehicle has been detained or seized by a police constable, for police purposes connected with such detention or seizure;

(*f*) where the vehicle has been removed, detained or seized or condemned as forfeited under any provision of the Customs and Excise Management Act 1979 for any purpose authorised by an officer of Customs and Excise;

(*g*) for the purpose of testing it by a motor trader as defined in section 16(8) of the Vehicles (Excise) Act 1971, to whom a trade licence has been issued under that section, during the course of, or after completion of repairs carried out to that vehicle by that motor trader.

(3) Pursuant to [section 47(7)] the Secretary of State hereby exempts from [section 47(1)] the use of a vehicle on any island in any area mainly surrounded by water, being an island or area from which motor vehicles, unless constructed for special purposes, can at no time be conveniently driven to a road in any other part of Great Britain by reason of the absence of any bridge, tunnel, ford or other way suitable for the passage of such motor vehicle:

Provided that this Regulation does not apply to any of the following islands, namely, the Isle of Wight, the islands of Arran, Bute, Great Cumbrae, Islay, Lewis, Mainland (Orkney), Mainland (Shetland), Mull, North Uist and Skye.

(4) The exemptions specified in paragraph (1)(xviii) and (xix) do not obtain unless the authority which issued the licence holds a certificate issued by the Secretary of State evidencing that he is satisfied that the issue of the licence is subject to the vehicle first passing an annual test relating to the prescribed statutory requirements; and, as from 1st January 1983,

(*a*) in the case of a vehicle of a kind mentioned in paragraph (1)(xviii) first used more than one year before the licence there mentioned was issued, or

(*b*) in the case of a vehicle of a kind mentioned in paragraph (1)(xix) first used more than three years before the licence there mentioned was issued

the authority which issued the licence also issued to the licensee a certificate recording that on the date on which the certificate was issued that authority was, as a result of a test, satisfied that the prescribed statutory requirements were satisfied.

(5) In this Regulation—

'private hire car' means a motor vehicle which is not a vehicle licensed to ply for hire under the provisions of the Metropolitan Public Carriage Act 1869, Town Police Clauses Act 1847, or any similar local statutory provision with respect to hackney carriages but which is kept for the purpose of being let out for hire with a driver for the carrying of passengers in such circumstances that it does not require to be licensed to ply for hire under the said provisions; and

'test' means an examination of a vehicle in relation to the prescribed statutory requirements conducted—

[(i) by a person appointed to act as an inspector under [section 45], or a person authorised as an examiner or acting on his behalf, or]

(ii) by a person on behalf of a police authority in England or Wales, or

(iii) *[Applies to Scotland.]*

[Regulation 6 is printed as amended by the Interpretation Act 1978, ss 17(2)(a) and 23(1); the Motor Vehicles (Tests) (Amendment) (No 2) Regulations 1983 (SI 1983 No 1434); the Road Traffic Regulation Act 1984, s 144(1) and Sched 10, para 2; the Motor Vehicles (Tests) (Amendment) Regulations 1985 (SI 1985 No 45).

Express references to Scottish legislation have been omitted from the text of reg 6(1)(xviii)(b) and (5).]

* * *

The Motor Vehicles (Third Party Risks) Regulations 1972

(SI 1972 No 1217)

[The text of these regulations is printed as amended by:

the Motor Vehicles (Third Party Risks) (Amendment) Regulations 1973 (SI 1973 No 1821) (1 January 1974);

the Motor Vehicles (Third Party Risks) (Amendment) Regulations 1974 (SI 1974 No 792) (27 May 1974);

the Motor Vehicles (Third Party Risks) (Amendment) (No 2) Regulations 1974 (SI 1974 No 2187) (31 January 1975); and

the Motor Vehicles (Third Party Risks) (Amendment) Regulations 1981 (SI 1981 No 1567) (1 December 1981).

The amending regulations are referred to in the notes to the main regulations only by their years and numbers. The dates referred to above are the dates on which the regulations came into force.]

1, 2. Commencement and citation *[Omitted.]*

3. Temporary use of existing forms *[Omitted.]*

4. Interpretation

(1) In these Regulations, unless the context otherwise requires, the following expressions have the meanings hereby respectively assigned to them:—

'the Act' means [the Road Traffic Act 1988];

'company' means an authorised insurer within the meaning of [Part VI] of the Act or a body of persons by whom a security may be given in pursuance of the said [Part VI];

'motor vehicle' has the meaning assigned to it by [sections 185, 186, 188 and 189 of the Act, but excludes any invalid carriage, tramcar or trolley vehicle to which [Part VI] of the Act does not apply;

'policy' means a policy of insurance in respect of third party risks arising out of the use of motor vehicles which complies with the requirements of [Part VI] of the Act and includes a covering note;

'security' means a security in respect of third party risks arising out of the use of motor vehicles which complies with the requirements of [Part VI] of the Act;

'specified body' means—

(*a*) any of the local authorities referred to in [paragraph (*a*) of section 144(2)] of the Act; or

(*b*) a Passenger Transport Executive established under an order made under section 9 of the Transport Act 1968, or a subsidiary of that Executive, being an Executive or subsidiary to whose vehicles [section 144(2)(*a*)] of the Act has been applied; or

(*c*) [*Lapsed.*]

(2) Any reference in these Regulations to a certificate in Form A, B, C, D, E or F shall be construed as a reference to a certificate in the form so headed and set out in Part 1 of the Schedule to these Regulations which has been duly made and completed subject to and in accordance with the provisions set out in Part 2 of the said Schedule.

(3) Any reference in these Regulations to any enactment shall be construed as a reference to that enactment as amended by any subsequent enactment.

(4) The Interpretation Act [1978] shall apply for the interpretation of these Regulations as it applies for the interpretation of an Act of Parliament, and as if for the purposes of [sections 16(1) and 17(2)(*a*)] of that Act these Regulations were an Act of Parliament and the Regulations revoked by Regulation 2 of these Regulations were Acts of Parliament thereby repealed.

[Regulation 4 is printed as amended by the Interpretation Act 1978, s 17(2)(a).]

5. Issue of certificates of insurance or security

(1) A company shall issue to every holder of a security or of a policy other than a covering note issued by the company:—

(*a*) in the case of a policy or security relating to one or more specified vehicles a certificate of insurance in Form A or a certificate of security in Form D in respect of each such vehicle;

(*b*) in the case of a policy or security relating to vehicles other than specified vehicles such number of certificates in Form B or Form D as may be necessary for the purpose of complying with the requirements of [section 165(1) and (2)] of the Act and of these Regulations as to the production of evidence that a motor vehicle is not being driven in contravention of [section 143] of the Act:

Provided that where a security is intended to cover the use of more than ten motor vehicles at one time the company by whom it was issued may, subject to the consent of the [Secretary of State for Transport], issue one certificate only, and where such consent has been given the holder of the security may issue duplicate copies of such certificate duly authenticated by him up to such number and subject to such conditions as the [Secretary of State for Transport] may determine.

(2) Notwithstanding the foregoing provisions of this Regulation, where as respects third party risks a policy or security relating to a specified vehicle extends also to the driving by the holder of other motor vehicles, not being specified vehicles, the certificate may be in Form A or Form D, as the case may be, containing a statement in either case that the policy or security extends to such driving of other motor vehicles. Where such a certificate is issued by a company they may, and shall in accordance with a demand made to them by the holder, issue to him a further such certificate or a certificate in Form B.

(3) Every policy in the form of a covering note issued by a company shall have printed thereon or on the back thereof a certificate of insurance in Form C.

[Regulation 5 is printed as amended by the Secretary of State for Transport Order 1976 (SI 1976 No 1775); the Interpretation Act 1978, s 17(2)(a) (cf reg 4(4) above); the Minister of Transport Order 1979 (SI 1979 No 571); the Transfer of Functions (Transport) Order 1981 (SI 1981 No 238).]

6. Every certificate of insurance or certificate of security shall be issued not later than four days after the date on which the policy or security to which it relates is issued or renewed.

7. Production of evidence as alternatives to certificates

The following evidence that a motor vehicle is not or was not being driven in contravention of [section 143] of the Act may be produced in pursuance of [section 165] of the Act as an alternative to the production of a certificate of insurance or a certificate of security:—

(1) a duplicate copy of a certificate of security issued in accordance with the proviso to sub-paragraph (*b*) of paragraph (1) of Regulation 5 of these Regulations;

(2) in the case of a motor vehicle of which the owner has for the time being deposited with the Accountant-General of the Supreme Court the sum of fifteen thousand pounds in accordance with the provisions of [section 144(1)] of the Act, a certificate in Form E signed by the owner of the motor vehicle or by some person authorised by him in that behalf that such sum is on deposit;

(3) in the case of a motor vehicle owned by a specified body, a police authority or the Receiver for the metropolitan police district, a certificate in Form F signed by some person authorised in that behalf by such specified body, police authority or Receiver as the case may be that the said motor vehicle is owned by the said specified body, police authority or Receiver.

[(4) in the case of a vehicle normally based [in the territory other than the United Kingdom and Gibraltar of a member state of the Communities or of [Austria, Czechoslovakia, Finland, the German Democratic Republic, Hungary, Norway, Sweden or Switzerland]] a document issued by the insurer of the vehicle which indicates the name of the insurer, the number or other identifying particulars of the insurance policy issued in respect of the vehicle and the period of the insurance cover. In this paragraph the territory of the state in which a vehicle is normally based is

(*a*) the territory of the state in which the vehicle is registered, or

(*b*) in cases where no registration is required for the type of vehicle, but the vehicle bears an insurance plate or distinguishing sign analogous to a registration plate, the territory of the state in which the insurance plate or the sign is issued, or

(*c*) in cases where neither registration plate nor insurance plate nor distinguishing sign is required for the type of vehicle, the territory of the state in which the keeper of the vehicle is permanently resident.]

[Regulation 7 is printed as amended by SI 1973 No 1821; SI 1974 No 792; SI 1974 No 2187; the Interpretation Act 1978, s 17(2)(a) (cf reg 4(4) above).]

8. Any certificate issued in accordance with paragraph (2) or (3) of the preceding Regulation shall be destroyed by the owner of the vehicle to which it relates before the motor vehicle is sold or otherwise disposed of.

* * *

12. Return of certificates to issuing company

(1) The following provisions shall apply in relation to the transfer of a policy or security with the consent of the holder to any other person:—

(*a*) the holder shall, before the policy or security is transferred, return any relative certificates issued for the purposes of these Regulations to the company by whom they were issued; and

(*b*) the policy or security shall not be transferred to any other person unless and until the certificates have been so returned or the company are satisfied that the certificates have been lost or destroyed.

(2) In any case where with the consent of the person to whom it was issued a policy or security is suspended or ceases to be effective, otherwise than by effluxion of time, in circumstances in which the provisions of [section 147(4)] of the Act (relating to the surrender of certificates) do not apply, the holder of the policy or security shall within

seven days from the date when it is suspended or ceases to be effective return any relative certificates issued for the purposes of these Regulations to the company by whom they were issued and the company shall not issue a new policy or security to the said holder in respect of the motor vehicle or vehicles to which the said first mentioned policy or security related unless and until the certificates have been returned to the company or the company are satisfied that they have been lost or destroyed.

(3) Where a policy or security is cancelled by mutual consent or by virtue of any provision in the policy or security, any statutory declaration that a certificate has been lost or destroyed made in pursuance of [section 147(4)] (which requires any such declaration to be made within a period of seven days from the taking effect of the cancellation) shall be delivered forthwith after it has been made to the company by whom the policy was issued or the security given.

(4) The provisions of the last preceding paragraph shall be without prejudice to the provisions of [paragraph (*c*) of subsection (1) of section 152] of the Act as to the effect for the purposes of that subsection of the making of a statutory declaration within the periods therein stated.

[Regulation 12 is printed as amended by the Interpretation Act 1978, s 17(2)(a) (cf reg 4(4) above).]

13. Issue of fresh certificates

Where any company by whom a certificate of insurance or a certificate of security has been issued are satisfied that the certificate has become defaced or has been lost or destroyed they shall, if they are requested to do so by the person to whom the certificate was issued, issue to him a fresh certificate. In the case of a defaced certificate the company shall not issue a fresh certificate unless the defaced certificate is returned to the company.

THE SCHEDULE

PART 1

Forms of Certificates

FORM A

Certificate of Motor Insurance

Certificate No .... Policy No .... (Optional)

1. Registration mark of vehicle.
2. Name of policy holder.
3. Effective date of the commencement of insurance for the purposes of the relevant law.
4. Date of expiry of insurance.
5. Persons or classes of persons entitled to drive.
6. Limitations as to use.

I/We hereby certify that the policy to which this certificate relates satisfies the requirements of the relevant law applicable in Great Britain.

....

Authorised Insurers

Note: For full details of the insurance cover reference should be made to the policy.

Form B

Certificate of Motor Insurance

Certificate No .... Policy No .... (Optional)

1. Description of vehicles.
2. Name of policy holder.
3. Effective date of the commencement of insurance for the purposes of the relevant law.
4. Date of expiry of insurance.
5. Persons or classes of persons entitled to drive.
6. Limitations as to use.

I/We hereby certify that the policy to which this certificate relates satisfies the requirements of the relevant law applicable in Great Britain.

....
Authorised Insurers

Note: For full details of the insurance cover
reference should be made to the policy.

Form C

Certificate of Motor Insurance

I/We hereby certify that this covering note satisfies the requirements of the relevant law applicable in Great Britain.

....
Authorised Insurers

Form D

Certificate of Security

Certificate No .... Security No .... (Optional)

1. Name of holder of security.
2. Effective date of the commencement of security for the purposes of the relevant law.
3. Date of expiry of security.
4. Conditions to which security is subject.

I/We hereby certify that the security to which this certificate relates satisfies the requirements of the relevant law applicable in Great Britain.

....
Persons giving security

Note: For full details of the cover
reference should be made to the security.

Form E

Certificate of Deposit

I/We hereby certify that I am/we are the owner(s) of the vehicle of which the registration mark is........................and that in pursuance of the relevant law applicable in Great Britain I/we have on deposit with the Accountant-General of the Supreme Court the sum of fifteen thousand pounds.

Signed ....
on behalf of ....

Form F

Certificate of Ownership

We hereby certify that the vehicle of which the registration mark is .... is owned by ....

Signed ....
on behalf of ....

PART 2

Provisions relating to the forms and completion of certificates

[1. Every certificate shall be printed and completed in black on white paper or similar material. This provision shall not prevent the reproduction of a seal or monogram or similar device referred to in paragraph 2 of this Part of this Schedule, or the presence of a background pattern (of whatever form and whether coloured or not) on the face of the form which does not materially affect the legibility of the certificate.]

[2. No certificate shall contain any advertising matter, either on the face or on the back thereof:

Provided that the name and address of the company by whom the certificate is issued, or a reproduction of the seal of the company or any monogram or similar device of the company, or the name and address of an insurance broker, shall not be deemed to be advertising matter for the purposes of this paragraph if it is printed or stamped at the foot or on the back of such certificate, or if it forms, or forms part of, any such background pattern as is referred to in the foregoing paragraph.]

3. The whole of each form as set out in Part 1 of this Schedule shall in each case appear on the face of the form, the items being in the order so set out and the certification being set out at the end of the form.

4. The particulars to be inserted on the said forms shall so far as possible appear on the face of the form, but where in the case of any of the numbered headings in Forms A, B, or D, this cannot conveniently be done, any part of such particulars may be inserted on the back of the form, provided that their presence on the back is clearly indicated under the relevant heading.

5. The particulars to be inserted on any of the said forms shall not include particulars relating to any exceptions purporting to restrict the insurance under the relevant policy or the operation of the relevant security which are by [subsections (1) and 2 of section 148] of the Act rendered of no effect as respects the third party liabilities required by [sections 145 and 146] of the Act to be covered by a policy or security.

6.(1) In any case where it is intended that a certificate of insurance, certificate of security or a covering note shall be effective not only in Great Britain, but also in any of the following territories, that is to say, Northern Ireland, the Isle of Man, the Island of Guernsey, the Island of Jersey or the Island of Alderney, Forms A, B, C and D may be modified by the addition thereto, where necessary, of a reference to the relevant legal provisions of such of those territories as may be appropirate.

(2) A certificate of insurance or a certificate of security may contain either on the face or on the back of the certificate a statement as to whether or not the policy or security to which it relates satisfies the requirements of the relevant law in any of the territories referred to in this paragraph.

7. Every certificate of insurance or certificate of security shall be duly authenticated by or on behalf of the company by whom it is issued.

8. A certificate in Form F issued by a subsidiary of a Passenger Transport Executive or by a wholly-owned subsidiary of the [London Regional Transport] shall indicate under the signature that the issuing body is such a subsidiary of an Executive, which shall there be specified.

[Part 2 of the Schedule is printed as amended by the Interpretation Act 1978, s 17(2)(a) (cf reg 4(4) above); SI 1981 No 1567; the London Regional Transport Act 1984, s 71(4).]

The Motor Vehicles (Type Approval) (EEC Manufacturers) Regulations 1981

(SI 1981 No 493)

1. Citation, commencement and interpretation

(1) *[Omitted.]*

(2) In these Regulations expressions which are also used in [Part II of the Road Traffic Act 1988] have the same meanings as in that Part.

[Regulation 1 is printed as amended by the Interpretation Act 1978, ss 17(2)(a) and 23(1).]

2. Application of provisions relating to type approval certificates and certificates of conformity

(1) Subject to paragraph (2), the provisions—

(*a*) of sections 47 to 50 of the Road Traffic Act 1972 [and sections 54 to 62 of the Road Traffic Act 1988] (approval of design, construction, etc, of vehicles and vehicle parts); and

(*b*) of regulations made thereunder before the coming into operation of these Regulations,

so far as relating to type approval certificates and certificates of conformity, shall apply in relation to vehicles and vehicle parts manufactured in a member State of the Economic Community (other than the United Kingdom) or in Northern Ireland as they apply in relation to vehicles and vehicle parts manufactured in Great Britain.

(2) Nothing in the said provisions as applied by paragraph (1) shall require the Secretary of State for Transport to issue a type approval certificate before the expiration of the period of 12 months beginning with the day on which these Regulations came into operation.

(3) In consequence of paragraph (1) above any reference in the said provisions to a vehicle or vehicle part (including a reference which is to be construed as including such a reference) shall be construed as including a reference to a vehicle or vehicle part manufactured in a member State of the Economic Community (other than the United Kingdom) or in Northern Ireland.

[Regulation 2 is printed as amended by the Road Traffic (Consequential Provisions) Act 1988, s 2(4).
These regulations came into operation on 27 April 1981; reg 1(1).]

The Motor Vehicles (Type Approval) (Great Britain) Regulations 1984

(SI 1984 No 981)

[The text of these regulations is printed as amended by:

the Motor Vehicles (Type Approval) (Great Britain) (Amendment) (No 2) Regulations 1984 (SI 1984 No 1761) (13 December 1984);

the Motor Vehicles (Type Approval) (Great Britain) (Amendment) Regulations 1985 (SI 1985 No 1651) (2 December 1985);

the Motor Vehicles (Type Approval) (Great Britain) (Amendment) Regulations 1987 (SI 1987 No 1509) (1 October 1987); and

the Motor Vehicles (Type Approval) (Great Britain) (Amendment) Regulations 1988 (SI 1988 No 1522) (1 October 1988).

The amending regulations are referred to in the notes to the main regulations only by their years and numbers. The dates referred to above are the dates on which the regulations came into force.

The main regulations were also corrected by a correction slip dated August 1984 and have been amended by the Motor Vehicles (Type Approval) (Great Britain) (Amendment) Regulations 1984 (SI 1984 No 1401) and the Motor Vehicles (Type Approval) (Great Britain) (Amendment) Regulations 1986 (SI 1986 No 739), but these do not affect the text of any regulation printed.]

1. Commencement and citation *[Omitted.]*

2. Interpretation

(1) In these Regulations—

'the Construction and Use Regulations' means the [Road Vehicles (Construction and Use) Regulations 1986] *[SI 1986 No 1078, qv]*;

. . .

'dual-purpose vehicle' means a vehicle constructed or adapted for the carriage both of passengers and of goods or burden of any description, being a vehicle of which the unladen weight does not exceed 2040 kilograms, and which satisfies the following conditions as to construction, namely:—

(*a*) the vehicle must be permanently fitted with a rigid roof, with or without a sliding panel;

(*b*) the area of the vehicle to the rear of the driver's seat must—

(i) be permanently fitted with at least one row of transverse seats (fixed or folding) for two or more passengers and those seats must be properly sprung or cushioned and provided with upholstered back-rests, attached either to the seats or to a side or the floor of the vehicle; and

(ii) be lit on each side and at the rear by a window or windows of glass or other transparent material having an area or aggregate area of not less than 1850 square centimetres on each side and not less than 770 square centimetres at the rear; and

(*c*) the distance between the rearmost part of the steering wheel and the back-rests of the row of transverse seats satisfying the requirements specified in sub-paragraph (*b*)(i) above or, if there is more than one such row of seats, the distance between the rearmost part of the steering wheel and the back-rests of the rearmost such row must, when the seats are ready for use, be not less than one-third of the distance between the rearmost part of the steering wheel and the rearmost part of the floor of the vehicle;

. . .

'maximum gross weight' means, in relation to a vehicle, the weight which it is designed or adapted not to exceed when in normal use and travelling on a road laden;

'motor ambulance' means a motor vehicle which is specially designed and constructed (and not merely adapted) for carrying, as equipment permanently fixed to the vehicle, equipment used for medical, dental or other health purposes and is used primarily for the carriage of persons suffering from illness, injury or disability;

'motor caravan' means a motor vehicle which is constructed or adapted for the carriage of passengers and their effects and which contains, as permanently installed equipment, the facilities which are reasonably necessary for enabling the vehicle to provide mobile living accommodation for its users;

. . .

'the prescribed type approval requirements', in relation to a vehicle or a vehicle part subject to type approval requirements, means the type approval requirements prescribed therefor by these Regulations;

'the type approval requirements' means the requirements with respect to the design, construction, equipment or marking of vehicles or vehicle parts which—

(*a*) relate to the items numbered in column (1) and listed in column (2) of Schedule 1, and

(*b*) are contained in instruments or other documents, and consist of the requirements, specified against each such item in column (3) of Schedule 1, and

. . .

(2) *[Omitted.]*

(3) For the purposes of these Regulations—

(*a*) a motor vehicle is to be regarded as being manufactured on or after a particular date if it is first assembled on or after that date, even if it includes one or more parts which were manufactured before that date, and

(*b*) the provisions of [regulation 3(3)] of the Construction and Use Regulations shall apply for determining when a motor vehicle is first used.

(4) Unless the context otherwise requires, any reference in these Regulations to—

(*a*) a numbered Regulation or Schedule is a reference to the Regulation of or Schedule to these Regulations bearing that number, and

(*b*) a numbered paragraph is a reference to the paragraph bearing that number in the Regulation in which that number appears, and

(*c*) a numbered section is a reference to a section having that number in [the Road Traffic Act 1988].

[Regulation 2 is printed as amended by the Interpretation Act 1978, ss 17(2)(a) and 23; SI 1987 No 1509.

In para (1), only selected definitions are included.]

3. Application

(1) Subject to paragraph (2) these Regulations apply to—

(*a*) every motor vehicle manufactured on or after 1st October 1977 and first used on or after 1st August 1978 which is constructed solely for the carriage of passengers and their effects or is a dual-purpose vehicle and in either case which—

(i) is adapted to carry not more than eight passengers exclusive of the driver and either has four or more wheels or, if having only three wheels, has a maximum gross weight of more than 1000 kilograms, or

(ii) has three wheels, a maximum gross weight not exceeding 1000 kilograms, and either a design speed exceeding [50 kilometres per hour] or an engine with a capacity exceeding 50 cubic centimetres, and is not a motor cycle with a side-car attached, and

(*b*) parts of any such motor vehicles.

(2) These Regulations do not apply to, or to parts of—

(*a*) a motor ambulance;

(*b*) a motor caravan;

(*c*) a motor vehicle brought temporarily into Great Britain by a person resident abroad;

(*d*) a vehicle in the service of a visiting force or of a headquarters (as defined in Article 8(6) of the Visiting Forces and International Headquarters (Application of Law) Order 1965) *[SI 1965 No 1536]*;

(*e*) a motor vehicle which is imported by an individual into Great Britain and in relation to which the following conditions are satisfied—

(i) the vehicle has been purchased outside Great Britain for the personal use of the individual importing it or of his dependants,

(ii) the vehicle has been so used by that individual or his dependants on roads outside Great Britain before it is imported,

(iii) the vehicle is intended solely for such personal use in Great Britain, and

(iv) the individual importing the vehicle intends, at the time when [application is first made for a licence for the vehicle under the Vehicles (Excise) Act 1971], to remain in Great Britain for not less than twelve months from that time;

(*f*) a motor vehicle which is to be exported from Great Britain and which—

(i) is exempt from car tax by virtue of [section 7(1) of the Car Tax Act 1983],

(ii) is a vehicle in relation to which there has been a remission of car tax by virtue of [section 7(2) and (3) of that Act], or

(iii) has been zero-rated under [Regulation 56 or 57 of the Value Added Tax (General) Regulations 1985] *[SI 1985 No 886, qv]*;

(*g*) a motor vehicle which is of a new or improved type, or is fitted with equipment of a new or improved type, and which has been constructed to that type, or fitted with that equipment, for the purposes of tests or trials or for use as a prototype, and—

(i) is not intended for general use on roads, and

(ii) in the case of a vehicle first used on a road on or after 21st August 1984, remains in the ownership and the use of—

(A) the manufacturer of the vehicle if the vehicle is of a new or improved type, or

(B) the manufacturer of the equipment if the vehicle is fitted with equipment of a new or improved type or the manufacturer of the vehicle on which that equipment is used;

(*h*) a motor vehicle which is of a new or improved type provided that—

(i) a final examination has been carried out in respect of a vehicle to which the vehicle is alleged to conform following a written application made either—

(A) in the manner approved in accordance with Regulation 5, for a type approval certificate for the type, or

(B) in the manner approved in accordance with Regulation 6, for a Minister's approval certificate,

and as a result of the examination the Secretary of State is satisfied that the relevant type approval requirements specified in Schedule 1 are complied with;

(ii) the Secretary of State has been notified of the vehicle identification number in a manner approved by him;

(iii) the vehicle is being used for no purpose other than for, or in connection with, publicity, demonstration or evaluation of that type of vehicle; and

(iv) until, following the examination mentioned in sub-paragraph (i) of this sub-paragraph, there has been issued a type approval certificate or, as the case may be, a Minister's approval certificate, the vehicle—

(A) remains in the ownership of the person who made the application referred to in the said sub-paragraph (i), and

(B) is not offered for sale or supply or sold or supplied by retail;

(*i*) a motor vehicle to which sections 45 to 51 and 61 have become applicable after a period of use on roads during which, by virtue of section 188(4) (which relates to vehicles in the public service of the Crown), those sections did not apply to that vehicle; or

(*j*) a motor vehicle constructed or assembled by a person not ordinarily engaged in the trade or business of manufacturing motor vehicles of that description[;]

[(*k*) a motor vehicle for which a first licence was granted under the Vehicles (Excise) Act (Northern Ireland) 1972 on or after 2nd December 1985; or]

[(*l*) a motor vehicle in respect of which there exists a certificate issued in accordance with the provisions of Article 31A of the Road Traffic (Northern Ireland) Order 1981 *[SI 1981 No 154]*.]

[Regulation 3 is printed as amended by the Interpretation Act 1978, ss 17(2)(a) and 23(1); SI 1984 No 1761; SI 1985 No 1651; SI 1987 No 1509.

References to the Car Tax Act 1983 have been inserted in reg 3(1)(b) to replace references to the Finance Act 1972, Sched 7; however, as Sched 7 to the 1972 Act had been repealed by the 1983 Act before these regulations were made, the Interpretation Act 1978 might not, strictly, be applicable.]

4. Type approval requirements—application

(1) Subject to paragraphs (2), (3), (4) and (5) and to the exemptions specified in column (4) of Schedule 1, the type approval requirements are hereby prescribed as requirements which are applicable—

(*a*) from the date specified in column (5) of Schedule 1, and

(*b*) in a case where a date is specified in column (6) of Schedule 1, until that date,

to vehicles to which these Regulations apply and to the relevant parts of such vehicles, before such vehicles are used on a road.

(2) If a vehicle or a vehicle part is manufactured on or after a date (other than 1st August 1978) specified in an item in column (5) of Schedule 1, the type approval

requirement specified in column (3) in that item shall not apply if the vehicle or, in the case of a vehicle part, the vehicle in which it is incorporated, is first used on a road within six months of that date.

(3) If a vehicle or a vehicle part is manufactured on or after a date specified in an item in column (6) of Schedule 1, the type approval requirement specified in column (3) in that item shall apply if the vehicle or, in the case of a vehicle part, the vehicle in which it is incorporated, is first used on a road within six months of that date.

(4) Where, in relation to an item listed in column (2) of Schedule 1, two or more instruments or other documents are specified in column (3) of Schedule 1 as alternatives, the requirements prescribed by paragraph (1) are the requirements contained in either or any of those instruments or documents, and subject to paragraphs (1), (2), (3), (5) and (6) where two or more items specified in column (1) of Schedule 1 have the same subject matter as is specified in column (2) of Schedule 1 the type approval requirements relate to either or, as the case may be, any of those items.

(5) Where, in relation to an item listed in column (2) of Schedule 1, a requirement contained in an instrument or other document specified in column (3) of Schedule 1 is shown, by an entry in division (*c*) of that column, as being varied for the purposes of these Regulations, that requirement as so varied is the requirement hereby prescribed.

(6) A vehicle to which, or to a part of which, any requirement mentioned in paragraph (1) is for the time being applicable by virtue of paragraphs (1) to (5) is referred to in these Regulations as 'a vehicle subject to type approval requirements', and a vehicle part to which any such requirement is so applicable is referred to in these Regulations as 'a vehicle part subject to type approval requirements'.

(7) Where a requirement is prescribed by these Regulations as a requirement applicable to a vehicle, or to a vehicle part, that requirement shall, for the purposes of these Regulations, be regarded as being applicable to that vehicle or vehicle part by virtue of paragraphs (1) to (5) notwithstanding that the same requirement may have been, or may hereafter be, applied to that vehicle or vehicle part by or under any provision of the European Communities Act 1972 or by or under any other statutory provision.

[(8) Subject to paragraph (9), where in relation to item [4B,] 14B, 14C or 14D in Schedule 1, a date is specified in column (6) of that Schedule (being a date of cessation of application of type approval reequirements), that date shall not apply to any vehicle for which, or for a model of which, there is a type approval certificate or (as the case may be) a Minister's approval certificate in force at the time but, in relation to any such vehicle, column (6) shall be read and shall have effect as if there appeared in that column a date one year later than the date specified therein.]

[(9) In relation to any vehicle—

(*a*) which has 5 or more forward gears and a maximum power to maximum gross weight ratio of not less than 75 kilowatts per tonne; and

(*b*) for which, or for a model of which, there is a type approval certificate or (as the case may be) a Minister's approval certificate in force on 30th September 1988,

notwithstanding the specification in item 14B or 14C in column (6) of Schedule 1 of any date, that column shall be read and have effect as if no date appeared therein.]

[(10) Schedule 1A shall have effect for the purpose of specifying, in relation to certain vehicles, dates which are to be read as if they appeared in column (5) of items 25 and 26 in Schedule 1.]

[Regulation 4 is printed as amended by SI 1987 No 1509; SI 1988 No 1522.]

* * *

The Motor Vehicles (Type Approval for Goods Vehicles) (Great Britain) Regulations 1982

(SI 1982 No 1271)

[The text of these regulations is printed as amended by:
the Motor Vehicles (Type Approval for Goods Vehicles) (Great Britain) (Amendment) Regulations 1984 (SI 1984 No 697) (20 June 1984);
the Motor Vehicles (Type Approval for Goods Vehicles) (Great Britain) (Amendment) Regulations 1985 (SI 1985 No 46) (1 March 1985);
the Motor Vehicles (Type Approval for Goods Vehicles) (Great Britain) (Amendment) Regulations 1986 (SI 1986 No 427) (4 April 1986); and
the Motor Vehicles (Type Approval for Goods Vehicles) (Great Britain) (Amendment) Regulations 1987 (SI 1987 No 1508) (except as otherwise indicated, 1 October 1987).
The amending regulations are referred to in the notes to the main regulations only by their year and number. The date referred to above is the date on which the regulations came into force.
In addition to the above, the main regulations have been amended by the Motor Vehicles (Type Approval for Goods Vehicles) (Great Britain) (Amendment) (No 2) Regulations 1986 (SI 1986 No 1089) and the Motor Vehicles (Type Approval for Goods Vehicles) (Great Britain) (Amendment) Regulations 1988 (SI 1988 No 1523); but these regulations do not affect the text of any provision printed in this work.]

1. Commencement and citation *[Omitted.]*

2. Interpretation

(1) In these regulations—

'the Construction and Use Regulations' means the [Road Vehicles (Construction and Use) Regulations 1986] *[SI 1986 No 1078, qv]*;

'the Great Britain Regulations' means the Motor Vehicles (Type Approval) (Great Britain) Regulations [1984] *[SI 1984 No 981, qv]*;

'the Plating and Testing Regulations' means the [Goods Vehicles (Plating and Testing) Regulations 1988] *[SI 1988 No 1478, qv]*;

'appropriate information document'—

(i) in relation to a vehicle subject to type approval requirements, means a document in the form set out in Part I of Schedule 2, and

(ii) in relation to a vehicle part subject to type approval requirements, means a document in the form set out in Part II of Schedule 2;

'bi-purpose vehicle' means a vehicle constructed or adapted for the carriage of both goods and not more than 8 passengers, not being a vehicle to which the Great Britain Regulations apply nor a motor ambulance or a motor caravan;

'break-down vehicle' has the meaning given in [Regulation 3(1) of] the Plating and Testing Regulations;

'dual-purpose vehicle' has the meaning given in [the Table in regulation 3(2)] of the Construction and Use Regulations;

['maximum gross weight' has the meaning given in the Table in regulation 3(2) of the Construction and Use Regulations;]

'motor ambulance' and 'motor caravan' have the meanings given respectively in Regulation 2(1) of the Great Britain Regulations;

'prescribed alteration' means an alteration to a vehicle to which these Regulations apply which varies the number or nominal diameter of the tyres or the wheels and which is made before the vehicle is first used;

'prescribed fee', in relation to any matter provided for in these Regulations, means the fee prescribed for such matter in Regulations under section 50(1);

'prescribed type approval requirements', in relation to a vehicle or vehicle part subject to type approval requirements, means the type approval requirements prescribed therefor by these Regulations;

'public works vehicle' has the meaning given in [the Table in regulation 3(2)] of the Construction and Use Regulations;

['recovery vehicle' has the meaning given in paragraph 8 of Schedule 3 to the Vehicles (Excise) Act 1971 [*qv (para 8 was inserted by the Finance Act 1987)*];]

'slow vehicle' means a vehicle incapable by reason of its construction of a speed of more than 25 kilometres per hour on the level under its own power;

'type approval requirements' means, in relation to any vehicle to which these Regulations apply, the determination of—

(*a*) the weights mentioned in Regulation 5;

(*b*) the requirements with respect to the design, construction, equipment or marking of such vehicles or their parts which—

(i) relate to the items numbered in column (1) and listed in column (2) of Schedule 1, and

(ii) are contained in instruments or other documents, and consist of the requirements, specified against each such item in column (3) of Schedule 1; and

'vehicle subject to type approval requirements' and 'vehicle part subject to type approval requirements' have the meanings given in Regulation 4.

(2), (3) *[Omitted.]*

(4) For the purposes of these Regulations—

(*a*) a vehicle is to be regarded as being manufactured on or after a particular date if it is assembled to the stage where it includes all the parts of the vehicle which it needs to have to comply with any one or more of the prescribed type approval requirements; and

(*b*) the date on which a vehicle is to be regarded as being first used is the date on which it is first registered under the Vehicles (Excise) Act 1971.

(5) *[Omitted.]*

[Regulation 2 is printed as amended by the Interpretation Act 1978, ss 17(2)(a) and 23(1); SI 1987 No 1508.

Regulation 5 of these regulations is concerned with plated weights.]

3. Application of Regulations

(1) Subject to paragraph (2), these Regulations apply to—

(*a*) every motor vehicle manufactured on or after 1st October 1982 and first used on or after 1st April 1983 and which

(i) has three or more wheels, and

(ii) is either a goods vehicle, the [tractive] unit of an articulated vehicle or a bi-purpose vehicle; and (*b*) parts of any such vehicles.

(2) These Regulations do not apply to, or to the parts of, any of the following vehicles, that is to say—

(*a*) a vehicle brought temporarily into Great Britain and which—

(i) displays a registration mark mentioned in [Regulation 5 of the Motor Vehicles (International Circulation) Regulations 1985] *[SI 1985 No 610]*, and

(ii) complies in every respect with the requirements relating to motor vehicles contained in:—

(A) Article 21 and paragraph (1) of Article 22 of the Convention on Road Traffic concluded at Geneva on 19th September 1949 *[Cmnd 7997]*, and Part I, Part II (so far as it relates to direction indicators and stop lights) and Part III of Annex 6 to that Convention; or

(B) paragraphs I, III and VIII of Article 3 of the International Convention relative to Motor Traffic concluded at Paris on 24th April 1926 *[TS No 11 (1930)]*

(*b*) a vehicle which is to be exported from Great Britain and which either—

(i) has not been used on a road in Great Britain for any purpose except that of proceeding from the place where it was manufactured to the place from which it is to be taken out of Great Britain, or

(ii) satisfies the criteria of—

(A) being exempt from car tax by virtue of [section 7(1) of the Car Tax Act 1983],

(B) being a vehicle in relation to which there has been a remission of car tax by virtue of [section 7(2) and (3) of that Act], or

(C) being zero-rated under [Regulation 56 or 57 of the Value Added Tax (General) Regulations 1985] *[SI 1985 No 886, qv]*,

(*c*) a vehicle in the service of a visiting force or of a headquarters (as defined in Article 8(6) of the Visiting Forces and International Headquarters (Application of Law) Order 1965 *[SI 1965 No 1536]*;

(*d*) a vehicle to which [sections 49 to 63 of the Road Traffic Act 1988] . . . have become applicable after a period of use on roads during which, by virtue of [section 183(2)] (which relates to vehicles in the public service of the Crown), those sections did not apply to that vehicle;

[(*e*) a motor vehicle which is of a new or improved type, or is fitted with equipment of a new or improved type, and which has been constructed to that type or fitted with that equipment, for the purposes of tests or trials or for use as a prototype, and—

(i) is not intended for general use on roads, and

(ii) in the case of a vehicle first used on a road on or after 20th June 1984, remains in the ownership and the use of—

(A) if the vehicle is of a new or improved type the manufacturer of the vehicle, or

(B) if the vehicle is fitted with equipment of a new or improved type the manufacturer of the equipment or the manufacturer of the vehicle on which that equipment is used;]

[(*ee*) a motor vehicle the unladen weight of which does not exceed 1525 kilograms which is of a new or improved type provided that—

(i) a final examination has been carried out in respect of a vehicle to which the vehicle is alleged to conform following a written application made either—

(A) in the manner approved in accordance with Regulation 7 for a type approval certificate for the type, or

(B) in the manner approved in accordance with Regulation 8 for a Minister's approval certificate in respect of a vehicle of the type,

and as a result of the examination the Secretary of State is satisfied that the relevant type approval requirements specified in Schedule 1 are complied with;

(ii) the Secretary of State has been notified of the vehicle identification number in a manner approved by him;

(iii) the vehicle is being used for no purpose other than for, or in connection with, publicity, demonstration or evaluation of that type of vehicle; and

(iv) until, following the examination mentioned in sub-paragraph (i), there has been issued a type approval certificate or, as the case may be, a Minister's approval certificate, the vehicle—

(A) remains in the ownership of the person who made the application referred to in sub-paragraph (i); and

(B) is not offered for sale or supply, or sold or supplied, by retail;]

(*f*) a motor tractor, a light locomotive and a heavy locomotive;

(*g*) [an agricultural motor vehicle, engineering plant], a pedestrian-controlled vehicle, a straddle carrier, a works truck and a vehicle which is track-laying (all as defined in [the Table in regulation 3(2)] of the Construction and Use Regulations);

(*h*) a vehicle [the use of which on a road is authorised by] Article 15, 17 or 18 of the Motor Vehicles (Authorisation of Special Types) General Order 1979 *[SI 1979 No 1198, qv]*;

(*i*) a tower wagon as defined in Schedule 4 to the Vehicles (Excise) Act 1971 [*qv*];

(*j*) a fire engine (including an air field crash tender);

(*k*) a road roller;

(*l*) a vehicle propelled by steam;

(*m*) a vehicle constructed for the purpose of preventing or reducing the effect of snow or ice on roads, either by spreading grit or other material, by scooping or sweeping, or by other means;

(*n*) a two-wheeled motor cycle, with or without a side-car;

(*o*) an electrically-propelled vehicle;

(*p*) a break-down vehicle;

(*q*) a vehicle the weight of which unladen does not exceed 1525 kilograms constructed or assembled by a person not ordinarily engaged in the trade or business or manufacturing vehicles of that description;

(*r*) a vehicle the weight of which unladen does not exceed 1525 kilograms imported by an individual into Great Britain and in relation to which the following conditions are satisfied—

(i) the vehicle has been purchased outside Great Britain for the personal use of the individual importing it or of his dependants,

(ii) the vehicle has been so used by that individual or his dependants on roads outside Great Britain before it is imported,

(iii) the vehicle is intended solely for such person's use in Great Britain, and

(iv) the individual importing the vehicle intends, at the time when the [application is first made for a licence for the vehicle under the Vehicles (Excise) Act 1971], to remain in Great Britain for not less than twelve months from that time;

(*s*) a motor ambulance; . . .

(*t*) a motor caravan;

[(*u*) a recovery vehicle first used before 1st January 1988.]

[Regulation 3 is printed as amended by the Interpretation Act 1978, ss 17(2)(a) and 23(1); SI 1984 No 697; SI 1985 No 46; SI 1986 No 427; SI 1987 No 1508 (which, inter alia, inserted reg 3(2)(u) with effect from 1st January 1988).]

* * *

The Motor Vehicles (Wearing of Seat Belts) Regulations 1982

(SI 1982 No 1203)

Note. The continuance in force of these regulations after the initial three years required approval by a resolution of each House of Parliament; see the Road Traffic Act 1972, s 199(2A)(c). This approval was given in January 1986 by both Houses; see The Times, *14 and 21 January 1986.*

1, 2. *[Omitted.]*

3. (1) In these Regulations—

'the Construction and Use Regulations' means the [Road Vehicles (Construction and Use) Regulations 1986] *[SI 1986 No 1078, qv]*;

'the Driving Licences Regulations' means the [Motor Vehicles (Driving Licences) Regulations 1987] *[SI 1987 No 1378, qv]*;

'disabled person's seat belt' has the same meaning as in [Regulation 47(8)] of the Construction and Use Regulations;

'disabled person's vehicle' means a vehicle which has been specially designed and constructed, or specially adapted, for the use of a person suffering from some physical defect or disability;

'private hire vehicle' means a motor vehicle constructed or adapted to seat fewer than 9 passengers, other than a taxi or a public service vehicle, which is provided for hire with the services of a driver for the purpose of carrying passengers and which displays a sign pursuant to either section 21 of the Vehicles (Excise) Act 1971 or section 48(2) of the Local Government (Miscellaneous Provisions) Act 1976 or any similar enactment;

'public service vehicle' has the same meaning as in section 1 of the Public Passenger Vehicles Act 1981 [*qv*];

'specified passenger's seat' has the same meaning as in [Regulation 47(8)] of the Construction and Use Regulations;

'taxi' has the same meaning as in section 64(3) of the Transport Act 1980 [*qv*];

'trade licence' has the same meaning as in section 38(1) of the Vehicles (Excise) Act 1971 [*qv*].

(2) In these Regulations a reference to any Act or subordinate legislation (as defined in section 21(1) of the Interpretation Act 1978) includes a reference to that Act or subordinate legislation as from time to time extended, amended, re-enacted or applied.

(3) In these Regulations, unless the context otherwise requires, any reference to a numbered Regulation is a reference to the Regulation bearing that number in these Regulations.

[Regulation 3 is printed as amended by the Interpretation Act 1978, ss 17(2)(a) and 23(1).]

4. Save as provided in Regulation 5, every person shall wear a seat belt of a description specified in Regulation 7 if he is—

(1) driving a motor vehicle of a class specified in Regulation 6; or

(2) riding in a motor vehicle of that class in—

(*a*) the specified passenger's seat, or

(*b*) a forward facing seat alongside the driver's seat which is not the specified passenger's seat and the specified passenger's seat is not occupied by another person (whether or not that person is over the age of 14 years).

5. The requirement specified in Regulation 4 does not apply to a person who is—

(*a*) using a vehicle constructed or adapted for the delivery or collection of goods or mail to consumers or addresses, as the case may be, whilst engaged in making local rounds of deliveries or collections;

(*b*) driving the vehicle whilst performing a manoeuvre which includes reversing;

(*c*) a qualified driver (as defined in [Regulation 9(6)] of the Driving Licences Regulations) and is supervising the holder of a provisional licence (as defined in [Regulation 3(1)] of those Regulations) while that holder is performing a manoeuvre which includes reversing;

(*d*) the holder of a valid certificate in a form supplied by the Secretary of State, containing the information required by it, and signed by a registered medical practitioner to the effect that it is inadvisable on medical grounds for him to wear a seat belt;

(*e*) a constable protecting or escorting another person;

(*f*) not a constable but is protecting or escorting another person by virtue of powers the same as or similar to those of a constable for that purpose;

(*g*) in the service of a fire brigade and is donning operational clothing or equipment;

(*h*) the driver of—

(i) a taxi which is being used for seeking hire, or answering a call for hire, or carrying a passenger for hire, or

(ii) a private hire vehicle which is being used to carry a passenger for hire;

(*i*) a person by whom, as provided in the Driving Licences Regulations, a test of competence to drive is being conducted and his wearing of a seat belt would endanger himself or any other person;

(*j*) occupying a seat for which the seat belt either—

(i) does not comply with the requirements of [Regulation 48] of the Construction and Use Regulations, or

(ii) has an inertia reel mechanism which is locked as a result of the vehicle being, or having been, on a steep incline; or

(*k*) riding on a vehicle, being used under a trade licence, for the purpose of investigating or remedying a mechanical fault in the vehicle.

[Regulation 5 is printed as amended by the Interpretation Act 1978, ss 17(2)(a) and 23(1).]

6. The classes of vehicle mentioned in Regulation 4 are—

(*a*) a vehicle to which [Regulation 46] of the Construction and Use Regulations applies; and

(*b*) a vehicle which is equipped with anchorage points and seat belts and to which that Regulation would apply if it were not for the circumstances that the vehicle—

(i) is proceeding to a port for export;

(ii) has been brought temporarily into Great Britain by a person resident abroad;

(iii) is within the provisions of [Regulation 4(4), item 3 in table,] of the Construction and Use Regulations (which relates to vehicles subject to certain tax exemptions by virtue of their impending export);

(iv) is in the service of a visiting force or headquarters (as defined in Article 8(6) of the Visiting Forces and International Headquarters (Application of Law) Order 1965 *[SI 1965 No 1536]*);

(v) is within the provisions of Regulation [4(4), item 5 in the table,] of the Construction and Use Regulations (which relates to vehicles subject to certain exemptions relating to tests of satisfactory conditions);

(vi) is being used under a trade licence; or

(vii) is not a vehicle to which the [Motor Vehicles (Type Approval) (Great Britain) Regulations 1984 *[SI 1984 No 981, qv]* applies but which is being driven from premises of the manufacturer by whom it was made, or of a distributor of vehicles or dealer in vehicles

— to premises of a distributor of or dealer in vehicles of the purchaser of the vehicle, or

— to premises of a person obtaining possession of the vehicle under a hiring agreement or hire-purchase agreement.

[Regulation 6 is printed as amended by the Interpretation Act 1978, ss 17(2)(a) and 23(1).]

7. The descriptions of seat belt referred to in Regulation 4 are—

(*a*) as regards a driver's seat or a specified passenger's seat in respect of which a seat belt is required to be fitted by [Regulation 47] of the Construction and Use Regulations—

(i) in the case of a disabled person's vehicle, a disabled person's seat belt;

(ii) in the case of any other vehicle to which that Regulation applies, a seat belt which complies with the requirements specified in [paragraphs (2), (3), (5) and (7)] of that Regulation;

(*b*) as regards a driver's seat or a specified passenger's seat in respect of which a seat belt is not required to be fitted by that Regulation, the seat belt fitted to the vehicle in respect of that seat;

(*c*) as regards a seat mentioned in Regulation 4(2)(*b*), the seat belt fitted to the vehicle in respect of that seat.

[Regulation 7 is printed as amended by the Interpretation Act 1978, ss 17(2)(a) and 23(1).

In respect of the paragraphs of reg 47 of the Construction and Use Regulations referred to in para (a)(ii) above, it should be noted that the wording of the 1986 Regulations does not correspond exactly with that of the 1978 Regulations; pending formal amendment of para (a)(ii) reference may be necessary to the text of the 1978 Regulations.]

The Motor Vehicles (Wearing of Seat Belts by Children) Regulations 1982

(SI 1982 No 1342)

1. *[Omitted.]*

2. In these Regulations—

'adult seat belt' means:—

(*a*) in the case where the seat belt is one mentioned in [paragraph (3) of Regulation 47] of the Construction and Use Regulations, one which complies with the requirements specified in [paragraphs (2), (3), (5) and (7)] of that Regulation;

(*b*) in a case where the seat belt is not one to which [paragraph (3)] of that Regulation applies, the belt fitted to the vehicle for the use by a person occupying the seat in question;

'the Construction and Use Regulations' means the [Road Vehicles (Construction and Use) Regulations 1986] *[SI 1986 No 1078, qv]*;

'restraining device for a young person' means a seat belt which is marked with a marking referred to in [Regulation 47(7)] of the Construction and Use Regulations; and

'seat belt' and 'specified passenger's seat' have the meanings respectively given to those expressions in [Regulation 47(8)] of the Construction and Use Regulations.

[Regulation 2 is printed as amended by the Interpretation Act 1978, ss 17(2)(a) and 23(1).

In respect of the paragraphs of reg 47 of the Construction and Use Regulations referred to in the above definitions, it should be noted that the wording of the 1986 Regulations does not correspond exactly with that of the 1978 Regulations; pending formal amendment of this regulation, reference may be necessary to the text of the 1978 Regulations.]

3. The provisions of [section 15(1) of the Road Traffic Act 1988] do not apply in respect of a child for whom there is a valid certificate in a form supplied by the Secretary of State, containing the information required by it, and signed by a registered medical practitioner to the effect that it is inadvisable on medical grounds for him to wear a seat belt.

[Regulation 3 is printed as amended by the Interpretation Act 1978, ss 17(2)(a) and 23(1).]

4. The provisions of the said [section 15(1)] apply only in respect of a vehicle which is of a class specified in Regulation 6 of the Motor Vehicles (Wearing of Seat Belts) Regulations 1982 *[SI 1982 No 1203, qv]* (which relates to vehicles to which seat belts for certain seats are required to be fitted and to vehicles to which, but for the use being made of them, that requirement would apply).

[Regulation 4 is printed as amended by the Interpretation Act 1978, ss 17(2)(a) and 23(1).]

5. The provisions of the said [section 15(1)] do not apply to a person driving on a road a motor vehicle in respect of a child who occupies either—

(*a*) a forward facing seat alongside the driver's seat if every other part of the vehicle which is designed to be used as a seat (including the specified passenger's seat and any seat which may be folded) is occupied by another person (whether a child or not); or

(*b*) a seat for which no restraining device for a young person is provided, and

(i) the seat belt provided for that seat is an adult seat belt which has an inertia reel mechanism which is locked as a result of the vehicle being or having been, on a steep incline, or

(ii) the seat belt provided for that seat is an adult seat belt which does not comply with the requirements of [Regulation 48] of the Construction and Use Regulations.

[Regulation 5 is printed as amended by the Interpretation Act 1978, ss 17(2)(a) and 23(1).]

6. The descriptions of seat belt prescribed for the purpose of the said [section 15(1)] are—

(*a*) for a child under 1 year of age, a restraining device for a young person appropriate to the weight of the child in accordance with the indication of weight shown on the marking referred to in [Regulation 47(7)] of the Construction and Use Regulations;

(*b*) for a child under 1 year of age or more who is not disabled, either any type of a restraining device for a young person or an adult seat belt;

(*c*) for a child of 1 year of age or more who is disabled, either—

(i) any type of a restraining device for a young person; or

(ii) an adult seat belt; or

(iii) a seat belt which has been specially designed and constructed, and not merely adapted, for use by a person suffering from some physical defect or disability.

[Regulation 6 is printed as amended by the Interpretation Act 1978, ss 17(2)(a) and 23(1).

As to the reference to reg 47(7) of the Construction and Use Regulations in para (a) above, see further the note to reg 2 of these regulations.]

The Motorways Traffic (England and Wales) Regulations 1982

(SI 1982 No 1163)

[The text of these regulations is printed as amended by;
the Motorways Traffic (England and Wales) (Amendment) Regulations 1983 (SI 1983 No 374) (16 April 1983); and
the Motorways Traffic (England and Wales) (Amendment) Regulations 1984 (SI 1984 No 1479) (17 October 1984).
The amending regulations are referred to in the notes to the main regulations only by their years and numbers. The dates referred to above are the dates on which the regulations came into force.]

ARRANGEMENT OF REGULATIONS

1. Commencement and citation *[Omitted.]*

2. Revocation *[Omitted.]*

3. Interpretation

(1) In these Regulations, the following expressions have the meanings hereby respectively assigned to them:—

(*a*) '[the Act of 1984]' means the [Road Traffic Regulation Act 1984];

(*b*) ['carriageway' means that part of a motorway which—

(i) is provided for the regular passage of vehicular motor traffic along the motorway; and

(ii) where a hard shoulder is provided, has the approximate position of its left-hand or near-side edge marked with a traffic sign of the type shown in diagram 1012.1 in Schedule 2 to the Traffic Signs Regulations and General Directions 1981 *[SI 1981 No 859]*.]

(*c*) 'central reservation' means that part of a motorway which separates the carriageway to be used by vehicles travelling in one direction from the carriageway to be used by vehicles travelling in the opposite direction;

(*d*) 'excluded traffic' means traffic which is not traffic of Classes I or II;

(*e*) 'hard shoulder' means a part of the motorway which is adjacent to and situated on the left hand or near side of the carriageway when facing in the direction in which vehicles may be driven in accordance with Regulation 6, and which is designed to take the weight of a vehicle;

(*f*) 'motorway' means any road or part of a road to which these Regulations apply by virtue of Regulation 4;

(*g*) 'verge' means any part of a motorway which is not a carriageway, a hard shoulder, or a central reservation.

(2) A vehicle shall be treated for the purposes of any provision of these Regulations as being on any part of a motorway specified in that provision if any part of the vehicle (whether it is at rest or not) is on the part of the motorway so specified.

(3) Any provision of these Regulations containing any prohibition or restriction relating to the driving, moving or stopping of a vehicle, or to its remaining at rest, shall be construed as a provision that no person shall use a motorway by driving, moving or stopping the vehicle or by causing or permitting it to be driven or moved, or to stop or remain at rest, in contravention of that prohibition or restriction.

(4) In these Regulations references to numbered classes of traffic are references to the classes of traffic set out in Schedule 4 to the Highways Act 1980 [*qv*].

[Regulation 3 is printed as amended by the Road Traffic Regulation Act 1984, s 144(1), and Sched 10, para 2, and SI 1984 No 1479.]

4. Application

These Regulations apply to every special road or part of a special road which can only be used by traffic of Classes I or II, but shall not apply to any part of any such road until such date as may be declared in accordance with the provisions of [section 1(4) of the Act of 1984] to be the date on which it is open for use as a special road.

[Regulation 4 is printed as amended by the Road Traffic Regulation Act 1984, s 144(1), and Sched 10, para 2.]

5. Vehicles to be driven on the carriageway only

Subject to the following provisions of these Regulations, no vehicle shall be driven on any part of a motorway which is not a carriageway.

6. Direction of driving

(1) Where there is a traffic sign indicating that there is no entry to a carriageway at a particular place, no vehicle shall be driven or moved onto that carriageway at that place.

(2) Where there is a traffic sign indicating that there is no left or right turn into a carriageway at a particular place, no vehicle shall be so driven or moved as to cause it to turn to the left or (as the case may be) to the right into that carriageway at that place.

(3) Every vehicle on a length of carriageway which is contiguous to a central reservation, shall be driven in such a direction that the central reservation is at all times on the right hand or offside of the vehicle.

(4) Where traffic signs are so placed that there is a length of carriageway (being a length which is not contiguous to a central reservation) which can be entered at one end only by vehicles driven in conformity with paragraph (1) of this Regulation, every vehicle on that length of carriageway shall be driven in such a direction only as to cause it to proceed away from that end of that length of carriageway towards the other end thereof.

(5) Without prejudice to the foregoing provisions of this Regulation, no vehicle which—

(*a*) is on a length of carriageway on which vehicles are required by any of the foregoing provisions of this Regulation to be driven in one direction only and is proceeding in or facing that direction, or

(*b*) is on any other length of carriageway and is proceeding in or facing one direction.

shall be driven or moved so as to cause it to turn and proceed in or face the opposite direction.

7. Restriction on stopping

(1) Subject to the following provisions of this Regulation, no vehicle shall stop or remain at rest on a carriageway.

(2) Whether it is necessary for a vehicle which is being driven on a carriageway to be stopped while it is on a motorway—

(*a*) by reason of a breakdown or mechanical defect or lack of fuel, oil or water, required for the vehicle; or

(*b*) by reason of any accident, illness or other emergency; or

(*c*) to permit any person carried in or on the vehicle to recover or move any object which has fallen onto a motorway; or

(*d*) to permit any person carried in or on the vehicle to give help which is required by any other person in any of the circumstances specified in the foregoing provisions of this paragraph,

the vehicle shall, as soon and in so far as is reasonably practicable, be driven or moved off the carriageway on to, and may stop and remain at rest on, any hard shoulder which is contiguous to that carriageway.

(3)(*a*) A vehicle which is at rest on a hard shoulder shall so far as is reasonably practicable be allowed to remain at rest on that hard shoulder in such a position only that no part of it or of the load carried thereby shall obstruct or be a cause of danger to vehicles using the carriageway.

(*b*) A vehicle shall not remain at rest on a hard shoulder for longer than is necessary in the circumstances or for the purposes specified in paragraph 2 of this Regulation.

(4) Nothing in the foregoing provisions of this Regulation shall preclude a vehicle from stopping or remaining at rest on a carriageway while it is prevented from proceeding along the carriageway by the presence of any other vehicle or any person or object.

8. Restriction on reversing

No vehicle on a motorway shall be driven or moved backwards except in so far as it is necessary to back the vehicle to enable it to proceed forwards or to be connected to any other vehicle.

9. Restriction on the use of hard shoulders

No vehicle shall be driven or stop or remain at rest on any hard shoulder except in accordance with paragraphs (2) and (3) of Regulation 7.

10. Vehicles not to use the central reservation or verge

No vehicle shall be driven or moved or stop or remain at rest on a central reservation or verge.

11. Vehicles not to be driven by learner drivers

No motor vehicle shall be driven on a motorway by a person who is authorised to drive that vehicle only by virtue of his being the holder of a provisional licence under [section 97(2) of the Road Traffic Act 1988], unless, since the date of coming into force of the said provisional licence that person has passed a test prescribed under [section 89 of the Road Traffic Act 1988] sufficient to entitle him under that Act to be granted a licence, other than a provisional licence, authorising him to drive that vehicle on a road.

[Regulation 11 is printed as amended by the Interpretation Act 1978, ss 17(2)(a) and 23(1).]

12. Restriction on use of right hand or off-side lane

[(1) This Regulation applies to—

(*a*) a goods vehicle which has an operating weight exceeding 7.5 tonnes.

(*b*) a motor vehicle constructed solely for the carriage of passengers and their effects the overall length of which exceeds 12 metres;

(*c*) a motor vehicle drawing a trailer, and

(*d*) a motor vehicle other than a motor vehicle constructed solely for the carriage of passengers and their effects which does not fall within sub-paragraphs (*a*), (*b*) or (*c*) and which is a heavy motor car, a motor tractor, a light locomotive or a heavy locomotive.

(2) Subject to the provisions of paragraph (3) below, no vehicle to which this Regulation applies shall be driven or moved or stop or remain at rest on the right hand or off-side lane of a length of carriageway which has three or more traffic lanes at any place where all the lanes are open for use by traffic proceeding in the same direction.

(3) The prohibition contained in paragraph (2) above shall not apply to a vehicle whilst it is being driven on any right hand or off-side lane such as is mentioned in that paragraph in so far as it is necessary for the vehicle to be driven to enable it to pass another vehicle which is carrying or drawing a load of exceptional width.

(4) In this Regulation—

'goods vehicle' and 'operating weight' have the same meanings as in [sections 138(3) and 138(2) respectively of the Act of 1984], and

'overall length' has the same meaning as in [Regulation 3(2)] of the [Road Vehicles (Construction and Use) Regulations 1986] *[SI 1986 No 1078, qv]]*.

[Regulation 12 is printed as substituted by SI 1983 No 374, and as subsequently amended by the

Interpretation Act 1978, ss 17(2)(a) and 23(1); the Road Traffic Regulation Act 1984, s 144(1) and Sched 10, para 2.]

13. Restrictions affecting persons on foot on a motorway

No person shall at any time while on foot go or remain on any part of a motorway other than a hard shoulder except in so far as it is necessary for him to do so to reach a hard shoulder or to secure compliance with any of these Regulations or to recover or move any object which has fallen on to a motorway or to give help which is required by any other person in any of the circumstances specified in paragraph (2) of Regulation 7.

14. Restrictions affecting animals carried in vehicles

The person in charge of any animal which is carried by a vehicle using a motorway shall, so far is practicable, secure that—

(*a*) the animal shall not be removed from or permitted to leave the vehicle while the vehicle is on a motorway, and

(*b*) if it escapes from, or it is necessary for it to be removed from, or permitted to leave, the vehicle—

(i) it shall not go or remain on any part of the motorway other than a hard shoulder, and

(ii) it shall whilst it is not on or in the vehicle be held on a lead or otherwise kept under proper control.

15. Use of motorway by excluded traffic

(1) Excluded traffic is hereby authorised to use a motorway on the occasions or in the emergencies and to the extent specified in the following provisions of this paragraph, that is to say—

(*a*) traffic of Classes III or IV may use a motorway for the maintenance, repair, cleaning or clearance of any part of a motorway or for the erection, laying, placing, maintenance, testing, alteration, repair or removal of any structure, works on apparatus in, on, under or over any part of a motorway;

(*b*) pedestrians may use a motorway—

(i) when it is necessary for them to do so as a result of an accident or emergency or of a vehicle being at rest on a motorway in any of the circumstances specified in paragraph (2) of Regulation 7, or

(ii) in any of the circumstances specified in sub-paragraphs (*b*), (*d*), (*e*) or (*f*) of paragraph (1) of Regulation 16.

(2) The Secretary of State may authorise the use of a motorway by any excluded traffic on occasion or in emergency or for the purpose of enabling such traffic to cross a motorway or to secure access to premises abutting on or adjacent to a motorway.

(3) Where by reason of any emergency the use of any road (not being a motorway) by any excluded traffic is rendered impossible or unsuitable the Chief Officer of Police of the police area in which a motorway or any part of a motorway is situated, or any officer of or above the rank of superintendent authorised in that behalf by that Chief Officer, may—

(*a*) authorise any excluded traffic to use that motorway or that part of a motorway as an alternative road for the period during which the use of the other road by such traffic continues to be impossible or unsuitable, and

(*b*) relax any prohibition or restriction imposed by these Regulations in so far as he considers it necessary to do so in connection with the use of that motorway or that part of a motorway by excluded traffic in pursuance of any such authorisation as aforesaid.

16. Exceptions and relaxations

(1) Nothing in the foregoing provisions of these Regulations shall preclude any person from using a motorway otherwise than in accordance with the provisions in any of the following circumstances, that is to say—

(*a*) where he does so in accordance with any direction or permission given by a constable in uniform or with the indication given by a traffic sign;

(*b*) where, in accordance with any permission given by a constable, he does so for the purpose of investigating any accident which has occurred on or near a motorway;

(*c*) where it is necessary for him to do so to avoid or prevent an accident or to obtain or give help required as the result of an accident or emergency, and he does so in such manner as to cause as little danger or inconvenience as possible to other traffic on a motorway,

(*d*) where he does so in the exercise of his duty as a constable or as a member of a fire brigade or of an ambulance service;

(*e*) where it is necessary for him to do so to carry out in an efficient manner—

(i) the maintenance, repair, cleaning, clearance, alteration or improvement of any part of a motorway, or

(ii) the removal of any vehicle from any part of a motorway, or

(iii) the erection, laying, placing, maintenance, testing, alteration, repair or removal of any structure, works or apparatus in, on, under or over any part of a motorway; or

(*f*) where it is necessary for him to do so in connection with any inspection, survey, investigation or census which is carried out in accordance with any general or special authority granted by the Secretary of State.

(2) Without prejudice to the foregoing provisions of these Regulations, the Secretary of State may relax any prohibition or restriction imposed by these Regulations.

The Passenger and Goods Vehicles (Recording Equipment) Regulations 1979

(SI 1979 No 1746)

[The text of these regulations is printed as amended by:

the Passenger and Goods Vehicles (Recording Equipment) (Amendment) Regulations 1984 (SI 1984 No 144) (13 March 1984);

the Community Drivers' Hours and Recording Equipment Regulations 1986 (SI 1986 No 1457) (29 September 1986); and

the Passenger and Goods Vehicles (Recording Equipment) (Amendment) Regulations 1986 (SI 1986 No 2076) (31 December 1986).

The amending regulations are referred to in the notes to the main regulations only by their year and number. The dates referred to above are the dates on which the regulations came into force.

As to SI 1984 No 144, reference should also be made to the note to Chapter VI of Annex I to Council Regulation (EEC) 3821/85 (qv).

The Passenger and Goods Vehicles (Recording Equipment) (Amendment) Regulations 1985 (SI 1985 No 1801) were revoked by SI 1986 No 2076.]

1. Commencement, citation, revocation and interpretation

(1), (2) *[Omitted.]*

(3) In these Regulations—

'the Act of 1968' means the Transport Act 1968;

['the Community Recording Equipment Regulation' means Council Regulation (EEC) No 3821/85 of 20 December 1985 on recording equipment in road transport [*qv*] as read with the Community Drivers' Hours and Recording Equipment (Exemptions and Supplementary Provisions) Regulations 1986 [*SI 1986 No 1456, qv*];]

[Regulation 1 is printed as amended by SI 1986 No 1457.]

2. Installation and use of recording equipment

[Substitutes ss 97–97B for s 97 of the Transport Act 1968 above and makes provision for their commencement.]

3. Consequential adaptations of enactments

[Amends the Transport Act 1968, ss 98, 99 and 103 above, and the Road Traffic (Foreign Vehicles) Act 1972, Sched 1.]

[4. Installation or repair of recording equipment, checks and inspections

(1) The Secretary of State shall be the competent authority in Great Britain—

(*a*) for the approval of fitters and workshops for the installation or repair of recording equipment in accordance with [Article 1] of the Community Recording Equipment Regulation; and

(*b*) for the nomination of bodies for the carrying out of checks and inspections of recording equipment in accordance with Chapter VI of Annex I to that Regulation.

(2) Any approval or nomination under this Regulation shall be in writing, shall specify its scope, shall provide for its withdrawal by the Secretary of State on notice given by him and, if the Secretary of State thinks fit, may contain conditions.

[(2A)(*a*) An approval or nomination shall be issued—

(i) in the case of an approval or nomination issued between 31st October and 31st December in any year, for a period ending on 31st January in the second year following the year of issue, and

(ii) in the case of any other approval or nomination, for a period ending on 31st January in the year following the year of issue.

(*b*) An approval or nomination issued and not withdrawn may, on application before the date of its expiry, be renewed for a further period ending on 31st January next following and thereafter for successive periods so ending.]

(3) Such conditions may in particular relate to—

(*a*) the fees to be charged for installing or repairing or, as the case may be, checking or inspecting recording equipment;

(*b*) the place where and equipment by means of which such activities are, or are to be, carried out;

(*c*) the procedure to be adopted in carrying out such activities;

(*d*) the records to be kept and the evidence to be furnished of the carrying out of such activities;

(*e*) the training of persons for carrying out such activities;

(*f*) the inspection by or on behalf of the Secretary of State of places where and equipment by means of which such activities are, or are to be, carried out; and

(*g*) the display, at the places where such activities are carried out, of signs indicating that such activities are carried out there by fitters or workshops approved or, as the case may be, bodies nominated, by the Secretary of State.

(4) The Secretary of State shall publish from time to time lists of—

(*a*) the fitters and workshops for the time being approved by him; and

(*b*) the bodies for the time being nominated by him;

and any list published under sub-paragraph (*a*) above shall specify the mark to be placed by each approved fitter or workshop on any seals which he or they affix to any recording equipment.

(5) In this Regulation 'recording equipment' means equipment for recording information as to the use of a vehicle.]

[Regulation 4 was substituted by SI 1984 No 144 (and a correction slip dated February 1984) and is printed as amended by SI 1986 No 2076.

As to approvals or nominations under para (2A)(b) and (c) above, see further the Passenger and Goods Vehicles (Recording Equipment) (Amendment) Regulations 1986 (SI 1986 No 2076), qv.]

5. *[Revoked by SI 1986 No 1457.]*

The Passenger and Goods Vehicles (Recording Equipment) (Amendment) Regulations 1986

(SI 1986 No 2076)

1. These Regulations may be cited as the Passenger and Goods Vehicles (Recording Equipment) (Amendment) Regulations 1986 and shall come into operation on 31st December 1986.

2. In these Regulations 'the 1979 Regulations' means the Passenger and Goods Vehicles (Recording Equipment) Regulations 1979 *[SI 1979 No 1746, qv]*.

3. *[Amends the Passenger and Goods Vehicles (Recording Equipment) Regulations 1979.]*

4.—(1) Any approval or nomination issued pursuant to the provisions of regulation 4(2A)(*b*) of the 1979 Regulations before the coming into operation of these Regulations—

(*a*) if issued before 30th September 1986 shall be treated as having been issued for a period ending on 31st January 1987, and

(*b*) if issued after 30th September 1986 shall be treated as having been issued for a period ending on 31st January 1988.

(2) Any approval or nomination renewed pursuant to the provisions of regulation 4(2A)(*c*) of the 1979 Regulations before the coming into operation of these Regulations shall be treated as having been renewed for a period ending on 31st January 1987.

5. *[Revocation.]*

The 'Pelican' Pedestrian Crossings Regulations and General Directions 1987

(SI 1987 No 16)

[The text of these regulations and directions is printed as corrected by a corrigendum dated March 1987.]

ARRANGEMENT

PART II

GENERAL

PART II

REGULATIONS

SCHEDULES TO PART II

PART III

General Directions

PART I

General

1. Citation and commencement

This Instrument may be cited as the 'Pelican' Pedestrian Crossings Regulations and General Directions 1987 and shall come into force on 18th February 1987.

2. Revocation *[Omitted.]*

3. Interpretation

(1) In this Instrument—

(*a*) any reference to a numbered regulation is a reference to the regulation bearing that number in the Regulations contained in Part II of this Instrument; and

(*b*) except where otherwise stated, any reference to a numbered Schedule is a reference to the Schedule to the Regulations contained in Part II of this Instrument bearing that number.

(2) In this Instrument the following expressions have the meanings hereby respectively assigned to them—

'the 1984 Act' means the Road Traffic Regulation Act 1984;

'the 1969 Regulations' means the 'Pelican' Pedestrian Crossing Regulations 1969;

'appropriate authority' means, in relation to a trunk road, the appropriate Secretary of State and, in relation to any other road, the local authority who established the crossing;

'appropriate Secretary of State' means, in relation to a crossing established or to be established on a road in—

(*a*) England, the Secretary of State for Transport;

(*b*) Scotland, the Secretary of State for Scotland; or

(*c*) Wales, the Secretary of State for Wales;

'carriageway' means—

(*a*) where it is in a highway, a way constituting or comprised in the highway being a way over which the public have a right of way for the passage of vehicles; and

(*b*) where it is in any other road to which the public has access, that part of the road to which vehicles have access, but does not, in either case, include any central reservation (whether within the limits of a crossing or not);

'central reservation' means any provision which separates one part of a carriageway from another part of that carriageway, and includes a refuge for pedestrians;

'crossing' means a crossing for pedestrians established either:—

(*a*) in the case of any road other than a trunk road, by a local authority under the provisions of section 23 of the 1984 Act; or

(*b*) in the case of a trunk road, by the appropriate Secretary of State in discharge of the duty imposed on him by section 24 of the 1984 Act;

'indicator for pedestrians' means the traffic sign of that description prescribed by regulation 2(1) and Schedule 1;

'one-way street' means any road on which the driving of vehicles otherwise than in one direction is prohibited at all times;

'pedestrian' means a foot passenger;

'pedestrian light signals' means the traffic signs of that description prescribed by regulation 2(1) and Schedule 1;

' "Pelican" crossing' means a crossing—

(*a*) at which there are traffic signs of the size, colour and type prescribed, or treated as if prescribed, by Regulation 2(1) and Schedule 1; and

(*b*) the presence and limits of which are indicated, or are treated as indicated, in accordance with regulation 2(2) and Schedule 2;

' "Pelican" controlled area' means, in relation to a 'Pelican' crossing, the area of the carriageway in the vicinity of the crossing and lying on both sides of the crossing or only one side of the crossing, the presence and limits of which are indicated, or are treated as indicated, in accordance with regulation 3 and Schedule 2;

'primary signal' means the traffic sign prescribed as a vehicular light signal by regulation 2(1) and Schedule 1 erected on or near the carriageway facing traffic approaching the 'Pelican' crossing and sited between the stop line and the line of studs indicating the limits of the crossing in accordance with Schedule 2 nearest to the stop line;

'refuge for pedestrians' means an area of a carriageway to which vehicles do not have access and on which pedestrians may wait after crossing one part of that carriageway and before crossing the other part;

'secondary signal' means the traffic sign prescribed as a vehicular light signal by regulation 2(1) and Schedule 1 erected on or near the carriageway facing traffic approaching the 'Pelican' crossing but sited beyond the furthest edge of the 'Pelican' crossing as viewed from the direction of travel of such traffic;

'stop line' means, in relation to the driver of a vehicle approaching a 'Pelican' crossing, the transverse white line which is parallel to the limits of the crossing as indicated in accordance with Schedule 2 and on the same side of the crossing as the driver;

'stud' means any mark or device on the carriageway, whether or not projecting above the surface thereof;

'a system of staggered crossings' means two 'Pelican' crossings provided on a road where there is a central reservation in the road, each separately constituted as a 'Pelican' crossing, one such crossing being on one side of the central reservation and the other such crossing being on the other side and which together do not form a straight line across the road.

(3) Any reference in this Instrument to a vehicular light signal is—

(*a*) where a primary signal has been erected without a secondary signal, a reference to the light signal displayed by the primary signal; and

(*b*) where a secondary signal has been erected as well as a primary signal, a reference to the light signal displayed by both the primary signal and the secondary signal or by either the primary signal operating without the secondary signal or by the secondary signal operating without the primary signal.

PART II

Regulations

1. Citation

The Regulations contained in this Part of this Instrument may be cited as the 'Pelican' Pedestrian Crossings Regulations 1987.

2. 'Pelican' crossings

(1) The provisions of Schedule 1 shall have effect as respects the size, colour and type of the traffic signs which are to be placed at or near a crossing for the purpose of constituting it a 'Pelican' crossing.

(2) The provisions of Schedule 2 shall have effect for regulating the manner in which the presence and limits of a crossing are to be indicated for the purpose of constituting it a 'Pelican' crossing.

(3) Any crossing which, immediately before the coming into operation of these Regulations, was constituted as a 'Pelican' crossing in accordance with the 1969 Regulations shall, notwithstanding the revocation of those Regulations, be treated as constituted in accordance with these Regulations for so long as the traffic signs situated at or near it and the manner in which its presence and limits are indicated comply with the 1969 Regulations.

3. 'Pelican' controlled areas

(1) The provisions of Schedule 2 shall have effect as respects the size, colour and type of the traffic signs which shall be placed in the vicinity of a 'Pelican' crossing for the purpose of constituting a 'Pelican' controlled area in relation to that crossing and of indicating the presence and limits of that area.

(2) A stop line shall indicate to vehicular traffic proceeding towards a 'Pelican' crossing the position at which a driver of a vehicle shall stop it for the purpose of complying with regulations 16 and 17.

(3) Where the appropriate authority is satisfied in relation to a particular area of carriageway in the vicinity of the 'Pelican' crossing that, by reason of the layout or character of the roads in the vicinity of the crossing, the application of such a prohibition as is mentioned in any of regulations 12, 13, 14, 19 and 20 to that particular area or the constitution of that particular area as a 'Pelican' controlled area by the placing of traffic signs in accordance with Schedule 2 would be impracticable, it shall not be necessary for that area to be constituted a 'Pelican' controlled area but if, by virtue of this paragraph, it is proposed that no area, on either side of the limits of a 'Pelican' crossing (not on a trunk road), is to be constituted a 'Pelican' controlled area by 18th

February 1989, a notice in writing shall be sent by the appropriate authority to the appropriate Secretary of State stating the reasons why it is proposed that no such area should be constituted.

(4) Where immediately before the coming into operation of these Regulations, the approach for vehicular traffic to a 'Pelican' crossing has been indicated by a pattern of studs placed and white lines marked on the carriageway in accordance with the provisions of paragraph 3 of Schedule 2 to the 1969 Regulations, then, notwithstanding the revocation effected by article 2 of Part I of this Instrument, that approach may until 18th February 1989 continue to be so indicated for so long as the said pattern of studs and white lines does not lie within a 'Pelican' controlled area or in the vicinity of such an area on the same side of the crossing as that pattern.

4. Variations in dimensions

(1) Any variation in—

(i) a dimension (other than as to the height of a letter) specified in any of the diagrams in Parts II and III of Schedule 1; or

(ii) a dimension as to the height of a letter specified in the diagram in Part III of that Schedule,

shall be treated as permitted by these Regulations if the variation—

(*a*) in the case of a dimension of less than 10 millimetres, does not exceed 1 millimetre;

(*b*) in the case of a dimension of 10 millimetres or more but less than 50 millimetres, does not exceed 10% of that dimension;

(*c*) in the case of a dimension of 50 millimetres or more but less than 300 millimetres, does not exceed $7\frac{1}{2}$% of that dimension; or

(*d*) in the case of a dimension of 300 millimetres or more, does not exceed 5% of that dimension.

(2) Any variation in a dimension specified in any of the diagrams in Schedule 2 shall be treated as permitted by these Regulations if the variation—

(*a*) in the case of a dimension of 300 millimetres or more, does not exceed 20% of that dimension; or

(*b*) in the case of a dimension of less than 300 millimetres, where the actual dimension exceeds the dimension so specified, does not exceed 30% of the dimension so specified, and where the actual dimension is less than the dimension so specified, does not exceed 10% of the dimension so specified.

5. Box for housing equipment

Apparatus designed to control or to monitor, or to control and monitor, the operation of the vehicular light signals and pedestrian light signals may be housed in one or more boxes attached to the post or other structure on which such signals are mounted.

6. Additional traffic signs

In addition to the traffic signs prescribed in regulation 2(1) and Schedule 1, the traffic signs specified in diagrams 610, 611, 612, 613 and 616 in Schedule 1 to the Traffic Signs Regulations 1981 *[SI 1981 No 859]* may be placed at or near a 'Pelican' crossing.

[Diagrams 610, 611, 612, 613 and 616 in Sched 1 to the Traffic Signs Regulations 1981 are signs indicating the direction in which traffic should proceed (diagram 610), that traffic may pass

either side of the sign (diagram 611), no right turn (diagram 612), no left turn (diagram 613) and no entry (diagram 616).]

7. Significance of traffic signs

Regulations 8 to 10 are made under section 64 of the 1984 Act and shall have effect for the purpose of prescribing the warnings, information, requirements and prohibitions which are to be conveyed to traffic by the traffic signs of the size, colour and type prescribed by regulations 2(1) and 6 and Schedule 1.

8. Significance of vehicular light signals

(1) The vehicular traffic light signal at a 'Pelican' crossing shall convey the following information, requirements and prohibitions—

(*a*) the steady green light shall convey the information that vehicular traffic may proceed across the crossing;

(*b*) except as provided in sub-paragraph (*d*) below, the steady amber light shall convey the prohibition that vehicular traffic shall not proceed beyond the stop line, or, if the stop line is not for the time being visible, beyond the post or other structure on which is mounted the primary signal facing such traffic on the side of the carriageway on which vehicles approach the crossing except in the case of any vehicle which when the steady amber light is first shown is so close to the stop line, post or structure that it cannot safely be stopped before passing the line, post or structure;

(*c*) except as provided in sub-paragraph (*d*) below, the red light shall convey the prohibition that vehicular traffic shall not proceed beyond the stop line, or, if the stop line is not for the time being visible, beyond the post or other structure on which is mounted the primary signal facing such traffic on the side of the carriageway on which vehicles approach the crossing;

(*d*) on any occasion when a vehicle is being used for fire brigade, ambulance or police purposes and the observance of the prohibitions conveyed by the steady amber and red lights (as specified in sub-paragraphs (*b*) and (*c*) above respectively) would be likely to hinder the use of the vehicle for the purpose in question, then sub-paragraphs (*b*) and (*c*) above shall not apply to that vehicle. In the circumstances described in the preceding part of this sub-paragraph, the steady amber light and the red light shall each convey the information that the vehicle may only proceed beyond the stop line or (as the case may be) the post or other structure if the driver—

(i) accords precedence to any pedestrian who is on that part of the carriageway which lies within the limits of the crossing or on a central reservation which lies between two crossings which do not form a system of staggered crossings; and

(ii) subject to sub-paragraph (i) above, does not proceed in such a manner or at such a time as is likely to cause danger to any other vehicle approaching or waiting at the crossing, or in such a manner as to compel the driver of any such vehicle to change its speed or course in order to avoid an accident; and

(*e*) the flashing amber light shall convey the information that vehicular traffic may proceed across the crossing but that every pedestrian if he is on the carriageway or a central reservation within the limits of that crossing (but not if he is on a central reservation which lies between two crossings which form a system of staggered crossings) before any part of a vehicle has entered those limits, has the right of precedence within those limits over that vehicle, and the requirement that the driver of a vehicle shall accord such precedence to any such pedestrian.

(2) Vehicular traffic passing the vehicular light signal in accordance with the foregoing provisions of this regulation shall proceed with due regard to the safety of other users of the road and subject to the direction of any police constable in uniform or traffic warden who may be engaged in the regulation of traffic.

9. Significance of pedestrian traffic signals

(1) The pedestrian traffic signal at a 'Pelican' crossing shall convey to pedestrians the warnings and information specified in the following paragraphs of this regulation.

(2) The pedestrian light signal shall convey to pedestrians the following warnings and information—

(*a*) the red light shall convey to a pedestrian the warning that he should not in the interests of safety use the crossing;

(*b*) the steady green light shall convey to a pedestrian the information that he may use the crossing and drivers of vehicles may not cause their vehicles to enter the limits of the crossing; and

(*c*) the flashing green light shall convey—

(i) to a pedestrian who is already on the crossing when the flashing green light is first shown the information that he may continue to use the crossing, and that if he is on the carriageway or on a central reservation within the limits of that crossing (but not if he is on a central reservation which lies between two crossings which form part of a system of staggered crossings) before any part of a vehicle has entered those limits he has the right of precedence within those limits over that vehicle; and

(ii) to a pedestrian who is not already on the crossing when the flashing green light is first shown the warning that he should not in the interests of safety start to cross the carriageway.

(3) When the word 'WAIT' shown by the indicator for pedestrians is illuminated it shall convey to a pedestrian the same warning as that conveyed by the red light shown by the pedestrian light signal, that is to say, that he should not in the interests of safety use the crossing.

(4) Any audible signal emitted by any device for emitting audible signals provided in conjunction with the steady green light for pedestrians, and any tactile signal made by any device for making tactile signals similarly provided, shall convey to a pedestrian the same information as that conveyed by the steady green light, that is to say, that he may use the crossing and drivers of vehicles may not cause their vehicle to enter the limits of the crossing.

10. Significance of additional traffic signs

The traffic signs referred to in regulation 6 shall convey the information, prohibitions or requirements mentioned in relation thereto in the captions to the diagrams in Schedule 1 to the Traffic Signs Regulations 1981 mentioned in that regulation.

11. Movement of traffic and precedence of pedestrians

Regulations 12 to 20 are made under section 25 of the 1984 Act and shall have effect with respect to the movement of traffic (including pedestrians) and the precedence of pedestrians over vehicles at and in the vicinity of a 'Pelican' crossing.

12. Prohibition on stopping in areas adjacent to 'Pelican' crossings

(1) For the purposes of this regulation and the next two following regulations, the expression 'vehicle' shall not include a pedal bicycle not having a sidecar attached thereto, whether additional means of propulsion by mechanical power are attached to the bicycle or not.

(2) Save as provided in regulations 13 and 14, and subject to regulation 15, the driver of a vehicle shall not cause the vehicle or any part thereof to stop in a 'Pelican' controlled area.

13. A vehicle shall not by regulation 12 be prevented from stopping in any length of road on any side thereof—

(*a*) if the driver has stopped for the purpose of complying with regulation 16, 17 or 19(*b*);

(*b*) if the driver is prevented from proceeding by circumstances beyond his control or it is necessary for him to stop in order to avoid an accident; or

(*c*) for so long as may be necessary to enable the vehicle, if it cannot be used for such purpose without stopping in that length of road, to be used for fire brigade, ambulance or police purposes or in connection with any building operation, demolition or excavation, the removal of any obstruction to traffic, the maintenance, improvement or reconstruction of that length of road, or the laying, erection, alteration, repair or cleaning in or near to that length of road of any sewer or of any main, pipe or apparatus for the supply of gas, water or electricity, or of any telecommunication apparatus kept installed for the purposes of a telecommunications code system or of any other telecommunication apparatus lawfully kept installed in any position.

14.—(1) A vehicle shall not by regulation 12 be prevented from stopping in a 'Pelican' controlled area—

(*a*) if the vehicle is stopped for the purpose of making a left or right turn; or

(*b*) if the vehicle is a public service vehicle being used—

(i) in the provision of a service which is a local service within the meaning of the Transport Act 1985; or

(ii) to carry passengers for hire or reward at separate fare otherwise than in the provision of a local service,

but excluding in each case any vehicle being used on an excursion or tour, and the vehicle is waiting, after having proceeded past the 'Pelican' crossing in relation to which the 'Pelican' controlled area is indicated, in order to take up or set down passengers.

(2) In sub-paragraph (*b*) of paragraph (1) of this regulation 'local service' and 'excursion or tour' have respectively the same meanings as in the Transport Act 1985.

15. Saving for crossings constituted in accordance with 1969 Regulations

In relation to any crossing which, immediately before the coming into operation of these Regulations, was constituted as a 'Pelican' crossing in accordance with the 1969 Regulations, for a period of two years commencing on the date these Regulations come into operation regulations 12, 13 and 14 shall not apply and regulation 9 of the 1969 Regulations shall, notwithstanding the repeal of those Regulations, continue to have effect but only for so long during that period as the crossing remains so constituted.

16. Prohibition against the proceeding of vehicles across a 'Pelican' crossing

When the vehicular traffic light signal is showing a red light, the driver of a vehicle shall not cause the vehicle or any part thereof to proceed beyond the stop line, or, if that line is not for the time being visible, beyond the post or other structure on which is mounted the primary signal facing the driver on the side of the carriageway on which vehicles approach the crossing.

17. Precedence of pedestrians over vehicles on a 'Pelican' crossing

When the vehicular traffic light signal at a 'Pelican' crossing is showing a flashing amber light, every pedestrian, if he is on the carriageway, or a central reservation within the limits of that crossing (but not if he is on a central reservation which lies between two crossings which form part of a system of staggered crossings) before any part of a vehicle has entered those limits, shall have precedence within those limits over that vehicle and the driver of a vehicle shall accord such precedence to any such pedestrian.

18. Prohibition against the waiting of vehicles and pedestrians on a 'Pelican' crossing

(1) The driver of a vehicle shall not cause the vehicle or any part thereof to stop within the limits of a 'Pelican' crossing unless either he is prevented from proceeding by circumstances beyond his control or it is necessary for him to stop in order to avoid an accident.

(2) No pedestrian shall remain on the carriageway within the limits of a 'Pelican' crossing longer than is necessary for the purpose of passing over the crossing with reasonable despatch.

19. Prohibition against overtaking at a 'Pelican' crossing

The driver of a vehicle while it or any part of it is in a 'Pelican' controlled area and it is proceeding towards the limits of a 'Pelican' crossing in relation to which the area is indicated (hereinafter referred to as 'the approaching vehicle') shall not cause that vehicle, or any part of it—

(*a*) to pass ahead of the foremost part of another moving motor vehicle being a vehicle proceeding in the same direction wholly or partly within that area; or

(*b*) subject to the next succeeding regulation, to pass ahead of the foremost part of a stationary vehicle on the same side of the crossing as the approaching vehicle, which stationary vehicle is stopped for the purpose of complying with regulation 16 or 17.

For the purposes of this regulation—

(i) the reference to another moving motor vehicle is, in a case where only one other motor vehicle is proceeding in the same direction in a 'Pelican' controlled area, a reference to that vehicle, and, in a case where more than one other motor vehicle is so proceeding, a reference to such one of those vehicles as is nearest to the limits of the crossing; and

(ii) the reference to a stationary vehicle is, in a case where only one other vehicle is stopped for the purpose of complying with regulation 16 or 17, a reference to that vehicle, and, in a case where more than one other vehicle is stopped for that purpose, a reference to such one of those vehicles as is nearest to the limits of the crossing.

20. Nothing in paragraph (*b*) of regulation 19 shall apply so as to prevent the approaching vehicle from passing ahead of the foremost part of a stationary vehicle within the meaning of that paragraph, if the stationary vehicle is stopped for the purpose of complying with regulation 16 or 17 in relation to a 'Pelican' crossing which is a separate crossing from the 'Pelican' crossing towards the limits of which the approaching vehicle is proceeding.

SCHEDULE 1

Regulation 2(1)

THE SIZE, COLOUR AND TYPE OF TRAFFIC SIGNS AT A 'PELICAN' CROSSING

PART I

1. Traffic signs

The traffic signs which are to be placed at or near a crossing for the purpose of constituting it a 'Pelican' crossing shall consist of a combination of—

(*a*) vehicular light signals;

(*b*) pedestrian light signals; and

(*c*) indicators for pedestrians,

of the size, colour and type prescribed by the following provisions of this Schedule, together with any additional traffic signs placed at or near the crossing pursuant to regulation 6.

2. Vehicular light signals

The vehicular light signals shall be as follows—

(*a*) three lights shall be used, one red, one amber, and one green;

(*b*) the lamps showing the aforesaid lights shall be arranged vertically, the lamp showing the red light being the uppermost and that showing the green light the lowermost;

(*c*) each lamp shall be separately illuminated and the effective diameter of the lens thereof shall be not less than 195 millimetres nor more than 220 millimetres;

(*d*) the height of the centre of the amber lens from the surface of the carriageway in the immediate vicinity shall, in the case of signals placed at the side of the carriageway or on a central reservation, be not less than 2.4 metres nor more than 4 metres and, in the case of signals placed elsewhere and over the carriageway, not less than 6.1 metres nor more than 9 metres;

(*e*) the centres of the lenses of adjacent lamps shall be not less than 305 millimetres nor more than 360 millimetres apart;

(*f*) the lamp showing the amber light shall be capable of showing a steady light or a flashing light such that it flashes at a rate of not less than 70 nor more than 90 flashes per minute; and

(*g*) no lettering or symbols shall be used upon the lens.

3. Pedestrian light signals

(1) The pedestrian light signals shall be of the size, colour and type shown in the diagrams in Part II of this Schedule.

(2) The height of the lower edge of the container enclosing the light signals from

the surface of the carriageway in the immediate vicinity shall be not less than 2.1 metres nor more than 2.6 metres.

(3) The said signals shall be so designed that—

(*a*) the red figure shown in the said diagrams can be internally illuminated by a steady light;

(*b*) the green figure shown in the said diagrams can be internally illuminated by a steady light or by a flashing light at a rate of not less than 70 nor more than 90 flashes per minute; and

(*c*) when one signal is illuminated the other signal is not illuminated.

(4) A device for emitting audible signals may be provided for use when the green figure is illuminated by a steady light.

4. Indicator for pedestrians

(1) The indicator for pedestrians shall be of the size, colour and type shown in the diagram in Part III of this Schedule.

(2) The indicator for pedestrians shall be so designed and constructed that 'WAIT' as shown on the diagram can be illuminated and that there is incorporated in the indicator a device, which may be a push button or pressure pad and which is hereinafter in this Schedule referred to as 'a push button', which can be used by pedestrians with the effect hereinafter described.

(3) The instruction for pedestrians shown in the diagram may be internally illuminated.

(4) A device for making tactile signals may be provided for use when the green figure shown in the diagram is illuminated by a steady light.

5. Sequence of signals

(1) The vehicular light signals and pedestrian light signals and the indicators for pedestrians when they are placed at or near any crossing shall be so designed and constructed that—

(*a*) before the signals and indicators are operated by the pressing of a push button or as described in paragraph 6 of this Schedule the vehicular light signal shows a steady green light, the pedestrian light signal shows a red light, the word 'WAIT' in the indicator for pedestrians is not illuminated, any device for making tactile signals is inactive, and any device for emitting audible signals is silent;

(*b*) when a push button is pressed—

(i) after the expiration of the vehicle period but before the vehicular light signals are showing a steady amber light, the signals and indicators, unless they are working as described in paragraph 6 of this Schedule, are caused to show lights in the sequences specified in descending order in column 1 in the case of vehicular light signals, in column 2 in the case of pedestrian light signals and in column 3 in the case of the indicators for pedestrians, of either Part IV or Part V of this Schedule;

(ii) when the vehicular light signals are showing a steady amber light or a red light when the signal to pedestrians shows a red or steady green light, there is no effect;

(iii) when the pedestrian light signals are showing a flashing green light, the word 'WAIT' in each of the indicators for pedestrians is illuminated immediately and the signals and indicators are caused to show lights in the sequence specified in sub-paragraph (i) of this paragraph at the end of the next vehicle period; and

(iv) after the pedestrian light signals have ceased to show a flashing green light and before the end of the next vehicle period, the word 'WAIT' in each of the indicators for pedestrians is illuminated immediately and the signals and indicators are caused to show lights in the sequence specified in sub-paragraph (i) of this paragraph at the end of the vehicle period;

(*c*) the periods during which lights are shown by the signals and the indicators, commence and terminate in relation to each other as shown in either Part IV or Part V of this Schedule as if each horizontal line therein represented one moment in time, subsequent moments occurring in descending order, but the distances between the horizontal lines do not represent the lengths of the periods during which the lights shown by the signals and the indicator are, or are not, lit.

(2) Where a device for emitting audible signals has been provided pursuant to paragraph 3(4) of this Schedule, it shall be so designed and constructed that a pulsed sound is emitted throughout every period when the pedestrian light signals are showing a steady green light, and at the same time the vehicular light signals are showing a red light, but only during such periods and at no other times, save that such a device need not operate during the hours of darkness.

(3) Where a device for making tactile signals has been provided pursuant to paragraph 4(4) of this Schedule, it shall be so designed and constructed that a regular movement perceptible to touch by pedestrians is made throughout every period when the pedestrian light signals are showing a steady green light, and at the same time the vehicular light signals are showing a red light, but only during such periods and at no other times.

(4) In this paragraph 'vehicle period' means such period as may be fixed from time to time in relation to a 'Pelican' crossing, which commences when the vehicular light signals cease to show a flashing amber light and during which the vehicular traffic light signals show a green light.

6. Operation by remote control

The vehicular light signals, pedestrian light signals, indicators for pedestrians, any device for making tactile signals, and any device for emitting audible signals, when they are placed at or near any crossing may also be so designed and constructed that they can by remote control be made to operate—

(*a*) as if a push button has been pressed; and

(*b*) so that the pressing of a push button has no effect, other than causing the word 'WAIT' in each of the indicators for the pedestrians to be illuminated, until normal operation is resumed.

PARTS II and III

* * *

PART IV

SEQUENCE OF OPERATION OF VEHICULAR AND PEDESTRIAN LIGHT SIGNALS AND INDICATOR FOR PEDESTRIANS (BUT NOT THE AUDIBLE SIGNALS)

Sequence of vehicular traffic light signals (1)	*Sequence of pedestrian signals*	
	Pedestrian light signals (2)	*Indicator for pedestrians* (3)
Green light	Red light	The word 'WAIT' is illuminated
Amber light		
Red light		
	Green light	The word 'WAIT' is not illuminated
Flashing amber light	Flashing green light	The word 'WAIT' is illuminated
	Red light	
Green light		

PART V

ALTERNATIVE SEQUENCE OF OPERATION OF VEHICULAR AND PEDESTRIAN LIGHT SIGNALS AND INDICATOR FOR PEDESTRIANS (BUT NOT THE AUDIBLE SIGNALS)

Sequence of vehicular traffic light signals (1)	*Sequence of pedestrian signals*	
	Pedestrian light signals (2)	*Indicator for pedestrians* (3)
Green light	Red light	The word 'WAIT' is illuminated
Amber light		
Red light		
	Green light	The word 'WAIT' is not illuminated
	Flashing green light	The word 'WAIT' is illuminated
Flashing amber light		
	Red light	
Green light		

Regulation 2(2)

SCHEDULE 2

THE MANNER OF INDICATING THE PRESENCE AND LIMITS OF A PELICAN CROSSING AND 'PELICAN' CONTROLLED AREA

1. General

In this Schedule, and except where otherwise stated, any reference to a numbered diagram is a reference to the diagram bearing that number in this Schedule.

2.—(1) Every crossing which is a 'Pelican' crossing on a road which is not a one-way street shall have its limits indicated, subject to the following provisions of this Schedule, by the pattern of studs on or in and lines on the carriageway in the manner shown—

(*a*) in diagram 1 where there is no central reservation;

(*b*) in diagram 2 where there is a central reservation, but the crossing does not form part of a system of staggered crossings; and

(*c*) in diagram 3 where the crossing forms part of a system of staggered crossings.

(2) Every crossing which is a 'Pelican' crossing on a road which is a one-way street shall have its limits indicated, subject to the following provisions of this Schedule, by the pattern of studs on or in and lines on the carriageway in the manner shown—

(*a*) in diagram 4 where there is no central reservation;

(*b*) in diagram 5 where there is a central reservation but the crossing does not form part of a system of staggered crossings; and

(*c*) in diagram 6 where the crossing forms part of a system of staggered crossings.

3. Manner of indicating the limits of the crossing

The limits of a 'Pelican' crossing shall be indicated by two lines of studs in the positions shown, and in accordance with the measurements in, the diagram corresponding to the type of crossing.

The two lines of studs indicating the limits of the crossing need not be at right angles to the edge of the carriageway, but shall form straight lines and shall as near as is reasonably practicable be parallel to each other.

5. Manner of indicating a 'Pelican' controlled area and provision as to placing the stop line

Subject to paragraph 8 of this Schedule, the presence and limits of a 'Pelican' controlled area shall be indicated by the pattern of lines placed in the positions shown, and in accordance with the measurements, in the diagram corresponding to the type of crossing, and in accordance with the provisions of paragraphs 6 and 7 of this Schedule.

6. Where the crossing is on a road which is not a one-way street the pattern of lines shall consist of—

(1) a stop line placed on the carriageway parallel to the nearer row of studs indicating the limits of the crossing and extending, in the manner indicated in the appropriate diagram, across the part of the carriageway used by vehicles approaching the crossing from the side on which the stop line is placed;

(2) two or more longitudinal white broken lines (hereinafter referred to as 'zig-zag lines') placed on the carriageway or, where the road is a dual-carriageway road, on each part of the carriageway, each zig-zag line containing not less than 8 nor more than 18 marks and extending away from the crossing in the manner indicated in the appropriate diagram;

(3) subject to sub-paragraph (4) of this paragraph, where a central reservation is provided the road marking shown in diagram 1040.1 in Schedule 2 to the Traffic Signs Regulations 1981 *[SI 1981 No 859]* may be placed on the carriageway between the zig-zag lines on the approaches to the central reservation;

(4) where a central reservation is provided connecting crossings which form part of a system of staggered crossings, the road markings mentioned in sub-paragraph (3) of this paragraph shall be placed on the carriageway in the manner indicated in diagram 3.

[Diagram 1040.1 in Sched 2 to the Traffic Signs Regulations 1981 is a sign on the carriageway (but not adjacent to either edge) indicating that traffic should not enter unless it is seen by the driver of the vehicle to be safe to do so.]

7. Where the crossing is on a road which is a one-way street the pattern of lines shall consist of:

(1) a stop line placed parallel to the nearer row of studs indicating the limits of the crossing and extending—

(*a*) in the case of a crossing of the type shown in diagram 4 or 5, from one edge of the carriageway to the other; and

(*b*) in the case of a crossing of the type shown in diagram 6, from the edge of the carriageway to the central reservation;

(2) two or more zig-zag lines placed on the carriageway, each containing not less than 8 and not more than 18 marks, and extending away from the crossing;

(3) subject to sub-paragraph (4) of this paragraph, where a central reservation is provided the road marking shown in diagram 1041 in Schedule 2 to the Traffic Signs Regulations 1981 may be placed on the carriageway between the zig-zag lines on the approaches to the central reservation; and

(4) where a central reservation is provided connecting crossings which form part of a system of staggered crossings, the road markings mentioned in sub-paragraph (3) of this paragraph shall be placed on the carriageway in the manner indicated in diagram 6.

[Diagram 1040 in Sched 2 to the Traffic Signs Regulations 1981 is a sign on the carriageway (adjacent to an edge) indicating that traffic should not enter unless it is seen by the driver of the vehicle to be safe to do so.]

8.—(1) Where the appropriate authority is satisfied in relation to a particular area of carriageway in the vicinity of a 'Pelican' crossing that by reason of the layout of, or character of, the roads in the vicinity of the crossing it would be impracticable to lay the pattern of lines as shown in the diagrams in, and in accordance with paragraphs 5 to 7 of this Schedule, any of the following variations as respects the pattern shall be permitted—

(*a*) the number of marks contained in each zig-zag line may be reduced from 8 to not less than 2; and

(*b*) a mark contained in a zig-zag line may be varied in length so as to extend for a distance not less than 1 metre and less than 2 metres, but where such a variation is made as respects a mark each other mark in each zig-zag line shall be of the same or substantially the same length as that mark, so however that the number of marks in each zig-zag line shall not be more than 8 nor less than 2.

(2) The angle of the stop line in relation to the nearer line of studs indicating the limits of a crossing may be varied, if the appropriate authority is satisfied that such variation is necessary having regard to the angle of the crossing in relation to the edge of the carriageway at the place where the crossing is situated.

(3) The maximum distance of 3 metres between the stop line and the nearer line of studs indicating the limits of the crossing shown in the diagrams in this Schedule may be increased to such greater distance, not in any case exceeding 10 metres, as the appropriate authority may decide.

(4) Where by reason of regulation 3(3) an area of carriageway in the vicinity of a 'Pelican' crossing is not constituted a 'Pelican' controlled area by the placing of a pattern of lines as provided in the foregoing provisions of this Schedule, a stop line shall nevertheless be placed on the carriageway as previously provided in this Schedule.

9. Colour and dimensions of road markings and studs

The road markings shown in the diagrams in this Schedule shall be white in colour, and may be illuminated by reflecting material.

10.—(1) The studs shown in the diagrams shall be either white, silver or light grey in colour and shall not be fitted with reflective lenses.

(2) The said studs shall be either circular in shape with a diameter of not more than 110 millimetres or less than 95 millimetres or square in shape with each side being not more than 110 millimetres or less than 95 millimetres.

(3) Any stud which is fixed or embedded in the carriageway shall not project more than 18 millimetres above the carriageway at its highest point nor more than 6 millimetres at its edges.

11. Where in any diagram in this Schedule a dimension or measurement is indicated in brackets against a dimension or measurement not indicated in brackets any dimension or measurement indicated in brackets may be treated as an alternative to the dimension or measurement not so indicated.

12. Supplementary

The foregoing provisions of this Schedule shall be regarded as having been complied with in the case of any pattern of studs or white lines if most of the studs or lengths of white lines comply notwithstanding that one or more studs or some of the lengths of white lines may not comply with those provisions by reason of discoloration, temporary removal, displacement or for some other reason so long as the general appearance of the pattern of studs or white lines is not thereby materially impaired.

[Diagrams 1 to 6 in Sched 2 are set out on pp 2/665–2/670]

Diagram 1

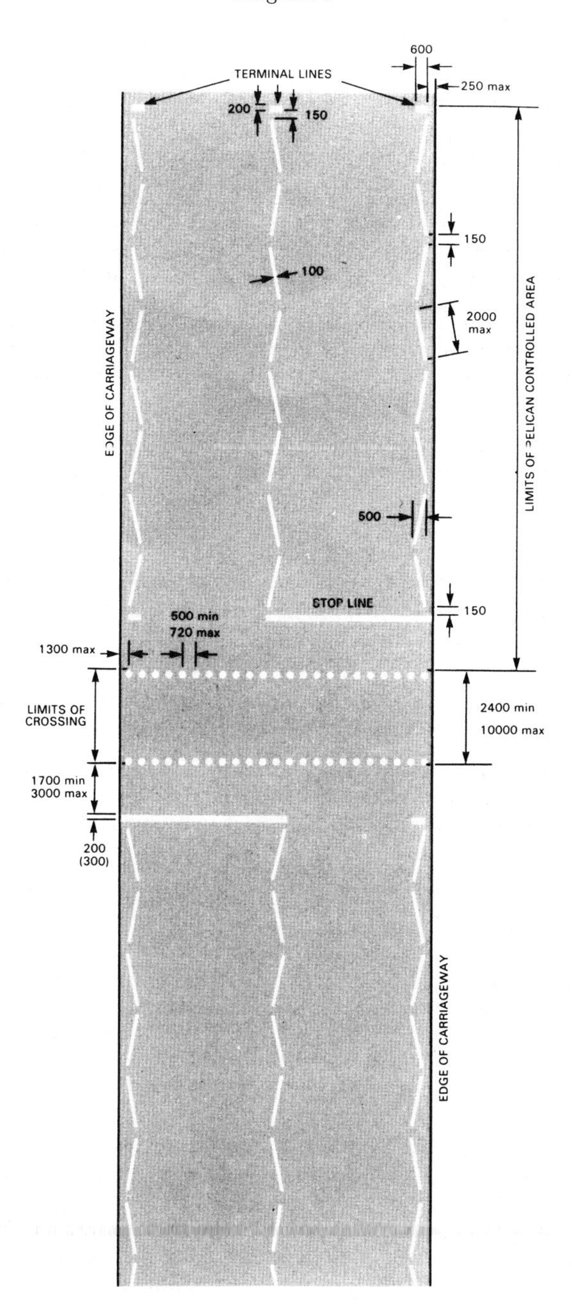

NOTE—Each zigzag line need not contain the same number of marks.
ALL DIMENSIONS IN MILLIMETRES.

Diagram 2

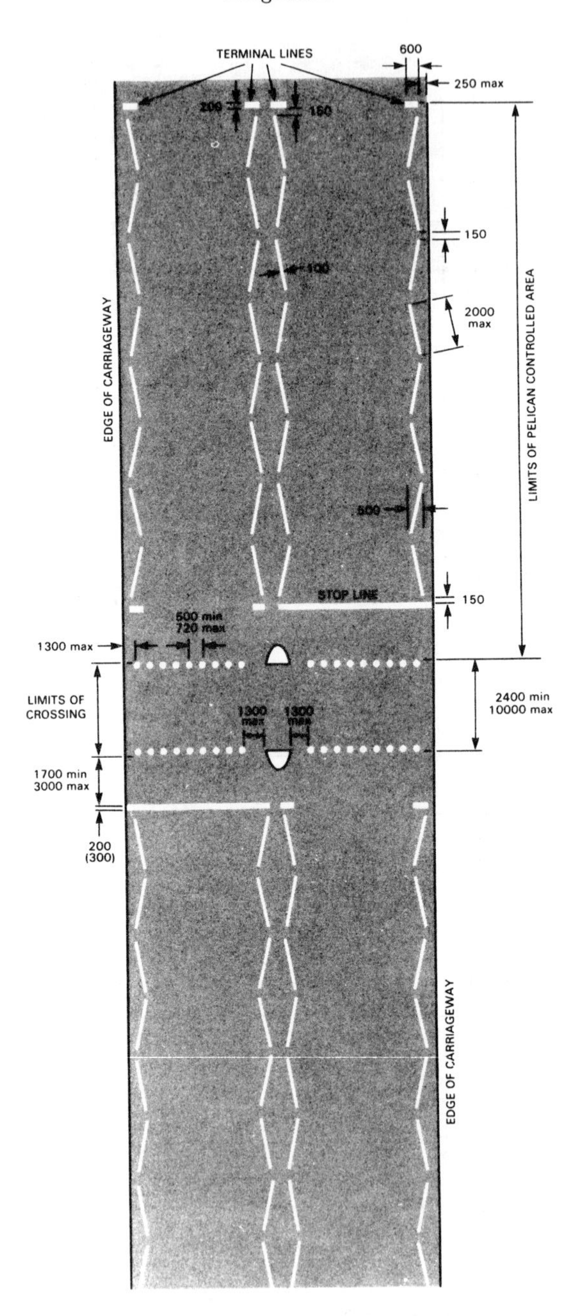

NOTE—Each zigzag line need not contain the same number of marks.
ALL DIMENSIONS IN MILLIMETRES.

Diagram 3

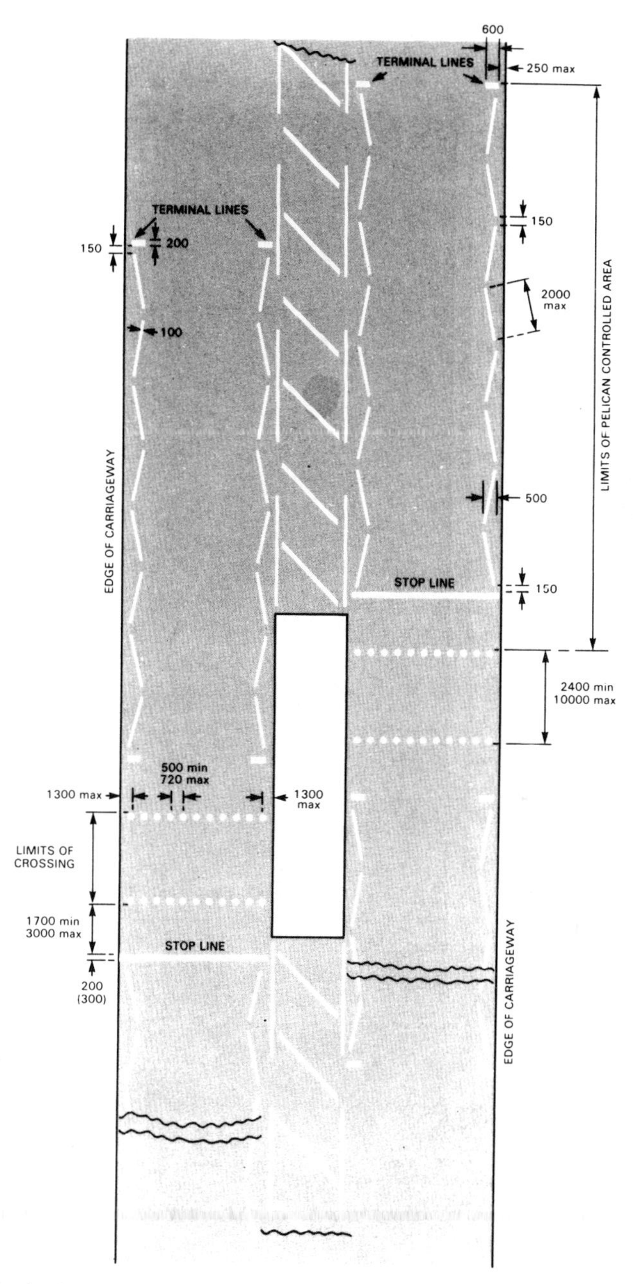

NOTE—Each zigzag line need not contain the same number of marks.
The stagger may be reversed as required.

ALL DIMENSIONS IN MILLIMETRES.

Diagram 4

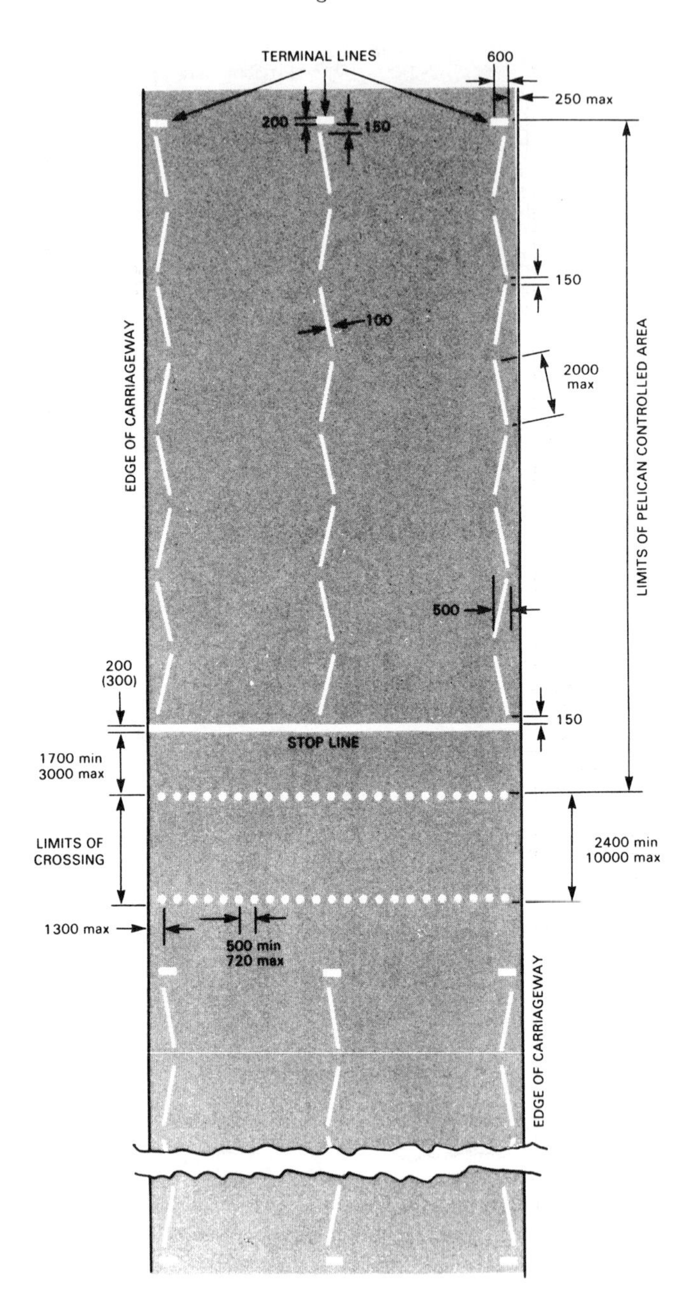

NOTE—Each zigzag line need not contain the same number of marks.
ALL DIMENSIONS IN MILLIMETRES.

Diagram 5

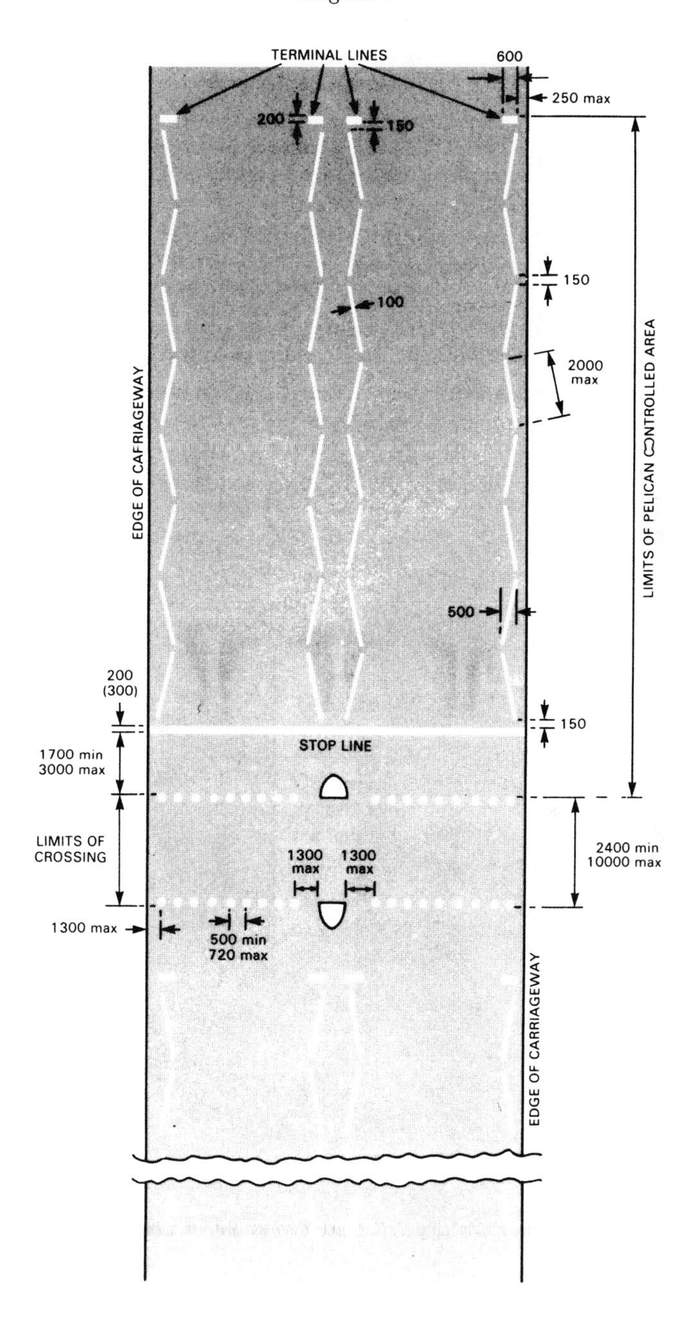

NOTE—Each zigzag line need not contain the same number of marks.
ALL DIMENSIONS IN MILLIMETRES

Diagram 6

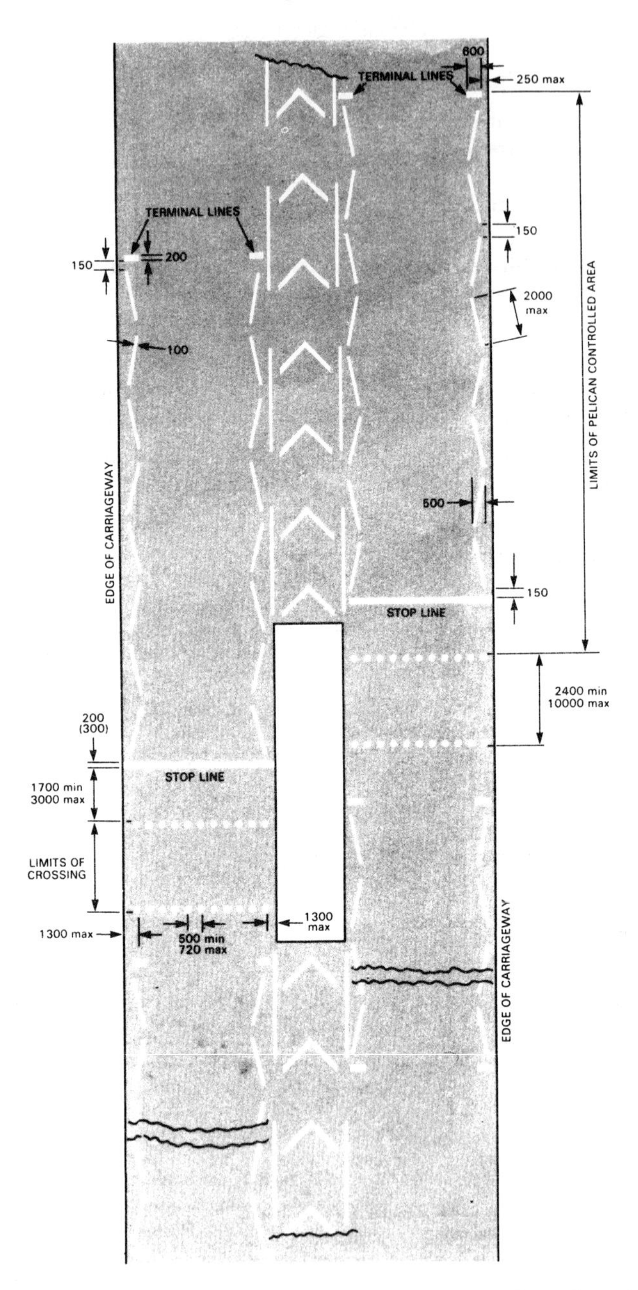

NOTE—Each zigzag line need not contain the same number of marks.
The stagger may be reversed as required.

ALL DIMENSIONS IN MILLIMETRES.

PART III

GENERAL DIRECTIONS

1. Citation

The Directions contained in this Part of this Instrument may be cited as the 'Pelican' Pedestrian Crossings General Directions 1987.

2. Number and manner of placing of vehicular light signals

(1) There shall be placed at a 'Pelican' crossing which is on a road which is not a one-way street and which is of the type specified in column 1 of Part 1 of the Table below, the vehicular light signals facing each direction of traffic specified in relation thereto in column 2 of Part I of the said Table.

(2) There shall be placed at a 'Pelican' crossing which is on a one-way street and which is of a type specified in column 1 of Part II of the said Table the vehicular light signals specified in relation thereto in column 2 of Part II of the said Table.

(3) The vehicular light signals referred to in paragraphs (1) and (2) shall be placed as primary signals or secondary signals as specified in column 2 of the said Table.

(4) One or more additional vehicular light signals may be placed either as a primary signal or as a secondary signal on the side of, or over, the carriageway or on any central reservation.

(5) Every vehicular light signal placed at a 'Pelican' crossing pursuant to the provisions of this direction shall face the stream of traffic which it is intended to control.

TABLE

PART I

PELICAN CROSSINGS ON ROADS WHICH ARE NOT ONE-WAY STREETS

1	2
Type of crossing	Vehicular light signals required facing each direction of traffic
Crossing on a road without a central reservation.	One primary signal on the side of the carriageway nearest to the direction of vehicular traffic and one secondary signal on the side of the carriageway furthest away from the direction of vehicular traffic.
Crossing on a road with a central reservation which does not form part of a system of staggered crossings.	One primary signal on the side of the carriageway nearest to the direction of vehicular traffic and one secondary signal on the central reservation.
Crossing which forms part of a system of staggered crossings.	One primary signal on the side of the carriageway nearest to the direction of vehicular traffic and one primary signal on the central reservation.

PART II

PELICAN CROSSINGS ON ROADS WHICH ARE ONE-WAY STREETS

1	2
Type of crossing	Vehicular light signals required
Crossing on a road without a central reservation.	One primary signal on each side of the carriageway.
Crossing on a road with a central reservation which does not form part of a system of staggered crossings.	One primary signal on each side of the carriageway and one secondary signal on the central reservation.
Crossing which forms part of a system of staggered crossings.	One primary signal on the side of the carriageway and one primary signal on the central reservation.

[The heading to Part II of the table is printed as corrected by the corrigendum dated March 1987.]

3. Number and manner of placing of pedestrian light signals and indicators for pedestrians

(1) At least one pedestrian light signal and at least one indicator for pedestrians shall be placed at each end of a 'Pelican' crossing.

(2) Where there is a central reservation in a crossing, one or more additional indicators for pedestrians shall be placed on the central reservation.

(3) Each pedestrian light signal at either end of the crossing shall be so placed as to be clearly visible to any person who is about to use the crossing at the other end of the crossing.

(4) Each indicator for pedestrians shall be so placed that the push button in the indicator is readily accessible to pedestrians who wish to press it.

4. Additional traffic signs

The traffic signs specified in diagrams 610 and 611 in Schedule 1 to the Traffic Signs Regulations 1981 shall be placed only on a central reservation in a crossing, or on a central reservation which lies between two crossings which form part of a system of staggered crossings.

[As to diagrams 610 and 611, see the note to reg 6, ante.]

5. Colouring of containers and posts

(1) The containers of the vehicular light signals and of the pedestrian light signals shall be coloured black and may be mounted with a backing board and if so mounted the backing board shall be coloured black and may have a white border not less than 45 millimetres nor more than 55 millimetres in width which may be of a reflective material.

(2) Where a vehicular light signal, a pedestrian light signal or an indicator for pedestrians is mounted on a post specially provided for the purpose, that part of the post which extends above ground level shall be coloured grey and may have one white

band not less than 140 millimetres nor more than 160 millimetres in depth, the lower edge of the band being not less than 1.5 metres nor more than 1.7 metres above the level of the surface of the ground in the immediate vicinity.

(3) Any box attached to a post or other structure on which pedestrian light signals or vehicular light signals are mounted and housing apparatus designed to control, or to monitor, or to control and monitor, the operation of such signals shall be coloured grey, yellow or black, or a combination of any of those colours.

6. Approval of mechanisms and sequence adjustments

(1) Vehicular light signals, pedestrian light signals and indicators for pedestrians may be placed at or near any 'Pelican' crossing only if the apparatus (including the content of all instructions stored in, or executable by, it) used to secure that the signals and indicators comply with the relevant provisions of the Regulations is of a type approved in writing by or on behalf of the Secretary of State.

(2) Such signals may be retained in place notwithstanding the subsequent withdrawal of any approval relating to any such apparatus.

7. Special Cases

Nothing in these Directions shall be taken to limit the power of the Secretary of State by any special direction to dispense with, add to or modify any of the requirements of the Directions in relation to any particular case.

The Prosecution of Offences Act 1985 (Specified Proceedings) Order 1985

(SI 1985 No 2010)

* * *

[The text of this order is printed as amended by:
the Prosecution of Offences Act 1985 (Specified Proceedings) (Amendment) Order 1988 (SI 1988 No 1121) (1 August 1988).
The amending order is referred to in the notes to the main order by its year and number. The date referred to above is the date on which the amending order came into force.]

2.—(1) Subject to paragraphs (2) and (3) below, proceedings for the offences mentioned in the Schedule to this Order are hereby specified for the purposes of section 3 of the Prosecution of Offences Act 1985 (which, amongst other things, places a duty on the Director of Public Prosecutions to take over the conduct of all criminal proceedings, other than specified proceedings, instituted on behalf of a police force).

(2) Where a summons has been issued in respect of an offence mentioned in the Schedule to this Order, proceedings for that offence cease to be specified when the summons is served on the accused unless the documents described in paragraphs (*a*) and (*b*) of section 12(1) of the Magistrates' Courts Act 1980 [*as amended*] (pleading guilty by post etc) are served upon the accused with the summons.

(3) Proceedings for an offence cease to be specified if at any time a magistrates' court begins to receive evidence in those proceedings, and for the purpose of this paragraph nothing read out before the court under section 12(4) of the Magistrates' Courts Act 1980 shall be regarded as evidence.

Article 2

SCHEDULE

OFFENCES PROCEEDINGS FOR WHICH ARE SPECIFIED BY ARTICLE 2(1)

1. Fixed penalty offences within the meaning of *[section 51(1) of the Road Traffic Offenders Act 1988]*.

2. The offence under section 8(1) of the Vehicles (Excise) Act 1971.

3. The offences under *[sections 17(2), 18(3), 24, 26(1) and (2), 29, 31, 42(1)(b), 47(1), 164(6) and (9), 165(3), 168 and 172(3) and (4) of the Road Traffic Act 1988]*.

4. All offences under the Road Traffic Regulations Act 1984 other than those under sections 35(5), 43(5) and (12), 47(3), 52(1), 108(3), 115(1) and (2), 116(1) and 129(3) and paragraph 6(3) of Schedule 12 or those mentioned in paragraph 1 above.

5. The offences arising by contravention of Regulations 3(9) (involving a pedal cycle) and 4(27), (28) and (30) of the Royal and other Parks and Gardens Regulations 1977 *[SI 1977 No 217]*.

[The Schedule is printed as amended by the Interpretation Act 1978, ss 17(2)(a) and 23(1); SI 1988 No 1121.

The provisions in the Acts referred to in the Schedule which are not set out in this work are: the Road Traffic Regulation Act 1984, s 35(5) (offence connected with misuse of apparatus for collecting off-street parking charges), s 43(5) (wrongful disclosure of information in connection with off-street parking in Greater London); s 43(12) (unlawful operation of off-street public parking place in Greater London), s 47(3) (interference etc with parking meter), s 52(1) (interference etc with parking devices etc), s 129(3) (failure to comply with order requiring attendance at inquiry etc), and Sched 12, para 6(3) (recklessly etc providing false information in response to fixed penalty notice).]

The Public Passenger Vehicles (Exemptions, and Appeals against Refusals to Issue Certificates or Remove Prohibitions) Regulations 1987

(SI 1987 No 1150)

1. Citation and commencement *[Omitted.]*

2. Interpretation

In these Regulations—

'the 1981 Act' means the Public Passenger Vehicles Act 1981 [*qv*];

'prohibition' means a prohibition under section 9(1) of the 1981 Act;

'public service vehicle examiner' has the same meaning as in sections 7 to 9 of the 1981 Act;

'referee' has the same meaning as in section 51(2) of the 1981 Act.

3. Exemptions from section 9(9) of the 1981 Act

(1) The following cases are prescribed for the purposes of section 9(9) of the 1981 Act (which makes it an offence to drive, or cause or permit to be driven, a public service vehicle or other large passenger vehicle in contravention of a prohibition)—

(*a*) the case of a vehicle being driven on a road solely for the purpose of submitting it by previous arrangement with a certifying officer or public service vehicle examiner at a specified time on a specified date for him to test the vehicle to ascertain whether or not he can remove a prohibition; and

(*b*) subject to paragraph (2) of this regulation, the case of a vehicle being driven on a road solely for the purpose of testing whether or not repairs which have been carried out as a result of a prohibition are likely to enable a certifying officer or public service vehicle examiner to remove the prohibition.

(2) The exemption given in paragraph (1)(*b*) of this regulation shall not apply to enable a vehicle to be driven on a road by a person other than a certifying officer or public service vehicle examiner at a distance greater than three miles, measured in a straight line, from the place where the repairs have been carried out.

4. Application of regulations 5 and 6 *[Omitted.]*

5. Prescribed time for appeal *[Omitted.]*

6. Prescribed manner of appeal *[Omitted.]*

7. Revocation *[Omitted.]*

The Public Service Vehicles (Carrying Capacity) Regulations 1984

(SI 1984 No 1406)

1. Commencement and citation *[Omitted.]*

2. Revocation *[Omitted.]*

3. Interpretation

(1) In these Regulations—

'the Act' means the Public Passenger Vehicles Act 1981 [*qv*];

'certificate of conformity' means a certificate issued in pursuance of section 10(2) of the Act;

'certificate of initial fitness' has the same meaning as in section 6(1) of the Act;

'certifying officer' has the same meaning as in section 7(1) of the Act;

'crew seat', 'deck', 'double-decked vehicle', 'gangway' and 'half-decked vehicle' have the meanings given to those expressions in Regulation 3(1) of the Public Service Vehicles (Conditions of Fitness, Equipment, Use and Certification) Regulations 1981 *[SI 1981 No 257, qv]*; and

'vehicle' means a public service vehicle to which section 1(1)(*a*) of the Act applies.

(2) Unless the context otherwise requires, any reference in these Regulations to—

(*a*) a numbered Regulation is a reference to the Regulation of these Regulations bearing that number;

(*b*) a numbered paragraph is a reference to the paragraph bearing that number in the Regulation in which the reference appears.

4. Maximum seating capacity *[Omitted.]*

5. Carriage of seated passengers

(1) Save as provided in paragraph (2), no person shall drive, or cause or permit to be driven, on a road a vehicle if the number of seated passengers exceeds the number of seats available for passengers.

(2) For the purposes of paragraph (1)—

(*a*) a child under 5 years of age who is not occupying a seat does not count as a passenger; and

(*b*) (i) until 1st September 1985 three seated children each of whom is under 15 years of age shall count as two passengers, and

(ii) on and after 1st September 1985 three seated children each of whom is under 14 years of age shall count as two passengers.

(3) For the purposes of paragraph (2)(*b*)(i) a child whose fifteenth birthday occurs during a term of a school which he attends shall be deemed to be under 15 years of age for the whole of that term. For the purposes of paragraph (2)(*b*)(ii) a child shall be

deemed to be under 14 years of age until the last day of August next following his fourteenth birthday.

6. Maximum standing capacity

(1) Save as provided in paragraph (2), the maximum standing capacity of a vehicle is—

(*a*) in a case where on or after 1st April 1981 there is issued in respect of the vehicle a certificate of initial fitness or a certificate of conformity, either—

(i) the number of standing passengers specified in such certificate, or

(ii) such greater or lesser number than that so specified as is authorised by a certifying officer either pursuant to a notification under Regulation 9 or otherwise;

(*b*) in a case where no certificate of a kind mentioned in sub-paragraph (*a*) is issued on or after 1st April 1981, either—

(i) one third of the number of passengers for which the vehicle, or, in the case of a double-deck vehicle, the lower deck, has seating capacity, or 8, whichever is the less; or

(ii) such greater or lesser number than that mentioned in sub-paragraph (i) as is authorised by a certifying officer either pursuant to a notification under Regulation 9 or otherwise.

(2) The maximum standing capacity of—

(*a*) a vehicle with a seating capacity for less than 13 passengers,

(*b*) a vehicle with a gangway any part of the height of which is less than 1.77 metres, and

(*c*) a half-decked vehicle

is nil.

7. Carriage of standing passengers

(1) No person shall drive, or cause or permit to be driven, on a road a vehicle if the number of standing passengers exceeds the maximum specified in relation to that vehicle in Regulation 6.

(2) No person shall stand on—

(*a*) the upper deck or on any step leading to the upper deck of any double-decked vehicle,

(*b*) any part of a gangway of a vehicle forward of the rearmost part of the driver's seat; or

(*c*) any part of a vehicle in which the operator has indicated by a notice, the letters on which are at least 10 millimetres tall and in a colour contrasting with the colour of their background, that no standing shall occur.

8. Markings on vehicles *[Omitted.]*

9. Notification of increase of seating or standing capacity *[Omitted.]*

10. Forms of certificate *[Omitted.]*

11. Exemptions

Nothing in these Regulations applies to a vehicle to which Part III of the Road Transport (International Passenger Services) Regulations 1980 *[SI 1980 No 1459]* or the Road Transport (Northern Ireland Passenger Services) Regulations 1980 *[SI 1980 No 1460]* applies.

[The Road Transport (International Passenger Services) Regulations 1980 were revoked and replaced by the Road Transport (International Passenger Services) Regulations 1984 (SI 1984 No 748) (qv) before these regulations were made.]

12. Appeals *[Omitted.]*

SCHEDULE

[Revocations—omitted.]

The Public Service Vehicles (Conditions of Fitness, Equipment, Use and Certification) Regulations 1981

(SI 1981 No 257)

[The text of these regulations is printed as amended by:

the Public Service Vehicles (Conditions of Fitness, Equipment, Use and Certification) (Amendment) Regulations 1982 (SI 1982 No 20) (22 February 1982);

the Public Service Vehicles (Conditions of Fitness, Equipment, Use and Certification) (Amendment) (No 2) Regulations 1982 (SI 1982 No 1058) (2 September 1982);

the Public Service Vehicles (Conditions of Fitness, Equipment, Use and Certification) (Amendment) (No 3) Regulations 1982 (SI 1982 No 1482) (22 November 1982); and

the Public Service Vehicles (Conditions of Fitness, Equipment, Use and Certification) (Amendment) (No 2) Regulations 1986 (SI 1986 No 1812) (26 November 1986).

The amending regulations are referred to in the notes to the main regulations only by their years and numbers. The dates referred to above are the dates on which the regulations came into force.

The main regulations have also been amended by the Public Service Vehicles (Conditions of Fitness, Equipment, Use and Certification) (Amendment) Regulations 1984 (SI 1984 No 1763), the Public Service Vehicles (Conditions of Fitness, Equipment, Use and Certification) (Amendment) Regulations 1986 (SI 1986 No 370), and the Public Service Vehicles (Conditions of Fitness, Equipment, Use and Certification) (Amendment) Regulations 1988 (SI 1988 No 340), but these do not affect the text of any regulation printed in this work.]

Note. As to the disapplication of the provisions of these regulations in respect of certain vehicles, see the Road Transport (International Passenger Services) Regulations 1984 (SI 1984 No 748), reg 23, below.

ARRANGEMENT OF REGULATIONS

PART I

Preliminary

PART II

Regulations Relating to the Conditions as to Fitness of Public Service Vehicles

PART III

REGULATIONS RELATING TO THE EQUIPMENT OF PUBLIC SERVICE VEHICLES

PART IV

REGULATIONS RELATING TO THE USE OF PUBLIC SERVICE VEHICLES

* * *

SCHEDULES

Schedule

1. Commencement and citation *[Omitted.]*

2. Revocation *[Omitted.]*

3. Interpretation

(1) In these Regulations, unless the context otherwise requires, the following exceptions have the meanings hereby respectively assigned to them:—

'the Act' means the [Public Passenger Vehicles Act 1981];

'articulated bus' means a passenger vehicle so constructed that—

(*a*) it can be divided into two parts, both of which are vehicles and one of which is a motor vehicle, but cannot be so divided without the use of facilities normally available only at a workshop; and

(*b*) passengers carried by it when not so divided can at all times pass from either part to the other;

'certificate of conformity' means a certificate issued by the Minister in pursuance of [section 10(2)] of the Act;

'certificate of initial fitness' has the same meaning as in [section 6(1)] of the . . . Act . . .

'the Commissioners' means the traffic commissioners for any traffic area constituted for the purposes of [Part I] of the Act;

['crew seat' means a seat fitted to a vehicle and intended for use by crew (other than the driver), including any arm rests and foot rest with which the vehicle is fitted in relation to the seat, and which complies with the requirements specified in Regulation 28A;]

'deck' means a floor or platform upon which seats are provided for the accommodation of passengers;

'double-decked vehicle' means a vehicle having two decks one of which is wholly or partly above the other and each deck of which is provided with a gangway serving seats on that deck only;

'ECE Regulation 36' means Regulation No 36 (uniform provisions concerning the construction of public service vehicles) which entered into force on 1st March 1976, annexed to the Agreement concerning the adoption of uniform conditions of approval and reciprocal recognition of approval for motor vehicle equipment and parts concluded at Geneva on 20th March 1958 [*Cmnd 2535*] as amended [*Cmnd 3562*], to which the United Kingdom is a party [*instrument of ratification deposited on 15 January 1961*];

'emergency exit' means an exit which is provided for use only in case of emergency;

'entrance' means any aperture or space provided to enable passengers to board the vehicle;

'exit' means any aperture or space provided to enable passengers to leave the vehicle;

'gangway' means the space provided for obtaining access from any entrance to the passengers' seats or from any such seat to an exit other than an emergency exit but does not include a staircase or any space in front of a seat or row of seats which is required only for the use of passengers occupying that seat or that row of seats;

'half-decked vehicle' means any vehicle not being a single-decked vehicle or a double-decked vehicle;

['minibus' means a motor vehicle which is constructed or adapted to carry more than 8 but not more than 16 seated passengers in addition to the driver;]

'permanent top' means any covering of a vehicle other than a hood made of canvas or other flexible material which is capable of being readily folded back so that no portion of such hood or any fixed structure of the roof remains vertically above any part of any seat of the vehicle, or, in the case of a double-decked vehicle, of any seat on the upper deck of the vehicle;

'registered' in relation to a vehicle, means registered under the Roads Act 1920 or, as the case may be, the Vehicles (Excise) Act 1949, the Vehicles (Excise) Act 1962 or the Vehicles (Excise) Act 1971 and references to a vehicle being registered are references to the date on which it was first so registered;

'safety glass', 'safety glazing' and 'specified safety glass' have the same meanings as are respectively assigned to them in [Regulation 32(13)] of the Road Vehicles (Construction and Use) Regulations 1986] *[SI 1986 No 1078, qv]*;

'single-decked vehicle' means a vehicle on which no part of a deck or gangway is placed vertically above another deck or gangway;

'type approval certificate' means a certificate issued by the Minister in pursuance of [section 10(1)] of the Act;

'vehicle' means a public service vehicle within [section 1(1)] of the . . . Act . . . ; and

'vehicle in the service of a visiting force or headquarters' has the same meaning as in Article 8(6) of the Visiting Forces and International Headquarters (Application of Law) Order 1965 [*SI 1965 No 1536*].

(2) For the purpose of these Regulations, the date when a motor vehicle is first used shall be taken to be such date as is the earlier of the undermentioned relevant dates applicable to that vehicle, that is to say—

(*a*) in the case of a vehicle registered under the Roads Act 1920, the Vehicles (Excise) Act 1949, the Vehicles (Excise) Act 1962 or the Vehicles (Excise) Act 1971 the relevant date is the date on which it was first so registered; and

(*b*) in each of the following cases, that is to say—

(i) in the case of a vehicle which is being or has been used under a trade licence within the meaning of section 16(1) of the Vehicles (Excise) Act 1971 (otherwise than for the purposes of demonstration or testing or of being delivered from premises of the manufacturer by whom it was made, or of a distributor of vehicles or dealer in vehicles to premises of a distributor of vehicles, dealer in vehicles or purchaser thereof, or to premises of a person obtaining possession thereof under a hiring agreement or hire purchase agreement);

(ii) in the case of a vehicle belonging, or which has belonged, to the Crown which is or was used or appropriated for use for naval, military or air force purposes;

(iii) in the case of a vehicle belonging, to which has belonged, to a visiting force or a headquarters within the meaning of Article 3 of the Visiting Forces and International Headquarters (Application of Law) Order 1965;

(iv) in the case of a vehicle which has been used on roads outside Great Britain and which has been imported into Great Britain; and

(v) in the case of a vehicle which has been used otherwise than on roads after being sold or supplied by retail and before being registered,

the relevant date is the date of manufacture of the vehicle.

In case (v) above 'sold or supplied by retail' means sold or supplied otherwise than to a person acquiring the vehicle solely for the purpose of resale or re-supply for valuable consideration.

(3) Unless the context otherwise requires, any reference in these Regulations—

(*a*) to a numbered Regulation or Schedule is a reference to the Regulation or Schedule bearing that number in these Regulations, and (*b*) to a numbered paragraph is to the paragraph bearing that number in the Regulation in which the reference occurs.

(4) The provisions of the Regulations in Part IV of these Regulations are in addition to, and not in derogation of, the provisions of any other Regulations made or having effect as if made under [section 41 of the Road Traffic Act 1988].

[Regulation 3 is printed as amended by the Interpretation Act 1978, ss 17(2)(a) and 23(1); SI 1982 No 1058; SI 1986 No 1812.

In relation to the definition of 'the Commissioners', it should be noted that since the substitution of ss 4 and 5 of the Public Passenger Vehicles Act 1981 by the Transport Act 1985, s 3, there has been only one Commissioner for each traffic area.]

[4. Exemptions—

(1) Part IV of these Regulations does not apply to any vehicle in the public service of the Crown or in the service of a visiting force or headquarters.

(2) Parts III and IV of these Regulations do not apply to a motor vehicle belonging to a local education authority and which is from time to time used by that authority to provide free school transport whether the vehicle is being used wholly or partly to provide such transport or to provide a local bus service.

[(2A) Notwithstanding regulation 5, regulations 6 to 33, 35 to 44 and 45A shall not apply to a minibus which either complies with, or is required to comply with, or is exempted from the requirements specified in regulations 41 to 43 of the Road Vehicles (Construction and Use) Regulations 1986 for a minibus first used within the meaning of those Regulations on or after 1st April 1988.]

(3) Regulation 43 does not apply to a motor vehicle not belonging to a local education authority at any time when that vehicle is being used by that authority to provide free school transport, and to carry as the only fare-paying passengers pupils other than those for whom free school transport is provided.

(4) In this Regulation:—

(*a*) 'free school transport' has the meaning given by section 46(3) of the Public Passenger Vehicles Act 1981 as regards England and Wales;

(*b*) 'pupil' has the meaning given by section 114(1) of the Education Act 1944 as regards England and Wales; and

(*c*) *[Applies to Scotland.]*]

[Regulation 4 is printed as substituted by SI 1982 No 20 and as amended by SI 1986 No 1812.

Words relating expressly and exclusively to Scotland have been omitted from subs (4)(a) and (b).

'Pupil' is defined in the Education Act 1944, s 114(1) (as amended by the Education Act 1980, s 24(3)), as a person of any age for whom education is required to be provided under that Act, and the term includes a junior pupil who has not attained the age of five years. The term 'junior pupil' is defined by s 114(1) as a child who has not attained the age of twelve years.]

PART II

Regulations Relating to the Conditions as to Fitness of Public Service Vehicles

5. Conditions of fitness *[Omitted.]*

6. Stability

(1) The stability of a vehicle shall be such that—

(*a*) in the case of a double-decked vehicle, the point at which overturning occurs would not be passed if, when the vehicle is complete, fully equipped for service and loaded with weights placed in the correct relative positions to represent the driver, a full complement of passengers on the upper deck only and a conductor (if carried), the surface on which the vehicle stands were tilted to either side to an angle of 28 degrees from the horizontal; and

(*b*) in the case of a single-decked vehicle and of a half-decked vehicle, the point at which overturning occurs would not be passed if, when the vehicle is complete, fully equipped for service and loaded with weights placed in the correct relative positions to represent [a full complement of passengers, a driver, any crew for whom a crew seat is provided, and any conductor intended to be carried on the vehicle otherwise than in a crew seat], the surface on which the vehicle stands were tilted to either side to an angle of 35 degrees from the horizontal.

(2) For the purpose of ascertaining whether the requirements of paragraph (1) have been complied with, the height of any stop used to prevent a wheel of the vehicle from slipping sideways shall not be greater than two-thirds of the distance between the surface upon which the vehicle stands before it is tilted and that part of the rim of that wheel which is nearest to that surface when the vehicle is loaded in accordance with the said requirements.

(3) For the purpose of this Regulation 63.5 kilograms shall be deemed to represent the weight of one person.

[Regulation 6 is printed as amended by SI 1982 No 1058.]

7–15. *[Omitted.]*

16. Artificial lighting

Subject to paragraph 4 of Schedule 2, adequate internal lighting shall be provided in every vehicle for the illumination—

(*a*) of each deck having a permanent top; and

(*b*) of any step or platform forming part of any entrance or exit other than an emergency exit;

and all lighting circuits shall be so arranged that an electrical failure of any lighting sub-circuit shall not be capable of extinguishing all the lights on any deck and at least one lamp shall be provided as near as practicable to the top of every staircase leading to an upper deck not having a permanent top.

17. Electrical equipment *[Omitted.]*

18. Body *[Omitted.]*

19. Height of sides of body *[Omitted.]*

20. Steps, platforms and stairs *[Omitted.]*

21. Number, position and size of entrances and exits

(1) For the purposes of this Regulation and Regulations 13, 22, 23, 24, 25 and 26—

(*a*) 'primary emergency exit' means an emergency exit being an exit provided in a single-decked vehicle or in the lower deck of a double-decked vehicle which, subject to paragraph 8 of Schedule 2—

(i) is situated so that passengers can step directly from the passage referred to in Regulation 26(1)(*g*) to the outside of the vehicle,

(ii) has a clear height—

(A) in the case of a vehicle which has a seating capacity not exceeding 14 passengers, of not less than 1.21 metres, and

(B) in the case of any other vehicle, of not less than 1.37 metres,

(iii) has a width of not less than 530 millimetres;

(*b*) 'secondary emergency exit' means an emergency exit of which the dimensions are not less than 910 millimetres by 530 millimetres and which does not satisfy all the requirements of a primary emergency exit and which is not in the roof of a vehicle;

(*c*) neither of the foregoing definitions shall apply in relation to an emergency exit as required by paragraphs (7) and (8) but the exit so required shall be of dimensions not less than 1.52 metres by 455 millimetres;

(*d*) references to the seating capacity of a vehicle shall, in the case of a double-decked vehicle, be treated as references to the seating capacity of its lower deck;

(*e*) references to the distance between the centres or between the nearest points of the openings of two exits in a vehicle are references to the distance between lines drawn at right-angles to the longitudinal axis of the vehicle and passing respectively through the centres or, as the case may be, the nearest points of the openings of the exists at gangway level; and

(*f*) the reference to the distance between the centre of an exit placed at the front end of a vehicle and the foremost part of the vehicle is a reference to the distance between lines drawn at right-angles to the longitudinal axis of the vehicle and passing through the centre of that exit and the said foremost part and the reference to the distance between the centre of an exit placed at the rear end of a vehicle and the rearmost part of the vehicle is a reference to the distance between lines drawn as aforesaid and passing through the centre of that exit and the said rearmost part.

(2) In this Regulation—

(*a*) 'pre-October 1981 vehicle' means a vehicle manufactured before 1st October 1981 or first used before 1st April 1982; and

(*b*) 'post-October 1981 vehicle' means a vehicle manufactured on or after 1st October 1981 and first used on or after 1st April 1982.

(3) Subject to paragraph 8 of Schedule 2, the following provisions of this Regulation shall apply with respect to the number and position of entrances and exits which shall be provided in a vehicle but a vehicle shall not be treated as failing to comply with any of those provisions by reason only that a number of exits is provided in a vehicle in excess of the number specified in relation to it by any provision of this Regulation.

(4) Subject to paragraphs (5) and (11), a vehicle which has a seating capacity for not more than 45 passengers shall be provided with two exits so placed as not to be on the same side of the vehicle, and

(*a*) in the case of a pre-October 1981 vehicle, one of which may be a primary emergency exit but neither of which shall be a secondary emergency exit;

(*b*) in the case of a post-October 1981 vehicle, one of which shall be a primary emergency exit and the other of which shall have dimensions which are not less than those specified in paragraph (1)(*a*) above in relation to a primary emergency exit;

Provided that this paragraph shall not apply in the case of a vehicle which has a seating capacity—

(i) exceeding 23 passengers and which is provided with an exit by virtue of its having a platform of a type described in Regulation 20(*a*) which communicates with a deck (being in the case of a double-decked vehicle, the lower deck) by means of a doorless opening and has a doorless opening on the nearside of the vehicle continuous with another such opening at the rear of the vehicle, these openings serving together as a means of entrance to or exit from the vehicle, and

(ii) not exceeding 12 passengers and of which the fuel tank is not placed behind the rear wheels if one exit of which, in the case of a post-October 1981 vehicle, the dimensions are not less than 1.21 metres in height by 530 millimetres in width is provided and is placed at the rear of the vehicle.

(5) Where the exits provided in accordance with paragraph (4) are so placed that the distance between their centres is—

(*a*) in the case of a vehicle first used before 1st January 1974 which has a seating capacity exceeding 30 passengers, less than 3.05 metres;

(*b*) in the case of a vehicle first used on or after 1st January 1974 which has a seating capacity exceeding 23 passengers, less than 3.05 metres;

(*c*) in the case of a vehicle first used on or after 1st January 1974 which has a seating capacity exceeding 14 but not exceeding 23 passengers, less than 2.44 metres,

a primary or secondary emergency exit shall be provided and placed so that there is a distance between the nearest points of the openings of that exit and one of the two exits mentioned in paragraph (4) of—

(i) in the cases mentioned in sub-paragraphs (*a*) and (*b*) above, not less than 3.05 metres, and

(ii) in the case mentioned in sub-paragraph (*c*) above, not less than 2.44 metres.

(6) Subject to paragraph (11), a vehicle which has a seating capacity exceeding 45 passengers shall be provided with three exits in respect of which the following provisions shall apply:—

(*a*) in the case of a pre-October 1981 vehicle one of the exits, but not more than one, may be a secondary emergency exit, and in the case of a post-October 1981 vehicle one of the exits shall be a primary emergency exit and any other exit (not being a secondary emergency exit) shall have dimensions not less than those specified in paragraph (1)(*a*) above in relation to primary emergency exits;

(*b*) two of the exits (neither being a secondary emergency exit) shall be so placed as not to be on the same side of the vehicle;

(*c*) where two exits are placed on the same side of the vehicle, the distance between their centres shall not be less than 3.05 metres; and

(*d*) one of the exits (not being a secondary emergency exit) shall be placed at the front end of the vehicle so that the distance between its centre and the foremost part of the vehicle is not more than 3.05 metres and another of the exits (not being a secondary emergency exit) shall be placed at the rear end of the vehicle so that the distance between its centre and the rearmost part of the vehicle is not more than 3.05 metres:

Provided that—

(i) in the case of a vehicle registered on or after 28th October 1964 and before 19th June 1968 the reference in sub-paragraph (*c*) above to 3.05 metres shall be replaced by a reference to 4.75 metres and sub paragraph (*d*) shall not apply, and

(ii) in the case of any other vehicle first used before 1st January 1974 sub-paragraph (*d*) above shall apply with the omission of the words '(not being a secondary emergency exit)' in both places where they occur.

(7) In the case of a half-decked vehicle an emergency exit shall be provided in the roof of the vehicle so placed that the transverse centre line of that exit lies within 610 millimetres of the mid-point between the front edges of the foremost and of the rear-most passenger seats in the vehicle.

(8) Where, in the case of a double-decked vehicle which has a permanent top, access to the upper-deck is obtained by means of an enclosed staircase, an emergency exit shall be provided on that deck and placed otherwise than on the nearside of the vehicle.

(9) Every entrance provided in a vehicle shall be placed on the nearside of the vehicle, but one or more entrances may be provided on the offside of the vehicle if—

(*a*) as respects any entrance so provided it is not also an exit provided in accordance with any of the foregoing provisions in this Regulation;

(*b*) every such entrance is fitted with a door which can be controlled only by the driver while sitting in his seat; and

(*c*) the device available to the driver for opening or closing that door is a separate and readily distinguishable device from that available to the driver for opening or closing any door fitted to the nearside of the vehicle:

Provided that this paragraph shall not apply in the case of any such vehicle as is mentioned in the proviso to paragraph (4).

(10) A grab handle shall be fitted to every entrance and exit (other than an emergency exit) to assist passengers to board or alight from the vehicle.

(11) In the case of a vehicle—

(*a*) being a post-October 1981 vehicle,

(*b*) having a seating capacity for more than 16 passengers, and

(*c*) being a single-decked vehicle or a half-decked vehicle,

there shall be at least one emergency exit which complies with the requirements specified in paragraph (12) and which is either—

(i) in the front face of the vehicle, or

(ii) in the rear face of the vehicle, or

(iii) in the roof of the vehicle.

(12) The requirements referred to in paragraph (11) are, in respect of each exit therein referred to, as follows:—

(*a*) the dimensions of the aperture shall be such that it has a total area of not less than 4,000 square centimetres and shall include a rectangular area the dimensions of which are not less than 70 centimetres by 50 centimetres;

(*b*) the exit shall be so constructed that it can be opened by means available to persons inside the vehicle, and it may be so constructed that it can be opened also be persons outside the vehicle; and

(*c*) the exit shall be—

(i) ejectable, or

(ii) constructed of specified safety glass which can be readily broken by the application of reasonable force so as to afford a clear aperture having the dimensions referred to in sub-paragraph (*a*) above, and provided in a position adjacent to the exit with a suitable means, readily available to persons inside the vehicle, for breaking the glass, or

(iii) except where the exit is an exit in the roof, hinged.

22. Width of entrances and exits *[Omitted.]*

23. Doors

(1) Subject to paragraph 9 of Schedule 2 and paragraph (4) the following conditions shall be complied with in the case of every vehicle:—

(*a*) means shall be provided for holding every entrance and exit door securely in the closed position and, where any such door is capable of remaining open when the vehicle is in motion or of being accidentally closed by the movement of the vehicle, means shall also be provided for holding that door securely in the open position;

(*b*) subject to paragraph (2), every entrance and exit door shall be provided with at least two devices (of which one may be a device provided for use in circumstances of normal operation only by a person authorised by the owner of the vehicle, and one, but not more than one, shall be provided on the outside of the vehicle) being in each case a device for operating the means for holding the door securely in the closed position, and every such device shall be so designed that a single movement of it will allow that door to be readily opened;

(*c*) the method of operation of any device mentioned in condition (*b*) above, the position of such a device where it is not placed on the door and the direction and points of application of any manual effort required to open any door, shall be clearly indicated; and there shall, in the case of a power-operated door, also be an indication that the said device may not be used by passengers except in an emergency;

(*d*) where any device mentioned in condition (*b*) above is not placed on the door, it shall be placed so as to be readily associated with that door and so that a person of normal height may conveniently operate the device without risk of being injured by movement of the door;

(*e*) in the case of every entrance and exit, any device mentioned in condition (*b*) above, other than such a device provided on the outside of an emergency exit on the upper deck of a double-decked vehicle or in the roof of a vehicle, shall be easily accessible to persons of normal height;

(*f*) the means and devices mentioned in conditions (*a*) and (*b*) above shall be so designed and fitted that they are unlikely to become dislodged or be operated accidentally but there shall be in the vehicle no means of a mechanical nature the operation of which would prevent the devices mentioned in the said condition (*b*) (devices for allowing entrance and exit doors to be opened in an emergency) when deliberately used, from allowing the entrance or exit doors for which they are provided to be readily opened;

(*g*) every door shall operate so as not to obstruct clear access to any entrance or exit from inside or outside the vehicle;

(*h*) being a vehicle having a power-operated door which, when open or being operated, projects laterally beyond the body of the vehicle at its widest point by more than 80 millimetres, shall be so constructed or adapted that it cannot move from rest under its own power when the door is open, and the door shall not be capable of being operated while the vehicle is in motion, except by the operation of such a device as is mentioned in condition (*b*) above;

(*i*) the storage and transmission system of the power for operating any power-operated door shall be such that operation of the doors does not adversely affect the efficient operation of the braking system of the vehicle and the apparatus shall be so designed and constructed that in the event of the system becoming inoperative the door shall be capable of being operated manually from inside and outside the vehicle; and

(*j*) the design of power-operated doors and their associated equipment at entrances and exits shall be such that, when opening or closing, the doors are unlikely to injure any passengers, and the vertical edges of any power-operated door which, when open or being operated, projects laterally beyond the body of the vehicle at its widest point by not more than 80 millimetres and which is installed in a vehicle not constructed or adapted as mentioned in condition (*h*) above shall be fitted with soft rubber.

(2) A vehicle shall not be deemed to fail to comply with condition (*b*) or (*f*) of paragraph (1) by reason only of the fact that, for the purposes of securing the vehicle when unattended, any entrance or exit door has been fitted with a supplementary lock with or without an actuating mechanism if the lock is so designed and constructed that a single movement of any device mentioned in condition (*b*) above, being a device provided on the inside of the vehicle, will at all times allow that door to be readily opened.

(3) In determining for the purposes of conditions (*h*) and (*j*) of paragraph (1) whether, or the distance by which, a power-operated door, when open or being operated, projects laterally beyond the body of the vehicle at its widest point any moulding on the outside of the vehicle shall be disregarded.

(4) The references to exits in paragraph (1) do not include an emergency exit provided in accordance with the provisions of Regulation 21(11) unless such exit is a primary emergency exit or a secondary emergency exit.

24. Marking, positioning and operation of emergency exits

(1) Subject to the provisions of paragraph 10 of Schedule 2, every emergency exit, other than an emergency exit with which a vehicle is required to be fitted under Regulation 21(11) shall comply with the following conditions—

(*a*) the emergency exit shall—

(i) be clearly marked as such inside and outside the vehicle;

(ii) be fitted with doors which open outwards or, in the case of a secondary emergency exit, be constructed of specified safety glass which can be readily broken by the application of reasonable force so as to afford a clear aperture of dimensions not less than those referred to in Regulation 21(1)(*b*);

(iii) except in the case of an emergency exit provided in the roof of a vehicle, be readily accessible to passengers;

(iv) in the case of a single-decked or half-decked vehicle or the lower deck of a double-decked vehicle, be so situated that passengers can step directly from the passage referred to in Regulation 26(1)(*g*) to the outside of the vehicle:

Provided that this requirement shall not apply in the case of an emergency exit provided in the roof of the vehicle or in the case of a secondary emergency exit;

(*b*) the means of operation of doors fitted to the emergency exit shall be clearly indicated;

(*c*) the doors of the emergency exit shall not be fitted with any system of power operation; and

(*d*) the means of operation of the doors of the emergency exit, other than those provided in the upper deck of a double-decked vehicle or in the roof of a vehicle, shall be readily accessible to persons of normal height standing at ground level outside the vehicle.

(2) Every emergency exit with which a vehicle is required to be fitted under Regulation 21(11) shall—

(*a*) be clearly marked as an emergency exit—
(i) on the inside of the vehicle, and
(ii) in a case where the emergency exit can be opened from the outside, on the outside of the vehicle;

(*b*) be accessible to persons inside the vehicle when the vehicle is tilted to either side through an angle of 99 degrees, measured from the normal vertical plane of the vehicle;

(*c*) be clearly marked with its means of operation;

(*d*) if hinged, open outwards; and

(*e*) if ejectable, be fitted with a restraint which will prevent the part of the emergency exit which is ejected from becoming completely detached from the vehicle but which will not prevent egress from the vehicle by persons within it.

25. Access to exits *[Omitted.]*

26. Width of gangways

(1) [Subject to paragraphs (2) and (3) and to paragraph 11 of Schedule 2], the following conditions shall be complied with in the case of every vehicle:—

(*a*) the width of every gangway shall be not less than—
(i) 305 millimetres up to a height of 765 millimetres above the level of the deck of the vehicle,
(ii) 355 millimetres at heights exceeding 765 millimetres but not exceeding 1.22 metres above the level of the deck of the vehicle, and
(iii) 455 millimetres at heights exceeding 1.22 metres above the level of the deck of the vehicle;

(*b*) a vertical line projected upwards from the centre line of any gangway at deck level shall, to the height prescribed in Regulation 27 as the height of the gangway, be laterally not less than 150 millimetres from any part of the vehicle other than the roof above the gangway;

(*c*) being a vehicle which has a seating capacity exceeding 12 passengers, no part of any gangway which is within 910 millimetres of an entrance or exit (other than an emergency exit) to which it provides access shall be less than 530 millimetres in width; and

(*d*) being a double-decked vehicle which has a seating capacity exceeding 12 passengers, one gangway in the vehicle which serves as a joint means of access—
  (i) to both the upper and lower decks from any entrance, or
  (ii) to any exit from both the upper and lower decks,

shall where it lies between an entrance or exit (other than an emergency exit) and a staircase, be, at every level, not less than 910 millimetres in width;

(*e*) where a part of a gangway which adjoins an entrance or exit is divided by a handrail, the width of that part of the gangway at any point on each side of the handrail shall not be less than 455 millimetres;

(*f*) where two seats (being either two seats each for one passenger only or two portions of a continuous seat, each of such portions being for one passenger only measured in accordance with condition (*b*) of Regulation 28(1)) are placed parallel to the longitudinal axis of a vehicle and face each other and the space between those seats is not required for the purpose of obtaining access from an entrance to any other seat or from any other seat to an exit (not being an emergency exit), that space shall not for the purposes of this Regulation and Regulation 27 be treated as forming part of the gangway;

(*g*) between every exit, not being either—
  (i) an emergency exit provided in the roof of a vehicle, or
  (ii) an exit provided in accordance with the provisions of Regulation 21(11) unless it be a primary or secondary emergency exit,

and a gangway there shall be a passage—

  A. of dimensions not less than those prescribed for a gangway in condition (*a*) of paragraph (1);

  B. so designed that a vertical line projected upwards from the centre line of the passage at floor level to a height of 760 millimetres from the level of the deck is laterally not less than 150 millimetres from any part of the vehicle (excluding any cowling or cover which projects not more than 230 millimetres from the bulkhead of the vehicle into the passage at floor level and not more than 230 millimetres above the deck level and the provision of which is required by the projection of part of the chassis or mechanism of the vehicle into the body);

  C. which has a clear height at every point along the centre line of the passage of 1.52 metres from the deck level:

    Provided that—

    (i) for the purposes of sub-paragraphs A and B of this paragraph a seat placed below or in front of an emergency exit, being such an exit provided on the upper deck of a double-decked vehicle or in the roof of a vehicle or which is a secondary emergency exit within the meaning of Regulation 21 shall be deemed to form part of such a passage, and

    (ii) sub-paragraph C of this paragraph shall not apply in the case of a passage leading to an emergency exit, being such an exit provided on the upper deck of a double-decked vehicle or in the roof of a vehicle or which is a secondary emergency exit within the meaning of Regulation 21, nor shall it apply in the case of a passage in a single-decked vehicle having a permanent top if the vehicle has a seating capacity not exceeding 14 passengers.

(2) Subject to paragraph 11 of Schedule 2, where any space in front of a seat in a

vehicle adapted to carry more than 12 passengers is required for the accommodation of seated passengers, the space within 225 millimetres of the seat shall not be taken into account in measuring the width of a gangway;

Provided that the provisions of this paragraph shall not apply in relation to paragraph (1)(*d*) above where—

(i) the floor of the gangway is free of any obstruction; and

(ii) there are no other intrusions into the gangway space above the level of the deck of the vehicle.

[(3) The provisions of paragraph (1)(*c*) and (*g*) do not apply as regards a crew seat occupied by crew.]

[Regulation 26 is printed as amended by SI 1982 No 1058.]

27. Height of gangways *[Omitted.]*

28. Seats

(1) Subject to paragraph 13 of Schedule 2, [the following conditions shall, as regards every passenger seat, be complied with] in the case of every vehicle—

(*a*) the supports of all seats shall be securely fixed in position;

(*b*) a length of at least 400 millimetres measured horizontally along the front of each seat shall be allowed for the accommodation of a seated passenger:

Provided that in the case of a continuous seat fitted with arms for the purpose of separating the seating spaces, being arms so constructed that they can be folded back or otherwise put out of use, the seat shall be measured for the purposes of this paragraph as though it were not fitted with arms;

(*c*) every seat shall have a back rest so closed or otherwise constructed as to prevent, as far as practicable, the pockets of passengers from being picked;

(*d*) all passenger seats shall be so fitted—

(i) that the distance between any part of the back rest of any seat placed lengthwise and the corresponding part of the back rest of the seat facing it shall be, in the case of a vehicle which has a seating capacity not exceeding 12 passengers, not less than 1.37 metres, and in any other case, not less than 1.60 metres, and

(ii) that there is a clear space of at least 610 millimetres in front of the back rest of any seat measured from the centre of each complete length of the seat allowed for the accommodation of a seated passenger in accordance with condition (*b*) above and a clear space of 200 millimetres in front of any part of that seat:

Provided that in the case of a seat for more than three passengers—

(*a*) in the case of a vehicle being used as a stage carriage, and

(*b*) in the case of any vehicle to which this regulation applies and which is first used on or after 1st April 1982

where access to that seat can be obtained only from one end of the seat, the said clear spaces shall respectively be at least 685 millimetres and 300 millimetres;

(*e*) there shall be a clear space of at least 480 millimetres between any part of the front edge of any transverse seat and any part of any other seat which faces it:

Provided that any support provided for a table shall be disregarded if there is a clear space of at least 225 millimetres between that support and the front edge of the nearest seat and the support is not in such a position as to cause discomfort to passengers occupying the seats;

(*f*) no seat shall be placed in such a position as to cause discomfort to passengers;

(*g*) there shall, as respects every seat, be a clear space measured vertically from the centre of each complete length of the seat allowed for the accommodation of a seated passenger in accordance with condition (*b*) above which shall be, in the case of a vehicle which has a seating capacity not exceeding 12 passengers, not less than 910 millimetres, and, in any other case, not less than 965 millimetres;

(*h*) where any seat is so placed that a passenger seated upon it is liable to be thrown through any entrance to or exit from the vehicle or down a stairway in the vehicle, an effective screen or guard shall be placed so as to afford adequate protection against that occurrence to a passenger occupying that seat; and

(*i*) the shortest distances between the edge of the well of any step in the vehicle and a vertical plane passing through the front edge of any seat shall be not less than 225 millimetres:

Provided that this condition shall not apply in the case of the well of a step provided as a means of obtaining access only to any forward-facing front passenger seat placed alongside the driver in a vehicle which has a seating capacity not exceeding 12 passengers.

(2) In this Regulation and in paragraph 13 of Schedule 2 the expression 'back rest' includes any part of the vehicle which is available for seated passengers to lean against.

[Regulation 28 is printed as amended by SI 1982 No 1058.

The expression 'stage carriage' was formerly defined in the Public Passenger Vehicles Act 1981, s 82(1), but the definition was revoked by the Transport Act 1985, s 139(3) and Sched 9; for the meaning of that expression, see now Sched 1, para 16, to the 1985 Act.]

[28A. Crew seats

(1) Every crew seat shall be so constructed and located that when it is in use—

(*a*) the person by whom it is occupied—

(i) is adequately protected by means of arm rests from falling sideways either to the left or the right,

(ii) may conveniently place his feet either on a deck of the vehicle or on a foot rest, and

(iii) does not impede the driving of the vehicle either by obstructing the driver's field of vision or otherwise; and

(*b*) a space of at least 300 millimetres exists, along the whole width of the seat, between the foremost edge of the seat and any other part of the vehicle.

(2) Every crew seat shall be so constructed and located that when it is not in use—

(*a*) no part of it impedes the driving of the vehicle either by obstructing the driver's field of vision or otherwise; and

(*b*) every part of it which, when the seat is ready for or in use, protrudes into a gangway so that the provisions of Regulation 26(1)(*c*) and (*g*) are not complied with, is, as a result of automatic mechanism, retracted so that those provisions are complied with.

(3) The words 'FOR CREW USE ONLY' shall be marked either on or near and in relation to every crew seat in letters not less than 10 millimetres tall and in a colour which contrasts with their background.

(4) The provisions of paragraph (1)(*a*) to (*f*) of Regulation 28 apply as respects a crew seat in the same manner as they apply as respects a seat to which that Regulation applies.]

[Regulation 28A was inserted by SI 1982 No 1058.]

29–34. *[Omitted.]*

PART III

Regulations Relating to the Equipment of Public Service Vehicles

35. Fire extinguishing apparatus

(1) There shall be carried by every vehicle being used before 31st December 1988 suitable and efficient apparatus for extinguishing fire which is of either one or more of the types specified in Part I of Schedule 4 or one or more of the types specified in Part II of Schedule 4, and by every vehicle being used on or after 31st December 1988 suitable and efficient apparatus for extinguishing fire which is of one or more of the types specified in Part II of Schedule 4.

(2) The apparatus referred to in paragraph (1) shall be—

(*a*) readily available for use,

(*b*) clearly marked with the appropriate British Standards Institution specification number, and

(*c*) maintained in good and efficient working order.

36. First aid equipment

(1) There shall be carried by every vehicle being used as an express carriage or as a contract carriage a receptacle which contains the items specified in Schedule 5.

(2) The receptacle referred to in paragraph (1) shall be—

(*a*) maintained in a good condition,

(*b*) suitable for the purpose of keeping the items referred to in the said paragraph in good condition,

(*c*) readily available for use, and

(*d*) prominently marked as a first aid receptacle.

(3) The items referred to in paragraph (1) shall be maintained in good condition and shall be of a good and reliable quality and of a suitable design.

[Section 82(1) of the Public Passenger Vehicles Act 1981 formerly included definitions of 'contract carriage' and 'express carriage'. These definitions were repealed by the Transport Act 1985, s 139(3) and Sched 8. For the meanings of these expressions, see now Sched 1, para 16, to the 1985 Act, above.]

PART IV

Regulations Relating to the Use of Public Service Vehicles

37. Obstruction of entrances, exits and gangways

No person shall, while passengers are being carried by a vehicle, cause or permit any unnecessary obstruction to any entrance or exit or gangway of the vehicle.

38. Obstruction of driver

No person shall cause or permit any unnecessary obstruction of the driver of a vehicle.

39. Body maintenance

No person shall use a vehicle while it is carrying passengers or cause or permit it to be so used unless the inside and the outside of the body of the vehicle and all windows and fittings and all passengers' seats are maintained in clean and good condition.

40. Lamps

(1) No person shall use a vehicle during the hours of darkness while it is carrying passengers or cause or permit it to be so used unless every lamp provided in compliance with Regulation 16 for the internal illumination of the vehicle is at all times during such use kept lighted to such extent as is necessary to provide adequate illumination of every access from any seat in the vehicle to every exit in the vehicle and of every such marking as is required by Regulation 24 to be provided in relation to every emergency exit in the vehicle:

Provided that it shall not be necessary to keep lighted any lamp provided on the upper deck of a double-decked vehicle if a barrier is secured across the bottom of all staircases leading to that deck so as effectively to prevent passengers using any such staircase.

(2) In this Regulation, 'hours of darkness' means the time between half-an-hour after sunset and half-an-hour before sunrise.

41. Use of device for operating power-operated doors

(1) Except as provided by paragraph (2), no person shall use or cause or permit to be used any device for operating the doors of a vehicle having power-operated doors, being a device such as is mentioned in condition (*b*) of Regulation 23(1) or, as the case may be, in paragraph 9(*b*)(ii) of Schedule 2.

(2) Paragraph (1) shall not apply—

(*a*) in an emergency, as to the use of a device by any person;

(*b*) otherwise than in an emergency, as to the use of a device by a person in accordance with an authorisation by the operator of the vehicle, save that no such use shall occur if—

(i) the vehicle is in motion, and

(ii) the doors, when fully opened, project more than 80 millimetres from the side of the vehicle.

42. Filling of petrol tank

While the engine of a vehicle is running no person shall cause or permit the filler cap fitted to the petrol tank of the vehicle to be removed or petrol to be put in its petrol tank.

43. Carriage of conductor

No person shall use or cause or permit to be used as a stage carriage any vehicle which has a seating capacity exceeding 20 passengers unless a person authorised to act as conductor of the vehicle is carried thereby:

Provided that this Regulation shall not apply—

(i) in the case of a single-decked vehicle which has a seating capacity not exceeding 32 passengers and which is provided with only one emergency exit, if that exit and the entrance to the vehicle are both placed at the front of the vehicle and are readily visible to the driver from his seat and means are provided for the driver to be aware if any person outside the vehicle has been trapped by the closure of any door provided at that entrance, or

(ii) in the case of any other vehicle, if a certifying officer has stated in writing that the construction and design of the vehicle is such that a conductor is not required for the purpose of the safety of the passengers.

44. Carriage of inflammable or dangerous substances

(1) No person shall use or cause or permit to be used any vehicle by which any highly inflammable or otherwise dangerous substance is carried unless that substance is carried in containers so designed and constructed, or unless the substance is so packed, that, notwithstanding an accident to the vehicle, it is unlikely that damage to the vehicle or injury to passengers carried by the vehicle will be caused by reason of the presence on it of that substance.

(2) The requirements of this Regulation are in addition to and not in derogation of the requirements of regulations made under the Petroleum (Consolidation) Act 1928 or under any other Act.

45. Markings

No vehicle in respect of which, by virtue of [section 6(1)] of the . . . Act . . . , a certificate of initial fitness, or a certificate under [section 10] of the . . . Act . . . , or a certificate under [section 57 of the Road Traffic Act 1988] is required shall be used on a road unless the vehicle is marked with clearly legible characters—

(i) not less than 25 millimetres tall,

(ii) in a conspicuous position on the nearside of the vehicle,

(iii) in colours which contrast with their background, and

(iv) indicating the name of the owner (as defined in [section 82(1)] of the . . . Act . . . in relation to a vehicle to which that definition applies) of the vehicle and the owner's principal place of business.

[Regulation 45 is printed as amended by the Interpretation Act 1978, ss 17(2)(a) and 23(1).]

[45A. Use of seats

(1) No passenger shall be permitted to use a seat provided for a passenger unless it complies with the requirements specified in Regulation 28.

(2) No crew shall be permitted to use a crew seat unless it complies with the requirements specified in Regulation 28A.]

[Regulation 45A was inserted by SI 1982 No 1058.]

PART V

Regulations Relating to Certificates of Initial Fitness, Approval as a Type Vehicle and Conformity to an Approved Type Vehicle

46–57. *[Omitted.]*

SCHEDULES

* * *

SCHEDULE 2

Exceptions from the Conditions Prescribed in Part II as Applicable to Vehicles Registered before Certain Dates

* * *

4. Regulation 16 (Artificial lighting) in so far as it consists of sub-paragraph (*b*), shall not apply in the case of a vehicle registered before 1st April 1959 and the requirements as to lighting circuits in that Regulation shall not apply in the case of a vehicle registered before 28th October 1964.

* * *

8. Regulation 21 (Number, position and size of entrances and exits) shall not apply—

(*a*) in so far as it consists of paragraphs (4) and (6) in the case of a vehicle registered before 1st April 1959 if it is provided with two exits so placed as not to be on the same side of the vehicle;

(*b*) in so far as it consists of paragraph (6) in the case of a vehicle registered on or after 1st April 1959 and before 28th October 1964 which has a seating capacity exceeding 45 passengers if—

(i) the vehicle is provided with two exits (of which neither is a secondary emergency exit) and those exits are not on the same side of the vehicle, and

(ii) in a case where those exits are so placed that the distance between their centres is less than 3.05 metres, a secondary emergency exit is provided in such a position that there is a distance of not less than 3.05 metres between the nearest points of the openings of that exit and of whichever of the exits mentioned in sub-paragraph (i) above is the nearer to that exit. For the purpose of this paragraph the reference to the distance between the centres and between the nearest points of the openings of the two exits there mentioned shall be construed in accordance with Regulation 21(1)(*e*);

(*c*) in so far as it consists of paragraph (9)—

(i) in the case of a vehicle registered before 1st April 1959 (not being a single-decked vehicle having a permanent top) if it is provided with two exits so placed as not to be on the same sides of the vehicle; or

(ii) in the case of a vehicle which—

A. is provided with a platform such as is mentioned in proviso (i) to Regulation 21(4); or

B. has a seating capacity not exceeding 14 passengers, if one means of exit and entrance is provided and is placed behind the rear wheels.

9. Regulation 23(1) (Doors) shall not apply—

(*a*) in so far as it consists of sub-paragraph (*j*) in the case of a vehicle registered before 1st August 1968;

(*b*) save in so far as it consists of sub-paragraph (*j*) in the case of a vehicle registered before 19th June 1968 if—

(i) every entrance door and every exit door can be readily opened from inside and outside the vehicle by one operation of the locking mechanism:

Provided that a vehicle shall not be deemed to fail to comply with this sub-paragraph by reason only of the fact that, for the purpose of securing the vehicle when unattended, any entrance or exit door has been fitted with a supplementary lock with or without an actuating mechanism if the lock is so designed and constructed that the door can at all times be opened by a person inside the vehicle by one operation of the ordinary locking mechanism;

(ii) except in the case of a vehicle registered before 1st April 1959, the device provided outside the vehicle for operating the locking mechanism of the door (not being a device provided in relation to an emergency exit on the upper deck of a double-decked vehicle or in the roof of a half-decked vehicle) is readily accessible to persons of normal height standing at ground level outside the vehicle;

(iii) except in the case of a vehicle registered before 1st April 1959, means are provided for holding every entrance and exit door securely in the closed position;

(iv) except in the case of a vehicle registered before 1st April 1959, all locks and fastenings fitted to entrance and exit doors are so designed and fitted that they are not likely to become dislodged or be operated accidentally, and, in the said excepted case, door handles or levers to door catches are so designed and fitted that they are not likely to become dislodged or be operated accidentally;

(v) where any entrances are provided with doors which are designed to remain open when the vehicle is in motion, suitable fastenings are provided to hold such doors securely in the opened position;

(vi) except in the case of a vehicle registered before 1st April 1959, every sliding door and every folding door fitted to an entrance or exit is provided with suitable fastenings to prevent it from being closed by any movement of the vehicle;

(vii) all doors can open so as not to obstruct clear access to any entrance or exit from inside or outside the vehicle; and

(viii) except in the case of a vehicle registered before 1st April 1959, the means by which a power-operated door may be opened are provided inside the vehicle on or adjacent to the door and their position is clearly indicated and there is also an indication that the said means may be used by passengers only in an emergency; and the storage and transmission system of the power for operating the door is such that operation of the doors does not adversely affect the efficient operation of the braking system of the vehicle and the apparatus is so designed and constructed that in the event of the system becoming inoperative the door can be operated manually from inside and outside the vehicle.

10. Regulation 24(1)(*b*)(iv) (Marking, positioning and operation of emergency exits) shall not apply in the case of a vehicle registered before 1st April 1959, being a vehicle which is provided with a rear platform, if an emergency exit (of which the clear height at the centre line is not less than 1.52 metres and of which the width is not

less than 455 millimetres) is provided from that platform to the rear of the vehicle and is enclosed by means of a door placed on the near side of that platform.

11. The provisions of Regulation 26 (Width of gangways) specified in column 1 of the Table below shall not apply in the case of a vehicle specified, in relation to those provisions, in column 2 of that Table.

TABLE

1	2
Paragraph (1)(*e*)	A vehicle registered before 19th June 1968.
Paragraph (1)(*d*)	A double-decked vehicle registered before 19th June 1969 if no part of any gangway which serves as a joint means of access from any entrance to the upper and lower decks is less than 910 millimetres in width.
Paragraph (1)(*a*), (*c*) and (*g*)c.	A vehicle registered before 1st April 1959 if the width of every gangway is not less than 305 millimetres up to a height of 765 millimetres above the level of the deck and not less than 355 millimetres above that height.
Paragraph 1(*c*)	A vehicle registered after 1st April 1959 and before 19th June 1968 if no part of any gangway which is within 915 millimetres of an exit (other than an emergency exit) to which it leads is less than 530 millimetres in width.

* * *

13. Regulation 28 (Seats) shall not apply—

(*a*) in so far as it consists of paragraph (1)(*d*) in the case of a vehicle registered before 1st April 1959 if all the passengers' seats in the vehicle are so fitted—

(a) that no part of the back rest of any seat placed lengthwise is less than 1.37 metres from the corresponding part of the back rest of the seat facing it; and

(b) there is in relation to every transverse seat in the vehicle a clear space of at least 660 millimetres in front of the whole length of the top of the back rest of that seat measured from the centre of each complete length of the seat allowed for the accommodation of a seated passenger in accordance with condition (*b*) of the said paragraph (1) but disregarding any handles or grips which do not project more than 105 millimetres from the back rest;

(*b*) in so far as it consists of paragraph (1)(*f*) and (*g*) in the case of a vehicle registered before 1st April 1959 if no seat placed over the arch of a wheel of the vehicle is in such a position as to cause discomfort to passengers;

(*c*) in so far as it consists of paragraph (1)(*h*) in the case of a vehicle registered before 1st April 1959 if, as respects any transverse seat in the vehicle which is so placed that a passenger seated upon it is liable to be thrown through any entrance to or exit from the vehicle or down a stairway in the vehicle, an effective screen or guard is placed so as to afford adequate protection against that occurrence to a passenger occupying that seat.

* * *

SCHEDULE 4 (see regulation 35)

FIRE EXTINGUISHING APPARATUS

PART I

(i) A foam-producing fire extinguisher complying in all respects with the specification issued by the British Standards Institution in respect of Portable Fire Extinguishers of the Foam Type (Chemical) and numbered B.S. 740: Part I: 1948.

(ii) A foam-producing fire extinguisher complying in all respects with the specification issued by the British Standards Institution in respect of Portable Fire Extinguishers of the Foam Type (Gas Pressure) and numbered B.S. 740: Part II: 1952.

(iii) A soda acid chemical fire extinguisher complying in all respects with the specification issued by the British Standards Institution in respect of Portable Fire Extinguishers of the Water Type (Soda Acid) and numbered B.S. 138: 1948.

(iv) A water fire extinguisher complying in all respects with the specification issued by the British Standards Institution in respect of Portable Fire Extinguishers of the Water Type (Gas Pressure) and numbered B.S. 1382: 1948.

(v) A bromochlorodifluoromethane (B.C.F.) fire extinguisher with a liquid capacity of at least 1·35 kilograms, or two such extinguishers having an aggregate such capacity, complying in all respects with the specification issued by the British Standards Institution in respect of Portable Fire Extinguishers of the Halogenated Hydrocarbon Type and numbered B.S. 1721: 1968.

[PART II

A fire extinguisher which complies in all respects with a specification for portable fire extinguishers issued by the British Standards Institution being either B.S. 5423: 1977 published on 31st December 1976 or B.S. 5423: 1980 which took effect on 31st December 1980 and which, in either case, either—

(*a*) contains water with a minimum test fire rating of 8A, or

(*b*) contains foam with a minimum test fire rating of 8A and 21B, or

(*c*) contains and is marked to indicate that it contains halon 1211 or halon 1301 with, in either case, a minimum test fire rating of 21B.]

[Schedule 4 is printed as amended by SI 1982 No 1482.]

SCHEDULE 5 (see regulation 36)

FIRST AID EQUIPMENT

(i) Ten antiseptic wipes, foil packed.

(ii) One conforming disposable bandage (not less than 7·5 centimetres wide).

(iii) Two triangular bandages.

(iv) One packet of 24 assorted adhesive dressings.

(v) Three large sterile unmedicated ambulance dressings (not less than 15·0 centimetres × 20·0 centimetres).

(vi) Two sterile eye pads, with attachments.

(vii) Twelve assorted safety pins.

(viii) One pair of rustless blunt-ended scissors.

SCHEDULE 6

Form of Certificate of Initial Fitness

[Omitted.]

SCHEDULE 7

Form of Type Approval Certificate

[Omitted.]

SCHEDULE 8

Form of Declaration of Conformity to an Approved Type Vehicle

[Omitted.]

SCHEDULE 9

Form of Certificate of Conformity

[Omitted.]

The Public Service Vehicles (Conduct of Drivers, Conductors and Passengers) Regulations 1936

(SR & O 1936 No 619)

[The text of these regulations is printed as amended by:

the Public Service Vehicles (Conduct of Drivers, Conductors and Passengers) (Amendment) Regulations 1975 (SI 1975 No 461) (16 April 1975); and

the Public Service Vehicles (Conduct of Drivers, Conductors and Passengers) (Amendment) Regulations 1980 (SI 1980 No 915) (31 July 1980).

The amending regulations are referred to in the notes to the regulations by their years and numbers. The dates referred to above are the dates on which the regulations came into force.]

PART I

* * *

2. In these Regulations unless the context otherwise requires the following expressions have the meanings hereby respectively assigned to them:—

'Vehicle' means public service vehicle;

'Driver' means a person licensed to drive a vehicle;

'Conductor' means a person [employed] to act as conductor of a vehicle or, in the case of a vehicle where there is no conductor, the driver;

'Authorised person' means any employee of the licensee (including the conductor) on duty or in connection with the vehicle;

'Stage Carriage', 'Express Carriage' and 'Contract Carriage' have the meanings assigned to them in the [Public Passenger Vehicles Act 1981].

['wireless telegraphy apparatus' has the meaning assigned to it by section 19 of the Wireless Telegraphy Act 1949 [*qv*].]

[Regulation 2 is printed as amended by the Road Traffic Act 1960, Sched XIX, para 3, SI 1975 No 461, SI 1980 No 915 and the Public Passenger Vehicles Act 1981, s 83(1).

Section 83(1) of the Public Passenger Vehicles Act 1981 has been amended by the Transport Act 1985, s 139(3) and Sched 8. As a result of that amendment, references in these regulations to 'stage carriage', 'express carriage' and 'contract carriage' should be construed in accordance with Sched 1, para 16, to the 1985 Act, qv].

3. The [Interpretation Act 1978] applies for the purpose of the interpretation of these Regulations as it applies for the interpretation of an Act of Parliament.

[Regulation 3 is printed as amended by the Interpretation Act 1978, s 17(2).]

PART II

Drivers and Conductors

4. A driver or a conductor, when acting as such,

(*a*) shall behave in a civil and orderly manner;

(*b*) shall not smoke in or on a vehicle during a journey or when it has passengers on board;

(*c*) shall take all reasonable precautions to ensure the safety of passengers in or on or entering or alighting from the vehicle;

(*d*) shall not wilfully deceive or refuse to inform any passenger or intending passenger as to the destination or route of the vehicle or as to the fare for any journey;

[(*e*) shall, if requested by any police constable or other person having reasonable cause, give particulars of his name, and the name and address of the person by whom he is employed and, in the case of a driver, of his licence;]

(*f*) shall not, at any reasonable time, obstruct or neglect to give all reasonable information and assistance to any person having authority to examine the vehicle.

[Regulation 4 is printed as amended by SI 1980 No 915.]

5. A driver, when acting as such, shall not when the vehicle is in motion speak to the conductor or any other person unless it is necessary to do so on grounds of safety.

[Provided that this Regulation shall not apply to any communication by the driver with an authorised person on operational matters or in an emergency by means of wireless telegraphy apparatus.]

[Regulation 5 is printed as amended by SI 1975 No 461.]

6. A conductor, when acting as such,

(*a*) shall not when the vehicle is in motion distract the driver's attention without reasonable cause or speak to him unless it is necessary to do so in order to give directions as to the stopping of the vehicle;

(*b*) shall take all reasonable precautions to ensure that every means provided for indicating the route fares and destination of the vehicle are clearly and correctly displayed;

(*c*) shall to the best of his ability take steps whenever necessary to enforce the provisions of these Regulations relating to the conduct of passengers.

7. A driver of a stage carriage or an express carriage, when acting as such,

(*a*) shall, when picking up or setting down passengers, stop the vehicle as close as may be to the left or near side of the road;

(*b*) shall not cause the vehicle to remain stationary on a road longer than is reasonably necessary to pick up or set down passengers except at a stand or place where such vehicles are permitted to stop for a longer time than is necessary for that purpose.

8. A conductor of a stage carriage or an express carriage, when acting as such, shall not, except for sufficient reason, by failing to signal to the driver to start, cause the vehicle to remain stationary on a road longer than is reasonably necessary to pick up or set down passengers except at a stand or place where the vehicle is permitted to stop for a longer time than is necessary for that purpose.

PART III

Passengers

9. When a public service vehicle is carrying passengers or waiting to pick up passengers a passenger or intending passenger shall not

(i) use obscene or offensive language or conduct himself in a riotous or disorderly manner;
(ii) enter or alight from the vehicle otherwise than by the doors or openings provided for the purpose;
(iii) when entering or attempting to enter the vehicle wilfully and unreasonably impede passengers seeking to enter the vehicle or to alight therefrom;
(iv) enter or remain in or on the vehicle when requested not to do so by an authorised person on the ground that the vehicle is carrying its full complement of passengers or that the operator is debarred from picking up passengers at the place in question by reason of the conditions attached to his road service licence;
(v) travel in or on the upper deck of the vehicle unless he occupies a seat provided for that purpose, or in or on any part of the vehicle not provided for the conveyance of passengers;
(vi) wilfully do or cause to be done with respect to any part of the vehicle or its equipment anything which is calculated to obstruct or interfere with the working of the vehicle or to cause injury or discomfort to any person;
(vii) when the vehicle is in motion distract the driver's attention without reasonable cause or speak to him unless it is necessary to do so in order to give directions as to the stopping of the vehicle;
(viii) give any signal which might be interpreted by the driver as a signal from the conductor to start;
(ix) spit upon or from or wilfully damage, soil or defile any part of the vehicle;
(x) when in or on the vehicle distribute printed or similar matter of any description or distribute any article for the purpose of advertising;
(xi) wilfully remove, displace or alter any number plate, notice board, fare table, route indicator, or destination board or any printed or other notice or advertisement in or on the vehicle;
(xii) when in or on the vehicle to the annoyance of other persons use or operate any noisy instrument or make or combine with any other person or persons to make any excessive noise by singing, shouting or otherwise;
(xiii) when in or on the vehicle throw any money to be scrambled for by any person on the road or footway; or throw out of the vehicle any bottle liquid or litter or any article or thing likely to annoy persons or to cause danger or injury to any person or property;
(xiv) throw any article from the vehicle or attach to or trail from the vehicle any streamer, balloon, flag or other article in such manner as to overhang the road;
(xv) wilfully obstruct or impede any authorised person;
(xvi) except in the case of a contract carriage, smoke or carry a lighted pipe, cigar or cigarette in or on any part of the vehicle in or on which a notice is exhibited that smoking is prohibited;
(xvii) except in the case of a contract carriage when in or on the vehicle beg, sell or offer for sale any article.

10. When a stage or express carriage is carrying passengers or is waiting to pick up passengers, a passenger or intending passenger shall not

(*a*) if his condition is such as to be offensive to passengers, or the condition of his dress or clothing is such that it may reasonably be expected to soil or injure the linings or cushions of the vehicle or the clothing of other passengers, enter or remain in or on the vehicle after an authorised person shall have requested him either not to enter or to leave the vehicle and in such latter case shall have tendered to him the amount of any fare previously paid;

(*b*) enter or travel in or on a vehicle with loaded firearms, or any dangerous or offensive article or, except with the consent of an authorised person, bring into or on to the vehicle any bulky or cumbersome article or place any such article elsewhere in or on the vehicle than as directed by an authorised person;

(*c*) bring any animal into or on to the vehicle without the consent of an authorised person or retain any animal in or on the vehicle after being requested by an authorised person to remove it or place any animal elsewhere in or on the vehicle than as directed by an authorised person.

[**11.** (*a*) No passenger on a stage or express carriage shall use or attempt to use in relation to the journey which he is taking or intending to take—

(i) any ticket which has been altered or defaced, or

(ii) any ticket which has been issued to another person if such ticket bears thereon an indication that it is not transferable; or

(iii) without reasonable excuse, any period or season ticket which has expired.

(*b*) Every passenger on a stage or express carriage shall—

(i) declare, if so requested by the driver or the conductor, the journey he has taken or intends to take:

(ii) where the vehicle is being operated by a driver without a conductor, immediately on boarding the vehicle, unless otherwise directed by an authorised person or by notice displayed on the vehicle, pay to the driver the fare for the journey he intends to take, or insert in any fare collection equipment provided on the vehicle coins of such denominations as may be required to pay that fare, and where the vehicle is not being so operated, if so requested by the conductor, pay the fare for the journey he intends to take or has taken, and in either case accept any ticket provided therefor:

Provided that this sub-paragraph shall not apply if the passenger is already the holder of a ticket in respect of the journey he intends to take or has taken and he complies with any directions on the ticket or by notice on the vehicle or given by an authorised person, as to the inspection, perforation, endorsement or cancellation of the ticket by such person;

(iii) produce his ticket, if any, when required to do so by an authorised person or, if he fails to produce his ticket, pay, by whichever of the means specified in sub-paragraph (ii) of this paragraph is appropriate, the fare for the journey he intends to take or has taken;

(iv) on completion of the journey for which he has paid the fare leave the vehicle if so requested by the driver or the conductor or pay, by whichever of the means specified in sub-paragraph (ii) of this paragraph is appropriate, the fare for any journey which he takes or intends to take on the vehicle by way of continuation of that journey, or, where so directed by an authorised person or by a notice on the vehicle, pay the fare for that further journey on leaving the vehicle;

(v) on demand by an authorised person surrender on completion of the journey any ticket issued to him in respect of the journey;

(vi) on demand by an authorised person surrender any period or season ticket held by him at the expiry of the period for which it was issued to him.

(*c*) No passenger shall without reasonable excuse leave or attempt to leave a stage or express carriage without having paid the fare for the journey he has taken.]

[Regulation 11 was substituted by SI 1975 No 461.]

12. (*a*) Any passenger contravening these Regulations may be removed from the vehicle by the driver or conductor or, on the request of the driver or conductor, by any police constable.

(*b*) A passenger in or on a vehicle who is reasonably suspected by the driver or conductor of contravening these Regulations shall give his name and address to a police constable or to the driver or conductor on demand.

The Public Service Vehicles (Operators' Licences) Regulations 1986

(SI 1986 No 1668)

1. Citation and commencement *[Omitted.]*

2. Revocation *[Omitted.]*

3. Interpretation

(1) In these Regulations, unless the context otherwise requires—

'the 1981 Act' means the Public Passenger Vehicles Act 1981;

'the 1985 Act' means the Transport Act 1985;

'the certifying officer' means an officer appointed under section 7(1);

'designated sporting event' has the same meaning as in the Sporting Events (Control of Alcohol) Act 1985;

'disc' means an operator's disc under section 18;

'holder' in relation to a licence means the individual, company or (in the case of a partnership) firm to whom that licence was granted;

'licence' means a PSV operator's licence and 'special licence' has the same meaning as in section 12(2) of the 1985 Act;

'local authority' has the meaning given by section 14A(4);

'Notices and Proceedings' has the same meaning as in regulation 3 of the Public Service Vehicles (Traffic Commissioners: Publications and Inquiries) Regulations 1986 [*SI 1986 No 1629*];

'public service vehicle examiner' means an examiner appointed under section 7(2); and

'traffic regulation conditions' has the meaning given by section 7(1) of the 1985 Act.

(2) Unless the context otherwise requires, any reference in these Regulations to:

(*a*) a numbered section is a reference to the section bearing that number in the 1981 Act;

(*b*) a numbered regulation is a reference to the regulation bearing that number in these Regulations;

(*c*) a numbered paragraph is a reference to the paragraph bearing that number in the regulation in which the reference appears.

4–9. *[Omitted.]*

10. Manner in which discs are to be fixed and exhibited

The holder of a licence (other than a special licence) shall, during such time as a vehicle is in use under it, cause a disc to be affixed to the vehicle either in a weatherproof container or on the inside of the vehicle and (in either case) in such a position that the disc:

(*a*) is adjacent to the licence under the Vehicles (Excise) Act 1971;

(*b*) does not interfere unduly with the driver's view; and

(*c*) can easily be read in daylight from the outside of the vehicle.

11. Form of and particulars to be contained on discs

(1) Every disc shall contain:

(*a*) the name of the holder of the licence in relation to which the disc has been issued;

(*b*) the code and number of the said licence and the date on which it will expire; and

(*c*) the words 'Public Service Operator's Identity Disc' or 'Public Service Vehicle Operator's Disc'.

(2) (*a*) If the licence under which the disc is being used is a standard licence which authorises use of the vehicle on which the disc is displayed on both national and international operations, the disc shall be green and contain, beneath the expiry date of the licence, the words 'standard international';

(*b*) If the licence under which the disc is being used is a standard licence which authorises the use of the vehicle on which the disc is displayed on national operations only, the disc shall be blue and contain beneath the expiry date of the licence, the words 'standard national' and

(*c*) If the licence under which the disc is being used is a restricted licence the disc shall be orange and contain, beneath the expiry date of the licence, the word 'restricted'.

12. Return of licences and discs

(1) In the event of the suspension, surrender or other termination of a licence prior to the date of expiry specified in it, the holder shall return that licence to the traffic commissioner by whom it was granted for retention during the time of the suspension, or for cancellation, as the case may be, and shall at the same time return to that commissioner any discs which have been issued in relation to the licence.

(2) On the removal of a suspension referred to in paragraph (1) the commissioner shall return any licence the period of validity of which has not expired together with any discs which were issued in relation to the licence.

(3) In the event of the period of validity of a licence being curtailed the holder shall return such licence to the traffic commissioner by whom it was granted, and that commissioner shall amend the licence as regards the curtailment and then return the same, and on the expiry of the licence as a result of a curtailment the holder shall return any discs which he then holds in respect of the licence.

(4) In the event of the traffic commissioner deciding to attach an additional condition or any traffic regulation conditions to a licence or to alter or remove a condition or any traffic regulation conditions attached to a licence, the holder shall return the licence to that commissioner and he shall amend the licence as regards the addition, alteration or removal and then return the same.

(5) In the event of the traffic commissioner deciding to vary one or more conditions attached to a licence under section 16(1), so reducing the maximum number of vehicles which may be used under the licence below the number of discs which have been issued to the holder, there shall be returned by the holder to that commissioner such number of discs as will leave the holder with only the same number of discs as is equal to the reduced maximum number of vehicles.

(6) The licence or discs (as the case may be) shall be returned within 14 days of the date on which the holder receives the notice from the traffic commissioner of the decision which requires such return.

(7) Any licence or disc required to be returned to the traffic commissioner under this regulation shall be produced at the address in the traffic area, and within the business hours, specified in the notice and if sent by post shall not be treated as having been returned until actually received by the traffic commissioner.

13. Issue of duplicate licences and discs *[Omitted.]*

14. Production of licences and discs for examination

(1) A licence or a disc shall be produced by the holder for examination if he is so required by any police constable, certifying officer or public service vehicle examiner or by any person authorised by the traffic commissioner for any traffic area to examine the licence or disc, and any such requirement shall be complied with in not more than 14 days.

(2) Any such requirement as is mentioned in paragraph (1) may be complied with by the holder producing the licence or disc within the traffic area of the traffic commissioner by whom the licence was granted at the operating centre or principal place of business of the holder.

15–20. *[Omitted.]*

21. Termination of licences held by companies

In a case where a licence is held by a company the events relating to the holder on the occurrence of which the licence is to terminate are as follows:

(*a*) the making of a winding up order; and

(*b*) the passing of a resolution for voluntary winding up.

22. Computation of time

Any day which is a bank holiday under the Banking and Financial Dealings Act 1971 [*qv*] shall be excluded from the computation of any period of a specified number of days prescribed in these Regulations.

23. Post Office

Section 16(1A) (limit on number of vehicles to be used under a restricted licence) shall not apply in respect of a licence held at any time by the Post Office.

The Recovery Vehicles (Prescribed Purposes) Regulations 1987

(SI 1987 No 2120)

1. *[Citation and commencement.]*

2. The purposes specified in the Schedule to these Regulations are hereby prescribed for the purposes of paragraph 8 of Part I of Schedule 3 to the Vehicles (Excise) Act 1971.

THE SCHEDULE

Regulation 2

PRESCRIBED PURPOSES

1. Repairing a disabled vehicle at the place where it became disabled or to which it has been moved in the interests of safety after becoming disabled.

2. Drawing or carrying one trailer if the trailer was immediately before a vehicle became disabled, being drawn or carried by the disabled vehicle.

The Removal and Disposal of Vehicles (Loading Areas) Regulations 1986

(SI 1986 No 184)

PART I

General

1. Citation, commencement and revocation *[Omitted.]*

2. Interpretation

In these Regulations—

'the 1984 Act' means the Road Traffic Regulation Act 1984;

'loading area' has the same meaning as in section 61 of the 1984 Act [*qv*];

'vehicle' has the same meaning as in section 99 of the 1984 Act [*qv*].

PART II

Removal of Vehicles

3. Power to require the removal of vehicles from loading areas

(1) This regulation applies to a vehicle which is in any part of a loading area while the parking of it in that part is prohibited by virtue of section 61 of the 1984 Act.

(2) Subject to paragraph (3) below, an officer of the local authority, duly authorised in writing by that authority, may require the owner, driver or other person in control or in charge of any vehicle to which this regulation applies to move it or cause it to be removed, and any such requirement may include a requirement that the vehicle shall be moved from the part of the loading area where it is to some other part of that loading area, or to a place on a highway, or to some other place which is not on a highway (being a place where the vehicle can be lawfully parked).

(3) When making any requirement under paragraph (2) above an officer of the local authority, if requested so to do by the owner, driver or other person in control or in charge of the vehicle, shall produce evidence of his authorisation.

(4) In this regulation and in regulation 4 below 'the local authority' means—

(*a*) in Greater London, the Council of the London borough or, as the case may be, the Common Council of the City,

(*b*) elsewhere in England, or in Wales, the council of the district in whose area is situated the part of the loading area where the vehicle in question is while parking is prohibited as mentioned in paragraph (1) above.

4. Power to remove vehicles

(1) Where, in the case of a vehicle to which regulation 3 above applies—

(*a*) the owner, driver or other person in control or in charge of the vehicle refuses or fails to comply with a requirement, made under that regulation by a duly authorised officer of the local authority, to move it or cause it to be moved, or (*b*) no person who is in control or in charge of the vehicle and who is capable of moving it or causing it to be moved is present on or in the vicinity of the vehicle,

an officer of the local authority (who need not be the officer who has made any requirement as respects the vehicle under regulation 3 above) may move or arrange for the removal of the vehicle to another part of the loading area, or may remove it or arrange for its removal from the loading area to some other place which is not on a highway.

(2) Any person removing or moving a vehicle under this regulation may do so by towing or driving the vehicle or in such other manner as he may think necessary, and may take such measures in relation to the vehicle as he may think necessary to enable him to remove or move it as aforesaid.

PART III

Disposal of Abandoned Vehicles

5. Disposal of abandoned vehicles *[Omitted.]*

The Removal and Disposal of Vehicles Regulations 1986

(SI 1986 No 183)

ARRANGEMENT OF REGULATIONS

PART I

GENERAL

PART II

REMOVAL OF VEHICLES

SCHEDULES

PART I

GENERAL

1. Commencement, citation and revocation *[Omitted.]*

2. Interpretation

In these Regulations, unless the contrary intention appears, the following expressions have the meanings hereby assigned to them respectively, that is to say:—

'the 1978 Act' means the Refuse Disposal (Amenity) Act 1978;

'the 1984 Act' means the Road Traffic Regulation Act 1984;

'motor vehicle' has the meaning assigned to it in section 11(1) of the 1978 Act;

'road', in England and Wales, means any highway and any other road to which the public has access;

'vehicle', in relation to any matter prescribed by these Regulations for the purposes of any provision in sections 3 and 4 of the 1978 Act, means a motor vehicle, and in relation to any matter prescribed by these Regulations for the purposes of any provision in sections 99 and 101 of the 1984 Act has the meaning assigned to it in section 99(5) of that Act, and, in relation to any matter prescribed by these Regulations for the purposes of section 99 of the 1984 Act, any reference to a vehicle which has been permitted to remain at rest or which has broken down includes a reference to a vehicle which has been permitted to remain at rest or which has broken down before the coming into force of these Regulations.

[Words relating expressly and exclusively to Scotland have been omitted from the definition of 'road' above.]

PART II

Removal of Vehicles

3. Power of constable to require removal of vehicles from roads

(1) Except as provided by regulation 7 of these Regulations, this regulation applies to a vehicle which—

(*a*) has broken down, or been permitted to remain at rest, on a road in such a position or in such condition or in such circumstances as to cause obstruction to persons using the road or as to be likely to cause danger to such persons, or

(*b*) has been permitted to remain at rest or has broken down and remained at rest on a road in contravention of a prohibition or restriction contained in, or having effect under, any of the enactments mentioned in Schedule 1 to these Regulations.

(2) A constable may require the owner, driver or other person in control or in charge of any vehicle to which this regulation applies to move or cause to be moved the vehicle and any such requirement may include a requirement that the vehicle shall be moved from that road to a place which is not on that or any other road, or that the vehicle shall not be moved to any such road or to any such position on a road as may be specified.

(3) A person required to move or cause to be moved a vehicle under this regulation shall comply with such requirement as soon as practicable.

4. Power of constable to remove vehicles

Except as provided by regulation 7 of these Regulations, where a vehicle—

(*a*) is a vehicle to which regulation 3 of these Regulations applies, or

(*b*) having broken down on a road or on any land in the open air, appears to a constable to have been abandoned without lawful authority, or

(*c*) has been permitted to remain at rest on a road or on any land in the open air in such a position or in such condition or in such circumstances as to appear to a constable to have been abandoned without lawful authority,

then, subject to the provisions of sections 99 and 100 of the 1984 Act, a constable may remove or arrange for the removal of the vehicle, and, in the case of a vehicle which is on a road, he may remove it or arrange for its removal from that road to a place which is not on that or any other road, or may move it or arrange for its removal to another position on that or another road.

5. Power of local authority to remove certain vehicles

(1) Except as provided by regulation 7 of these Regulations, where a vehicle (other than a motor vehicle which a local authority have a duty to remove under section 3 of the 1978 Act)—

(*a*) having broken down on a road or on any land in the open air in the area of a local authority, appears to them to have been abandoned without lawful authority, or

(*b*) has been permitted to remain at rest on a road or on any land in the open air in the area of a local authority in such a position or in such condition or in such circumstances as to appear to them to have been abandoned without lawful authority,

the local authority may, subject to the provisions of sections 99 and 100 of the 1984 Act, remove or arrange for the removal of the vehicle to a place which is not on any road.

(2) In this regulation 'local authority' means, in the case of a vehicle situate at a place—

(*a*) in England, the council of the district or of the London borough, or the Common Council of the City of London;

(*b*) *[Applies to Scotland]*; or

(*c*) in Wales, the council of the district,

within whose area is situate that place.

6. Method of removing vehicles

Any person removing or moving a vehicle under the last two preceding regulations may do so by towing or driving the vehicle or in such other manner as he may think necessary and may take such measures in relation to the vehicle as he may think necessary to enable him to remove or move it as aforesaid.

7. Exception for Severn Bridge

Regulations 3, 4 and 5 of these Regulations shall not apply in relation to any vehicle while on the central section of the specified carriageways (as defined in section 1 of the Severn Bridge Tolls Act 1965) of a road which crosses the Rivers Severn and Wye.

8. Manner of giving notice to occupier of land before removing a vehicle therefrom *[Omitted.]*

9. Manner and period during which occupier of land may object *[Omitted.]*

10. Period before which notice must be affixed to a vehicle in certain cases before removing it for destruction

For the purposes of section 3(5) of the 1978 Act and section 99(4) of the 1984 Act, the period before the commencement of which a notice must be caused to be affixed to a vehicle by an authority who propose to remove it, before they remove it, being a vehicle which in the opinion of the authority is in such a condition that it ought to be destroyed, shall be seven days.

PART III

Disposal of Abandoned Vehicles

11–16. *[Omitted.]*

SCHEDULE 1

Regulation 3

Certain Enactments by or under which are Imposed Prohibitions or Restrictions on the Waiting of Vehicles on Roads

Section 52 of the Metropolitan Police Act 1839 and section 22 of the local Act of the second and third year of the reign of Queen Victoria, chapter 94 (relating to the prevention of obstruction in streets in London).

Section 21 of the Town Police Clauses Act 1847 (relating to the prevention of obstructions in streets in England and Wales elsewhere than in London).

Section 2 of the Parks Regulation (Amendment) Act 1926 (authorising the marking of regulations as to Royal Parks).

[Section 36 of the Road Traffic Act 1988] (which makes it an offence to fail to conform to the indications given by certain traffic signs).

Section 1 of the 1984 Act (which authorises the making of orders regulating traffic on roads outside Greater London).

Section 6 of the 1984 Act (authorising the making of orders regulating traffic on roads in Greater London).

Section 9 of the 1984 Act (authorising the making of experimental traffic orders).

Section 12 of the 1984 Act (relating to experimental traffic schemes in Greater London).

Section 14 of the 1984 Act (which provides for the restriction or prohibition of the use of roads in consequence of the execution of works).

Section 17 of the 1984 Act (authorising the making of regulations with respect to the use of special roads).

Section 25 of the 1984 Act (authorising the making of regulations for crossings for foot passengers).

Sections 35 and 45 to 49 of the 1984 Act (relating to parking places for vehicles).

Section 57 of the 1984 Act (relating to the provision of parking places in England and Wales for bicycles and motor cycles).

Sections 66 and 67 of the 1984 Act (which empower the police to place traffic signs relating to local traffic regulations and temporary signs for dealing with traffic congestion and danger).

Any enactment in any local Act for the time being in force, and any byelaw having effect under any enactment for the time being in force, being an enactment or byelaw imposing or authorising the imposition of a prohibition or restriction similar to any prohibition or restriction which is or can be imposed by or under any of the abovementioned enactments.

[Schedule 1 is printed as amended by the Interpretation Act 1978, ss 17(2)(a) and 23(1). References to Scottish legislation have been omitted from Sched 1.]

SCHEDULE 2

Form of Notice to Occupier of Land before Removing Abandoned Vehicles

[Omitted.]

The Road Transport (International Passenger Services) Regulations 1984

(SI 1984 No 748)

[The text of these regulations is printed as amended by:
the Road Transport (International Passenger Services) (Amendment) Regulations 1987 (SI 1987 No 1755) (1 November 1987); and
the Road Transport (International Passenger Services) (Amendment) Regulations 1988 (SI 1988 No 1809) (18 November 1988).
The amending regulations are referred to in the notes to the regulations by their years and numbers. The dates referred to above are the dates on which the regulations came into force.]

ARRANGEMENT OF REGULATIONS

PART I

GENERAL

Regulation

PART II

MODIFICATIONS OF THE ACT OF 1981 IN RELATION TO VEHICLES REGISTERED IN THE UNITED KINGDOM WHEN USED FOR THE INTERNATIONAL CARRIAGE OF PASSENGERS

PART III

MODIFICATIONS OF THE ACT OF 1981 IN RELATION TO VEHICLES REGISTERED OUTSIDE THE UNITED KINGDOM

PART IV

APPLICATIONS FOR ISSUE OF AUTHORISATIONS AND OTHER DOCUMENTS AND FEES IN RESPECT THEREOF

PART V

PENALTIES, ENFORCEMENT, SUPPLEMENTARY AND CONSEQUENTIAL

SCHEDULES

PART I

GENERAL

1. Citation, commencement and revocation *[Omitted.]*

2. Interpretation

(1) In these Regulations—

(*a*) the references to the following provisions, that is to say—

Council Regulation No 117/66 [*qv*]
Council Regulation No 516/72
Council Regulation No 517/72 and
Commission Regulation No 1016/68

are references, respectively, to the Community provisions more particularly described in Schedule 1 and references to 'the Council Regulations' or 'the Commission Regulation' shall be construed accordingly;

(*b*) 'ASOR' means the Agreement on the International Carriage of Passengers by Road by means of Occasional Coach and Bus Services (ASOR) [*qv*], approved on behalf of the Economic Community pursuant to Council Decision (EEC) of 20th July 1982 concluding the Agreement [*OJ L 230, 5 August 1982, p 38*], entering into force for the Economic Community on 1st December 1983, as read with Council Regulation (EEC) No 56/83 on measures implementing the Agreement [*OJ L10, 13 January 1983, p 1*].

(*c*) 'ASOR State' means—

(i) a state, not being a member State, which is a Contracting Party to ASOR and to which the provision of Sections II and III of ASOR apply in accordance with Article 18 thereof; or

(ii) the Economic Community;

(*d*) 'ASOR regulated' means, in relation to the carriage of passengers, the international carriage of passengers by road to which ASOR applies, namely in the circumstances specified in Article 1 thereof, that is to say, by means of occasional services (within the meaning of that Agreement) effected—

(i) between the territories of two ASOR States, or starting and finishing in the territory of the same ASOR State; and

(ii) should the need arise during such services, in transit through the territory of another ASOR State or through the territory of a state which is not an ASOR State; and

(iii) using vehicles registered in the territory of an ASOR State which by virtue of their construction and their equipment, are suitable for carrying more than nine persons, including the driver, and are intended for that purpose

and references to the carriage of passengers which is ASOR regulated include unladen journeys of the vehicles concerned with such carriage;

(*e*) 'Community regulated' means, in relation to the carriage of passengers, the international carriage of passengers by road to which Council Regulation No 117/66 applies, namely in the circumstances mentioned in Article 4(1) thereof, that is to say—

(i) where the place of departure is in the territory of a member State and the destination is in the territory of the same or another member State; and

(ii) the vehicle is registered in a member State and in construction and equipment is suitable for carrying more than nine persons, including the driver, and is intended for that purpose,

and references to the carriage of passengers which is Community regulated include unladen journeys of the vehicles concerned with such carriage;

(*f*) 'ECMT State' means a State which is a member of the European Conference of Ministers of Transport of the 17th November 1953 but not a member State or an ASOR State;

(*g*) 'the Secretary of State' means the Secretary of State for Transport;

(*h*) 'examiner' has the same meaning as in section 7(1) of the Road Traffic (Foreign Vehicles) Act 1972 [*qv*];

(*i*) 'public service vehicle' shall be construed in accordance with section 1 of the Act of 1981 [*qv*];

(*j*) 'the Act of 1981' means the Public Passenger Vehicles Act 1981;

(2) Any reference in these Regulations to a numbered Regulation or Schedule is a reference to the Regulations or Schedule bearing that number in these Regulations.

3. Extent

These Regulations do not extend to Northern Ireland.

PART II

MODIFICATIONS OF THE ACT OF 1981 IN RELATION TO VEHICLES REGISTERED IN THE UNITED KINGDOM WHEN USED FOR THE INTERNATIONAL CARRIAGE OF PASSENGERS

4. Community regulated regular, shuttle and works services by vehicles registered in the United Kingdom

(1) This Regulation applies to a vehicle registered in the United Kingdom which is being used for Community regulated carriage of passengers in so far as the vehicle—

(*a*) is used to provide any service for the carriage of passengers such as is mentioned in Article 1, 2 or 6 of Council Regulation No 177/66; and

(*b*) is so used in accordance with such of the requirements of the Council Regulations as apply in relation to the service in question.

(2) The provisions of the Act of 1981 shall have effect as if—

(*a*) *[Lapsed.]*

(*b*) in relation to a vehicle to which this Regulation applies registered in Northern Ireland, sections 6, 12, 18, 22 . . . of the Act of 1981 were omitted.

[Regulation 4 is printed as it has effect after the repeal of s 30 of the Public Passenger Vehicles Act 1981.]

5. Non-Community regulated regular and shuttle services by public service vehicles registered in the United Kingdom

(1) This Regulation applies to a public service vehicle registered in the United Kingdom which is being used for the international carriage of passengers by road which is not Community regulated but where the vehicle is being used to provide a service for the carriage of passengers of a description such as is mentioned in Article 1 or 2 of Council Regulation 117/66 (that is to say, a regular service, a special regular service or a shuttle service as defined in those Articles).

(2) The provisions of the Act of 1981 [and Parts I and II of the Transport Act 1985] shall have effect as if—

(*a*) in relation to a vehicle to which this Regulation applies registered in Northern Ireland, sections 6, 12, 18 and 22 of the Act of 1981 were omitted; and

(*b*) in relation to a vehicle to which this Regulation applies registered in Great Britain or in Northern Ireland, for [section 6 of the Transport Act 1985 there shall be substituted the following section and section 35 of that Act shall be omitted]:—

'[**6.**]—(1) No person shall cause or permit a public service vehicle to be used on a road for the international carriage of passengers unless there is in force in relation to the use of the vehicle, and is carried on the vehicle, an international passenger transport authorisation.

(2) A certifying officer or a public service vehicle examiner may at any time, on production if so required of his authority, require the operator or the driver of any

such vehicle as is referred to in subsection (1) above, to produce and to permit him to inspect and copy an international passenger transport authorisation relating to the use of the vehicle, and for that purpose may require the vehicle to be stopped and may detain the vehicle for such time as is requisite for the purpose of inspecting and copying the authorisation.

(3) A person who—

(*a*) without reasonable excuse contravenes subsection (1) of this section, or

(*b*) without reasonable excuse fails to comply with a requirement of a certifying officer or public service vehicle examiner, or wilfully obstucts such officer or examiner, in the exercise of his powers under subsection (2) of this section,

shall be guilty of an offence and shall be liable on summary conviction to a fine not exceeding level 3 on the standard scale (within the meaning of section 75 of the Criminal Justice Act 1982).

(4) In this section "international passenger transport authorisation" means a licence, permit, authorisation or other document issued by the Secretary of State in pursuance of an international agreement or arrangement to which the United Kingdom is for the time being a party.'.

[Regulation 5 is printed as amended by SI 1987 No 1755.]

6. Occasional services by vehicles registered in the United Kingdom (whether ASOR or Community regulated or not)

(1) This Regulation applies to a vehicle registered in the United Kingdom which is being used for the international carriage of passengers by road—

(*a*) in so far as the vehicle is used to provide a service for the carriage of passengers which is Community regulated and is such as is mentioned—

(i) in paragraph 1(*a*) of Article 3 of Council Regulation No 117/66 (that is to say, an occasional service described in that paragraph as a closed-door tour), or

(ii) in paragraph 1(*b*) of the said Article 3 (that is to say, an occasional service described in that paragraph where the passengers are carried on the outward journey and the return journey is made unladen), or

(iii) in paragraph 1(*c*) of the said Article 3 (that is to say, an occasional service, as mentioned in that paragraph, of any other description); or

(*b*) in so far as the vehicle is used to provide a service for the carriage of passengers which is ASOR regulated; or

(*c*) in so far as the vehicle is used as a public service vehicle for the carriage of passengers which is not ASOR regulated or Community regulated but is a service of a description such as is mentioned in any of the paragraphs of Article 3 of Council Regulation No 117/66.

(2) The provision of the Act of 1981 [and Parts I and II of the Transport Act 1985] shall have effect as if—

(*a*) in relation to a vehicle to which this Regulation applies registered in Northern Ireland, sections 6, 12, 18 and 22 of the Act of 1981 were omitted; and

(*b*) in relation to a vehicle to which this Regulation applies registered in Great Britain or in Northern Ireland, for [section 6 of the Transport Act 1985 there shall be substituted the following section and section 35 of that Act shall be omitted]:—

'[**6.**]—(1) No person shall cause or permit a vehicle to be used on a road for the international carriage of passengers unless—

(*a*) in relation to the use of the vehicle, in the case of such carriage which is ASOR regulated, the requirements of Articles 7, 8 and 9 of, and the Annex to, ASOR (which provide for the completion by the person by whom, or on whose behalf, a vehicle is used to provide an occasional service of a passenger waybill in respect of the service in question and for the carrying of the top copy of such waybill on the vehicle at all times while it is used on that service) are complied with and, in the case of any other such carriage, the requirements of Articles 2, 3 and 4 of, and of Annex 2 to, Commission Regulation No 1016/68 (which provide as aforesaid) are complied with, or would be complied with if those provisions applied to the service; and

(*b*) the vehicle is used on the service in question in circumstances which accord in all respects with the particulars which have been specified in the said passenger waybill as applicable to that service.

(2) A certifying officer or a public service vehicle examiner may, at any time which is reasonable having regard to the circumstances of the case, enter any premises from which he has reason to believe that a vehicle is or is to be operated on a service for the international carriage of passengers and may, on production if so required of his authority, require the operator of the vehicle to produce and to permit him to inspect and copy a control document duly completed for the service, in the case of ASOR regulated carriage, in accordance with Articles 7, 8 and 9 of, and the Annex to, ASOR and, in the case of any other such carriage, in accordance with Articles 2, 3, and 4 of, and Annex 2 to, Commission Regulation No 1016/68.

(3) A certifying officer or a public service vehicle examiner may, on production if so required of his authority—

(*a*) require the driver of a vehicle used for the international carriage of passengers to produce and to permit him to inspect and copy and to mark with an official stamp, in the case of a vehicle used for ASOR regulated carriage, the document required by Article 8(2) of ASOR and, in the case of any other such carriage, the document required by Article 3(2) of Commission Regulation No 1016/68, to be kept on a vehicle to which that Article applies; and

(*b*) detain the vehicle for such time as is required for the purpose of inspecting, copying and marking the document.

(4) A person who—

(*a*) without reasonable excuse contravenes subsection (1) above, or

(*b*) without reasonable excuse fails to comply with a requirement of an officer or examiner, under subsection (2) or (3) above, or

(*c*) wilfully obstructs an officer or examiner in the exercise of his powers under either of those subsections,

shall be guilty of an offence and shall be liable on summary conviction to a fine not exceeding level 3 on the standard scale (within the meaning of section 75 of the Criminal Justice Act 1982).

(5) In this section—

'ASOR' means the Agreement on the International Carriage of Passengers by Road by means of Occasional Coach and Bus Services (ASOR) approved on behalf of the Economic Community pursuant to Council Decision (EEC) of 20th July 1982 concluding the Agreement entering into force for the Economic Community on 1st December 1983 [*qv*], as read with Council Regulation (EEC) No 56/83 on measures implementing the Agreement;

'ASOR State' means—

(*a*) a state, not being a member State, which is a Contracting Party to ASOR and to which the provisions of Section II and III of ASOR apply in accordance with Article 18 thereof; or

(*b*) the Economic Community;

'ASOR regulated' means, in relation to the carriage of passengers, the international carriage of passengers by road to which ASOR applies namely in the circumstances specified in Article 1 thereof, that is to say, by means of occasional services (within the meaning of that Agreement) effected—

(*a*) between the territories of two ASOR States, or starting and finishing in the territory of the same ASOR State: and

(*b*) should the need arise during such services, in transit through the territory of another ASOR State or through the territory of a state which is not an ASOR State; and

(*c*) using vehicles registered in the territory of an ASOR State which, by virtue of their construction and their equipment, are suitable for carrying more than nine persons, including the driver, and are intended for that purpose,

and references to the carriage of passengers which is ASOR regulated include unladen journeys of the vehicles concerned with such carriage;

'Commission Regulation No 1016/68' means Regulation (EEC) No 1016/68 of the Commission of 9th July 1968 prescribing the model control documents referred to in Articles 6 and 9 of Council Regulation No 117/66/EEC as amended by and as read with Regulation (EEC) No 2485/82 of the Commission of 13th September 1982; and

'Council Regulation No 117/66' means Regulation No 117/66/EEC of the Council of 28th July 1966 on the introduction of common rules for the international carriage of passengers by coach and bus [*qv*].'.

[Regulation 6 is printed as amended by SI 1987 No 1755.]

PART III

Modifications of the Act of 1981 in Relation to Vehicles Registered outside the United Kingdom

7. Small vehicles registered outside the United Kingdom visiting Great Britain temporarily

(1) This Regulation applies to a public service vehicle registered outside the United Kingdom which—

(*a*) in construction and equipment is suitable for carrying not more than nine persons, including the driver, and is intended for that purpose;

(*b*) is brought into Great Britain for the purpose of carrying passengers who are travelling to Great Britain from a place outside the United Kingdom, or who are travelling from the United Kingdom to any such place; and

(*c*) remains in Great Britain for a period not exceeding three months from the date of its entry therein.

(2) The provisions of the Act of 1981 shall, in relation to a vehicle to which this Regulation applies, have effect as if sections 6, 12, 18, 22 . . . of the Act of 1981 were omitted.

[Regulation 7 is printed as it has effect after the repeal of s 30 of the Public Passenger Vehicles Act 1981.]

8. Community regulated regular, shuttle and works services by vehicles registered outside the United Kingdom

(1) This Regulation applies to a vehicle registered outside the United Kingdom which is being used for Community regulated carriage of passengers in so far as the vehicle—

(*a*) is being used to provide any service for the carriage of passengers such as is mentioned in Article 1, 2 or 6 of Council Regulation 117/66; and

(*b*) is being so used in accordance with such of the requirements of the Council Regulations or, as the case may be, the Commission Regulation as apply to the service in question.

(2) The provisions of the Act of 1981 shall, in relation to a vehicle to which this Regulation applies, have effect as if sections 6, 12, 18, 22 . . . of the Act of 1981 were omitted.

[Regulation 8 is printed as it has effect after the repeal of s 30 of the Public Passenger Vehicles Act 1981.]

9. Non-Community regulated regular and shuttle services by vehicles registered outside the United Kingdom

(1) This Regulation applies to a public service vehicle registered outside the United Kingdom which is being used for the international carriage of passengers which is not Community regulated in so far as the vehicle—

(*a*) is being used to provide a service for the carriage of passengers of a description such as is mentioned in Article 1 or 2 of Council Regulation 117/66 (that is to say, a regular service, a special regular service or a shuttle service as defined in those Articles), and

(*b*) is so used by or on behalf of a person who is authorised, under the law of the country in which the vehicle is registered, to use the vehicle for the carriage of passengers on the journey in question or such parts thereof as are situated within that country.

(2) The provisions of the Act of 1981 shall in relation to a vehicle to which this Regulation applies, have effect as if sections 6, 18, 22 . . . of the Act of 1981 were omitted, and as if for section 12 of the Act of 1981 there were substituted the section set out in Schedule 2.

[Regulation 9 is printed as it has effect after the repeal of s 30 of the Public Passenger Vehicles Act 1981.]

10. ASOR or Community regulated occasional services by vehicles registered outside the United Kingdom

(1) This Regulation applies to a vehicle registered outside the United Kingdom which is being used for ASOR or Community regulated carriage of passengers—

(*a*) in so far as the vehicle is used to provide a service for the carriage of passengers such as is mentioned—

(i) in paragraph 1(*a*) of Article 2 of ASOR or paragraph 1(*a*) of Article 3 of Council Regulation No 117/66 (that is to say, an occasional service described in that paragraph as a closed-door tour), or

(ii) in paragraph 1(*b*) of each of those Articles (that is to say an occasional service as described in that paragraph where passengers are carried on the outward journey and the return journey is made unladen), or

(iii) in paragraph 1(*c*) of each of those Articles (that is to say, an occasional service as mentioned in that paragraph of any other description); and

(*b*) in so far as, in relation to the use of the vehicle—

(i) in the case of a vehicle being used for ASOR regulated carriage, the requirements of Articles 7, 8 and 9 of, and Annex to, ASOR (which provides for the completion, by the person by whom or on whose behalf a vehicle is used to provide such an occasional service as aforesaid, of a passenger waybill in respect of the service in question and for the carrying of the top copy of such waybill on the vehicle at all times while it is used on that service) and in the case of a vehicle being used for Community regulated carriage, the requirements of Articles 2, 3 and 4 of, and Annex 2 to, Commission Regulation No 1016/68 (which provides as aforesaid), have been complied with, and

(ii) the vehicle is used on the service in question in circumstances which accord in all respects with particulars which, in pursuance of the said requirements, have been specified in the said passenger waybill as applicable to that service.

(2) In relation to a vehicle to which this Regulation applies, the provisions of the Act of 1981 shall have effect as if sections 6, 18, 22 . . . of the Act of 1981 were omitted and—

(*a*) in so far as the vehicle is used to provide a service for the carriage of passengers such as is mentioned—

(i) in Article 2(1)(*a*) or (*b*) of ASOR or Article 3(1)(*a*) or (*b*) of Council Regulation No 117/66, or

(ii) in a case where the service is ASOR regulated and all the conditions mentioned in Article 5(2) of ASOR are fulfilled, in Article 2(1)(*c*) of ASOR, or

(iii) in a case where the service is Community regulated and all the conditions mentioned in Article 5(2) of the said Council Regulation are fulfilled, in Article 2(1)(*c*) of that Regulation,

as if section 12 of the Act of 1981 were omitted; and

(*b*) in so far as the vehicle is used as a public service to provide a service for the carriage of passengers such as is mentioned in Article 2(1)(*c*) of ASOR or Article 2(1)(*c*) of the said Council Regulation and—

(i) in a case where the service is ASOR regulated any of the conditions mentioned in Article 5(2) of ASOR are not fulfilled, or

(ii) in a case where the service is Community regulated, any of the conditions mentioned in Article 5(2) of the said Council Regulation are not fulfilled,

as if for the said section 12 there were substituted the section set out in Schedule 2.

[Regulation 10 is printed as it has effect after the repeal of s 30 of the Public Passenger Vehicles Act 1981.]

11. Certain occasional services by vehicles registered in ECMT States

(1) This Regulation applies to a public service vehicle—

(*a*) which is registered in the territory of a State which is an ECMT State;

(*b*) which is brought into Great Britain for the purpose of carrying passengers who are making only a temporary stay therein or are in transit; and

(*c*) which remains in Great Britain for a period not exceeding three months from the date of its entry therein,

in so far as the vehicle—

(i) is used to provide a service for the carriage of passengers which is not ASOR or Community regulated but which is of a description such as is mentioned in Article 3(1)(*a*), (*b*) or (*c*) of Council Regulation No 117/66, where the journey made by the vehicle in providing that service starts from a place situated in the territory of an ECMT State and ends at a place situated in the territory of such a State or in Great Britain, and

(ii) is so used by or on behalf of a person who is authorised, under the law in force in the State, in the territory of which it is registered to use the vehicle for the carriage of passengers on the journey in question or such part thereof as lies within the territory of that State.

(2) In relation to a vehicle to which this Regulation applies, the provisions of the Act of 1981 shall have effect as if sections 6, 18, 22 . . . of the Act of 1981 were omitted and as if—

(*a*) in so far as the vehicle is used to provide a service for the carriage of passengers such as is mentioned in paragraph 1(*a*) and 1(*b*) of Article 3 of Council Regulation No 117/66, for section 12 of the Act of 1981 there were substituted the following sections [*sic*]:—

> '**12.** No person shall cause or permit a public service vehicle to be used on a road for the international carriage of passengers unless there is in force in relation to the use of the vehicle, and is carried on the vehicle, a document which is issued by the competent authority of the country in which the vehicle is registered in the form set out in Schedule 3 to the Road Transport (International Passenger Service) Regulations 1984 and which is duly completed.';

and

(*b*) in so far as the vehicle is used for the carriage of passengers such as is mentioned in paragraph 1(*c*) of the said Article 3, for section 12 of the Act of 1981 there were substituted the section set out in Schedule 2.

[Regulation 11 is printed as it has effect after the repeal of s 30 of the Public Passenger Vehicles Act 1981.]

12. Certain occasional services by vehicles not registered in a member State, an ASOR State or an ECMT State

(1) This Regulation applies to a public service vehicle—

(*a*) which is registered in the territory of a State which is not a member State, an ASOR State or an ECMT State;

(*b*) which is brought into Great Britain for the purpose of carrying passengers who are making only a temporary stay therein or are in transit, being passengers who commenced their journey from the state in the territory of which the vehicle is registered or, as the case may be, from Northern Ireland; and

(*c*) which remains in Great Britain for a period not exceeding three months from the date of its entry therein,

in so far as the vehicle—

(i) is used to provide a service for the carriage of passengers which is not Community regulated but which is of a description such as is mentioned in Article 3(1)(*a*), (*b*) or (*c*) of Regulation No 117/66, and

(iii) is so used by or on behalf of a person who is authorised, under the law in force in the state in the territory of which it is registered to use the vehicle for the carriage of passengers on the journey in question or such parts thereof as lie within the territory of that state.

(2) The provisions of the Act of 1981 shall, in relation to a vehicle to which this Regulation applies, have effect as if sections 6, 18, 22 . . . of the Act of 1981 were omitted and as if for section 12 of the Act of 1981 there were substituted

[(*a*) in the case of a public service vehicle registered in the Union of Soviet Socialist Republics used to provide a service of a description such as is mentioned in article 3(1)(*a*) or (*b*) of Regulation No 117/66, the following section;—

12. No person shall cause or permit a public service vehicle to be used on a road for the international carriage of passengers unless there is carried on the vehicle a list of the passengers carried by the vehicle; and

(*b*) in any other case, the section set out in Schedule 2.]

[Regulation 12 is printed as it has effect after the repeal of s 30 of the Public Passenger Vehicles Act 1981; and as subsequently amended by SI 1988 No 1809.]

PART IV

Applications for Issue of Authorisations and other Documents and Fees in respect thereof

* * *

15. Applications for, and issue of, certificates and control documents for works and occasional services

(1)–(3) *[Omitted.]*

(4) The top copy of every passenger waybill (being the document which, as mentioned in Article 7 of ASOR or Article 2 of the Commission Regulation is the document applicable in respect of the provision of a service for the carriage of passengers such as is mentioned in Article 2 of ASOR or Article 3 of Council Regulation No 117/66), shall be retained, after the service in question has been provided, by the person by whom or on whose behalf it was provided and shall be sent to the Secretary of State so as to reach him not later than 31st March next following the end of the calendar year in which the service to which the waybill relates was provided.

(5) The duplicate of every such passenger waybill (being the duplicate which, by virtue of Article 7(1) of ASOR or Article 2(1) of Commission Regulation No 1016/68 is required to be contained in a control document such as is mentioned in those Articles shall not be detached from that document at any time during its period of validity.

PART V

Penalties, Enforcement, Supplementary and Consequential

16. Production, inspection and copying of documents in relation to ASOR or Community regulated services

(1) Paragraph (2) below shall have effect in relation to a vehicle where it appears to an examiner that the vehicle—

(*a*) is being used for the provision of an ASOR regulated or Community regulated service; and

(*b*) is being used, or has been brought into Great Britain for the purpose of being used, in such circumstances as, by virtue of any of the provisions specified in paragraph (3) below, to require a document of a description referred to in that provision to be kept or carried on the vehicle.

(2) An examiner may, on production if so required of his authority—

(*a*) require the driver of a vehicle referred to in paragraph (1) above to produce the document and to permit him to inspect and copy it and (in the case of a document of a description referred to in any of the provisions specified in paragraph (3)(*c*) or (*e*) below) to mark it with an official stamp; and

(*b*) may detain the vehicle for such time as is required for the purpose of inspecting, copying and marking the document.

(3) The provisions referred to in paragraph (1) above as being specified in this paragraph are—

(*a*) Article 17 of Council Regulation No 517/72 (which provides, inter alia, that the authorisation required by that Regulation for the use of a vehicle to provide a service for the carriage of passengers such as is mentioned in Article 1 thereof shall be carried on the vehicle);

(*b*) Articles 17 and 18 of Council Regulation No 516/72 (which respectively provide, inter alia, that the authorisation required by that Regulation for the use of a vehicle to provide a service for the carriage of passengers such as is mentioned in Article 1 thereof shall be carried on the vehicle and that passengers using that service shall be provided with a ticket throughout the journey in question);

(*c*) Article 8(2) of ASOR and Article 3(2) of Commission Regulation No 1016/68 (which provide that the top copy of the passenger waybill being the document which, by virtue of Article 7 of ASOR or Article 2 of Commission Regulation No 1016/68, has been detached from the control document such as is mentioned in those Articles, and is the document applicable in respect of the provision of a service for the carriage of passengers such as is mentioned in Article 2 of ASOR or Article 3 of Council Regulation No 117/66, shall be kept on the vehicle);

(*d*) Article 11(3) of ASOR and Article 5a(3) of Commission Regulation No [1016/68] (which provide that the model document with stiff green covers referred to in Article 11 of ASOR must be carried on the vehicle); and

(*e*) Regulation 17.

17. Carriage on the vehicle of certificate issued under Article 6 of Council Regulation No 117/66

(1) In relation to a vehicle being used to provide a Community regulated service for the carriage of passengers such as is mentioned in Article 6 of Council Regulation

No 117/66 there shall be carried on the vehicle, at all times while it is being used, the certificate specified in Article 1 of Commission Regulation No 1016/68, being the certificate which, by virtue of the said Article 6, is required to be in force in respect of the provision of that service.

(2) An examiner may, on production if so required of his authority—

(*a*) require the driver of a vehicle referred to in paragraph (1) above to produce the document and to permit him to inspect and copy it and to mark it with an official stamp; and

(*b*) may detain the vehicle for such time as is required for the purpose of inspecting, copying and marking the document.

18. Withdrawal of regular, special regular and shuttle service authorisations

(1) If the Secretary of State is at any time satisfied that a holder of a regular, special regular or shuttle service authorisation issued by him—

(*a*) has failed to comply with the relevant Council Regulation, with the authorisation or any conditions specified therein; or

(*b*) has failed to operate, or is no longer operating, a service under the authorisation,

he may, by notice in writing to the holder, withdraw the authorisation.

(2) Where the Secretary of State decides to withdraw an authorisation in exercise of his powers under Council Regulation No 516/72 or Council Regulation No 517/72 he may do so by notice in writing to the holder of the authorisation.

(3) The withdrawal of an authorisation in accordance with this Regulation shall take effect on the date specified in the notice which shall be not earlier than 28 days after the date of the notice.

(4) Where an authorisation is withdrawn in accordance with this Regulation it shall be of no effect and the holder shall forthwith surrender the authorisation to the Secretary of State.

(5) At any time that is reasonable having regard to the circumstances of the case, an examiner may, on production if so required of his authority, enter any premises of the holder of an authorisation which has been withdrawn in accordance with this Regulation and may require the holder to produce the authorisation and, on its being produced, may seize it and deliver it to the Secretary of State.

(6) Where it appears to an examiner that a document produced to him in pursuance of Regulation 16 is an authorisation which has been withdrawn in accordance with this Regulation he may seize it and deliver it to the Secretary of State.

(7) In paragraph 1 of this Regulation 'relevant Council Regulation' means in the case of a regular or special regular service authorisation Council Regulation No 517/72 and in the case of a shuttle service authorisation Council Regulation No 516/72.

19. Penalty for contravention of ASOR, the Council Regulations or the Commission Regulation

(1) A person is guilty of an offence under this Regulation if without reasonable excuse, he uses a vehicle for Community regulated carriage of passengers by road or causes or permits such a vehicle to be used—

(*a*) to provide a service for the carriage of passengers such as is mentioned in Article 1 of Council Regulation No 117/66 (that is to say, a regular service or a special regular service as defined in that Article), not being, in either such case, a service such as is mentioned in Article 6 of that Regulation, otherwise than under and in accordance with the terms of an authorisation issued under Article 2 of Council Regulation No 517/72; or

(*b*) to provide a service for the carriage of passengers such as is mentioned in Article 2 of Council Regulation No 117/66 (that is to say, a shuttle service as defined in that Article), not being a service such as is mentioned in Article 6 of that Regulation, otherwise than under and in accordance with the terms of an authorisation issued under Article 2 of Council Regulation No 516/72; or

(*c*) to provide a service for the carriage of passengers such as is mentioned in Article 6 of Council Regulation No 117/66 (that is to say, a service provided by an undertaking for its own workers in relation to which the conditions mentioned in paragraph 1(*a*) and (*b*) of that Article are fulfilled) without there being in force in relation to the service a certificate issued under Article 1 of Commission Regulation No 1016/68.

(2) A person shall be guilty of an offence under this Regulation if, without reasonable excuse, he uses a vehicle for ASOR regulated or Community regulated carriage by road, or causes or permits a vehicle to be so used, to provide a service for the carriage of passengers such as is mentioned in paragraph 1 of Article 2 of ASOR or Article 3 of Council Regulation No 117/66 when there is not duly and correctly completed for the vehicle a passenger waybill, or when the top copy of the passenger waybill is not kept on the vehicle throughout the journey to which it refers, as required, in the case of a vehicle being used for ASOR regulated carriage, by Articles 7 and 8 of ASOR and, in the case of a vehicle being used for Community regulated carriage, by Articles 2 and 3 of Council Regulation No 1016/68.

(3) A person guilty of an offence under this Regulation shall be liable on summary conviction to a fine not exceeding [level 3 on the standard scale].

[Regulation 19 is printed as amended by the Criminal Justice Act 1988, s 52.]

20. Penalty relating to documents required in respect of ASOR and Community regulated services

A person who—

(*a*) without reasonable excuse contravenes, or fails to comply with a requirement imposed by or under Regulation 15(4) or (5), 16(2)(*a*), 17(1) or (2), or 18(4) or (5), or by or under any provision of ASOR, the Council Regulations or the Commission Regulation referred to in any of those provisions; or

(*b*) wilfully obstructs an examiner in the exercise of his powers under Regulation 16(2), 17(1) or (2), or 18(5) or (6), or under any provision of ASOR, the Council Regulations or Commission Regulation referred to in any of those provisions

shall be liable on summary conviction to a fine not exceeding [level 3 on the standard scale].

[Regulation 20 is printed as amended by the Criminal Justice Act 1988, s 52.]

21. Forgery and false statements, etc

In sections 65(1)(*a*) (forgery) and 66(*a*) (false statements) of the Act of 1981 the references to a licence under any Part of that Act shall include references to an authorisation, certificate or other document required by ASOR, any of the Council Regulations or the Commission Regulation, or by these Regulations, or by the Act of 1981 as modified by these Regulations, to be in force in relation to a vehicle, or to be kept or carried on a vehicle, used for the international carriage of passengers.

22. *[Amended the Road Traffic (Foreign Vehicles) Act 1972.]*

23. Disapplication of requirements as to fitness, equipment type approval and certification of public service vehicles

None of the provisions of Parts II, III, IV and V of the Public Service Vehicles (Conditions of Fitness, Equipment Use and Certification) Regulations 1981 [*SI 1981 No 257, as amended (qv)*] shall have effect in relation to a vehicle to which any provision of Part III of these Regulations applies or to a vehicle registered in Northern Ireland to which any provision of Part II of these Regulations applies.

SCHEDULE 1 (see regulation 2)

THE COUNCIL REGULATIONS AND THE COMMISSION REGULATION

'Council Regulation No 117/66' means Regulation No 117/66/EEC of the Council of 28th July 1966 on the introduction of common rules for the international carriage of passengers by coach and bus [*OJ 147, 9 August 1966, p 2688)*];

'Council Regulation No 516/72' means Regulations (EEC) No 516/72 of the Council of 28th February 1972 on the introduction of common rules for shuttle services by coach and bus between Member States [*OJ L67, 20 March 1972, p 13*];

'Council Regulation No 517/72' means Regulation (EEC) No 517/72 of the Council of 28th February 1972 on the introduction of common rules for regular and special regular services by coach and bus between Member States [*OJ L67, 20 March 1972, p 19*] as amended by Regulation (EEC) No 1301/78 of the Council of 12th June 1978 [*OJ L158, 16 June 1978, p 1*].

'Commission Regulation No 1016/68' means Regulations (EEC) No 1016/68 of the Commission of 9th July 1968 prescribing the model control documents referred to in Articles 6 and 9 of Council Regulation No 117/66 EEC [*OJ L173, 22 July 1968, p 8*] as amended by and as read with Regulation (EEC) No 2485/82 of the Commission of 13th September 1982 [*OJ L265, 15 September 1982, p 5*].

SCHEDULE 2 (see regulations 9, 10 and 11)

'**12.**—(1) No person shall cause or permit a public service vehicle to be used on a road for the international carriage of passengers unless there is in force and is carried on the vehicle, an international passenger transport authorisation.

(2) An authorisation under this section may authorise the use of the vehicle or vehicles to which it relates on a specified occasion or during a specified period.

(3) In this section—

'specified' means specified in the authorisation; and

'international passenger transport authorisation' means a licence, permit, authorisation or other document issued by the Secretary of State in pursuance of an international agreement or arrangement to which the United Kingdom is for the time being a party.'

SCHEDULE 3 (see regulation 11(2))

WAYBILL *[Omitted.]*

The Road Vehicles (Construction and Use) Regulations 1986

(SI 1986 No 1078)

[The text of these regulations is printed as amended by:

the Road Vehicles (Construction and Use) (Amendment) Regulations 1986 (SI 1986 No 1597) (10 October 1986);

the Road Vehicles (Construction and Use) (Amendment) Regulations 1987 (SI 1987 No 676) (except as otherwise indicated, 6 May 1987);

the Road Vehicles (Construction and Use) (Amendment) (No 2) Regulations 1987 (SI 1987 No 1133) (31 July 1987);

the Road Vehicles (Construction and Use) (Amendment) Regulations 1988 (SI 1988 No 271) (18 March 1988);

the Road Vehicles (Construction and Use) (Amendment) (No 4) Regulations 1988 (SI 1988 No 1178) (25 July 1988);

the Road Vehicles (Construction and Use) (Amendment) (No 5) Regulations 1988 (SI 1988 No 1287) (1 January 1989);

the Road Vehicles (Construction and Use) (Amendment) (No 6) Regulations 1988 (SI 1988 No 1524) (1 October 1988); and

the Road Vehicles (Construction and Use) (Amendment) (No 7) Regulations 1988 (SI 1988 No 1871) (1 January 1989).

The amending regulations are referred to in the notes to the main regulations only by their years and numbers. The dates referred to above are the dates on which the regulations came into force.

The Road Vehicles (Construction and Use) (Amendment) (No 2) Regulations 1988 (SI 1988 No 1102) were revoked on 12 July 1988 (before they were due to take effect) by the Road Vehicles (Construction and Use) (Amendment) (No 3) Regulations 1988 (SI 1988 No 1177); reg 3 of the latter regulations expressly stated that the principal regulations should have effect as if the Amendment No 2 regulations had never been made. The Amendment No 2 regulations have, in effect, been replaced by the Amendment No 4 regulations (see above) and hence neither the Amendment No 2 regulations nor the Amendment No 3 regulations are referred to in the notes to the principal regulations.

Note. These regulations revoked and replaced the Motor Vehicles (Construction and Use) (Track Laying Vehicles) Regulations 1955, as amended, and the Motor Vehicles (Construction and Use) Regulations 1978, as amended, on 11 August 1986. The 1986 Regulations are set out in a new presentation with more extensive use of tabulations, more logical arrangement of material and simplified language. Because of these changes, it is not possible to identify with precision the provisions in the 1986 Regulations which correspond to those in the revoked regulations. A table of comparison may be found at 3 RTLB 55; but where exact comparison is necessary, reference should be made to the actual provisions of the revoked regulations.

ARRANGEMENT OF REGULATIONS

PART I

Preliminary

PART II

Regulations governing the Construction, Equipment and Maintenance of Vehicles

A *Dimensions and manoeuvrability*

B *Brakes*

C *Wheels, Springs, Tyres and Tracks*

D *Steering*

PART III

Plates, Markings, Testing and Inspection

PART IV

Conditions relating to Use

A *Laden Weight*

B *Dimensions of Laden Vehicles*

C *Trailers and Sidecars*

D *Use of Gas Propulsion Systems and Gas-fired Appliances*

E *Control of Noise*

F *Avoidance of Danger*

SCHEDULES

Schedule

PART I

Preliminary

1. Commencement and citation *[Omitted.]*

2. Revocation *[Omitted.]*

3. Interpretation

(1) In these Regulations, unless the context otherwise requires—

(*a*) any reference to a numbered regulation or a numbered Schedule is a reference to the regulation or Schedule bearing that number in these Regulations,

(*b*) any reference to a numbered or lettered paragraph or sub-paragraph is a reference to the paragraph or sub-paragraph bearing that number or letter in the regulation or Schedule or (in the case of a sub-paragraph) paragraph in which the reference occurs, and

(*c*) any reference to a Table, or to a numbered Table, is a reference to the Table, or to the Table bearing that number, in the regulation or Schedule in which that reference occurs.

(2) In these Regulations, unless the context otherwise requires, the expressions specified in column 1 of the Table have the meaning, or are to be interpreted in accordance with the provisions, specified for them in column 2 of the Table.

Table

(regulation 3(2))

1	2
Expression	Meaning
The 1971 Act	The Vehicles (Excise) Act 1971.
The [1988 Act]	The [Road Traffic Act 1988].
The 1981 Act	The Public Passenger Vehicles Act 1981.
The 1984 Act	The Road Traffic Regulation Act 1984.
The Approval Marks Regulations	The Motor Vehicles (Designation of Approval Marks) Regulations 1979 [*SI 1979 No 1088, as amended*].
The Lighting Regulations	The Road Vehicles Lighting Regulations 1984 [*SI 1984 No 812, as amended (qv)*].
The Plating and Testing Regulations	The [Goods Vehicles (Plating and Testing) Regulations 1988] [*SI 1988 No 1478 (qv)*].
The Type Approval Regulations	The Motor Vehicles (Type Approval) Regulations 1980 [*SI 1980 No 1182, as amended*].
The Type Approval (Great Britain) Regulations	The Motor Vehicles (Type Approval) (Great Britain) Regulations 1984 [*SI 1984 No 981, as amended (qv)*].
The Type Approval for Goods Vehicles Regulations	The Motor Vehicles (Type Approval for Goods Vehicles) (Great Britain) Regulations 1982 [*SI 1982 No 1271, as amended (qv)*].
The Type Approval for Agricultural Vehicles Regulations	The Agricultural or Forestry Tractors and Tractor Components (Type Approval) Regulations 1979 [*SI 1979 No 221, as amended*].

1	2
Expression	Meaning
The Act of Accession	the Treaty concerning the Accession of the Kingdom of Denmark, Ireland, the Kingdom of Norway and the United Kingdom of Great Britain and Northern Ireland to thc European Economic Community and the European Atomic Energy Community [*Cmnd 5179–I*].
agricultural motor vehicle	a motor vehicle which is constructed or adapted for use off roads for the purpose of agriculture, horticulture or forestry and which is primarily used for one or more of those purposes, not being a dual-purpose vehicle.
agricultural trailer	a trailer which is constructed or adapted for the purpose of agriculture, horticulture or forestry and which is only used for one or more of those purposes, not being an agricultural trailed appliance.
agricultural trailed appliance	a trailer— (*a*) which is an implement constructed or adapted— (i) for use off roads for the purpose of agriculture, horticulture or forestry and which is only used for one or more of those purposes, and (ii) so that, save in the case of an appliance manufactured before 1st December 1985, or a towed roller, its maximum gross weight is not more than twice its unladen weight; but (*b*) which is not— (i) a vehicle which is used primarily as living accommodation by one or more persons, and which carries no goods or burden except those needed by such one or more persons for the purpose of their residence in the vehicle; or (ii) an agricultural, horticultural or forestry implement rigidly but not permanently mounted on any vehicle whether or not any of the weight of the implement is supported by one or more of its own wheels; so however that such an implement is an agricultural trailed appliance if —part of the weight of the implement is supported by one or more of its own wheels, and —the longitudinal axis of the greater part of the implement is capable of articulating in the horizontal plane in relation to the longitudinal axis of the rear portion of the vehicle which is mounted.
agricultural trailed appliance conveyor	an agricultural trailer which— (*a*) has an unladen weight which does not exceed 510 kg;

1	2
Expression	Meaning
	(*b*) is clearly and indelibly marked with its unladen weight; (*c*) has a pneumatic tyre fitted to each one of its wheels; (*d*) is designed and constructed for the purpose of conveying one agricultural trailed appliance or one agricultural, horticultural or forestry implement.
articulated bus	a bus so constructed that— (*a*) it can be divided into two parts, both of which are vehicles and one of which is a motor vehicle, but cannot be so divided without the use of facilities normally available only at a workshop; and (*b*) passengers carried by it can at all times pass from either part to the other.
articulated vehicle	a heavy motor car or motor car, not being an articulated bus, with a trailer so attached that part of the trailer is superimposed on the drawing vehicle and, when the trailer is uniformly loaded, not less than 20% of the weight of its load is borne by the drawing vehicle.
axle	any reference to the number of axles of a vchiclc is to be interpreted in accordance with paragraph (8).
axle weight	in relation to each axle of a vehicle, the sum of the weights transmitted to the road surface by all the wheels of that axle, having regard to the provisions of paragraph (8).
braking efficiency	the maximum braking force capable of being developed by the brakes of a vehicle, expressed as a percentage of the weight of the vehicle including any persons or load carried in the vehicle.
braking system	is to be interpreted in accordance with paragraph (6).
bus	a motor vehicle which is constructed or adapted to carry more than eight seated passengers in addition to the driver.
cc	cubic centimetre(s).
close-coupled	in relation to wheels on the same side of a trailer, fitted so that at all times while the trailer is in motion they remain parallel to the longitudinal axis of the trailer, and that the distance between the centres of their respective areas of contact with the road surface does not exceed 1 m.
closely-spaced	(i) in the case of two axles, that they are spaced at a distance apart of not more that 2.5 m and not less than 1.02 m; and (ii) in the case of three axles, that the outermost axles are spaced at a distance apart of 3.25 m or less and no one of those three axles has a plated weight of more than 7500 kg; the said distance being obtained as provided in paragraph (10).
cm	centimetre(s).

1	2
Expression	Meaning
cm^2	square centimetre(s).
[coach	a large bus with a maximum gross weight of more than 7.5 tonnes and with a maximum speed exceeding 60 mph.]
Community Directive, followed by a number	the Directive adopted by the Council or the Commission of the European Communities of which identifying particulars are given in the item in column 3 of Table I in Schedule 2 in which that number appears in column 2; where such a Directive amends a previous Directive mentioned in column 3(d) of the Table the reference to it means that previous Directive as so amended. Any reference to a Directive which has been amended by the Act of Accession is a reference to the Directive as so amended.
the Community Recording Equipment Regulation	Council Regulation (EEC) 1463/70 of 20th July 1970 on the introduction of recording equipment in road transport [*OJ L164, 27.7.1970, p 1*], as amended by Council Regulations (EEC) 1787/73 [*OJ L181, 4.7.1973, p 1*] and 2828/77 [*OJ L334, 24.12.1977, p 5*], and as read with the Community Road Transport Rules (Exemption) Regulations 1978 [*SI 1978 No 1158*] and the Community Road Transport Rules (Exemptions) (Amendment) Regulations 1980 [*SI 1980 No 266*].
composite trailer	a combination of a converter dolly and a semi-trailer.
container	an article of equipment, not being a motor vehicle or trailer, having a volume of at least 8 cubic metres, constructed wholly or mostly of metal and intended for repeated use for the carriage of goods or burden.
converter dolly	a trailer which is— (*a*) equipped with two or more wheels, (*b*) designed to enable a semi-trailer to move without any part of its weight being directly superimposed on the drawing vehicle, and (*c*) not itself a part either of the semi-trailer or of the drawing vehicle.
Council Regulation (EEC), followed by a number	the Regulation adopted by the Council of the European Communities.
deck	a floor or platform on which seats are provided for the accommodation of passengers.
design weight	in relation to the gross weight, each axle weight or the train weight of a motor vehicle or trailer, the weight at or below which in the opinion of the Secretary of State or of a person authorised in that behalf by the Secretary of State the vehicle could safely be driven on roads.
double-decked vehicle	a vehicle having two decks one of which is wholly or partly above the other and each of which is provided with a gangway serving seats on that deck only.

1	2
Expression	Meaning
dual-purpose vehicle	a vehicle constructed or adapted for the carriage both of passengers and of goods or burden of any description, being a vehicle of which the unladen weight does not exceed 2040 kg, and which either— (i) is so constructed or adapted that the driving power of the engine is, or by the appropriate use of the controls of the vehicle can be, transmitted to all the wheels of the vehicle; or (ii) satisfies the following conditions as to construction, namely— (*a*) the vehicle must be permanently fitted with a rigid roof, with or without a sliding panel; (*b*) the area of the vehicle to the rear of the driver's seat must— (i) be permanently fitted with at least one row of transverse seats (fixed or folding) for two or more passengers and those seats must be properly sprung or cushioned and provided with upholstered back-rests, attached either to the seats or to a side or the floor of the vehicle; and (ii) be lit on each side and at the rear by a window or windows of glass or other transparent material having an area or aggregate area of not less that 1850 square centimetres on each side and not less than 770 square centimetres at the rear; and (*c*) the distance between the rearmost part of the steering wheel and the back-rests of the row of transverse seats satisfying the requirements specified in head (i) of sub-paragraph (*b*) (or, if there is more than one such row of seats, the distance between the rearmost part of the steering wheel and the back-rests of the rearmost such row) must, when the seats are ready for use, be not less than one-third of the distance between the rearmost part of the steering wheel and the rearmost part of the floor of the vehicle.
ECE Regulation, followed by a number	the Regulation, annexed to the Agreement concerning the adoption of uniform conditions of approval for Motor Vehicles Equipment and Parts and reciprocal recognition thereof concluded at Geneva on 20th March 1958 [*Cmnd 2535*] as amended [*Cmnd 3562*], to which the United Kingdom is party [*instrument of accession dated 14 January 1963 deposited with the Secretary-General of the United Nations on 15*

1	2
Expression	Meaning
	January 1963], of which identifying particulars are given in the item in column (3)(*a*), (*b*) and (*c*) of Table II in Schedule 2 in which that number appears in column (2); and where that number contains more than two digits, it refers to that Regulation with the amendments in force at the date specified in column (3)(*d*) in that item.
engine power in kilowatts (kW)	the maximum net power ascertained in accordance with Community Directive 80/1269.
engineering plant	(*a*) movable plant or equipment being a motor vehicle or trailer specially designed and constructed for the special purposes of engineering operations, and which cannot, owing to the requirements of those purposes, comply with all the requirements of these Regulations and which is not constructed primarily to carry a load other than a load being either excavated materials raised from the ground by apparatus on the motor vehicle or trailer or materials which the vehicle or trailer is specially designed to treat while carried thereon; or (*b*) a mobile crane which does not comply in all respects with the requirements of these Regulations.
exhaust system	a complete set of components through which the exhaust gases escape from the engine unit of a motor vehicle including those which are necessary to limit the noise caused by the escape of those gases.
first used	is to be interpreted in accordance with paragraph (3).
gangway	the space provided for obtaining access from any entrance to the passengers' seats or from any such seat to an exit other than an emergency exit, but excluding a staircase and any space in front of a seat which is required only for the use of passengers occupying that seat or a seat in the same row of seats.
gas	any fuel which is wholly gaseous at 17.5°C under a pressure of 1.013 bar absolute.
gas-fired appliance	a device carried on a motor vehicle or trailer when in use on a road, which consumes gas and which is neither— (*a*) a device owned or operated by or with the authority of the British Gas Corporation for the purpose of detecting gas, nor (*b*) an engine for the propulsion of a motor vehicle, nor (*c*) a lamp which consumes acetylene gas.
goods vehicle	a motor vehicle or trailer constructed or adapted for use for the carriage or haulage of goods or burden of any description.
gritting trailer	a trailer which is used on a road for the purpose of spreading grit or other matter so as to avoid or reduce the effect of ice or snow on the road.

1	2
Expression	Meaning
gross weight	(*a*) in relation to a motor vehicle, the sum of the weights transmitted to the road surface by all the wheels of the vehicle. (*b*) in relation to a trailer, the sum of the weights transmitted to the road surface by all the wheels of the trailer and of any weight of the trailer imposed on the drawing vehicle.
heavy motor car	a mechanically propelled vehicle, not being a locomotive, a motor tractor, or a motor car, which is constructed itself to carry a load or passengers and the weight of which unladen exceeds 2540 kg.
indivisible load	a load which cannot without undue expense or risk of damage be divided into two or more loads for the purpose of conveyance on a road.
industrial tractor	a tractor, not being an agricultural motor vehicle, which— (*a*) has an unladen weight not exceeeding 7370 kg, (*b*) is designed and used primarily for work off roads, or for work on roads in connection only with road construction or maintenance (including any such tractor when fitted with an implement or implements designed primarily for use in connection with such work, whether or not any such implement is of itself designed to carry a load), and (*c*) has a maximum speed not exceeding 20 mph.
invalid carriage	a mechanically propelled vehicle the weight of which unladen does not exceed 254 kg and which is specially designed and constructed, and not merely adapted, for the use of a person suffering from some physical defect or disability and is solely used by such a person.
kerbside weight	the weight of a vehicle when it carries— (*a*) in the case of a motor vehicle, (i) no person; and (ii) a full supply of fuel in its tank, an adequate supply of other liquids incidental to its propulsion and no load other than the loose tools and equipment with which it is normally equipped; (*b*) in the case of a trailer, no person and is otherwise unladen.
kg	kilogram(s).
km/h	kilometre(s) per hour.
kW	kilowatt(s).
[large bus	a vehicle constructed or adapted to carry more than 16 seated passengers in addition to the driver.]
living van	a vehicle used primarily as living accommodation by one or more persons, and which is not also used for the carriage of goods or burden which are not needed by such one or more persons for the purpose of their residence in the vehicle.

1	2
Expression	Meaning
locomotive	a mechanically propelled vehicle which is not constructed itself to carry a load other than the following articles, that is to say, water, fuel, accumulators and other equipment used for the purpose of propulsion, loose tools and loose equipment, and the weight of which unladen exceeds 7370 kg.
longitudinal plane	a vertical plane parallel to the longitudinal axis of a vehicle.
m	metre(s).
m^2	square metre(s).
m^3	cubic metre(s).
maximum gross weight	(*a*) in the case of a vehicle equipped with a Ministry plate in accordance with regulation 70, the design gross weight shown in column (3) of that plate or, if no such weight is shown, the gross weight shown in column (2) of that plate; (*b*) in the case of a vehicle not equipped with a Ministry plate, but which is equipped with a plate in accordance with regulation 66, the maximum gross weight shown on the plate in respect of item 7 of Part 1 of Schedule 8 in the case of a motor vehicle and item 6 of Part II of Schedule 8 in the case of a trailer; (*c*) in any other case, the weight which the vehicle is designed or adapted not to exceed when the vehicle is travelling on a road.
maximum speed	the speed which a vehicle is incapable, by reason of its construction, of exceeding on the level under its own power when fully laden.
minibus	a motor vehicle which is constructed or adapted to carry more than 8 but not more than 16 seated passengers in addition to the driver.
Ministry plate	a plate issued by the Secretary of State for a goods vehicle following the issue or amendment of a plating certificate and in the form in, and containing the particulars required by, Schedule 10 [or Schedule 10A].
mm	millimetre(s).
motor ambulance	a motor vehicle which is specially designed and constructed (and not merely adapted) for carrying, as equipment permanently fixed to the vehicle, equipment used for medical, dental, or other health purposes and is used primarily for the carriage of persons suffering from illness, injury or disability.
motor car	a mechanically propelled vehicle, not being a motor tractor, a motor cycle or an invalid carriage, which is constructed itself to carry a load or passengers and the weight of which unladen— (*a*) if it is constructed solely for the carriage of passengers and their effects and is adapted to carry

1	2
Expression	Meaning
	not more than seven passengers exclusive of the driver does not exceed 3050 kg; (*b*) if it is constructed for use for the conveyance of goods or burden of any description, does not exceed 3050 kg; (*c*) does not exceed 2540 kg in a case falling within neither of the foregoing paragraphs.
[motor caravan	a motor vehicle which is constructed or adapted for the carriage of passengers and their effects and which contains, as permanently installed equipment, the facilities which are reasonably necessary for enabling the vehicle to provide mobile living accommodation for its users.]
motor cycle	a mechanically propelled vehicle, not being an invalid carriage, having less than four wheels and the weight of which unladen does not exceed 410 kg.
motor tractor	a mechanically propelled vehicle which is not constructed itself to carry a load, other than the following articles, that is to say, water, fuel, accumulators and other equipment used for the purpose of propulsion, loose tools and loose equipment, and the weight of which unladen does not exceed 7370 kg.
motor vehicle	a mechanically propelled vehicle intended or adapted for use on roads.
mph	mile(s) per hour.
N/mm^2	newton(s) per square millimetre.
overall height	the vertical distance between the ground and the point on the vehicle which is furthest from the ground, calculated when— (*a*) the tyres of the vehicle are suitably inflated for the use to which it is being put; (*b*) the vehicle is at its unladen weight; and (*c*) the surface of the ground under the vehicle is reasonably flat; but, in the case of a trolley bus, exclusive of the power collection equipment mounted on the roof of the vehicle.
overall length	in relation to a vehicle, the distance between transverse planes passing through the extreme forward and rearward projecting points of the vehicle inclusive of all parts of the vehicle, of any receptacle which is of a permanent character and accordingly strong enough for repeated use, and any fitting on, or attached to, the vehicle except— (i) for all purposes— (*a*) any driving mirror; (*b*) any expanding or extensible contrivance forming part of a turntable fire escape fixed to a vehicle; (*c*) any snow-plough fixed in front of a vehicle; (*d*) any receptacle specially designed to hold

1	2
Expression	Meaning
	and keep secure a seal issued for the purposes of customs clearance; (*e*) any tailboard which is let down while the vehicle is stationary in order to facilitate its unloading; (*f*) any tailboard which is let down in order to facilitate the carriage of, but which is not essential for the support of, loads which are in themselves so long as to extend at least as far as the tailboard when upright; (*g*) any fitting attached to a part of, or to a receptacle on, a vehicle which does not increase the carrying capacity of the part or receptacle but which enables it to be —transferred from a road vehicle to a railway vehicle or from a railway vehicle to a road vehicle, —secured to a railway vehicle by a locking device, and —carried on a railway vehicle by the use of stanchions: (*h*) any plate, whether rigid or movable, fitted to a trailer constructed for the purpose of carrying other vehicles and designed to bridge the gap between that trailer and a motor vehicle constructed for that purpose and to which the trailer is attached so that, while the trailer is attached to the motor vehicle, vehicles which are to be carried by the motor vehicle may be moved from the trailer to the motor vehicle before a journey begins, and vehicles which have been carried on the motor vehicle may be moved from it to the trailer after a journey ends; (*i*) any sheeting or other readily flexible means of covering or securing a load; (*j*) any receptacle with an external length, measured parallel to the longitudinal axis of the vehicle, not exceeding 2.5 m; (*k*) any empty receptacle which itself forms a load; (*l*) any receptacle which contains an indivisible load of exceptional length; (*m*) any receptacle manufactured before 30th October 1985, not being a maritime container (namely a container designed primarily for carriage on sea transport without an accompanying road vehicle); or

1	2
Expression	Meaning
	(*n*) any special appliance or apparatus as described in regulation 81(*c*) which does not itself increase the carrying capacity of the vehicle; (ii) for the purposes of regulation 7— (*a*) any part of a trailer (not being in the case of an agricultural trailed appliance a drawbar or other thing with which it is equipped for the purpose of being towed) designed primarily for use as a means of attaching it to another vehicle and any fitting designed for use in connection with any such part; (*b*) the thickness of any front or rear wall on a semi-trailer and of any part forward of such front wall or rearward of such rear wall which does not increase the vehicle's load-carrying space.
overall width	the distance between longitudinal planes passing through extreme lateral projecting points of the vehicle inclusive of all parts of the vehicle, of any receptacle which is of permanent character and accordingly strong enough for repeated use, and any fitting on, or attached to, the vehicle except— (*a*) any driving mirror; (*b*) any snow-plough fixed in front of the vehicle; (*c*) so much of the distortion of any tyre as is caused by the weight of the vehicle; (*d*) any receptacle specially designed to hold and keep secure a seal issued for the purpose of customs clearance; (*e*) any lamp or reflector fitted to the vehicle in accordance with the Lighting Regulations; (*f*) any sideboard which is let down while the vehicle is stationary in order to facilitate its loading or unloading; (*g*) any fitting attached to part of, or to a receptacle on, a vehicle which does not increase the carrying capacity of the part or receptacle but which enables it to be —transferred from a road vehicle to a railway vehicle or from a railway vehicle to a road vehicle; —secured to a railway vehicle by a locking device; and —carried on a railway vehicle by the use of stanchions; (*h*) any sheeting or other readily flexible means of covering or securing a load;

1	2
Expression	Meaning
	(*i*) any receptacle with an external width, measured at right angles to the longitudinal axis of the vehicle, which does not exceed 2.5 m; (*j*) any empty receptacle which itself forms a load; (*k*) any receptacle which contains an indivisible load of exceptional width; (*l*) any receptacle manufactured before 30th October 1985, not being a maritime container (namely a container designed primarily for carriage on sea transport without an accompanying road vehicle); or (*m*) any special appliance or apparatus as described in regulation 81(*c*) which does not itself increase the carrying capacity of the vehicle.
overhang	the distance measured horizontally and parallel to the longitudinal axis of a vehicle between two transverse planes passing through the following two points— (*a*) the rearmost point of the vehicle exclusive of— (i) any expanding or extensible contrivance forming part of a turntable fire escape fixed to a vehicle; (ii) in the case of a motor car constructed solely for the carriage of passengers and their effects and adapted to carry not more than eight passengers exclusive of the driver, any luggage carrier fitted to the vehicle; and (*b*) (i) in the case of a motor vehicle having not more than three axles of which only one is not a steering axle, the centre point of that axle; (ii) in the case of a motor vehicle having three axles of which the front axle is the only steering axle and of a motor vehicle having four axles of which the two foremost are the only steering axles, a point 110 mm behind the centre of a straight line joining the centre points of the two rearmost axles; and (iii) in any other case a point situated on the longitudinal axis of the vehicle and such that a line drawn from it at right angles to that axis will pass through the centre of the minimum turning circle of the vehicle.
passenger vehicle	a vehicle constructed solely for the carriage of passengers and their effects.
pedestrian-controlled vehicle	a motor vehicle which is controlled by a pedestrian and not constructed or adapted for use or used for the carriage of a driver or passenger.
pneumatic tyre	a tyre which—

1	2
Expression	Meaning
	(*a*) is provided with, or together with the wheel upon which it is mounted forms, a continuous closed chamber inflated to a pressure substantially exceeding atmospheric pressure when the tyre is in the condition in which it is normally used, but is not subjected to any load; (*b*) is capable of being inflated and deflated without removal from the wheel or vehicle; and (*c*) is such that, when it is deflated and is subjected to a normal load, the sides of the tyre collapse.
public works vehicle	a mechanically propelled vehicle which is specially designed for use on a road by or on behalf of any statutory undertaking (as defined in section 262(13) of the Local Government Act 1972), highway authority, local authority, water authority, the Post Office, British Telecommunications plc or any police force for the purpose of works which such undertaking, authority or other body has a duty or a power to carry out, but excluding the carriage of persons other than crew or of goods other than goods needed for the works in respect of which the vehicle is being used.
recut pneumatic tyre	a pneumatic tyre in which all or part of its original tread pattern has been cut deeper or burnt deeper or a different tread pattern has been cut deeper or burnt deeper than the original tread pattern.
refuse vehicle	a vehicle designed for use and used solely in connection with street cleansing, the collection or disposal of refuse, or the collection or disposal of the contents of gullies or cesspools.
registered	registered under any of the following enactments— (*a*) the Roads Act 1920 (*b*) the Vehicles (Excise) Act 1949 (*c*) the Vehicles (Excise) Act 1962, or (*d*) the 1971 Act and, in relation to the date on which a vehicle was registered, the date on which it was first registered under any of those enactments.
relevant braking requirement	a requirement that the brakes of a motor vehicle (as assisted, where a trailer is being drawn, by the brakes on the trailer) comply— (i) in a case to which item 1 in Table 1 in regulation 18 applies, with the requirements specified in regulation 18(3) for vehicles falling in that item; (ii) in any other case, with the requirements specified in regulation 18(3) for vehicle classes (a) and (b) in item 2 of that Table

1	2
Expression	Meaning
	(whatever the date of first use of the motor vehicle and the date of manufacture of any trailer drawn by it may be).
resilient tyre	a tyre, not being a pneumatic tyre, which is of soft or elastic material, having regard to paragraph (5).
rigid vehicle	a motor vehicle which is not constructed or adapted to form part of an articulated vehicle or articulated bus.
secondary braking system	a braking system of a vehicle applied by a secondary means of operation independent of the service braking system or by one of the sections comprised in a split braking system.
service braking system	the braking system of a vehicle which is designed and constructed to have the highest braking efficiency of any of the braking systems with which the vehicle is equipped.
semi-trailer	a trailer which is constructed or adapted to form part of an articulated vehicle [including (without prejudice to the generality of that) a vehicle which is not itself a motor vehicle but which has some or all of its wheels driven by the drawing vehicle].
silencer	a contrivance suitable and sufficient for reducing as far as may be reasonable the noise caused by the escape of exhaust gases from the engine of a motor vehicle.
single-decked vehicle	a vehicle upon which no part of a deck or gangway is vertically above another deck or gangway.
split braking system	in relation to a motor vehicle, a braking system so designed and constructed that— (*a*) it comprises two independent sections of mechanism capable of developing braking force such that, excluding the means of operation, a failure of any part (other than a fixed member or a brake shoe anchor pin) of one of the said sections will not cause a decrease in the braking force capable of being developed by the other section; (*b*) the said two sections are operated by a means of operation which is common to both sections; (*c*) the braking efficiency of either of the said two sections can be readily checked.
[staircase	a staircase by means of which passengers on a double-decked vehicle may pass to and from the upper deck of the vehicle.]
stored energy	in relation to a braking system of a vehicle, energy (other than the muscular energy of the driver or the mechanical energy of a spring) stored in a reservoir for the purpose of applying the brakes under the control of the driver, either directly or as a supplement to his muscular energy.
straddle carrier	a motor vehicle constructed to straddle and lift its load for the purpose of transportation.

1	2
Expression	Meaning
statutory power of removal	a power conferred by or under any enactment to remove or move a vehicle from any road or from any part of a road.
temporary use spare tyre	a pneumatic tyre which is designed for use on a motor vehicle only— (*a*) in the event of a failure of one of the tyres normally fitted to a wheel of the vehicle, and (*b*) at a speed lower than that for which such normally fitted tyres are designed.
three-wheeled motor cycle	a motor cycle having three wheels, not including a two-wheeled motor cycle with a sidecar attached.
towing implement	a device on wheels designed for the purpose of enabling a motor vehicle to draw another vehicle by the attachment of that device to that other vehicle in such a manner that part of that other vehicle is secured to and either rests on or is suspended from the device and some but not all of the wheels on which that other vehicle normally runs are raised off the ground.
track-laying	in relation to a vehicle, so designed and constructed that the weight thereof is transmitted to the road surface either by means of continuous tracks or by a combination of wheels and continuous tracks in such circumstances that the weight transmitted to the road surface by the tracks is not less than half the weight of the vehicle.
trailer	means a vehicle drawn by a motor vehicle and is to be interpreted in accordance with paragraphs (9) and (11).
train weight	in relation to a motor vehicle which may draw a trailer, the maximum laden weight for the motor vehicle together with any trailer which may be drawn by it.
transverse plane	a vertical plane at right angles to the longitudinal axis of a vehicle.
trolley bus	a bus adapted for use on roads without rails and moved by power transmitted thereto from some external source.
unbraked trailer	any trailer other than one which, whether or not regulation 15 or 16 applies to it, is equipped with a braking system in accordance with one of those regulations.
unladen weight	the weight of a vehicle or trailer inclusive of the body and all parts (the heavier being taken where alternative bodies or parts are used) which are necessary to or ordinarily used with the vehicle or trailer when working on a road, but exclusive of the weight of water, fuel or accumulators used for the purpose of the supply of power for the propulsion of the vehicle or, as the case may be, of any vehicle by which the trailer is drawn, and of loose tools and loose equipment.
vehicle in the service of a visiting force or of a headquarters	a vehicle so described in Article 8(6) of the Visiting Forces and International Headquarters (Application of Law) Order 1965 [*SI 1965 No 1536*].

1	2
Expression	Meaning
wheel	a wheel the tyre or rim of which when the vehicle is in motion on a road is in contact with the ground; two wheels are to be regarded as one wheel in the circumstances specified in paragraph (7).
wheeled	in relation to a vehicle, so constructed that the whole weight of the vehicle is transmitted to the road surface by means of wheels.
wide tyre	a pneumatic tyre of which the area of contact with the road surface is not less than 300 mm in width when measured at right angles to the longitudinal axis of the vehicle.
works trailer	a trailer designed for use in private premises and used on a road only in delivering goods from or to such premises to or from a vehicle on a road in the immediate neighbourhood, or in passing from one part of any such premises to another or to other private premises in the immediate neighbourhood or in connection with road works while at or in the immediate neighbourhood of the site of such works.
works truck	a motor vehicle (other than a straddle carrier) designed for use in private premises and used on a road only in delivering goods from or to such premises to or from a vehicle on a road in the immediate neighbourhood, or in passing from one part of any such premises to another or to other private premises in the immediate neighbourhood or in connection with road works while at or in the immediate neighbourhood of the site of such works.

(3) For the purpose of these Regulations, the date on which a motor vehicle is first used is—

(*a*) in the case of a vehicle not falling within sub-paragraph (*b*) and which is registered, the date on which it was registered;

(*b*) in each of the following cases—

(i) a vehicle which is being or has been used under a trade licence as defined in section 16 of the 1971 Act (otherwise than for the purposes of demonstration or testing or of being delivered from premises of the manufacturer by whom it was made or of a distributor of vehicles, or dealer in vehicles, to premises of a distributor of vehicles, dealer in vehicles or purchaser thereof or to premises of a person obtaining possession thereof under a hiring agreement or hire purchase agreement);

(ii) a vehicle belonging, or which has belonged, to the Crown and which is or was used or appropriated for use for naval, military or air force purposes;

(iii) a vehicle belonging, or which has belonged, to a visiting force or a headquarters or defence organisation to which in each case the Visiting Forces and International Headquarters (Application of Law) Order 1965 applies;

(iv) a vehicle which has been used on roads outside Great Britain before being imported into Great Britain; and

(v) a vehicle which has been used otherwise than on roads after being sold or supplied by retail and before being registered;

the date of manufacture of the vehicle.

In sub-paragraph (*b*)(v) of this paragraph 'sold or supplied by retail' means sold or supplied otherwise than to a person acquiring it solely for the purpose of resale or re-supply for a valuable consideration.

(4) The date of manufacture of a vehicle to which the Type Approval for Goods Vehicles Regulations apply shall be the date of manufacture described in regulation 2(4)(*a*) of those Regulations.

(5) Save where otherwise provided in these Regulations a tyre shall not be deemed to be of soft or elastic material unless the said material is either—

(*a*) continuous round the circumference of the wheel; or

(*b*) fitted in sections so that so far as reasonably practicable no space is left between the ends thereof,

and is of such thickness and design as to minimise, so far as reasonably possible, vibration when the vehicle is in motion and so constructed as to be free from any defect which might in any way cause damage to the surface of a road.

(6) For the purpose of these Regulations a brake drum and a brake disc shall be deemed to form part of the wheel and not of the braking system.

(7) For the purpose of these Regulations other than regulations 26 and 27 any two wheels of a motor vehicle or trailer shall be regarded as one wheel if the distance between the centres of the areas of contact between such wheels and the road surface is less than 460 mm.

(8) For the purpose of these Regulations other than regulations 26 and 27 in counting the number of axles of, and in determining the sum of the weights transmitted to the road surface by any one axle of, a vehicle, all the wheels of which the centres of the areas of contact with the road surface can be included between any two transverse planes less than 1.02 m apart shall be treated as constituting one axle.

(9) The provisions of these Regulations relating to trailers do not apply to any part of an articulated bus.

(10) For the purpose of regulations 51, [76, 77 and 79] and Schedule 11 and of the definition in paragraph (2) of the expression 'closely-spaced', the distance between any two axles shall be obtained by measuring the shortest distance between the line joining the centres of the areas of contact with the road surface of the wheels of one axle and the line joining the centres of the areas of contact with the road surface of the wheels of the other axle.

(11) For the purpose of the following provisions only, a composite trailer shall be treated as one trailer (not being a semi-trailer or a converter dolly)—

(*a*) regulations 7, 76 and 83;

(*b*) paragraph (2) of, and items 3 and 10 in the Table in, regulation 75;

(*c*) item 2 in the Table in regulation 78.

[Regulation 3 is printed as amended by the Interpretation Act 1978, ss 17(2)(a) and 23(1), SI 1987 Nos 676 and 1133; SI 1988 No 1287.

Council Regulation (EEC) 1463/70, as amended (see definition of 'the Community Recording Equipment Regulation' in the table to reg 3(2)), has been repealed and replaced by Council Regulation (EEC) 3821/85, qv. The Community Road Transport Rules (Exemptions) Regulations 1978, as amended (referred to in the same definition), have been revoked and replaced by the Community

Drivers' Hours and Recording Equipment (Exemptions and Supplementary Provisions) Regulations 1986 (SI 1986 No 1456), qv.]

4. Application and exemptions

(1) Save where the context otherwise requires, these Regulations apply to both wheeled vehicles and track-laying vehicles.

(2) Where a provision is applied by these Regulations to a motor vehicle first used on or after a specified date it does not apply to that vehicle if it was manufactured at least six months before that date.

(3) Where an exemption from, or relaxation of, a provision is applied by these Regulations to a motor vehicle first used before a specified date it shall also apply to a motor vehicle first used on or after that date if it was manufactured at least six months before that date.

(4) The regulations specified in an item in column 3 of the Table do not apply in respect of a vehicle of a class specified in that item in column 2.

TABLE

(regulation 4(4))

1	2	3
Item	Class of vehicle	Regulations which do not apply
1	A vehicle proceeding to a port for export.	The regulations in Part II in so far as they relate to construction and equipment, except regulations 16 (insofar as it concerns parking brakes), 20, 30, 34, 37, 53 and 57(3) and (4). Regulations 66 to 69 and 71.
2	A vehicle brought temporarily into Great Britain by a person resident abroad, provided that the vehicle complies in every respect with the requirements relating to motor vehicles or trailers contained in— (*a*) article 21 and paragraph (1) of article 22 of the Convention on Road Traffic concluded at Geneva on 19th September 1949 [*Cmnd 7997*] and [Part I,] Part II (so far as it relates to direction indicators and stop lights) and Part III of Annex 6 to that Convention; or	The regulations in Part II in so far as they relate to construction and equipment except regulations 7, 8, 9(2), 10, 40, 53 and 57(3) and (4). Regulations 66 to 69 and 71.

1	2	3
Item	Class of vehicle	Regulations which do not apply
	(*b*) paragraphs I, III and VIII of article 3 of the International Convention relative to Motor Traffic concluded at Paris on 24th April 1926 [*Treaty Series No 11 (1930)*]	
3	A vehicle manufactured in Great Britain which complies with the requirements referred to in item 2 above and contained in the Convention of 1949, or, as the case may be, 1926 referred to in that item as if the vehicle had been brought temporarily into Great Britain, and either— (*a*) is exempt from car tax by virtue of [section 7(1), (2) and (3) of the Car Tax Act 1983], or (*b*) has been zero rated under [regulation 56 or 57 of the Value Added Tax (General) Regulations 1985] [*SI 1985 No 886, qv*]	The regulations in Part II in so far as they relate to construction and equipment, except regulations 7, 8, 9(2), 10, 40, 53 and 57(3) and (4). Regulations 66 to 69 and 71.
4	A vehicle in the service of a visiting force or of a headquarters.	The regulations in Part II in so far as they relate to construction and equipment, except regulations 9(2), 16 (in so far as it concerns parking brakes), 21, 53, 57(3) and (4), and 61. Regulations 66 to 69, 71 and 75 to 79.
5	A vehicle which has been submitted for an examination under [section 45 or section 67A of the 1988 Act] while it is being used on a road in connection with the carrying out of that examination and is being so used by a person who is empowered under that section to carry out that examination, or by a person acting under the direction of a person so empowered.	The regulations in Part II except regulations 57(3) and (4). Regulations 75 to 79 and 100.

1	2	3
Item	Class of vehicle	Regulations which do not apply
6	A motor car or a motor cycle in respect of which a certificate has been issued by the Officer in Charge of a National Collections of Road Transport, the Science Museum, London SW7, that it was designed before 1st January 1905 and constructed before 31st December 1905.	Regulations 16 (except in so far as it applies requirements 3 and 6 in Schedule 3), 21, 37(4), 63 and 99(4).
7	(*a*) A towing implement which is being drawn by a motor vehicle while it is not attached to any vehicle except the one drawing it if— (i) the towing implement is not being so drawn during the hours of darkness, and (ii) the vehicle by which it is being so drawn is not driven at a speed exceeding 20 mph; or (*b*) a vehicle which is being drawn by a motor vehicle in the exercise of a statutory power of removal.	The regulations in Part II in so far as they relate to the construction and equipment of trailers, except regulation 20.

(5) Any reference to a broken down vehicle shall include a reference to any towing implement which is being used for the drawing of any such vehicle.

(6) The Secretary of State is satisfied that it is requisite that the provisions of regulation 40(2) should apply, as from the date on which these Regulations come into operation, to track-laying vehicles registered before the expiration of one year from the making of these Regulations; and that, notwithstanding that those provisions will then apply to these vehicles, no undue hardship or inconvenience will be caused thereby.

[Regulation 4 is printed as corrected by a corrigendum dated October 1986 and as amended by the Interpretation Act 1978, ss 17(2)(a) and 23(1); SI 1988 No 271.]

5. Trade Descriptions Act 1968

Nothing in any provision of these Regulations whereby any vehicle or any of its parts or equipment is required to be marked with a specification number or the registered certification trade mark of the British Standards Institution or with an approval mark, or whereby such a marking is treated as evidence of compliance with a standard to which the marking relates, shall be taken to authorise any person to apply any such marking to the vehicle, part or equipment in contravention of the Trade Descriptions Act 1968.

6. Compliance with Community Directives and ECE Regulations

(1) For the purpose of any regulation which requires or permits a vehicle to comply with the requirements of a Community Directive or an ECE Regulation, a vehicle shall be deemed so to have complied at the date of its first use only if—

(*a*) one of the certificates referred to in paragraph (2) has been issued in relation to it; or

(*b*) the marking referred to in paragraph (3) has been applied; or

(*c*) it was, before it was used on a road, subject to a relevant type approval requirement as specified in paragraph (4).

(2) The certificates mentioned in paragraph (1) are—

(*a*) a type approval certificate issued by the Secretary of State under regulation 5 of the Type Approval Regulations or of the Type Approval for Agricultural Vehicles Regulations;

(*b*) a certificate of conformity issued by the manufacturer of the vehicle under regulation 6 of either of those Regulations; or

(*c*) a certificate issued under a provision of the law of any member state of the European Economic Community which corresponds to the said regulations 5 or 6,

being in each case a certificate issued by reason of the vehicle's conforming to the requirements of the Community Directive in question.

(3) The marking mentioned in paragraph (1) is a marking designated as an approval mark by regulation 4 of the Approval Marks Regulations, being in each case a mark shown in column 2 of an item in Schedule 2 to those Regulations which refers, in column 5, to the ECE Regulation in question, applied as indicated in column 4 in that item.

(4) A relevant type approval requirement is a requirement of the Type Approval (Great Britain) Regulations or that Type Approval for Goods Vehicles Regulations which appears—

(*a*) in column 4 of Table 1 in Schedule 2 in that item in which the Community Directive in question appears in column 3, or

(*b*) in column 4 of Table II in Schedule 2 in the item in which the ECE Regulation in question appears in column 3.

PART II

Regulations governing the Construction, Equipment and Maintenance of Vehicles

A *Dimensions and Manoeuvrability*

7. Length

(1) Subject to paragraphs (2) to (6), the overall length of a vehicle or combination of vehicles of class specified in an item in column 2 of the Table shall not exceed the maximum length specified in that item in column 3 of the Table, the overall length in the case of a combination of vehicles being calculated in accordance with regulation 81(*g*) and (*h*).

TABLE

(regulation 7(1))

1	2	3
Item	Class of vehicle	Maximum length (metres)
	Vehicle Combinations	
1	A motor vehicle drawing one trailer not being a semi-trailer.	18
2	An articulated bus.	18
3	An articulated vehicle.	15.5
	Motor vehicles	
4	A wheeled motor vehicle.	12
5	A track-laying motor vehicle.	9.2
	Trailers	
6	An agricultural trailed appliance manufactured on or after 1st December 1985.	15
7	A semi-trailer manufactured on or after 1st May 1983.	12.2
8	A trailer with at least 4 wheels which is— (*a*) drawn by a goods vehicle being a motor vehicle having a maximum gross weight exceeding 3500 kg; or (*b*) an agricultural trailer.	12
9	Any other trailer not being an agricultural trailed appliance or a semi-trailer.	7

(2) In the case of a motor vehicle drawing one trailer where—

(*a*) the motor vehicle is a showman's vehicle as defined in paragraph 7 of Schedule 3 to the 1971 Act [*qv*]; and

(*b*) the trailer is used primarily as living accommodation by one or more persons and is not also used for the carriage of goods or burden which are not needed for the purpose of such residence in the vehicle,

item 1 in the Table applies with the substitution of 22 m for 18 m.

(3) The provisions of paragraph (1) do not apply to—

(*a*) a vehicle combination or trailer which is constructed and normally used for the conveyance of indivisible loads of exceptional length;

(*b*) a wheeled semi-trailer which is constructed and normally used for the purpose of carrying at least two other wheeled vehicles;

(*c*) a broken down vehicle which is being drawn by a motor vehicle in consequence of a breakdown; or

(*d*) a trailer being drying or mixing plant designed for the production of asphalt or of bituminous or tar macadam and used mainly for the construction, repair or maintenance of roads, or a road planing machine so used.

(4) Where a motor vehicle is drawing—

(*a*) two trailers, then only one of those trailers may exceed an overall length of 7 m;

(*b*) three trailers, then none of those trailers shall exceed an overall length of 7 m.

(5) Where a motor vehicle is drawing—

(*a*) two or more trailers; or

(*b*) one trailer constructed and normally used for the conveyance of indivisible loads of exceptional length—

then—

(i) the overall length of that motor vehicle shall not exceed 9.2 m; and

(ii) the overall length of the combination of vehicles, calculated in accordance with regulation 81(*g*) and (*h*), shall not exceed 25.9 m, unless the conditions specified in paragraphs 1 and 2 of Schedule 12 have been complied with.

(6) Item 7 in the Table does not apply to a semi-trailer which is normally used on international journeys any part of which takes place outside the United Kingdom.

8. Width

(1) Save as provided in paragraph (2), overall width of a vehicle of a class specified in an item in column 2 of the Table shall not exceed the maximum width specified in column 3 in that item.

TABLE

(regulation 8(1))

1	2	3
Item	Class of vehicle	Maximum width (metres)
1	A locomotive, other than an agricultural motor vehicle.	2.75
2	A refrigerated vehicle.	[2.60]
3	Any other motor vehicle.	2.5
4	A trailer drawn by a motor vehicle having a maximum gross weight (determined as provided in Part I of Schedule 8 to these Regulations) exceeding 3500 kg.	2.5
5	An agricultural trailer.	2.5
6	An agricultural trailed appliance.	2.5
7	Any other trailer drawn by a vehicle other than a motor cycle.	2.3
8	A trailer drawn by a motor cycle.	1.5

(2) Paragraph (1) does not apply to a broken down vehicle which is being drawn in consequence of the breakdown.

(3) No person shall use or cause or permit to be used on a road a wheeled agricultural motor vehicle drawing a wheeled vehicle trailer if, when the longitudinal axes of

the vehicles are parallel but in different vertical planes, the overall width of the two vehicles, measured as if they were on one vehicle, exceeds 2.5 metres.

(4) In this regulation 'refrigerated vehicle' means any vehicle which is specially designed for the carriage of goods at a low temperature and of which the thickness of each of the side walls, inclusive of insulation, is at least 45mm.

[Regulation 8 is printed as amended by SI 1988 No 1871.]

9. Height

(1) The overall height of a bus shall not exceed 4.57 m.

(2) Save as provided in paragraph (3), no person shall use or cause or permit to be used on a road any semi-trailer if—

(*a*) any part of the structure of the vehicle is more than 4.2 m from the ground when the vehicle is on level ground; and

(*b*) the total laden weight of the semi-trailer and the vehicle by which it is drawn exceeds 32,520 kg.

(3) For the purpose of paragraph (2) the structure of a vehicle includes any detachable structure attached to the vehicle for the purpose of containing any load, but does not include any load which is not a detachable structure or any sheeting or other flexible means of covering or securing a load.

The provisions of paragraph (2) do not apply in respect of any vehicle while it is being loaded or unloaded.

10. Indication of overall travelling height

(1) This regulation applies to every motor vehicle which is—

(*a*) constructed or adapted so as to be capable of hoisting and carrying a skip;

(*b*) carrying a container;

(*c*) drawing a trailer or semi-trailer carrying a container;

(*d*) engineering plant;

(*e*) carrying engineering equipment; or

(*f*) drawing a trailer or semi-trailer carrying engineering equipment.

(2) No person shall use or cause or permit to be used on a road a vehicle to which this regulation applies if the overall travelling height exceeds 3.66 m unless there is carried in the vehicle in the manner specified in paragraph (3) a notice clearly indicating in feet and inches and in figures not less than 40 mm tall, the overall travelling height.

(3) The notice referred to in paragraph (2) shall be attached to the vehicle in such a manner that it can be read by the driver when in the driving position.

(4) In this regulation—

'engineering equipment' means engineering plant and any other plant or equipment designed and constructed for the purpose of engineering operations;

'overall travelling height' means not less than and not above 25 mm more than the distance between the ground and the point on the motor vehicle, or on any trailer drawn by it, or on any load which is being carried by or any equipment which is fitted to the said motor vehicle or trailer, which is farthest from the ground, and for the purpose of determining the overall travelling height—

(*a*) the tyres of the motor vehicle and of any trailer which it is drawing shall be suitably inflated for the use to which the vehicle or combination of vehicles is being put; and

(*b*) the surface under the motor vehicle and any trailer which it is drawing and any load which is being carried on and any equipment which is fitted to any part of the said vehicle or combination of vehicles and which projects beyond any part of the said vehicle or combination of vehicles shall be reasonably flat; and

(*c*) any equipment which is fitted to the motor vehicle or any trailer which it is drawing shall be stowed in the position in which it is to proceed on the road;

'skip' means an article of equipment designed and constructed to be carried on a road vehicle and to be placed on a road or other land for the storage of materials, or for the removal and disposal of rubble, waste, household or other rubbish or earth.

11. Overhang

(1) The overhang of a wheeled vehicle of a class specified in an item in column 2 of the Table *[see table at p 2/764]* shall not, subject to any exemption specified in that item in column 4, exceed the distance specified in that item in column 3.

(2) In the case of an agricultural motor vehicle the distance measured horizontally and parallel to the longitudinal axis of the rear portion of the vehicle between the transverse planes passing through the rearmost point of the vehicle and through the centre of the rear or the rearmost axle should not exceed 3 m.

12. Minimum ground clearance

(1) Save as provided in paragraph (2), a wheeled trailer which is—

(*a*) a goods vehicles; and

(*b*) manufactured on or after 1st April 1984,

shall have a minimum ground clearance of not less than 160 mm if the trailer has an axle interspace of more than 6 m but less than 11.5 m, and a minimum ground clearance of not less than 190 mm if the trailer has an axle interspace of 11.5 m or more.

(2) Paragraph (1) shall not apply in the case of a trailer—

(*a*) which is fitted with a suspension system with which, by the operation of a control, the trailer may be lowered or raised, while that system is being operated to enable the trailer to pass under a bridge or other obstruction over a road provided that at such time the system is operated so that no part of the trailer (excluding any wheel) touches the ground or is likely to do so; or

(*b*) while it is being loaded or unloaded.

(3) In this regulation—

'axle interspace' means—

(*a*) in the case of a semi-trailer, the distance between the point of support of the semi-trailer at its forward end and, if it has only one axle, the centre of that axle or, if it has more than one axle, the point halfway between the centres of the foremost and rearmost of those axles; and

(*b*) in the case of any other trailer, the distance between the centre of its front axle or, if it has more than one axle at the front, the point halfway between the centres of the foremost and rearmost of those axles, and the centre of its rear axle or, if it has more than one axle at the rear, the point halfway between the centre of the foremost and rearmost of those axles; and

TABLE

(regulation 11(1))

1 Item	2 Class of vehicle	3 Maximum overhang	4 Exemptions
1	Motor tractor	1.83 m.	(*a*) a track-laying vehicle (*b*) an agricultural motor vehicle
2	Heavy motor car and motor car	60% of the distance between the transverse plane which passes through the centre or centres of the foremost wheel or wheels and the transverse plane which passes through the foremost point from which the overhang is to be measured as provided in regulation 3(2).	(*a*) a bus (*b*) a refuse vehicle (*c*) a works truck (*d*) a track-laying vehicle (*e*) an agricultural motor vehicle (*f*) a motor car which is an ambulance (*g*) a vehicle designed to dispose of its load to the rear, if the overhang does not exceed 1.15 m (*h*) a vehicle first used before 2nd January 1933 (*i*) a vehicle first used before 1st January 1966 if— (i) the distance between the centres of the rearmost and foremost axles does not exceed 2.29 m, and (ii) the distance specified in column 3 is not exceeded by more than 767 mm (*j*) heating plant on a vehicle designed and mainly used to heat the surface of a road or other similar surface in the process of construction, repair or maintenance shall be disregarded.

'ground clearance' means the shortest distance between the ground and the lowest part of that portion of the trailer (excluding any part of a suspension, steering or braking system attached to any axle, any wheel and any air skirt) which lies within the area formed by the overall width of the trailer and the middle 70% of the axle interspace, such distance being ascertained when the trailer—

(*a*) is fitted with suitable tyres which are inflated to a pressure recommended by the manufacturer, and

(*b*) is reasonably horizontal and standing on ground which is reasonably flat.

13. Turning circle

(1) This regulation applies to a bus first used on or after 1st April 1982.

(2) Every vehicle to which this regulation applies shall be able to move on either lock so that no part of it projects outside the area contained between concentric circles with radii of 12 m and 5.3 m.

(3) When a vehicle to which this regulation applies moves forward from rest, on either lock, so that its outermost point describes a circle of 12 m radius, no part of the vehicle shall project beyond the longitudinal plane which, at the beginning of the manoeuvre, defines the overall width of the vehicle on the side opposite to the direction in which it is turning by more than—

(*a*) 0.8 m if it is a rigid vehicle; or

(*b*) 1.2 m if it is an articulated bus.

(4) For the purpose of paragraph (3) the two rigid portions of an articulated bus shall be in line at the beginning of the manoeuvre.

14. Connecting section and direction-holding of articulated buses

(1) This regulation applies to every articulated bus first used on or after 1st April 1982.

(2) The connecting section of the two parts of every articulated bus to which this regulation applies shall be constructed so as to comply with the provisions relating to such a section specified in paragraph 5.9 in ECE Regulation 36 as regards vehicles within the scope of that Regulation.

(3) Every articulated bus to which this regulation applies shall be constructed so that when the vehicle is moving in a straight line the longitudinal median planes of its two parts coincide and form a continuous plane without any deflection.

B *Brakes*

15. Braking systems of certain vehicles first used on or after 1st April 1983

(1) Save as provided in paragraphs (2), (3) [except in sub-paragraph (*b*)(ii)] and (4), the braking system of every wheeled vehicle of a class specified in an item in column 2 of the Table which is first used on or after 1st April 1983 shall comply with the construction, fitting, and performance requirements specified in Annexes I, II and VII to Community Directive 79/489, and if relevant, Annexes III, IV, V, VI and VIII to that Directive, in relation to the category of vehicles specified in that item in column 3.

Provided that it shall be lawful for any vehicle of such a class which was first used before 1st April 1983 to comply with the said requirements instead of complying with regulations 16 and 17.

TABLE

(regulation 15(1))

1	2	3
Item	Class of vehicle	Vehicle category in the Community Directive
1	Passenger vehicles and dual-purpose vehicles which have 3 or more wheels except— (*a*) dual-purpose vehicles constructed and adapted to carry not more than 2 passengers exclusive of the driver; (*b*) motor cycles with sidecar attached; (*c*) vehicles having 3 wheels, and not exceeding a maximum gross weight of 1000 kg, a design speed of 40 km/h and an engine capacity of 50 cc; (*d*) buses.	M1
2	Buses having a maximum gross weight which does not exceed 5000 kg.	M2
3	Buses having a maximum gross weight which exceeds 5000 kg.	M3
4	Dual-purpose vehicles not within item 1(*a*); and goods vehicles, having a maximum gross weight which does not exceed 3500 kg, and not being motor cycles with a sidecar attached.	N1
	Goods vehicles with a maximum gross weight which—	
5	exceeds 3500 kg but does not exceed 12,000 kg.	N2
6	exceeds 12,000 kg.	N3
	Trailers of which the sum of the axle weights—	
7	does not exceed 750 kg.	O1
8	exceeds 750 kg but does not exceed 3500 kg.	O2
9	exceeds 3500 kg but does not exceed 10,000 kg.	O3
10	exceeds 10,000 kg.	O4

[(1A) Save as provided in paragraphs (2), (3)(*b*) and(*c*), (3A) and (5), the braking system of every wheeled vehicle of a class specified in an item in column 2 of the Table which is first used on or after the relevant date shall comply with the construction, fitting and performance requirements specified in Annexes I, II and VII to Community Directive 85/647, and if relevant, Annexes III, IV, V, VI, VIII, X, XI and

XII to that Directive, in relation to the category of vehicles specified in that item in column 3.

Provided that it shall be lawful for any vehicle of such a class which was first used before 1st April 1989 to comply with the said requirements instead of complying with regulations 15(1), 16 and 17.]

[(1B) In paragraph (1A), the relevant date in relation to a vehicle in category M1, M2 or N1 is 1st April 1990, and in relation to a vehicle in any other category is 1st April 1989.]

(2) The requirements specified in [paragraphs (1) and (1A)] do not apply to—

(*a*) an agricultural trailer or agricultural trailed appliance that is not, in either case, drawn at a speed exceeding 20 mph;

(*b*) a locomotive;

(*c*) a motor tractor;

(*d*) an agricultural motor vehicle unless it is first used after 1st June 1986 and is driven at more than 20 mph;

(*e*) a vehicle which has a maximum speed not exceeding 25 km/h;

(*f*) a works trailer;

(*g*) a works truck;

(*h*) a public works vehicle;

(*i*) a trailer designed and constructed, or adapted, to be drawn exclusively by a vehicle to which sub-paragraph (*b*), (*c*), (*e*), (*g*) or (*h*) of this paragraph applies;

(*j*) a trailer mentioned in regulation 16(3)(*b*), (*d*), (*e*), (*f*) and (*g*); or

(*k*) a vehicle manufactured by Leyland Vehicles Limited and known as the Atlantean Bus, if first used before 1st October 1984.

(3) The requirements specified in [paragraphs (1) and (1A)] shall apply to the classes of vehicles specified in the Table so that—

(*a*) in items 2 and 3 the testing requirements specified in paragraphs 1.5.1 and 1.5.2 of Annex II to [Community Directive 79/489] shall not apply in relation to a double-decked vehicle first used before 1st October 1983;

(*b*) in items 2 and 3—

(i) the requirements specified in paragraph 1.1.4.2 of Annex II to Community Directive 79/489; and

(ii) sub-note (2) to paragraph 1.17.2 of Annex I to Community Directive 85/647,

shall not apply;]

(*c*) in items 1, 2, 3, 4, 5 and 6, in the case of vehicles constructed or adapted for use by physically handicapped drivers, the requirement in paragraph 2.1.2.1 of Annex I to [Community Directive 79/489] that the driver must be able to achieve the braking action mentioned in that paragraph from his driving seat without removing his hands from the steering control shall be modified so as to require that the driver is able to achieve that action while one of his hands remains on the steering control; and

(*d*) in items 1, 4, 5, 6, 7, 8, 9 and 10 the requirement specified in paragraph 1.1.4.2 of Annex II to [Community Directive 79/489] shall not apply to a vehicle if either—

(i) following a test in respect of which the fee numbered 1360C, 1361Z or 1362W, prescribed in Schedule 1 to the Motor Vehicles (Type Approval and Approval Marks) (Fees) Regulations 1984 [*SI 1984 No 1404, as amended*] has been paid, a document is issued by the Secretary of State indicating that, at the date of manufacture of the vehicle, the type to which it belongs complies with the requirements specifed in Annex 13 to ECE Regulation 13.03, 13.04 or 13.05; or

(ii) as a result of a notifiable alteration to the vehicle, within the meaning of regulation 3 of the Plating and Testing Regulations, a fitment has been approved as complying with the requirements mentioned in sub-paragraph (i).

[(3A) The requirements specified in paragraph (1A) shall apply to a road tanker subject to the exclusion of paragraph 4.3 of Annex X to Community Directive 85/647.]

(4) Instead of complying with [paragraph (1)] of this regulation, a vehicle to which this regulation applies may comply with Community Directive 79/489 or with ECE Regulation 13.03, 13.04 or 13.05, so, however, that a vehicle on which a notifiable alteration referred to in paragraph (3)(*d*) has been carried out shall not be treated as so complying unless the fitment installed in it has been approved as mentioned in that paragraph.

[(5) Instead of complying with paragraph (1A) of this regulation, a vehicle to which this regulation applies may comply with Community Directive 85/647 or ECE Regulation 13.05.]

[(6) In paragraph (3A) the expression 'road tanker' means any vehicle or trailer which carries liquid fuel in a tank forming part of the vehicle or trailer other than that containing the fuel which is used to propel the vehicle, and also includes any tank with a capacity exceeding $3m^3$ carried on a vehicle.]

[(7) In this regulation, and in relation to the application to any vehicle of any provision of Community Directive 85/647, the definitions of 'semi-trailer', 'full trailer' and 'centre-axle trailer' set out in that Directive shall apply and the meaning of 'semi-trailer' in column 2 of the Table in regulation 3(2) shall not apply.]

[Regulation 15 is printed as amended by SI 1987 No 676.

The following definitions (which are referred to in reg 15(7)) are taken from Commission Directive 85/647/EEC:

'Semi-trailer' means a towed vehicle in which the axle(s) is (are) positioned behind the centre of gravity of the vehicle (when uniformly loaded) and which is equipped with a connecting device permitting horizontal and vertical forces to be transmitted to the drawing vehicle.

'Full trailer' means a towed vehicle having at least two axles, and equipped with a towing device which can move vertically (in relation to the trailer) and controls the direction of the front axle(s), but which transmits no significant static load to the drawing vehicle.

'Centre-axle trailer' means a towed vehicle equipped with a towing device which cannot move vertically (in relation to the trailer), and in which the axle(s) is (are) positioned close to the centre of gravity of the vehicle (when uniformly loaded) such that only a small static vertical load, not exceeding 10% of the maximum mass of the trailer or 1,000 kg (whichever is the lesser) is transmitted to the drawing vehicle.

The maximum mass to be taken into consideration when classifying a centre-axle trailer shall be the mass tansmitted to the ground by the axle(s) of the centre-axle trailer when coupled to the drawing vehicle and laden with a maximum load.]

16. Braking systems of vehicles to which regulation 15 does not apply

(1) Save as provided in paragraphs (2) and (3), this regulation applies to every vehicle to which regulation 15 does not apply.

(2) Paragraph (4) of this regulation does not apply to a vehicle which complies with regulation 15 by virtue of the proviso to regulation 15(1) [or 1(A)], or which complies with Community Directive 79/489 [or 85/647] or ECE Regulation 13.03, 13.04 or 13.05.

(3) This regulation does not apply to the following vehicles, except in the case of a vehicle referred to in (*a*) in so far as the regulation concerns parking brakes (requirements 16 to 18 in Schedule 3)—

(*a*) a locomotive first used before 2nd January 1933, propelled by steam, and with an engine which is capable of being reversed;

(*b*) a trailer which—

(i) is designed for use and used for street cleansing and does not carry any load other than its necessary gear and equipment;

(ii) has axle weights of which the sum does not exceed 750 kg;

(iii) is an agricultural trailer manufactured before 1st July 1947 drawn by a motor tractor or an agricultural vehicle if the trailer—

(A) has a laden weight not exceeding 4070 kg; and

(B) is the only trailer being drawn; and

(C) is drawn at a speed not exceeding 10 mph; and

(iv) is drawn by a motor cycle in accordance with regulation 84;

(*c*) an agricultural trailed appliance;

(*d*) an agricultural trailed appliance conveyor;

(*e*) a broken down vehicle;

(*f*) before 1st October 1986—

(i) a trailer with an unladen weight not exceeding 102 kg which was manufactured before 1st October 1982; and

(ii) a gritting trailer; or

(*g*) on or after 1st October 1986, a gritting trailer with a maximum gross weight not exceeding 2000 kg.

(4) Save as provided in paragraph (7), a vehicle of a class specified in an item in column 2 of the Table shall comply with the requirements shown in column 3 in that item, subject to any exemptions or modifications shown in column 4 in that item, reference to numbers in column 3 being references to the requirements so numbered in Schedule 3.

Provided that wheeled agricultural motor vehicles not driven at more than 20 mph are excluded from all items other than items 21 to 23.

TABLE

(regulation 16(4))

1	2	3	4
Item	Class of vehicle	Requirement in Schedule 3	Exemptions or modifications
	Motor cars		
1	First used before 1st January 1915.	3, 6, 7, 13, 16	Requirements 13 and 16 do not apply to a motor car with less than 4 wheels.
2	First used on or after 1st January 1915 but before 1st April 1938.	1, 4, 6, 7, 9, 16	A works truck within items 1 to 11 is not subject to requirements 1, 2, 3 or 4 if it is equipped with one braking system with one means of operation
3	First used on or after 1st April 1938 and being either a track-laying vehicle or a vehicle first used before 1st January 1968.	1, 4, 6, 7, 8, 9, 16	
4	Wheeled vehicles first used on or after 1st January 1968.	1, 4, 6, 7, 8, 9, 18	
	Heavy motor cars		
5	First used before 15th August 1928.	1, 6, 16	
6	First used on or after 15th August 1928 but before 1st April 1938.	1, 4, 6, 7, 8, 16	
7	First used on or after 1st April 1938 and being either a track-laying vehicle or a vehicle first used before 1st January 1968.	1, 4, 6, 7, 8, 9, 16	
8	Wheeled vehicles first used on or after 1st January 1968.	1, 4, 6, 7, 8, 9, 18	
	Motor cycles		
9	First used before 1st January 1927.	3, and, in the case of three-wheeled vehicles, 16	
10	First used on or after 1st January 1927 but before 1st January 1968.	2, 7, and, in the case of three-wheeled vehicles, 16	
11	First used on or after 1st January 1968 and not being a motor cycle to which paragraph (5) applies.	2, 7, and, in the case of three-wheeled vehicles, 18	

1	2	3	4
Item	Class of vehicle	Requirement in Schedule 3	Exemptions or modifications
	Locomotives		
12	Wheeled vehicles first used before 1st June 1955.	3, 6, 12, 16	
13	Wheeled vehicles first used on or after 1st June 1955 but before 1st January 1968.	3, 4, 6, 7, 8, 9, 18	
14	Wheeled vehicles first used on or after 1st January 1968.	3, 4, 6, 7, 8, 9, 18	
15	Track-laying vehicles.	3, 6, 16	
	Motor tractors		
16	Wheeled vehicles first used before 14th January 1931 and track-laying vehicles first used before 1st April 1938.	3, 4, 6, 7, 16	Industrial tractors within items 16 to 19 are subject to requirement 5 instead of requirement 4.
17	Wheeled vehicles first used on or after 14th January 1931 but before 1st April 1938.	3, 4, 6, 7, 9, 16	
18	Wheeled vehicles first used on or after 1st April 1938 but before 1st January 1968.	3, 4, 7, 8, 9, 16	
19	Wheeled vehicles first used on or after 1st January 1968.	3, 4, 6, 7, 8, 9, 18	
20	Track-laying vehicles first used on or after 1st April 1938.	3, 4, 6, 7, 8, 16	
	Wheeled agricultural motor vehicles not driven at more than 20 mph		
21	First used before 1st January 1968.	3, 4, 6, 7, 8, 16	
22	First used on or after 1st January 1968 but before 9th February 1980.	3, 4, 6, 7, 8, 18	
23	First used on or after 9th February 1980.	3, 5, 6, 7, 8, 18	
	Invalid carriages		
24	Whenever first used.	3, 13	
	Trailers		
25	Manufactured before 1st April 1938.	3, 10, 14, 17	

1	2	3	4
Item	Class of vehicle	Requirement in Schedule 3	Exemptions or modifications
26	Manufactured on or after 1st April 1938 and being either a track-laying vehicle, an agricultural trailer or a vehicle manufactured before 1st January 1968.	3, 8, 10, 14, 17	Agricultural trailers are not subject to requirement 8.
27	Wheeled vehicles manufactured on or after 1st January 1968, not being an agricultural trailer.	3, 4, 8, 11, 15, 18	Trailers equipped with brakes which come into operation on the overrun of the vehicle are not subject to requirement 15.

(5) Save as provided in paragraph (6), the braking system of every motor cycle with two wheels (with or without a sidecar) first used on or after 1st April 1987 shall comply with ECE Regulation 13.05.

(6) Paragraph (5) does not apply to a works truck or to a vehicle constructed or assembled by a person not ordinarily engaged in the business of manufacturing vehicles of that description.

(7) Instead of complying with the provisions of paragraph (4) of this Regulation an agricultural motor vehicle may comply with Community Directive 76/432.

[Regulation 16 is printed as amended by SI 1987 No 676.]

17. Vacuum or pressure brake warning devices

(1) Save as provided in paragraph (2), every motor vehicle which is equipped with a braking system which embodies a vacuum or pressure reservoir or reservoirs shall be equipped with a device so placed as to be readily visible to the driver of the vehicle and which is capable of indicating any impending failure of, or deficiency in, the vacuum or pressure system.

(2) The requirement specified in paragraph (1) does not apply in respect of—

(*a*) a vehicle to which [paragraph (1) or (1A) of] regulation 15 applies, or which complies with the requirements of that regulation, of Community Directive 79/489 [or 85/647] or of ECE Regulation 13.03, 13.04 or 13.05;

(*b*) an agricultural motor vehicle which complies with Community Directive 76/432;

(*c*) a vehicle with an unladen weight not exceeding 3050 kg propelled by an internal combustion engine, if the vacuum in the reservoir or reservoirs is derived directly from the inclusion system of the engine, and if, in the event of a failure of, or deficiency in, the vacuum system, the brakes of that braking system are sufficient under the most adverse conditions to bring the vehicle to rest within a reasonable distance; or

(*d*) a vehicle first used before 1st October 1937.

[Regulation 17 is printed as amended by SI 1987 No 676.]

18. Maintenance and efficiency of brakes

(1) Every part of every braking system and of the means of operation thereof fitted to a vehicle shall be maintained in good and efficient working order and be properly adjusted.

(2) Paragraph (3) applies to every wheeled motor vehicle except—

(*a*) an agricultural motor vehicle which is not driven at more than 20 mph;

(*b*) a works truck; and

(*c*) a pedestrian-controlled vehicle.

(3) Every vehicle to which this paragraph applies and which is of a class specified in an item in column 2 of Table I shall, subject to any exemption shown for that item in column 4, be so maintained that—

(*a*) its service braking system has a total braking efficiency not less than that shown in column (3)(a) for that item; and

(*b*) if the vehicle is a heavy motor car, a motor car first used on or after 1st January 1915 or a motor-cycle first used on or after 1st January 1927, its secondary braking system has a total braking efficiency not less than that shown in column 3(b) for those items.

Provided that a reference in Table I to a trailer is a reference to a trailer required by regulation 15 or 16 to be equipped with brakes.

TABLE

(regulation 18(3))

1	2	3		4
Item	Class of vehicle	Efficiencies % (a)	(b)	Exemptions
1	A vehicle to which regulation 15 applies or which complies in all respects other than its braking efficiency with the requirements of that regulation or with Community Directive 79/489 [or 85/647] or with ECE Regulation 13.03, 13.04 or 13.05—			A motor cycle.
	(*a*) when not drawing a trailer;	50	25	
	(*b*) When drawing a trailer	45	25	
2	A vehicle, not included in item 1 and not being a motor cycle, which is first used on or after 1st January 1968—			
	(*a*) when not drawing a trailer	50	25	
	(*b*) when drawing a trailer manufactured on or after 1st January 1968;	50	25	
	(*c*) when drawing a trailer manufactured before 1st January 1968	40	15	

1	2	3		4
Item	Class of vehicle	Efficiencies % (a)	(b)	Exemptions
3	Goods vehicles first used on or after 15th August 1928 but before 1st January 1968 having an unladen weight exceeding 1525 kg being—			
	(*a*) rigid vehicles with 2 axles not constructed to form part of an articulated vehicle—			
	(i) when not drawing a trailer	45	20	
	(ii) when drawing a trailer	40	15	
	(*b*) other vehicles, including vehicles constructed to form part of an articulated vehicle, whether or not drawing a trailer	40	15	
4	Vehicles not included in items 1 to 3—			(*a*) a bus;
	(*a*) having at least one means of operation applying to at least 4 wheels;	50	25	(*b*) an articulated vehicle;
	(*b*) having 3 wheels and at least one means of operation applying to all 3 wheels and not being a motor cycle with sidecar attached			(*c*) a vehicle constructed or adapted to form part of an articulated vehicle;
	(i) when not drawing a trailer	40	25	(*d*) a heavy motor car which is a goods vehicle first used before 15th August 1928.
	(ii) in the case of a motor cycle when drawing a trailer	40	25	
	(*c*) other			
	(i) when not drawing a trailer	30	25	
	(ii) in the case of a motor cycle when drawing a trailer.	30	25	

(4) A goods vehicle shall not be deemed to comply with the requirements of paragraph (3) unless it is capable of complying with those requirements both at the laden weight at which it is operating at any time and when its laden weight is equal to—

(*a*) if a plating certificate has been issued and is in force for the vehicle, the design gross weight shown in column (3) of that certificate or, if no such weight is so shown, the gross weight shown in column (2) of that certificate; and

(*b*) in any other case, the design gross weight of the vehicle.

Provided that in the case of a goods vehicle drawing a trailer, references in this paragraph to laden weight refer to the combined laden weight of the drawing vehicle and the trailer and references to gross weight and design gross weight are to be taken as references to train weight and design train weight respectively.

(5) The brakes of every agricultural motor vehicle which is first used on or after 1st June 1986 and is not driven at more than 20 mph, and of every agricultural trailer manufactured on or after 1st December 1985 shall be capable of achieving a braking efficiency of not less than 25% when the weight of the vehicle is equal to the total maximum axle weights which the vehicle is designed to have.

(6) Every vehicle or combination of vehicles specified in an item in column 2 of Table II shall be so maintained that its brakes are capable, without the assistance of stored energy, of holding it stationary on a gradient of at least the percentage specified in column 3 in that item.

TABLE II

(regulation 18(6))

1	2	3
Item	Class of vehicle or combination	Percentage gradient
1	A vehicle specified in item 1 of Table I— (*a*) when not drawing a trailer (*b*) when drawing a trailer	 16 12
2	A vehicle to which requirement 18 in Schedule 3 applies by virtue of regulation 16.	16
3	A vehicle, not included in item 1, drawing a trailer manufactured on or after 1st January 1968 and required, by regulation 15 or 16, to be fitted with brakes.	16

(7) For the purpose of this regulation the date of manufacture of a trailer which is a composite trailer shall be deemed to be the same as the date of manufacture of the semi-trailer which forms part of the composite trailer.

(8) A vehicle which is subject to, and which complies with the requirements in, item 1 and Tables I and II shall not be treated as failing, by reason of its braking efficiency, to comply with regulation 15 or with Community Directive 79/489 [or 85/647] or ECE Regulation 13.03, 13.04 or 13.05.

[Regulation 18 is printed as amended by SI 1987 No 676.]

19. Application of brakes of trailers

Where a trailer is drawn by a motor vehicle the driver (or in the case of a locomotive one of the persons employed in driving or tending the locomotive) shall be in a position readily to operate any brakes required by these Regulations to be fitted to the trailer as well as the brakes of the motor vehicle unless a person other than the driver is in a position and competent efficiently to apply the brakes of the trailer.

Provided that this regulation shall not apply to a trailer which—

(*a*) in compliance with these Regulations, is fitted with brakes which automatically come into operation on the overrun of the trailer; or

(*b*) which is a broken down vehicle being drawn, whether or not in consequence of a breakdown, in such a manner that it cannot be steered by its own steering gear.

C *Wheels, Springs, Tyres and Tracks*

20. General requirements as to wheels and tracks

Every motor cycle and invalid carriage shall be a wheeled vehicle, and every other motor vehicle and every trailer shall be either a wheeled vehicle or a track-laying vehicle.

21. Diameter of wheels

All wheels of a wheeled vehicle which are fitted with tyres other than pneumatic tyres shall have a rim diameter of not less than 670 mm.

Provided that this regulation does not apply to—

(*a*) a motor vehicle just used on or before 2nd January 1933;

(*b*) a trailer manufactured before 1st January 1933;

(*c*) a wheel fitted to a motor car first used on or before 1st July 1936, if the diameter of the wheel inclusive of the tyre is not less than 670 mm;

(*d*) a works truck or works trailer;

(*e*) a refuse vehicle;

(*f*) a pedestrian-controlled vehicle;

(*g*) a mobile crane;

(*h*) an agricultural trailed appliance;

(*i*) a broken down vehicle which is being drawn by a motor vehicle in consequence of the breakdown; or

(*j*) an electrically propelled goods vehicle the unladen weight of which does not exceed 1270 kg.

22. Springs and resilient material

(1) Save as provided in paragraphs (3) and (4), every motor vehicle and every trailer be equipped with suitable and sufficient springs between each wheel and the frame of the vehicle.

(2) Save as provided in paragraphs (3) and (4), in the case of a track-laying vehicle—

(*a*) resilient material shall be interposed between the rims of the weight-carrying rollers and the road surface so that the weight of the vehicle, other than that borne by any wheel, is supported by the resilient material, and

(*b*) where the vehicle is a heavy motor car, motor car, or trailer it shall have suitable springs between the frame of the vehicle and the weight-carrying rollers.

(3) This regulation does not apply to—

(*a*) a wheeled vehicle with an unladen weight not exceeding 4070 kg and which is—

(i) a motor tractor any unsprung wheel of which is fitted with a pneumatic tyre;

(ii) a motor tractor used in connection with railway shunting and which is used on a road only when passing from one railway track to another in connection with such use;

(iii) a vehicle specially designed, and mainly used, for work on rough ground or unmade roads and every wheel of which is fitted with a pneumatic tyre and which is not driven at more than 20 mph;

(iv) a vehicle constructed or adapted for, and being used for, road sweeping and every wheel of which is fitted with either a pneumatic tyre or a resilient tyre and which is not driven at more than 20 mph;

(*b*) an agricultural motor vehicle which is not driven at more than 20 mph;

(*c*) an agricultural trailer, or an agricultural trailed appliance;

(*d*) a trailer used solely for the haulage of felled trees;

(*e*) a motor cycle;

(*f*) a mobile crane;

(*g*) a pedestrian-controlled vehicle all the wheels of which are equipped with pneumatic tyres;

(*h*) a road roller;

(*i*) a broken down vehicle; or

(*j*) a vehicle first used on or before 1st January 1932.

(4) Paragraphs (1) and (2)(*b*) do not apply to a works truck or a works trailer.

23. Wheel loads

(1) Subject to paragraph (2) this regulation applies to—

(*a*) a semi-trailer with more than 2 wheels;

(*b*) a track-laying vehicle with more than 2 wheels; and

(*c*) any other vehicle with more than 4 wheels.

(2) This regulation does not apply to a road roller.

(3) Save as provided in paragraphs (4) and (5), every vehicle to which this regulation applies shall be fitted with a compensating arrangement which will ensure that under the most adverse conditions every wheel will remain in contact with the road and will not be subject to abnormal variations of load.

(4) Paragraph (3) does not apply in respect of a steerable wheel on which the load does not exceed—

(*a*) if it is a wheeled vehicle, 3560kg; and

(*b*) if it is a track laying vehicle, 2540kg.

(5) In the application of paragraph (3) to an agricultural motor vehicle, wheels which are in line transversely on one side of the longitudinal axis of the vehicle shall be regarded as one wheel.

24. Tyres

(1) Save as provided in paragraph (2), every wheel of a vehicle of a class specified in an item in column 2 of the Table shall be fitted with a tyre of a type specified in that item in column 3 which complies with any conditions specified in that item in column 4.

(2) The requirements referred to in paragraph (1) do not apply to a road-roller and are subject, in the case of any item in the Table, to the exemptions specified in that item in column 5.

TABLE

(regulation 24(1))

1	2	3	4	5
Item	Class of vehicle	Type of tyre	Conditions	Exemptions
1	Locomotives not falling in item 6	Pneumatic or resilient		

1	2	3	4	5
Item	Class of vehicle	Type of tyre	Conditions	Exemptions
2	Motor tractors not falling in item 6	Pneumatic or resilient	No re-cut pneumatic tyre shall be fitted to any wheel of a vehicle with an unladen weight of less than 2540 kg unless the diameter of the rim of the wheel is at least 405 mm	
3	Heavy motor cars not falling in item 6	Pneumatic		The following, if every wheel not fitted with a pneumatic tyre is fitted with a resilient tyre— (*a*) a vehicle mainly used for work on rough ground; (*b*) a tower wagon; (*c*) a vehicle fitted with a turntable fire escape; (*d*) a refuse vehicle; (*e*) a works truck; (*f*) a vehicle first used before 3rd January 1933.
4	Motor cars not falling in item 6	Pneumatic	No re-cut tyre shall be fitted to any wheel of a vehicle unless it is— (*a*) an electrically propelled goods vehicle or, (*b*) a goods vehicle with an unladen weight of at least 2540 kg and the diameter of the rim of the wheel is at least 405 mm.	The following, if every wheel not fitted with a pneumatic tyre is fitted with a resilient tyre— (*a*) a vehicle mainly used for work on rough ground; (*b*) a refuse vehicle; (*c*) a works truck; (*d*) a vehicle with an unladen weight not exceeding— (i) 1270 kg if electrically propelled; (ii) 1020 kg in any other case; (*e*) a tower wagon; (*f*) a vehicle fitted with a turntable fire escape; (*g*) a vehicle first used before 3rd January 1933.

1	2	3	4	5
Item	Class of vehicle	Type of tyre	Conditions	Exemptions
5	Motor cycles	Pneumatic	No re-cut tyre shall be fitted	The following, if every wheel not fitted with a pneumatic tyre is fitted with a resilient tyre— (*a*) a works truck; (*b*) a pedestrian-controlled vehicle
6	Agricultural motor vehicles which are not driven at more than 20 mph	Pneumatic or resilient	The same as for item 2	The requirement in column 3 does not apply to a vehicle of which— (*a*) every steering wheel is fitted with a smooth soled tyre which is not less than 60 mm wide where it touches the road; and (*b*) in the case of a wheeled vehicle, every driving wheel is fitted with a smooth-soled tyre which— (i) is not less than 150 mm wide if the unladen weight of the vehicle exceeds 3050 kg, or 76 mm wide in any other case, and either (ii) is shod with diagonal cross-bars not less than 76 mm wide or more than 20 mm thick extending the full breadth of the tyre and so arranged that the space between adjacent bars is not more than 76 mm; or (iii) is shod with diagonal cross-bars of resilient material not less than 60 mm wide extending the full breadth of the tyre and so arranged that the space between adjacent bars is not more than 76 mm.

1	2	3	4	5
Item	Class of vehicle	Type of tyre	Conditions	Exemptions
7	Trailers	Pneumatic	Except in the case of a trailer mentioned in paragraph (*d*) of column 5, no re-cut tyre shall be fitted to any wheel of a trailer drawn by a heavy motor car or a motor car if the trailer— (*a*) has an unladen weight not exceeding— (i) if it is a living van, 2040 kg; or (ii) in any other case, 1020 kg; or (*b*) is not constructed or adapted to carry any load, other than plant or other special appliance which is a permanent or essentially permanent fixture and has a gross weight not exceeding 2290 kg	(*a*) an agricultural trailer manufactured before 1st December 1985; (*b*) an agricultural trailed appliance; (*c*) a trailer used to carry water for a road roller being used in connection with road works; (*d*) the following if every wheel which is not fitted with a pneumatic tyre is fitted with a resilient tyre— (i) a works trailer; (ii) a refuse vehicle; (iii) a trailer drawn by a heavy motor car every wheel of which is not required to be fitted with a pneumatic tyre; (iv) a broken down vehicle; or (v) a trailer drawn by a vehicle which is not a heavy motor car or a motor car.

(3) Save as provided in paragraph (4) a wheel of a vehicle may not be fitted with a temporary use spare tyre unless either—

(*a*) the vehicle is a passenger vehicle (not being a bus) first used before 1st April 1987; or

(*b*) the vehicle complies at the time of its first use with ECE Regulation 64.

(4) Paragraph (3) does not apply to a vehicle constructed or assembled by a person not ordinarily engaged in the trade or business of manufacturing vehicles of that description.

25. Tyre loads and speed ratings

(1) This regulation applies—

(*a*) to a goods vehicle first used before 1st April 1987 in respect of which a plating certificate has been issued;

(*b*) to a vehicle first used on or after 1st April 1987, which is a goods vehicle, a bus or trailer; and,

(*c*) from 1st April 1990 to every vehicle, whenever first used, which is a goods vehicle, a bus or trailer.

(2) Each axle of a vehicle to which this regulation applies solely by virtue of paragraph 1(*a*) shall be equipped with tyres which, as respects strength, are designed and maintained adequately to support the maximum axle weight for that axle.

(3) Each axle of a vehicle to which this regulation applies by virtue of paragraph (1)(*b*) or (*c*) shall be equipped with tyres which are designed and maintained adequately to support the maximum axle weight for that axle when the vehicle is driven at the speed shown in column 3 in the Table in the item in which the vehicle is described in column 2 (the lowest relevant speed being applicable to a vehicle which is described in more than one item).

TABLE

(regulation 25(3))

1	2	3
Item	Class of vehicle	Speed
1	A vehicle of a class for which a maximum speed is prescribed by the 1984 Act.	The speed so prescribed
2	An electrically propelled vehicle having a maximum speed less than 70 mph.	The maximum speed
3	A bus which is not driven at more than 50 mph.	50 mph
4	A low platform trailer, or a municipal vehicle, or a multi-stop local collection and delivery vehicle.	40 mph
5	A vehicle not falling in items 1 to 4.	70 mph

(4) In this regulation—

'low platform trailer' means a trailer fitted with tyres of 20 rim diameter and below carrying a rectangular plate 7″ × 9″ carrying two letters 'L' each 5″ high and $3\frac{1}{2}$″ wide with a stroke width of $\frac{1}{2}$″ the letters being black on a white ground.

'maximum axle weight' means—

(*a*) in the case of a vehicle equipped with a Ministry plate in accordance with regulation 70 the axle weight shown in column (2) of that place;

(*b*) in the case of a vehicle not equipped with a Ministry plate, but which is equipped with a plate in accordance with regulation 66, the maximum axle weight shown on the plate in respect of item 9 of Part I of Schedule 8 in the case of a motor vehicle and item 7 of Part II of Schedule 8 in the case of a trailer;

(*c*) in any other case, the weight which the axle is designed or adapted not to exceed when the vehicle is travelling on a road.

'municipal vehicle' means a motor vehicle or trailer limited at all times to use by a local authority, or a person acting in pursuance of a contract with a local authority, for road cleansing, road watering or the collection and disposal of refuse, night soil or the contents of cesspools, or the purposes of the enactments relating to weights and measures or the sale of food and drugs.

'multi-stop local collection and delivery vehicle' means a motor vehicle or trailer used for multi-stop collection and delivery services to be used only within a radius of 25 miles from the permanent base at which it is normally kept.

26. Mixing of tyres

(1) Save as provided in paragraph (5) pneumatic tyres of different types of structure shall not be fitted to the same axle of a wheeled vehicle.

(2) Save as provided in paragraphs (3) or (5), a wheeled motor vehicle having only two axles each of which is equipped with one or two single wheels shall not be fitted with—

(*a*) a diagonal-ply tyre or a bias-belted tyre on its rear axle if a radial-ply tyre is fitted on its front axle; or

(*b*) a diagonal-ply tyre on its rear axle if a bias-belted tyre is fitted on the front axle.

(3) Paragraph (2) does not apply to a vehicle to an axle of which there are fitted wide tyres not specially constructed for use on engineering plant or to a vehicle which has a maximum speed not exceeding 30 mph.

(4) Save as provided in paragraph (5) pneumatic tyres fitted to—

(*a*) the steerable axles of a wheeled vehicle; and

(*b*) the driven axles of a wheeled vehicle, not being steerable axles,

shall all be of the same type of structure.

(5) Paragraphs (1), (2), and (4) do not prohibit the fitting of a temporary use spare tyre to a wheel of a passenger vehicle (not being a bus) unless it is driven at a speed exceeding 50 mph.

(6) In this regulation—

'axle' includes—

(i) two or more stub axles which are fitted on opposite sides of the longitudinal axis of the vehicle so as to form—

(*a*) a pair in the case of two stub axles; and

(*b*) pairs in the case of more than two stub axles; and

(ii) a single stub axle which is not one of a pair;

'a bias-belted tyre' means a pneumatic tyre, the structure of which is such that the ply cords extend to the bead so as to be laid at alternate angles of substantially less than 90 degrees to the peripheral line of the tread, and are constrained by a circumferential belt comprising two or more layers of substantially inextensible cord material laid at alternate angles smaller than those of the ply cord structure;

'a diagonal-ply tyre' means a pneumatic tyre, the structure of which is such that the ply cords extend to the bead so as to be laid at alternate angles of substantially less than 90 degrees to the peripheral line of the tread, but not being a bias-belted tyre;

'a driven axle' means an axle through which power is transmitted from the engine of a vehicle to the wheels on that axle;

'a radial-ply tyre' means a pneumatic tyre, the structure of which is such that the ply cords extend to the bead so as to be laid at an angle of substantially 90 degrees to the peripheral line of the tread, the ply cord structure being stabilised by a substantially inextensible circumferential belt;

'stub-axle' means an axle on which only one wheel is mounted; and

'type of structure', in relation to a tyre, means a type of structure of a tyre of a kind defined in the foregoing provisions of this paragraph.

27. Condition and maintenance of tyres

(1) Save as provided in paragraphs (2), (3) and (4), a wheeled motor vehicle or trailer a wheel of which is fitted with a pneumatic tyre shall not be used on a road, if—

(*a*) the tyre is unsuitable having regard to the use to which the motor vehicle or trailer is being put or to the types of tyres fitted to its other wheels;

(*b*) the tyre is not so inflated as to make it fit for the use to which the motor vehicle or trailer is being put;

(*c*) the tyre has a cut in excess of 25 mm or 10% of the section width of the tyre, whichever is the greater, measured in any direction on the outside of the tyre and deep enough to reach the ply or cord;

(*d*) the tyre has any lump, bulge or tear caused by separation or partial failure of its structure;

(*e*) the tyre has any of the ply or cord exposed;

(*f*) the base of any groove which showed in the original tread pattern of the tyre is not clearly visible;

(*g*) either—

(i) the grooves of the tread pattern of the tyre do not have a depth of at least 1 mm throughout a continuous band measuring at least three-quarters of the breadth of the tread and round the entire outer circumference of the tyre; or;

(ii) if the grooves of the original tread pattern of the tyre did not extend beyond three-quarters of the breadth of the tread, any groove which showed in the original tread pattern does not have a depth of at least 1 mm; or

(*h*) the tyre is not maintained in such condition as to be fit for the use to which the vehicle or trailer is being put or has a defect which might in any way cause damage to the surface of the road or damage to persons on or in the vehicle or to other persons using the road.

(2) Paragraph (1) does not prohibit the use on a road of a motor vehicle or trailer by reason only of the fact that a wheel of the vehicle or trailer is fitted with a tyre which is deflated or not fully inflated and which has any of the defects described in sub-paragraph (*c*), (*d*) or (*e*) of paragraph (1), if the tyre and the wheel to which it is fitted are so constructed as to make the tyre in that condition fit for the use to which the motor vehicle or trailer is being put and the outer sides of the wall of the tyre are so marked as to enable the tyre to be identified as having been constructed to comply with the requirements of this paragraph.

(3) Paragraph (1)(*a*) does not prohibit the use on a road of a passenger vehicle (not being a bus) by reason only of the fact that a wheel of the vehicle is fitted with a temporary use spare tyre, unless the vehicle is driven at a speed exceeding 50 mph.

(4) (*a*) Nothing in paragraph (1)(*a*) to (*g*) applies to—

(i) an agricultural motor vehicle that is not driven at more than 20 mph;

(ii) an agricultural trailer;

(iii) an agricultural trailed appliance; or

(iv) a broken down vehicle or a vehicle proceeding to a place where it is to be broken up, being drawn, in either case, by a motor vehicle at a speed not exceeding 20 mph.

(*b*) Nothing in paragraph (1)(*f*) and (*g*) applies to—

(i) a three-wheeled motor cycle the unladen weight of which does not exceed 102 kg and which has a maximum speed of 12 mph; or

(ii) a pedestrian-controlled works truck.

(*c*) Nothing in paragraph (1)(*g*) applies to a motorcycle with an engine capacity which does not exceed 50 cc.

(5) A recut pneumatic tyre shall not be fitted to any wheel of a motor vehicle or trailer if—

(*a*) its ply or cord has been cut or exposed by the recutting process; or

(*b*) it has been wholly or partially recut in a pattern other than the manufacturer's recut tread pattern.

(6) (*a*) In this regulation—

'breadth of tread' means the breadth of that part of the tyre which can contact the road under normal conditions of use measured at 90 degrees to the peripheral line of the tread;

'original tread pattern' means in the case of—

a re-treaded tyre, the tread pattern of the tyre immediately after the tyre was re-treaded;

a wholly recut tyre, the manufacture's recut tread pattern;

a partially recut tyre, on that part of the tyre which has been recut, the manufacturer's recut tread pattern, and on the other part, the tread pattern of the tyre when new; and

any other tyre, the tread pattern of the tyre when the tyre was new.

'tie-bar' means any part of a tyre moulded in the tread pattern of the tyre for the purpose of bracing two or more features of such tread pattern;

'tread pattern' means the combination of plain surfaces and grooves extending across the breadth of the tread and round the entire outer circumference of the tyre but excludes any—

(i) tie bars or tread wear indicators;

(ii) features which are designed to wear out substantially before the rest of the pattern under normal conditions of use; and

(iii) other minor features; and

'tread wear indicator' means any bar, not being a tie-bar, projecting from the base of a groove of the tread pattern of a tyre and moulded between two or more features of the tread pattern of a tyre for the purpose of indicating the extent of the wear of such tread pattern.

(*b*) The references in paragraph (1)(*g*)(i) to grooves are references—

if a tyre has been recut, to the grooves of the manufacturer's recut tread pattern; and

if a tyre has not been recut, to the grooves which showed when the tyre was new.

28. Tracks

(1) Every part of every track of a track-laying vehicle which comes into contact with the road shall be flat and have a width of not less than 12.5 mm.

(2) The area of the track which is in contact with the road shall not at any time be

less than 225 cm^2 in respect of every 1000kg of the total weight which is transferred to the roads by the tracks.

(3) The tracks of a vehicle shall not have any defect which might damage the road or cause danger to any person on or in the vehicle or using the road, and shall be properly adjusted and maintained in good and efficient working order.

D *Steering*

29. Maintenance of steering gear

All steering gear fitted to a motor vehicle shall at all times while the vehicle is used on a road be maintained in good and efficient working order and be properly adjusted.

E *Vision*

30. View to the front

(1) Every motor vehicle shall be so designed and constructed that the driver thereof while controlling the vehicle can at all times have a full view of the road and traffic ahead of the motor vehicle.

(2) Instead of complying with the requirement of paragraph (1) a vehicle may comply with Community Directive 77/649, 81/643 or, in the case of an agricultural motor vehicle, 79/1073.

(3) All glass or other transparent material fitted to a motor vehicle shall be maintained in such condition that it does not obscure the vision of the driver while the vehicle is being driven on a road.

31. Glass

(1) This regulation applies to a motor vehicle which is—

(*a*) a wheeled vehicle, not being a caravan, first used before 1st June 1978;

(*b*) a caravan first used before 1st September 1978; or

(*c*) a track-laying vehicle.

(2) The glass fitted to any window specified in an item in column 3 of the Table of a vehicle of a class specified in that item in column 2 shall be safety glass.

TABLE

(regulation 31(2))

1	2	3
Item	Class of vehicle	Windows
1	Wheeled vehicles first used on or after 1st January 1959, being passenger vehicles or dual-purpose vehicles.	Windscreens and all outside windows.
2	Wheeled vehicles first used on or after 1st January 1959, being goods vehicles (other than dual-purpose vehicles), locomotives or motor tractors.	Windscreens and all windows in front of and on either side of the driver's seat.

1	2	3
Item	Class of vehicle	Windows
3	Wheeled vehicles not mentioned in item 1 or 2.	Windscreens and windows facing to the front on the outside, except glass fitted to the upper decks of a double-decked vehicle.
4	Track-laying vehicles.	Windscreens and windows facing to the front.

(3) For the purposes of this regulation any windscreen or window at the front of the vehicle the inner surface of which is at an angle exceeding 30 degrees to the longitudinal axis of the vehicle shall be deemed to face to the front.

[(4) In this regulation and in regulation 32—

'caravan' means a trailer which is constructed (and not merely adapted) for human habitation; and

'safety glass' means glass so constructed or treated if fractured it does not fly into fragments likely to cause severe cuts.]

[Regulation 31 is printed as amended by SI 1987 No 676.]

32.—(1) This regulation applies to—

(*a*) a caravan first used on or after 1st September 1978, and

(*b*) a wheeled motor vehicle and a wheeled trailer, not being a caravan, first used on or after 1st June 1978.

(2) Save as provided in paragraphs (3) to (9) the windows specified in column 2 of Table I in relation to a vehicle of a class specified in that column shall be constructed of the material specified in column 3 of the Table.

TABLE I

(regulation 32(2))

1	2	3
Item	Window	Material
1	Windscreens and other windows wholly or partly on either side of the driver's seat fitted to motor vehicles first used on or after 1st April 1985.	Specified safety glass (1980).
2	Windscreens and other windows wholly or partly on either side of the driver's seat fitted to a motor vehicle first used before 1st April 1985.	Specified safety glass, or specified safety glass (1980).
3	All other windows.	Specified safety glass, specified safety glass (1980), or safety glazing.

(3) The windscreens and all other windows of security vehicles or vehicles being used for police purposes shall not be subject to the requirements specified in paragraph (2), but shall be constructed of either safety glass or safety glazing.

(4) The windscreens of motorcycles not equipped with an enclosed compartment for the driver or for a passenger shall not be subject to the requirements specified in paragraph (2), but shall be constructed of safety glazing.

(5) Any windscreens or other windows which are wholly or partly in front of or on either side of the driver's seat, and which are temporarily fitted to motor vehicles to replace any windscreens or other windows which have broken, shall—

(*a*) be constructed of safety glazing; and

(*b*) be fitted only while the vehicles are being driven or towed either to premises where new windscreens or other windows are to be permanently fitted to replace the windscreens or other windows which have broken, or to complete the journey in the course of which the breakage occurred.

(6) Windows forming all or part of a screen or door in the interior of a bus first used on or after 1st April 1988, shall be constructed either of safety glazing or of specified safety glass (1980).

(7) Windows being—

(*a*) windows (other than windscreens) of motor-vehicles being engineering plant, industrial tractors, agricultural motor vehicles (other than agricultural motor vehicles first used on or after 1st June 1986 and driven at more than 20 mph) which are wholly or partly in front of or on either side of the driver's seat;

(*b*) windows of the upper deck of a double-decked bus; or

(*c*) windows in the roof of a vehicle,

shall be constructed of either specified safety glass, specified safety glass (1980) or safety glazing.

(8) In the case of motor vehicles and trailers which have not at any time been fitted with permanent windows and which are being driven or towed to a place where permanent windows are to be fitted, any temporary windscreens and any other temporary windows shall be constructed of either specified safety glass, specified safety glass (1980) or safety glazing.

(9) No requirement in this regulation that a windscreen or other window shall be constructed of specified safety glass or of specified glass (1980) shall apply to a windscreen or other window which is—

(*a*) manufactured in France;

(*b*) marked with a marking consisting of the letters 'TP GS' or 'TP GSE'; and

(*c*) fitted to a vehicle first used before 1st October 1986.

(10) Save as provided in paragraph (11), the windscreens or other windows constructed in accordance with the foregoing provisions of this regulation of specified safety glass, specified safety glass (1980) or safety glazing and specified in column 3 of Table II in relation to a vehicle of a class specified in column 2 of that Table shall have a visual transmission for light of not less than the percentage specified in relation to those windows in column 4 when measured perpendicular to the surface in accordance with the procedure specified in a document specified in relation to those windows in column 5.

TABLE II

(regulation 32(10))

1	2	3	4	5
Item	Class of vehicle	Windows	Percentage	Documents specifying procedure
1	Motor vehicles first used before 1st April 1985	All windows	70	British Standard Specification No. 857 or No. 5282
2	Motor vehicles first used on or after 1st April 1985 and trailers	(*a*) Wind-screens (*b*) All other windows	75 70	The documents mentioned in sub-paragraph (i), (ii) or (iii) of the definition in paragraph (13) of 'specified safety glass (1980).'

(11) Paragraph (10) does not apply to—

(*a*) any part of any windscreen which is ouside the vision reference zone;

(*b*) windows through which the driver when in the driver's seat is unable at any time to see any part of the road on which the vehicle is waiting or proceeding;

(*c*) windows in any motor ambulance which are not wholly or partly in front of or on either side of any part of the driver's seat; or

(*d*) windows in any bus, goods vehicle, locomotive, or motor tractor other than windows which—

(i) are wholly or partly in front of or on either side of any part of the driver's seat;

(ii) face the rear of the vehicle; or

(iii) form the whole or part of a door giving access to or from the exterior of the vehicle.

(12) For the purposes of this regulation any window at the rear of the vehicle is deemed to face the rear of the vehicle if the inner surface of such window is at an angle exceeding 30 degrees to the longitudinal axis of the vehicle.

(13) In this regulation, unless the context otherwise requires—

'British Standard Specification No 857' means the British Standard Specification for Safety Glass for Land Transport published on 30th June 1967 under the number BS 857 as amended by Amendment Slip No 1 published on 15th January 1973 under the number AMD 1088;

'British Standard Specification No 5282' means the British Standard Specification for Road Vehicle Safety Glass published in December 1975 under the number BS 5282 as amended by Amendment Slip No 1 published on 31st March 1976 under the number AMD 1927, and as amended by Amendment Slip No 2 published on 31st January 1977 under the number AMD 2185;

'British Standard Specification BS AU 178' means the British Standard Specification for Road Vehicle Safety Glass published on 28th November 1980 under the number BS AU 178;

. . .

'safety glazing' means material (other than glass) which is so constructed or treated that if fractured it does not fly into fragments likely to cause severe cuts;

'security vehicle' means a motor vehicle which is constructed (and not merely adapted) for the carriage of either—

(i) persons who are likely to require protection from any criminal offence involving violence; or

(ii) dangerous substances, bullion, money, jewellery, documents or other goods or burden which, by reason of their nature or value, are likely to require protection from any criminal offence;

'specified safety glass' means glass complying with the requirements of either—

(i) British Standard Specification No 857 (including the requirements as to marking); or

(ii) British Standard Specification No 5282 (including the requirements as to marking);

'specified safety glass (1980)' means glass complying with the requirements of either—

(i) the British Standard Specification for Safety Glass for Land Transport published on 30th June 1967 under the number BS 857 as amended by Amendment Slip No 1 published on 15th January 1973 under the number AMD 1088, Amendment Slip No 2 published on 30th September 1980 under the number AMD 3402, and Amendment Slip 4 published on 15th February 1981 under the number AMD 3548 (including the requirements as to marking); or

(ii) British Standard Specification BS AU 178 (including the requirements as to marking); or

(iii) ECE Regulation 43 (including the requirements as to marking).

'vision reference zone' means either—

(i) the primary vision area as defined in British Standard Specification No 857;

(ii) Zone 1, as defined in British Standard Specification No 5282;

(iii) Zone B (as regards passenger vehicles other than buses) and Zone 1 (as regards all other vehicles) as defined in British Standard Specification BS AU 178 and in ECE Regulation 43; and

'windscreen' includes a windshield;

[Regulation 32 is printed as amended by SI 1987 No 676.]

33. Mirrors

(1) Save as provided in paragraphs (5) and (6), a motor vehicle (not being a road roller) which is of a class specified in an item in column 2 of Table shall be fitted with such mirror or mirrors, if any, as are specified in that item in column 3; and any mirror which is fitted to such a vehicle shall, whether or not it is required to be fitted, comply with the requirements, if any, specified in that item in column 4.

(2) Save as provided in paragraph (5), each exterior mirror with which a vehicle is required to be fitted in accordance with item 2 or 6 of the Table shall, if the vehicle has a technically permissible maximum weight (as mentioned in Annex 1 to Community Directive 71/127) exceeding 3500 kg, be a Class II mirror (as described in

that Annex) and shall in any other case be a Class II or a Class III mirror (as described in that Annex).

(3) Save as provided in paragraph (5), in the case of a wheeled motor vehicle described in item 1, 2, 7 or 8 of the Table which is first used on or after 1st April 1969 the edges of any mirror fitted internally shall be surrounded by some material such as will render it unlikely that severe cuts would be caused if the mirror or that material were struck by any occupant of the vehicle.

(4) Save as provided in paragraph (5), in the case of a motor vehicle falling within paragraph (*a*) in column 4 of items 1 and 5, or within item 6, of the Table—

(*a*) each mirror shall be fixed to the vehicle in such a way that it remains steady under normal driving conditions;

(*b*) each exterior mirror on a vehicle fitted with windows and a windscreen shall be visible to the driver, when in his driving position, through a side window or through the portion of the windscreen which is swept by the windscreen wiper;

(*c*) where the bottom edge of an exterior mirror is less than 2 m above the road surface when the vehicle is laden, that mirror shall not project more than 20 cm beyond the overall width of the vehicle or, in a case where the vehicle is drawing a trailer which has an overall width greater than that of the drawing vehicle, more than 20 cm beyond the overall width of the trailer;

(*d*) each interior mirror shall be capable of being adjusted by the driver when in his driving position; and

(*e*) except in the case of a mirror which, if knocked out of its alignment, can be returned to its former position without needing to be adjusted, each exterior mirror on the driver's side of the vehicle shall be capable of being adjusted by the driver when in his driving position, but this requirement shall not prevent such a mirror from being locked into position from the outside of the vehicle.

TABLE

(regulation 33(1))

1	2	3	4
Item	Class of vehicle	Mirrors to be fitted	Requirements to be complied with by any mirrors fitted
1	A motor vehicle which is— (*a*) drawing a trailer, if a person is carried on the trailer so that he has an uninterrupted view to the rear and has an efficient means of communicating to the driver the effect of signals given by the drivers of other vehicles to the rear; (*b*) (i) a works truck; (ii) a track-laying agricultural motor vehicle; and (iii) a wheeled agricultural motor vehicle first used before 1st June 1978,	No requirement	(*a*) If the vehicle is a wheeled vehicle first used on or after 1st June 1978, item 2 of Annex I to Community Directive 71/127 or 79/795 or Annex II to Community Directive [86/562] and paragraph (4) of this regulation. (*b*) In other cases, none, except as specified in paragraph (3).

1	2	3	4
Item	Class of vehicle	Mirrors to be fitted	Requirements to be complied with by any mirrors fitted
	if, in each case, the driver can easily obtain a view to the rear; (*c*) a pedestrian-controlled vehicle; (*d*) a chassis being driven from the place where it has been manufactured to the place where it is to receive a vehicle body; or (*e*) an agricultural motor vehicle which has an unladen weight exceeding 7370 kg and which— (i) is a track-laying vehicle or (ii) is a wheeled vehicle first used before 1st June 1978		
2	A motor vehicle, not included in item 1, which is— (*a*) a wheeled locomotive or a wheeled motor tractor first used in either case on or after 1st June 1978; (*b*) an agricultural motor vehicle, not being a track-laying vehicle with an unladen weight not exceeding 7370 kg (which falls in item 8) or a wheeled agricultural motor vehicle first used after 1st June 1986 which is driven at more than 20 mph (which falls in item (6)); or (*c*) a works truck.	At least one mirror fitted externally on the offside	None except as specified in paragraphs (2) and (3).
3	A wheeled motor vehicle not included in item 1 first used on or after 1st April 1983 which is— (*a*) a bus; or (*b*) a goods vehicle with a maximum gross weight exceeding 3500 kg (not being an agricultural motor vehicle or one which is not driven at more than 20 mph) other than a vehicle described in item 4.	Mirrors complying with item 3 of Annex I to Community Directive 79/795 or with paragraph 2.1 of Annex III to Community Directive [86/562] or, except in the case of a goods vehicle first used on or after 1st April 1985, mirrors as required in the entry in this column in item 6	Item 2 of Annex I to Community Directive 71/127 or 79/795 or Annex II to Community Directive [86/562].

1	2	3	4
Item	Class of vehicle	Mirrors to be fitted	Requirements to be complied with by any mirrors fitted
4	A goods vehicle not being an agricultural motor vehicle with a maximum gross weight exceeding 12,000 kg which is first used on or after 1st October 1988	Mirrors complying with paragraph 2.1 of Annex III to Community Directive [86/562]	Annex II to Community Directive [86/562].
5	A two-wheeled motor cycle with or without a sidecar attached	No requirement	(*a*) If the vehicle is first used on or after 1st October 1978, item 2 of Annex I to Community Directive 71/127, 79/795 or 80/780 or Annex II to Community Directive [86/562] and paragraph (4) of this regulation. (*b*) In other cases, none.
6	A wheeled motor vehicle not in items 1 to 5, which is first used on or after 1st June 1978 (or, in the case of a Ford Transit motor car, 10th July 1978)	(i) At least one mirror fitted externally on the offside of the vehicle; and (ii) at least one mirror fitted internally, unless a mirror so fitted would give the driver no view to the rear of the vehicle; and (iii) at least one mirror fitted externally on the nearside of the vehicle unless a mirror which gives the driver an adequate view to the rear is fitted internally	Item 2 of Annex I to Community Directive 71/127 or 79/795 or Annex II to Community Directive [86/562] and paragraphs (2) and (4) of this regulation.
7	A wheeled motor vehicle, not in items 1 to 5, first used before 1st June 1978 (or in the case of a Ford Transit motor car, 10th July 1978) and a track-laying motor vehicle which is not an agricultural motor vehicle first	At least one mirror fitted externally on the offside of the vehicle and at least one mirror fitted either	None, except as specified in paragraph (3).

1	2	3	4
Item	Class of vehicle	Mirrors to be fitted	Requirements to be complied with by any mirrors fitted
	used on or after 1st January 1958, which in either case is— (*a*) a bus; (*b*) a dual-purpose vehicle; or (*c*) a goods vehicle.	internally or externally on the near-side of the vehicle	
8	A motor vehicle, whether wheeled or track-laying, not in items 1 to 7	At least one mirror fitted either internally or externally	None, except as specified in paragraph (3).

[(5) Instead of complying with paragraphs (1) to (4) a vehicle may comply—

(*a*) if it is a goods vehicle with a maximum gross weight exceeding 3500 kg first used on or after 1st April 1985 and before 1st August 1989, with Community Directive 79/795, 85/205 or 86/562;

(*b*) if it is a goods vehicle first used on or after 1st August 1989—

(i) in the case of a vehicle with a maximum gross weight exceeding 3500 kg but not exceeding 12,000 kg with Community Directive 79/795, 85/205 or 86/562; and

(ii) in the case of a vehicle with a maximum gross weight exceeding 12,000 kg with Community Directive 85/205 or 86/562;

(*c*) if it is an agricultural motor vehicle with Community Directive 71/127, 74/346, 79/795, 85/205 or 86/562;

(*d*) if it is a two-wheeled motor cycle with or without a side-car with Community Directive 71/127, 79/795, 80/780, 85/205 or 86/562; and

(*e*) if it is any other vehicle with Community Directive 71/127, 79/795, 85/205 or 86/562.]

(6) Instead of complying with the provisions of column 4 in items 3, 5 or 6 of the Table a mirror may comply with the requirements as to construction and testing set out either in Annex I to Community Directive 71/127, excluding paragraphs 2.3.4 and 2.6, or in Annex I to Community Directive 79/795, excluding paragraphs 2.3.3 and 2.6.

(7) In this regulation 'mirror' means a mirror to assist the driver of a vehicle to become aware of traffic—

(i) if it is an internal mirror, to the rear of the vehicle; and

(ii) if it is an external mirror fitted on one side of the vehicle, rearwards on that side of the vehicle.

In the case of an agricultural motor vehicle described in items 2 or 6 in the Table when drawing a trailer, the references to a vehicle in sub-paragraphs (i) and (ii) include references to the trailer so drawn.

[Regulation 33 is printed as amended by SI 1988 No 1178.]

34. Windscreen wipers and washers

(1) Subject to paragraphs (4) and (5), every vehicle fitted with a windscreen shall, unless the driver can obtain an adequate view to the front of the vehicle without looking through the windscreen, be fitted with one or more efficient automatic windscreen wipers capable of clearing the windscreen so that the driver has an adequate view of the road in front of both sides of the vehicle and to the front of the vehicle.

(2) Save as provided in paragraphs (3), (4) and (5), every wheeled vehicle required by paragraph (1) to be fitted with a wiper or wipers shall also be fitted with a windscreen washer capable of cleaning, in conjunction with the windscreen wiper, the area of the windscreen swept by the wiper of mud or similar deposit.

(3) The requirement specified in paragraph (2) does not apply in respect of—

(*a*) an agricultural motor vehicle (other than a vehicle first used on or after 1st June 1986 which is driven at more than 20 mph);

(*b*) a track-laying vehicle;

(*c*) a vehicle having a maximum speed not exceeding 20 mph; or

(*d*) a vehicle being used to provide a local service, as defined in the Transport Act 1985.

(4) Instead of complying with paragraphs (1) and (2), a vehicle may comply with Community Directive 78/318.

(5) Instead of complying with paragraph (1) an agricultural motor vehicle may comply with Community Directive 79/1073.

(6) Every wiper and washer fitted in accordance with this regulation shall at all times while a vehicle is being used on a road be maintained in efficient working order and be properly adjusted.

F *Instruments and Equipment*

35. Speedometers

(1) Save as provided in paragraphs (2) and (3), every motor vehicle shall be fitted with a speedometer which, if the vehicle is first used on or after 1st April 1984, shall be capable of indicating speed in both miles per hour and kilometers per hour, either simultaneously or, by the operation of a switch, separately.

(2) Paragraph (1) does not apply to—

(*a*) a vehicle having a maximum speed not exceeding 25 mph;

(*b*) a vehicle which is at all times unlawful to drive at more than 25 mph;

(*c*) an agricultural motor vehicle which is not driven at more than 20 mph;

(*d*) a motor cycle first used before 1st April 1984 the engine of which has a cylinder capacity not exceeding 100 cc;

(*e*) an invalid carriage first used before 1st April 1984;

(*f*) a works truck first used before 1st April 1984;

(*g*) a vehicle first used before 1st October 1937; or

(*h*) a vehicle equipped with recording equipment marked with a marking designated as an approval mark by regulation 5 of the Approval Marks Regulations and shown at item 3 in Schedule 4 to those Regulations (whether or not the vehicle is required to be equipped with that equipment) and which, as regards the visual indications given by that equipment of the speed of the vehicle, complies with the requirements relating to the said indications and installations specified in the Community Recording Equipment Regulation.

(3) Instead of complying with paragraph (1) a vehicle may comply with Community Directive 75/443 or with ECE Regulation 39.

36. Maintenance of speedometers

(1) Every instrument for indicating speed fitted to a motor vehicle—

(*a*) in compliance with the requirements of regulation 35(1) or (3); or

(*b*) to which regulation 35(2)(*h*) relates and which is not, under the Community Recording Equipment Regulation, required to be equipped with the recording equipment mentioned in that paragraph,

shall be kept free from any obstruction which might prevent it being easily read and shall at all material times be maintained in good working order.

(2) In this regulation 'all material times' means all times when the motor vehicle is in use on a road except when—

(*a*) the vehicle is being used on a journey during which, as a result of a defect, the instrument ceased to be in good working order; or

(*b*) as a result of a defect, the instrument has ceased to be in good working order and steps have been taken to have the vehicle equipped with all reasonable expedition, by means of repairs or replacement, with an instrument which is in good working order.

36A. Speed limiters

(1) This regulation applies to every coach first used on or after 1st April 1974 and which has, or if a speed limiter were not fitted to it would have, a maximum speed exceeding 70 mph.

(2) A vehicle to which this regulation applies and which is first used on a date included in an item in column 2 of the Table shall not be used on a road on or after the date specified in column 3 in that item unless it has been fitted with a speed limiter.

TABLE

(regulation 36A (2))

1	2	3
Item	Date of first use	Date from which requirement applies
1	1st April 1974 to 31st March 1984	1st April 1991
2	1st April 1984 to 31st March 1989	1st April 1990
3	On or after 1st April 1989	Date of first use

(3) Every speed limiter fitted in accordance with paragraph (2) shall—

(*a*) unless it is fitted before 1st October 1988, comply with Part I of the British Standard;

(*b*) be calibrated to a set speed not exceeding 70 mph;

(*c*) be sealed in such a manner as to protect the limiter against any improper interference or adjustment and against any interruption of its power supply; and

(*d*) be maintained in good and efficient working order.

(4) A vehicle to which a speed limiter has been fitted in accordance with paragraphs (2) and (3) shall not be driven on a road unless the speed limiter is functioning except for the purpose of—

(*a*) completing a journey in the course of which the speed limiter has accidentally ceased to function; or

(*b*) taking the vehicle to a place where the speed limiter is to be repaired or replaced.

(5) In this regulation—

'Part I of the British Standard' means the British Standard for Maximum Road Speed Limiters for Motor Vehicles which was published by the British Standards Institution under the number BSAU 217: Part I: 1987 and which came into effect on 29th May 1987 [as amended by Amendment Slip No 1 under the number AMD 5969 which was published and came into effect on 30th June 1988];

'set speed' has the same meaning as in clause 2.2 of Part I of the British Standard;

'speed limiter' means a device designed to limit the maximum speed of a motor vehicle by controlling the engine power of the vehicle.]

[Regulation 36A was inserted by SI 1988 No 271 and is printed as subsequently amended by SI 1988 No 1524.]

37. Audible warning instruments

(1) (*a*) Subject to sub-paragraph (*b*), every motor vehicle which has a maximum speed of more than 20 mph shall be fitted with a horn, not being a reversing alarm or a two-tone horn.

(*b*) Sub-paragraph (*a*) shall not apply to an agricultural motor vehicle, unless it is being driven at more than 20 mph.

(2) Subject to paragraph (6), the sound emitted by any horn, other than a reversing alarm or a two-tone horn, fitted to a wheeled vehicle first used on or after 1st August 1973 shall be continuous and uniform and not strident.

(3) A reversing alarm fitted to a wheeled vehicle shall not be strident.

(4) Subject to paragraphs (5), (6) and (7) no motor vehicle shall be fitted with a bell, gong, siren or two-tone horn.

(5) The provisions of paragraph (4) shall not apply to motor vehicles—

(*a*) used for fire brigade, ambulance or police purposes;

(*b*) owned by a body formed primarily for the purposes of fire salvage and used for those or similar purposes;

(*c*) owned by the Forestry Commission or by local authorities and used from time to time for the purposes of fighting fires;

(*d*) owned by the Secretary of State for Defence and used for the purposes of the disposal of bombs or explosives;

(*e*) used for the purposes of the Blood Transfusion Service provided under the

National Health Service Act 1977 or under the National Health Service (Scotland) Act 1947;

(*f*) used by her Majesty's Coastguard or the Coastguard Auxiliary Service to aid persons in danger or vessels in distress on or near the coast;

(*g*) owned by the National Coal Board and used for the purposes of rescue operations at mines;

(*h*) owned by the Secretary of State for Defence and used by the Royal Air Force Mountain Rescue Service for the purposes of rescue operations in connection with crashed aircraft or any other emergencies; or

(*i*) owned by the Royal National Lifeboat Institution and used for the purposes of launching lifeboats.

(6) The provisions of paragraphs (2) and (4) shall not apply so as to make it unlawful for a motor vehicle to be fitted with an instrument or apparatus (not being a two-tone horn) designed to emit a sound for the purpose of informing members of the public that goods are on the vehicle for sale.

(7) Subject to paragraph (8), the provisions of paragraph (4) shall not apply so as to make it unlawful for a vehicle to be fitted with a bell, gong or siren—

(*a*) if the purpose thereof is to prevent theft or attempted theft of the vehicle or its contents; or

(*b*) in the case of a bus, if the purpose thereof is to summon help for the driver, the conductor or an inspector.

(8) Every bell, gong or siren fitted to a vehicle by virtue of paragraph (7)(*a*), and every device fitted to a motor vehicle first used on or after 1st October 1982 so as to cause a horn to sound for the purpose mentioned in paragraph (7)(*a*), shall be fitted with a device designed to stop the bell, gong, siren or horn emitting noise for a continuous period of more than five minutes; and every such device shall at all times be maintained in good working order.

(9) Instead of complying with paragraphs (1), (2) and (4) to (8), a vehicle may comply with Community Directive 70/388 or ECE Regulation 28 or, if the vehicle is an agricultural motor vehicle, with Community Directive 74/151.

(10) In this regulation and in regulation 99—

(*a*) 'horn' means an instrument, not being a bell, gong or siren, capable of giving audible and sufficient warning of the approach or position of the vehicle to which it is fitted;

(*b*) references to a bell, gong or siren include references to any instrument or apparatus capable of emitting a sound similar to that emitted by a bell, gong or siren;

(*c*) 'reversing alarm' means a device fitted to a motor vehicle and designed to warn persons that the vehicle is reversing or is about to reverse; and

(*d*) 'two-tone horn' means an instrument which, when operated, automatically produces a sound which alternates at regular intervals between two fixed notes.

38. Motor cycle sidestands

(1) No motor cycle first used on or after 1st April 1986 shall be fitted with any sidestand which is capable of—

(*a*) disturbing the stability of direction of the motor cycle when it is in motion under its own power; or (*b*) closing automatically if the angle of the inclination of the motor cycle is inadvertently altered when it is stationary.

(2) In this regulation 'sidestand' means a device fitted to a motor cycle which, when fully extended or pivoted to its open position, supports the vehicle from one side only and so that both the wheels of the motor cycle are on the ground.

G *Fuel*

39. Petrol tanks

(1) Subject to paragraph (2), every tank containing petroleum spirit (as defined in section 23 of the Petroleum (Consolidation) Act 1928) which is fitted to a wheeled vehicle first used on or after 1st July 1973, and is used either for the propulsion of the vehicle or for driving an ancillary engine or equipment forming part of the vehicle shall be—

(*a*) made only of metal;

(*b*) fixed in such a position and so maintained as to be reasonably secure from damage; and

(*c*) constructed and maintained so that the leakage of any liquid or vapour from the tank is adequately prevented, so, however, that the tank may be fitted with a device which, by the intake of air or the emission of vapour, relieves changes of pressure in the tank.

(2) Instead of complying with the requirements of paragraph (1) as to construction, a vehicle may comply with the requirements of Community Directive 70/221 (in so far as they relate to fuel tanks) or ECE Regulation 34 or 34.01 or, if the vehicle is an agricultural motor vehicle, of Community Directive 74/151.

[**39A.** (1) Every vehicle to which this regulation applies shall be designed and constructed for running on unleaded petrol.

(2) No person shall use or cause or permit to be used a vehicle to which this regulation applies on a road if it—

(*a*) has been deliberately altered or adjusted for running on leaded petrol, and

(*b*) as a direct result of such alteration or adjustment it is incapable of running on unleaded petrol.

(3) Subject to paragraph (4) this regulation applies to every motor vehicle which is—

(*a*) propelled by a spark ignition engine which is capable of running on petrol, and

(*b*) is first used on or after the 1st April 1991.

(4) Part I of Schedule 3A shall have effect for the purpose of excluding certain vehicles first used before specified dates from the application of this legislation.

(5) In this regulation 'petrol', 'leaded petrol' and 'unleaded petrol' have the same meaning as in Community Directive 85/210.

(6) A vehicle shall be regarded for the purposes of this regulation as incapable of running on unleaded petrol at any particular time if and only if in its state of adjustment at that time prolonged continuous running on such petrol would damage the engine.]

[Regulation 39A was inserted by SI 1988 No 1524.

'Petrol' is defined by Council Directive 85/210, art 1, as 'any volatile mineral oil intended for the operation of internal combustion spark-ignited engines used for the propulsion of vehicles'. 'Unleaded petrol' is defined by art 1 as 'any petrol the contamination of which by lead compounds calculated in terms of lead, does not exceed 0.013 g Pb/1'.]

[39B. (1) Subject to paragraph (2), every fuel tank fitted to a vehicle to which regulation 39A applies shall be so constructed and fitted that it cannot readily be filled from a petrol pump delivery nozzle which has an external diameter of 23.6mm or greater without the aid of a device (such as a funnel) not fitted to the vehicle.

(2) Paragraph (1) does not apply to a vehicle in respect of which both of the following conditions are satisfied, that is to say—

(*a*) that at the time of its first use the vehicle is so designed and constructed that prolonged continuous running on leaded petrol would not cause any device designed to control the emission of carbon monoxide, hydrocarbons or nitrogen oxides to malfunction, and

(*b*) that it is conspicuously and legibly marked in a position immediately visible to a person filling the fuel tank with—

(i) the word 'UNLEADED', or

(ii) the symbol shown in Part II of Schedule 3A.

(3) In this regulation 'fuel tank', in relation to a vehicle, means a fuel tank used in connection with the propulsion of the vehicle.]

[Regulation 39B was inserted by SI 1988 No 1524.]

40. Gas propulsion systems and gas-fired appliances

(1) A vehicle which is—

(*a*) a motor vehicle which first used gas as a fuel for its propulsion before 19th November 1982; or

(*b*) a trailer manufactured before 19th November 1982 to which there is fitted a gas container,

shall be so constructed that it complies either with the provisions of Schedule 4 or with the provisions of Schedule 5.

(2) A vehicle which is—

(*a*) a motor vehicle which first used gas as a fuel for its propulsion on or after 19th November 1982; or

(*b*) a motor vehicle first used on or after 1st May 1984 or a trailer manufactured on or after 19th November 1982 which is in either case equipped with a gas container or a gas-fired appliance,

shall comply with the provisions of Schedule 5.

(3) The requirements of this regulation are in addition to, and not in derogation from, the requirements of any regulations made under powers conferred by the Petroleum (Consolidation) Act 1928, the Health and Safety at Work etc Act 1974, the Control of Pollution Act 1974 or any other Act or of any codes of practice issued under the Health and Safety at Work etc Act 1974.

(4) In this regulation 'gas container' has the meaning given in Schedule 4 where compliance with the provisions of that Schedule is concerned and otherwise has the meaning given in Schedule 5.

H *Minibuses*

41. Minibuses

The requirements specified in Schedule 6 shall apply to every minibus first used on or after 1st April 1988 except a vehicle—

(*a*) manufactured by Land Rover UK Limited and known as the Land Rover; or

(*b*) constructed or adapted for the secure transport of prisoners.

42. Fire-extinguishing apparatus

(1) No person shall use, or cause or permit to be used, on a road a minibus first used on or after 1st April 1988 unless it carries suitable and efficient apparatus for extinguishing fire which is of a type specified in Part I of Schedule 7.

(2) The apparatus referred to in paragraph (1) above shall be—

(*a*) readily available for use;

(*b*) clearly marked with the appropriate British Standards Institution specification number; and

(*c*) maintained in good and efficient working order.

(3) This regulation does not apply to a vehicle manufactured by Land Rover UK Limited and known as the Land Rover.

43. First-aid equipment

(1) No person shall use, or cause or permit to be used, on a road a minibus first used on or after 1st April 1988 unless it carries a receptacle which contains the items specified in Part II of Schedule 7.

(2) The receptacle referred to in paragraph (1) above shall be—

(*a*) maintained in a good condition;

(*b*) suitable for the purpose of keeping the items referred to in the said paragraph in good condition;

(*c*) readily available for use; and

(*d*) prominently marked as a first aid receptacle.

(3) The items referred to in paragraph (1) above shall be maintained in good condition and shall be of a good and reliable quality and of a suitable design.

(4) This regulation does not apply to a vehicle manufactured by Land Rover UK Limited and known as the Land Rover.

44. Carriage of dangerous substances

(1) Save as provided in paragraph (2), no person shall use or cause or permit to be used on a road a minibus by which any highly inflammable or otherwise dangerous substance is carried unless that substance is carried in containers so designed and constructed, and unless the substance is so packed, that, notwithstanding an accident to the vehicle, it is unlikely that damage to the vehicle or injury to passengers in the vehicle will be caused by the substance.

(2) Paragraph (1) shall not apply in relation to the electrolyte of a battery installed in an electric wheelchair provided that the wheelchair is securely fixed to the vehicle.

(3) This regulation does not apply to a vehicle manufactured by Land Rover UK Limited and known as the Land Rover.

I *Power-to-Weight Ratio*

45. Power-to-weight ratio

(1) Save as provided in paragraph (2), every wheeled vehicle which is propelled by a compression ignition engine and which is required to be equipped with a plate by regulation 66(1) shall be so constructed that the power of its engine, calculated in accordance with paragraph 1 of Part III of Schedule 8, is at least 4.4 kW for every 1000 kg of the relevant weight.

(2) Paragraph (1) does not apply to—

(*a*) a heavy motor car or motor car first used before 1st April 1973;

(*b*) a vehicle manufactured before 1st April 1973 and powered by a Perkins 6.354 engine; or

(*c*) a bus.

(3) Every vehicle to which this regulation applies shall—

(*a*) if it is equipped with machinery or apparatus forming part of the vehicle or mounted on it and used for purposes not connected with the driving of the vehicle;

(*b*) if that machinery or apparatus is designed for use, or is likely to be used, when the vehicle is in motion on a road at a speed exceeding 5 mph; and

(*c*) if the power absorbed by that use is provided by the engine propelling the vehicle,

be so constructed that, when that machinery or apparatus is being used, the power of the engine remaining available to drive the vehicle is at least 4.4 kW for every 1000 kg of the relevant weight.

(4) In this regulation 'relevant weight' means—

(*a*) if the vehicle is equipped with a plate in accordance with regulation 66(2)(*a*), the maximum train weight shown at item 8 on that plate or, if no such weight is shown, the maximum gross weight in Great Britain shown at item 10 on that plate; or

(*b*) if the vehicle is equipped with a plate in accordance with regulation 66(2)(*b*) and—

(i) is constructed to draw a trailer, the higher of the weights referred to in column 3 in item 2.1.5 in the Table in regulation 66; or

(ii) is not constructed to draw a trailer, the higher of the weights for motor vehicles referred to in columns 3 and 4 in item 2.1.4 in the Table in regulation 66.

J *Protective Systems*

[46. Seat belt anchorage points

(1) Save as provided by paragraph (2), this regulation applies to—

(*a*) every wheeled motor car first used on or after 1st January 1965;

(*b*) every three-wheeled motor cycle the unladen weight of which exceeds 255 kg and which was first used on or after 1st September 1970; and

(*c*) every heavy motor car first used on or after 1st October 1988.

(2) This regulation does not apply to—

(*a*) a goods vehicle (other than a dual-purpose vehicle) which was first used—

(i) before 1st April 1967; or

(ii) on or after 1st April 1980 and before 1st October 1988 and has a maximum gross weight exceeding 3500 kg; or

(iii) before 1st April 1980 or, if the vehicle is of a model manufactured before 1st October 1979, was first used before 1st April 1982 and in either case, has an unladen weight exceeding 1525 kg;

(*b*) a bus, being—

(i) a minibus—

(A) if first used before 1st October 1988, constructed or adapted to carry more than twelve passengers; or

(B) if first used on or after 1st October 1988, having a maximum gross weight exceeding 3500 kg; or

(ii) a large bus (other than a coach first used on or after 1st October 1988);

(*c*) an agricultural motor vehicle;

(*d*) a motor tractor;

(*e*) a works truck;

(*f*) an electrically-propelled goods vehicle first used before 1st October 1988;

(*g*) a pedestrian-controlled vehicle;

(*h*) a vehicle which has been used on roads outside Great Britain and has been imported into Great Britain, whilst it is being driven from the place where it has arrived in Great Britain to a place of residence of the owner or driver of the vehicle, or from any such place to a place where, by previous arrangement, it will be provided with such anchorage points as are required by this regulation and such seat belts as are required by regulation 47;

(*i*) a vehicle having a maximum speed not exceeding 16 mph;

(*j*) a motor cycle equipped with a driver's seat of a type requiring the driver to sit astride it, and which is constructed or assembled by a person not ordinarily engaged in the trade or business of manufacturing vehicles of that description; or

(*k*) a locomotive.

(3) A vehicle which was first used before 1st April 1982 shall be equipped with anchorage points which are designed to hold securely in position on the vehicle seat belts for the driver's seat and specified passenger's seat (if any).

(4) Save as provided in paragraph (4A) or (4B) a vehicle which is first used on or after 1st April 1982 shall be equipped with anchorage points which—

(*a*) are designed to hold securely in position on the vehicle seat belts for—

(i) in the case of a minibus, motor ambulance or a motor caravan—

(A) if first used before 1st October 1988, the driver's seat and the specified passenger's seat (if any); or

(B) if first used on or after 1st October 1988, the driver's seat and any forward-facing front seat; and

(ii) in the case of any other passenger or dual-purpose vehicle, every forward-facing seat constructed or adapted to accommodate one adult;

(iii) in every other case, every forward-facing front seat and every non-protected seat, and

(*b*) comply with the technical and installation requirements of Community Directive 76/115 or 81/575 or 82/318 or ECE Regulation 14 whether or not those instruments apply to the vehicle, so however, that the requirements in those instruments which relate to testing shall not apply.

(4A) The requirements specified in paragraph (4) shall not apply to—

(*a*) a goods vehicle first used on or after 1st October 1988 and having a maximum gross weight exceeding 3500 kg, but any such vehicle shall be equipped with two belt anchorages designed to hold securely in position on the vehicle lap belts for the driver's seat and each forward-facing front seat; or

(*b*) a coach equipped with anchorage points which are designed to hold securely in position on the vehicle seat belts for all exposed forward-facing seats and which—

(i) comply with the requirements in paragraph (4)(*b*); or

(ii) in any case where the anchorage points form part of a seat, do not when a forward horizontal force is applied to them become detached from the seat of which they form part before that seat becomes detached from the vehicle.

(4B) Instead of complying with the requirements in paragraph (4), a vehicle may comply with Community Directive 76/115 or 81/575 or 82/318 or ECE Regulation 14.

(5) Save as provided in paragraph (5A), a vehicle of a type mentioned in paragraphs (4), (4A) and (4B) which is fitted with anchorage points other than those required by those paragraphs shall comply with the requirements in paragraph (4)(*b*), or in the case of a coach the requirements in paragraph (4A)(*b*)(ii), in respect of any additional anchorage points as well as in respect of the anchorage points required by paragraph (4), (4A) or (4B) to be provided.

(5A) The requirements in paragraph (5) shall not apply in respect of any additional anchorage points first fitted before 1st April 1986 in the case of a vehicle of a type mentioned in paragraph (4)(*a*)(i)(A), or before 1st October 1988 in the case of a vehicle of any other type.

(6) In this regulation—

(*a*) the expressions 'exposed forward-facing seat', 'forward-facing seat', 'forward-facing front seat', 'lap belt', 'seat-belt' and 'specified passenger's seat' have the same meaning as in regulation 47(8); and

(*b*) the expression 'non-protected seat' means a seat other than a front seat which does not satisfy the requirements of section 4.3.3 of Annex 1 to Community Directive 81/575.]

[Regulation 46 was substantially amended by SI 1987 No 1133. The text of reg 46, as so amended, was set out in the Schedule to SI 1987 No 1133 and the above text is the text so printed.]

[47. Seat belts

(1) This regulation applies to every vehicle to which regulation 46 applies.

(2) Save as provided in paragraph (4) a vehicle to which—

(*a*) this regulation applies which was first used before 1st April 1981 shall be provided with—

(i) a body-restraining belt, designed for use by an adult, for the driver's seat; and

(ii) a body-restraining belt for the specified passenger's seat (if any);

(*b*) this regulation applies which is first used on or after 1st April 1981 shall be provided with three-point belts for the driver's seat and for the specified passenger's seat (if any);

(*c*) regulation 46(4)(*a*)(ii) or (iii) applies which is first used on or after 1st April 1987 shall be fitted with seat belts additional to those required by sub-paragraph (*b*) as follows—

(i) for any forward-facing front seat alongside the driver's seat, not being a specified passenger's seat, a seat belt which is a three-point belt, or a lap belt installed in accordance with paragraph 3.1.2.1 of Annex 1 to Community Directive 77/541 or a disabled person's belt;

(ii) in the case of a passenger or dual-purpose vehicle having not more than two forward-facing seats behind the driver's seat with either—

(A) an inertia reel belt for at least one of those seats, or

(B) a three-point belt, a lap belt, a disabled person's belt or a child restraint for each of those seats;

(iii) in the case of a passenger or dual-purpose vehicle having more than two forward-facing seats behind the driver's seat, with either—

(A) an inertia reel belt for one of those seats being an outboard seat and a three-point belt, a lap belt, a disabled person's belt or a child restraint for at least one other of those seats;

(B) a three-point belt for one of those seats and either a child restraint or a disabled person's belt for at least one other of those seats; or

(C) a three-point belt, a lap belt, a disabled person's belt or a child restraint for each of those seats.

(*d*) regulation 46(4)(*a*)(i)(B) applies shall be fitted with seat belts as follows—

(i) for the driver's seat and the specified passenger's seat (if any) a three-point belt; and

(ii) for any forward-facing front seat which is not a specified passenger's seat, a three-point belt or a lap belt installed in accordance with the provisions of sub-paragraph (*c*)(i);

(*e*) regulation 46(4A)(*b*) applies shall be equipped with seat belts which shall be three-point belts, lap belts or disabled person's belts.

Where a lap belt is fitted to a forward-facing front seat of a minibus, a motor ambulance or a motor caravan, or to an exposed forward-facing seat of a coach (other than the driver's seat) either—

(i) there shall be provided padding to a depth of not less than 50 millimetres on the surface of any bar or partition which is, or any part of which is, forward of and within 1 metre of the intersection of the back rest and the cushion of the seat in question and such padding shall extend for not less than 150 mm on either side of that point on the bar or partition which would be bisected by a prolongation of the longitudinal centreline of the seat; or

(ii) the technical and installation requirements of Annex 4 to ECE Regulations 21 shall be met.

(3) Every seat belt for an adult, other than a disabled person's belt, provided for a vehicle in accordance with paragraph (2)(*b*), (*c*), (*d*) or (*e*) shall, except as provided in paragraph (6), comply with the installation requirements specified in paragraph 3.2.2 to 3.3.4 of Annex I to Community Directive 77/541 whether or not that Directive applies to the vehicle.

(4) The requirements specified in paragraph (2) do not apply—

(*a*) to a vehicle while it is being used under a trade licence within the meaning of section 16 of the 1971 Act;

(*b*) to a vehicle, not being a vehicle to which the Type Approval (Great Britain) Regulations apply, while it is being driven from premises of the manufacturer by whom it was made, or of a distributor of vehicles or dealer in vehicles—

(i) to premises of a distributor of or dealer in vehicles or of the purchaser of the vehicle, or

(ii) to premises of a person obtaining possession of the vehicle under a hiring agreement or hire-purchase agreement;

(*c*) in relation to any seat for which there is provided—

(i) a seat belt which bears a mark including the specification number of the British Standard for Passive Belt Systems, namely BSAU 183:1983 and including the registered certification trade mark of the British Standards Institution; or

(ii) a seat belt designed for use by an adult which is a harness belt comprising a lap belt and shoulder straps which bears a British Standard mark or a mark including the specification number for the British Standard for Seat Belt Assemblies for Motor Vehicles, namely BS 3254:1960 or BS AU 160c and including the registered certification trade mark of the British Standards Institution, or the marking designated in item 16 in Schedule 2 to the Approval Marks Regulations;

(*d*) in relation to the driver's seat or the specifed passenger's seat (if any) of a vehicle which has been specially designed and constructed, or specially adapted, for the use of a person suffering from some physical defect or disability, in a case where a disabled person's belt for an adult person is provided for use for that seat;

(*e*) to a vehicle to which regulation 46(4A)(*a*) applies.

(5) Every seat belt provided in pursuance of paragraph (2) shall be properly secured to the anchorage points provided for it in accordance with regulation 46; or, in the case of a child restraint, to anchorages specially provided for it or, in the case of a disabled person's belt, secured to the vehicle or to the seat which is being occupied by the person wearing the belt.

(6) Paragraph (3), in so far as it relates to the second paragraph of paragraph 3.3.2 of the Annex there mentioned (which concerns the locking or releasing of a seat belt by a single movement) does not apply in respect of a seat belt fitted for—

(*a*) a seat which is treated as a specified passenger's seat by virtue of the provisions of sub-paragraph (ii) in the definition of 'specified passenger's seat' in paragraph (8); or

(*b*) any forward-facing seat for a passenger alongside the driver's seat of a goods vehicle which has an unladen weight of more than 915 kg and has more than one such seat, any such seats for passengers being joined together in a single structure; or

(*c*) any seat (other than the driver's seat) fitted to a coach.

(7) Every seat belt, other than a disabled person's belt or a seat belt of a kind mentioned in paragraph 4(*c*)(i) or (ii) above, provided for any person in a vehicle to which this regulation applies shall be legibly and permanently marked—

(*a*) if the vehicle was first used before 1st April 1981 or if the belt is a child restraint, with a British Standard mark or a designated approval mark;
or

(*b*) in any other case, with a designated approval mark.

Provided this paragraph shall not operate so as to invalidate the exception permitted in paragraph (6).

(8) In this regulation—

'body-restraining belt' means a seat belt designed to provide restraint for both the upper and lower parts of the trunk of the wearer in the event of an accident to the vehicle;

'British Standard mark' means a mark consiting of—

(i) the specification number of one of the following British Standards for Seat Belt Assemblies for Motor Vehicles, namely—

(*a*) if it is a seat belt for an adult, BS 3254:1960 and BS AU 160a or 160b; or

(*b*) if it is a child restraint, BS 3254:1960, or BS 3254:1960 as amended by Amendment No 16 published on 31st July 1986 under the number AMD 5210, BS AU 157 or 157a, BS AU 185, BS AU 186 or 186a, BS AU 202; and, in either case,

(ii) the registered certification trade mark of the British Standards Institution;

'child restraint' means a seat belt for the use of a young person which is designed either to be fitted directly to a suitable anchorage or to be used in conjunction with a seat belt for an adult and held in place by the restraining action of that belt;

Provided that for the purposes of paragraph (2)(*c*)(ii)(B) and (2)(*c*)(iii) it means only such seat belts fitted directly to a suitable anchorage and excludes belts marked with the specification numbers BS AU 185 and BS AU 186 or 186a.

'crew seat' has the same meaning as in regulation 3(1) of the Public Service Vehicles (Conditions of Fitness, Equipment, Use and Certification) Regulations 1981;

'designated approval mark' means

(*a*) if it is a seat belt other than a child restraint, the marking designated as an approval mark by regulation 4 of the Approval Marks Regulations and shown at item 16 of Schedule 2 to those Regulations or the marking designated as an approval mark by regulation 5 of those Regulations and shown at item 23 and 23A in Schedule 4 to those Regulations and

(*b*) if it is a child restraint, either of the markings designated as approval marks by regulation 4 of those Regulations and shown at item 44 and 44A in Schedule 2 to those Regulations.

'disabled person's belt' means a seat belt which has been specially designed or adapted for use by an adult or young person suffering from some physical defect or disability and which is intended for use solely by such a person;

'exposed forward-facing seat' means—

(i) a forward-facing front seat (including any crew seat) and the driver's seat; and

(ii) any other forward-facing seat which is not immediately behind and on the same horizonal plane as a forward-facing high-backed seat;

'forward-facing seat' means a seat which is attached to a vehicle so that it faces towards the front of the vehicle in such a manner that a line passing through the centre of both the front and the back of the seat is at an angle of 30° or less to the longitudinal axis of the vehicle;

'forward-facing front seat' means—

(i) any forward-facing seat alongside the driver's seat; or

(ii) if the vehicle normally has no seat which is a forward-facing front seat under sub-paragraph (i) of this definition, each forward-facing seat for a passenger which is foremost in the vehicle;

'forward-facing high-backed seat' means a forward-facing seat which is also a high-backed seat;

'high-backed seat' means a seat the highest part of which is at least 1 metre above the deck of the vehicle;

'inertia reel belt' means a three-point belt of either of the types required for a front outboard seating position by paragraph 3.1.1 of Annex 1 to Community Directive 77/541;

'lap belt' means a seat belt which passes across the front of the wearer's pelvic region and which is designed for use by an adult;

'seat' includes any part designed for the accommodation of one adult of a continuous seat designed for the accommodation of more than one adult;

'seat belt' means a belt intended to be worn by a person in a vehicle and designed to prevent or lessen injury to its wearer in the event of an accident to the vehicle and includes, in the case of a child restraint, any special chair to which the belt is attached;

'specified passenger's seat' means—

(i) in the case of a vehicle which has one forward-facing front seat alongside the driver's seat, that seat, and in the case of a vehicle which has more than one such seat, the one furthest from the driver's seat; or

(ii) if the vehicle normally has no seat which is the specified passenger's seat under sub-paragraph (i) of this definition the forward-facing front seat for a passenger which is the foremost in the vehicle and furthest from the driver's seat, unless there is a fixed partition separating that seat from the space in front of it alongside the driver's seat; and

'three-point belt' means a seat belt which—

(i) restrains the upper and lower parts of the torso;

(ii) includes a lap belt;

(iii) is anchored at not less than three points; and

(iv) is designed for use by an adult.]

[Regulation 47 was substantially amended by SI 1987 No 1133. The text of reg 47, as so amended, was set out in the Schedule to SI 1987 No 1133 and the above text is the text so printed.]

48. Maintenance of seat belts and anchorage points

(1) This regulation applies to every seat belt with which a motor vehicle is required to be provided in accordance with regulation 47 and to the anchorages, fastenings, adjusting device and retracting mechanism (if any) of every such seat belt [and also to every anchorage with which a goods vehicle is required to be provided in accordance with regulation 46(4A)(*a*)] .

(2) For the purposes of this regulation the anchorages and anchorage points of a seat belt shall, in the case of a seat which incorporates integral seat belt anchorages, include the system by which the seat assembly itself is secured to the vehicle structure.

(3) The anchorage points provided for seat belts shall be used only as anchorages for the seat belts for which they are intended to be used or capable of being used.

(4) Save as provided in paragraph (5) below—

(*a*) all load-bearing members of the vehicle structure or panelling within 30 cm of each anchorage point shall be maintained in a sound condition and free from serious corrosion, distortion or fracture;

(*b*) the adjusting device and (if fitted) the retracting mechanism of the seat belt shall be so maintained that the belt may be readily adjusted to the body of the wearer, either automatically or manually, according to the design of the device and (if fitted) the retracting mechanism;

(*c*) the seat belt and its anchorages, fastenings and adjusting device shall be maintained free from any obvious defect which would be likely to affect adversely the performance by the seat belt of the function of restraining the body of the wearer in the event of an accident to the vehicle;

(*d*) the buckle or other fastening of the seat belt shall—

(i) be so maintained that the belt can be readily fastened or unfastened;

(ii) be kept free from any temporary or permanent obstruction; and

(iii) except in the case of a disabled person's seat belt, be readily accessible to a person sitting in the seat for which the seat belt is provided;

(*e*) the webbing or other material which forms the seat belt shall be maintained free from cuts or other visible faults (as, for example, extensive fraying) which would be likely to affect adversely the performance of the belt when under stress;

(*f*) the ends of every seat belt, other than a disabled person's seat belt, shall be securely fastened to the anchorage points provided for them; and

(*g*) the ends of every disabled person's seat belt shall, when the seat belt is being used for the purpose for which it was designed and constructed, be securely fastened either to some part of the structure of the vehicle or to the seat which is being occupied by the person wearing the belt so that the body of the person wearing the belt would be restrained in the event of an accident to the vehicle.

(5) No requirement specified in paragraph (4) above applies if the vehicle is being used—

(*a*) on a journey after the start of which the requirement ceased to be complied with; or

(*b*) after the requirement ceased to be complied with and steps have been taken for such compliance to be restored with all reasonable expedition.

(6) Expressions which are used in this regulation and are defined in regulation 47 have the same meaning in this regulation as they have in regulation 47.

[Regulation 48 is printed as amended by SI 1987 No 1133.]

49. Rear under-run protection

(1) Save as provided in paragraph (2), this regulation applies to a wheeled goods vehicle being either—

(*a*) a motor vehicle with a maximum gross weight which exceeds 3500 kg and which was first used on or after 1st April 1984; or

(*b*) a trailer manufactured on or after 1st May 1983 with an unladen weight which exceeds 1020 kg.

(2) This regulation does not apply to—

(*a*) a motor vehicle which has a maximum speed not exceeding 15 mph;

(*b*) a motor car or a heavy motor car constructed or adapted to form part of an articulated vehicle;

(*c*) an agricultural trailer;

(*d*) engineering plant;

(*e*) a fire engine;

(*f*) an agricultural motor vehicle;

(*g*) a vehicle fitted at the rear with apparatus specially designed for spreading material on a road;

(*h*) a vehicle so constructed that it can be unloaded by part of the vehicle being tipped rearwards;

(*i*) a vehicle owned by the Secretary of State for Defence and used for naval, military or air force purposes;

(*j*) a vehicle to which no bodywork has been fitted and which is being driven or towed—

(i) for the purpose of a quality or safety check by its manufacturer or a dealer in, or distributor of, such vehicles; or

(ii) to a place where, by previous arrangement, bodywork is to be fitted or work preparatory to the fitting of bodywork is to be carried out; or

(iii) by previous arrangement to premises of a dealer in, or distributor of, such vehicles;

(*k*) a vehicle which is being driven or towed to a place where by previous arrangement a device is to be fitted so that it complies with this regulation;

(*l*) a vehicle specially designed and constructed, and not merely adapted, to carry other vehicles loaded onto it from the rear;

(*m*) a trailer specially designed and constructed, and not merely adapted, to carry round timber, beams or girders, being items of exceptional length;

(*n*) a vehicle fitted with a tail lift so constructed that the lift platform forms part of the floor of the vehicle and this part has a length of at least 1 m measured parallel to the longitudinal axis of the vehicle;

(*o*) a trailer having a base or centre in a country outside Great Britain from which it normally starts its journeys, provided that a period of not more than 12 months has elapsed since the vehicle was last brought into Great Britain;

(*p*) a vehicle specially designed, and not merely adapted, for the carriage and mixing of liquid concrete;

(*q*) a vehicle designed and used solely for the delivery of coal by means of a special conveyor which is carried on the vehicle and when in use is fitted to the rear of the vehicle so as to render its being equipped with a rear under-run protective device impracticable; or

(*r*) an agricultural trailed appliance.

(3) Subject to the provisions of paragraphs (4), (5) and (6), every vehicle to which this regulation applies shall be equipped with a rear under-run protective device.

(4) A vehicle to which this regulation applies and which is fitted with a tail lift, bodywork or other part which renders its being equipped with a rear under-run protective device impracticable shall instead be equipped with one or more devices which do not protrude beyond the overall width of the vehicle (excluding any part of the device or the devices) and which comply with the following requirements—

(*a*) where more than one device is fitted, not more than 50 cm shall lie between one device and the device next to it;

(*b*) not more than 30 cm shall lie between the outermost end of a device nearest to the outermost part of the vehicle to which it is fitted and a longitudinal plane passing through the outer end of the rear axle of the vehicle on the same side of the vehicle or, in a case where the vehicle is fitted with more than one rear axle, through the outer end of the widest rear axle on the same side of the vehicle, and paragraph II. 5.4.2 in the Annex to Community Directive 79/490 shall not have effect in a case where this requirement is met; and (*c*) the device or, where more than one device is fitted, all the devices together, shall have the characteristics specified in paragraphs II.5.4.5.1 to II.5.4.5.5.2 in the Annex to the said Directive save—

(i) as provided in sub-paragraphs (*a*) and (*b*) above;

(ii) that for the reference in paragraph II.5.4.5.1 in that Annex to 30 cm there is substituted a reference to 35 cm; and

(iii) that the distance of 40 cm specified in paragraph II.5.4.5 in that Annex may be measured exclusive of the said tail-lift, bodywork or other part.

(5) The provisions of paragraph (3) shall have effect so that in the case of—

(*a*) a vehicle which is fitted with a demountable body, the characteristics specified in paragraph II.5.4.2 in the Annex to the said Directive have effect as if the reference to 10 cm were a reference to 30 cm and as if in paragraph II.5.4.5.1 the reference to 30 cm were a reference to 35 cm; and

(*b*) a trailer with a single axle to two close-coupled axles, the height of 55 cm referred to in paragraph II.5.4.5.1 in that Annex is measured when the coupling of the trailer to the vehicle by which it is drawn is at the height recommended by the manufacturer of the trailer.

(6) Instead of complying with paragraphs (3) to (5) a vehicle may comply with Community Directive 79/490.

(7) In this regulation—

'rear under-run protective device' means a device within the description given in paragraph II.5.4 in the Annex to Community Directive 79/490.

50. Maintenance of rear under-run protective device

Every device fitted to a vehicle in compliance with the requirements of regulation 49 shall at all times when the vehicle is on a road be maintained free from any obvious defect which would be likely to affect adversely the performance of the device in the function of giving resistance in the event of an impact from the rear.

51. Sideguards

(1) Save as provided in paragraph (2), this regulation applies to a wheeled goods vehicle being—

(*a*) a motor vehicle first used on or after 1st April 1984 with a maximum gross weight which exceeds 3500 kg; or

(*b*) a trailer manufactured on or after 1st May 1983 with an unladen weight which exceeds 1020 kg; or

(*c*) a semi-trailer manufactured before 1st May 1983 which has a relevant plate showing a gross weight exceeding 26,000 kg and which forms part of an articulated vehicle with a relevant train weight exceeding 32,520 kg.

(2) This regulation does not apply to—

(*a*) a motor vehicle which has a maximum speed not exceeding 15 mph;

(*b*) an agricultural trailer;

(*c*) engineering plant;

(*d*) a fire engine;

(*e*) an agricultural motor vehicle;

(*f*) a vehicle so constructed that it can be unloaded by part of the vehicle being tipped sideways or rearwards;

(*g*) a vehicle owned by the Secretary of State for Defence and used for naval, military or air force purposes;

(*h*) a vehicle to which no bodywork has been fitted and which is being driven or towed—

(i) for the purpose of a quality or safety check by its manufacturer or a dealer in, or distributor of, such vehicles;

(ii) to a place where, by previous arrangement, bodywork is to be fitted or work preparatory to the fitting of bodywork is to be carried out; or

(iii) by previous arrangement to premises of a dealer in, or distributor of, such vehicles;

(*i*) a vehicle which is being driven or towed to a place where by previous arrangement a sideguard is to be fitted so that it complies with this regulation;

(*j*) a refuse vehicle;

(*k*) a trailer specially designed and constructed, and not merely adapted, to carry round timber, beams or girders, being items of exceptional length;

(*l*) a motor car or a heavy motor car constructed or adapted to form part of an articulated vehicle;

(*m*) a vehicle specially designed and constructed, and not merely adapted, to carry other vehicles loaded onto it from the front or the rear;

(*n*) a trailer with a load platform—

(i) no part of any edge of which is more than 60 mm inboard from the tangential plane; and

(ii) the upper surface of which is not more than 750 mm from the ground throughout that part of its length under which a sideguard would have to be fitted in accordance with paragraph (5)(*d*) to (*g*) if this exemption did not apply to it;

(*o*) a trailer having a base or centre in a country outside Great Britain from which it normally starts its journeys, provided that a period of not more than 12 months has elapsed since the vehicle was last brought into Great Britain; or

(*p*) an agricultural trailed appliance.

[(2A) This regulation also applies to a wheeled goods vehicle, whether of a description falling within paragraph (2) or not, which is a semi-trailer some or all of the wheels of which are driven by the drawing vehicle.]

(3) Every vehicle to which this regulation applies shall be securely fitted with a sideguard to give protection on any side of the vehicle where—

(*a*) if it is a semi-trailer, the distance between the transverse planes passing through the centre of its foremost axle and through the centre of its king pin or, in the case of a vehicle having more than one king pin, the rearmost one, exceeds 4.5 m; or

(*b*) if it is any other vehicle, the distance between the centres of any two consecutive axles exceeds 3 m.

(4) Save as provided in paragraphs (6) and (7), a sideguard with which a vehicle is by this regulation required to be fitted shall comply with all the specifications listed in paragraph (5).

(5) Those specifications are—

(*a*) the outermost surface of every sideguard shall be smooth, essentially rigid and either flat or horizontally corrugated, save that—

(i) any part of the surface may overlap another provided that the overlapping edges face rearwards or downwards;

(ii) a gap not exceeding 25 mm measured longitudinally may exist between any two adjacent parts of the surface provided that the foremost edge of the rearward part does not protrude outboard of the rearmost edge of the forward part; and

(iii) domed heads of bolts or rivets may protrude beyond the surface to a distance not exceeding 10 mm;

(*b*) no part of the lowest edge of a sideguard shall be more than 550 mm above the ground when the vehicle to which it is fitted is on level ground and, in the case of a semi-trailer, when its load platform is horizontal;

(*c*) in a case specified in an item in column 2 of the Table the highest edge of a sideguard shall be as specified in that item in column 3;

(*d*) the distance between the rearmost edge of a sideguard and the transverse plane passing through the foremost part of the tyre fitted to the wheel of the vehicle nearest to it shall not exceed 300 mm;

(*e*) the distance between the foremost edge of a sideguard fitted to a semi-trailer and a transverse plane passing through the centre of the vehicle's king pin or, if the vehicle has more than one king pin, the rearmost one, shall not exceed 3 m;

(*f*) the foremost edge of a sideguard fitted to a semi-trailer with landing legs shall, as well as complying with sub-paragraph (*e*), not be more than 250 mm to the rear of a transverse plane passing through the centre of the leg nearest to that edge;

(*g*) the distance between the foremost edge of a sideguard fitted to a vehicle other than a semi-trailer and a transverse plane passing through the rearmost part of the tyre fitted to the wheel of the vehicle nearest to it shall not exceed 300 mm if the vehicle is a motor vehicle and 500 mm if the vehicle is a trailer;

(*h*) the external edges of a sideguard shall be rounded at a radius of at least 2.5 mm;

(*i*) no sideguard shall be more than 30 mm inboard from the tangential plane;

(*j*) no sideguard shall project beyond the longitudinal plane from which, in the absence of a sideguard, the vehicle's overall width would fall to be measured;

(*k*) every sideguard shall cover an area extending to at least 100 mm upwards from its lowest edge 100 mm downwards from its highest edge, and 100 mm rearwards and inwards from its foremost edge, and no sideguard shall have a vertical gap measured more than 300 mm nor any vertical surface measuring less than 100 mm; and

(*l*) except in the case of a vehicle described in paragraph (1)(*c*) every sideguard shall be capable of withstanding a force of 2 kilonewtons applied perpendicularly to any part of its surface by the centre of a ram the face of which is circular and not more than 220 mm in diameter, and during such application—

(i) no part of the sideguard shall be deflected by more than 150 mm, and

(ii) no part of the sideguard which is less than 250 mm from its rearmost part shall be deflected by more than 30 mm.

TABLE

(regulation 51(5))

1	2	3
Item	Case	Requirement about highest edge of sideguard
1	Where the floor of the vehicle to which the side-guard is fitted— (i) extends laterally outside the tangential plane; (ii) is not more than 1.85 m from the ground; (iii) extends laterally over the whole of the length of the sideguard with which the vehicle is required by this regulation to be fitted; and (iv) is wholly covered at its edge by a side-rave the lower edge of which is not more than 150 mm below the underside of the floor.	Not more than 350 mm below the lower edge of the side-rave.
2	Where the floor of the vehicle to which the sideguard is fitted— (i) extends laterally outside the tangential plane; and (ii) does not comply with all of the provisions specified in sub-paragraphs (ii), (iii) and (iv) in item 1 above, and any part of the structure of the vehicle is cut within 1.85 m of the ground by the tangential plane.	Not more than 350 mm below the structure of the vehicle where it is cut by the tangential plane.
3	Where— (i) no part of the structure of the vehicle is cut within 1.85 m of the ground by the tangential plane; and (ii) the upper surface of the load carrying structure of the vehicle is less than 1.5 m from the ground.	Not less than the height of the upper surface of the load carrying structure of the vehicle.
4	A vehicle specially designed, and not merely adapted, for the carriage and mixing of liquid concrete.	Not less than 1 m from the ground.
5	Any other case.	Not less than 1.5 m from the ground.

(6) The provisions of paragraph (4) apply—

(*a*) in the case of an extendible trailer when it is, by virtue of the extending mechanism, extended to a length greater than its minimum, so as not to require, in respect of any additional distance solely attributed to the extension, compliance with the specifications mentioned in paragraph (5)(*d*) to (*g*);

(*b*) in the case of a vehicle designed and constructed, and not merely adapted, to be fitted with a demountable body or to carry a container, when it is not fitted with a demountable body or carrying such a container as if it were fitted with such a body or carrying such a container; and

(*c*) only so far as it is practicable in the case of—

(i) a vehicle designed solely for the carriage of a fluid substance in a closed tank which is permanently fitted to the vehicle and provided with valves and hose or pipe connections for loading or unloading; and

(ii) a vehicle which requires additional stability during loading or unloading or while being used for operations for which it is designed or adapted and is fitted on one or both sides with an extendible device to provide such stability.

(7) In the case of a motor vehicle to which this regulation applies and which is of a type which was required to be approved by the Type Approval for Goods Vehicles Regulations before 1st October 1983—

(*a*) if the bodywork of the vehicle covers the whole of the area specified as regards a sideguard in paragraph (5)(*b*), (*c*), (*d*) and (*g*) above the other provisions of that paragraph do not apply to that vehicle; and

(*b*) if the bodywork of the vehicle covers only part of that area the part of that area which is not so covered shall be fitted with a sideguard which complies with the provisions of paragraph (5) above save that there shall not be a gap between—

(i) the rearmost edge of the sideguard or the rearmost part of the bodywork (whichever is furthest to the rear) and the transverse plane mentioned in paragraph (5)(*d*) of more than 300 mm;

(ii) the foremost edge of the sideguard or the foremost part of the bodywork (whichever is furthest to the front) and the transverse plane mentioned in paragraph (5)(*g*) of more than 300 mm; or

(iii) any vertical or sloping edge of any part of the bodywork in question and the edge of the sideguard immediately forwards or rearwards thereof of more than 25 mm measured horizontally.

(8) In this regulation

'relevant plate' means a Ministry plate, where fitted, and in other cases a plate fitted in accordance with regulation 66;

'relevant train weight' means the train weight shown in column 2 of the Ministry plate, where fitted, and in other cases the maximum train weight shown at item 8 of the plate fitted in accordance with regulation 66; and

'tangential plane', in regulation to a sideguard, means the vertical plane tangential to the external face of the outermost part of the tyre (excluding any distortion caused by the weight of the vehicle) fitted to the outermost wheel at the rear and on the same side of the vehicle.

[Regulation 51 is printed as amended by SI 1987 No 676.]

52. Maintenance of sideguards

Every sideguard fitted to a vehicle in compliance with the requirements of regulation 51 shall at all times when the vehicle is on a road be maintained free from any obvious defect which would be likely to affect adversely its effectiveness.

53. Mascots

(1) Subject to paragraph (2), no mascot, emblem or other ornamental object shall be carried by a motor vehicle first used on or after 1st October 1937 in any position

where it is likely to strike any person with whom the vehicle may collide unless the mascot is not liable to cause injury to such person by reason of any projection thereon.

(2) Instead of complying with the requirements of paragraph (1) a vehicle may comply with Community Directive 74/483 or 79/488 or ECE Regulation 26.01.

[53A. Strength of superstructure

(1) This regulation applies to every coach which is—

(*a*) a single decked vehicle;

(*b*) equipped with a compartment below the deck for the luggage of passengers; and

(*c*) first used on or after 1st April 1990.

(2) Every vehicle to which this regulation applies shall comply with the requirements of ECE Regulation 66.]

[Regulation 53A was inserted by SI 1987 No 1133.]

[53B. Additional exits from double decked coaches

(1) This regulation applies to every coach which is—

(*a*) a double-decked vehicle; and

(*b*) first used on or after 1st April 1990.

(2) Subject to the following provisions of this regulation, every vehicle to which this regulation applies shall be equipped with two staircases, one of which shall be located in one half of the vehicle and the other in the other half of the vehicle.

(3) Instead of being equipped with two staircases in accordance with paragraph (2), a vehicle to which this regulation applies may be equipped in accordance with the following provisions of this regulation with a hammer or other similar device with which in case of emergency any side window of the vehicle may be broken.

(4) Where a vehicle is equipped with–

(*a*) a staircase located in one half of the vehicle; and

(*b*) an emergency exit complying with regulation 21(8) of the Public Service Vehicles (Conditions of Fitness, Equipment, Use and Certification) Regulations 1981 *[SI 1981 No 257, qv]* located in the same half of the upper deck of the vehicle;

the hammer or other similar device shall be located in the other half of that deck.

(5) Any hammer or other similar device with which a vehicle is equipped pursuant to this regulation shall be located in a conspicuous and readily accessible position in the upper deck of the vehicle.

(6) There shall be displayed, in a conspicuous position in close proximity to the hammer or other similar device, a notice which shall contain in clear and indelible lettering—

(*a*) in letters not less than 25 mm high, the heading 'IN EMERGENCY'; and

(*b*) in letters not less than 10 mm high, instructions that in case of emergency the hammer or device is to be used first to break any side window by striking the glass near the edge of the window and then to clear any remaining glass from the window aperture.

(7) For the purposes of this regulation a staircase, emergency exit, hammer or other similar device (as the case may be) shall be considered to be located in the other

half of the vehicle if the shortest distance between any part of that staircase, exit, hammer or device (as the case may be) and any part of any other staircase, emergency exit, hammer or device is not less than one half of the overall length of the vehicle.]

[*Regulation 53B was inserted by SI 1987 No 1133.*]

K *Control of Emissions*

54. Silencers

(1) Every vehicle propelled by an internal combustion engine shall be fitted with an exhaust system including a silencer and the exhaust gases from the engine shall not escape into the atmosphere without first passing through the silencer.

(2) Every exhaust system and silencer shall be maintained in good and efficient working order and shall not be altered so as to increase the noise made by the escape of exhaust gases.

(3) Instead of complying with paragraph (1) a vehicle may comply with Community Directive 77/212, 81/334, 84/372 or 84/424 or, in the case of a motor cycle other than a moped, 78/1015.

(4) In this regulation 'moped' has the meaning given to it in paragraph (5) of Schedule 9.

55. Noise limits—general

(1) Save as provided in paragraph (2) and regulation 59, this regulation applies to every wheeled motor vehicle having at least three wheels and first used on or after 1st October 1983 which is—

(*a*) a vehicle, not falling within sub-paragraph (*b*) or (*c*), with or without bodywork;

(*b*) a vehicle not falling within sub-paragraph (*c*) which is—

(i) engineering plant;

(ii) a locomotive other than an agricultural motor vehicle;

(iii) a motor tractor other than an industrial tractor or an agricultural motor vehicle;

(iv) a public works vehicle;

(v) a works truck; or

(vi) a refuse vehicle; or

(*c*) a vehicle which—

(i) has a compression ignition engine;

(ii) is so constructed or adapted that the driving power of the engine is, or by appropriate use of the controls can be, transmitted to all wheels of the vehicle; and

(iii) falls within category I.1.1, I.1.2, or I.1.3 specified in Article 1 of Community Directive 77/212.

(2) This regulation does not apply to—

(*a*) a motor cycle with a sidecar attached;

(*b*) an agricultural motor vehicle which is first used before 1st June 1986 or which is not driven at more than 20 mph;

(*c*) an industrial tractor;

(*d*) a road roller;

(*e*) a vehicle specially constructed, and not merely adapted, for the purposes of fighting fires or salvage from fires at or in the vicinity of airports, and having an engine power exceeding 220 kW;

(*f*) a vehicle which runs on rails; or

(*g*) a vehicle manufactured by Leyland Vehicles Ltd. and known as the Atlantean Bus, if first used before 1st October 1984.

(3) Save as provided in paragraphs (4) and (5), every vehicle to which this regulation applies shall be so constructed that it complies with the requirements set out in item 1, 2, 3 or 4 of the Table *[see table on pp 2/818–19]*; a vehicle complies with those requirements if—

(*a*) its sound level does not exceed the relevant limit specified in column 2(*a*), (*b*) or (*c*), as the case may be, in the relevant item when measured under the conditions specified in column 3 in that item and by the method specified in column 4 in that item using the apparatus prescribed in paragraph (6); and

(*b*) in the case of a vehicle referred to in paragraph 1(*a*) (other than one having less than four wheels or a maximum speed not exceeding 25 km/h) or 1(*c*), the device designed to reduce the exhaust noise meets the requirements specified in column 5 in that item.

(4) Save as provided in paragraph (5), paragraph (3) applies to every vehicle to which this regulation applies and which is first used on or after 1st April 1990, unless it is equipped with 5 or more forward gears and has a maximum power to maximum gross weight ratio not less than 75 kW per 1000 kg, and is of a type in respect of which a type approval certificate has been issued under the Type Approval (Great Britain) Regulations as if, for the reference to items 1, 2, 3 or 4 of the Table there were substituted a reference to item 4 of the Table.

(5) Paragraph (4) does not apply to a vehicle in category 5.2.2.1.3 as defined in Annex I to Directive 84/424 and equipped with a compression ignition engine, a vehicle in category 5.2.2.1.4 as defined in that Annex, or a vehicle referred to in paragraph 1(*b*) unless it is first used on or after 1st April 1991.

(6) The apparatus prescribed for the purposes of paragraph 3(*a*) and regulations 56(2)(*a*) and 57(2)(*a*) is a sound level meter of the type described in Publication No 179 of the International Electrotechnical Commission, in either its first or second edition, a sound level meter complying with the specification for Type 0 or Type 1 in Publication No 651 (1979) 'Sound Level Meters' of the International Electrotechnical Commission, or a sound level meter complying with the specifications of the British Standard Number BS 5969: 1981 which came into effect on 29th May 1981.

(7) Instead of complying with the preceding provisions of this regulation a vehicle may comply at the time of its first use with Community Directive 77/212, 81/334, 84/372 or 84/424.

56. Noise limits—agricultural motor vehicles and industrial tractors

(1) Save as provided in regulation 59, this regulation applies to every wheeled vehicle first used on or after 1st April 1983 being an agricultural motor vehicle or an industrial tractor, other than—

(*a*) an agricultural motor vehicle which is first used on or after 1st June 1986 and which is driven at more than 20 mph; or

(*b*) a road roller.

(2) Every vehicle to which this regulation applies should be so constructed—

(*a*) that its sound level does not exceed—

[*continued on p 2/820*]

TABLE

(regulation 55(3))

1	2			3	4	5
Item	Limits of sound level			Conditions of measurement	Method of measurement	Requirements for exhaust device
	(a) Vehicle referred to in paragraph (1)(*a*)	(b) Vehicle referred to in paragraph (1)(*c*)	(c) Vehicle referred to in paragraph (1)(*c*)			
1	Limits specified in paragraph I.1 of the Annex to Community Directive 77/212.	89dB(A)	82dB(A)	Conditions specified in paragraph I.3 of the Annex to Community Directive 77/212	Method specified in paragraph I.4.1 of the Annex to Community Directive 77/212	Requirements specified in heading II of the Annex to Community Directive 77/212 (except paragraphs II.2 and II.5).
2	Limits specified in paragraph 5.2.2.1 of Annex I to Community Directive 81/334.	89dB(A)	82dB(A)	Conditions specified in paragraph 5.2.2.3 of Annex I to Community Directive 81/334.	Method specified in paragraph 5.2.2.4 of Annex I to Community Directive 81/334. Interpretation of results as specified in paragraph 5.2.2.5 of that Annex.	Requirements specified in section 3 and paragraphs 5.1 and 5.3.1 of Annex I to Community Directive 81/334.
3	Limits specified in paragraph 5.2.2.1 of Annex I to Community Directive 84/372	89dB(A)	82dB(A)	Conditions specified in paragraph 5.2.2.3 of Annex I to Community Directive 84/372	Method specified in paragraph 5.2.2.4 of Annex I to Community Directive 84/372, except that vehicles with 5 or more	Requirements specified in section 3 and paragraphs 5.1 and 5.3.1 of Annex I to Community Directive 84/372.

					forward gears and a maximum power to maximum gross weight ratio not less than 75 kW per 1000 kg may be tested in 3rd gear only. Interpretation of results as specified in paragraph 5.2.2.5 of that Annex.	
4	Limits specified in paragraph 5.2.2.1 of the Annex I to Community Directive 84/424	Vehicles with engine power— –less than 75kW –84dB(A) –not less than 75kW –86dB(A)	Limits specified in paragraph 5.2.2.1 of Annex I to Community Directive 84/424.	Conditions specified in paragraph 5.2.2.3 of Annex I to Community Directive 84/424	Method specified in paragraph 5.2.2.4 of Annex I to Community Directive 84/424, except that vehicles with 5 or more forward gears and a maximum power to maximum gross weight ratio not less than 75 kW per 1000 kg may be tested in 3rd gear only. Interpretation of results as specified in paragraph 5.2.2.5 of that Annex	Requirements specified in section 3 and paragraphs 5.1 and 5.3.1 of Annex I to Community Directive 84/424.

(i) if it is a vehicle with engine power of less than 65kW, 89 dB(A);
(ii) if it is a vehicle with engine power of 65kW or more, and first used before 1st October 1991, 92 dB(A); or
(iii) if it is a vehicle with engine power of 65kW or more, and first used on or after 1st October 1991, 89 dB(A),

when measured under the conditions specified in paragraph I.3 of Annex VI of Community Directive 74/151 by the method specified in paragraph I.4.1 of that Annex using the apparatus prescribed in regulation 55(6); and

(*b*) that the device designed to reduce the exhaust noise meets the requirements specified in paragraph II.1 of the Annex and, if fibrous absorbent material is used, the requirements specified in paragraphs II.4.1 to II.4.3 of that Annex.

57. Noise limits—motor cycles

(1) Save as provided in regulations 59, paragraph (2) of this regulation applies to every motor vehicle first used on or after 1st April 1983 which is—

(*a*) a moped; or

(*b*) a two-wheeled motor cycle, whether or not with sidecar attached, which is not a moped.

(2) Every vehicle to which this paragraph applies shall be so constructed that—

(*a*) its sound level does not exceed the relevant limit specified in column 2(*a*) or (*b*), as the case may be, in item 1 of the Table when measured under the conditions specified in column 3 in that item by the method specified in column 4 in that item using the apparatus prescribed in regulation 55(6); and

(*b*) the device designed to reduce the exhaust noise meets the requirements specified in column 5.

(3) The silencer which forms part of the exhaust system of a motor cycle first used on or after 1st January 1985 shall be either—

(*a*) that with which the vehicle was fitted when it was manufactured; or

(*b*) clearly and indelibly marked with either—
(i) the British Standard marking indicating that it has been tested in accordance with test 2; or
(ii) a reference to its make and type specified by the manufacturer of the vehicle.

(4) A motor cycle shall not be used on a road if it is fitted with an exhaust system any part of which is marked with the words 'NOT FOR ROAD USE' or words to the like effect.

(5) Instead of complying with the provisions of paragraph (2), a vehicle referred to in paragraph (1)(*b*) may comply at the time of its first use with Community Directive 78/1015.

(6) In this regulation—

'British Standard marking' means a marking specified in paragraph 6.1 of the British Standard Specification for replacement motor cycle and moped exhaust systems, which came into effect on 30th September 1983, issued by the British Standards Institution under reference BS AU 193:1983, and 'test 2' means the test so described in that Specification and therein specified; and

'moped' has the meaning given to it in paragraph 5 of Schedule 9.

TABLE

(regulation 57(2))

1	2		3	4	5
Item	Limits of sound level		Conditions of measurement	Method of measurement	Requirements for exhaust device
	Vehicle referred to in paragraph (1)(*a*)	Vehicle referred to in paragraph (1)(*b*)			
1	73dB(A)	Limits specified in paragraph 2.1.1 of Annex I to Community Directive 78/1015	Conditions specified in paragraph 2.1.3 of Annex I to Community Directive 78/1015	Method specified in paragraph 2.1.4 of Annex I to Community Directive 78/1015. Interpretation of results as in paragraphs 2.1.5.2, 2.1.5.3 and 2.1.5.4 of that Annex	Requirements as specified in paragraph 3 of Annex I to Community Directive 78/1015 except for sub-paragraph 3.2.

58. Noise limits—vehicles not subject to regulations 55 to 57, first used on or after 1st April 1970

(1) Save as provided in paragraph (2) and in regulation 59, every wheeled motor vehicle which was first used on or after 1st April 1970 and which is not subject to regulations 55, 56 or 57 shall be so constructed that the sound level (A weighting) in decibels does not exceed the maximum permitted level shown in column 2 of the Table for the relevant class of vehicle shown in column 1, when the noise emitted by it is measured under the specified conditions using the prescribed apparatus.

(2) A vehicle to which this regulation applies is not required to comply with paragraph (1) if at the time of its first use it complied with Community Directive 70/157, 73/350 or 77/212 or, in the case of an agricultural motor vehicle, 74/151, or if it is—

(*a*) a road roller;

(*b*) a vehicle specially constructed, and not merely adapted, for the purposes of fighting fires or salvage from fires at or in the vicinity of airports, and having an engine power exceeding 220 kW;

(*c*) a vehicle propelled by a compression ignition engine and which is of a type in respect of which a type approval certificate has been issued under the Type Approval (Great Britain) Regulations;

(*d*) a motor cycle first used on or after 1st October 1980, with an engine capacity not exceeding 50 cc which complies with the requirements specified in regulation 57(2); or

(*e*) an agricultural motor vehicle manufactured on or after 7th February 1975 which complies with the requirements specified in regulation 56(2).

(3) The definition of sound level (A weighting) in decibels contained in clause 2 of the British Standard Specification for Sound Level Meters published by the British Standards Institution on 7th September 1962 under the number BS 3539:1962, as amended by Amendment Slip No 1, numbered AMD22 and published on 1st July 1968, applies for the purposes of this regulation.

(4) In this regulation, 'the specified conditions' means the method described by the British Standard Method for the Measurement of Noise Emitted by Motor Vehicles published on 24th June 1966 under the number BS 3425:1966.

(5) In this regulation 'the prescribed apparatus' means a noise meter—

(*a*) which is in good working order and complies with the requirements laid down for vehicle noise meters in Part I of the said British Standard Specification numbered BS 3539:1962, as amended by the said Amendment Slip No 1;

(*b*) which has, not more than 12 months before the date of the measurement made in accordance with paragraph (1), undergone all the tests for checking calibration applicable in accordance with the Appendix to the said British Standard Specification; and

(*c*) in respect of which there has been issued by the National Physical Laboratory, the British Standards Institution or the Secretary of State a certificate recording the date on which as a result of those tests the meter was found to comply with the requirements of clauses 8 and 9 of the said British Standard Specification.

TABLE

(regulation 58(1))

1	2	3
Item	Class of vehicle	Maximum permitted sound level in dB(A)
1	Motor cycle of which the cylinder capacity of the engine does not exceed 50 cc	77
2	Motor cycle of which the cylinder capacity of the engine exceeds 50 cc but does not exceed 125 cc	82
3	Motor cycle of which the cylinder capacity of the engine exceeds 125 cc	86
4	Goods vehicle to which regulation 66 applies and which is equipped with a plate complying with the requirements of regulation 66 and showing particulars of a maximum gross weight of more than 3560 kg	89
5	Motor car not being a goods vehicle of the kind described in item 4 above	85
6	Motor tractor	89
7	Locomotive	89
8	Agricultural motor vehicle	89
9	Works truck	89
10	Engineering plant	89
11	Passenger vehicle constructed for a carriage of more than 12 passengers exclusive of the driver	89
12	Any other passenger vehicle	84
13	Any other vehicle	85

59. Exceptions to regulations 55 to 58

Regulations 55, 56, 57(2) and 58 do not apply to a motor vehicle which is—

(*a*) proceeding to a place where, by previous arrangement—

(i) noise emitted by it is about to be measured for the purpose of ascertaining whether or not the vehicle complies with such of those provisions as apply to it; or

(ii) the vehicle is about to be mechanically adjusted, modified or equipped for the purpose of securing that it so complies; or

(*b*) returning from such a place immediately after the noise has been so measured.

60. Radio interference suppression

(1) Save as provided in paragraph (2), every wheeled motor vehicle first used on or after 1st April 1974 which is propelled by a spark ignition engine shall comply at the time of its first use with Community Directive 72/245 or ECE Regulation 10 or 10.01 or, in the case of an agricultural motor vehicle, Community Directive 75/322.

(2) This regulation does not apply to a vehicle constructed or assembled by a person not ordinarily engaged in the trade or business of manufacturing vehicles of that description, but nothing in this paragraph affects the application to such vehicles of the Wireless Telegraphy (Control of Interference from Ignition Apparatus) Regulations 1973 *[SI 1973 No 1217]*.

61. Emission of smoke, vapour, gases, oily substances, etc

(1) Subject to paragraph (4), every vehicle shall be constructed so as not to emit any avoidable smoke or avoidable visible vapour.

(2) Every motor vehicle using solid fuel shall be fitted with—

(*a*) a tray or shield to prevent ashes and cinders from falling onto the road; and

(*b*) an efficient appliance to prevent any emission of sparks or grit..

(3) Subject to paragraph (4) and to the exemptions specified in an item in column 4 of the Table *[see table on pp 2/826–7]*, every wheeled vehicle of a class specified in that item in column 2 shall be constructed so as to comply with the requirements specified in that item in column 3.

(4) Instead of complying with such provisions of paragraph (1) and items 1, 2 and 3 in the Table as apply to it, a vehicle may at the time of its first use comply—

(*a*) if it is propelled by a compression ignition engine, with Community Directive 72/306 (or, in the case of an agricultural vehicle, 77/537) or ECE Regulation 24.01, 24.02 or 24.03; or

[(*b*) if it is propelled by a spark ignition engine—

(i) in a case where the first use is before 1st April 1991, with Community Directive 78/665, 83/351 or 88/76, or ECE Regulation 15.03 or 15.04; or

(ii) in any other case, with Community Directive 83/351 or 88/76, or ECE Regulation 15.04.]

(5) No person shall use, or cause a permit to be used, on a road any motor vehicle—

(*a*) from which any smoke, visible vapour, grit, sparks, ashes, cinders or oily substance is emitted if that emission causes, or is likely to cause, damage to any property or injury or danger to any person who is, or who may reasonably be expected to be, on the road;

(*b*) which is subject to the requirement in item 2 of the Table (whether or not it is deemed to comply with that requirement by virtue of paragraph (4)), if the fuel injection equipment, the engine speed governor or any other parts of the engine by which it is propelled have been altered or adjusted so as to increase the emission of smoke; or

(*c*) which is subject to the requirement in item 1 of the Table if the device mentioned in column 2 in that item is used while the vehicle is in motion.

(6) No person shall use, or cause a permit to be used, on a road a motor vehicle to

which item 3 of the Table applies unless it is so maintained that the means specified in column 3 of that item are in good working order.

[*Regulation 61 is printed as amended by SI 1988 No 1524.*]

62. Closets, etc

(1) No wheeled vehicle first used after 15th January 1931 shall be equipped with any closet or urinal which can discharge directly on to a road.

(2) Every tank into which a closet or urinal with which a vehicle is equipped empties, and every closet or urinal which does not empty into a tank, shall contain chemicals which are non-inflammable and non-irritant and provide an efficient germicide.

63. Wings

(1) Save as provided in paragraph (4), this regulation applies to—

(*a*) invalid carriages;

(*b*) heavy motor cars, motor cars and motor cycles, not being agricultural motor vehicles or pedestrian-controlled vehicles;

(*c*) agricultural motor vehicles driven at more than 20 mph; and

(*d*) trailers.

(2) Subject to paragraphs (3) and (5), every vehicle to which this regulation applies shall be equipped with wings or other similar fittings to catch, so far as practicable, mud or water thrown up by the rotation of its wheels or tracks.

(3) The requirements specified in paragraph (2) apply, in the case of a trailer with more than two wheels, only in respect of the rearmost two wheels.

(4) Those requirements do not apply in respect of—

(*a*) a works truck;

(*b*) a living van;

(*c*) a water cart;

(*d*) an agricultural trailer drawn by a motor vehicle which is not driven at a speed in excess of 20 mph;

(*e*) an agricultural trailed appliance;

(*f*) an agricultural trailed appliance conveyor;

(*g*) a broken down vehicle;

(*h*) a heavy motor car, motor car or trailer in an unfinished condition which is proceeding to a workshop for completion;

(*i*) a trailer used for or in connection with the carriage of round timber and the rear wheels of any heavy motor car or motor car drawing a semi-trailer so used; or

(*j*) a trailer drawn by a motor vehicle the maximum speed of which is restricted to 20 mph or less under Schedule 6 to the 1984 Act.

(5) Instead of complying with paragraph (2) a vehicle may comply with Community Directive 78/549.

64. Spray suppression devices

(1) Save as provided in paragraph (2), this regulation applies to every wheeled goods vehicle which is—

(*a*) a motor vehicle first used on or after 1st April 1986 having a maximum gross weight exceeding 12,000 kg;

[*continued on p 2/828*]

TABLE

(regulation 61(3))

1	2	3	4
Item	Class of vehicle	Requirements	Exemptions
1	Vehicles propelled by a compression ignition engine and equipped with a device designed to facilitate starting the engine by causing it to be supplied with excess fuel.	Provision shall be made to ensure the device cannot readily be operated by a person inside the vehicle.	(*a*) a works truck; (*b*) a vehicle on which the device is so designed and maintained that— (i) its use after the engine has started cannot cause the engine to be supplied with excess fuel, or (ii) it does not cause any increase in the smoke or visible vapour emitted from the vehicle.
2	Vehicles first used on or after 1st April 1973 and propelled by a compression ignition engine.	The engine of the vehicle shall be of a type for which there has been issued by a person authorised by the Secretary of State a type test certificate in accordance with the British Standard Specification for the Performance of Diesel Engines for Road Vehicles published on 19th May 1971 under number BS AU 141a: 1971. In the case of an agricultural motor vehicle (other than one which is first used after 1st June 1986 and is driven at more than 20 mph), an industrial tractor, a works truck or engineering plant, for the purposes of that Specification as to the exhaust gas opacity, measurements shall be made with the engine running at 80%	(*a*) a vehicle manufactured before 1st April 1973 and propelled by an engine known as the Perkins 6.354 engine; (*b*) a vehicle propelled by an engine having not more than 2 cylinders and being an agricultural motor vehicle (other than one which is first used on or after 1st June 1986 and which is driven at more than 20 mph), an industrial tractor, a works truck or engineering plant.

		of its full load over the speed range from maximum speed down to the speed at which maximum torque occurs as declared by the manufacturer of the vehicle for those purposes.	
3	Vehicles first used on or after 1st January 1972 and propelled by a spark ignition engine other than a 2-stroke engine.	The engine shall be equipped with means sufficient to ensure that, while the engine is running, any vapours or gases in the engine crank case, or in any other part of the engine to which vapours or gases may pass from that case, are prevented, so far as is reasonably practicable, from escaping into the atmosphere otherwise than through the combustion chamber of the engine.	(*a*) a two-wheeled motor cycle with or without a sidecar attached; (*b*) a vehicle to which item 4 below applies.
4	Vehicles first used on or after 1st October 1982 and propelled by a spark ignition engine.	The vehicle shall comply at the time of its first use with Community Directive 78/665 or 83/351 or ECE Regulation 15.03 or 15.04.	(*a*) a vehicle with a maximum gross weight exceeding 3500 kg; (*b*) a vehicle which has only two wheels; (*c*) a vehicle with an unladen weight of less than 400 kg; (*d*) a vehicle with less than 4 wheels and having a maximum speed not exceeding 30 mph.

(*b*) a trailer manufactured on or after 1st May 1985 having a maximum gross weight exceeding 3500 kg; or

(*c*) a trailer, whenever manufactured, having a maximum gross weight exceeding 16,000 kg and 2 or more axles.

(2) This regulation does not apply to—

(*a*) a motor vehicle so constructed that the driving power of its engine is, or can by use of its controls be, transmitted to all the wheels on at least one front axle and on at least one rear axle;

(*b*) a motor vehicle of which no part which lies within the specified area is less than 400 mm vertically above the ground when the vehicle is standing on reasonably flat ground;

(*c*) a works truck;

(*d*) a works trailer;

(*e*) a broken down vehicle;

(*f*) a motor vehicle which has a maximum speed not exceeding 30 mph;

(*g*) a vehicle of a kind specified in sub-paragraphs (*b*), (*c*), (*d*), (*e*), (*f*), (*g*), (*h*), (*j*), (*o*) or (*p*) or regulation 51(2);

(*h*) a vehicle specially designed, and not merely adapted, for the carriage and mixing of liquid concrete; or

(*i*) a vehicle which is being driven or towed to a place where by previous arrangement a device is to be fitted so that it complies with the requirements specified in paragraph (3).

(3) A vehicle to which this regulation applies and which is of a class specified in an item in column 2 of the Table shall not be used on a road on or after the date specified in column 3 in that item, unless it is fitted in relation to the wheels on each of its axles, with such containment devices as satisfy the technical requirements and other provisions about containment devices specified in the British Standard Specification, provided that in the case of a containment device fitted before 1st January 1985 the said requirements shall be deemed to be complied with if that containment device substantially conforms to those requirements.

TABLE

(regulation 64(3))

1	2	3
Item	Class of vehicle	Date
1	A trailer manufactured before 1st January 1975	1st October 1987
2	A trailer manufactured on or after 1st January 1975 but before 1st May 1985	1st October 1986
3	A trailer manufactured on or after 1st May 1985	1st May 1985
4	A motor vehicle	1st April 1986

(4) In this regulation—

['the British Standard Specification' means—

(*a*) in relation to a containment device fitted before 1st May 1987, Part 1a of the amended Specification and Part 2 of the original Specification; and

(*b*) in relation to a containment device fitted on or after 1st May 1987, Part 1a and Part 2a of the amended Specification;]

['the original Specification' means the British Standard Specification for Spray Reducing Devices for Heavy Goods Vehicles published under the reference BS AU 200: Part 1: 1984 and BS AU 200: Part 2: 1984;]

['the amended Specification' means the original Specification as amended and published under the reference BS AU 200: Part 1a: 1986 and BS AU 200: Part 2a: 1986;]

['containment device' means any device so described in the original Specification or the amended Specification;]

'the specified area' means the area formed by the overall length of the vehicle and the middle 80% of the shortest distance between the inner edges of any two wheels on opposite sides of the vehicle (such distance being ascertained when the vehicle is fitted with suitable tyres inflated to a pressure recommended by the manufacturer, but excluding any bulging of the tyres near the ground).

(5) Nothing in this regulation derogates from any requirement in regulation 63.

[Regulation 64 is printed as amended by SI 1986 No 1597.]

65. Maintenance of spray suppression devices

Every part of every containment device with which a vehicle is required to be fitted by the provisions of regulation 64 shall at all times when the vehicle is on a road be maintained free from any obvious defect which would be likely to affect adversely the effectiveness of the device.

PART III

PLATES, MARKINGS, TESTING AND INSPECTION

66. Plates for goods vehicles and buses

(1) This regulation applies to—

(*a*) a wheeled heavy motor car or motor car first used on or after 1st January 1968 not being—

- (i) a dual-purpose vehicle;
- (ii) an agricultural motor vehicle;
- (iii) a works truck;
- (iv) a pedestrian-controlled vehicle; or
- (v) save as provided in sub-paragraph (*b*) below, a passenger vehicle;

(*b*) a bus (whether or not it is an articulated bus) first used on or after 1st April 1982;

(*c*) a wheeled locomotive or motor tractor first used on or after 1st April 1973 not being—

- (i) an agricultural motor vehicle;
- (ii) an industrial tractor;
- (iii) a works truck;
- (iv) engineering plant; or
- (v) a pedestrian-controlled vehicle;

(*d*) a wheeled trailer manufactured on or after 1st January 1968 which exceeds 1020 kg in weight unladen not being—

(i) a trailer not constructed or adapted to carry any load, other than plant or special appliances or apparatus which is a permanent or essentially permanent fixture, and not exceeding 2290 kg in total weight;

(ii) a living van not exceeding 2040 kg in weight unladen and fitted with pneumatic tyres;

(iii) a works trailer;

(iv) a trailer mentioned in regulation 16(3)(*b*) to (*g*); or

(v) a trailer which was manufactured and used outside Great Britain before it was first used in Great Britain; and

(*e*) a converter dolly manufactured on or after 1st January 1979.

(2) Every vehicle to which this regulation applies shall be equipped with a plate securely attached to the vehicle in a conspicuous and readily accessible position which either—

(*a*) contains the particulars required, in the case of a motor vehicle by Part I of Schedule 8 or, in the case of a trailer, by Part II of that Schedule and complies with the provisions of Part III of that Schedule; or

(*b*) complies with the requirements specified in the Annex to Community Directive 78/507 or, in the case of a vehicle first used before 1st October 1982, in the Annex to Community Directive 76/114, such requirements being in any case modified as provided in paragraph (3).

(3) Instead of the particulars required by items 2.1.4 to 2.1.7 of that Annex, the plate required by paragraph (2)(*b*) shall show, for a vehicle of a class specified in column 2 of the Table against an item of that Annex so specified in column 1, the following particulars—

(*a*) the maximum permitted weight for that class, if any, shown in column 3 of the Table;

(*b*) where the maximum weight shown in column 4 of the Table exceeds the maximum permitted weight, the maximum weight in a column on the plate to the right of the maximum permitted weight; and

(*c*) if no weight is shown in column 3 of the Table, the maximum weight shown in column 4 of the Table, in the right hand column of the plate.

TABLE

(regulation 66(3))

1	2	3	4
Item in Annex to Directive	Class of vehicle	Maximum permitted weight	Maximum weight
2.1.4 (Laden weight of vehicle)	(i) Motor vehicles	The maximum gross weight in Great Britain referred to in item 10 in Part I of Schedule 8.	The maximum gross weight referred to in item 7 in Part I of Schedule 8.
	(ii) Trailers, other than semi-trailers	The maximum gross weight in Great Britain referred to in item 8 in Part II of Schedule 8.	The maximum gross weight referred to in item 6 in Part II of Schedule 8.

1	2	3	4
Item in Annex to Directive	Class of vehicle	Maximum permitted weight	Maximum weight
	(iii) Semi-trailers		The maximum gross weight referred to in item 6 in Part II of Schedule 8.
2.1.5 (Train weight of motor vehicle)	Motor vehicles constructed to draw a trailer	The lower of— (*a*) the maximum train weight referred to in item 8 in Part I of Schedule 8; and (*b*) the maximum laden weight specified, in the case of vehicles constructed to form part of an articulated vehicle, in regulation 77, and, in other cases, in regulation 76.	The maximum train weight referred to in item 8 in Part 1 of Schedule 8.
2.1.6 (Axle weight of vehicle)	(i) Motor vehicles	The maximum weight in Great Britain for each axle referred to in item 9 in Part I of Schedule 8.	The maximum weight for each axle referred to in item 6 in Part I of Schedule 8.
	(ii) Trailers	The maximum weight in Great Britain for each axle referred to in item 7 in Part II of Schedule 8.	The maximum weight for each axle referred to in item 4 in Part II of Schedule 8.
2.1.7 (Load imposed by semi-trailer)	Semi-trailers		The maximum load imposed on the drawing vehicle referred to in item 5 in Part II of Schedule 8.

(4) Part III of Schedule 8 applies for determining the relevant weights to be shown on a plate in accordance with this regulation.

67. Vehicle identification numbers

(1) This regulation applies to a wheeled vehicle which is first used on or after 1st April 1980 and to which the Type Approval (Great Britain) Regulations apply.

(2) A vehicle to which this regulation applies shall be equipped with a plate which is in a conspicuous and readily accessible position, is affixed to a vehicle part which is not normally subject to replacement and shows clearly and indelibly—

(*a*) the vehicle identification number in accordance with the requirements specified—

(i) in the case of a vehicle first used before 1st April 1987, in paragraphs 3.1.1 and 3.1.2 of the Annex to Community Directive 76/114/EEC; or

(ii) in any case, in sections 3 and 4 of the Annex to Community Directive 78/507/EEC;

(*b*) the name of the manufacturer; and

(*c*) the approval reference number of either—

(i) the type approval certificate which relates to the vehicle model or the model variant of the vehicle model, as the case may be, issued in accordance with the provisions of regulation 9(1) of, and Part I of Schedule 3 to, the Type Approval (Great Britain) Regulations; or

(ii) the Minister's approval certificate which relates to the vehicle, issued in accordance with the provisions of regulation 9(2) of, and Part 1A of Schedule 4 to, the said Regulations.

Provided that the information required under sub-paragraph (*c*) above may be shown clearly and indelibly on an additional plate which is fitted in a conspicuous and readily accessible position and which is affixed to a vehicle part which is not normally subject to replacement.

(3) The vehicle identification number of every vehicle to which this regulation applies shall be marked on the chassis, frame or other similar structure, on the offside of the vehicle, in a clearly visible and accessible position, and by a method such as hammering or stamping, in such a way that it cannot be obliterated or deteriorate.

68. Plates—agricultural trailed appliances

(1) Save as provided in paragraph (3) below, every wheeled agricultural trailed appliance manufactured on or after 1st December 1985 shall be equipped with a plate affixed to the vehicle in a conspicuous and readily accessible position and which is clearly and indelibly marked with the particulars specified in paragraph (2) below.

(2) Those particulars are—

(*a*) the name of the manufacturer of the appliance;

(*b*) the year in which the appliance was manufactured;

(*c*) the maximum gross weight;

(*d*) the unladen weight; and

(*e*) the maximum load which would be imposed by the appliance on the drawing vehicle.

(3) In the case of a towed roller consisting of several separate rollers used in combination, a single plate shall satisfy the requirements specified in paragraph (2) above.

69. Plates—motor cycles

(1) This regulation applies to every motor cycle first used on or after 1st August 1977 which is not—

(*a*) propelled by an internal combustion engine with a cylinder capacity exceeding 150 cc if the vehicle was first used before 1st January 1982 or 125 cc if it was first used on or after 1st January 1982;

(*b*) a mowing machine; or

(*c*) a pedestrian-controlled vehicle.

(2) Every vehicle to which this regulation applies shall be equipped with a plate which is securely affixed to the vehicle in a conspicuous and readily accessible position and which complies with the requirements of Schedule 9.

70. Ministry plates

(1) Every goods vehicle to which the Plating and Testing Regulations apply and in respect of which a plating certificate has been issued shall, from the date specified in paragraph (2), be equipped with a Ministry plate securely affixed, so as to be legible at all times, in a conspicuous and readily accessible position, and in the cab of the vehicle if it has one.

(2) That date is in the case of—

(*a*) a vehicle to which the Type Approval for Goods Vehicles Regulations apply, the date of the fourteenth day after the plate was issued; or

(*b*) any other vehicle, the date by which it is required, by the said Regulations, to be submitted for examination for plating.

[70A. Speed limiters—plates

(1) Paragraph (2) applies to every vehicle to which regulation 36A (speed limiters) applies and which is fitted with a speed limiter which complies with Part I of the British Standard.

(2) Every vehicle to which this paragraph applies shall be equipped with a plate which is in a conspicuous and readily accessible position within the driving compartment and which shows clearly and indelibly the particulars specified in clause 10 of Part I of the British Standard.

(3) Paragraph (4) applies to every vehicle to which regulation 36A applies and which is fitted with a speed limiter which does not comply with Part I of the British Standard.

(4) Every vehicle to which this paragraph applies shall be equipped with a plate which is in a conspicuous and readily accessible position within the driving compartment and which shows clearly and indelibly—

(*a*) the words 'SPEED LIMITER FITTED';

(*b*) the set speed in mph to which the limiter is calibrated; and

(*c*) the name or trade mark of the [limiter calibrator].

(5) In this regulation—

(*a*) 'Part I of the British Standard' and 'speed limiter' have the same meanings respectively as in regulation 36A;

(*b*) '[limiter calibrator]' and 'set speed' have the same meanings respectively as in Part I of the British Standard; and

(*c*) 'trade mark' has the same meaning as in the Trade Marks Act 1938 [*qv*].]

[*Regulation 70A was inserted by SI 1988 No 271 and is printed as subsequently amended by SI 1988 No 1524.*]

71. Marking of weights on certain vehicles

(1) This regulation applies to a vehicle (other than an agricultural motor vehicle which is either a track-laying vehicle not exceeding 3050 kg in unladen weight or a wheeled vehicle) which is—

(*a*) a locomotive;

(*b*) a motor tractor;

(*c*) a heavy motor car which is registered under the 1971 Act (or any enactment repealed thereby) if the unladen weight of the vehicle is not shown on its Ministry plate; or (*d*) an unbraked wheeled trailer, other than one mentioned in regulation 16(3)(*b*)(i), (iii), (iv) or (v) or (*c*) to (*g*).

(2) There shall be plainly marked in a conspicuous place on the outside of a vehicle to which this regulation applies, on its near side—

(*a*) if it is a vehicle falling in paragraph (1)(*a*), (*b*) or (*c*), its unladen weight; and

(*b*) if it is a vehicle falling in paragraph (1)(*d*), its maximum gross weight.

72. Additional markings

(1) This regulation applies to every goods vehicle to which the Plating and Testing Regulations apply and for which a plating certificate has been issued.

(2) Without prejudice to the provisions of regulation 70, any weight which by virtue of regulation 80 may not be exceeded in the case of a goods vehicle to which this regulation applies may be marked on either side, or on both sides, of the vehicle.

(3) Where at any time by virtue of any provision contained in regulation 75 a goods vehicle to which this regulation applies may not be used in excess of a weight which is less than the gross weight which may not be exceeded by that vehicle by virtue of regulation 80, the first mentioned weight may be marked on either side, or on both sides, of the vehicle.

(4) Where at any time by virtue of any provision contained in regulation 76 and 77 a goods vehicle to which this regulation applies is drawing, or being drawn by, another vehicle and those vehicles may not be used together in excess of a laden weight applicable to those vehicles by virtue of any such provision, that weight may be marked on either side, or on both sides, of that goods vehicle.

73. Test date discs

(1) Every Ministry test date disc which is issued, following the issue of a goods vehicle test certificate, in respect of a trailer to which the Plating and Testing Regulations apply and for which a plating certificate has been issued shall be carried on the trailer in a legible condition and in a conspicuous and readily accessible position in which it is clearly visible by daylight from the near side of the road, from the date of its issue until but not beyond the date of expiry of that test certificate or the date of issue of a further test certificate for that trailer, whichever date is the earlier.

(2) In this regulation 'Ministry test date disc' means a plate issued by the Secretary of State for a goods vehicle, being a trailer, following the issue of a goods vehicle test certificate for that trailer under the Plating and Testing Regulations and containing the following particulars—

(*a*) the identification mark allotted to that trailer and shown in that certificate;

(*b*) the date until which that certificate is valid; and

(*c*) the number of the vehicle testing station shown in that certificate.

74. Testing and inspection

(1) Subject to the conditions specified in paragraph (2), the following persons are hereby empowered to test and inspect the brakes, silencers, steering gear and tyres of any vehicle, on any premises where that vehicle is located—

(*a*) a police constable in uniform;

(*b*) a person appointed by the Commissioner of Police of the Metropolis to inspect public carriages for the purposes of the Metropolitan Public Carriage Act 1869;

(*c*) a person appointed by the police authority for a police area to act for the purposes of [section 67 of the 1988 Act];

(*d*) a goods vehicle examiner as defined in [section 68 of the 1988 Act];

(*e*) a certifying officer as defined in section 7(1) of the 1981 Act; and

(*f*) a public service vehicle examiner appointed as mentioned in section 7(2) of the 1981 Act.

(2) Those conditions are—

(*a*) any person empowered as there mentioned shall produce his authorisation if required to do so;

(*b*) no such person shall enter any premises unless the consent of the owner of those premises has first been obtained;

(*c*) no such person shall test or inspect any vehicle on any premises unless—

(i) the owner of the vehicle consents thereto;

(ii) notice has been given to that owner personally or left at his address not less than 48 hours before the time of the proposed test or inspection, or has been sent to him at least 72 hours before that time by the recorded delivery service to his address last known to the person giving the notice; or

(iii) the test or inspection is made within 48 hours of an accident to which [section 170 of the 1988 Act] applies and in which the vehicle was involved.

(3) For the purposes of this regulation, the owner of the vehicle shall be deemed to be in the case of a vehicle—

(*a*) which is for the time being registered under the 1971 Act, and is not being used under a trade licence under that Act the person appearing as the owner of the vehicle in the register kept by the Secretary of State under that Act;

(*b*) used under a trade licence, the holder of the licence; or

(*c*) exempt from excise duty by virtue of the Motor Vehicles (International Circulation) Order 1975 [*SI 1975 No 1208, qv*], the person resident outside the United Kingdom who has brought the vehicle into Great Britain;

and in cases (*a*) and (*b*) the address of the owner as shown on the said register or, as the case may be, on the licence may be treated as his address.

PART IV

Conditions relating to Use

A *Laden Weight*

75. Maximum permitted laden weight of a vehicle

(1) Save as provided in paragraph (2), the laden weight of the vehicle of a class specified in an item in column 2 of the Table shall not exceed the maximum permitted laden weight specified in that item in column 3.

(2) The maximum permitted laden weight of a vehicle first used before 1st June 1973 which falls in item 1 or 2 shall not be less than would be the case if the vehicle fell in item 9.

TABLE

(regulation 75(1))

1	2	3
Item	Class of vehicle	Maximum permitted laden weight (kg)
1	A wheeled heavy motor car or motor car which is not described in items 2, 4 or 5 and which complies with the relevant braking requirement	The weight specified in column (5) of Part I of Schedule 11 in the item which is appropriate, having regard to columns (2), (3) and (4) in that Part
2	A wheeled heavy motor car or motor car (not being an agricultural motor vehicle) which forms part of an articulated vehicle and which complies with the relevant braking requirement	The weight specified in column (5) in Part II of Schedule 11 in the item which is appropriate having regard to columns (2), (3) and (4) in that Part
3	A wheeled trailer, including a composite trailer, but not including a semi-trailer, which is drawn by a motor tractor, heavy motor car or motor car which complies with the relevant braking requirement, other than a trailer described in items 6, 7, 8 or 11	As for item 1
4	A bus	The weight specified in column (5) of Part I of Schedule 11 in the item which is appropriate having regard to columns (2), (3) and (4) in that Part, the laden weight of the bus being calculated in the manner described in regulation 78(3) to (5)
5	A wheeled agricultural motor vehicle	As for item 1, but subject to a maximum of 24,390
6	A balanced agricultural trailer, as defined in paragraph (4), which is not described in items 8, 11 or 16	As for item 1, but subject to a maximum of 18,290
7	An unbalanced agricultural trailer, as defined in paragraph (4) which is not described in items 8, 11 or 16	18,290 inclusive of the weight imposed by the trailer on the drawing vehicle

1	2	3
Item	Class of vehicle	Maximum permitted laden weight (kg)
8	A wheeled trailer manufactured on or after 27th February 1977 and fitted with brakes which automatically come into operation on the over-run of the trailer (whether or not it is fitted with any other brake), except an agricultural trailer which is being drawn by an agricultural motor vehicle, which complies with the requirements specified in items 3, 14 and 17 of Schedule 3 and of which the brakes can be applied either by the driver of the drawing vehicle or by some other person on that vehicle or on the trailer	3,500
9	A wheeled heavy motor car or motor car not described in items 1, 2, 4 or 5— (*a*) with not more than 4 wheels (*b*) with more than 4 but not more than 6 wheels (*c*) with more than 6 wheels	 14,230 20,330 24,390
10	A wheeled trailer not described in items 3, 6, 7, 8 or 11 having less than 6 wheels, and not forming part of an articulated vehicle; and an agricultural trailed appliance	14,230
11	A trailer manufactured before 27th February 1977 and having no brakes other than— (i) a parking brake and (ii) brakes which come into operation on the over-run of the trailer	3,560
12	A wheeled locomotive, not described in item 5, which is equipped with suitable and sufficient springs between each wheel and the vehicle's frame and with a pneumatic tyre or a tyre of soft or elastic material fitted to each wheel—	

1	2	3
Item	Class of vehicle	Maximum permitted laden weight (kg)
	(*a*) if having less than 6 wheels (*b*) if having 6 wheels (*c*) if having more than 6 wheels	22,360 26,420 30,490
13	A track-laying locomotive with resilient material interposed between the rims of the weight-carrying rollers and the road so that the weight of the vehicle (other than that borne by any wheels and the portion of the track in contact with the road) is supported by the resilient material	22,360
14	A locomotive not described in items 5, 12 or 13	20,830
15	A track-laying heavy motor car or motor car	22,360
16	A track-laying trailer	13,210

(3) The maximum total weight of all trailers, whether laden or unladen, drawn at any one time by a locomotive shall not exceed 40,650 kg.

(4) In this regulation and regulation 76—

'balanced agricultural trailer' means an agricultural trailer the whole of the weight of which is borne by its own wheels; and

'unbalanced agricultural trailer' means an agricultural trailer of which some, but not more than 35%, of the weight is borne by the drawing vehicle and the rest of the weight is borne by its own wheels.

76. Maximum permitted laden weight of a vehicle and trailer, other than an articulated vehicle

(1) The total laden weight of a motor vehicle and the trailer or trailers (other than semi-trailers) drawn by it shall not, in a case specified in an item in column 2 of the Table, exceed the maximum permitted train weight specified in that item in column 3.

(2) In this regulation the expression 'unbalanced agricultural trailer' has the meaning given to it in regulation 75.

TABLE

(regulation 76(1))

1	2	3
Item	Vehicle combination	Maximum permitted train weight (kg)
1	A wheeled trailer which is drawn by a wheeled motor tractor, heavy motor car or motor car (not being in any case an agricultural motor vehicle) and which— (*a*) is fitted with power-assisted brakes which can be operated by the driver of the drawing vehicle and are not rendered ineffective by the non-rotation of its engine; and (*b*) is drawn by a vehicle which is equipped with a warning device so placed as to be readily visible to the driver when in the driving seat in order to indicate an impending deficiency or failure in the vacuum or pressure system	32,520
2	A wheeled agricultural motor vehicle drawing a wheeled unbalanced agricultural trailer, if the distance between the rearmost axle of the trailer and the rearmost axle of the drawing vehicle does not exceed 2.9 m	20,000
3	A wheeled trailer or trailers drawn by a wheeled motor tractor, heavy motor car, motor car or agricultural motor vehicle, not being a combination of vehicles mentioned in items 1 or 2	24,390
4	A track-laying trailer drawn by a motor tractor, heavy motor car or motor car, whether wheeled or track-laying and a wheeled trailer, drawn by a track-laying vehicle being a motor tractor, heavy motor car or motor car	22,360

77. Maximum permitted laden weight of an articulated vehicle

(1) Except as provided in paragraph (2), the laden weight of an articulated vehicle of a class specified in an item in column 2 of the Table shall not exceed the weight specified in column 3 in that item.

TABLE

(regulation 77(1))

1	2	3
Item	Class of vehicle	Maximum permitted laden weight (kg)
1	An articulated vehicle which complies with the relevant braking requirement	Whichever is the lower of— (*a*) the weight specified in column (3) of Part III of Schedule 11 in the item in which the spacing between the rearmost axles of the motor vehicle and the semi-trailer is specified in column (2), provided that the weights in items 13 to 18 shall not apply unless the overall length of the articulated vehicle is at least that specified in column (4) in those items; and (*b*) if the vehicle is of a description specified in an item in column (2) of Part IV of Schedule 11, the weight specified in column (3) of that item
2	An articulated vehicle which does not comply with the relevant braking requirement if the trailer has— (*a*) less than 4 wheels (*b*) 4 wheels or more	 20,330 24,390

(2) This regulation does not apply to an agricultural motor vehicle, an agricultural trailer or an agricultural trailed appliance.

78. Maximum permitted wheel and axle weights

(1) The weight transmitted to the road by one or more wheels of a vehicle as mentioned in an item in column 2 of the Table shall not exceed the maximum permitted weight specified in that item in column 3.

(2) The Parts of the Table have the following application—

(*a*) Part I applies to wheeled heavy motor cars, motor cars and trailers which comply with the relevant braking requirement and to wheeled agricultural motor vehicles, agricultural trailers and agricultural trailed appliances; items 1(*b*) and 2 also apply to buses;

(*b*) Part II applies to wheeled heavy motor cars, motor cars and trailers which do not fall in Part I;

(*c*) Part III applies to wheeled locomotives; and

(*d*) Part IV applies to track-laying vehicles.

TABLE

(regulation 78(1))

PART I

(wheeled heavy motor cars, motor cars and trailers which comply with the relevant braking requirement and wheeled agricultural motor vehicles, agricultural trailers and agricultural trailed appliances; and, in respect of items 1(*b*) and 2, buses)

1	2	3
Item	Wheel criteria	Maximum permitted weight (kg)
1	Two wheels in line transversely each of which is fitted with a wide tyre or with two pneumatic tyres having the centres of their areas of contact with the road not less than 300 mm apart, measured at right angles to the longitudinal axis of the vehicle—	
	(*a*) if the wheels are on the sole driving axle of a motor vehicle [not being a bus],	10,500
	(*b*) if the vehicle is a bus which has 2 axles and of which the weight transmitted to the road surface by its wheels is calculated in accordance with regulation 78(5),	10,500
	(*c*) in any other case	10,170
2	Two wheels in line transversely otherwise than as mentioned in item 1	9,200
3	More than two wheels in line transversely—	
	(*a*) in the case of a vehicle manufactured before 1st May 1983 if the wheels are on one axle of a group of two closely spaced axles or on one of three adjacent axles as mentioned in regulation 79(4),	10,170
	(*b*) in the case of a vehicle manufactured on or after 1st May 1983,	10,170
	(*c*) in any other case	11,180

1	2	3
Item	Wheel criteria	Maximum permitted weight (kg)
4	One wheel not transversely in line with any other wheel—	
	(*a*) if the wheel is fitted as described in item 1,	5,090
	(*b*) in any other case	4,600

Part II

(wheeled heavy motor cars, motor cars and trailers not falling in Part I)

1	2	3
Item	Wheel criteria	Maximum permitted weight (kg)
5	More than two wheels transmitting weight to a strip of the road surface on which the vehicle rests contained between two parallel lines at right angles to the longitudinal axis of the vehicle—	
	(*a*) less than 1.02 m apart,	11,180
	(*b*) 1.02 m or more apart but less than 1.22 m apart,	16,260
	(*c*) 1.22 m or more apart but less than 2.13 m apart	18,300
6	Two wheels in line transversely	9,200
7	One wheel, where no other wheel is in the same line transversely	4,600

PART III

(wheeled locomotives)

1	2	3
Item	Wheel criteria	Maximum permitted weight (kg)
8	Two wheels in line transversely (except in the case of a road roller, or a vehicle with not more than four wheels first used before 1st June 1955)	11,180
9	Any two wheels in the case of a wheeled locomotive having not more than four wheels first used before 1st June 1955 (not being a road roller or an agricultural motor vehicle which is not driven at more than 20 mph)	Three quarters of the total weight of the locomotive

PART IV

(track-laying vehicles)

1	2	3
Item	Wheel criteria	Maximum permitted weight (kg)
10	The weight of a heavy motor car, motor car or trailer transmitted to any strip of the road surface on which the vehicle rests contained between two parallel lines 0.6 m apart at right angles to the longitudinal axis of the vehicle	10,170
11	Two wheels in line— (*a*) heavy motor cars or motor cars with 2 wheels, (*b*) heavy motor cars or motor cars with more than 2 wheels	 8,130 7,630
12	One wheel, where no other wheel is in the same line transversely, on a heavy motor car or a motor car	4,070

(3) In the case of an articulated bus, or, subject to paragraph (4), of a bus first used before 1st April 1988, the laden weight, for the purposes of item 4 in the Table in regulation 75, and the weight transmitted to the road surface by wheels of the vehicle, for the purposes of items 1 and 2 of the Table in this regulation, shall be calculated with reference to the vehicle when it is complete and fully equipped for service with—

(*a*) a full supply of water, oil and fuel; and

(*b*) weights of 63.5 kg for each person (including crew)—

(i) for whom a seat is provided in the position in which he may be seated; and

(ii) who may by or under any enactment be carried standing, the total of such weights being reasonably distributed in the space in which such persons may be carried, save that in the case of a bus (not being an articulated bus) only the number of such persons exceeding 8 shall be taken into account.

(4) The weights for the purposes referred to in paragraph (3) may, in the case of a bus to which that paragraph applies, be calculated in accordance with paragraph (5) instead of paragraph (3).

(5) In the case of a bus first used on or after 1st April 1988, the weights for the purposes referred to in paragraph (3) shall be calculated with reference to the vehicle when it is complete and fully equipped for service with—

(*a*) a full supply of water, oil and fuel;

(*b*) a weight of 65 kg for each person (including crew)—

(i) for whom a seat is provided, in the position in which he may be seated; and

(ii) who may by or under any enactment be carried standing, the total of such weights being reasonably distributed in the space in which such persons may be so carried, save that in the case of a bus (not being an articulated bus) only the number of such persons exceeding 4 shall be taken intó account;

(*c*) all luggage space within the vehicle but not with the passenger compartment loaded at the rate of 100 kg per m^3 or 10 kg per person mentioned in sub-paragraph (*b*) above, whichever is the less; and

(*d*) any area of the roof of the vehicle constructed or adapated for the storage of luggage loaded with a uniformly distributed load at the rate of 75 kg per m^2.

[*Regulation 78 is printed as amended by SI 1987 No 676 (with effect from 1 April 1988).*]

79. Maximum permitted weights for certain closely spaced axles, etc

(1) This regulation applies to—

(*a*) a wheeled motor vehicle which complies with the relevant braking requirement;

(*b*) a wheeled trailer which is drawn by such a motor vehicle; and

(*c*) an agricultural motor vehicle, an agricultural trailer and an agricultural trailed appliance.

(2) Save as provided in paragraph (5), where two closely spaced axles of a vehicle to which this regulation applies are spaced at a distance specified in an item in column 2 of Part V of Schedule 11, the total weight transmitted to the road surface by all wheels of those axles shall not exceed in a case—

(*a*) where the weight transmitted to the road surface by all the wheels of either of the axles does not in either case exceed one-half of the weight specified in that item in column 3, the weight so specified;

(*b*) where the weight transmitted to the road surface by all the wheels of one of the axles exceeds one-half of the weight shown in that item in column 3 of that Part but does not exceed 10,170 kg, the weight specified in that item in column 4; or (*c*) other than one mentioned in sub-paragraph (*a*) or (*b*) above, the weight specified in that item in column 5.

(3) Save as provided in [paragraphs (5) and (6)], where any two adjoining axles of three closely spaced axles of a vehicle to which this regulation applies are spaced at such a distance apart as is specified in an item in column 2 of Part VI of Schedule 11, the weight transmitted to the road surface by all the wheels of each of those axles shall not exceed the weight shown in that item in column 3.

(4) Save as provided in [paragraphs (5) and (6)], where—

(*a*) the weight transmitted to the road surface by all the wheels of any one of three adjacent axles of a semi-trailer to which this regulation applies exceeds 7,500 kg;

(*b*) the foremost and rearmost of the three adjacent axles are spaced at a distance specified in an item in column 2 of Part VII of Schedule 11; and

(*c*) the weight transmitted to the road surface by all the wheels of the intermediate axle does not exceed the weight shown in column 3 in that item,

the total weight transmitted to the road surface by all the wheels of those axles shall not exceed the weight shown in column 4 in that item.

(5) Nothing in paragraphs (2), (3) or (4) of this regulation shall apply so as to prevent a vehicle first used before 1st June 1973 from being used on a road at a weight as respects those axles at which it could be used if it fell within item 5 in the Table in regulation 78 and nothing in paragraph (3) of this regulation shall apply so as to prevent a vehicle being used on a road with axle weights shown on the plating certificate issued for the vehicle current on 30th April 1983.

[(6) Nothing in paragraphs (3) or (4) shall apply so as to prevent a semi-trailer being used on a road if—

(*a*) it is a semi-trailer to which this paragraph applies; and

(*b*) the weight transmitted to the road surface by all the wheels of any axle of the semi-trailer does not exceed the relevant weight.]

[(7) Paragraph (6) applies to a semi-trailer if—

(*a*) it has a total of three axles;

(*b*) the outermost axles are spaced at a distance apart of at least 0.7m but not more than 3.25m, such distances being obtained as provided in regulation 3(10);

(*c*) each axle is fitted with suspension devices in which air springs are used to support a substantial part of the weight borne on that axle; and

(*d*) the devices are so interconnected and maintained that under any relevant condition of load the weight transmitted to the road surface by all the wheels of any one axle does not exceed the total weight transmitted to the road surface by all the wheels of any other axle by more than 500 kg.]

[(8) For the purposes of paragraphs (6) and (7), in relation to a semi-trailer any two adjoining axles of which are spaced at such a distance apart as is specified in an item in column 2 of Part VI of Schedule 11

(*a*) 'air spring' means a spring operated by means of air or other compressible fluid under pressure;

(*b*) 'relevant condition of load' means a condition of load which causes the weight transmitted to the road surface by all the wheels of any one axle to exceed the weight shown in column 3 of that item;

(*c*) 'relevant weight' means the weight shown in column 4 of that item.]

[*Regulation 79 is printed as amended by SI 1988 No 1287.*]

80. Over-riding weight restrictions

(1) Subject to paragraph (2), no person shall use, or cause or permit to be used, on a road a vehicle—

(*a*) fitted with a plate in accordance with regulation 66, but for which no plating certificate has been issued, if any of the weights shown on the plate is exceeded;

(*b*) for which a plating certificate has been issued, if any of the weights shown in column (2) of the plating certificate is exceeded; or

(*c*) required by regulation 68 to be fitted with a plate, if the maximum gross weight referred to in paragraph (2)(*c*) of that regulation is exceeded.

(2) Where any two or more axles are fitted with a compensating arrangement in accordance with regulation 23 the sum of the weights shown for them in the plating certificate shall not be exceeded. In a case where a plating certificate has not been issued the sum of the weights referred to shall be that shown for the said axles in the plate fitted in accordance with regulation 66.

(3) Nothing in regulations 75 to 79 shall permit any such weight as is mentioned in the preceding provisions of this regulation to be exceeded and nothing in this regulation shall permit any weight prescribed by regulations 75 to 79 in relation to the vehicle in question to be exceeded.

B *Dimensions of Laden Vehicles*

81. Restrictions on use of vehicles carrying wide or long loads or having fixed appliances or apparatus

For the purpose of this regulation, regulation 82 and Schedule 12—

(*a*) 'lateral projection', in relation to a load carried by a vehicle, means that part of the load which extends beyond a side of the vehicle;

(*b*) the width of any lateral projection shall be measured between longitudinal planes passing through the extreme projecting point of the vehicle on that side on which the projection lies and the part of the projection furthest from that point;

(*c*) references to a special appliance or apparatus, in relation to a vehicle, are references to any crane or other special appliance or apparatus fitted to the vehicle which is a permanent or essentially permanent fixture;

(*d*) 'forward projection' and 'rearward projection'—

(i) in relation to a load carried in such a manner that its weight rests on only one vehicle, mean respectively that part of the load which extends beyond the foremost point of the vehicle and that part which extends beyond the rearmost point of the vehicle;

(ii) in relation to a load carried in such a manner that part of its weight rests on more than one vehicle, mean respectively that part of the load which extends beyond the foremost point of the foremost vehicle by which the load is carried except where the context otherwise requires and that part of the load which extends beyond the rearmost point of the rearmost vehicle by which the load is carried; and

(iii) in relation to any special appliance or apparatus, mean respectively that part of the appliance or apparatus which, if it were deemed to be a load carried by the vehicle, would be a part of a load extending beyond the foremost point of the vehicle and that part which would be a part of a load extending beyond the rearmost point of the vehicle,

and references in regulation 82 and Schedule 12 to a forward projection or to a rearward projection in relation to a vehicle shall be construed accordingly;

(*e*) the length of any forward projection or of any rearward projection shall be measured between transverse planes passing—

(i) in the case of a forward projection, through the foremost point of the vehicle and that part of the projection furthest from that point; and

(ii) in the case of a rearward projection, through the rearmost point of the vehicle and that part of the projection furthest from that point.

In this and the foregoing sub-paragraph 'vehicle' does not include any special appliance or apparatus or any part thereof which is a forward projection or a rearward projection;

(*f*) references to the distance between vehicles, in relation to vehicles carrying a load, are references to the distance between the nearest points of any two adjacent vehicles by which the load is carried, measured when the longitudinal axis of each vehicle lies in the same vertical plane.

For the purposes of this sub-paragraph, in determining the nearest point of two vehicles any part of either vehicle designed primarily for use as a means of attaching the one vehicle to the other and any fitting designed for use in connection with any such part shall be disregarded;

(*g*) references to a combination of vehicles, in relation to a motor vehicle which is drawing one or more trailers, are references to the motor vehicle and the trailer or trailers drawn thereby, including any other motor vehicle which is used for the purpose of assisting in the propulsion of the trailer or the trailers on the road;

(*h*) the overall length of a combination of vehicles shall be taken as the distance between the foremost point of the drawing vehicle comprised in the combination and the rearmost point of the rearmost vehicle comprised therein, measured when the longitudinal axis of each vehicle comprised in the combination lies in the same vertical plane;

(*i*) the extreme projecting point of a vehicle is the point from which the overall width of the vehicle is calculated in accordance with the definition of overall width contained in regulation 3(2);

(*j*) without prejudice to sub-paragraph (*e*) the foremost or, as the case may be, the rearmost point of a vehicle is the foremost or rearmost point from which the overall length of the vehicle is calculated in accordance with the definition of overall length contained in regulation 3(2); and

(*k*) an agricultural, horticultural or forestry implement rigidly but not permanently mounted on an agricultural motor vehicle, agricultural trailer or agricultural trailed appliance, whether or not part of its weight is supported by one or more of its own wheels, shall not be treated as a load, or special appliance, on that vehicle.

82. (1) No load shall be carried on a vehicle so that the overall width of the vehicle together with the width of any lateral projections or projection of its load exceeds 4.3m.

(2) Subject to the following provisions of this regulation, no load shall be carried on a vehicle so that—

(*a*) the load has a lateral projection or projections on either side exceeding 305 mm; or

(*b*) the overall width of the vehicle and of any lateral projection or projections of its load exceeds 2.9 m.

Provided that this paragraph does not apply to the carriage of—

(i) loose agricultural produce not baled or crated; or

(ii) an indivisible load if—

(A) it is not reasonably practicable to comply with this paragraph and the conditions specified in paragraph 1 of Schedule 12 are complied with; and

(B) where the overall width of the vehicle together with the width of any lateral projection or projections of its loads exceeds 3.5 m, the conditions specified in paragraph 2 of Schedule 12 are complied with.

(3) Where a load is carried so that its weight rests on a vehicle or vehicles, the length specified in paragraph (5) shall not exceed 27.4 m.

(4) Where a load is so carried and either—

(*a*) the length specified in paragraph (5) exceeds 18.3 m; or

(*b*) the load rests on a trailer or trailers and the length specified in paragraph (6) exceeds 25.9 m,

the conditions specified in paragraphs 1 and 2 of Part I of Schedule 12 shall be complied with.

(5) The length referred to in paragraphs (3) and (4)(*a*) is—

(*a*) where the load rests on a single vehicle, the overall length of the vehicle together with the length of any forward and rearward projection of the load;

(*b*) where the load rests on a motor vehicle and one trailer, whether or not forming an articulated vehicle, the overall length of the trailer together with the length of any projection of the load in front of the foremost point of the trailer and of any rearward projection of the load; and

(*c*) in any other case, the overall length of all the vehicles on which the load rests, together with the length of any distance between them and of any forward or rearward projection of the load.

(6) The length referred to in paragraph (4)(*b*) is the overall length of the combination of vehicles, together with the length of any forward or rearward projection of the load.

(7) Subject to the following provisions of this regulation no person shall use, or cause or permit to be used, on a road a vehicle, not being a straddle carrier, carrying a load or fitted with a special appliance or apparatus if the load, appliance or apparatus has a forward projection of a length specified in an item in column 2 of the Table, or rearward projection of a length specified in an item in column 3, unless the conditions specified in that item in column 4 are complied with.

TABLE

(regulation 82(7))

1	2	3	4	
Item	Length of forward projection	Length of rearward projection	Conditions to be complied with	
			(a) if the load consists of a racing boat propelled solely by oars	(b) in any other case
1	Exceeding 1 m but not exceeding 2 m	—	Para 4 of Schedule 12	—
2	Exceeding 2 m but not exceeding 3.05 m	—	Para 4 of Schedule 12	Paras 2 and 3 of Schedule 12
3	Exceeding 3.05 m	—	Paras 1 and 4 of Schedule 12	Paras 1, 2 and 3 of Schedule 12
4	—	Exceeding 1 m but not exceeding 2 m	Para 4 of Schedule 12	Para 4 of Schedule 12
5	—	Exceeding 2 m but not exceeding 3.05 m	Para 4 of Schedule 12	Para 3 of Schedule 12
6	—	Exceeding 3.05 m	Paras 1 and 4 of Schedule 12	Paras 1, 2 and 3 of Schedule 12

(8) Subject to the following provisions of this regulation, no person shall use, or cause or permit to be used, on a road a straddle carrier carrying a load if—

(*a*) the load has a rearward projection exceeding 1 m unless the conditions specified in paragraph 4 of Schedule 12 are met;

(*b*) the load has a forward projection exceeding 2 m or a rearward projection exceeding 3 m; or

(*c*) the overall length of the vehicle together with the length of any forward projection and of any rearward projection of its load exceeds 12.2 m

Provided that—

(i) sub-paragraph (*a*) does not apply to a vehicle being used in passing from one part of private premises to another part thereof or to other private premises in the immediate neighbourhood;

(ii) sub-paragraphs (*b*) and (*c*) do not apply to a vehicle being used as in proviso (i) above if—

(A) the vehicle is not being driven at a speed exceeding 12 mph; and

(B) where the overall length of the vehicle together with the length of any forward projection and of any rearward projection of its load exceeds 12.2 m, the conditions specified in paragraphs 1 and 2 of Schedule 12 are complied with.

(9) Where another vehicle is attached to that end of a vehicle from which a projection extends, then for the purposes of any requirement in this regulation to comply

with paragraph 3 or 4 of Schedule 12, that projection shall be treated as a forward or rearward projection only if, and to the extent that it extends beyond the foremost point or, as the case may be, the rearmost point, of that other vehicle, measured when the longitudinal axis of each vehicle lies in the same vertical plane.

(10) In the case of a vehicle being used—

(*a*) for fire brigade, ambulance or police purposes or for defence purposes (including civil defence purposes); or

(*b*) in connection with the removal of any obstruction to traffic,

if compliance with any provision of this regulation would hinder or be likely to hinder the use of the vehicle for the purpose for which it is being used, that provision does not apply to that vehicle while it is being so used.

(11) No person shall use, or cause or permit to be used, on a road an agricultural, horticultural or forestry implement rigidly, but not permanently, mounted on a wheeled agricultural motor vehicle, agricultural trailer, or agricultural trailed appliance, whether or not part of its weight is supported by one or more of its own wheels if—

(*a*) the overall width of the vehicle together with the lateral projection of the implement exceeds 2.5 m; or

(*b*) the implement projects more than 1 m forwards or rearwards of the vehicle,

so however, that this restriction shall not apply in a case where—

(i) part of the weight of the implement is supported by one or more of its own wheels; and

(ii) the longitudinal axis of the greater part of the implement is capable of articulating in the horizontal plane in relation to the longitudinal axis of the rear portion of the vehicle.

C *Trailers and Sidecars*

83. Number of trailers

(1) No person shall use, or cuase or permit to be used, on a road a wheeled vehicle of a class specified in an item in column 2 of the Table drawing a trailer, subject to any exceptions which may be specified in that item in column 3.

TABLE

(regulation 83(1))

1	2	3
Item	Class of vehicles	Exceptions
1	A straddle carrier	—
2	An invalid carriage	—
3	An articulated bus	—
4	A bus not being an articulated bus or a mini-bus	(*a*) 1 broken down bus where no person other than the driver is carried in either vehicle or

1	2	3
Item	Class of vehicles	Exceptions
		(*b*) 1 trailer having an overall length, including the draw-bar, not exceeding 5 m provided that the overall length of the combination does not exceed 15 m
5	A locomotive	3 trailers
6	A motor tractor	1 trailer if laden, 2 trailers if neither is laden
7	A heavy motor car or a motor car not described in items 1, 3 or 4	2 trailers if one of them is a towing implement and part of the other is secured to and either rests on or is suspended from that implement 1 trailer in any other case
8	An agricultural motor vehicle	(*a*) in respect of trailers other than agricultural trailers and agricultural trailed appliances, such trailers as are permitted under items 5, 6 or 7 above, as the case may be; or (*b*) in respect of agricultural trailers and agricultural trailed appliances— (i) 2 unladen agricultural trailers, or (ii) 1 agricultural trailer and 1 agricultural trailed appliance, or (iii) 2 agricultural trailed appliances

(2) For the purposes of items 5, 6 and 7 of the Table—

(*a*) an unladen articulated vehicle, when being drawn by another motor vehicle because it has broken down, shall be treated as a single trailer; and

(*b*) a towed roller used for the purposes of agriculture, horticulture or forestry and consisting of several separate rollers shall be treated as one agricultural trailed appliance.

(3) No track-laying motor vehicle which exceeds 8 m in overall length shall draw a trailer other than a broken down vehicle which is being drawn in consequence of the breakdown.

[(4) For the purpose of this regulation, the word 'trailer' does not include a vehicle which is drawn by a steam powered vehicle and which is used solely for carrying water for the purpose of the drawing vehicle.]

[*Regulation 83 is printed as amended by SI 1987 No 676.*]

84. Trailers drawn by motor cycles

(1) Save as provided in paragraph (2), no person shall use, or cause or permit to be used, on a road a motor cycle—

(*a*) drawing behind it more than one trailer;

(*b*) drawing behind it any trailer carrying a passenger;

(*c*) drawing behind it a trailer with an unladen weight exceeding 254 kg;

(*d*) with not more than 2 wheels, without a sidecar, and with an engine capacity which does not exceed 125 cc, drawing behind it any trailer; or

(*e*) with not more than 2 wheels, without a sidecar and with an engine capacity exceeding 125 cc, drawing behind it any trailer unless—

(i) the trailer has an overall width not exceeding 1 m;

(ii) the distance between the rear axle of the motor cycle and the rearmost part of the trailer does not exceed 2.5 m;

(iii) the motor cycle is clearly and indelibly marked in a conspicuous and readily accessible position with its kerbside weight;

(iv) the trailer is clearly and indelibly marked in a conspicuous and readily accessible position with its unladen weight; and

(v) the laden weight of the trailer does not exceed 150 kg or two-thirds of the kerbside weight of the motor cycle, whichever is the less.

(2) The provisions of paragraph (1)(*b*), (*d*) and (*e*) do not apply if the trailer is a broken down motor cycle and one passenger is riding it.

85. Trailers drawn by agricultural motor vehicles

(1) No person shall use, or cause or permit to be used, on a road a wheeled agricultural motor vehicle drawing one or more wheeled trailers if the weight of the drawing vehicle is less than a quarter of the weight of the trailer or trailers, unless the brakes fitted to each trailer in compliance with regulation 15 or 16 are operated directly by the service braking systems fitted to the motor vehicle.

(2) No person shall use, or cause or permit to be used, on a road any motor vehicle drawing an agricultural trailer of which—

(*a*) more than 35% of the weight is borne by the drawing vehicle; or

(*b*) the gross weight exceeds 14,230 kg, unless it is fitted with brakes as mentioned in paragraph (1).

(3) No person shall use, or cause or permit to be used, on a road an agricultural trailer manufactured on or after 1st December 1985 which is drawn by a motor vehicle first used on or after 1st June 1986 unless the brakes fitted to the trailer—

(*a*) in accordance with regulation 15 can be applied progressively by the driver of the drawing vehicle, from his normal driving position and while keeping proper control of that vehicle, using a means of operation mounted on the drawing vehicle; or

(*b*) automatically come into operation on the over-run of the trailer.

86. Distance between motor vehicles and trailers

(1) Where a trailer is attached to the vehicle immediately in front of it solely by means of a rope or chain, the distance between the trailer and that vehicle shall not in any case exceed 4.5 m; and shall not exceed 1.5 m unless the rope or chain is made clearly visible to any other person using the road within a reasonable distance from either side.

(2) For the purpose of determining the said distance any part of either vehicle designed primarily for use as a means of attaching the one vehicle to the other and any fitting designed for use in connection with any such part shall be disregarded.

87. Unbraked trailers

(1) Save as provided in paragraph (2), no person shall use, or cause or permit to be used, on a road an unbraked wheeled trailer if—

(*a*) its laden weight exceeds its maximum gross weight; or

(*b*) it is drawn by a vehicle of which the kerbside weight is less than twice the sum of the unladen weight of the trailer and the weight of any load which the trailer is carrying.

(2) This regulation does not apply to—

(*a*) an agricultural trailer; or

(*b*) a trailer mentioned in [paragraphs (*b*) (excluding sub-paragraph (ii)) to (*g*) of regulation 16(3)].

[*Regulation 87 is printed as amended by SI 1987 No 676.*]

88. Use of bridging plates between motor vehicle and trailer

(1) Save as provided in paragraph (2), no person shall use or cause or permit to be used on a road a motor vehicle constructed for the purpose of carrying other vehicles or any trailer constructed for that purpose so that while such vehicle or trailer is on a road any part of the weight of any vehicle which is being carried rests on a plate of a kind mentioned in paragraph (*h*) in the definition in regulation 3(2) of 'overall length'.

(2) The provisions of paragraph (1) do not apply—

(*a*) while the motor vehicle or trailer constructed for the purpose of carrying other vehicles is being loaded or unloaded; or

(*b*) if the plate is folded or withdrawn so that it does not bridge the gap between the motor vehicle and the trailer.

89. Leaving trailers at rest

No person in charge of a motor vehicle, or trailer drawn thereby, shall cause or permit such trailer to stand on a road when detached from the drawing vehicle unless one at least of the wheels of the trailer is (or, in the case of a track-laying trailer, its tracks are) prevented from revolving by the setting of the brake or the use of a chain, chock or other efficient device.

90. Passengers in trailers

(1) Save as provided in paragraph (2), no person shall use, or cause or permit to be used, on a road any trailer for the carriage of passengers for hire or reward.

(2) The provisions of paragraph (1) do not apply in respect of a wheeled trailer which is, or is carrying, a broken down motor vehicle if—

(*a*) the trailer is drawn at a speed not exceeding 30 mph; and

(*b*) where the trailer is, or is carrying, a broken down bus, it is attached to the drawing vehicle by a rigid draw bar.

(3) Save as provided in paragraph (4), no person shall use, or cause or permit to be used, on a road a wheeled trailer in which any person is carried and which is a living van having either—

(*a*) less than 4 wheels; or

(*b*) 4 wheels consisting of two close-coupled wheels on each side.

(4) The provisions of paragraph (3) do not apply in respect of a trailer which is being tested by—

(*a*) its manufacturer;

(*b*) a person by whom it has been, or is being, repaired; or

(*c*) a distributor of, or dealer in, trailers.

91. Attendants on trailers and certain other vehicles *[Revoked by the Road Traffic (Consequential Provisions) Act 1988.]*

92. Attachment of sidecars

Every sidecar fitted to a motor cycle shall be so attached that the wheel thereof is not wholly outside the space between transverse planes passing through the extreme projecting points at the front and at the rear of the motor cycle.

93. Use of sidecars

No person shall use or cause or permit to be used on a road any two-wheeled motor cycle registered on or after 1st August 1981, not being a motor cycle brought temporarily into Great Britain by a person resident abroad, if there is a sidecar attached to the right (or off) side of the motor cycle.

D *Use of Gas Propulsion Systems and Gas-fired Appliances*

94. Use of gas propulsion systems

(1) No person shall use, or cause or permit to be used, on a road a vehicle with a gas propulsion system unless the whole of such system is in a safe condition.

(2) No person shall use, or cause or permit to be used, in any gas supply system for the propulsion of a vehicle when the vehicle is on a road any fuel except liquefied petroleum gas.

(3) No person shall use, or cause or permit to be used, on a road a vehicle which is propelled by gas unless the gas container in which such fuel is stored is on the motor vehicle, and not on any trailer, and in the case of an articulated vehicle on the portion of the vehicle to which the engine is fitted.

(4) In this regulation and in regulation 95 'liquefied petroleum gas' means—

(*a*) butane gas in any phase which meets the requirements contained in the specification of commercial butane and propane issued by the British Standards Institution under the number BS4250:1975 published on 29th August 1975; or

(*b*) propane gas in any phase which meets the requirements contained in the said specification; or

(*c*) any mixture of such butane gas and such propane gas.

95. Use of gas-fired appliances—general

(1) No person shall use, or cause or permit to be used, in or on a vehicle on a road any gas-fired appliance unless the whole of such appliance and the gas system attached thereto is in an efficient and safe condition.

(2) No person shall use, or cause or permit to be used, in any gas-fired appliance in or on a vehicle on a road any fuel except liquefied petroleum gas as defined in regulation 94(4).

(3) No person shall use, or cause or permit to be used, in or on a vehicle on a road any gas-fired appliance unless the vehicle is so ventilated that—

(*a*) an ample supply of air is available for the operation of the appliance;

(*b*) the use of the appliance does not adversely affect the health or comfort of any person using the vehicle; and

(*c*) any unburnt gas is safely disposed of to the outside of the vehicle.

(4) No person shall use, or cause or permit to be used, on a road a vehicle in or on which there is—

(*a*) one gas-fired appliance unless the gas supply for such appliance is shut off at the point where it leaves the container or containers at all times when the appliance is not in use;

(*b*) more than one gas-fired appliance each of which has the same supply of gas unless the gas supply for such appliances is shut off at the point where it leaves the container or containers at all times when none of such appliances is in use; or

(*c*) more than one gas-fired appliance each of which does not have the same supply of gas unless each gas supply for such appliances is shut off at the point where it leaves the container or containers at all times when none of such appliances which it supplies is in use.

96. Use of gas-fired appliances when a vehicle is in motion

(1) Subject to paragraph (2), this regulation applies to every motor vehicle and trailer.

(2) Paragraphs (3) and (4) do not apply to a vehicle constructed or adapted for the conveyance of goods under controlled temperatures.

(3) No person shall use, or cause or permit to be used, in any vehicle to which this paragraph applies, while the vehicle is in motion on a road, any gas-fired appliance except—

(*a*) a gas-fired appliance which is fitted to engineering plant while the plant is being used for the purposes of the engineering operations for which it was designed;

(*b*) a gas-fired appliance which is permanently attached to a bus, provided that any appliance for heating or cooling the interior of the bus for the comfort of the driver and any passengers does not expose a naked flame on the outside of the appliance; or

(*c*) in any other vehicle, a refrigerating appliance or an appliance which does not expose a naked flame on the outside of the appliance and which is permanently attached to the vehicle and designed for the purpose of heating any part of the interior of the vehicle for the comfort of the driver and any passengers.

(4) No person shall use, or cause or permit to be used, in any vehicle to which this paragraph applies, while the vehicle is in motion on a road, any gas-fired appliance to which—

(*a*) sub-paragraph (3)(*a*) refers, unless the appliance complies with the requirements specified in paragraphs 12 and 13 Schedule 5 and the gas system to which it is attached complies with the requirements specified in paragraphs 2 to 9 and 15 of Schedule 5; or

(*b*) sub-paragraph (3)(*b*) refers, unless the appliance complies with the requirements specified in paragraphs 12, 13 and 14 of Schedule 5 and the gas system to which it is attached complies with the requirements specified in paragraphs 2 to 9, 11 and 15 of Schedule 5; or

(*c*) sub-paragraph (3)(*c*) refers, unless the appliance complies—

(i) if it is fitted to a motor vehicle, with the requirements specified in paragraphs 12, 13 and 14 of Schedule 5; and

(ii) in any other case, with the requirements specified in paragraphs 12 and 13 of Schedule 5;

and the gas system to which the appliance is attached complies with the requirements specified in paragraphs 2 to 9 and 15 of Schedule 5.

(5) No person shall use, or cause or permit to be used, in a vehicle to which this regulation applies which is in motion on a road any gas-fired appliance unless it is fitted with a valve which stops the supply of gas to the appliance if the appliance fails to perform its function and causes gas to be emitted.

E *Control of Noise*

97. Avoidance of excessive noise

No motor vehicle shall be used on a road in such manner as to cause any excessive noise which could have been avoided by the exercise of reasonable care on the part of the driver.

98. Stopping of engine when stationary

(1) Save as provided in paragraph (2), the driver of a vehicle shall, when the vehicle is stationary, stop the action of any machinery attached to or forming part of the vehicle so far as may be necessary for the prevention of noise.

(2) The provisions of paragraph (1) do not apply—

(*a*) when the vehicle is stationary owing to the necessities of traffic;

(*b*) so as to prevent the examination or working of the machinery where the examination is necessitated by any failure or derangement of the machinery or where the machinery is required to be worked for a purpose other than driving the vehicle; or

(*c*) in respect of a vehicle propelled by gas produced in plant carried on the vehicle, to such plant.

99. Use of audible warning instruments

(1) Subject to the following paragraphs, no person shall sound, or cause or permit to be sounded, any horn, gong, bell or siren fitted to or carried on a vehicle which is—

(*a*) stationary on a road, at any time, other than at times of danger due to another moving vehicle on or near the road; or

(*b*) in motion on a restricted road, between 23.30 hours and 07.00 hours in the following morning.

(2) The provisions of paragraph (1)(*a*) do not apply in respect of the sounding of a reversing alarm when the vehicle to which it is fitted is about to move backwards and its engine is running.

(3) No person shall sound, or cause or permit to be sounded, on a road any reversing alarm fitted to a vehicle—

(*a*) unless the vehicle is a goods vehicle which has a maximum gross weight not less than 2000 kg, a bus, engineering plant, [a refuse vehicle,] or a works truck; or (*b*) if the sound of the alarm is likely to be confused with a sound emitted in the operation of a pedestrian crossing established, or having effect as if established, under Part III of the 1984 Act.

(4) Subject to the provisions of the following paragraphs, no person shall sound, or cause or permit to be sounded a gong, bell, siren or two-tone horn, fitted to or otherwise carried on a vehicle (whether it is stationary or not).

(5) Nothing in paragraph (1) or (4) shall prevent the sounding of—

(*a*) an instrument or apparatus fitted to, or otherwise carried on, a vehicle at a time when the vehicle is being used for one of the purposes specified in regulation 37(5) and it is necessary or desirable to do so either to indicate to other road users the urgency of the purposes for which the vehicle is being used, or to warn other road users of the presence of the vehicle on the road; or

(*b*) a horn (not being a two-tone horn), bell, gong or siren—

(i) to raise alarm as to the theft or attempted theft of the vehicle or its contents, or

(ii) in the case of a bus, to summon help for the driver, the conductor or an inspector.

(6) Subject to the provisions of section 62 of the Control of Pollution Act 1974 and notwithstanding the provisions of paragraphs (1) and (4) above, a person may, between 12.00 hours and 19.00 hours, sound or cause or permit to be sounded an instrument or apparatus, other than a two-tone horn, fitted to or otherwise carried on a vehicle, being an instrument or apparatus designed to emit a sound for the purpose of informing members of the public that the vehicle is conveying goods of sale, if when the apparatus or instrument is sounded, it is sounded only for that purpose.

(7) For the purposes of this regulation the expressions which are referred to in regulation 37(10) have the meanings there given to them and the expression 'restricted road' in paragraph (1) means a road which is a restricted road for the purpose of section 81 of the 1984 Act [*qv*].

[Regulation 99 is printed as amended by SI 1987 No 676.
The Control of Pollution Act 1974, s 62, regulates the use of loudspeakers in streets.]

F *Avoidance of Danger*

100. Maintenance and use of vehicle so as not to be a danger, etc

(1) A motor vehicle, every trailer drawn thereby and all parts and accessories of such vehicle and trailer shall at all times be in such condition, and the number of passengers carried by such vehicle or trailer, the manner in which any passengers are carried in or on such vehicle or trailer, and the weight, distribution, packing and adjustment of the load of such vehicle or trailer shall at all times be such, that no danger is caused or is likely to be caused to any person in or on the vehicle or trailer or on a road.

Provided that the provisions of this regulation with regard to the number of passengers carried shall not apply to a vehicle to which the Public Service Vehicles (Carrying Capacity) Regulations 1984 [*SI 1984 No 1406, qv*] apply.

(2) The load carried by a motor vehicle or trailer shall at all times be so secured, if necessary by physical restraint other than its own weight, and be in such a position, that neither danger nor nuisance is likely to be caused to any person or property by reason of the load or any part thereof falling or being blown from the vehicle or by reason of any other movement of the load or any part thereof in relation to the vehicle.

(3) No motor vehicle or trailer shall be used for any purpose for which it is so

unsuitable as to cause or be likely to cause danger or nuisance to any person in or on the vehicle or trailer or on a road.

101. Parking in darkness

(1) Save as provided in paragraph (2) no person shall, except with the permission of a police officer in a uniform, cause or permit any motor vehicle to stand on a road at any time between half an hour after sunset and half an hour before sunrise unless the near side of the vehicle is as close as may be to the edge of the carriageway.

(2) The provisions of paragraph (1) do not apply in respect of any motor vehicle—

(*a*) being used for fire brigade, ambulance or police purposes or for defence purposes (including civil defence purposes) if compliance with those provisions would hinder or be likely to hinder the use of the vehicle for the purpose for which it is being used on that occasion;

(*b*) being used in connection with—

(i) any building operation or demolition;

(ii) the repair of any other vehicle;

(iii) the removal of any obstruction to traffic;

(iv) the maintenance, repair or reconstruction of any road; or

(v) the laying, erection, alteration or repair in or near to any road of any sewer, main pipe or apparatus for the supply of gas, water or electricity, of any telecommunication apparatus as defined in Schedule 2 to the Telecommunication Act 1984 [*qv*] or of the apparatus of any electric transport undertaking;

if, in any such case, compliance with those provisions would hinder or be likely to hinder the use of the vehicle for the purpose for which it is being used on that occasion;

(*c*) on any road in which vehicles are allowed to proceed in one direction only;

(*d*) standing on a part of a road set aside for the parking of vehicles or as a stand for hackney carriages or as a stand for buses or as a place at which such vehicles may stop for a longer time than is necessary for the taking up and setting down of passengers where compliance with those provisions would conflict with the provisions of any order, regulations or byelaws governing the use of such part of a road for that purpose; or

(*e*) waiting to set down or pick up passengers in accordance with regulations made or directions given by a chief officer of police in regard to such setting down or picking up.

102. Passengers on motor cycles

If any person in addition to the driver is carried astride a two-wheeled motor cycle on a road (whether a sidecar is attached to it or not) suitable supports or rests for the feet shall be available on the motor cycle for that person.

103. Obstruction

No person in charge of a motor vehicle or trailer shall cause or permit the vehicle to stand on a road so as to cause any unnecessary obstruction of the road.

104. Driver's control

No person shall drive or cause or permit any other person to drive, a motor vehicle on a road if he is in such a position that he cannot have proper control of the vehicle or have a full view of the road and traffic ahead.

105. Opening of doors

No person shall open, or cause or permit to be opened, any door of a vehicle on a road so as to injure or endanger any person.

106. Reversing

No person shall drive, or cause or permit to be driven, a motor vehicle backwards on a road further than may be requisite for the safety or reasonable convenience of the occupants of the vehicle or other traffic, unless it is a road roller or is engaged in the construction, maintenance or repair of the road.

107. Leaving motor vehicles unattended

(1) Save as provided in paragraph (2), no person shall leave or cause or permit to be left, on a road a motor vehicle which is not attended by a person licensed to drive it unless the engine is stopped and any parking brake with which the vehicle is required to be equipped is effectively set.

(2) The requirement specified in paragraph (1) as to the stopping of the engine shall not apply in respect of a vehicle—

(*a*) being used for ambulance, fire brigade or police purposes; or

(*b*) in such a position and condition as not to be likely to endanger any person or property and engaged in an operation which requires its engine to be used to—

(i) drive machinery forming part of, or mounted on, the vehicle and used for purposes other than driving the vehicle; or

(ii) maintain the electrical power of the batteries of the vehicle at a level required for driving that machinery or apparatus.

(3) In this regulation 'parking brake' means a brake fitted to a vehicle in accordance with requirement 16 or 18 in Schedule 3.

108. Securing of suspended implements

Where a vehicle is fitted with any apparatus or appliance designed for lifting and part of the apparatus or appliance consists of a suspended implement, the implement shall at all times while the vehicle is in motion on a road and when the implement is not attached to any load supported by the appliance or apparatus be so secured either to the appliance or apparatus or to some part of the vehicle that no danger is caused or is likely to be caused to any person on the vehicle or on the road.

109. Television sets

(1) No person shall drive, or cause or permit to be driven, a motor vehicle on a road, if the driver is in such a position as to be able to see, whether directly or by reflection, a television receiving apparatus or other cinematographic apparatus used to display anything other than information—

(*a*) about the state of the vehicle or its equipment;

(*b*) about the location of the vehicle and the road on which it is located;

(*c*) to assist the driver to see the road adjacent to the vehicle; or

(*d*) to assist the driver to reach his destination.

(2) In this regulation 'television receiving apparatus' means any cathode ray tube carried on a vehicle and on which there can be displayed an image derived from a television broadcast, a recording or a camera or computer.

SCHEDULE 1

REGULATIONS REVOKED BY REGULATION 2 *[Omitted.]*

SCHEDULE 2 (See regulation 3)

Community Directives and ECE Regulations

Table I

Community Directives

1	2	3				4	
Item	Reference No	Community Directives				Item No in Schedule 1 to—	
		(a) Date	(b) Official Journal Reference	(c) Subject matter	(d) Previous Directives included	(a) The Type Approval (Great Britain) Regulations	(b) The Type Approval for Goods Vehicles Regulations
1	70/157	6.2.70	L42, 23.2.70, p. 16	The permissible sound level and the exhaust system of motor vehicles			
2	70/220	20.3.70	L76, 6.4.70, p. 1	Measures to be taken against air pollution by gases from spark ignition engines of motor vehicles			
3	70/221	20.3.70	L76, 6.4.70, p. 23	Liquid fuel tanks and rear protective devices for motor vehicles and their trailers			
4	70/388	27.7.70	L176, 10.8.70, p. 12	Audible warning devices for motor vehicles			
5	71/127	1.3.71	L68, 22.3.71, p. 1	The rear-view mirrors of motor vehicles		10	
6	71/320	26.9.71	L202, 6.9.71, p. 37	The braking devices of certain categories of motor vehicles and their trailers			

7	72/245	20.6.72	L152, 6.7.72, p. 15	The suppression of radio interference produced by spark ignition engines fitted to motor vehicles		2A	5A
8	72/306	2.8.72	L190, 20.8.72, p. 1	The emission of pollutants from diesel engines for use in vehicles		5	3
9	73/350	7.11.73	L321, 22.11.73, p. 33	The permissible sound level and the exhaust system of motor vehicles	70/157		4A
10	74/132	11.2.74	L74, 19.3.74, p. 7	The braking devices of certain categories of motor vehicles and their trailers	71/320		
11	74/151	4.3.74	L84, 28.3.74, p. 25	Parts and characteristics of agricultural motor vehicles (see Note 1)			
12	74/290	28.5.74	L159, 15.6.74, p. 61	Measures to be taken against air pollution by gases from spark ignition engines for motor vehicles	70/220		
13	74/346	25.6.74	L191, 15.7.74, p. 1	Rear view mirrors for agricultural motor vehicles (see Note 1)			
14	74/347	25.6.74	L191, 15.7.74, p. 1	Field of vision and windscreen wipers for agricultural motor vehicles (see Note 1)			
15	74/483	17.9.74	L266, 2.10.74, p. 4	External projections of motor vehicles		19	
16	75/322	20.5.75	L147, 9.6.75, p. 28	Suppression of radio interference from spark ignition engines of agricultural motor vehicles (see Note 1)			

1	2	3				4	
Item	Reference No	Community Directives				Item No in Schedule 1 to—	
		(a) Date	(b) Official Journal Reference	(c) Subject matter	(d) Previous Directives included	(a) The Type Approval (Great Britain) Regulations	(b) The Type Approval for Goods Vehicles Regulations
17	75/443	26.6.75	L196, 26.7.75, p. 1	Reverse and speedometer equipment of motor vehicles		20	
18	75/524	25.7.75	L236, 8.9.75, p. 3	The braking devices of certain categories of motor vehicles and their trailers	71/320 as amended by 74/132	13A	
19	76/114	18.12.75	L24, 30.1.76, p. 1	Statutory plates and inscriptions for motor vehicles and trailers			
20	76/115	18.12.75	L24, 30.1.76, p. 6	Anchorages for motor vehicle seat belts		12A	
21	76/432	6.4.76	L122, 8.5.76, p. 1	Braking devices of agricultural vehicles (see Note 1)			
22	77/102	30.11.76	L32, 3.2.77, p. 32	Measures to be taken against air pollution by gases from spark ignition engines of motor vehicles	70/220 as amended by 74/290		
23	77/212	8.3.77	L66, 12.3.77, p. 33	The permissible sound level and the exhaust system of motor vehicles	70/157 as amended by 73/350	14B	4B, 4C, 4D
24	77/537	28.6.77	L220, 29.8.77, p. 38	Emission of pollution from diesel engines for agricultural motor vehicles (see Note 1)			

25	77/541	28.6.77	L220, 29.8.77, p. 95	Seat belts and restraint systems for motor vehicles		12A	
26	77/649	27.9.77	L267, 19.10.77, p. 1	Field of vision of motor vehicle drivers			
27	78/318	21.12.77	L81, 28.3.78, p. 49	Wiper and washer systems of motor vehicles		22	
28	78/507	19.5.78	L155, 13.6.78, p. 31	Statutory plates and inscriptions for motor vehicles and trailers	76/114		
29	78/549	12.6.78	L168, 26.6.78, p. 45	Wheel guards of motor vehicles			
30	78/665	14.7.78	L223, 14.8.78, p. 48	Measures to be taken against air pollution by gases from spark ignition engines of motor vehicles	70/220 as amended by 74/290 and 77/102	4B, 4C	2
31	78/1015	23.11.78	L349, 13.12.78, p. 21	The permissible sound level and exhaust system of motorcycles			
32	79/488	18.4.79	L128, 26.5.79, p. 1	External projections of motor vehicles	74/483	19A	
33	79/489	18.4.79	L128, 26.5.79, p. 12	The braking devices of certain categories of motor vehicles and their trailers	71/320 as amended by 74/132 and 75/524	13B	
34	79/490	18.4.79	L128, 26.5.79, p. 22	Liquid fuel tanks and rear under-run protection	70/221		6, 6C
35	79/795	20.7.79	L239, 22.9.79, p. 1	The rear-view mirrors of motor vehicles	71/127	10A	
36	79/1073	22.11.79	L331, 27.12.79, p. 20	Field of vision and windscreen wipers for agricultural motor vehicles	74/347		

1	2	3				4	
Item	Reference No	Community Directives				Item No in Schedule 1 to—	
		(a) Date	(b) Official Journal Reference	(c) Subject matter	(d) Previous Directives included	(a) The Type Approval (Great Britain) Regulations	(b) The Type Approval for Goods Vehicles Regulations
37	80/780	22.7.80	L229, 30.8.80, p. 49	Rear view mirrors for motor cycles			
38	80/1269	16.12.80	L375, 31.12.80, p. 46	The engine power of motor vehicles			
39	81/334	13.4.81	L131, 18.5.81, p. 6	The permissible sound level and exhaust system of motor vehicles	70/157 as amended by 73/350 and 77/212	14C	4B, 4C, 4D
40	81/575	29.7.81	L209, 29.7.81, p. 30	Anchorages for motor vehicle seat belts	76/115	12A	
41	81/576	29.7.81	L209, 29.7.81, p. 32	Seat belts and restraint systems for motor vehicles	77/541	12A	
42	81/643	29.7.81	L231, 15.8.81, p. 41	Field of vision of motor vehicle drivers	77/649		
43	82/318	2.4.82	L139, 19.5.82, p. 9	Anchorages for motor vehicle seat belts	76/115 as amended by 81/575	12A	
44	82/319	2.4.82	L139, 19.5.82, p. 17	Seat belts and restraint systems for motor vehicles	77/541 as amended by 81/576	12A	
45	82/890	17.12.82	L378, 31.12.82, p. 45	Agricultural motor vehicles			

46	83/351	16.6.83	L197, 20.7.82, p. 1	Air pollution by gases from positive ignition engines of motor vehicles	70/220 as amended by 74/290, 77/102 and 78/665	4C	
47	84/372	3.7.84	L196, 26.7.84, p. 47	The permissible sound level and exhaust system of motor vehicles	70/157 as amended by 73/350, 77/212 and 81/334		
48	84/424	3.9.84	L238, 6.9.84, p. 31	The permissible sound level and exhaust system of motor vehicles	70/157 as amended by 73/350, 77/212, 81/334 and 84/372		
49	85/205	18.2.85	L90, 29.3.85, p. 1	Mirrors	71/127 as amended by 79/795	10B	
[49A	85/210	20.3.85	L96, 3.4.85, p. 25	The lead content of petrol]			
[50	85/657	23.12.85	L380, 31.12.85, p. 1	The braking devices of certain motor vehicles and their trailers	71/320 as amended by 74/132, 75/524 and 79/489]		
[51	86/562	6.11.86	L327, 27.11.86, p. 49	Mirrors	71/127 as amended by 79/795 and 85/205]		

1	2	3				4	
Item	Reference No	Community Directives				Item No in Schedule 1 to—	
		(a) Date	(b) Official Journal Reference	(c) Subject matter	(d) Previous Directives included	(a) The Type Approval (Great Britain) Regulations	(b) The Type Approval for Goods Vehicles Regulations
[52	88/76	3.12.87	L36, 9.2.88, p. 1	Measures to be taken against air pollution by gases from the engines of motor vehicles	70/220 as amended by 74/290, 77/102, 78/665, and 83/351	4D	2B]

NOTE 1. This item is to be interpreted as including reference to the amendments made by Community Directive 82/890 (item 45).

[*Table I in Sched 2 is printed as amended by SI 1987 No 676; SI 1988 Nos 1178 and 1524.*]

Table II

ECE REGULATIONS

1	2	3				4	
Item	Reference No	ECE Regulations				Item No in Schedule 1 to—	
		(a) Number	(b) Date	(c) Subject matter	(d) Date of amendment	(a) The Type Approval (Great Britain) Regulations	(b) The Type Approval for Goods Vehicles Regulations
1	10	10	17.12.68	Radio interference suppression	—	2	5
2	10.01	10	17.12.68	Radio interference suppression	19.3.78	2A	5A
3	13.03	13	29.5.69	Brakes	4.1.79	13C, 13D	6A, 6B, 6D
4	13.04	13	29.5.69	Brakes	11.8.81	13C, 13D	6A, 6B, 6D
5	13.05	13	29.5.69	Brakes	26.11.84	—	—
6	14.01	14	30.1.70	Anchorages for seat belts	28.4.76	12A	—
7	15.03	15	11.3.70	Emission of gaseous pollutants	6.3.78	4B	—
8	15.04	15	11.3.70	Emission of gaseous pollutants	20.10.81	4C	2
9	16.03	16	14.8.70	Seat belts and restraint systems	9.12.79	12A	2
10	24.01	24	23.8.71	Emission of pollutants by a diesel engine	11.9.73	5	—
11	24.02	24	23.8.71	Emission of pollutants by a diesel engine	11.2.80	5A	3
12	24.03	24	23.8.71	Emission of pollutants by a diesel engine	20.4.86	—	3A
13	26.01	26	28.4.72	External projections	11.9.73	19	—
14	34	34	25.7.75	Prevention of fire risks	—	—	—
15	34.01	34	25.7.75	Prevention of fire risks	18.1.79	—	—
16	36	36	21.11.75	Construction of public service vehicles	—	—	—
17	39	39	11.7.78	Speedometers	—	20	—
18	43	43	15.9.80	Safety glass and glazing materials	—	15B	—
19	43.0[illegible]	43	15.9.80	Safety glass and glazing materials	12.11.82	15B	—
20	44	44	1.2.81	Child restraints	—	—	—
21	44.0[illegible]	44	1.2.81	Child restraints	1.2.84	—	—
22	64	64	1.8.85	Vehicles with temporary-use spare wheels/tyres	—	—	—

SCHEDULE 3 (see regulation 16)

Braking Requirements

1. The braking requirements referred to in regulation 16(4) are set out in the Table and are to be interpreted in accordance with paragraphs 2 to 5 of this Schedule.

Table

(Schedule 3)

Number	Requirement
1	The vehicle shall be equipped with— (*a*) one efficient braking system having two means of operation; (*b*) one efficient split braking system having one means of operation; or (*c*) two efficient braking systems each having a separate means of operation, and in the case of a vehicle first used on or after 1st January 1968, no account shall be taken of a multi-pull means of operation unless, at first application, it operates a hydraulic, electric or pneumatic device which causes the application of brakes with total braking efficiency not less than 25%.
2	The vehicle shall be equipped with— (*a*) one efficient braking system having two means of operation; or (*b*) two efficient braking systems each having a separate means of operation.
3	The vehicle shall be equipped with an efficient braking system.
4	The braking system shall be so designed that in the event of failure of any part (other than a fixed member or a brake shoe anchor pin) through or by means of which the force necessary to apply the brakes is transmitted, there shall still be available for application by the driver brakes sufficient under the most adverse conditions to bring the vehicle to rest within a reasonable distance. The brakes so available shall be applied to— (*a*) in the case of a track-laying vehicle, one track on each side of the vehicle; (*b*) in the case of a wheeled motor vehicle, one wheel if the vehicle has 3 wheels and otherwise to at least half the wheels; and (*c*) in the case of a wheeled trailer, at least one wheel if it has only 2 wheels and otherwise at least 2 wheels. This requirement applies to the braking systems of both a trailer and the vehicle by which it is being drawn except that if the drawing vehicle complies with regulation 15, Community Directive 79/489 [or 85/647] or ECE Regulation 13.03, 13.04, or 13.05, the requirement applies only to the braking system of the drawing vehicle. It does not apply to vehicles having split braking systems (which are subject to regulation 18(3)(*b*)) or to road rollers. (The expressions 'part' and 'half the wheels' are to be interpreted in accordance with paragraphs (3) and (4) respectively.)

Number	Requirement
5	The braking system shall be so designed and constructed that, in the event of the failure of any part thereof, there shall still be available for application by the driver a brake sufficient under the most adverse conditions to bring the vehicle to rest within a reasonable distance.
6	The braking system of a vehicle, when drawing a trailer which complies with regulation 15, Community Directive 79/489 [or 85/647] or ECE Regulation 13.03, 13.04 or 13.05, shall be so constructed that, in the event of a failure of any part (other than a fixed member or brake shoe anchor pin) of the service braking system of the drawing vehicle (excluding the means of operation of a split braking system) the driver can still apply brakes to at least one wheel of the trailer, if it has only 2 wheels, and otherwise to at least 2 wheels, by using the secondary braking system of the drawing vehicle. (The expression 'part' is to be interpreted in accordance with paragraph 3.)
7	The application of any means of operation of a braking system shall not affect or operate the pedal or hand lever of any other means of operation.
8	The braking system shall not be rendered ineffective by the non-rotation of the engine of the vehicle or, in the case of a trailer, the engine of the drawing vehicle (steam-propelled vehicles, other than locomotives and buses, are excluded from this requirement).
9	At least one means of operation shall be capable of causing brakes to be applied directly, and not through the transmission gear, to at least half the wheels of the vehicle. This requirement does not apply to a works truck with an unladen weight not exceeding 7370 kg, or to an industrial tractor; and it does not apply to a vehicle with more than 4 wheels if— (*a*) the drive is transmitted to all wheels other than the steering wheels without the interposition of a differential driving gear or similar mechanism between the axles carrying the driving wheels; and (*b*) the brakes applied by one means of operation apply directly to 2 driving wheels on opposite sides of the vehicle; and (*c*) the brakes applied by another means of operation act directly on all the other driving wheels. (The expression 'half the wheels' is to be interpreted in accordance with paragraph (4).)
10	The brakes of a trailer shall come into operation automatically on its overrun or, in the case of a track-laying trailer drawn by a vehicle having steerable wheels at the front or a wheeled trailer, the driver of, or some other person on, the drawing vehicle or on the trailer shall be able to apply the brakes on the trailer.
11	The brakes of a trailer shall come into operation automatically on its overrun or the driver of the drawing vehicle shall be able to apply brakes to all the wheels of the trailer, using the means of operation which applies the service brakes of the drawing vehicle.

Number	Requirement
12	The brakes of the vehicle shall apply to all wheels other than the steering wheels.
13	The brakes of the vehicle shall apply to at least 2 wheels.
14	The brakes of the vehicle shall apply in the case of a wheeled vehicle to at least 2 wheels if the vehicle has no more than 4 wheels and to at least half the wheels if the vehicle has more than 4 wheels; and in the case of a track-laying vehicle to all the tracks.
15	The brakes shall apply to all the wheels.
16	The parking brake shall be so designed and constructed that— (*a*) in the case of a wheeled heavy motor car or motor car, its means of operation is independent of the means of operation of any split braking system with which the vehicle is fitted; (*b*) in the case of a motor vehicle other than a motor cycle or an invalid carriage, either— (i) it is capable of being applied by direct mechanical action without the intervention of any hydraulic, electric or pneumatic device; or (ii) the vehicle complies with requirement 15; and (*c*) it can at all times when the vehicle is not being driven or is left unattended be set so as— (i) in the case of a track-laying vehicle, to lock the tracks; and (ii) in the case of a wheeled vehicle, to prevent the rotation of at least one wheel in the case of a three wheeled vehicle and at least two wheels in the case of a vehicle with more than three wheels.
17	The parking brake shall be capable of being set so as effectively to prevent two at least of the wheels from revolving when the trailer is not being drawn.
18	The parking brake shall be so designed and constructed that— (*a*) in the case of a motor vehicle, its means of operation (whether multi-pull or not) is independent of the means of operation of any braking system required by regulation 18 to have a total braking efficiency of not less than 50%; and (*b*) in the case of a trailer, its brakes can be applied and released by a person standing on the ground by a means of operation fitted to the trailer; and (*c*) in either case, its braking force, when the vehicle is not being driven or is left unattended (and in the case of a trailer, whether the braking force is applied by the driver using the service brakes of the drawing vehicle or by a person standing on the ground in the manner indicated in sub-paragraph (*b*)) can at all times be maintained in operation by direct mechanical action without the intervention of any hydraulic, electric or pneumatic device and, when so maintained, can hold the vehicle stationary on a gradient of at least 16% without the assistance of stored energy.

[Paragraph 1 of Sched 3 is printed as amended by SI 1987 No 676.]

2. For the purposes of requirement 3 in the Table, in the case of a motor car or heavy motor car propelled by steam and not used as a bus, the engine shall be deemed to be an efficient braking system with one means of operation if the engine is capable of being reversed and, in the case of a vehicle first used on or after 1st January 1927, is incapable of being disconnected from any of the driving wheels of the vehicle except by the sustained effort of the driver.

3. For the purpose of requirements 4 and 6 in the Table, in the case of a wheeled motor car and of a vehicle first used on or after 1st October 1938 which is a locomotive, a motor tractor, a heavy motor car or a track-laying motor car, every moving shaft which is connected to or supports any part of a braking system shall be deemed to be part of the system.

4. For the purpose of [requirements 4, 9 and 14] in the Table, in determining whether brakes apply to at least half the wheels of a vehicle, not more than one front wheel shall be treated as a wheel to which brakes apply unless the vehicle is—

(*a*) a locomotive or motor tractor with more than 4 wheels;

(*b*) a heavy motor car or motor car first used before 1st October 1938;

(*c*) a motor car with an unladen weight not exceeding 1020 kg;

(*d*) a motor car which is a passenger vehicle but is not a bus;

(*e*) a works truck;

(*f*) a heavy motor car or motor car with more than 3 wheels which is equipped in respect of all its wheels with brakes which are operated by one means of operation; or

(*g*) a track-laying vehicle.

[Paragraph 4 of Sched 3 is printed as amended by SI 1987 No 676.]

5. In this Schedule a 'multi-pull means of operation' means a device forming part of a braking system which causes the muscular energy of the driver to apply the brakes of that system progressively as a result of successive applications of that device by the driver.

[SCHEDULE 3A (see regulations 39A and 39B)

Exclusion of Certain Vehicles from the Application of Regulation 39A

PART I

1.—(1) In this Part—

'EEC type approval certificate' means a certificate issued by a member state of the European Economic Community in accordance with Community Directive 70/220 as originally made or with any amendments which have from time to time been made before 5th Spetember 1988;

'engine capacity' means in the case of a reciprocating engine, the nominal swept volume and, in the case of a rotary engine, double the nominal swept volume;

'off-road vehicle' has the meaning given by Annex I to Council Directive 70/156/EEC of 6th February 1970 *[OJ L 42, 23.2.70, p 1]* as amended at 5th September 1988 *[Council Directive 87/403/EEC (OJ L 220, 8.8.87, p 44)]*;

'relevant authority' means—

(*a*) in relation to an EEC type approval certificate issued by the United Kingdom, the Secretary of State, and

(*b*) in relation to an EEC type approval certificate issued by any other member state of the European Economic Community, the authority having power under the law of that state to issue that certificate.

(2) The reference in this Schedule to a M1 category vehicle is reference to a vehicle described as M1 in Council Directive 70/156/EEC of 6th February 1970 as amended at 5th September 1988.

[2. There is no paragraph numbered '2' in this Schedule.]

3. A vehicle of a description specified in column 2 of the Table below is excluded from the application of regulation 39A if it is first used before the date specified in column 3 and the conditions specified in paragraph 3 are satisfied in respect to it on that date.

[The reference to 'paragraph 3' appears to have been intended to be a reference to 'paragraph 4'.]

4. The conditions referred to in paragraph 2 are—

(*a*) that the vehicle is a model in relation to which there is in force an EEC type approval certificate issued before 1st October 1989;

(*b*) that the manufacturer of the vehicle has supplied to the relevant authority which issued the EEC type approval certificate, a certificate stated that adapting vehicles of that model to the fuel requirements specified in the Annexes to Community Directive 88/76 would entail a change in material specification of the inlet or exhaust valve seats or a reduction in the compression ratio or an increase in the engine capacity to compensate for loss of power; and

(*c*) that the relevant authority has accepted the certificate referred to in sub-paragraph (*b*).

TABLE

Item (1)	*Description of vehicle* (2)	*Date before which vehicle must be first used* (3)
1.	Vehicles with an engine capacity of less than 1400cc.	1.4.92
2.	Vehicles with an engine capacity of not less than 1400cc and not more than 2000cc.	1.4.94
3.	M1 category vehicles with an engine capacity of more than 2000cc and which— (*a*) are constructed or adapted to carry not more than 5 passengers excluding the driver, or (*b*) have a maximun gross weight of not more than 2500kg not being in either case, an off-road vehicle.	1.4.93

[The reference to 'paragraph 2' appears to have been intended to be a reference to 'paragraph 3'.]

PART II

SYMBOL INDICATING THAT VEHICLE CAN RUN ON UNLEADED PETROL

[Omitted.]]

[Schedule 3A was inserted by SI 1988 No 1524.]

SCHEDULE 4 (see regulation 40)

GAS CONTAINERS

PART I

Definitions relating to gas containers

1. In this Schedule, unless the context otherwise requires, the following expressions have the meanings hereby assigned to them respectively, that is to say—

'gas container' means a container fitted to a motor vehicle or a trailer and intended for the storage of gaseous fuel for the purpose of the propulsion of the vehicle or the drawing vehicle as the case may be;

'gas cylinder' means a container fitted to a motor vehicle or a trailer and intended for the storage of compressed gas for the purpose of the propulsion of the vehicle or the drawing vehicle as the case may be;

'compressed gas' means gaseous fuel under a pressure exceeding 1.0325 bar above atmospheric pressure;

'pipe line' means all pipes connecting a gas container or containers—

(*a*) to the engine or the mixing device for the supply of a mixture of gas and air to the engine; and

(*b*) to the filling point on the vehicle;

'pressure pipe line' means any part of a pipe line intended for the conveyance of compressed gas; and

'reducing valve' means an apparatus which automatically reduces the pressure of the gas passing through it.

Gas containers

2. Every gas container shall—

(*a*) be securely attached to the vehicle in such manner as not to be liable to displacement or damage due to vibration or other cause; and

(*b*) be so placed or insulated as not to be adversely affected by the heat from the exhaust system.

Pipelines

3.—(1) Every pipeline shall be supported in such manner as to be protected from excessive vibration and strain.

(2) No part of a pipeline shall be in such a position that it may be subjected to undue heat from the exhaust system.

(3) Every pressure pipeline shall be made of steel solid drawn.

(4) The maximum unsupported length of a pressure pipeline shall not exceed 920 mm.

Unions

4.—(1) Every union shall be so constructed and fitted that it will—

(*a*) not be liable to work loose or develop leakage when in use; and

(*b*) be readily accessible for inspection and adjustment.

(2) No union on a pressure pipeline or on a gas cylinder shall contain a joint other than a metal to metal joint.

Reducing valves

5. Every reducing valve shall be—

(*a*) so fitted as to be readily accessible; and

(*b*) so constructed that there can be no escape of gas when the engine is not running.

Valves and cocks

6.—(1) Every valve or cock intended to be subjected to a pressure exceeding 6.8948 bar shall be of forged steel or of brass or bronze complying with the specification contained in Part II of this Schedule.

(2) A valve or cock shall be fitted to the pipe line to enable the supply of gas from the container or containers to the mixing device to be shut off.

(3)(*a*) In the case of a pressure pipe line the valve or cock shall be placed between the reducing valve and the container and shall be readily visible and accessible from the outside of the vehicle and a notice indicating its position and method of operation shall be affixed in a conspicuous position on the outside of the vehicle carrying the gas container or containers.

(*b*) In other cases, if the valve or cock is not so visible and accessible as aforesaid, a notice indicating its position shall be affixed in a conspicuous position on the outside of the vehicle carrying the container or containers.

Pressure gauges

7. Every pressure gauge connected to a pressure pipe line shall be so constructed as not to be liable to deterioration under the action of the particular gases employed and shall be so constructed and fitted that—

(*a*) in the event of failure of such pressure gauge no gas can escape into any part of the vehicle.

(*b*) it is not possible owing to leakage of gas into the casing of the pressure gauge for pressure to increase therein to such extent as to be liable to cause a breakage of the glass thereof; and

(*c*) in the event of failure of such pressure gauge the supply of gas thereto may be readily cut off.

Charging connections

8.—(1) Every connection for charging a gas container shall be outside the vehicle and in the case of a public service vehicle no such connection shall be within 610 mm of any entrance or exit.

(2) An efficient shut-off valve shall be fitted as near as practicable to the filling point.

Provided that in cases where compressed gas is not used a cock or an efficient non-return valve may be fitted in lieu thereof.

(3) Where compressed gas is used an additional emergency shut-off valve shall be fitted adjacent to the valve referred to in sub-paragraph (2) of this paragraph.

(4) A cap shall be fitted to the gas filling point on the vehicle and where compressed gas is used this cap shall be made of steel with a metal to metal joint.

Trailers

9.—(1) Where a trailer is used for the carriage of a gas cylinder, a reducing valve shall be fitted on the trailer.

(2) No pipe used for conveying gas from a trailer to the engine of a vehicle shall contain compressed gas.

Construction, etc, of system

10. Every part of a gas container propulsion system shall be—

(*a*) so placed or protected as not to be exposed to accidental damage and shall be soundly and properly constructed of suitable and well-finished materials capable of withstanding the loads and stresses likely to be met with in operation and shall be maintained in an efficient, safe and clean condition, and

(*b*) so designed and constructed that leakage of gas is not likely to occur under normal working conditions, whether or not the engine is running.

PART II

Specification for Brass or Bronze Valves

Manufacture of valves

1. The stamping or pressing from which each valve is manufactured shall be made from bars produced by (*a*) extrusion, (*b*) rolling, (*c*) forging, (*d*) extrusion and drawing, or (*e*) rolling and drawing.

Heat treatment

2. Each stamping or pressing shall be heat treated so as to produce an equiaxed microstructure in the material.

Freedom from defects

3. All stampings or pressings and the bars from which they are made shall be free from cracks, laminations, hard spots, segregated materials and variations in composition.

Tensile test

4. Tensile tests shall be made on samples of stampings or pressings taken at random from any consignment. The result of the tensile test shall conform to the following conditions—

Yield Stress.—Not less than 231.6 N/mm^2.
Ultimate Tensile Stress.—Not less than 463.3 N/mm^2.
Elongation on 50 mm gauge length.—Not less than 25%.

Note.—When the gauge length is less than 50 mm the required elongation shall be proportionately reduced.

The fractured test piece shall be free from piping and other defects (see paragraph 3 of this Part of this Schedule).

SCHEDULE 5 (see regulations 40 and 96)

Gas Systems

Definitions

1. In this Schedule—

'check valve' means a device which permits the flow of gas in one direction and prevents the flow of gas in the opposite direction;

'design pressure' means the pressure which a part of a gas system has been designed and constructed safely to withstand;

'double-check valve' means a device which consists of two check valves in series and which permits the flow of gas in one direction and prevents the flow of gas in the opposite direction;

'excess flow valve' means a device which automatically and instantaneously reduces to a minimum the flow of gas through the valve when the flow rate exceeds a set value;

'fixed gas container' means a gas container which is attached to a vehicle permanently and in such a manner that the container can be filled without being moved;

'gas container' means any container, not being a container for the carriage of gas as goods, which is fitted to or carried on a motor vehicle or trailer and is intended for the storage of gas for either—

(*a*) the propulsion of the motor vehicle, or

(*b*) the operation of a gas-fired appliance;

'high pressure' means a pressure exceeding 1.0325 bar absolute;

'high pressure pipeline' means a pipeline intended to contain gas at high pressure;

'pipeline' means any pipe or passage connecting any two parts of a gas propulsion system of a vehicle or of a gas-fired appliance supply system on a vehicle or any two points on the same part of any such system;

'portable gas container' means a gas container which may be attached to a vehicle but which can readily be removed;

'pressure relief valve' means a device which opens automatically when the pressure in the part of the gas system to which it is fitted exceeds a set value, reaches its maximum flow capacity when the set value is exceeded by 10% and closes automatically when the pressure falls below a set value; and

'reducing valve' means a device which automatically reduces the pressure of the gas passing through it, and includes regulator devices.

Gas containers

2.—(1) Every gas container shall—

(*a*) be capable of withstanding the pressure of the gas which may be stored in the container at the highest temperature which the gas is likely to reach,

(*b*) if fitted inside the vehicle be so arranged as to prevent so far as is practicable the possibility of gas entering the engine, passenger or living compartments due to leaks or venting from the container or valves connections and gauges immediately adjacent to it, and the space containing those components shall be so ventilated and drained as to prevent the accumulation of gas, (*c*) be securely attached to the vehicle in such a manner as not to be liable to displacement or damage due to vibration or other cause, and

(*d*) be so placed and so insulated or shielded as not to suffer any adverse effect from the heat of the exhaust system of any engine or any other source of heat.

(2) Every portable gas container shall be either—

(*a*) hermetically sealed, or

(*b*) fitted with a valve or cock to enable the flow of gas from the container to be stopped.

(3) Every fixed gas container shall—

(*a*) be fitted with—

(i) at least one pressure relief valve, and

(ii) at least one manually operated valve which may be extended by an internal dip tube inside the gas container so as to indicate when the container has been filled to the level corresponding to the filling ratio specified in the British Standards Institution Specification for Filling Ratios and Developed Pressure for Liquefiable and Permanent Gases (as defined, respectively, in paragraphs 3.2 and 3.5 of the said Specification) published in May 1976 under the number BS 5355, and

(*b*) be conspicuously and permanently marked with its design pressure.

(4) If any fixed gas container is required to be fitted in a particular attitude or location, or if any device referred to in sub-paragraph (3) above requires the container to be fitted in such a manner, then it shall be conspicuously and permanently marked to indicate that requirement.

(5) If the operation of any pressure relief valve or other device referred to in sub-paragraph (3) above may cause gas to be released from the gas container an outlet shall be provided to lead such gas to the outside of the vehicle so as not to suffer any adverse effect from the heat of the exhaust system of any engine or any other source of heat, and that outlet from the pressure relief valve shall not be fitted with any other valve or cock.

Filling systems for fixed gas containers

3.—(1) Every connection for filling a fixed gas container shall be on the outside of the vehicle.

(2) There shall be fitted to every fixed gas container either—

(*a*) a manually operated shut-off valve and an excess flow valve, or

(*b*) a manually operated shut-off valve and a single check valve, or

(*c*) a double-check valve,

and all parts of these valves in contact with gas shall be made entirely of suitable metal except that they may contain non-metal washers and seals provided that such washers and seals are supported and constrained by metal components.

(3) In every case where a pipe is attached to a gas container for the purpose of filling the gas container there shall be fitted to the end of the pipe furthest from the gas container a check valve or a double-check valve.

(4) There shall be fitted over every gas filling point on a vehicle a cap which shall—

(*a*) prevent any leakage of gas from the gas filling point,

(*b*) be secured to the vehicle by a chain or some other suitable means, (*c*) be made of suitable material; and

(*d*) be fastened to the gas filling point by either a screw thread or other suitable means.

Pipelines

4.—(1) Every pipeline shall be fixed in such a manner and position that—

(*a*) it will not be adversely affected by the heat of the exhaust system of any engine or any other source of heat,

(*b*) it is protected from vibration and strain in excess of that which it can reasonably be expected to withstand, and

(*c*) in the case of a high pressure pipeline it is so far as is practicable accessible for inspection.

(2) Save as provided in sub-paragraph (4) below, every high pressure pipeline shall be—

(*a*) a rigid line of steel, copper or copper alloy of high pressure hydraulic grade, suitable for service on road vehicles and designed for a minimum service pressure rating of not less than 75 bar absolute, and

(*b*) effectively protected against, or shielded from, or treated so as to be resistant to, external corrosion throughout its length unless it is made from material which is corrosion resistant under the conditions which it is likely to encounter in service.

(3) No unsupported length of any high pressure pipeline shall exceed 600 mm.

(4) Flexible hose may be used in a high pressure pipeline if—

(*a*) it is reinforced either by stainless steel wire braid or by textile braid,

(*b*) its length does not exceed 500 mm, and

(*c*) save in the case of a pipeline attached to a gas container for the purpose of filling that container the flexibility which it provides is necessary for the construction or operation of the gas system of which it forms a part.

(5) If a high pressure pipeline or part of such a pipeline is so constructed or located that it may, in the course of its normal use (excluding the supply of fuel from a gas container), contain liquid which is prevented from flowing, a relief valve shall be incorporated in that pipeline.

Unions and joints

5.—(1) Every union and joint on a pipeline or gas container shall be so constructed and fitted that it will—

(*a*) not be liable to work loose or leak when in use, and

(*b*) be readily accessible for inspection and maintenance.

(2) Every union on a high pressure pipeline or on a gas container shall be made of suitable metal but such a union may contain non-metal washers and seals provided that such washers and seals are supported and constrained by metal components.

Reducing valves

6. Every reducing valve shall be made of suitable materials and be so fitted as to be readily accessible for inspection and maintenance.

Pressure relief valves

7.—(1) Every pressure relief valve which is fitted to any part of a gas system (including a gas container) shall—

(*a*) be made entirely of suitable metal and so constructed and fitted as to ensure that the cooling effect of the gas during discharge shall not prevent its effective operation,

(*b*) be capable, under the most extreme temperatures likely to be met (including exposure to fire), of a discharge rate which prevents the pressure of the contents of the gas system from exceeding its design pressure,

(*c*) have a maximum discharge pressure not greater than the design pressure of the gas container,

(*d*) be so designed and constructed as to prevent unauthorised interference with the relief pressure setting during service, and

(*e*) have outlets which are—

(i) so sited that so far as is reasonably practicable in the event of an accident the valve and its outlets are protected from damage and the free discharge from such outlets is not impaired, and

(ii) so designed and constructed as to prevent the collection of moisture and other foreign matter which could adversely affect their performance.

(2) The pressure at which a pressure relief valve is designed to start lifting shall be clearly and permanently marked on every such valve.

(3) Every pressure relief valve which is fitted to a gas container shall communicate with the vapour space in the gas container and not with any liquefied gas.

Valves and cocks

8.—(1) A valve or cock shall be fitted to every supply pipeline as near as practicable to every fixed gas container and such valve or cock shall by manual operation enable the supply of gas from the gas container to the gas system to be stopped, and save as provided in sub-paragraph (2) below, shall—

(*a*) if fitted on the outside of the vehicle, be readily visible and accessible from the outside of the vehicle, or

(*b*) if fitted inside the vehicle be readily accessible for operation and be so arranged as to prevent so far as is practicable the possibility of gas entering the engine, passenger or living compartments due to leaks, and the space containing the valve or cock shall be so ventilated and drained as to prevent the accumulation of gas in that space.

(2) Where a fixed gas container supplies no gas system other than a gas propulsion system and the gas container is so located that it is not practicable to make the valve or cock referred to in sub-paragraph (1) above readily accessible there shall be fitted an electrically-operated valve which shall either be incorporated in the valve or cock referred to in sub-paragraph (1) above or be fitted immediately downstream from it and shall—

(*a*) be constructed so as to open when the electric power is applied and to close when the electric power is cut off,

(*b*) be so fitted as to shut off the supply of gas from the gas container to the gas system when the engine is not running, and

(*c*) if fitted inside the vehicle be so arranged as to prevent as far as is practicable the possibility of gas entering the engine, passenger or living compartments due to leaks, and the space containing the valve shall be so ventilated and drained as to prevent the accumulation of gas in that space.

(3) A notice clearly indicating the position, purpose and method of operating every valve or cock referred to in sub-paragraphs (1) and (2) above shall be fixed—

(*a*) in all cases, in a conspicuous position on the outside of the vehicle, and

(*b*) if every case where the valve or cock is located inside the vehicle in a conspicuous position adjacent to the gas container.

(4) In the case of a high pressure pipeline for the conveyance of gas from the gas container an excess flow valve shall be fitted as near as practicable to the gas container and such valve shall operate in the event of a fracture of the pipeline or other similar failure.

(5) All parts of every valve or cock referred to in this paragraph which are in contact with gas shall be made of suitable metal, save that they may contain non-metal washers and seals provided that such washers and seals are supported and constrained by metal components.

Gauges

9. Every gauge connected to a gas container or to a pipeline shall be so constructed as to be unlikely to deteriorate under the action of the gas used or to be used and shall be so constructed and fitted that—

(*a*) no gas can escape into any part of the vehicle as a result of any failure of the gauge, and

(*b*) in the event of any failure of the gauge the supply of gas to the gauge can be readily stopped.

Provided that the requirement specified in sub-paragraph (*b*) above shall not apply in respect of a gauge as an integral part of a gas container.

Propulsion systems

10.—(1) Every gas propulsion system shall be so designed and constructed that—

(*a*) the supply of gas to the engine is automatically stopped by the operation of a valve when the engine is not running at all or is not running on the supply of gas, and,

(*b*) where a reducing valve is relied on to comply with sub-paragraph (*a*) above, the supply of gas to the engine is automatically stopped by the operation of an additional valve when the engine is switched off.

(2) Where the engine of a vehicle is constructed or adapted to run on one or more fuels as alternatives to gas, the safety and efficiency of the engine and any fuel system shall not be impaired by the presence of any other fuel system.

Special requirements for buses

11. In the case of a bus there shall be fitted as near as practicable to the gas container a valve which shall stop the flow of gas into the gas supply pipeline in the event of—

(*a*) the angle of tilt of the vehicle exceeding that referred to in regulation 6 of the Public Services Vehicles (Conditions of Fitness, Equipment, Use and Certification) Regulations 1981 *[SI 1981 No 257, qv]*, and

(*b*) the deceleration of the vehicle exceeding 5g.

Gas-fired appliances

12. Every part of a gas-fired appliance shall be—

(*a*) so designed and constructed that leakage of gas is unlikely to occur, and

(*b*) constructed of materials which are compatible both with each other and with the gas used.

13. Every gas-fired appliance shall be—

(*a*) so located as to be easily inspected and maintained,

(*b*) so located and either insulated or shielded that its use shall not cause or be likely to cause danger due to the presence of any flammable material,

(*c*) so constructed and located as not to impose undue stress on any pipe or fitting, and

(*d*) so fastened or located as not to work loose or move in relation to the vehicle.

14. With the exception of catalytic heating appliances, every appliance of the kind described in regulation 96(3)(*b*) or (*c*) which is fitted to a motor vehicle shall be fitted with a flue which shall be—

(*a*) connected to an outlet which is on the outside of the vehicle,

(*b*) constructed and located so as to prevent any expelled matter from entering the vehicle, and

(*c*) located so that it will not cause any adverse effect to, or suffer any adverse effect from, the exhaust outlet of any engine or any other source of heat.

General requirements

15. Every part of a gas propulsion system or a gas-fired appliance system, excluding the appliance itself, shall be—

(*a*) so far as is practicable so located or protected as not to be exposed to accidental damage,

(*b*) soundly and properly constructed of materials which are compatible with one another and with the gas used or to be used and which are capable of withstanding the loads and stresses likely to be met in operation, and

(*c*) so designed and constructed that leakage of gas is unlikely to occur.

SCHEDULE 6 (see regulation 41)

CONSTRUCTION OF MINIBUSES

The requirements referred to in regulation 41 are as follows—

Exhaust pipes

1. The outlet of every exhaust pipe fitted to a minibus shall be either at the rear or on the off side of the vehicle.

Doors—number and position

2.—(1) Every minibus shall be fitted with at least—

(*a*) one service door on the near side of the vehicle; and

(*b*) one emergency door either at the rear or on the off side of the vehicle so, however, that any emergency door fitted on the off side of the vehicle shall be in addition to the driver's door and there shall be no requirement for an emergency door on a minibus if it has a service door at the rear in addition to the service door on the near side.

(2) No minibus shall be fitted with any door on its off side other than a driver's door and an emergency door.

Emergency doors

3. Every emergency door fitted to a minibus, whether or not required pursuant to these Regulations, shall—

(*a*) be clearly marked, in letters not less than 25 mm high, on both the inside and the outside, 'EMERGENCY DOOR' or 'FOR EMERGENCY USE ONLY', and the means of its operation shall be clearly indicated on or near the door;

(*b*) if hinged, open outwards;

(*c*) be capable of being operated manually; and

(*d*) when fully opened, give an aperture in the body of the vehicle not less than 1210 mm high nor less than 530 mm wide.

Power-operated doors

4.—(1) Every power-operated door fitted to a minibus shall—

(*a*) incorporate transparent panels so as to enable a person immediately inside the door to see any person immediately outside the door;

(*b*) be capable of being operated by a mechanism controlled by the driver of the vehicle when in the driving seat;

(*c*) be capable, in the event of an emergency or a failure of the supply of power for the operation of the door, of being opened from both inside and outside the vehicle by controls which—

(i) over-ride all other controls;

(ii) are placed on, or adjacent to, the door, and

(iii) are accompanied by markings which clearly indicate their position and method of operation and state that they may not be used by passengers except in an emergency;

(*d*) have a soft edge so that a trapped finger is unlikely to be injured; and

(*e*) be controlled by a mechanism by virtue of which if the door, when closing, meets a resistance exceeding 150 Newtons, either

—the door will cease to close and begin to open, or

—the closing force will cease and the door will become capable of being opened manually.

(2) No minibus shall be equipped with a system for the storage or transmission of energy in respect of the opening or closing of any door which, either in normal operation or if the system fails, is capable of adversely affecting the operation of the vehicle's braking system.

Locks, handles and hinges of doors

5. No minibus shall be fitted with—

(*a*) a door which can be locked from the outside unless, when so locked, it is capable of being opened from inside the vehicle when stationary;

(*b*) a handle or other device for opening any door, other than the driver's door, from inside the vehicle unless the handle or other device is designed so as to prevent, so far as is reasonably practicable, the accidental opening of the door, and is fitted with a guard or transparent cover or so designed that it must be raised to open the door;

(*c*) a door which is not capable of being opened, when not locked, from inside and outside the vehicle by a single movement of the handle or other device for opening the door;

(*d*) a door in respect of which there is not a device capable of holding the door closed so as to prevent any passenger falling through the doorway;

(*e*) a side door which opens outwards and is hinged at the edge nearest the rear of the vehicle except in the case of a door having more than one rigid panel;

(*f*) a door, other than a power-operated door, in respect of which there is not either—

(i) a slam lock of the two-stage type; or

(ii) a device by means of which the driver, when occupying the driver's seat, is informed if the door is not securely closed, such device being operated by movement of the handle or other device for opening the door or, in the case of a handle or other device with a spring-return mechanism, by movement of the door as well as of the handle or other device.

Provided that the provisions of sub-paragraphs (*a*), (*c*), (*d*) and (*f*) of this paragraph shall not apply in respect of a near side rear door forming part of a pair of doors fitted at the rear of a vehicle if that door is capable of being held securely closed by the other door of that pair.

View of doors

6.—(1) Save as provided in sub-paragraph (2), every minibus shall be fitted with mirrors or other means so that the driver, when occupying the driver's seat, can see clearly the area immediately inside and outside every service door of the vehicle.

(2) The provisions of sub-paragraph (1) shall be deemed to be satisfied in respect of a rear service door if a person 1.3 metres tall standing 1 metre behind the vehicle is visible to the driver when occupying the driver's seat.

Access to doors

7.—(1) Save as provided in sub-paragraph (2), there shall be unobstructed access from every passenger seat in a minibus to at least two doors one of which must be on the nearside of the vehicle and one of which must be either at the rear or on the offside of the vehicle.

(2) Access to one only of the doors referred to in sub-paragraph (1) may be obstructed by either or both of—

(*a*) a seat which when tilted or folded does not obstruct access to that door, and

(*b*) a lifting platform or ramp which—

(i) does not obstruct the handle or other device on the inside for opening the door with which the platform or ramp is associated, and

(ii) when the door is open, can be pushed or pulled out of the way from the inside so as to leave the doorway clear for use in an emergency.

Grab handles and hand rails

8. Every minibus shall be fitted as respects every side service door with a grab handle or a hand rail to assist passengers to get on or off the vehicle.

Seats

9.—(1) No seat shall be fitted to any door of a minibus.

(2) Every seat and every wheelchair anchorage fitted to a minibus shall be fixed to the vehicle.

(3) No seat, other than a wheelchair, fitted to a minibus shall be less than 400 mm wide, and in ascertaining the width of a seat no account shall be taken of any arm-rests, whether or not they are folded back or otherwise put out of use.

(4) No minibus shall be fitted with an anchorage for a wheelchair in such a manner that a wheelchair secured to the anchorage would face either side of the vehicle.

(5) No minibus shall be fitted with a seat—

(*a*) facing either side of the vehicle and immediately forward of a rear door unless the seat is fitted with an arm-rest or similar device to guard against a passenger on that seat falling through the doorway; or

(*b*) so placed that a passenger on it would, without protection, be liable to be thrown through any doorway which is provided with a power-operated door or down any steps, unless the vehicle is fitted with a screen or guard which affords adequate protection against that occurrence.

Electrical equipment and wiring

10.—(1) Save as provided in sub-paragraph (2) no minibus shall be fitted with any—

(*a*) electrical circuit which is liable to carry a current exceeding that for which it was designed;

(*b*) cable for the conduct of electricity unless it is suitably insulated and protected from damage;

(*c*) electrical circuit, other than a charging circuit, which includes any equipment other than—

(i) a starter motor,
(ii) a glow plug,
(iii) an ignition circuit, and
(iv) a device to stop the vehicle's engine,

unless it includes a fuse or circuit breaker so, however, that one fuse or circuit breaker may serve more than one circuit; or

(*d*) electrical circuit with a voltage exceeding 100 volts unless there is connected in each pole of the main supply of electricity which is not connected to earth a manually-operated switch which is—

(i) capable of disconnecting the circuit, or, if there is more than one, every circuit, from the main supply,
(ii) not capable of disconnecting any circuit supplying any lamp with which the vehicle is required to be fitted, and
(iii) located inside the vehicle in a position readily accessible to the driver.

(2) The provisions of sub-paragraph (1) do not apply in respect of a high tension ignition circuit or a circuit within a unit of equipment.

Fuel tanks

11. No minibus shall be fitted with a fuel tank or any apparatus for the supply of fuel which is in the compartments or other spaces provided for the accommodation of the driver or passengers.

Lighting of steps

12. Every minibus shall be provided with lamps to illuminate every step at a passenger exit or in a gangway.

General construction and maintenance

13. Every minibus, including all bodywork and fittings, shall be soundly and properly constructed of suitable materials and maintained in good and serviceable condition, and shall be of such design as to be capable of withstanding the loads and stresses likely to be met in the normal operation of the vehicle.

Definitions

14. In this Schedule—

'driver's door' means a door fitted to a minibus for use by the driver;

'emergency door' means a door fitted to a minibus for use by passengers in an emergency; and

'service door' means a door fitted to a minibus for use by passengers in normal circumstances.

SCHEDULE 7

Fire-extinguishing Apparatus and First-aid Equipment for Minibuses

PART I

(see regulation 42)

Fire Extinguishing Apparatus

A fire extinguisher which complies in all respects with the specification for portable fire extinguishers issued by the British Standards Institution numbered BS 5423:1980 as amended by Amendment No. 1 (reference number AMD 4110 published on 31st December 1982) and Amendment No. 2 (reference number AMD 4544 published on 30th April 1984) and which—

(*a*) contains water with a minimum test fire rating of 8A, or

(*b*) contains foam with a minimum test fire rating of 8A and 21B, or

(*c*) contains, and is marked to indicate that it contains, halon 1211, or halon 1301, with a minimum test fire rating of 21B.

PART II

(see regulation 43)

First Aid Equipment

(i) Ten antiseptic wipes, foil packed;

(ii) One conforming disposable bandage (not less than 7.5 cm wide);

(iii) Two triangular bandages;

(iv) One packet of 24 assorted adhesive dressings;

(v) Three large sterile unmedicated ambulance dressings (not less than 15.0 cm × 20.0 cm);

(vi) Two sterile eye pads, with attachments;

(vii) Twelve assorted safety pins; and

(viii) One pair of rustless blunt-ended scissors.

SCHEDULE 8 (see regulation 66)

Plates for Certain Vehicles

PART I

Particulars to be shown on plate for motor vehicles (including motor vehicles forming part of articulated vehicles)

1. Manufacturer's name.
2. Vehicle type.
3. Engine type and power (*a*).
4. Chassis or serial number.
5. Number of axles.
6. Maximum axle weight for each axle (*b*).
7. Maximum gross weight (*c*).
8. Maximum train weight (*d*).
9. Maximum weight in Great Britain for each axle (*b*), (*e*).
10. Maximum gross weight in Great Britain (*c*), (*e*).

(*a*) The power need not be shown in the case of a motor vehicle manufactured before 1st October 1972 (hereinafter in this Schedule referred to as 'an excepted vehicle') and shall not be shown in the case of any motor vehicle which is propelled otherwise than by a compression ignition engine.

(*b*) This weight as respects each axle is the sum of the weights to be transmitted to the road surface by all the wheels of that axle.

(*c*) This weight is the sum of the weights to be transmitted to the road surface by all the wheels of the motor vehicle (including any load imposed by a trailer, whether forming part of an articulated vehicle or not, on the motor vehicle).

(*d*) This weight is the sum of the weights to be transmitted to the road surface by all the wheels of the motor vehicle and of any trailer drawn, but this item need not be completed where the motor vehicle is not constructed to draw a trailer.

(*b*), (*c*), (*d*) References to the weights to be transmitted to the road surface by all or any of the wheels of the vehicle or any trailer drawn are references to the weights so to be transmitted both of the vehicle or trailer and of any load or persons carried by it.

(*e*) This item need not be completed in the case of an excepted vehicle or in the case of a vehicle which is a locomotive or motor tractor.

PART II

Particulars to be shown on plate for trailers (including trailers forming part of articulated vehicles)

1. Manufacturer's name.
2. Chassis or serial number.
3. Number of axles.
4. Maximum weight for each axle (*a*).
5. Maximum load imposed on drawing vehicle (*b*).
6. Maximum gross weight (*c*).
7. Maximum weight in Great Britain for each axle (*a*), (*e*).
8. Maximum gross weight in Great Britain (*c*), (*f*).

9. Year of manufacture (*d*).

(*a*) This weight as respects each axle is the sum of the weights to be transmitted to the road surface by all the wheels of that axle.

(*b*) Only for trailers forming part of articulated vehicles or where some of the weight of the trailer or its load is to be imposed on the drawing vehicle. This item need not be completed in the case of a converter dolly.

(*c*) This weight is the sum of the weights to be transmitted to the road surface by all the wheels of the trailer, including any weight of the trailer to be imposed on the drawing vehicle.

(*a*), (*b*), (*c*) References to the weights to be transmitted to the road surface by all or any of the wheels of the trailer are references to the weight so to be transmitted both of the trailer and of any load or persons carried by it and references to the weights to be imposed on the drawing vehicle are references to the weights so to be imposed both of the trailer and of any load or persons carried by it except where only the load of the trailer is imposed on the drawing vehicle.

(*d*) This item need not be completed in the case of a trailer manufactured before 1st April 1970.

(*e*) This item need not be completed in the case of a trailer manufactured before 1st October 1972.

(*f*) This item need not be completed in the case of a trailer manufactured before 1st October 1972 or which forms part of an articulated vehicle.

PART III

1. The power of an engine, which is to be shown only in the case of a compression ignition engine on the plate in respect of item 3 in Part I of this Schedule, shall be the amount in kilowatts equivalent to the installed power output shown in a type test certificate issued—

(*a*) by a person authorised by the Secretary of State for the type of engine to which the engine conforms; and

(*b*) in accordance with either—

(i) the provisions relating to the installed brake power output specified in the British Standard Specification for the Performance of Diesel Engines for Road Vehicles published on 19th May 1971 under the number BS AU 141a:1971;

(ii) the provisions relating to the net power specified in Community Directive 80/1269 but after allowance has been made for the power absorbed by such equipment, at its minimum power setting, driven by the engine of the vehicle as is fitted for the operation of the vehicle (other than its propulsion) such power being measured at the speed corresponding to the engine speed at which maximum engine power is developed; or

(iii) the provisions of Annex 10 of ECE Regulations 24.02 as further amended with effect from 15th February 1984 relating to the method of measuring internal combustion engine net power, but after allowance has been made for the power absorbed by any disconnectable or progressive cooling fan, at its maximum setting, and by any other such equipment, at its minimum power setting, driven by the engine of the vehicle as is fitted for the operation of the vehicle (other than its propulsion), such power being measured at the speed corresponding to the engine speed at which maximum engine power is developed.

2.—(1) The weights to be shown on the plate in relation to items 6, 7 and 8 in Part I and in relation to items 4, 5 and 6 in Part II shall be the weight limits at or below which the vehicle is considered fit for use, having regard to its design, construction and equipment and the stresses to which it is likely to be subject in use, by the Secretary of State if the vehicle is one to which the Type Approval for Goods Vehicles Regulations apply, and by the manufacturer if the vehicle is one to which those Regulations do not apply.

Provided that, where alterations are made to a vehicle which may render the vehicle fit for use at weights which exceed those referred to above in this paragraph and shown on the plate—

(*a*) there may be shown on the plate, in place of any of those weights, such new weights as the manufacturer of the vehicle or any person carrying on business as a manufacturer of motor vehicles or trailers (or a person duly authorised on behalf of that manufacturer or any such person) or a person authorised by the Secretary of State considers to represent the weight limits at or below which the vehicle will then be fit for use, having regard to its design, construction and equipment and to those alterations and to the stresses to which it is likely to be subject in use; and

(*b*) the name of the person who has determined the new weights shall be shown on the plate as having made that determination and, where he is a person authorised by the Secretary of State, his appointment shall be so shown.

(2) In relation to a vehicle manufactured on or after 1st October 1972, in the foregoing paragraph—

(*a*) the references to equipment shall not be treated as including a reference to the type of tyres with which the vehicle is equipped; and

(*b*) for the words 'weight limits at or below' in both places where they occur there shall be substituted the words 'maximum weights at'.

3. The weights to be shown on the plate in respect of—

(*a*) item 9 in Part I of this Schedule shall be the weights shown at item 6 in that Part and in respect of item 7 in Part II of this Schedule shall be the weights shown at item 4 in that Part, in each case reduced so far as necessary to indicate the maximum weight applicable to each axle of the vehicle, if the vehicle is not to be used in contravention of regulations 23, 75, 78 or 79, and if the tyres with which the vehicle is equipped are not, as respects strength, to be inadequate to support the weights to be so shown at item 9 and item 7;

(*b*) item 10 in the said Part I shall be the weight shown at item 7 in that Part and in respect of item 8 in the said Part II shall be the weight shown at item 6 in that Part, in each case reduced so far as necessary to indicate the maximum permissible weight applicable if the vehicle is not to be used in contravention of regulation 75 if the tyres with which the vehicle is equipped are not, as respects strength, to be inadequate to support the weights to be so shown at item 10 and item 8.

4.—(1) Subject to sub-paragraph (2) of this paragraph weights on plates first affixed to a vehicle on or after 1st October 1972 shall be shown in kilograms and weights on plates first so affixed before that date shall be shown in tons and decimals thereof.

(2) Where a new weight if first shown on a plate by virtue of the proviso to paragraph 2(1) the weight shall be shown as if it was on a plate first affixed to a vehicle on the date it was first shown.

5. All letters and figures shown on the plate shall be not less than 6 mm in height.

6. In this Schedule references to the manufacturer of a motor vehicle or trailer are in relation to—

(*a*) a vehicle constructed with a chassis which has not previously formed part of another vehicle, references to the person by whom that chassis was made;

(*b*) any other vehicle, references to the person by whom that vehicle was constructed.

SCHEDULE 9 (see regulation 69)

Plates for Motor Cycles

1. The plate required by regulation 69 shall be firmly attached to a part of the motor cycle which is not normally subject to replacement during the life of the motor cycle.

2. The plate shall be in the form shown in the diagram in this paragraph, shall have dimensions not less than those shown in that diagram and shall show the information provided for in that diagram and detailed in the Notes below.

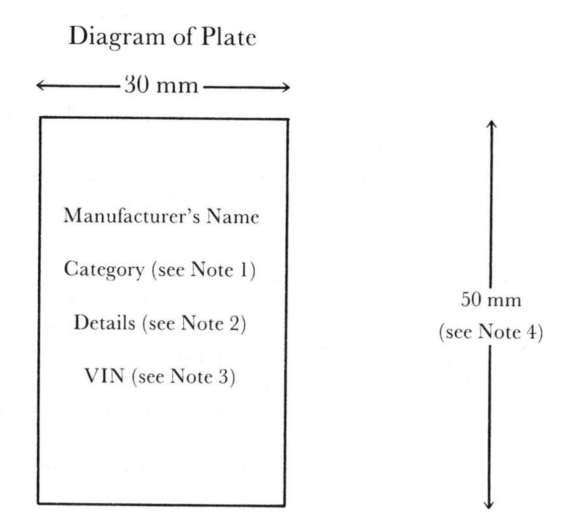

Notes:

1. The categories are 'standard motor cycle' and 'moped'

2. The details are—

(*a*) for standard motor cycles—

(i) the engine capacity,

(ii) the maximum engine power, and

(iii) the power to weight ratio,

provided that the details under (ii) and (iii) need not be shown for a vehicle first used before 1st January 1982;

(*b*) for mopeds—
  (i) the engine capacity,
  (ii) the kerbside weight, and
  (iii) the maximum speed.

3. The vehicle identification number (VIN) shall be marked in the form used by the manufacturer to identify any one individual vehicle.

4. In the case of a plate fitted to a vehicle first used before 1st January 1982 or to a moped this dimension shall be 40 mm.

3. The information on the plate shall be shown in characters not less than 4 mm in height and in the positions on the plate indicated in the diagram above.

4. No information, other than that provided for in the diagram above, shall be marked within the rectangle which is shown in that diagram.

5. In this Schedule and, in respect of the definition of 'moped', in regulations 54 and 57—

'maximum engine power' means the maximum net power the motor cycle engine will develop, in kilowatts, when measured in accordance with the test conditions specified in the International Standard number ISO 4106 developed by the technical committee of the International Organisation for Standardisation, and approved by member bodies, including the United Kingdom, and published under the reference ISO 1978 4106–09–01;

'moped' means a motor cycle which—

(*a*) has a kerbside weight not exceeding 250 kg, and

(*b*) if propelled by an internal combustion engine, has an engine with a cylinder capacity which does not exceed 50 cc, and

(*c*) is designed to have a maximum speed not exceeding 30 mph when driven under the conditions set out in paragraph 6.

'power to weight ratio' means the ratio of the maximum engine power to the kerbside weight of the vehicle measured, as regards the maximum engine power, in kilowatts and, as regards the kerbside weight, in 1000 kg;

'standard motor cycle' means a motor cycle which is not a moped.

6. A motor cycle shall be regarded as complying with paragraph (*c*) of the definition of 'moped' in paragraph 5 if it cannot exceed 35 mph when tested under the following conditions—

(*a*) the surface on which it is tested shall be dry asphalt or concrete;

(*b*) the rider shall be a person not exceeding 75 kg in weight;

(*c*) no passenger or load shall be carried;

(*d*) the test route shall be so located that acceleration to, and deceleration from, maximum speed can take place elsewhere than on the test route itself;

(*e*) the test route shall not have a gradient exceeding 5%;

(*f*) the motor cycle shall be ridden in opposite directions along the test route and the speed recorded for the purpose of the test shall (in order to minimise the effect of wind resistance and gradient) be the average of speeds shown for each direction;

(*g*) when being driven along the test route, the motor cycle shall be driven in such manner and in such gear as to achieve the maximum speed of which it is capable; and

(*h*) if the motor cycle is fitted with a device which can, without the use of specialist tools or equipment, be readily modified or removed so as to increase its maximum speed, the test shall be carried out with the device in the modified condition or, as the case may be, without the device.

SCHEDULE 10 (see regulation 70)

Ministry Plate

<table>
<tr><td colspan="2">PLATE</td><td colspan="3">DEPARTMENT OF TRANSPORT
[Road Traffic Act 1988, Sections 41 and 54]
Examination of Goods Vehicles</td><td>Serial No.
DTp REF. No.</td></tr>
<tr><td colspan="2">REGISTRATION/IDENTIFICATION MARK</td><td>YEAR OF ORIGINAL REGISTRATION</td><td>YEAR OF MANUFACTURE</td><td>FUNCTION</td><td rowspan="2">MAKE AND MODEL</td></tr>
<tr><td colspan="3">CHASSIS/SERIAL No.</td><td colspan="2">UNLADEN WEIGHT</td></tr>
<tr><td colspan="2" rowspan="2">(1) DESCRIPTION OF WEIGHTS APPLICABLE TO VEHICLE</td><td>(2) WEIGHTS NOT TO BE EXCEEDED IN GREAT BRITAIN</td><td colspan="2">(3) DESIGN WEIGHTS (if higher than shown in col (2))</td><td rowspan="6">DATE OF ISSUE</td></tr>
<tr><td>KILOGRAMS</td><td colspan="2">KILOGRAMS</td></tr>
<tr><td rowspan="4">AXLE WEIGHT (Axles numbered from front to rear)</td><td>AXLE 1</td><td></td><td colspan="2"></td></tr>
<tr><td>AXLE 2</td><td></td><td colspan="2"></td></tr>
<tr><td>AXLE 3</td><td></td><td colspan="2"></td></tr>
<tr><td>AXLE 4</td><td></td><td colspan="2"></td></tr>
<tr><td colspan="2">GROSS WEIGHT (see warning opposite)</td><td></td><td colspan="2"></td><td rowspan="2">WARNING
1. A reduced gross weight may apply in certain cases to a vehicle towing or being towed by another.
2. A reduced train weight may apply depending on the type of trailer drawn.
3. All weights shown are subject to fitting of correct tyres.</td></tr>
<tr><td colspan="2">TRAIN WEIGHT (see warning opposite)</td><td></td><td colspan="2"></td></tr>
</table>

NOTES: 1. A Ministry plate may contain the words 'MINISTRY OF TRANSPORT' or 'DEPARTMENT OF THE ENVIRONMENT' instead of the words 'DEPARTMENT OF TRANSPORT', and may contain the words 'Road Safety Act 1967, Sections 8 and 9' or the words 'Road Traffic Act 1972, Sections 40 and 45' [or the words 'Road Traffic Act 1988, Sections 41 and 49']. (In a case where the Type Approval for Goods Vehicles Regulations do not apply.) It may also contain additional columns in Columns (2) and (3) showing the weights in tons.

2. Entries in respect of train weight are required in the case of—(*a*) a motor vehicle constructed or adapted to form part of an articulated vehicle; and (*b*) a rigid vehicle which is constructed or adapted to draw a trailer and is first used on or after 1st April 1983.

3. A Ministry plate shows the unladen weight and function of the vehicle in a case where the Type Approval for Goods Vehicles Regulations apply.

4. A Ministry plate may have separate spaces for the 'make' and 'model' of the vehicle.

5. A Ministry plate may have no 'Reference Number' or may refer to the 'Department of the Environment Reference No'.

[SCHEDULE 10A (see regulation 70)

MINISTRY PLATE

PLATE VTG 6A	DEPARTMENT OF TRANSPORT [Road Traffic Act 1988, Sections 41, 49 and 54 Examination of Goods Vehicles			SERIAL NUMBER		
				UNLADEN WEIGHT	DTp REF No	
				5. VEHICLE DIMENSIONS		
REGISTRATION/ IDENTIFICATION MARK	YEAR OF ORIGINAL REG	YEAR OF MANUFACTURE	FUNCTION	LENGTH (L)		
MANUFACTURER/MODEL				WIDTH (W)		
TYPE APPROVAL/ VARIANT No				a. (See Note 1) COUPLING CENTRE TO VEHICLE FOREMOST PART	**MAXIMUM**	**MINIMUM**
VEHICLE IDENTIFICATION No						
(1) DESCRIPTION OF WEIGHTS APPLICABLE TO VEHICLE	(2) WEIGHT NOT TO BE EXCEEDED IN Gt. BRITAIN	(3) EEC MAXIMUM PERMITTED WEIGHTS (See Note 4)	(4) DESIGN WEIGHTS (if higher than shown in column 2)	b. (See Note 2) COUPLING CENTRE TO VEHICLE REARMOST PART	**MAXIMUM**	**MINIMUM**
GROSS WEIGHT (See warning below)						
TRAIN WEIGHT (See warning below)						
MAXIMUM TRAIN WEIGHT (See Note 3)						
AXLE WEIGHTS (Axles numbered from front to rear) Axle 1						
Axle 2						
Axle 3						
Axle 4						
MAXIMUM KINGPIN LOAD (Semi-trailers only)				DATE OF ISSUE		
N.B. ALL WEIGHTS IN KILOGRAMS/ALL DIMENSIONS IN MILLIMETRES.						

[*continued on next page*]

WARNING

a. A reduced gross weight may apply in certain cases to a vehicle towing or being towed by another.
b. All reduced train weight may apply depending on the type of trailer drawn.
c. All weights shown are subject to the fitting of correct tyres.

NOTES

NOTES

1. This dimension only applies to drawing vehicles of trailers and semi-trailers.
2. This dimension only applies to trailers and semi-trailers.
3. This weight only applies to a 3 axle tractor with a 2 or 3 axle semi-trailer carrying a 40 foot ISO container as a combined transport operation.
4. Where there is no weight shown in the EEC maximum permitted weights column this is because there is no EEC standard relating to that weight.

NOTES

1. Entries in respect of train weight are required in the case of—(a) a motor vehicle constructed or adapted to form an articulated vehicle; and (b) a rigid vehicle which is constructed or adapted to draw a trailer and is first used on or after 1st April 1983.
2. A Ministry plate shows the unladen weight and function of the vehicle in a case where the Type Approval for Goods Vehicles Regulations apply.
3. A Ministry plate may have no 'Reference Number'.]

[*Schedule 10A was inserted by SI 1987 No 676 and is printed as amended by the Interpretation Act 1978, ss 17(2)(a) and 23(1).*]

SCHEDULE 11 (see regulations 75, 77 and 79)

MAXIMUM PERMITTED WEIGHTS, ETC.

PART I (see regulation 75)

Maximum permitted laden weights for heavy motor cars and motor cars and trailers in each case not forming part of articulated vehicles

1	2	3	4	5
Item	No. of axles	Distance between foremost and rearmost axles (metres)	Weight not exceeded by any axle (kg)	Maximum permitted laden weight (kg)
1	2	Less than 2.65	The maximum weight permitted by Regulation 78 (items 1 to 5)	14,230 (unless item 2 applies)
2	2	Closely spaced on a trailer where the distance between the foremost axle of the trailer and the rear axle of the drawing vehicle is at least 4.2		16,260
3	2	At least 2.65		16,260
4	2	At least 3.0 if the vehicle is a bus the laden weight of which is calculated in accordance with regulation 78(5) [or a goods vehicle]		17,000
5	2	At least 3.0 if the vehicle is a trailer		18,000
6	3	Less than 3.0	10,170	16,260
7	3	At least 3.0	10,170	18,290
8	3	At least 3.2	8,130	20,330
9	3	At least 3.9	10,170	20,330
10	3	At least 3.9	8,640	22,360
11	3	At least 4.6	10,170	22,360
12	3	At least 4.9	9,400	24,390
13	3	At least 5.1	10,170	24,390
14	4 or more	Less than 3.7	10,170	18,290
15	4 or more	At least 3.7	8,640	20,330
16	4 or more	At least 4.6	8,640	22,360
17	4 or more	At least 4.7	8,640	24,390
18	4 or more	At least 5.0	9,150	24,390
19	4 or more	At least 5.6	9,150	26,420
20	4 or more	At least 6.0	9,660	26,420
21	4 or more	At least 5.9	9,150	28,450
22	4 or more	At least 6.3	9,660	28,450
23	4 or more	At least 6.3	9,400	30,490
24	4 or more	At least 6.5	9,660	30,490

[Part I of Sched 11 is printed as amended by SI 1987 No 676 (with effect from 1 April 1988).]

PART II (see regulation 75)

Maximum permitted laden weights for heavy motor cars and motor cars forming part of articulated vehicles

1	2	3	4	5
Item	No of axles	Distance between foremost and rearmost axles (metres)	Weight not exceeded by any axle not being the foremost or rearmost (kg)	Maximum permitted laden weight (kg)
1	2	At least 2.0	—	14,230
2	2	At least 2.4	—	16,260
3	2	At least 2.7	—	17,000 . . .
4	3 or more	At least 3.0	8,390	20,330
5	3 or more	At least 3.8	8,640	22,360
6	3 or more	At least 4.0	10,500	22,500
7	3 or more	At least 4.3	9,150	24,390
8	3 or more	At least 4.9	10,500	24,390

[Part II of Sched 11 is printed as amended by SI 1987 No 676 (with effect from 1 April 1988).]

PART III (see regulation 77)

Maximum permitted laden weight of articulated vehicles

1	2		3	4
Item	Relevant axle spacing (metres)		Maximum weight (kg)	Minimum overall length (metres)
	(a) Where motor vehicle has 2 axles	(b) Where motor vehicle has more than 2 axles		
1	At least 2.0	At least 2.0	20,330	—
2	At least 2.2	At least 2.2	22,360	—
3	At least 2.6	At least 2.6	23,370	—
4	At least 2.9	At least 2.9	24,390	—
5	At least 3.2	At least 3.2	25,410	—
6	At least 3.5	At least 3.5	26,420	—
7	At least 3.8	At least 3.8	27,440	—
8	At least 4.1	At least 4.1	28,450	—
9	At least 4.4	At least 4.4	29,470	—
10	At least 4.7	At least 4.7	30,490	—
11	At least 5.0	At least 5.0	31,500	—
12	At least 5.3	At least 5.3	32,520	—
13	At least 5.5	At least 5.4	33,000	10.0
14	At least 5.8	At least 5.6	34,000	10.3
15	At least 6.2	At least 5.8	35,000	10.5
16	At least 6.5	At least 6.0	36,000	11.0
17	At least 6.7	At least 6.2	37,000	11.5
18	At least 6.9	At least 6.3	38,000	12.0

PART IV (see regulation 77)

Maximum permitted laden weight of articulated vehicles

1	2	3
Item	Type of articulated vehicle	Maximum permitted weight (kg)
1	Motor vehicle and semi-trailer having a total of 3 axles	24,390
2	Motor vehicle and semi-trailer having a total of 4 axles or motor vehicle first used before 1st April 1973 and semi-trailer having a total of 5 or more axles	32,520
3	Motor vehicle first used on or after 1st April 1973 and semi-trailer having a total of 5 or more axles	38,000

PART V (see regulation 79(2))

Maximum permitted weights of two closely-spaced axles

1	2	3	4	5
Item	Distance between axles (metres)	Maximum permitted weight when weight of neither axle exceeds one half of the specified weight (kg)	Maximum permitted weight in cases not within column (3) when weight of neither axle exceeds 10170 kg (kg)	Maximum permitted weight in cases not within column (3) or (4) (kg)
1	At least 1.02	16,260	12,200	10,500
2	At least 1.05	17,280	15,260	10,500
3	At least 1.20	18,300	16,270	15,260
4	At least 1.35	18,800	17,280	16,500
5	At least 1.50	19,320	18,300	18,000
6	At least 1.80	20,000	19,000	19,000
7	At least 1.85	20,340	19,320	19,320

[PART VI (see regulation 79(3), (6) and (8))

Maximum permitted weights of three closely-spaced axles, and semi-trailer axles where regulation 79(6) applies

1	2	3	4
Item	Smallest distance between any adjoining axles (metres)	Maximum permitted weight of each axle in the case of three closely-spaced axles where regulation 79(6) does not apply (kg)	Maximum permitted weight of each axle in the case of a semi-trailer to which regulation 79(6) applies (kg)
1	At least 0.70	6000	6000
2	At least 0.80	6200	6200
3	At least 0.90	6400	6400
4	At least 1.00	6600	6600
5	At least 1.10	6900	7000
6	At least 1.20	7100	7300
7	At least 1.30	7500	8000]

[Part VI of Sched 11 is printed as substituted by SI 1988 No 1287.]

PART VII (see regulation 79(4))

Maximum permitted weight of three adjacent axles

1	2	3	4
Item	Distance between foremost and rearmost axles (metres)	Maximum intermediate axle weight (kg)	Maximum permitted total weight (kg)
1	Less than 3.0	10,170	18,290
2	At least 3.0	8,390	20,330
3	At least 3.8	8,640	22,360
4	At least 4.6	9,150	24,390

SCHEDULE 12 (see regulations 81 and 82)

CONDITIONS TO BE COMPLIED WITH IN RELATION TO THE USE OF VEHICLES CARRYING WIDE OR LONG LOADS OR VEHICLES CARRYING LOADS OR HAVING FIXED APPLIANCES OR APPARATUS WHICH PROJECT

PART I

Advance notice to police

1. (*a*) Before using on a road a vehicle or vehicles to which this paragraph applies, the owner shall give notice of the intended use to the Chief Officer of Police for any area in which he proposes to use the vehicle or vehicles. The notice shall be given so that it is received by the date after which there

are at least two working days before the date on which the use of the vehicle or vehicles is to begin, and shall include the following details—
(i) time, date and route of the proposed journey, and
(ii) in a case to which regulation 82(2) applies, the overall length and width of the vehicle by which the load is carried and the width of the lateral projection or projections of its load,
(iii) in a case to which regulation 82(4)(*a*) applies, the overall length and width of each vehicle by which the load is carried, the length of any forward or rearward projection and, where the load rests on more than one vehicle, the distance between the vehicles,
(iv) in a case to which regulation 82(4)(*b*) applies, the overall length of the combination of vehicles and the length of any forward or rearward projection of the load, and
(v) in a case to which regulation 82(7) and (8) applies, the overall length of the vehicle and the length of any forward or rearward projection of the load or special appliance or apparatus.

The Chief Officer of Police for any police area may, at his discretion, accept a shorter period of notice or fewer details.

(*b*) The vehicle or vehicles shall be used only in accordance with the details at (*a*) subject to any variation in the time, date or route which may be directed by—
(i) any such Chief Officer of Police to the owner of the vehicle or vehicles, or
(ii) a police constable to the driver in the interests of road safety or in order to avoid undue traffic congestion by halting the vehicle or vehicles in a place on or adjacent to the road on which the vehicle or vehicles are travelling.

(*c*) In this paragraph—
(i) 'Chief Officer of Police' has, in relation to England and Wales, the same meaning as in the Police Act 1964 *[qv]*,
(ii) 'working day' means a day which is not a Sunday, a bank holiday, Christmas Day or Good Friday, and
(iii) 'bank holiday' means a day which is a bank holiday by or under the Banking and Financial Dealings Act 1971 *[qv]*, either generally or in the locality in which the road is situated.

[Words relating expressly and exclusively to Scotland have been omitted from para 1(c) above.]

Attendants

2. At least one person in addition to the person or persons employed in driving a motor vehicle to which this paragraph applies shall be employed—

(*a*) in attending to that vehicle and its load and any other vehicle or vehicles drawn by that vehicle and the load or loads carried on the vehicle or vehicles so drawn, and

(*b*) to give warning to the driver of the said motor vehicle and to any person of any danger likely to be caused to any such person by reason of the presence of the said vehicle or vehicles on the road.

Provided that, where three or more vehicles as respects which the conditions in this paragraph are applicable are travelling together in convoy, it shall be a sufficient compliance with this paragraph if only the foremost and rearmost vehicles in the convoy are attended in the manner prescribed in this paragraph.

For the purpose of this paragraph when a motor vehicle is drawing a trailer or trailers—

(i) any person employed in pursuance of section 34 of the 1972 Act in attending that vehicle or any such trailer shall be treated as being an attendant required by this paragraph so long as he is also employed to discharge the duties mentioned in this paragraph; and

(ii) when another motor vehicle is used for the purpose of assisting in their propulsion on the road, the person or persons employed in driving that other motor vehicle shall not be treated as a person or persons employed in attending to the first-mentioned vehicle or any vehicle or vehicles drawn thereby.

[Section 34 of the Road Traffic Act 1972 (to which reference is made in para 2 of Sched 12 above) was repealed by the Road Traffic (Consequential Provisions) Act 1988 but not re-enacted. It seems therefore that para 2(i) above has lapsed.]

Marking of longer projections

3. (*a*) Every forward and rearward projection to which this paragraph applies shall be fitted with—

(i) an end marker, except in the case of a rearward projection which is fitted with a rear marking in accordance with the Lighting Regulations, and

(ii) where required by sub-paragraphs (*c*) and (*d*) of this paragraph, two or more side markers;

which shall be of the size, shape and colour described in Part II of this Schedule.

(*b*) the end marker shall be so fitted that—

(i) it is as near as is practicable in a transverse plane,

(ii) it is not more than 0.5 m from the extreme end of the projection,

(iii) the vertical distance between the lowest point of the marker and the road surface is not more than 2.5 m,

(iv) it, and any means by which it is fitted to the projection, impedes the view of the driver as little as possible, and

(v) it is clearly visible within a reasonable distance to a person using the road at the end of the vehicle from which the projection extends;

(*c*) where the forward projection exceeds 2 m or the rearward projection exceeds 3 m, one side marker shall be fitted on the right hand side and one on the left hand side of the projection so that—

(i) each marker is as near as is practicable in a longitudinal plane,

(ii) no part extends beyond the end of the projection,

(iii) the vertical distance between the lowest part of each marker and the surface of the road is not more than 2.5 m,

(iv) the horizontal distance between each marker and the end marker or as the case may be, the rear marking carried in accordance with the Lighting Regulations does not exceed 1 m, and

(v) each marker is clearly visible within a reasonable distance to a person using the road on that side of the projection;

(*d*) where—

(i) a forward projection exceeds 4.5 m, or

(ii) a rearward projection exceeds 5 m

extra side markers shall be fitted on either side of the projection so that the horizontal distance between the extreme projecting point of the vehicle from which the projection extends and the nearest point on any side marker from that point, and between the nearest points of any adjacent side markers on the same side does not exceed—

2.5 m in the case of a forward projection, or
3.5 m in the case of a rearward projection.

For the purposes of this sub-paragraph the expression 'the vehicle' shall not include any special appliance or apparatus or any part thereof which is a forward projection or a rearward projection within the meaning of regulation 81;

(*e*) the extra side markers required by this sub-paragraph shall also meet the requirements of (i), (iii) and (v) of sub-paragraph (*c*);

(*f*) every marker fitted in accordance with this paragraph shall be kept clean and unobscured and during the hours of darkness be illuminated by a lamp which renders it readily visible from a reasonable distance and which is so shielded that its light, except as reflected from the marker, is not visible to other persons using the road.

Marking of shorter projections

4. A projection to which this paragraph applies shall be rendered clearly visible to other persons using the road within a reasonable distance, in the case of a forward projection, from the front thereof or, in the case of a rearward projection, from the rear thereof and, in either case, from either side thereof.

PART II

Projection Markers

(see paragraph 3(*a*) of this Schedule)

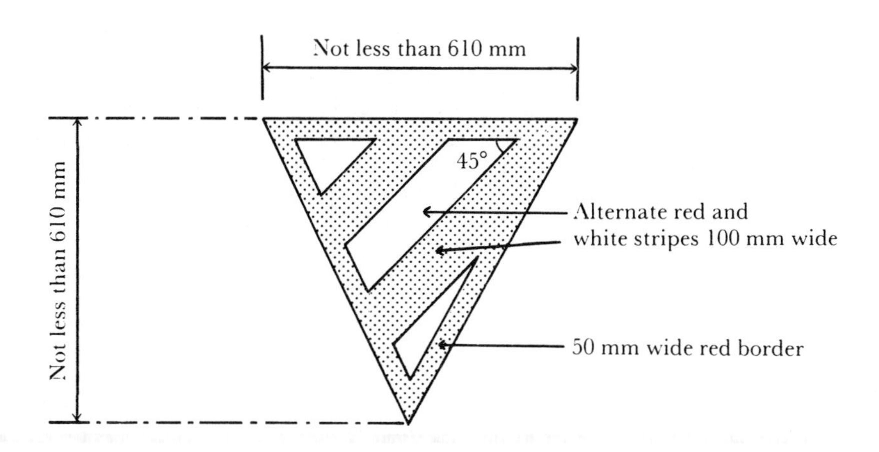

DIAGRAM OF SIDE MARKER SURFACE

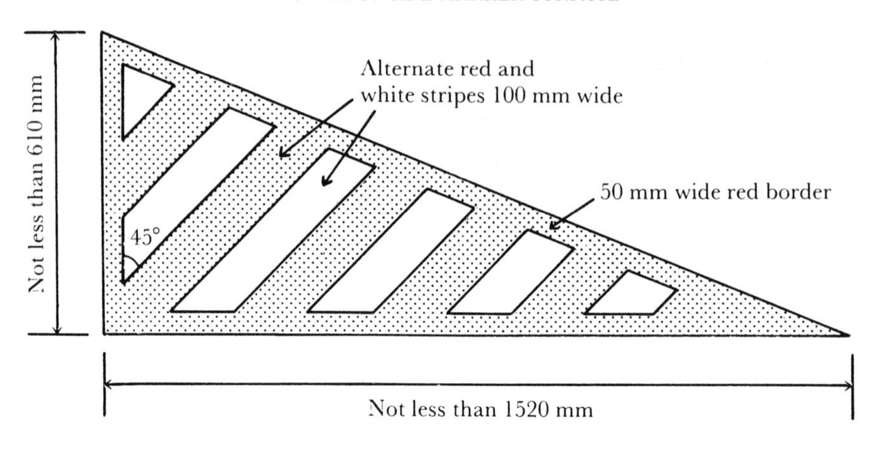

The Road Vehicles (Exemptions from Duty) Regulations 1986

(SI 1986 No 1467)

* * *

2.—(1) In these Regulations—

'the 1971 Act' means the Vehicles (Excise) Act 1971;

'dependant' means any of the following members of an entitled person's household, namely, his spouse, or any other person wholly or mainly maintained by him or in his custody, charge or care;

'entitled person' means a person falling within paragraph (*a*) or (*b*) of regulation 3;

'member of a visiting force' means a person for the time being appointed to serve with any body, contingent or detachment of the forces of any country specified in Part I of the Schedule to these Regulations, which is for the time being present in the United Kingdom on the invitation of Her Majesty's Government, and shall include a person for the time being recognised by the Secretary of State as a member of a civilian component of such force;

'member of a headquarters or organisation' means a member of any country's military forces, except a member of Her Majesty's United Kingdom forces, who is for the time being appointed to serve in the United Kingdom under the orders of any headquarters or organisation specified in Part II of the Schedule to these Regulations, and shall include a person for the time being recognised by the Secretary of State as a civilian member of such headquarters or organisation.

(2) Any reference in these Regulations to a numbered regulation is a reference to the regulation having that number in these Regulations, except where otherwise expressly provided.

3. Exemption from duty

Subject to regulations 4 and 5, a mechanically propelled vehicle shall not be chargeable with any duty under the 1971 Act if it has been imported into any part of the United Kingdom other than Northern Ireland by or on behalf of—

(*a*) a member of a visiting force;

(*b*) a member of a headquarters or organisation; or

(*c*) a dependant of a person falling within paragraph (*a*) or (*b*) of this regulation,

and if there is produced in relation to the vehicle evidence that the person importing it has not been required to pay any duty or tax chargeable in respect of its import.

4. Period of exemption

An exemption from duty pursuant to regulation 3 shall subsist only for a period of 12 months commencing on the date on which the first vehicle licence is issued under the 1971 Act for the vehicle in respect of which the exemption is claimed.

5. Conditions to be observed during period of exemption

During the period prescribed by regulation 4, the owner of or, as the case may be, the person keeping the vehicle in respect of which the exemption is claimed shall comply with the provisions of Part II and Part III of the Road Vehicles (Registration and Licensing) Regulations 1971 *[SI 1971 No 450, as amended (qv)]* (being provisions as to the licensing and registration of mechanically propelled vehicles, and as to the exhibition of licences and the form and display of registration marks).

6. Cessation of exemption

An exemption from duty pursuant to regulation 3 shall cease to apply if, at any time during the period prescribed by regulation 4, the person who imported the vehicle in respect of which the exemption is claimed becomes liable to pay any duty or tax chargeable in respect of the import of that vehicle.

regulation 2(1)

SCHEDULE

PART I

List of Countries

Antigua and Barbuba
Australia
Bahamas
Bangladesh
Barbados
Belgium
Belize
Botswana
Burma
Canada
Cyprus
Denmark
Dominica
Fiji
France
Gambia
Germany, Federal Republic of
Ghana
Greece
Grenada
Guyana
Iceland
India
Italy
Jamaica
Jordan
Kenya
Kiribati
Lesotho
Luxembourg
Malawi
Malaysia
Malta
Mauritius
Nauru
Netherlands
New Zealand
Nigeria
Norway
Pakistan
Papua New Guineau
Portugal
Saint Lucia
Saint Vincent and the Grenadines
Seychelles
Sierra Leone
Singapore
Spain
Solomon Islands
South Africa
Sri Lanka
Swaziland
Tanzania
Tonga
Trinidad and Tobago
Turkey
Tuvalu

Uganda
United States of America
Vanuatu
Western Samoa
Zambia
Zimbabwe

PART II

List of Headquarters and Organisations

The Supreme Headquarters Allied Powers Europe (SHAPE)
The Headquarters of the Supreme Allied Commander, Europe (SACEUR)
The Headquarters of the Supreme Allied Commander Atlantic (SACLANT)
The Headquarters of the Allied Commander in Chief Channel (CINCHAN)
The Channel Committee (CHANCOMTEE)
The Headquarters of the Commander of the Allied Maritime Air Force, Channel (COMMAIRCHAN)
The Headquarters of the Commander in Chief of the Eastern Atlantic Area (CINCEASTLANT)
The Headquarters of the Commander in Chief United Kingdom Air (CINCUKAIR)
The Headquarters of the Commander of the Maritime Air Eastern Atlantic Area (COMMAIREASTLANT)
The Headquarters of the Commander Submarines, East Atlantic (COMSUBEASTLANT)

The Road Vehicles (Prescribed Regulations for the Purposes of Increased Penalties) Regulations 1987

(SI 1987 No 2085)

1. [*Citation and commencement*]

2. Prescribing of regulations

The regulations of the Road Vehicles (Registration and Licensing) Regulations 1971 *[SI 1971 No 450, as amended (qv)]* specified in column (1) of the Table below, the subject matter of which is briefly described in column (2) of the Table, are hereby prescribed for the purposes of paragraph (*a*) of section 37(3) of the Vehicles (Excise) Act 1971 (as set out in paragraph 24 of Part I of Schedule 7 to that Act).

TABLE

PRESCRIBED REGULATIONS

(1) *Regulation*	(2) *Subject matter of regulation*
10	Notification of alteration of vehicles
12(1)	Notification of change of ownership by previous owner of vehicle
12(2)	Notification of change of ownership by new owner of vehicle
13	Notification of change of address of owner of vehicle
14	Notification of destruction or permanent export of vehicle
24(7)	Notification of acquisition of vehicle by the Crown, or of transfer of vehicle from one Government Department to another
24(9)	Notification of disposal, or destruction or permanent export, of vehicle by the Crown
30	Notification of change of name of business, or of business address, by holder of trade licence
31(2)	Return of trade plates
33	Exhibition of trade plates and licences
34*	Restriction on use of trade plates and licences

* Regulation 34 as amended by SI 1986 No 2101.

The Road Vehicles (Registration and Licensing) Regulations 1971

(SI 1971 No 450)

[The text of these regulations is printed as amended by:

the Road Vehicles (Registration and Licensing) (Amendment) Regulations 1972 (SI 1972 No 1865) (29 December 1972);

the Road Vehicles (Registration and Licensing) (Amendment) (No 2) Regulations 1975 (SI 1975 No 1342) (1 September 1975);

the Road Vehicles (Registration and Licensing) (Amendment) Regulations 1976 (SI 1976 No 1680) (9 November 1976);

the Road Vehicles (Registration and Licensing) (Amendment) Regulations 1983 (SI 1983 No 1248) (14 September 1983);

the Road Vehicles (Registration and Licensing) (Amendment) Regulations 1984 (SI 1984 No 814) (1 August 1984);

the Road Vehicles (Registration and Licensing) (Amendment) (No 3) Regulations 1986 (SI 1986 No 2101) (1 January 1987); and

the Road Vehicles (Registration and Licensing) (Amendment) Regulations 1987 (SI 1987 No 2123) (1 January 1988).

The amending regulations are referred to in the notes by their years and numbers. The dates referred to above are the dates on which the regulations came into force.

The main regulations have also been amended by the Road Vehicles (Registration and Licensing) (Amendment) Regulations 1973 (SI 1973 No 870); the Road Vehicles (Registration and Licensing) (Amendment) Regulations 1975 (SI 1975 No 1089); the Road Vehicles (Registration and Licensing) (Amendment) (No 2) Regulations 1976 (SI 1976 No 2089); the Road Vehicles (Registration and Licensing) (Amendment) Regulations 1977 (SI 1977 No 230); the Road Vehicles (Registration and Licensing) (Amendment) Regulations 1978 (SI 1978 No 1536); the Road Vehicles (Registration and Licensing) (Amendment) Regulations 1986 (SI 1986 No 607); the Road Vehicles (Registration and Licensing) (Amendment) (No 2) Regulations 1986 (SI 1986 No 1177); but these do not affect the text of any regulation set out in this work.]

* * *

ARRANGEMENT OF REGULATIONS

PART I

PRELIMINARY

PART II

LICENSING AND REGISTRATION

PART III

Exhibition of Licences and Registration Marks

* * *

PART V

Trade Licences

* * *

PART I

Preliminary

1. Commencement and citation *[Omitted.]*

2. Revocation, savings and transitional provisions *[Omitted.]*

3. Interpretation

(1) In these Regulations, unless the context otherwise requires, the following expressions have the meanings hereby respectively assigned to them, that is to say:—

'the Act' means the Vehicles (Excise) Act 1971;

'agricultural machine' has the same meaning as in Schedule 3 to the Act;

'bicycle' means a mechanically propelled bicycle (including a motor scooter, a bicycle with an attachment for propelling it by mechanical power and a mechanically propelled bicycle used for drawing a trailer or sidecar) not exceeding 8 hundredweight in weight unladen;

. . .

['invalid carriage'] means a mechanically propelled vehicle (including a cycle with an attachment for propelling it by mechanical power) which does not exceed [10] hundredweight in weight unladen and is adapted and used or kept on a road for an invalid or invalids;

'owner' in relation to a vehicle means the person by whom the vehicle is kept . . . and the expression 'ownership' shall be construed accordingly;

'pedestrian controlled vehicle' means a mechanically propelled vehicle with three or more wheels which does not exceed 8 hundredweight in weight unladen and which is neither constructed nor adapted for use nor used for the carriage of a driver or passenger;

. . .

'road' has the same meaning as in [section 192 of the Road Traffic Act 1988];

'trade licence' has the meaning assigned to it by section 16 of the Act;

'trade plates' has the meaning assigned thereto in Regulation 31 of these Regulations;

'tricycle' means a mechanically propelled tricycle (including a motor scooter and a tricycle with an attachment for propelling it by mechanical power) not exceeding 8 hundredweight in weight unladen and not being a pedestrian controlled vehicle;

['valeting' means the thorough cleaning of a vehicle prior to its first registration by the Secretary of State including removing wax and grease from the exterior, engine and interior, and 'valeted' shall be construed accordingly;]

'works truck' means a mechanically propelled vehicle designed for use in private premises and used on a road only in delivering goods from or to such premises to or from a vehicle on a road in the immediate neighbourhood, or in passing from one part of any such premises to another or to other private premises in the immediate neighbourhood or in connection with road works while at or in the immediate neighbourhood of the site of such works.

(2) Any reference in these Regulations to any enactment shall be construed as a reference to that enactment as amended by or under any subsequent enactment.

(3) The [Interpretation Act 1978] shall apply for the interpretation of these Regulations as it applies for the interpretation of an Act of Parliament, and as if for the purposes of [section 17] of that Act these Regulations were an Act of Parliament and the Regulations revoked by Regulation 2 of these Regulations were Acts of Parliament thereby repealed.

[Regulation 3 is printed as amended by the Road Traffic Act 1972, Sched 10, para 3; SI 1972 No 1865; SI 1975 No 1342; the Interpretation Act 1978, s 17(2)(a); SI 1986 No 2101.
Selected definitions only are reproduced in para (1).]

[3A. Exclusion for electrically assisted pedal cycles

The provisions of Parts II and III of these Regulations do not apply to an electrically assisted pedal cycle for the time being prescribed for the purposes of [section 140 of the Road Traffic Regulation Act 1984] and [section 189 of the Road Traffic Act 1088].]

[Regulation 3A was inserted by SI 1983 No 1248 and is printed as amended by the Road Traffic Regulation Act 1984, s 144(1) and Sched 10, para 2; the Interpretation Act 1978, s 17(2)(a).]

* * *

PART II

Licensing and Registration

* * *

12. Notification of change of ownership

(1) On a change of ownership of a mechanically propelled vehicle the previous owner of the vehicle shall deliver the registration book issued in respect of the vehicle and may deliver any current licence issued in respect of the vehicle to the new owner and shall notify in writing forthwith the change of ownership to the [Secretary of State for Transport] stating the registration mark of the vehicle, its make and class and the name and address of the new owner.

(2) Upon acquiring the vehicle the new owner shall—

(*a*) if he intends to use or keep the vehicle upon public roads otherwise than under a trade licence, forthwith insert his name and address in the appropriate part of the registration book and deliver it to the [Secretary of State for Transport];

(*b*) if he does not intend to use or keep the vehicle upon public roads, forthwith notify the [Secretary of State for Transport] in writing that he is the owner of the vehicle, and he shall state in such notification the registration mark of the vehicle, its make and class, the name and address of the previous owner and the fact that he does not intend to use or keep the vehicle on public roads;

(*c*) if he intends to use the vehicle upon public roads solely under a trade licence, at the expiration of three months from the date when he became the owner of the vehicle or, if a further change of ownership occurs, on the date of that change, whichever is the sooner, notify the [Secretary of State for Transport] in writing of his name and address and those of the previous owner.

[Regulation 12 is printed as amended by the Minister of Transport Order 1979 (SI 1979 No 571) and the Transfer of Functions (Transport) Order 1981 (SI 1981 No 238).

The 1971 Regulations were made under in part under the Vehicles (Excise) Act 1971, s 23, as substituted by s 39 of and Sched 7, Part I, para 20, to that Act. Section 23 (as so substituted) was amended by the Finance Act 1987. Under s 2(6) and (8) of, and Sched 1, Part III, para 16(4), to the 1987 Act, reg 12(1) is deemed as from 15 May 1987 to have effect as if the amendments effected to s 23 of the 1971 Act by the 1987, s 2(6) and (8) and Sched 1, Part III, para 16(3), had been in force when reg 12(1) was made.

Contravention of either reg 12(1) or (2) is a summary offence for which the offender is liable to a fine on level 3 of the standard scale under the Vehicles (Excise) Act 1971, s 37(3)(a) and the Road Vehicles (Prescribed Regulations for the Purposes of Increased Penalties) Regulations 1987 (SI 1987 No 2085) (qv).]

13. Notification of change of address of owner

If the owner of a mechanically propelled vehicle changes his address he shall forthwith enter particulars of his new address in the space provided in the registration book issued in respect of the vehicle and send the book to the [Secretary of State for Transport].

[Regulation 13 is printed as amended by the Minister of Transport Order 1979 (SI 1979 No 571) and the Transfer of Functions (Transport) Order 1981 (SI 1981 No 238).

Contravention of reg 13 is a summary offence for which the offender is liable to a fine on level 3 of the standard scale under the Vehicle (Excise) Act 1971, s 37(3)(a), and the Road Vehicles (Pre-

scribed Regulations for the Purposes of Increased Penalties) Regulations 1987 (SI 1987 No 2085) (qv).]

* * *

PART III

Exhibition of Licences and Registration Marks

16. Exhibition of licences

(1) Every licence issued under the Act and in force for a mechanically propelled vehicle, excepting a tramcar, shall be fixed to and exhibited on the vehicle in accordance with the provisions of this Regulation at all times while the vehicle is being used or kept on a public road:

Provided that when such a licence is delivered up with an application for a new licence to [any post office authorised for the time being to issue vehicle licences in accordance with arrangements for that purpose made between the Post Office and the [Secretary of State for Transport]], no licence shall be required to be fixed to and exhibited on the vehicle until the new licence is obtained, when that licence shall be deemed to be the licence in force for the vehicle for the purposes of this Regulation.

(2) Each such licence shall be fixed to the vehicle in a holder sufficient to protect the licence from any effects of the weather to which it would otherwise be exposed.

(3) The licence shall be exhibited on the vehicle:—

(*a*) in the case of an invalid vehicle, tricycle or bicycle, other than a case specified in sub-paragraph (*b*) or (*c*) of this paragraph, on the near side of the vehicle in front of the driving seat so that all the particulars thereon are clearly visible by daylight from the near side of the road;

(*b*) in the case of a bicycle drawing a side-car or to which a side-car is attached when the bicycle is being kept on a public road, on the near side of the handlebars of the bicycle or on the near side of the side-car in front of the driving seat so that all the particulars thereon are clearly visible by daylight from the near side of the road;

(*c*) in the case of any vehicle fitted with a glass windscreen in front of the driver extending across the vehicle to its near side, on or adjacent to the near side . . . of the windscreen, so that all particulars thereon are clearly visible by daylight from the near side of the road;

(*d*) in the case of any other vehicle, if the vehicle is fitted with a driver's cab containing a near side window, on such window, or on the near side of the vehicle in front of the driver's seat or towards the front of the vehicle in the case of a pedestrian controlled vehicle and not less than 2 feet 6 inches and not more than 6 feet above the surface of the road, so that in each case all the particulars thereon are clearly visible by daylight from the near side of the road.

[Regulation 16 is printed as amended by SI 1972 No 1865, SI 1976 No 1680, the Minister of Transport Order 1979 (SI 1979 No 571) and the Transfer of Functions (Transport) Order 1981 (SI 1981 No 238).]

* * *

[19.—(1) Save as provided in paragraph (2) below, no person shall use or cause or permit to be used on a road during the hours of darkness any motor vehicle unless every letter and number of the registration mark displayed on the back of—

(*a*) the motor vehicle if it is not drawing a trailer, or

(*b*) the trailer if the motor vehicle is drawing one trailer, or

(*c*) the rearmost trailer if the motor vehicle is drawing more than one trailer,

is illuminated so as to be easily legible in the absence of fog from every part of the relevant area, the diagonal of the square governing that area being—

(i) 15 metres in the case of a bicycle, an invalid vehicle and a pedestrian controlled vehicle, and

(ii) 18 metres in the case of any other vehicle.

(2) The provisions of paragraph (1) above do not apply in respect of:—

(*a*) a works truck; or

(*b*) a vehicle which is not required to be fitted with a rear registration plate.]

[Regulation 19 is printed as substituted by SI 1984 No 814.]

* * *

22. Trailers

(1) Subject to paragraph (3) of this Regulation, where one or more trailers are attached to a mechanically propelled vehicle the owner of the vehicle shall ensure that there is displayed on the trailer or rearmost trailer (as the case may be) the registration mark of the mechanically propelled vehicle, and that such registration mark is fixed to and displayed on the trailer as if the trailer were a vehicle of the same class or description as the mechanically propelled vehicle.

(2) Where the registration mark of a mechanically propelled vehicle is fixed to and displayed on a trailer attached to it in accordance with the foregoing paragraph, the requirements of these Regulations as to the fixing to and display of a registration mark on the back of a mechanically propelled vehicle shall not apply to the vehicle drawing the trailer.

(3) Where the mechanically propelled vehicle is a restricted vehicle, the registration mark fixed to and displayed on the trailer in accordance with paragraph (1) of this Regulation may, instead of being that of the vehicle to which the trailer is attached, be that of any other restricted vehicle belonging to the owner of the vehicle to which the trailer is attached, and in such a case the duty in the said paragraph (1) as to fixing and display shall apply as if the other restricted vehicle were the vehicle to which the trailer was attached.

(4) In this Regulation 'restricted vehicle' means a vehicle mentioned in section 7(1) of the Act or paragraph 2(1) of Schedule 3 thereto.

* * *

PART V

Trade Licences

* * *

[28A. Descriptions of businesses

The prescribed descriptions of businesses for the purposes of the definition of a 'motor trader' in section 16(8) of the Act are those of modifying vehicles (whether by fitting accessories or otherwise) prior to their first registration by the Secretary of State and of valeting vehicles.]

[Regulation 28A was inserted by SI 1986 No 2101.]

* * *

30. Notification of change of address etc

If the holder of a trade licence changes the name of his business or his business address he shall notify this fact and the new name or address forthwith to the [Secretary of State for Transport] and shall at the same time send to the [Secretary of State for Transport] the licence for any necessary amendment.

[Regulation 30 is printed as amended by the Minister of Transport Order 1979 (SI 1979 No 571) and the Transfer of Functions (Transport) Order 1981 (SI 1981 No 238).

Contravention of reg 30 is a summary offence for which the offender is liable to a fine on level 3 of the standard scale under the Vehicles (Excise) Act 1971, s 37(3)(a), and the Road Vehicles (Prescribed Regulations for the Purposes of Increased Penalties) Regulations 1987 (SI 1987 No 2085) (qv).]

31. Issue of trade plates and replacements therefor

(1) The [Secretary of State for Transport] shall issue to every holder of a trade licence in respect of that licence two plates (in these Regulations referred to as 'trade plates') appropriate to the class of vehicles on which they will be used showing the general registration mark assigned to the holder of the licence, and one of the plates so issued shall contain means whereby the licence may be fixed thereto:

Provided that where the holder of a trade licence satisfies the [Secretary of State for Transport] that the vehicles which he will use by virtue of the licence include vehicles which would otherwise be liable to duty under Schedule 1 to the Act and other vehicles he shall be entitled to be issued free of charge with two additional trade plates in respect of the vehicles first mentioned in this proviso.

(2) Each trade plate shall remain the property of the [Secretary of State for Transport] and shall be returned forthwith to the [Secretary of State for Transport] if the person to whom it was issued no longer holds a trade licence which is in force or if that person ceases to be a motor trader or a vehicle tester.

(3) *[Omitted.]*

(4) In the case of the loss of any trade plate, if at any time after the issue of a replacement the original plate is found, the holder of the trade licence, if the plate is in his possession, shall forthwith return it to the [Secretary of State for Transport], or if it is not in his possession but he becomes aware that it is found, shall take all reasonable steps to obtain possession of it and if successful shall forthwith return it to the [Secretary of State for Transport], so, however, that if possession is not obtained, such fact shall be notified to the [Secretary of State for Transport] by the holder of the licence.

[Regulation 31(1), (2) and (4) is printed as amended by the Minister of Transport Order 1979 (SI 1979 No 571); the Transfer of Functions (Transport) Order 1981 (SI 1981 No 238).

Contravention of reg 31(2) is a summary offence for which the offender is liable to a fine on level 3 of the standard scale under the Vehicles (Excise) Act 1971, s 37(3)(a), and the Road Vehicles

(Prescribed Regulations for the Purposes of Increased Penalties) Regulations 1987 (SI 1987 No 2085) (qv).]

32. Alteration of trade plates and similar offences

(1) No person shall alter, deface, mutilate or add anything to any trade plate or exhibit upon any mechanically propelled vehicle any trade plate which has been altered, defaced, mutilated or added to as aforesaid or upon which the figures or particulars have become illegible or the colour has become altered by fading or otherwise.

(2) No person shall exhibit on any mechanically propelled vehicle anything which could be mistaken for a trade plate.

33. Exhibition of trade plates and licences

No person shall use a vehicle on a public road by virtue of a trade licence except in accordance with the following provisions, that is to say—

(*a*) there shall be fixed to and displayed on the vehicle the trade plates issued by the [Secretary of State for Transport] in such a manner that, if the trade plates contained a registration mark assigned to the vehicle, the provisions of Regulations 18 and 19 of these Regulations would be complied with, notwithstanding the vehicle may not have been first registered on or after 1st October 1938 or it is a works truck or an agricultural machine; and

(*b*) where in accordance with the provisions of the preceding paragraph a trade plate is required to be fixed to the front of a vehicle, the trade plate so fixed shall be that containing means for fixing the licence thereto, and the trade licence shall be fixed to the vehicle by means of that plate and exhibited on that plate so as to be at all times clearly visible by daylight.

[Regulation 33 is printed as amended by the Minister of Transport Order 1979 (SI 1979 No 571) and the Transfer of Functions (Transport) Order 1981 (SI 1981 No 238).

Contravention of reg 33 is a summary offence for which the offender is liable to a fine on level 3 of the standard scale under the Vehicles (Excise) Act 1971, s 37(3)(a), and the Road Vehicles (Prescribed Regulations for the Purposes of Increased Penalties) Regulations 1987 (SI 1987 No 2085) (qv).]

34. Restriction on use of trade plates and licences

No person, not being the holder of a trade licence, shall use on a public road a vehicle on which there is displayed a trade plate or a trade licence, so, however, that nothing in this Regulation shall apply so as to prevent a person with the consent of the holder of the trade licence from driving a vehicle when the vehicle is being used on a public road by virtue of a trade licence [for a purpose prescribed in regulations 35 to 37 of these Regulations] and by the holder thereof.

[Regulation 34 is printed as amended by SI 1986 No 2101.

Contravention of reg 34 is a summary offence for which the offender is liable to a fine on level 3 of the standard scale under the Vehicles (Excise) Act 1971, s 37(3)(a), and the Road Vehicles (Prescribed Regulations for the Purposes of Increased Penalties) Regulations 1987 (SI 1987 No 2085) (qv).]

Purposes for which a vehicle may be used

35.—(1) In this Regulation, 'business purpose', in relation to a motor trader, means—

(*a*) a purpose connected with his business as a manufacturer or repairer of or dealer in mechanically propelled vehicles, . . .

(*b*) a purpose connected with his business as a manufacturer or repairer of or dealer in trailers carried on in conjunction with his business as a motor trader,

[(*c*) a purpose connected with his business of modifying vehicles prior to their first registration by the Secretary of State or of valeting vehicles.]

(2) For the purposes of sub-paragraphs (*a*) to (*k*) of paragraph (4) of this Regulation, where a mechanically propelled vehicle is used on a public road by virtue of a trade licence and that vehicle is drawing a trailer, the vehicle and trailer shall be deemed to constitute a single vehicle.

(3) Save as provided in Regulation 36 of these Regulations, no person, being a motor trader and the holder of a trade licence, shall use any mechanically propelled vehicle on a public road by virtue of that licence unless it is a vehicle which is temporarily in his possession in the course of his business as a motor trader . . .

(4) Save as provided in the said Regulation 36 and without derogation from the provisions of the last preceding paragraph of this Regulation, no person, being a motor trader and the holder of a trade licence, shall use any mechanically propelled vehicle on a public road by virtue of that licence for a purpose other than a business purpose and other than one of the following purposes:—

(*a*) for its test or trial or the test or trial of its accessories or equipment in the ordinary course of construction [modification] or repair or after completion in either such case;

(*b*) for proceeding to or from a public weighbridge for ascertaining its unladen weight or to or from any place for its registration or inspection by a person acting on behalf of the [Secretary of State for Transport];

(*c*) for its test or trial for the benefit of a prospective purchaser, for proceeding at the instance of a prospective purchaser to any place for the purpose of such test or trial, or for returning after such test or trial;

(*d*) for its test or trial for the benefit of a person interested in promoting publicity in regard to it, for proceeding at the instance of such a person to any place for the purpose of such test or trial, or for returning after such test or trial;

(*e*) for delivering it to the place where the purchaser intends to keep it;

(*f*) for demonstrating its operation or the operation of its accessories or equipment when being handed over to the purchaser;

(*g*) for delivering it from one part of his premises to another part of his premises, or for delivering it from his premises to the premises of, or between parts of premises of, another manufacturer or repairer of or dealer in mechanically propelled vehicles or removing it from the premises of another manufacturer or repairer of or dealer in mechanically propelled vehicles direct to his own business;

(*h*) for proceeding to or returning from a workshop in which a body or a special type of equipment or accessory is to be or has been fitted to it or in which it is to be or has been painted [valeted] or repaired;

(*i*) for proceeding from the premises of a manufacturer or repairer of or dealer in mechanically propelled vehicles to a place from which it is to be transported by train, ship or aircraft or for proceeding to the premises of such a manufacturer, repairer or dealer from a place to which it has been so transported;

(*j*) for proceeding to or returning from any garage, auction room or other place at which vehicles are usually stored or usually or periodically offered for sale and at which the vehicle is to be or has been stored or is to be or has been offered for sale as the case may be;

(*k*) for proceeding to or returning from a place where it is to be or has been tested, or for proceeding to a place where it is to be broken up or otherwise dismantled; or

(*l*) *[Revoked.]*

[Regulation 35 is printed as amended by the Minister of Transport Order 1979 (SI 1979 No 571); the Transfer of Functions (Transport) Order 1981 (SI 1981 No 238); SI 1986 No 2101; SI 1987 No 2123.]

36. No person, being a motor trader and who is a manufacturer of mechanically propelled vehicles and the holder of a trade licence, shall use any mechanically propelled vehicle, kept by him solely for the purposes of conducting research and development in the course of his business as such a manufacturer, on a public road by virtue of that licence except for such a purpose.

37. No person, being a vehicle tester and the holder of a trade licence, shall use any mechanically propelled vehicle on a public road by virtue of that licence for any purpose other than testing it or any trailer drawn thereby or any of the accessories or equipment on such vehicle or trailer in the course of his business as a vehicle tester.

Conveyance of goods or burden

38.—(1) No person, being a motor trader and the holder of a trade licence, shall use a mechanically propelled vehicle on a public road by virtue of that licence for the conveyance of goods or burden of any description other than—

(*a*) a load which is carried by a vehicle being used for a relevant purpose and is carried solely for the purpose of testing or demonstrating the vehicle or any of its accessories or equipment and which is returned to the place of loading without having been removed from the vehicle except for such last mentioned purpose or in the case of accident [or when the load consists of water, fertiliser or refuse.]:

In this sub-paragraph 'relevant purpose' means a purpose mentioned in Regulation 35(4)(*a*), (*c*), (*d*) and (*f*) of these Regulations; or

(*b*) *[Revoked.]*

(*c*) any load built in as part of the vehicle or permanently attached thereto: or

(*d*) a load consisting of parts, accessories or equipment designed to be fitted to the vehicle and of tools for so fitting them, the vehicle being used for a relevant purpose;

In this sub-paragraph 'relevant purpose' means a purpose mentioned in Regulation 35(4)(*g*), (*h*) or (*i*) of these Regulations; or

(*e*) a load consisting of a trailer, the vehicle carrying the trailer being used for a relevant purpose:

In this sub-paragraph 'relevant purpose' means a purpose mentioned in Regulation 35(4)(*e*), (*h*) or (*i*) of these Regulations.

(2) No person, being a motor trader and who is a manufacturer of mechanically propelled vehicles and the holder of a trade licence, shall use any mechanically propelled vehicle, kept by him solely for the purpose of conducting research and development in the course of his business as such a manufacturer, on a public road by virtue of that licence for the conveyance of goods or burden of any description other than—

(*a*) a load which is carried solely for the purpose of testing the vehicle or any of its accessories or equipment and which is returned to the place of loading without having been removed from the vehicle except for such purpose or in the case of accident; or

(*b*) any load built in as part of the vehicle or permanently attached thereto,

and nothing in the last preceding paragraph of this Regulation shall be taken as applying to a mechanically propelled vehicle the use of which is restricted by this paragraph.

(3) For the purposes of this Regulation and the next succeeding Regulation, where a vehicle is so constructed that a trailer may by partial superimposition be attached to the vehicle in such a manner as to cause a substantial part of the weight of the trailer to be borne by the vehicle, the vehicle and the trailer shall be deemed to constitute a single vehicle.

[Regulation 38 is printed as amended by SI 1986 No 2101; SI 1987 No 2123.]

39. No person, being a vehicle tester and the holder of a trade licence, shall use a mechanically propelled vehicle on a public road by virtue of that licence for the conveyance of goods or burden of any description other than—

(*a*) a load which is carried solely for the purpose of testing or demonstrating the vehicle or any of its accessories or equipment and which is returned to the place of loading without having been removed from the vehicle except for such purpose or in the case of accident; or

(*b*) any load built in as part of the vehicle or permanently attached thereto.

40. Carriage of passengers

[No person, being the holder of a trade licence, shall use a mechanically propelled vehicle on a public road by virtue of that licence for carrying any person on the vehicle or on any trailer drawn by it except a person carried in connection with a purpose for which the holder of the trade licence may use the vehicle on the public road by virtue of that licence.]

[Regulation 40 is printed as substituted by SI 1986 No 2101.]

* * *

The Road Vehicles Lighting Regulations 1984

(SI 1984 No 812)

[The text of these regulations is printed as amended by:
the Road Vehicles Lighting (Amendment) Regulations 1987 (SI 1987 No 1315) (1 January 1988).
The amending regulations are referred to in the notes to the main regulations by their year and number. The date referred to above is the date on which those regulations came into force.]

ARRANGEMENT OF REGULATIONS

PART I—Preliminary

PART II—Regulations Governing the Fitting of Lamps, Reflectors, Rear Markings and Devices

PART III—Regulations Governing the Maintenance and Use of Lamps, Reflectors, Rear Markings and Devices

PART IV—TESTING AND INSPECTION OF LIGHTING EQUIPMENT AND REFLECTORS

SCHEDULES

. . . .

The Secretary of State for Transport in exercise of powers

(i) s 40(1), (2A) and (3) of the Road Traffic Act 1972 as regards vehicles, other than cycles not being motor vehicles;

(ii) s 66(1) and (3) of that Act as regards cycles not being motor vehicles; and

(iii) s 41(3) of that Act as regards the provisions referred to in Regulation 1(2) below

all of which powers are now vested in him, and of all other enabling powers, and after consultation with representative organisations in accordance with section 199(2) of that Act, hereby makes the following Regulations:—

[Although the Road Traffic Act 1972 has been repealed, the references to that Act have been retained in the recital of enabling powers for historical reasons.

Section 40(1), (2A) and (3) of the 1972 Act has been re-enacted as s 41(1), (2), (4) and (5) of the Road Traffic Act 1988; s 66(1) and (3) of the 1972 Act has become s 81(1), (2) and (4) of the 1988 Act; and s 41(3) of the 1972 Act has become s 43(3) of the 1988 Act.]

PART I

Preliminary

1. Commencement, citation and exercise of powers *[Omitted.]*

2. Revocation *[Omitted.]*

3. Interpretation

(1) Unless the context otherwise requires, any references in these Regulations—

(*a*) to a numbered Regulation or Schedule is a reference to the Regulation or Schedule bearing that number in these Regulations,

(*b*) to a numbered paragraph is to the paragraph bearing that number in the Regulation or Schedule in which the reference occurs,

(*c*) to a numbered or lettered sub-paragraph is to the sub-paragraph bearing that number or letter in the paragraph in which the reference occurs.

(2) In these Regulations, unless the context otherwise requires—

'the Act' means the [Road Traffic Act 1988];

'the Construction and Use Regulations' means the [Road Vehicles (Construction and Use) Regulations 1986] *[SI 1986 No 1078, qv]*;

'the Designation of Approval Marks Regulations' means the Motor Vehicles (Designation of Approval Marks) Regulations 1979 *[SI 1979 No 1088, as amended]*;

'articulated bus', 'articulated vehicle', 'dual-purpose vehicle', 'engineering plant', 'industrial tractor', 'large passenger-carrying vehicle', 'overall length', 'overall width', 'passenger vehicle, 'pedestrian-controlled vehicle', 'vehicle in the service of a visiting force or of a headquarters', 'wheel', 'wheeled', 'works trailer' and 'works truck' have the meanings given respectively by [Regulation 3(2)] of the Construction and Use Regulations;

'agricultural vehicle' means a vehicle constructed or adapted for agriculture, grass cutting, forestry, land levelling, dredging or similar operations and primarily used for one or more of these purposes, and includes any trailer drawn by an agricultural vehicle;

'angles of visibility' means the horizontal and vertical angles throughout which the whole of the apparent surface of a lamp or reflector is visible, disregarding any part of the apparent surface which may be obscured by any part of the vehicle, provided that the lamp or reflector remains visible throughout the angles specified in the relevant Schedule below;

'apparent surface' means the orthogonal projection of a light-emitting surface in a plane perpendicular to the direction of observation;

'breakdown vehicle' means a vehicle used to attend an accident or breakdown or to draw a broken down vehicle;

'Chief Officer of Police' and 'police area', in relation to England and Wales, have the same meanings as in the Police Act 1964 *[qv]*;

'circuit-closed tell-tale' means a light showing that a device has been switched on;

'combat vehicle' means a vehicle of a type described at item 1, 2 or 3 in column 1 of Schedule 1 to the Motor Vehicles (Authorisation of Special Types) General Order 1979) *[SI 1979 No 1198, qv]*;

'daytime hours' means the time between half an hour before sunrise and half an hour after sunset;

'dim-dip lighting device' means a device which complies with the requirements specified in Part I of Schedule 3;

'dipped beam' means a beam of light emitted by a lamp which illuminates the road ahead of the vehicle without causing undue dazzle or discomfort to oncoming drivers or other road users;

'direction indicator' means a lamp on a vehicle used to indicate to other road users that the driver intends to change direction to the right or to the left;

'emergency vehicle' means—

(*a*) a motor vehicle used for fire brigade or police purposes;

(*b*) an ambulance, being a motor vehicle (other than an invalid carriage) which is constructed or adapted for the purposes of conveying sick, injured or disabled persons and which is used for such purposes;

(*c*) a motor vehicle owned by a body formed primarily for the purposes of fire salvage and used for those or similar purposes;

(*d*) a motor vehicle owned by the Forestry Commission or by a local authority and used from time to time for the purposes of fighting fires;

(*e*) a motor vehicle owned by the Secretary of State for Defence and used—

(i) for the purposes of the disposal of bombs or explosives,

(ii) by the Naval Emergency Monitoring Organisation for the purposes of a nuclear accident or an accident involving radio-activity,

(iii) by the Royal Air Force Mountain Rescue Service for the purposes of rescue operations or any other emergencies; or

(iv) by the Royal Air Force Armament Support Unit;

(*f*) a motor vehicle primarily used for the purposes of the Blood Transfusion Service provided under the National Health Service Act 1977;

(*g*) a motor vehicle used by Her Majesty's Coastguard or Coastguard Auxiliary Service for the purposes of giving aid to persons in danger or vessels in distress on or near the coast;

(*h*) a motor vehicle owned by the National Coal Board and used for the purposes of rescue operations at mines;

(*i*) a motor vehicle owned by the Royal National Lifeboat Institution and used for the purposes of launching lifeboats, and

(*j*) a motor vehicle primarily used for the purposes of conveying any human tissue for transplanting or similar purposes;

'extreme outer edge', in relation to a side of a vehicle, means the plane parallel with the median longitudinal plane of the vehicle, and coinciding with its lateral outer edge, disregarding the projection of—

(*a*) so much of the distortion of any tyre as is caused by the weight of the vehicle,
(*b*) any connections for tyre pressure gauges,
(*c*) any anti-skid devices which may be mounted on the wheels,
(*d*) rear-view mirrors,
(*e*) lamps and reflectors,
(*f*) customs seals affixed to the vehicle, and devices for securing and protecting such seals, and
(*g*) special equipment;

'front fog lamp' means a lamp used to improve the illumination of the road in front of a motor vehicle in conditions of seriously reduced visibility;

'front position lamp' means a lamp used to indicate the presence and width of a vehicle when viewed from the front;

'hazard warning signal device' means a device which is capable of operating simultaneously all the direction indicators with which a vehicle, or a combination of vehicles, is fitted for the purpose of warning other persons of a temporary obstruction on the road;

'headlamp' means a lamp used to illuminate the road in front of a vehicle and which is not a front fog lamp;

'home forces' means the naval, military or air forces of Her Majesty raised in the United Kingdom;

'home forces vehicle' means a vehicle owned by, or in the service of, the home forces and used for naval, military or air forces purposes;

'horse-drawn', in relation to a vehicle, means that the vehicle is drawn by a horse or other animal;

'hours of darkness' means the time between half an hour after sunset and half an hour before sunrise;

'illuminated area', in relation to a lamp, means the area of the orthogonal projection of the light-emitting surface on a vertical plane (touching the surface of the lamp) at right angles to the longitudinal axis of the vehicle to which it is fitted, such projection being bounded by the edges of straight-edged screens situated in that plane and each allowing only 98 per cent of the total intensity of the light to be shown in the direction parallel to the longitudinal axis of the vehicle and, for the purposes of determining the lower, upper and lateral edges of a lamp, only screens having a horizontal or vertical edge shall be considered;

'installation and performance requirements', in relation to any lamp, reflector, rear marking or device, means the requirements specified in the Schedule hereto relating to that lamp, reflector, rear marking or device;

'kerbside weight' means—
(*a*) in relation to a motor vehicle, the weight of the vehicle when it carries—
(i) no person,
(ii) a full supply of fuel in its tank, an adequate supply of other liquids incidental to its propulsion and no load other than the loose tools and equipment with which the vehicle is normally equipped, and
(*b*) in relation to a trailer, the weight of the trailer when it carries no person and it is otherwise unladen;

'light-emitting surface', in relation to a lamp, means that part of the exterior surface of the lens through which light is emitted when the lamp is lit, and in relation to a reflex reflector means that part of the exterior surface of the reflex reflector through which light can be reflected;

'main beam' means a beam of light emitted by a lamp which illuminates the road over a long distance ahead of the vehicle;

'matched pair', in relation to lamps, means a pair of lamps in respect of which—

(*a*) both lamps emit light of substantially the same colour and intensity; and

(*b*) both lamps are of the same size and of such a shape that they are symmetrical to one another;

'maximum distance from the side of the vehicle' means the maximum distance from that side (the side being determined by reference to 'extreme outer edge') to the nearest edge of the illuminated area in the case of a lamp or the reflecting area in the case of a reflex reflector;

'maximum height above the ground' means the height above which no part of the illuminated area in the case of a lamp, or the reflecting area in the case of a reflex reflector, extends when the vehicle is at its kerbside weight and when each tyre with which the vehicle is fitted is inflated to the pressure recommended by the manufacturer of the vehicle;

'maximum speed' means, in relation to a motor vehicle, the maximum speed the vehicle can attain on the level under its own power;

'minimum height above the ground' means the height below which no part of the illuminated area in the case of a lamp, or the reflecting area in the case of a reflex reflector, extends when the vehicle is at its kerbside weight and when each tyre with which the vehicle is fitted is inflated to the pressure recommended by the manufacturer of the vehicle;

'motor bicycle combination' means a combination of a solo motor bicycle and a sidecar;

'movable platform' means a platform which is attached to, and may be moved by means of, an extensible boom;

'obligatory', in relation to a lamp, reflector, rear marking or device, means a lamp, reflector, rear marking or device with which a vehicle, its load or equipment is required by these Regulations to be fitted;

'operational tell-tale' means a warning device readily visible or audible to the driver and showing whether a device that has been switched on is operating correctly or not;

'optional', in relation to a lamp, reflector, rear marking or device, means a lamp, reflector, rear marking or device with which a vehicle, its load or equipment is not required by these Regulations to be fitted;

'pair', in relation to lamps, reflectors or rear markings, means a pair of lamps, reflectors or rear markings, one on each side of the vertical plane passing through the longitudinal axis of the vehicle, in respect of which—

(*a*) each lamp, reflector or rear marking is at the same height above the ground; and

(*b*) each lamp, reflector or rear marking is at the same distance from the said vertical plane,

these requirements being complied with so far as practicable in the case of an asymmetric vehicle;

'pedal cycle' means a vehicle which is not constructed or adapted to be propelled by mechanical power and which is equipped with pedals, including an electrically-assisted pedal cycle prescribed for the purposes of [section 189] of the Act and [section 140 of the Road Traffic Regulation Act 1984];

'pedal reflex reflector' means a reflex reflector attached to or incorporated in the pedals of a pedal cycle or motor bicycle;

'rear fog lamp' means a lamp used to render a vehicle more readily visible from the rear in conditions of seriously reduced visibility;

'rear marking' means a marking of the size, colour and type indicated in Part I, Section B of Schedule 18;

'rear position lamp' means a lamp used to indicate the presence and width of a vehicle when viewed from the rear;

'rear reflex reflector' means a reflex reflector used to indicate the presence and width of a vehicle when viewed from the rear;

'rear registration plate lamp' means a lamp used to illuminate the rear registration plate;

'reflecting area' means, in relation to a reflex reflector fitted to a vehicle, the area of the orthogonal projection on a vertical plane—

(*a*) at right angles to the longitudinal axis of the vehicle of that part of the reflector designed to reflect light in the case of a rear reflex reflector, and

(*b*) parallel to the longitudinal axis of the vehicle of that part of the reflector designed to reflect light in the case of a side reflex reflector;

'reversing lamp' means a lamp used to illuminate the road to the rear of a vehicle for the purpose of reversing and to warn other road users that the vehicle is reversing or about to reverse;

'road clearance vehicle' means a mechanically propelled vehicle used for dealing with frost, ice or snow on roads;

'separation distance' between two lamps or two reflex reflectors means, except where otherwise specified, the distance between the orthogonal projections in a plane perpendicular to the longitudinal axis of the vehicle of the illuminated areas of the two lamps or the reflecting areas of the two reflectors;

'side marker lamp' means a lamp fitted to the side of a vehicle or its load and used to render the vehicle more visible to other road users;

'side reflex reflector' means a reflector fitted to the side of a vehicle or its load and used to render the vehicle more visible from the side;

'solo motor bicycle' means a motor bicycle without a sidecar;

'special equipment' means the movable platform of a vehicle fitted with such a platform, the apparatus for moving the platform and any jacks fitted to the vehicle for stabilising it while the movable platform is in use;

'special warning lamp' means a lamp, fitted to the front or rear of an emergency vehicle, capable of emitting a blue flashing light and not any other kind of light;

'stop lamp' means a lamp used to indicate to road users that the brakes of a vehicle or combination of vehicles are being applied;

'trailer' means a vehicle constructed or adapted to be drawn by another vehicle;

'vehicle' means a vehicle of any description and includes a machine or implement of any kind drawn or propelled along roads whether by hand, horse or mechanical power;

'visiting vehicle' has the meaning given by [Regulation 3 of the Motor Vehicles (International Circulation) Regulations 1985] *[SI 1985 No 610]*;

'warning beacon' means a lamp that is capable of emitting a flashing or rotating beam of light throughout 360° in the horizontal plane;

'work lamp' means a lamp used to illuminate a working area or the scene of an accident, breakdown or roadworks in the vicinity of the vehicle to which it is fitted.

(3) Material designed primarily to reflect light is, when reflecting light, to be treated for the purposes of these Regulations as showing a light, and material capable of reflecting an image is not, when reflecting the image of a light, to be so treated.

(4) In these Regulations—

(*a*) except in the case of a dipped-beam headlamp, a main-beam headlamp and a front fog lamp, a reference to one lamp includes any combination of two or more lamps, whether identical or not, having the same function and emitting light of the same colour, if it comprises devices the projection of the aggregate illuminated areas of which in a vertical plane perpendicular to the median longitudinal plane of the vehicle occupies 60 per cent or more of the area of the smallest rectangle circumscribing the projections of those illuminated areas; and

(*b*) a reference to two lamps includes—

(i) a single illuminated area which

(A) is placed symmetrically in relation to the median longitudinal plane of the vehicle,

(B) extends on both sides to within 400 millimetres of the extreme outer edge of the vehicle,

(C) is not less than 800 millimetres long, and

(D) is illuminated by not less than two sources of light, and

(ii) any number of illuminated areas which—

(A) are juxtaposed,

(B) if on the same transverse plane have illuminated areas which occupy not less than 60 per cent of the area of the smallest rectangle circumscribing the projections of their illuminated areas,

(C) are placed symmetrically in relation to the median longitudinal plane of the vehicle,

(D) extend on both sides to within 400 millimetres of the extreme outer edge of the vehicle,

(E) do not have a total length of less than 800 millimetres, and

(F) are illuminated by not less than two sources of light.

(5) The angles of visibility specified in the Schedules to these Regulations shall be treated as being satisfied if they are satisfied when every door, tailgate, boot lid, engine cover or cab is in the closed position, provided that at all times every front and rear position lamp, direction indicator and rear reflector, in each case being an obligatory lamp or reflector, remains visible to the front or rear as appropriate.

(6) For the purposes of these Regulations, in determining when a motor vehicle is first used, the date of such first use shall be taken to be the date which is prescribed as the date of first use by [Regulation 3(3)] of the Construction and Use Regulations for the purposes of those Regulations. In the case of a motor bicycle combination, the date of manufacture or first use of the sidecar shall be disregarded.

(7) Any reference in these Regulations to a vehicle having any number of wheels is a reference to a vehicle having that number of wheels the tyres or rims of which are in contact with the ground when the vehicle is in motion on a road and any two such wheels shall be treated as one wheel if the distance between the centres of the areas of contact between them and the ground is less than 460 millimetres.

(8) For the purposes of these Regulations, the unladen weight of a motor vehicle shall be calculated in accordance with [section 190] of the Act.

(9) For the purposes of these Regulations, maximum gross weight shall be determined in accordance with the provisions of [Part I of Schedule 8] to the Construction and Use Regulations in the case of a motor vehicle, and [Part II of Schedule 8] to those Regulations in the case of a trailer.

[Regulation 3 is printed as amended by the Interpretation Act 1978, ss 17(2)(a) and 23(1); the Road Traffic Regulation Act 1984, s 144(1) and Sched 10, para 2.

The term 'visiting vehicle' is defined in the Motor Vehicles (International Circulation) Regulations 1985 (SI 1985 No 610), reg 3(1), as 'a vehicle brought temporarily into Great Britain by a person resident outside the United Kingdom'; and a 'vehicle' is there defined as 'a mechanically propelled vehicle intended or adapted for use on roads'.

Words relating expressly and exclusively to Scottish legislation have been omitted from reg 3(2) (definitions of 'Chief Officer of Police' and 'emergency vehicle').]

4. Exemptions—General

(1) Where a provision is applied by these Regulations to a motor vehicle first used on or after a specified date it does not apply to that vehicle if it was manufactured at least six months before that date.

(2) Where an exemption from, or relaxation to, a provision is applied by these Regulations to a motor vehicle first used before a specified date it shall also apply to a motor vehicle first used on or after that date if it was manufactured at least six months before that date.

(3) Nothing in these Regulations shall require any lamp or reflector to be fitted during daytime hours to—

(*a*) a vehicle not fitted with any front or rear position lamp,

(*b*) an incomplete vehicle proceeding to a works for completion,

(*c*) a pedal cycle,

(*d*) a pedestrian-controlled vehicle,

(*e*) a horse-drawn vehicle,

(*f*) a vehicle drawn or propelled by hand, or

(*g*) a combat vehicle.

(4) For the purposes of these Regulations, a lamp shall not be treated as being a lamp if it is—

(*a*) so painted over or masked that it is not capable of being immediately used or readily put to use; or

(*b*) an electric lamp which is not provided with any system of wiring by means of which that lamp is, or can readily be, connected with a source of electricity.

5. Exemptions—Temporarily imported vehicles and vehicles proceeding to a port for export

Part II of these Regulations does not apply to—

(*a*) any vehicle having a base or centre in a country outside Great Britain from which it normally starts its journeys, provided that a period of not more than 12 months has elapsed since the vehicle was last brought into Great Britain;

(*b*) a visiting vehicle;

(*c*) any combination of two or more vehicles, one of which is drawing the other or others, if the combination includes any vehicle of the type mentioned in paragraph 5(*a*) or (*b*); or

(*d*) a vehicle proceeding to a port for export

if in each case the vehicle or combination of vehicles complies in every respect with the requirements about lighting equipment and reflectors relating thereto contained in a Convention mentioned in [item 2 of the table to Regulation 4(4)] of the Construction and Use Regulations.

[Regulation 5 is printed as amended by the Interpretation Act 1978, ss 17(2)(a) and 23(1).]

6. Exemptions—Vehicles towing or being towed

(1) No motor vehicle first used before 1st April 1986 and no pedal cycle or trailer manufacturerd before 1st October 1985 is required by Regulation 16 to be fitted with any rear position lamp, stop lamp, rear direction indicator, rear fog lamp or rear reflector whilst a trailer fitted with any such lamp or reflector is attached to its rear.

(2) No trailer manufacturerd before 1st October 1985 is required by Regulation 16 to be fitted with—

(*a*) any front position lamp whilst being drawn by a passenger vehicle or a dual-purpose vehicle;

(*b*) any stop lamp, rear fog lamp or rear direction indicator whilst being drawn by a motor vehicle which is not required by Regulation 16 to be fitted with any such lamp.

(3) No trailer is required by Regulation 16 to be fitted with any stop lamp or direction indicator whilst being drawn by a motor vehicle fitted with one or two stop lamps and two or more direction indicators if the dimensions of the trailer are such that when the longitudinal axes of the drawing vehicle and the trailer lie in the same vertical plane such stop lamps and at least one direction indicator on each side of the vehicle are visible to an observer in that vertical plane from a point 6 metres behind the rear of the trailer whether it is loaded or not.

(4) No rear marking is required to be fitted to any vehicle by Regulation 16 if another vehicle in a combination of which it forms part would obscure any such marking.

(5) In the case of any lamp, reflector or rear marking fitted to a vehicle forming part of a combination of vehicles, the angles of visibility specified in the Schedules to these Regulations shall be treated as being satisfied if they would have been satisfied but for the presence of other vehicles in the combination.

(6) No broken down vehicle whilst being drawn is required by these Regulations either to be fitted with any lamp, reflector or rear marking, except rear position lamps and rear reflectors, when on a road during the hours of darkness or, if fitted, to be maintained in accordance with Regulation 20.

7. Exemptions—Military vehicles

(1) Regulation 16 does not apply to a home forces' vehicle or to a vehicle in the service of a visiting force or of a headquarters whilst being used

(*a*) in connection with training which is certified in writing for the purposes of this Regulation by a person duly authorised in that behalf to be training on a special occasion and of which not less than 48 hours' notice has been given by that person to the Chief Officer of Police of every police area in which the place selected for the training is wholly or partly situated; or (*b*) on manoeuvres within such limits and during such period as may from time to time be specified by Order in Council under the Manoeuvres Act 1958.

(2) Where not less than 6 nor more than 12 vehicles being home forces' vehicles or vehicles of a visiting force or of a headquarters are proceeding together in a convoy on tactical or driving exercises which are authorised in writing by a person duly authorised in that behalf, and of which not less than 48 hours' notice in writing has been given by that person to the Chief Officer of Police of every police area through which it is intended that the convoy shall pass and the interval between any two vehicles in such a convoy does not exceed 20 metres—

(*a*) front position lamps shall be required only on the vehicle leading the convoy;

(*b*) rear position lamps shall be required only on the rearmost vehicle provided that every other vehicle in the convoy carries a bright light under the vehicle illuminating either a part of the vehicle or anything attached to the vehicle or the road surface beneath the vehicle, in such a manner that the presence of the vehicle can be detected from the rear.

(3) No lamp is required to be fitted to any home forces' vehicle or any vehicle in the service of a visiting force or of a headquarters if the vehicle is constructed or adapted for combat and is such that compliance with these provisions is impracticable and is fitted with two red rear position lamps and two red reflex reflectors when on a road during the hours of darkness. Such lamps and reflectors need not meet any of the requirements specified in Schedules 10 and 17.

(4) Part II of these Regulations does not apply to a vehicle in the service of a visiting force or of a headquarters if the vehicle complies in every respect with the requirements as to lighting equipment and reflectors relating thereto contained in a Convention referred to in Regulation 5.

8. Exemptions—Invalid carriages

The provisions of Regulation 6 of the Use of Invalid Carriages on Highways Regulations 1970 *[SI 1970 No 1391, qv]* apply for the purposes of these Regulations as they apply for the purposes of the said Regulations of 1970.

[The Use of Invalid Carriages on Highways Regulations 1970 have been revoked except so far as they apply to invalid carriages which were manufactured before 30 January 1989 by the Use of Invalid Carriages on Highways Regulations 1988 (SI 1988 No 2268), qv. As to the requirements regarding lighting in the 1988 Regulations, see ibid, reg 9 below.]

9. Exemptions—Vehicles drawn or propelled by hand

A vehicle drawn or propelled by hand which has an overall width, including any load, not exceeding 800 millimetres is required by these Regulations to be fitted with lamps and reflectors only when it is used on the carriageway of a road during the hours of darkness otherwise than—

(*a*) close to the near side or left hand edge of the carriageway, or

(*b*) to cross the road.

10. Provision as respects Trade Descriptions Act 1968

Where by any provision in these Regulations any vehicle or any of its parts or equipment is required to be marked with a specification number or a registered certification trade mark of the British Standards Institution or with any approval mark, nothing in that provision shall be taken to authorise any person to apply any such number or mark to the vehicle, part or equipment in contravention of the Trade Descriptions Act 1968.

PART II

[REGULATIONS GOVERNING THE FITTING OF LAMPS, REFLECTORS, REAR MARKINGS AND DEVICES]

11. Colour of light shown by lamps and reflectors

(1) No person shall use, or cause or permit to be used, on a road a vehicle which is readily capable of showing a red light to the front, except red light from—

(*a*) a red and white chequered domed lamp, or a red and white segmented mast-mounted flashing beacon, fitted to a fire service control vehicle and intended for use at the scene of an emergency;

(*b*) reflex reflective material or a reflex reflector designed primarily to reflect light to one or both sides of the vehicle and attached to or incorporated in any wheel or tyre of—

(i) a pedal cycle and any sidecar attached to it;

(ii) a solo motor bicycle or motor bicycle combination; or

(iii) an invalid carriage; or

(*c*) a traffic sign which is attached to a vehicle and prescribed as authorised for that purpose under [section 64 of the Road Traffic Regulation Act 1984].

(2) No person shall use, or cause or permit to be used, on a road a vehicle which is readily capable of showing any light to the rear, other than a red light, except—

(*a*) amber light from a direction indicator;

(*b*) white light from a reversing lamp;

(*c*) white light from a work lamp;

(*d*) light to illuminate the interior of a vehicle;

(*e*) light from an illuminated rear registration plate;

(*f*) light for the purposes of illuminating a taxi meter;

(*g*) in the case of a large passenger-carrying vehicle, light for the purposes of illuminating a route indicator;

(*h*) blue light and white light from a chequered domed lamp fitted to a police control vehicle and intended for use at the scene of an emergency;

(*i*) white light from a red and white chequered domed lamp, or a red and white segmented mast-mounted flashing beacon, fitted to a fire service control vehicle and intended for use at the scene of an emergency;

(*j*) blue light from a warning beacon or rear special warning lamp fitted to an emergency vehicle;

(*k*) amber light from a warning beacon fitted to—

(i) a road clearance vehicle;

(ii) a vehicle constructed or adapted for the purpose of collecting refuse;

(iii) a breakdown vehicle;

(iv) a vehicle having a maximum speed not exceeding 25 miles per hour [or any trailer drawn by such a vehicle];

(v) a vehicle having an overall width exceeding 2.9 metres;

(vi) a vehicle used for the purposes of testing, maintaining, improving, cleansing or watering roads or for any purpose incidental to any such use;

(vii) a vehicle used for the purpose of inspecting, cleansing, maintaining, adjusting, renewing or installing any apparatus which is in, on, under or over a road, or for any purpose incidental to any such use;

(viii) a vehicle used for or in connection with any purpose for which it is authorised to be used on roads by an Order under [section 44] of the Act and any vehicle used to escort such a vehicle;

(ix) a vehicle used by Her Majesty's Customs and Excise for the purpose of testing fuels;

(*l*) green light from a warning beacon fitted to a vehicle used by a medical practitioner registered by the General Medical Council (whether with full, provisional or limited registration);

(*m*) yellow light from a warning beacon fitted to a vehicle for use at airports;

(*n*) reflected light from amber pedal reflex reflectors;

(*o*) reflected light of any colour from reflex reflective material or a reflex reflector designed primarily to reflect light to one or both sides of the vehicle and attached to or incorporated in any wheel or type of—

(i) a pedal cycle and any sidecar attched to it;

(ii) a solo motor bicycle or motor bicycle combination; or

(iii) an invalid carriage;

(*p*) reflected light from amber reflex reflective material on a road clearance vehicle;

(*q*) reflected light from yellow reflex reflective registration plates;

(*r*) reflected light from yellow reflex reflective material incorporated in a rear marking of a type specified in Part I Section B of Schedule 18 and fitted to—

(i) a motor vehicle having a maximum gross weight exceeding 7500 kilograms;

(ii) a motor vehicle first used before 1st August 1982 having an unladen weight exceeding 3000 kilograms;

(iii) a trailer having a maximum gross weight exceeding 3500 kilograms;

(iv) a trailer manufactured before 1st August 1982 having an unladen weight exceeding 1000 kilograms;

(v) a trailer which forms part of a combination of vehicles one of which is of a typc mentioned in a previous item of this sub-paragraph; or

(vi) a load carried by any vehicle of a type mentioned in this sub-paragraph; or

(*s*) light of any colour from a traffic sign attached to a vehicle and authorised as mentioned in Regulation 11(1)(*c*).

[Regulation 11 is printed as amended by the Interpretation Act 1978, ss 17(2)(a) and 23(1); the Road Traffic Regulation Act 1984, s 144(1) and Sched 10, para 2; SI 1987 No 1315.]

12. Movement of lamps and reflectors

(1) Save as provided in paragraph (2), no person shall use, or cause or permit to be used, on a road any vehicle to which, or to any load or equipment of which, there is fitted a lamp, reflector or marking which is capable of being moved by swivelling, deflecting or otherwise while the vehicle is in motion.

(2) Paragraph (1) does not apply in respect of—

(*a*) a headlamp which can be dipped only by the movement of the headlamp or its reflector;

(*b*) a headlamp which is capable of adjustment so as to compensate for the effect of the load carried by the vehicle;

(*c*) a lamp or reflector which can be deflected to the side by the movement of, although not necessarily through the same angle as, the front wheel or wheels of the vehicle when turned for the purpose of steering the vehicle;

(*d*) a headlamp or front fog lamp which can be wholly or partially retracted or concealed;

(*e*) a direction indicator fitted to a motor vehicle first used before 1st April 1986;

(*f*) a work lamp;

(*g*) a warning beacon;

(*h*) an amber pedal reflex reflector; or

(*i*) reflex reflective material or a reflex reflector of any colour which is fitted so as to reflect light primarily to one or both sides of the vehicle and is attached to or incorporated in any wheel or tyre of—

(i) a pedal cycle and any sidecar attached to it;

(ii) a solo motor bicycle or motor bicycle combination; or

(iii) an invalid carriage.

13. Lamps to show a steady light

(1) Save as provided in paragraph (2), no person shall use, or cause or permit to be used, on a road any vehicle which is fitted with a lamp which emits a flashing light.

(2) Paragraph (1) does not apply in respect of—

(*a*) a direction indicator;

(*b*) a headlamp being flashed manually to signal the presence of the vehicle to which it is fitted;

(*c*) a warning beacon or special warning lamp;

(*d*) a lamp or illuminated sign fitted to a vehicle used for police purposes; or

(*e*) a green warning lamp used as an anti-lock brake indicator.

14. Filament lamps

No person shall use, or cause or permit to be used, on a road any motor vehicle first used on or after 1st April 1986 or any trailer manufactured on or after 1st October 1985, equipped with any lamp of a type that is required by any Schedule to these Regulations to be marked with an approval mark, unless every such lamp is fitted with a filament lamp referred to in the Designation of Approval Marks Regulations in—

(1) Regulation 4 and Schedule 2, items 2 or 2A, 8, 20, 37 or 37A; or

(2) Regulation 5 and Schedule 4, item 18.

15. Restrictions on fitting of warning beacons, special warning lamps and similar devices

(1) Save as provided in [regulations 11 and 15A], no person shall use, or cause or permit to be used, on a road any vehicle which is fitted with—

(*a*) a warning beacon or a special warning lamp, or

(*b*) a device which resembles a warning beacon or a special warning lamp.

(2) The provisions of paragraph (1) apply in respect of a device, warning beacon or special warning lamp whether the same is in working order or not.

[Regulation 15 is printed as amended by SI 1987 No 1315.]

[15A. Obligatory warning beacons

(1) Subject to paragraph (2), no person shall use, or cause or permit to be used, on an unrestricted dual-carriageway road any motor vehicle with four or more wheels having a maximum speed not exceeding 25 miles per hour unless it or any trailer being drawn by it is fitted with at least one warning beacon showing an amber light.

(2) Paragraph (1) shall not apply in relation to—

(*a*) any motor vehicle first used before 1st January 1947; and

(*b*) any motor vehicle, or any trailer being drawn by it, to which paragraph (1) would otherwise apply, when that vehicle or trailer is on any carriageway of any unrestricted dual-carriageway road for the purpose only of crossing that road in the quickest manner practicable in the circumstances.

(3) Warning beacons fitted in accordance with paragraph (1) shall comply with Schedule 15.

(4) A road is an unrestricted road for the purposes of this regulation and of regulation 22A if any motor vehicle may lawfully be driven on it at a speed exceeding 50 miles per hour.

(5) In this regulation and in regulation 22A 'dual-carriageway road' has the same meaning as in Schedule 6 to the Road Traffic Regulation Act 1984 *[qv]*.]

[Regulation 15A was inserted by SI 1987 No 1315.]

16. Obligatory lamps, reflectors, rear markings and devices

(1) Save as provided in the foregoing provisions of these Regulations and in paragraph (2), no person shall use, or cause or permit to be used, on a road any vehicle of a class specified in an item in column 2 of Schedule 1 unless it is equipped with lamps, reflectors, rear markings and devices which—

(*a*) are of a type specified in that item in column 3 of that Schedule, and

(*b*) comply with the relevant installation and performance requirements referred to in that item in column 4 of that Schedule.

(2) The requirements specified in paragraph (1) do not apply in respect of a lamp, reflector, rear marking or device of a type specified in an item in column 3 of Schedule 1 in the case of a vehicle specified in column 5 of that Schedule, nor to any lamp, reflector, rear marking or device to which Regulation 17 applies.

(3) The requirements specified in paragraph (1) apply without prejudice to any additional requirement specified in Regulation 18 or 19.

17. Optional lamps, reflectors, rear markings and devices

No person shall use, or cause or permit to be used, on a road any vehicle which is fitted with an optional lamp, reflector, rear marking or device specified in an item in column 2 of the Table below unless it complies with the provisions or, in the case of a direction indicator, the relevant provisions, contained in the Schedule, or part of the Schedule, referred to in that item in column 3 of that Table.

TABLE

1	2	3
Item No	Type of lamp, reflector, rear marking or device	Schedule, or Part of Schedule containing provisions with which compliance is required
1	Front position lamp	Schedule 2, Part II
2	Dim-dip lighting device	Schedule 3, Part II
3	Dipped-beam headlamp	Schedule 4, Part II
4	Main-beam headlamp	Schedule 5, Part II
5	Front fog lamp	Schedule 6
6	Director indicator	Schedule 7, Parts I and II
7	Hazard warning signal device	Schedule 8, Part II
8	Side marker lamp	Schedule 9, Part II
9	Rear position lamp	Schedule 10, Part II
10	Rear fog lamp	Schedule 11, Part II
11	Stop lamp	Schedule 12, Part II
12	Reversing lamp	Schedule 13
13	Warning beacon	Schedule 15
14	Side reflex reflector	Schedule 16, Part II
15	Rear reflex reflector	Schedule 17, Part II
16	Rear marking	Schedule 18, Part II
17	Pedal reflex reflector	Schedule 19, Part II

18. Projecting trailers and vehicles carrying overhanging or projecting loads or equipment

(1) No person shall use, or cause or permit to be used, on a road in the circumstances mentioned in paragraph (2)—

(*a*) any trailer which forms part of a combination of vehicles which projects laterally beyond any preceding vehicle in the combination; or

(*b*) any vehicle or combination of vehicles which carries a load or equipment

in either case under the conditions specified in an item in column 2 of the Table below, unless the vehicle or combination of vehicles complies with the requirements specified in that item in column 3 of that Table.

TABLE *[ie table to reg 18(1)]*

1	2	3
Item No	Conditions	Requirements
1	A trailer which is not fitted with front position lamps and which projects laterally on any side so that the distance from the outermost part of the projection to the outermost part of the illuminated area of the obligatory front position lamp on that side fitted to any preceding vehicle in the combination exceeds 400 millimetres.	A lamp showing white light to the front shall be fitted to the trailer so that the outermost part of the illuminated area is not more than 100 millimetres from the outermost projection of the trailer. The installation and performance requirements relating to front position lamps do not apply to any such lamp.

1	2	3
Item No	Conditions	Requirements
2	A trailer which is not fitted with front position lamps and which carries a load or equipment which projects laterally on any side of the trailer so that the distance from the outermost projection of the load or equipment to the outermost part of the illuminated area of the obligatory front position lamp on that side fitted to any preceding vehicle in the combination exceeds 400 millimetres.	A lamp showing white light to the front shall be fitted to the trailer or the load or equipment so that the outermost part of the illuminated area is not more than 400 millimetres from the outermost projection of the load or equipment. The installation and performance requirements relating to front position lamps do not apply to any such lamp.
3	A vehicle which carries a load or equipment which projects laterally on any side of the vehicle so that the distance from the outermost part of the load or equipment to the outermost part of the illuminated area of the obligatory front or rear position lamp on that side exceeds 400 millimetres.	Either— (*a*) the obligatory front or rear position lamp shall be transferred from the vehicle to the load or equipment; or (*b*) an additional front or rear position lamp shall be fitted to the vehicle, load or equipment. All the installation, performance and maintenance requirements relating to front or rear position lamps shall in either case be complied with except that for the purpose of determining the lateral position of such lamps any reference to the vehicle shall be taken to include the load or equipment except special equipment on a vehicle fitted with a movable platform or the jib of any crane.
4	A vehicle which carries a load or equipment which projects beyond the rear of the vehicle or, in the case of a combination of vehicles, beyond the rear of the rearmost vehicle in the combination, more than— (*a*) 2 metres in the case of an agricultural vehicle or a vehicle carrying a fire escape; or (*b*) 1 metre in the case of any other vehicle.	An additional rear lamp capable of showing red light to the rear visible from a reasonable distance shall be fitted to the vehicle or the load in such a position that the distance between the lamp and the rearmost projection of the load or equipment does not exceed 2 metres in the case mentioned in sub-paragraph (*a*) in column 2 of this item or 1 metre in any other case. The installation and performance requirements relating to rear position lamps do not apply to any such additional lamp.
5	A vehicle which carries a load or equipment which obscures any obligatory lamp, reflector or rear marking.	Either— (*a*) the obligatory lamp, reflector or rear marking shall be transferred to a position on the vehicle, load or equipment where it is not obscured; or (*b*) an additional lamp, reflector or rear marking shall be fitted to the vehicle, load or equipment. All the installation, performance and maintenance requirements relating to obligatory lamps, reflectors or rear markings shall in either case be complied with.

(2) The circumstances referred to in paragraph (1) are—

(*a*) as regards item 5 in the Table, in so far as it relates to obligatory stop lamps and direction indicators, all circumstances; and

(*b*) as regards items 1 to 4 in the Table and item 5 in the Table, except in so far as it relates to obligatory stop lamps and direction indicators, the circumstances of hours of darkness and of seriously reduced visibility.

19. Additional side marker lamps

(1) Save as provided in paragraph (2), no person shall use, or cause or permit to be used, on a road during the hours of darkness, or in seriously reduced visibility during daytime hours, any vehicle or combination of vehicles of a type specified in an item in column 2 of the Table below unless each side of the vehicle or combination of vehicles is fitted with the side marker lamps specified in that item in column 3 and those lamps are kept lit.

TABLE *[ie table to reg 19(1)]*

1	2	3
Item No	Vehicle or combination of vehicles	Side marker lamps
1	A vehicle or a combination of vehicles the overall length of which (including any load) exceeds 18.3 metres.	(*a*) One lamp no part of the light-emitting surface of which is more than 9.15 metres from the foremost part of the vehicle or vehicles (in either case inclusive of any load); (*b*) One lamp no part of the light-emitting surface of which is more than 3.05 metres from the rearmost part of the vehicle or vehicles (in either case inclusive of any load); and (*c*) Such other lamps as are required to ensure that not more than 3.05 metres separates any part of the light-emitting surface of one lamp and any part of the light-emitting surface of the next lamp.
2	A combination of vehicles the overall length of which (including any load) exceeds 12.2 metres but does not exceed 18.3 metres and carrying a load supported by any two of the vehicles but not including a load carried by an articulated vehicle.	(*a*) One lamp no part of the light-emitting surface of which is forward of, or more than 1530 millimetres rearward of, the rearmost part of the drawing vehicle; (*b*) If the supported load extends more than 9.15 metres rearward of the rearmost part of the drawing vehicle, one lamp no part of the light-emitting surface of which is forward of, or more than 1530 millimetres rearward of, the centre of the length of the load.

(2) The requirements specified in paragraph (1) do not apply to

(*a*) a combination of vehicles where any vehicle being drawn in that combination has broken down; or

(*b*) a vehicle (not being one of a combination of vehicles)—

(i) having a special appliance or apparatus of a kind specified in [Regulation 82(5)] of the Construction and Use Regulations; or

(ii) carrying a load of a kind specified in [Regulation 82(7) or (8)(*a*)] of those Regulations

if the conditions specified in [paragraph 3] (which provides for the special marking of projections from vehicles) of [Schedule 12] to those Regulations are complied with in relation to the special appliance or load as if the said conditions had been expressed in the said [Regulation 82] to apply in the case of every special appliance or apparatus or load of a kind specified in [paragraph (5), (7) or (8)(*a*)] of that Regulation.

(3) Every side marker lamp fitted in accordance with this Regulation shall comply with Schedule 9.

[Regulation 19 has been amended by the Interpretation Act 1978, ss 17(2)(a) and 23(1).

The wording of the Road Vehicles (Construction and Use) Regulations 1986 (SI 1986 No 1078), above, does not correspond exactly with that of the revoked regulations of 1978. Until these regulations are formally amended it may be necessary to refer to the text of the 1978 Regulations to determine precisely which provisions of the 1986 Regulations are referred to in this regulation.]

PART III

Regulations Governing the Maintenance and Use of Lamps, Reflectors, Rear Markings and Devices

20. Maintenance of lamps, reflectors, rear markings and devices

(1) Save as provided in paragraph (4), no person shall use, or cause or permit to be used, on a road any vehicle unless every front position lamp, rear position lamp, headlamp, rear registration plate lamp, side marker lamp, rear fog lamp, reflex reflector and rear marking with which it is required by these Regulations to be fitted and every stop lamp and direction indicator with which it is fitted is clean and in good working order.

(2) No person shall use, or cause or permit to be used, on a road any vehicle which is required by these Regulations to be fitted with a hazard warning signal device unless that device is in good working order.

(3) No person shall use, or cause or permit to be used, on a road any vehicle fitted with a dipped-beam headlamp, front fog lamp, rear fog lamp or reversing lamp, whether or not the lamp is required by these Regulations to be fitted to the vehicle, unless the lamp is maintained so that its aim will not cause undue dazzle or inconvenience to other persons using the road.

(4) The provisions of paragraph (1) do not apply in respect of—

(*a*) a rear fog lamp on a vehicle which is part of a combination of vehicles any part of which is not required by these Regulations to be fitted with a rear fog lamp;

(*b*) a rear fog lamp on a motor vehicle drawing a trailer;

(*c*) a defective lamp or reflector fitted to a vehicle in use on a road during daytime hours if such a lamp or reflector became defective during the journey which is in progress or if arrangements have been made to remedy the defect with all reasonable expedition; or

(*d*) a lamp, reflector or rear marking which, during daytime hours, is fitted to a combat vehicle.

21. Requirements about the use of front and rear position lamps, rear registration plate lamps and side marker lamps

(1) Save as provided in paragraphs (2) and (3), no person shall—

(*a*) use, or cause or permit to be used, on a road any vehicle during the hours of darkness or any vehicle which is in motion during daytime hours in seriously reduced visibility; or

(*b*) allow to maintain at rest, or cause or permit to be allowed to remain at rest, on a road any vehicle during the hours of darkness

unless every front position lamp, rear position lamp, rear registration plate lamp and side marker lamp with which the vehicle is required by these Regulations to be fitted is kept lit and, in the case of—

(i) a motor bicycle combination which is only fitted with a front position lamp on the sidecar, or a trailer to the front of which no other vehicle is attached and which is not required to be fitted with front position lamps, a pair of front position lamps is fitted and kept lit; or

(ii) a solo motor bicycle which is not required to be fitted with a front position lamp, a front position lamp is fitted and kept lit.

(2) The provisions of paragraph (1) do not apply in respect of a vehicle of a class specified in paragraph (4) which is parked on a road on which a speed limit of 30 miles per hour or less is in force and the vehicle is parked—

(*a*) in a parking place for which provision is made under [section 6], or which is authorised under [section 32] or designated under [section 45, of the Road Traffic Regulation Act 1984], or which is set apart as a parking place under some other enactment or instrument and the vehicle is parked in a manner which does not contravene the provision of any enactment or instrument relating to the parking place; or

(*b*) in a lay-by—

(i) the limits of which are indicated by a traffic sign consisting of the road marking shown in diagram 1010 in Schedule 2 of the Traffic Signs Regulations and General Directions 1981 *[SI 1981 No 859]*; or

(ii) the surface of which is a colour or texture which is different from that of the part of the carriageway of the road used primarily by through traffic; or

(iii) the limits of which are indicated by a continuous strip of surface of a different colour or texture from that of the surface of the remainder of the carriageway of the road; or

(*c*) elsewhere than in such a parking place or lay-by if—

(i) the vehicle is parked on—

(A) a road on which the driving of vehicles otherwise than in one direction is prohibited at all times and its left or near side is as close as may be and parallel to the left-hand edge of the carriageway or its right or off side is as close as may be and parallel to the right-hand edge of the carriageway, or

(B) a road on which such a prohibition does not exist and its left or near side is as close as may be and parallel to the edge of the carriageway, and

(ii) no part of the vehicle is less than 10 metres from the junction of any part of the carriageway of any road with the carriageway of the road on which it is parked whether that junction is on the same side of the road as that on which the vehicle is parked or not.

(3) The provisions of paragraph (1) do not apply in respect of—

(*a*) a solo motor bicycle or a pedal cycle being pushed along the left-hand edge of a carriageway;

(*b*) a pedal cycle waiting to proceed provided it is kept to the left-hand or near side edge of a carriageway; or

(*c*) a vehicle which is parked in an area outlined by lamps or traffic signs so as to prevent the presence of the vehicle, its load or equipment being a danger to persons using the road.

(4) The classes of vehicles referred to in paragraph (2) are—

(*a*) a motor vehicle being a goods vehicle the unladen weight of which does not exceed 1525 kilograms;

(*b*) a passenger vehicle other than a large passenger-carrying vehicle;

(*c*) an invalid carriage; and

(*d*) a motor cycle or a pedal cycle in either case with or without a sidecar.

Provided that this paragraph does not include—

(i) a vehicle to which a trailer is attached; or

(ii) a vehicle or a vehicle carrying a load which in either case is required to be fitted with lamps by Regulation 18.

[Regulation 21 is printed as amended by the Road Traffic Regulation Act 1984, s 144(1) and Sched 10, para 2.]

22. Requirements about the use of headlamps and front fog lamps

(1) Save as provided in paragraph (2), no person shall use, or cause or permit to be used, on a road a vehicle which is fitted with obligatory dipped-beam headlamps unless every such lamp is kept lit—

(*a*) during the hours of darkness, except on a road which is a restricted road for the purposes of [section 81 of the Road Traffic Regulation Act 1984] by virtue of a system of street lighting when it is lit; and

(*b*) in seriously reduced visibility.

(2) The provisions of paragraph (1) do not apply—

(*a*) in the case of a motor vehicle fitted with one obligatory dipped-beam head-lamp or a solo motor bicycle or motor bicycle combination fitted with a pair of obligatory dipped-beam headlamps, if a main-beam headlamp or a front fog lamp is kept lit;

(*b*) in the case of a motor vehicle, other than a solo motor bicycle or motor bicycle combination, fitted with a pair of obligatory dipped-beam headlamps, if—

(i) a pair of main-beam headlamps is kept lit; or

(ii) a pair of front fog lamps which is so fitted that the outermost part of the illuminated area of each lamp in the pair is not more than 400 milli-metres from the outer edge of the vehicle is kept lit;

(*c*) to a vehicle being drawn by another vehicle;

(*d*) to a vehicle while being used to propel a snow plough; or

(*e*) to a vehicle which is parked.

(3) No light provided by a dim-dip lighting device shall be deemed to satisfy the requirements of this Regulation.

[Regulation 22 is printed as amended by the Road Traffic Regulation Act 1984, s 144(1) and Sched 10, para 2.]

[22A. Requirements about the use of warning beacons

No person shall use, or cause or permit to be used, on an unrestricted dual-carriageway road a vehicle which is required to be fitted with at least one warning beacon by regulaiton 15A unless every such beacon is kept lit.]

[Regulation 22A was inserted by SI 1987 No 1315.]

23. Restrictions on the use of lamps other than those to which Regulation 21 refers

No person shall use, or cause or permit to be used, on a road any vehicle on which any lamp, hazard warning signal device or warning beacon of a type specified in an item in column 2 of the Table below is used in a manner specified in column 3 in that item.

TABLE

1	2	3
Item No	Type of lamp, hazard warning signal device or warning beacon	Manner of use prohibited
1	Headlamp	(*a*) Used so as to cause undue dazzle or discomfort to other persons using the road. (*b*) Used so as to be lit when a vehicle is parked.
2	Front fog lamp	(*a*) Used so as to cause undue dazzle or discomfort to other persons using the road. (*b*) Used so as to be lit at any time other than in conditions of seriously reduced visibility. (*c*) Used so as to be lit when a vehicle is parked.
3	Rear fog lamp	(*a*) Used so as to cause undue dazzle or discomfort to the driver of a following vehicle. (*b*) Used so as to be lit at any time other than in conditions of seriously reduced visibility. (*c*) Save in the case of an emergency vehicle, used so as to be lit when a vehicle is parked.
4	Reversing lamp	Used so as to be lit except for the purpose of reversing the vehicle.
5	Hazard warning signal device	Used other than for the purpose of— (i) warning persons using the road of a temporary obstruction when the vehicle is at rest; or (ii) in the case of a large passenger-carrying vehicle, for the purpose of summoning assistance for the driver or any person acting as a conductor or inspector on the vehicle.
6	Warning beacon emitting blue light and special warning lamp	Used so as to be lit except— (i) at the scene of an emergency; or (ii) when it is necessary or desirable

1	2	3
Item No	Type of lamp, hazard warning signal device or warning beacon	Manner of use prohibited
		either to indicate to persons using the road the urgency of the purpose for which the vehicle is being used, or to warn persons of the presence of the vehicle or a hazard on the road.
7	Warning beacon emitting amber light	Used so as to be lit except— (i) at the scene of an emergency; (ii) when it is [required or necessary or desirable] to warn persons of the presence of the vehicle; and (iii) in the case of a breakdown vehicle, while it is being used in connection with, and in the immediate vicinity of, an accident or breakdown, or while it is being used to draw a broken-down vehicle.
8	Warning beacon emitting green light	Used so as to be lit except whilst occupied by a medical practitioner registered by the General Medical Council (whether with full, provisional or limited registration) and used for the purposes of an emergency.
9	Warning beacon emitting yellow light	Used so as to be lit on a road.
10	Work lamp	(*a*) Used so as to cause undue dazzle or discomfort to the driver of any vehicle. (*b*) Used so as to be lit except for the purpose of illuminating a working area, accident, breakdown or works in the vicinity of the vehicle.
11	Any other lamp	Used so as to cause undue dazzle or discomfort to other persons using the road.

[Regulation 23 is printed as amended by SI 1987 No 1315.]

PART IV

Testing and Inspection of Lighting Equipment and Reflectors

24. Testing and inspection of lighting equipment and reflectors

The provisions of [Regulation 74] of the Construction and Use Regulations apply in respect of lighting equipment and reflectors with which a vehicle is required by these Regulations to be fitted in the same way as they apply in respect of brakes, silencers, steering gear and tyres.

[Regulation 24 is printed as amended by the Interpretation Act 1978, ss 17(2)(a) and 23(1).]

SCHEDULE 1

(see Regulation 16)

Obligatory Lamps, Reflectors, Rear Markings and Devices

1	2	3	4	5
Item No	Class of Vehicle	Type of lamp, reflector, rear marking or device	Schedule in which relevant installation and performance requirements are specified	Exceptions
1	Motor vehicle having three or more wheels not being a vehicle to which any other item in this Schedule applies	Front position lamp	Schedule 2: Part I	None.
		Dim-dip lighting device	Schedule 3: Part I	A vehicle having a maximum speed not exceeding 25 miles per hour; A vehicle first used before 1st April 1987; A home forces' vehicle
		Dipped-beam headlamp	Schedule 4: Part I	A vehicle having a maximum speed not exceeding 15 miles per hour; A vehicle first used before 1st April 1986 being an agricultural vehicle or a works truck; A vehicle first used before 1st January 1931.

1	2	3	4	5
Item No	Class of Vehicle	Type of lamp, reflector, rear marking or device	Schedule in which relevant installation and performance requirements are specified	Exceptions
		Main-beam headlamp	Schedule 5: Part I	A vehicle having a maximum speed not exceeding 25 miles per hour; A vehicle first used before 1st April 1986 being an agricultural vehicle or a works truck; A vehicle first used before 1st January 1931.
		Direction indicator	Schedule 7: Parts I and II	A vehicle having a maximum speed not exceeding 15 miles per hour; An agricultural vehicle having an unladen weight not exceeding 255 kilograms; A vehicle first used before 1st April 1986 being an agricultural vehicle, an industrial tractor or a works truck; A vehicle first used before 1st January 1936.

		Hazard warning signal device	Schedule 8: Part I	A vehicle not required to be fitted with direction indicators;
				A vehicle first used before 1st April 1986.
		Rear position lamp	Schedule 10: Part I	None.
		Rear fog lamp	Schedule 11: Part I	A vehicle having a maximum speed not exceeding 25 miles per hour;
				A vehicle first used before 1st April 1986 being an agricultural vehicle or a works truck;
				A vehicle first used before 1st April 1980;
				A vehicle having an overall width which does not exceed 1300 millimetres.
		Stop lamp	Schedule 12: Part I	A vehicle having a maximum speed not exceeding 25 miles per hour;
				A vehicle first used before 1st April 1986 being an agricultural vehicle or a works truck;
				A vehicle first used before 1st January 1936.
		Rear registration plate lamp	Schedule 14	A vehicle not required to be fitted with a rear registration plate.

1	2	3	4	5
Item No	Class of Vehicle	Type of lamp, reflector, rear marking or device	Schedule in which relevant installation and performance requirements are specified	Exceptions
		Side reflex reflector	Schedule 16: Part I	A vehicle having a maximum speed not exceeding 25 miles per hour; A goods vehicle— (*a*) first used on or after 1st April 1986 the overall length of which does not exceed 6 metres; or (*b*) first used before 1st April 1986 the overall length of which does not exceed 8 metres; A passenger vehicle; An incomplete vehicle proceeding to a works for completion or to a place where it is to be stored or displayed for sale; A vehicle primarily constructed for moving excavated material and being used by virtue of an Order under [Section 44] of the Act;

				A mobile crane or engineering plant.
		Rear reflex reflector	Schedule 17: Part I	None
		Rear marking	Schedule 18: Part I	A vehicle having a maximum speed not exceeding 25 miles per hour;
				A vehicle first used before 1st August 1982 the unladen weight of which does not exceed 3050 kilograms;
				A vehicle the maximum gross weight of which does not exceed 7500 kilograms;
				A passenger vehicle not being an articulated bus;
				A tractive unit for an articulated vehicle;
				An incomplete vehicle proceeding to a works for completion or to a place where it is to be stored or displayed for sale;
				A vehicle first used before 1st April 1986 being an agricultural vehicle, a works truck or engineering plant;

1	2	3	4	5
Item No	Class of Vehicle	Type of lamp, reflector, rear marking or device	Schedule in which relevant installation and performance requirements are specified	Exceptions
				A vehicle first used before 1st January 1940; A home forces' vehicle; A vehicle constructed or adapted for— (*a*) fire fighting or fire salvage; (*b*) servicing or controlling aircraft; (*c*) heating and dispensing tar or other material for the construction or maintenance of roads; or (*d*) transporting two or more vehicles or vehicle bodies or two or more boats.
2	Solo motor bicycle and motor bicycle combination	Front position lamp	Schedule 2: Part I	A solo motor bicycle fitted with a headlamp.
		Dipped-beam headlamp	Schedule 4: Part I	A vehicle first used before 1st January 1931.

		Main-beam headlamp	Schedule 5: Part I	A vehicle having a maximum speed not exceeding 25 miles per hour; A vehicle first used before 1st January 1972 and having an engine with a capacity of less than 50 cubic centimetres; A vehicle first used before 1st January 1931.
		Direction indicator	Schedule 7: Parts I and II	A vehicle having a maximum speed not exceeding 25 miles per hour; A vehicle first used before 1st April 1986; A vehicle which can carry only one person or which, in the case of a motor bicycle combination, can carry only the rider and one passenger in the sidecar and which is constructed or adapted primarily for use off roads (whether by reason of its tyres, suspension, ground clearance or otherwise).
		Rear position lamp	Schedule 10: Part I	None.
		Stop lamp	Schedule 12: Part I	A vehicle having a maximum speed not exceeding 25 miles per hour;

1	2	3	4	5
Item No	Class of Vehicle	Type of lamp, reflector, rear marking or device	Schedule in which relevant installation and performance requirements are specified	Exceptions
				A vehicle first used before 1st April 1986 and having an engine capacity of less than 50 cubic centimetres;
				A vehicle first used before 1st January 1936.
		Rear registration plate lamp	Schedule 14	A vehicle not required to be fitted with a rear registration plate.
		Rear reflex reflector	Schedule 17: Part I	None.
3	Pedal cycle	Front position lamp	Schedule 2: Part I	None.
		Rear position lamp	Schedule 10: Part I	None.
		Rear reflex reflector	Schedule 17: Part I	None.
		Pedal reflex reflector	Schedule 19: Part I	A pedal cycle manufactured before 1st October 1985.
4	Pedestrian-controlled vehicle, horse-drawn vehicle and track-laying vehicle	Front position lamp	Schedule 2: Part I	None.
		Rear position lamp	Schedule 10: Part I	None.

		Rear reflex reflector	Schedule 17: Part I	None.
5	Vehicle drawn or propelled by hand	Front position lamp	Schedule 2: Part I	None.
		Rear position lamp	Schedule 10: Part I	A vehicle fitted with a rear reflex reflector.
		Rear reflex reflector	Schedule 17: Part I	A vehicle fitted with a rear position lamp.
6	Trailer drawn by a motor vehicle	Front position lamp	Schedule 2: Part I	A trailer with an overall width not exceeding 1600 millimetres;
				A trailer manufactured before 1st October 1985 the overall length of which, excluding any drawbar and any fitting for its attachment, does not exceed 2300 millimetres.
		Direction indicator	Schedule 7: Parts I and II	A trailer manufactured before 1st September 1965;
				An agricultural vehicle or a works trailer.
		Side marker lamp	Schedule 9: Part I	A trailer the overall length of which, excluding any drawbar and any fitting for its attachment, does not exceed 9.15 metres.
		Rear position lamp	Schedule 10: Part I	None.
		Rear fog lamp	Schedule 11: Part I	A trailer manufactured before 1st April 1980;

1	2	3	4	5
Item No	Class of Vehicle	Type of lamp, reflector, rear marking or device	Schedule in which relevant installation and performance requirements are specified	Exceptions
				A trailer the overall width of which does not exceed 1300 millimetres;
				An agricultural vehicle or a works trailer.
		Stop lamp	Schedule 12: Part I	An agricultural vehicle or a works trailer.
		Rear registration plate lamp	Schedule 14	A trailer not required to be fitted with a rear registration plate.
		Side reflex reflector	Schedule 16: Part I	A trailer the overall length of which, excluding any draw-bar, does not exceed 5 metres;
				An incomplete trailer proceeding to a works for completion or to a place where it is to be stored or displayed for sale;
				Engineering plant;

				A trailer primarily constructed for moving excavated material and which is being used by virtue of an order under [section 44] of the Act.
		Rear reflex reflector	Schedule 17: Part I	None.
		Rear marking	Schedule 18: Part I	A trailer manufactured before 1st August 1982 the unladen weight of which does not exceed 1020 kilograms; A trailer the maximum gross weight of which does not exceed 3500 kilograms; An incomplete trailer proceeding to a works for completion or to a place where it is to be stored or displayed for sale; An agricultural vehicle, a works trailer or engineering plant; A trailer drawn by a large passenger-carrying vehicle; A home forces' vehicle; A trailer constructed or adapted for—

1	2	3	4	5
Item No	Class of Vehicle	Type of lamp, reflector, rear marking or device	Schedule in which relevant installation and performance requirements are specified	Exceptions
				(*a*) fire fighting or fire salvage; (*b*) servicing or controlling aircraft; (*c*) heating and dispensing tar or other material for the construction or maintenance of roads; (*d*) carrying asphalt or macadam, in each case being mixing or drying plant; or (*e*) transporting two or more vehicles or vehicle bodies or two or more boats.
7	Trailer drawn by a pedal cycle	Rear position lamp	Schedule 10: Part I	None.
		Rear reflex reflector	Schedule 17: Part I	None.

SCHEDULE 2

(See Regulations 16 and 17)

PART I

Front Position Lamps to which Regulation 16 applies

1. Number—	
(*a*) Any vehicle not covered by sub-paragraph (*b*), (*c*), (*d*), (*e*) or (*f*):	Two
(*b*) A pedal cycle with less than four wheels and without a sidecar:	One
(*c*) A solo motor bicycle:	One
(*d*) A motor bicycle combination with a headlamp on the motor bicycle:	One, on the sidecar
(*e*) A vehicle drawn or propelled by hand which has an overall width including any load not exceeding 1250 millimetres:	One
(*f*) An invalid carriage:	One
2. Position:	
(*a*) Longitudinal:	No requirement
(*b*) Lateral—	
(i) Where two front position lamps are required to be fitted—	
(A) Maximum distance from the side of the vehicle—	
(1) A motor vehicle first used on or after 1st April 1986:	400 millimetres
(2) A trailer manufactured on or after 1st October 1985:	150 millimetres
(3) Any other vehicle manufactured on or after 1st October 1985:	400 millimetres
(4) A motor vehicle first used before 1st April 1986 and any other vehicle manufactured before 1st October 1985:	510 millimetres
(B) Minimum separation distance between front position lamps:	No requirement
(ii) Where one front position lamp is required to be fitted—	
(A) A sidecar forming part of a motor bicycle combination:	On the centre-line of the sidecar or on the side of the sidecar furthest from the motor bicycle
(B) Any other vehicle:	On the centre line or offside of the vehicle
(*c*) Vertical—	
(i) Maximum height above the ground—	
(A) Any vehicle not covered by sub-paragraph (B), (C) or (D):	1500 millimetres or, if the structure of the vehicle

	makes this impracticable, 2100 millimetres
(B) A motor vehicle first used before 1st April 1986 and a trailer manufactured before 1st October 1985;	2300 millimetres
(C) A motor vehicle, first used on or after 1st April 1986, having a maximum speed not exceeding 25 miles per hour;	2100 millimetres
(D) A large passenger-carrying vehicle and a road clearance vehicle:	No requirement
(ii) Minimum height above the ground:	No requirement
3. Angles of visibility—	
(*a*) A motor vehicle (not being a motor bicycle combination or an agricultural vehicle) first used on or after 1st April 1986 and a trailer manufactured on or after 1st October 1985—	
(i) Horizontal—	
(A) Where one lamp is required to be fitted:	80° to the left and to the right
(B) Where two lamps are required to be fitted:	Either 80° outwards and 45° inwards or 45° outwards and 80° inwards
(ii) Vertical—	
(A) Any case not covered by sub-paragraph (B):	15° above and below the horizontal
(B) Where the highest part of the illuminated area of the lamp is less than 750 millimetres above the ground:	15° above and 5° below the horizontal
(*b*) Any other vehicle:	Visible to the front
4. Markings—	
(*a*) A motor vehicle (other than a solo motor bicycle or a motor bicycle combination) first used on or after 1st January 1972 and a trailer manufactured on or after 1st October 1985:	An approval mark
(*b*) A solo motor bicycle and a motor bicycle combination in either case first used on or after 1st April 1986:	An approval mark
(*c*) Any other vehicle:	No requirement
5. Size of illuminated area:	No requirement
6. Colour:	White or, if incorporated in a headlamp which is capable of emitting only a yellow light, yellow
7. Wattage:	No requirement

8. Intensity—

(*a*) A front position lamp bearing any of the markings mentioned in paragraph 4:	No requirement
(*b*) Any other front position lamp:	Visible from a reasonable distance
9. Electrical connections:	No requirement
10. Tell-tale:	No requirement

11. Other requirements—

(*a*) Except in the case of a vehicle covered by sub-paragraph (*b*), where two front position lamps are required to be fitted they shall form a pair.

(*b*) In the case of a trailer manufactured before 1st October 1985 and a motor bicycle combination, where two front position lamps are required to be fitted they shall be fitted on each side of the longitudinal axis of the vehicle.

12. Definitions—

In this Schedule—

'approval mark' means—

(*a*) in relation to a solo motor bicycle or a motor bicycle combination, a marking designated as an approval mark by Regulation 4 of the Designation of Approval Marks Regulations and shown at item 50A of Schedule 2 to those Regulations, and

(*b*) in relation to any other motor vehicle or any trailer, either—

(i) a marking designated as an approval mark by Regulation 5 of the Designation of Approval Marks Regulations and shown at item 5 of Schedule 4 to those Regulations, or

(ii) a marking designated as an approval mark by Regulation 4 of the Designation of Approval Marks Regulations and shown at item 7 of Schedule 2 to those Regulations.

PART II

Front Position Lamps to which Regulation 17 applies

Any number may be fitted, and the only requirement prescribed by these Regulations in respect of any which are fitted is that specified in paragraph 6 as regards front position lamps to which Regulation 16 applies.

SCHEDULE 3

(See Regulations 16 and 17)

PART I

Dim-Dip Lighting Devices to which Regulation 16 applies

1. Every dim-dip lighting device shall whenever the obligatory front lamps of the vehicle are switched on and either—

(i) the engine of the vehicle is running, or

(ii) the key or devices which control the starting or stopping of the engine are in the normal position for driving the vehicle

automatically supply sufficient current to cause to be emitted either—

(A) lights as specified in paragraph 2 below, or
(B) lights as specified in paragraph 3 below.

2. The lights referred to in paragraph 1(A) above are a light to the front from the dipped-beam filament of each of a pair of obligatory headlamps, each such light having, so far as is reasonably practicable, an intensity—

(*a*) in the case of a halogen filament lamp, of 10 per cent of the normal intensity of the dipped beam, or

(*b*) in the case of any other type of filament lamp, of 15 per cent of the normal intensity of the dipped beam.

3. The lights referred to in paragraph 1(B) above are a white light to the front from each lamp of any pair of front lamps each of which has an illuminated area of not less than 150 square centimetres and which are fitted in a position in which obligatory headlamps emitting a dipped beam may lawfully be fitted, each such light having an intensity of not less than 200 candelas, measured from directly in front of the centre of the lamp in a direction parallel to the longitudinal axis of the vehicle, and not more than 400 candelas in any direction.

PART II

Dim-Dip Lighting Devices to which Regulation 17 applies

The requirements prescribed by these Regulations in respect of a dim-dip lighting device which is fitted are all those specified in this Schedule as regards a dim-dip lighting device to which Regulation 16 applies.

SCHEDULE 4

(See Regulations 16 and 17)

PART I

Dipped-beam Headlamps to which Regulation 16 applies

1. Number—

(*a*) Any vehicle not covered by sub-paragraph (*b*), (*c*), (*d*) or (*e*):	Two
(*b*) A solo motor bicycle and a motor bicycle combination:	One
(*c*) A motor vehicle with three wheels, other than a motor bicycle combination, first used before 1st January 1972:	One
(*d*) A motor vehicle with three wheels, other than a motor bicycle combination, first used on or after 1st January 1972 and which has an unladen weight of not more than 400 kilogrammes and an overall width of not more than 1300 millimetres:	One

(*e*) A large passenger-carrying vehicle first used before 1st October 1969:	One

2. Position—

(*a*) Longitudinal:	No requirement
(*b*) Lateral—	
(i) Where two dipped-beam headlamps are required to be fitted—	
(A) Maximum distance from the side of the vehicle—	
(1) Any vehicle not covered by sub-paragraph (2) or (3):	400 millimetres
(2) A vehicle first used before 1st January 1972:	No requirement
(3) An agricultural vehicle, engineering plant and an industrial tractor:	No requirement
(B) Minimum separation distance between a pair of dipped-beam headlamps:	No requirement
(ii) Where one dipped-beam headlamp is required to be fitted—	
(A) Any vehicle not covered by sub-paragraph (B):	(i) On the centre-line of the motor vehicle (disregarding any sidecar forming part of a motor bicycle combination), or (ii) At any distance from the side of the motor vehicle (disregarding any sidecar forming part of a motor bicycle combination) provided that a duplicate lamp is fitted on the other side so that together they form a matched pair. In such a case, both lamps shall be regarded as obligatory lamps.
(B) A large passenger-carrying vehicle first used before 1st October 1969:	No requirement
(*c*) Vertical—	
(i) Maximum height above the ground—	
(A) Any vehicle not covered by sub-paragraph (B):	1200 millimetres
(B) A vehicle first used before 1st January 1952, an agricultural vehicle, a road clearance vehicle, an aerodrome fire tender, an aerodrome runway sweeper, an industrial tractor, engineering plant and a home forces' vehicle:	No requirement

(ii) Minimum height above the ground—	
(A) Any vehicle not covered by sub-paragraph (B):	500 millimetres
(B) A vehicle first used before 1st January 1956:	No requirement
3. Angles of visibility:	No requirement
4. Markings—	
(*a*) Any vehicle not covered by sub-paragraph (*b*), (*c*) or (*d*):	An approval mark or a British Standard mark
(*b*) A motor vehicle first used before 1st April 1986:	No requirement
(*c*) A three-wheeled motor vehicle, not being a motor bicycle combination, first used on or after 1st April 1986 and having a maximum speed not exceeding 50 miles per hour:	No requirement
(*d*) A solo motor bicycle and a motor bicycle combination:	No requirement
5. Size of illuminated area:	No requirement
6. Colour:	White or yellow
7. Wattage—	
(*a*) A motor vehicle with four or more wheels first used on or after 1st April 1986:	No requirement
(*b*) A three-wheeled motor vehicle, not being a motor bicycle combination, first used on or after 1st April 1986—	
(i) having a maximum speed not exceeding 50 miles per hour:	24 watts minimum
(ii) having a maximum speed exceeding 50 miles per hour:	No requirement
(*c*) A motor vehicle with four or more wheels first used before 1st April 1986:	30 watts minimum
(*d*) A three-wheeled motor vehicle, not being a motor bicycle combination, first used before 1st April 1986:	24 watts minimum
(*e*) A solo motor bicycle and a motor bicycle combination—	
(i) having an engine not exceeding 250 cubic centimetres and a maximum speed not exceeding 25 miles per hour:	10 watts minimum
(ii) having an engine not exceeding 250 cubic centimetres and a maximum speed exceeding 25 miles per hour:	15 watts minimum
(iii) having an engine exceeding 250 cubic centimetres:	24 watts minimum

8. Intensity:	No requirement
9. Electrical connections:	No requirement
10. Tell-tale:	No requirement

11. Other requirements—

(*a*) Every dipped-beam headlamp shall be so constructed that the direction of the beam of light emitted therefrom can be adjusted whilst the vehicle is stationary.

(*b*) Where two dipped-beam headlamps are required to be fitted, they shall form a matched pair and shall be capable of being switched on and off simultaneously and not otherwise.

12. Definitions—

In this Schedule—

'approval mark' means either—

(*a*) a marking designated as an approval mark by Regulation 5 of the Designation of Approval Marks Regulations and shown at item 12 or 13 or 14 or 16 or, in the case of a vehicle having a maximum speed not exceeding 25 miles per hour, 27 or 28 of Schedule 4 to those Regulations, or

(*b*) a marking designated as an approved mark by Regulation 4 of the Designation of Approval Marks Regulations and shown at item 1A or 1B or 1C or 1E or 5A or 5B or 5C or 5E or 8C or 8E or 8F or 8G or 8H or 8K or 8L or 20C or 20D or 20E or 20F or 20G or 20H or 20K or 20L or 31A or 31C or, in the case of a vehicle having a maximum speed not exceeding 25 miles per hour, 1H or 1I or 5H or 5I of Schedule 2 to those Regulations; and

'British Standard mark' means the specification for sealed beam headlamps published by the British Standards Institution under the reference BS AU 40: Part 4a: 1966 as amended by Amendment AMD 2188 published in December 1976, namely 'B.S. AU 40'.

PART II

Dipped-beam headlamps to which Regulation 17 applies

Any number may be fitted, and the only requirements prescribed by these Regulations in respect of any which are fitted are those specified in paragraphs 2(*c*), 6 and 11(*a*) as regards dipped-beam headlamps to which Regulation 16 applies.

SCHEDULE 5

(See Regulations 16 and 17)

PART I

Main-beam Headlamps to which Regulation 16 applies

1. Number—

(*a*) Any vehicle not covered by sub-paragraph (*b*), (*c*) or (*d*):	Two

(*b*) A solo motor bicycle and motor bicycle combination:	One
(*c*) A motor vehicle with three wheels, other than a motor bicycle combination, first used before 1st January 1972:	One
(*d*) A motor vehicle with three wheels, other than a motor bicycle combination, first used on or after 1st January 1972 and which has an unladen weight of not more than 400 kilogrammes and an overall width of not more than 1300 millimetres:	One
2. Position—	
(*a*) Longitudinal	No requirement
(*b*) Lateral—	
(i) Where two main-beam headlamps are required to be fitted—	
(A) Maximum distance from the side of the vehicle:	The outer edges of the illuminated areas must in no case be closer to the side of the vehicle than the outer edges of the illuminated areas of the obligatory dipped-beam headlamps.
(B) Maximum separation distance between a pair of main-beam headlamps:	No requirement
(ii) Where one main-beam headlamp is required to be fitted:	(i) On the centre-line of the motor vehicle (disregarding any sidecar forming part of a motor bicycle combination), or (ii) At any distance from the side of thc vchiclc (disrcgarding any sidecar forming part of a motor bicycle combination) provided that a duplicate lamp is fitted on the other side so that together they form a matched pair. In such a case, both lamps shall be treated as obligatory lamps.
(*c*) Vertical:	No requirement
3. Angles of visibility:	No requirement
4. Markings—	
(*a*) Any vehicle not covered by sub-paragraph (*b*), (*c*) or (*d*):	An approval mark or a British Standard mark

(*b*) A motor vehicle first used before 1st April 1986:	No requirement
(*c*) A three-wheeled motor vehicle, not being a motor bicycle combination, first used on or after 1st April 1986 and having a maximum speed not exceeding 50 miles per hour:	No requirement
(*d*) A solo motor bicycle and a motor bicycle combination:	No requirement
5. Size of illuminated area:	No requirement
6. Colour:	White or yellow
7. Wattage—	
(*a*) A motor vehicle, other than a solo motor bicycle or motor bicycle combination, first used on or after 1st April 1986:	No requirement
(*b*) A motor vehicle, other than a solo motor bicycle or a motor bicycle combination, first used before 1st April 1986:	30 watts minimum
(*c*) A solo motor bicycle and a motor bicycle combination—	
(i) having an engine not exceeding 250 cubic centimetres:	15 watts minimum
(ii) having an engine exceeding 250 cubic centimetres:	30 watts minimum
8. Intensity:	No requirement
9. Electrical connections:	Every main-beam headlamp shall be so constructed that the light emitted therefrom— (*a*) can be deflected at the will of the driver to become a dipped beam, or (*b*) can be extinguished by the operation of a device which at the same time either— (i) causes the lamp to emit a dipped beam, or (ii) causes another lamp to emit a dipped beam.
10. Tell-tale—	
(*a*) Any vehicle not covered by sub-paragraph (*b*):	A circuit-closed tell-tale shall be fitted
(*b*) A motor vehicle first used before 1st April 1986:	No requirement

11. Other requirements—

(*a*) Every main-beam headlamp shall be so constructed that the direction of the beam of light emitted therefrom can be adjusted whilst the vehicle is stationary.

(*b*) Except in the case of a large passenger-carrying vehicle first used before 1st October 1969, where two main-beam headlamps are required to be fitted, they shall form a matched pair and shall be capable of being switched on and off simultaneously and not otherwise.

12. Definitions—

In this Schedule—

'approval mark' means—

(*a*) a marking designated as an approval mark by Regulation 5 of the Designation of Approval Marks Regulations and shown at item 12 or 13 or 17 of Schedule 4 to those Regulations; or

(*b*) a marking designated as an approval mark by Regulation 4 of the Designation of Approval Marks Regulations and shown at item 1A or 1B or 1F or 5A or 5B or 5F or 8C or 8D or 8E or 8F or 8M or 8N or 20C or 20D or 20E or 20F or 20M or 20N or 31A or 31D of Schedule 2 to those Regulations; and

'British Standard mark' means the specification for sealed beam headlamps published by the British Standards Institution under the reference BS AU 40: Part 4a: 1966 as amended by Amendment AMD 2188 published in December 1976, namely 'B.S. AU 40'.

PART II

Main-beam Headlamps to which Regulation 17 applies

Any number may be fitted, and the only requirements prescribed by these Regulations in respect of any which are fitted are those specified in paragraphs 6, 9 and 11(a) as regards main-beam headlamps to which Regulation 16 applies.

SCHEDULE 6

(See Regulation 17)

Front Fog Lamps to which Regulation 17 applies

1. Number: No requirement

2. Position—

(*a*) Longitudinal: No requirement

(*b*) Lateral—

(i) Where a pair of front fog lamps is used in conditions of seriously reduced visibility in place of the obligatory dipped beam headlamps—
Maximum distance from side of vehicle: 400 millimetres

(ii) In all other cases:	No requirement
(*c*) Vertical—	
(i) Maximum height above the ground—	
(A) Any vehicle not covered by sub-paragraph (B):	1200 millimetres
(B) An agricultural vehicle, a road clearance vehicle, an aerodrome fire tender, an aerodrome runway sweeper, an industrial tractor, engineering plant and a home forces' vehicle:	No requirement
(ii) Minimum height above the ground:	No requirement
3. Angles of visibility:	No requirement
4. Markings—	
(*a*) A vehicle first used on or after 1st April 1986:	An approval mark
(*b*) A vehicle first used before 1st April 1986:	No requirement
5. Size of illuminated area:	No requirement
6. Colour:	White or yellow
7. Wattage:	No requirement
8. Intensity:	No requirement
9. Electrical connections:	No requirement
10. Tell-tale:	No requirement

11. Definitions—

In this Schedule 'approval mark' means either—

(*a*) a marking designated as an approval mark by Regulation 5 of the Designation of Approval Marks Regulations and shown at item 19 of Schedule 4 to those Regulations, or

(*b*) a marking designated as an approval mark by Regulation 4 of the Designation of Approval Marks Regulations and shown at item 19 or 19A of Schedule 2 to those regulations.

SCHEDULE 7

(See Regulations 16 and 17)

Direction Indicators to which either Regulation 16 or 17 applies

PART I

General Requirements

1. Number—

The minimum and maximum number of direction indicators fitted on each side of a vehicle, whether required to be so fitted or not, is as follows—

(*a*) A motor vehicle with three or more wheels, not being a motor bicycle combination, first used on or after 1st April 1986:	A single front indicator (Category 1), one or two (but not more than two) rear indicators (Category 2) and at least one side repeater indicator (Category 5) or, in the case of a motor vehicle having a maximum speed not exceeding 25 miles per hour, a single front indicator (Category 1) and one or two (but not more than two) rear indicators (Category 2). Additional indicators may be fitted to the side (excluding the front and rear) of any motor vehicle.
(*b*) A trailer manufactured on or after 1st October 1985 drawn by a motor vehicle:	One or two (but not more than two) rear indicators (Category 2) or, in the case of a trailer towed by a solo motor bicycle or a motor bicycle combination, one or two (but not more than two) rear indicators (Category 12). Additional indicators may be fitted to the side (excluding the front and rear) of any trailer.
(*c*) A solo motor bicycle first used on or after 1st April 1986:	A single front indicator (Category 1 or 11) and a single rear indicator (Category 2 or 12). Additional indicators may be fitted to the side (excluding the front and rear) of any solo motor bicycle.

(*d*) A motor bicycle combination first used on or after 1st April 1986:	A single front indicator (Category 1 or 11) and a single rear indicator (Category 2 or 12). Additional indicators may be fitted to the side (excluding the front and rear) of any motor bicycle combination.
(*e*) A motor vehicle first used on or after 1st January 1936 and before 1st April 1986, a trailer manufactured on or after 1st January 1936 and before 1st October 1985, a pedal cycle with or without a sidecar or trailer, a horse-drawn vehicle and a vehicle drawn or propelled by hand:	Any arrangement of indicators so as to satisfy the requirements for angles of visibility in paragraph 3. However, not more than one front indicator and not more than two rear indicators may be fitted. Additional indicators may be fitted to the side (excluding the front and rear) of any vehicle.
(*f*) A motor vehicle first used before 1st January 1936 and any trailer manufactured before that date:	Any arrangement of indicators so as to make the intention of the driver clear to other road users.

2. Position—

(*a*) Longitudinal—	
(i) A side repeater indicator which is required to be fitted in accordance with paragraph 1(a)(i):	Within 2600 millimetres of the front of the vehicle
(ii) Any other indicator:	No requirement
(*b*) Lateral—	
(i) Maximum distance from the side of the vehicle—	
(A) Any vehicle not covered by sub-paragraph (B):	400 millimetres. However, where the vertical distance between the illuminated areas of any rear indicator and any rear position lamp is less than 300 millimetres, the distance between the outer edge of the vehicle and the outer edge of the illuminated area of the said indicator shall not exceed by more than 50 millimetres the distance between the extreme outer edge of the vehicle and the outer edge of the illuminated area of the said rear position lamp.

(B) A motor vehicle first used before 1st April 1986, a trailer manufactured before 1st October 1985, a solo motor bicycle, a pedal cycle, a horse-drawn vehicle and a vehicle drawn or propelled by hand:	No requirement
(ii) Minimum separation distance between indicators on opposite sides of a vehicle—	
(A) A motor vehicle, other than a solo motor bicycle or a motor bicycle combination, first used on or after 1st April 1986, a trailer manufactured on or after 1st October 1985, a horse-drawn vehicle, a pedestrian-controlled vehicle and a vehicle drawn or propelled by hand:	500 millimetres or, if the overall width of the vehicle is less than 1400 millimetres, 400 millimetres
(B) A solo motor bicycle having an engine exceeding 50 cubic centimetres and first used on or after 1st April 1986—	
(1) Front indicators:	300 millimetres
(2) Rear indicators:	240 millimetres
(3) Side repeater indicators:	No requirement
(C) A solo motor bicycle having an engine not exceeding 50 cubic centimetres and first used on or after 1st April 1986 and a pedal cycle—	
(1) Front indicators:	240 millimetres
(2) Rear indicators:	180 millimetres
(3) Side repeater indicators:	No requirement
(D) A motor bicycle combination first used on or after 1st April 1986:	400 millimetres
(E) A motor vehicle first used before 1st April 1986 and a trailer manufactured before 1st October 1985:	No requirement
(iii) Minimum separation distance between a front indicator and any dipped-beam headlamp or front fog lamp—	
(A) Every front indicator fitted to a motor vehicle, other than a solo motor bicycle or a motor bicycle combination, first used on or after 1st April 1986:	40 millimetres. However, this shall not apply if the luminous intensity in the reference axis of the indicator is at least 400 candelas.
(B) Every front indicator fitted to a solo motor bicycle or a motor bicycle combination in either case first used on or after 1st April 1986:	100 millimetres
(C) Any front indicator fitted to any other vehicle:	No requirement

(*c*) Vertical—	
(i) Maximum height above the ground—	
(A) Any vehicle not covered by sub-paragraph (B) or (C):	1500 millimetres or, if the structure of the vehicle makes this impracticable, 2300 millimetres. However, if two pairs of rear indicators are fitted, one pair may be mounted at any height.
(B) A motor vehicle first used before 1st April 1986 and a trailer manufactured before 1st October 1985:	No requirement
(C) A motor vehicle having a maximum speed not exceeding 25 miles per hour:	No requirement
(ii) Minimum height above the ground:	350 millimetres

3. Angles of visibility—

(*a*) A motor vehicle first used on or after 1st April 1986 and a trailer manufactured on or after 1st October 1985—	
(i) Horizontal (see diagrams in Part II of this Schedule)—	
(A) Every front or rear indicator fitted to a motor vehicle, other than a solo motor bicycle or a motor bicycle combination, having a maximum speed of not less than 25 miles per hour and every rear indicator fitted to a trailer:	80° outwards and 45° inwards
(B) Every front or rear indicator fitted to a solo motor bicycle or a motor bicycle combination:	80° outwards and 20° inwards
(C) Every front or rear indicator fitted to a motor vehicle, other than a solo motor bicycle or a motor bicycle combination, having a maximum speed not exceeding 25 miles per hour:	80° outwards and 3° inwards
(D) Every side repeater indicator fitted to a motor vehicle or a trailer:	Between rearward angles of 5° outboard and 60° outboard or, in the case of a motor vehicle having a maximum speed not exceeding 25 miles per hour where it is impracticable to comply with the 5° angle, this may be replaced by 10°.
(ii) Vertical—	
(A) Any vehicle not covered by sub-paragraph (B) or (C):	15° above and below the horizontal

(B) A motor vehicle having a maximum speed not exceeding 25 miles per hour where the highest part of the illuminated area of the lamp is less than 1900 millimetres above the ground:	15° above and 10° below the horizontal
(C) Where the highest part of the illuminated area of the lamp is less than 750 millimetres above the ground:	15° above and 5° below the horizontal
(*b*) A motor vehicle first used before 1st April 1986, a trailer manufactured before 1st October 1985, a pedal cycle, horse-drawn vehicle and a vehicle drawn or propelled by hand:	Such that at least one (but not necessarily the same) indicator on each side is plainly visible to the rear in the case of a trailer and both to the front and rear in the case of any other vehicle.
4. Markings—	
(*a*) A motor vehicle, other than a solo motor bicycle or a motor bicycle combination, first used on or after 1st April 1986 and a trailer, other than a trailer drawn by a solo motor bicycle or a motor bicycle combination, manufactured on or after 1st October 1985:	An approval mark and, above such mark, the following numbers— (*a*) in the case of a front indicator, '1'; (*b*) in the case of a rear indicator, '2'; (*c*) in the case of a side repeater indicator, '5'.
(*b*) A solo motor bicycle and a motor bicycle combination in either case first used on or after 1st April 1986, a trailer, manufactured on or after 1st October 1985, drawn by such a solo motor bicycle or a motor bicycle combination, a pedal cycle, a horse-drawn vehicle and a vehicle drawn or propelled by hand:	An approval mark and, above such mark, the following numbers— (*a*) in the case of a front indicator, '1' or '11'; (*b*) in the case of a rear indicator, '2' or '12'; (*c*) in the case of a side repeater indicator, '5'.
(*c*) A motor vehicle first used before 1st April 1986 and a trailer manufactured before 1st October 1985:	No requirement
5. Size of illuminated area:	No requirement
6. Colour—	
(*a*) Any vehicle not covered by sub-paragraph (*b*):	Amber
(*b*) Any indicator fitted to a motor vehicle first used before 1st September 1965 and any trailer drawn thereby—	
(i) if it shows only the front:	White or amber
(ii) if it shows only the rear:	Red or amber
(iii) if it shows both to the front and to the rear:	Amber

7. Wattage—

(*a*) Any front or rear indicator which emits a flashing light and does not bear an approval mark:	15 to 36 watts
(*b*) Any other indicator:	No requirement

8. Intensity—

(*a*) An indicator bearing an approval mark:	No requirement
(*b*) An indicator not bearing an approval mark:	Such that the light is plainly visible from a reasonable distance

9. Electrical connections—

(*a*) All indicators on one side of a vehicle together with all indicators on that side of any trailer drawn by the vehicle, while so drawn, shall be operated by one switch.

(*b*) All indicators on one side of a vehicle or combination of vehicles showing a flashing light shall flash in phase, except that in the case of a solo motor bicycle, a motor bicycle combination and a pedal cycle, the front and rear direction indicators on one side of the vehicle may flash alternately.

10. Tell-tale—

(*a*) One or more indicators on each side of a vehicle to which indicators are fitted shall be so designed and fitted that the driver when in his seat can readily be aware when it is in operation; or

(*b*) The vehicle shall be equipped with an operational tell-tale for front and rear indicators (including any rear indicator on the rearmost of any trailers drawn by the vehicle).

11. Other requirements—

(*a*) Every indicator (other than a semaphore arm, that is an indicator in the form of an illuminated sign which when in operation temporarily alters the outline of the vehicle to the extent of at least 150 millimetres measured horizontally and is visible from both the front and rear of the vehicle) shall when in operation show a light which flashes constantly at the rate of not less than 60 nor more than 120 flashes per minute. However, in the event of a failure, other than a short-circuit, of an indicator, any other indicator on the same side of the vehicle or combination of vehicles may continue to flash, but the rate may be less than 60 or more than 120 flashes per minute. Every indicator shall when in operation perform efficiently regardless of the speed of the vehicle.

(*b*) Where two front or rear direction indicators are fitted to a motor vehicle first used on or after 1st April 1986, and two rear direction indicators are fitted to a trailer manufactured on or after 1st October 1985, in each case they shall be fitted so as to form a pair. Where four rear direction indicators are fitted to a motor vehicle first used on or after 1st April 1986 and to a trailer manufactured on or after 1st October 1985, they shall be fitted so as to form two pairs.

12. Definitions—

In this Schedule 'approval mark' means either—

(*a*) a marking designated as an approval mark by Regulation 5 of the Designation of Approval Marks Regulations and shown at item 9 of Schedule 4 to those Regulations; or

(*b*) a marking designated as an approval mark by Regulation 4 of the Designation of Approval Marks Regulations and shown at item 6 or, in the case of a solo motor bicycle or a motor bicycle combination, a pedal cycle, a horse-drawn vehicle, or a vehicle drawn or propelled by hand, at item 50 of Schedule 2 to those Regulations.

[Part II of Sched 7 is set out on p 2/971]

PART II

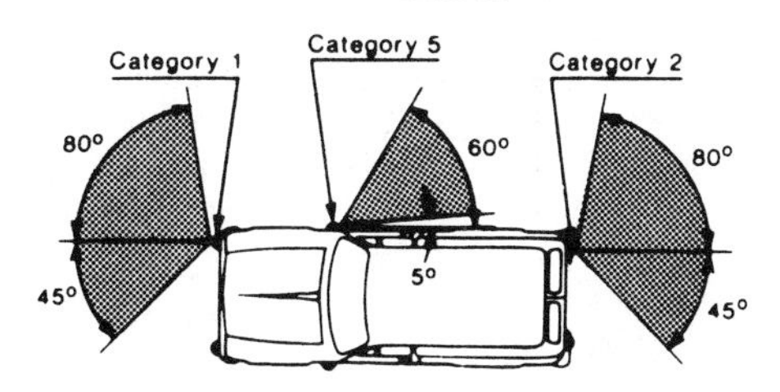
Category 1
Category 5
Category 2
80°
60°
80°
5°
45°
45°

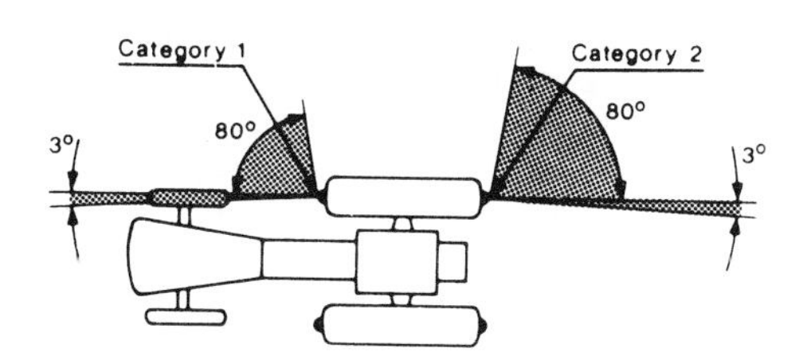
Category 1
Category 2
80°
80°
3°
3°

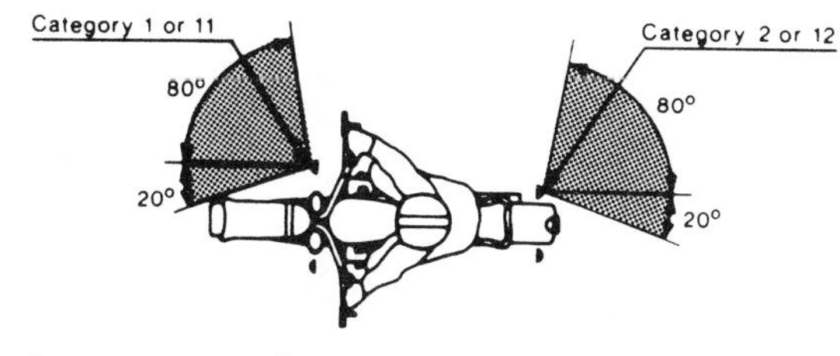
Category 1 or 11
Category 2 or 12
80°
80°
20°
20°

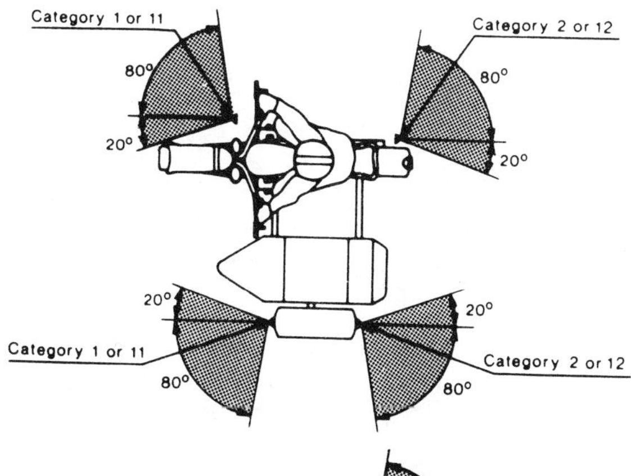
Category 1 or 11
Category 2 or 12
80°
80°
20°
20°
20°
20°
Category 1 or 11
Category 2 or 12
80°
80°

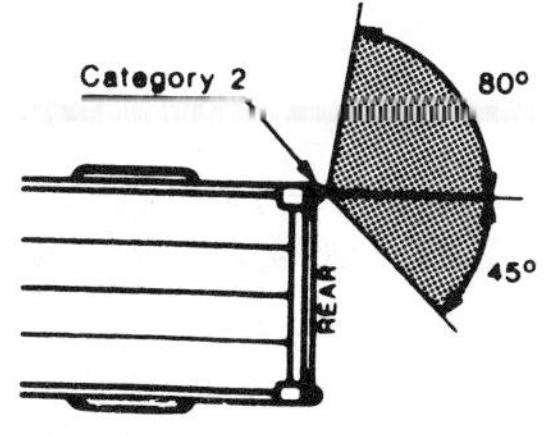
Category 2
80°
45°
REAR

SCHEDULE 8

(See Regulations 16 and 17)

PART I

Hazard Warning Signal Devices to which Regulation 16 applies

Every hazard warning signal device shall—

(*a*) be operated by one switch,

(*b*) cause all the direction indicators with which a vehicle or a combination of vehicles is equipped to flash in phase,

(*c*) be provided with a closed-circuit tell-tale in the form of a flashing light which may operate in conjunction with any direction indicator tell-tale, and

(*d*) be able to function even if the device which controls the starting and stopping of the engine is in a position which makes it impossible to start the engine.

PART II

Hazard Warning Signal Devices to which Regulation 17 applies

The requirements prescribed by these Regulations in respect of a hazard warning signal device which is fitted are all those specified in this Schedule as regards a hazard warning signal device to which Regulation 16 applies.

SCHEDULE 9

(See Regulations 16, 17 and 19)

PART I

Side Marker Lamps to which Regulation 16 or 19 applies

1. Number—	
(*a*) Any trailer not covered by sub-paragraph (*b*):	One on each side
(*b*) Long vehicles and vehicle combinations to which Regulation 19 applies:	The numbers required by Regulation 19
2. Position—	
(*a*) Longitudinal—	
(i) Any trailer not covered by sub-paragraph (ii):	Such that no part of the light-emitting surface is forward of, or more than 1530 millimetres to the rear of, the centre point of the overall length of the trailer.
(ii) Long vehicles and vehicle combinations, including any loads, to which Regulation 19 applies:	As specified in Regulation 19
(*b*) Lateral:	No requirement

(*c*) Vertical—

(i) Maximum height above the ground:	2300 millimetres
(ii) Minimum height above the ground:	No requirement

3. Angles of visibility—

(*a*) Horizontal:	70° to the left and to the right when viewed in a direction at right angles to the longitudinal axis of the vehicle
(*b*) Vertical:	No requirement
4. Markings:	No requirement
5. Size of light-emitting surface:	Not less than 490 square millimetres in the case of each of the surfaces through which the red light or the white light is emitted
6. Colour:	White when viewed from the front and red when viewed from the rear
7. Wattage:	7 watts maximum
8. Intensity:	Visible from a reasonable distance
9. Electrical connections:	No requirement
10. Tell-tale:	No requirement

PART II

Side Marker Lamps to which Regulation 17 applies

Any number may be fitted, and the only requirement prescribed by these Regulations in respect of any which are fitted is that specified in paragraph 6 as regards side marker lamps to which Regulation 16 or 19 applies.

SCHEDULE 10

(See Regulations 16 and 17)

PART I

Rear Position Lamps to which Regulation 16 applies

1. Number—

(*a*) Any vehicle not covered by sub-paragraph (*b*), (*c*), (*d*), (*e*), (*f*) or (*g*):	Two
(*b*) A large passenger-carrying vehicle first used before 1st April 1955:	One

(*c*) A solo motor bicycle:	One
(*d*) A pedal cycle with less than four wheels and without a sidecar:	One
(*e*) A trailer drawn by a pedal cycle and a trailer, the overall width of which does not exceed 800 millimetres, drawn by a solo motor bicycle or by a motor bicycle combination:	One
(*f*) A vehicle drawn or propelled by hand:	One
(*g*) A motor vehicle having three or more wheels and a maximum speed not exceeding 25 miles per hour and a trailer drawn by any such vehicle if, in either case, the structure of the vehicle makes it impracticable to meet all of the relevant requirements of paragraphs 2 and 3 below with two lamps:	Four

2. Position:

(*a*) Longitudinal:	At or near the rear
(*b*) Lateral—	
(i) Where two lamps are required to be fitted—	
(A) Maximum distance from the side of the vehicle—	
(1) Any vehicle not covered by sub-paragraph (2):	400 millimetres
(2) A motor vehicle first used before 1st April 1986 and any other vehicle manufactured before 1st October 1985:	800 millimetres
(B) Minimum separation distance between pair of rear position lamps—	
(1) Any vehicle not covered by sub-paragraph (2):	500 millimetres or, if the overall width of the vehicle is less than 1400 millimetres, 400 millimetres.
(2) A motor vehicle first used before 1st April 1986 and any other vehicle manufactured before 1st October 1985:	No requirement
(ii) Where one lamp is required to be fitted:	On the centre-line or off side of the vehicle
(iii) Where four lamps are required to be fitted—	
(A) Maximum distance from the side of the vehicle—	
(1) One pair of lamps:	Such that they satisfy the relevant requirements in sub-paragraph 2(*b*)(i)(A)
(2) The other pair of lamps:	No requirement
(B) Minimum separation distance between rear position lamps—	

(1) One pair of lamps:	Such that they satisfy the relevant requirements in sub-paragraph 2(*b*)(i)(B)
(2) The other pair of lamps:	No requirement
(*c*) Vertical—	
(i) Maximum height above the ground where one or two rear position lamps are required to be fitted—	
(A) Any vehicle not covered by sub-paragraph (B) or (C):	1500 millimetres or, if the structure of the vehicle makes this impracticable, 2100 millimetres
(B) A large passenger-carrying vehicle first used before 1st April 1986:	No requirement
(C) A motor vehicle first used before 1st April 1986 not being a large passenger-carrying vehicle, a trailer manufactured before 1st October 1985, an agricultural vehicle, a horse-drawn vehicle, an industrial tractor and engineering plant:	2100 millimetres
(ii) Maximum height above the ground where four rear position lamps are required to be fitted—	
(A) One pair of lamps:	Such that they satisfy the relevant requirements in paragraph 2(*c*)(i)
(B) The other pair of lamps:	No requirement
(iii) Minimum height above the ground—	
(A) A vehicle not covered by sub-paragraph (B):	350 millimetres
(B) A motor vehicle first used before 1st April 1986 and any other vehicle manufactured before 1st October 1985:	No requirement
3. Angles of visibility—	
(*a*) A motor vehicle, other than a motor bicycle combination, first used on or after 1st April 1986 and a trailer manufactured on or after 1st October 1985—	
(i) Horizontal—	
(A) Where two lamps are required to be fitted:	Either 45° inwards and 80° outwards or 80° inwards and 45° outwards
(B) Where one lamp is required to be fitted:	80° to the left and to the right
(C) Where four lamps are required to be fitted—	
(1) The outer pair of lamps:	0° inwards and 80° outwards
(2) The inner pair of lamps:	Either 45° inwards and 80° outwards or 80° inwards and 45° outwards

(ii) Vertical—	
(A) Where one or two rear position lamps are required to be fitted—	
(1) Any vehicle not covered by sub-paragraph (2) or (3):	15° above and below the horizontal
(2) Where the highest part of the illuminated area of the lamp is less than 1500 millimetres above the ground:	15° above and 10° below the horizontal
(3) Where the highest part of the illuminated area of the lamp is less than 750 millimetres above the ground:	15° above and 5° below the horizontal
(B) Where four rear position lamps are required to be fitted—	
(1) One pair of lamps:	Such that they satisfy the relevant requirements in paragraph 3(*a*)(ii)(A)
(2) The other pair of lamps:	Visible to the rear
(*b*) A motor vehicle, other than a motor vehicle combination, first used before 1st April 1986 and any other vehicle manufactured before 1st October 1985:	Visible to the rear
(*c*) A vehicle drawn or propelled by hand, a pedal cycle, a horse-drawn vehicle and a motor bicycle combination:	Visible to the rear
4. Markings—	
(*a*) A motor vehicle or a trailer not covered by sub-paragraph (*b*), (*c*) or (*d*):	An approval mark
(*b*) A motor vehicle first used before 1st January 1974 and a trailer, other than a trailer drawn by a pedal cycle, manufactured before that date:	No requirement
(*c*) A solo motor bicycle and a motor bicycle combination, in each case first used before 1st April 1986, and a trailer manufactured before 1st October 1985 and drawn by a solo motor bicycle or a motor bicycle combination:	No requirement
(*d*) A pedal cycle, a trailer drawn by a pedal cycle, a horse-drawn vehicle and a vehicle drawn or propelled by hand:	A British Standard mark
5. Size of illuminated area:	No requirement
6. Colour:	Red
7. Wattage:	No requirement
8. Intensity—	
(*a*) A rear position lamp bearing any of the markings mentioned in paragraph 4:	No requirement
(*b*) Any other rear position lamp:	Visible from a reasonable distance

9. Electrical connections: No requirement

10. Tell-tale: No requirement

11. Other requirements—

Except in the case of a motor vehicle first used before 1st April 1986, any other vehicle manufactured before 1st October 1985 and a motor bicycle combination, where two rear position lamps are required to be fitted they shall form a matched pair and where four rear position lamps are required to be fitted they shall form two matched pairs and each pair shall be capable of being switched on and off simultaneously and not otherwise.

12. Definitions—

In this Schedule—

'approval mark' means—

(*a*) in relation to a solo motor bicycle, a motor bicycle combination and a trailer drawn by a solo motor bicycle or a motor bicycle combination, a marking designated as an approval mark by Regulation 4 of the Designation of Approval Marks Regulations and shown at item 50A of Schedule 2 to those Regulations, and

(*b*) in relation to any other motor vehicle or any trailer, either—

(i) a marking designated as an approval mark by Regulation 5 of the Designation of Approval Marks Regulations and shown at item 6 or, if combined with a stop lamp, at item 8 of Schedule 4 to those Regulations, or

(ii) a marking designated as an approval mark by Regulation 4 of the Designation of Approval Marks Regulations and shown at item 7A or, if combined with a stop lamp, at item 7C of Schedule 2 to those Regulations; and

'British Standard mark' means the specification for cycle rear lamps published by the British Standards Institution under the reference 3648:1963 as amended by Amendment PD 6137 published in May 1967, namely 'B.S. 3648'.

PART II

Rear Position Lamps to which Regulation 17 applies

Any number may be fitted, and the only requirement prescribed by these Regulations in respect of any which are fitted is that specified in paragraph 6 as regards rear position lamps to which Regulation 16 applies.

SCHEDULE 11

(See Regulations 16 and 17)

PART I

Rear Fog Lamps to which Regulation 16 applies

1. Number:	One
2. Position—	
(*a*) Longitudinal:	At or near the rear of the vehicle
(*b*) Lateral—	
(i) Where one rear fog lamp is fitted:	On the centre-line or off side of the vehicle (disregarding any sidecar forming part of a motor bicycle combination)
(ii) Where two lamps are fitted:	No requirement
(*c*) Vertical—	
(i) Maximum height above the ground—	
(A) Any vehicle not covered by sub-paragraph (B):	1000 millimetres
(B) An agricultural vehicle, engineering plant and a motor tractor:	2100 millimetres
(ii) Minimum height above the ground:	250 millimetres
(*d*) Minimum separation distance between a rear fog lamp and a stop lamp—	
(i) In the case of a rear fog lamp which does not share a common lamp body with a stop lamp:	A distance of 100 millimetres between the light-emitting surfaces of the lamps when viewed in a direction parallel to the longitudinal axis of the vehicle
(ii) In the case of a rear fog lamp which shares a common lamp body with a stop lamp:	100 millimetres
3. Angles of visibility—	
(*a*) Horizontal:	25° inwards and outwards. However, where two rear fog lamps are fitted it shall suffice if throughout the sector so defined at least one lamp (but not necessarily the same lamp) is visible.
(*b*) Vertical:	5° above and below the horizontal
4. Markings:	An approval mark
5. Size of illuminated area:	No requirement

6. Colour:	Red
7. Wattage:	No requirement
8. Intensity:	No requirement
9. Electrical connections:	No rear fog lamp shall be fitted to any vehicle so that it can be illuminated by the application of any braking system on the vehicle.
10. Tell-tale:	A circuit-closed tell-tale shall be fitted.

11. Other requirements—

Where two rear fog lamps are fitted to a motor vehicle first used on or after 1st April 1986 or to a trailer manufactured on or after 1st October 1985 they shall form a matched pair.

12. Definitions—

In this Schedule 'approval mark' means either—

(*a*) a marking designated as an approval mark by Regulation 5 of the Designation of Approval Marks Regulations and shown at item 20 of Schedule 4 to those Regulations, or

(*b*) a marking designated as an approval mark by Regulation 4 of the Designation of Approval Marks Regulations and shown at item 38 of Schedule 2 to those Regulations.

PART II

Rear Fog Lamps to which Regulation 17 applies

1. In the case of a motor vehicle first used before 1st April 1980 and any other vehicle manufactured before 1st October 1979, any number may be fitted and the only requirements prescribed by these Regulations in respect of any which are fitted are those specified in paragraphs 2(*d*), 6 and 9 as regards rear fog lamps to which Regulation 16 applies.

2. In the case of a motor vehicle first used on or after 1st April 1980 and any other vehicle manufactured on or after 1st October 1979, not more than two may be fitted and the requirements prescribed by these Regulations in respect of any which are fitted are all those specified in this Schedule as regards rear fog lamps to which Regulation 16 applies except those specified in paragraph 1.

SCHEDULE 12

(See Regulations 16 and 17)

PART I

Stop Lamps to which Regulation 16 applies

1. Number—	
(*a*) Any vehicle not covered by sub-paragraph (*b*) or (*c*):	Two
(*b*) A solo motor bicycle, a motor bicycle combination, an invalid carriage and a trailer drawn by a solo motor bicycle or a motor bicycle combination:	One
(*c*) Any other motor vehicle first used before 1st January 1971 and any other trailer manufactured before that date:	One
2. Position—	
(*a*) Longitudinal:	At or towards the rear of the vehicle
(*b*) Lateral—	
(i) Maximum distance from the side of the vehicle—	
(A) Where two or more stop lamps are fitted:	At least one on each side of the longitudinal axis of the vehicle
(B) Where only one stop lamp is fitted:	On the centre-line or off side of the vehicle (disregarding any sidecar forming part of a motor bicycle combination)
(ii) Minimum separation distance between two obligatory stop lamps:	400 millimetres
(*c*) Vertical—	
(i) Maximum height above the ground—	
(A) Any vehicle not covered by sub-paragraph (B):	1500 millimetres or, if the structure of the vehicle makes this impracticable, 2100 millimetres
(B) A motor vehicle first used before 1st January 1971, a trailer manufactured before that date and a motor vehicle having a maximum speed not exceeding 25 miles per hour:	No requirement
(ii) Minimum height above the ground—	
(A) Any vehicle not covered by sub-paragraph (B):	350 millimetres
(B) A motor vehicle first used before 1st January 1971 and a trailer manufactured before that date:	No requirement

3. Angles of visibility—

(*a*) A motor vehicle first used on or after 1st January 1971 and a trailer manufactured on or after that date—	
(i) Horizontal:	45° to the left and to the right
(ii) Vertical—	
(A) Except in a case specified in sub-paragraph (B) or (C):	15° above and below the horizontal
(B) Where the highest part of the illuminated area of the lamp is less than 1500 millimetres above the ground:	15° above and 10° below the horizontal
(C) Where the highest part of the illuminated area of the lamp is less than 750 millimetres above the ground:	15° above and 5° below the horizontal
(*b*) A motor vehicle first used before 1st January 1971 and a trailer manufactured before that date:	Visible to the rear

4. Markings—

(*a*) Any vehicle not covered by sub-paragraph (*b*) or (*c*):	An approval mark
(*b*) A motor vehicle first used before 1st February 1974 and a trailer manufactured before that date:	No requirement
(*c*) A solo motor bicycle and a motor bicycle combination, in each case first used before 1st April 1986, and a trailer manufactured before 1st October 1985 drawn by a solo motor bicycle or a motor bicycle combination:	No requirement

5. Size of illuminated area:	No requirement
6. Colour:	Red

7. Wattage—

(*a*) A stop lamp fitted to a motor vehicle first used before 1st January 1971 or a trailer manufactured before that date and a stop lamp bearing an approval mark:	No requirement
(*b*) Any other stop lamp:	15 to 36 watts

8. Intensity:	No requirement

9. Electrical connections—

(*a*) Every stop lamp fitted to

(i) a solo motor bicycle or a motor bicycle combination first used on or after 1st April 1986 shall be operated both by the application of the front braking system and by the application of the rear braking system;

(ii) any other motor vehicle, shall be operated by the application of a braking system.

(*b*) The braking systems mentioned in paragraph (*a*) are those which are designed to be used to bring the vehicle when in motion to a halt.

(*c*) Every stop lamp fitted to a trailer drawn by a motor vehicle shall be operated by the application of the braking system of that motor vehicle.

10. Tell-tale: No requirement

11. Other requirements—

Where two stop lamps are required to be fitted, they shall form a pair.

12. Definitions—

In this Schedule 'approval mark' means—

(*a*) in relation to a solo motor bicycle, a motor bicycle combination or a trailer drawn by a solo motor bicycle or a motor bicycle combination, a marking designated as an approval mark by Regulation 4 of the Designation of Approval Marks Regulations and shown at item 50A of Schedule 2 to those Regulations, and

(*b*) in relation to any other vehicle, either—

(i) a marking designated as an approval mark by Regulation 5 of the Designation of Approval Marks Regulations and shown at item 7 or, if combined with a rear position lamp, at item 8 of Schedule 4 to those Regulations; or

(ii) a marking designated as an approval mark by Regulation 4 of the Designation of Approval Marks Regulations and shown at item 7B or, if combined with a rear position lamp, at item 7C of Schedule 2 to those Regulations.

PART II

STOP LAMPS TO WHICH REGULATION 17 APPLIES

Any number may be fitted, and the requirements prescribed by these Regulations in respect of any which are fitted are all those specified in this Schedule as regards stop lamps to which Regulation 16 applies except those specified in paragraphs 1 and 2(*b*)(ii).

SCHEDULE 13

(See Regulation 17)

REVERSING LAMPS TO WHICH REGULATION 17 APPLIES

1. Number: Not more than two

2. Position: No requirement

3. Angles of visibility: No requirement

4. Markings—

(*a*) A motor vehicle first used on or after 1st April 1986 and a trailer manufactured on or after 1st October 1985: An approval mark

(*b*) A motor vehicle first used before 1st April 1986 and a trailer manufactured before 1st October 1985: No requirement

5. Size of illuminated area:	No requirement
6. Colour:	White
7. Wattage—	
(*a*) A reversing lamp bearing an approval mark:	No requirement
(*b*) A reversing lamp not bearing an approval mark:	The total wattage of any one reversing lamp shall not exceed 24 watts.
8. Intensity:	No requirement
9. Electrical connections:	No requirement
10. Tell-tale—	
(*a*) A motor vehicle first used on or after 1st July 1954, provided that the electrical connections are such that the reversing lamp or lamps cannot be illuminated other than automatically by the selection of the reverse gear of the vehicle:	No requirement
(*b*) Any other motor vehicle first used on or after 1st July 1954:	A circuit-closed tell-tale shall be fitted.
(*c*) A motor vehicle first used before 1st July 1954:	No requirement
(*d*) Any vehicle which is not a motor vehicle:	No requirement

11. Definitions—

In this Schedule 'approval mark' means either—

(*a*) a marking designated as an approval mark by Regulation 5 of the Designation of Approval Marks Regulations and shown at item 21 of Schedule 4 to those Regulations, or

(*b*) a marking designated as an approval mark by Regulation 4 of the Designation of Approval Marks Regulations and shown at item 23 or 23A of Schedule 2 to those Regulations.

SCHEDULE 14

(See Regulation 16)

Rear Registration Plate Lamps to which Regulation 16 applies

1. Number:	At least one
2. Position:	Such that the lamp or lamps are capable of adequately illuminating the rear registration plate
3. Angles of visibility:	No requirement

4. Markings—

(*a*) A motor vehicle first used on or after 1st April 1986 and a trailer manufactured on or after 1st October 1985:	An approval mark
(*b*) A motor vehicle first used before 1st April 1986 and a trailer manufactured before 1st October 1985:	No requirement
5. Size of illuminated area:	No requirement
6. Colour:	No requirement
7. Wattage:	No requirement
8. Intensity:	No requirement
9. Electrical connections:	No requirement
10. Tell-tale:	No requirement

11. Definitions—

In this Schedule 'approval mark' means—

(*a*) in relation to a solo motor bicycle, a motor bicycle combination and a trailer drawn by a solo motor bicycle or a motor bicycle combination, a marking designated as an approval mark by Regulation 4 of the Designation of Approval Marks Regulations and shown at item 50A of Schedule 2 to those Regulations, and

(*b*) in relation to any other motor vehicle and any other trailer, either—

(i) a marking designated as an approval mark by Regulation 5 of the Designation of Approval Marks Regulations and shown at item 10 of Schedule 4 to those Regulations, or

(ii) a marking designated as an approval mark by Regulation 4 of the Designation of Approval Marks Regulations and shown at item 4 of Schedule 2 to those Regulations.

SCHEDULE 15

(See Regulation 17)

Warning Beacons to which Regulation 17 applies

1. Number:	No requirement

2. Position—

Every warning beacon shall be so mounted on the vehicle that the centre of the lamp is at a height not less than 1200 millimetres above the ground.

3. Angles of visibility—

The light shown from at least one beacon (but not necessarily the same beacon) shall be visible from any point at a reasonable distance from the vehicle [or any trailer being drawn by it].

4. Markings:	No requirement
5. Size of illuminated area:	No requirement
6. Colour:	Blue, amber, green or yellow in accordance with Regulation 11
7. Wattage:	No requirement
8. Intensity:	No requirement
9. Electrical connections:	No requirement
10. Tell-tale:	No requirement

11. Other requirements—

The light shown by any one warning beacon shall be displayed not less than 60 nor more than 240 equal times per minute and the intervals between each display of light shall be constant.

[Schedule 15 is printed as amended by SI 1987 No 1315.]

SCHEDULE 16

(See Regulations 16 and 17)

PART I

Side Reflex Reflectors to which Regulation 16 applies

1. Number—

(*a*) A motor vehicle first used on or after 1st April 1986 and a trailer manufactured on or after 1st October 1985:	On each side: two and as many more as are sufficient to satisfy the requirements of paragraph 2(*a*)
(*b*) A motor vehicle first used before 1st April 1986 and a trailer manufactured before 1st October 1985:	On each side: Two

2. Position—

(*a*) Longitudinal—

(i) A motor vehicle first used on or after 1st April 1986 and a trailer manufactured on or after 1st October 1985—

(A) Maximum distance from the front of the vehicle, including any drawbar, in respect of the foremost reflector on each side:	3 metres
(B) Maximum distance from the rear of the vehicle in respect of the rearmost reflector on each side:	1 metre

(C) Maximum separation distance between the reflecting areas of adjacent reflectors on the same side of the vehicle:	3 metres
(ii) A motor vehicle first used before 1st April 1986 and a trailer manufactured before 1st October 1985—	
(A) Maximum distance from the rear of the vehicle in respect of the rearmost reflector on each side:	1 metre
(B) The other reflector on each side of the vehicle:	Towards the centre of the vehicle
(*b*) Lateral:	No requirement
(*c*) Vertical—	
(i) Maximum height above the ground—	
(A) A motor vehicle first used on or after 1st April 1986 and a trailer manufactured on or after 1st October 1985:	900 millimetres or, if the structure of the vehicle makes this impracticable, 1500 millimetres
(B) A motor vehicle first used before 1st April 1986 and a trailer manufactured before 1st October 1985:	1500 millimetres
(ii) Minimum height above the ground:	350 millimetres
(*d*) Alignment:	Vertical and facing squarely to the side
3. Angles of visibility—	
(*a*) A motor vehicle first used on or after 1st April 1986 and a trailer manufactured on or after 1st October 1985—	
(i) Horizontal:	45° to the left and to the right when viewed in a direction at right angles to the longitudinal axis of the vehicle
(ii) Vertical—	
(A) Except in a case specified in sub-paragraph (B):	15° above and below the horizontal
(B) Where the highest part of the reflecting area is less than 750 millimetres above the ground:	15° above and 5° below the horizontal
(*b*) A motor vehicle first used before 1st April 1986 and a trailer manufactured before 1st October 1985:	Plainly visible to the side
4. Markings:	An approval mark
5. Size of reflecting area:	No requirement
6. Colour—	
(*a*) Any vehicle not covered by sub-paragraph (*b*):	Amber

(*b*) A solo motor bicycle, a motor bicycle combination, a pedal cycle with or without a sidecar attached thereto or an invalid carriage:	No requirement

7. Other requirements:	No side reflex reflector shall be triangular.

8. Definitions—

(*a*) In this Schedule 'approval mark' means either—

(i) a marking designated as an approval mark by Regulation 4 of the Designation of Approval Marks Regulations and shown at item 3 of Schedule 2 to those Regulations and which includes the Roman numeral I, or

(ii) a marking designated as an approval mark by Regulation 5 of the Designation of Approval Marks Regulations and shown at item 4 of Schedule 4 to those Regulations and which includes the Roman numeral I; and

(*b*) In this Schedule references to 'maximum distance from the front of the vehicle' and 'maximum distance from the rear of the vehicle' are references to the maximum distance from that end of the vehicle (as determined by reference to the overall length of the vehicle exclusive of any special equipment) beyond which no part of the reflecting area of the side reflex reflector extends.

PART II

Side Reflex Reflectors to which Regulation 17 applies

Any number may be fitted, and the only requirements prescribed by these Regulations in respect of any which are fitted are those specified in paragraphs 6 and 7 as regards side reflex reflectors to which Regulation 16 applies.

SCHEDULE 17

(See Regulations 16 and 17)

PART I

Rear Reflex Reflectors to which Regulation 16 applies

1. Number—

(*a*) Any vehicle not covered by sub-paragraph (*b*) or (*c*):	Two
(*b*) A solo motor bicycle, a pedal cycle with less than four wheels and with or without a sidecar, a trailer drawn by a pedal cycle, a trailer the overall width of which does not exceed 800 millimetres drawn by a solo motor bicycle or a motor bicycle combination and a vehicle drawn or propelled by hand:	One
(*c*) A motor vehicle having three or more wheels and a maximum speed not exceeding 25 miles per hour and a trailer drawn by any such vehicle if, in either case, the structure of the vehicle makes it impracticable to meet all of the requirements of paragraphs 2 and 3 below with two reflectors:	Four

2. Position—

(*a*) Longitudinal:	At or near the rear
(*b*) Lateral—	
(i) Where two rear reflectors are required to be fitted—	
(A) Maximum distance from the side of the vehicle—	
(1) Any vehicle not covered by sub-paragraph (2), (3) or (4):	400 millimetres
(2) A large passenger-carrying vehicle first used before 1st October 1954 and a horse-drawn vehicle manufactured before 1st October 1985:	No requirement
(3) A vehicle constructed or adapted for the carriage of round timber:	765 millimetres
(4) Any other motor vehicle first used before 1st April 1986 and any other vehicle manufactured before 1st October 1985:	610 millimetres
(B) Minimum separation distance between a pair of rear reflectors—	
(1) Any vehicle not covered by sub-paragraph (2):	600 millimetres or, if the overall width of the vehicle is less than 1300 millimetres, 400 millimetres
(2) A motor vehicle first used before 1st April 1986 and any other vehicle manufactured before 1st October 1985:	No requirement
(ii) Where one rear reflector is required to be fitted:	On the centre-line or off side of the vehicle
(iii) Where four rear reflectors are required to be fitted—	
(A) Maximum distance from the side of the vehicle—	
(1) One pair of reflectors:	Such that they satisfy the relevant requirements in sub-paragraph 2(*b*)(i)(A)
(2) The other pair of reflectors:	No requirement
(B) Minimum separation distance between rear reflectors—	
(1) One pair of reflectors:	Such that they satisfy the relevant requirements in sub-paragraph 2(*b*)(i)(B)
(2) The other pair of reflectors:	No requirement
(*c*) Vertical—	
(i) Maximum height above the ground where one or two rear reflectors are required to be fitted—	

(A) Any vehicle not covered by sub-paragraph (B):	900 millimetres or, if the structure of the vehicle makes this impracticable, 1200 millimetres
(B) A motor vehicle first used before 1st April 1986 and any other vehicle manufactured before 1st October 1985:	1525 millimetres
(ii) Maximum height above the ground where four rear reflectors are required to be fitted—	
(A) One pair of reflectors:	Such that they satisfy the relevant requirements in paragraph 2(*c*)(i)
(B) The other pair of reflectors:	2100 millimetres
(iii) Minimum height above the ground—	
(A) Any vehicle not covered by sub-paragraph (B):	350 millimetres
(B) A motor vehicle first used before 1st April 1986 and any other vehicle manufactured before 1st October 1985:	No requirement
(*d*) Alignment:	Vertical and facing squarely to the rear
3. Angles of visibility—	
(*a*) A motor vehicle (not being a motor bicycle combination) first used on or after 1st April 1986 and a trailer manufactured on or after 1st October 1985—	
(i) Where one or two rear reflectors are required to be fitted—	
(A) Horizontal—	
(1) Where two rear reflectors are required to be fitted:	30° inwards and outwards
(2) Where one rear reflector is required to be fitted:	30° to the left and to the right
(B) Vertical—	
(1) Except in a case specified in sub-paragraph (2)	15° above and below the horizontal
(2) Where the highest part of the reflecting area is less than 750 millimetres above the ground:	15° above and 5° below the horizontal
(ii) Where four rear reflectors are required to be fitted—	
(A) One pair of reflectors:	Such that they satisfy the relevant requirements in paragraph 3(*a*)(i)
(B) The other pair of reflectors:	Plainly visible to the rear
(*b*) A motor vehicle (not being a motor bicycle combination) first used before 1st April 1986 and a trailer manufactured before 1st October 1985:	Plainly visible to the rear

(*c*) A motor bicycle combination, a pedal cycle, a sidecar attached to a pedal cycle, a horse-drawn vehicle and a vehicle drawn or propelled by hand:	Plainly visible to the rear
4. Markings—	
(*a*) A motor vehicle first used—	
(i) On or after 1st April 1986:	(A) An approval mark incorporating 'I' or 'IA', or (B) A British Standard mark which is specified in sub-paragraph (i) of the definition of 'British Standard mark' below followed by 'LI' or 'LIA'.
(ii) On or after 1st July 1970 and before 1st April 1986:	(A) Any of the markings mentioned in sub-paragraph (*a*)(i) above, or (B) In the case of a vehicle manufactured in Italy, an Italian approved marking.
(iii) Before 1st July 1970:	No requirement
(*b*) A trailer (other than a broken-down motor vehicle) manufactured—	
(i) On or after 1st October 1985:	(A) An approval mark incorporating 'III' or 'IIIA', or (B) A British Standard mark which is specified in sub-paragraph (i) of the definition of 'British Standard mark' below followed by 'LIII' or 'LIIIA'.
(ii) On or after 1st July 1970 and before 1st October 1985:	(A) Any of the markings mentioned in sub-paragraph (*b*)(i) above, or (B) In the case of a vehicle manufactured in Italy, an Italian approved marking.
(iii) Before 1st July 1970:	No requirement
(*c*) A pedal cycle manufactured—	
(i) On or after 1st July 1970:	(A) An approval mark incorporating 'I' or 'IA', or (B) A British Standard mark which is specified in sub-paragraph (i) of the definition of 'British Standard mark' below followed by 'LI' or 'LIA', or

(C) A British Standard mark which is specified in sub-paragraph (ii) of the definition of 'British Standard mark' below.

(ii) Before 1st July 1970: No requirement

(*d*) A horse-drawn vehicle and a vehicle drawn or propelled by hand in either case manufactured—

(i) On or after 1st July 1970: (A) An approval mark incorporating 'I' or 'IA', or (B) A British Standard mark which is specified in sub-paragraph (i) of the definition of 'British Standard mark' followed by 'LI' or 'LIA'.

(ii) Before 1st July 1970: No requirement

5. Size of reflecting area: No requirement

6. Colour: Red

7. Other requirements—

(*a*) Except in the case of a motor vehicle used before 1st April 1986, any other vehicle manufactured before 1st October 1985 and a motor bicycle combination, where two rear reflectors are required to be fitted they shall form a pair. Where four rear reflectors are required to be fitted they shall form two pairs.

(*b*) No vehicle, other than a trailer or a broken-down motor vehicle being towed, may be fitted with triangular-shaped rear reflectors.

8. Definitions—

In this Schedule—

(*a*) 'approval mark' means either—

(i) a marking designated as an approval mark by Regulation 4 of the Designation of Approval Marks Regulations and shown at item 3 or 3A or 3B of Schedule 2 to those Regulations, or

(ii) a marking designated as an approval mark by Regulation 5 of the Designation of Approval Marks Regulations and shown at item 4 of Schedule 4 to those Regulations;

(*b*) 'British Standard mark' means either—

(i) the specification for reflex reflectors for vehicles, including cycles, published by the British Standards Institution under the reference B.S. AU 40: Part 2: 1965, namely 'AU 40', or

(ii) the specification for photometric and physical requirements of reflective devices published by the British Standards Institution under the reference BS 6102: Part 2: 1982, namely 'BS 6102/2'; and

(*c*) 'Italian approved marking' means—

a mark approved by the Italian Ministry of Transport, namely, one including two separate groups of symbols consisting of 'IGM' or 'DGM' and 'C.1' or 'C.2'.

PART II

Rear Reflex Reflectors to which Regulation 17 applies

Any number may be fitted, and the only requirements prescribed by these Regulations in respect of any which are fitted are those specified in paragraphs 6 and 7(*b*) as regards rear reflex reflectors to which Regulation 16 applies.

SCHEDULE 18

(See Regulations 16 and 17)

PART I

Rear Markings to which Regulation 16 applies

SECTION A

General requirements

1. Number—	
(*a*) A motor vehicle the overall length of which—	
(i) does not exceed 13 metres:	A rear marking shown in diagram 1, 2 or 3 in Section B of this Schedule
(ii) exceeds 13 metres:	A rear marking shown in diagram 4 or 5 in Section B of this Schedule
(*b*) A trailer if it forms part of a combination of vehicles the overall length of which—	
(i) does not exceed 11 metres:	A rear marking shown in diagram 1, 2 or 3 in Section B of this Schedule
(ii) exceeds 11 metres but does not exceed 13 metres:	A rear marking shown in diagram 1, 2, 3, 4 or 5 in Section B of this Schedule
(iii) exceeds 13 metres:	A rear marking shown in diagram 4 or 5 in Section B of this Schedule
2. Position—	
(*a*) Longitudinal:	At or near the rear of the vehicle
(*b*) Lateral—	
(i) A rear marking shown in diagram 2, 3 or 5 in Section B of this Schedule:	Each part shall be fitted as near as practicable to the outermost edge of the vehicle on the side thereof on which it is fitted so that no part of the marking projects beyond the outermost part of the vehicle on either side.

(ii) A rear marking shown in diagram 1 or 4 in Section B of this Schedule:	The marking shall be fitted so that the vertical centre-line of the marking lies on the vertical plane through the longitudinal axis of the vehicle and no part of the marking projects beyond the outermost part of the vehicle on either side.
(*c*) Vertical:	The lower edge of every rear marking shall be at a height of not more than 1700 millimetres nor less than 400 millimetres above the ground whether the vehicle is laden or unladen.
(*d*) Alignment:	The lower edge of every rear marking shall be fitted horizontally. Every part of a rear marking shall lie within 20° of a transverse vertical plane at right angles to the longitudinal axis of the vehicle.
3. Angles of visibility:	Plainly visible to the rear, except while the vehicle is being loaded or unloaded.
4. Markings:	A British Standard mark
5. Size:	In accordance with Sections B and C of this Schedule
6. Colour:	Red fluorescent material in the stippled areas shown in any of the diagrams in Section B of this Schedule and yellow reflex reflecting material in any of the areas so shown, being areas not stippled and not constituting a letter. All letters shall be coloured black.

7. Other requirements—

The two parts of every rear marking shown in diagrams 2, 3 or 5 in Section B of this Schedule shall form a pair.

8. Definitions—

In this Schedule 'British Standard mark' means the specification for rear marking plates for vehicles published by the British Standards Institution under the reference BS AU 152:1970, namely 'BS AU 152'.

SECTION B

Size, Colour and Type of Rear Markings

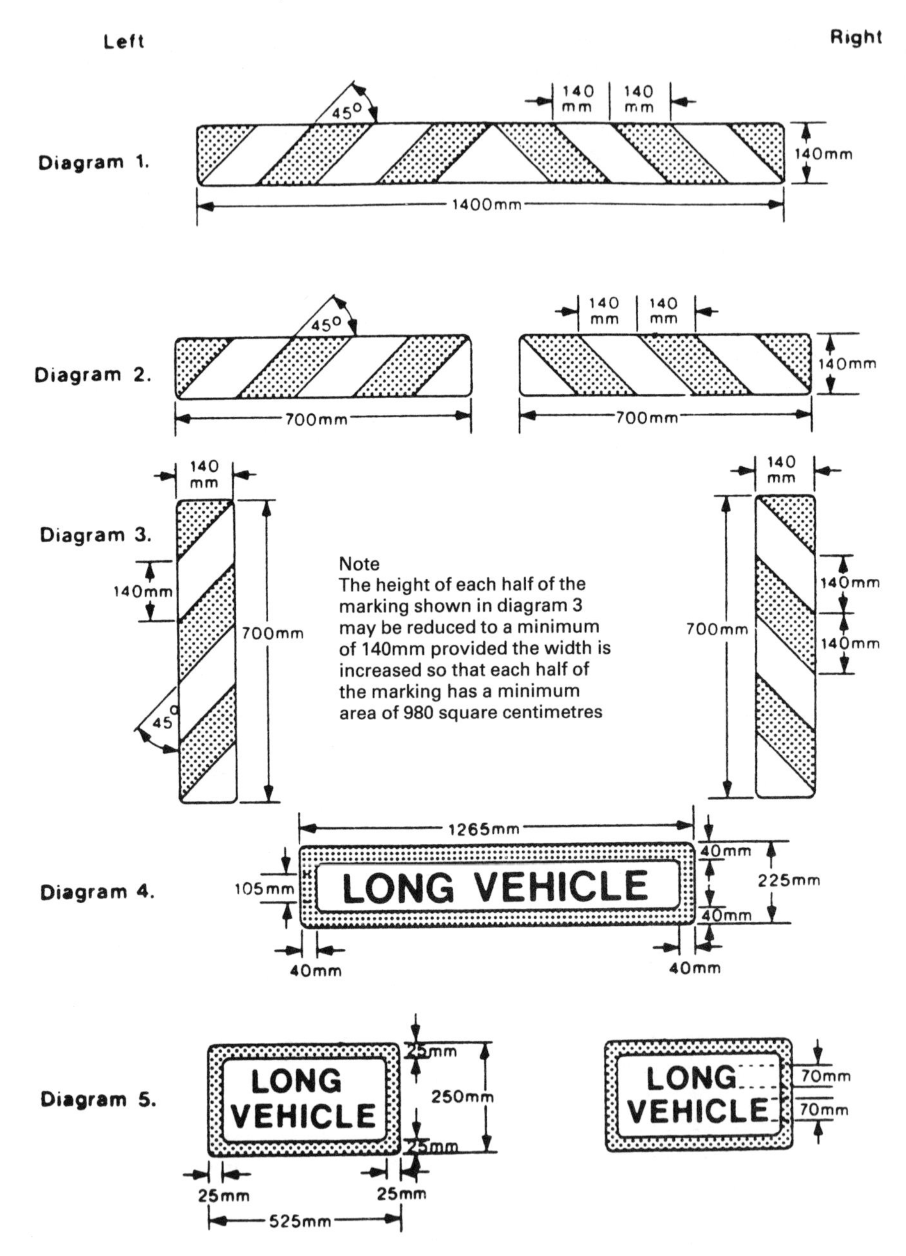

SECTION C

Additional Provisions Relating to the Size and Form of Rear Markings

1. Any variation in a dimension (other than as to the height of a letter) specified in any of the diagrams in Section B of this Schedule shall be treated as permitted for the purposes of these Regulations if the variation—

(*a*) in the case of a dimension so specified as 250 millimetres or as over 250 millimetres does not exceed 2.5 per cent of that dimension;

(*b*) in the case of a dimension so specified as 40 millimetres or as over 40 millimetres but as under 250 millimetres does not exceed 5 per cent of that dimension; or

(*c*) in the case of a dimension so specified as under 40 millimetres does not exceed 10 per cent of that dimension.

2. Any variation in a dimension as to the height of a letter specified in any of the said diagrams shall be treated as permitted for the purposes of these Regulations if the variation—

(*a*) in the case of a dimension so specified as 105 millimetres does not exceed 2·5 per cent of that dimension; or

(*b*) in the case of a dimension so specified as 70 millimetres does not exceed 5 per cent of that dimension.

3. Any variation in a dimension as to the angle of hatching specified in any of the said diagrams shall be treated as permitted for the purposes of these Regulations if the variation does not exceed 5 degrees.

4. Every rear marking shown in diagrams 1 or 4 of Section B of this Schedule shall be constructed in the form of a single plate, and every rear marking shown in diagrams 2, 3 or 5 of Section B of this Schedule shall be constructed in the form of two plates of equal size and shape.

5. All letters incorporated in any rear marking shall have the proportions and form of letters as shown in Part V of Schedule 7 to the Traffic Signs Regulations 1981 *[SI 1981 No 859]*.

PART II

Rear Markings to which Regulation 17 applies

1. Number—

The following requirements are prescribed as regards the number of rear markings to which Regulation 17 applies—

(i) Any motor vehicle the maximum gross weight of which exceeds 7500 kilograms or the unladen weight of which exceeds 3000 kilograms:	Any number of rear markings may be fitted appropriate to the length of the vehicle as in paragraph 1(*a*) of Part I, Section A of this Schedule.

(ii) Any trailer the maximum gross weight of which exceeds 3500 kilograms or the unladen weight of which exceeds 1000 kilograms:	Any number of rear markings may be fitted appropriate to the length of the combination of vehicles as in paragraph 1(*b*) of Section A of Part I of this Schedule.
(iii) Any trailer which is being drawn by a vehicle which is itself required or permitted to be fitted with a rear marking:	Any number of rear markings may be fitted appropriate to the length of the combination of vehicles as in paragraph 1(*b*) of Section A of Part I of this Schedule.
(iv) Any other vehicle:	No rear marking may be fitted.

2. Other provisions—

The requirements specified in relation to rear markings to which Regulation 16 applies in paragraphs 2 to 7 of Section A of Part I of this Schedule and in Sections B and C of that Part are prescribed as regards rear markings to which Regulation 17 applies.

SCHEDULE 19

(See Regulations 16 and 17)

PART I

Pedal Reflex Reflectors to which Regulation 16 applies

1. Number:	Two reflectors on each pedal
2. Position—	
(*a*) Longitudinal:	On the leading edge and the trailing edge of each pedal.
(*b*) Lateral:	No requirement
(*c*) Vertical:	No requirement
3. Angles of visibility:	Such that the reflector on the leading edge of each pedal is plainly visible to the front and the reflector on the trailing edge of each pedal is plainly visible to the rear.
4. Markings:	A British Standard mark
5. Size of reflecting area:	No requirement
6. Colour:	Amber

7. Definitions—

In this Schedule 'British Standard mark' means the specification for photometric and physical requirements of reflective devices published by the British Standards Institution under the references BS 6102: Part 2: 1982, namely 'BS 6102/2'.

PART II

Pedal Reflex Reflectors to which Regulation 17 applies

Any number may be fitted, and the only requirement prescribed by these Regulations in respect of any which are fitted is that specified in paragraph 6 as regards pedal reflex reflectors to which Regulation 16 applies.

* * *

The 70 miles per hour, 60 miles per hour and 50 miles per hour (Temporary Speed Limit) Order 1977

[This order was varied by the 70 miles per hour, 60 miles per hour and 50 miles per hour (Temporary Speed Limit) (Variation) Order 1978 with effect from 23 August 1978. This order, which would otherwise have expired on 30 November 1978, was continued in force indefinitely by the 70 miles per hour (Temporary Speed Limit) (Continuation) Order 1978 (SI 1978 No 1548).]

* * *

2. Subject to Article 4 below, no person shall during the period of this Order drive a motor vehicle—

(*a*) at a speed exceeding 50 miles per hour on the lengths of dual carriageway road specified in Part I of Schedule 1 to this Order.

(*b*) at a speed exceeding 60 miles per hour on the lengths of dual carriageway road specified in Schedule 2 to this Order, or

(*c*) at a speed exceeding 70 miles per hour on any other length of dual carriageway road.

3. Subject to Article 4 below, no person shall during the period of this Order drive a motor vehicle—

(*a*) at a speed exceeding 50 miles per hour on the lengths of single carriageway road specified in Part II of Schedule 1 to this Order, or

(*b*) at a speed exceeding 60 miles per hour on any length of single carriageway road.

4. Nothing in this Order shall prohibit a person from driving a motor vehicle on a length of road at a speed exceeding that which would apply to that length under Article 2 or 3 above in a case where a higher speed limit is, after the coming into operation of this Order, prescribed in relation to that length by means of an Order under [section 84 of the Road Traffic Regulation Act 1984].

[Article 4 is printed as amended by the Road Traffic Regulation Act 1984, s 144(1) and Sched 10, para 2.]

SCHEDULE 1

PART I

LENGTHS OF DUAL CARRIAGEWAY ROAD FOR WHICH A 50 MILES PER HOUR SPEED LIMIT IS PRESCRIBED

Any dual carriageway sections of any of the lengths of road described in Part II of this Schedule.

PART II

LENGTHS OF SINGLE CARRIAGEWAY ROAD FOR WHICH A 50 MILES PER HOUR SPEED LIMIT IS PRESCRIBED

[In certain instances the lengths of road described below in this Part of this Schedule include short sections of dual carriageway road. These sections are covered by Part I of this Schedule.]

A *Trunk Roads*

* * *

B *Other Roads*

* * *

SCHEDULE 2

LENGTHS OF DUAL CARRIAGEWAY ROAD FOR WHICH A 60 MILES PER HOUR SPEED LIMIT IS PRESCRIBED

A *Trunk Roads*

* * *

B *Other Roads*

* * *

The Traffic Signs Regulations and General Directions 1981

(SI 1981 No 859)

ARRANGEMENT OF REGULATIONS

[The text of these regulations and general directions is printed as amended by:
the Traffic Signs (Amendment) Regulations 1982 (SI 1982 No 1879) (10 February 1983);
the Traffic Signs General (Amendment) Directions 1982 (SI 1982 No 1880) (10 February 1983); and
the Traffic Signs General (Amendment) Directions 1983 (SI 1983 No 1086) (25 August 1983);
the Traffic Signs (Amendment) Regulations 1983 (SI 1983 No 1088) (25 August 1983);
the Traffic Signs (Amendment) Regulations and General Directions 1984 (SI 1984 No 966) (13 August 1984);
the Traffic Signs (Amendment) Regulations 1986 (SI 1986 No 1859) (1 December 1986); and
the Traffic Signs General (Amendment) Directions 1987 (SI 1987 No 1706) (15 October 1987).
The amending regulations are referred to in the notes by their years and numbers. The dates referred to above are the dates on which the regulations and directions came into force.]

PART I

TRAFFIC SIGNS REGULATIONS

* * *

SECTION II

Miscellaneous General Provisions

SECTION III

Traffic Signs shown in Schedule 1

. . . .

11. Signs shown in diagrams 601.1, 602, 602.1 and 649.1, and their significance
12. Permitted variants
13. Dimensions
14. Proportions and form of letters and numerals
15,16. Illumination of signs by steady lighting

. . . .

18. Illumination of signs by reflecting material

. . . .

SECTION IV

Traffic Signs shown in Schedule 2

20. Road markings
21–23. Particular road markings
24. Colour of road markings
25. Use on road markings of reflecting material and studs with reflectors

. . . .

SECTION V

Miscellaneous Traffic Signs

27. Certain temporary signs

. . . .

31,32. Light signals for control of vehicular traffic
33. Portable light signals for control of vehicular traffic
34. Significance of light signals

. . . .

36. Light signals for lane control of vehicular traffic.

* * *

PART II

GENERAL DIRECTIONS

Direction

. . . .

5.

. . . .

10–12.

. . . .

17–20.

. . . .

24,25.

. . . .

30.

. . . .

34.

. . . .

36.

. . . .

42,43.

PART III

General Citation and Commencement

* * *

PART I

Traffic Signs Regulations

* * *

Section II

Miscellaneous General Provisions

6. Authorisations by the Secretary of State

Nothing in these Regulations shall be taken to limit the powers of the Secretary of State under [section 64 of the Road Traffic Regulation Act 1984] to authorise the erection or retention of traffic signs of a character not prescribed by these Regulations.

[Regulation 6 is printed as amended by the Road Traffic Regulation Act 1984, s 144(1) and Sched 10, para 2.]

7. Application of [section 36 of the Road Traffic Act 1988] to signs and disqualification for offences

(1) [Section 36 of the Road Traffic Act 1988] shall apply—

(*a*) to signs of the typc shown in any of the diagrams 601.1, 602, 603, 606, 610, 616 and [649.2] and to the sign of the type shown in diagram 602 when used in combination with that shown in diagram 602.1,

(*b*) to the red signal when shown by the light signals prescribed by Regulation 31, by Regulation 31 as varied by Regulation 32, or by Regulation 33,

(*c*) to the road marking shown in diagram 1013.1 insofar as that marking conveys the requirements specified in Regulation 23(2),

(*d*) *[Revoked.]*

[(*e*) until 1st January 1985 to any sign of the type shown in diagram 649 in Schedule 1 to the 1975 Regulations or in diagram 649.1 in Schedule 1 to these Regulations, and]

(*f*) to any sign which in accordance with Regulation 3(2) is treated as if prescribed by these Regulations, if it is a road marking of the type shown in the diagram numbered 1013 in Schedule 2 to the Regulations of 1964 insofar as that marking conveys the requirements specified in Regulation 23(2) thereof.

(2) The signs specified hereby for the purposes of the paragraph appearing in col-

umn 5 of Part I of Schedule 4 to the said Act of 1972 in relation to section 22 thereof, are:—

(*a*) the sign shown in the diagram numbered in 601.1,

(*b*) the sign shown in the diagram numbered [649.2],

(*c*) the red signal when shown by light signals prescribed by Regulation 31, by Regulation 31 as varied by Regulation 32, or by Regulation 33,

(*d*) the road marking shown in the diagram numbered 1013.1 insofar as that marking conveys the requirements specified in Regulation 23(2),

(*e*) *[Revoked.]*

[(*f*) until 1st January 1985 any sign of the type shown in diagram 649 in Schedule 1 to the Regulations of 1975 or in diagram 649.1 in Schedule 1 to these Regulations, and]

(*g*) the road marking shown in the diagram numbered 1013 in Schedule 2 to the Regulations of 1964 insofar as it conveys the requirements specified in Regulation 23(2) thereof which marking is in accordance with Regulation 3(2) treated as if prescribed by these Regulations.

[Regulation 7 is printed as amended by the Interpretation Act 1978, ss 17(2)(a) and 23(1); SI 1984 No 966.]

8. Variations in dimensions

(1) Any variation in a dimension (other than a dimension as to the height of a letter or expressed as being the maximum or, as the case may be, minimum) specified in any of the diagrams in Schedule 1 or Schedule 3 to 6 shall be treated as permitted by these Regulations if the variation—

(*a*) in the case of a dimension so specified as 300 millimetres or as over 300 millimetres, does not exceed 5% of that dimension,

(*b*) in the case of a dimension so specified as 50 millimetres or as over 50 millimetres but as under 300 millimetres, does not exceed 7.5% of that dimension, or

(*c*) in the case of a dimension so specified as under 50 millimetres, does not exceed 10% of that dimension.

(2) Any variation in a dimension as to the height of a letter specified in any of the diagrams in Schedule 1 shall be treated as permitted by these Regulations if the variation—

(*a*) in the case of a dimension so specified as 100 millimetres or as over 100 millimetres does not exceed 5% of that dimension, or

(*b*) in the case of a dimension so specified as under 100 millimetres, does not exceed 7.5% of that dimension.

(3) Without prejudice to the next following paragraph, any variation in a dimension (other than a dimension expressed in diagrams 1003.4, 1013.1, 1027.1, 1040 to 1045 or 1055 as being the maximum, or as the case may be, minimum) specified in any of the diagrams in Schedule 2 shall be treated as permitted by these Regulations if the variation—

(*a*) in the case of a dimension so specified as 3 metres or as over 3 metres, does not exceed 15% of that dimension,

(*b*) in the case of a dimension so specified as 300 millimetres or as over 300 millimetres but as under 3 metres, does not exceed 20% of that dimension, or

(c) in the case of a dimension so specified as under 300 millimetres, does not exceed 30% of the dimension so specified, and is not less than 20% of the dimension so specified.

(4) Any variation in a dimension as to the angle of hatching specified in any of the diagrams in Schedule 2 except diagrams 1043 to 1045 shall be treated as permitted by these Regulations if the variation does not exceed 5 degrees.

Section III

Traffic Signs shown in Schedule 1

9. Signs to be of the sizes, colours and types shown in diagrams

Subject to the provisions of these Regulations, a traffic sign for conveying—

(a) to vehicular traffic on roads a warning of the description specified in or under a diagram in Part I of Schedule 1 shall be of the size, colour and type shown in the diagram relating to that warning;

(b) to vehicular traffic on roads a requirement, prohibition or restriction specified in or under a diagram in Part II of Schedule 1 (other than a requirement shown in diagram 601.1, 602, 602.1, [649.1 or 649.2]) shall be of the size, colour and type shown in the diagram relating to that requirement, prohibition or restriction;

(c) to traffic on a road other than a motorway information of a directional nature of the description specified in or under a diagram in Part III of Schedule 1 shall be of the size, colour and type shown in the diagram relating to that information;

(d) to traffic on roads information of the description specified in or under a diagram in Part IV of Schedule 1 shall be of the size, colour and type shown in the diagram relating to that information:

Provided that until 1st January 1992 a traffic sign indicating a stopping place for stage or scheduled express carriages may, notwithstanding that it is not of the size, colour and type shown in any of the diagrams 845 to 852, be of a circular or rectangular shape of not less than 30 square centimetres on which the lettering shall be shown coloured black, dark brown, dark blue or dark red on a white or yellow background, or white or yellow on a red, blue, green, brown or black background if such sign so indicating is situated on or near any road immediately after the coming into operation of these Regulations;

(e) to traffic on a motorway information of a directional or other nature specified in or under a diagram in Part V of Schedule 1 shall be of the size, colour and type shown in the diagram relating to that information.

[Regulation 9 is printed as amended by SI 1984 No 966.
These regulations came into operation on 13 August 1981; see Part III.]

9A. Sign shown in diagram 610 and its significance

(1) Subject to the provisions of these Regulations, a traffic sign for conveying to vehicular traffic on roads the requirement specified in paragraph (2) or (3) shall be of the size, colour and type shown in diagram 610.

(2) Except as provided in paragraph (3) the requirement conveyed by the sign shown in diagram 610 shall be that vehicular traffic passing the sign must keep to the

left of the sign when the arrow is pointed downwards to the left, or to the right of the sign where the arrow is pointed downwards to the right.

(3) On an occasion when a vehicle is being used for fire brigade, ambulance or police purposes and the observance of the requirement specified in paragraph (2) would be likely to hinder the use of that vehicle for the purpose for which it is being used on that occasion, then, instead of that requirement, the requirement conveyed by the traffic sign in question shall be that the vehicle shall not proceed beyond that sign in such a manner or at such a time—

(i) as is likely to cause danger to the driver of any vehicle proceeding on or from another road or on or from another part of the same road; or

(ii) as is likely to cause danger to non-vehicular traffic proceeding on or from another road or on or from another part of the same road.

10. *[Revoked.]*

[**11.**—(1) The requirements conveyed by a sign of the size, colour and type shown in a diagram of a type specified in an item in column 2 of the Table below are specified in that item in column 3 of that Table *[see table on pp 2/1006–7]*.

(2) In this Regulation—

'abnormal transport unit' means—

(*a*) a motor vehicle or a vehicle combination—

(i) the overall length of which, inclusive of the load (if any) on the vehicle or the combination, exceeds 55 feet;

(ii) the overall width of which, inclusive of the load (if any) on the vehicle or the combination, exceeds 9 feet 6 inches; or

(iii) the maximum gross weight of which exceeds 38 tonnes; or

(*b*) a motor vehicle, or a vehicle combination, which in either case is incapable of proceeding, or is unlikely to proceed, over an automatic half-barrier level crossing or an automatic open crossing (R) at a speed exceeding 5 miles per hour;

'automatic half-barrier level crossing' means a level crossing where a road is crossed by a railway and where barriers are installed to descend automatically across part of the road when a train approaches;

'automatic open crossing (R)' means a level crossing without automatic barriers where a road is crossed by a railway and where light signals are so installed as to be operated automatically by the trains approaching the crossing and the operation of the signals is monitored remotely from the crossing;

'driver', in relation to an abnormal transport unit, means where that unit is a single motor vehicle the driver of that vehicle and, where that unit is a vehicle combination, the driver of the only or the foremost motor vehicle forming part of that combination;

'major road' means the road at a road junction into which road there emerges vehicular traffic from a minor road;

'minor road' means a road at a road junction on which road there is placed the sign shown in diagram 601.1 or 602; and

'vehicle combination' means a combination of vehicles made up of one or more motor vehicles and one or more trailers all of which are linked together when travelling.]

[Regulation 11 is printed as substituted by SI 1984 No 966.]

TABLE *[ie table in reg 11(1)]*

1 Item No.	2 Type of diagram of sign	3 Requirements of sign
1.	601.1	(i) Every vehicle shall stop before crossing the transverse line shown in diagram 1002.1 or, if that line is not clearly visible, before entering the major road in respect of which the sign shown in diagram No. 601.1 has been provided; (ii) no vehicle shall proceed past the transverse line shown in diagram 1002.1 or, if that line is not clearly visible, enter the major road in respect of which the sign shown in diagram No. 601.1 has been provided, so as to be likely to cause danger to the driver of any other vehicle on the major road or to cause that driver to change the speed or course of his vehicle so as to avoid an accident.
2.	602	No vehicle shall cross the transverse line shown in diagram 1003 nearest to the major road at the side of which that line is drawn, or if that line is not clearly visible, enter that major road, so as to be likely to cause danger to the driver of any other vehicle or to cause that driver to change the speed or course of his vehicle so as to avoid an accident.
3.	602 when used with 602.1	No vehicle shall cross the transverse line shown in diagram 1003 nearest to the level crossing at the side of which that line is drawn or, if that line is not clearly visible, enter that level crossing, so as to be likely to cause danger to the driver of any railway vehicle or to cause the driver to change the speed or course of his vehicle so as to avoid an accident.
4.	649.1 and 649.2	No abnormal transport unit or, in relation to sign 649.1, no motor vehicle or vehicle combination which would be an abnormal transport unit if in sub-paragraph (*a*)(iii) of the definition of that expression in paragraph (2) below the reference to 38 tonnes

1 Item No.	2 Type of diagram of sign	3 Requirements of sign
		were a reference to 32.5 tonnes, shall proceed onto or over an automatic half-barrier level crossing or an automatic open crossing (R) unless— (*a*) the driver of the unit has used a telephone provided at or near the crossing for the purpose of obtaining from a person, authorised in that behalf by the railway authority, permission for the unit to proceed; (*b*) that permission has been obtained before the unit proceeds; and (*c*) the unit proceeds in accordance with any terms attached to that permission. Provided that sub-paragraphs (*b*) and (*c*) above shall not apply if— (i) on the use by the driver of the telephone placed at or near the crossing he receives an indication for not less than two minutes that the telephone at the other end of the telephone line is being called, but no duly authorised person answers it or he receives no indication at all due to a fault or malfunction of the telephone; and (ii) the driver then drives the unit on to the crossing with the reasonable expectation of crossing it within times specified in a railway notice at that telephone as being times between which trains do not normally travel over that crossing.

12. Permitted variants

(1) Where the circumstances so require, the indications given by the signs shown in the diagrams in Schedule 1 shall or may be varied as hereinafter provided in this paragraph—

(*a*) any indication given by such a sign may be varied in the respect (if any) in which it is shown below the diagram relating to that sign that the indication may be varied;

[Wherever an indication in metric units may be substituted for one in imperial units under this sub-paragraph and the sign in which the substitution is permitted is incorporated as a symbol in another sign, the indication given by the symbol so incorporated may be varied in the same manner as the variation permitted for the sign which it symbolises;]

(*b*) in the signs shown in diagrams 502, 503, 523.1, 524.1, 530, 532.1, 534.1 to 535.1, 556.4, 626.1, 628.1 to 629.2, 712.1, 719.3A and 729.2 the numerals shall be varied to accord with the circumstances except that no fractions of a number shall be used;

(*c*) in the signs shown in diagrams 527, 565.4, 571, 715, 724, 724.2, [728.1, 728.2, 729,] 730 to [733, 742.5, 742.6,] 838.2, 911, 915 and 916, the numerals shall be varied to accord with the circumstances, distances being expressed in miles to the nearest mile except that in the case of any of the signs so shown other than a sign shown in diagram 715, 724.2, 732.2 or 911 the fractions $\frac{3}{4}$, $\frac{1}{2}$ and $\frac{1}{4}$ may be used for distances of less than 3 miles;

(*d*) in the sign shown in diagram 572 the numerals shall be varied to accord with the circumstances, distances being expressed in yards to the nearest 50 yards;

(*e*) in the signs shown in diagrams 534.2, 547.3, 556.4, [557.2, 557.3,] 569.2, 570, 573, [734.8, 735.1,] 746.2 to 753.1, 759, 818.1, 818.2, and 841 to 842.4, the numerals indicating distance shall be varied to accord with the circumstances, distances of less than $\frac{1}{2}$ mile being expressed in yards to the nearest 50 yards, distances of $\frac{1}{2}$ mile or more but less than 3 miles being expressed in miles so long as no fractions other than $\frac{3}{4}$, $\frac{1}{2}$ or $\frac{1}{4}$ are used, and distances of 3 miles or more being expressed in miles to the nearest mile;

(*f*) in the sign shown in any diagram in Schedule 1, any numerals which indicate route numbers shall be so varied as to indicate the route number for the time being appropriate to the route to which the indication refers and when a route number has been superseded by a new route number, any such numerals indicating the old route number may be retained in the said sign so long as those numerals so indicating are cancelled by a red bar to indicate that that route number has been superseded;

(*g*) in the signs shown in diagrams 618, 638 to 641, [646, 656.1,] 660.2, 662, 801.5, 805, 806.1, 806.3, [807 and 812.4] the legend shall be varied, so far as respects any reference to a period of time, time of day or day of the week, and may be supplemented by a reference to days of the month or months of the year, so as to accord with the prohibition or restriction imposed in relation to vehicular traffic;

(*h*) in the signs shown in diagrams 515, 534.2, 553, 556.4, [557.3, 557.4,] 567.1, 567.2, 569, 573, 580, 606 (through either 90° or 180° above horizontal), 639, 640, 640.2A, 644, 703.1, 703.2, 705, 714, 718.1, 718.2, 720, 721.1, 723, 724.1, 727, 727.2, 728.1, [730, 730.1, 732.1, 732.5,] 733.1, 734.2, 734.4, 734.9, [734.10, 735.2,] 741.1, 742.2, [742.4, 742.5,] 754, 755, 756, 757, 810, 842.2, 844, 855, 910.1 and 912, the direction of any arrow or chevron shown therein shall be varied to accord with the circumstances, so however that no chevron shown in diagrams 515 or 569 and no arrow shown in diagram 553, [557.3, 557.4,] 639, 640, 640.2A, 644, 810, 842.2, 855 or 912 shall point otherwise than horizontally either to the left or to the right, and so that from the signs shown in [diagrams 557.4, 639,] [640, 742.5, 757,] and 842.2, the arrows may be omitted;

(*i*) in any of the signs shown in diagrams 637, 641, 651, 662, 758, 805, 818.2, 841 and 842.4, an arrow pointing in the appropriate direction horizontally left or right may be included;

(*j*) in the signs shown in diagrams 713, 714, 724.1, [729.1 to 729.3] and [741 to 742.4] an indication of distance may be expressed to the nearest mile, in the signs shown in diagrams 734.1 to 734.4, 734.6, 736, 736.1, 739 to [739.5] and

756 such an indication as aforesaid may be expressed to the nearest mile for a distance greater than 3 miles, to the nearest $\frac{1}{4}$ mile for a distance less than 3 miles but greater than $\frac{1}{2}$ mile, and to the nearest 50 yards for a distance of 800 yards or less, and in the signs shown in diagrams 724, 728.1, 728.2, 729, 730 to 732.1, 733, [734.8, 742.5, 742.6,] 749, 759, 841, 842.2 and 842.4 the distance may be omitted;

(*k*) in the signs shown in diagrams 713, 724, 728, 728.2, 728.3, 732, 732.4, 733, 734.1, 734.3, 734.5 to [734.8, 735.1,] 736, 736.1, 737.1, [739 to 739.5,] 741, 742.1, [742.3, 742.6,] 749, 751, 753, 753.1, 755.1, 756.1, 759, 841.1, 842.1, 842.3, 903.1 and 904.1 the direction in which they point shall be reversed;

(*l*) in the signs shown in diagrams 703.1 to 705, 708 to 711.1, 712.1, 718, 723 and 728.1, where a junction with a motorway is to be indicated, the appropriate panel or panels shall be blue with a white legend and the route number of the motorway shown in characters of the proportion and form shown in Parts I, II and III of Schedule 7; in the signs shown in diagrams 718 to 723 and 728.1 where a non-primary route joins a primary route the primary route number shall be shown in yellow on a green panel; and without prejudice to the foregoing provisions of this sub-paragraph, whenever a motorway route number is indicated on a sign shown in any of the diagrams 701 to 715, 718 to 724.2 and 728, that number shall be shown in white on a blue panel;

(*m*) in the signs shown in diagrams 701 to 716, 718 to 725, 727 to 733.1, [734.8, 735.1,] 737.1, [739, 739.4,] 737.1, 739, 741 to 744.1, 747 to [761,], 818.1, 818.2, 838.1, 841 to 842.4, 903.1 to 911 and 915 to 916.1 the route numbers, place names, route symbols, junction numbers and distances (other than the mileages in diagrams 702, [702.1, 703.2, 718.2,] 905, 906, 906.2, 908.1 and 908.2) shall, subject to the preceding provisions of this paragraph, be varied, where appropriate and the words 'Other routes' or as the case may be, 'Ring road' may be substituted for the place name, having regard to the place where any such sign is erected;

(*n*) in the signs shown in diagrams [727, 728, 728.1, 728.2 and 729 to 732.1,] there may be substituted for, or added to the place name the words 'Tourist information', 'Toilets', 'Ladies toilet', 'Mens toilet', 'Airport', 'Station', 'Bus Station', 'Coach Station', 'Country park' or 'Public Telephone', or any of the following symbols, that is to say, the aircraft shown in diagram 733, the white on red symbol indicating British Railways and shown in diagram 734.1, the red circle and bar on white indicating London Transport and shown in diagram 734.4, the parking symbol shown in diagram 734.8, the telephone handset shown in diagram 734.6, the disabled person symbol shown in diagram [736.1, the red rose symbol shown in diagram 742.5 or the variant symbol permitted by that sign], the building shown in diagram 747, the building shown in diagram 748, the tent and caravan symbol shown in diagram 750, the youth hostel symbol shown in diagram 752, the picnic site symbol shown in diagram 752.1, the black on white letter 'i' shown in diagram 758, or the white on blue letter 'H' shown in diagram 827;

(*o*) without prejudice to the next following paragraph, the white lorry symbol in diagram 727.2 may be incorporated on a black panel in the signs shown in diagrams 718 to 724.1, 728.1, 728.2 and 729 to 732.1 when those signs are placed on or near a road . . . to indicate that the route with which the symbol is associated on the sign is a route suitable for goods vehicles;

(*p*) the aircraft symbol shown in diagram 733 either with or without the name of an airport may be substituted for, or added to, a place name shown on any of the signs shown in diagrams 701 to 714, 718 to 724.1 and 903.1 to 910.1 to indicate the site of an airport.

(2) Where overall dimensions are shown in Schedule 1 for any such sign as is mentioned in the preceding paragraph and where the legend on that sign may be varied and the sign is varied in accordance with that paragraph, the overall dimensions or the number of lines filled by the legend or both may be varied in so far as is necessary to give effect to that variation.

[(2A) Where the sign shown in diagram 812 in Schedule 1 is varied in accordance with the indication given below that diagram the overall dimensions of the sign may be varied so far as is necessary to give effect to the variation.]

(3) In the sign shown in diagram 536 the number of bells shall be increased or decreased according to the width of the road over which it is placed, and in each of the signs shown in diagrams 534.1 to 535.1 the safe height shown on the sign shall be varied where necessary so that it is between 1 foot 6 inches and 2 feet less than the height of the lowest part of the overhead wire, of which it gives warning, over the highest part of the surface of the carriageway beneath the said wire.

(4) The signs shown in diagrams 732, 733, 734.8, [735.1,] 736 to 731.1, 739, [739.4,] 741 to 742.4, 743.1, 744.1, 805 (except when varied to convey a condition), 814, 820 to 822, 833 to 836 and 916.1, when erected in Wales may show the information contained on the sign in both the English and Welsh languages:

Provided that—

(*a*) except in the case of the signs shown in diagrams 743.1 and 744.1 names indicating the location of a place shall be those in common usage in the English language;

(*b*) all information shown on any such sign as is mentioned in this paragraph shall be shown in both the English and Welsh languages;

(*c*) one language version of each item of information shall be placed immediately above the other language version of that item; and

(*d*) the same size lettering shall be used for each language version of each item of information.

(5) Where a sign shown in diagrams 743.1, 744.1, 805, 814, 820 to 822 and 833 to 836 is varied in accordance with the last preceding paragraph, the overall dimensions as shown in the said diagrams may be varied in so far as is necessary to give effect to that variation.

(6) Where a sign shown in any diagram in Part III of Schedule 1 other than any of the diagrams 742.1 to 759 indicates a road or a route, and that road or route is temporarily closed, there may be affixed to the sign or to that part of the sign where that road or route is indicated, so as to cancel temporarily the indication, a board coloured red and on which are inscribed in white characters the words 'road temporarily closed' or 'route temporarily closed'.

[Regulation 12 is printed as amended by SI 1980 No 1879; SI 1983 No 1088; SI 1986 No 1859.]

13. Dimensions

(1) Where as respects any diagram in Schedule 1 a dimension for the sign shown in the diagram is indicated in one or more sets of brackets against a dimension not indi-

cated in brackets, any dimension indicated in a set of brackets may be treated as an alternative to the dimension not so indicated.

(2) Where a sign shown in any of the diagrams 606 to 614, 616 or 637 to 645 is placed temporarily on a road by a constable or a person acting under the instructions (whether general or specific) of the chief officer of police for the purposes of a temporary statutory provision any dimension specified for the sign in such a diagram may be reduced so long as any dimension shown in the diagram for measurement horizontally is not reduced to less than 200 millimetres.

(3) A sign shown in a diagram in Part III of Schedule 1 other than in diagrams 717, 726, 734.7 and 754 and a sign shown in a diagram in Part V of that Schedule other than in any of the diagrams 901.1, 910, 912 to 915, and 916.1 to 920 shall be of such dimensions having regard to the character of the road and the speed of the vehicular traffic generally using it as are necessary to accommodate any place name, route symbol, route number, arrow, any indication of distance, or any other indication which in accordance with these Regulations may be shown therein and it is appropriate to show for the purpose for which the sign is placed on a road.

[(4) In any diagram in Schedule 1 and, subject to Regulation 20(2), in Schedule 2, any alternative dimension adopted for a sign shall be so selected that that alternative is matched by the selection of the alternative for every other dimension for which an indication is given in the said diagrams and which corresponds in numerical ascending or descending order with that alternative so adopted.]

[Regulation 13 is printed as amended by SI 1982 No 1879.]

14. Proportions and form of letters and numerals

(1) Subject to the provisions of paragraphs (2) to (4) of this Regulation, and without prejudice to Regulation 12(1)(*l*) (variant requirements to signs there specified), all letters incorporated in the signs shown in the diagrams in Schedule 1 other than in diagrams 742.1 to 742.4, 828.1 and 849 to 852 shall have the proportions and form shown in either Part I, Part II, Part V or Part VI of Schedule 7, all numerals incorporated in the signs shown in the diagrams in Schedule 1 shall have the proportions and form shown in Part III or Part VII of Schedule 7 and all other characters incorporated in the signs shown in the diagrams in Schedule 1 shall have the proportions and form shown in Part IV or Part VIII of Schedule 7.

(2) Letters and numerals used for the purposes of indicating a route number on the sign shown in diagram 757 and on any sign shown in a diagram in Part V of Schedule 1 shall have the proportions and form shown in Part IX of Schedule 7.

(3) Any arrow to be used in any of the signs shown in diagrams 703.3, 718.3 or 908.2 when those signs are erected over the carriageway on structures on which there is also mounted equipment for displaying the signs shown in diagram 6021 in Schedule 6 shall have the proportion and form of the arrow shown in the last diagram in Part IV of Schedule 7 and any such arrow to be used in any of the signs first abovementioned when those signs are erected over the carriageway on structures on which no such equipment is also mounted shall have the proportion and form of the arrow shown in the penultimate diagram in the said Part IV.

(4) Subject to and within the limits of any dimension specified as maximum or minimum in diagrams 743.1 and 744.1 any letters, numerals or other characters incorporated in those diagrams may have proportions and form other than the proportions and form shown in any Part of Schedule 7.

15. Illumination of signs by steady lighting

(1) In this Regulation (except in paragraph (6) as respects the sign shown in diagram 828.1) and in Regulations 16 and 17 the references to lighting shall be construed as references to steady lighting.

(2) Subject to the provisions of paragraph (7), this paragraph applies to the signs shown in diagrams 606, 609 to 616, 617 (except when used with the sign shown in diagram 618), 619, 619.1, 621 to 622.2 [622.4 and 625] in constructing the following sub-paragraphs—

(*a*) when the signs shown in diagrams 606 and 612 to 614 are fixed to light signals prescribed by Regulation 31, or by Regulation 31 as varied by Regulation 32, they shall be illuminated by a means of internal lighting at all times except when the light signals to which they are fixed are being maintained or repaired;

(*b*) when the signs shown in diagrams 606, 609 to 611 [616 and 625] are mounted in a bollard fitted with a means of lighting them internally, they shall be illuminated throughout the hours of darkness by that means of internal lighting;

(*c*) without prejudice to the next following sub-paragraph, if a sign specified in sub-paragraph (*a*) above when not so fixed, or a sign specified in sub-paragraph (*b*) above when not so mounted, or any other sign to which this paragraph applies is erected on a road within 50 metres of any lamp lit by electricity which forms part of a system of street-lighting furnished by means of at least three such lamps placed not more than 183 metres apart, that sign shall be illuminated by a means of internal or external lighting either for so long as the said system is illuminated, or throughout the hours of darkness, unless it is erected temporarily for any of the following reasons—

(i) for the purpose of a temporary statutory provision,

(ii) by reason of some emergency, or,

(iii) if that road is a road subject to a speed limit of 30 m.p.h. or under, by reason of the execution of works, or of any obstruction on the road;

(*d*) any sign to which this paragraph applies and is either not so fixed as provided in sub-paragraph (*a*) or is erected in such a manner that it is not illuminated regularly throughout the hours of darkness by a means of internal or external lighting, shall be illuminated by the use of reflecting material in accordance with the provisions of Regulation 18(3) and (4).

(3) Subject to the provisions of paragraph (7), this paragraph applies to any sign shown in diagrams 501, 504.1 to 510, 512, 513, 516, 517, 520 to 524.1, 528 to 532.1, 533, 537, 538, 543, 544 to [544.3], 555, 556, 564, 564.5 to 566, 567.2, 569.2, 569.3, 601.1, 602, 626.1, 628.1 to 632, 642 (if the diameter of that sign is more than 450 millimetres), 649.1, [649.2], 652 to [654.1], 701 to 712.1, 714, 718.2, 718.3, 727.2, 818 to 819.2, 837.1 to 838.2, 858 to 858.2, 901.1 to 911, 915 to 916.1, 918.1 and 919.1 in construing the following sub-paragraphs—

(*a*) without prejudice to the next following sub-paragraph, if a sign to which this paragraph applies is erected on a road within 50 metres of any such lamp as is described in sub-paragraph (*c*) of paragraph (2) that sign shall be illuminated by a means of internal or external lighting as is therein provided unless it is erected temporarily for such a reason as is therein specified;

(*b*) any sign to which this paragraph applies which is erected in such a manner that it is not illuminated regularly throughout the hours of darkness by a means of internal or external lighting, shall be illuminated by the use of reflecting material as provided by paragraph (2)(*d*).

(4) Any sign shown in diagrams 515, 539 to 542.2, 545, 548 to 552, 554, 554.1, 557 to 559, 562, 569, 569.1, 569.4, 574, 577, 578, 580, 633 to 635, 642 (if the diameter of that sign is 450 millimetres or less), 646, 647, 655, 713, 715 to 718.1, 719 to 727, 728 to 737.1, 746.2, 754 to 757, 760, 761, 801, 806 to 806.3, 808.1, 808.3, 811 to [812.2, 812.5 and 812.6], 819.3 to 825, 827, 828.2, 830 to 832.2, 838.3, 838.4, 854 to 856, 861 to 863, 912, 917, 920 and 925 may be illuminated by a means of internal or external lighting, but if not so illuminated throughout the hours of darkness, shall be illuminated by the use of reflecting material in accordance with the provisions of Regulation 18(3) and (4).

(5) The signs shown in diagrams [557.1] 603, 604 and 814, shall be illuminated throughout the hours of darkness by a means of internal or external lighting.

(6) The sign shown in diagram 828.1 shall be illuminated by an intermittent light flashing at a rate of not less than 54 nor more than 90 flashes per minute during such times only as it is necessary that the sign shall be illuminated for the purpose of indicating the information shown in diagram 828.1.

(7) Where a sign to which any of the foregoing paragraphs applies is placed on or near a road for the purpose of conveying a warning or informtion from time to time to vehicular traffic, or in connection with a statutory prohibition, restriction or requirement which relates to such traffic but does not apply at all times, that sign shall be illuminated in accordance with such of the foregoing provisions of this Regulation as apply to it but only during such times as, for the said purpose or in the said connection, it is necessary that the sign shall be visible from a reasonable distance to drivers of approaching motor vehicles, any other provision of this Regulation to the contrary notwithstanding.

(8) Subject to the foregoing paragraphs of this Regulation and to Regulation 19, any sign shown in a diagram in Schedule 1 may be illuminated by a means of internal or external lighting and where, subject as aforesaid, the means of lighting any such sign is external, then that means of lighting shall be either fitted to the sign or to the structure on which it is mounted or otherwise specially provided.

[Regulation 15 is printed as amended by SI 1982 No 1879, SI 1983 No 1088, and SI 1984 No 966.]

16. Where a sign shown in a diagram in Schedule 1 (not being a sign consisting of a plate) is illuminated by a means of lighting in accordance with the provisions of Regulation 15 and a plate shown in a diagram in that Schedule is used in conjunction with that sign, the said plate shall, unless the means of lighting provided for the illumination of the sign adequately illuminates the plate, be illuminated, during such times as the sign is illuminated, by a means of lighting and that means of lighting shall accord with that one of the methods of lighting, namely, internal or external adopted for the illumination of the sign.

17. Illumination of signs shown is diagrams 560 and 561 by reflectors, etc *[Omitted.]*

18. Illumination of signs by reflecting material

(1) Nothing in this Regulation shall apply to the signs shown in diagrams 536, 560, 561 and 828.1.

(2) Subject to the provisions of Regulation 15 and paragraph (1) above any sign

shown in a diagram in Schedule 1 shall be illuminated by the use of reflecting material in accordance with the following provisions of this Regulation.

(3) Subject to paragraph (4) where reflecting material is used on any sign shown in a diagram in Schedule 1 it shall be of the same colour as that of, and extend throughout, that part of the sign to which it is applied:

Provided that no reflecting material shall be applied to—

(*a*) any part of a sign coloured black, or

(*b*) any part of the sign shown in diagram 605.1 which is coloured fluorescent yellow unless the reflecting material is applied to that part in horizontal strips each such strip being 3 millimetres wide, spaced at intervals of 6 millimetres from each other, the centre of the sign being located at a point in one such interval equidistant from the strips so spaced.

In this paragraph the word 'part', in relation to a sign, means any part of the surface of that sign uniformly coloured and bounded by parts of a different colour.

(4) (*a*) Where in accordance with the last paragraph, different colours of reflecting material are used next to one another on the same sign being a traffic sign to which this paragraph applies in accordance with the next following subparagraph, a gap of not more than 20 millimetres in width may be left between the different colours of reflecting material.

(*b*) This paragraph applies only to traffic signs which being circular in shape have a diameter of at least 1.2 metres, being triangular in shape have a height of at least 1.2 metres along the perpendicular from apex to base, or being rectangular in shape have a side which is at least 1.2 metres in length.

19. *[Omitted.]*

Section IV

Traffic Signs shown in Schedule 2

20. Road markings

(1) Subject to the provisions of these Regulations, a traffic sign consisting of a line or mark on a road (in these Regulations referred to as a 'road marking') for conveying to traffic on roads a warning, a requirement or information of the description specified under a diagram (other than diagrams 1003 and 1013.1) in Schedule 2 shall be of the size and type shown in the diagram relating to that warning, requirement or information.

(2) In any diagram in Schedule 2, the dimensions indicated in brackets against dimensions not so indicated may be treated as an alternative to the last mentioned dimensions.

(3) Where the circumstances so require, the indication given by any of the signs shown in the diagrams in Schedule 2 shall or may be varied as hereinafter provided in this paragraph:—

(*a*) any indication given by such a sign may be varied in the respect (if any) in which it is shown below the diagram relating to that sign that the indication may be varied;

(*b*) in the sign shown in diagram 1035 route numbers place names and the direction in which any arrow-head points shall be varied and interchangeable to accord with the circumstances but the words 'turn left', 'ahead' or 'turn right' shall not appear as a part of the said sign.

21. Particular road markings

A road marking for conveying to vehicular traffic the requirement specified in paragraph (2) of the next succeeding Regulation shall be of the size and type shown in diagram 1003.

22.—(1) For the purposes of this Regulation—

'minor road' means a road at a road junction on which road there are placed the transverse lines shown in diagram 1003;

'major road' means the road at a road junction into which road there emerges vehicular traffic from a minor road.

(2) Except as provided by the next following paragraph, the requirement conveyed by the said transverse lines, whether or not they are used in conjunction with the sign shown in diagram 602, shall be that no vehicle shall proceed past such one of those lines as is nearest to the major road into that road in such a manner or at such a time as is likely to cause danger to the driver of any other vehicle on the major road or as to necessitate the driver of any such other vehicle to change its speed or course in order to avoid an accident with the first-mentioned vehicle.

(3) Whenever the said transverse lines are used in conjunction with the sign shown in diagram 602 and that sign is at the same time used in combination with the sign shown in diagram 602.1 at a level crossing where a road is crossed by a railway then the said requirement shall be that no vehicle shall proceed past such one of those lines as is nearest to the said level crossing in such a manner or at such a time as is likely to cause the driver of any railway vehicle to change its speed to avoid collision with the vehicle first above-mentioned in this paragraph.

23.—(1) A road marking for conveying the requirements specified in the next succeeding paragraph and the warning specified in paragraph (5) shall be of the size and type shown in diagram 1013.1.

(2) The requirements conveyed by the road marking mentioned in the last preceding paragraph shall be that—

(*a*) subject to the provisions of paragraph (3), no vehicle shall stop on any length of road along which the marking has been placed at any point between the two ends of the marking; and

(*b*) subject to the provisions of paragraph (4), every vehicle proceeding on any length of road along which the marking has been so placed that, as viewed in the direction of travel of the vehicle, the continuous line is on the left of a dotted line or of another continuous line, shall be so driven as to keep the first-mentioned continuous line on the right hand or off side of the vehicle.

(3) Nothing in sub-paragraph (*a*) of the last preceding paragraph shall apply—

(*a*) so as to prevent a vehicle stopping on any length of road so long as may be necessary—

(i) to enable a person to board or alight from the vehicle,

(ii) to enable goods to be loaded on to or to be unloaded from the vehicle; or

(iii) to enable the vehicle, if it cannot be used for such purpose without stopping on that length of road, to be used in connection with any building operation or demolition, the removal of any obstruction to traffic, the maintenance, improvement or reconstruction of that length of road, or the laying, erection, alteration or repair in or near to that length of road of any sewer or of any main, pipe or apparatus for the supply of gas, water or electricity, or of any telegraphic line as defined in the Telegraph Act 1978,

so, however, that no vehicle shall be enabled by virtue of this sub-paragraph to stop for any of the purposes at (i), (ii) or (iii) above on a part of that length of road, not being a lay-by or a road verge, if it is reasonably practicable to stop the vehicle for that purpose on a part of that length of road, being a lay-by or a road verge;

(*b*) to a vehicle used for fire brigade, ambulance or police purposes;

(*c*) to a pedal bicycle not having a sidecar attached thereto, whether additional means of propulsion by mechanical power are attached to the bicycle or not;

(*d*) to a vehicle stopping in any case where the person in control of the vehicle is required by law to stop, or is obliged to do so in order to avoid an accident, or is prevented from proceeding by circumstances outside his control; or

(*e*) to anything done with the permission of a police constable in uniform or in accordance with the direction of a traffic warden.

(4) Nothing in sub-paragraph (*b*) of paragraph (2) shall apply so as to prevent a vehicle crossing or straddling the continuous line first mentioned in that sub-paragraph for the purpose of obtaining access to any other road joining the length of road along which the line is placed or to land or premises situated on or adjacent to the said length of road or if it is necessary to do so—

(*a*) in order to pass a stationary vehicle, or owing to circumstances outside the control of the driver or in order to avoid an accident, or

(*b*) for the purposes of complying with any direction of a police constable in uniform or a traffic warden.

(5) The warning conveyed by the road marking mentioned in paragraph (1) shall be that no vehicle while travelling next to a dotted line placed on the left, as viewed in the direction of travel of the vehicle, of a continuous line should cross or straddle the first mentioned line unless it is seen by the driver of the vehicle to be safe to do so.

[The Telegraph Act 1878, s 2, defined 'telegraphic line' as 'telegraphs, posts, and any work (within the meaning of the Telegraph Act 1863) and also any cables, apparatus, pneumatic or other tube, pipe, or thing whatsoever used for the purpose of transmitting telegraphic messages or maintaining telegraphic communication, and includes any portion of a telegraphic line as defined by this Act', In the definition of 'telegraphic line' the words from 'and also' to 'communication' were repealed by the British Telecommunications Act 1981, s 89(1), and Sched 6, Part I. The Telegraph Act 1863, s 3, defined 'telegraph' as 'a wire or wires used for the purpose of telegraphic communication, with any casing, coating, tube, or pipe inclosing the same, and any apparatus connected therewith for the purpose of telegraphic communication'; 'post' as 'a post, pole, standard, stay, strut, or other above-ground contrivance for carrying, suspending, or supporting a telegraph'; and 'work' as including telegraphs and posts. The Telegraph Act 1878 and s 3 of the Telegraph Act 1863 were repealed by the Telecommunications Act 1984, s 109(6) and Sched 7.]

24. Colour of road markings

(1) Except as otherwise provided by this Regulation, the road markings shown in the diagrams in Schedule 2 shall be white.

(2) Road markings shown in diagrams 1016.1 to 1021, 1027.1 and 1043 to 1045 shall be yellow.

(3) In the road markings shown in the diagrams 1025.1 and 1025.3 the line shown therein as coloured yellow and having a width of 200 or 300 millimetres shall be yellow.

(4) The road markings shown in diagrams 1025 and 1025.2 and when displaying the word 'Taxis' in diagram 1028.1 shall be yellow in the following but in no other circumstances, that is to say, where those markings are placed in a part of the carriageway which is subject to restrictions on waiting or on waiting, loading and unloading for at least 8 hours during the period from 7 a.m. to 7 p.m. on at least 4 days, none of them being a Sunday, in any week by all vehicles, other than stage and express carriages in the case of the markings shown in diagrams 1025 or 1025.2 and other than hackney carriages in the case of the marking shown in diagram 1028.1.

(5) Road markings shown in diagram 1055 consisting of marks arranged in transverse lines may be either white or silver or light grey in colour.

(6) In this Regulation, 'hackney carriage' has the same meaning as in the Vehicles (Excise) Act 1971.

[The term 'hackney carriage' is defined in s 38(1) of the Vehicles (Excise) Act 1971 (qv).]

25. Use on road markings of reflecting material and studs with reflectors

(1) (*a*) The road markings shown in diagrams 1011 to 1014 shall be illuminated with reflecting material; and

(*b*) studs incorporating reflectors and spaced so as to form a single line of studs at intervals of not less than 3·6 nor more than 4·4 metres apart shall be fitted between the two lines constituting the marking shown in diagram 1013.1 unless that marking—

(i) is placed on any automatic railway level crossing, or

(ii) is placed on a length of the road falling within a distance of 90 metres measured from the transverse stop line provided in association with any such crossing and in conformity with diagram 1001, or

(iii) is so placed that the continuous lines shown in diagram 1013.1 are more than 175 millimetres apart and are separated by an area of cross-hatching so shown.

(*c*) Where the marking shown in diagram 1013.1 is placed as described in any of the cases in sub-paragraph (*b*)(i) to (iii) above, then such studs as aforesaid and so spaced as aforesaid shall be fitted either within the width of each of the said two lines or between them.

In this paragraph the expression 'automatic railway level crossing' means an automatic half-barrier level crossing, and an automatic open crossing (R) as both those crossings are defined for the purposes of Regulation 11(2) and includes a level crossing which is the same as an automatic open crossing (R) except that the operation of the light signals is monitored at or near the crossing by the driver of the train instead of remotely from the crossing.

(2) Subject to the foregoing provisions of this Regulation, any road marking may be illuminated with reflecting material and studs incorporating reflectors may be fitted to the markings shown in diagrams 1003.4 to 1012.1, 1025.2, 1025.3 and 1040 to 1042 in such a manner that any such stud shall not be fitted to any mark coloured white and forming part of any of the markings so shown as aforesaid but shall be applied to the surface of the carriageway in the gap between any two such marks:

Provided that in the case of the markings shown in diagram 1011 or 1012.1, the said studs shall, if fitted, be applied to the surface of the carriageway at the side of and adjacent to the line shown in the diagram.

[(2A) The road markings shown in diagram 1060 including the permitted variants shall be illuminated with reflecting material.]

(3) Reflectors incorporated in studs shall be white except that in the case of reflectors fitted to the markings shown in diagrams 1009 to 1012.1, 1025.2, 1025.3, 1041 and 1042 they may be—

(*a*) red where the near side edge of a carriageway is indicated to drivers of approaching motor vehicles, or when fitted to the markings shown in diagrams 1041 and 1042 to indicate the offside edge of a carriageway.

(*b*) amber to indicate the offside edge of a carriageway which is contiguous to a central reservation or which carries traffic in one direction only, and

(*c*) green when fitted to the markings shown in diagrams 1009, 1010, 1025.2 and 1025.3 where the edge of any part of the carriageway available for through traffic at a road junction, a lay-by or a parking place is so indicated as aforesaid.

In this Regulation 'central reservation' means any provision made in a road (not being the provision of a street refuge) for dividing the road for the safety or guidance of vehicular traffic.

[Regulation 25 is printed as amended by SI 1983 No 1088.]

26. Height of road markings and size of studs *[Omitted.]*

27. Certain temporary signs

(1) Notwithstanding the provisions of Regulation 9 and subject to the succeeding paragraphs of this Regulation, signs placed temporarily on or near a road—

(*a*) for conveying to traffic—

(i) information as respects deviations of, or alternative traffic routes,

(ii) information as respects the route which may conveniently be followed on the occasion of a sports meeting, exhibition or other public gathering, in each case attracting a considerable volume of traffic,

(iii) information as to the date from which works are to be executed on or near a road, or

[(iv) information or warnings as to the avoidance of any temporary hazards occasioned by works being executed on or near a road, by adverse weather conditions or other natural causes, by the failure of street lighting or by malfunction of or damage to any apparatus, equipment, or facility used in connection with the road or any thing situated on near or under it or by damage to the road itself.]

(*b*) for conveying to vehicular traffic any prohibition, restriction or requirement of a description required for the purposes of a temporary statutory provision; or

(*c*) pending the erection of any permanent sign prescribed by these Regulations, for conveying to traffic the indication which such a permanent sign indicates,

may be of such size, colour and type as is specified in the following provisions of this Regulation.

(2) Every such sign placed as aforesaid (hereinafter referred to as a 'temporary sign') shall be of a shape which—

(*a*) is rectangular;

(*b*) is rectangular, but with the corners rounded; or

(*c*) is rectangular, but with one end pointed.

(3) Every temporary sign shall be of such size as is necessary to accommodate the wording, numerals, arrows or chevrons and any symbol taken from any diagram shown in Schedule 1 appropriate to the purpose for which the sign is placed as aforesaid and to accommodate any arms, badge, device, words or letters incorporated in the sign in accordance with the provisions of paragraph (6).

(4) Every letter and numeral incorporated in a temporary sign other than any letter incorporated in the sign in accordance with the provisions of paragraph (6) shall be not less than 40 nor more than 250 millimetres in height, and every arrow so incorporated shall be not less than 250 nor more than 500 millimetres in length except that where an arrow is incorporated in the index part of a sign with a pointed end such arrow shall be not less than 100 nor more than 200 millimetres in length.

(5) Every letter, numeral, arrow, chevron or symbol incorporated in a temporary sign shall be—

(*a*) black on a background of white, or yellow; or

(*b*) white on a blue background[; or]

[(*c*) if the sign conveys information or warnings as to the avoidance of any temporary hazards such as are mentioned in paragraph (1)(*a*)(iv) above, white on a red background.]

(6) There may be incorporated in, or attached to, a temporary sign the arms, badge or other device of a highway authority, police authority or an organisation representative of road users, or words or letters indicating the highway authority, or that the sign is a police sign.

(7) No sign shall by virtue of this Regulation convey to traffic any information, warning, requirement, restriction or prohibition of a description which can be so conveyed either by a sign shown in a diagram in Part I, Part II, or Part IV of Schedule 1 or by a sign so shown used in combination with or in conjunction with another sign shown in such a diagram.

[Regulation 27 is printed as amended by SI 1982 No 1879.]

28. Flashing beacons and flags *[Omitted.]*

29. Cones and cylinders *[Omitted.]*

30. Refuge indicator lamps *[Omitted.]*

31.—(1) Light signals may be used for the control of vehicular traffic and shall be of the size, colour and type prescribed by paragraph (2), by paragraph (3) or by paragraph 2(4).

(2) The size, colour and type of light signals prescribed by this paragraph shall be as follows:—

(*a*) three lights shall be used, one red, one amber and one green;

(*b*) the lamps showing the coloured lights aforesaid shall be arranged vertically, the lamp showing a red light being the uppermost and that showing a green light the lowermost;

(*c*) each lamp shall be separately illuminated and the effective diameter of the lens thereof shall be not less than 195 nor more than 220 millimetres unless the lens is a lens of the kind shown in diagram 3001 when instead the said diameter may be not less than 290 nor more than 310 millimetres;

(*d*) the height of the centre of the amber lens from the surface of the carriageway in the immediate vicinity shall be in the case of signals placed at the side of the carriageway or on a street refuge not less than 2·4 nor more than 4 metres and in the case of signals placed elsewhere and over the carriageway not less than 6·1 nor more than 9 metres;

(*e*) the centres of adjacent lenses shall be not less than 305 nor more than 360 millimetres apart;

(*f*) no lettering shall be used upon the lenses or in connection with a light signal;

(*g*) the sequence of the lights shown for the purpose of controlling vehicular traffic shall be as follows:—

(i) red,
(ii) amber and red together,
(iii) green,
(iv) amber.

(3) The size, colour and type of light signals prescribed by this paragraph shall be as follows:—

(*a*) Four lamps each showing an intermittent red light shall be used.

(*b*) The lamps shall be so fitted as to enclose a rectangular area bounded by the one pair of sides extending horizontally and terminating as to each side in the centres of each pair of lenses (in these Regulations called 'the horizontal pairs') and by the other pair of sides extending vertically in relation to the ground and terminating as to each side in the centres of each pair of lenses (in these Regulations called 'the vertical pairs').

(*c*) When the four lamps are erected beside the carriageway, the distance between the centres of the lenses for each of the horizontal pairs shall be not less than 945 nor more than 955 millimetres and for each of the vertical pairs shall be not less than 695 nor more than 705 millimetres in accordance with the arrangement shown in diagram 6032.

(*d*) When the four lamps are erected over the carriageway, the distance between the said centres for each of the horizontal pairs shall be not less than 1395 nor more than 1405 millimetres and for each of the vertical pairs not less than 545 nor more than 555 millimetres in accordance with the arrangement shown in diagram 6031.

(*e*) Subject to the provisions of the next following sub-paragraph, each lamp shall be separately illuminated and the effective diameter of the lens thereof shall be not less than 120 nor more than 130 millimetres.

(*f*) When the signal is operated, each lamp shall show its intermittent red light at a rate of flashing of not less than 60 nor more than 90 flashes per minute, and in such a manner that the lights of one of the vertical pairs are always shown when the lights of the other vertical pair are not shown.

(*g*) The height of the centres of the lenses comprising the lower of the horizontal pairs from the surface of the carriageway in the immediate vicinity shall be in the case of signals placed at the side of the carriageway not less than 1·8 nor more than 3·2 metres and in the case of signals placed over the carriageway not less than 5·8 nor more than 6·8 metres.

(*h*) No lettering of any kind shall be used upon any of the lenses.

(4) The size, colour and type of light signals prescribed by this paragraph shall be as follows:—

(*a*) two lamps each showing an intermittent red light and one lamp showing a steady amber light shall be used;

(*b*) the lamps showing an intermittent red light shall be arranged horizontally so that there is a distance of not less than 585 nor more than 665 millimetres between the centres of the lenses of the lamps;

(*c*) the lamp showing the amber light shall be placed below the red lenses in such a position that a vertical line passing through the centre of the lamp is horizontally equidistant from the vertical lines passing through the centre of each red lens and that the vertical distance between a horizontal line passing through the centres of the red lenses is not less than 235 nor more than 345 millimetres;

(*d*) each lamp shall be separately illuminated and the effective diameter of the lens thereof shall be not less than 195 nor more than 220 millimetres;

(*e*) when the lamps showing an intermittent red light are operated, each such lamp shall show a red light at a rate of flashing of not less than 60 nor more than 90 flashes per minute, and in such a manner that the light of one lamp is always shown at a time when the light of the other lamp is not shown;

(*f*) the height of the centre of the amber lens from the surface of the carriageway in the immediate vicinity shall be in the case of signals placed at the side of the carriageway or on a street refuge not less than 2·4 nor more than 4 metres and in the case of signals placed elsewhere and over the carriageway not less than 6·1 nor more than 9 metres;

(*g*) the lenses shall be provided with a rectangular backing board having an overall width of not less than 1·3 metres and extending not less than 300 millimetres above the centre of each of the red lenses and not less than 300 millimetres below the centre of the amber lens, which board shall be coloured black, save for a white border having a width of not less than 80 nor more than 100 millimetres on the side from which the lamps show;

(*h*) the sequence of the signal lights under this paragraph shown for the purpose of controlling vehicular traffic shall be amber followed by red;

(*i*) no lettering of any kind shall appear on any of the lenses.

(5) Light signals prescribed by paragraph (4) may be surmounted by a cross of the size, colour and type shown in diagrams 542 and 542.1.

32.—(1) Subject to the next following paragraph, a lens or lenses of the size and colour shown in diagram 3001 in Schedule 3, which, when illuminated, shows a green arrow—

(*a*) may be substituted for the lens showing the green light in the light signals referred to in Regulation 31(2) in any of the methods shown in diagrams 3003, 3005, 3006 and 3011 in the said Schedule;

(*b*) may be affixed to the light signals referred to in Regulation 31(2) or to those signals as altered in accordance with the preceding sub-paragraph in any of the methods shown in diagram 3002 and diagrams 3004 to 3011 in the said Schedule.

In this paragraph, the substitution authorised in sub-paragraph (*a*) thereof in the method shown in the said diagram 3011 shall be treated as having been effected by means of the upper arrow shown in that diagram, the lower arrow shown therein being treated as affixed in accordance with sub-paragraph (*b*) thereof.

(2) When a lens is, or lenses are, so affixed as provided in paragraph (1)(*b*) and any one lens so affixed is of the larger of the two sizes specified in diagram 3001 in the said Schedule, the distance between the centre of that lens and the centre of any other lens affixed next in position immediately above, below or to the side of that first mentioned lens shall be not less than 415 nor more than 440 millimetres.

(3) The direction in which the arrow shown in diagram 3003 in the said Schedule points may be varied so as to be—

(*a*) a direction which lies straight upright, or

(*b*) a direction which lies at any angle between 90 degrees either to the left or to the right of the said upright direction.

(4) The direction in which any arrow shown in any of the diagrams 3002, 3004 to 3006, 3009 and 3010 in the said Schedule points may be varied so as to be—

(*a*) a direction which lies straight upright, or

(*b*) a direction which lies between the direction shown in the diagram showing that arrow and the said upright direction.

(5) The direction in which the upper arrow shown in diagram 3007 of the said Schedule points may be varied so as to be a direction which lies at any angle from the upright position shown to an angle of 45 degrees to the left and the direction in which the upper arrow shown in diagram 3008 in that Schedule points may be so varied as aforesaid to an angle of 45 degrees to the right.

(6) The direction in which the lower arrow shown in each of the said diagrams 3007 and 3008 points may be varied so as to be a direction which lies at any angle from the position shown in each such diagram respectively to an angle of 45 degrees towards the upright position as shown for the upper arrow in each such diagram.

(7) When both arrows shown in diagram 3011 of the said Schedule are illuminated and extinguished simultaneously the direction in which the upper arrow shown in that diagram points may be varied so as to be a direction which lies at any angle from the position so shown for that arrow to an angle of 45 degrees to the right passing through an arc of 135 degrees and the direction in which the lower arrow so shown points may be varied so as to be a direction which lies at any angle from the position so shown for that arrow to an angle of 45 degrees towards the upright position or alternatively so as to be a direction lying at any angle from a position in which that arrow faces in the opposite direction from that so shown to an angle 45 degrees towards the upright position.

(8) When both arrows shown in the said diagram 3011 are illuminated and extinguished independently of each other, the direction of each such arrow may be varied so as to be a direction which lies at any angle between 90 degrees either to the left or to the right of the upright position.

33. Portable light signals for control of vehicular traffic

(1) Portable light signals may be used for the control of vehicular traffic in the circumstances specified at (*a*) to (*c*) of this paragraph—

[(*a*) on a length of road having no junction along its length with any other road carrying vehicular traffic to or from it and where the width of the carriageway of that length of road is temporarily restricted so that it will carry only one line of traffic,] (*b*) at a level crossing where a road is crossed by a railway when work in relation to that crossing is being carried out, or

(*c*) during the progress of temporary schemes of traffic control, if the signals are being operated and maintained by, and under the regular supervision of, the police or have been erected at a site approved in writing by the highway authority.

[(2) Such light signals shall comply with—

(*a*) the provisions of Regulation 31(2)(*a*), (*b*), (*c*), (*f*) and (*g*), or if appropriate, those provisions as varied by Regulation 32(1), and

(*b*) the provisions of Regulation 31(2)(*e*), or if appropriate, those provisions as varied by Regulation 32(2) as if for '305' there appeared '270'.]

[Regulation 33 is printed as amended by SI 1982 No 1879.]

34. Significance of light signals

(1) The significance of the light signals prescribed by Regulation 31(2) or by Regulation 33 shall be as follows:—

(*a*) except as provided in the next following sub-paragraph, the red signal shall convey the prohibition that vehicular traffic shall not proceed beyond the stop line on the carriageway provided in conjunction with the signals or, if that line is not for the time being visible or there is no stop line, beyond the post or other structure on or in which the primary signals are mounted;

(*b*) on an occasion when a vehicle is being used for fire brigade, ambulance or police purposes and the observance of the prohibition conveyed by the red signal as provided by the last preceding sub-paragraph would be likely to hinder the use of that vehicle for the purpose for which it is being used on that occasion, then the said sub-paragraph shall not apply to that vehicle; but instead the prohibition conveyed to that vehicle by the red signal shall be that that vehicle shall not proceed beyond the stop line, or as the case may be as provided by the said sub-paragraph, beyond the said post or other structure in such a manner or at such a time—

(i) as is likely to cause danger to the driver of any other vehicle proceeding on or from another road or on or from another part of the same road in accordance with the indications of the light signals operating there in association with the said red signal or as to necessitate the driver of any other such vehicle to change its speed or course in order to avoid an accident, or

(ii) in the case of any traffic which is not vehicular, as is likely to cause danger to that traffic proceeding on or from another road or on or from another part of the same road;

(*c*) the amber-with-red signal shall be taken to denote an impending change in the indication given by the signals from red to green but shall not alter the prohibition conveyed by the red signal;

(*d*) the green signal shall indicate that vehicular traffic may pass the signals and proceed straight on or to the left or to the right;

(*e*) the amber signal shall, when shown alone, convey the prohibition that vehicular traffic shall not proceed beyond the stop line or, if that line is not for the time being visible or there is no stop line, beyond the said post or other structure, except in the case of any vehicle which when the signal first appears is so close to the said line, post or structure that it cannot safely be stopped before passing the line, post or structure.

(2) The significance of the light signals prescribed by Regulation 31(2) as varied in accordance with the provisions of Regulation 32, shall be as follows:—

(*a*) subject as provided in sub-paragraph (*d*) of this paragraph, the red signal shall convey the prohibition that vehicular traffic shall not proceed beyond the stop line on the carriageway provided in conjunction with the signals or if the stop line is not for the time being visible or there is no stop line, beyond the post or other structure on or in which the primary signals are mounted, except that when a vehicle is being used on such an occasion as is specified in paragraph (1)(*b*), the foregoing prohibition prescribed by this sub-paragraph shall not then apply to that vehicle but instead the prohibition conveyed to it on that occasion by the red signal shall be the same as that provided by paragraph (1)(*b*) in relation to the vehicle mentioned in that paragraph;

(*b*) subject as provided in sub-paragraph (*d*) of this paragraph, the amber-with-red signal shall denote an impending change in the indication given by the signals from red to green (where a green signal is provided) or from red to a green arrow or arrows but shall not alter the prohibition conveyed by the red signal;

(*c*) the green signal (where a green signal is provided) shall indicate that vehicular traffic may pass the signals and proceed straight on or to the left or to the right;

(*d*) any green arrow during such time as it is illuminated shall indicate that vehicular traffic may pass the signals and proceed in the direction indicated by the arrow notwithstanding any other indication given by the signals;

(*e*) the amber signal shall, when shown alone, convey the prohibition that vehicular traffic shall not proceed beyond the stop line, or if the stop line is not for the time being visible or there is no stop line, beyond the said post or other structure, except in the case of any vehicle which when the signal first appears is so close to the said line, post or structure that it cannot safely be stopped before passing the line, post or structure.

(3) Vehicular traffic passing any light signals in accordance with the foregoing provisions of this Regulation shall proceed with due regard to the safety of other users of the road and subject to the direction of any police constable in uniform or other duly authorised person who may be engaged in the regulation of traffic.

(4) The significance of the light signals prescribed in Regulation 31(3) shall be that the intermittent red lights when displayed at the side of the carriageway convey the prohibition that vehicular traffic shall not proceed beyond those lights and when displayed over the carriageway so as to operate in relation to vehicular traffic proceeding in the traffic lane (as defined by Regulation 36(1)) situated immediately beneath them, the said lights convey the prohibition that such vehicular traffic as aforesaid shall not proceed beyond those lights:

Provided that this paragraph shall not apply to a vehicle when it is being used on such an occasion as is specified in Regulation 34(1)(*b*); and for that vehicle when it is being so used, the intermittent red lights whether so displayed at the side of or over the carriageway shall have no significance.

(5) The significance of the light signals prescribed by Regulation 31(4) shall be as follows:—

(*a*) the amber signal shall convey the prohibition that vehicular traffic shall not proceed beyond the stop line of the carriageway provided in conjunction with the signal or, if that line is not for the time being visible or there is no stop line beyond the post or other structure on or in which the primary signals are mounted, except in the case of any vehicle which when the signal first appears is so close to the said post or structure, that it cannot safely be stopped before passing the post or structure; and

(*b*) the intermittent red signals shall convey the prohibition that vehicular traffic shall not proceed beyond the stop line on the carriageway provided in conjunction with the signals or, if that line is not for the time being visible or there is no stop line, beyond the said post or structure.

(6) In this Regulation,

(*a*) the expression 'Stop line' means the road marking shown in diagram 1001 placed on the carriageway in conjunction with light signals being either primary signals alone, or secondary signals alone or both primary and secondary signals;

(*b*) any reference to light signals, to the signals or to a signal of a particular colour, is, where secondary signals have been erected as well as primary signals, a reference to the light signals, signals or particular signal displayed by both the primary signals and the secondary signals or by either the primary signals operating without the secondary signals, or by the secondary signals operating without the primary signals;

(*c*) the expression 'primary signals' means light signals erected on or near the carriageway of a road and sited in the vicinity of either one end or both ends of the stop line or, if there is no stop line, sited at either or both edges of the carriageway or part of that carriageway which is in use by the traffic approaching and controlled by the signals; and

(*d*) the expression 'secondary signals' means light signals erected on or near the carriageway facing approaching traffic in the same direction as the primary signals but sited beyond those signals as viewed from the direction of travel of such traffic.

35. Light signals for pedestrians *[Omitted.]*

36. Light signals for lane control of vehicular traffic

(1) In this Regulation the expression 'traffic lane' means, in relation to a road, a part of the carriageway having as a boundary which separates it from another such part, a road marking of the type shown either in diagram 1004, 1005, 1007 or 1013.1.

(2) Light signals placed above the carriageway and facing the direction of the oncoming vehicular traffic may be used for the control of that traffic proceeding along the traffic lane over and in relation to which those signals have been so placed and, subject to the provisions of this Regulation, shall be of the size, colour and type shown in diagrams [5001 to 5004].

(3) The height of the centre of each such signal from the surface of the carriageway in the immediate vicinity shall be not less than 5.5 metres or more than 9 metres.

(4) The said signals shall be so designed that—

(*a*) the red cross shown in diagrams 5003 and 5004 (hereinafter referred to as 'the red cross') can be internally illuminated in such a manner as to show a steady red light,

(*b*) the white arrow shown in diagrams 5001 and 5002 (hereinafter referred to as 'the white downward arrow') can be internally illuminated by a steady white light, and

(*c*) whenever the red cross is illuminated above a traffic lane, the white downward arrow above that traffic lane is not also then illuminated and whenever the white downward arrow is illuminated above that same lane, the red cross is not also then illuminated.

(5) The significance of the light signals prescribed by this Regulation shall be—

(*a*) the red cross conveys to vehicular traffic proceeding in the traffic lane above and in relation to which it is displayed the prohibition that such traffic shall not proceed beneath or beyond the red cross in the said traffic lane in the direction opposite to that in which the red cross faces until that prohibition is cancelled by a display over that traffic lane of the white downward arrow or by the display over that traffic lane or beside the carriageway of the traffic sign shown in diagram 6001 or of a traffic sign bearing the legend 'End of lane control'; and

(*b*) the white downward arrow conveys to such traffic proceeding in the traffic lane above and in relation to which it is displayed the information that that traffic may proceed or continue so to do in the said lane beneath or beyond the said arrow and in the direction opposite to that in which that arrow faces.

[Regulation 36 is printed as amended by SI 1982 No 1879.]

37. School crossing patrol signs and warning lights *[Omitted.]*

38, 39. Light signals for motorways *[Omitted.]*

40. Road danger lamps *[Omitted.]*

PART II

General Directions

* * *

5. Without prejudice to [section 77 of the Road Traffic Regulation Act 1984]—

(1) whenever a sign shown in diagram 734.7 or in any of the diagrams 837.1 to 838.2 is to be placed for the first time at any given site on or near a primary route, that sign shall not be so placed unless the site shall have first been approved in writing by or on behalf of the Secretary of State; and

(2) whenever the sign shown in diagram 601.1 is to be placed for the first time at any given site on or near any road whatsoever, that sign shall not be so placed unless the site shall have first been so approved as aforesaid, except that if the said site shall already have been duly so approved for placing the sign shown in diagram 601 in Schedule 1 to the Regulations of 1964, its replacement by the sign shown in diagram 601.1 shall be treated as a placing otherwise than for the first time for the purposes of this sub-paragraph.

[Direction 5 is printed as amended by the Road Traffic Regulation Act 1984, s 144(1), and Sched 10, para 2.]

* * *

10. The traffic signs shown in the diagrams whose numbers appear in column 1 of the table set out in this paragraph shall not be used on a road unless so used in conjunction with the road markings shown in the diagrams whose numbers appear in column 2 of that table opposite to the number in column 1 to which they relate:

Provided that the provisions of this paragraph requiring the use of the signs shown in diagrams 601.1, 602, 611.1 and 650 in conjunction with a road marking shall not apply during the execution of works on a road in the vicinity of the place where any of those signs is erected, if those works necessitate the temporary removal of that marking, and shall not apply if any of those signs is erected only temporarily in connection with the execution of works on a road.

TABLE

Column 1 Sign diagram number	*Column 2* Road marking diagram number
601.1	both 1002.1 and 1022
602	both 1003 and 1023
611.1	[if used in conjunction with diagram 602, 1003.4; in any other case both 1003.3 and 1003.4]
650	either 1025.1 or 1025.3
653	both 1048 and 1049
654	both 1048 and 1049
[625.3	1057]
[654.1	both 1049 varied to a width of 150 millimetres, and 1057

Any reference in this paragraph and in the next following paragraph to a traffic sign shown in diagram 601.1 and to the number of that diagram in the said table shall be treated as a reference until the [31st December 1982] inclusive of that date to any sign which can be treated as if prescribed by the Regulations until that date if it is a sign of the type shown in the diagram numbered 601 in Schedule 1 to the Traffic Signs Regulations 1964.

References in this paragraph to the road marking shown in diagram number 1002.1 specified in column 2 of the table above include, until the 31st December 1983 inclusive of that date, references to any road marking which can be treated until that date as if prescribed by the Regulations if it is a sign of the type shown in diagram 1002 in Schedule 2 to the Regulations of 1975.

[Direction 10 is printed as amended by SI 1982 No 1880.]

11.—(1) The sign shown in diagram 501 shall not be used unless used either in combination with a plate of the type shown in diagram 502 and in conjunction with the sign shown in diagram 601.1 or in combination with a plate of the type shown in diagram 503 and in conjunction with the sign shown in diagram 602.

(2) The sign shown in diagram 545 shall not be used unless used in combination with any of the following, that is to say, with a plate of the type shown in diagram 546 to 547.3, or the traffic sign (warning lights) prescribed by Regulation 37(2) of the Regulations.

(3) The traffic signs shown in the diagrams whose numbers appear in column 1 of the table set out at the end of this paragraph shall not be used unless used in combination with a plate of the type shown in the diagrams whose numbers appear in column 2 of that table opposite to the number in column 1 to which the relate.

(4) Where the indications given by any of the signs shown in diagrams 530, 532.1 and 629 to 629.2 are varied in accordance with Regulation 12(1)(*a*) of the Regulations, the sign whose indications shall have been so varied shall not be used displaying the permitted variant unless used in combination with another sign of the same type whose indications have not been so varied as aforesaid and which gives the indications prescribed in the relevant diagram without the permitted variant.

[When the signs shown in the diagrams specified in this paragraph are incorporated as symbols displayed by other signs incorporating them and the indications given by those symbols are so varied, this paragraph shall apply to those other signs incorporating the varied symbols in the same way as it applied to the said signs so symbolised.]

TABLE

Column 1 Sign diagram number	*Column 2* Plate diagram number
533	either 534.1 or 534.2 or 535.1
544.2	547.4
562	either 537.3 or 563
617	either 618 or 618.1
632	either 570 or 645
[557.1	557.2, 557.3 or 557.4]

[Direction 11 is printed as amended by SI 1982 No 1880 and SI 1983 No 1086.]

12. A plate of the type shown in diagrams 502, 503, 511, 518, 519, 519.1, 525 to 527, 534.1, 534.2, 535.1, 537.1 to 537.4, 546, [547.1 to 547.5], 553, 556.3, 556.4, [557.2, 557.3, 557.4] 563, 564.1, 570 to 573, 575, 579, 602.1, 607, 608, 618, 618.1, 619.3, 619.4, 620, 620.1, 622.3, 625.2, 627, 636.1, 642.1, 643 to 645, 656, 656.1, 660.2, 662, 802.1 to 805, 807, 812.3, 812.4 and 817.1 shall not be used unless used in combination with the signs which are specified beneath the diagrams showing the plate.

[Direction 12 is printed as amended by SI 1983 No 1086; SI 1987 No 1706.]

* * *

17. The signs shown in diagrams 564, 564.1, 564.5 to 569.1, 754 to 756.1 and the signs shown in diagrams 858 to 858.2 when those last-mentioned signs are displayed on the yellow but not on the blue permitted backgrounds may be placed on or near a road only in connection with the execution of works thereon, or a temporary obstruction thereon, and any such sign so placed and any other sign shown in a diagram in Schedule 1 to the Regulations so placed as aforesaid shall not be retained on or near the road after the completion of the works or the removal of the obstruction, as the case may be, unless—

(i) it is a sign of the type shown in diagram 565.1 and if so, that sign may be retained on or near a road after the completion of the works for so long as the highway authority concerned sees fit, or

(ii) it is a sign of the type shown in diagram 565.2 bearing the words 'Give way markings erased', or 'stop markings erased' and if so, that sign shall have been removed as soon as the road markings have been replaced and in any event not later than 28 days from the date of completion of the works.

18.—(1) Signs shown in diagrams 603 and 604 may be used only where one-way working is necessary owing to a temporary closure to vehicular traffic of a width of the carriageway of a road.

(2) The signs shown in diagrams 615 and 811 shall not be used unless used in conjunction with one another and shall not be used at all in conjunction with the signs shown in diagrams 603 or 604.

(3) The signs shown in diagrams 634 and 635 may be used only by a constable in uniform or a person acting under the instructions or authority of the chief officer of police for the police area in which the signs are to be placed.

19. The sign shown in diagram 569.2 or 569.3 may be placed on or near a road only in connection with works involving an alteration in the layout of the carriageway or involving the removal of or change in the road markings or other traffic signs placed on or near a road at cross roads or other junctions (including in the case of the sign shown in the diagram 569.3 an automatic railway level crossing within the meaning of Regulation 25(1) of the Regulations), and shall be retained for not more than 3 months from the date of the completion of those works.

20. Signs shown in diagrams 830, 830.1, 831 and 832 (except when varied to contain the words 'weight check') may be used only in connection with a traffic census the taking of which on a road has been approved by the highway authority for that road, by the chief officer of police of the police area in which the road is situate, and by or on behalf of the Secretary of State.

* * *

24.—(1) The road marking shown in diagram 1001 shall not be placed on a road unless it is so placed for use in conjunction with the light signals prescribed by paragraph (2) or paragraph (4) of Regulation 31 of the Regulations or with the light signals prescribed by the said paragraph (2) as varied in accordance with Regulation 32 of the Regulations or unless it is so placed at a site where vehicular traffic is from time to time controlled by the police.

(2) Where both primary and secondary signals within the meaning of Regulation 34(6) of the Regulations have been erected, the reference in sub-paragraph (1) above to light signals prescribed by the said paragraph (2) or paragraph (4) of Regulation 31 or by the said paragraph 2 as so varied as aforesaid shall be construed as a reference to both the primary and the secondary signals or if either the primary or

secondary signals are not operating, to the primary signals operating alone or to the secondary signals operating alone as the case may be.

25. The road markings shown in diagrams 1002.1 and 1022 shall not be placed on a road unless they are so placed for use in conjunction with the sign shown in diagram 601.1 or until the [31st December 1982] inclusive of that date, with any sign which can be treated as if prescribed by the Regulations until that date if it is a sign of the type shown in the diagram numbered 601 in Schedule 1 to the Traffic Signs Regulations 1964; and the road marking shown in diagram 1003.4 shall not be so placed as aforesaid unless it is placed for use in conjunction with the sign shown in diagram 611.1.

[Direction 25 is printed as amended by SI 1982 No 1880.]

* * *

30.—(1) The road markings shown in diagram 1023 shall not be placed on a road unless so placed for use in conjunction with the road marking shown in diagram 1003.

(2) The road markings shown in diagrams 1025.1 and 1025.3 shall not be placed on a road unless so placed for use in conjunction with at least one sign of the type shown in diagram 650 which shall have been erected on or near the same side of the road as that on which the marking is placed.

(3) The road marking shown in diagram 1048 shall not be placed on a road unless so placed for use in conjunction with the marking shown in diagram 1049 and either the traffic sign shown in diagram 653 or that shown in diagram 654; and the marking shown in diagram 1049 shall not be placed on a road unless so placed for the use in conjunction with the marking shown in diagram 1048 and either the sign shown in diagram 653 or that shown in diagram 654.

[(4) No road marking of a kind shown in diagrams 1003, 1023 or 1049 when varied in size to conform with any of the smaller alternative dimensions prescribed for it shall be placed on the carriageway except for use in conjunction with the marking shown in diagram 1057 and also with one or more of the signs shown in diagrams 625, 625.3, 654.1 or 815.]

[(5) No roadmarking of the kind shown in diagram 1009 when varied in size to conform with the smallest alternative dimensions prescribed for it shall be placed on the carriageway except to mark the junction of a cycle track and another road, in conjunction with road markings of the smallest alternative dimensions prescribed for diagrams 1003 and 1023.]

[(6) No roadmarking of a kind shown in diagram 1057 shall be placed on a road except in conjunction with at least one of the signs shown in diagrams 625, 625.3, 654.1 or 815 erected along that road.]

[(7) The road markings shown in diagrams 1058 or 1059 shall not be placed on a road unless so placed for use in conjunction with at least one road marking of the kind shown in diagram 1057.]

[Direction 30 is printed as amended by SI 1982 No 1880.]

* * *

34.—(1) Light signals such as are prescribed by Regulations 31 to 33, 35, 36,

37(2), 38 and 39 of the Regulations may be placed on or near a road only if the following conditions are satisfied, that is to say—

(*a*) the said signals are so placed that they face the stream of traffic to which they are intended to convey respectively the warning, information, requirements, restrictions or prohibitions prescribed by the Regulations;

(*b*) the apparatus (including the content of all instructions stored in, or executable by it) used in connection with the said signals is of a type which has been approved in writing by or on behalf of the Secretary of State; and

(*c*) if the light signals are light signals prescribed by Regulation 31(4) of the Regulations and are to be erected at or near a level crossing (where a road is crossed by a railway) otherwise than in pursuance of an Order made by the Secretary of State under section 66 of the British Transport Commission Act 1957 (which empowers the Secretary of State to authorise special arrangements at public level crossings), [an] Order so made under section 124 of the Transport Act 1968 (British Railways Board's obligations at level crossings with roads other than public carriage roads), [or of an order under section 1 of the Level Crossings Act 1983 (which empowers the Secretary of State to provide for the protection of those using the level crossing)] the site for, and the number and disposition of, those signals shall first have been approved in writing by or on behalf of the Secretary of State after consideration of such plans for the site and such other information as he may require for the purposes of his function in this condition.

(2) If, after any light signals such as are mentioned in sub-paragraph (1) of this paragraph have been placed on or near a road, the apparatus used in connection with the said signals is altered so as to enable any further instructions to be stored in, or made executable by, the apparatus, the said signals shall not be further used unless that alteration is of a type which has been approved in writing by or on behalf of the Secretary of State.

(3) The light signals prescribed by Regulation 31(2) and (4) of the Regulations or those light signals as varied in accordance with Regulation 32 thereof shall not be used unless used in conjunction with the road marking shown in diagram 1001, except that this sub-paragraph shall not apply while works which necessitate the temporary removal of that road marking are being executed on a road in the vicinity of the place where the said light signals are erected.

(4) The containers enclosing the lamps of each of the kinds of light signals mentioned in sub-paragraph (1) of this paragraph shall be coloured black, except that if those containers enclose lamps of the light signals prescribed by Regulation 31(3), 36, 37(2) or 39 of the Regulations, they may be coloured grey instead of black.

(5) Any of the kinds of light signals mentioned in sub-paragraph (1) of this paragraph other than the signals prescribed by Regulation 35 of the Regulations may be mounted with a backing board and if so mounted, the backing board shall be coloured black and may have a white border not less than 85 nor more than 95 millimetres in width in the case of signals prescribed by Regulation 31(4) of the Regulations and not less than 45 nor more than 55 millimetres in width in the case of the other kinds of light signals which may be so mounted.

(6) Without prejudice to the next following sub-paragraph, where light signals prescribed by any of the Regulations specified in sub-paragraph (1) of this paragraph are mounted on a post specially provided for the purpose, that part of the post which extends above ground level shall be coloured [grey or black] and may have one white

band not less than 140 nor more than 160 millimetres in depth, the lower edge of the band being not less than 1.5 nor more than 1.7 metres above the level of the surface of the ground in the immediate vicinity.

(7) In the case of light signals prescribed by Regulation 33 of the Regulations, instead of being mounted on a post coloured in accordance with the provisions of the last preceding sub-paragraph, they may be mounted on either a post coloured yellow (but having no such white band as therein specified) or, alternatively on a tripod coloured yellow.

[Direction 34 is printed as amended by SI 1984 No 966 (the word '[an]' has been added editorially in para 1(c) following that amendment); SI 1987 No 1706.]

* * *

36.—(1) The back of any sign shown in a diagram in Schedule 1, other than a sign in diagram 569.1, of any backing board or other fitting provided for the assembly of such a sign, including any container enclosing apparatus for the illumination of that sign, shall be coloured—

(*a*) black, if the sign is mounted on the same post as that on which light signals prescribed by Regulation 31(2) of the Regulations or those signals as varied by Regulation 32 thereof, or prescribed by Regulation 33 of the Regulations are mounted, and

(*b*) [grey or black] in any other case except that information about sites for placing the sign may be indicated on the back of the sign in characters not exceeding 15 millimetres in height.

(2) The back of a sign of the type shown in diagram 569.1 in Schedule 1 shall be coloured either grey or white.

[(3) The containers enclosing the road danger lamps prescribed by Regulation 40 shall be coloured yellow.]

[(4) The front of any backing board for a sign mounted otherwise than as described in sub-paragraph (*a*) of paragraph (1) shall be coloured either grey or yellow.]

[Direction 36 is printed as amended by SI 1982 No 1880; SI 1987 No 1706.]

* * *

42. At least one road marking of the kind shown in diagram 1014 shall be placed for use in conjunction with a road marking of the kind shown in diagram 1013.1 on the length of carriageway which extends backwards from the commencement of any continuous line marked on the carriageway as a part of the last mentioned road marking so shown, such commencement being viewed in the direction of travel of a vehicle driven so as to have and keep that continuous line on the right hand or offside thereof in accordance with Regulation 23(2)(*b*) of the Regulations, and if more than one road marking of the kind first above-mentioned is placed on the said length of carriageway then those road markings shall be so spaced apart that one follows in *[sic]* in line in front of the other.

43. Nothing in these Directions shall be taken to limit the power of the Secretary of State acting as the appropriate Minister by any special Direction to dispense with, add to or modify any of the requirements of these Directions in their application to any particular case.

PART III

General Citation and Commencement

* * *

The Traffic Signs (Welsh and English Language Provisions) Regulations and General Directions 1985

(SI 1985 No 713)

The Secretary of State for Wales, in exercise of the powers conferred by section 28(4) of the Road Traffic Regulation Act 1984 (hereinafter referred to as 'the Act of 1984') and the Secretary of State for Wales, the Secretary of State for Transport and the Secretary of State for Scotland acting jointly in exercise of the powers conferred by section 64(1) and 65(1) of the Act of 1984 and by the provision in column 5 of Part I of Schedule 4 to the Road Traffic Act 1972 which relates to section 22 of that Act as that provision is amended by paragraph 9 of Schedule 3 to the Secretary of State for Transport Order 1976 *[SI 1976 No 1775]* and in exercise of the powers conferred by section 2(2) and (3) of the Welsh Language Act 1967 and now vested in them and all other enabling powers, and after consultation with representative organisations in accordance with section 134(2) of the Act of 1984 and section 199(2) of the Road Traffic Act 1972 hereby make these Regulations and give these Directions.

[Although the Road Traffic Act 1972 has been repealed, the references to that Act in the recital of enabling powers have been retained for historical reasons. For ss 22 and 199(2) of the 1972 Act, see now ss 36 and 195(2), respectively, of the Road Traffic Act 1988; for Sched 4, Part I, column 5, to the 1972 Act, see now Sched 2, Part I, column 5, to the Road Traffic Offenders Act 1988.]

PART I

TRAFFIC SIGNS REGULATIONS

* * *

2. Interpretation

(1) In these Regulations the Main Regulations means the Traffic Signs Regulations 1981 *[SI 1981 No 859, qv]* as amended and a reference in Schedule 1 to these Regulations and Directions to 'Main Regulations' or to 'Prif Reolau' is similarly a reference to the Traffic Signs Regulations 1981 amended as aforesaid.

(2) References in these Regulations to a numbered Regulation or numbered Schedule shall be construed, unless the context otherwise requires, as a reference to the Regulation bearing that number in these Regulations or to the Schedule bearing that number in these Regulations and Directions.

(3) References in these Regulations to a sign shown in a diagram in Schedule 1 shall include references to a variant of the sign which is specified in Schedule 1 as being a permitted variant.

(4) References in Schedule 1 to a sign without the prefix 'W' before a diagram number are references to the sign bearing the same diagram number in Parts I and II of Schedule I to the Main Regulations and references in Schedule I to a sign with the prefix 'W' before a diagram number are references to the sign bearing the same diagram number which is prescribed for use in Wales by regulation 4(1).

(5) Nothing in these Regulations shall have effect so as to authorise any person not otherwise authorised to do so to place on or near a road any object or device for warning traffic of a temporary obstruction.

3. Authorisation by the Secretary of State

Nothing in these Regulations shall be taken to limit the power of the Secretary of State under section 64 of the Act of 1984 to authorise the erection or retention of traffic signs of a character not prescribed by these Regulations.

4. Traffic Signs shown in Schedule 1

(1) A sign shown in a diagram in Schedule 1 with the prefix 'W' followed by a diagram number may be used in Wales in place of a sign bearing the same diagram number without the prefix 'W' in Parts I or II of Schedule 1 to the Main Regulations.

(2) In the signs shown in the diagrams in Schedule 1, other than the signs shown in diagrams W605.1 and W629.1 and other than the signs therein which specifically prescribe the manner in which the two texts are to be displayed, either the Welsh or English text shall be placed above the other text.

[Diagram W605.1 is the sign exhibited by a school crossing patrol and diagram W629.1 is the sign prohibiting vehicles or combinations of vehicles exceeding the length indicated.]

5. Application of the Main Regulations

(1) Subject to the provisions of this Regulation, the provisions of the Main Regulations shall apply to a sign shown in a diagram in Schedule 1 with the prefix 'W' followed by a diagram number as if it were a sign bearing the same diagram number without the prefix 'W' in Schedule 1 to the Main Regulations.

Provided that:—

(*a*) except as provided in paragraph (2) of this Regulation, references in subparagraphs (*c*), (*d*) and (*e*) of Regulation 12(1) of the Main Regulations to the signs specified in those subparagraphs showing distances in miles or in yards shall be construed as references to such signs in Schedule 1 showing distances in both the Welsh and English texts;

(*b*) references in subparagraph (*g*) of Regulation 12(1) of the Main Regulations to signs showing a period of time, day of the week, days of the month or months of the year shall be construed as references to such signs in Schedule 1 indicating these matters in both the Welsh and English texts;

(*c*) where, in accordance with the provisions of Regulation 12(1) of the Main Regulations, the indication given by a sign shown in a diagram in Schedule 1 is varied, the variation shall be made to both the Welsh and English texts of the sign; and

(*d*) Regulation 28(1) of the Main Regulations shall not apply to the sign shown in diagram 562 of Schedule 1 to the Main Regulations when used as directed in proviso (*a*) to Direction 3 in Part II of this Instrument in combination with any of the signs shown in diagrams W552, W554 and W554.1 in Schedule 1.

(2) A reference in Regulation 12(1)(*c*) of the Main Regulations to the sign shown in diagram 564.4 of Schedule 1 to the Main Regulations expressing distances in miles shall be construed as a reference to the sign showing distances by means of the letter 'm' in diagram W564.4 in Schedule 1 and a similar reference in Regulation 12(1)(*e*) of the Main Regulations to the signs shown in diagrams 557.2 and 557.3 expressing distances in miles or yards shall be construed as references to the signs showing distances by means of the letters 'm' or 'yds' in diagrams W557.2 and W557.3 in Schedule 1.

(3) The provisions of Regulation 14 of and Schedule 7 to the Main Regulations shall apply as if in that Part of Schedule 7 specified in Column 1 of the following Table there were inserted the characters shown in that Part of Schedule 2 to these Regulations specified in Column 2 of the said Table opposite the Part in Column 1 to which it relates.

TABLE

Column 1 Part of Schedule 7 to Main Regulations	Column 2 Part of Schedule 2 to these Regulations to be inserted
Part I	Part A
Part II	Part B
Part IV	Part C
Part V	Part D
Part VI	Part E
Part VIII	Part F

[Diagrams 557.2 and 557.3 are plates for use in connection with diagram 557.1 (road hump ahead); diagram 562 is a warning sign of other danger ahead; diagrams W552 (cattle grid), W554 (snow drifts) and W554.1 (try your brakes) are plates for use in connection with diagram 562; and diagrams W557.2 and W557.3 are plates for use in connection with diagram 557.1]

6. Application of other enactments

A reference in any enactment to a traffic sign shown in a numbered diagram in the Main Regulations shall be construed as including a reference to a sign bearing the same diagram number with the prefix 'W' in Schedule 1.

SCHEDULE 1

[Warning and regulating signs; omitted.]

SCHEDULE 2

[Proportion and form of letters, numerals and other characters; omitted.]

PART II

GENERAL DIRECTIONS

* * *

2. Interpretation

(1) References in these Directions to 'Schedule 1' shall be construed as references to Schedule 1 to these Regulations and Directions.

(2) In these Directions 'the Main Regulations' means the Traffic Signs Regulations 1981 as amended; 'the Main Directions' means the Traffic Signs General Directions 1981 *[SI 1981 No 859, qv]* as amended and a reference in Schedule 1 to these

Regulations and Directions to 'Main Directions' or to 'Prif Gyfarwyddiadau' is similarly a reference to the Traffic Signs General Directions 1981 as amended.

(3) References in these Directions to a sign in a diagram in Schedule 1 shall include references to a variant of the sign which is specified in Schedule 1 as being a permitted variant.

(4) Nothing in these Directions shall have effect so as to authorise any person not otherwise authorised to do so to place on or near a road any object or device for warning traffic of a temporary obstruction.

3. Application of the Main Directions

The Main Directions shall apply to a sign shown in a diagram in Schedule 1 with the prefix 'W' followed by a diagram number as if it were a sign bearing the equivalent diagram number without the prefix 'W' in Schedule 1 to the Main Regulations and the reference in Direction 12 of the Main Directions to signs which are specified beneath the diagrams showing the plates referred to in Direction 12 shall be construed as references to such signs beneath the corresponding diagrams in Schedule 1. Provided that:

(*a*) notwithstanding anything to the contrary contained in Direction 11(3) of the Main Directions the plates shown in diagrams W552, W554 and W554.1 in Schedule 1 shall be used only in combination with the sign shown in diagram 562 of Schedule 1 to the Main Regulations; and

(*b*) the references in Direction 17(ii) of the Main Directions to the sign shown in diagram 565.2 in Schedule 1 to the Main Regulations bearing words in the English language shall be construed as a reference to such sign in Schedule 1 in both the Welsh and English texts.

[Diagram 565.2 is a warning sign (slow—wet tar; and a number of specified variants). As to the other diagrams mentioned in direction 3, see the note to reg 5.]

The Use of Invalid Carriages on Highways Regulations 1970

(SI 1970 No 1391)

Note. Although these regulations have been revoked by the Use of Invalid Carriages on Highways Regulations 1988 (SI 1988 No 2268), they continue to apply to invalid carriages which were manufactured before 30 January 1989; see ibid, reg 2(2), below. In consequence, the provisions of these regulations as to the use of invalid carriages have been retained in this edition; reference should be made to the 13th edition of this publication for the text of the regulations relating to the construction of such invalid carriages.

1. Commencement, citation and interpretation

(1) *[Omitted.]*

(2) The [Interpretation Act 1978] shall apply for the interpretation of these Regulations as it applies for the interpretation of an Act of Parliament.

[Regulation 1 is printed as amended by the Interpretation Act 1978, ss 17(2)(a) and 23(1).]

2. Prescribed requirements and conditions for purposes of section 20(1) of the said Act of 1970

The requirements with which an invalid carriage (within the meaning of subsection (2) of the said section 20) must comply, and the conditions in accordance with which it must be used, in order that the modifications of the statutory provisions mentioned in subsection (1) of that section shall have effect in the case of the vehicle (being modifications of certain statutory provisions which relate to the use of vehicles on footways and roads) shall be—

(*a*) that the vehicle is being used by a person for whose use it was constructed or adapted, being a person suffering from some physical defect or disability, or by some other person for the purposes only of taking the vehicle to or bringing it away from any place where work of maintenance or repair is to be or has been carried out to the vehicle; and

(*b*) the requirements (subject to the exceptions specified in relation thereto) as set out in Regulations 3 to 6 below.

[The reference to s 20 of the 'said Act of 1970' and that to the 'said section 20' are references to s 20 of the Chronically Sick and Disabled Persons Act 1970, to which reference is made in the recital of enabling powers.]

3. Unladen weight *[Omitted.]*

4. Limit of speed *[Omitted.]*

5. Brakes

(1) *[Omitted.]*

(2) Every part of the braking system and of the means of operation thereof fitted to

the vehicle shall be maintained in good and efficient working order and be properly adjusted.

(3) *[Omitted.]*

6. Lighting

(1) Subject to paragraph (3) below, an invalid carriage when on the carriageway of any road shall during the hours of darkness carry—

(*a*) one lamp showing to the front a white light visible from a reasonable distance;

(*b*) one lamp showing to the rear a red light visible from a reasonable distance; and

(*c*) one unobscured and efficient red reflector facing to the rear.

(2) Every such lamp shall be kept properly trimmed, lighted, and in a clean and efficient condition, and every such lamp and reflector shall be attached to the vehicle in such position and manner, and shall comply with such conditions with respect thereto, as are specified in the Schedule to these Regulations.

(3) The foregoing provisions of this Regulation shall not apply in relation to a vehicle when it is on the carriageway of a road for the purpose only of crossing that carriageway in the quickest manner practicable in the circumstances.

(4) In this Regulation,—

(*a*) 'road' means any highway and any other road to which the public has access not being (in either case) a footway within the meaning of section 20(2) of the said Act of 1970, and

(*b*) 'hours of darkness' means the time between half-an-hour after sunset and half-an-hour before sunrise.

[As to the 'said Act of 1970', see the note to reg 2, above.]

SCHEDULE

(see regulation 6)

Conditions as to Lamps and Reflectors

1. The lamp showing a white light to the front shall be fixed on the centre line or offside of the vehicle.

2. The lamp showing a red light to the rear shall be so fixed that—

(*a*) its lateral position is on the centre line or off side of the vehicle,

(*b*) its longitudinal position is not more than 20 inches from the extreme rear of the vehicle,

(*c*) the maximum height from the ground of the highest part of the illuminated area of the lamp is 3 feet 6 inches, and

(*d*) the minimum height from the ground of the lowest part of the said area is 12 inches,

and shall be marked—

(i) with the specification number of the British Standard for Cycle Rear Lamps, namely BS 3648, and

(ii) with the name, trade mark or other means of identification of the manufacturer of the lamp.

3. The reflector shall be so fixed that—

(*a*) its lateral position is on the centre line or off side of the vehicle,

(*b*) its longitudinal position is not more than 20 inches from the extreme rear of the vehicle,

(*c*) the maximum height from the ground of the highest part of the reflecting area of the reflector is 3 feet 6 inches, and

(*d*) the minimum height from the ground of the lowest part of the said area is 12 inches,

and shall be marked—

(i) with the specification number of the British Standard for Reflex Reflectors for Vehicles, namely, AU 40 followed by a marking 'LI' or 'LIA' and with the registered trade name or trade mark of the manufacturer of the reflector, or

(ii) with an approval mark (that is to say, a marking designated as an approval mark by the [Motor Vehicles (Designation of Approval Marks) Regulations 1979] *[SI 1979 No 1088]*) incorporating the roman numeral I.

[The Schedule is printed as amended by the Interpretation Act 1978, ss 17(2)(a) and 23(1).]

The Use of Invalid Carriages on Highways Regulations 1988

(SI 1988 No 2268)

1. Citation and commencement

These Regulations may be cited as the Use of Invalid Carriages on Highways Regulations 1988 and shall come into force on 30th January 1989.

2. Revocation and saving

(1) Subject to paragraph (2), the Use of Invalid Carriages on Highways Regulations 1970 *[SI 1970 No 1391, qv]* ('the 1970 Regulations') are hereby revoked.

(2) Nothing in these Regulations shall apply to invalid carriages manufactured before 30th January 1989, and the 1970 Regulations shall continue to apply to such invalid carriages as if these Regulations had not been made.

3. Interpretation

In these Regulations—

the '1970 Act' means the Chronically Sick and Disabled Persons Act 1970;

the '1986 Regulations' means the Road Vehicles (Construction and Use) Regulations 1986 *[SI 1986 No 1078, qv]*;

a 'Class 1 invalid carriage' means an invalid carriage which is not mechanically propelled;

a 'Class 2 invalid carriage' means a mechanically propelled invalid carriage which is so constructed or adapted as to be incapable of exceeding a speed of 4 miles per hour on the level under its own power;

a 'Class 3 invalid carriage' means a mechanically propelled invalid carriage which is so constructed or adapted as to be capable of exceeding a speed of 4 miles per hour but incapable of exceeding a speed of 8 miles per hour on the level under its own power;

'horn' has the meaning given by regulation 37(10)(*a*) of the 1986 Regulations;

'reversing alarm' has the meaning given by regulation 37(10)(*c*) of the 1986 Regulations;

'road' has the meaning given by section 142(1) of the Road Traffic Regulation Act 1984 *[qv]*;

'two-tone horn' has the meaning given by regulation 37(10)(*d*) of the 1986 Regulations.

4. Prescribed conditions for purposes of section 20(1) of the 1970 Act

The conditions in accordance with which an invalid carriage must be used, in order that the modifications of the statutory provisions mentioned in subsection (1) of section 20 of the 1970 Act *[qv]* shall have effect in the case of the invalid carriage (being modifications of certain statutory provisions which relate to the use of vehicles on footways and roads) shall be—

(*a*) in the case of Class 1, Class 2 and Class 3 invalid carriages that the invalid carriage must be used—
(i) by a person falling within a class of persons for whose use it was constructed or adapted, being a person suffering from some physical defect or physical disability;
(ii) by some other person for the purposes only of taking the invalid carriage to or bringing it away from any place where work of maintenance or repair is to be or has been carried out to the invalid carriage;
(iii) by a manufacturer for the purposes only of testing or demonstrating the invalid carriage;
(iv) by a person offering to sell the invalid carriage for the purpose only of demonstrating it; or
(v) by a person giving practical training in the use of the invalid carriage for that purpose only;

(*b*) in the case of Class 1, Class 2 and Class 3 invalid carriages, that any horn fitted to it must not be sounded in the circumstances set out in regulation 5;

(*c*) in the case of Class 3 invalid carriages only—
(i) that the invalid carriage must not be used by a person who is aged under 14 years;
(ii) that, when being used on a footway, the invalid carriage must not be driven at a speed greater than 4 miles per hour;
(iii) that the invalid carriage must not be used on a footway unless the device fitted in accordance with regulation 10(1)(*a*) is operating; and
(iv) that the invalid carriage must not be used at any time unless the speed indicator fitted to it in accordance with regulation 10(1)(*b*) is operating.

5. The circumstances referred to in regualtion 4(*b*) are that the invalid carriage is either—

(*a*) stationary on a road, at any time, other than at times of danger due to another moving vehicle on or near the road; or

(*b*) in motion on a road which is a restricted road for the purposes of section 81 of the Road Traffic Regulation Act 1984 between 23.30 hours and 07.00 hours in the following morning.

6. Prcscribed requirements for purposes of section 20(1) of the 1970 Act

The requirements with which an invalid carriage must comply in order that the modifications of the statutory provisions mentioned in subsection (1) of section 20 of the 1970 Act *[qv]* shall have effect in the case of the invalid carriage (being modifications of certain statutory provisions which related to the use of vehicles on footways and roads) shall be—

(*a*) that it shall be a Class 1, Class 2 or Class 3 invalid carriage; and

(*b*) the requirements specified in regulations 7 to 14.

7. Unladen weight

(1) The unladen weight of a Class 1 or Class 2 invalid carriage shall not exceed 113.4 kilograms.

(2) The unladen weight of a Class 3 invalid carriage shall not exceed 150 kilograms.

(3) In this regulation 'unladen weight' means the weight of the invalid carriage inclusive of the weight of water, fuel or accumulators used for the purpose of the

supply of power for its propulsion and of loose tools, but exclusive of the weight of any other load or of a person carried by the invalid carriage.

8. Means of stopping

(1) A Class 2 or Class 3 invalid carriage shall be so constructed and maintained that it meets the requirements set out in paragraphs (2) to (4).

(2) The invalid carriage shall be capable of being brought to rest in all conditions of use with reasonable directional stability and within a reasonable distance.

(3) When the invalid carriage is not being propelled or is left unattended it shall be capable of being held stationary indefinitely in all conditions of use on a gradient of at least 1 in 5.

(4) The requirements of paragraphs (2) and (3) shall not be regarded as met unless the necessary braking effect can be achieved by the appropriate use—

(*a*) of the invalid carriage's propulsion unit transmission gear or of both the propulsion unit and transmission gear;

(*b*) of a separate system fitted to the vehicle (which may be a system which operates upon the propulsion unit or transmission gear); or

(*c*) of a combination of the means of achieving a braking effect referred to in sub-paragraphs (*a*) and (*b*);

and in the case of paragraph (3) without depending upon any hydraulic or pneumatic device or on the flow of electrical current.

9. Lighting

A Class 2 or Class 3 invalid carriage when on the carriageway of any road shall comply with the requirements specified in the Road Vehicles Lighting Regulations 1984 *[SI 1984 No 812, qv]* as if it was a motor vehicle within the meaning of [the Road Traffic Act 1988] and as if any reference to an invalid carriage in those Regulations included an invalid carriage within the meaning of the 1970 Act.

[Regulation 9 is printed as amended by the Interpretation Act 1978, ss 17(2)(a) and 23(1).]

10. Speed device and speed indicator

(1) A Class 3 invalid carriage shall be fitted with—

(*a*) a device which is capable of limiting the maximum speed of the invalid carriage to 4 miles per hour on the level under its own power and which can be put into operation by the user; and

(*b*) a speed indicator.

(2) A speed indicator fitted in accordance with this regulation shall be kept free from any obstruction which might prevent it being easily seen by the user of the invalid carriage and shall be maintained in efficient working order.

(3) In this regulation, 'speed indicator' means a device fitted to an invalid carriage for the purpose of indicating to the user of the invalid carriage whether the device referred to in paragraph (1)(*a*) is in operation.

11. Width

The overall width of a Class 3 invalid carriage shall not exceed 0.85 metres.

12. Audible warning instrument

(1) A Class 3 invalid carriage shall be fitted with a horn, not being a reversing alarm or a two-tone horn.

(2) The sound emitted by any horn fitted to an invalid carriage shall be continuous and uniform and not strident.

13. Vision

(1) A Class 2 or Class 3 invalid carriage shall be so constructed that the user of the invalid carriage can at all times have a full view of the road and traffic ahead when controlling the invalid carriage.

(2) Any windscreen or window fitted to a Class 2 or Class 3 invalid carriage shall be made of safety glass or safety glazing and shall be maintained in such condition that it does not obscure the vision of the user of the invalid carriage while the invalid carriage is being driven.

(3) In this regulation—

'safety glass' means glass so manufactured or treated that if fractured it does not fly into fragments likely to cause severe cuts; and

'safety glazing' means material other than glass so manufactured or treated that if fractured it does not fly into fragments likely to cause severe cuts.

14. Rear view mirrors

(1) A Class 3 invalid carriage shall be fitted either internally or externally with a rear view mirror.

(2) Any rear view mirror fitted to an invalid carriage shall be so constructed or treated that if fractured it does not fly into fragments likely to cause severe cuts.

(3) In this regulation 'rear view mirror' means a mirror to assist the user of the invalid carriage to become aware of traffic to the rear of the invalid carriage.

The Value Added Tax (General) Regulations 1985

(SI 1985 No 886)

* * *

56. The Commissioners may, on application by an overseas visitor who intends to depart from the United Kingdom within 15 months and remain outside the United Kingdom for a period of at least 6 months, permit him within 12 months of his intended departure to acquire, from a manufacturer, a new motor vehicle without payment of tax, for subsequent export, and its supply, subject to such conditions as they may impose, shall be zero-rated.

57. The Commissioners may, on application by any person who intends to depart from the United Kingdom within 9 months and remain outside the United Kingdom for a period of at least 6 months, permit him within 6 months of his intended departure to acquire, from a manufacturer, a new motor vehicle without payment of tax, for subsequent export, and its supply, subject to such conditions as they may impose, shall be zero-rated.

[Regulations 56 and 57 above are incorporated by reference into various other instruments, eg the Motor Vehicles (Type Approval for Goods Vehicles) (Great Britain) Regulations 1982 (SI 1982 No 1271), reg 3, and the Motor Vehicles (Type Approval) (Great Britain) Regulations 1984 (SI 1984 No 981), reg 3, qv.]

* * *

The Various Trunk Roads (Prohibition of Waiting) (Clearways) Order 1963)

(SI 1963 No 1172)

* * *

3. Interpretation

(1) In this Order the following expressions have the meanings hereby respectively assigned to them:—

'the [Act of 1984]' means the [Road Traffic Regulation Act 1984];

'main carriageway', in relation to a trunk road, means any carriageway of that road used primarily by through traffic and excludes any lay-by;

'lay-by', in relation to a main carriageway of a trunk road, means any area intended for use for the waiting of vehicles, lying at a side of the road and bounded partly by a traffic sign consisting of a yellow dotted line on the road, or of a white dotted line and the words 'lay-by' on the road, authorised by the [Secretary of State for Transport] under subsection (2) of [section 64 of the Road Traffic Regulation Act 1984], and partly by the outer edge of that carriageway on the same side of the road as that on which the sign is placed;

'verge' means any part of a road which is not a carriageway.

(2) The [Interpretation Act 1978] shall apply for the interpretation of this Order as it applies for the interpretation of an Act of Parliament and as if for the purposes of [section 17] of that Act this Order were an Act of Parliament and the Orders revoked by Article 2 were Acts of Parliament thereby repealed.

[Article 3 is printed as amended by the Road Traffic Regulation Act 1967, Sched 8, para 2, the Interpretation Act 1978, s 17(2), the Minister of Transport Order 1979 (SI 1979 No 571), the Transfer of Functions (Transport) Order 1981 (SI 1981 No 238), and the Road Traffic Regulation Act 1984, s 144(1), and Sched 10, para 2.]

4. Prohibition of waiting on main carriageways

Save as provided in Article 5 of this Order no person shall, except upon the direction or with the permission of a police constable in uniform, cause or permit any vehicle to wait on any of those main carriageways forming part of trunk roads which are specified in Schedule 1 to this Order.

5. Exceptions to Article 4

Nothing in Article 4 of this Order shall apply—

(*a*) so as to prevent a vehicle waiting on any main carriageway specified in Schedule 1 to this Order for so long as may be necessary to enable the vehicle, if it cannot be used for such purpose without waiting on that carriageway, to be used in connection with any building operation or demolition, the removal of any obstruction or potential obstruction to traffic, the maintenance, improvement or reconstruction of the road comprising that carriageway, or the erection, laying, placing, maintenance, testing, alteration, repair or removal of any structure, works, or apparatus in, on, under or over that road;

(*b*) to a vehicle being used for fire brigade, ambulance or police purposes;

(*c*) to a vehicle being used for the purposes of delivering or collecting postal packets as defined in section 87 of the Post Office Act 1953;

(*d*) so as to prevent a vehicle being used by or on behalf of a local authority from waiting on any main carriageway specified in Schedule 1 to this Order for so long as may be necessary to enable the vehicle, if it cannot be used for such a purpose without waiting on that carriageway to be used for the purpose of the collection of household refuse from, or the clearing of cesspools at, premises situated on or adjacent to the road comprising that carriageway;

(*e*) to a vehicle waiting on any main carriageway specified in Schedule 1 to this Order while any gate or other barrier at the entrance to premises to which the vehicle requires access or from which it has emerged is opened or closed, if it is not reasonably practicable for the vehicle to wait otherwise that on that carriageway while such gate or barrier is being opened or closed;

(*f*) to a vehicle waiting in any case where the person in control of the vehicle:—

(i) is required by law to stop;

(ii) is obliged to do so in order to avoid accident; or

(iii) is prevented from proceeding by circumstances outside his control and it is not reasonably practicable for him to drive or move the vehicle to a place not on any main carriageway specified in Schedule 1 to this Order.

6. Restriction of waiting on verges, etc

No person shall cause or permit any vehicle to wait on any verge or lay-by immediately adjacent to a main carriageway specified in Schedule 1 to this Order for the purpose of selling goods from that vehicle unless the goods are immediately delivered at or taken into premises adjacent to the vehicle from which sale is effected.

* * *

The Vehicle and Driving Licences Records (Evidence) Regulations 1970

(SI 1970 No 1997)

* * *

3. Matters prescribed for [s 13(5) of the Road Traffic Offenders Act 1988]

The following matters are prescribed for the purposes of [section 13(5) of the Road Traffic Offenders Act 1988]—

(1) in connection with the licensing of drivers under [Part III of the Road Traffic Act 1988]—

(*a*) a document being, forming part of, or submitted in connection with, an application for a driving licence;

(*b*) a driving licence;

(*c*) a certificate of competence to drive;

(*d*) the conviction of an offence specified in [Part I of Schedule 2 to the Road Traffic Offenders Act 1988 or the offence of manslaughter (or culpable homicide) specified in Part II of that Schedule] of any person or any order made by the Court as a result of any such conviction;

(2) in connection with the licensing and registration of mechanically propelled vehicles under the [Vehicles (Excise) Act 1971]—

(*a*) a document being, forming part of, or submitted in connection with, an application for—

(i) a vehicle licence;

(ii) a trade licence;

(iii) a repayment of duty under [section 17 of the 1971 Act] or the recovery of underpayments or overpayments of duty under [section 30] of that Act;

(*b*) a vehicle licence, trade licence, registration book or registration mark;

(*c*) a document containing a declaration and particulars such as are prescribed under the [1971 Act] in relation to vehicles exempted from duty under that Act;

(*d*) the conviction of an offence under the [1971 Act] of any person;

(3) in connection with the examination of a goods vehicle under regulations under [section 49 of the Road Traffic Act 1988]—

(*a*) an application for an examination of a vehicle under the said regulations;

(*b*) a notifiable alteration made to a vehicle and required by the said regulations to be notified to the [Secretary of State for Transport];

(*c*) a plating certificate, goods vehicle test certificate, notification of the refusal of a goods vehicle test certificate, Ministry plate, Ministry test date disc or certificate of temporary exemption.

[Regulation 3 is printed as amended by the Vehicles (Excise) Act 1971, Sched 7, para 11, the

Road Traffic Act 1972, Sched 10, para 3, the Minister of Transport Order 1979 (SI 1979 No 751) and the Transfer of Functions (Transport) Order 1981 (SI 1981 No 238).

For the regulations under s 49 of the Road Traffic Act 1988, see the Goods Vehicles (Plating and Testing) Regulations 1988 (SI 1988 No 1478), above.]

* * *

The Vehicle Licences (Duration and Rate of Duty) Order 1980

(SI 1980 No 1183)

1. Citation and commencement *[Omitted.]*

2. Interpretation and application

(1) In this Order 'the Act of 1971' means the Vehicles (Excise) Act 1971.

(2) *[Omitted.]*

3. Commencement and duration of licences

Vehicle licences (other than licences for one calendar year) may be taken out—

(*a*) in the case of any vehicle licence, for any period of twelve months running from the beginning of the month in which the licence first has effect;

(*b*) in the case of any vehicle the annual rate of duty applicable to which exceeds £18, for any period of six months running from the beginning of the month in which the licence first has effect;

(*c*) in the case of a goods vehicle which is authorised to be used on roads by virtue of an order made under [section 44(1) of the Road Traffic Act 1988], and the unladen weight of which exceeds eleven tons, for any period of seven consecutive days.

[Article 3 is printed as amended by the Interpretation Act 1978, ss 17(2)(a) and 23(1).]

The Motor Vehicles (Authorisation of Special Types) General Order 1979 (SI 1979 No 1198) (qv) have effect as if made under s 44(1) of the Road Traffic Act 1988.]

4. Rate of duty

The duty payable on a vehicle licence for a vehicle of any description shall—

(*a*) if the licence is taken out for a period of twelve months, be paid at the annual rate of duty applicable to vehicles of that description under section 1 of the Act of 1971;

(*b*) if the licence is taken out for a period of six months, be paid at a rate equal to one half of the said annual rate plus ten per cent, of that amount;

(*c*) if the licence is taken out for a period of seven consecutive days, be paid at a rate equal to one fifty-second of the said annual rate plus ten per cent of that amount;

and in computing the rate of duty in accordance with paragraph (*b*) or paragraph (*c*) above, any fraction of 5p shall be treated as 5p if it exceeds 2.5p and shall otherwise be disregarded.

5. Amendment of section 2 of the Act of 1971 *[Omitted.]*

The 'Zebra' Pedestrian Crossings Regulations 1971

(SI 1971 No 1524)

ARRANGEMENT OF REGULATIONS

PART I

GENERAL

1. Commencement and citation *[Omitted.]*

2. Revocation and savings *[Omitted.]*

3. Interpretation

(1) In these Regulations, unless the context otherwise requires, the following expressions have the meanings hereby respectively assigned to them:—

'the appropriate Secretary of State' means, in relation to a crossing established on a road in England excluding Monmouthshire, the [Secretary of State for Transport], in relation to a crossing established on a road in Scotland, the Secretary of State for Scotland, and, in relation to a crossing established on a road in Wales or Monmouthshire, the Secretary of State for Wales;

'appropriate authority' means, in relation to a crossing on a trunk road, the appropriate Secretary of State, and in relation to any other crossing the local authority in whose scheme submitted and approved under [section 23 of the Road Traffic Regulation Act 1984] the crossing is for the time being included;

'carriageway' does not include that part of any road which consists of a street refuge or central reservation, whether within the limits of a crossing or not;

'central reservation' means any provision, not consisting of a street refuge, made in a road for separating one part of the carriageway of that road from another part of that carriageway for the safety or guidance of vehicular traffic using that road;

'crossing' means a crossing for foot passengers established either—

(*a*) by a local authority in accordance with the provisions for the time being in force of a scheme submitted and approved under [section 23 of the Road Traffic Regulation Act 1984], or

(*b*) in the case of a trunk road, by the appropriate Secretary of State in the discharge of the duty imposed on him by [section 24 of the Road Traffic Regulation Act 1984]; but does not include a 'Pelican' crossing within the meaning of the ['Pelican' Pedestrian Crossings Regulations 1987] *[SI 1987 No 16 (qv)]*;

'dual-carriageway road' means a length of road on which a part of the carriageway thereof is separated from another part thereof by a central reservation;

'give-way line' has the meaning assigned to it by paragraph 2 of Schedule 3;

'one-way street' means any road in which the driving of all vehicles otherwise than in one direction is prohibited at all times;

'stud' means a mark or device on the carriageway, whether or not projecting above the surface thereof;

'zebra controlled area' means, in relation to a zebra crossing, the area of the carriageway in the vicinity of the crossing and lying on both sides of the crossing or only one side of the crossing, being an area the presence and limits of which are indicated in accordance with Schedule 3;

'zebra crossing' means a crossing the presence and limits of which are indicated in accordance with the provisions of Schedule 2;

'uncontrolled zebra crossing' means a zebra crossing at which traffic is not for the time being controlled by a police constable in uniform or by a traffic warden.

(2) Any reference in these Regulations to a numbered Regulation or Schedule is a reference to the Regulation or Schedule bearing that number in these Regulations except where otherwise expressly provided.

(3) Any reference in these Regulations to any enactment shall be construed as a reference to that enactment as amended by any subsequent enactment.

(4) The [Interpretation Act 1978] shall apply for the interpretation of these Regu-

lations as it applies for the interpretation of an Act of Parliament, and as if for the purposes of [section 17] of that Act these Regulations were an Act of Parliament and the Regulations revoked by Regulation 2 were Acts of Parliament thereby repealed.

[Regulation 3 is printed as amended by the Interpretation Act 1978, s 17(2)(a); the Minister of Transport Order 1979 (SI 1979 No 571); the Transfer of Functions (Transport) Order 1981 (SI 1981 No 238); the Road Traffic Regulation Act 1984, s 144(1), and Sched 10, para 2.]

PART II

Marks, Signs and other Particulars as Respects Zebra Crossings

4. Zebra crossings

(1) The provisions of Part I of Schedule 2 shall have effect for regulating the manner in which the presence and limits of a crossing are to be indicated by marks or studs on the carriageway for the purpose of constituting it a zebra crossing.

(2) The provisions of Part II of Schedule 2 shall have effect as respects the size, colour and type of the traffic signs which are to be placed at or near a crossing for the purpose of constituting it a zebra crossing.

5. Zebra controlled areas and give-way lines

(1) Subject to paragraph (3) of this Regulation, the provisions of Schedule 3 shall have effect as respects the size, colour and type of the traffic signs which shall be placed in the vicinity of a zebra crossing for the purpose of constituting a zebra controlled area in relation to that crossing and of indicating the presence and limits of that area.

(2) A give-way line (included among the said signs) shall, where provided, also convey to vehicular traffic proceeding towards a zebra crossing the position at or before which a driver of a vehicle should stop it for the purpose of complying with Regulation 8.

(3) Where the appropriate authority is satisfied in relation to a particular area of carriageway in the vicinity of a zebra crossing that, by reason of the layout of, or character of, the roads in the vicinity of the crossing, the application of such a prohibition as is mentioned in Regulation 10 or 12 to that particular area or the constitution of that particular area as a zebra controlled area by the placing of traffic signs in accordance with Schedule 3 would be impracticable, it shall not be necessary for that area to be constituted a zebra controlled area but, if by virtue of this paragraph it is proposed that no area, on either side of the limits of a zebra crossing (not on a trunk road), is to be constituted a zebra controlled area by the 30th November 1973, a notice in writing shall be sent by the appropriate authority before that date to the appropriate Secretary of State stating the reasons why it is proposed that no such area should be so constituted.

6. Variations in dimensions shown in Schedule 3

Any variations in a dimension specified in the diagram in Schedule 3 or otherwise specified in that Schedule shall be treated as permitted by these Regulations if the variation—

(*a*) in the case of a dimension of 300 millimetres or more, does not exceed 20% of that dimension; or

(*b*) in the case of a dimension of less than 300 millimetres, where the actual dimension exceeds the dimension so specified, does not exceed 30% of the dimension so specified, and where the actual dimension is less than the dimension so specified, does not exceed 10% of the dimension so specified.

7. Lamps for illumination of pedestrians at crossings *[Omitted.]*

PART III

Regulations governing use of Zebra Crossings and Zebra Controlled Areas

8. Precedence of pedestrians over vehicles

Every foot passenger on the carriageway within the limits of an uncontrolled zebra crossing shall have precedence within those limits over any vehicle and the driver of the vehicle shall accord such precedence to the foot passenger, if the foot passenger is on the carriageway within those limits before the vehicle or any part thereof has come on to the carriageway within those limits.

For the purpose of this Regulation, in the case of such a crossing on which there is a street refuge or central reservation the parts of the crossing which are situated on each side of the street refuge or central reservation as the case may be shall each be treated as a separate crossing.

9. Prohibition against the waiting of vehicles and pedestrians on zebra crossings

(1) The driver of a vehicle shall not cause the vehicle or any part thereof to stop within the limits of a zebra crossing unless either he is prevented from proceeding by circumstances beyond his control or it is necessary for him to stop in order to avoid an accident.

(2) No foot passenger shall remain on the carriageway within the limits of a zebra crossing longer than is necessary for the purpose of passing over the crossing with reasonable despatch.

Prohibition against overtaking at zebra crossings

10. The driver of a vehicle while it or any part of it is in a zebra controlled area and it is proceeding towards the limits of an uncontrolled zebra crossing in relation to which that area is indicated (which vehicle is in this and the next succeeding Regulation referred to as 'the approaching vehicle') shall not cause the vehicle, or any part of it—

(*a*) to pass ahead of the foremost part of another moving motor vehicle, being a vehicle proceeding in the same direction wholly or partly within that area, or

(*b*) subject to the next succeeding Regulation, to pass ahead of the foremost part of a stationary vehicle on the same side of the crossing as the approaching vehicle, which stationary vehicle is stopped for the purpose of complying with Regulation 8.

For the purposes of this Regulation—

(i) the reference to another moving motor vehicle is, in a case where only one other motor vehicle is proceeding in the same direction in a zebra controlled area, a reference to that vehicle, and, in a case where more than one other motor vehicle is so proceeding, a reference to such one of those vehicles as is nearest to the limits of the crossing;

(ii) the reference to a stationary vehicle is, in a case where only one other vehicle is stopped for the purpose of complying with Regulation 8, a reference to that vehicle and, in a case where more than one other vehicle is stopped for the purpose of complying with that Regulation, a reference to such one of those vehicles as is nearest to the limits of the crossing.

11.—(1) For the purposes of this Regulation, in the case of an uncontrolled zebra crossing, which is on a road, being a one-way street, and on which there is a street refuge or central reservation, the parts of the crossing which are situated on each side of the street refuge or central reservation as the case may be shall each be treated as a separate crossing.

(2) Nothing in paragraph (*b*) of the last preceding Regulation shall apply so as to prevent the approaching vehicle from passing ahead of the foremost part of a stationary vehicle within the meaning of that paragraph, if the stationary vehicle is stopped for the purpose of complying with Regulation 8 in relation to an uncontrolled zebra crossing which by virtue of this Regulation is treated as a separate crossing from the uncontrolled zebra crossing towards the limits of which the approaching vehicle is proceeding.

Prohibition on stopping in areas adjacent to zebra crossings

12.—(1) For the purposes of this Regulation and the next two following Regulations, the expression 'vehicle' shall not include a pedal bicycle not having a sidecar attached thereto, whether additional means of propulsion by mechanical power are attached to the bicycle or not.

(2) Save as provided in Regulations 14 and 15, the driver of a vehicle shall not cause the vehicle or any part thereof to stop in a zebra controlled area.

13. *[Omitted.]*

14. A vehicle shall not by Regulation 12 or 13 be prevented from stopping in any length of road on any side thereof—

(*a*) if the driver has stopped for the purpose of complying with Regulation 8 or Regulation 10(*b*);

(*b*) if the driver is prevented from proceeding by circumstances beyond his control or it is necessary for him to stop in order to avoid an accident; or

(*c*) for so long as may be necesary to enable the vehicle, if it cannot be used for such purpose without stopping in that length of road, to be used for fire brigade, ambulance or police purposes or in connection with any building operation, demolition or excavation, the removal of any obstruction to traffic, the maintenance, improvement or reconstruction of that length of road, or the laying, erection, alteration, repair or cleaning in or near to that length of road of any traffic sign or sewer or of any main, pipe or apparatus for the supply of gas, water or electricity, or of any telegraph or telephone wires, cables, posts or supports.

15. A vehicle shall not by Regulation 12 be prevented from stopping in a zebra controlled area—

(*a*) if the vehicle is stopped for the purpose of making a left or right turn;

(*b*) if the vehicle is a public service vehicle, being a stage carriage or an express carriage being used otherwise than on an excursion or tour within the meaning of section 159(1) of the Transport Act 1968, and the vehicle is waiting, after having proceeded past the zebra crossing in relation to which the zebra controlled area is indicated, for the purpose of enabling persons to board or alight from the vehicle.

[The Transport Act 1968, s 159(1) (as amended by the Transport Act 1980, s 43(1), and Sched 5, Part II; see reg 3(3) of these regulations), defined 'excursion or tour' as meaning 'a stage or express carriage service on which the passengers travel together on a journey, with or without breaks, from one or more places to one or more other places and back'.

The definition of 'excursion or tour' in the Transport Act 1968, s 159(1), has been repealed by the Transport Act 1985, s 139(3) and Sched 8.]

SCHEDULE 1

Regulations Revoked

[Omitted.]

SCHEDULE 2

Manner of Indicating Presence and Limits of Zebra Crossings

PART I

Studs and Marks

1.—(1) Every crossing and its limits shall be indicated by two lines of studs placed across the carriageway in accordance with the following provisions of this paragraph.

(2) Each line formed by the outside edges of the studs shall be so separated from the other line so formed that no point on one line shall be less than 2.4 metres nor more than 5 metres or such greater distance (not being more than 10.1 metres) as the appropriate Secretary of State may authorise in writing in the case of any particular crossing from the nearest point on the other line:

Provided that the preceding provisions of this sub-paragraph shall be regarded as having been complied with in the case of any crossing which for the most part complies with those provisions notwithstanding that those provisions may not be so complied with as respects the distance from one or more points on one line to the nearest point on the other line, so long as the general indication of the lines is not thereby materially impaired.

(3) The studs of which each line is constituted shall be so placed that the distance from the centre of any one stud to the centre of the next stud in the line is not less than 250 millimetres nor more than 715 millimetres, and a distance of not more than 1.3 metres is left between the edge of the carriageway at either end of the line and the centre of the stud nearest thereto:

Provided that the preceding provisions of this sub-paragraph shall be regarded as having been complied with in the case of any line where most of the studs constituting it comply with those provisions notwithstanding that those provisions may not be complied with as respects one or more such studs, so long as the general indication of the line is not thereby materially impaired.

(4) Studs shall not be fitted with reflecting lenses and shall be—

(*a*) white, silver or light grey in colour;

(*b*) square or circular in plan, the sides of a square stud not being less than 95 millimetres nor more than 110 millimetres in length and the diameter of a circular stud not being less than 95 millimetres nor more than 110 millimetres, and

(*c*) so fixed that they do not project more than 16 millimetres above the carriageway at their highest points nor more than 7 millimetres at their edges.

2. A crossing or its limits shall not be deemed to have ceased to be indicated in accordance with the preceding provisions of this Part of this Schedule by reason only of the discoloration or temporary removal or displacement of one or more studs in any line so long as the general indication of the line is not thereby materially impaired.

3. Without derogation from the provisions of the preceding paragraphs of this Part of this Schedule, every crossing shall be further indicated in accordance with the following provisions of this Part and of Part II of this Schedule.

4.—(1) The carriageway shall be marked within the limits of every such crossing with a pattern of alternate black and white stripes:

Provided that where the colour of the surface of the carriageway provides a reasonable contrast with the colour of white that surface may itself be utilised for providing stripes which would otherwise be required to be black.

(2) Every stripe shall—

(*a*) extend along the carriageway from one line formed by the inside edges of the studs or from a part of the crossing which is not more than 155 millimetres from that line to the other line so formed or to a part of the crossing which is not more than 155 millimetres from that line; and

(*b*) be of a width of not less than 500 millimetres or of such smaller width not being less than 380 millimetres as in the case of any particular crossing the appropriate authority may consider necessary having regard to the layout of the carriageway and, in the case of the first stripe at each end of the crossing, not more than 1.3 metres, or in the case of any other stripe, not more than 715 millimetres or of such greater width not being more than 840 millimetres as in the case of any particular crossing the appropriate authority may consider necessary having regard to the layout of the carriageway.

(3) The preceding provisions of this paragraph shall be regarded as having been complied with in the case of any crossing which for the most part complies with those provisions notwithstanding that those provisions may not be complied with as respects one or more stripes and a crossing shall not be deemed to have ceased to be indicated in accordance with those provisions by reason only of the imperfection, discoloration or partial displacement of one or more of the stripes, so long as the general appearance of the pattern of stripes is not materially impaired.

PART II

Traffic Signs

1. The traffic signs which are to be placed at or near a crossing for the purpose of constituting it and indicating it as a zebra crossing shall consist of globes in relation to which the following provisions in this Part of this Schedule are complied with.

2.—(1) At or near each end of every crossing there shall be placed, and in the case of a crossing on which there is a street refuge or central reservation there may be placed on the refuge or reservation, in accordance with the following provisions of this paragraph globes mounted on posts or brackets.

(2) Globes shall be—

(*a*) yellow in colour;

(*b*) not less than 275 millimetres nor more than 335 millimetres in diameter; and

(*c*) so mounted that the height of the lowest part of the globe is not less than 2.1 metres nor more than 3.1 metres above the surface of the ground in the immediate vicinity.

(3) Globes shall be illuminated by a flashing light or, where the appropriate Secretary of State so authorises in writing in the case of any particular crossing, by a constant light.

(4) Where globes are mounted on or attached to posts specially provided for the purpose, every such post shall, in so far as it extends above ground level, be coloured black and white in alternate horizontal bands, the lowest band visible to approaching traffic being coloured black and not less than 275 millimetres nor more than 1 metre in width and each other band being not less than 275 millimetres nor more than 335 millimetres in width:

Provided that nothing in this sub-paragraph shall apply to any container fixed on any such post which encloses the apparatus for providing the illumination of a globe.

3. A crossing shall not be deemed to have ceased to be indicated in accordance with the preceding provisions of this Part of this Schedule by reason only of—

(*a*) the imperfection, discoloration or disfigurement of any of the globes, posts or brackets; or

(*b*) the failure of the illumination of any of the globes:

Provided that this sub-paragraph shall not apply unless at least one globe is illuminated in accordance with the provisions of sub-paragraph (3) of the last preceding paragraph.

SCHEDULE 3

MANNER OF INDICATING ZEBRA CONTROLLED AREA AND PROVISION AS TO PLACING OF GIVEWAY LINE

PART I

Traffic Signs

1. Subject to the provisions of Regulation 5(3), the traffic signs which are to be placed on a road in the vicinity of a zebra crossing for the purpose of constituting a zebra controlled area lying on both sides of the limits of the crossing or on only one side of such limits and indicating the presence and limits of such an area shall consist of a pattern of lines of the size and type shown in the diagram in Part II of this Schedule and so placed as hereinafter provided.

2. A pattern of lines shall, subject as hereinafter provided, consist of:—

(*a*) a transverse white broken line (hereinafter referred to as a 'give-way line') placed on the carriageway 1 metre from and parallel to the nearer line of studs indicating the limits of the crossing and shall extend across the carriageway in the manner indicated in the said diagram; and

(*b*) two or more longitudinal white broken lines (hereinafter referred to as 'zig-zag lines') placed on the carriageway or, where the road is a dual-carriageway road, on each part of the carriageway, each zig-zag line containing not less than 8 nor more than 18 marks and extending away from the crossing at a point 150 millimetres from the nearest part of the give-way line on the same side of the crossing to a point 150 millimetres from the nearest part of a terminal line of the size and type shown in the said diagram (hereinafter referred to as a 'terminal line').

3. Where the appropriate authority is satisfied in relation to a particular area of carriageway in the vicinity of a zebra crossing that by reason of the layout of, or character of, the roads in the vicinity of the crossing it would be impracticable to lay the pattern of lines as shown in the diagram in Part II of this Schedule and in accordance with the preceding paragraph any of the following variations as respects the pattern shall be permitted—

(*a*) the number of marks contained in each zig-zag line may be reduced from 8 to not less than 2;

(*b*) a mark contained in a zig-zag line may be varied in length so as to extend for a distance not less than 1 metre and less than 2 metres, but where such a variation is made as respects a mark each other mark in each zig-zag line shall be of the same or substantially the same length as that mark, so however that the number of marks in each zig-zag line shall not be more than 8 nor less than 2.

4. The angle of the give-way line (if any) in relation to and its distance from the nearer line of studs indicating the limits of a crossing may be varied, if the appropriate authority is satisfied that such variation is necessary having regard to the angle of the crossing in relation to the edge of the carriageway at the place where the crossing is situated.

5. Where by reason of Regulation 5(3) an area of carriageway in the vicinity of a zebra crossing is not constituted a zebra controlled area by the placing of a pattern of lines as provided in the foregoing provisions of this Schedule, a give-way line shall nevertheless be placed on the carriageway as previously provided in this Schedule unless the appropriate authority is satisfied that by reason of the position of that crossing it is impracticable so to place the line.

6. Each mark contained in a give-way line or in a zig-zag line and each terminal line may be illuminated by the use of reflecting material.

7. A zebra controlled area or its limits shall not be deemed to have ceased to be indicated in accordance with the provisions of this Schedule by reason only of the imperfection, discoloration or partial displacement of either a terminal line or one or more of the marks comprised in a give-way line or a zig-zag line, so long as the general indication of any such line is not thereby materially impaired.

Section C

European Community Regulations

Regulation 117/66/EEC
of 28 July 1966

on the introduction of common rules for the international carriage of passengers by coach and bus

[The text of this Regulation is printed as amended by:
Regulation (EEC) 517/72 (OJ L 67, 20 March 1972, p 19 (S Edn 1972 (I), p 143)).
As to the date on which the amendments take effect, see the note to art 1.]

Note. Various provisions of this Regulation have been incorporated by reference into the Road Transport (International Passenger Services) Regulations 1984 (SI 1984 No 748) (*qv*).

THE COUNCIL OF THE EUROPEAN ECONOMIC COMMUNITY,

Having regard to the Treaty establishing the European Economic Community, and in particular Article 75 thereof;

Having regard to the proposal from the Commission;

Having regard to the Opinion of the European Parliament;

Having regard to the Opinion of the Economic and Social Committee;

Whereas the adoption of a common transport policy requires that common rules be laid down for the international carriage of passengers by road;

Whereas such rules can only be laid down on the basis of standard definitions of the various types of passenger transport service;

Whereas the lapse of a period of time to allow the necessary work to be carried out would facilitate the adoption and application of common rules for regular services and shuttle services; whereas, in any case, it would appear necessary to fix in this Regulation the date for the drawing up of those rules;

Whereas the application of common rules for occasional services cannot create difficulties for that type of transport service; whereas liberalisation measures for closed door tours and for occasional services operated 'outward laden/return unladen' can easily be applied forthwith; whereas, in respect of certain occasional services operated 'outward unladen/ return laden', liberalisation measures can also be applied without difficulty in the near future;

Whereas the liberalisation of certain transport services operated by undertakings for their own workers would not appear to create any difficulties in the transport market; whereas it is therefore possible to relax the rules applicable to such services by substituting for the system of authorisation a system of certification subject to the fulfilment of specific conditions;

Whereas, as soon as common rules for regular services and shuttle services have been laid down, it will be possible to adopt common rules, with a view to extending the measures provided for in this Regulation to international carriage of passengers by road to or from a third country:

Whereas traffic between the Member States of the Community would be facilitated by simplifying the control formalities for occasional services and harmonising administrative procedures; whereas for this purpose a single control document should be introduced, replacing the existing documents;

HAS ADOPTED THIS REGULATION:

SECTION I

Definitions and Scope

Article 1

1. Regular services are services which provide for the carriage of passenagers at specified intervals along specified routes, passengers being taken up and set down at predetermined stopping points.

2. *Rules governing the operation of services or documents taking the place thereof, approved by the competent authorities of Member States and published by the carrier before coming into operation, shall specify the conditions of carriage and in particular the frequency of services, timetables and the obligation to accept passengers for carriage, in so far as such conditions are not prescribed by any law or regulation.*

3. Services, by whomsoever organised, which provide for the carriage of specified categories of passengers to the exclusion of other passengers, in so far as such services are operated under the conditions specified in paragraph 1, shall be deemed to be regular services. Such services, in particular those providing for the carriage of workers to and from their place of work or of schoolchildren to and from school, are hereinafter called 'special regular services'.

The fact that a service may be varied according to the needs of those concerned shall not affect its classification as a regular service.

[Article 1(2) has been prospectively repealed by Regulation (EEC) 517/72, art 5(2). The repeal will take effect on the entry into force of model rules adopted by the EC Council under ibid, art 5(1).]

Article 2

1. Shuttle services are services whereby, by means of repeated outward and return journeys, previously formed groups of passengers are carried from a single place of departure to a single destination. Each group of passengers who have made the outward journey together shall subsequently be carried back to the place of departure.

Place of departure and destination mean respectively the place where the journey begins and the place where the journey ends, together with, in each case, the surrounding locality.

2. Passengers shall not be taken up or down during the journey.

3. The first return journey and the last outward journey shall be made unladen.

4. The following shall be defined under the provisions of Article 8:

— the conditions under which certain passengers may be authorised, by way of exception to paragraph 1, to make the return journey with another group;

— the conditions under which exceptions to the provisions of paragraph 2 may be authorised;

— the conditions under which exceptions to the provisions of paragraph 3 may be authorised;

— the authorities competent to authorise these exceptions.

Article 3

1. Occasional services are services falling neither within the definition of a regular service in Article 1, nor within the definition of a shuttle service in Article 2. They include:

(*a*) closed-door tours, that is to say services whereby the same vehicle is used to carry the same group of passengers throughout the journey and to bring them back to the place of departure;

(*b*) services which make the outward journey carrying passengers and the return journey unladen;

(*c*) all other services.

2. Save for exceptions authorised by the competent authorities of the Member State concerned, occasional services shall not take up or set down passengers during the journey. Such services may be operated with some degree of frequency without thereby ceasing to be occasional services.

Article 4

1. The provisions of this Regulation shall apply to international carriage of passengers by road where:

— the place of departure is in the territory of a Member State and the destination is in the territory of the same or another Member State;

— the vehicles used are registered in a Member State and in construction and equipment are suitable for carrying more than 9 persons, including the driver, and are intended for that purpose.

2. The Community shall enter into any negotiations with third countries which may be found necessary for the purpose of implementing this Regulation.

3. When the common rules provided for in Articles 7 and 8 have been laid down, the Council shall, as soon as possible and on a proposal from the Commission, lay down the common rules necessary in order to enable application of this Regulation to be extended to international carriage of passengers by road to or from third countries.

SECTION II

Common Rules

Article 5

1. From 1 January 1967 the occasional services referred to in Article 3(1)(*a*) and (*b*) shall not require authorisation by any Member State other than the State where the vehicle is registered.

2. From 1 January 1969 the occasional services referred to in Article 3(1)(*c*) shall not require authorisation by any Member State other than the State where the vehicle is registered, provided that:

— the outward journey is made unladen and all the passengers are taken up in the same place; and

— the passengers:

(*a*) constitute groups formed under contracts of carriage made before their arrival in the country where they are to be taken up; or

(*b*) have been previously brought by the same carrier, in the circumstances provided for in Article 3(1)(*b*), into the country where such passengers are again taken up, and such passengers are carried out of that country; or

(*c*) have been invited to travel to another Member State, the cost of transport being borne by the person issuing the invitation. Such passengers shall constitute a single group, which shall not have been formed solely with a view to undertaking that particular journey.

3. Where, in the case of occasional services falling within Article 3(1)(*c*), the conditions laid down in paragraph 2 of this Article are not satisfied, Member States may make such services subject to authorisation:

4. The provisions of this Article shall not be applied in so far as existing rules made under bilateral or multilateral arrangements between Member States provide for more liberal treatment.

Article 6

1. From 1 January 1967 road services operated by an undertaking for its own workers shall not require authorisation but shall be subject to a system of certification, provided that the following conditions are fulfilled:

(*a*) passengers must be carried in vehicles which are owned by the undertaking or which have been obtained by it on deferred terms and which are driven by its own employees;

(*b*) the purpose of such services must be:
- — to carry workers to and from their place of work;
- — to carry workers between the various places of work of the undertaking.

2. The certificates provided for in paragraph 1 shall be issued by the competent authority of the Member State where the vehicle is registered and shall be valid for the whole of the journey, including any transit section. The certificates shall conform to a model to be prescribed by the Commission by reguation after consulting the Member States.

Article 7

Before 1 January 1968 the Council shall, in accordance with the provisions of Article 75 of the Treaty, lay down common rules for regular services.

Article 8

Before 1 January 1968 the Council shall, in accordance with the provisions of Article 75 of the Treaty, lay down common rules for shuttle services.

SECTION III

Control Procedures and Penalties

Article 9

1. Carriers operating occasional services within the meaning of Article 3 of this Regulation shall, whenever required to do so by any authorised inspecting officer produce a control document supplied by the competent authorities of the Member State where the vehicle is registered or by any duly authorised agency. This document, made out in the name of the carrier, must be completed by the latter for each journey.

The Commission shall, after consulting the Member States, prescribe the model for the control document and the way in which the control document is to be used.

2. Without prejudice to the provisions of Article 11, this control document shall replace existing control documents.

Article 10

Member States shall, within a reasonable time and after consulting the Commission, adopt such laws, regulations or administrative provisions as may be necessary for the implementation of this Regulation.

Such measures, shall cover, inter alia, the organisation of, procedure for and means of control, and the penalties for any breach.

SECTION IV

Final Provisions

Article 11

Article 5 of this Regulation shall not affect the conditions imposed by Member States on their own nationals engaged in the operations referred to in that Article.

This Regulation shall be binding in its entirety and directly applicable in all Member States.

Regulation (EEC) 543/69 of the Council
of 25 March 1969

on the harmonisation of certain social legislation relating to road transport

[The text of the provisions of this Regulation which are reproduced is printed as amended by:
Regulation (EEC) 514/72 (OJ L 67/1, 20 March 1972, p 124) (28 February 1972);
Regulation (EEC) 515/72 (OJ L 67/11, 20 March 1972, p 134) (28 February 1972); and
Regulation (EEC) 2827/77 (OJ L 334, 24 December 1977, p 1) (1 January 1978).
The dates referred to above are the dates on which the Regulations took effect.

The main Regulation was also amended by Regulation (EEC) 2829/77, but this Regulation did not amend any provision of the main Regulation which is reproduced.]

Note. Regulation (EEC) 543/69, as amended, has been repealed by Regulation (EEC) 3820/85, art 18(1) (*qv*). However, arts 4 and 15 of Regulation 543/69 continue to apply in particular circumstances until 31 December 1989 and are reproduced below together with the appropriate ancillary provisions of that Regulation.

THE COUNCIL OF THE EUROPEAN COMMUNITIES,

Having regard to the Treaty establishing the European Economic Community, and in particular Article 75 thereof;

Having regard to the Council Decision of 13 May 1965 *[OJ No 88, 24.5.1965, p 1500/65]* on the harmonisation of certain provisions affecting competition in transport by rail, road and inland waterway, and in particular Section III thereof;

Having regard to the proposal from the Commission;

Having regard to the Opinion of the European Parliament;

Having regard to the Opinion of the Economic and Social Committee;

Whereas, in the case of road transport, it is a matter of some urgency to bring into operation the social legislation referred to in the above-mentioned Decision; whereas it is also desirable to take account as far as possible of the needs deriving from the prescribed approximation of such provisions as between the three modes of transport;

Whereas for this purpose priority should be given to necessary measures which deal with manning, driving time and rest periods;

Whereas the provisions of the Regulation dealing with working conditions cannot be allowed to prejudice the right of the two sides of industry to lay down, by collective bargaining or otherwise, provisions more favourable to workers; whereas, in order not only to promote social progress but also to improve road safety, each Member State must retain the right to adopt certain appropriate measures; whereas, accordingly, the Commission must keep the development of the situation in Member States under review and submit reports thereon to the Council at regular intervals so that any adaptation of the Regulation to the developments thus noted may be effected;

Whereas provision must be made for this Regulation to be applied uniformly to all carriage in vehicles circulating within the territory of Member States, whether such vehicles are registered in a Member State or in a third country;

Whereas certain transport operations may be exempted from the application of this Regulation;

Whereas it is desirable to lay down provisions concerning the minimum ages for drivers engaged in the carriage of goods or of passengers—bearing in mind here certain vocational training requirements—and concerning also the minimum age for drivers' mates and conductors;

Whereas for journeys exceeding a certain distance and for certain vehicles, it is necessary to lay down manning requirements; whereas it is desirable that undertakings should be left free to choose between arranging for the presence of two drivers on board the vehicle and arranging for relief drivers;

Whereas, with regard to driving periods, it is desirable to set limits on continuous driving time and on daily driving time, but without prejudice to any national rules whereby drivers are prohibited from driving for longer than they can with complete safety;

Whereas, with regard to driving periods, it is nevertheless desirable to provide that the requirements laid down in the Regulation be brought into operation only by stages whereas for this purpose there must be transitional provisions, laying down the rules to be applied during an initial two-year stage; where it is nevertheless desirable, for reasons of road safety and other reasons, to provide that, from the entry into force of this Regulation, more restrictive provisions should be applied to certain long and heavy vehicles;

Whereas, with regard to rest periods, it is desirable to lay down the minimum duration of and other conditions governing the daily and weekly rest periods of crew members;

Whereas it is desirable, in order to make it possible to check that the provisions of this Regulation are being observed, that each member of the crew be required to have an individual control book; whereas, however, in the case of crews of vehicles used for regular services, a copy of the timetable and an extract from the undertaking's duty roster may replace the individual control book;

Whereas it is desirable to provide for the replacement, wherever possible, of the individual control book by mechanical recording equipment; whereas, for this purpose, it is desirable that the technical characteristics and the methods of using such equipment should be settled at Community level within a set time limit;

Whereas, in order that this Regulation may be applied and that compliance therewith may be checked, it is appropriate for Member States to give each other assistance;

Whereas it is desirable, in order to enable undertakings to adjust their operations so as to conform to the provisions of this Regulation, that during an initial phase such provisions should apply only to international transport between Member States and that their application should be extended in a second phase to all the transport operations referred to in this Regulation.

HAS ADOPTED THIS REGULATION:

SECTION I

Definitions

Article 1

In this Regulation:

1. 'carriage by road' means any journey by road of a vehicle, whether laden or not, used for the carriage of passengers or goods;

2. 'vehicles' means motor vehicles, tractors, trailers and semi-trailers, defined as follows:

(*a*) 'motor vehicle': any mechanically self-propelled vehicle circulating on the road, other than a vehicle running on rails, and normally used for carrying passengers or goods;

(*b*) 'tractor': any mechanically self-propelled vehicle circulating on the road, other than a vehicle running on rails, and specially designed to pull, push or move trailers, semi-trailers, implements or machines;

(*c*) 'trailer'; any vehicle designed to be coupled to a motor vehicle or tractor;

(*d*) 'semi-trailer': a trailer without a front axle coupled in such a way that a substantial part of its weight and of the weight of its load is borne by the tractor or motor vehicle;

3. 'crew member' means the driver, driver's mate, and conductor, defined as follows:

(*a*) 'driver': any person who drives the vehicle even for a short period, or who is carried in the vehicle in order to be available for driving if necessary;

(*b*) 'driver's mate': any person accompanying the driver of a vehicle in order to assist him in certain manoeuvres and habitually taking an effective part in the transport operations, but not being a driver within the meaning of (*a*);

(*c*) 'conductor': any person who accompanies the driver of a vehicle used for the carriage of passengers and has the particular duty of issuing and checking tickets;

4. 'week' means any period of seven consecutive days;

5. 'daily rest period' means any uninterrupted period of at least eight hours during which the crew members may freely dispose of their time and are entirely free to move about as they please;

6. (*a*) 'regular goods services' means transport services operated at specified intervals along specified routes, goods being loaded and unloaded at predetermined stopping points;

(*b*) 'regular passenger services' means the services defined in Article 1 of Regulation (EEC) No 117/66 *[qv]*;

7. 'permissible maximum weight' means the maximum authorised operating weight of the vehicle fully laden.

[Article 1 has been repealed by Regulation (EEC) 3820/85, art 18(1) (qv). The text of art 1 is reproduced, however, as it is needed for the interpretation of arts 4 and 15 of this Regulation which are continued in operation for limited purposes until 31 December 1989.]

SECTION II

Scope

* * *

Article 4

This Regulation shall not apply to carriage by:

1. vehicles which in construction and equipment are suitable for carrying not more than nine persons including the driver and are intended for that purpose;

2. vehicles used for the carriage of goods, the permissible maximum weight of which, including any trailer or semi-trailer, does not exceed 3·5 metric tons;

3. vehicles used for the carriage of passengers on regular services where the route covered by the service in question does not exceed 50 km;

[4. vehicles used by the police, gendarmerie, armed forces, fire brigades, civil defence, drainage or flood prevention authorities, water, gas or electricity services, highway authorities and refuse collection, telegraph or telephone services, by the postal authorities for the carriage of mail, by radio or television services or for the detection of radio or television transmitters or receivers, or vehicles which are used by other public authorities for public services and which are not in competition with professional road hauliers;

5. vehicles used for the carriage of sick or injured persons and for carrying rescue material, and any other specialized vehicles used for medical purposes;]

6. tractors with a maximum authorised speed not exceeding 30 kilometres per hour;

[7. tractors and other machines used exclusively for local agricultural and forestry work;

8. vehicles used to transport circus and fun-fair equipment;

9. specialized breakdown vehicles.]

[Article 4 is continued in force until 31 December 1989 for the purposes specified in Regulation (EEC) 3820/85, art 18(2), (qv).
Article 4 is printed as amended by Regulation (EEC) 515/72 and Regulation (EEC) 2827/77.]

* * *

SECTION VII

Control Procedures and Penalties

Article 14

1. *[Omitted.]*

2. Members of the crew shall from day to day enter in the daily sheets of the individual control book details of the following periods:

(*a*) under the symbol [bed symbol] : daily rest periods;

(*b*) under the symbol [chair symbol] : breaks from work of not less than fifteen minutes;

(*c*) under the symbol [steering wheel symbol] : driving periods;

(*d*) under the symbol ☐ : other periods of attendance at work.

3. Each Member State may prescribe, in respect of individual control books issued in its territory, that the periods covered by paragraph 2(*d*) should be subdivided so as to show separately:

(*a*) under the symbol ☒ :

— waiting time, that is to say the period during which crew members must be at their place of work only for the purpose of answering any calls to carry out or resume any of the duties covered by paragraph 2(*c*) or by subparagraph (*b*) of this paragraph;
— time spent beside the driver while the vehicle is on the move;
— time spent on a bunk while the vehicle is on the move;

(*b*) under the symbol ⚒ : all other working periods.

4–9. *[Omitted.]*

[Article 14 has been repealed by Regulation (EEC) 3820/85, art 18(1) (qv). The text of art 14(2) and (3) is incorporated by reference into art 15 of this Regulation which is continued in operation for limited purposes until 31 December 1989.
Article 14 is printed as amended by Regulation (EEC) 514/72 and Regulation (EEC) 515/72.]

* * *

Article 15

1. All operators of regular services shall draw up a service timetable and a duty roster.

2. The duty roster shall show, in respect of each crew member, the name, date of birth, place where based and the schedule, which shall have been laid down in advance, for the various periods of time covered by Article 14(2) and (3).

3. The duty roster shall include all the particulars specified in paragraph 2 for a minimum period covering both the current week and the weeks immediately preceding and following that week.

4. The duty roster shall be signed by the head of the undertaking or by a person authorised to represent him.

5. Each crew member assigned to a regular service shall carry an extract from the duty roster and a copy of the service timetable.

[Article 15 is continued in force until 31 December 1989 for the purposes specified in Regulation (EEC) 3820/85, art 18(2) (qv).]

* * *

Regulation (EEC) 1463/70 of the Council
of 20 July 1970

on the introduction of recording equipment in road transport

[The text of the provisions of this Regulation which are reproduced is printed as amended by:
Regulation (EEC) 2828/77 (OJ L 334, 24 December 1977, p 5) (1 January 1978).
The date referred to above is the date on which the Regulation took effect.
The main Regulation was also corrected in accordance with a corrigendum which was published at OJ L 110, 27 April 1973, p 39, and amended by Regulation (EEC) 1787/73; but neither the correction nor the amendment affected any provision of the main Regulation which is reproduced.]

Note. Regulation (EEC) 1463/70, as amended, has been repealed by Regulation (EEC) 3821/85, art 29 (*qv*). However, art 3(1) of Regulation 1463/70 continues to apply in particular circumstances until 31 December 1989 and is reproduced below together with the appropriate ancillary provisions of that Regulation.

THE COUNCIL OF THE EUROPEAN COMMUNITIES,

Having regard to the Treaty establishing the European Economic Community, and in particular Article 75 thereof;

Having regard to Council Regulation (EEC) No 543/69 of 25 March 1969 on the harmonisation of certain social legislation relating to road transport, and in particular Article 16 thereof;

Having regard to the proposal from the Commission;

Having regard to the Opinion of the European Parliament;

Having regard to the Opinion of the Economic and Social Committee;

Whereas Article 16 of Regulation (EEC) No 543/69 provides for the determination of the technical characteristics of recording equipment to replace as far as possible the individual control book and for the determination at the same time of the details concerning the approval, use and testing of such equipment and the dates from which vehicles are to be fitted with such equipment;

Whereas in the current state of technical knowledge it is possible to envisage the development and production of types of recording equipment capable of replacing entirely the individual control book while ensuring that an effective check is kept on all periods of time referred to in Regulation (EEC) No 543/69 concerning the activities and rest of the crews of vehicles;

Whereas a certain period of time will be needed to develop and produce recording equipment and to set up the services necessary for the installation, repair and testing of such equipment; whereas it is furthermore appropriate to provide for installation to be staggered over a certain period of time in order to maintain stability on the market, while giving priority to installation in vehicles which enter into service for the first time on or after a certain date and to installation in vehicles used for the carriage of dangerous goods;

Whereas the obligation to introduce such recording equipment can be imposed only for vehicles registered in Member States; whereas furthermore certain of such vehicles may, without giving rise to difficulty, be excluded from the scope of this Regulation;

Whereas, in order to ensure effective checking, the equipment must be reliable in operation, easy to use and designed in such a way as to minimise any possibility of fraudulent use; whereas to this end recording equipment should in particular be capable of providing, on separate sheets for each crew member and in a sufficiently precise and easily readable form, recorded details of the various periods of time;

Whereas automatic recording of other details of a vehicle's journey, such as speed and distance covered, will contribute significantly to road safety and will encourage sensible driving of the vehicle; whereas, consequently, it appears appropriate to provide for the equipment also to record those details;

Whereas, in certain Member States, there are as yet no rules concerning recording equipment in motor vehicles and whereas among the other Member States rules differ; whereas such omissions and differences are liable to hinder the free circulation of motor vehicles within the Community and to bring about distortions in the conditions of competition;

Whereas to remedy this situation it is necessary to lay down sufficiently detailed Community standards for construction and installation; whereas, in order to avoid any impediment to the registration of vehicles fitted with such recording equipment or any impediment to their entry into service or use, or to such equipment being used throughout the territory of the Member States, it is necessary to provide for an EEC approval procedure;

Whereas, in order to ensure that recording equipment functions reliably and correctly, it is advisable to lay down uniform requirements for the periodic checks and inspections to which the equipment is to be subject after installation;

Whereas, in order to achieve the aims hereinbefore mentioned of keeping a check on work and rest periods, it is necessary that employers and crew members be responsible for seeing that the equipment functions correctly and that they perform with due care the operations prescribed;

Whereas, in the interests of road safety and of keeping a more effective check on compliance with the provisions of Regulation (EEC) No 543/69 it is appropriate to lay down transitional provisions for the period preceding the compulsory introduction of recording equipment, so as to enable each Member State, in respect of vehicles registered in its territory, either to bring forward the dates specified in this Regulation for the installation of recording equipment complying with its terms, or to prescribe the use of recording equipment conforming to a type which has received national approval;

Whereas exercise by a Member State of the latter option is compatible with the measures provided for in Article 14(4) and (5) of Regulation (EEC) No 543/69; whereas, in the interests of economy, it is desirable to avoid replacing too soon recording equipment conforming to a type which has received national approval and, therefore, the date from which the vehicles concerned must be fitted with recording equipment complying with the terms of this Regulation should be deferred for a certain time;

HAS ADOPTED THIS REGULATION:

CHAPTER I

Principles and Scope

* * *

Article 2

For the purposes of this Regulation the definitions set out in Article 1 of Regulation (EEC) No 543/69 shall apply.

[Article 2 has been repealed by Regulation (EEC) 3821/85, art 20 (qv). The text of art 2 is reproduced, however, as it is needed for the interpretation of art 3(1) of this Regulation which is continued in operation for limited purposes until 31 December 1989.
For Regulation (EEC) 543/69, art 1, see above.]

Article 3

[1.] Recording equipment shall be installed and used in vehicles used for the carriage for passengers or goods by road and registered in a Member State, with the exception of the vehicles referred to in Article 4 of Regulation (EEC) No 543/69 and of vehicles used for the carriage of passengers on regular services where the route covered by the service in question exceeds 50 kilometres.

[2. However, after consulting the Commission, Member States may exempt from the application of this Regulation vehicles mentioned in Article 14a(2) of Regulation (EEC) No 543/69.]

[3. Member States may, after authorisation from the Commission, exempt from the application of this Regulation vehicles mentioned in Article 14a(3)(*a*) of Regulation (EEC) No 543/69.]

[Article 3(1) is continued in force until 31 December 1989 for the purposes specified in Regulation (EEC) 3821/85, art 20 (qv).
Article 3(1) is printed as amended by Regulation (EEC) 2828/77.]

* * *

Regulation (EEC) 3820/85
of 20 December 1985

on the harmonisation of certain social legislation relating to road transport

THE COUNCIL OF THE EUROPEAN COMMUNITIES,

Having regard to the Treaty establishing the European Economic Community, and in particular Article 75 thereof;

Having regard to the Council Decision of 13 May 1965 on the harmonisation of certain provisions affecting competition in transport by rail, road and inland waterway *[OJ No 88, 24 May 1965, p 1500/65]*, and in particular Section III thereof,

Having regard to the proposal from the Commission *[OJ C 100, 12 April 1984, p 3, OJ C 223, 3 September 1985, p 5]*,

Having regard to the opinion of the European Parliament *[OJ C 122, 20 May 1985, p 168]*,

Having regard to the opinion of the Economic and Social Committee *[OJ C 104, 25 April 1985, p 4, OJ C 303, 25 November 1985, p 29]*,

Whereas in the field of road transport, Community social legislation is set out in Regulation (EEC) No 543/69 *[OJ L 77, 29 March 1969, p 49]* as last amended by Regulation (EEC) No 2829/77 *[OJ L 334, 24 December 1977, p 1]*; whereas that legislation aims at the harmonisation of conditions of competition between methods of inland transport, especially with regard to the road sector and the improvement of working conditions and road safety; whereas progress made in these fields must be safeguarded and extended; whereas, however, it is necessary to make the provisions of the said Regulation more flexible without undermining their objectives;

Whereas, taking into account the amendments set out hereinafter, in order to clarify matters, all the relevant provisions should be brought together in a single text, and in consequence thereof, Regulation (EEC) No 543/69 should be repealed; whereas, however, the exemptions set out in Article 4 for certain vehicles and the provisions of Article 15 for certain passenger transport operations should be maintained in force for a certain time;

Whereas the provisions of this Regulation dealing with working conditions cannot be allowed to prejudice the right of the two sides of industry to lay down, by collective bargaining or otherwise, provisions more favourable to workers; whereas, in order not only to promote social progress but also to improve road safety, each Member State must retain the right to adopt certain appropriate measures;

Whereas in view of the fall in the number of drivers' mates and conductors it is no longer necessary to regulate the rest periods of crew members other than the driver;

Whereas the replacement of the flexible week by a fixed week would make it easier for drivers to organize their work and improve checking;

Whereas a system should be defined to apply to international road transport operations to or from a third country or between two countries in transit through the territory of a Member State; whereas the provisions of the European Agreement concerning the Work of Crews of Vehicles engaged in International Road Transport (AETR) *[qv]* of 1 July 1970 should apply to those transport operations; whereas in the case of vehicles registered in a State which is not a Contracting Party to AETR, those provisions will only apply to that part of the journey effected within the Community;

Whereas, since the subject matter of the AETR Agreement falls within the scope of this Regulation, the power to negotiate and conclude the Agreement lies with the Community; whereas, however, the particular circumstances in which the AETR negotiations took place warrant, by way of exception, a procedure whereby the Member States of the Community individually deposit the instruments of ratification or accession in a concerted action but nonetheless act in the interest and on behalf of the Community;

Whereas, in order to ensure the supremacy of Community law in intra-Community transport, Member States should enter a reservation when depositing their instruments of ratification or accession whereby international transport operations between Member States are not to be regarded as international transport operations within the meaning of the Agreement;

Whereas the possibilities provided for in the Agreement itself for bilateral agreements between Contracting Parties derogating from the said Agreement as regards frontier zone and transit transport operations are a matter which in principle fall within the competence of the Community;

Whereas, if an amendment to the internal Community rules in the field in question necessitates a corresponding agreement to the Agreement, the Member States will act jointly to obtain such an amendment to the Agreement in accordance with the procedure laid down therein;

Whereas certain transport operations may be exempted from the application of this Regulation;

Whereas it is desirable to amplify and clarify certain definitions and to bring up to date certain provisions, in particular concerning the exceptions for certain categories of vehicles;

Whereas it is desirable to lay down provisions concerning the minimum ages for drivers engaged in the carriage of goods or of passengers—bearing in mind here certain vocational training requirements—and concerning also the minimum age for drivers' mates and conductors; whereas for the purposes of vocational training, Member States must be able to reduce the approved minimum age for drivers' mates to 16 years;

Whereas, with regard to driving periods, it is desirable to set limits on continuous driving time and on daily driving time, but without prejudice to any national rules whereby drivers are prohibited from driving for longer than they can with complete safety;

Whereas a longer driving day, together with a shorter driving time over a two-week period is likely to facilitate the management of transport undertakings and to contribute to social progress;

Whereas the provisions on breaks in driving should be adjusted because of the longer daily driving time;

Whereas, with regard to rest periods, it is desirable to lay down the minimum duration of and other conditions governing the daily and weekly rest periods of crew members;

Whereas trips would be made easier if the driver were able to split up his daily rest period, in particular to avoid his having to take a meal and lodging in the same place;

Whereas it is beneficial to social progress and to road safety to lengthen weekly rest periods, while enabling these periods to be shortened, provided that the driver can compensate for parts of his rest period which have not been taken in a place of his choosing within a given time;

Whereas many road transport operations within the Community involve transport by ferryboat or by rail for part of the journey; whereas provisions regarding daily rest periods and breaks which are appropriate to such operations should therefore be provided for in the rules;

Whereas, in the interests of road safety, the payment of bonuses for distance travelled and/or tonnage carried which might endanger road safety must be prohibited;

Whereas it is desirable to provide that exceptions may be made from this Regulation for certain national transport operations with special characteristics; whereas in the event of exceptions Member States should ensure that the standard of social protection and road safety is not jeopardised;

Whereas it is justified, given the specific nature of passenger transport, to redefine the category of vehicles that the Member States may exempt from application of the Regulation in the field of national transport;

Whereas the Member States should be entitled, with the Commission's authorisation, to grant exceptions from the provisions of the Regulation in exceptional circumstances; whereas in urgent cases, it should be possible to grant these exceptions for a limited time without prior authorisation from the Commission;

Whereas in the case of drivers of vehicles used for regular passenger services, a copy of the timetable and an extract from the undertaking's duty roster may replace the recording equipment; whereas it would be useful for the application of this Regulation and the prevention of abuse, to have delivered to drivers who so request extracts from their duty rosters;

Whereas it is desirable, in the interest of effective control, that regular international passenger services, with the exception of certain border services should no longer be exempt from the obligation to install and use recording equipment;

Whereas it is desirable to emphasise the importance of and the need for compliance with this Regulation by employers and drivers;

Whereas the Commission should monitor the way the situation with Member States develops and submit to the Council and to the European Parliament a report on the application of the rules every two years;

Whereas, in order that this Regulation may be applied and that compliance therewith may be checked, it is appropriate for Member States to give each other assistance.

HAS ADOPTED THIS REGULATION:

SECTION I

Definitions

Article 1

In this Regulation:

1. 'carriage by road' means any journey made on roads open to the public of a vehicle, whether laden or not, used for the carriage of passengers or goods;

2. 'vehicles' means motor vehicles, tractors, trailers and semi-trailers, defined as follows:

(*a*) 'motor vehicle': any mechanically self-propelled vehicle circulating on the road, other than a vehicle running on rails, and normally used for carrying passengers or goods;

(*b*) 'tractor': any mechanically self-propelled vehicle circulating on the road, other than a vehicle running on rails, and specially designed to pull, push or move trailers, semi-trailers, implements or machines;

(*c*) 'trailer': any vehicle designed to be coupled to a motor vehicle or a tractor;

(*d*) 'semi-trailer': a trailer without a front axle coupled in such a way that a substantial part of its weight and of the weight of its load is borne by the tractor or motor vehicle;

3. 'driver' means any person who drives the vehicle even for a short period, or who is carried in the vehicle in order to be available for driving if necessary;

4. 'week' means the period between 00.00 hours on Monday and 24.00 hours on Sunday;

5. 'rest' means any uninterrupted period of at least one hour during which the driver may freely dispose of his time;

6. 'permissible maximum weight' means the maximum authorised operating weight of the vehicle fully laden;

7. 'regular passenger services' means national and international services as defined in Article 1 of Council Regulation No 117/66/EEC of 28 July 1966 on the introduction of common rules for the international carriage of passengers by coach and bus *[qv]*.

SECTION II

Scope

Article 2

1. This Regulation applies to carriage by road, as defined in Article 1(1), within the Community.

2. The European Agreement concerning the Work of Crews of Vehicles engaged in International Road Transport (AETR) [*qv*] shall apply instead of the present rules to international road transport operations;

— to and/or from third countries which are Contracting Parties to the Agreement, or in transit through such countries, for the whole of the journey where such operations are carried out by vehicles registered in a Member State or in one of the said third countries;

— to and/or from a third country which is not a Contracting Party to the Agreement in the case of any journey made within the Community where such operations are carried out by vehicles registered in one of those countries.

Article 3

The Community shall enter into any negotiations with third countries which may prove necessary for the purpose of implementing this Regulation.

Article 4

This Regulation shall not apply to carriage by:

1. vehicles used for the carriage of goods where the maximum permissible weight of the vehicle, including any trailer or semi-trailer, does not exceed 3.5 tonnes;

2. vehicles used for the carriage of passengers which, by virtue of their construction and equipment, are suitable for carrying not more than nine persons, including the driver, and are intended for that purpose;

3. vehicles used for the carriage of passengers on regular services where the route covered by the service in question does not exceed 50 kilometres;

4. vehicles with a maximum authorised speed not exceeding 30 kilometres per hour;

5. vehicles used by or under the control of the armed services, civil defence, fire services, and forces responsible for maintaining public order;

6. vehicles used in connection with the sewerage, flood protection, water, gas and electricity services, highway maintenance and control, refuse collection and disposal, telegraph and telephone services, carriage of postal articles, radio and television broadcasting and the detection of radio or television transmitters or receivers;

7. vehicles used in emergencies or rescue operations;

8. specialised vehicle used for medical purposes;

9. vehicles transporting circus and fun-fair equipment;

10. specialised breakdown vehicles;

11. vehicles undergoing road tests for technical development, repair or maintenance purposes, and new or rebuilt vehicles which have not yet been put into service;

12. vehicles used for non-commercial carriage of goods for personal use;

13. vehicles used for milk collection from farms and the return to farms of milk containers or milk products for animal feed.

SECTION III

Crew

Article 5

1. The minimum ages for drivers engaged in the carriage of goods shall be as follows:

(*a*) for vehicles, including, where appropriate, trailers or semi-trailers, having a permissible maximum weight of not more than 7.5 tonnes, 18 years;

(*b*) for other vehicles:

— 21 years, or

— 18 years provided that the person concerned holds a certificate of professional competence recognised by one of the Member States confirming that he has completed a training course for drivers of vehicles intended for the carriage of goods by road, in conformity with Community rules on the minimum level of training for road transport drivers.

2. Any driver engaged in the carriage of passengers shall have reached the age of 21 years.

Any driver engaged in the carriage of passengers on journeys beyond a 50 kilometre radius from the place where the vehicle is normally based must also fulfil one of the following conditions:

(*a*) he must have worked for at least one year in the carriage of goods as a driver of vehicles with a permissible maximum weight exceeding 3.5 tonnes;

(*b*) he must have worked for at least one year as a driver of vehicles used to provide passenger services on journeys within a 50 kilometre radius from the place where the vehicle is normally based, or other types of passenger services not subject to this Regulation, provided the competent authority considers that he has by so doing acquired the necessary experience;

(*c*) he must hold a certificate of professional competence recognised by one of the Member States confirming that he has completed a training course for drivers of vehicles intended for the carriage of passengers by road, in conformity with Community rules on the minimum level of training for road transport drivers.

3. The minimum age for drivers' mates and conductors shall be 18 years.

4. A driver engaged in the carriage of passengers shall not be subject to the conditions laid down in paragraph 2, second paragraph, (*a*), (*b*) and (*c*) if he has carried on that occupation for at least one year prior to 1 October 1970.

5. In the case of internal transport operations carried out within a 50 kilometre radius of the place where the vehicle is based, including local administrative areas the centres of which are situated within that radius, Member States may reduce the minimum age for drivers' mates to 16 years, on condition that this is for purposes of vocational training and subject to the limits imposed by their national law in employment matters.

SECTION IV

Driving Periods

Article 6

1. The driving period between any two daily rest periods or between a daily rest period and a weekly rest period, hereinafter called 'daily driving period', shall not exceed nine hours. It may be extended twice in any one week to 10 hours.

A driver must, after no more than six daily driving periods, take a weekly rest period as defined in Article 8(3).

The weekly rest period may be postponed until the end of the sixth day if the total driving time over the six days does not exceed the maximum corresponding to six daily driving periods.

In the case of the international carriage of passengers, other than on regular services, the terms 'six' and 'sixth' in the second and third sub-paragraphs shall be replaced by 'twelve' and 'twelfth' respectively.

Member States may extend the application of the previous sub-paragraph to national passenger services within their territory, other than regular services.

2. The total period of driving in any one fortnight shall not exceed 90 hours.

[For the extension of the application of art 6(1) to national passenger services, see the Community Drivers' Hours and Recording Equipment (Exemptions and Supplementary Provisions) Regulations 1986 (SI 1986 No 1456), reg 3(1), above.]

SECTION V

Breaks and Rest Periods

Article 7

1. After four-and-a-half hours' driving, the driver shall observe a break of at least 45 minutes, unless he begins a rest period.

2. This break may be replaced by breaks of at least 15 minutes each distributed over the driving period or immediately after this period in such a way as to comply with the provisions of paragraph 1.

3. By way of exception from paragraph 1, in the case of national carriage of passengers on regular services Member States may fix the minimum break at not less than 30 minutes after a driving period not exceeding four hours. Such exceptions may be granted only in cases where breaks in driving over 30 minutes could hamper the flow of urban traffic and where it is not possible for drivers to take a 15-minute break within four-and-a-half hours of driving prior to a 30-minute break.

4. During these breaks, the driver may not carry out any other work. For the purposes of this Article, the waiting time and time not devoted to driving spent in a vehicle in motion, a ferry, or a train shall not be regarded as 'other work'.

5. The breaks observed under this Article may not be regarded as daily rest periods.

[For exceptions under national legislation in accordance with art 7(3), see the Community Drivers' Hours and Recording Equipment (Exemptions and Supplementary Provisions) Regulations 1986 (SI 1986 No 1456), reg 3(2), above.]

Article 8

1. In each period of 24 hours, the driver shall have a daily rest period of at least 11 consecutive hours, which may be reduced to a minimum of nine consecutive hours not more than three times in any one week, on condition that an equivalent period of rest be granted as compensation before the end of the following week.

On days when the rest is not reduced in accordance with the first sub-paragraph, it may be taken in two or three separate periods during the 24-hour period, one of which must be of at least eight consecutive hours. In this case the minimum length of the rest shall be increased to 12 hours.

2. During each period of 30 hours when a vehicle is manned by at least two drivers, each driver shall have a rest period of not less than eight consecutive hours.

3. In the course of each week, one of the rest periods referred to in paragraphs 1 and 2 shall be extended, by way of weekly rest, to a total of 45 consecutive hours. This rest period may be reduced to a minimum of 36 consecutive hours if taken at the place where the vehicle is normally based or where the driver is based, or to a minimum of 24 consecutive hours if taken elsewhere. Each reduction shall be compensated by an equivalent rest taken *en bloc* before the end of the third week following the week in question.

4. A weekly rest period which begins in one week and continues into the following week may be attached to either of these weeks.

5. In the case of the carriage of passengers to which Article 6(1), fourth or fifth sub-

paragraph applies, the weekly rest period may be postponed until the week following that in respect of which the rest is due and added on to that second week's weekly rest.

6. Any rest taken as compensation for the reduction of the daily and/or weekly rest periods must be attached to another rest of at least eight hours and shall be granted, at the request of the person concerned, at the vehicle's parking place or driver's base.

7. The daily rest period may be taken in a vehicle, as long as it is fitted with a bunk and is stationary.

Article 9

Notwithstanding Article 8(1) where a driver engaged in the carriage of goods or passengers accompanies a vehicle which is transported by ferryboat or train, the daily rest period may be interrupted not more than once, provided the following conditions are fulfilled:

— that part of the daily rest period spent on land must be able to be taken before or after the portion of the daily rest period taken on board the ferryboat or train,

— the period between the two portions of the daily rest period must be as short as possible and may on no account exceed one hour before embarkation or after disembarkation, customs formalities being included in the embarkation or disembarkation operations,

— during both portions of the rest period the driver must be able to have access to a bunk or couchette.

The daily rest period, interrupted in this way, shall be increased by two hours.

SECTION VI

Prohibition of Certain Types of Payment

Article 10

Payments to wage-earning drivers, even in the form of bonuses or wage supplements, related to distances travelled and/or the amount of goods carried shall be prohibited, unless these payments are of such a kind as not to endanger road safety.

SECTION VII

Exceptions

Article 11

Each Member may apply higher minima or lower maxima than those laid down in Articles 5 to 8 inclusive. Nevertheless, the provisions of this Regulation shall remain applicable to drivers engaged in international transport operations on vehicles registered in another Member State.

Article 12

Provided that road safety is not thereby jeopardised and to enable him to reach a suitable stopping place, the driver may depart from the provisions of this Regulation to the extent necessary to ensure the safety of persons, of the vehicle or of its load. The driver shall indicate the nature of and reason for his departure from those provisions on the record sheet of the recording equipment or in his duty roster.

Article 13

1. Each Member State may grant exceptions on its own territories or, with the agreement of the States concerned, on the territory of another Member State from any provision of this Regulation applicable to carriage by means of a vehicle belonging to one or more of the following categories:

(*a*) vehicles used for carrying passengers, which by virtue of their construction and equipment are suitable for carrying not more than 17 persons, including the driver, and are intended for that purpose;

(*b*) vehicles used by public authorities to provide public services which are not in competition with professional road hauliers;

(*c*) vehicles used by agricultural, horticultural, forestry or fishery undertakings for carrying goods within a 50 kilometre radius of the place where the vehicle is normally based, including local administrative areas the centres of which are situated within that radius;

(*d*) vehicles used for carrying animal waste or carcases which are not intended for human consumption;

(*e*) vehicles used for carrying live animals from farms to the local markets and vice versa or from markets to the local slaughterhouses;

(*f*) vehicles used as shops at local markets or for door-to-door selling, or used for mobile banking, exchange or saving transactions, for worship, for the lending of books, records or cassettes, for cultural events or exhibitions, and specially fitted for such uses;

(*g*) vehicles carrying material or equipment for the driver's use in the course of his work within a 50 kilometre radius of the place where the vehicle is normally based, provided that driving the vehicle does not constitute the driver's main activity and that the exception does not seriously prejudice the objectives of the Regulation. The Member States may make such exceptions subject to individual authorisation;

(*h*) vehicles operating exclusively on islands not exceeding 2,300 square kilometres in areas which are not linked to the rest of the national territory by a bridge, ford or tunnel open for use by motor vehicles;

(*i*) vehicles used for the carriage of goods and propelled by means of gas produced on the vehicle or of electricity or equipped with a governor in so far as such vehicles are regarded, under the legislation of the Member State of registration, as equivalent to vehicles propelled by a petrol or diesel engine, the maximum weight of which, including the weight of trailers or semi-trailers, does not exceed 3.5 tonnes;

(*j*) vehicles used for driving instruction with a view to obtaining a driving licence;

(*k*) tractors used exclusively for agricultural and forestry work.

Member States shall inform the Commission of the exceptions granted under this paragraph.

2. Member States may, after authorisation by the Commission, grant exceptions from the application of the provisions of this Regulation to transport operations carried out in exceptional circumstances, if such exceptions do not seriously jeopardise the objectives of the Regulation.

In urgent cases they may grant a temporary exception for a period not exceeding 30 days, which shall be notified immediately to the Commission.

The Commission shall notify the other Member States of any exception granted pursuant to this Regulation.

[For exemptions under national legislation in accordance with art 13(1), see the Community Drivers' Hours and Recording Equipment (Exemptions and Supplementary Provisions) Regulations 1986 (SI 1986 No 1456), reg 2 and Schedule, above.

Exemptions under national legislation in accordance with art 13(2) are likely to be of short duration. The Community Drivers' Hours (Passenger Vehicles) (Temporary Exemption) Regulations 1986 (SI 1986 No 1542), exempted any vehicle engaged in the national carriage of passengers on regular services from the application (other than art 5) of Regulation (EEC) 3820/85 from 29 September to 26 October 1986. The Community Drivers' Hours (Passenger and Goods Vehicles) (Temporary Exception) Regulations 1987 (SI 1987 No 27) provided (with effect from 17 January 1987) that Regulation 3820/85 should apply with the exception of arts 6, 8 and 9, until 16 February 1987 (reg 2 of the 1987 Regulations). The 1987 Regulations were revoked on 2 February by the Community Drivers' Hours (Passenger and Goods Vehicles) (Temporary Exception) (Revocation) Regulations 1987 (SI 1987 No 97), reg 2(1). Regulation 2(2) of the latter regulations provided that, on and after 2 February 1987, no account should be taken of any time spent driving or on duty before that date for the purpose of the application of art 6, art 8 or art 9 of Regulation 3820/85.]

SECTION VIII

Control Procedures and Penalties

Article 14

1. In the case of

— regular national passenger services, and

— regular international passenger services whose route terminals are located within a distance of 50 kilometres as the crow flies from a frontier between two Member States and whose route length does not exceed 100 kilometres;

which are subject to this Regulation, a service timetable and a duty roster shall be drawn up by the undertaking.

2. The duty roster shall show, in respect of each driver, the name, place where based and the schedule laid down in advance for various periods of driving, other work and availability.

3. The duty roster shall include all the particulars specified in paragraph 2 for a minimum period covering both the current week and the weeks immediately preceding and following that week.

4. The duty roster shall be signed by the head of the undertaking or by a person authorised to represent him.

5. Each driver assigned to a service referred to in paragraph 1 shall carry an extract from the duty roster and a copy of the service timetable.

6. The duty roster shall be kept by the undertaking for one year after expiry of the period covered. The undertaking shall give an extract from the roster to the drivers concerned who request it.

7. This Article shall not apply to the drivers of vehicles fitted with recording equipment used in accordance with the provisions of Council Regulation (EEC) No 3821/85 of 20 December 1985 on recording equipment in road transport *[qv]*.

Article 15

1. The transport undertaking shall organise drivers' work in such a way that drivers are able to comply with the relevant provisions of this Regulation and of Regulation (EEC) No 3821/85.

2. The undertaking shall make periodic checks to ensure that the provisions of these two Regulations have been complied with. If breaches are found to have occurred, the undertaking shall take appropriate steps to prevent their repetition.

Article 16

1. The Commission shall produce a report every two years on the implementation of this Regulation by Member States and developments in the fields in question. The Commission shall forward the report to the Council and the European Parliament within 13 months of expiry of the two-year period covered by the report.

2. To enable the Commission to draw up the report referred to in paragraph 1, Member States shall communicate the necessary information to the Commission every two years, using a standard form. This information must reach the Commission not later than 30 September following the date on which the two-year period covered by the report expires.

3. The Commission shall draw up the standard form after consulting the Member States.

Article 17

1. Member States shall, in due time and after consulting the Commission, adopt such laws, regulations or administrative provisions as may be necessary for the implementation of this Regulation.

Such measures shall cover, inter alia, the organisation of, procedure for and means of control and the penalties to be imposed in case of breach.

2. Member States shall assist each other in applying this Regulation and in checking compliance therewith.

3. Within the framework of this mutual assistance the competent authorities of the Member States shall regularly send one another all available information concerning:

— breaches of this Regulation committed by non-residents and any penalties imposed for such breaches;

— penalties imposed by a Member State on its residents for such breaches committed in other Member States.

SECTION IX

FINAL PROVISIONS

Article 18

1. Regulation (EEC) No 543/69 is hereby repealed.

However:

— Article 4 of the said Regulation shall, until 31 December 1989, continue to apply to vehicles used by public authorities for public services which do not compete with commercial transport undertakings and to tractors used solely for local agricultural and forestry work. A Member State may, nevertheless, provide that this Regulation will apply to such national transport operations within its territory from an earlier date.

— Article 15 of the said Regulation shall, until 31 December 1989, continue to apply to vehicles and drivers employed in regular international passenger services in so far as the vehicles used for such services are not fitted with recording equipment used as prescribed in Regulation (EEC) No 3821/85.

2. References to the Regulation repealed under paragraph 1 shall be construed as references to this Regulation.

Article 19

This Regulation shall enter into force on 29 September 1986.

This Regulation shall be binding in its entirety and directly applicable in all Member States.

Regulation (EEC) 3821/85
of 20 December 1985
on recording equipment in road transport

THE COUNCIL OF THE EUROPEAN COMMUNITIES,

Having regard to the Treaty establishing the European Economic Community, and in particular Article 75 thereof,

Having regard to the proposal from the Commission *[OJ C 100, 12 April 1984, p 3, OJ C 223, 3 September 1985, p 5]*,

Having regard to the opinion of the European Parliament *[OJ C 122, 20 May 1985, p 168]*,

Having regard to the opinion of the Economic and Social Committee *[OJ C 104, 25 April 1985, p 4, OJ C 303, 25 November 1985, p 29]*,

Whereas Regulation (EEC) No 1463/70 *[OJ L 164, 27 July 1970, p 1]* as last amended by Regulation (EEC) No 2828/77 *[OJ L 334, 24 December 1977, p 11]* introduced recording equipment in road transport;

Whereas, taking into account the amendments set out hereinafter, in order to clarify matters, all the relevant provisions should be brought together in a single text, and in consequence thereof, Regulation (EEC) No 1463/70 of the Council should be repealed; whereas, however, the exemptions set out in Article 3(1) for certain passenger services should be maintained in force for a certain time;

Whereas the use of recording equipment that may indicate the periods of time referred to in Regulation (EEC) No 3820/85 on the harmonisation of certain social legislation relating to road transport *[qv]* is intended to ensure effective checking on that social legislation;

Whereas the obligation to use such recording equipment can be imposed only for vehicles registered in Member States; whereas furthermore certain of such vehicles may, without giving rise to difficulty, be excluded from the scope of this Regulation;

Whereas the Member States should be entitled with the Commission's authorisation, to grant certain vehicles exemptions from the provisions of the Regulation in exceptional circumstances; whereas, in urgent cases, it should be possible to grant these exemptions for a limited time without prior authorisation from the Commission;

Whereas, in order to ensure effective checking, the equipment must be reliable in operation, easy to use and designed in such a way as to minimise any possibility of fraudulent use; whereas to this end recording equipment should in particular be capable of providing, on separate sheets for each driver and in a sufficiently precise and easily readable form, recorded details of the various periods of time;

Whereas automatic recording of other details of a vehicle's journey, such as speed and distance covered, will contribute significantly to road safety and will encourage sensible driving of the vehicle; whereas, consequently, it appears appropriate to provide for the equipment also to record those details;

Whereas it is necessary to set Community construction and installation standards for recording equipment and to provide for an EEC approval procedure, in order to avoid throughout the territory of the Member States any impediment to the registration of vehicles fitted with such recording equipment, to their entry into service or use, or to such equipment being used;

Whereas, in the event of differences of opinion between Member States concerning cases of EEC type approval, the Commission should be empowered to take a decision on a dispute within six months if the States concerned have been unable to reach a settlement;

Whereas it would be helpful in implementing this Regulation and preventing abuses to issue drivers who so request with a copy of their record sheets;

Whereas, in order to achieve the aims hereinbefore mentioned of keeping a check on work and rest periods, it is necessary that employers and drivers be responsible for seeing that the equipment functions correctly and that they perform with due care the operations described;

Whereas the provisions governing the number of records sheets that a driver must keep with him must be amended following the replacement of the flexible week by a fixed week;

Whereas technical progress necessitates rapid adaptation of the technical specifications set out in the Annexes to this Regulation; whereas, in order to facilitate the implementation of the measures necessary for this purpose, provision should be made for a procedure establishing close co-operation between the Member States and the Commission within an Advisory Committee;

Whereas Member States should exchange the available information on breaches established;

Whereas, in order to ensure that recording equipment functions reliably and correctly, it is advisable to lay down uniform requirements for the periodic checks and inspections to which the equipment is to be subject after installation,

HAS ADOPTED THIS REGULATION:

CHAPTER I

Principles and Scope

Article 1

Recording equipment within the meaning of this Regulation shall, as regards construction, installation, use and testing, comply with the requirements of this Regulation and of Annexes I and II thereto, which shall form an integral part of this Regulation.

Article 2

For the purposes of this Regulation the definitions set out in Article 1 of Regulation (EEC) No 3820/85 *[qv]* shall apply.

Article 3

1. Recording equipment shall be installed and used in vehicles registered in a Member State which are used for the carriage of passengers or goods by road, except the vehicles referred to in Articles 4 and 14(1) of Regulation (EEC) No 3820/85.

2. Member States may exempt vehicles mentioned in Article 13(1) of Regulation

(EEC) No 3820/85 from application of this Regulation. Member States shall inform the Commission of any exemption granted under this paragraph.

3. Member States may, after authorisation by the Commission, exempt from application of this Regulation vehicles used for the transport operations referred to in Article 13(2) of Regulation (EEC) No 3820/85. In urgent cases they may grant a temporary exemption for a period not exceeding 30 days, which shall be notified immediately to the Commission. The Commission shall notify the other Member States of any exemption granted pursuant to this paragraph.

4. In the case of national transport operations, Member States may require the installation and use of recording equipment in accordance with this Regulation in any of the vehicles for which its installation and use are not required by paragraph 1.

[For exemptions under national legislation in accordance with art 3(2), see the Community Drivers' Hours and Recording Equipment (Exemptions and Supplementary Provisions) Regulations 1986 (SI 1986 No 1456), reg 4 and Schedule, above.

For the extension under national legislation in accordance with art 3(4) of the application of Regulation (EEC) 3821/85 to vehicles used for the carriage of postal articles on national transport operations, see SI 1986 No 1456, reg 5, above.]

CHAPTER II

Type Approval

Article 4

Applications for EEC approval of a type of recording equipment or of a model record sheet shall be submitted, accompanied by the appropriate specifications, by the manufacturer or his agent to a Member State. No application in respect of any one type of recording equipment or of any one model record sheet may be submitted to more than one Member State.

Article 5

A Member State shall grant EEC approval to any type of recording equipment or to any model record sheet which conforms to the requirements laid down in Annex I to this Regulation, provided the Member State is in a position to check that production models conform to the approved prototype.

Any modifications or additions to an approved model must receive additional EEC type approval from the Member State which granted the original EEC type approval.

Article 6

Member States shall issue to the applicant an EEC approval mark, which shall conform to the model shown in Annex II, for each type of recording equipment or model record sheet which they approve pursuant to Article 5.

Article 7

The competent authorities of the Member State to which the application for type approval has been submitted shall, in respect of each type of recording equipment or model record sheet which they approve or refuse to approve, either send within one month to the authorities of the other Member States a copy of the approval certificate accompanied by copies of the relevant specifications, or, if such is the case, notify those authorities that approval has been refused; in cases of refusal they shall communicate the reasons for their decision.

Article 8

1. If a Member State which has granted EEC type approval as provided for in Article 5 finds that certain recording equipment or record sheets bearing the EEC type approval mark which it has issued do not conform to the prototype which it has approved, it shall take the necessary measures to ensure that production models conform to the approved prototype. The measures taken may, if necessary, extend to withdrawal of EEC type approval.

2. A Member State which has granted EEC type approval shall withdraw such approval if the recording equipment or record sheet which has been approved is not in conformity with this Regulation to its Annexes or displays in use any general defect which makes it unsuitable for the purpose for which it is intended.

3. If a Member State which has granted EEC type approval is notified by another Member State of one of the cases referred to in paragraphs 1 and 2, it shall also, after consulting the latter Member State, take the steps laid down in those paragraphs, subject to paragraph 5.

4. A Member State which ascertains that one of the cases referred to in paragraph 2 has arisen may forbid until further notice the placing on the market and putting into service of the recording equipment or record sheets. The same applies in the cases mentioned in paragraph 1 with respect to recording equipment or record sheets which have been exempted from EEC initial verification, if the manufacturer, after due warning, does not bring the equipment into line with the approved model or with the requirements of this Regulation.

In any event, the competent authorities of the Member States shall notify one another and the Commission, within one month, of any withdrawal of EEC type approval or of any other measures taken pursuant to paragraphs 1, 2 and 3 shall specify the reasons for such action.

5. If a Member State which has granted an EEC type approval disputes the existence of any of the cases specified in paragraphs 1 or 2 notified to it, the Member States concerned shall endeavour to settle the dispute and the Commission shall be kept informed.

If talks between the Member States have not resulted in agreement within four months of the date of the notification referred to in paragraph 3 above, the Commission, after consulting experts from all Member States and having considered all the relevant factors, eg economic and technical factors, shall within six months adopt a decision which shall be communicated to the Member States concerned and at the same time to the other Member States. The Commission shall lay down in each instance the time limit for implementation of its decision.

Article 9

1. An applicant for EEC type approval of a model record sheet shall state on his application the type or types of recording equipment on which the sheet in question is designed to be used and shall provide suitable equipment of such type or types for the purpose of testing the sheet.

2. The competent authorities of each Member State shall indicate on the approval certificate for the model record sheet the type or types of recording equipment on which that model sheet may be used.

Article 10

No Member State may refuse to register any vehicle fitted with recording equipment, or prohibit the entry into service or use of such vehicle for any reason connected with the fact that the vehicle is fitted with such equipment, if the equipment bears the EEC approval mark referred to in Article 6 and the installation plaque referred to in Article 12.

Article 11

All decisions pursuant to this Regulation refusing or withdrawing approval of a type of recording equipment or model record sheet shall specify in detail the reasons on which they are based. A decision shall be communicated to the party concerned, who shall at the same time be informed of the remedies available to him under the laws of the Member States and of the time-limits for the exercise of such remedies.

CHAPTER III

Installation and Inspection

Article 12

1. Recording equipment may be installed or repaired only by fitters or workshops approved by the competent authorities of Member States for that purpose after the latter, should they so desire, have heard the views of the manufacturers concerned.

2. The approved fitter or workshop shall place a special mark on the seals which it affixes. The competent authorities of each Member State shall maintain a register of the marks used.

3. The competent authorities of the Member States shall send each other their lists of approved fitters or workshops and also copies of the marks used.

4. For the purpose of certifying that installation of recording equipment took place in accordance with the requirements of this Regulation an installation plaque affixed as provided in Annex I shall be used.

CHAPTER IV

Use of Equipment

Article 13

The employer and drivers shall be responsible for seeing that the equipment functions correctly.

Article 14

1. The employer shall issue a sufficient number of record sheets to drivers, bearing in mind the fact that these sheets are personal in character, the length of the period of service and the possible obligation to replace sheets which are damaged, or have been taken by an authorised inspecting officer. The employer shall issue to drivers only sheets of an approved model suitable for use in the equipment installed in the vehicle.

2. The undertaking shall keep the record sheets in good order for at least a year after their use and shall give copies to the drivers concerned who request them. The sheets shall be produced or handed over at the request of any authorised inspecting officer.

Article 15

1. Drivers shall not use dirty or damaged record sheets. The sheets shall be adequately protected on this account.

In case of damage to a sheet bearing recordings, drivers shall attach the damaged sheet to the spare sheet used to replace it.

2. Drivers shall use the record sheets every day on which they are driving, starting from the moment they take over the vehicle. The record sheet shall not be withdrawn before the end of the daily working period unless its withdrawal is otherwise authorised. No record sheet may be used to cover a period longer than that for which it is intended.

When, as a result of being away from the vehicle, a driver is unable to use the equipment fitted to the vehicle, the periods of time indicated in paragraph 3, second indent (*b*), (*c*) and (*d*) below shall be entered on the sheet, either manually, by automatic recording or other means, legibly and without dirtying the sheet.

Drivers shall amend the record sheets as necessary should there be more than one driver on board the vehicle, so that the information referred to in Chapter II(1) to (3) of Annex I is recorded on the record sheet of the driver who is actually driving.

3. Drivers shall:

— ensure that the time recorded on the sheet agrees with the official time in the country of registration of the vehicle,

— operate the switch mechanisms enabling the following periods of time to be recorded separately and distinctly:

(*a*) under the sign [driving sign] : driving time;

(*b*) under the sign [work sign] : all other periods of work;

(*c*) under the sign [availability sign] : other periods of availability, namely:

— waiting time, ie the period during which drivers need remain at their posts only for the purpose of answering any calls to start or resume driving or to carry out other work,

— time spent beside the driver while the vehicle is in motion,

— time spent on a bunk while the vehicle is in motion;

(*d*) under the sign [rest sign] : breaks in work and daily rest periods.

4. Each Member State may permit all the periods referred to in paragraph 3, second indent (*b*) and (*c*) to be recorded under the sign [availability sign] on the record sheets used on vehicles registered in its territory.

5. Each crew member shall enter the following information on his record sheet:

(*a*) on beginning to use the sheet—his surname and first name;

(*b*) the date and place where use of the sheet begins and the date and place where such use ends;

(*c*) the registration number of each vehicle to which he is assigned, both at the start of the first journey recorded on the sheet and then, in the event of a change of vehicle, during the use of the sheet;

(*d*) the odometer reading:

— at the start of the first journey recorded on the sheet;
— at the end of the last journey recorded on the sheet;
— in the event of a change of vehicle during a working day (reading on the vehicle to which he was assigned and reading on the vehicle to which he is to be assigned);

(*e*) the time of any change of vehicle.

6. The equipment shall be so designed that it is possible for an authorised inspecting officer, if necessary after opening the equipment, to read the recordings relating to the nine hours preceding the time of the check without permanently deforming, damaging or soiling the sheet.

The equipment shall, furthermore, be so designed that it is possible, without opening the case, to verify that recordings are being made.

7. Whenever requested by an authorised officer to do so, the driver must be able to produce record sheets for the current week, and in any case for the last day of the previous week on which he drove.

Article 16

1. In the event of breakdown or faulty operation of the equipment, the employer shall have it repaired by an approved fitter or workshop, as soon as circumstances permit.

If the vehicle is unable to return to the premises within a period of one week calculated from the date of the breakdown or of the discovery of defective operation, the repair shall be carried out en route.

Measures taken by Member States pursuant to Article 19 may give the competent authorities power to prohibit the use of the vehicle in cases where breakdown or faulty operation has not been put right as provided in the foregoing subparagraphs.

2. While the equipment is unserviceable or operating defectively, drivers shall mark on the record sheet or sheets, or on a temporary sheet to be attached to the record sheet, all information for the various periods of time which is not recorded correctly by the equipment.

CHAPTER V

Final Provisions

Article 17

The amendments necessary to adapt the Annexes to technical progress shall be adopted in accordance with the procedure laid down in Article 18.

Article 18

1. A Committee for the adaptation of this Regulation to technical progress (hereinafter called 'the Committee') is hereby set up; it shall consist of representatives of the Member States, and a representative of the Commission shall be chairman.

2. The Committee shall adopt its own rules of procedure.

3. Where the procedure laid down in this Article is to be followed, the matter shall be referred to the Committee by the chiarman, either on his own initiative or at the request of the representative of a Member State.

4. The Commission representative shall submit to the Committee a draft of the measures to be taken. The Committee shall give its opinion on that draft within a

time limit set by the chairman having regard to the urgency of the matter. Opinions shall be delivered by a qualified majority in accordance with Article 148(2) of the Treaty. The chairman shall not vote.

5. (*a*) The Commission shall adopt the envisaged measures where they are in accordance with the opinion of the Committee.

(*b*) Where the measures envisaged are not in accordance with the opinion of the Committee or if no opinion is delivered, the Commission shall without delay submit to the Council a proposal on the measures to be taken. The Council shall act by a qualified majority.

(*c*) If the Council has not acted within three months of the proposal being submitted to it, the proposed measures shall be adopted by the Commission.

Article 19

1. Member States shall, in good time and after consulting the Commission, adopt such laws, regulations or administrative provisions as may be necessary for the implementation of this Regulation.

Such measures shall cover, inter alia, the re-organisation of, procedure for, and means of carrying out, checks on compliance and the penalties to be imposed in case of breach.

2. Member States shall assist each other in applying this Regulation and in checking compliance therewith.

3. Within the framework of this mutual assistance the competent authorities of the Member States shall regularly send one another all available information concerning:

— breaches of this Regulation committed by non-residents and any penalties imposed for such breaches,

— penalties imposed by a Member State on its residents for such breaches committed in other Member States.

Article 20

Regulation (EEC) No 1463/70 shall be repealed.

However, Article 3(1) of the said Regulation shall, until 31 December 1989, continue to apply to vehicles and drivers employed in regular international passenger services in so far as the vehicles used for such services are not fitted with recording equipment used as prescribed in this Regulation.

Article 21

This Regulation shall enter into force on 29 September 1986.

This Regulation shall be binding in its entirety and directly applicable in all Member States.

ANNEX I

Requirements for Construction, Testing, Installation and Inspection

I Definitions

In this Annex:

(a) Recording equipment means:

equipment intended for installation in road vehicles to show and record automatically or semi-automatically details of the movement of those vehicles and of certain working periods of their drivers;

(b) Record sheet means:
a sheet designed to accept and retain recorded data, to be placed in the recording equipment and on which the marking devices of the latter inscribe a continuous record of the information to be recorded;

(c) The constant of the recording equipment means:
the numerical characteristics giving the value of the input signal required to show and record a distance travelled of one kilometre; this constant must be expressed either in revolutions per kilometre (k = . . . rev/km), or in impulses per kilometre (k = . . . imp/km);

(d) Characteristic coefficient of the means:
the numerical characteristic giving the value of the output signal emitted by the part of the vehicle linking it with the recording equipment (gearbox output shaft or axle) while the vehicle travels a distance of one measured kilometre under normal test conditions (see Chapter VI, point 4 of this Annex). The characteristic coefficient is expressed either in revolutions per kilometre (w = . . . rev/km) or in impulses per kilometre (w = . . . imp/km);

(e) Effective circumference of wheel tyres means:
the average of the distances travelled by the several wheels moving the vehicle (driving wheels) in the course of one complete rotation. The measurement of these distances must be made under normal test conditions (see Chapter VI, point 4 of this Annex) and is expressed in the form: 1 = . . . mm.

II General Characteristics and Functions of Recording Equipment

The equipment must be able to record the following:

1. distance travelled by the vehicle;
2. speed of the vehicle;
3. driving time;
4. other periods of work or of availability;
5. breaks from work and daily rest periods;
6. opening of the case containing the record sheet.

For vehicles used by two drivers the equipment must be capable of recording simultaneously but distinctly and on two separate sheets details of the periods listed under 3, 4 and 5.

III Construction Requirements for Recording Equipment

(a) General points

1. *Recording equipment shall include the following*:

1.1. Visual instruments showing:
- distance travelled (distance recorder),
- speed (speedometer),
- time (clock).

1.2. Recording instruments comprising:
- a recorder of the distance travelled,

— a speed recorder,
— one or more time recorders satisfying the requirements laid down in Chapter III (c) 4.

1.3. A marking device showing on the record sheet each opening of the case containing that sheet.

2. Any inclusion in the equipment of devices additional to those listed above must not interfere with the proper operation of the mandatory devices or with the reading of them.

The equipment must be submitted for approval complete with any such additional devices.

3. *Materials*

3.1. All the constituent parts of the recording equipment must be made of materials with sufficient stability and mechanical strength and stable electrical and magnetic characteristics.

3.2. Any modification in a constituent part of the equipment or in the nature of the materials used for its manufacture must, before being applied in manufacture, be submitted for approval to the authority which granted type approval for the equipment.

4. *Measurement of distance travelled*

The distances travelled may be measured and recorded either:

— so as to include both forward and reverse movement; or
— so as to include only forward movement.

Any recording of reversing movements must on no account affect the clarity and accuracy of the other recordings.

5. *Measurement of speed*

5.1. The range of speed measurement shall be as stated in the type approval certificate.

5.2. The natural frequency and the damping of the measuring device must be such that the instruments showing and recording the speed can, within the range of measurement, follow acceleration changes of up to 2 m/s^2, within the limits of accepted tolerances.

6. *Measurement of time (clock)*

6.1. The control of the mechanism for resetting the clock must be located inside a case containing the record sheet; each opening of that case must be automatically recorded on the record sheet.

6.2. If the forward movement mechanism of the record sheet is controlled by the clock, the period during which the latter will run correctly after being fully wound must be greater by at least 10% than the recording period corresponding to the maximum sheet-load of the equipment.

7. *Lighting and protection*

7.1. The visual instruments of the equipment must be provided with adequate non-dazzling lighting.

7.2. For normal conditions of use, all the internal parts of the equipment must be protected against damp and dust. In addition they must be made proof against tampering by means of casings capable of being sealed.

(b) Visual instruments

1. *Distance travelled indicator (distance recorder)*

1.1. The value of the smallest grading on the instrument showing distance travelled must be 0.1 kilometres. Figures showing hectometres must be clearly distinguishable from those showing whole kilometres.

1.2. The figures on the distance recorder must be clearly legible and must have an apparent height of at least 4 mm.

1.3. The distance recorder must be capable of reading up to at least 99,999.9 kilometres.

2. *Speed indicators (speedometer)*

2.1. Within the range of measurement, the speed scale must be uniformly graduated by 1, 2, 5 or 10 kilometres per hour. The value of a speed graduation (space between two successive marks) must not exceed 10% of the maximum speed shown on the scale.

2.2. The range indicated beyond that measured need not be marked by figures.

2.3. The length of each space on the scale representing a speed difference of 10 kilometres per hour must not be less than 10 millimetres.

2.4. On an indicator with a needle, the distance between the needle and the instrument face must not exceed three millimetres.

3. *Time indicator (clock)*

The time indicator must be visible from outside the equipment and give a clear, plain and unambiguous reading.

(c) Recording instruments

1. *General points*

1.1. All equipment, whatever the form of the record sheet (strip or disc) must be provided with a mark enabling the record sheet to be inserted correctly, in such a way as to ensure that the time shown by the clock and the time-marking on the sheet correspond.

1.2. The mechanism moving the record sheet must be such as to ensure that the latter moves without play and can be freely inserted and removed.

1.3. For record sheets in disc form, the forward movement device must be controlled by the clock mechanism. In this case, the rotating movement of the sheet must be continuous and uniform, with a minimum speed of seven millimetres per hour measured at the inner border of the ring marking the edge of the speed recording area.

In equipment of the strip type, where the forward movement device of the sheets is controlled by the clock mechanism the speed of rectilinear forward movement must be at least 10 millimetres per hour.

1.4. Recording of the distance travelled, of the speed of the vehicle and of any opening of the case containing the record sheet or sheets must be automatic.

2. *Recording distance travelled*

2.1. Every kilometre of distance travelled must be represented on the record by a variation of at least one millimetre on the corresponding coordinate.

2.2. Even at speeds reaching the upper limit of the range of measurement, the record of distances must still be clearly legible.

3. *Recording speed*

3.1. Whatever the form of the record sheet, the speed recording stylus must normally move in a straight line and at right angles to the direction of travel of the record sheet.

However, the movement of the stylus may be curvilinear, provided the following conditions are satisfied:

— the trace drawn by the stylus must be perpendicular to the average circumference (in the case of sheets in disc form) or to the axis (in the case of sheets in strip from) of the area reserved for speed recording,

— the ratio between the radius of curvature of the trace drawn by the stylus and the width of the area reserved for speed recording must be not less than 2.4 to 1 whatever the form of the record sheet,

— the markings on the time-scale must cross the recording area in a curve of the same radius as the trace drawn by the stylus. The spaces between the markings on the time-scale must represent a period not exceeding one hour.

3.2. Each variation in speed of 10 kilometres per hour must be represented on the record by a variation of at least 1.5 millimetres on the corresponding coordinate.

4. *Recording time*

4.1. Recording equipment must be so constructed that it is possible, through the operation where necessary of a switch device, to record automatically and separately four periods of time as indicated in Article 15 of the Regulations.

4.2. It must be possible, from the characteristics of the traces, their relative positions and if necessary the signs laid down in Article 15 of the Regulation to distinguish clearly between the various periods of time.

The various periods of time should be differentiated from one another on the record by differences in the thickness of the relevant traces, or by any other system of at least equal effectiveness from the point of view of legibility and ease of interpretation of the record.

4.3. In the case of vehicles with a crew consisting of more than one driver, the recordings provided for in point 4.1 must be made on two separate sheets, each sheet being allocated to one driver. In this case, the forward movement of the separate sheets must be effected either by a single mechanism or by separate synchronised mechanisms.

(d) Closing device

1. The case containing the record sheet or sheets and the control of the mechanism for resetting the clock must be provided with a lock.

2. Each opening of the case containing the record sheet or sheets and the control of the mechanism for resetting the clock must be automatically recorded on the sheet or sheets.

(e) Markings

1. The following markings must appear on the instrument face of the equipment:

— close to the figure shown by the distance recorder, the unit of measurement of distance, indicated by the abbreviation 'km',

— near the speed scale, the marking 'km/h',

— the measurement range of the speedometer in the form 'Vmin . . . km/h, Vmax . . . km/h'. This marking is not necessary if it is shown on the descriptive plaque of the equipment.

However, these requirements shall not apply to recording equipment approved before 10 August 1970.

2. The descriptive plaque must be built into the equipment and must show the following markings, which must be visible on the equipment when installed:

— name and address of the manufacturer of the equipment,
— manufacturer's number and year of construction,
— approval mark for the equipment type,
— the constant of the equipment in the form 'k = . . . rev/km' or 'k = . . . imp/km',
— optionally, the range of speed measurement, in the form indicated in point 1,
— should the sensitivity of the instrument to the angle of inclination be capable of affecting the readings given by the equipment beyond the permitted tolerances, the permissible angle expressed as:

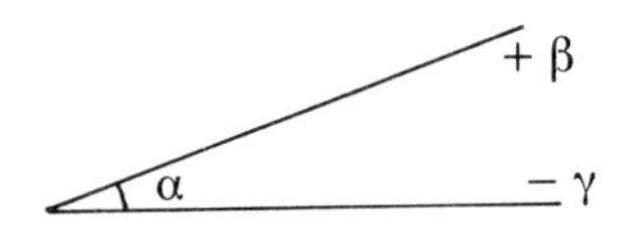

where α is the angle measured from the horizontal position of the front face (fitted the right way up) of the equipment for which the instrument is calibrated, while β and γ represent respectively the maximum permissible upward and downward deviations from the angle of calibration α.

(f) Maximum tolerances (visual and recording instruments)

1. On the test bench before installation:

(a) distance travelled:
1% more or less than the real distance, where that distance is at least one kilometre;

(b) speed:
3 km/h more or less than the real speed;

(c) time:
± two minutes per day with a maximum of 10 minutes per seven days in cases where the running period of the clock after rewinding is not less than that period.

2. On installation:

(a) distance travelled:
2% more or less than the real distance, where that distance is at least one kilometre;

(b) speed;
4 km/h more or less than the real speed;

(c) time:
± two minutes per day, or
± 10 minutes per seven days.

3. In use:

(a) distance travelled:

4% more or less than the real distance, where that distance is at least one kilometre;

(b) speed:
6 km/h more or less than the real speed;

(c) time:
± two minutes per day, or
± 10 minutes per seven days.

4. The maximum tolerances set out in points 1, 2 and 3 are valid for temperatures between 0° and 40°C, temperatures being taken in close proximity to the equipment.

5. Measurement of the maximum tolerances set out in points 2 and 3 shall take place under the conditions laid down in Chapter VI.

IV Record Sheets

(a) General points

1. The record sheets must be such that they do not impede the normal functioning of the instrument and that the records which they contain are indelible and easily legible and identifiable;

The record sheets must retain their dimensions and any records made on them under normal conditions of humidity and temperature.

In addition it must be possible to write on the sheets, without damaging them and without affecting the legibility of the recordings, the information referred to in Article 15(5) of the Regulation.

Under normal conditions of storage, the recordings must remain clearly legible for at least one year.

2. The minimum recording capacity of the sheets, whatever their form, must be 24 hours.

If several discs are linked together to increase the continuous recording capacity which can be achieved without intervention by staff, the links between the various discs must be made in such a way that there are no breaks in or overlapping of recordings at the point of transfer from one disc to another.

(b) Recording areas and their graduation

1. The record sheets shall include the following recording areas:

- an area exclusively reserved for data relating to speed,
- an area exclusively reserved for data relating to distance travelled,
- one or more areas for data relating to driving time, to other periods of work and availability to breaks from work and to rest periods for drivers.

2. The area for recording speed must be scaled off in divisions of 20 kilometres per hour or less. The speed corresponding to each marking on the scale must be shown in figures against that marking. The symbol 'km/h' must be shown at least once within the area. The last marking on the scale must coincide with the upper limit of the range of measurement.

3. The area for recording distance travelled must be set out in such a way that the number of kilometres travelled may be read without difficulty.

4. The area or areas reserved for recording the periods referred to in point 1 must be so marked that it is possible to distinguish clearly between the various periods of time.

(c) Information to be printed on the record sheets

Each sheet must bear, in printed form, the following information:

— name and address or trade name of the manufacturer,
— approval mark for the model of the sheet,
— approval mark for the type or types of equipment in which the sheet may be used,
— upper limit of the speed measurement range, printed in kilometres per hour.

By way of minimal additional requirements, each sheet must bear, in printed form a time-scale graduated in such a way that the time may be read directly at intervals of fifteen minutes while each five minute interval may be determined without difficulty.

(d) Free space for handwritten insertions

A free space must be provided on the sheets such that drivers may as a minimum write in the following details:

— surname and first name of the driver,
— date and place where use of the sheet begins and date and place where such use ends,
— the registration number or numbers of the vehicle or vehicles to which the driver is assigned during the use of the sheet,
— odometer readings from the vehicle or vehicles to which the driver is assigned during the use of the sheet,
— the time at which any change of vehicle takes place.

V INSTALLATION OF RECORDING EQUIPMENT

1. Recording equipment must be positioned in the vehicle in such a way that the driver has a clear view from his seat of speedometer, distance recorder and clock while at the same time all parts of those instruments, including driving parts, are protected against damage.

2. It must be possible to adapt the constant of the recording equipment to the characteristic coefficient of the vehicle by means of a suitable device, to be known as an adaptor.

Vehicles with two or more rear axle ratios must be fitted with a switch device whereby these various ratios may be automatically brought into line with the ratio for which the equipment has been adapted to the vehicle.

3. After the equipment has been checked on installation, an installation plaque shall be affixed to the vehicle beside the equipment or in the equipment itself and in such a way as to be clearly visible. After every inspection by an approved fitter or workshop requiring a change in the setting of the installation itself, a new plaque must be affixed in place of the previous one.

The plaque must show at least the following details:

— name, address or trade name of the approved fitter or workshop,
— characteristic coefficient of the vehicle, in the form 'w= . . . rev/km' or 'w= . . . imp/km',
— effective circumference of the wheel tyres in the form '1= . . . mm',
— the dates on which the characteristic coefficient of the vehicle was determined and the effective measured circumference of the wheel tyres.

4. *Sealing*

The following parts must be sealed:

(a) the installation plaque, unless it is attached in such a way that it cannot be removed without the markings thereon being destroyed;
(b) the two ends of the link between the recording equipment proper and the vehicle;
(c) the adaptor itself and the point of its insertion into the circuit;
(d) the switch mechanism for vehicles with two or more axle ratios;
(e) the links joining the adaptor and the switch mechanism to the rest of the equipment;
(f) the casings required under Chapter III (a) 7.2.

In particular cases, further seals may be required on approval of the equipment type and a note of the positioning of these seals must be made on the approval certificate.

Only the seals mentioned in (b), (c) and (e) may be removed in cases of emergency; for each occasion that these seals are broken a written statement giving the reasons for such action must be prepared and made available to the competent authority.

VI CHECKS AND INSPECTIONS

The Member States shall nominate the bodies which shall carry out the checks and inspections.

1. *Certification of new or repaired instruments*

Every individual device, whether new or repaired, shall be certified in respect of its correct operation and the accuracy of its readiness and recordings, within the limits laid down in Chapter III (f) 1, by means of sealing in accordance with Chapter V (4)(f).

For this purpose the Member States may stipulate an initial verification, consisting of a check on and confirmation of the conformity of a new or repaired device with the type-approved model and/or with the requirements of the Regulation and its Annexes, or may delegate the power to certify to the manufacturers or to their authorised agents.

2. *Installation*

When being fitted to a vehicle, the equipment and the whole installation must comply with the provisions relating to maximum tolerances laid down in Chapter III (f) 2. The inspection tests shall be carried out by the approved fitter or workshop on his or its responsibility.

3. *Periodic inspections*

(a) Periodic inspections of the equipment fitted to vehicles shall take place at least every two years and may be carried out in conjunction with roadworthiness tests of vehicles.

These inspections shall include the following checks:

— that the equipment is working correctly,
— that the equipment carries the type approval mark,
— that the installation plaque is affixed,
— that the seals on the equipment and on the other parts of the installation are intact,
— the actual circumference of the tyres.

(b) An inspection to ensure compliance with the provision of Chapter III (f) 3 on the maximum tolerances in use shall be carried out at least once every six years, although each Member State may stipulate a shorter interval or such inspection in respect of vehicles registered in its territory. Such inspections must include replacement of the installation plaque.

4. *Measurement of errors*
The measurement of errors on installation and during use shall be carried out under the following conditions, which are to be regarded as constituting standard test conditions:

— vehicle unladen, in normal running, order
— tyre pressures in accordance with the manufacturer's instructions,
— tyre wear within the limits allowed by law,
— movement of the vehicle: the vehicle must proceed, driven by its own engine, in a straight line and on a level surface, at a speed of 50 ± 5 km/h; provided that it is of comparable accuracy, the test may also be carried out on an appropriate test bench.

ANNEX II

Approval Mark and Certificate

I Approval Mark

1. The approval mark shall be made up of:

— a rectangle, within which shall be placed the letter 'e' followed by a distinguishing number or letter for the country which has issued the approval in accordance with the following conventional signs:

Belgium	6,
Denmark	18,
Germany	1,
Greece	GR,
Spain	9,
France	2,
Ireland	IRL,
Italy	3,
Luxembourg	13,
Netherlands	4,
Portugal	21,
United Kingdom	11,

and

— an approval number corresponding to the number of the approval certificate drawn up for prototype of the recording equipment or the record sheet, placed at any point within the immediate proximity of this rectangle.

2. The approval mark shall be shown on the descriptive plaque of each set of equipment and on each record sheet. It must be indelible and must always remain clearly legible.

3. The dimensions of the approval mark drawn below are expressed in millimetres, these dimensions being minima. The ratios between the dimensions must be maintained.

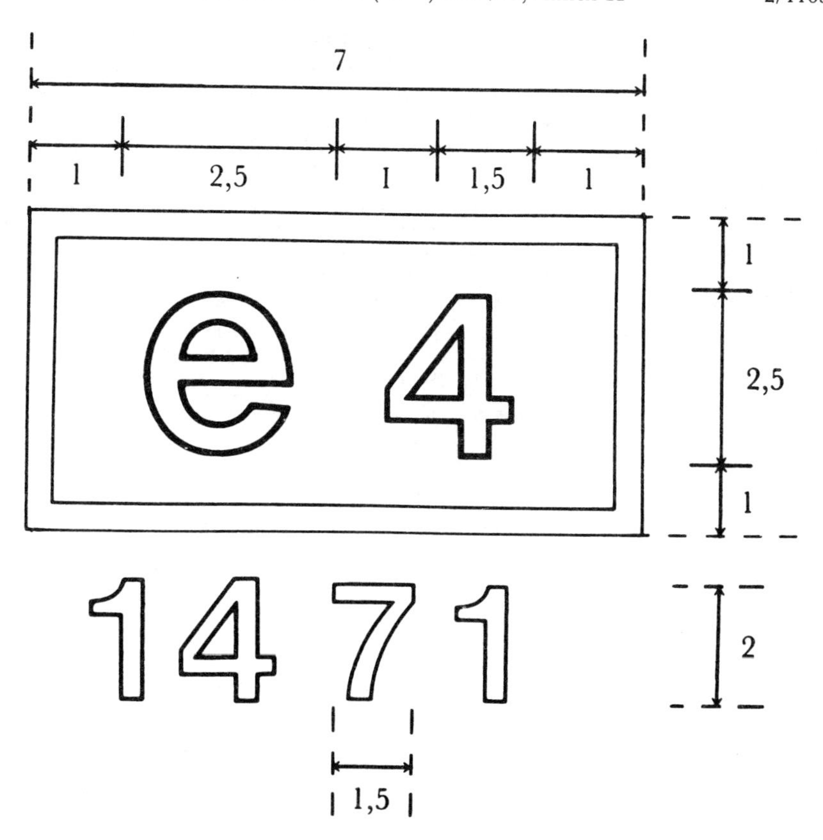

[The characters 'e 4' and '1471' are stated to be for guidance only.]

II Approval Certificate

A State having granted approval shall issue the applicant with an approval certificate, the model for which is given below. When informing other Member States of approvals issued or, if the occasion should arise, withdrawn, a Member State shall use copies of that certificate.

APPROVAL CERTIFICATE

Name of competent administration ....

Notification concerning [*the items which are not applicable should be deleted*]:

— approval of a type of recording equipment

— withdrawal of approval of a type of recording equipment

— approval of a model record sheet

— withdrawal of approval of a record sheet

....

Approval No ....

1. Trade mark or name ....
2. Name of type or model ....
3. Name of manufacturer ....
4. Address of manufacturer ....
   ....
5. Submitted for approval on ....
6. Tested at ....
7. Date and number of test report ....
8. Date of approval ....
9. Date of withdrawal of approval ....
10. Type or types of recording equipment in which sheet is designed to be used
    ....
11. Place ....
12. Date ....
13. Descriptive documents annexed ....
14. Remarks ....

....

(Signature)

Section D

International Agreements

Agreement on the International Carriage of Passengers by Road by means of Occasional Coach and Bus Services (ASOR)

[THE CONTRACTING PARTIES]

Desiring to promote the development of international transport and especially to facilitate the organization and operation thereof;

Whereas some international carriage of passengers by road by means of occasional coach and bus services are liberalised as far as the European Economic Community is concerned by Council Regulation No 117/66/EEC of 28 July 1966 on the introduction of common rules for the international carriage of passengers by coach and bus *[OJ L 147, 9 August 1966, p 2688/66]* and by Regulation (EEC) No 1016/68 of the Commission of 9 July 1968 prescribing the model control documents referred to in Articles 6 and 9 of Council Regulation No 117/66/EEC *[OJ L 173, 22 July 1968, p 8]*;

Whereas in addition, the European Conference of Ministers of Transport (ECMT) adopted on 16 December 1969 resolution No 20 concerning the formulation of general rules for international coach and bus transport *[volume of ECMT resolutions, 1969, p 67; volume of ECMT resolutions, 1971 p 133]* which also concerns the liberalisation of some international carriage of passengers by road by means of occasional coach and bus services;

Whereas it is desirable to provide for harmonised liberalisation measures for occasional international services for passengers by road and to simplify inspection procedures by introducing a single document;

Whereas it is desirable to assign some administrative tasks concerned with the Agreement to the Secretariat of the European Conference of Ministers of Transport;

Have decided to establish uniform rules for the international carriage of passengers by road by means of occasional coach and bus services,

AND . . . HAVE AGREED AS FOLLOWS:

SECTION I

SCOPE AND DEFINITIONS

Article 1

1. This Agreement shall apply:

(*a*) to the international carriage of passengers by road by means of occasional services effected:

— between the territories of two Contracting Parties, or

— starting and finishing in the terriotry of the same Contracting Party,

and, should the need arise during such services, in transit through the territory of another Contracting Party or through the territory of a non contracting State, and

— using vehicles registered in the territory of a Contracting Party which by virtue of their construction and their equipment, are suitable for carrying more than nine persons, including the driver, and are intended for that purpose;

(*b*) to unladen journeys of the vehicles concerned with these services.

2. For the purpose of this Agreement, international services are understood to be services which cross the territory of at least two Contracting Parties.

3. For the purposes of this Agreement, the term 'territory of a Contracting Party' covers, as far as the European Economic Community is concerned, those territories where the Treaty establishing that Community is applied and under the conditions laid down in that Treaty.

Article 2

1. For the purposes of this Agreement, occasional services shall mean services falling neither within the definition of a regular service in Article 3 nor within the definition of a shuttle service in Article 4. They include:

(*a*) closed-door tours, that is to say services whereby the same vehicle is used to carry the same group of passengers throughout the journey and to bring them back to the place of departure;

(*b*) services which make the outward journey laden and the return journey unladen;

(*c*) all other services.

2. Save for exemptions authorised by the competent authorities of the Contracting Party concerned, in the course of occasional services no passenger may be taken up or set down during the journey. Such services may be operated with some degree of frequency without thereby ceasing to be occasional services.

Article 3

1. For the purposes of this Agreement regular services shall mean services which provide for the carriage of passengers according to a specified frequency and along specified routes, whereby passengers may be taken up or set down at pre-determined stopping points. Regular services can be subject to the obligation to respect previously established timetables and tariffs.

2. For the purposes of this Agreement, services, by whomsoever organised, which provide for the carriage of specified categories of passengers to the exclusion of other passengers, in so far as such services are operated under the conditions set out in paragraph 1, shall also be considered to be regular services. Such services, in particular those providing for the carriage of workers to and from their place of work or of school children to and from school, are called 'special regular services'.

3. The fact that a service may be varied according to the needs of those concerned shall not affect its classification as a regular service.

Article 4

1. For the purposes of this Agreement, shuttle services shall mean services whereby, by means of repeated outward and return journeys, previously formed groups of passengers are carried from a single place of departure to a single destination. Each group, consisting of the passengers who made the outward journey, shall be carried back to the place of departure on a later journey.

Place of departure and destination shall mean respectively the place where the journey begins and the place where the journey ends, together with, in each case, the surrounding locality.

2. In the course of shuttle services, no passenger may be taken up or set down during the journey.

3. The first return journey and the last outward journey in a series of shuttles shall be made unladen.

4. However, the classification of a transport operation as a shuttle service shall not be affected by the fact that, with the agreement of the competent authorities in the Contracting Party or Parties concerned:
— passengers, notwithstanding the provisions of paragraph 1, make the return journey with another group,
— passengers, notwithstanding the provisions of paragraph 2, are taken up or set down along the way,
— the first outward journey and the last return journey of the series of shuttles are, notwithstanding the provisions of paragraph 3, made unladen.

SECTION II

Liberalisation Measures

Article 5

1. The occasional services referred to in Article 2(1)(*a*) and (*b*) shall be exempted from the need for any transport authorisation on the territory of any Contracting Party other than that in which the vehicle is registered.

2. The occasional services referred to in Article 2(1)(*c*) shall be exempted from the need for any transport authorisation on the territory of any Contracting Party other than that in which the vehicle is registered where they are characterised by the following:
— the outward journey is made unladen and all the passengers are taken up in the same place, and
— the passengers:
(*a*) — constitute groups, in the territory of a non-Contracting Party or a Contracting Party other than that in which the vehicle is registered or that where the passengers are taken up, formed under contracts of carriage made before their arrival in the territory of the latter Contracting Party, and
— are carried in the territory of the Contracting Party in which the vehicle is registered; or
(*b*) — have been previously brought, by the same carrier in the circumstances provided for under Article 2(1)(*b*), into the territory of the Contracting Party where they are taken up again and carried into the territory of the Contracting Party in which the vehicle is registered; or
(*c*) — have been invited to travel into the territory of another Contracting Party, the cost of transport being borne by the person issuing the invitation. Such passengers must constitute a homogeneous group, which has not been formed solely with a view to undertaking that particular journey and which is brought into the territory of the Contracting Party where the vehicle is registered.

3. In so far as the conditions laid down in paragraph 2 are not satisfied, in the case

of occasional services referred to in Article 2(1)(*c*), such services may be made subject to a transport authorisation in the territory of the Contracting Party concerned.

SECTION III

CONTROL DOCUMENT

Article 6

Carriers operating occasional services within the meaning of this Agreement shall, whenever required to do so by any authorised inspecting officer, produce a passenger waybill which forms part of a control document issued by the competent authorities in the Contracting Party where the vehicle is registered or by any duly authorised agency. This control document shall replace the existing control documents.

Article 7

1. The control document referred to in Article 6 shall consist of detachable passenger waybills in duplicate in books of 25. The control documents shall conform to the model shown in the Annex to this Agreement. This Annex shall form an integral part of the Agreement.

2. Each book and its component passenger waybills shall bear a number. The passenger waybills shall also be numbered consecutively, running from 1 to 25.

3. The wording on the cover of the book and that on the passenger waybills shall be printed in the official language or several official languages of the Member State of the European Economic Community or of any other Contracting Party in which the vehicle used is registered.

Article 8

1. The book referred to in Article 7 shall be made out in the name of the carrier; it not shall not be transferable.

2. The top copy of the passenger waybill shall be kept on the vehicle throughout the journey to which it refers.

3. The carrier shall be responsible for seeing that passenger waybills are duly and correctly completed.

Article 9

1. The passenger waybill shall be completed in duplicate by the carrier for each journey before the start of the journey.

2. For the purpose of providing the names of passengers, the carrier may use a list already completed on a separate sheet, which shall be firmly stuck in the place provided for it under item No 6 in the passenger waybill. The carrier's stamp or, where appropriate, the carrier's signature or that of the driver of the vehicle shall be placed across both the list and the passenger waybill.

3. For the services involving an outward journey unladen referred to in Article 5(2) of this Agreement, the list of passengers may be completed as provided in paragraph 2 at the time when the passengers are taken up.

Article 10

The competent authorities in two or more Contracting Parties may agree bilaterally or multilaterally that the list of passengers under item No 6 of the passenger waybill need not be drawn up. In that case, the number of passengers must be shown.

Article 11

1. A model with stiff green covers and containing the text of the model cover page recto verso of the control document shown in the Annex to this Agreement in each official language of all the Contracting Parties must be kept on the vehicle.

2. The following shall be printed on the front cover of the model in capital letters and in the official language or several official languages of the State in which the vehicle used is registered:

> 'Text of the model control document in Danish, Dutch, English, Finnish, French, German, Greek, Italian, Norwegian, Portuguese, Spanish, Swedish and Turkish'.

3. This model shall be produced whenever required by any authorised inspecting officer.

Article 12

Notwithstanding the provisions of Article 6, control documents used for occasional services before the entry into force of this Agreement may be used for two years after the entry into force of the said Agreement pursuant to Article 18(2).

SECTION IV

General and Final Provisions

Articles 13, 14 *[Omitted.]*

Article 15

The provisions of Articles 5 and 6 shall not be applied to the extent that Agreements or other arrangements in force or to be concluded between two or more Contracting Parties provide for more liberal treatment. The terms 'Agreements or other arrangements in force between two or more Contracting Parties' shall cover, as far as the European Economic Community is concerned, the Agreements and other arrangements which have been concluded by the Member States of that Community.

Articles 16, 17 *[Omitted.]*

Article 18

1. *[Omitted.]*

2. This Agreement shall enter into force, when five Contracting Parties including the European Economic Community have approved or ratified it, on the first day of the third month following the date on which the fifth instrument of approval or ratification is deposited.

3. This Agreement shall enter into force, for each Contracting Party which approves or ratifies it after the entry into force provided for under paragraph 2, on the first day of the third month following the date on which the Contracting Party

concerned has deposited its instrument of approval or ratification with the ECMT Secretariat.

4. The provisions of Section II and III of this Agreement shall apply seven months after the entry into force of the Agreement as specified in paragraphs 2 and 3 respectively.

Articles 19–21 *[Omitted.]*

ANNEX

(green-coloured paper: DIN A4 = 29·7 x 21 cm)

(Front cover — recto)

(To be worded in the official language or several of the official languages of the State where the vehicle is registered)

State in which the control document is issued
— Distinguishing sign of the country —

Competent authority or duly authorized agency

Book No ....

BOOK OF PASSENGER WAYBILLS

for the international carriage of passengers by road by means of occasional coach and bus services **established pursuant to:**

- **ASOR (Agreement on the International Carriage of Passengers by Road by means of Occasional Coach and Bus Services) and**
- **Regulation No 117/66/EEC (Council Regulation on the introduction of common rules for the international carriage of passengers by coach and bus)**

Name and first name of carrier or trade name: ....

....

Address: ....

....

....
(Place and date of issue of book)

....
(Signature and stamp of the authority or agency issuing the book)

(green-coloured paper: DIN A4 — 29·7 x 21 cm)

(Flyleaf of the book of waybills — recto)

(To be worded in the official language or several of the official languages of the State where the vehicle is registered)

IMPORTANT NOTICE

I. TRANSPORT WITHIN THE JURISDICTION OF ASOR

Pursuant to Article 5 (1) and (2) of ASOR, the following shall be exempted from the need for any transport authorization on the territory of any Contracting Party other than that in which the vehicle is registered:

(a) certain occasional international services carried out by means of a vehicle registered in the territory of a Contracting Party:
- between the territories of the Contracting Parties, or
- starting and finishing in the territory of the same Contracting Party,

and, should the need arise, during such services, in transit through the territory of another Contracting Party or through the territory of a non-contracting State,

(b) unladen journeys of the vehicles concerned with these services.

The occasional services covered by the above provisions are as follows:

A. closed-door tours, i.e. services whereby the same vehicle is used to carry the same group of passengers throughout the journey and to bring them back to the place of departure, this place being situated on the territory of the Contracting Party where the vehicle is registered,

B. services which make the outward journey laden and the return journey unladen,

C. services where the outward journey is made unladen and where:

- all the passengers are taken up in the same place to be carried into the territory in which the vehicle is registered, and
- the passengers:

C.1. constitute groups in the territory either of a non-Contracting Party or of a Contracting Party other than that in which the vehicle is registered or than that where the passengers are taken up, formed under contracts of carriage made before their arrival on the territory of the latter Contracting Party, or

C.2. have been previously brought, by the same carrier, on a service referred to in B above, into the territory of the Contracting Party where they are taken up again, or

C.3. have been invited to travel into the territory of another Contracting Party, the cost of transport being borne by the person issuing the invitation. Such passengers must constitute a homogeneous group, which has not been formed solely with a view to undertaking that particular journey.

II. TRANSPORT WITHIN THE JURISDICTION OF REGULATION No 117/66/EEC

Pursuant to Article 5 (1) and (2) of Council Regulation No 117/66/EEC of 28 July 1966, certain international occasional services whose place of departure is in the territory of a Member State and whose destination is in the territory of the same or another Member State and which are operated using a vehicle registered in a Member State do not require authorization by any Member State other than the State where the vehicle is registered. For journeys in transit over the territory of an ASOR Contracting Party other than the Community, the ASOR provisions apply.

The occasional services covered by this provision are as follows:

A. closed-door tours, i.e. services whereby the same vehicle is used to carry the same group of passengers throughout the journey and to bring them back to the place of departure,

B. services which make the outward journey laden and the return journey unladen,

C. services where the outward journey is made unladen, provided that all the passengers are taken up in the same place and that the passengers:

C.1. constitute groups formed under contracts of carriage made before their arrival in the country where they are to be taken up, or

C.2. have been previously brought by the same carrier, on a service referred to in B above, into the country where such passengers are taken up again and carried out of that country, or

C.3. have been invited to travel to another Member State, the cost of transport being borne by the person issuing the invitation. Such passengers must constitute a homogeneous group, which has not been formed solely with a view to undertaking that particular journey.

III. COMMON PROVISIONS APPLICABLE TO ALL INTERNATIONAL SERVICES WITHIN THE SCOPE OF ASOR OR REGULATION No 117/66/EEC

1. For each journey carried out as an occasional service the carrier must complete a passenger waybill in duplicate, before the start of the journey.

   For the purpose of providing the names of passengers, the carrier may use a list already completed on a separate sheet, which must be firmly stuck in the place provided for it under item No 6 in the passenger waybill. The carrier's stamp or, where appropriate, the carrier's signature or that of the driver of the vehicle must be placed across both the list and the passenger waybill.

   For services where the outward journey is made unladen, the list of passengers may be completed as provided above at the time when the passengers are taken up.

   The top copy of the passenger waybill must be kept on board the vehicle throughout the journey and be produced whenever required by any authorized inspecting officer.

2. A model with stiff green covers and containing the text of the model cover page recto/verso, in each official language of all the Contracting Parties to ASOR, must be kept on the vehicle.

3. For services where the outward journey is made unladen, referred to in C, the carrier must attach the following supporting documents to the passenger waybill:

   - in cases mentioned under C.1: the copy of the contract of carriage in so far as some countries require it, or any other equivalent document which establishes the essential data of this contract (especially place, country and date of conclusion, place, country and date when passengers are taken up, place and country of destination);
   - in the case of services falling within C.2.: the passenger waybill which accompanied the vehicle during the corresponding journey made by the carrier outward laden/return unladen in order to bring the passengers into the territory either of the Contracting Party or the EEC Member State where they are taken up again;
   - in the case of services falling within C.3: the letter of invitation from the person issuing the invitation or a photocopy thereof.

4. Occasional services not falling within points I and II may be made subject to transport authorization on the territory of the Contracting Party or of the Member State of the EEC concerned. For these services, a cross must be placed in the appropriate box, under point 4D of the waybill, showing whether a transport authorization is or is not required. If a transport authorization is required it must be attached to the waybill. If no transport authorization is required justification must be given.

5. In the course of occasional services no passenger may be taken up or set down during the journey, save for exemption authorized by the competent authorities. This authorization must also be attached.

6. The carrier is responsible for seeing that passenger waybills are duly and correctly completed. They shall be completed in block letters and in indelible ink.

7. The book of waybills is not transferable.

(Flyleaf of the book of waybills – verso)

(To be worded in the official language or several of the official languages of the State of registration of the vehicle)

Explanation of symbols used in the passenger waybill and instructions on how to fill it in

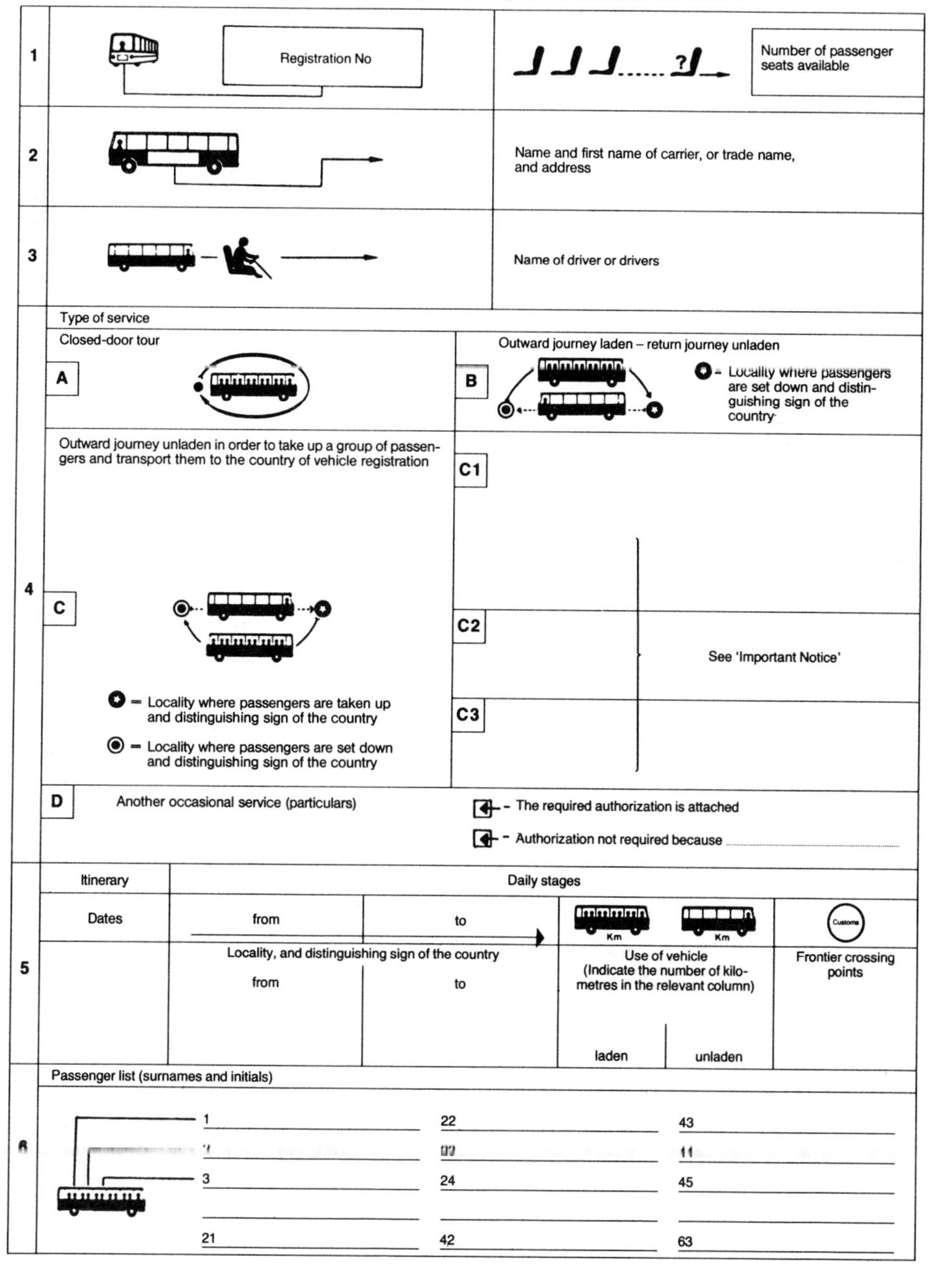

1 — Registration No — Number of passenger seats available

2 — Name and first name of carrier, or trade name, and address

3 — Name of driver or drivers

4 — Type of service

A — Closed-door tour

B — Outward journey laden – return journey unladen

Locality where passengers are set down and distinguishing sign of the country

C — Outward journey unladen in order to take up a group of passengers and transport them to the country of vehicle registration

Locality where passengers are taken up and distinguishing sign of the country

Locality where passengers are set down and distinguishing sign of the country

C1, C2, C3 — See 'Important Notice'

D — Another occasional service (particulars)

– The required authorization is attached

– Authorization not required because ....

5 — Itinerary — Daily stages

Dates	from	to	Km (laden)	Km (unladen)	Customs
	Locality, and distinguishing sign of the country: from	to	Use of vehicle (Indicate the number of kilometres in the relevant column): laden	unladen	Frontier crossing points

6 — Passenger list (surnames and initials)

1 ______	22 ______	43 ______
2 ______	23 ______	44 ______
3 ______	24 ______	45 ______
______	______	______
21 ______	42 ______	63 ______

(Passenger waybill – recto) (Green coloured paper – DIN A4 = 29·7 x 21 cm)

(To be worded in the official language or several of the official languages of the State of vehicle registration)

Book No ....

Waybill No ....

(State in which the document is issued) — Distinguishing sign of the country

1

2

3

1 ______

2 ______

3 ______

4

Type of service (put a cross in the appropriate box and add the required supplementary information)

A

B

C

Outward journey unladen in order to take up a group of passengers and transport them to the country of vehicle registration.

C1 The passengers were assembled, under a contract of carriage made on .... with .... (travel agency, association, etc.).
They arrive(d) on ....

☐ in the territory of the Contracting Party where they are to be taken up,

☐ in the Member State of the EEC where they are to be taken up (for EEC vehicles only),

☐ copy of the contract of carriage or equivalent document (cf. Important Notice under III.3) is attached.

C2 previously brought by the same carrier on a service referred to in B, to the country where they are to be taken up again.
The passenger waybill for the previous outward laden journey and unladen return journey is attached.

C3 invited to travel to ....
Cost of transport being borne by the person issuing the invitation and the passengers constitute a homogeneous group which has not been formed solely with a view to undertaking that particular journey. The letter of invitation (or a photocopy thereof) is attached.

D Another occasional service (particulars):

☐ – The required authorization is attached

☐ – Authorization not required because ....

5

Itinerary					
Dates	from	to	Km	Km	Customs
		Total	+	=	

(Passenger waybill – verso)

6	1	22	43
	2	23	44
	3	24	45
	4	25	46
	5	26	47
	6	27	48
	7	28	49
	8	29	50
	9	30	51
	10	31	52
	11	32	53
	12	33	54
	13	34	55
	14	35	56
	15	36	57
	16	37	58
	17	38	59
	18	39	60
	19	40	61
	20	41	62
	21	42	63

7	Date of completion of waybill	Signature of carrier

8	Unforeseen changes

9	Control stamps if any					

SIGNATURES

[The Agreement was signed in Dublin on 26 May 1982 on behalf of:

the Council of the European Communities
Austria
Finland
Norway
Portugal
Spain
Sweden
Switzerland
Turkey

Regulation (EEC) 56/83 imposed responsibility for the implementation of ASOR on the Member States of the European Communities. The ASOR was approved on behalf of the European Communities by Decision 82/505/EEC and entered into force within the Community on 1 December 1983; see the Road Transport (International Passenger Services) Regulations 1984 (SI 1984 No 748), reg 2(1)(b), above. The ASOR entered into force for Austria on 1 January 1987.]

DECLARATION BY THE CONTRACTING PARTIES ON THE APPLICATION OF THE AGREEMENT

The Contracting Parties agree that the liberalisation measures provided under Articles 5(2) of the Agreement shall only be enforceable between the Contracting Parties who apply the provisions of the European Agreement concerning the work of crews of vehicles engaged in International Road Transport (AETR) from 1 July 1970, or equivalent conditions to those provided under the AETR, to the occasional services governed by this Agreement.

Each Contracting Party which intends, for the reasons set out above, to adopt measures for the non-application or the suspension of the liberalisation provisions under Article 5(2) of the Agreement, declares itself ready to consult the relevant Contracting Party before the possible adoption of these measures.

DECLARATION BY THE EUROPEAN ECONOMIC COMMUNITY CONCERNING ARTICLE 5 OF THE AGREEMENT

With regard to Article 5, the European Economic Community declares that the liberalisation measures laid down for the entry of an unladen vehicle into another Contracting Party with a view to taking up passengers for the return journey to the territory of the Contracting Party where the vehicle is registered shall only apply, where the return to the territory of the European Economic Community is concerned, to return journeys to the Member State in which the vehicle used is registered.

* * *

European Agreement concerning the Work of Crews of Vehicles engaged in International Road Transport (AETR)

(Cmnd 7401)

[The text of this agreement is printed as amended by amendments published as Cmnd 9037 (which took effect on 3 August 1983).]

THE CONTRACTING PARTIES,

Being desirous of promoting the development and improvement of the international transport of passengers and goods by road,

Convinced of the need to increase the safety of the road traffic, to make regulations governing certain conditions of employment in international road transport in accordance with the principles of the International Labour Organisation, and jointly to adopt certain measures to ensure the observance of those regulations,

HAVE AGREED AS FOLLOWS,

Article 1: Definitions

For the purposes of this Agreement

(*a*) 'vehicle' means any motor vehicle or trailer; this term includes any combination of vehicles;

(*b*) 'motor vehicle' means any self-propelled road vehicle which is normally used for carrying persons or goods by road or for drawing, on the road, vehicles used for the carriage of persons or goods; this term does not include agricultural tractors;

(*c*) 'trailer' means any vehicle designed to be drawn by a motor vehicle and includes semi-trailers;

(*d*) 'semi-trailer' means any trailer designed to be coupled to a motor vehicle in such a way that part of it rests on the motor vehicle and that a substantial part of its weight and of the weight of its load is borne by the motor vehicle;

(*e*) 'combination of vehicles' means coupled vehicles which travel on the road as a unit;

(*f*) 'permissible maximum weight' means the maximum weight of the laden vehicle declared permissible by the competent authority of the State in which the vehicle is registered;

(*g*) 'road transport' ['carriage by road'] means

(i) any journey by road of a vehicle, whether laden or not, intended for the carriage of passengers and having more than eight seats in addition to the driver's seat;

(ii) any journey by road of a vehicle, whether laden or not, intended for the carriage of goods;

(iii) any journey which involves both a journey as defined in either (i) or (ii) of this definition and immediately before or after the said journey, the conveyance of the vehicle by sea, rail, air or inland waterway;

(*h*) 'international road transport' ['international carriage by road'] means road transport which involves the crossing of at least one frontier;

(*i*) 'regular passenger services' means services for the transport of passengers at specified intervals on specified routes; such services may take up or set down passengers at predetermined stopping points.

Terms of carriage covering in particular operating schedules (timetable, frequency), tariffs and the obligation to carry shall be specified in operating rules or equivalent documents approved by the competent public authorities of the Contracting Parties and published by the carrier before they are put into effect, in so far as such terms are not already laid down in laws and regulations or in administrative provisions.

Any service by whatever person organized catering only for specific categories of passengers to the exclusion of others, such as a service for the carriage of workers to and from their place of work and of schoolchildren to and from school, shall also be treated as a regular service in so far as it complies with the conditions set out in the first sub-paragraph of this definition.

(*j*) 'driver' means any person, whether wage-earning or not, who drives the vehicle even for a short period, or who is carried on the vehicle in order to be available for driving if necessary;

(*k*) 'crew member' means the driver or either of the following, whether wage-earning or not

(i) a driver's mate, *i.e.* any person accompanying the driver in order to assist him in certain manoeuvres and habitually taking an effective part in the transport operations, though not a driver in the sense of paragraph (*j*) of this article;

(ii) a conductor, *i.e.* any person who accompanies the driver of a vehicle engaged in the carriage of passengers and is responsible in particular for the issue or checking of tickets or other documents entitling passengers to travel on the vehicle;

(*l*) 'week' means any period of seven consecutive days;

(*m*) 'daily rest period' means any uninterrupted period in accordance with article 6 of this Agreement during which a crew member may freely dispose of his time;

(*n*) 'off-duty period' means any uninterrupted period of at least fifteen minutes, other than the daily rest period, during which a crew member may freely dispose of his time:

(*o*) 'occupational activities' means the activities represented by items 6, 7 and 7a in the daily sheet of the individual control book shown in the annex to this Agreement.

[In art 1, the square brackets used in the definitions of 'road transport' and 'international road transport' occur in the text of the agreement and (unlike the use of square brackets elsewhere in this work) do not denote amendments to the text.

The Annex to the agreement is not reproduced. Items 6, 7 and 7a in the daily sheet of the individual control book (referred to in the definition of 'occupational activities') concern driving periods, periods of occupational activities other than driving, and actual work other than driving, respectively.

On depositing their instruments of accession to or ratification of this agreement, the governments of Belgium, Denmark, France, Luxembourg, the Netherlands and the United Kingdom each made the following declaration: 'Transport operations between Member States of the European Economic Community shall be regarded as national transport operations within the meaning of the AETR in so far as such operations do not pass in transit through the territory of a third State which is a contracting party to the AETR'. (cf art 2(2) of Council Regulation (EEC) 2829/77).]

Article 2: Scope

1. This Agreement shall apply in the territory of each Contracting Party to all international road transport performed by any vehicle registered in the territory of the said Contracting Party or in the territory of any other Contracting Party.

2. Nevertheless,

(*a*) if, in the course of an international road transport operation one or more crew members do not leave the national territory in which they normally exercise their occupational activities, the Contracting Party for that territory shall be free not to apply to him or them the provisions of this Agreement;

(*b*) unless the Contracting Parties whose territory is used agree otherwise, this Agreement shall not apply to the international road transport of goods performed by a vehicle having a permissible maximum weight not exceeding 3·5 tons;

(*c*) two Contracting Parties with adjoining territories may agree that the provisions of the domestic laws and regulations of the State in which the vehicle is registered and the provisions of arbitral awards and collective agreements in force in that State shall alone be applicable to international road transport confined to their two territories if the vehicle concerned:

— does not while in one of those territories travel beyond a zone contiguous to the frontier and defined by agreement between the two Contracting Parties as a *frontalier* zone, or

— crosses one of those territories in transit only;

(*d*) Contracting Parties may agree that the provisions of the domestic laws and regulations of the State in which the vehicle is registered and the provisions of arbitral awards and collective agreements in force in that State shall alone be applicable to certain international road transport operations confined to their territories and covering a distance of less than 100 km from the point of departure to the point of arrival of a vehicle, and to regular passenger services.

[Agreements to be reached with third countries under art 2(2) will be concluded, on behalf of Member States of the EEC, by the Communtiy; see Council Regulation (EEC) 2829/77, art 3.]

Article 3: Application of some provisions of the Agreement to road transport performed by vehicles registered in the territories of non-contracting States

1. Each Contracting Party shall apply in its territory, in respect of international road transport performed by any vehicle registered in the territory of a State which is not a Contracting Party to this Agreement, [provisions not less strict than those laid down in articles 5, 6, 7, 8, 9, 10, 11, in article 12 paragraphs 1, 2, 6 and 7 and in article 12*bis* of this Agreement].

2. However, any Contracting Party shall be free not to apply the provisions of paragraph 1 of this article.

(*a*) to the international carriage of goods by road by a vehicle whose permissible maximum weight does not exceed 3·5 tons.

(*b*) to international road transport confined to its territory and to the territory of an adjoining State which is not a Contracting Party to this Agreement if the vehicle concerned does not while in its territory travel beyond a zone contiguous to the frontier and defined as a *frontalier* zone or if it crosses its territory in transit only.

[Article 3 is printed as amended by Cmnd 9037.
The measures provided for under art 3(2) will be adopted by the Council of the European Communities on a proposal from the Commission; see Council Regulation (EEC) 2829/77, art 3.]

Article 4: General principles

1. In all international road transport to which this Agreement applies, the undertaking and crew members shall observe in the matter of rest periods, driving periods and manning, the rules laid down by domestic laws and regulations in the district of the State in which the crew member normally exercises his occupational activities and by arbitral awards or collective agreements in force in that district: the rest periods and driving periods shall be calculated in conformity with the said laws and regulations, arbitral awards or collective agreements. In so far as the rules thus applicable are not at least as strict as the provisions of articles 6, 7, 8, 9, 10 and 11 of this Agreement the latter provisions shall be observed.

2. Except by special agreement between the Contracting Parties concerned or except to the extent that pursuant to article 2, paragraph 2, of this Agreement certain provisions of this Agreement are not applied, no Contracting Party shall enforce observance of the provisions of its domestic laws and regulations regarding the matters dealt with in this Agreement by undertakings of another Contracting Party, or by crew members of vehicles registered by another Contracting Party, in cases where the said provisions are stricter than those of this Agreement.

[When signing the agreement, the Contracting Parties agreed the following statement on art 4 which was set out in the Protocol of Signature to the agreement:

'The provisions of article 4, paragraph 1, shall not be construed as rendering applicable, outside the State in which the vehicle performing the transport operation is registered, any prohibition of traffic on certain days or at certain hours which may apply in that State to certain categories of vehicles. The provisions of article 4, paragraph 2, shall not be construed as preventing a Contracting Party from enforcing in its territory the provisions of its domestic laws and regulations which prohibit certain categories of vehicle traffic on certain days or at certain hours.

'Every Contracting Party which, being a Party to a special agreement as referred to in article 4, paragraph 2, of this Agreement, authorizes international transport operations beginning and ending in the territories of the Parties to the said special agreement by vehicles registered in the territory of a State which, being a Contracting Party to this Agreement, is not a Party to the said special agreement may make it a condition for the conclusion of bilateral or multilateral agreements authorizing such transport operations that the crews performing those operations shall, in the territories of States Parties to the said special agreement, comply with the provisions of the said special agreement.']

Article 5: Conditions to be fulfilled by drivers

1. The minimum age of drivers engaged in the international road transport of goods shall be:

(*a*) for vehicles of a permissible maximum weight not exceeding 7·5 tons, 18 years;

(*b*) for other vehicles:

(i) 21 years; or

(ii) 18 years where the person concerned holds a certificate of professional competence recognized by the Contracting Party in whose territory the vehicle is registered and confirming the completion of a training course for drivers of vehicles intended for the carriage of goods by road. However, in the case of drivers whose age is less than 21 years any Contracting Party may:

— prohibit them from driving such vehicles in its territory even if they hold the certificate aforesaid; or
— restrict permission to drive such vehicles to those who hold certificates which it recognizes as having been issued after the completion of a training course for drivers of vehicles intended for the carriage of goods by road equivalent to the course prescribed by its own domestic laws and regulations.

2. If under the provisions of article 10 of this Agreement two drivers are required to be on board, one of the drivers shall have reached the age of 21 years.

3. Drivers engaged in the international road transport of passengers shall have reached the age of 21 years.

4. Drivers of vehicles shall be responsible and trustworthy. They shall possess sufficient experience and the qualifications essential to that performance of the services required.

[In relation to art 5, the Government of Spain (on depositing its instrument of accession) has started that it 'avails itself of the first of the options provided for in article 5, paragraph 1(b)(ii) of the agreement whereby persons whose age is less than 21 years may be prohibited from driving in its territory vehicles of a permissible maximum weight exceeding 7.5 tons'.]

Article 6: Daily rest period

1. (*a*) Except in the cases referred to in paragraphs 3 and 4 of this article, every crew member assigned to the international road transport of goods shall have had a daily rest period of not less than eleven consecutive hours in the period of twenty-four hours preceding any time when he is exercising one of his occupational activities.

(*b*) The daily rest period referred to in sub-paragraph (*a*) of this paragraph may, not more than twice in the course of any one week, be reduced to not less than nine consecutive hours provided that the rest period can be taken at the crew member's normal place of residence; or not more than twice in the course of any one week, to not less than eight consecutive hours in cases where for operational reasons the rest period cannot be taken at the crew member's normal place of residence.

2. (*a*) Except in the cases referred to in paragraphs 3 and 4 of this article, every crew member assigned to the international road transport of passengers shall have had, in the period of twenty-four hours preceding any time when he is exercising one of his occupational activities, either:

(i) a daily rest period of not less than ten consecutive hours, which shall not be reduced during the week; or

(ii) a daily rest period of not less than eleven consecutive hours, which may be reduced twice a week to not less than ten consecutive hours and twice a week to not less than nine consecutive hours, provided that in the latter two cases the transport operation shall include a scheduled break of not less than four consecutive hours, or two scheduled breaks each of not less than two consecutive hours and that during these breaks the crew member shall neither exercise any of his operational activities nor perform any other work as an occupation.

(*b*) The individual control book referred to in article 12 of this Agreement shall contain particulars showing the daily rest system applied during the current week to the crew member assigned to the international road transport of passengers.

3. If the vehicle is manned by two drivers and has no bunk enabling crew members to lie down comfortably, each crew member shall have had a daily rest period of not less than ten consecutive hours during the period of twenty-seven hours preceding any time when he is exercising one of his occupational activities.

4. If the vehicle is manned by two drivers and has a bunk enabling crew members to lie down comfortably, each crew member shall have had a daily rest period of not less than eight consecutive hours during the period of thirty hours preceding any time when he is exercising one of his occupational activities.

5. The rest periods specified in this article shall be taken outside the vehicle; however, if the vehicle has a bunk enabling crew members to lie down comfortably, the rest periods may be taken on that bunk provided that the vehicle is stationary.

[Article 6*bis*: Interruption of the daily rest period in the course of combined transport operations

Where a crew member engaged in the carriage of goods or passengers accompanies a vehicle which is transported by ferryboat or train, the daily rest period may be interrupted not more than once, provided the following conditions are fulfilled:

(*a*) that part of the daily rest period spent on land may be taken before or after the portion of the daily rest period taken on board the ferryboat or the train,

(*b*) the period between the two portions of the daily rest period must be as short as possible and may on no account exceed one hour before embarkation or after disembarkation, customs formalities being included in the embarkation or disembarkation operations,

(*c*) during both portions of the rest period the crew member must have access to a bunk or couchette.

(*d*) where a daily rest period is interrupted in this way, it shall be increased by two hours.

(*e*) any time spent on board a ferryboat or a train and not counted as part of the daily rest period shall be regarded as a break as defined in article 8.]

[Article 6bis was inserted by Cmnd 9037.]

Article 7: Daily driving period, maximum weekly and fortnightly driving period

1. The total driving time between two consecutive daily rest periods as prescribed by article 6 of this Agreement, which driving time is hereinafter referred to as the 'daily driving period', shall not exceed eight hours.

2. In the case of drivers of vehicles other than vehicles as referred to in article 10 of this Agreement the daily driving period may, by derogation from the provisions of paragraph 1 of this article, be extended to nine hours not more than twice in one week.

3. The driving time may not exceed forty-eight hours in one week or ninety-two hours in one fortnight.

Article 8: Maximum continuous driving periods

1. (*a*) No continuous driving period shall exceed four hours except where the driver cannot reach a convenient stopping place or his destination; in such a case the driving period may be extended by not more than thirty minutes, provided that the use of this option does not result in a breach of the provisions of article 7 of this Agreement.

(*b*) Any driving period which is interrupted only by breaks not meeting at least the provisions of paragraph 2 or paragraph 3 of this article shall be deemed to be continuous.

2. (*a*) For drivers of vehicles as referred to in article 10 of this Agreement, driving shall be interrupted for not less than one hour at the end of the period referred to in paragraph 1 of this article.

(*b*) This break may be replaced by two uninterrupted breaks of not less than thirty minutes each, spaced out over the daily driving period in such a way that the provisions of paragraph 1 of this article are complied with.

3. (*a*) For drivers of vehicles other than vehicles as referred to in article 10 of this Agreement, and where the daily driving period does not exceed eight hours, driving shall be interrupted for not less than thirty consecutive minutes at the end of the period referred to in paragraph 1 of this article.

(*b*) This break may be replaced by two uninterrupted breaks of not less than twenty minutes each or by three uninterrupted breaks of not less than fifteen minutes each, which may all be spaced out over the driving period referred to in paragraph 1 of this article or may in part fall within that period and in part immediately follow it.

(*c*) If the daily driving period exceeds eight hours the driver shall be required to discontinue driving during not less than two uninterrupted periods of thirty minutes.

4. During breaks as referred to in paragraphs 2 or 3 of this article the driver shall not engage in any occupational activity other than supervision of the vehicle and its load. However, if the vehicle is manned by two drivers the requirements of paragraphs 2 or 3 of this article shall be deemed to be met if the driver who is having his break does not engage in any of the activities falling under item 7a in the daily sheet of the individual control book referred to in article 12 of this Agreement.

[The reference in art 8, para 4, to item 7a in the daily sheet of the individual control book is to the item concerning actual work other than driving. (The individual control book is set out in the Annex to this agreement which is not reproduced in this work.)]

Article 9: Weekly rest period

1. In addition to the daily rest periods referred to in article 6 of this Agreement, every crew member shall have a weekly rest period of not less than twenty-four consecutive hours which shall be immediately preceded or followed by a daily rest period conforming to the provisions of the said article 6.

2. (*a*) However, during the period from 1 April to 30 September inclusive the weekly rest period referred to in paragraph 1 of this article may be replaced, for crew members of vehicles used for the international road transport of passengers, by a rest period of not less than sixty consecutive hours to be taken in full before the expiry of any maximum period of fourteen consecutive days. This rest period shall be immediately preceded or followed by a daily rest period conforming to the provisions of article 6 of this Agreement.

(*b*) The provisions of this paragraph shall not apply to crew members of vehicles used on regular passenger services.

Article 10: Manning

[Subject to the provisions of article 12*bis* paragraph 2 of this Agreement, in the case of]

(*a*) a combination of vehicles including more than one trailer or semi-trailer; or of

(*b*) a combination of vehicles used for the carriage of passengers where the permissible maximum weight of the trailer or semi-trailer exceeds 5 metric tons; or of

(*c*) a combination of vehicles used for the carriage of goods where the permissible maximum weight of the combination of vehicles exceeds 20 metric tons,

the driver shall be accompanied by another driver from the start of the journey, or be replaced by another driver after 450 km, if the distance to be travelled between two consecutive daily rest periods exceeds 450 km.

[Article 10 is printed as amended by Cmnd 9037.]

Article 11: Exceptional cases

Provided that there is no detriment to road safety, the driver may depart from the provisions of articles 6, 7, 8 and 10 of this Agreement in case of danger, in case of *force majeure*, to render aid, or as a result of a breakdown, to the extent necessary to ensure the safety of persons, of the vehicle or of its load and to enable him to reach a suitable stopping place or, according to circumstances, the end of his journey. The driver [shall record in the individual control book or in the case mentioned in article 12*bis*, as appropriate, in the record sheet and/or in the other control documents envisaged under paragraph 1 of that article, the nature of and] reason for his departure from those provisions.

[Article 11 is printed as amended by Cmnd 9037.]

Article 12: Individual control book

1. Every driver or driver's mate shall enter in an individual control book, as the day proceeds, a record of his occupational activities and rest periods. He shall keep the book with him and produce it whenever required by the control authorities.

2. The specifications with which the control book must comply and the requirements to be met in keeping the records are set out in the annex to this Agreement.

3. The Contracting Parties shall take all necessary measures concerning the issue and control of individual control books, and, in particular, measures required to prevent the simultaneous use of two such books by the same crew member.

4. Every undertaking shall keep a register of the individual control books it uses; the register shall show at least the name of the driver or driver's mate to whom the book is issued, the driver's or driver's mate's signature in the margin, the number of the book, the date of issue to the driver or driver's mate and the date of the last daily sheet completed by the driver or driver's mate before final return of the control book to the undertaking after use.

5. Undertakings shall keep the used books for a period of not less than twelve months after the date of the last entry and shall produce them together with the registers of issue, at the request of the control authorities.

6. At the beginning of an international road transport operation every driver or

driver's mate shall have with him an individual control book conforming to the specifications in the annex to this Agreement, in which the data relating to the seven days preceding that on which the transport operation begins shall be entered. However, if domestic laws and regulations of the State where the driver or driver's mate exercises his occupational activities do not prescribe the obligation to use an individual control book conforming to the specifications in the annex to this Agreement for road transport operations which are not international, it will suffice if the data relating to the 'uninterrupted rest period before coming on duty' and the 'daily driving periods' during the seven days concerned appear against items 12 and 13 of the daily sheets or in the weekly report of the individual control book conforming to the specifications in the annex to this Agreement.

7. It shall be open to any Contracting Party, in the case of a vehicle registered in a State which is not a Contracting Party to this Agreement, merely to require, in lieu of an individual control book conforming to the specifications in the annex to this Agreement, papers made out in the same form as the daily sheets of the said book.

[The references in art 12, para 6, to 'items 12 and 13 of the daily sheets . . . of the individual control book' relate to the total duration of the rest period before going on duty and to the driving period, respectively. (The Annex to the agreement which sets out the individual control book is not reproduced.)

On signing the agreement, the Contracting Parties agreed the following statement which was set out in the Protocol of Signature to the agreement: 'The undersigned undertake to discuss after the Agreement has entered into force the insertion therein, by means of an amendment, of a clause providing for the use of a control device of approved type which when placed on the vehicle would so far as possible replace the individual control book'.]

[Article 12*bis*: Control device

1. If a Contracting Party describes or authorises the installation and use on vehicles registered in its territory of a mechanical control device, such device may give rise to complete or partial exemption from the filling in of the individual control book mentioned in article 12, under the following conditions:

(*a*) The control device must be of a type either approved or recognised by one of the Contracting Parties;

(*b*) If the crew includes more than one person and if the recording is not made on separate sheets but on only one sheet, this must show clearly the part of the recording corresponding to each of the persons;

(*c*) If the device provides for the recording of crew members' driving times, times spent performing occupational activities other than driving, and rest periods as well as vehicle speeds and distance covered, the keeping of the individual control book may be entirely dispensed with;

(*d*) If the device provides only for recording driving time, time during which the vehicle is stationary, speed and distance covered, the exemption will only be partial and limited to the entries in the daily sheets of the said control book, the crew members being obliged to complete daily the appropriate columns of a weekly report conforming to the model sheet (*e*) appearing in the annex to the Agreement;

(*e*) If the normal and appropriate use of a control device installed on a vehicle is not possible, each crew member shall enter by hand, using the appropriate graphic representation, the details corresponding to his occupational activities and rest periods on a record sheet, or on a daily sheet conforming to the model sheet (*c*) appearing in the annex to the Agreement;

(*f*) When, by reason of their being away from the vehicle, the crew members are unable to make use of the device, they shall insert by hand, using the appropriate graphic representation, in the record sheet or a daily sheet conforming to the model sheet (*c*) envisaged in the annex to this Agreement, the various times corresponding to their occupational activities while they were away;

(*g*) The crew members must always have available, and be able to present for inspection, as appropriate, the record sheets and/or the other control documents filled in as provided under (*c*), (*d*), (*e*) and (*f*) of this paragraph, relating to the previous seven days;

(*h*) The crew members must ensure that the control device be activated and handled correctly and that, in case of malfunctioning, it be repaired as soon as possible.

2. If the control device within the meaning of paragraph 1 is installed and used on a vehicle registered in the territory of one of the Contracting Parties, the application of the provisions of article 10 of this Agreement to that vehicle shall not be required by the other Contracting Parties.

3. Undertakings shall keep, as appropriate, the record sheets and/or the other control documents filled in as provided under (*c*), (*d*) and (*e*) of paragraph 1 of this Article, for a period of not less than twelve months after the date of the last entry and shall produce them at the request of the control authorities.]

[Article 12bis was inserted by Cmnd 9037.]

Articles 13–26 [*Not reproduced.*]

* * *

SIGNATURES

[The following States have signed and ratified the agreement:

Austria
Belgium
Federal Republic of Germany (including West Berlin)
France
Luxembourg
the Netherlands
Norway
Portugal
Sweden and
the United Kingdom (including the Isle of Man)

The following States which signed the agreement have not yet ratified it (ratification being required under art 16, para 2):

Italy
Poland and
Switzerland

The agreement came into operation, in accordance with art 16, para 4, on 5 January 1976; it came into operation in the United Kingdom on 18 August 1978.

On signature of the agreement, the Contracting States agreed the following declaration which was set out in the Protocol of Signature to the agreement: 'The Contracting Parties declare that this Agreement is without prejudice to such provisions as may, if appropriate, subsequently be drawn up in the matter of the duration and spread-over of work.']

ACCESSIONS

[The following countries have acceded to the agreement:

Czechoslovakia
Democratic Republic of Germany
Denmark
Greece
Spain
Union of Soviet Socialist Republics and
Yugoslavia]

ANNEX

Individual Control Book

* * *

PROTOCOL OF SIGNATURE

* * *